Amiga

ROM Kernel Reference Manual:

Includes and Autodocs

Amiga

ROM Kernel Reference Manual:

Includes and Autodocs

Commodore-Amiga, Incorporated

Amiga Technical Reference Series

Addison-Wesley Publishing Company, Inc.

Reading, Massachusetts Menlo Park, California New York
Don Mills, Ontario Wokingham, England Amsterdam Bonn
Sydney Singapore Tokyo Madrid San Juan

This manual corresponds to the V1.3 system software release.

Material written by:

Steve Beats, David Berezowski, Robert Burns, Eric Cotton, Sam Dicker, Andy Finkel, Larry Hildenbrand, Randell Jesup, Neil Katin, Dale Luck, Jim Mackraz, R.J. Mical, Bryce Nesbitt, Bob Pariseau, Rob Peck, Tom Pohorsky, Carl Sassenrath, Carolyn Scheppner, Stan Shepard, and Bart Whitebrook

Manual compiled by:

Bryce Nesbitt, Robert Burns, Carolyn Scheppner, and Nancy Rains. C cross-reference created by John Toebes using Lattice C Version 5.0 by Lattice, Inc.

This book is dedicated to all those "busy guys" who made Amiga and who are Amiga.

Commodore item number: 327271-06

ISBN 0-201-18177-0
ABCDEFG-AL-909
First printing, January 1989

TABLE OF CONTENTS

Error Reports

In a complex technical manual, errors are often found after publication. When errors in this manual are found, they will be corrected in the following printing. Updates will be published in the AmigaMail technical support publication.

Bug reports can be sent to Commodore electronically or by mail. Submitted reports must be clear, complete, and concise. Reports must include a telephone number and enough information so that the bug can be quickly verified from your report. (I.e. please describe the bug *and* the steps that preceded it.)

Amiga Software Engineering Group
ATTN: BUG REPORTS
Commodore Business Machines
1200 Wilson Drive
West Chester, PA 19380
USA

BIX: afinkel
USENET: bugs@commodore.COM or uunet!cbmvax!bugs

About this book

The Amiga Technical Reference Series is the official guide to programming the Commodore-Amiga computers. This revised edition has been updated for version 1.3 of the Amiga operating system and the new Amiga computer systems. The series has been reorganized into three volumes. This volume, the *Amiga ROM Kernel Reference Manual: Includes and Autodocs*, contains alphabetically organized autodoc function summaries, listings of the Amiga system include files, and the IFF Interchange File Format specifications and listings. This is the essential quick reference for all Amiga programmers.

The other manuals in this series are the *Amiga ROM Kernel Reference Manual: Libraries and Devices*, with tutorial-style chapters on the use of each Amiga system library and device, and the *Amiga Hardware Reference Manual*, a guide to hardware level programming of the Amiga custom and peripheral chips.

This manual contains:

- Summaries for system library functions
- Summaries for system device commands
- Summaries for system resource calls
- C Language Include Files
- Assembly Language Include Files
- Documentation on "Amiga.lib" and reference source code
- Updated sample library and device
- Handy Charts designed to ease debugging and exploring
- Documentation on the Interchange File Format standard (IFF)

The manual is a perfect companion for programming the Amiga.

About the examples

Except as noted, 68000 assembly language examples have been assembled under the Metacomco assembler V11.0, the Inovatronics CAPE assembler V2.0, and the HiSoft Devpac assembler V1.2. No substantial changes should be required to switch between assemblers.

C examples have been compiled under Lattice C, version 4.01 and Manx Aztec C68K, version 3.6a. Default compiler options are used in both cases. All the C examples assume that the automatic CTRL-C feature of the compiler has been disabled. With the exception of those examples in Section A, this code *must* be added to each example to complete it:

For Aztec C

```
Compile with:   cc <filename>.c
                ln <filename.o> -lc

/* Add this near the top */
      #include "functions.h"

/* Add this before main() */
      extern int Enable_Abort;   /* reference abort enable */

/* Add this after main(), as the first active line in the program */
      Enable_Abort=0;            /* turn off CTRL-C */
```

For Lattice C revisions 4.0 and greater

```
Compile with:        lc -L <filename>.c

/* Add this function before main(). This overrides the default
 * Lattice CTRL-C trap. If this function  returns zero, then the
 * CTRL-C event will be ignored */
int CXBRK()
{
      return(0);
}
```

General Amiga Development Guidelines

The environment of the Amiga computer is quite different than that of many older computers. The Amiga is multitasking, which means multiple programs must share the same machine without interfering with each other. It also means that certain guidelines must be followed during programming.

- Always make sure you actually GET what you ask for. This applies to memory allocations, windows, screens, file handles, libraries, devices, ports, etc. Where an error value or return is possible, ensure that there is a reasonable failure path. Many poorly written programs will *appear* to be reliable, until some error condition (such as memory full or a disk problem) causes the program to continue with an invalid or null pointer, or branch to untested error handling code.

- Always clean up after yourself. This applies for both normal program exit and program termination due to error conditions. Anything that was opened must be closed, anything allocated must be deallocated. It is generally correct to do closes and deallocations in reverse order of the opens and allocations. Be sure to check your development language manual and startup code; some items may be closed or deallocated automatically, especially in abort conditions. If you write in the C language, make sure that when CTRL-C is pressed, your program gracefully closes down and exits.

- Remember that memory, peripheral configurations, and ROMs differ between models and between individual systems. Do not make assumptions about memory address ranges, storage device names, or the locations of system structures or code. Do not jump into the ROM directly. Do not assume library bases or structures will exist at any particular memory location. The only absolute in the system is address 0x00000004, which contains a pointer to the exec.library base.

- Do not assume that programs can access hardware resources directly. Most hardware is controlled by system software and resources that will not respond well to interference. Shared hardware requires programs to use the proper sharing protocols. Using the defined interface enhances the probability that your software will continue to operate on future Amiga computers.

- Do not access shared data structures directly without the proper mutual exclusion (locking). Remember that other tasks may be accessing the same structures.

- The system does not monitor the size of a program's stack. Take care that your program does not cause stack overflow, and provide enough leeway for the possibility that future revisions of system functions might require additional stack space.

- If your program waits for external events like menu selection or key-strokes, do not bog down the multitasking system by busy-waiting in a loop. Instead, let your task go to sleep by Wait()ing on its signal bits. For example:

```
signals = (ULONG)Wait((1<<windowPtr->UserPort->mp_SigBit) |
                      (1<<consoleMsgPortPtr->mp_SigBit) );
```

  This turns the signal bit number for each port into a mask, then combines them as the argument for the exec.library/Wait() function. When your task is awakened, handle all of the messages at each port where the SigBit is set. There may be more than one message per port, or no messages at the port. Make sure that you ReplyMsg() to all messages that are not replies themselves.

- Tasks (and Processes) execute in 68000 processor user mode. Supervisor mode is reserved for interrupts, traps, and task dispatching. Take extreme care if your code executes in supervisor mode. Exceptions while in supervisor mode are deadly.

- Most system functions require a particular execution environment. All DOS functions and any functions that might call DOS (such as the opening of a disk-resident library, font, or device) can only be executed from a process. A task is not sufficient. Most other ROM Kernel functions may be executed from tasks. Only a few may be executed from interrupts.

- Do not disable interrupts or multitasking for long periods. If you use Forbid() or Disable(), you should be aware that execution of any system function that WAITS will temporarily suspend the Forbidden or Disabled state, and allow multitasking and interrupts to occur. Such functions include almost all forms of DOS and device IO, including common "stdio" functions like "printf".

- Do not tie up system resources unless it is absolutely necessary. For example, if your program does not require constant use of the printer, open the printer.device only when you need it. This will allow other tasks to use the printer while your program is running. You must provide a reasonable error response if a resource is not available when you need it.

- Check for memory loss. Operate your program, then exit. Write down the amount of free memory. Repeat the operation of your program and exit. The amount of free memory remaining should be *exactly* the same. Any difference may signal some serious problem in your cleanup. A useful tool for memory testing is the "LoadWB -debug" command; this will start the Workbench tool with a special invisible debug menu. The "flushlibs" option of this menu can cause unused libraries and devices to be flushed out of memory. (The "debug" option invokes the ROM debugger, RomWack, on the serial port at 9600 baud.)

- All data for the custom chips *must* reside in CHIP type memory. This includes bitplanes, sound samples, trackdisk buffers, and images for sprites, bobs, pointers, and gadgets. The AllocMem() call takes a flag for specifying CHIP type memory.

  On machines with expansion (FAST) memory, the default location for memory allocations is FAST memory. A developer with only CHIP memory may fail to notice the memory was incorrectly specified. (On the current generation of machines, CHIP memory is the lowest 512K of memory in the system.)

  Most compilers have options to mark specific data structures or object modules so that they will load into CHIP ram. Some older compilers provide the Atom utility for marking object modules. If this method is unacceptable, use the AllocMem() call to dynamically allocate CHIP memory, and copy your data there.

- Do not use software delay loops! Under the multitasking operating system, the time spent in a loop can be better used by other tasks. Even ignoring the effect of multitasking, timing loops are inaccurate and will wait varying amounts of time depending on the specific model of computer. The timer.device provides precision timing for use under the multitasking system. The AmigaDOS Delay() function provides a simple interface for longer delays.

The 8520 I/O chips provide timers for developers who are bypassing the operating system (see the *Amiga Hardware Reference Manual* for more information).

- Obey structure conventions!
  - All non-byte fields must be word aligned.
  - All address pointers should be 32 bits (not 24 bits). The upper byte must never be used for data.
  - Fields that are not defined to contain particular initial values *must* be initialized to zero. This includes pointer fields.
  - All reserved or unused fields *must* be initialized to zero for future compatibility.
  - Data structures to be accessed by the custom chips, public data structures (such as a task control block), and structures which must be longword aligned must NOT be allocated on a program's stack.
  - Dynamic allocation of structures with AllocMem provides longword aligned memory of a specified type with optional initialization to zero, which is useful in the allocation of structures.

Additional Assembler Development Guidelines

- Do not use the "TAS" instruction on the Amiga. System DMA can conflict with this instruction's special indivisible read-modify-write cycle .

- System functions must be called with A6 containing the library or device base. Libraries and devices assume A6 is valid at the time of any function call. Even if a particular function does not currently require its base register, you must provide it for compatibility with future system software releases.

- Except as noted, system library functions use registers D0, D1, A0, and A1 as scratch registers and you must consider their former contents to be lost after a system library call. The contents of all other registers will be preserved. System functions which provide a result will return the result in D0.

- System functions that return a result may not necessarily affect the processor condition codes. The caller must test the returned value before acting on a condition code. This is usually done with a TST or MOVE instruction.

- For 68010/68020/68030/68040 compatibility:

- Do not use the "MOVE SR,..." instruction! This 68000 instruction acts differently on other members of the 68000 family. If you wish a copy of the processor condition codes, use the exec.library/GetCC() function.
- Do not use the upper 8 bits of a pointer for storing unrelated information. The 68020 uses all 32 bits for addressing.
- Do not use signed variables or signed math for addresses.
- Do not execute code on your stack.
- The stack frame used for exceptions is different on each member of the 68000 family. The type identification in the frame must be checked!
- Do not use self modifying code.

Commodore-Amiga Technical Support (CATS)

Commodore maintains a technical support group dedicated to helping developers achieve their goals with the Amiga. Available technical support programs are tailored both to the needs of smaller independent developers and larger corporations. Subscription to the support publication *AmigaMail* is available to anyone with an interest in the latest news, Commodore software and hardware changes, and tips for developers.

To request an application for the Commodore-Amiga Developer Programs, lists of CATS technical publications, or information regarding electronic developer support, send a self-addressed, stamped, 9" x 12" envelope to:

CATS-Information
1200 West Wilson Drive
West Chester, PA 19380-4231

Section A

Library Summaries

This section contains summaries for the shared library routines that are built into the Amiga operating system software. These documents have been automatically extracted from the original source code and are often called **autodocs**.

Most of the Amiga operating system is divided into functional groups called libraries. Libraries may exist in the Kickstart ROM or on disk. Each library may be individually opened and closed. When a library is open, any of its functions may be called. When all openers of a library have closed, the library becomes a candidate for purging from the system memory.

These documentation files are organized alphabetically by library, one document per function call. Tutorial information for each of the libraries and a description of the library mechanism is available in the *Amiga ROM Kernel Manual: Libraries and Devices*. Only a brief introduction will be given here.

The "exec.library" is the system's master library and is always open. This library controls the lowest levels of the multitasking operating system. One of exec's functions, **OpenLibrary()**, is used to open the other libraries. Usage is as follows:

```
struct LibBase *LibBase;
LibBase = OpenLibrary("library.name",version);
```

library.name
is a string that describes the name of the library you wish to open.

version
should be set to the earliest acceptable library version. A value of 0 matches any version. A value of 33, for example, means you require version 33 of the library or a later version if 33 is not available. For the system libraries, the following table applies:

0 = Any version
30 = Kickstart V1.0 (obsolete)
31 = Kickstart V1.1 (NTSC only - obsolete)
32 = Kickstart V1.1 (PAL only - obsolete)
33 = Kickstart V1.2 (the oldest revision still in use)
34 = Kickstart V1.3 (adds autoboot to Kickstart V1.2)

If you specify a higher version number than is installed in the system, the open will fail. Except as noted, all functions documented in this manual will work with Kickstart V33 and greater. Since V34 Kickstart is nearly identical to V33, it is generally NOT wise to require it.

If the library is disk-resident, it is loaded and initialized. The **OpenLibrary()** function returns the address of the library base, which you must assign to a **specific** variable. (Case is important.) This base is used to access the functions of the library. Zero is returned if something goes wrong with the open.

Library bases represent a midpoint in the library. Below the base are the function vectors, above the base is a data area:

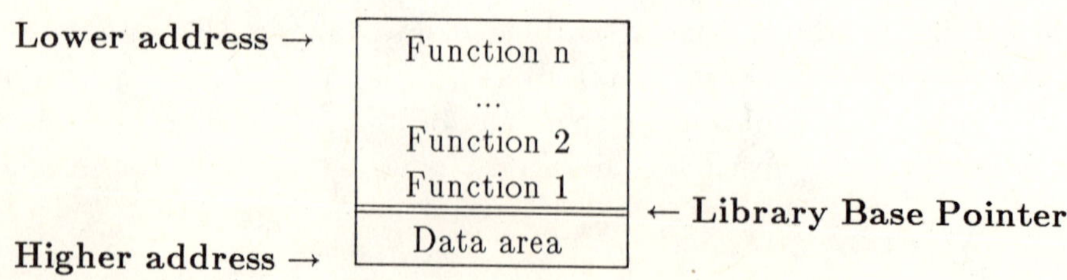

The names of the libraries that are currently part of the Amiga software and associated library base pointer names are as follows:

Library Name	Library Base Pointer Name
diskfont.library	DiskfontBase
dos.library	DOSBase† ‡
exec.library	SysBase†
graphics.library	GfxBase
icon.library	IconBase
intuition.library	IntuitionBase
layers.library	LayersBase
mathffp.library	MathBase
mathtrans.library	MathTransBase
mathieeedoubbas.library	MathIeeeDoubBasBase
mathieeedoubtrans.library	MathIeeeDoubTransBase
romboot.library	(V1.3 system private)
translator.library	TranslatorBase
version.library	(system private)

†Automatically opened by the standard C startup module
‡ dos library is documented in the *AmigaDOS Manual*

All Amiga libraries accept parameters in registers, and return the result in data register D0. All routines return a full 32 bit longword, even if fewer bits are significant. This allows programs and functions that are written in assembler to communicate quickly. It also eliminates the dependence on the stack frame conventions of any particular language. Some C language compilers for the Amiga can generate parameters directly into registers, others translate any Amiga library call into a stub routine that moves parameters from the stack to registers. See the "amiga.lib" appendix for more details.

Complete examples follow:

```c
/*
 * A complete ready-to-compile example of library use.
 * The library is opened, checked, used and closed.
 * See the intuition.library document for a description
 * of what the DisplayBeep() function does.
 *
 */
struct Library *OpenLibrary();            /* declare return type */

struct IntuitionBase *IntuitionBase;      /* get storage for base */

void main()
{
    IntuitionBase=(struct IntuitionBase *)
                  OpenLibrary("intuition.library",33L);
    if(!IntuitionBase)  /* check if it actually opened */
        exit(20);

    DisplayBeep(0L);    /* use the library function */

    CloseLibrary(IntuitionBase);
}
```

```
************************************************************************
*
* A complete ready-to-assemble example of library use.   The intuition
* library is opened, checked, used, and closed.  See the intuition
* document for a description of what the DisplayBeep() function does.
*
* When calling an Amiga library, the base pointer *must* be in
* A6... the library is free to depend on this.  Registers D0,D1,A0
* and A1 may be destroyed by the library, all others will be preserved.
*
* Normally the constants _AbsExecBase, _LVOOpenLibrary,
* _LVOCloseLibrary, and _LVODisplayBeep would be resolved by the linker
* from the file "amiga.lib".  For this minimal example we define them
* explicitly.
*
_AbsExecBase            EQU  4          ;Where exec's library base is
_LVOOpenLibrary         EQU -552        ;Offset from base for OpenLibrary
_LVOCloseLibrary        EQU -414        ;  "
_LVODisplayBeep         EQU -96         ;  "

        move.l  _AbsExecBase,a6         ;Move exec.library base to a6
        lea.l   IntuiName(pc),a1        ;Pointer to "intuition.library"
        moveq   #33,d0                  ;Version
        jsr     _LVOOpenLibrary(a6)     ;Call exec's OpenLibrary()
        tst.l   d0
        bne.s   open_ok
        moveq   #20,d0                  ;Set failure code
        rts                             ;Failed exit

open_ok move.l  d0,a6                   ;Put IntuitionBase in a6.
        suba.l  a0,a0                   ;Load zero into a0
        jsr     _LVODisplayBeep(a6)     ;Call intuition's DisplayBeep()

        move.l  a6,a1                   ;Put IntuitionBase into a1
        move.l  _AbsExecBase,a6
        jsr     _LVOCloseLibrary(a6)    ;Call exec's CloseLibrary()
        moveq   #0,d0                   ;Set return code
        rts

IntuiName:      dc.b 'intuition.library',0
        END
```

TABLE OF CONTENTS

TABLE OF CONTENTS

```
diskfont.library/AvailFonts                      diskfont.library/AvailFonts

   NAME
        AvailFonts - build an array of all fonts in memory / on disk

   SYNOPSIS
        error = AvailFonts(buffer, bufBytes, types);
                           A0      D0        D1

   FUNCTION
        AvailFonts fills a user supplied buffer with the structure,
        described below, that contains information about all the
        fonts available in memory and/or on disk.  Those fonts
        available on disk need to be loaded into memory and opened
        via OpenDiskFont, those already in memory are accessed via
        OpenFont.  The TextAttr structure required by the open calls
        is part of the information AvailFonts supplies.

        When AvailFonts fails, it returns the number of extra bytes
        it needed to complete the command.  Add this number to your
        current buffer size, allocate a new buffer, and try again.
        If the second AvailFonts call fails, abort the operation.

   INPUTS
        buffer - memory to be filled with struct AvailFontsHeader
                followed by an array of AvailFonts elements, which
                contains entries for the available fonts and their
                names.
        bufBytes - the number of bytes in the buffer
        types - AFF_MEMORY is set to search memory for fonts to fill
                the structure, AFF_DISK is set to search the disk for
                fonts to fill the structure.  Both can be specified.

   RESULTS
        buffer - filled with struct AvailFontsHeader followed by the
                AvailFonts elements, There will be duplicate entries
                for fonts found both in memory and on disk, differing
                only by type.  The existance of a disk font in the
                buffer indicates that it exists as an entry in a font
                contents file -- the underlying font file has not been
                checked for validity, thus an OpenDiskFont of it may
                fail.
        error - if non-zero, this indicates the number of bytes needed
                for AvailFonts in addition to those supplied.  Thus
                structure elements were not returned because of
                insufficient bufBytes.
```

```
diskfont.library/DisposeFontContents

   NAME
        DisposeFontContents - free the result from NewFontContents

   SYNOPSIS
        DisposeFontContents(fontContentsHeader)
                            A1

   FUNCTION
        This function frees the array of FontContents entries
        returned by NewFontContents.

   INPUTS
        fontContentsHeader - a struct FontContentsHeader pointer
            returned by NewFontContents.

   EXCEPTIONS
        This command was first made available as of version 34.

        A fontContentsHeader other than one acquired by a call
        NewFontContents will crash.

   SEE ALSO
        NewFontContents to get structure freed here.
```

diskfont.library/NewFontContents

```
diskfont.library/NewFontContents          diskfont.library/NewFontContents

   NAME
       NewFontContents - create a FontContents structs for a font

   SYNOPSIS
        fontContentsHeader = NewFontContents(fontsLock,fontName)
       D0                                    A0        A1

   FUNCTION
        This function creates a new array of FontContents entries
        that describe all the fonts associated with the fontName,
        specifically, all those in the font directory whose name
        is that of the font sans the ".font" suffix.

   INPUTS
        fontsLock - a DOS lock on the FONTS: directory (or other
            directory where the font contents file and associated
            font directory resides).
        fontName - the font name, with the ".font" suffix, which
            is also the name of the font contents file.

   RESULT
        fontContentsHeader - a struct FontContentsHeader pointer.

   EXCEPTIONS
        This command was first made available as of version 34.

        D0 is zero if the fontName is does not have a ".font" suffix,
        or a DOS error occurred, or memory could not be allocated for
        the fontContentsHeader.

   SEE ALSO
        DisposeFontContents to free the structure acquired here.
```

diskfont.library/OpenDiskFont

```
diskfont.library/OpenDiskFont                  diskfont.library/OpenDiskFont

   NAME
       OpenDiskFont - load and get a pointer to a disk font.

   SYNOPSIS
       font = OpenDiskFont(textAttr)
       D0                  A0

   FUNCTION
       This function finds the font with the specified textAttr on
       disk, loads it into memory, and returns a pointer to the font
       that can be used in subsequent SetFont and CloseFont calls.
       It is important to match this call with a corresponding
       CloseFont call for effective management of font memory.

       If the font is already in memory, the copy in memory is used.
       The disk copy is not reloaded.

   INPUTS
       textAttr - a TextAttr structure that describes the text font
               attributes desired.

   RESULTS
       D0 is zero if the desired font cannot be found.

   BUGS
       This routine will not work well with font names whose file
        name components are longer than the maximum allowed
        (30 characters).
```

TABLE OF CONTENTS

```
NAME
     AbortIO - attempt to abort an in-progress I/O request

SYNOPSIS
     error = AbortIO(iORequest)
     D0              A1
     BYTE AbortIO(struct IORequest *);

FUNCTION
     Ask a device to abort a previously started IORequest.  This is done
     by calling the device's ABORTIO vector, with your given IORequest.


     AbortIO is a request that device that may or may not grant.  If
     successful, the device will stop processing the IORequest, and
     reply to it earlier than it would otherwise have done.

NOTE
     AbortIO() does NOT remove the IORequest from your ReplyPort, OR
     wait for it to complete.  After an AbortIO() you must wait normally
     for the reply message before actually reusing the request [see
     WaitIO()].

     If a request has already completed when AbortIO() is called, no
     action is taken.

EXAMPLE
         AbortIO(timer_request);
         WaitIO (timer_request);
         /* Message is free to be reused */

RESULTS
     error - Depending on the device and the state of the request, it
             may not be possible to abort a given I/O request.  If for
             some reason the device cannot abort the request, it should
             return an error code in D0.

INPUTS
     iORequest - pointer to an I/O request block.

RESULTS
     error - zero if successful, else an error is returned

SEE ALSO
     WaitIO, DoIO, SendIO, CheckIO
```



```
NAME
     AddDevice -- add a device to the system

SYNOPSIS
     AddDevice(device)
               A1
     void AddDevice(struct Device *);

FUNCTION
     This function adds a new device to the system device list, making
     it available to other programs.  The device must be ready to be
     opened at this time.

INPUTS
     device - pointer to a properly initialized device node

SEE ALSO
     RemDevice, OpenDevice, CloseDevice, MakeLibrary
```

```
NAME
     AddHead -- insert node at the head of a list

SYNOPSIS
     AddHead(list, node)
             A0    A1
     void AddHead(struct List *, struct Node *)

FUNCTION
     Add a node to the head of a doubly linked list. Assembly
     programmers may prefer to use the ADDHEAD macro from
     "exec/lists.i".

WARNING
     This function does not arbitrate for access to the list.  The
     calling task must be the owner of the involved list.

INPUTS
     list - a pointer to the target list header
     node - the node to insert at head

SEE ALSO
     AddTail, Enqueue, Insert, Remove, RemHead, RemTail
```



```
NAME
     AddIntServer -- add an interrupt server to the system

SYNOPSIS
     AddIntServer(intNum, interrupt)
                  D0-0:4  A1
     void AddIntServer(ULONG, struct Interrupt *);

FUNCTION
     This function adds a new interrupt server to a given server chain.
     The node is located on the chain in a priority dependent position.
     If this is the first server on a particular chain, interrupts will
     be enabled for that chain.

     Each link in the chain will be called in priority order until the
     chain ends or one of the servers returns with the 68000's Z
     condition code clear (indicating non-zero).  Servers on the chain
     should return with the Z flag clear if the interrupt was
     specifically for that server, and no one else.  VERTB servers
     should always return Z set.  (Take care with High Level
     Language servers, the language may not have a mechanism for
     reliably setting the Z flag on exit).

     Servers are called with the following register conventions:

         D0 - scratch
         D1 - scratch

         A0 - scratch
         A1 - server is_Data pointer (scratch)

         A5 - jump vector register (scratch)
         A6 - scratch

         all other registers - must be preserved

INPUTS
     intNum - the Portia interrupt bit number (0 through 14). Processor
              level seven interrupts (NMI) are encoded as intNum 15.
              The PORTS, VERTB, COPER and EXTER and NMI interrupts are
              set up as server chains.
     interrupt - pointer to an interrupt server node

BUGS
     The graphics library's VBLANK server incorrectly assumes that
     address register A0 will contain a pointer to the custom chips.  If
     you add a server at a priority of 10 or greater, you must
     compensate for this by providing the expected value ($DFF000).

SEE ALSO
     RemIntServer, SetIntVector, hardware/intbits.h
```

```
NAME
     AddLibrary -- add a library to the system

SYNOPSIS
     AddLibrary(library)
                A1
     void AddLibrary(struct Library *);

FUNCTION
     This function adds a new library to the system, making it available
     to other programs.  The library should be ready to be opened at
     this time.  It will be added to the system library name list, and
     the checksum on the library entries will be calculated.

INPUTS
     library - pointer to a properly initialized library structure

SEE ALSO
     RemLibrary, CloseLibrary, OpenLibrary, MakeLibrary
```



```
NAME
     AddMemList - add memory to the system free pool

SYNOPSIS
     AddMemList( size, attributes, pri, base, name )
                 D0    D1          D2   A0    A1
     void AddMemList(ULONG, ULONG, LONG, APTR, char *);

FUNCTION
     Add a new region of memory to the system free pool.  The first few
     bytes will be used to hold the MemHeader structure.  The remainder
     will be made available to the rest of the world.

INPUTS
     size - the size (in bytes) of the memory area
     attributes - the attributes word that the memory pool will have
     pri  - the priority for this memory.  CHIP memory has a pri of -10,
            16 bit expansion memory has a priority of 0.  The higher the
            priority, the closer to the head of the memory list it will
            be placed.
     base - the base of the new memory area
     name - the name that will be used in the memory header, or NULL
            if no name is to be provided.  This name is not copied, so it
            must remain valid for as long as the memory header is in the
            system.

SEE ALSO
     AllocMem, exec/memory.h
```

exec.library/AddPort

NAME
    AddPort -- add a public message port to the system

SYNOPSIS
```
AddPort(port)
        A1
void AddPort(struct MsgPort *);
```

FUNCTION
    This function attaches a message port structure to the system's public message port list, where it can be found by the FindPort() function. The name and priority fields of the port structure must be initialized prior to calling this function. If the user does not require the priority field, it should be initialized to zero.

    Only ports that will be searched for with FindPort() need to be added to the system list. In addition, adding ports is often useful during debugging. If the port will be searched for, the priority field should be at least 1 (to avoid the large number of inactive ports at priority zero). If the port will be searched for often, set the proritiry in the 50-100 range (so it will be before other less used ports).

    Once a port has been added to the naming list, you must be careful to remove the port from the list (via RemPort) before deallocating its memory.

NOTE
    A point of confusion is that clearing a MsgPort structure to all zeros is not enough to prepare it for use. As mentioned in the Exec chapter of the ROM Kernel Manual, the List for the MsgPort must be initialized. This is automatically handled by AddPort(), and amiga.lib/CreatePort. This initialization can be done manually with amiga.lib/NewList or the assembly NEWLIST macro.

INPUTS
    port - pointer to a message port

SEE ALSO
    RemPort, FindPort, amiga.lib/CreatePort, amiga.lib/NewList

exec.library/AddResource

NAME
    AddResource -- add a resource to the system

SYNOPSIS
```
AddResource(resource)
            A1
void AddResource(APTR);
```

FUNCTION
    This function adds a new resource to the system and makes it available to other users. The resource must be ready to be called at this time.

    Resources currently have no system-imposed structure, other than starting with a standard Exec node or Library structure.

INPUTS
    resource - pointer an initialized resource node

SEE ALSO
    RemResource, OpenResource

```
NAME
     AddSemaphore -- add a signal semaphore to the system

SYNOPSIS
     AddSemaphore(signalSemaphore)
                  A1
     void AddSemaphore(struct SignalSemaphore *);

FUNCTION
     This function attaches a signal semaphore structure to the system's
     public signal semaphore list.  The name and priority fields of the
     semaphore structure must be initialized prior to calling this
     function.  If you do not want to let others rendezvous with this
     semaphore, use InitSemaphore() instead.

     If a semaphore has been added to the naming list, you must be
     careful to remove the semaphore from the list (via RemSemaphore)
     before deallocating its memory.

     Semaphores that are linked together in an allocation list (which
     ObtainSemaphoreList() would use) may not be added to the system
     naming list, because the facilities use the link field of the
     signal semaphore in incompatible ways

INPUTS
    signalSemaphore -- an signal semaphore structure

BUGS
     Does not work in Kickstart V33/34.  Instead use this code:

         #include "exec/execbase.h"
             ...
         void AddSemaphore(s)
         struct SignalSemaphore *s;
         {
             InitSemaphore(s);
             Forbid();
             Enqueue(&SysBase->SemaphoreList,s);
             Permit();
         }

SEE ALSO
     RemSemaphore, FindSemaphore, InitSemaphore
```



```
NAME
     AddTail -- append node to tail of a list

SYNOPSIS
     AddTail(list, node)
             A0    A1
     void AddTail(struct List *, struct Node *);

FUNCTION
     Add a node to the tail of a doubly linked list.  Assembly
     programmers may prefer to use the ADDTAIL macro from
     "exec/lists.i".

WARNING
     This function does not arbitrate for access to the list.  The
     calling task must be the owner of the involved list.

INPUTS
     list - a pointer to the target list header
     node - a pointer to the node to insert at tail of the list

SEE ALSO
     AddHead, Enqueue, Insert, Remove, RemHead, RemTail
```

```
NAME
     AddTask -- add a task to the system

SYNOPSIS
     AddTask(task, initialPC, finalPC)
             A1    A2         A3
     void AddTask(struct Task *, APTR, APTR);

FUNCTION
     Add a task to the system.  A reschedule will be run; the task with
     the highest priority in the system will start to execute (this may
     or may not be the new task).

     Certain fields of the task control block must be initialized and a
     stack allocated prior to calling this function.  The absolute
     smallest stack that is allowable is something in the range of 100
     bytes, but in general the stack size is dependent on what
     subsystems are called. In general 256 bytes is sufficient if only
     Exec is called, and 4K will do if anything in the system is called.
     DO NOT UNDERESTIMATE.  If you use a stack sniffing utility,
     leave a healthy pad above the minimum value.

     This function will temporarily use space from the new task's stack
     for the task's initial set of registers.  This space is allocated
     starting at the SPREG location specified in the task control block
     (not from SPUPPER).  This means that a task's stack may contain
     static data put there prior to its execution.  This is useful for
     providing initialized global variables or some tasks may want to
     use this space for passing the task its initial arguments.

     A task's initial registers are set to zero (except the PC).

     The TC_MEMENTRY field of the task structure may be extended by
     the user to hold additional MemLists (as returned by AllocEntry()).
     These will be automatically be deallocated at RemTask() time.
     If the code you have used to start the task has already added
     something to the MEMENTRY list, simply use AddHead to add your
     new MemLists in.  If no initialization has been done, a NewList will
     need to be performed.

NOTE
     AddTask clears out TC_FLAGS.

INPUTS
     task - pointer to the task control block (TCB)
     initialPC - the initial entry point's address
     finalPC - the finalization code entry point's address.  If zero,
               the system will use a general finalizer. This pointer is
               placed on the stack as if it were the outermost return
               address.

WARNING
     Tasks are a low-level building block, and are unable to call
     dos.library, or any system routine that might call dos.library.
     See the AmigaDOS CreateProc() for information on Processes.

SEE ALSO
     RemTask, FindTask, amiga.lib/CreateTask, dos/CreateProc,
     amiga.lib/NewList
```



```
NAME
     Alert -- alert the user of an error

SYNOPSIS
     Alert(alertNum, parameters)
           D7        A5
     void Alert(ULONG, APTR);

FUNCTION
     Alerts the user of a serious system problem.  This function will
     bring the system to a grinding halt, and do whatever is necessary
     to present the user with a message stating what happened.
     Interrupts are disabled, and an attempt to post the alert is made.
     If that fails, the system is reset.  When the system comes up
     again, Exec notices the cause of the failure and tries again to
     post the alert.

     If the Alert is a recoverable type, this call MAY return.

     This call may be made at any time, including interrupts.

INPUT
     alertNum - a number indicating the particular alert
     parameters - currently points to the number that forms the
                  second part of a "Guru meditation" message. Typically
                  this is a pointer to the task that was active at the
                  time of the problem.

NOTE
     Much more needs to be said about this function and its implications.

SEE ALSO
     exec/alerts.h
```

```
NAME
     AllocAbs -- allocate at a given location

SYNOPSIS
     memoryBlock = AllocAbs(byteSize, location)
     D0                     D0        A1
     void *AllocAbs(ULONG, APTR);

FUNCTION
     This function attempts to allocate memory at a given absolute
     memory location.  Often this is used by boot-surviving entities
     such as recoverable ram-disks.  If the memory is already being
     used, or if there is not enough memory to satisfy the request,
     AllocAbs will return NULL.

     This block may not be exactly the same as the requested block
     because of rounding, but if the return value is non-zero, the block
     is guaranteed to contain the requested range.

INPUTS
     byteSize - the size of the desired block in bytes
                This number is rounded up to the next larger
                block size for the actual allocation.
     location - the address where the memory MUST be.


RESULT
     memoryBlock - a pointer to the newly allocated memory block, or
                   NULL if failed.

NOTE
     If the free list is corrupt, the system will panic with alert
     AN_MemCorrupt, $81000005.

SEE ALSO
     AllocMem, FreeMem
```



```
NAME
     Allocate - allocate a block of memory

SYNOPSIS
     memoryBlock=Allocate(MemHeader, byteSize)
     D0                   A0         D0
     void *Allocate(struct MemHeader *, ULONG);

FUNCTION
     This function is used to allocate blocks of memory from a given
     private free memory pool (as specified by a MemHeader and its
     memory chunk list).  Allocate will return the first free block that
     is greater than or equal to the requested size.

     All blocks, whether free or allocated, will be block aligned;
     hence, all allocation sizes are rounded up to the next block even
     value (e.g. the minimum allocation resolution is currently 8
     bytes).

     This function can be used to manage an application's internal data
     memory.  Note that no arbitration of the MemHeader and associated
     free chunk list is done.  You must be the owner before calling
     Allocate.

INPUTS
     freeList - points to the memory list header
     byteSize - the size of the desired block in bytes

RESULT
     memoryBlock - a pointer to the just allocated free block.
            If there are no free regions large enough to satisfy the
            request, return zero.

EXAMPLE
     #include "exec/types.h"
     #include "exec/memory.h"
     void *AllocMem();
     #define BLOCKSIZE 4000L /* Or whatever you want */

     void main()
     {
     struct MemHeader *mh;
     struct MemChunk  *mc;
     APTR   block1;
     APTR   block2;

         /* Get the MemHeader needed to keep track of our new block */
         mh = (struct MemHeader *)
              AllocMem((long)sizeof(struct MemHeader), MEMF_CLEAR );
         if( !mh )
             exit(10);

         /* Get the actual block the above MemHeader will manage */
         mc = (struct MemChunk *)AllocMem( BLOCKSIZE, 0L );
         if( !mc )
             {
             FreeMem( mh, (long)sizeof(struct MemHeader) ); exit(10);
             }

         mh->mh_Node.ln_Type = NT_MEMORY;
         mh->mh_Node.ln_Name = "myname";
         mh->mh_First = mc;
         mh->mh_Lower = (APTR) mc;
         mh->mh_Upper = (APTR) ( BLOCKSIZE + (ULONG) mc );
         mh->mh_Free  = BLOCKSIZE;

         /* Set up first chunk in the freelist */
         mc->mc_Next  = NULL;
         mc->mc_Bytes = BLOCKSIZE;
```

```
        block1 = (APTR) Allocate( mh, 20L );
        block2 = (APTR) Allocate( mh, 314L );
        printf("mh=$%lx mc=$%lx\n",mh,mc);
        printf("Block1=$%lx, Block2=$%lx\n",block1,block2;;

        FreeMem( mh, (long)sizeof(struct MemHeader) );
        FreeMem( mc, BLOCKSIZE );
    }
```

NOTE
    If the free list is corrupt, the system will panic with alert AN_MemCorrupt, $81000005.

SEE ALSO
    Deallocate

NAME
    AllocEntry -- allocate many regions of memory

SYNOPSIS

```
    memList = AllocEntry(memList)
    D0                   A0
    struct MemList *AllocEntry(struct MemList *);
```

FUNCTION
    This routine takes a memList structure and allocates enough memory to hold the required memory as well as a MemList structure to keep track of it.

    These MemList structures may be linked together in a task control block to keep track of the total memory usage of this task. (See the description of TC_MEMENTRY under RemTask).

INPUTS
    memList -- A MemList structure filled in with MemEntry structures.

RESULTS
    memList -- A different MemList filled in with the actual memory allocated in the me_Addr field, and their sizes in me_Length. If enough memory cannot be obtained, then the requirements of the allocation that failed is returned and bit 31 is set.

EXAMPLES
    The user wants five regions of 2, 4, 8, 16, and 32 bytes in size with requirements of MEMF_CLEAR, MEMF_PUBLIC, MEMF_CHIP!MEMF_CLEAR, MEMF_FAST!MEMF_CLEAR, and MEMF_PUBLIC!MEMF_CLEAR respectively. The following code fragment would do that:

```
    MemListDecl:
        DS.B    LN_SIZE                 * reserve space for list node
        DC.W    5                       * number of entries
        DC.L    MEMF_CLEAR                      * entry #0
        DC.L    2
        DC.L    MEMF_PUBLIC                     * entry #1
        DC.L    4
        DC.L    MEMF_CHIP!MEMF_CLEAR            * entry #2
        DC.L    8
        DC.L    MEMF_FAST!MEMF_CLEAR            * entry #3
        DC.L    16
        DC.L    MEMF_PUBLIC!MEMF_CLEAR          * entry #4
        DC.L    32

    start:
        LEA.L   MemListDecl(PC),A0
        JSR     _LVOAllocEntry(a6)
        BCLR.L  #31,D0
        BEQ.S   success

        ------- Type of memory that we failed on is in D0
```

BUGS
    If any one of the allocations fails, this function fails to back out fully. This is fixed by the "SetPatch" program on V1.3 Workbench disks.

SEE ALSO
    exec/memory.h

```
NAME
     AllocMem -- allocate memory given certain requirements

SYNOPSIS
     memoryBlock = AllocMem(byteSize, attributes)
     D0                     D0        D1
     void *AllocMem(ULONG, ULONG);

FUNCTION
     This is the memory allocator to be used by system code and
     applications.  It provides a means of specifying that the allocation
     should be made in a memory area accessible to the chips, or
     accessible to shared system code.

     Memory is allocated based on requirements and options.  Any
     "requirement" must be met by a memory allocation, any "option" will
     be applied to the block regardless.  AllocMem will try all memory
     spaces until one is found with the proper requirements and room for
     the memory request.

INPUTS
     byteSize - the size of the desired block in bytes.  This number is
             rounded up to the next larger memory chunk size for the
             actual allocation.  The chunk size is guaranteed to be
             at least 8.


     attributes -
         requirements

             MEMF_CHIP:      Only certain parts of memory are reachable
                             by the special chip sets' DMA circuitry.
                             Anything that will use on-chip DMA *MUST*
                             be in memory with this attribute. DMA
                             includes screen memory, things that are
                             blitted, audio blocks, sprites and
                             trackdisk.device buffers.

             MEMF_FAST:      This is non-chip memory.  It is possible
                             for the processor to get locked out of chip
                             memory under certain conditions. If one
                             cannot accept these delays, then one should
                             use FAST memory (by default the system will
                             allocate from FAST memory first anyway).

                             This is rarely specified, since it would
                             cause incompatibility with non-expanded
                             machines.

             MEMF_PUBLIC:    Memory must not be mapped, swapped,
                             or otherwise made non-addressable. ALL
                             MEMORY THAT IS REFERENCED VIA INTERRUPTS
                             AND/OR BY OTHER TASKS MUST BE EITHER PUBLIC
                             OR LOCKED INTO MEMORY! This includes both
                             code and data.

         options

             MEMF_CLEAR:     The memory will be initialized to all
                             zeros.


RESULT
     memoryBlock - a pointer to the newly allocated block. If there are
             no free regions large enough to satisfy the request (or if
             the amount of requested memory is invalid), return zero.

WARNING
     The result of any memory allocate MUST be checked, and a viable
     error handling path taken.  ANY allocation may fail if memory has
     been filled.

EXAMPLES
     AllocMem(321,MEMF_CHIP) - private chip memory
     AllocMem(25,MEMF_PUBLIC|MEMF_CLEAR) - a cleared "public" system
                         structure that does not require chip memory.

NOTE
     If the free list is corrupt, the system will panic with alert
     AN_MemCorrupt, $81000005.

     This function may not be called from interrupts.

SEE ALSO
     FreeMem
```

```
NAME
     AllocSignal -- allocate a signal bit

SYNOPSIS
     signalNum = AllocSignal(signalNum)
     D0                      D0
     BYTE AllocSignal(LONG);

FUNCTION
     Allocate a signal bit from the current tasks' pool.  Either a
     particular bit, or the next free bit may be allocated.  The signal
     associated with the bit will be properly initialized (cleared).  At
     least 16 user signals are available per task.  Signals should be
     deallocated before the task exits.

     If the signal is already in use (or no free signals are available)
     a -1 is returned.

     This function can only be used by the currently running task.

WARNING
     Signals may not be allocated or freed from exception handling code.

INPUTS
     signalNum - the desired signal number {of 0..31} or -1 for no
                 preference.

RESULTS
     signalNum - the signal bit number allocated {0..31}. If no signals
                 are available, this function returns -1.

SEE ALSO
     FreeSignal
```



```
NAME
     AllocTrap -- allocate a processor trap vector

SYNOPSIS
     trapNum = AllocTrap(trapNum)
     D0                  D0
     LONG AllocTrap(LONG);

FUNCTION
     Allocate a trap number from the current task's pool.  These trap
     numbers are those associated with the 68000 TRAP type instructions.
     Either a particular number, or the next free number may be
     allocated.

     If the trap is already in use (or no free traps are available) a -1
     is returned.

     This function only affects the currently running task.

     Traps are sent to the trap handler pointed at by tc_TrapCode.
     Unless changed by user code, this points to a standard trap
     handler.  The stack frame of the exception handler will be:

             0(SP) = Exception vector number.  This will be in the
                     range of 32 to 47 (corresponding to the
                     Trap #1...Trap #15 instructions).
             4(SP) = 68000/68010/68020/68030, etc. exception frame

     tc_TrapData is not used.


WARNING
     Traps may not be allocated or freed from exception handling code.
     You are not allowed to write to the exception table yourself.  In
     fact, on some machines you will have trouble finding it - the VBR
     register may be used to remap its location.

INPUTS
     trapNum - the desired trap number {of 0..15} or -1
               for no preference.

RESULTS
     trapNum - the trap number allocated {of 0..15}.  If no traps are
               available, this function returns -1.  Instructions of the
               form "Trap #trapNum" will be sent to the task's trap
               handler.

SEE ALSO
     FreeTrap
```

exec.library/AttemptSemaphore exec.library/AttemptSemaphore

```
NAME
     AttemptSemaphore -- try to obtain without blocking

SYNOPSIS
     success = AttemptSemaphore(signalSemaphore)
     D0                         A0
     LONG AttemptSemaphore(struct SignalSemaphore *);

FUNCTION
     This call is similar to ObtainSemaphore(), except that it will not
     block if the semaphore could not be locked.

INPUT
    signalSemaphore -- an initialized signal semaphore structure

RESULT
     success -- TRUE if the semaphore was locked, false if some
         other task already possessed the semaphore.

SEE ALSO
     ObtainSemaphore(), ReleaseSemaphore(), exec/semaphores.h
```

exec.library/AvailMem exec.library/AvailMem

```
NAME
     AvailMem -- memory available given certain requirements

SYNOPSIS
     size = AvailMem(attributes)
     D0              D1
     ULONG AvailMem(ULONG);

FUNCTION
     This function returns the amount of free memory given certain
     attributes.

     To find out what the largest block of a particular type is, add
     MEMF_LARGEST into the requirements argument.

WARNING
     Due to the effect of multitasking, the value returned may not
     actually be the amount of free memory available at that instant.

INPUTS
     requirements - a requirements mask as specified in AllocMem.  Any
                    of the AllocMem bits are valid, as is MEMF_LARGEST
                    which returns the size of the largest block matching
                    the requirements.

RESULT
     size - total free space remaining (or the largest free block).

EXAMPLE
     AvailMem(MEMF_CHIP|MEMF_LARGEST);
     /* return size of largest available chip memory chunk */

SEE ALSO
     exec/memory.h
```

```
NAME
    Cause -- cause a software interrupt

SYNOPSIS
    Cause(interrupt)
          A1
    void Cause(struct Interrupt *);

FUNCTION
     This function causes a software interrupt to occur.  If it is
     called from user mode (and processor level 0), the software
     interrupt will preempt the current task.  This call is often used
     by high-level hardware interrupts to defer medium-length processing
     down to a lower interrupt level.  Note that a software interrupt is
     still a real interrupt, and must obey the same restrictions on what
     system routines it may call.

     Currently only 5 software interrupt priorities are implemented:
     -32, -16, 0, +16, and +32.  Priorities in between are truncated,
     values outside the -32/+32 range are not allowed.

NOTE
     When setting up the Interrupt structure, set the node type to
     NT_INTERRUPT.

IMPLEMENTATION
     1> Checks if the node type is NT_SOFTINT.  If so does nothing since
        the softint is already pending.  No nest count is maintained.
     2> Sets the node type to NT_SOFTINT.
     3> Links into one of the 5 priority queues.
     4> Pokes the hardware interrupt bit used for softints.

     The node type returns to NT_INTERRUPT after removal from the list.

INPUTS
     interrupt - pointer to a properly initialized interrupt node
```



```
NAME
     CheckIO -- get the status of an IORequest

SYNOPSIS
     result = CheckIO(iORequest)
     D0                A1
     BOOL CheckIO(struct IORequest *);

FUNCTION
     This function determines the current state of an I/O request and
     returns FALSE if the I/O has not yet completed.  This function
     effectively hides the internals of the I/O completion mechanism.

     CheckIO will NOT remove the returned IORequest from the reply port.
     This is best performed with WaitIO(). If the request has already
     completed, WaitIO() will return quickly. Use of the Remove()
     function is dangerous, since other tasks may still be adding things
     to your message port; a Disable() would be required.

     This function should NOT be used to busy loop (looping until IO is
     complete).  WaitIO() is provided for that purpose.

INPUTS
     iORequest - pointer to an I/O request block

RESULTS
     result - null if I/O is still in progress.  Otherwise
              D0 points to the IORequest block.

SEE ALSO
     DoIO, SendIO, WaitIO, AbortIO
```

NAME
CloseDevice -- conclude access to a device

SYNOPSIS
```
CloseDevice(iORequest)
            A1
void CloseDevice(struct IORequest *);
```

FUNCTION
This function informs the device that access to a device/unit previously opened has been concluded. The device may perform certain house-cleaning operations.

The user must ensure that all outstanding IORequests have been returned before closing the device. The AbortIO function can kill any stragglers.

After a close, the I/O request structure is free to be reused.

INPUTS
iORequest - pointer to an I/O request structure

SEE ALSO
OpenDevice

NAME
CloseLibrary -- conclude access to a library

SYNOPSIS
```
CloseLibrary(library)
             A1
void CloseLibrary(struct Library *);
```

FUNCTION
This function informs the system that access to the given library has been concluded. The user must not reference the library or any routine in the library after this close.

INPUTS
library - pointer to a library node

SEE ALSO
OpenLibrary

NAME
    CopyMem - general purpose memory copy routine

SYNOPSIS
```
CopyMem( source, dest, size )
         A0      A1    D0
void CopyMem(APTR,APTR,ULONG);
```

FUNCTION
    CopyMem is a general purpose, fast memory copy routine. It can deal with arbitrary lengths, with its pointers on arbitrary alignments. It attempts to optimize larger copies with more efficient copies, it uses byte copies for small moves, parts of larger copies, or the entire copy if the source and destination are misaligned with respect to each other.

    Arbitrary overlapping copies are not supported.

    The internal implementation of this routine will change from system to system, and may be implemented via hardware DMA.

INPUTS
    source - a pointer to the source data region
    dest - a pointer to the destination data region
    size - the size (in bytes) of the memory area

SEE ALSO
    CopyMemQuick

NAME
    CopyMemQuick - optimized memory copy routine

SYNOPSIS
```
CopyMemQuick( source, dest, size )
              A0      A1    D0
void CopyMem(ULONG *,ULONG *,ULONG);
```

FUNCTION
    CopyMemQuick is a highly optimized memory copy routine, with restrictions on the size and alignment of its arguments. Both the source and destination pointers must be longword aligned. In addition, the size must be an integral number of longwords (e.g. the size must be evenly divisible by four).

    Arbitrary overlapping copies are not supported.

    The internal implementation of this routine will change from system to system, and may be implemented via hardware DMA.

INPUTS
    source - a pointer to the source data region, long aligned
    dest - a pointer to the destination data region, long aligned
    size - the size (in bytes) of the memory area

SEE ALSO
    CopyMem

NAME
    Deallocate -- deallocate a block of memory

SYNOPSIS

```
Deallocate(MemHeader, memoryBlock, byteSize)
           A0         A1           D0
void Deallocate(struct MemHeader *,APTR,ULONG);
```

FUNCTION

This function deallocates memory by returning it to the appropriate private free memory pool. This function can be used to free an entire block allocated with the above function, or it can be used to free a sub-block of a previously allocated block. Sub-blocks must be an even multiple of the memory chunk size (currently 8 bytes).

This function can even be used to add a new free region to an existing MemHeader, however the extent pointers in the MemHeader will no longer be valid.

If memoryBlock is not on a block boundary (MEM_BLOCKSIZE) then it will be rounded down in a manner compatible with Allocate(). Note that this will work correctly with all the memory allocation routines, but may cause surprises if one is freeing only part of a region. The size of the block will be rounded up, so the freed block will fill to an even memory block boundary.

INPUTS
    freeList - points to the free list
    memoryBlock - memory block to return
    byteSize - the size of the desired block in bytes. If NULL, nothing happens.

SEE ALSO
    Allocate

NAME
    Debug -- run the system debugger

SYNOPSIS

```
void Debug(0L);
           D0
```

FUNCTION

This function calls the system debugger. By default this debugger is "ROM-WACK". Other debuggers are encouraged to take over this entry point (via SetFunction()) so that when an application calls Debug(), the alternative debugger will get control. Currently a zero is passed to allow future expansion.

NOTE

The Debug() call may be made when the system is in a questionable state; if you have a SetFunction() patch, make few assumptions, be prepared for Supervisor mode, and be aware of differences in the Motorola stack frames on the 68000,'10,'20, and '30.

SEE ALSO
    SetFunction
    your favorite debugger's manual
    the ROM-WACK chapter of the ROM Kernel Manual

```
exec.library/Disable                                   exec.library/Disable

    NAME
        Disable -- disable interrupt processing.

    SYNOPSIS
        Disable();

        void Disable(void);

    FUNCTION
        Prevents interrupts from being handled by the system, until a
        matching Enable() is executed.  Disable() implies Forbid().

    RESULTS
        All interrupt processing is deferred until the task executing makes
        a call to Enable() or is placed in a wait state.  Normal task
        rescheduling does not occur while interrupts are disabled.  In order
        to restore normal interrupt processing, the programmer must execute
        exactly one call to Enable() for every call to Disable().

        IMPORTANT REMINDER:

        It is important to remember that there is a danger in using
        disabled sections.  Disabling interrupts for more than ~250
        microseconds will prevent vital system functions (especially serial
        I/0) from operating in a normal fashion.

        Think twice before using Disable(), then think once more.
        After all that, think again.  With enough thought, the need
        for a Disable() can often be eliminated.
        Do not use a macro for Disable(), insist on the real thing.

        This call may be made from interrupts, it will have the effect
        of locking out all higher-level interrupts (lower-level interrupts
        are automatically disabled by the CPU).

    WARNING
        In the event of a task entering a Wait after disabling interrupts,
        the system "breaks" the forbidden state and runs normally until the
        task which called Forbid() is rescheduled.

        If caution is not taken, this can cause subtle bugs, since any
        device or DOS call will (in effect) cause your task to wait.

    SEE ALSO
        Forbid, Permit, Enable
```

```
exec.library/DoIO                                         exec.library/DoIO

    NAME
        DoIO -- perform an I/O command and wait for completion

    SYNOPSIS
        error = DoIO(iORequest)
        D0           A1
        BYTE DoIO(struct IORequest *);

    FUNCTION
        This function requests a device driver to perform the I/O command
        specified in the I/O request.  This function will always wait until
        the I/O request is fully complete.

    IMPLEMENTATION
        This function first tries to complete the IO via the "Quick I/O"
        mechanism.  The io_Flags field is always set to IOF_QUICK (0x01)
        before the internal device call.

    INPUTS
        iORequest - pointer to an IORequest initialized by OpenDevice()

    RESULTS
        error - a sign-extended copy of the io_Error field of the
                IORequest.  Most device commands require that the error
                return be checked.

    SEE ALSO
        SendIO, CheckIO, WaitIO, AbortIO, amiga.lib/BeginIO
```

exec.library/Enable

```
exec.library/Enable                                         exec.library/Enable

   NAME
        Enable -- permit system interrupts to resume.

   SYNOPSIS
        Enable();

        void Enable(void);

   FUNCTION
        Allow system interrupts to again occur normally, after a matching
        Disable() has been executed.

   RESULTS
        Interrupt processing is restored to normal operation. The
        programmer must execute exactly one call to Enable() for every call
        to Disable().

   SEE ALSO
        Forbid, Permit, Disable
```

exec.library/Enqueue

```
exec.library/Enqueue                                        exec.library/Enqueue

   NAME
        Enqueue -- insert or append node to a system queue

   SYNOPSIS
        Enqueue(list, node)
                A0    A1
        void Enqueue(struct List *, struct Node *);

   FUNCTION
        Insert or append a node into a system queue.  The insert is
        performed based on the node priority -- it will keep the list
        properly sorted.  New nodes will be inserted in front of the first
        node with a lower priority.   Hence a FIFO queue for nodes of equal
        priority

   WARNING
        This function does not arbitrate for access to the list.  The
        calling task must be the owner of the involved list.

   INPUTS
        list - a pointer to the system queue header
        node - the node to enqueue

   SEE ALSO
        AddHead, AddTail, Insert, Remove, RemHead, RemTail
```

```
NAME
     FindName -- find a system list node with a given name

SYNOPSIS
     node = FindName(start, name)
     D0              A0     A1
     struct Node *FindName(struct List *,char *);

FUNCTION
     Traverse a system list until a node with the given name is found.
     To find multiple occurrences of a string, this function may be
     called with a node starting point.

     No arbitration is done for access to the list!  If multiple tasks
     access the same list, an arbitration mechanism such as
     SignalSemaphores must be used.

INPUTS
     start - a list header or a list node to start the search
             (if node, this one is skipped)
     name - a pointer to a name string terminated with null

RESULTS
     node - a pointer to the node with the same name else
         zero to indicate that the string was not found.
```



```
NAME
     FindPort -- find a given system message port

SYNOPSIS
     port = FindPort(name)
     D0              A1
     struct MsgPort *FindPort(char *);

FUNCTION
     This function will search the system message port list for a port
     with the given name.  The first port matching this name will be
     returned.  No arbitration of the port list is done.  This function
     MUST be protected with A Forbid()/Permit() pair!

EXAMPLE
     #include "exec/types.h"
     struct MsgPort *FindPort();

     ULONG SafePutToPort(message, portname)
     struct Message *message;
     char           *portname;
     {
     struct MsgPort *port;

         Forbid();
             port = FindPort(portname);
             if (port)
                 PutMsg(port,message);
         Permit();
         return((ULONG)port); /* If zero, the port has gone away */
     }

INPUT
     name - name of the port to find

RETURN
     port - a pointer to the message port, or zero if
             not found.
```

```
NAME
    FindResident - find a resident module by name

SYNOPSIS
    resident = FindResident(name)
    D0                      A1
    struct Resident *FindResident(char *);

FUNCTION
    Find the resident tag with the given name.  If found return a
    pointer to the resident tag structure, else return zero.

    Resident modules are used by the system to pull all its parts
    together at startup.  Resident tags are also found in disk based
    devices and libraries.

INPUTS
    name - pointer to name string

RESULT
    resident - pointer to the resident tag structure or
            zero if none found.

SEE ALSO
    exec/resident.h
```



```
NAME
    FindSemaphore -- find a given system signal semaphore

SYNOPSIS
    signalSemaphore = FindSemaphore(name)
    D0                              A1
    struct SignalSemaphore *FindSemaphore(char *);

FUNCTION
    This function will search the system signal semaphore list for a
    semaphore with the given name.  The first semaphore matching this
    name will be returned.

INPUT
    name - name of the semaphore to find

RESULT
    semaphore - a pointer to the signal semaphore, or zero if not
            found.

BUGS
    This routine does not arbitrate for access to the semaphore list,
    surround the call with a Forbid()/Permit() pair.
```

exec.library/FindTask

```
NAME
     FindTask -- find a task with the given name or find oneself

SYNOPSIS
     task = FindTask(name)
     D0              A1
     struct Task *FindTask(char *);

FUNCTION
     This function will check all task queues for a task with the given
     name, and return a pointer to its task control block.  If a NULL
     name pointer is given a pointer to the current task will be
     returned.

     Finding oneself with a NULL for the name is very quick.  Finding a
     task by name is very system expensive, and will disable interrupts
     for a long time.

INPUT
     name - pointer to a name string

RESULT
     task - pointer to the task (or Process)
```

exec.library/Forbid

```
NAME
    Forbid -- forbid task rescheduling.

SYNOPSIS
    Forbid()

    void Forbid(void);

FUNCTION
    Prevents other tasks from being scheduled to run by the dispatcher,
    until a matching Permit() is executed, or this task is scheduled to
    Wait.  Interrupts are NOT disabled.

RESULTS
    The current task will not be rescheduled as long as it is ready to
    run.  In the event that the current task enters a wait state, other
    tasks may be scheduled.  Upon return from the wait state, the original
    task will continue to run without disturbing the Forbid().

    Calls to Forbid() nest. In order to restore normal task rescheduling,
    the programmer must execute exactly one call to Permit() for every
    call to Forbid().

WARNING
    In the event of a task entering a Wait after a Forbid(), the system
    "breaks" the forbidden state and runs normally until the task which
    called Forbid() is rescheduled.
    If caution is not taken, this can cause subtle bugs, since any
    device or DOS call will (in effect) cause your task to wait.

    Forbid() is not useful or safe from within an interrupt routine
    (Since interrupts are always higher priority than tasks, and
    since interrupts are allowed interrupt a Forbid()).

SEE ALSO
    Permit, Disable
```

```
exec.library/FreeEntry                                  exec.library/FreeEntry

   NAME
        FreeEntry -- free many regions of memory

   SYNOPSIS
        FreeEntry(memList)
                  A0
        void FreeEntry(struct MemList *);

   FUNCTION
        This routine takes a memList structure (as returned by AllocEntry)
        and frees all the entries.

   INPUTS
        memList -- pointer to structure filled in with MemEntry
                   structures

   SEE ALSO
        AllocEntry
```

```
exec.library/FreeMem                                      exec.library/FreeMem

   NAME
        FreeMem -- deallocate with knowledge

   SYNOPSIS
        FreeMem(memoryBlock, byteSize)
                A1           D0
        void FreeMem(void *,ULONG);

   FUNCTION
        Free a region of memory, returning it to the system pool from which
        it came.  Freeing partial blocks back into the system pool is
        unwise.

   NOTE
        If a block of memory is freed twice, the system will GURU. The
        Alert is AN_FreeTwice ($81000009). Future versions may add more
        sanity checks to the memory lists.

   INPUTS
        memoryBlock - memory block to free
                If the memoryBlock previously returned by an allocation
                routine.
        byteSize - the size of the block in bytes

   SEE ALSO
        AllocMem
```

NAME
    FreeSignal -- free a signal bit

SYNOPSIS
```
FreeSignal(signalNum)
           D0
FreeSignal(ULONG);
```

FUNCTION
    This function frees a previously allocated signal bit for reuse. This call must be performed while running in the same task in which the signal was allocated.

WARNING
    Signals may not be allocated or freed from exception handling code.

INPUTS
    signalNum - the signal number to free {0..31}

NAME
    FreeTrap -- free a processor trap

SYNOPSIS
```
FreeTrap(trapNum)
         D0
void FreeTrap(ULONG);
```

FUNCTION
    This function frees a previously allocated trap number for reuse. This call must be performed while running in the same task in which the trap was allocated.

WARNING
    Traps may not be allocated or freed from exception handling code.

INPUTS
    trapNum - the trap number to free {of 0..15}

```
NAME
     GetCC -- get condition codes in a 68010 compatible way.

SYNOPSIS
     conditions = GetCC()
       D0
     UWORD = GetCC(void);

FUNCTION
     The 68000 processor has a "MOVE SR,<ea>" instruction which gets a
     copy of the processor condition codes.

     On the 68010,20 and 30 CPUs, "MOVE SR,<ea>" is privileged.  User
     code will trap if it is attempted.  These processors need to use
     the "MOVE CCR,<ea>" instruction instead.

     This function provides a means of obtaining the CPU condition codes
     in a manner that will make upgrades transparent.  This function is
     very short and quick.

RESULTS
     conditions - the 680XX condition codes
```



```
NAME
     GetMsg -- get next message from a message port

SYNOPSIS
     message = GetMsg(port)
     D0               A0
     struct Message *GetMsg(struct MsgPort *);

FUNCTION
     This function receives a message from a given message port. It
     provides a fast, non-copying message receiving mechanism. The
     received message is removed from the message port.

     This function will not wait.  If a message is not present this
     function will return zero.  If a program must wait for a message,
     it can Wait() on the signal specified for the port or use the
     WaitPort() function.  There can only be one task waiting for any
     given port.

     Getting a message does not imply to the sender that the message is
     free to be reused by the sender.  When the receiver is finished
     with the message, it may ReplyMsg() it back to the sender.


     Getting a signal does NOT always imply a message is ready.  More
     than one message may arrive per signal, and signals may show up
     without messages.  Typically you must loop to GetMsg() until it
     returns zero, then Wait() or WaitPort().

INPUT
     port - a pointer to the receiver message port

RESULT
     message - a pointer to the first message available.  If
               there are no messages, return zero.
               Callers must be prepared for zero at any time.

SEE ALSO
     PutMsg, ReplyMsg, WaitPort, Wait, exec/ports.h
```

```
NAME
     InitCode - initialize resident code modules

SYNOPSIS
     InitCode(startClass, version)
              D0          D1
     void InitCode(ULONG,ULONG);

FUNCTION
     Initialize all resident modules with the given startClass and with
     versions equal or greater than that specified. Modules are
     initialized in a prioritized order.

     Resident modules are used by the system to pull all its parts
     together at startup.  Resident tags are also found in disk based
     devices and libraries.

INPUTS
     startClass - the class of code to be initialized: coldstart,
                  coolstart, warmstart, ...
     version    - a major version number

SEE ALSO
     exec/resident.h
```



```
NAME
     InitResident - initialize resident module

SYNOPSIS
     InitResident(resident, segList)
                  A1        D1
     void InitResident(struct Resident *,BPTR);

FUNCTION
     Initialize a module (these are also called "ROM-tags").  This includes
     interpreting the fields of the ROM-tag, and calling the initialization
     hooks.

     An automatic method of library/device base and vector table
     initialization is also provided through the use of a such a ROM-tag
     (Resident) structure.  In this case, the initial code hunk of the
     library or device should contain "MOVEQ #-1,d0; RTS;".  Following
     that must be an initialized Resident structure including RTF_AUTOINIT
     in rt_Flags, and an rt_Init pointer which points to four longwords as
     follows:

         - Size of your library/device base structure including initial
           Library or Device structure.
         - Pointer to a longword table of standard, then library
           specific function offsets, terminated with -1L.
         - Pointer to data table in exec/InitStruct format for
           initialization of Library or Device structure.
         - Pointer to library initialization routine, which will receive
           library/device base in d0, segment in a0, and must return
           non-zero to link the library/device into the device/library
           list.

SEE ALSO
     exec/resident.h
```

```
NAME
     InitSemaphore -- initialize a signal semaphore

SYNOPSIS
     InitSemaphore(signalSemaphore)
                   A0
     void InitSemaphore(struct SignalSemaphore *);

FUNCTION
     This function initializes a signal semaphore and prepares it for
     use.  It does not allocate anything, but does initialize list
     pointers and the semaphore counters.

     Semaphores are often used to protect critical data structures
     or hardware that can only be accessed by one task at a time.
     After initialization, the address of the SignalSemaphore may be
     made available to any number of tasks.  Typically a task will
     try to ObtainSemaphore(), passing this address in.  If no other
     task owns the semaphore, then the call will lock and return
     quickly.  If more tasks try to ObtainSemaphore(), they will
     be put to sleep.  When the owner of the semaphore releases
     it, the next waiter in turn will be woken up.

     Semaphores are often preferable to the old-style Forbid()/Permit()
     type arbitration.  With Forbid()/Permit() *all* other tasks are
     prevented from running.  With semaphores, only those tasks that
     need access to whatever the semaphore protects are subject
     to waiting.

INPUT
     signalSemaphore -- a signal semaphore structure (with all fields
                        set to zero before the call)

SEE ALSO
     ObtainSemaphore(), AttemptSemaphore(), ReleaseSemaphore()
     exec/semaphores.h
```



```
NAME
     InitStruct - initialize memory from a table

SYNOPSIS
     InitStruct(initTable, memory, size);
                A1         A2      D0
     void InitStruct(struct InitStruct *, APTR, ULONG);

FUNCTION
     Clear a memory area except those words whose data and offset values
     are provided in the initialization table.  Typically only assembly
     programs take advantage of this, and only with the macros defined
     in "exec/initializers.i".

     The initialization table has byte commands to

          |a    ||byte|      |given||byte|         |once         |
     load |count||word| into |next ||rptr| offset, |repetitively |
                 |long|

     Not all combinations are supported.  The offset, when specified, is
     relative to the memory pointer provided (Memory), and is initially
     zero.  The initialization data (InitTable) contains byte commands
     whose 8 bits are interpreted as follows:

     ddssnnnn
         dd  the destination type (and size):
             00  next destination, nnnn is count
             01  next destination, nnnn is repeat
             10  destination offset is next byte, nnnn is count
             11  destination offset is next rptr, nnnn is count
         ss  the size and location of the source:
             00  long, from the next two aligned words
             01  word, from the next aligned word
             10  byte, from the next byte
             11  ERROR - will cause an ALERT (see below)
       nnnn  the count or repeat:
          count  the (number+1) of source items to copy
         repeat  the source is copied (number+1) times.

     initTable commands are always read from the next even byte. Given
     destination offsets are always relative to memory (A2).

     The command 00000000 ends the InitTable stream: use 00010001 if you
     really want to copy one longword.

     24 bit APTR not supported for 68020 compatibility -- use long.

INPUTS
     initTable - the beginning of the commands and data to init
             Memory with.  Must be on an even boundary unless only
             byte initialization is done.
     memory - the beginning of the memory to initialize.  Must be
             on an even boundary if size is specified.
     size - the size of memory, which is used to clear it before
             initializing it via the initTable.  If Size is zero,
             memory is not cleared before initializing.

             We recommend an EVEN number for size; odd byte sizes
             may be truncated.

SEE ALSO
     exec/initializers.i
```

```
exec.library/Insert                                    exec.library/Insert

   NAME
       Insert -- insert a node into a list

   SYNOPSIS
       Insert(list, node, listNode)
              A0    A1    A2
       void Insert(struct List *, struct Node *, struct Node *);

   FUNCTION
       Insert a node into a doubly linked list AFTER a given node
       position.  Insertion at the head of a list is possible by passing a
       zero value for listNode, though the AddHead function is slightly
       faster for that special case.

   WARNING
       This function does not arbitrate for access to the list.  The
       calling task must be the owner of the involved list.

   INPUTS
       list - a pointer to the target list header
       node - the node to insert
       listNode - the node after which to insert

    SEE ALSO
       AddHead, AddTail, Enqueue, RemHead, Remove, RemTail
```

```
exec.library/MakeFunctions                      exec.library/MakeFunctions

   NAME
       MakeFunctions -- construct a function jump table

   SYNOPSIS
       tableSize = MakeFunctions(target, functionArray, funcDispBase)
       D0                        A0      A1             A2
       ULONG MakeFunctions(APTR,APTR,APTR);

   FUNCTION
       This function constructs a function jump table of the type used by
       resources, libraries, and devices.  It allows the table to be built
       anywhere in memory, and can be used both for initialization and
       replacement. This function also supports function pointer
       compression by expanding relative displacements into absolute
       pointers.

   INPUT
       destination - the target address for the high memory end of the
               function jump table.  Typically this will be the library
               base pointer.

       functionArray - pointer to an array of function pointers or
               function displacements.  If funcDispBase is zero, the array
               is assumed to contain absolute pointers to functions. If
               funcDispBase is not zero, then the array is assumed to
               contain word displacements to functions.  In both cases,
               the array is terminated by a -1 (of the same size as the
               actual entry.

       funcDispBase - pointer to the base about which all function
               displacements are relative.  If zero, then the function
               array contains absolute pointers.

   RESULT
       tableSize - size of the new table in bytes.

   SEE ALSO
       exec/MakeLibrary
```

```
NAME
     MakeLibrary -- construct a library

SYNOPSIS
     library = MakeLibrary(vectors, structure, init, dSize, segList)
     D0                    A0       A1         A2    D0     D1
     struct Library *MakeLibrary
                          (APTR,struct InitStruct *,APTR,ULONG,BPTR);

FUNCTION
     This function is used for constructing a library vector and data
     area.  The same call is used to make devices.  Space for the library
     is allocated from the system's free memory pool. The size fields of
     the library are filled.  The data portion of the library is
     initialized.  init may point to a library specific entry point,
     or NULL if no call is to be made.

INPUTS
     vectors - pointer to an array of function pointers or function
               displacements.  If the first word of the array is -1, then
               the array contains relative word displacements (based off
               of vectors); otherwise, the array contains absolute
               function pointers. The vector list is terminated by a -1
               (of the same size as the pointers).

     structure - points to an "InitStruct" data region.  If NULL,
               then it will not be used.

     init -    an entry point that will be called before adding the
               library to the system.  If null, it will not be called. When
               it is called, it will be called with the libAddr in D0 and
               the segList parameter in A0. The result of the init function
               will be the result returned by MakeLibrary.
               A Forbid()/Permit() pair surrounds this call.

     dSize - the size of the library data area, including the
               standard library node data.

    segList - pointer to an AmigaDOS SegList (segment list).
               This is passed to a library's init code, and is used later
               for removing the library from memory.

RESULT
     library - the reference address of the library.  This is the
               address used in references to the library, not the
               beginning of the memory area allocated.  If the library
               vector table require more system memory than is
               available, this function will return NULL.

SEE ALSO
     InitStruct, InitResident, exec/initializers.i
```



```
NAME
     ObtainSemaphore -- gain exclusive access to a semaphore

SYNOPSIS
     ObtainSemaphore(signalSemaphore)
                     A0
     void ObtainSemaphore(struct SignalSemaphore *);

FUNCTION
     Signal semaphores are used to gain exclusive access to an object.
     ObtainSemaphore is the call used to gain this access.  If another
     user currently has the semaphore locked the call will block until
     the object is available.

     If the current task already has locked the semaphore and attempts to
     lock it again the call will still succeed.  A "nesting count" is
     incremented each time the current owning task of the semaphore calls
     ObtainSemaphore().  This counter is decremented each time
     ReleaseSemaphore() is called.  When the counter returns to zero the
     semaphore is actually released, and the next waiting task is called.

     A queue of waiting tasks is maintained on the stacks of the waiting
     tasks.  Each will be called in turn as soon as the current task
     releases the semaphore.

     Signal Semaphores are different than Procure()/Vacate() semaphores.
     The former requires less CPU time, especially if the semaphore is
     not currently locked.  They require very little set up and user
     thought.  The latter flavor of semaphore make no assumptions about
     how they are used -- they are completely general.  Unfortunately
     they are not as efficient as signal semaphores, and require the
     locker to have done some setup before doing the call.

INPUT
    signalSemaphore -- an initialized signal semaphore structure

SEE ALSO
     InitSemaphore(), ReleaseSemaphore()
     AttemptSemaphore(), ObtainSemaphoreList()
```

```
NAME
     ObtainSemaphoreList -- get a list of semaphores.

SYNOPSIS
     ObtainSemaphoreList(list)
                         A0
     void ObtainSemaphoreList(struct List *);

FUNCTION
     Signal semaphores may be linked together into a list. This routine
     takes a list of these semaphores and attempts to lock all of them at
     once. This call is preferable to applying ObtainSemaphore() to each
     element in the list because it attempts to lock all the elements
     simultaneously, and won't deadlock if someone is attempting to lock
     in some other order.

     This routine assumes that only one task at a time will attempt to
     lock the entire list of semaphores.  In other words, there needs to
     be a higher level lock (perhaps another signal semaphore...) that is
     used before someone attempts to lock the semaphore list via
     ObtainSemaphoreList().

     Note that deadlocks may result if this call is used AND someone
     attempts to use ObtainSemaphore() to lock more than one semaphore on
     the list.  If you wish to lock more than semaphore (but not all of
     them) then you should obtain the higher level lock (see above)

INPUT
    list -- a list of signal semaphores

SEE ALSO
    ObtainSemaphore(), ReleaseSemaphore(), ReleaseSemaphoreList()
```



```
NAME
     OldOpenLibrary -- obsolete OpenLibrary

SYNOPSIS
     library = OldOpenLibrary(libName)
     D0                       A1
     struct Library *OldOpenLibrary(APTR);

FUNCTION
     The 1.0 release of the Amiga system had an incorrect version of
     OpenLibrary that did not check the version number during the
     library open.  This obsolete function is provided so that object
     code compiled using a 1.0 system will still run.

     This exactly the same as "OpenLibrary(libName,0L);"

INPUTS
     libName - the name of the library to open

RESULTS
     library - a library pointer for a successful open, else zero

SEE ALSO
     CloseLibrary
```

```
NAME
     OpenDevice -- gain access to a device

SYNOPSIS
     error = OpenDevice(devName, unitNumber, ioRequest, flags)
     D0                 A0       D0          A1         D1
     BYTE OpenDevice(char *,ULONG,struct IORequest *,ULONG);

FUNCTION
     This function opens the named device/unit and initializes the given
     I/O request block.  Specific documentation on opening procedures
     may come with certain devices.

     The device may exist in memory, or on disk; this is transparent to
     the OpenDevice caller.

     A full path name for the device name is legitimate.  For example
     "test:devs/fred.device".  This allows the use of custom devices
     without requiring the user to copy the device into the system's
     DEVS: directory.

NOTE
     All calls to OpenDevice should have matching calls to CloseDevice!

INPUTS
     devName - requested device name

     unitNumber - the unit number to open on that device.  The format of
             the unit number is device specific.  If the device does
             not have separate units, send a zero.

     ioRequest - the I/O request block to be returned with
             appropriate fields initialized.

     flags - additional driver specific information.  This is sometimes
             used to request opening a device with exclusive access.

RESULTS
     error - Returns a sign-extended copy of the io_Error field
             of the IORequest.  Zero if successful, else an error code
             is returned.

BUGS
     AmigaDOS file names are not case sensitive, but Exec lists are.  If
     the library name is specified in a different case than it exists on
     disk, unexpected results may occur.

     Tasks should not be allowed to make OpenDevice calls that will
     cause the device to be loaded from disk (since tasks are not
     allowed to make dos.library calls).

SEE ALSO
     CloseDevice, DoIO, SendIO, CheckIO, AbortIO, WaitIO
```



```
NAME
     OpenLibrary -- gain access to a library

SYNOPSIS
     library = OpenLibrary(libName, version)
     D0                    A1       D0
     struct Library *OpenLibrary(char *,ULONG);

FUNCTION
     This function returns a pointer to a library that was previously
     installed into the system.  If the requested library is exists, and
     if the library version is greater than or equal to the requested
     version, then the open will succeed.

     The device may exist in memory, or on disk; this is transparent to
     the OpenDevice caller.  Only Processes are allowed to call
     OpenLibrary (since OpenLibrary may in turn call dos.library).

     A full path name for the library name is legitimate.  For example
     "wp:libs/wp.library".  This allows the use of custom libraries
     without requiring the user to copy the library into the system's
     LIBS: directory.

NOTE
     All calls to OpenLibrary should have matching calls to CloseLibrary!

INPUTS
     libName - the name of the library to open

     version - the version of the library required.

RESULTS
     library - a library pointer for a successful open, else zero

BUGS
     AmigaDOS file names are not case sensitive, but Exec lists are. If
     the library name is specified in a different case than it exists on
     disk, unexpected results may occur.

     Tasks should not be allowed to make OpenLibrary calls that will
     cause the library to be loaded from disk (since tasks are not
     allowed to make dos.library requests).

SEE ALSO
     CloseLibrary
```

exec.library/OpenResource

NAME
    OpenResource -- gain access to a resource

SYNOPSIS
```
resource = OpenResource(resName)
D0                      A1
APTR OpenResource(char *);
```

FUNCTION
    This function returns a pointer to a resource that was previously installed into the system.

    There is no CloseResource() function.

INPUTS
    resName - the name of the resource requested.

RESULTS
    resource - if successful, a resource pointer, else NULL

exec.library/Permit

NAME
    Permit -- permit task rescheduling.

SYNOPSIS
```
Permit()

void Permit(void);
```

FUNCTION
    Allow other tasks to be scheduled to run by the dispatcher, after a matching Forbid() has been executed.

RESULTS
    Other tasks will be rescheduled as they are ready to run. In order to restore normal task rescheduling, the programmer must execute exactly one call to Permit() for every call to Forbid().

SEE ALSO
    Forbid, Disable, Enable

```
NAME
     Procure -- bid for a message lock (semaphore)

SYNOPSIS
     result = Procure(semaphore, bidMessage)
     D0               A0         A1
     BYTE Procure(struct Semaphore *, struct Message *);

FUNCTION
     This function is used to obtain a message based semaphore lock.  If
     the lock is immediate, Procure() returns a true result, and the
     bidMessage is not used.   If the semaphore is already locked,
     Procure() returns false, and the task must wait for the bidMessage
     to arrive at its reply port.

     Straight "Semaphores" use the message system.  They are therefore
     queueable, and users may wait on several of them at the same time.
     This makes them more powerful than "Signal Semaphores"

INPUT
     semaphore - a semaphore message port.  This port is used to queue
     all pending lockers.  This port should be initialized with the
     PA_IGNORE option, as the MP_SigTask field is used for a pointer to
     the current locker message (not a task). New semaphore ports must
     also have the SM_BIDS word initialized to -1.  If the semaphore is
     public, it should be named, its priority set, and the added with
     AddPort. Message port priority is often used for anti-deadlock
     locking conventions.

RESULT
     result - true when the semaphore is free.  In such cases no waiting
     needs to be done.  If false, then the task should wait at its
     bidMessage reply port.

BUGS
     Procure() and Vacate() do not have proven reliability.

SEE ALSO
     Vacate()
```



```
NAME
     PutMsg -- put a message to a message port

SYNOPSIS
     PutMsg(port, message)
            A0    A1
     void PutMsg(struct MsgPort *, struct Message *);

FUNCTION
     This function attaches a message to a given message port. It
     provides a fast, non-copying message sending mechanism.

     Messages can be attached to only one port at a time.  The message
     body can be of any size or form.  Because messages are not copied,
     cooperating tasks share the same message memory.  The sender task
     should not recycle the message until it has been replied by the
     receiver.  Of course this depends on the message handling conventions
     setup by the involved tasks.  If the ReplyPort field is non-zero,
     when the message is replied by the receiver, it will be sent back to
     that port.

     Any one of the following actions can be set to occur when a message
     is put:

             1. no special action
             2. signal a given task (specified by MP_SIGTASK)
             3. cause a software interrupt (specified by MP_SIGTASK)

     The action is selected depending on the value found in the MP_FLAGS
     of the destination port.

IMPLEMENTATION
     1.  Sets the LN_TYPE field to "NT_MESSAGE".
     2.  Attaches the message to the destination port.
     3.  Performs the specified arrival action at the destination.

INPUT
     port - pointer to a message port
     message - pointer to a message

SEE ALSO
     GetMsg, ReplyMsg, exec/ports.h
```

```
   NAME
        RawDoFmt -- format data into a character stream.

   SYNOPSIS
        RawDoFmt(FormatString, DataStream, PutChProc, PutChData);
                 A0            A1          A2         A3
        void(char *,APTR,void (*)(),APTR);

   FUNCTION
        perform "C"-language-like formatting of a data stream, outputting
        the result a character at a time.  Where % formatting commands are
        found in the FormatString, they will be replaced with the
        corresponding element in the DataStream.  %% must be used in the
        string if a % is desired in the output.

   INPUTS
        FormatString - a "C"-language-like null terminated format string,
        with the following supported % options:

             %[flags][width.limit][length]type

           flags  - only one allowed. '-' specifies left justification.
           width  - field width.  If the first character is a '0', the
                    field will be padded with leading 0's.
             .    - must follow the field width, if specified
           limit  - maximum number of characters to output from a string.
                    (only valid for %s).
           length - size of input data defaults to WORD, 'l' changes this
                    to long.
           type   - supported types are:
                        d - decimal
                        x - hexadecimal
                        s - string
                        c - character

        DataStream - a stream of data that is interpreted according to
                     the format string.  Often this is a pointer into
                     the task's stack.
        PutChProc  - the procedure to call with each character to be
                     output, called as:

            PutChProc(Char,  PutChData);
                      D0-0:8 A3

                the procedure is called with a null Char at the end of
                the format string.

        PutChData - a value that is passed through to the PutChProc
                    procedure.  This is untouched by RawDoFmt, and may be
                    modified by the PutChProc.

  EXAMPLE
;
; Simple version of the C "sprintf" function.  Assumes C-style
; stack-based function conventions.
;
;   long eyecount;
;   eyecount=2;
;   sprintf(string,"%s have %ld eyes.","Fish",eyecount);
;
; would produce "Fish have 2 eyes." in the string buffer.
;
                XDEF _sprintf
_sprintf:       ; ( string, format, {values} )
                movem.l a2/a3/a6,-(sp)

                move.l  5*4(sp),a3        ;Get the output string pointer
                move.l  6*4(sp),a0        ;Get the FormatString pointer
                lea.l   7*4(sp),a1        ;Get the pointer to the DataStream
                lea.l   stuffChar(pc),a2
                move.l  _AbsExecBase,a6
                jsr     _LVORawDoFmt(a6)

                movem.l (sp)+,a2/a3/a6
                rts

;------ PutChProc function used by RawDoFmt -----------
stuffChar:      move.b  d0,(a3)+          ;Put data to output string
                rts

   WARNING
        This is the only Amiga ROM function that accepts word inputs. If
        your compiler defaults to longs, you will need to add a "l" to your
        % specification.  This can get strange for characters, which must
        look like "%lc".

   SEE ALSO
        Documentation on the C language "printf" call in any C language
        reference book.
```

NAME
    ReleaseSemaphore -- make signal semaphore available to others

SYNOPSIS
```
ReleaseSemaphore(signalSemaphore)
                 A0
void ReleaseSemaphore(struct SignalSemaphore *);
```

FUNCTION
    ReleaseSemaphore() is the inverse of ObtainSemaphore(). It makes the semaphore lockable to other users. If tasks are waiting for the semaphore and this this task is done with the semaphore then the next waiting task is signalled.

    Each ObtainSemaphore() call must be balanced by exactly one ReleaseSemaphore() call. This is because there is a nesting count maintained in the semaphore of the number of times that the current task has locked the semaphore. The semaphore is not released to other tasks until the number of releases matches the number of obtains.

    Needless to say, havoc breaks out if the task releases more times than it has obtained.

INPUT
    signalSemaphore -- an initialized signal semaphore structure

SEE ALSO
    ObtainSemaphore(), AttemptSemaphore()

NAME
    ReleaseSemaphoreList -- make a list of semaphores available

SYNOPSIS
```
ReleaseSemaphoreList(list)
                     A0
void ReleaseSemaphoreList(struct List *);
```

FUNCTION
    ReleaseSemaphoreList() is the inverse of ObtainSemaphoreList(). It releases each element in the semaphore list.

    Needless to say, havoc breaks out if the task releases more times than it has obtained.

INPUT
    list -- a list of signal semaphores

SEE ALSO
    ObtainSemaphore(), ReleaseSemaphore(), ObtainSemaphoreList()
    AttemptSemaphore()

NAME
RemDevice -- remove a device from the system

SYNOPSIS
```
void RemDevice(device)
               A1
void RemDevice(struct Device *);
```

FUNCTION
This function calls the device's EXPUNGE vector, which requests that a device delete itself. The device may refuse to do this if it is busy or currently open. This is not typically called by user code.

There are certain, limited circumstances where it may be appropriate to attempt to specifically flush a certain device. Example:

```
/* Attempts to flush the named device out of memory. */
#include "exec/types.h"
#include "exec/execbase.h"

void FlushDevice(name)
char  *name;
{
struct Device *result;

   Forbid();
   if(result=(struct Device *)FindName(&SysBase->DeviceList,name))
       RemDevice(result);
   Permit();
}
```

INPUTS
device - pointer to a device node

SEE ALSO
AddLibrary

NAME
RemHead -- remove the head node from a list

SYNOPSIS
```
node = RemHead(list)
D0             A0
struct Node *RemHead(struct List *);
```

FUNCTION
Get a pointer to the head node and remove it from the list. Assembly programmers may prefer to use the REMHEAD macro from "exec/lists.i".

WARNING
This function does not arbitrate for access to the list. The calling task must be the owner of the involved list.

INPUTS
list - a pointer to the target list header

RESULT
node - the node removed or zero when empty list

SEE ALSO
AddHead, AddTail, Enqueue, Insert, Remove, RemTail

```
NAME
     RemIntServer -- remove an interrupt server

SYNOPSIS
     RemIntServer(intNum, interrupt)
                  D0      A1
     void RemIntServer(ULONG,struct Interrupt *);

FUNCTION
     This function removes an interrupt server node from the given
     server chain.

     If this server was the last one on this chain, interrupts for this
     chain are disabled.

INPUTS
     intNum - the Portia interrupt bit (0..14)
     interrupt - pointer to an interrupt server node

BUGS
     Under V33/34 Kickstart, the feature that disables the interrupt
     does not function.  For most server chains this does not
     cause a problem.

SEE ALSO
     AddIntServer, hardware/intbits.h
```



```
NAME
     RemLibrary -- remove a library from the system

SYNOPSIS
     void RemLibrary(library)
                     A1
     void RemLibrary(struct Library *);

FUNCTION
     This function calls the library's EXPUNGE vector, which requests
     that a library delete itself.  The library may refuse to do this if
     it is busy or currently open. This is not typically called by user
     code.

     There are certain, limited circumstances where it may be
     appropriate to attempt to specifically flush a certain Library.
     Example:

      /* Attempts to flush the named library out of memory. */
      #include "exec/types.h"
      #include "exec/execbase.h"

      void FlushLibrary(name)
      char  *name;
      {
      struct Library *result;

         Forbid();
         if(result=(struct Library *)FindName(&SysBase->LibList,name))
             RemLibrary(result);
         Permit();
      }

INPUTS
     library - pointer to a library node structure
```

NAME
    Remove -- remove a node from a list

SYNOPSIS
```
Remove(node)
       A1
void Remove(struct Node *);
```

FUNCTION
    Remove a node from whatever list it is in. Nodes that are not part of a list must not be Removed! Assembly programmers may prefer to use the REMOVE macro from "exec/lists.i".

WARNING
    This function does not arbitrate for access to the list. The calling task must be the owner of the involved list.

INPUTS
    node - the node to remove

SEE ALSO
    AddHead, AddTail, Enqueue, Insert, RemHead, RemTail

NAME
    RemPort -- remove a message port from the system

SYNOPSIS
```
RemPort(port)
        A1
void RemPort(struct MsgPort *);
```

FUNCTION
    This function removes a message port structure from the system's message port list. Subsequent attempts to rendezvous by name with this port will fail.

INPUTS
    port - pointer to a message port

SEE ALSO
    AddPort, FindPort

```
exec.library/RemResource                                  exec.library/RemResource

   NAME
        RemResource -- remove a resource from the system

   SYNOPSIS
        RemResource(resource)
                    A1
        void RemResource(APTR);

   FUNCTION
        This function removes an existing resource from the system resource
        list.

   INPUTS
        resource - pointer to a resource node

   SEE ALSO
        AddResource
```

```
exec.library/RemSemaphore                                exec.library/RemSemaphore

   NAME
        RemSemaphore -- remove a signal semaphore from the system

   SYNOPSIS
        RemSemaphore(signalSemaphore)
                     A1
        void RemSemaphore(struct SignalSemaphore *);

   FUNCTION
        This function removes a signal semaphore structure from the
        system's signal semaphore list.  Subsequent attempts to
        rendezvous by name with this semaphore will fail.

   INPUTS
       signalSemaphore -- an initialized signal semaphore structure

   SEE ALSO
        AddSemaphore, FindSemaphore
```

```
NAME
     RemTail -- remove the tail node from a list

SYNOPSIS
     node = RemTail(list)
     D0             A0
     struct Node *RemTail(struct List *);

FUNCTION
     Remove the last node from a list, and return a pointer to it. If
     the list is empty, return zero. Assembly programmers may prefer to
     use the REMTAIL macro from "exec/lists.i".

WARNING
     This function does not arbitrate for access to the list.  The
     calling task must be the owner of the involved list.

INPUTS
     list - a pointer to the target list header

RESULT
     node - the node removed or zero when empty list

SEE ALSO
     AddHead, AddTail, Enqueue, Insert, Remove, RemHead, RemTail
```



```
NAME
     RemTask -- remove a task from the system

SYNOPSIS
     RemTask(task)
             A1
     void RemTask(struct Task *);

FUNCTION
     This function removes a task from the system.  Deallocation of
     resources should have been performed prior to calling this
     function.  Removing some other task is very dangerous.  Generally
     is is best to arrange for tasks to call RemTask(0L) on themselves.

     RemTask will automagically free any memory lists attached to the
     task's TC_MEMENTRY list.

INPUTS
     task - pointer to the task node representing the task to be
            removed.  A zero value indicates self removal, and will
            cause the next ready task to begin execution.

SEE ALSO
     AddTask, exec/AllocEntry, amiga.lib/DeleteTask
```

```
exec.library/ReplyMsg                                   exec.library/ReplyMsg

   NAME
        ReplyMsg -- put a message to its reply port

   SYNOPSIS
        ReplyMsg(message)
                 A1
        void ReplyMsg(struct Message *);

   FUNCTION
        This function sends a message to its reply port.  This is usually
        done when the receiver of a message has finished and wants to
        return it to the sender (so that it can be re-used or deallocated,
        whatever).

        This call may be made from interrupts.

   INPUT
        message - a pointer to the message

   IMPLEMENTATION
        1> Places "NT_REPLYMSG" into LN_TYPE.
        2> Puts the message to the port specified by MN_REPLYPORT
           If there is no replyport, sets LN_TYPE to "NT_FREEMSG".

   SEE ALSO
        GetMsg, PutMsg, exec/ports.h
```

```
exec.library/SendIO                                       exec.library/SendIO

   NAME
        SendIO -- initiate an I/O command

   SYNOPSIS
        SendIO(iORequest)
               A1
        void SendIO(struct IORequest *);

   FUNCTION
        This function requests the device driver start processing the given
        I/O request.  The device will return control without waiting for
        the I/O to complete.

        The io_Flags field of the IORequest will be set to zero before the
        request is sent.

   INPUTS
        iORequest - pointer to an I/O request, or a device specific
                    extended IORequest.

   SEE ALSO
        DoIO, CheckIO, WaitIO, AbortIO
```

```
exec.library/SetExcept                                   exec.library/SetExcept

    NAME
        SetExcept -- define certain signals to cause exceptions

    SYNOPSIS
        oldSignals = SetExcept(newSignals, signalMask)
        D0                     D0          D1
        ULONG SetExcept(ULONG,ULONG);

    FUNCTION
        This function defines which of the task's signals will cause a
        private task exception.  When any of the signals occurs the task's
        exception handler will be dispatched.  If the signal occurred prior
        to calling SetExcept, the exception will happen immediately.

        The user function pointed to by the task's tc_ExceptCode gets
        called as:

            newExcptSet = <exceptCode>(signals, exceptData),SysBase
            D0                         D0       A1          A6

            signals - The set of signals that caused this exception.  These
                Signals have been disabled from the current set of signals
                that can cause an exception.

            exceptData - A copy of the task structure tc_ExceptData field.

            newExcptSet - The set of signals in NewExceptSet will be re-
                enabled for exception generation.  Usually this will be the
                same as the Signals that caused the exception.

        All registers are preserved by the system before the call.


    INPUTS
        newSignals - the new values for the signals specified in
                signalMask.
        signalMask - the set of signals to be effected

    RESULTS
        oldSignals - the prior exception signals

    EXAMPLE
        Get the current state of all exception signals:
            SetExcept(0,0)
        Change a few exception signals:
            SetExcept($1374,$1074)

    SEE ALSO
        Signal, SetSignal
```

```
exec.library/SetFunction                               exec.library/SetFunction

    NAME
        SetFunction -- change a function vector in a library

    SYNOPSIS
        oldFunc = SetFunction(library, funcOffset, funcEntry)
        D0                    A1       A0.W        D0
        APTR SetFunction(struct Library *,LONG,APTR);

    FUNCTION
        SetFunction is a functional way of changing where vectors in a
        library point.  They are changed in such a way that the
        checksumming process will never falsely declare a library to be
        invalid.

    NOTE
        SetFunction cannot be used on non-standard libraries like
        dos.library.  Here you must manually Forbid(), preserve all 6
        original bytes, set the new vector, SumLibrary(), then Permit().

    INPUTS
        library    - a pointer to the library to be changed
        funcOffset - the offset of the function to be replaced
        funcEntry  - pointer to new function

    RESULTS
        oldFunc    - pointer to the old function that was just replaced
```

```
NAME
     SetIntVector -- set a system interrupt vector

SYNOPSIS
     oldInterrupt = SetIntVector(intNumber, interrupt)
     D0                          D0-0:4     A1
     struct Interrupt *SetIntVector(ULONG, struct Interrupt *);

FUNCTION
     This function provides a mechanism for setting the system interrupt
     vectors.  These are non-sharable, setting something here
     disconnects the old handler.

     Both the code and data pointers of the vector are set to the new
     values.  A pointer to the old interrupt structure is returned. When
     the system calls the specified interrupt code the registers are
     setup as follows:

         D0 - scratch
         D1 - scratch (on entry: active portia
                       interrupts -> equals INTENA & INTREQ)

         A0 - scratch (on entry: pointer to base of custom chips
                       for fast indexing)
         A1 - scratch (on entry: interrupt's is_Data pointer)

         A5 - jump vector register (scratch on call)
         A6 - Exec library base pointer (scratch on call)

         all other registers - must be preserved

INPUTS
     intNum - the Portia interrupt bit number (0..14)
     interrupt - a pointer to an Interrupt structure containing
         the handler's entry point and data segment pointer. It is a
         good idea to give the node a name so that other users may
         identify who currently has control of the interrupt.

RESULT
     A pointer to the prior interrupt node which had control
     of this interrupt.

SEE ALSO
     AddIntServer, exec/interrupts.h, exec/hardware.h
```



```
NAME
     SetSignal -- define the state of this task's signals

SYNOPSIS
     oldSignals = SetSignal(newSignals, signalMask)
     D0                     D0          D1
     ULONG SetSignal(ULONG,ULONG);

FUNCTION
     This function defines the states of the task's signals.
     Setting the state of signals is considered dangerous.
     Reading the state of signals is safe.

INPUTS
     newSignals - the new values for the signals specified in
                  signalSet.
     signalMask - the set of signals to be affected

RESULTS
     oldSignals - the prior values for all signals

EXAMPLES
     Get the current state of all signals:
         SetSignal(0,0);
     Clear all signals:
         SetSignal(0,0xFFFFFFFFL);
     Clear the CTRL-C signal:
         SetSignal(0,SIGBREAKF_CTRL_C);


     Check if the CTRL-C signal was pressed:

         #include "libraries/dos.h"

         if(SetSignal(0L,0L) & SIGBREAKF_CTRL_C)
             printf("CTRL-C pressed!\n");

SEE ALSO
     Signal, Wait
```

```
NAME
     SetSR -- get and/or set processor status register

SYNOPSIS
     oldSR = SetSR(newSR, mask)
     D0            D0     D1
     ULONG SetSR(ULONG, ULONG);

FUNCTION
     This function provides a means of modifying the CPU status register
     in a "safe" way (well, how safe can a function like this be
     anyway?).  This function will only affect the status register bits
     specified in the mask parameter.  The prior content of the entire
     status register is returned.

INPUTS
     newSR - new values for bits specified in the mask.
         All other bits are not effected.
     mask - bits to be changed

RESULTS
     oldSR - the entire status register before new bits

EXAMPLES
     To get the current SR:
         currentSR = SetSR(0,0);
     To change the processor interrupt level to 3:
         oldSR = SetSR($0300,$0700);
     Set processor interrupts back to prior level:
         SetSR(oldSR,$0700);
```



```
NAME
     SetTaskPri -- get and set the priority of a task

SYNOPSIS
     oldPriority = SetTaskPri(task, priority)
     D0-0:8                   A1    D0-0:8
     BYTE SetTaskPri(struct Task *,LONG);

FUNCTION
     This function changes the priority of a task regardless of its
     state.  The old priority of the task is returned.  A reschedule is
     performed, and a context switch may result.

     To change the priority of the currently running task, pass the
     result of FindTask(0); as the task pointer.

INPUTS
     task - task to be affected
     priority - the new priority for the task

RESULT
     oldPriority - the tasks previous priority
```

NAME
    Signal -- signal a task

SYNOPSIS
```
Signal(task, signals)
       A1    D0
void Signal(struct Task *,ULONG);
```

FUNCTION
    This function signals a task with the given signals. If the task is currently waiting for one or more of these signals, it will be made ready and a reschedule will occur. If the task is not waiting for any of these signals, the signals will be posted to the task for possible later use. A signal may be sent to a task regardless of whether its running, ready, or waiting.

    This function is considered "low level". Its main purpose is to support multiple higher level functions like PutMsg.

    This function is safe to call from interrupts.

INPUT
    task - the task to be signalled
    signals - the signals to be sent

SEE ALSO
    Wait, SetSignal

NAME
    SumKickData -- compute the checksum for the Kickstart delta list

SYNOPSIS
```
void SumKickData(void)
```

FUNCTION
    The Amiga system has some ROM (or Kickstart) resident code that provides the basic functions for the machine. This code is unchangeable by the system software. This routine is part of a support system to modify parts of the ROM.

    The ROM code is linked together at run time via ROM-tags (also known as Resident structures, defined in exec/resident.h). These tags tell Exec's low level boot code what subsystems exist in which regions of memory. The current list of ROM-tags is contained in the ResModules field of ExecBase. By default this list contains any ROM-tags found in the address ranges $FC0000-$FFFFFF and $F00000-$F7FFFF.

    There is also a facility to selectively add or replace modules to the ROM-tag list. These modules can exist in RAM, and the memory they occupy will be deleted from the memory free list during the boot process. SumKickData() plays an important role in this run-time modification of the ROM-tag array.

    Three variables in ExecBase are used in changing the ROM-tag array: KickMemPtr, KickTagPtr, and KickCheckSum. KickMemPtr points to a linked list of MemEntry structures. The memory that these MemEntry structures reference will be allocated (via AllocAbs) at boot time. The MemEntry structure itself must also be in the list.

    KickTagPtr points to a long-word array of the same format as the ResModules array. The array has a series of pointers to ROM-tag structures. The array is either null terminated, or will have an entry with the most significant bit (bit 31) set. The most significant bit being set says that this is a link to another long-word array of ROM-tag entries. This new array's address can be found by clearing bit 31.

    KickCheckSum has the result of SumKickData(). It is the checksum of both the KickMemPtr structure and the KickTagPtr arrays. If the checksum does not compute correctly then both KickMemPtr and KickTagPtr will be ignored.

    If all the memory referenced by KickMemPtr can't be allocated then KickTagPtr will be ignored.

    There is one more important caveat about adding ROM-tags. All this ROM-tag magic is run very early on in the system -- before expansion memory is added to the system. Therefore any memory in this additional ROM-tag area must be addressable at this time. This means that your ROM-tag code, MemEntry structures, and resident arrays cannot be in expansion memory. There are two regions of memory that are acceptable: one is chip memory, and the other is "Ranger" memory (memory in the range between $C00000-$D80000).

    Remember that changing an existing ROM-tag entry falls into the "heavy magic" category -- be very careful when doing it. The odd are that you will blow yourself out of the water.

NOTE
    SumKickData was introduced in the 1.2 release

SEE ALSO
    InitResident, FindResident

```
NAME
     SumLibrary -- compute and check the checksum on a library

SYNOPSIS
     SumLibrary(library)
                A1
     void SumLibrary(struct Library *);

FUNCTION
     SumLibrary computes a new checksum on a library.  It can also be
     used to check an old checksum.  If an old checksum does not match,
     and the library has not been marked as changed, then the system
     will call Alert().

     This call could also be periodically made by some future
     system-checking task.

INPUTS
     library - a pointer to the library to be changed

NOTE
     An alert will occur if the checksum fails.

SEE ALSO
     SetFunction
```



```
NAME
     SuperState -- enter supervisor state with user stack

SYNOPSIS
     oldSysStack = SuperState()
     D0
     APTR SuperState(void);

FUNCTION
     Enter supervisor mode while running on the user's stack. The user
     still has access to user stack variables.  Be careful though, the
     user stack must be large enough to accommodate space for all
     interrupt data -- this includes all possible nesting of interrupts.
     This function does nothing when called from supervisor state.

RESULTS
     oldSysStack - system stack pointer; save this.  It will come in
                   handy when you return to user state.  If the system
                   is already in supervisor mode, oldSysStack is zero.

SEE ALSO
     UserState
```

NAME
    TypeOfMem -- determine attributes of a given memory address

SYNOPSIS
```
attributes = TypeOfMem(address)
D0                     A1
ULONG TypeOfMem(void *);
```

FUNCTION
    Given a RAM memory address, search the system memory lists and return its memory attributes. The memory attributes are similar to those specified when the memory was first allocated: (eg. MEMF_CHIP and MEMF_FAST).

    This function is usually used to determine if a particular block of memory is within CHIP space.

    If the address is not in known-space, a zero will be returned. (Anything that is not RAM, like the ROM or expansion area, will return zero. Also the first few bytes of a memory area are used up by the MemHeader.)

INPUT
    address - a memory address

RESULT
    attributes - a long word of memory attribute flags.
    If the address is not in known RAM, zero is returned.

SEE ALSO
    AllocMem()

NAME
    UserState -- return to user state with user stack

SYNOPSIS
```
UserState(sysStack)
          D0
void UserState(APTR);
```

FUNCTION
    Return to user state with user stack, from supervisor state with user stack. This function is normally used in conjunction with the SuperState function above.

    This function must not be called from the user state.

INPUT
    sysStack - supervisor stack pointer

BUGS
    This function is broken in V33/34 Kickstart.

SEE ALSO
    SuperState

NAME
    Vacate -- release a message lock (semaphore)

SYNOPSIS
```
Vacate(semaphore)
       A0
void Vacate(struct Semaphore *);
```

FUNCTION
    This function releases a previously locked semaphore (see the Procure() function). If another task is waiting for the semaphore, its bidMessage will be sent to its reply port.

INPUT
    semaphore - the semaport message port representing the semaphore to be freed.

BUGS
    Procure() and Vacate() do not have proven reliability.

SEE ALSO
    Procure

NAME
    Wait -- wait for one or more signals

SYNOPSIS
```
signals = Wait(signalSet)
D0             D0
ULONG Wait(ULONG);
```

FUNCTION
    This function will cause the current task to suspend waiting for one or more signals. When one or more of the specified signals occurs, the task will return to the ready state, and those signals will be cleared.

    If a signal occurred prior to calling Wait, the wait condition will be immediately satisfied, and the task will continue to run without delay.

CAUTION
    This function cannot be called while in supervisor mode or interrupts! This function will break the action of a Forbid() or Disable() call.

INPUT
    signalSet - The set of signals for which to wait. Each bit represents a particular signal.

RESULTS
    signals - the set of signals that were active

```
NAME
     WaitIO -- wait for completion of an I/O request

SYNOPSIS
     error = WaitIO(iORequest)
     D0             A1
     BYTE WaitIO(struct IORequest *);

FUNCTION
     This function waits for the specified I/O request to complete, then
     removes it from the replyport.  If the I/O has already completed,
     this function will return immediately.

     This function should be used with care, as it does not return until
     the I/O request completes; if the I/O never completes, this
     function will never return, and your task will hang.  If this
     situation is a possibility, it is safer to use the Wait() function.
     Wait() will return return when any of a specified set of signal is
     received.  This is how I/O timeouts can be properly handled.

WARNING
     If this IORequest was "Quick" or otherwise finished BEFORE this
     call, this function drops though immediately, with no call to
     Wait().  A side effect is that the signal bit related the port may
     remain set.  Expect this.

INPUTS
     iORequest - pointer to an I/O request block

RESULTS
     error - zero if successful, else an error is returned
             (a sign extended copy of io_Error).

SEE ALSO
     DoIO, SendIO, CheckIO, AbortIO
```



```
NAME
     WaitPort -- wait for a given port to be non-empty

SYNOPSIS
     message = WaitPort(port)
     D0                 A0
     struct Message *WaitPort(struct MsgPort *);

FUNCTION
     This function waits for the given port to become non-empty.  If
     necessary, the Wait function will be called to wait for the port
     signal.  If a message is already present at the port, this function
     will return immediately.  The return value is always a pointer to
     the first message queued (but it is not removed from the queue).

CAUTION
     More than one message may be at the port when this returns.  It is
     proper to call the GetMsg() function in a loop until all messages
     have been handled, then wait for more to arrive.

     To wait for more than one port, combine the signal bits from each
     port into one call to the Wait() function, then use a GetMsg() loop
     to collect any and all messages.  It is possible to get a signal
     for a port WITHOUT a message showing up.  Plan for this.

INPUT
     port - a pointer to the message port

RETURN
     message - a pointer to the first available message

SEE ALSO
     GetMsg
```

TABLE OF CONTENTS


```
   NAME
       AddDosNode -- mount a disk to the system

   SYNOPSIS
       ok = AddDosNode( bootPri, flags, deviceNode )
       D0               D0       D1     A0

   FUNCTION
       This routine makes sure that your disk device (or a device
       that wants to be treated as if it was a disk...) will be
       entered into the system.  If the dos is already up and
       running, then it will be entered immediately.  If the dos
       has not yet been run then the data will be recorded, and the
       dos will get it later.

       We hope to eventually try and boot off a disk device.  We will
       try and boot off of each device in turn, based on priority,
       iff there is no boot floppy in the floppy disk drive.  As of
       this writing that facility does not yet exist.

       There is only one additional piece of magic done by AddDosNode.
       If there is no executable code specified in the deviceNode
       structure (e.g. dn_SegList, dn_Handler, and dn_Task are all
       null) then the standard dos file handler is used for your
       device.

       Documentation note: a "task" as used here is a dos-task, not
       an exec-task.  A dos-task, in the strictest sense, is the
       address of an exec-style message port.  In general, it is
       a pointer to a process's pr_MsgPort field (e.g. a constant
       number of bytes after an exec port).

   INPUTS
       bootPri -- a BYTE quantity with the boot priority for this disk.
           This priority is only for which disks should be looked at:
           the actual disk booted from will be the first disk with
           a valid boot block.  If no disk is found then the "bootme"
           hand will come up and the bootstrap code will wait for
           a floppy to be inserted.  Recommend priority assignments are:

               +5 -- unit zero for the floppy disk.  The floppy should
                   always be highest priority to allow the user to
                   abort out of a hard disk boot.
               0 -- the run of the mill hard disk
               -5 -- a "network" disk (local disks should take priority).
               -128 -- don't even bother to boot from this device.

       flags -- additional flag bits for the call:
           ADN_STARTPROC (bit 0) -- start a handler process immediately.
               Normally the process is started only when the device node
               is first referenced.  This bit is meaningless if you
               have already specified a handler process (non-null dn_Task).

       deviceNode -- a legal DOS device node, properly initialized.
           Typically this will be the result of a MakeDosNode()
           call, but feel free to manufacture your own if you need
           to.  If deviceNode is null then AddDosNode does nothing.


   RESULTS
       ok - non-zero everything went ok, zero if we ran out of memory
           or some other weirdness happened.

   EXAMPLES


       /* enter a bootable disk into the system.  Start a file handler
       ** process immediately.
       */
       AddDosNode( 0, ADNF_STARTPROC, MakeDosNode( paramPacket ) );
```

BUGS

The flexible boot strategy is only that -- strategy. It still needs to be reflected in code somewhere.

SEE ALSO

MakeDosNode

BUGS

NAME

MakeDosNode -- construct dos data structures that a disk needs

SYNOPSIS

```
deviceNode = MakeDosNode( parameterPkt )
D0                        A0
```

FUNCTION

This routine manufactures the data structures needed to enter a dos disk device into the system. This consists of a DeviceNode, a FileSysStartupMsg, a disk environment vector, and up to two bcpl strings. See the libraries/dosextens and libraries/filehandler include files for more information.

MakeDosNode will allocate all the memory it needs, and then link the various structure together. It will make sure all the structures are long-word aligned (as required by the DOS). It then returns the information to the user so he can change anything else that needs changing. Typically he will then call AddDosNode() to enter the new device into the dos tables.

INPUTS

parameterPkt - a longword array containing all the information needed to initialize the data structures. Normally I would have provided a structure for this, but the variable length of the packet caused problems. The two strings are null terminated strings, like all other exec strings.

longword	description
0	string with dos handler name
1	string with exec device name
2	unit number (for OpenDevice)
3	flags (for OpenDevice)
4	# of longwords in rest of enviroment
5-n	file handler environment (see libraries/filehandler.h)

RESULTS

deviceNode - pointer to initialize device node structure, or null if there was not enough memory.

EXAMPLES

```
/* set up a 3.5" amiga format floppy drive for unit 1 */

char execName[] = "trackdisk.device";
char dosName[] = "df1";

ULONG parmPkt[] = {
    (ULONG) dosName,
    (ULONG) execName,
    1,                  /* unit number */
    0,                  /* OpenDevice flags */

    /* here is the environment block */
    11,                 /* table upper bound */
    512>>2,             /* # longwords in a block */
    0,                  /* sector origin -- unused */
    2,                  /* number of surfaces */
    1,                  /* secs per logical block -- unused */
    11,                 /* secs per track */
    2,                  /* reserved blocks -- 2 boot blocks */
    0,                  /* ?? -- unused */
    0,                  /* interleave */
    0,                  /* lower cylinder */
    79,                 /* upper cylinder */
    5,                  /* number of buffers */
};

struct Device Node *node, *MakeDosNode();
```

```
     node = MakeDosNode( parmPkt );

BUGS

SEE ALSO
     AddDosNode
```

expansion.library/AddConfigDev

```
NAME
     AddConfigDev - add a new ConfigDev structure to the system

SYNOPSIS
     AddConfigDev( configDev )
                   A0

FUNCTION
     This routine adds the specified ConfigDev structure to the
     list of Configuration Devices in the system.

INPUTS
     configDev - a valid ConfigDev structure.

RESULTS

EXCEPTIONS

SEE ALSO
     RemConfigDev

BUGS
```

```
expansion.library/AllocBoardMem

   NAME
        AllocBoardMem - allocate standard device expansion memory

   SYNOPSIS
        startSlot = AllocBoardMem( slotSpec )
        D0                         D0

   FUNCTION
        This function allocates numslots of expansion space (each slot
        is E_SLOTSIZE bytes).  It returns the slot number of the
        start of the expansion memory.  The EC_MEMADDR macro may be
        used to convert this to a memory address.

        AllocBoardMem() knows about the intracacies of expansion
        board hardware and will allocate the proper expansion
        memory for each board type.

   INPUTS
        slotSpec - the memory size field of the Type byte of
                an expansion board

   RESULTS
        startSlot - the slot number that was allocated, or -1 for error.

   EXAMPLES

                struct ExpansionRom *er;
                slot = AllocBoardMem( er->er_Type & ERT_MEMMASK )

   EXCEPTIONS
        Not typically called by user code.

   SEE ALSO
        AllocExpansionMem, FreeExpansionMem, FreeBoardMem

   BUGS
```

```
expansion.library/AllocConfigDev

   NAME
        AllocConfigDev - allocate a ConfigDev structure

   SYNOPSIS
        configDev = AllocConfigDev()
        D0

   FUNCTION
        This routine returns the address of a ConfigDev structure.
        It is provided so new fields can be added to the structure
        without breaking old, existing code.  The structure is cleared
        when it is returned to the user.

   INPUTS

   RESULTS
        configDev - either a valid ConfigDev structure or NULL.

   EXCEPTIONS

   SEE ALSO
        FreeConfigDev

   BUGS
```

```
expansion.library/AllocExpansionMem

   NAME
        AllocExpansionMem - allocate expansion memory

   SYNOPSIS
        startSlot = AllocExpansionMem( numSlots, slotOffset )
        D0                             D0        D1

   FUNCTION
        This function allocates numslots of expansion space (each slot
        is E_SLOTSIZE bytes).  It returns the slot number of the
        start of the expansion memory.  The EC_MEMADDR macro may be
        used to convert this to a memory address.

        Boards that fit the expansion architecture have alignment
        rules.  Normally a board must be on a binary boundary of its
        size.  Four and Eight megabyte boards have special rules.
        User defined boards might have other special rules.

        The routine AllocBoardMem() knows about all the allocation
        rules for standard boards.  Most users will want to use
        that routine if they want memory for a standard expansion
        device.

        If AllocExpansionMem() succeeds, the startSlot will satisfy
        the following equation:

                (startSlot - slotOffset) MOD slotAlign = 0

   INPUTS
        numSlots - the number of slots required.
        slotOffset - an offset from that boundary for startSlot.

   RESULTS
        startSlot - the slot number that was allocated, or -1 for error.

   EXAMPLES

                AllocExpansionMem( 2, 0 )

        Tries to allocate 2 slots on a two slot boundary.

                AllocExpansionMem( 64, 32 )

        This is the allocation rule for 4 meg boards.  It allocates
        4 megabytes (64 slots) on an odd 2 meg boundary.

   EXCEPTIONS
        Not typically called by user code.

   SEE ALSO
        FreeExpansionMem, AllocBoardMem, FreeBoardMem

   BUGS
```

```
expansion.library/ConfigBoard

   NAME
        ConfigBoard - configure a board

   SYNOPSIS
        error = ConfigBoard( board, configDev )
        D0                   A0     A1

   FUNCTION
        This routine configures an expansion board.  The board
        will generally live at E_EXPANSIONBASE, but the base is
        passed as a parameter to allow future compatibility.
        The configDev parameter must be a valid configDev that
        has already had ReadExpansionRom() called on it.

        ConfigBoard will allocate expansion memory and place
        the board at its new address.  It will update configDev
        accordingly.  If there is not enough expansion memory
        for this board then an error will be returned.

   INPUTS
        board - the current address that the expansion board is
                responding.
        configDev - an initialized ConfigDev structure.

   RESULTS
        error - non-zero if there was a problem configuring this board

   EXCEPTIONS
        Not normally called by user code

   SEE ALSO
        FreeConfigDev

   BUGS
```

```
expansion.library/ConfigChain

   NAME
        ConfigChain - configure the whole damn system

   SYNOPSIS
        error = ConfigChain( baseAddr )
        D0                   A0

   FUNCTION
        This is the big one!  This routine will take a base address
        (generally E_EXPANSIONBASE) and configure all the devices that
        live there.  This routine will call all the other routines
        that might need to be called.  All boards that are found will
        be linked into the configuration list.

   INPUTS
        baseAddr - the base address to start looking for boards.

   RESULTS
        error - non-zero if something went wrong.

   EXCEPTIONS
        Not normally called by user code

   SEE ALSO
        FreeConfigDev

   BUGS
```

```
expansion.library/FindConfigDev

   NAME
        FindConfigDev - find a matching ConfigDev entry

   SYNOPSIS
        configDev = FindConfigDev( oldConfigDev, manufacturer, product )
        D0                         A0            D0            D1

   FUNCTION
        This routine searches the list of existing ConfigDev
        structures in the system and looks for one that has
        the specified manufacturer and product codes.

        If the oldConfigDev is NULL the the search is from the
        start of the list of configuration devices.  If it is
        not null then it searches from the first configuration
        device entry AFTER oldConfigDev.

        A code of -1 is treated as a wildcard -- e.g. it matches
        any manufacturer (or product)

   INPUTS
        oldConfigDev - a valid ConfigDev structure, or NULL to start
                from the start of the list.
        manufacturer - the manufacturer code being searched for, or
                -1 to ignore manufacturer numbers.
        product - the product code being searched for, or -1 to
                ignore product numbers.

   RESULTS
        configDev - the next ConfigDev entry that matches the
                manufacturer and product codes, or NULL if there
                are no more matches.

   EXCEPTIONS

   EXAMPLES
        /* to find all configdevs of the proper type */
        struct ConfigDev *cd = NULL;

        while( cd = FindConfigDev( cd, MANUFACTURER, PRODUCT ) ) {
                /* do something with the returned ConfigDev */
        }

   SEE ALSO

   BUGS
```

```
expansion.library/FreeBoardMem

   NAME
        FreeBoardMem - allocate standard device expansion memory

   SYNOPSIS
        FreeBoardMem( startSlot, slotSpec )
                      D0         D1

   FUNCTION
        This function frees numslots of expansion space (each slot
        is E_SLOTSIZE bytes).  It is the inverse function of
        AllocBoardMem().

   INPUTS
        startSlot - a slot number in expansion space.
        slotSpec - the memory size field of the Type byte of
                an expansion board

   RESULTS

   EXAMPLES

        struct ExpansionRom *er;
        int startSlot;
        int slotSpec;

        slotSpec = er->er_Type & ERT_MEMMASK;
        startSlot = AllocBoardMem( er->er_Type & ERT_MEMMAK );

        if( startSlot != -1 ) {
            FreeBoardMem( startSlot, slotSpec );
        }

   EXCEPTIONS
        If the caller tries to free a slot that is already in the
        free list, FreeBoardMem will Alert() (e.g. crash the
        system).

        Not normally called by user code

   SEE ALSO
        AllocExpansionMem, FreeExpansionMem, AllocBoardMem

   BUGS
```

```
expansion.library/FreeConfigDev

   NAME
        FreeConfigDev - allocate a ConfigDev structure

   SYNOPSIS
        FreeConfigDev( configDev )
                       A0

   FUNCTION
        This routine frees a ConfigDev structure as returned by
        AllocConfigDev.

   INPUTS
        configDev - a valid ConfigDev structure.

   RESULTS

   EXCEPTIONS

   SEE ALSO
        AllocConfigDev

   BUGS
```

expansion.library/FreeExpansionMem

```
NAME
     FreeExpansionMem - allocate standard device expansion memory

SYNOPSIS
     FreeExpansionMem( startSlot, numSlots )
                       D0         D1

FUNCTION
     This function allocates numslots of expansion space (each slot
     is E_SLOTSIZE bytes).  It is the inverse function of
     AllocExpansionMem().

INPUTS
     startSlot - the slot number that was allocated, or -1 for error.
     numSlots - the number of slots to be freed.

RESULTS

EXAMPLES

EXCEPTIONS
     If the caller tries to free a slot that is already in the
     free list, FreeExpansionMem will Alert() (e.g. crash the
     system).

     Not normally called by user code

SEE ALSO
     AllocExpansionMem, AllocBoardMem, FreeBoardMem

BUGS
```

expansion.library/GetCurrentBinding

```
NAME
     GetCurrentBinding - sets static board configuration area

SYNOPSIS
     actual = GetCurrentBinding( currentBinding, size )
                                 A0              D0:16

FUNCTION
     This function writes the contents of the "currentBinding"
     structure out of a private place.  It may be set via
     SetCurrentBinding().  This is really a kludge, but it is
     the only way to pass extra arguments to a newly configured
     device.

     A CurrentBinding structure has the name of the currently
     loaded file, the product string that was associated with
     this driver, and a pointer to the head of a singly linked
     list of ConfigDev structures (linked through the cd_NextCD
     field).

     Many devices may not need this information; they have hard
     coded into themselves their manufacture number.  It is
     recommended that you at least check that you can deal with
     the product code in the linked ConfigDev structures.

INPUTS
     currentBinding - a pointer to a CurrentBinding structure

     size - the size of the user's binddriver structure.  No
         more than this much data will be copied.  If size is
            larger than the libraries idea a CurrentBinding size,
            then the structure will be null padded.


RESULTS
     actual - the true size of a CurrentBinding structure is returned.

EXAMPLES

EXCEPTIONS

SEE ALSO
     GetCurrentBinding

BUGS
```

```
expansion.library/ObtainConfigBinding

   NAME
        ObtainConfigBinding - try to get permission to bind drivers

   SYNOPSIS
        ObtainConfigBinding()


   FUNCTION
        ObtainConfigBinding gives permission to bind drivers to
        ConfigDev structures.  It exists so two drivers at once
        do not try and own the same ConfigDev structure.  This
        call will block until it is safe proceed.

        Individual drivers to not need to call this routine.  It
        is intended for BindDriver program, and others like it.
        If your drivers won't be loaded via the standard method,
        you may need to lock out others.

        It is crucially important that people lock out others
        before loading new drivers.  Much of the data that is used
        to configure things is statically kept, and others need
        to be kept from using it.

        This call is build directly on Exec SignalSemaphore code
        (e.g. ObtainSemaphore).

   INPUTS

   RESULTS

   EXCEPTIONS

   SEE ALSO
        ReleaseConfigBinding

   BUGS
```

```
expansion.library/ReadExpansionByte

   NAME
        ReadExpansionByte - read a byte nybble by nybble.

   SYNOPSIS
        byte = ReadExpansionByte( board, offset )
        D0                        A0     D0

   FUNCTION
        ReadExpansionByte reads a byte from a new-style expansion
        board.  These boards have their readable data organized
        as a series of nybbles in memory.  This routine reads
        two nybbles and returns the byte value.

        In general, this routine will only be called by ReadExpansionRom.

        The offset is a byte offset into a ExpansionRom structure.
        The actual memory address read will be four times larger.
        The macros EROFFSET and ECOFFSET are provided to help get
        these offsets from C.

   INPUTS
        board - a pointer to the base of a new style expansion board.
        offset - a logical offset from the board base

   RESULTS
        byte - a byte of data from the expansion board, or -1 if there
                was an error reading from the board.

   EXAMPLES
        byte = ReadExpansionByte( cd->BoardAddr, EROFFSET( er_Type ) );
        ints = ReadExpansionByte( cd->BoardAddr, ECOFFSET( ec_Interrupt ) );

   EXCEPTIONS
        Not typically called by user code.

   SEE ALSO
        WriteExpansionByte, ReadExpansionRom

   BUGS
```

expansion.library/ReadExpansionRom

```
NAME
     ReadExpansionRom - read a boards configuration rom space

SYNOPSIS
     error = ReadExpansionRom( board, configDev )
     D0                        A0     A1

FUNCTION
     ReadExpansionRom reads a the rom portion of an expansion
     device in to cd_Rom portion of a ConfigDev structure.
     This routine knows how to detect whether or not there is
     actually a board there,

     In addition, the Rom portion of a new style expansion board
     is encoded in ones-complement format (except for the first
     two nybbles -- the er_Type field).  ReadExpansionRom knows
     about this and un-complements the appropriate fields.

INPUTS
     board - a pointer to the base of a new style expansion board.
     configDev - the ConfigDev structure that will be read in.
     offset - a logical offset from the configdev base

RESULTS
     error - If the board address does not contain a valid new style
             expansion board, then error will be non-zero.

EXAMPLES

     configDev = AllocConfigDev();
     if( ! configDev ) panic();

     error = ReadExpansionBoard( board, configDev );
     if( ! error ) {
             configDev->cd_BoardAddr = board;
             ConfigBoard( configDev );
     }

EXCEPTIONS
     Not typically called by user code.

SEE ALSO
     ReadExpansionByte, WriteExpansionByte

BUGS
```

expansion.library/ReleaseConfigBinding

```
NAME
     ReleaseConfigBinding - allow others to bind to drivers

SYNOPSIS
     ReleaseConfigBinding()


FUNCTION
     This call should be used when you are done binding drivers
     to ConfigDev entries.  It releases the SignalSemaphore; this
     allows others to bind their drivers to ConfigDev structures.

INPUTS

RESULTS

EXAMPLES

EXCEPTIONS

SEE ALSO
     ObtainConfigBinding

BUGS
```

expansion.library/RemConfigDev

NAME
    RemConfigDev - remove a ConfigDev structure from the system

SYNOPSIS

```
RemConfigDev( configDev )
              A0
```

FUNCTION
    This routine removes the specified ConfigDev structure from the list of Configuration Devices in the system.

INPUTS
    configDev - a valid ConfigDev structure.

RESULTS

EXCEPTIONS

SEE ALSO
    AddConfigDev

BUGS

expansion.library/SetCurrentBinding

NAME
    SetCurrentBinding - sets static board configuration area

SYNOPSIS

```
SetCurrentBinding( currentBinding, size )
                   A0              D0:16
```

FUNCTION
    This function records the contents of the "currentBinding" structure in a private place. It may be read via GetCurrentBinding(). This is really a kludge, but it is the only way to pass extra arguments to a newly configured device.

A CurrentBinding structure has the name of the currently loaded file, the product string that was associated with this driver, and a pointer to the head of a singly linked list of ConfigDev structures (linked through the cd_NextCD field).

Many devices may not need this information; they have hard coded into themselves their manufacture number. It is recommended that you at least check that you can deal with the product code in the linked ConfigDev structures.

INPUTS
    currentBinding - a pointer to a CurrentBinding structure

size - the size of the user's binddriver structure. No more than this much data will be copied. If size is larger than the libraries idea a CurrentBinding size, then the structure will be null padded.

RESULTS

EXAMPLES

EXCEPTIONS

SEE ALSO
    GetCurrentBinding

BUGS

```
expansion.library/WriteExpansionByte

    NAME
        WriteExpansionByte - write a byte nybble by nybble.

    SYNOPSIS
        error = WriteExpansionByte( board, offset, byte )
        D0                          A0     D0      D1

    FUNCTION
        WriteExpansionByte write a byte to a new-style expansion
        board.  These boards have their writeable data organized
        as a series of nybbles in memory.  This routine writes
        two nybbles in a very carefull manner to work with all
        types of new expansion boards.

        To make certain types of board less expensive, an expansion
        board's write registers may be organized as either a
        byte-wide or nybble-wide register.  If it is nybble-wide
        then it must latch the less significant nybble until the
        more significant nybble is written.  This allows the
        following algorithm to work with either type of board:

                write the low order nybble to bits D15-D12 of
                        byte (offset*4)+2

                write the entire byte to bits D15-D8 of
                        byte (offset*4)

        The offset is a byte offset into a ExpansionRom structure.
        The actual memory address read will be four times larger.
        The macros EROFFSET and ECOFFSET are provided to help get
        these offsets from C.

    INPUTS
        board - a pointer to the base of a new style expansion board.
        offset - a logical offset from the configdev base
        byte - the byte of data to be written to the expansion board.

    RESULTS
        error - the routine will return a zero on success, non-zero if
                there was a problem.

    EXAMPLES
        err = WriteExpansionByte( cd->BoardAddr, ECOFFSET( ec_Shutup ),  0 );
        err = WriteExpansionByte( cd->BoardAddr, ECOFFSET( ec_Interrupt ), 1 );

    EXCEPTIONS
        Not typically called by user code.

    SEE ALSO
        ReadExpansionByte, ReadExpansionRom

    BUGS
```

TABLE OF CONTENTS

```
NAME
   AddAnimOb  --  Add an AnimOb to the linked list of AnimObs.

SYNOPSIS
   AddAnimOb(anOb, anKey, rp)
             a0    a1     a2

    struct AnimOb *anOb,**anKey;
    struct RastPort *rp;

FUNCTION
   Links this AnimOb into the current list pointed to by animKey.
   Initializes all the Timers of the AnimOb's components.
   Calls AddBob with each component's Bob.
    rp->GelsInfo must point to an initialized GelsInfo structure.

INPUTS
   anOb = pointer to the AnimOb structure to be added to the list
   anKey = address of a pointer to the first AnimOb in the list
        (anKey = NULL if there are no AnimObs in the list so far)
   rp = pointer to a valid RastPort

BUGS

SEE ALSO
  Animate graphics/rastport.h graphics/gels.h
```



```
NAME
   AddBob  --  Adds a Bob to current gel list.

SYNOPSIS
   AddBob(Bob, rp)
          a0   a1

    struct Bob *Bob;
    struct RastPort *rp;

FUNCTION
   Sets up the system Bob flags, then links this gel into the list
       via AddVSprite.

INPUTS
   Bob = pointer to the Bob structure to be added to the gel list
   rp = pointer to a RastPort structure

BUGS

SEE ALSO
   InitGels  AddVSprite  graphics/gels.h  graphics/rastport.h
```

```
NAME
     AddFont -- add a font to the system list

SYNOPSIS
     AddFont(textFont)
             a1

     struct TextFont *textFont;

FUNCTION
     This function adds the text font to the system, making it
     available for use by any application.  The font added must be
     in public memory, and remain until successfully removed.

INPUTS
     textFont - a TextFont structure in public ram.

BUGS

SEE ALSO
     SetFont RemFont graphics/text.h
```



```
NAME
   AddVSprite -- Add a VSprite to the current gel list.

SYNOPSIS
   AddVSprite(vs, rp)
              a0  a1

    struct VSprite *vs;
    struct RastPort *rp;

FUNCTION
   Sets up the system VSprite flags
   Links this VSprite into the current gel list using its Y,X

INPUTS
   vs = pointer to the VSprite structure to be added to the gel list
   rp = pointer to a RastPort structure

BUGS

SEE ALSO
    InitGels  graphics/rastport.h  graphics/gels.h
```

```
NAME
    AllocRaster -- Allocate space for a bitplane.

SYNOPSIS
    planeptr = AllocRaster( width, height )
      d0                    d0:16  d1:16

     PLANEPTR planeptr;
     USHORT  width,height;

FUNCTION
    This function calls the memory allocation routines
    to allocate memory space for a bitplane width bits
     wide and height bits high.

INPUTS
     width - number of bits wide for bitplane
    height - number of rows in bitplane

RESULT
    planeptr - pointer to first word in bitplane
         If unable to allocate space then planeptr will be NULL.

BUGS

SEE ALSO
    FreeRaster graphics/gfx.h
```



```
NAME
     AndRectRegion -- Perform 2d AND operation of rectangle
                      with region, leaving result in region.

SYNOPSIS
     AndRectRegion(region,rectangle)
                   a0     a1

     struct Region *region;
     struct Rectangle *rectangle;

FUNCTION
     Clip away any portion of the region that exists outside
     of the rectangle. Leave the result in region.

INPUTS
     region - pointer to Region structure
     rectangle - pointer to Rectangle structure

BUGS

SEE ALSO
     AndRegionRegion OrRectRegion graphics/regions.h
```

graphics.library/AndRegionRegion graphics.library/AndRegionRegion

```
NAME
    AndRegionRegion -- Perform 2d AND operation of one region
                with second region, leaving result in second region.

SYNOPSIS
    status = AndRegionRegion(region1,region2)
      d0                       a0      a1

     BOOL status;
     struct Region *region1, *region2;

FUNCTION
    Remove any portion of region2 that is not in region1.

INPUTS
    region1 - pointer to Region structure
    region2 - pointer to Region structure to use and for result

RESULTS
     status - return TRUE if successful operation
              return FALSE if ran out of memory

BUGS

SEE ALSO
     OrRegionRegion AndRectRegion graphics/regions.h
```

graphics.library/Animate graphics.library/Animate

```
NAME
   Animate  --  Processes every AnimOb in the current animation list.

SYNOPSIS
   Animate(anKey, rp)
           a0     a1

    struct AnimOb **anKey;
    struct RastPort *rp;

FUNCTION
   For every AnimOb in the list
       - update its location and velocities
       - call the AnimOb's special routine if one is supplied
       - for each component of the AnimOb
           - if this sequence times out, switch to the new one
           - call this component's special routine if one is supplied
           - set the sequence's VSprite's y,x coordinates based
              on whatever these routines cause

INPUTS
   key = address of the variable that points to the head AnimOb
   rp  = pointer to the RastPort structure

BUGS

SEE ALSO
    AddAnimOb graphics/gels.h graphics/rastport.h
```

```
NAME
    AreaCircle -- add a circle to areainfo list for areafill.


SYNOPSIS
    error = (int) AreaCircle( rp,  cx,  cy, radius)
    D0                        A1   D0   D1  D2

    LONG error;
    struct RastPort *rp;
    SHORT cx, cy;
    SHORT radius;

FUNCTION
    Add circle to the vector buffer.

INPUTS
    rp - pointer to a RastPort structure

    (cx, cy) - are coordinates of a "centerpoint" in the raster
    radius is the radius of the circle to draw around the centerpoint

    This function is a macro which calls
        AreaEllipse(rp,cx,cy,radius,radius).

RESULTS
    0 if no error
    -1 if no space left in vector list

SEE ALSO
   AreaMove, AreaDraw, AreaCircle, InitArea, AreaEnd, graphics/rastport.h
    graphics/gfxmacros.h
```



```
NAME
    AreaDraw -- Add a point to a list of end points for areafill.


SYNOPSIS
    error = AreaDraw( rp,  x,     y)
      d0                   A1 D0:16 D1:16

     LONG error;
     struct RastPort *rp;
     SHORT   x,y;

FUNCTION
    Add point to the vector buffer.


INPUTS
    rp - points to a RastPort structure
    x,y -  are coordinates of a point in the raster

RETURNS
    0 if no error
     -1 if no space left in vector list

BUGS

SEE ALSO
    AreaMove InitArea AreaEnd graphics/rastport.h
```

```
NAME
    AreaEllipse -- add a ellipse to areainfo list for areafill.


SYNOPSIS
    error = AreaEllipse( rp, cx,   cy,   a,    b    )
    d0                   a1  d0:16 d1:16 d2:16 d3:16

    LONG error;
    struct RastPort *rp;
    SHORT cx, cy;
    SHORT a, b;

FUNCTION
    Add ellipse to the vector buffer.

INPUTS
    rp - pointer to a RastPort structure
    cx - x coordinate of the centerpoint relative to the rastport.
    cy - y coordinate of the centerpoint relative to the rastport.
    a - the horizontal radius of the ellipse (note: a must be > 0)
    b - the vertical radius of the ellipse (note: b must be > 0)

RESULTS
    0 if no error
    -1 if no space left in vector list

SEE ALSO
    AreaMove, AreaDraw, AreaCircle, InitArea, AreaEnd, graphics/rastport.h
```



```
NAME
        AreaEnd -- Process table of vectors and produce areafill.


SYNOPSIS
        error = AreaEnd(rp)
   d0           Al

    LONG error;
    struct RastPort *rp;

FUNCTION
        Trigger the filling operation.
        Process  the vector buffer and  generate  required
        fill  into  the raster planes.  After the fill  is
        complete reinitialize for the next AreaMove.   Use
        the raster set up by InitTmpRas when generating an
        areafill mask.

 RESULT
        Fill the area enclosed by the definitions in the vector table.
        Returns -1 if an error occured anywhere.
        Returns 0 if no error.

INPUTS
        rp points to a RastPort structure

BUGS

SEE ALSO
        InitArea AreaMove AreaDraw AreaEllipse graphics/rastport.h
```

```
graphics.library/AreaMove                          graphics.library/AreaMove

   NAME
       AreaMove -- Define a new starting point for a new
                   shape in the vector list.


   SYNOPSIS
       error =  AreaMove( rp,   x,     y)
         d0                 a1  d0:16  d1:16

        LONG error;
        struct RastPort *rp;
        SHORT   x,y;

   FUNCTION
       Close  the last polygon and start another  polygon
       at  (x,y).    Enter  necessary  points  in  vector
       buffer. Cosing a polygon may result in the generation
        of another AreaDraw() to close previous polygon.
        Remember to have an initialized AreaInfo structure attached
        to the RastPort.

   INPUTS
       rp - points to a RastPort structure
       x,y - positions in the raster

   RETURNS
       0 if no error
        -1 if no space left in vector list

   BUGS

   SEE ALSO
       InitArea AreaDraw AreaEllipse AreaEnd graphics/rastport.h
```

```
graphics.library/AskFont                            graphics.library/AskFont

   NAME
        AskFont -- get the text attributes of the current font

   SYNOPSIS
        AskFont(rp, textAttr)
                a1        a0

        struct RastPort *rp;
        struct TextAttr *textAttr;

   FUNCTION
        This function fills the text attributes structure with the
        attributes of the current font in the RastPort.

   INPUTS
        rp - the RastPort from which the text attributes are extracted
        textAttr - the TextAttr structure to be filled

   BUGS

   SEE ALSO
        graphics/text.h
```

```
graphics.library/AskSoftStyle                    graphics.library/AskSoftStyle

   NAME
        AskSoftStyle -- Get the soft style bits of the current font.

   SYNOPSIS
        enable = AskSoftStyle(rp)
          d0                    a1

        ULONG enable;
        struct RastPort *rp;

   FUNCTION
        This function returns those style bits of the current font
        that are not intrinsic in the font itself, but
        algorithmically generated.  These are the bits that are
        valid to set in the enable mask for SetSoftStyle

   INPUTS
        rp - the RastPort from which the font and style are extracted.

   RESULTS
        enable - those bits in the style algorithmically generated
            Style bits that are not defined are also set.

   BUGS

   SEE ALSO
        SetSoftStyle    graphics/text.h
```

```
graphics.library/AttemptLockLayerRom
                                      *
   NAME
        AttemptLockLayerRom -- Attempt to Lock Layer structure
                                         by rom(gfx lib) code

   SYNOPSIS
        gotit = AttemptLockLayerRom( layer )
         d0                           a5

        BOOLEAN gotit;
        struct Layer *layer;

   FUNCTION
        Query the current state of the lock on this Layer. If it is
        already locked then return FALSE, could not lock. If the
        Layer was not locked then lock it and return TRUE.
        This call does not destroy any registers.
        This call nests so that callers in this chain will not lock
        themselves out.

   INPUTS
        layer - pointer to Layer structure

    RESULT
        returns TRUE or FALSE depending on whether the Layer is now
        locked by the caller.

SEE ALSO
        LockLayerRom UnlockLayerRom
```

```
NAME
     BltBitMap -- Move a rectangular region of bits in a BitMap.

SYNOPSIS
     planecnt = BltBitMap(SrcBitMap, SrcX, SrcY, DstBitMap,
     D0                   A0         D0:16 D1:16  A1
                DstX, DstY, SizeX, SizeY, Minterm, Mask [, TempA])
                D2:16 D3:16 D4:16  D5:16  D6:8     D7:8    [A2]

     ULONG planecnt;
     struct BitMap *SrcBitMap,*DstBitMap;
     SHORT SrcX,SrcY;
     SHORT DstX,DstY;
     SHORT SizeX,SizeY;
     UBYTE MinTerm,Mask;
     CPTR  TempA;    /*optional */

FUNCTION
     Perform non-destructive blits to move a rectangle from one
     area in a BitMap to another area, which can be on a different
     BitMap.
     This blit is assumed to be friendly: no error conditions (e.g.
     a rectangle outside the BitMap bounds) are tested or reported.

INPUTS
     SrcBitMap, DstBitMap - the BitMap(s) containing the
             rectangles
         - the planes copied from the source to the destination are
           only those whose plane numbers are identical and less
           than the minimum Depth of either BitMap and whose Mask
           bit for that plane is non-zero.
         - SrcBitMap and DstBitMap can be identical
     SrcX, SrcY - the x and y coordinates of the upper left corner
         of the source rectangle.  Valid range is positive
         signed integer such that the raster word's offset
         0..(32767-Size)
     DstX, DstY - the x and y coordinates of the upper left
         corner of the destination for the rectangle.  Valid
         range is as for Src.
     SizeX, SizeY - the size of the rectangle to be moved.  Valid
         range is (X: 1..976; Y: 1..1023 such that final raster
         word's offset is 0..32767)
     Minterm - the logic function to apply to the rectangle when
         A is non-zero (i.e. within the rectangle).  B is the
         source rectangle and C, D is the destination for the
         rectangle.
         - $0C0 is a vanilla copy
         - $030 inverts the source before the copy
         - $050 ignores the source and inverts the destination
         - see the hardware reference manual for other combinations
     Mask - the write mask to apply to this operation.  Bits set
         indicate the corresponding planes (if not greater than
         the minimum plane count) are to participate in the
         operation.  Typically this is set to 0xff.
     TempA - If the copy overlaps exactly to the left or right
         (i.e. the scan line addresses overlap), and TempA is
         non-zero, it points to enough chip accessable memory
         (MAXBYTESPERROW) to hold a line of A source for the blit.
         BitBitMap will allocate the needed TempA if none is
         provided and one is needed. If the blit does not overlap;
         SrcBitMap != DstBitMap then TempA need not be supplied.

RESULTS
     planecnt - the number of planes actually involved in the blit.

BUGS
     This routine uses over 300 bytes of stack when it really does
      not need to. It calculates all blits ahead of time and then
      sits in a loop doing the blits when it should overlap blits
      with calculations.

SEE ALSO
     ClipBlit graphics/gfx.h hardware/blit.h
```

```
NAME
     BltBitMapRastPort -- Blit from source bitmap to destination rastport.

SYNOPSIS
     BltBitMapRastPort
         (srcbm,srcx,srcy,destrp,destX,destY,sizeX,sizeY,minterm)
          a0    d0   d1   a1     d2    d3    d4    d5    d6

     struct BitMap *srcbm;
     SHORT srcx,srcy;
     struct RastPort *destrp;
     SHORT destX,destY;
     SHORT sizeX,sizeY;
     UBYTE minterm;

FUNCTION
     Blits from source bitmap to position specified in destination rastport
      using minterm.

INPUTS
     srcbm - a pointer to the source bitmap
     srcx  - x offset into source bitmap
     srcy  - y offset into source bitmap
     destrp - a pointer to the destination rastport
     destX - x offset into dest rastport
     destY - y offset into dest rastport
     sizeX - width of blit in pixels
     sizeY - height of blit in rows
     minterm - minterm to use for this blit

RETURNS
     TRUE

BUGS

SEE ALSO
     BltMaskBitMapRastPort graphics/gfx.h graphics/rastport.h
```



```
NAME

     BltClear - Clear a block of memory words to zero.

SYNOPSIS
     BltClear( memBlock, bytecount, flags )
                 a1         d0        d1

     APTR memBlock;
     ULONG   bytecount;
     ULONG   flags;

FUNCTION
     For memory that is local and blitter accessable
    the most efficient way to clear a range of memory locations is
    to use the system's most efficient data mover, the blitter.
    This command accepts the starting location and count and clears
    that block to zeros.

INPUTS
     memBloc - pointer to local memory to be cleared
             memBlock is assumed to be even.
     flags   set bit 0 to force function to wait until blit
             is done.
             set bit1 to use row/bytesperrow
     bytecount       if (flags & 2) == 0 then
                             even number of bytes to clear.
                     else
                             low 16 bits is taken as number of bytes
                             per row and upper 16 bits taken as
                             number of rows.

     This function is somewhat hardware dependant. In the
     rows/bytesperrow mode, rows must be <=1024.
     In bytecount mode multiple runs of the blitter
     may be used to clear all the memory.
may be used to clear all the memory.
  RESULT
     The block of memory is set to zeros.

  BUGS

  SEE ALSO
```

```
NAME

     BltMaskBitMapRastPort -- blit from source bitmap to destination rastport
                              with masking of source image.

SYNOPSIS

     BltMaskBitMapRastPort
         (srcbm,srcx,srcy,destrp,destX,destY,sizeX,sizeY,minterm,bltmask)
          a0    d0   d1   a1     d2    d3    d4    d5    d6      a2

     struct BitMap *srcbm;
     SHORT srcx,srcy;
     struct RastPort *destrp;
     SHORT destX,destY;
     SHORT sizeX,sizeY;
     UBYTE   minterm;
     APTR    bltmask;          * chip memory *

FUNCTION
     Blits from source bitmap to position specified in destination rastport
     using bltmask to determine where source overlays destination, and
     minterm to determine whether to copy the source image "as is" or
     to "invert" the sense of the source image when copying. In either
     case, blit only occurs where the mask is non-zero.


INPUTS
     srcbm - a pointer to the source bitmap
     srcx  - x offset into source bitmap
     srcy  - y offset into source bitmap
     destrp - a pointer to the destination rastport
     destX - x offset into dest rastport
     destY - y offset into dest rastport
     sizeX - width of blit in pixels
     sizeY - height of blit in rows
     minterm - either (ABC|ABNC|ANBC) if copy source and blit thru mask
               or     (ANBC)        if invert source and blit thru mask
     bltmask - pointer to the single bit-plane mask, which must be the
               same size and dimensions as the planes of the
               source bitmap.

RETURNS

BUGS

SEE ALSO
BltBitMapRastPort    graphics/gfx.h graphics/rastport.h
```



```
NAME
     BltPattern --  Using standard drawing rules for areafill,
                                     blit through a mask.

SYNOPSIS
    BltPattern(rp, mask, xl, yl, maxx, maxy, bytecnt)
               al,  a0   d0  dl   d2   d3     d4

     struct RastPort *rp;
     APTR    mask;
     SHORT   xl,yl,maxx,maxy;
     SHORT bytecnt;

FUNCTION
    Blit using drawmode,areafill pattern, and mask
    at position rectangle (xl,yl) (maxx,maxy).

INPUTS
    rp -  points to RastPort
    mask -  points to 2 dimensional mask if needed
            if mask == NULL then use a rectangle.
    xl,yl - upper left of rectangular region in RastPort
    maxx,maxy - points to lower right of rectangular region in RastPort
    bytecnt - BytesPerRow for mask

RETURNS

SEE ALSO
     AreaEnd
```

```
NAME
     BltTemplate -- Cookie cut a shape in a rectangle to the RastPort.

SYNOPSIS
     BltTemplate(SrcTemplate, SrcX, SrcMod, rp,
                 a0           d0:16 d1:16  a1
                 DstX,  DstY, SizeX, SizeY)
                 d2:16  d3:16 d4:16  d5:16

     CPTR    SrcTemplate;
     SHORT   SrcX;
     SHORT   SrcMod;
     struct  RastPort *rp;
     SHORT   DstX,DstY;
     SHORT   SizeX,SizeY;

FUNCTION
     This function draws the image in the template into the
     RastPort in the current color and drawing mode at the
     specified position.  The template is assumed not to overlap
     the destination.
     If the template falls outside the RastPort boundary, it is
     truncated to that boundary.

     Note: the SrcTemplate pointer should point to the "nearest" word
        (rounded down) of the template mask. Fine alignment of the mask
        is acheived by setting the SrcX bit offseet within the range
        of 0 to 15 decimal.

INPUTS
     SrcTemplate - pointer to the first (nearest) word of the template mask.
     SrcX - x bit offset into the template mask (range 0..15).
     SrcMod - number of bytes per row in template mask.
     rp - pointer to destination RastPort.
     DstX, DstY - x and y coordinates of the upper left
         corner of the destination for the blit.
     SizeX, SizeY - size of the rectangle to be used as the
         template.

BUGS
     The destination rastport (rp) must have an associated
     Layer structure or srcX will be ignored.

SEE ALSO
     BltPattern      graphics/rastport.h
```



```
NAME
     CBump -  increment user copper list pointer (bump to next position in list).

SYNOPSIS
     CBump( c )
            a1

     struct UCopList *c;

FUNCTION
     Increment pointer to space for next instruction in user copper list.

INPUTS
     c - pointer to UCopList structure

RESULTS
     User copper list pointer is incremented to next position.
     Pointer is repositioned to next user copperlist instruction block
     if the current block is full.

         Note: CBump is usually invoked for the programmer as part of the
               macro definitions CWAIT or CMOVE.

BUGS

SEE ALSO
     CINIT CWAIT CMOVE CEND graphics/copper.h
```

```
graphics.library/CEND                                    graphics.library/CEND
   NAME
      CEND -- Terminate user copper list.

   SYNOPSIS
      CEND( c )

      struct UCopList *c;

   FUNCTION
      Add instruction to terminate user copper list.

   INPUTS
      c - pointer to UCopList structure

   RESULTS
      This is actually a macro that calls the macro CWAIT(c,10000,255).
      10000 is a magical number that the graphics library uses.
      I hope display technology doesn't catch up too fast!

   BUGS

   SEE ALSO
      CINIT CWAIT CMOVE graphics/copper.h
```

```
graphics.library/ChangeSprite                    graphics.library/ChangeSprite

   NAME
      ChangeSprite -- Change the sprite image pointer.

   SYNOPSIS
      ChangeSprite( vp, s, newdata)
                    a0  a1   a2

       struct ViewPort *vp;
       struct SimpleSprite *s;
       APTR    newdata;         /* chip memory */

   FUNCTION
       The sprite image is changed to use the data starting at newdata

   INPUTS
      vp - pointer to ViewPort structure that this sprite is
                relative to.
                or 0 if relative only top of View
       s - pointer to SimpleSprite structure
       newdata - pointer to data structure of the following form.
               struct spriteimage
               {
                   UWORD    posctl[2]; /* used by simple sprite machine*/
                   UWORD    data[height][2];   /* actual sprite image */
                   UWORD    reserved[2];       /* initialized to */
                                                    /*  0x0,0x0 */
               };
       Programmer must initialize reserved[2].  Spriteimage must be
       in CHIP memory. The height subfield of the SimpleSprite structure
       must be set to reflect the height of the new spriteimage BEFORE
       calling ChangeSprite. The programmer may allocate two sprites to
       handle a single attached sprite.  After GetSprite, ChangeSprite,
       the programmer can set the SPRITE_ATTACHED bit in posctl[1] of the
       odd numbered sprite.
       If you need more than 8 sprites look up VSprites in the
       graphics documentation.

   RESULTS

   BUGS

   SEE ALSO
       FreeSprite ChangeSprite MoveSprite AddVSprite graphics/sprite.h
```

```
NAME
     CINIT -- Initialize user copperlist to accept intermediate
             user copper instructions.

SYNOPSIS
     ucl = CINIT( c , n )

     UCopperListInit( c , n )
                      a0  d0

     struct UCopList *ucl;
     struct UCopList *c;
     short n;

FUNCTION
     Allocates and/or initialize copperlist structures/buffers.
     This is a macro that calls UCopListLinit. CINIT will
     allocate a new UCopList if c==0. If (c != 0) it will
     initialize the data structures to begin new copperlist
     without allocating more memory and it ignores n.

INPUTS
     c - pointer to UCopList structure
     n - number of instructions buffer must hold

RESULTS
     An initialize list to accept intermediate copper instructions.

BUGS
     CINIT will not actually allocate a new copperlist if c==0.
     Instead you must allocate a 12 byte MEMF_PUBLIC|MEMF_CLEAR block,
     and pass it to this function.  The system's FreeVPortCopLists
     function will take care of deallocating it.

SEE ALSO
```



```
NAME
     ClearEOL - Clear from current position to end of line.

SYNOPSIS
     ClearEOL( rp )
               a1

     struct RastPort *rp;

FUNCTION
     Clear a rectangular swath from the current position to the
     right edge of the rastPort.  The height of the swath is taken
     from that of the current text font, and the vertical
     positioning of the swath is adjusted by the text baseline,
     such that text output at this position would lie wholly on
     this newly cleared area
     Clearing consists of setting the color of the swath to zero,
     or, if the DrawMode is 2, to the BgPen.

INPUTS
     rp - pointer to RastPort structure

BUGS

SEE ALSO
     Text ClearScreen SetRast graphics/text.h graphics/rastport.h
```

graphics.library/ClearRectRegion graphics.library/ClearRectRegion

```
NAME
     ClearRectRegion -- Perform 2d CLEAR operation of rectangle
                        with region, leaving result in region.

SYNOPSIS
     status = ClearRectRegion(region,rectangle)
      d0                       a0      a1

     BOOL error;
     struct Region *region;
     struct Rectangle *rectangle;

FUNCTION
     Clip away any portion of the region that exists inside
     of the rectangle. Leave the result in region.

INPUTS
     region - pointer to Region structure
     rectangle - pointer to Rectangle structure

RESULTS
     status - return TRUE if successful operation
              return FALSE if ran out of memory

BUGS

SEE ALSO
     AndRectRegion graphics/regions.h
```

graphics.library/ClearRegion graphics.library/ClearRegion

```
NAME
     ClearRegion -- Remove all rectangles from region.

SYNOPSIS
     ClearRegion(region)
                  a0

      struct Region *region;

FUNCTION
     Clip away all rectangles in the region leaving nothing.

INPUTS
     region - pointer to Region structure

BUGS

SEE ALSO
      NewRegion graphics/regions.h
```

```
graphics.library/ClearScreen                    graphics.library/ClearScreen

   NAME
        ClearScreen - Clear from current position to end of RastPort.

   SYNOPSIS
        ClearScreen( rp )
                     a1

        struct RastPort *rp;

   FUNCTION
        Clear a rectangular swath from the current position to the
        right edge of the rastPort with ClearEOL, then clear the rest
        of the screen from just beneath the swath to the bottom of
        the rastPort.
        Clearing consists of setting the color of the swath to zero,
        or, if the DrawMode is 2, to the BgPen.

   INPUTS
        rp - pointer to RastPort structure

   BUGS

   SEE ALSO
       ClearEOL Text SetRast graphics/text.h graphics/rastport.h
```

```
graphics.library/ClipBlit                          graphics.library/ClipBlit

NAME

   ClipBlit  --  Calls BltBitMap() after accounting for windows

SYNOPSIS

   ClipBlit(Src, SrcX, SrcY, Dest, DestX, DestY, XSize, YSize, Minterm );
            a0   d0    d1    a1    d2     d3     d4     d5     d6

FUNCTION
   Performs the same function as BltBitMap(), except that it
   takes into account the Layers and ClipRects of the layer library,
   all of which are (and should be) transparent to you.  So, whereas
   BltBitMap() requires pointers to BitMaps, ClipBlit requires pointers to
   the RastPorts that contain the Bitmaps, Layers, et cetera.

   If you are going to blit blocks of data around via the RastPort of your
   Intuition Window, you must call this routine (rather than BltBitMap()).

   Either the Src RastPort, the Dest RastPort, both, or neither, can have
   Layers.  This routine takes care of all cases.

   See BltBitMap() for a thorough explanation.

INPUTS

   Src = pointer to the RastPort of the source for your blit
   SrcX, SrcY = the topleft offset into Src for your data
   Dest = pointer to the RastPort to receive the blitted data
   DestX, DestY = the topleft offset into the destination RastPort
   XSize = the width of the blit
   YSize = the height of the blit
   Minterm = the boolean blitter function, where SRCB is associated with the
             Src RastPort and SRCC goes to the Dest RastPort

RESULT

   None

BUGS

   None

SEE ALSO

   BltBitMap();
```

```
NAME
     CloseFont -- Release a pointer to a system font.

SYNOPSIS
     CloseFont(font)
               a1

     struct TextFont *font;

FUNCTION
     This function indicates that the font specified is no longer
     in use.  It is used to close a font opened by OpenFont, so
     that fonts that are no longer in use do not consume system
     resources.

INPUTS
     font -  a font pointer as returned by OpenFont or OpenDiskFont

BUGS

SEE ALSO
     OpenFont diskfont.library/OpenDiskFont graphics/text.h
```



```
NAME
     CMOVE -- append copper move instruction to user copper list.

SYNOPSIS
     CMOVE( c , a , v )

     CMove( c , a , v )
           a1  d0  d1
     CBump( c )
           a1

     struct UCopList *c;
     APTR    a;
     SHORT   v;

FUNCTION
     Add instruction to move value v to hardware register a.

INPUTS
     c - pointer to UCopList structure
     a - hardware register
     v - 16 bit value to be written

RESULTS
     This is actually a macro that calls CMove(c,&a,v)
     and then calls CBump(c) to bump the local pointer
     to the next instruction. Watch out for macro side affects.

BUGS

SEE ALSO
     CINIT CMOVE CWAIT graphics/copper.h
```

```
NAME
     CopySBitMap --   Syncronize Layer window with contents of
                                               Super BitMap

SYNOPSIS
     CopySBitMap( layer )
                  a0

      struct Layer *layer;

FUNCTION
      This is the inverse of SyncSBitMap.
     Copy all bits from SuperBitMap to Layer bounds.
      This is used for those functions that do not
      want to deal with the ClipRect structures but do want
      to be able to work with a SuperBitMap Layer.

INPUTS

      layer - pointer to a SuperBitMap Layer
          The Layer must already be locked by the caller.

BUGS

SEE ALSO
      LockLayerRom SyncSBitMap
```



```
NAME
     CWAIT -- Append copper wait instruction to user copper list.

SYNOPSIS
     CWAIT( c , v , h )

     CWait( c , v , h )
            al  d0  dl
     CBump( c )
           al

     struct UCopList *c;
     short v,h;

FUNCTION
     Add instruction to wait for vertical beam position v and
     horizontal position h to this intermediate copper list.

INPUTS
     c - pointer to UCopList structure
     v - vertical beam position (relative to top of viewport)
     h - horizontal beam position

RESULTS
     this is actually a macro that calls CWait(c,v,h)
     and then calls CBump(c) to bump the local pointer
     to the next instruction.

BUGS
     User waiting for horizontal values of greater than 222 decimal is illegal.

SEE ALSO
     CINIT CMOVE CEND graphics/copper.h
```

graphics.library/DisownBlitter

```
graphics.library/DisownBlitter                  graphics.library/DisownBlitter

NAME
       DisownBlitter - return blitter to free state.


SYNOPSIS
       DisownBlitter()

FUNCTION
               Free blitter up for use by other blitter users.

INPUTS

RETURNS

SEE ALSO
       OwnBlitter
```

graphics.library/DisposeRegion

```
graphics.library/DisposeRegion                  graphics.library/DisposeRegion

   NAME
       DisposeRegion -- Return all space for this region to free
                        memory pool.

   SYNOPSIS
       DisposeRegion(region)
                      a0

        struct Region *region;

   FUNCTION
       Free all RegionRectangles for this Region then
        free the Region itself.

   INPUTS
       region - pointer to Region structure

   BUGS

   SEE ALSO
        NewRegion graphics/regions.h
```

```
NAME
   DoCollision -- Test every gel in gel list for collisions.

SYNOPSIS
   DoCollision(rp)
               a1

    struct RastPort *rp;

FUNCTION
   Tests each gel in gel list for boundary and gel-to-gel collisions.
   On detecting one of these collisions, the appropriate collision-
    handling routine is called.  See the documentation for a thorough
    description of which collision routine is called. This routine
    expects to find the gel list correctly sorted in Y,X order.
   The system routine SortGList performs this function for the user

INPUTS
   rp = pointer to a RastPort

BUGS

SEE ALSO
   InitGels  SortGList  graphics/gels.h  graphics/gels.h
```



```
NAME
    Draw -- Draw a line between the current pen position
                    and the new x,y position.

SYNOPSIS
    Draw( rp,   x,     y)
          a1  d0:16  d1:16

     struct RastPort *rp;
     SHORT x,y;

FUNCTION
    Draw a line from the current pen position to (x,y).

INPUTS

     rp - pointer to a RastPort
    x,y - point in the RastPort to end the line.

BUGS

SEE ALSO
     Move graphics/rastport.h
```

graphics.library/DrawEllipse graphics.library/DrawEllipse

```
NAME
    DrawEllipse -- Draw an ellipse centered at cx,cy with vertical
       and horizontal radii of a,b respectively.

SYNOPSIS
    DrawEllipse( rp, cx, cy, a, b )
                 a1  d0  d1  d2 d3

    struct RastPort *rp;
    SHORT cx, cy;
    SHORT a, b;

FUNCTION
   Create an elliptical outine within the rectangular region
    specified by the parameters, using the current foreground pen color.

INPUTS
    rp - pointer to the RastPort into which the ellipse will be drawn.
    cx - x coordinate of the centerpoint relative to the rastport.
    cy - y coordinate of the centerpoint relative to the rastport.
    a - the horizontal radius of the ellipse (note: a must be > 0)
    b - the vertical radius of the ellipse (note: b must be > 0)

    Note: this routine does not clip the ellipse to a non-layered rastport.

BUGS

SEE ALSO
    DrawCircle, graphics/rastport.h
```

graphics.library/DrawGList graphics.library/DrawGList

```
NAME
   DrawGList -- Process the gel list, queueing VSprites, drawing Bobs.

SYNOPSIS
   DrawGList(rp, vp)
             a1  a0

    struct RastPort *rp;
    struct ViewPort *vp;

FUNCTION
   Performs one pass of the current gel list.
      - If nextLine and lastColor are defined, these are
            initialized for each gel.
       - If it's a VSprite build it into the copper list.
       - If it's a Bob, draw it into the current raster.
      - Copy the save values into the "old" variables,
            double-buffering if required.

INPUTS
   rp = pointer to the RastPort where Bobs will be drawn
    vp = pointer to the ViewPort for which VSprites will be created

BUGS
   MUSTDRAW isn't implemented yet.

SEE ALSO
    InitGels  graphics/gels.h graphics/rastport.h  graphics/view.h
```

```
NAME
     Flood -- Flood rastport like areafill.

SYNOPSIS
     error = Flood( rp, mode, x, y)
     d0             a1   d2  d0  d1

     BOOLEAN error;
     struct RastPort rp;
     ULONG mode;
     SHORT x,y;

FUNCTION
     Search the BitMap starting at (x,y). Fill all adjacent pixels
     if they are:
     a: arenot the same as AOLPen      Mode 0
     b: same as the one at (x,y)           Mode 1
     When actually doing the fill use the modes that apply to
     standard areafill routine such as drawmodes and patterns.

INPUTS
     rp - pointer to RastPort
     (x,y) - coordinate in BitMap
     mode -  0 fill all adjacent pixels searching for border
             1 fill all adjacent pixels that have same pen number
                     as (x,y)

     Note: in order to use Flood, the destination RastPort must
             have a valid TmpRas raster whose size is as large as
             that of the RastPort.

SEE ALSO
     AreaEnd graphics/rastport.h
```



```
NAME
    FreeColorMap -- Free the ColorMap structure and return memory
                                              to free memory pool.

SYNOPSIS
    FreeColorMap( colormap )
                  a0

     struct ColorMap *colormap;

FUNCTION
     Return the memory to the free memory pool that was allocated
         with GetColorMap.

INPUTS
     colormap - pointer to ColorMap allocated with GetColorMap

RESULT
     The space is made available for others to use.

BUGS

SEE ALSO
    SetRGB4 GetColorMap graphics/view.h
```

graphics.library/FreeCopList graphics.library/FreeCopList

```
NAME
       FreeCopList -- deallocate intermediate copper list

SYNOPSIS
       FreeCopList(coplist)
                   a0

        struct CopList *coplist;

FUNCTION
        Deallocate all memory associated with this copper list.

INPUTS
       coplist  - pointer to structure CopList

RESULTS
        memory returned to memory manager

BUGS

SEE ALSO
        graphics/copper.h
```

graphics.library/FreeCprList graphics.library/FreeCprList

```
NAME
    FreeCprList -- deallocate hardware copper list

SYNOPSIS
    FreeCprList(cprlist)
                a0

     struct cprlist *cprlist;

FUNCTION
    return cprlist to free memory pool

INPUTS
    cprlist - pointer to cprlist structure

RESULTS
     memory returned and made available to other tasks

BUGS

SEE ALSO
     graphics/copper.h
```

```
NAME
   FreeGBuffers -- Deallocate memory obtained by GetGBufers.

SYNOPSIS
   FreeGBuffers(anOb, rp, db)
                a0    a1  d0

    struct AnimOb *anOb;
    struct RastPort *rp;
    BOOL db;

FUNCTION
   For each sequence of each component of the AnimOb,
    deallocate memory for:
       SaveBuffer
       BorderLine
       CollMask and ImageShadow (point to same buffer)
       if db is set (user had used double-buffering) deallocate:
           DBufPacket
           BufBuffer

INPUTS
   anOb = pointer to the AnimOb structure
   rp = pointer to the current RastPort
   db = double-buffer indicator (set TRUE for double-buffering)

BUGS

SEE ALSO
   GetGBuffers  graphics/gels.h  graphics/rastport.h
```



```
NAME
      FreeRaster -- Release an allocated area to the system free memory pool.


SYNOPSIS
      FreeRaster( p, width, height)
                  a0   d0:16  d1:16

       PLANEPTR p;
       USHORT width,height;

   FUNCTION
       Return the memory associated with this PLANEPTR of size
       width and height to the MEMF_CHIP memory pool.

INPUTS
      p  =  a pointer to a memory space  returned  as  a
                    result of a call to AllocRaster.

       width - the width in bits of the bitplane.
       height - number of rows in bitplane.

      the same values of width and height with which  you
      called AllocRaster in the first  place,  when  the
      pointer p returned.   This defines the size of the
      memory  space which is to be returned to the  free
      memory pool.

   BUGS

   SEE ALSO
       AllocRaster graphics/gfx.h
```

```
graphics.library/FreeSprite                              graphics.library/FreeSprite

    NAME
        FreeSprite -- Return sprite for use by others and virtual
                                      sprite machine.


    SYNOPSIS
        FreeSprite( pick )
                    d0

         SHORT pick;

    FUNCTION
         Mark sprite as available for others to use.
        These sprite routines are provided to ease sharing of sprite
         hardware and to handle simple cases of sprite usage and
         movement.  It is assumed the programs that use these routines
         do want to be good citizens in their hearts. ie: they will
         not FreeSprite unless they actually own the sprite.
         Virtual Sprite machine may ignore simple sprite machine.

    INPUTS
        pick - number in range of 0-7

    RESULTS
         sprite made available for subsequent callers of GetSprite
         as well as use by Virtual Sprite Machine

    BUGS

    SEE ALSO
        GetSprite ChangeSprite MoveSprite graphics/sprite.h
```

```
graphics.library/FreeVPortCopLists              graphics.library/FreeVPortCopLists

    NAME
        FreeVPortCopLists -- deallocate all intermediate copper lists and
        their headers from a viewport

    SYNOPSIS
        FreeVPortCopLists(vp)
                          a0

         struct ViewPort *vp;

    FUNCTION
        Search display, color, sprite, and user copper
        lists and call FreeMem() to deallocate them from memory

    INPUTS
        vp - pointer to ViewPort structure

    RESULTS
        vp->DspIns = NULL; vp->SprIns = NULL; vp->ClrIns = NULL;
        vp->UCopIns = NULL;

    BUGS
        none known

    SEE ALSO
         graphics/view.h
```

```
NAME
    GetColorMap -- allocate and initialize Colormap


SYNOPSIS
    cm = GetColorMap( entries )
    d0                d0

     struct ColorMap *cm;
     LONG entries;

FUNCTION
    Allocates, initializes and returns a pointer to a ColorMap
    data structure, later enabling calls to SetRGB4
    and LoadRGB4 to load colors for a view port. The ColorTable
     pointer in the ColorMap structure points to a hardware
     specific colormap data structure. You should not count on
     it being anything you can understand. Use GetRGB4() to
     query it or SetRGB4CM to set it directly.

INPUTS
     entries - number of entries for this colormap

 RESULT
     The pointer value returned by this routine, if nonzero,
    may be stored into the ViewPort.ColorMap pointer.
    If a value of 0 is returned, the system was unable
    to allocate enough memory space for the required
    data structures.

BUGS

SEE ALSO
    SetRGB4 FreeColorMap
```



```
NAME
   GetGBuffers -- Attempt to allocate ALL buffers of an entire AnimOb.

SYNOPSIS
   status = GetGBuffers(anOb, rp, db)
     d0                 a0    a1  d0

    BOOL status;
    struct AnimOb *anOb;
    struct RastPort *rp;
    BOOL db;

FUNCTION
   For each sequence of each component of the AnimOb, allocate memory for:

       SaveBuffer
       BorderLine
       CollMask and ImageShadow (point to same buffer)
       if db is set TRUE (user wants double-buffering) allocate:
           DBufPacket
           BufBuffer

INPUTS
   anOb = pointer to the AnimOb structure
   rp = pointer to the current RastPort
   db = double-buffer indicator (set TRUE for double-buffering)

RESULT
   status = TRUE if the memory allocations were all successful, else FALSE


BUGS
    If any of the memory allocations fail it does not free the partial
    allocations that did succeed.

SEE ALSO
    FreeGBuffers graphics/gels.h
```

```
NAME
    GetRGB4 -- Inquire value of entry in ColorMap.

SYNOPSIS
    value = GetRGB4( colormap, entry )
     d0               a0        d0

      ULONG value;
      struct ColorMap *colormap;
      LONG entry;

FUNCTION
      Read and format a value from the ColorMap.

INPUTS
      colormap - pointer to ColorMap structure
      entry - index into colormap

RESULT
      returns -1 if no valid entry
      return UWORD RGB value 4 bits per gun right justified

BUGS

SEE ALSO
     SetRGB4 LoadRGB4 GetColorMap FreeColorMap graphics/view.h
```



```
NAME
     GetSprite -- Attempt to get a sprite for the simple sprite
                                         manager.

SYNOPSIS
     Sprite_Number = GetSprite( sprite, pick )
       d0                        a0      d0

     SHORT Sprite_Number;
     struct SimpleSprite *sprite;
     SHORT pick;

FUNCTION
     Attempt to allocate one of the eight sprites for private use
     with the simple sprite manager. This must be done before using
     further calls to simple sprite machine. If the programmer
     wants to use 15 color sprites you must allocate both sprites
     and set the 'SPRITE_ATTACHED' bit in the odd sprite's posctldata
     array.

INPUTS
     sprite - ptr to programmers SimpleSprite structure.
     pick - number in the range of 0-7 or
       -1 if programmer just wants the next one.

RESULTS
     If pick is 0-7 attempt to allocate the sprite. If the sprite
     is already allocated then return -1.
     If pick -1 allocate the next sprite starting search at 0.
     If no sprites are available return -1 and fill -1 in num entry
     of SimpleSprite structure.
     If the sprite is available for allocation, mark it allocated
     and fill in the 'num' entry of the SimpleSprite structure.
     If successful return the sprite number.

BUGS

SEE ALSO
     FreeSprite ChangeSprite MoveSprite GetSprite graphics/sprite.h
```

NAME

InitArea -- Initialize vector collection matrix

SYNOPSIS

```
InitArea( areainfo, buffer, maxvectors )
          a0        a1      d0

struct AreaInfo *areainfo;
APTR buffer;
SHORT maxvectors;
```

FUNCTION

This function provides initialization for the vector collection matrix such that it has a size of (max vectors). The size of the region pointed to by buffer (short pointer) should be five (5) times as large as maxvectors. This size is in bytes. Areafills done by using AreaMove, AreaDraw, and AreaEnd must have enough space allocated in this table to store all the points of the largest fill. AreaEllipse takes up two vectors for every call. If AreaMove/Draw/Ellipse detect too many vectors going into the buffer they will return -1.

INPUTS

areainfo - pointer to AreaInfo structure
buffer - pointer to chunk of memory to collect vertices
maxvectors - max number of vectors this buffer can hold

RESULT

Pointers are set up to begin storage of vectors done by AreaMove, AreaDraw, and AreaEllipse.

BUGS

SEE ALSO

AreaEnd AreaMove AreaDraw AreaEllipse graphics/rastport.h

NAME

InitBitMap -- Initialize bit map structure with input values.

SYNOPSIS

```
InitBitMap( bm, depth, width, height )
            a0  d0     d1     d2

struct BitMap *bm;
BYTE depth;
SHORT width, height;
```

FUNCTION

Initialize various elements in the BitMap structure to correctly reflect depth, width, and height.
Must be used before use of BitMap in other graphics calls.
The Planes[8] are not initialized and need to be set up by the caller. The Planes table was put at the end of the structure so that it may be truncated to conserve space, as well as extended. All routines that use BitMap should only depend on existence of depth number of bitplanes.

INPUTS

bm - pointer to a BitMap structure (gfx.h)
depth - number of bitplanes that this bitmap will have
width - number of bits (columns) wide for this BitMap
height- number of bits (rows) tall for this BitMap

BUGS

SEE ALSO

graphics/gfx.h

```
NAME
    InitGels -- initialize a gel list; must be called before using gels.

SYNOPSIS
    InitGels(head, tail, GInfo)
             a0    a1    a2

     struct VSprite *head, *tail;
     struct GelsInfo *GInfo;

FUNCTION
    Assigns the VSprites as the head and tail of the gel list in GfxBase.
    Links these two gels together as the keystones of the list.
    If the collHandler vector points to some memory array, sets
     the BORDERHIT vector to NULL.

INPUTS
    head = pointer to the VSprite structure to be used as the gel list head

    tail = pointer to the VSprite structure to be used as the gel list tail

    GInfo = pointer to the GelsInfo structure to be initialized

BUGS

SEE ALSO
     graphics/gels.h   graphics/rastport.h
```



```
NAME
    InitGMasks -- Initialize all of the masks of an AnimOb.

SYNOPSIS
    InitGMasks(anOb)
               a0

     struct AnimOb *anOb;

FUNCTION
    For every sequence of every component call InitMasks.

INPUTS
    anOb = pointer to the AnimOb

BUGS

SEE ALSO
     InitMasks graphics/gels.h
```

```
NAME
   InitMasks -- Initialize the BorderLine and CollMask masks of a VSprite.


SYNOPSIS
   InitMasks(vs)
             a0

    struct VSprite *vs;

FUNCTION
   Creates the appropriate BorderLine and CollMask masks of the VSprite.
   Correctly detects if the VSprite is actually a Bob definition, handles
   the image data accordingly.

INPUTS
   vs = pointer to the VSprite structure

BUGS

SEE ALSO
   InitGels  graphics/gels.h
```



```
NAME
     InitRastPort -- Initialize raster port structure

SYNOPSIS
     InitRastPort( rp )
                   a1

     struct RastPort *rp;

FUNCTION
    Initialize  a RastPort structure to standard values.
    The struct Rastport describes a control  structure
    for a write-able raster.   The RastPort  structure
    describes  how a complete single playfield display
    will be written into. A  RastPort   structure   is
    referenced   whenever   any drawing  or   filling
    operations  are  to be performed on a  section  of
    memory.

    The section of memory which is being used in  this
    way  may  or  may not be presently a part  of  the
    current actual onscreen display memory.   The name
    of  the actual memory section which is  linked  to
    the  RastPort is referred to here as a "raster" or
    as a bitmap.

    NOTE:    Calling   the   routine InitRastPort only
    establishes    various   defaults.    It  does   NOT
    establish  where,   in  memory,  the  rasters  are
    located. To do graphics with this RastPort the user
     must set up the BitMap pointer in the RastPort.

INPUTS
     rp      = pointer to a RastPort structure.

RESULT
     all entries in RastPort get zeroed out.
     exceptions:
             The following get -1:
                     Mask,FgPen,AOLPen,LinePtrn
             DrawMode = JAM2
             The font is set to the standard system font

BUGS

SEE ALSO
     graphics/rastport.h
```

```
NAME
     InitTmpRas -- Initialize area of local memory for usage by
                   areafill, floodfill, text.

SYNOPSIS
     InitTmpRas(tmpras, buffer, size)
                a0      a1      d0

     struct TmpRas *tmpras;
     APTR buffer;
     LONG size;

FUNCTION
     The area of memory pointed to by buffer is set up to be used
     by RastPort routines that may need to get some memory for
     intermediate operations in preparation to putting the graphics
     into the final BitMap.
     Tmpras is used to control the usage of buffer.

INPUTS
     tmpras - pointer to a TmpRas structure to be linked into
             a RastPort
     buffer - pointer to a contguous piece of chip memory.
     size - size in bytes of buffer

RESULT
     makes buffer available for users of RastPort

BUGS
     Would be nice if RastPorts could share one TmpRas.

SEE ALSO
     AreaEnd Flood Text graphics/rastport.h
```



```
NAME
InitView - Initialize View structure.

SYNOPSIS
     InitView( view )
               a1

     struct View *view;

FUNCTION
     Initialize View structure to default values.

INPUTS
     view - pointer to a View structure

RESULT
     View structure set to all 0's. (1.0,1.1.1.2)
     Then values are put in DxOffset,DyOffset to properly position
     default display about .5 inches from top and left on monitor.
     InitView pays no attention to previous contents of view.

BUGS

SEE ALSO
     MakeVPort graphics/view.h
```

```
graphics.library/InitVPort                          graphics.library/InitVPort

   NAME
        InitVPort - Initialize ViewPort structure.

   SYNOPSIS
        InitVPort( vp )
                   a0

        struct ViewPort *vp;

   FUNCTION
        Initialize ViewPort structure to default values.

   INPUTS
        vp - pointer to a ViewPort structure

   RESULT

   BUGS

   SEE ALSO
        MakeVPort graphics/view.h
```

```
graphics.library/LoadRGB4                            graphics.library/LoadRGB4

NAME
        LoadRGB4 -- Load RGB color values from table.

SYNOPSIS
        LoadRGB4( vp, colors , count )
                  a0     a1     d0:16

        struct ViewPort *vp;
        UWORD colors[];
        SHORT count;

FUNCTION
        load the count words of the colormapper from table starting at
        entry 0.

INPUTS
        vp - pointer to ViewPort, whos colors you want to change
        colors - pointer to table of RGB values set up as an array
                  of USHORTS
                        background--  0x0RGB
                        color1    --  0x0RGB
                        color2    --  0x0RGB
                         etc.         UWORD per value.
                The colors are interpreted as 15 = maximum intensity.
                                   0 = minimum intensity.
        count   = number of UWORDs in the table to load into the
          colormap starting at color 0(background) and proceeding
          to the next higher color number

RESULTS
        The ViewPort should have a pointer to a valid ColorMap to store
        the colors in.
        Update the hardware copperlist to reflect the new colors.
        Update the intermediate copperlist with the new colors.

BUGS

SEE ALSO
        SetRGB4 GetRGB4 GetColorMap graphics/view.h
```

graphics.library/LoadView   graphics.library/LoadView

```
NAME
    LoadView -- Use a (possibly freshly created) coprocessor instruction
                list to create the current display.

SYNOPSIS
    LoadView( View )
              A1

     struct View *View;

FUNCTION
     Install a new view to be displayed during the next display
     refresh pass.
    Coprocessor instruction list has been created by
    InitVPort, MakeView, and MrgCop.

INPUTS
    View - a pointer to the View structure which contains the
    pointer to the constructed coprocessor instructions list.

RESULT
    The new View is displayed, according to your instructions.
     The vertical blank routine will pick this pointer up and
     direct the copper to start displaying this View.

BUGS

SEE ALSO
    InitVPort MakeVPort MrgCop intuition/RethinkDisplay graphics/view.h
```

graphics.library/LockLayerRom   graphics.library/LockLayerRom
*

```
NAME
    LockLayerRom -- Lock Layer structure by rom(gfx lib) code.

SYNOPSIS
    LockLayerRom( layer )
                  a5

    struct Layer *layer;

FUNCTION
    Return when the layer is locked and no other task may
    alter the ClipRect structure in the Layer structure.
    This call does not destroy any registers.
    This call nests so that callers in this chain will not lock
    themselves out.
    Do not have the Layer locked during a call to intuition.
    There is a potential deadlock problem here, if intuition
    needs to get other locks as well.
    Having the layer locked prevents other tasks from using the
    layer library functions, most notably intuition itself. So
    be brief.
    layer.library's LockLayer is identical to LockLayerRom.

INPUTS
    layer - pointer to Layer structure

RESULTS
    The layer is locked and the task can render assuming the
    ClipRects will not change out from underneath it until
    an UnlockLayerRom is called.

SEE ALSO
    UnlockLayerRom graphics/clip.h
```

```
NAME
     MakeVPort -- generate display copper list.

SYNOPSIS
     MakeVPort( view, viewport )
                a0    a1

     struct View *view;
     struct ViewPort *viewport;

FUNCTION
     Use information in the View, ViewPort, ViewPort->RasInfo;
     construct intermediate copper list for this ViewPort.

INPUTS
     view - pointer to View structure
     viewport - pointer to ViewPort structure
         The viewport must have valid pointer to a RasInfo.

RESULTS
     constructs intermediate copper list and puts pointers in
     viewport.DspIns
     If the ColorMap ptr in ViewPort is NULL then it uses colors
     from the default color table.
     If DUALPF in Modes then there must be a second RasInfo pointed
     to by the first RasInfo

BUGS

SEE ALSO
     InitVPort MrgCop graphics/view.h
     Intuition's MakeScreen RemakeDisplay and RethinkDisplay
```



```
NAME
     Move -- Move graphics pen position.

SYNOPSIS
     Move( rp,   x,    y)
           a1  d0:16 d1:16

     struct RastPort *rp;
     SHORT x,y;

FUNCTION
     Move graphics pen position to (x,y) relative to upper left (0,0)
     of RastPort.
     Note: Text uses the same position.

INPUTS
     rp - pointer to a RastPort structure
     x,y - point in the RastPort

RESULTS

BUGS

SEE ALSO
     Draw graphics/rastport.h
```

```
NAME
       MoveSprite -- Move sprite to a point relative to top of viewport.

SYNOPSIS
       MoveSprite( vp, sprite, x, y )
                   a0  a1      d0 d1

         struct ViewPort *vp;
         struct SimpleSprite *sprite;
         SHORT   x,y;

FUNCTION
         Move sprite image to new place on display.

INPUTS
         vp - pointer to ViewPort structure
              if vp = 0, sprite is positioned relative to View.
         sprite - pointer to SimpleSprite structure
         (x,y) - new position relative to top of viewport or view.

RESULTS
         Calculate the hardware information for the sprite and
         place it in the posctldata array. During next video display
         the sprite will appear in new position.

BUGS
         Sprites really appear one pixel to the left of the position you specify.
         This bug affects the apparent display position of the sprite on the screen,
    but does not affect the numeric position relative to the viewport or view.

SEE ALSO
       FreeSprite ChangeSprite GetSprite graphics/sprite.h
```



```
NAME
    MrgCop -- Merge together coprocessor instructions.

SYNOPSIS
    MrgCop( View )
            A1

     struct View *View;

FUNCTION
    Merge together the display, color, sprite and user coprocessor
    instructions into a single coprocessor instruction stream.  This
    essentially creates a per-display-frame program for the coprocessor.
    This function MrgCop is used, for example, by the graphics animation
    routines which effectively add information into an essentially
    static background display.  This changes some of the user
    or sprite instructions, but not those which have formed the
    basic display in the first place.  When all forms of coprocessor
    instructions are merged together, you will have a complete per-
    frame instruction list for the coprocessor.

    Restrictions:  Each of the coprocessor instruction lists MUST be
    internally sorted in min to max Y-X order.  The merge routines
    depend on this!
             Each list must be terminated using CEND(copperlist)

INPUTS
    View - a pointer to the view structure whose coprocessor
           instructions are to be merged.

RESULT

    The view structure will now contain a complete, sorted/merged
    list of instructions for the coprocessor, ready to be used by
    the display processor.  The display processor is told to use
    this new instruction stream through the instruction LoadView().

BUGS

SEE ALSO
    InitVPort MakeVPort LoadView graphics/view.h
             Intuition's RethinkDisplay
```

```
NAME
     NewRegion -- Get a clear region.

SYNOPSIS
     region = NewRegion()
      d0

      struct Region *region;

FUNCTION
      Create a Region structure, initialize it to empty and return
      a pointer it.

RESULTS
      region - pointer to initialized region. If it could not allocate
              required memory region = NULL.

INPUTS
      none

BUGS

SEE ALSO
      graphics/regions.h
```



```
NAME
     OpenFont -- Get a pointer to a system font.

SYNOPSIS
     font = OpenFont(textAttr)
     d0              a0

     struct TextFont *font;
     struct TextAttr *textAttr;

FUNCTION
     This function searches the system font space for the graphics
     text font that best matches the attributes specified.  The
     pointer to the font returned can be used in subsequent
     SetFont and CloseFont calls.  It is important to match this
     call with a corresponding CloseFont call for effective
     management of ram fonts.

INPUTS
     textAttr - a TextAttr structure that describes the text font
         attributes desired

RESULTS
     font is zero if the desired font cannot be found.  If the named
     font is found, but the size and style specified are not
     available, a font with the nearest attributes is returned.

BUGS

SEE ALSO
     CloseFont SetFont diskfont.library/OpenDiskFont graphics/text.h
```

```
graphics.library/OrRectRegion                    graphics.library/OrRectRegion

    NAME
        OrRectRegion -- Perform 2d OR operation of rectangle
                        with region, leaving result in region.

    SYNOPSIS
        status = OrRectRegion(region,rectangle)
          d0                    a0       a1

         BOOL status
         struct Region *region;
         struct Rectangle *rectangle;

    FUNCTION
        If any portion of rectangle is not in the region then add
        that portion to the region.

    INPUTS
        region - pointer to Region structure
        rectangle - pointer to Rectangle structure

    RESULTS
         status - return TRUE if successful operation
                  return FALSE if ran out of memory

    BUGS

    SEE ALSO
         AndRectRegion OrRegionRegion graphics/regions.h
```

```
graphics.library/OrRegionRegion                graphics.library/OrRegionRegion

    NAME
        OrRegionRegion -- Perform 2d OR operation of one region
                          with second region, leaving result in second region

    SYNOPSIS
        status = OrRegionRegion(region1,region2)
          d0                      a0      a1

         BOOL status;
         struct Region *region1, *region2;

    FUNCTION
        If any portion of region1  is not in the region then add
        that portion to the region2

    INPUTS
        region1 - pointer to Region structure
        region2 - pointer to Region structure

    RESULTS
         status - return TRUE if successful operation
                  return FALSE if ran out of memory

    BUGS

    SEE ALSO
         OrRectRegion graphics/regions.h
```

graphics.library/OwnBlitter

```
NAME
    OwnBlitter -- get the blitter for private usage

SYNOPSIS
    OwnBlitter()

FUNCTION
     If blitter is available return immediately with the blitter
     locked for your exclusive use. If the blitter is not available
     put task to sleep. It will be awakened as soon as the blitter
     is available. When the task first owns the blitter the blitter
     may still be finishing up a blit for the previous owner. You
     must do a WaitBlit before actually using the blitter registers.

     Calls to OwnBlitter() not nest. If a task that owns the
     blitter calls OwnBlitter() again, a lockup will result.
     (Same situation if the task calls a system function
     that tries to own the blitter).

INPUTS
     NONE

RETURNS

SEE ALSO
     DisownBlitter
```

graphics.library/PolyDraw

```
NAME
        PolyDraw -- Draw lines from table of (x,y) values.

SYNOPSIS
        PolyDraw( rp, count , array )
                  a1   d0      a0

        struct RastPort *rp;
        SHORT count;
        SHORT   array[];

FUNCTION
        starting with the first pair draw connected lines to
        it and every succeeding pair.

INPUTS
        rp - pointer to RastPort structure
        count -  number of points in array (x,y) pairs
        array - pointer to first (x,y) pair

BUGS

SEE ALSO
        Draw Move graphics/rastport.h
```

NAME

QBlit -- Queue up a request for blitter usage

SYNOPSIS

```
QBlit( bp )
       a1

struct bltnode *bp;
```

FUNCTION

Link a request for the use of the blitter to the end of the current blitter queue. The pointer bp points to a blit structure containing, among other things, the link information, and the address of your routine which is to be called when the blitter queue finally gets around to this specific request. When your routine is called, you are in control of the blitter ... it is not busy with anyone else's requests. This means that you can directly specify the register contents and start the blitter. See the description of the blit structure and the uses of QBlit in the section titled Graphics Support in the OS Kernel Manual. Your code must be written to run either in supervisor or user mode on the 68000.

INPUTS

bp - pointer to a blit structure

RESULT

Your routine is called when the blitter is ready for you. In general requests for blitter usage through this channel are put in front of those who use the blitter via OwnBlitter and DisownBlitter. However for small blits there is more overhead using the queuer than Own/Disown Blitter.

BUGS

SEE ALSO

QBSBlit hardware/blit.h

NAME

QBSBlit -- Synchronize the blitter request with the video beam.

SYNOPSIS

```
QBSBlit( bsp )
         a1

struct bltnode *bsp;
```

FUNCTION

Call a user routine for use of the blitter, enqueued separately from the QBlit queue. Calls the user routine contained in the blit structure when the video beam is located at a specified position onscreen. Useful when you are trying to blit into a visible part of the screen and wish to perform the data move while the beam is not trying to display that same area. (prevents showning part of an old display and part of a new display simultaneously). Blitter requests on the QBSBlit queue take precedence over those on the regular blitter queue. The beamposition is specified the blitnode.

INPUTS

bsp - pointer to a blit structure. See description in the Graphics Support section of the manual for more info.

RESULT

User routine is called when the QBSBlit queue reaches this request AND the video beam is in the specified position. If there are lots of blits going on and the video beam has wrapped around back to the top it will call all the remaining bltnodes as fast as it can to try and catch up.

BUGS

Not very smart when getting blits from different tasks. They all get put in same queue so there are unfortunately some interdependencies with the beam syncing.

SEE ALSO

QBlit hardware/blit.h

```
NAME
    ReadPixel -- read the pen number value of the pixel at a
                 specified x,y location within a certain RastPort.

SYNOPSIS
    penno = ReadPixel( rp,    x,    y )
      d0               a1  d0:16 d1:16

     LONG    penno;
     struct RastPort *rp;
     SHORT   x,y;

FUNCTION
    Combine the bits from each of the bit-planes used to describe
    a particular RastPort into the pen number selector which that
    bit combination normally forms for the system hardware selection
    of pixel color.

INPUTS
    rp -  pointer to a RastPort structure
    (x,y) a point in the RastPort

RESULT
    Pen - (0..255) number at that position is returned.
             -1 is returned if cannot read that pixel

BUGS

SEE ALSO
    WritePixel       graphics/rastport.h
```



```
NAME
    RectFill -- Fill a defined rectangular area with
            the current drawing pen color, outline color,
            secondary color, and pattern.

SYNOPSIS
             RectFill( rp, xmin, ymin, xmax, ymax)
              a1  d0:16 d1:16 d2:16 d3:16

     struct RastPort *rp;
     SHORT xmin,ymin;
     SHORT xmax,ymax;

FUNCTION
             Fill  the  rectangular  region  specified  by  the
             parameters  with the chosen pen  colors,  areafill
             pattern, and drawing mode. If no areafill pattern is
             specified, fill the rectangular region with the FgPen
             color, taking into account the drawing mode.

INPUTS
             rp - pointer to a RastPort structure
             (xmin,ymin) (xmax,ymax) are the coordinates of the upper
             left corner and the lower right corner, respectively, of the
    rectangle.
             The following relation MUST be true:
             (xmax >= xmin) and (ymax >= ymin)

BUGS
             Complement mode with FgPen complements all bitplanes.

SEE ALSO
     AreaEnd graphics/rastport.h
```

```
graphics.library/RemBob                                   graphics.library/RemBob

    NAME
       RemBob -- Remove a Bob from the gel list.

    SYNOPSIS
       RemBob(bob)

        struct Bob *bob;

    FUNCTION
       Marks a Bob as no-longer-required.  The gels internal code then
        removes the Bob from the list of active gels the next time
        DrawGList is executed.   This is implemented as a macro.
        If the user is double-buffering the Bob, it could take two
        calls to DrawGList before the Bob actually disappears from
        the RastPort.

    INPUTS
       Bob = pointer to the Bob to be removed

    BUGS

    SEE ALSO
       RemIBob  DrawGList  graphics/gels.h  graphics/gfxmacros.h
```

```
graphics.library/RemFont                                  graphics.library/RemFont

    NAME
        RemFont -- Remove a font from the system list.

    SYNOPSIS
        RemFont(textFont)
                al

        struct TextFont *textFont;

    FUNCTION
        This function removes a font from the system, ensuring that
        access to it is restricted to those applications that
        currently have an active pointer to it: i.e. no new SetFont
        requests to this font are satisfied.

    INPUTS
        textFont - the TextFont structure to remove.

    BUGS

    SEE ALSO
        SetFont AddFont graphics/text.h
```

```
NAME
   RemIBob -- Immediately remove a Bob from the gel list and the RastPort.


SYNOPSIS
   RemIBob(bob, rp, vp)
           a0   a1  a2

    struct Bob *bob;
    struct RastPort *rp;
    struct ViewPort *vp;

FUNCTION
   Removes a Bob immediately by uncoupling it from the gel list and
    erases it from the RastPort.

INPUTS
   bob = pointer to the Bob to be removed
   rp = pointer to the RastPort if the Bob is to be erased
   vp = pointer to the ViewPort for beam-synchronizing

BUGS

SEE ALSO
   InitGels  RemVSprite  graphics/gels.h
```



```
NAME
   RemVSprite -- Remove a VSprite from the current gel list.

SYNOPSIS
   RemVSprite(vs)
              a0

    struct VSprite *vs;

FUNCTION
   Unlinks the VSprite from the current gel list.

INPUTS
   vs = pointer to the VSprite structure to be removed from the gel list

BUGS

SEE ALSO
   InitGels  RemIBob  graphics/gels.h
```

```
NAME
     ScrollRaster -- Push bits in rectangle in raster around by
                     dx,dy towards 0,0 inside rectangle.
SYNOPSIS
     ScrollRaster( rp, dx, dy, xmin, ymin, xmax, ymax)
                   a1  d0  d1   d2    d3    d4    d5

     struct RastPort *rp;
     SHORT dx,dy;
     SHORT xmin,ymin;
     SHORT xmax,ymax;

FUNCTION
     Move the bits in the raster by (dx,dy) towards (0,0)
     The space vacated is RectFilled with BGPen.
     Limit the scroll operation to the rectangle defined
     by (xmin,ymin)(xmax,ymax). Bits outside will not be
     affected. If xmax,ymax is outside the rastport then use
     the lower right corner of the rastport.
     If you are dealing with a SimpleRefresh layered RastPort you
     should check rp->Layer->Flags & LAYER_REFRESH to see if
     there is any damage in the damage list.  If there is you should
     call the appropriate BeginRefresh(Intuition) or BeginUpdate(graphics)
     routine sequence.

INPUTS
    rp - pointer to a RastPort structure
    dx,dy are integers that may be postive, zero, or negative
     xmin,ymin - upper left of bounding rectangle
     xmax,ymax - lower right of bounding rectangle

EXAMPLE
    ScrollRaster(rp,0,1)    /* shift raster up by one row */
    ScrollRaster(rp,-1,-1)  /* shift raster down and to the right by 1 pixel

BUGS
     In 1.2/V1.3 if you ScrollRaster a SUPERBITMAP exactly left or right,
     and there is no TmpRas attached to the RastPort, the system will
     allocate one for you, but will never free it or record its location.
     The only workaround is to attach a valid TmpRas of size at least
     MAXBYTESPERROW to the RastPort before the call.

     ScrollRaster does not add the shifted areas into the damage list.
     This can cause difficulties for SIMPLE_REFRESH windows.

SEE ALSO
     graphics/rastport.h
```



```
NAME
     ScrollVPort -- Reinterpret RasInfo information in ViewPort.

SYNOPSIS
     ScrollVPort( vp )
                  a0

     struct ViewPort *vp;

FUNCTION
     After the programmer has adjusted the Offset values in
     the RasInfo structures of ViewPort, change the
     the copper lists to reflect the the Scroll positions.
     Changing the BitMap ptr in RasInfo and not changing the
     the Offsets will effect a double buffering affect.

INPUTS
    vp - pointer to a ViewPort structure
             that is currently be displayed.
RESULTS
     modifies hardware and intermediate copperlists to reflect
     new RasInfo

BUGS
    pokes not fast enough to avoid some visible hashing of display

SEE ALSO
     MakeVPort MrgCop LoadView  graphics/view.h
```

```
graphics.library/SetAPen                                graphics.library/SetAPen

    NAME
        SetAPen -- Set primary pen

    SYNOPSIS
        SetAPen( rp, pen )
                 a1  d0

        struct RastPort *rp;
        UBYTE pen;

    FUNCTION
        Set the primary drawing pen for lines, fills, and text.

    INPUTS
        rp - pointer to RastPort structure.
        pen - (0-255)

    RESULT
        Changes the minterms in the RastPort to reflect new primary pen.
        Set line drawer to restart pattern.

    BUGS

SEE ALSO
        SetBPen graphics/rastport.h
```

```
graphics.library/SetBPen                                graphics.library/SetBPen

    NAME
        SetBPen -- Set secondary pen

    SYNOPSIS
        SetBPen( rp, pen )
                 a1  d0

        struct RastPort *rp;
        UBYTE pen;

    FUNCTION
        Set the secondary drawing pen for lines, fills, and text.

    INPUTS
        rp - pointer to RastPort structure.
        pen - (0-255)

    RESULT
        Changes the minterms in the RastPort to reflect new secondary pen.
        Set line drawer to restart pattern.

    BUGS

SEE ALSO
        SetAPen graphics/rastport.h
```

```
graphics.library/SetCollision                  graphics.library/SetCollision

   NAME
      SetCollision -- Set a pointer to a user collision routine.

   SYNOPSIS
      SetCollision(num, routine, GInfo)
                   d0   a0       a1

       ULONG num;
       VOID (*routine)();
       struct GelsInfo *GInfo;

   FUNCTION
      Sets a specified entry (num) in the user's collision vectors table
       equal to the address of the specified collision routine.

   INPUTS
      num = collision vector number
      routine = pointer to the user's collision routine
      GInfo = pointer to a GelsInfo structure

   BUGS

   SEE ALSO
      InitGels  graphics/gels.h  graphics/rastport.h
```

```
graphics.library/SetDrMd                            graphics.library/SetDrMd

   NAME
        SetDrMd -- Set drawing mode

   SYNOPSIS
        SetDrMd( rp, mode )
                 a1  d0:8

        struct RastPort *rp;
        UBYTE mode;

   FUNCTION
        Set the drawing mode for lines, fills and text.
        Get the bit definitions from rastport.h

   INPUTS
        rp - pointer to RastPort structure.
        mode - 0-255, some combinations may not make much sense.

   RESULT
        The mode set is dependant on the bits selected.
        Change minterms to reflect new drawing mode.
        Set line drawer to restart pattern.

   BUGS

   SEE ALSO
        SetAPen graphics/rastport.h
```

graphics.library/SetFont graphics.library/SetFont

```
NAME
     SetFont -- Set the text font and attributes in a RastPort.

SYNOPSIS
     SetFont(rp, font)
             a1   a0

     struct RastPort *rp;
     struct TextFont *font;

FUNCTION
     This function sets the font in the RastPort to that described
     by font, and updates the text attributes to reflect that
     change.  If font is zero, this call leaves the RastPort
     with no font.  This function clears the effect of any previous
     soft styles.

INPUTS
     rp - the RastPort in which the text attributes are to be changed
     font - pointer to a TextFont structure returned from OpenFont
         or OpenDiskFont

BUGS

SEE ALSO
     OpenFont diskfont.library/OpenDiskFont graphics/text.h
```

graphics.library/SetOPen graphics.library/SetOPen

```
NAME
     SetOPen -- Change the Area OutLine pen and turn on Outline
                mode for areafills.

SYNOPSIS
     SetOPen(rp, pen)

     struct RastPort *rp;
     UBYTE pen;

FUNCTION
     This is implemented as a c-macro.
     Pen is the pen number that will be used to draw a border
     around an areafill during AreaEnd().

INPUTS
     rp = pointer to RastPort structure
     pen = number  between 0-255

BUGS

SEE ALSO
     AreaEnd() graphics/gfxmacros.h graphics/rastport.h
```

graphics.library/SetRast

```
graphics.library/SetRast                          graphics.library/SetRast

   NAME
       SetRast - Set an entire drawing area to a specified color.

   SYNOPSIS
       SetRast( rp, pen )
                al  d0

        struct RastPort *rp;
        UBYTE pen;

   FUNCTION
       Set the entire contents of the specified RastPort to the
       specified pen.

   INPUTS
       rp - pointer to RastPort structure
       pen - the pen number (0-255) to jam into bitmap

   RESULT
       The drawing area becomes the selected pen number.

   BUGS

   SEE ALSO
        RectFill graphics/rastport.h
```

graphics.library/SetRGB4

```
graphics.library/SetRGB4                          graphics.library/SetRGB4

   NAME
      SetRGB4 -- Set one color register for this viewport.

   SYNOPSIS
      SetRGB4(  vp, n,   r,    g,    b)
                a0  d0  d1:4  d2:4  d3:4

       struct ViewPort *vp;
       SHORT n;
       UBYTE r,g,b;

   FUNCTION
       Change the color look up table so that this viewport displays
       the color (r,g,b) for pen number n.

   INPUTS
       vp - pointer to  viewport structure
      n - the color number (range from 0 to 31)
      r - red level
      g - green level
      b - blue level

   RESULT
       If there is a ColorMap for this viewport store the value in
       in the structure ColorMap.
      The selected color register is changed to match your specs.
       If the color value is unused then nothing will happen.

   BUGS

   SEE ALSO
      LoadRGB4 GetRGB4 graphics/view.h
```

```
NAME
    SetRGB4CM -- Set one color register for this ColorMap.

SYNOPSIS
    SetRGB4CM(  cm,  n,   r,    g,    b)
                a0  d0  d1:4  d2:4  d3:4

    struct ColorMap *cm;
    SHORT n;
    UBYTE r,g,b;

INPUTS
     cm = colormap
    n = the color number (range from 0 to 31)
    r = red level
    g = green level
    b = blue level

RESULT
     Store the (r,g,b) triplet at index n of the ColorMap structure.
    This function can be used to set up a ColorMap before before
     linking it into a viewport.

BUGS

SEE ALSO
    GetColorMap GetRGB4 SetRGB4 graphics/view.h
```



```
NAME
     SetSoftStyle -- Set the soft style of the current font.

SYNOPSIS
     newStyle = SetSoftStyle(rp, style, enable)
       d0                    a1  d0      d1

     ULONG   newStyle;
     struct RastPort *rp;
     ULONG   style;
     ULONG   enable;

FUNCTION
     This function alters the soft style of the current font.  Only
     those bits that are also set in enable are affected.  The
     resulting style is returned, since some style request changes
     will not be honored when the implicit style of the font
     precludes changing them.

INPUTS
     rp - the RastPort from which the font and style are extracted.
     style - the new font style to set, subject to enable.
     enable - those bits in style to be changed.  Any set bits here
         that would not be set as a result of AskSoftStyle will
         be ignored, and the newStyle result will not be as
         expected.

RESULTS
     newStyle - the resulting style, both as a result of previous
         soft style selection, the effect of this function, and
         the style inherent in the set font.

BUGS

SEE ALSO
     AskSoftStyle graphics/text.h
```

```
graphics.library/SortGList                          graphics.library/SortGList

   NAME
      SortGList -- Sort the current gel list, ordering its y,x coordinates.

   SYNOPSIS
      SortGList(rp)
                a1

   FUNCTION
      Sorts the current gel list according to the gels' y,x coordinates.
      This sorting is essential before calls to DrawGList or DoCollision.

   INPUTS
      rp = pointer to the RastPort structure containing the GelsInfo

   BUGS

   SEE ALSO
      InitGels  DoCollision  DrawGList  graphics/rastport.h
```

```
graphics.library/SyncSBitMap                      graphics.library/SyncSBitMap

   NAME
       SyncSBitMap --   Syncronize Super BitMap with whatever is
                        in the standard Layer bounds.

   SYNOPSIS
       SyncSBitMap( layer )
                      a0

        struct Layer *layer;

   FUNCTION
       Copy all bits from ClipRects in Layer into Super BitMap
        BitMap.  This is used for those functions that do not
        want to deal with the ClipRect structures but do want
        to be able to work with a SuperBitMap Layer.

   INPUTS
        layer - pointer to a Layer that has a SuperBitMap
                The Layer should already be locked by the caller.

   RESULT
        A bitmap that the programmer can now diddle with the bits.
        After diddling the programmer should call CopySBitMap to
        copy the bits back into the onscreen layer.

   BUGS

   SEE ALSO
        CopySBitMap graphics/clip.h
```

```
NAME
     Text -- Write text characters (no formatting).

SYNOPSIS
     Text(rp, string, count)
          a1   a0     d0-0:16

     struct  RastPort *rp;
     STRPTR  string;
     SHORT   count;

FUNCTION
     This graphics function writes printable text characters to the
     specified RastPort at the current position.  No control meaning
     is applied to any of the characters, and only text on the
     current line is output.
     If the characters displayed run past the RastPort boundary,
     the current position is truncated to the boundary, and
     thus does not represent the true position.

INPUTS
     rp - a pointer to the RastPort which describes where the
         text is to be output
     count - the string length.  If zero, there are no characters
          to be output.
     string - the address of string to output

BUGS

     The maximum string length (in pixels) is limited to (1024 - 16 = 1008)
         pixels wide.

     Text is clipped to the width of the rastport even if the Text() write
         was made starting to the left of the rastport.

SEE ALSO
     Move TextLength graphics/text.h graphics/rastport.h
```



```
NAME
     TextLength -- Determine raster length of text data.

SYNOPSIS
     length = TextLength(rp, string, count)
     d0:16               a1    a0    d0:16

     SHORT length;
     struct RastPort *rp;
     STRPTR string;
     SHORT count;

FUNCTION
     This graphics function determines the length that text data
     would occupy if output to the specified RastPort with the
     current attributes.  The length is specified as the number of
     raster dots: to determine what the current position would be
     after a Write using this string, add the length to cp_x
     (cp_y is unchanged by Write).

INPUTS
     rp - a pointer to the RastPort which describes where the
         text attributes reside.
     string - the address of string to determine the length of
     count - the string length.  If zero, there are no characters
         in the string.

RESULTS
     length - the number of pixels in x this text would occupy, not
         including any negative kerning that may take place at
         the beginning of the text string, nor taking into
         account the effects of any clipping that may take
         place.

BUGS
     A length that would overflow single word arithmatic is not
     calculated correctly.

SEE ALSO
     Text graphics/text.h graphics/rastport.h
```

```
graphics.library/UnlockLayerRom                graphics.library/UnlockLayerRom
                              *
   NAME
        UnlockLayerRom -- Unlock Layer structure by rom(gfx lib) code.

   SYNOPSIS
        UnlockLayerRom( layer )
                         a5

   FUNCTION
        Release the lock on this layer. If the same task has called
        LockLayerRom more than once than the same number of calls to
        UnlockLayerRom must happen before the layer is actually freed
        so that other tasks may use it.
        This call does destroy scratch registers.
        This call is identical to UnlockLayer (layers.library).

   INPUTS
        layer - pointer to Layer structure

   BUGS

   SEE ALSO
        LockLayerRom graphics/clip.h
                                *
```

```
graphics.library/VBeamPos                            graphics.library/VBeamPos

   NAME
        VBeamPos -- Get vertical beam position at this instant.

   SYNOPSIS
        pos = VBeamPos()
         d0

        LONG pos;

   FUNCTION
        Get the vertical beam position from the hardware.

   INPUTS
        none

   RESULT
        interrogates hardware for beam position and returns value.
        valid results in the range of 0-511
        Because of multitasking, the actual value returned may have
        no use. If you are the highest priority task then the value
        returned should be close, within 1 line.

   BUGS

   SEE ALSO
```

graphics.library/WaitBlit graphics.library/WaitBlit

NAME
WaitBlit -- Wait for the blitter to be finished before proceeding with anything else.

SYNOPSIS
```
WaitBlit()
```

FUNCTION
WaitBlit returns when the blitter is idle. This function should normally only be used when dealing with the blitter in a synchronous manner, such as when using OwnBlitter and DisownBlitter. WaitBlit does not wait for all blits queued up using QBlit or QBSBlit. You should call WaitBlit if you are just about to free some memory that you have used with the blitter.

Note that many graphics calls fire up the blitter, and let it run. The CPU does not need to wait for the blitter to finish before returning. When examining bits with the CPU right after a blit, or when freeeing temorary memory used by the blitter, a WaitBlit() may be required.

INPUTS
none

RESULT
Your program waits until the blitter is finished. Unlike most Amiga rom routines, the CPU registers D0/D1/A0 and A1 are preserved by this call.

BUGS
There is a bug in the older revisions of the Agnus chip that can cause the BUSY bit to indicate the blit has finished when the blitter has, in fact, not started the blit yet (even though BltSize has been written). This most often occurs in a heavily loaded systen with extended memory, HIRES, and 4 bitplanes. WaitBlit currently tries to avoid the Agnus problem by testing the BUSY bit multiple times to make sure the blitter has started, there is no need for further action on the part of the WaitBlit user. Also this pig busy waits. (sigh)

The hardware bug was fixed as of the first "Fat Agnus" chip, as used in all A500 and A2000 computers.

SEE ALSO
OwnBlitter DisownBlitter hardware/blit.h

graphics.library/WaitBOVP graphics.library/WaitBOVP

*

NAME
WaitBOVP -- Wait till vertical beam reached bottom of this viewport.

SYNOPSIS
```
WaitBOVP( vp )
          a0
```

FUNCTION
Returns when vertical beam reaches bottom of this viewport

INPUTS
vp - pointer to ViewPort structure

RESULT
This function will return sometime after the beam gets beyond the bottom of the viewport. Depending on the multitasking load of the system, the actual beam position may be different than what would be expected in a lightly loaded system.

BUGS
Horrors! This function currently busy waits waiting for the beam to get to the right place. It should use the copper interrupt to trigger and send signals like WaitTOF does.

SEE ALSO
WaitTOF VBeamPos

```
NAME
    WaitTOF -- Wait for the top of the next video frame.

SYNOPSIS
    WaitTOF()

FUNCTION
    Wait  for vertical blank to occur and all vertical blank
    interrupt routines to complete before returning to caller.

INPUTS
    none

RESULT
     Place this task on the TOF wait queue. When vertical blank
     interupt comes around the interrupt service routine fires off
     signals to all the tasks doing WaitTOF. The highest priority task
     ready gets to run then.

BUGS

SEE ALSO
     exec/Wait exec/Signal
```



```
NAME
    WritePixel -- Change the pen num of one specific pixel in a
                  specified RasterPort.

SYNOPSIS
    error = WritePixel(  rp, x,  y)
      d0                 al D0  Dl

     LONG error;
     struct RastPort *rp;
     SHORT x,y;

FUNCTION
    Changes the pen number of the selected pixel in the specified
    RastPort to that currently specified by PenA, the primary
    drawing pen. Obey minterms in RastPort.

INPUTS
    rp - a pointer to the RastPort structure
    (x,y) - point within the RastPort at which the selected
        pixel is located.

RESULT
    error = 0 if pixel succesfully changed
          = -1 if (x,y) is outside the RastPort

BUGS

SEE ALSO
    ReadPixel graphics/rastport.h
```

```
NAME
    XorRectRegion -- Perform 2d XOR operation of rectangle
                     with region, leaving result in region

SYNOPSIS
    status = XorRectRegion(region,rectangle)
      d0                     a0      a1

     BOOL status;
     struct Region *region;
     struct Rectangle *rectangle;

FUNCTION
     Add portions of rectangle to region if they are not in
     the region.
     Remove portions of rectangle from region if they are
     in the region.

INPUTS
    region - pointer to Region structure
    rectangle - pointer to Rectangle structure

RESULTS
     status - return TRUE if successful operation
              return FALSE if ran out of memory

BUGS

SEE ALSO
     OrRegionRegion AndRegionRegion graphics/regions.h
```



```
NAME
    XorRegionRegion -- Perform 2d XOR operation of one region
                       with second region, leaving result in second region

SYNOPSIS
    status = XorRegionRegion(region1,region2)
      d0                       a0      a1

     BOOL status;
     struct Region *region1, *region2;

FUNCTION
     Join the regions together. If any part of region1 overlaps
     region2 then remove that from the new region.

INPUTS
         region1     = pointer to Region structure
         region2     = pointer to Region structure

RESULTS
     status - return TRUE if successful operation
              return FALSE if ran out of memory

BUGS
```

TABLE OF CONTENTS


```
   NAME
       AddFreeList - add memory to the free list

   SYNOPSIS
       status = AddFreeList( free, mem, len )
       D0                    A0    A1   A2

   FUNCTION
       This routine adds the specified memory to the free list.
        The free list will be extended (if required).  If there
        is not enough memory to complete the call, a null is returned.

        Note that AddFreeList does NOT allocate the requested memory.
        It only records the memory in the free list.

   INPUTS
        free -- a pointer to a FreeList structure
        mem -- the base of the memory to be recorded
        len -- the length of the memory to be recorded

   RESULTS
        status -- nonzero if the call succeeded.

   EXCEPTIONS

   SEE ALSO
        AllocEntry, FreeEntry, FreeFreeList

   BUGS
```

```
NAME
     BumpRevision - reformat a name for a second copy

SYNOPSIS
     result = BumpRevision( newbuf, oldname  )
     D0                     A0      A1

FUNCTION
      BumpRevision takes a name an turns it into a "copy of name".
      It knows how to deal with copies of copies.  The routine
      will truncate the new name to the maximum dos name size
      (currently 30 characters).

INPUTS
      newbuf - the new buffer that will receive the name (it must
              be at least 31 characters long).
      oldname - the original name

RESULTS
      result - a pointer to newbuf

EXCEPTIONS

EXAMPLE
      oldname                           newbuf
      --------                          ------

      "foo"                             "copy of foo"
      "copy of foo"                     "copy 2 of foo"
      "copy 2 of foo"                   "copy 3 of foo"
      "copy 199 of foo"                 "copy 200 of foo"
      "copy foo"                        "copy of copy foo"
      "copy 0 of foo"                   "copy 1 of foo"
      "012345678901234567890123456789" "copy of 0123456789012345678901"

SEE ALSO

BUGS
```



```
NAME
     FindToolType - find the value of a ToolType variable

SYNOPSIS
     value = FindToolType( toolTypeArray, typeName  )
     D0                    A0             A1

FUNCTION
     This function searches a tool type array for a given entry,
      and returns a pointer to that entry.  This is useful for
      finding standard tool type variables.  The returned
      value is not a new copy of the string but is only
      a pointer to the part of the string after typeName.

INPUTS
      toolTypeArray - an array of strings
      typeName - the name of the tooltype entry

RESULTS
      value - a pointer to a string that is the value bound to
          typeName, or NULL if typeName is not in
          the toolTypeArray.

EXCEPTIONS

EXAMPLE
      Assume the tool type array has two strings in it:
          "FILETYPE=text"
          "TEMPDIR=:t"

      FindToolType( toolTypeArray, "FILETYPE" ) returns "text"
      FindToolType( toolTypeArray, "TEMPDIR" )  returns ":t"
      FindToolType( toolTypeArray, "MAXSIZE" )  returns NULL

SEE ALSO
      MatchToolValue

BUGS
```

```
NAME
    FreeDiskObject - free all memory in a Workbench disk object

SYNOPSIS
    FreeDiskObject( diskobj )
                    A0

FUNCTION
    This routine frees all memory in a Workbench disk object, and the
     object itself.  It is implemented via FreeFreeList().

     GetDiskObject() takes care of all the initialization required
     to set up the objects free list.  This procedure may ONLY
     be called on DiskObject allocated via GetDiskObject().

INPUTS
     diskobj -- a pointer to a DiskObject structure

RESULTS

EXCEPTIONS

SEE ALSO
     GetDiskObject, FreeFreeList

BUGS
```



```
NAME
    FreeFreeList - free all memory in a free list

SYNOPSIS
    FreeFreeList( free )
                  A0

FUNCTION
    This routine frees all memory in a free list, and the
     free list itself.  It is useful for easily getting
     rid of all memory in a series of structures.  There is
     a free list in a Workbench object, and this contains
     all the memory associated with that object.

     A FreeList is a list of MemList structures.  See the
     MemList and MemEntry documentation for more information.

     If the FreeList itself is in the free list, it must be
     in the first MemList in the FreeList.

INPUTS
     free -- a pointer to a FreeList structure

RESULTS

EXCEPTIONS

SEE ALSO
     AllocEntry, FreeEntry, AddFreeList

BUGS
```

```
NAME
    GetDiskObject - read in a Workbench disk object

SYNOPSIS
    diskobj = GetDiskObject( name )
    D0                       A0

FUNCTION
    This routine reads in a Workbench disk object in from disk.  The
     name parameter will have a ".info" postpended to it, and the
     info file of that name will be read.  If the call fails,
     it will return zero.  The reason for the failure may be obtained
     via IoErr().

     Using this routine protects you from any future changes to
     the way icons are stored within the system.

     A FreeList structure is allocated just after the DiskObject
     structure; FreeDiskObject makes use of this to get rid of the
     memory that was allocated.

INPUTS
     name -- name of the object

RESULTS
     diskobj -- the Workbench disk object in question

EXCEPTIONS

SEE ALSO
     FreeDiskObject

BUGS
```



```
NAME
    MatchToolValue - check a tool type variable for a particular value

SYNOPSIS
    result = MatchToolValue( typeString, value  )
    D0                       A0          A1

FUNCTION
     MatchToolValue is useful for parsing a tool type value for
     a known value.  It knows how to parse the syntax for a tool
     type value (in particular, it knows that '|' separates
     alternate values).

INPUTS
     typeString - a ToolType value (as returned by FindToolType)
     value - you are interested if value appears in typeString

RESULTS
     result - a one if the value was in typeString

EXCEPTIONS

EXAMPLE
     Assume there are two type strings:
         type1 = "text"
         type2 = "a|b|c"

     MatchToolValue( type1, "text" ) returns 1
     MatchToolValue( type1, "data" ) returns 0
     MatchToolValue( type2, "a" ) returns 1
     MatchToolValue( type2, "b" ) returns 1
     MatchToolValue( type2, "d" ) returns 0
     MatchToolValue( type2, "a|b" ) returns 0

SEE ALSO
     FindToolType

BUGS
```

```
NAME
    PutDiskObject - write out a DiskObject to disk

SYNOPSIS
    status = PutDiskObject( name, diskobj )
    D0                      A0    A1

FUNCTION
    This routine writes out a DiskObject structure, and its
     associated information.  The file name of the info
     file will be the name parameter with a
     ".info" postpended to it.  If the call fails, a zero will
     be returned.  The reason for the failure may be obtained
     via IoErr().

     Using this routine protects you from any future changes to
     the way icons are stored within the system.

INPUTS
     name -- name of the object
     diskobj -- a pointer to a DiskObject

RESULTS
     status -- non-zero if the call succeeded

EXCEPTIONS

SEE ALSO
     GetDiskObject, FreeDiskObject

BUGS
```

TABLE OF CONTENTS

```
NAME
    ActivateGadget -- Activate a (String) Gadget.

SYNOPSIS
    Success = ActivateGadget(Gadget, Window, Request)
    D0                       A0      A1      A2

    BOOL   Success;
    struct Gadget *Gadget;
    struct Window *Window;
    struct Requester *Request;

FUNCTION
    Activates a String Gadget.  If successful, this means that the user
    does not need to click in the gadget before typing.

    The Window parameter must point to the window which contains the Gadget.
    If the gadget is actually in a Requester, the Window must contain
    the Requester, and a pointer to the Requester must also be
    passed. The Requester parameter must only be valid if the Gadget
    has the REQGADGET flag set, a requirement for all Requester Gadgets.

    The success of this function depends on a rather complex set
    of conditions.  The intent is that the user is never interrupted from
    what interactions he may have underway.

    The current set of conditions includes:
    -   The Window must be active. (Use the ACTIVEWINDOW IDCMP).
    -   No other gadgets may be in use.  This includes system gadgets,
        such as those for window sizing, dragging, etc.
    -   If the gadget is in a Requester, that Requester must
        be active. (Use the REQSET and REQCLEAR IDCMP).
    -   The right mouse button cannot be held down (e.g. menus

INPUTS
    Gadget = pointer to the Gadget that you want activated.
    Window = pointer to a Window structure containing the Gadget.
    Requester = pointer to a Requester (may by NULL if this isn't
       a Requester Gadget (i.e. REQGADGET is not set)).

RESULT
    If the conditions above are met, and the Gadget is in fact a String
    Gadget, then this function will return TRUE, else FALSE.

BUGS

SEE ALSO
```



```
NAME
    ActivateWindow  --  Activate an Intuition Window.

SYNOPSIS
    ActivateWindow(Window)
                   A0

    struct Window *Window;

FUNCTION
    Activates an Intuition Window.

    Note that this call may have its action deferred: you cannot assume
    that when this call is made the selected window has become active.
    This action will be postponed while the user plays with gadgets and menus,
    or sizes and drags windows.  You may detect when the window actually
    has become active by the ACTIVEWINDOW IDCMP Message.

    This call is intended to provide flexibility but not to confuse the
    user.  Please call this function synchronously with some action
    by the user.

INPUTS
    Window = a pointer to a Window structure

RESULT
    None

BUGS
    Calling this function in a tight loop can blow out Intuition's deferred
    action queue.

SEE ALSO
    OpenWindow(), and the ACTIVATE Window Flag
```

NAME
    AddGadget -- Add a Gadget to the Gadget list of the Window or Screen.

SYNOPSIS

```
RealPosition = AddGadget(Window, Gadget, Position)
D0                       A0      A1      D0

USHORT RealPosition;
struct Window *Window;
struct Gadget *Gadget;
USHORT Position;
```

FUNCTION

Adds the specified Gadget to the Gadget list of the given Window, linked in at the position in the list specified by the Position argument (that is, if Pos == 0, the Gadget will be inserted at the head of the list, and if Position == 1 then the Gadget will be inserted after the first Gadget and before the second). If the Position you specify is greater than the number of Gadgets in the list, your Gadget will be added to the end of the list.

Calling AddGadget() does not cause your gadget do be redisplayed. The benefit of this is that you may add several gadgets without having the gadget list be redrawn every time.

This procedure returns the position at which your Gadget was added.

NOTE: A relatively safe way to add the Gadget to the end of the list is to specify a Position of -1 (i.e., (USHORT) ~0). That way, only the 65536th (and multiples of it) will be inserted at the wrong position. The return value of the procedure will tell you where it was actually inserted.

NOTE: The System Window Gadgets are initially added to the front of the Gadget List. The reason for this is: If you position your own Gadgets in some way that interferes with the graphical representation of the system Gadgets, the system's ones will be "hit" first by User. If you then start adding Gadgets to the front of the list, you will disturb this plan, so beware. On the other hand, if you don't violate the design rule of never overlapping your Gadgets, there's no problem.

NOTE: You may not add your own gadgets to a Screen. Gadgets may be added to backdrop windows, however, which can be visually similar, but also provide an IDCMP channel for gadget input messages.

INPUTS

```
Window = pointer to the Window to get your Gadget
Gadget = pointer to the new Gadget
Position = integer position in the list for the new Gadget (starting from
      zero as the first position in the list)
```

RESULT
    Returns the position of where the Gadget was actually added.

BUGS

SEE ALSO
    AddGList(), RemoveGadget()

NAME
    AddGList -- add a linked list of gadgets to a Window or Requester

SYNOPSIS

```
RealPosition =  AddGList(Window, Gadget, Position, Numgad, Requester);
D0                       A0      A1      D0        D1      A2

USHORT RealPosition;
struct Window *Window;
struct Gadget *Gadget;
USHORT Position;
USHORT Numgad;
struct Requester *Requester;
```

FUNCTION

Adds the list of Gadgets to the Gadget list of the given Window or Requester linked in at the position in the list specified by the Position argument.

See AddGadget() for more information about gadget list position.

The Requester parameter will be ignored unless the REQGADGET bit is set in the GadgetType field of the first Gadget in the list. In that case, the gadget list is added to the Requester gadgets. NOTE: be sure that REQGADGET is either set of cleared consistently for all gadgets in the list. NOTE ALSO: The Window parameter should point to the Window that the Requester (will) appear in.

Will add 'Numgad' gadgets from gadget list linked by the field NextGadget, or until some NextGadget field is found to be NULL. Does not assume that the Numgad'th gadget has NextGadget equal to NULL.

NOTE WELL: In order to link your gadget list in, the NextGadget field of the Numgad'th (or last) gadget will be modified. Thus, if you are adding the first 3 gadgets from a linked list of five gadgets, this call will sever the connection between your third and fourth gadgets.

INPUTS

```
Window = pointer to the Window to get your Gadget
Gadget = pointer to the first Gadget to be added
Position = integer position in the list for the new Gadget
    (starting from zero as the first position in the list)
Numgad = the number of gadgets from the linked list to be added
    if Numgad equals -1, the entire null-terminated list of
    gadgets will be added.
Requester = the requester the gadgets will be added to if the
    REQGADGET GadgetType flag is set for the first gadget in the list
```

RESULT
    Returns the position of where the first Gadget in the list was actually added.

BUGS

SEE ALSO
    AddGadget(), RemoveGadget()

```
NAME
    AllocRemember  --  AllocMem and create a link node to make FreeMem easy.

SYNOPSIS
    MemBlock = AllocRemember(RememberKey, Size, Flags)
    D0                       A0           D0    D1

    CPTR MemBlock;
    struct Remember **RememberKey;
    ULONG Size;
    ULONG Flags;

FUNCTION
    This routine calls the EXEC AllocMem() function for you, but also links
    the parameters of the allocation into a master list, so that
    you can simply call the Intuition routine FreeRemember() at a later
    time to deallocate all allocated memory without being required to
    remember the details of the memory you've allocated.

    This routine will have two primary uses:
  -   Let's say that you're doing a long series of allocations in a
      procedure (such as the Intuition OpenWindow() procedure).
      If any one of the allocations fails for lack of memory, you
      need to abort the procedure.  Abandoning ship correctly involves
      freeing up what memory you've already allocated.  This procedure
      allows you to free up that memory easily, without being required
      to keep track of how many allocations you've already done, what the
      sizes of the allocations were, or where the memory was allocated.

  -   Also, in the more general case, you may do all of the allocations
      in your entire program using this routine.  Then, when your
      program is exiting, you can free it all up at once with a
      simple call to FreeRemember().

    You create the "anchor" for the allocation master list by creating
    a variable that's a pointer to struct Remember, and initializing
    that pointer to NULL.  This is called the RememberKey.  Whenever
    you call AllocRemember(), the routine actually does two memory
    allocations, one for the memory you want and the other for a copy
    of a Remember structure.  The Remember structure is filled in
    with data describing your memory allocation, and it's linked
    into the master list pointed to by your RememberKey.  Then, to
    free up any memory that's been allocated, all you have to do is
    call FreeRemember() with your RememberKey.

    Please read the FreeRemember() function description, too.  As you will
    see, you can select either to free just the link nodes and keep all the
    allocated memory for yourself, or to free both the nodes and your memory
    buffers.


INPUTS
    RememberKey = the address of a pointer to struct Remember.  Before the
    very first call to AllocRemember, initialize this pointer to NULL.

    Size = the size in bytes of the memory allocation.  Please refer to the
        exec.library/AllocMem function for details.
    Flags = the specifications for the memory allocation.  Please refer to
        the exec.library/AllocMem function for details.

EXAMPLE
    struct Remember *RememberKey;
    RememberKey = NULL;
    AllocRemember(&RememberKey, BUFSIZE, MEMF_CHIP);
    FreeRemember(&RememberKey, TRUE);

RESULT
    If the memory allocation is successful, this routine returns the byte
    address of your requested memory block.  Also, the node to your block
    will be linked into the list pointed to by your RememberKey variable.
    If the allocation fails, this routine returns NULL and the list pointed
    to by RememberKey, if any, will be undisturbed.

BUGS

SEE ALSO
    FreeRemember(), exec.library/AllocMem()
```

NAME
    AutoRequest -- Automatically build and get response from a Requester.

SYNOPSIS
```
Response = AutoRequest(Window, BodyText, PositiveText, NegativeText,
D0                     A0      A1        A2            A3
                       PositiveFlags, NegativeFlags, Width, Height)
                       D0             D1             D2     D3

BOOL Response;
struct Window *Window;
struct IntuiText *BodyText, *PositiveText, *NegativeText;
ULONG PositiveFlags, NegativeFlags;
SHORT Width, Height;
```

FUNCTION

This procedure automatically builds a Requester for you and then waits for a response from the user, or for the system to satisfy your request. If the response is positive, this procedure returns TRUE. If the response is negative, this procedure returns FALSE.

An IDCMPFlag specification is creates by bitwise "or'ing" your PositiveFlags, NegativeFlags, and the IDCMP classes GADGETUP and RAWKEY. You may specify zero flags for either the PositiveFlags or NegativeFlags arguments.

The IntuiText arguments, and the Width and Height values, are passed directly to the BuildSysRequest() procedure along with your Window pointer and the IDCMP flags. Please refer to BuildSysRequest() for a description of the IntuiText that you are expected to supply when calling this routine. It's an important but long-winded description that need not be duplicated here.

If the BuildSysRequest() procedure does not return a pointer to a Window, it will return TRUE or FALSE (not valid structure pointers) instead, and these BOOL values will be returned to you immediately.

On the other hand, if a valid Window pointer is returned, that Window will have had its IDCMP Ports and flags initialized according to your specifications. AutoRequest() then waits for IDCMP messages on the UserPort, which satisfies one of four requirements:

- either the message is of a class that matches one of your PositiveFlags arguments (if you've supplied any), in which case this routine returns TRUE. Or
- the message class matches one of your NegativeFlags arguments (if you've supplied any), in which case this routine returns FALSE. Or
- the IDCMP message is of class GADGETUP, which means that one of the two Gadgets, as provided with the PositiveText and NegativeText arguments, was selected by the user. If the TRUE Gadget was selected, TRUE is returned. If the FALSE Gadget was selected, FALSE is returned.
- Lastly, two RAWKEY messages may satisfy the request: those for the V and B keys with the left Amiga key depressed. These keys, satisfy the gadgets on the left or right side of the Requester--TRUE or FALSE--, respectively.

When the dust has settled, this routine calls FreeSysRequest() if necessary to clean up the Requester and any other allocated memory.

INPUTS

Window = pointer to a Window structure
BodyText = pointer to an IntuiText structure
PositiveText = pointer to an IntuiText structure, may be NULL.
NegativeText = pointer to an IntuiText structure, MUST be valid!
PositiveFlags = flags for the IDCMP
NegativeFlags = flags for the IDCMP
Width, Height = the sizes to be used for the rendering of the Requester

RESULT

The return value is either TRUE or FALSE. See the text above for a complete description of the chain of events that might lead to either of these values being returned.

BUGS

SEE ALSO
    BuildSysRequest()

NAME
    BeginRefresh -- Sets up a Window for optimized refreshing.

SYNOPSIS
```
BeginRefresh(Window)
             A0

struct Window *Window;
```

FUNCTION
    This routine sets up your Window for optimized refreshing.

It's role is to provide Intuition integrated access to the Layers library function BeginUpdate(). Its additional contribution is to be sure that locking protocols for layers are followed, by locking both layers of a GIMMEZEROZERO window only after the parent Layer_Info has been locked. Also, the WINDOWREFRESH flag is set in your window, for your information.

The purpose of BeginUpdate(), and hence BeginRefresh(), is to restrict rendering in a Window (Layer) to the region in that needs refreshing after an operation such as window sizing or uncovering. This restriction to the "Damage Region" persists until you call EndRefresh().

For instance, if you have a SIMPLE_REFRESH Window which is partially concealed and the user brings it to the front, you may receive a message asking you to refresh your display. If you call BeginRefresh() before doing any of the rendering, then the layer that underlies your Window will be arranged such that the only rendering that will actually take place will be that which goes to the newly-revealed areas. This is very performance-efficient, and visually attractive.

After you have performed your refresh of the display, you should call EndRefresh() to reset the state of the layer and the Window. Then you may proceed with rendering to the Window as usual.

You learn that your Window needs refreshing by receiving either a message of class REFRESHWINDOW through the IDCMP, or an input event of class IECLASS_REFRESHWINDOW through the Console Device. Whenever you are told that your Window needs refreshing, you should call BeginRefresh() and EndRefresh() to clear the refresh-needed state, even if you don't plan on doing any rendering. You may relieve yourself of even this burden by setting the NOCAREREFRESH Flag when opening your window.

INPUTS
    Window = pointer to the Window structure which needs refreshing

RESULT
    None

BUGS

SEE ALSO
    EndRefresh(), layers.library/BeginUpdate(), OpenWindow()
    The "Windows" chapter of the Intuition Reference Manual

NAME
    BuildSysRequest -- Build and display a system Requester.

SYNOPSIS
```
ReqWindow = BuildSysRequest(Window, BodyText, PositiveText, NegativeText,
D0                          A0      A1        A2            A3
                    IDCMPFlags, Width, Height)
                    D0          D2     D3

struct Window *ReqWindow;
struct Window *Window;
struct IntuiText *BodyText;
struct IntuiText *PositiveText;
struct IntuiText *NegativeText;
ULONG  IDCMPFlags;
SHORT  Width, Height;
```

FUNCTION
    This procedure builds a Requester based on the supplied information. If all goes well and the Requester is constructed, this procedure returns a pointer to the Window in which the Requester appears. That Window will have the IDCMP UserPort and WindowPort initialized to reflect the flags found in the IDCMPFlags argument. You may then Wait() on those ports to detect the user's response to your Requester, which response may include either selecting one of the Gadgets or causing some other event to be noticed by Intuition (like DISKINSERTED, for instance). After the Requester is satisfied, you should call the FreeSysRequest() procedure to remove the Requester and free up any allocated memory.

The requester used by this function has the NOISYREQ flag bit set, which means that the set of IDCMPFlags that may be used here include RAWKEY, MOUSEBUTTONS, and others.

If it isn't possible to construct the Requester for any reason, this procedure will instead use the text arguments to construct a text string for a call to the DisplayAlert() procedure, and then will return either a TRUE or FALSE depending on whether DisplayAlert() returned a FALSE or TRUE respectively.

If the Window argument you supply is equal to NULL, a new Window will be created for you in the Workbench Screen. If you want the Requester created by this routine to be bound to a particular Window, you should not supply a Window argument of NULL.

The text arguments are used to construct the display. Each is a pointer to an instance of the structure IntuiText.

The BodyText argument should be used to describe the nature of the Requester. As usual with IntuiText data, you may link several lines of text together, and the text may be placed in various locations in the Requester. This IntuiText pointer will be stored in the ReqText variable of the new Requester.

The PositiveText argument describes the text that you want associated with the user choice of "Yes, TRUE, Retry, Good." If the Requester is successfully opened, this text will be rendered in a Gadget in the lower-left of the Requester, which Gadget will have the GadgetID field set to TRUE. If the Requester cannot be opened and the DisplayAlert() mechanism is used, this text will be rendered in the lower-left corner of the Alert display with additional text specifying that the left mouse button will select this choice. This pointer can be set to NULL, which specifies that there is no TRUE choice that can be made.

The NegativeText argument describes the text that you want associated with the user choice of "No, FALSE, Cancel, Bad." If the Requester is successfully opened, this text will be rendered in a Gadget in the lower-right of the Requester, which Gadget will have the GadgetID field set to FALSE. If the Requester cannot be opened and

```
    the DisplayAlert() mechanism is used, this text will be rendered in
    the lower-right corner of the Alert display with additional text
    specifying that the right mouse button will select this choice.  This
    pointer cannot be set to NULL.  There must always be a way for the
    user to cancel this Requester.

    The Positive and Negative Gadgets created by this routine have
    the following features:
      - BOOLGADGET
      - RELVERIFY
      - REQGADGET
      - TOGGLESELECT

    When defining the text for your Gadgets, you may find it convenient
    to use the special constants used by Intuition for the construction
    of the Gadgets.  These include defines like AUTODRAWMODE, AUTOLEFTEDGE,
    AUTOTOPEDGE and AUTOFRONTPEN.  You can find these in your local
    intuition.h (or intuition.i) file.

    The Width and Height values describe the size of the Requester.  All
    of your BodyText must fit within the Width and Height of your
    Requester.  The Gadgets will be created to conform to your sizes.

    VERY IMPORTANT NOTE:  for this release of this procedure, a new Window
    is opened in the same Screen as the one containing your Window.
    Future alternatives will be provided as a function distinct from this
    one.

INPUTS
    Window = pointer to a Window structure
    BodyText = pointer to an IntuiText structure
    PositiveText = pointer to an IntuiText structure
    NegativeText = pointer to an IntuiText structure
    IDCMPFlags = the IDCMP flags you want used for the initialization of the
       IDCMP of the Window containing this Requester
    Width, Height = the size required to render your Requester

RESULT
    If the Requester was successfully rendered in a Window, the value
    returned by this procedure is a pointer to the Window in which the
    Requester was rendered.  If, however, the Requester cannot be rendered
    in the Window, this routine will have called DisplayAlert() before
    returning and will pass back TRUE if the user pressed the left mouse
    button and FALSE if the user pressed the right mouse button.

BUGS
    This procedure currently opens a Window as wide as the Screen in
    which it was rendered, and then opens the Requester within that
    Window.  Also, if DisplayAlert() is called, the PositiveText and
    NegativeText are not rendered in the lower corners of the Alert.

SEE ALSO
    FreeSysRequest(), DisplayAlert(), ModifyIDCMP(), exec.library/Wait(),
    Request(), AutoRequest()
```



```
    NAME
        ClearDMRequest -- clears (detaches) the DMRequest of the Window.

    SYNOPSIS
        Response = ClearDMRequest(Window)
        D0                        A0

        BOOL Response;
        struct Window *Window;

    FUNCTION
        Attempts to clear the DMRequester from the specified window,
        that is detaches the special Requester that you attach to
        the double-click of the menu button which the user can then
        bring up on demand.  This routine WILL NOT clear the DMRequester
        if it's active (in use by the user). The IDCMP message class REQCLEAR
        can be used to detect that the requester is not in use,
        but that message is sent only when the last of perhaps several
        requesters in use in a window is terminated.

    INPUTS
        Window = pointer to the window from which the DMRequest is to be cleared.

    RESULT
        If the DMRequest was not currently in use, zeroes out the DMRequest
        pointer in the Window and returns TRUE.
pointer in the Window and returns TRUE.
        If the DMRequest was currently in use, doesn't change the pointer
        and returns FALSE.

    BUGS

    SEE ALSO
        SetDMRequest(), Request()
```

```
NAME
    ClearMenuStrip  --  Clears (detaches) the Menu strip from the Window

SYNOPSIS
    ClearMenuStrip(Window)
                   A0

    struct Window *Window;

FUNCTION
    Detaches the current menu strip from the Window; menu strips
    are attached to windows using the SetMenuStrip() function.

    If the menu is in use (for that matter if any menu is in use)
    this function will block (Wait()) until the user has finished.

    Call this function before you make any changes to the data
    in a Menu or MenuItem structure which is part of a menu
    strip linked into a window.

INPUTS
    Window = pointer to a Window structure

RESULT
    None

BUGS

SEE ALSO
    SetMenuStrip()
```



```
NAME
    ClearPointer  --  clears the Mouse Pointer definition from a Window.

SYNOPSIS
    ClearPointer(Window)
                 A0

    struct Window *Window;

FUNCTION
    Clears the Window of its own definition of the Intuition mouse pointer.
    After calling ClearPointer(), every time this Window is the active
    one the default Intuition pointer will be the pointer displayed
    to the user.  If your Window is the active one when this routine
    is called, the change will take place immediately.

    Custom definitions of the mouse pointer which this function clears
    are installed by a call to SetPointer().

INPUTS
    Window = pointer to the Window to be cleared of its Pointer definition

RESULT
    None

BUGS

SEE ALSO
    SetPointer()
```

```
NAME
    CloseScreen  --  Closes an Intuition Screen.

SYNOPSIS
    CloseScreen(Screen)
                A0

    struct Screen *Screen;

FUNCTION
    Unlinks the Screen, unlinks the ViewPort, deallocates everything that
    Intuition allocated when the screen was opened (using OpenScreen()).
    Doesn't care whether or not there are still any Windows attached to the
    Screen.  Doesn't try to close any attached Windows; in fact, ignores them
    altogether.  If this is the last Screen to go, attempts to reopen
    Workbench.

INPUTS
    Screen = pointer to the Screen to be closed.

RESULT
    None

BUGS

SEE ALSO
    OpenScreen()
```



```
NAME
    CloseWindow  --  Closes an Intuition Window.

SYNOPSIS
    CloseWindow(Window)
                A0

    struct Window *Window;

FUNCTION
    Closes an Intuition Window.  Unlinks it from the system, unallocates
    its memory, and if its Screen is a system one that would be empty
    without the Window, closes the system Screen too.

    When this function is called, all IDCMP messages which have been sent
    to your window are deallocated.  If the window had shared a Message Port
    with other windows, you must be sure that there are no unreplied messages
    for this window in the message queue.  Otherwise, your program will
    try to make use of a linked list (the queue) which contains free
    memory (the old messages).  This will give you big problems.
memory (the old messages).  This will give you big problems.
    NOTE:  If you have added a Menu strip to this Window (via
    a call to SetMenuStrip()) you must be sure to remove that Menu strip
    (via a call to ClearMenuStrip()) before closing your Window.

    NOTE: This function may block until it is safe to delink and free
    your window.  Your program may thus be suspended while the user
    plays with gadgets, menus, or window sizes and position.

INPUTS
    Window = a pointer to a Window structure

RESULT
    None

BUGS

SEE ALSO
    OpenWindow(), CloseScreen()
```

```
intuition.library/CloseWorkBench            intuition.library/CloseWorkBench

    NAME
        CloseWorkBench  --  Closes the Workbench Screen.

    SYNOPSIS
        Success =  CloseWorkBench()
        D0

        BOOL Success;

    FUNCTION
        This routine attempts to close the Workbench.  The actions taken are:
       -   Test whether or not any applications have opened Windows on the
           Workbench, and return FALSE if so.  Otherwise ...
       -   Clean up all special buffers
       -   Close the Workbench Screen
       -   Make the Workbench program mostly inactive (it will still
           monitor disk activity)
       -   Return TRUE

    INPUTS
        None

    RESULT
        TRUE if the Workbench Screen closed successfully
        FALSE if the Workbench was not open, or if it has windows
            open which are not Workbench drawers.

    BUGS

    SEE ALSO
        OpenWindow()
```

```
intuition.library/CurrentTime                  intuition.library/CurrentTime

    NAME
        CurrentTime  --  Get the current time values.

    SYNOPSIS
        CurrentTime(Seconds, Micros)
                    A0       A1

        ULONG *Seconds, *Micros;

    FUNCTION
        Puts copies of the current time into the supplied argument pointers.

        This time value is not extremely accurate, nor is it of a very fine
        resolution.  This time will be updated no more than sixty times a
        a second, and will typically be updated far fewer times a second.

    INPUTS
        Seconds = pointer to a LONG variable to receive the current seconds value
        Micros = pointer to a LONG variable for the current microseconds value

    RESULT
        Puts the time values into the memory locations specified by the arguments
        Return value is not defined.

    BUGS

    SEE ALSO
        timer.device/TR_GETSYSTIME
```

```
NAME
    DisplayAlert  --  Create the display of an Alert message.

SYNOPSIS
    Response = DisplayAlert(AlertNumber, String, Height)
    D0                      D0           A0      D1

    BOOL  Response;
    ULONG AlertNumber;
    UBYTE *String;
    SHORT Height;

FUNCTION
    Creates an Alert display with the specified message.

    If the system can recover from this Alert, its a RECOVERY_ALERT and
    this routine waits until the user presses one of the mouse buttons,
    after which the display is restored to its original state and a
    BOOL value is returned by this routine to specify whether or not
    the User pressed the LEFT mouse button.

    If the system cannot recover from this Alert, it's a DEADEND_ALERT
    and this routine returns immediately upon creating the Alert display.
    The return value is FALSE.

    NOTE THIS: Starting with Version 1.2, if Intuition can't get enough
    memory to display a RECOVERY_ALERT, the value FALSE will be returned.

    The AlertNumber is a LONG value, historically related to the value
    sent to the Alert() routine.  But the only bits that are pertinent to
    this routine are the ALERT_TYPE bit(s).  These bits must be set to
    either RECOVERY_ALERT for Alerts from which the system may safely
    recover, or DEADEND_ALERT for those fatal Alerts.  These states are
    described in the paragraph above.

    The String argument points to an AlertMessage string.  The AlertMessage
    string is comprised of one or more substrings, each of which is
    comprised of the following components:
       - first, a 16-bit x-coordinate and an 8-bit y-coordinate,
         describing where on the Alert display you want this string
         to appear.  The y-coordinate describes the offset to the
         baseline of the text.
       - then, the bytes of the string itself, which must be
         null-terminated (end with a byte of zero)
       - lastly, the continuation byte, which specifies whether or
         not there's another substring following this one.  If the
         continuation byte is non-zero, there IS another substring
         to be processed in this Alert Message.  If the continuation
         byte is zero, this is the last substring in the message.

    The last argument, Height, describes how many video lines tall you
    want the Alert display to be.

INPUTS
    AlertNumber = the number of this Alert Message.  The only pertinent bits
       of this number are the ALERT_TYPE bit(s).  The rest of the
       number is ignored by this routine
    String = pointer to the Alert message string, as described above
    Height = minimum display lines required for your message

RESULT
    A BOOL value of TRUE or FALSE.  If this is a DEADEND_ALERT, FALSE
    is always the return value.  If this is a RECOVERY_ALERT. The return
    value will be TRUE if the User presses the left mouse button in
    response to your message, and FALSE if the User presses the right hand
    button is response to your text, or if the alert could not
    be posted.

BUGS
    If the system is worse off than you think, the level of your Alert
    may become DEADEND_ALERT without you ever knowing about it.

SEE ALSO
```

```
intuition.library/DisplayBeep                    intuition.library/DisplayBeep

    NAME
        DisplayBeep  --  flashes the video display.

    SYNOPSIS
        DisplayBeep(Screen)
                    A0

        struct Screen *Screen;

    FUNCTION
        "Beeps" the video display by flashing the background color of the
        specified Screen.  If the Screen argument is NULL, every Screen
        in the display will be beeped.  Flashing everyone's Screen is not
        a polite thing to do, so this should be reserved for dire
        circumstances.

        The reason such a routine is supported is because the Amiga has
        no internal bell or speaker.  When the user needs to know of
        an event that is not serious enough to require the use of a Requester,
        the DisplayBeep() function may be called.

    INPUTS
        Screen = pointer to a Screen.  If NULL, every Screen in the display
           will be flashed

    RESULT
        None

    BUGS

    SEE ALSO
```

```
intuition.library/DoubleClick                    intuition.library/DoubleClick

    NAME
        DoubleClick  --  Test two time values for double-click timing.

    SYNOPSIS
        IsDouble = DoubleClick(StartSecs, StartMicros, CurrentSecs, CurrentMicros)
        A0                     D0         D1           D2           D3

        BOOL IsDouble;
        LONG StartSecs, StartMicros;
        LONG CurrentSecs, CurrentMicros;

    FUNCTION
        Compares the difference in the time values with the double-click
        timeout range that the user has set (using the "Preferences" tool) or
        some other program has configured into the system.  If the
        difference between the specified time values is within the current
        double-click time range, this function returns TRUE, else it
        returns FALSE.

       These time values can be found in InputEvents and IDCMP Messages.
       The time values are not perfect; however, they are precise enough for
       nearly all applications.

    INPUTS
        StartSeconds, StartMicros = the timestamp value describing the start of
          the double-click time period you are considering
        CurrentSeconds, CurrentMicros = the timestamp value describing
          the end of the double-click time period you are considering

    RESULT
        If the difference between the supplied timestamp values is within the
        double-click time range in the current set of Preferences, this
        function returns TRUE, else it returns FALSE

    BUGS

    SEE ALSO
        CurrentTime()
```

```
NAME
    DrawBorder  --  draws the specified Border into the RastPort.

SYNOPSIS
    DrawBorder(RastPort, Border, LeftOffset, TopOffset)
               A0        A1      D0          D1

    struct RastPort *RastPort;
    struct Border   *Border;
    SHORT  LeftOffset, TopOffset;

FUNCTION
    First, sets up the DrawMode and Pens in the RastPort according to the
    arguments of the Border structure.  Then, draws the vectors of
    the Border argument into the RastPort, offset by the Left and Top Offsets.
    As with all graphics rendering routines, the border will be clipped to
    to the boundaries of the RastPort's layer, if it exists.  This is
    the case with Window RastPorts.

    If the NextBorder field of the Border argument is non-zero,
    the next Border is rendered as well, and so on until some NextBorder
    field is found to be NULL.

INPUTS
    RastPort = pointer to the RastPort to receive the border rendering
    Border = pointer to a Border structure
    LeftOffset = the offset which will be added to each vector's x coordinate
    TopOffset = the offset which will be added to each vector's y coordinate

RESULT
    None

BUGS

SEE ALSO
```



```
NAME
    DrawImage  --  draws the specified Image into the RastPort.

SYNOPSIS
    DrawImage(RastPort, Image, LeftOffset, TopOffset)
              A0        A1     D0          D1

    struct RastPort *RastPort;
    struct Image    *Image;
    SHORT  LeftOffset, TopOffset;

FUNCTION
    First, sets up the DrawMode and Pens in the RastPort according to the
    arguments of the Image structure.  Then, moves the image data of
    the Image argument into the RastPort, offset by the Left and Top Offsets.
    This routine does window layer clipping as appropriate -- if you
    draw an image outside of your Window, your imagery will be
    clipped at the Window's edge.

    If the NextImage field of the Image argument is non-zero,
    the next Image is rendered as well, and so on until some
    NextImage field is found to be NULL.

INPUTS
    RastPort = pointer to the RastPort to receive image rendering
    Image = pointer to an Image structure
    LeftOffset = the offset which will be added to the Image's x coordinate
    TopOffset = the offset which will be added to the Image's y coordinate

RESULT
    None

BUGS

SEE ALSO
```

```
NAME
    EndRefresh  --  Ends the optimized refresh state of the Window.

SYNOPSIS
    EndRefresh(Window, Complete)
               A0      D0

    struct Window *Window;
    BOOL Complete;

FUNCTION
    This function gets you out of the special refresh state of your
    Window.  It is called following a call to BeginRefresh(), which
    routine puts you into the special refresh state.  While your Window
    is in the refresh state, the only rendering that will be wrought in
    your Window will be to those areas which were recently revealed and
    need to be refreshed.

    After you've done all the refreshing you want to do for this Window,
    you should call this routine to restore the Window to its
    non-refreshing state.  Then all rendering will go to the entire
    Window, as usual.

    The Complete argument is a boolean TRUE or FALSE value used to
    describe whether or not the refreshing you've done was all the
    refreshing that needs to be done at this time.  Most often, this
    argument will be TRUE.  But if, for instance, you have multiple
    tasks or multiple procedure calls which must run to completely
    refresh the Window, then each can call its own Begin/EndRefresh()
    pair with a Complete argument of FALSE, and only the last calls
    with a Complete argument of TRUE.

    For your information, this routine calls the Layers library function
    EndUpdate(), unlocks your layers (calls UnlockLayerRom()), clears
    the LAYERREFRESH bit in your Layer Flags, and clears the WINDOWREFRESH
    bit in your window flags.

INPUTS
    Window = pointer to the Window currently in optimized-refresh mode
    Complete = Boolean TRUE or FALSE describing whether or not this
       Window is completely refreshed

RESULT
    None

BUGS

SEE ALSO
    BeginRefresh(), layers.library/EndUpdate(), layers.library/UnlockLayerRom()
```



```
NAME
    EndRequest  --  Ends the Request and resets the Window.

SYNOPSIS
    EndRequest(Requester, Window);
               A0         A1

FUNCTION
    Ends the Request by erasing the Requester and resetting the Window.
    Note that this doesn't necessarily clear all Requesters from the Window,
    only the specified one.  If the Window labors under other Requesters,
    they will remain in the Window.

INPUTS
    Requester = pointer to the Requester to be removed
    Window = pointer to the Window structure with which this Requester
       is associated

RESULT
    None

BUGS

SEE ALSO
    Request()
```

```
intuition.library/FreeRemember                    intuition.library/FreeRemember

    NAME
        FreeRemember  --  Free memory allocated by calls to AllocRemember().

    SYNOPSIS
        FreeRemember(RememberKey, ReallyForget)
                     A0           D0

        struct Remember **RememberKey;
        BOOL   ReallyForget;

    FUNCTION
        This function frees up memory allocated by the AllocRemember() function.
        It will either free up just the Remember structures, which supply the
        link nodes that tie your allocations together, or it will deallocate
        both the link nodes AND your memory buffers too.

        If you want to deallocate just the Remember structure link nodes,
        you should set the ReallyForget argument to FALSE.  However, if you
        want FreeRemember to really deallocate all the memory, including
        both the Remember structure link nodes and the buffers you requested
        via earlier calls to AllocRemember(), then you should set the
        ReallyForget argument to TRUE.

    INPUTS
        RememberKey = the address of a pointer to struct Remember.  This
           pointer should either be NULL or set to some value (possibly
           NULL) by a call to AllocRemember().
        ReallyForget = a BOOL FALSE or TRUE describing, respectively,
           whether you want to free up only the Remember nodes or
           if you want this procedure to really forget about all of
           the memory, including both the nodes and the memory buffers
           referenced by the nodes.

    EXAMPLE
        struct Remember *RememberKey;
        RememberKey = NULL;
        AllocRemember(&RememberKey, BUFSIZE, MEMF_CHIP);
        FreeRemember(&RememberKey, TRUE);

    RESULT
        None

    BUGS

    SEE ALSO
        AllocRemember(), exec.library/FreeMem()
```

```
intuition.library/FreeSysRequest                intuition.library/FreeSysRequest

    NAME
        FreeSysRequest -- Frees resources used by a call to BuildSysRequest().

    SYNOPSIS
        FreeSysRequest(Window)
                       A0

        struct Window *Window;

    FUNCTION
        This routine frees up all memory allocated by a successful call to
        the BuildSysRequest() procedure.  If BuildSysRequest() returned a
        pointer to a Window, then you are able to Wait() on the message port
        of that Window to detect an event which satisfies the Requester.
        When you want to remove the Requester, you call this procedure.  It
        ends the Requester and deallocates any memory used in the creation
        of the Requester.  It also closes the special window that was opened
        for your System Requester.

       NOTE:  if BuildSysRequest() did not return a pointer to a Window,
       you should not call FreeSysRequest()!

    INPUTS
        Window = value of the Window pointer returned by a successful call to
           the BuildSysRequest() procedure

    RESULT
        None

    BUGS

    SEE ALSO
        BuildSysRequest(), AutoRequest(), CloseWindow(), exec.library/Wait()
```

```
NAME
    GetDefPrefs  --  Get a copy of the the Intuition default Preferences.

SYNOPSIS
    Prefs = GetDefPrefs(PrefBuffer, Size)
    D0                  A0          D0

    struct Preferences *Prefs;
    struct Preferences *PrefBuffer;
    SHORT  Size;

FUNCTION
    Gets a copy of the Intuition default preferences data.  Writes the
    data into the buffer you specify.  The number of bytes you want
    copied is specified by the Size argument.

    The default Preferences are those that Intuition uses when it
    is first opened.  If no preferences file is found, these are
    the preferences that are used.  These would also be the startup
    Preferences in an AmigaDOS-less environment.

    It is legal to take a partial copy of the Preferences structure.
    The more pertinent Preferences variables have been grouped near
    the top of the structure to facilitate the memory conservation
    that can be had by taking a copy of only some of the Preferences
    structure.

INPUTS
    PrefBuffer = pointer to the memory buffer to receive your copy of the
            Intuition Preferences
    Size = the number of bytes in your PrefBuffer, the number of bytes
      you want copied from the system's internal Preference settings

RESULT
    Returns your parameter PrefBuffer.

BUGS

SEE ALSO
    GetPrefs()
```



```
NAME
    GetPrefs  --  Get the current setting of the Intuition Preferences.

SYNOPSIS
    Prefs = GetPrefs(PrefBuffer, Size)
    D0               A0          D0

    struct Preferences *Prefs;
    struct Preferences *PrefBuffer;

FUNCTION
    Gets a copy of the current Intuition Preferences data.  Writes the
    data into the buffer you specify.  The number of bytes you want
    copied is specified by the Size argument.

    It is legal to take a partial copy of the Preferences structure.
    The more pertinent Preferences variables have been grouped near
    the top of the structure to facilitate the memory conservation
    that can be had by taking a copy of only some of the Preferences
    structure.

INPUTS
    PrefBuffer = pointer to the memory buffer to receive your copy of the
       Intuition Preferences
    Size = the number of bytes in your PrefBuffer, the number of bytes
       you want copied from the system's internal Preference settings

RESULT
    Returns your parameter PrefBuffer.

BUGS

SEE ALSO
    GetDefPrefs(), SetPrefs()
```

```
NAME
    GetScreenData -- Get copy of a screen data structure.

SYNOPSIS
   Success = GetScreenData(Buffer, Size, Type, Screen )
    D0                      A0      D0    D1     A1

    BOOL   Success;
    CPTR   Buffer;
    USHORT Size;
    USHORT Type;
    struct Screen *Screen;

FUNCTION
    This function copies into the caller's buffer data from a Screen structure
    Typically, this call will be used to find the size, title bar height, and
    other values for a standard screen, such as the Workbench screen.

    To get the data for the Workbench screen, one would call:
        GetScreenData(buff, sizeof(struct Screen), WBENCHSCREEN, NULL)

    NOTE: if the requested standard screen is not open, this function
    will have the effect of opening it.

INPUTS
    Buffer = pointer to a buffer into which data can be copied
    Size   = the size of the buffer provided, in bytes
    Type   = the screen type, as specified in OpenWindow (WBENCHSCREEN,
        CUSTOMSCREEN, ...)
    Screen = ignored, unless type is CUSTOMSCREEN, which results only in
        copying 'size' bytes from 'screen' to 'buffer'

RESULT
    TRUE if successful
    FALSE if standard screen of Type 'type' could not be opened.

BUGS

SEE ALSO
    OpenWindow()
```



```
NAME
    InitRequester  --  initializes a Requester structure.

SYNOPSIS
    InitRequester(Requester)
                  A0

    struct Requester *Requester;

FUNCTION
    Initializes a requester for general use.  After calling InitRequester,
    you need fill in only those Requester values that fit your needs.
    The other values are set to NULL--or zero--states.

INPUTS
    Requester = a pointer to a Requester structure

RESULT
    None

BUGS

SEE ALSO
```

NAME
    IntuiTextLength -- Returns the length (pixel-width) of an IntuiText.

SYNOPSIS

```
IntuiTextLength(IText)
                D0

struct IntuiText *IText;
```

FUNCTION
    This routine accepts a pointer to an instance of an IntuiText structure, and returns the length (the pixel-width) of the string which that instance of the structure represents.

    NOTE: if the Font pointer of your IntuiText structure is set to NULL, you'll get the pixel-width of your text in terms of the current system default font. You may wish to be sure that the field IText->ITextFont for 'default font' text is equal to the Font field of the screen it is being measured for.

INPUTS
    IText = pointer to an instance of an IntuiText structure

RESULT
    Returns the pixel-width of the text specified by the IntuiText data

BUGS
    Would do better to take a RastPort as argument, so that a NULL in the Font pointer would lead automatically to the font for the intended target RastPort.

SEE ALSO
    OpenScreen()

NAME
    ItemAddress -- Returns the address of the specified MenuItem.

SYNOPSIS

```
Item = ItemAddress(MenuStrip, MenuNumber)
D0                 A0         D0

struct MenuItem *ItemAddress;
struct Menu     *MenuStrip;
USHORT MenuNumber;
```

FUNCTION
    This routine feels through the specified MenuStrip and returns the address of the Item specified by the MenuNumber. Typically, you will use this routine to get the address of a MenuItem from a MenuNumber sent to you by Intuition after User has played with a Window's Menus.

    This routine requires that the arguments are well-defined. MenuNumber may be equal to MENUNULL, in which case this routine returns NULL. If MenuNumber doesn't equal MENUNULL, it's presumed to be a valid Item number selector for your MenuStrip, which includes:
    - a valid Menu number
    - a valid Item Number
    - if the Item specified by the above two components has a SubItem, the MenuNumber may have a SubItem component too

    Note that there must be BOTH a Menu number and an Item number. Because a SubItem specifier is optional, the address returned by this routine may point to either an Item or a SubItem.

INPUTS
    MenuStrip = a pointer to the first Menu in your MenuStrip
    MenuNumber = the value which contains the packed data that selects the Menu and Item (and SubItem). See the Intuition Reference Manual for information on Menu Numbers.

RESULT
    If MenuNumber == MENUNULL, this routine returns NULL, else this routine returns the address of the MenuItem specified by MenuNumber.

BUGS

SEE ALSO
    The "Menus" chapter of the Intuition Reference Manual, for more information about "Menu Numbers."

```
intuition.library/LockIBase                    intuition.library/LockIBase

    NAME
        LockIBase -- Intuition user's access to Intuition Locking

    SYNOPSIS
        Lock = LockIBase(LockNumber)
        D0               D0

        ULONG Lock;
        ULONG LockNumber;

    FUNCTION

        Grabs Intuition internal semaphore so that caller may examine
        IntuitionBase safely.

        The idea here is that you can get the locks Intuition needs before
        such IntuitionBase fields as ActiveWindow and FirstScreen are
        changed, or linked lists of windows and screens, are changed.

        Do Not Get Tricky with this entry point, and do not hold these locks
        for long, as all Intuition input processing will wait for you to
        surrender the lock by a call to UnlockIBase().

        NOTE WELL: A call to this function MUST be paired with a subsequent
        call to UnlockIBase(), and soon, please.

    INPUTS

        A long unsigned integer, LockNumber, specifies which of Intuition's internal
        locks you want to get.  This parameter should be zero for all forseeable
        uses of this function, which will let you examine Active fields and linked
        lists of screens and windows with safety.

    RESULT

        Returns another ULONG which should be passed to UnlockIBase() to surrender
        the lock gotten by this call.

    BUGS
        This function should not be called while holding any other system locks
        such as Layer or LayerInfo locks.

    SEE ALSO
        UnlockIBase(), layers.library/LockLayerInfo, exec.library/ObtainSemaphore
```

```
intuition.library/MakeScreen                  intuition.library/MakeScreen

    NAME
        MakeScreen  --  Do an Intuition-integrated MakeVPort() of a custom screen

    SYNOPSIS
        MakeScreen(Screen)
                   A0

        struct Screen *Screen;

    FUNCTION
        This procedure allows you to do a MakeVPort() for the ViewPort of your
        Custom Screen in an Intuition-integrated way.  This allows you to
        do your own Screen manipulations without worrying about interference
        with Intuition's usage of the same ViewPort.

        The operation of this function is as follows:
            - Block until the Intuition View is not in use.
            - Set the View Modes correctly to reflect if there is a (visible)
              interlaced screen.
            - call MakeVPort, passing the Intuition View and your Screen's
              ViewPort.
            - Unlocks the Intuition View.

        After calling this routine, you can call RethinkDisplay() to
        incorporate the new ViewPort of your custom screen into the
        Intuition display.

    INPUTS
        Screen = address of the Custom Screen structure

    RESULT
        None

    BUGS

    SEE ALSO
        RethinkDisplay(), RemakeDisplay(), graphics.library/MakeVPort()
```

```
NAME
    ModifyIDCMP  --  Modify the state of the Window's IDCMPFlags.

SYNOPSIS
    ModifyIDCMP(Window, IDCMPFlags)
                A0      D0

    struct Window *Window;
    ULONG  IDCMPFlags;

FUNCTION
    This routine modifies the state of your Window's IDCMP (Intuition Direct
    Communication Message Port).  The state is modified to reflect your
    desires as described by the flag bits in the value IDCMPFlags.

    The four actions that might be taken are:

   - if there is currently no IDCMP in the given Window, and IDCMPFlags
     is NULL, nothing happens
   - if there is currently no IDCMP in the given Window, and any of the
     IDCMPFlags is selected (set), then the IDCMP of the Window is
     created, including allocating and initializing the message ports
     and allocating a Signal bit for your Port.  See the "Input and
     Output Methods" chapter of the Intuition Reference Manual for full
      details
   - if the IDCMP for the given Window exists, and the
     IDCMPFlags argument is NULL, this says that you want
     Intuition to close the Ports, free the buffers and free
     your Signal bit.  You MUST be the same Task that was active
     when this Signal bit was allocated
   - if the IDCMP for the given Window is opened, and the IDCMPFlags
     argument is not NULL, this means that you want to change the
     state of which events will be broadcast to you through the IDCMP

    NOTE:  You can set up the Window->UserPort to any Port of your own
    before you call ModifyIDCMP().  If IDCMPFlags is non-null but
    your UserPort is already initialized, Intuition will assume that
    it's a valid Port with Task and Signal data preset and Intuition
    won't disturb your set-up at all, Intuition will just allocate
    the Intuition Message Port half of it.  The converse is true
    as well:  if UserPort is NULL when you call here with
    IDCMPFlags == NULL, Intuition will deallocate only the Intuition
    side of the Port.

    This allows you to use a Port that you already have allocated:
   - OpenWindow() with IDCMPFlags equal to NULL (open no ports)
   - set the UserPort variable of your Window to any valid Port of your
     own choosing
   - call ModifyIDCMP with IDCMPFlags set to what you want
   - then, to clean up later, set UserPort equal to NULL before calling
     CloseWindow() (leave IDCMPFlags alone)  BUT FIRST: you must make
      sure that no messages sent your window are queued at the port,
      since they will be returned to the memory free pool.

INPUTS
    Window = pointer to the Window structure containing the IDCMP Ports
    IDCMPFlags = the flag bits describing the new desired state of the IDCMP

RESULT
    None

BUGS
    Method for closing a window with a shared port needs to be better
    documented somewhere, or provided as an Intuition call, or both.
    At the present, the technique is available through developer support
    newsletters as a function called CloseWindowSafely().  See, for
    example, Amiga Mail, vol.2.

SEE ALSO
    OpenWindow(), CloseWindow()
```



```
NAME
    ModifyProp  --  Modify the current parameters of a Proportional Gadget.

SYNOPSIS
    ModifyProp(Gadget, Window, Requester,
               A0      A1      A2
                Flags, HorizPot, VertPot, HorizBody, VertBody)
                D0     D1        D2       D3         D4

    struct Gadget *Gadget;
    struct Window *Window;
    struct Requester *Requester;
    USHORT Flags;
    USHORT HorizPot, VertPot;
    USHORT HorizBody, VertBody;

FUNCTION
    Modifies the parameters of the specified Proportional Gadget.  The
    Gadget's internal state is then recalculated and the imagery
    is redisplayed in the Window or Requester that contains the gadget.

    The Requester variable can point to a Requester structure.  If the
    Gadget has the REQGADGET flag set, the Gadget is in a Requester
    and the Window pointer must point to the window of the Requester.
    If this is not the Gadget of a Requester, the Requester argument may
    be NULL.

    NOTE: this function causes all gadgets from the proportional
    gadget to the end of the gadget list to be refreshed, for
    reasons of compatibility.
    For more refinded display updataing, use NewModifyProp

INPUTS
    PropGadget = pointer to a Proportional Gadget
    Window = pointer to the window containing the gadget or the Window
        containing the Requester containing the Gadget.
    Requester = pointer to a Requester (may be NULL if this isn't
        a Requester Gadget)
    Flags = value to be stored in the Flags variable of the PropInfo
    HorizPot = value to be stored in the HorizPot variable of the PropInfo
    VertPot = value to be stored in the VertPot variable of the PropInfo
    HorizBody = value to be stored in the HorizBody variable of the PropInfo
    VertBody = value to be stored in the VertBody variable of the PropInfo

RESULT
    None

BUGS

SEE ALSO
    NewModifyProp()
    The Intuition Reference Manual contains more information on
    Proportional Gadgets.
```

```
NAME
    MoveScreen  --  attempts to move the Screen by increments provided.

SYNOPSIS
    MoveScreen(Screen, DeltaX, DeltaY);
               A0      D0      D1

    struct Screen *Screen;
    SHORT  DeltaX, DeltaY;

FUNCTION
    Moves the screen the specified increment.

    Currently, only the DeltaY coordinate is significant; you should
    pass zero for DeltaX.

    Screens are constrained now only by the top and bottom of the
    Intuition View, which is not guaranteed to be the same in all
    versions of the software.

   If the DeltaX and DeltaY variables you specify would move the Screen
   in a way that violates any restrictions, the Screen will be moved
   as far as possible.  You may examine the LeftEdge and TopEdge fields
    of the Screen Structure to see where the screen really ended up.

    In operation, this function determines what the actual increments
    that are actually to be used, sets these values up, and calls
    RethinkDisplay().

INPUTS
    Screen = pointer to a Screen structure
    DeltaX = amount to move the screen on the x-axis
             Note that DeltaX should be set to zero.
    DeltaY = amount to move the screen on the y-axis

RESULT
    None

BUGS

SEE ALSO
    RethinkDisplay()
```



```
NAME
    MoveWindow  --  Ask Intuition to move a Window.

SYNOPSIS
    MoveWindow(Window, DeltaX, DeltaY)
               A0      D0      D1

    struct Window *Window;
    SHORT  DeltaX, DeltaY;

FUNCTION
    This routine sends a request to Intuition asking to move the Window
    the specified distance.  The delta arguments describe how far to
    move the Window along the respective axes.

    Note that the Window will not be moved immediately, but rather
    will be moved the next time Intuition receives an input event,
    which happens currently at a minimum rate of ten times per second,
    and a maximum of sixty times a second.

    This routine does no error-checking.  If your delta values specify
    some far corner of the Universe, Intuition will attempt to move
    your Window to the far corners of the Universe.  Because of the
    distortions in the space-time continuum that can result from this,
    as predicted by special relativity, the result is generally not
    a pretty sight.

    You are thus advised to consider the dimensions of your Window's screen
    and the current position of your window before calling this function.

INPUTS
    Window = pointer to the structure of the Window to be moved
    DeltaX = signed value describing how far to move the Window on the x-axis
    DeltaY = signed value describing how far to move the Window on the y-axis

RESULT
    None

BUGS

SEE ALSO
    SizeWindow(), WindowToFront(), WindowToBack()
```

```
NAME
    NewModifyProp  --  ModifyProp, but with Selective Update

SYNOPSIS
    NewModifyProp(Gadget, Window, Requester, Flags
                  A0      A1      A2         D0
                  HorizPot, VertPot, HorizBody, VertBody, NumGad)
                  D1        D2       D3         D4        D5

    struct Gadget *Gadget;
    struct Window *Window;
    struct Requester *Requester;
    USHORT Flags;
    USHORT HorizPot, VertPot;
    USHORT HorizBody, VertBody;
    int    NumGad;

FUNCTION
    Performs the function of ModifyProp(), but can update a
    subset of the entire gadget list.  The starting position
    and gadget count are specified as parameters.  If NumGad = -1,
    updates are made until the end of the list is reached.

NOTE
    Under V33/34, NewModifyProp() has the side effect of redrawing
    the entire gadget.  In the future this function may only update
    that parts that changed.  To cause a full draw operation, use
    RefreshGList().

INPUTS
    PropGadget = pointer to a Proportional Gadget
    Window = pointer to the window containing the gadget or the Window
        containing the Requester containing the Gadget.
    Requester = pointer to a Requester (may be NULL if this isn't
        a Requester Gadget)
    Flags = value to be stored in the Flags variable of the PropInfo
    HorizPot = value to be stored in the HorizPot variable of the PropInfo
    VertPot = value to be stored in the VertPot variable of the PropInfo
    HorizBody = value to be stored in the HorizBody variable of the PropInfo
    VertBody = value to be stored in the VertBody variable of the PropInfo
    NumGad = number of gadgets to be refreshed after propgadget internals
        have been adjusted.  -1 means "to end of list."

RESULT
    None

BUGS

SEE ALSO
    ModifyProp()
    The Intuition Reference Manual contains more information on Proportional
    Gadgets.
```



```
NAME
    OffGadget  --  disables the specified Gadget.

SYNOPSIS
    OffGadget(Gadget, Window, Requester)
              A0      A1      A2

    struct Gadget *Gadget;
    struct Window *Window;
    struct Requester *Requester;

FUNCTION
    This command disables the specified Gadget.  When a Gadget is
    disabled, these things happen:
         - its imagery is displayed ghosted
         - the GADGDISABLED flag is set
         - the Gadget cannot be selected by User

    The Window parameter must point to the window which contains the Gadget,
    or which contains the Requester that contains the Gadget
    The Requester parameter must only be valid if the Gadget has the
    REQGADGET flag set, a requirement for all Requester Gadgets.

   NOTE:  it's never safe to tinker with the Gadget list yourself.  Don't
   supply some Gadget that Intuition hasn't already processed in
   the usual way.

    NOTE: for compatibility reasons, this function will refresh all
    gadgets in a requester, and all gadgets from Gadget to the
    end of the gadget list if Gadget is in a window.

INPUTS
    Gadget = pointer to the Gadget that you want disabled
    Window = pointer to a Window structure containing the Gadget or
        containing the Requester which contains the Gadget
    Requester = pointer to a Requester (may by NULL if this isn't
       a Requester Gadget (i.e. REQGADGET is not set)).

RESULT
    None

BUGS

SEE ALSO
    AddGadget(), RefreshGadgets()
```

```
NAME
    OffMenu  --  disables the given menu or menu item.

SYNOPSIS
    OffMenu(Window, MenuNumber)
            A0      D0

    struct Window *Window;
    USHORT MenuNumber;

FUNCTION
    This command disables a sub-item, an item, or a whole menu.
    This depends on the contents of the data packed into MenuNumber,
    which is described in the Intuition Reference Manual.

INPUTS
    Window = pointer to the window
    MenuNumber = the menu piece to be disabled

RESULT
    None

BUGS

SEE ALSO
```



```
NAME
    OnGadget  --  enables the specified Gadget.

SYNOPSIS
    OnGadget(Gadget, Window, Requester)
             A0      A1      A2

    struct Gadget *Gadget;
    struct Window *Window;
    struct Requester *Requester;

FUNCTION
    This command enables the specified Gadget.  When a Gadget is
    enabled, these things happen:
    - its imagery is displayed normally (not ghosted)
    - the GADGDISABLED flag is cleared
    - the Gadget can thereafter be selected by the user

    The Window parameter must point to the window which contains the Gadget,
    or which contains the Requester that contains the Gadget
    The Requester parameter must only be valid if the Gadget has the
    REQGADGET flag set, a requirement for all Requester Gadgets.

    NOTE:  it's never safe to tinker with the Gadget list yourself.  Don't
    supply some Gadget that Intuition hasn't already processed in
    the usual way.

    NOTE: for compatibility reasons, this function will refresh all
    gadgets in a requester, and all gadgets from Gadget to the
    end of the gadget list if Gadget is in a window.

INPUTS
    Gadget = pointer to the Gadget that you want disabled
    Window = pointer to a Window structure containing the Gadget or
        containing the Requester which contains the Gadget
    Requester = pointer to a Requester (may by NULL if this isn't
       a Requester Gadget (i.e. REQGADGET is not set)).

RESULT
    None

BUGS

SEE ALSO
```

```
NAME
    OnMenu  --  enable the given menu or menu item.

SYNOPSIS
    OnMenu(Window, MenuNumber)
           A0      D0

    struct Window *Window;
    USHORT MenuNumber;

FUNCTION
    This command enables a sub-item, an item, or a whole menu.
    This depends on the contents of the data packed into MenuNumber,
    which is described in the Intuition Reference Manual.

INPUTS
    Window = pointer to the window
    MenuNumber = the menu piece to be enables

RESULT
    None

BUGS

SEE ALSO
```



```
NAME
    OpenScreen  --  Open an Intuition Screen.

SYNOPSIS
    Screen = OpenScreen(NewScreen)
    D0                  A0

    struct Screen *Screen;
    struct NewScreen *NewScreen;

FUNCTION
    Opens an Intuition Screen according to the specified parameters
    found in the NewScreen structure.

    Does all the allocations, sets up the Screen structure and all
    substructures completely, and links this Screen's ViewPort into
    Intuition's View structure.

    Before you call OpenScreen(), you must initialize an instance of
    a NewScreen structure.  NewScreen is a structure that contains
    all of the arguments needed to open a Screen.  The NewScreen
    structure may be discarded immediately after OpenScreen() returns.

    The SHOWTITLE flag is set to TRUE by default when a Screen is opened.
    To change this, you must call the routine ShowTitle().

INPUTS
    NewScreen = pointer to an instance of a NewScreen structure.
    That structure is initialized with the following information:
    -------------------------------------------------------------------------
    Left = initial x-position of your Screen (should be zero currently)
    Top = initial y-position of the opening Screen
    Width = the width for this Screen's RastPort.
    Height = the height for his Screen's RastPort, or the constant
             STDSCREENHEIGHT to get current local maximum (at this time
             guaranteed to be at least 200).  The actual height the screen
             opended to can be found in the returned Screen structure.
    The "normal" width and height for a particular system is stored by
    the graphics.library in GfxBase->NormalDisplayRows and
    GfxBase->NormalDisplayColumns.  These values will be different
    depending on factors such as PAL video and overscan.

    Depth = number of BitPlanes
    DetailPen = pen number for details (like gadgets or text in title bar)
    BlockPen = pen number for block fills (like title bar)
    Type = Screen type
        Set these flag bits as desired from the set:
        CUSTOMSCREEN -- this is your own Screen, not a System screen.
        CUSTOMBITMAP -- this custom screen has bit maps supplied
            in the BitMap field of the NewScreen structure.  Intuition is
            not to allocate any Raster BitMaps.
        SCREENBEHIND -- your screen will be created behind all other open
            screens.  This allows a program to prepare imagery in the
            screen, change it's colors, and so on, bringing it to the front
            when it is presentable.
        SCREENQUIET -- Intuition will not render system screen gadgets or
            screen title.  In concert with the RMBTRAP flag on all your
            screen's windows, this flag will prevent Intuition from rendering
            into your screen's bitplanes.  Without RMBTRAP (or using MENUVERIFY
            IDCMP facility to cancel menu operations), this flag will
            prevent Intuition from clearing your menu bar, which is probably
            unacceptable.  The title bar layer may still overwrite your
            bitmap on open.
    ViewModes = the appropriate argument for the data type ViewPort.Modes.
          these might include:
                HIRES for this screen to be HIRES width.
                INTERLACE for the display to switch to interlace.
                SPRITES for this Screen to use sprites (pointer comes anyway).
                DUALPF for dual-playfield mode (not supported yet)
    Font = pointer to the default TextAttr structure for text in this Screen
```

and all Windows that open in this Screen. Text that uses this TextAttr includes title bars of both Screen and Windows, String Gadgets, and Menu titles. Of course, IntuiText that specifies a NULL TextAttr field will use the Screen/Window default Fonts.

DefaultTitle = pointer to a line of text that will be displayed along the Screen's Title Bar. Null terminated, or just a NULL pointer to get no text

Gadgets = This field should be set to NULL, since no user Gadgets may be attached to a Screen.

CustomBitMap = if you're not supplying a custom BitMap, this value is ignored. However, if you have your own display memory that you want used for this Screen, the CustomBitMap argument should point to the BitMap that describes your display memory. See the "Screens" chapter and the "Amiga ROM Kernel Manual" for more information about BitMaps.

RESULT

If all is well, returns the pointer to your new Screen
If anything goes wrong, returns NULL

NOTE

By default AmigaDOS requesters related to your Process are put on the workbench screen (these are messages like "Disk Full"). If you wish them to show up on custom screens, DOS must be told. This fragment shows the procedure. More information is availble in the AmigaDOS books. Sample code fragment:

```
----------- cut here ----------
#include "libraries/dosextens.h"
        ...
struct Process *process;
struct Window  *window;
APTR           temp;
        ...
    process=(struct Process *)FindTask(0L);
    temp=process->pr_WindowPtr;         /* save old value */
    process->pr_WindowPtr=(APTR)window;
    /* set a pointer to any open window on your screen */
        ...
        your code goes here
        ...
    process->pr_WindowPtr=temp;
    /* restore value _before_ CloseWindow */
    CloseWindow(window);
------- cut here ------
```

BUGS

SEE ALSO

OpenWindow(), PrintIText(), CloseScreen(), The Intuition Reference Manual

NAME

OpenWindow -- Opens an Intuition Window

SYNOPSIS

```
OpenWindow(NewWindow);
where the NewWindow structure is initialized with:
    Left, Top, Width, Height, DetailPen, BlockPen, Flags,
    IDCMPFlags, Gadgets, CheckMark, Text, Type, Screen, BitMap,
    MinWidth, MinHeight, MaxWidth, MaxHeight
```

FUNCTION

Opens an Intuition window of the given height, width and depth, including the specified system Gadgets as well as any of your own. Allocates everything you need to get going.

Before you call OpenWindow(), you must initialize an instance of a NewWindow structure. NewWindow is a structure that contains all of the arguments needed to open a Window. The NewWindow structure may be discarded immediately after it is used to open the Window.

If Type == CUSTOMSCREEN, you must have opened your own Screen already via a call to OpenScreen(). Then Intuition uses your screen argument for the pertinent information needed to get your Window going. On the other hand, if type == one of the Intuition's standard Screens, your screen argument is ignored. Instead, Intuition will check to see whether or not that Screen already exists: if it doesn't, it will be opened first before Intuition opens your window in the Standard Screen.
If the flag SUPER_BITMAP is set, the bitmap variable must point to your own BitMap.
The DetailPen and the BlockPen are used for system rendering; for instance, the Title bar is first filled using the BlockPen, and then the Gadgets and text are rendered using DetailPen. You can either choose to supply special pens for your Window, or, by setting either of these arguments to -1, the Screen's Pens will be used instead.

INPUTS

NewWindow = pointer to an instance of a NewWindow structure. That structure is initialized with the following data:

Left = the initial x-position for your window
Top = the initial y-position for your window
Width = the initial width of this window
Height = the initial height of this window
DetailPen = pen number (or -1) for the rendering of Window details (like gadgets or text in title bar)
BlockPen = pen number (or -1) for Window block fills (like Title Bar)
Flags = specifiers for your requirements of this window, including:

- which system Gadgets you want attached to your window:
    - WINDOWDRAG allows this Window to be dragged
    - WINDOWDEPTH lets the user depth-arrange this Window
    - WINDOWCLOSE attaches the standard Close Gadget
    - WINDOWSIZING allows this Window to be sized. If you ask the WINDOWSIZING Gadget, you must specify one or both of the flags SIZEBRIGHT and SIZEBBOTTOM below; if you don't, the default is SIZEBRIGHT. See the following items SIZEBRIGHT and SIZEBBOTTOM for extra information.
    - SIZEBRIGHT is a special system Gadget flag that you set to specify whether or not you want the RIGHT Border adjusted to account for the physical size of the Sizing Gadget. The Sizing Gadget must, after all, take up room in either the right or bottom border (or both, if you like) of the Window. Setting either this or the SIZEBBOTTOM flag selects which edge will take up the slack. This will be particularly useful to applications that want to use the extra space for other Gadgets (like a Proportional Gadget and two Booleans done up to look like scroll bars) or, for

```
                for instance, applications that want every possible
                horizontal bit and are willing to lose lines vertically.
                NOTE:  if you select WINDOWSIZING, you must select
                either SIZEBRIGHT or SIZEBBOTTOM or both.  If you select
                neither, the default is SIZEBRIGHT.
              - SIZEBBOTTOM is a special system Gadget flag that
                you set to specify whether or not you want the
                BOTTOM Border adjusted to account for the physical size
                of the Sizing Gadget.  For details, refer to
                SIZEBRIGHT above.
                NOTE:  if you select WINDOWSIZING, you must select
                either SIZEBRIGHT or SIZEBBOTTOM or both.  If you select
                neither, the default is SIZEBRIGHT.
          - GIMMEZEROZERO for easy but expensive output
          - what type of window raster you want, either:
              - SIMPLE_REFRESH
              - SMART_REFRESH
              - SUPER_BITMAP
            If the type is SMART_REFRESH, and you do not handle
            REFRESHWINDOW type messages, also set the NOCAREREFRESH
            flag.
          - BACKDROP for whether or not you want this window to be one
            of Intuition's special backdrop windows.  See BORDERLESS
            as well.
          - REPORTMOUSE for whether or not you want to "listen" to
            mouse movement events whenever your Window is the active
            one.  After you've opened your Window, if you want to change
            you can later change the status of this via a call to
            ReportMouse().  Whether or not your Window is listening to
            Mouse is affected by Gadgets too, since they can cause
            you to start getting reports too if you like.
            The mouse move reports (either InputEvents or messages on
            the IDCMP) that you get will have the x/y coordinates of the
            current mouse position, relative to the upper-left corner
            of your Window (GIMMEZEROZERO notwithstanding).
            This flag can work in conjunction with the IDCMP Flag
            called MOUSEMOVE, which allows you to listen via the
            IDCMP.
          - BORDERLESS should be set if you want a Window with no
            Border padding.  Your Window may have the Border variables
            set anyway, depending on what Gadgetry you've requested for
            the Window, but you won't get the standard border lines and
            spacing that comes with typical Windows.
            This is a good way to take over the entire Screen, since you
            can have a Window cover the entire width of the Screen using
            this flag.  This will work particularly well in
            conjunction with the BACKDROP flag (see above), since it
            allows you to open a Window that fills the ENTIRE Screen.
            NOTE:  this is not a flag that you want to set casually,
            since it may cause visual confusion on the Screen.  The
            Window borders are the only dependable visual division
            between various Windows and the background Screen.  Taking
            away that Border takes away that visual cue, so make sure
            that your design doesn't need it at all before you
            proceed.
          - ACTIVATE is the flag you set if you want this
            Window to automatically become the active Window.
            The active Window is the one that receives input from
            the keyboard and mouse.  It's usually a good idea to
            to have the Window you open when your application
            first starts up be an ACTIVATED one, but all others
            opened later not be ACTIVATED (if the user is off
            doing something with another Screen, for instance, your
            new Window will change where the input is going, which
            would have the effect of yanking the input rug from
            under the user).  Please use this flag thoughtfully and
            carefully.
          - RMBTRAP, when set, causes the right mouse button events
            to be trapped and broadcast as events.  You can receive
            these events through either the IDCMP or the Console.
IDCMPFlags = IDCMP is the acronym for Intuition Direct Communications
        Message Port.  It's Intuition's sole acronym, given in honor of
        all hack-heads who love to mangle our brains with maniacal names,
        and fashioned especially cryptic and unpronounceable to make them
        squirm with sardonic delight.  Here's to you, my chums.  Meanwhile,
        I still opt (and argue) for simplicity and elegance.
            If any of the IDCMP Flags is selected, Intuition will create
        a pair of messageports and use them for direct communications with
        the Task opening this Window (as compared with broadcasting
        information via the Console Device).  See the "Input and Output
        Methods" chapter of the intuition manual for complete details.
            You request an IDCMP by setting any of these flags.  Except
         for the special VERIFY flags, every other flag you set
        tells me that if a given event occurs which your
        program wants to know about, I'm to broadcast the details
        of that event through the IDCMP rather than via the Console device.
        device.  This allows a program to interface with Intuition
        directly, rather than going through the Console device.
            Remember, if you are going to open both an IDCMP and
        a Console, it will be far better to get most of the event
        messages via the Console.  Reserve your usage of the IDCMP
        for special performance cases; that is, when you aren't going
        to open a Console for your Window and you do want to learn
        about a certain set of events (for instance, CLOSEWINDOW); another
        example would be SIZEVERIFY, which is a function that you get
        ONLY through the use of the IDCMP (because the Console doesn't
        give you any way to talk to Intuition directly).
            On the other hand, if the IDCMPFlags argument is equal to
        zero, no IDCMP is created and the only way you can learn about any
        Window event for this Window is via a Console opened for
        this Window.  And you have no way to SIZEVERIFY.
            If you want to change the state of the IDCMP some time after
        you've opened the Window (including opening or closing the IDCMP)
        you call the routine ModifyIDCMP().
            The flags you can set are:
              - REQVERIFY is the flag which, like SIZEVERIFY and(see
                MENUVERIFY (see immediately below), specifies that you
                want to make sure that your graphical state is quiescent
                before something extraordinary happens.  In this
                case, the extraordinary event is that a rectangle of
                graphical data is about to be blasted into your Window.
                If you're drawing into that Window, you probably will
                wish to make sure that you've ceased drawing before
                the user is allowed to bring up the DMRequest you've set
                up, and the same for when system has a request for the
                user.  Set this flag to ask for that verification step.
              - REQCLEAR is the flag you set to hear about it when the
                last Requester is cleared from your Window and
                it's safe for you to start output again (presuming you're
                using REQVERIFY)
              - REQSET is a flag that you set to receive a broadcast
                when the first Requester is opened in your Window.
                Compare this with REQCLEAR above.  This function is
                distinct from REQVERIFY.  This functions merely tells you
                that a Requester has opened, whereas REQVERIFY requires
                you to respond before the Requester is opened.
              - MENUVERIFY is the flag you set to have Intuition stop
                and wait for you to finish all graphical output to your
                Window before rendering the menus.  Menus are currently
                rendered in the most memory-efficient way, which
                involves interrupting output to all Windows in the
                Screen before the Menus are drawn.  If you need to
                finish your graphical output before this happens,
                you can set this flag to make sure that you do.
              - SIZEVERIFY means that you will be doing output to your
                Window which depends on a knowledge of the current size
                of the Window.  If the user wants to resize the
                Window,  you may want to make sure that any queued
                output completes before the sizing takes place
                (critical Text, for instance).  If this is the case,
                set this flag.   Then, when the user wants to size,
                Intuition will send you the SIZEVERIFY message and
                Wait() until you reply that it's OK to proceed with
                the sizing. NOTE:  when I say that Intuition will
```

Wait() until you reply, what I'm really saying is that User will WAIT until you reply, which suffers the great negative potential of User-Unfriendliness. So remember: use this flag sparingly, and, as always with any IDCMP Message you receive, Reply to it promptly! Then, after User has sized the Window, you can find out about it using NEWSIZE:

With all of the "VERIFY" functions, it is not safe to leve them enabled at any time when you task may not be able to respond for a long period.

It is NEVER safe to call AmigaDOS, directly or indirectly, when a "VERIFY" function is active. If AmigaDOS needs to put up a disk requester for you, your task might end up waiting for the requester to be satisfied, at the same time as Intuition is waiting for your response. The result is a complete machine lockup. USE ModifyIDCMP TO TURN OFF ANY VERIFY MESSAGES BEFORE CALLING AmigaDOS!!!

- NEWSIZE is the flag that tells Intuition to send an IDCMP Message to you after the user has resized your Window. At this point, you could examine the size variables in your Window structure to discover the new size of the Window
- REFRESHWINDOW when set will cause a Message to be sent whenever your Window needs refreshing. This flag makes sense only with SIMPLE_REFRESH and SMART_REFRESH Windows.
- MOUSEBUTTONS will get reports about Mouse-button Up/Down events broadcast to you (Note: only the ones that don't mean something to Intuition. If the user clicks the Select button over a Gadget, Intuition deals with it and you don't find out about it through here).
- MOUSEMOVE will work only if you've set the flag REPORTMOUSE above, or if one of your Gadgets has the flag FOLLOWMOUSE set. Then all mouse movements will be reported here.
- GADGETDOWN means that when the User "selects" a Gadget you've created with the GADGIMMEDIATE flag set, the fact will be broadcast through the IDCMP.
- GADGETUP means that when the User "releases" a Gadget that you've created with the RELVERIFY flag set, the fact will be broadcast through the IDCMP.
- MENUPICK selects that MenuNumber data will come this way
- CLOSEWINDOW means broadcast the CLOSEWINDOW event through the IDCMP rather than the Console
- RAWKEY selects that all RAWKEY events are transmitted via the IDCMP. Note that these are absolutely RAW keycodes, which you will have to massage before using. Setting this and the MOUSE flags effectively eliminates the need to open a Console Device to get input from the keyboard and mouse. Of course, in exchange you lose all of the Console features, most notably the "cooking" of input data and the systematic output of text to your Window.

- VANILLAKEY is for developers who don't want the hassle of RAWKEYS. This flag will return all the keycodes after translation via the current country-dependant keymap. When you set this flag, you will get IntuiMessages where the Code field has a decoded ASCII character representing the key struck on the keyboard. Only codes that map to one character are returned, you can't read such keys as HELP or the Function keys with VANILLAKEY.

- INTUITICKS gives you simple timer events from Intuition when your window is the active one; it may help you avoid opening and managing the timer device. With this flag set, you will get only one queued-up INTUITICKS message at a time. If Intuition notices that you've been sent an INTUITICKS message and haven't replied to it, another message will not be sent. Intuition receives timer events ten times a second (approximately).

- DELTAMOVE gives raw (unscaled) input event delta X/Y values. This is so you can detect mouse motion regardless of screen/window/display boundaries. Note that MOUSEBUTTONS messages will also be affected.

- NEWPREFS indicates you wish to be notified when the system-wide preferences changes.

- Set ACTIVEWINDOW and INACTIVEWINDOW to get messages when those events happen to your window. Take care not to confuse this "ACTIVEWINDOW" with the remarkably familiar sounding, but totally different "WINDOWACTIVE" flag.

Gadgets = the pointer to the first of a linked list of the your own Gadgets which you want attached to this Window. Can be NULL if you have no Gadgets of your own

CheckMark = a pointer to an instance of the struct Image where can be found the imagery you want used when any of your MenuItems is to be checkmarked. If you don't want to supply your own imagery and you want to just use Intuition's own checkmark, set this argument to NULL

Text = a null-terminated line of text to appear on the title bar of your window (may be null if you want no text)

Type = the Screen type for this window. If this equal CUSTOMSCREEN, you must have already opened a CUSTOMSCREEN (see text above). Types available include:
- WBENCHSCREEN
- CUSTOMSCREEN

Screen = if your type is one of Intuition's Standard Screens, then this argument is ignored. However, if Type == CUSTOMSCREEN, this must point to the structure of your own Screen

BitMap = if you have specified SUPER_BITMAP as the type of refreshing you want for this Window, then this value points to a instance of the struct BitMap. However, if the refresh type is NOT SUPER_BITMAP, this pointer is ignored

MinWidth, MinHeight, MaxWidth, MaxHeight = the size limits for this that the minimums cannot be greater than the current size, nor can the maximums be smaller than the current size.

The maximums may be LARGER than the current size, or even larger than the current screen. The maximums should be set to the highest value your application can handle. This allows users with larger display devices to take full advantage of your software. If there is no good reason to limit the size, then don't. -1 or ~0 indicates the maximum available.

Any one of these can be initialized to zero, which means that limit will be set to the current dimension of that axis. The limits can be changed after the Window is opened by calling the WindowLimits() routine.

RESULT

If all is well, returns the pointer to your new Window
If anything goes wrong, returns NULL

BUGS

SEE ALSO

OpenScreen()
ModifyIDCMP()
WindowTitles()

```
NAME
    OpenWorkBench  --  Opens the WorkBench Screen

SYNOPSIS
    WBScreen =  OpenWorkBench()
    D0

    struct Screen *WBScreen;

FUNCTION
    This routine attempts to reopen the WorkBench.  The actions taken are:
        - general good stuff and nice things, and then return a non-null
          pointer to the Workbench Screen.
        - find that something has gone wrong, and return NULL

    The return value, if not NULL, is indeed the address of the Workbench
    Screen, although you should not use it as such.  This is because the
    Workbench may be closed by other programs, which can invalidate
    the address at any time.  We suggest that you regard the return
    value as a BOOL indication that the routine has succeeded, if
    you pay any attention to it at all.

INPUTS
    None

RESULT
    non-FALSE if WorkBench Screen opened successfully, or was already opened
    FALSE if anything went wrong and the WorkBench Screen isn't out there

BUGS

SEE ALSO
```



```
NAME
    PrintIText  --  prints the text according to the IntuiText argument

SYNOPSIS
    PrintIText(RastPort, IText, LeftOffset, TopOffset)
               A0        A1     D0          D1

    struct RastPort *RastPort;
    struct IntuiText *IText;
    SHORT LeftOffset, TopOffset;

FUNCTION
    Prints the IntuiText into the specified RastPort.  Sets up the RastPort
    as specified by the IntuiText values, then prints the text into the
    RastPort at the IntuiText x/y coordinates offset by the left/top
    arguments.  Note, though, that the IntuitText structure itself
    may contain further text position coordinates: those coordinates
    and the Left/TopOffsets are added to obtain the true position of
    the text to be rendered.

    This routine does window layer clipping as appropriate -- if you
    print text outside of your Window, your characters will be
    clipped at the Window's edge.

    If the NextText field of the IntuiText argument is non-NULL,
    the next IntuiText is rendered as well, and so on until some
    NextText field is NULL.

    IntuiText with the ITextAttr field NULL are displayed in the
    font of the RastPort.  If the RastPort font is also NULL, the
    system default font, as set via the Preferences tool, will be used.

INPUTS
    RastPort = the RastPort destination of the text
    IText = pointer to an instance of the structure IntuiText
    LeftOffset = left offset of the IntuiText into the RastPort
    TopOffset = top offset of the IntuiText into the RastPort

RESULT
    None

BUGS

SEE ALSO
```

NAME
    RefreshGadgets -- Refresh (redraw) the Gadget display

SYNOPSIS
```
    RefreshGadgets(Gadgets, Window, Requester)
                   A0       A1      A2
```

FUNCTION
    Refreshes (redraws) all of the Gadgets in the Gadget List starting from the specified Gadget.

    The Window parameter must point to the window which contains the Gadget, or which contains the Requester that contains the Gadget The Requester parameter must only be valid if the Gadget has the REQGADGET flag set, a requirement for all Requester Gadgets.

    The Pointer argument points a Window structure.

    The two main reasons why you might want to use this routine are: first, that you've modified the imagery of the Gadgets in your display and you want the new imagery to be displayed; secondly, if you think that some graphic operation you just performed trashed the Gadgetry of your display, this routine will refresh the imagery for you.

    Note that to modify the imagery of a gadget, you must first remove that gadget from the Window's Gadget list, using RemoveGadget() (or RemoveGList()). After changing the Image, Border, Text (including Text for a String Gadget), the gadget is replaced in the Gadget List (using AddGadget() or AddGList()). Adding gadgets does not cause them to be displayed (refreshed), so this function, or RefreshGList() is typically called.

    A common technique is to set or reset the SELECTED flag of a Boolean Gadget and then call RefreshGadgets() to see them displayed highlighted if and only if SELECTED is set. If you wish to do this and be completely proper, you must RemoveGadget(), change SELECTED flag, AddGadget(), and RefreshGadgets(), or the equivalent.

    The Gadgets argument can be a copy of the FirstGadget variable in either the Screen or Window structure that you want refreshed: the effect of this will be that all Gadgets will be redrawn. However, you can selectively refresh just some of the Gadgets by starting the refresh part-way into the list: for instance, redrawing your Window non-GIMMEZEROZERO Gadgets only, which you've conveniently grouped at the end of your Gadget list.

    Even more control is available using the RefreshGList routine which enables you to refresh a single gadget, or number of your choice.

    NOTE: It's never safe to tinker with the Gadget list yourself. Don't supply some Gadget list that Intuition hasn't already processed in the usual way.

INPUTS
    Gadgets = pointer to the first in the list of Gadgets wanting refreshment
    Window = pointer to the Window containing the Gadget or its Requester
    Requester = pointer to a Requester (ignored if Gadget is not attached to a Requester).

RESULT
    None

BUGS

SEE ALSO
    RefreshGList(), RemoveGadget(), RemoveGList(), AddGadget(), AddGList()

NAME
    RefreshGList -- Refresh (redraw) a chosen number of gadgets.

SYNOPSIS
```
    RefreshGList(Gadgets, Window, Requester, NumGad)
                 A0       A1      A2         D0

    struct Gadget *Gadget;
    struct Window *Window;
    struct Requester *Requester;
    SHORT  NumGad;
```

FUNCTION
    Refreshes (redraws) Gadgets in the Gadget List starting from the specified Gadget. At most NumGad gadgets are redrawn. If NumGad is -1, all gadgets until a terminating NULL value in the NextGadget field is found will be refreshed, making this routine a superset of RefreshGadgets().

    The Requester variable can point to a Requester structure. If the first Gadget in the list has the REQGADGET flag set, the Gadget list refers to Gadgets in a Requester and the Pointer must necessarily point to a Window. If these are not the Gadgets of a Requester, the Requester argument may be NULL.

    Be sure to see the RefreshGadgets() function description, as this function is simple an extension of that.

INPUTS
    Gadgets = pointer to the first in the list of Gadgets wanting refreshment
    Window = pointer to the Window containing the Gadget or its Requester
    Requester = pointer to a Requester (ignored if Gadget is not attached to a Requester).
    NumGad = maximum number of gadgets to be refreshed. A value of -1 will cause all gadgets to be refreshed from Gadget to the end of the list. A value of -2 will also do this, but if Gadget is a Requester Gadget (REQGADGET) ALL gadgets in the requester will be refreshed (this is a mode compatible with v1.1 RefreshGadgets().

RESULT
    None

BUGS

SEE ALSO
    RefreshGadgets()

```
intuition.library/RefreshWindowFrame

    NAME
        RefreshWindowFrame -- Ask Intuition to redraw your window border/gadgets

    SYNOPSIS
        RefreshWindowFrame(Window)
                           A0

        struct Window *Window;

    FUNCTION
        Refreshes the border of a window, including title region and all
        of the window's gadgets.

        You may use this call if you wish to update the display of your borders.
        The expected use of this is to correct unavoidable corruption.

    INPUTS
        Window = a pointer to a Window structure

    RESULT
        None

    BUGS

    SEE ALSO
```

```
intuition.library/RemakeDisplay                    intuition.library/RemakeDisplay

    NAME
        RemakeDisplay  --  Remake the entire Intuition display

    SYNOPSIS
        RemakeDisplay()

    FUNCTION
        This is the big one.

        This procedure remakes the entire Intuition display.  It does
        the equivalent of MakeScreen() for every Screen in the system,
        and then it calls RethinkDisplay().

        WARNING:  This routine can take several milliseconds to run, so
        do not use it lightly.  RethinkDisplay() (called by this routine)
        does a Forbid() on entry and a Permit() on exit, which can seriously
        degrade the performance of the multi-tasking Eexecutive.

    INPUTS
        None

    RESULT
        None

    BUGS

    SEE ALSO
        MakeScreen(), RethinkDisplay(), graphics.library/MakeVPort
```

```
NAME
    RemoveGadget  --  removes a Gadget from a Window

SYNOPSIS
    Position = RemoveGadget(Window, Gadget)
    D0                      A0      A1

    USHORT Position;
    struct Window *Window;
    struct Gadget *Gadget;

FUNCTION
    Removes the given Gadget from the Gadget list of the specified
    Window.  Returns the ordinal position of the removed Gadget.

    If the Gadget is in a Requester attached the the window, this
    routine will look for it and remove it if it is found.

    If the Gadget pointer points to a Gadget that isn't in the
    appropriate list, -1 is returned.  If there aren't any Gadgets in the
    list, -1 is returned.  If you remove the 65535th Gadget from the list
    -1 is returned.

INPUTS
    Window = pointer to the Window containing the Gadget or the Requester
        containing the Gadget to be removed.
    Gadget = pointer to the Gadget to be removed.  The Gadget itself describes
        whether this is a Gadget that should be removed from the Window
        or some Requester.

RESULT
    Returns the ordinal position of the removed Gadget.  If the Gadget
    wasn't found in the appropriate list, or if there are no Gadgets in
    the list, returns -1.

BUGS

SEE ALSO
    AddGadget(), RemoveGList()
```



```
NAME
    RemoveGList  --  removes a sublist of Gadgets from a Window.

SYNOPSIS
    Position =  RemoveGList(Window, Gadget, Numgad)
    D0                      A0      A1      D0

    struct Window *Window;
    struct Gadget *Gadget;
    SHORT  Numgad;

FUNCTION
    Removes 'Numgad' Gadgets from the Gadget list of the specified
    Window.  Will remove Gadgets from a Requester if the first
    Gadget's GadgetType flag REQGADGET is set.

    Otherwise identical to RemoveGadget().

NOTE
    The last gadget in the list does NOT have it's link zeroed.

INPUTS
    Window = pointer to the Window containing the Gadget or the Requester
        containing the Gadget to be removed.
    Gadget = pointer to the Gadget to be removed.  The Gadget itself
       describes whether this is a Gadget that should be removed
       from the Window or some Requester.
    Numgad = number of gadgets to be removed.  If -1, remove all gadgets
        to end of Window Gadget List

RESULT
    Returns the ordinal position of the removed Gadget.  If the Gadget
    wasn't found in the appropriate list, or if there are no Gadgets in
    the list, returns -1.

BUGS

SEE ALSO
    RemoveGadget(), AddGadget()
```

```
NAME
    ReportMouse  --  tells Intuition whether to report mouse movement.

SYNOPSIS
    ReportMouse(Boolean, Window)
                D0       A0          <-note
    BOOL   Boolean;
    struct Window *Window;

SPECIAL NOTE
    Some compilers and link files switch the arguments to this function about
    in unpredictable ways.  The call will take one of two forms:

            ReportMouse(Window, (ULONG)Boolean);
                    -or-
            ReportMouse(Boolean, Window);

    The Manx Aztec compiler prefers the second form.  From assembler the
    interface is always the same:  Boolean in D0, Window in A0

    Also, it is still endorsed to simply set the REPORTMOUSE flag bit
    in Window->Flags, or reset it, on your own.  Make the operation
    an atomic assembly instruction (e.g.: OR.W #REPORTMOUSE,wd_Flags+2(A0)
    where A0 contains your window pointer).  Most compilers will produce
    an atomic operation when faced with:
                    Window->Flags |= REPORTMOUSE;
                    Window->Flags &=~REPORTMOUSE;
    or else bracket the operation between Forbid/Permit().

FUNCTION
    Tells Intuition whether or not to broadcast mouse-movement events to
    your Window when it's the active one.  The Boolean value specifies
    whether to start or stop broadcasting position information of
    mouse-movement.  If the Window is the active one, mouse-movement reports
    start coming immediately afterwards.  This same routine will change
    the current state of the FOLLOWMOUSE function of a
    currently-selected Gadget too.

    Note that calling ReportMouse() when a Gadget is selected will only
    temporarily change whether or not mouse movements are reported while
    that Gadget remains selected; the next time the Gadget is selected, its
    FOLLOWMOUSE flag is examined anew.

    Note also that calling ReportMouse() when no Gadget is currently
    selected will change the state of the Window's REPORTMOUSE flag, but
    will have no effect on any Gadget that may be subsequently selected.

    The ReportMouse() function is first performed when OpenWindow()
    is first called; if the flag REPORTMOUSE is included among
    the options, then all mouse-movement events are reported
    to the opening task and will continue to be reported
    until ReportMouse() is called with a Boolean value of FALSE.
    If REPORTMOUSE is not set, then no mouse-movement reports will
    be broadcast until ReportMouse() is called with a Boolean of TRUE.

    Note that the REPORTMOUSE flag, as managed by this routine, determines
    IF mouse messages are to be broadcast.  Determining HOW they are to
    be broadcast is determined by the MOUSEMOVE IDCMPFlag.

INPUTS
    Window = pointer to a Window structure associated with this request
    Boolean = TRUE or FALSE value specifying whether to turn this
          function on or off

RESULT
    None

BUGS
    See above

SEE ALSO
    The Input and Output section of the Intuition Reference Manual
```

```
NAME
    Request  --  Activates a Requester.

SYNOPSIS
    Success = Request(Requester, Window);
    D0                A0         A1

    BOOL Success;
    struct Requester *Requester;
    struct Window *Window;

FUNCTION
    Links in and displays a Requester into the specified Window.

    This routine ignores the Window's REQVERIFY flag.

INPUTS
    Requester = pointer to the Requester to be displayed
    Window = pointer to the Window into which this Requester goes

RESULT
    If the Requester is successfully opened, TRUE is returned.  Otherwise,
    if the Requester could not be opened, FALSE is returned.

BUGS
    POINTREL requesters not currently supported, by THIS call, but
    are now supported for Double-Menu Requesters.

SEE ALSO
    The Requesters section of the Intuition Reference Manual
```



```
NAME
    RethinkDisplay  --  the grand manipulator of the entire Intuition display

SYNOPSIS
    RethinkDisplay()

FUNCTION
    This function performs the Intuition global display reconstruction.  This
    includes rethinking about all of the  ViewPorts and their relationship to
    another and reconstructing the entire display based on the results of this
    rethinking.

    Specifically, and omitting some internal details, the operation consists
    of this:

        Determine which ViewPorts are invisible and set their VP_HIDE
        ViewPort Mode flag.

        If a change to a viewport height or changing interlace needs
        require, MakeVPort() is called for specific ViewPorts.  After
        this phase, the Copper lists for each Screen's ViewPort are
        correctly set up.

        MrgCop() and LoadView() are then called to get these copper lists
        in action, thus establishing the new state of the Intuition
        display.

    You may perform a MakeScreen() on your Custom Screen before calling this
    routine.  The results will be incorporated in the new display, but
    changing the INTERLACE ViewPort mode for one screens must be reflected
    in the Intuition View, which is best left to Intuition.

    WARNING:  This routine can take several milliseconds to run, so
    do not use it lightly.  RethinkDisplay() does a Forbid() on entry
    and a Permit() on exit, which can seriously degrade the performance
    of the multi-tasking Eexecutive.

INPUTS
    None

RESULT
    None

BUGS

SEE ALSO
    RemakeDisplay(), graphics.library/MakeVPort(), graphics.library/MrgCop(),
    graphics.library/LoadView(), MakeScreen()
```

```
NAME
    ScreenToBack  --  send the specified Screen to the back of the display.

SYNOPSIS
    ScreenToBack(Screen)
                 A0

    struct Screen *Screen;

FUNCTION
    Sends the specified Screen to the back of the display.

INPUTS
    Screen = pointer to a Screen structure

RESULT
    None

BUGS

SEE ALSO
```



```
NAME
    ScreenToFront  --  brings the specified Screen to the front of the display

SYNOPSIS
    ScreenToFront(Screen)
                  A0

FUNCTION
    Brings the specified Screen to the front of the display.

INPUTS
    Screen = a pointer to a Screen structure

RESULT
    None

BUGS

SEE ALSO
```

```
NAME
    SetDMRequest  --  sets the DMRequest of the Window.

SYNOPSIS
    SetDMRequest(Window, DMRequester)
                 A0      A1

    struct Window *Window;
    struct Requester *DMRequester;

FUNCTION
    Attempts to set the DMRequester into the specified window.
    The DMRequester is the special Requester that you attach to
    the double-click of the menu button which the user can then
    bring up on demand.  This routine WILL NOT set the DMRequester
    if it's already set and is currently active (in use by the user).
    After having called SetDMRequest(), if you want to change the
    DMRequester, the correct way to start is by calling ClearDMRequest()
    until it returns a value of TRUE; then you can call SetDMRequest()
    with the new DMRequester.

    If the POINTREL flag is set, the DMR will open as close to the
    pointer as possible.  The RelLeft/Top fields are for fine-tuning
    the position.

INPUTS
    Window = pointer to the window from which the DMRequest is to be set
    DMRequester = a pointer to a Requester

RESULT
    If the current DMRequest was not in use, sets the DMRequest
        pointer into the Window and returns TRUE.
    If the DMRequest was currently in use, doesn't change the pointer
        and returns FALSE

BUGS

SEE ALSO
    ClearDMRequest(), Request()
```



```
NAME
    SetMenuStrip  --  Attaches the Menu strip to the Window.

SYNOPSIS
    Success = SetMenuStrip(Window, Menu)
    D0                     A0      A1

    BOOL   Success;
    struct Window *Window;
    struct Menu *Menu;

FUNCTION
    Attaches the Menu strip to the Window.  After calling this routine,
    if the user presses the menu button, this specified menu strip
    will be displayed and accessible by the user.

    Menus with zero MenuItems are not allowed.

    NOTE:  You should always design your Menu strip changes to be a
    two-way operation, where for every Menu strip you add to your
    Window you should always plan to clear that strip sometime.  Even
    in the simplest case, where you will have just one Menu strip for
    the lifetime of your Window, you should always clear the Menu strip
    before closing the Window.  If you already have a Menu strip attached
    to this Window, the correct procedure for changing to a new Menu
    strip involves calling ClearMenuStrip() to clear the old first.
    The sequence of events should be:
       - OpenWindow()
       - zero or more iterations of:
         - SetMenuStrip()
         - ClearMenuStrip()
       - CloseWindow()

INPUTS
    Window = pointer to a Window structure
    Menu = pointer to the first Menu in the Menu strip

RESULT
    TRUE if there were no problems.  TRUE always, since this routine
    will Wait until it is OK to proceed.

BUGS

SEE ALSO
    ClearMenuStrip()
```

```
NAME
    SetPointer  --  sets a Window with its own Pointer

SYNOPSIS
    SetPointer(Window, Pointer, Height, Width, XOffset, YOffset)
               A0      A1       D0      D1     D2       D3

    struct Window *Window;
    USHORT  *Pointer;
    SHORT Height, Width;
    SHORT XOffset, YOffset;

FUNCTION
    Sets up the Window with the sprite definition for the Pointer.
    Then whenever the Window is the active one, the Pointer
    image will change to its version of the Pointer.  If the
    Window is the active one when this routine is called, the
    change takes place immediately.

    The XOffset and YOffset are used to offset the top-left corner
    of the hardware sprite imagery from what Intuition regards as
    the current position of the Pointer.  Another way of describing
    it is as the offset from the "hot spot" of the Pointer to the
    top-left corner of the sprite.  For instance, if you specify
    offsets of zero, zero, then the top-left corner of your sprite
    image will be placed at the Pointer position.  On the other hand,
    if you specify an XOffset of -7 (remember, sprites are 16 pixels
    wide) then your sprite will be centered over the Pointer position.
    If you specify an XOffset of -15, the right-edge of the sprite
    will be over the Pointer position.

INPUTS
    Window = pointer to the Window to receive this Pointer definition
    Pointer = pointer to the data definition of a Sprite
    Height = the height of the Pointer
    Width = the Width of the sprite (must be less than or equal to sixteen)
    XOffset = the offset for your sprite from the Pointer position
    YOffset = the offset for your sprite from the Pointer position

RESULT
    None

BUGS

SEE ALSO
    ClearPointer()
```



```
NAME
    SetPrefs  --  Set Intuition Preferences.

SYNOPSIS
    Prefs = SetPrefs(PrefBuffer, Size, Inform)
    D0               A0          D0    D1

    struct Preferences *Prefs;
    struct Preferences *PrefBuffer;
    int    Size;
    BOOL   Inform;

FUNCTION
    Sets new Preferences values.  Copies the first 'Size' bytes
    from your Preferences buffer to the system Preferences table,
    and puts them into effect.

    The 'Inform' parameter, if TRUE, indicates that a NEWPREFS
    message is to be sent to all Windows that have the NEWPREFS
    IDCMPFlag set.

    It is legal to set a partial copy of the Preferences structure.
    The most frequently changed values are grouped at the beginning
    of the Preferences structure.

INPUTS
    PrefBuffer = pointer to the memory buffer which contains your
        desired settings for Intuition Preferences
    Size = the number of bytes in your PrefBuffer, the number of bytes
       you want copied to the system's internal Preference settings
    Inform = whether you want the information of a new Preferences
        setting propogated to all windows.

RESULT
    Returns your parameter PrefBuffer.

BUGS

SEE ALSO
    GetDefPrefs(), GetPrefs()
```

```
NAME
    SetWindowTitles  --  Sets the Window's titles for both Window and Screen

SYNOPSIS
    SetWindowTitles(Window, WindowTitle, ScreenTitle)
                    A0      A1           A2

    struct Window *Window;
    UBYTE *WindowTitle, *ScreenTitle;

FUNCTION
    Allows you to set the text which appears in the Window and/or Screen
    title bars.

    The Window Title appears at all times along the Window Title Bar.
    The Window's Screen Title appears at the Screen Title Bar whenever
    this Window is the active one.

    When this routine is called, your Window Title will be changed
    immediately.  If your Window is the active one when this routine is
    called, the Screen Title will be changed immediately.

    You can specify a value of -1 (i.e. (struct Window *) ~0) for either of
    the title pointers.  This designates that you want to Intuition to leave
    the current setting of that particular title alone, and modify
    only the other one.  Of course, you could set both to -1.

    Furthermore, you can set a value of 0 (zero) for either of the
    title pointers.  Doing so specifies that you want no title to
    appear (the title bar will be blank).

    Both of the titles are rendered in the default font of the Window's
    Screen, as set using OpenScreen().

    In setting the Window's title, Intuition may do some other rendering
    in the top border of your window.  If your own rendering sometimes appears
    in your window border areas, you may want to restore the entire
    window border frame.  The function SetWindowTitles() does not do this
    in the newer versions.  The function RefreshWindowFrame() is provided
    to do this kind of thing for you.

INPUTS
    Window = pointer to your Window structure
    WindowTitle = pointer to a null-terminated text string, or set to
       either the value of -1 (negative one) or 0 (zero)
    ScreenTitle = pointer to a null-terminated text string, or set to
       either the value of -1 (negative one) or 0 (zero)

RESULT
    None

BUGS

SEE ALSO
    OpenWindow(), RefreshWindowFrame(), OpenScreen()
```



```
NAME
    ShowTitle  --  Set the Screen title bar display mode

SYNOPSIS
    ShowTitle(Screen, ShowIt)
              A0      D0

    struct Screen *Screen;
    BOOL   ShowIt;

FUNCTION
    This routine sets the SHOWTITLE flag of the specified Screen, and
    then coordinates the redisplay of the Screen and its Windows.

    The Screen title bar can appear either in front of or behind BACKDROP
    Windows.  This is contrasted with the fact that non-BACKDROP Windows
    always appear in front of the Screen Title Bar.  You specify whether
    you want the Screen Title Bar to be in front of or behind the
    Screen's BACKDROP Windows by calling this routine.

    The ShowIt argument should be set to either TRUE or FALSE.  If TRUE,
    the Screen's Title Bar will be shown in front of BACKDROP Windows.
    If FALSE, the Title Bar will be rendered behind all Windows.

    When a Screen is first opened, the default setting of the SHOWTITLE
    flag is TRUE.

INPUTS
    Screen = pointer to a Screen structure
    ShowIt = Boolean TRUE or FALSE describing whether to show or hide the
       Screen Title Bar

RESULT
    None

BUGS

SEE ALSO
```

```
NAME
    SizeWindow  --  Ask Intuition to size a Window.

SYNOPSIS
    SizeWindow(Window, DeltaX, DeltaY)
               A0      D0      D1

    struct Window *Window;
    SHORT  DeltaX, DeltaY;

FUNCTION
    This routine sends a request to Intuition asking to size the Window
    the specified amounts.  The delta arguments describe how much to
    size the Window along the respective axes.

    Note that the Window will not be sized immediately, but rather
    will be sized the next time Intuition receives an input event,
    which happens currently at a minimum rate of ten times per second,
    and a maximum of sixty times a second.  You can discover when
    you Window has finally been sized by setting the NEWSIZE flag
    of the IDCMP of your Window.  See the "Input and Output Methods"
    chapter of The Intuition Reference Manual for description of the IDCMP.

    This routine does no error-checking.  If your delta values specify
    some far corner of the Universe, Intuition will attempt to size
    your Window to the far corners of the Universe.  Because of the
    distortions in the space-time continuum that can result from this,
    as predicted by special relativity, the result is generally not
    a pretty sight.

INPUTS
    Window = pointer to the structure of the Window to be sized
    DeltaX = signed value describing how much to size the Window on the x-axis
    DeltaY = signed value describing how much to size the Window on the y-axis

RESULT
    None

BUGS

SEE ALSO
    MoveWindow(), WindowToFront(), WindowToBack()
```



```
NAME
    UnlockIBase -- surrender an Intuition lock gotten by LockIBase()

SYNOPSIS
    UnlockIBase(Lock)
                A0

    ULONG Lock;

FUNCTION

    Surrenders lock gotten by LockIBase().

    Calling this function when you do not own the specified lock will
    immediately crash the system.

INPUTS
    The value returned by LockIBase() should be passed to this function,
    to specify which internal lock is to be freed.

    Note that the parameter is passed in A0, not D0, for historical reasons.

RESULT
    None

BUGS

SEE ALSO
    LockIBase()
```

intuition.library/ViewAddress

NAME
ViewAddress -- Returns the address of the Intuition View structure.

SYNOPSIS
```
ViewAddress()
```

FUNCTION
Returns the address of the Intuition View structure. If you want to use any of the graphics, text, or animation primitives in your Window and that primitive requires a pointer to a View, this routine will return the address of the View for you.

INPUTS
None

RESULT
Returns the address of the Intuition View structure

BUGS

SEE ALSO
graphics.library

intuition.library/ViewPortAddress

NAME
ViewPortAddress -- Returns the address of a Window's ViewPort structure.

SYNOPSIS
```
ViewPortAddress(Window)
                A0

struct Window *Window;
```

FUNCTION
Returns the address of the ViewPort associated with the specified Window. The ViewPort is actually the ViewPort of the Screen within which the Window is displayed. If you want to use any of the graphics, text, or animation primitives in your Window and that primitive requires a pointer to a ViewPort, you can use this call.

INPUTS
Window = pointer to the Window for which you want the ViewPort address

RESULT
Returns the address of the Intuition View structure

BUGS

SEE ALSO
graphics.library

```
intuition.library/WBenchToBack                         intuition.library/WBenchToBack

    NAME
        WBenchToBack  --  Sends the WorkBench Screen in back of all Screens.

    SYNOPSIS
        Success = WBenchToBack()
        D0

        BOOL Success;

    FUNCTION
        Causes the WorkBench Screen, if it's currently opened, to go to
        the background.  This does not 'move' the Screen up or down, instead
        only affects the depth-arrangement of the Screen.

        If the WorkBench Screen was opened, this function returns TRUE, otherwise
        it returns FALSE.

    INPUTS
        None

    RESULT
        If the WorkBench Screen was opened, this function returns TRUE, otherwise
        it returns FALSE.

    BUGS

    SEE ALSO
        WBenchToFront(), ScreenToFront()
```

```
intuition.library/WBenchToFront                       intuition.library/WBenchToFront

    NAME
        WBenchToFront  --  Brings the WorkBench Screen in front of all Screens.

    SYNOPSIS
        Success = WBenchToFront()
        D0

        BOOL Success;

    FUNCTION
        Causes the WorkBench Screen, if it's currently opened, to come to
        the foreground.  This does not 'move' the Screen up or down, instead
        only affects the depth-arrangement of the Screen.

        If the WorkBench Screen was opened, this function returns TRUE, otherwise
        it returns FALSE.

    INPUTS
        None

    RESULT
        If the WorkBench Screen was opened, this function returns TRUE, otherwise
        it returns FALSE.

    BUGS

    SEE ALSO
        WBenchToBack(), ScreenToBack()
```

```
NAME
    WindowLimits  --  Set the minimum and maximum limits of the Window.

SYNOPSIS
    Success = WindowLimits(Window, MinWidth, MinHeight, MaxWidth, MaxHeight)
    D0                     A0      D0        D1         D2        D3

    BOOL   Success;
    struct Window *Window;
    SHORT  MinWidth, MinHeight;
    USHORT MaxWidth, MaxHeight;

FUNCTION
    Sets the minimum and maximum limits of the Window's size.  Until this
    routine is called, the Window's size limits are equal to the Window's
    initial size, which means that the user won't be able to size it at all.
    After the call to this routine, the Window will be able to be sized
    to any dimensions within the specified limits.

    If you don't want to change any one of the dimensions, set the limit
    argument for that dimension to zero.  If any of the limit arguments
    is equal to zero, that argument is ignored and the initial setting
    of that parameter remains undisturbed.

    If any of the arguments is out of range (minimums greater than the
    current size, maximums less than the current size), that limit
    will be ignored, though the others will still take effect if they
    are in range.  If any are out of range, the return value from this
    procedure will be FALSE.  If all arguments are valid, the return
    value will be TRUE.

    If you want your window to be able to become "as large as possible"
    you may put -1 (i.e. ~0) in either or both Max arguments.  But
    please note: screen sizes may vary for several reasons, and you
    must be able to handle any possible size of window you might end
    up with if you use this method.  Note that you can use the function
    GetScreenData() to find out how big the screen your window appears in
    is.  That function is particularly useful if your window is in
    the Workbench Screen.

    If the user is currently sizing this Window, the new limits will
    not take effect until after the sizing is completed.

INPUTS
    Window = pointer to a Window structure
    MinWidth, MinHeight, MaxWidth, MaxHeight = the new limits for the size
        of this Window.  If any of these is set to zero, it will
        be ignored and that setting will be unchanged.

RESULT
    Returns TRUE if everything was in order.  If any of the parameters was
    out of range (minimums greater than current size, maximums less than
    current size), FALSE is returned and the errant limit request is
    not fulfilled (though the valid ones will be).

BUGS

SEE ALSO
    GetScreenData()
```



```
NAME
    WindowToBack  --  Ask Intuition to send this Window to the back

SYNOPSIS
    WindowToBack(Window)
                 A0

FUNCTION
    This routine sends a request to Intuition asking to send the Window
    in back of all other Windows in the Screen.

    Note that the Window will not be depth-arranged immediately, but rather
    will be arranged the next time Intuition receives an input event,
    which happens currently at a minimum rate of ten times per second,
    and a maximum of sixty times a second.

    Remember that BACKDROP Windows cannot be depth-arranged.

INPUTS
    Window = pointer to the structure of the Window to be sent to the back

RESULT
    None

BUGS

SEE ALSO
    MoveWindow(), SizeWindow(), WindowToFront()
```

```
NAME
    WindowToFront  --  Ask Intuition to bring this Window to the front.

SYNOPSIS
    WindowToFront(Window)

FUNCTION
    This routine sends a request to Intuition asking to bring the Window
    in front of all other Windows in the Screen.

    Note that the Window will not be depth-arranged immediately, but rather
    will be arranged the next time Intuition receives an input event,
    which happens currently at a minimum rate of ten times per second,
    and a maximum of sixty times a second.

    Remember that BACKDROP Windows cannot be depth-arranged.

INPUTS
    Window = pointer to the structure of the Window to be brought to front

RESULT
    None

BUGS

SEE ALSO
    MoveWindow(), SizeWindow(), WindowToBack()
```

TABLE OF CONTENTS

layers.library/BeginUpdate   layers.library/BeginUpdate

```
NAME
    BeginUpdate -- Prepare to repair damaged layer.

SYNOPSIS
    result = BeginUpdate( l )
    d0                    a0

    BOOLEAN result;
    struct Layer *l;

FUNCTION
    Convert damage list to ClipRect list and swap in for
    programmer to redraw through. This routine simulates
    the ROM library environment. The idea is to only render in the
    "damaged" areas, saving time over redrawing all of the layer.
    The layer is locked against changes made by the layer library.

INPUTS
    l - pointer to a layer

RESULTS
    result - TRUE if damage list converted to ClipRect list sucessfully.
             FALSE if list conversion aborted. (probably out of memory)

BUGS
    If BeginUpdate returns FALSE, programmer must abort the attempt to
    refresh this layer and instead call EndUpdate( l, FALSE ) to restore
    original ClipRect and damage list.

SEE ALSO
    EndUpdate, graphics/layers.h, graphics/clip.h
```

```
NAME
    BehindLayer -- Put layer behind other layers.

SYNOPSIS
    result = BehindLayer( dummy, l )
    d0                    a0     a1

    BOOLEAN result;
    LONG dummy;
    struct Layer *l;

FUNCTION
    Move this layer to the most behind position swapping bits
    in and out of the display with other layers.
    If other layers are REFRESH then collect their damage lists and
    set the LAYERREFRESH bit in the Flags fields of those layers that
    may be revealed.  If this layer is a backdrop layer then
    put this layer behind all other backdrop layers.
    If this layer is NOT a backdrop layer then put in front of the
    top backdrop layer and behind all other layers.

    Note: this operation may generate refresh events in other layers
       associated with this layer's Layer_Info structure.

INPUTS
    dummy - unused
    l - pointer to a layer

RESULTS
    result - TRUE    if operation successful
             FALSE   if operation unsuccessful (probably out of memory)

BUGS

SEE ALSO
   graphics/layers.h, graphics/clip.h
```



```
NAME
    CreateBehindLayer -- Create a new layer behind all existing layers.

SYNOPSIS
    result = CreateBehindLayer(li,bm,x0,y0,x1,y1,flags [,bm2])
    d0                         a0 a1 d0 d1 d2 d3   d4   [ a2 ]

    struct Layer *result;
    struct Layer_Info *li;
    struct BitMap *bm;
    LONG x0,y0,x1,y1;
    LONG flags;
    struct BitMap *bm2;

FUNCTION
    Create a new Layer of position and size (x0,y0)->(x1,y1)
    Make this layer of type found in flags.
    If SuperBitMap, use bm2 as pointer to real SuperBitMap,
    and copy contents of Superbitmap into display layer.
    If this layer is a backdrop layer then place it behind all
    other layers including other backdrop layers. If this is
    not a backdrop layer then place it behind all nonbackdrop
    layers.

    Note: when using SUPERBITMAP, you should also set LAYERSMART flag.

INPUTS
    li - pointer to LayerInfo structure
    bm - pointer to common BitMap used by all Layers
    x0,y0 - upper left hand corner of layer
    x1,y1 - lower right hand corner of layer
    flags - various types of layers supported as bit sets.
        (for bit definitions, see graphics/layers.h )
    bm2 - pointer to optional Super BitMap

RESULTS
    result - pointer to Layer structure if successful
             NULL if not successful

BUGS

SEE ALSO
    DeleteLayer, graphics/layers.h, graphics/clip.h, graphics/gfx.h
```

```
NAME
    CreateUpfrontLayer -- Create a new layer on top of existing layers.

SYNOPSIS
    result = CreateUpfrontLayer(li,bm,x0,y0,x1,y1,flags [,bm2])
    d0                          a0 a1 d0 d1 d2 d3   d4  [ a2 ]

    struct Layer *result;
    struct Layer_Info *li;
    struct BitMap *bm;
    LONG x0,y0,x1,y1;
    LONG flags;
    struct BitMap *bm2;

FUNCTION
    Create a new Layer of position and size (x0,y0)->(x1,y1)
    and place it on top of all other layers.
    Make this layer of type found in flags
    if SuperBitMap, use bm2 as pointer to real SuperBitMap.
    and copy contents of Superbitmap into display layer.

    Note: when using SUPERBITMAP, you should also set LAYERSMART flag.

INPUTS
    li - pointer to LayerInfo structure
    bm - pointer to common BitMap used by all Layers
    x0,y0 - upper left hand corner of layer
    x1,y1 - lower right hand corner of layer
    flags - various types of layers supported as bit sets.
    bm2 - pointer to optional Super BitMap

RESULTS
    result - pointer to Layer structure if successful
             NULL if not successful

BUGS

SEE ALSO
   DeleteLayer, graphics/layers.h, graphics/clip.h, graphics/gfx.h
```



```
NAME
    DeleteLayer -- delete layer from layer list.

SYNOPSIS
    result = DeleteLayer( dummy, l )
    d0                    a0,    a1

    BOOLEAN result;
    LONG dummy;
    struct Layer *l;

FUNCTION
    Remove this layer from the list of layers.  Release memory
    associated with it.  Restore other layers that may have been
    obscured by it.  Trigger refresh in those that may need it.
    If this is a superbitmap layer make sure SuperBitMap is current.
    The SuperBitMap is not removed from the system but is available
    for program use even though the rest of the layer information has
    been deallocated.

INPUTS
    dummy - unused
    l - pointer to a layer

RESULTS
    result - TRUE if this layer successfully deleted from the system
             FALSE if layer not deleted. (probably out of memory )

BUGS

SEE ALSO
    graphics/layers.h, graphics/clip.h
```

```
NAME
    DisposeLayerInfo -- Return all memory for LayerInfo to memory pool

SYNOPSIS
    DisposeLayerInfo(li)
                     a0

    struct Layer_Info *li;

FUNCTION
    return LayerInfo and any other memory attached to this LayerInfo
    to memory allocator.

    Note: if you wish to delete the layers associated with this Layer_Info
        structure, remember to call DeleteLayer() for each of the layers
        before calling DisposeLayerInfo().

INPUTS
    li - pointer to LayerInfo structure

EXAMPLE

    -- delete the layers associated this Layer_Info structure --

    DeleteLayer(li,simple_layer);
    DeleteLayer(li,smart_layer);

    -- see documentation on DeleteLayer about deleting SuperBitMap layers --
    my_super_bitmap_ptr = super_layer->SuperBitMap;
    DeleteLayer(li,super_layer);

    -- now dispose of the Layer_Info structure itself --
    DisposeLayerInfo(li);


BUGS

SEE ALSO
    DeleteLayer, graphics/layers.h
```



```
NAME
    EndUpdate -- remove damage list and restore state of layer to normal.

SYNOPSIS
    EndUpdate( l, flag )
               a0  d0

    struct Layer *l;
    USHORT flag;

FUNCTION
    After the programmer has redrawn his picture he calls this
    routine to restore the ClipRects to point to his standard
    layer tiling. The layer is then unlocked for access by the
    layer library.

    Note: use flag = FALSE if you are only making a partial update.
        You may use the other region functions (graphics functions such as
        OrRectRegion, AndRectRegion, and XorRectRegion ) to clip adjust
        the DamageList to reflect a partial update.

INPUTS
    l - pointer to a layer
    flag - use TRUE if update was completed. The damage list is cleared.
           use FALSE if update not complete. The damage list is retained.

EXAMPLE

    -- begin update for first part of two-part refresh --
    BeginUpdate(my_layer);

    -- do some refresh, but not all --
    my_partial_refresh_routine(my_layer);

    -- end update, false (not completely done refreshing yet) --
    EndUpdate(my_layer, FALSE);

    -- begin update for last part of refresh --
    BeginUpdate(my_layer);

    -- do rest of refresh --
    my_complete_refresh_routine(my_layer);

    -- end update, true (completely done refreshing now) --
    EndUpdate(my_layer, TRUE);

BUGS

SEE ALSO
    BeginUpdate, graphics/layers.h, graphics/clip.h
```

layers.library/FattenLayerInfo layers.library/FattenLayerInfo

```
NAME
    FattenLayerInfo -- convert 1.0 LayerInfo to 1.1 LayerInfo
    OBSOLETE OBSOLETE OBSOLETE OBSOLETE OBSOLETE

SYNOPSIS
    OBSOLETE OBSOLETE OBSOLETE OBSOLETE OBSOLETE
    FattenLayerInfo(li)
                    a0

    struct Layer_Info *li;
    OBSOLETE OBSOLETE OBSOLETE OBSOLETE OBSOLETE

FUNCTION
    V1.1 software and any later releases need to have more info in the
    Layer_Info structure. To do this in a 1.0 supportable manner requires
    allocation and deallocation of the memory whenever most
    layer library functions are called.  To prevent unnecessary
    allocation/deallocation FattenLayerInfo will preallocate the
    necessary data structures and fake out the layer library into
    thinking it has a LayerInfo gotten from NewLayerInfo.
    NewLayerInfo is the approved method for getting this structure.
    When a program needs to give up the LayerInfo structure it
    must call ThinLayerInfo before freeing the memory. ThinLayerInfo
    is not necessary if New/DisposeLayerInfo are used however.

INPUTS
    li - pointer to LayerInfo structure

BUGS

SEE ALSO

    NewLayerInfo, ThinLayerInfo, DisposeLayerInfo, graphics/layers.h
```

layers.library/InitLayers layers.library/InitLayers

```
NAME
    InitLayers -- Initialize Layer_Info structure
    OBSOLETE OBSOLETE OBSOLETE OBSOLETE OBSOLETE

SYNOPSIS
    OBSOLETE OBSOLETE OBSOLETE OBSOLETE OBSOLETE
    InitLayers(li)
               a0

    struct Layer_Info *li;
    OBSOLETE OBSOLETE OBSOLETE OBSOLETE OBSOLETE

FUNCTION
    Initialize Layer_Info structure in preparation to use
    other layer operations on this list of layers.
    Make the Layers unlocked (open), available to layer operations.

INPUTS
    li - pointer to LayerInfo structure

BUGS

SEE ALSO
    NewLayerInfo, DisposeLayerInfo, graphics/layers.h
```

```
NAME
    InstallClipRegion -- Install clip region in layer

SYNOPSIS
    oldclipregion = InstallClipRegion( l,  region )
    d0                                 a0  a1

    struct Region *oldclipregion;
    struct Layer *l;
    struct Region *region;

FUNCTION
    Installs a transparent Clip region in the layer. All
    subsequent graphics calls will be clipped to this region.
    You MUST remember to call InstallClipRegion(l,NULL) before
    calling DeleteLayer(l) or the Intuition function CloseWindow()
    if you have installed a non-NULL ClipRegion in l.

INPUTS
    l - pointer to a layer
    region - pointer to a region

RESULTS
    oldclipregion - The pointer to the previous ClipRegion that
        was installed. Returns NULL if no previous ClipRegion installed.

        Note: If the system runs out of memory while computing the
            resulting ClipRects the LAYERS_CLIPRECTS_LOST bit will
            be set in l->Flags.

BUGS
    If the system runs out of memory during normal layer operations,
    the ClipRect list may get swept away and not restored.
    As soon as there is enough memory and the layer library
    gets called again the ClipRect list will be rebuilt.

SEE ALSO
    BeginUpdate EndUpdate,
    graphics/layers.h, graphics/clip.h, graphics/regions.h
```



```
NAME
    LockLayer -- Lock layer to make changes to ClipRects.

SYNOPSIS
    LockLayer( dummy, l )
               a0     a1

    LONG dummy;
    struct Layer *l;

FUNCTION
    Make this layer unavailable for other tasks to use.
    If another task is already using this layer then wait for
    it to complete and then reserve the layer for your own use.
    (this function does the same thing as graphics.library/LockLayerRom)

    Note: if you wish to lock MORE THAN ONE layer at a time, you
        must call LockLayerInfo() before locking those layers and
        then call UnlockLayerInfo() when you have finished. This
        is to prevent system "deadlocks".

    Further Note: while you hold the lock on a layer, Intuition will block
        on operations such as windowsizing, dragging, menus, and depth
        arranging windows in this layer's screen.  It is recommended that
        YOU do not make Intuition function calls while the layer is locked.

INPUTS
    dummy - unused
    l - pointer to a layer

BUGS

SEE ALSO
    UnlockLayer, LockLayerInfo, UnlockLayerInfo,
    graphics.library/LockLayerRom, graphics/layers.h, graphics/clip.h
```

```
layers.library/LockLayerInfo                    layers.library/LockLayerInfo

    NAME
        LockLayerInfo -- Lock the LayerInfo structure.

    SYNOPSIS
        LockLayerInfo( li )
                       a0

        struct Layer_Info *li;

    FUNCTION
        Before doing an operation that requires the LayerInfo
        structure, make sure that no other task is also using the
        LayerInfo structure.  LockLayerInfo() returns when the
        LayerInfo belongs to this task.  There should be
        an UnlockLayerInfo for every LockLayerInfo.

        Note: All layer routines presently LockLayerInfo() when they
        start up and UnlockLayerInfo() as they exit.  Programmers
        will need to use these Lock/Unlock routines if they wish
        to do something with the LayerStructure that is not
        supported by the layer library.

    INPUTS
        li - pointer to Layer_Info structure

    BUGS

    SEE ALSO
        UnlockLayerInfo, graphics/layers.h
```

```
layers.library/LockLayers                          layers.library/LockLayers

    NAME
        LockLayers -- lock all layers from graphics output.

    SYNOPSIS
        LockLayers( li )
                    a0

        struct Layer_Info *li;

    FUNCTION
        First calls LockLayerInfo()
        Make all layers in this layer list locked.

    INPUTS
        li - pointer to Layer_Info structure

    BUGS

    SEE ALSO
        LockLayer, LockLayerInfo, graphics/layers.h
```

```
    NAME
        MoveLayer -- Move layer to new position in BitMap.

    SYNOPSIS
        result = MoveLayer( dummy, l, dx, dy )
        d0                  a0     a1 d0  d1

        BOOLEAN result;
        LONG dummmy;
        struct Layer *l;
        LONG dx,dy;

    FUNCTION
        Move this layer to new position in shared BitMap.
        If any refresh layers become revealed, collect damage and
        set REFRESH bit in layer Flags.

    INPUTS
        dummy - unused
        l - pointer to a nonbackdrop layer
        dx - delta to add to current x position
        dy - delta to add to current y position

    RETURNS
        result - TRUE if operation successful
                 FALSE if failed (out of memory)

    BUGS
        May not handle (dx,dy) which attempts to move the layer ouside the
        layer's RastPort->BitMap bounds .

    SEE ALSO
        graphics/layers.h, graphics/clip.h
```



```
    NAME
        MoveLayerInFrontOf-- Put layer in front of another layer.

    SYNOPSIS
        result = MoveLayerInFrontOf( layertomove, targetlayer )
                                     a0           a1

        BOOLEAN result;
        struct Layer *layertomove;
        struct Layer *targetlayer;

    FUNCTION
        Move this layer in front of target layer, swapping bits
        in and out of the display with other layers.
        If this is a refresh layer then collect damage list and
        set the LAYERREFRESH bit in layer->Flags if redraw required.

        Note: this operation may generate refresh events in other layers
           associated with this layer's Layer_Info structure.

    INPUTS
        layertomove - pointer to layer which should be moved
        targetlayer - pointer to target layer in front of which to move layer

    RESULTS
        result = TRUE    if operation successful
                 FALSE   if operation unsuccessful (probably out of memory)

    BUGS

    SEE ALSO
        graphics/layers.h
```

```
    NAME
        NewLayerInfo -- Allocate and Initialize full Layer_Info structure.

    SYNOPSIS
        result = NewLayerInfo()
        d0

        struct Layer_Info *result;

    FUNCTION
        Allocate memory required for full Layer_Info structure.
        Initialize Layer_Info structure in preparation to use
        other layer operations on this list of layers.
        Make the Layer_Info unlocked (open).

    INPUTS
        None

RESULT
        result- pointer to Layer_Info structure if successful
                NULL if not enough memory

BUGS

SEE ALSO
        graphics/layers.h
```



```
    NAME
        ScrollLayer -- Scroll around in a superbitmap, translate coordinates
                       in non-superbitmap layer.

    SYNOPSIS
        ScrollLayer( dummy, l, dx, dy )
                     a0     a1 d0  d1

        LONG dummy;
        struct Layer *l;
        LONG dx,dy;

    FUNCTION
        For a SuperBitMap Layer:
        Update the SuperBitMap from the layer display, then copy bits
        between Layer and SuperBitMap to reposition layer over different
        portion of SuperBitMap.
        For nonSuperBitMap layers, all (x,y) pairs are adjusted by
        the scroll(x,y) value in the layer.  To cause (0,0) to actually
        be drawn at (3,10) use ScrollLayer(-3,-10). This can be useful
        along with InstallClipRegion to simulate Intuition GZZWindows
        without the overhead of an extra layer.

    INPUTS
        dummy - unused
        l - pointer to a layer
        dx - delta to add to current x scroll value
        dy - delta to add to current y scroll value

    BUGS
        May not handle (dx,dy) which attempts to move the layer ouside the
        layer's SuperBitMap bounds.

    SEE ALSO
        graphics/layers.h
```

```
NAME
    SizeLayer -- Change the size of this nonbackdrop layer.

SYNOPSIS
    result = SizeLayer( dummy, l, dx, dy )
    d0                  a0     a1 d0  d1

    BOOLEAN result;
    LONG dummy;
    struct Layer *l;
    LONG dx, dy;

FUNCTION
    Change the size of this layer by (dx,dy). The lower right hand
    corner is extended to make room for the larger layer.
    If there is SuperBitMap for this layer then copy pixels into
    or out of the layer depending on whether the layer increases or
    decreases in size.  Collect damage list for those layers that may
    need to be refreshed if damage occurred.

INPUTS
    dummy - unused
    l - pointer to a nonbackdrop layer
    dx - delta to add to current x size
    dy - delta to add to current y size

RESULTS
    result - TRUE if operation successful
             FALSE if failed (out of memory)

BUGS

SEE ALSO
    graphics/layers.h, graphics/clip.h
```



```
NAME
    SwapBitsRastPortClipRect -- Swap bits between common bitmap
                                and obscured ClipRect

SYNOPSIS
    SwapBitsRastPortClipRect( rp, cr )
                              a0  a1

    struct RastPort *rp;
    struct ClipRect *cr;

FUNCTION
    Support routine useful for those that need to do some
    operations not done by the layer library.  Allows programmer
    to swap the contents of a small BitMap with a subsection of
    the display. This is accomplished without using extra memory.
    The bits in the display RastPort are exchanged with the
    bits in the ClipRect's BitMap.

    Note: the ClipRect structures which the layer library allocates are
    actually a little bigger than those described in the graphics/clip.h
    include file.  So be warned that it is not a good idea to have
    instances of cliprects in your code.

INPUTS
   rp - pointer to rastport
   cr - pointer to cliprect to swap bits with

BUGS

SEE ALSO
    graphics/clip.h, graphics/rastport.h, graphics/clip.h
```

```
NAME
    ThinLayerInfo -- convert 1.1 LayerInfo to 1.0 LayerInfo.
    OBSOLETE OBSOLETE OBSOLETE OBSOLETE OBSOLETE

SYNOPSIS
    OBSOLETE OBSOLETE OBSOLETE OBSOLETE OBSOLETE
    ThinLayerInfo(li)
                  a0

    struct Layer_Info *li;
    OBSOLETE OBSOLETE OBSOLETE OBSOLETE OBSOLETE

FUNCTION
    return the extra memory needed that was allocated with
    FattenLayerInfo. This is must be done prior to freeing
    the Layer_Info structure itself. V1.1 software should be
    using DisposeLayerInfo.

INPUTS
    li - pointer to LayerInfo structure

BUGS

SEE ALSO
    DisposeLayerInfo, FattenLayerInfo, graphics/layers.h
```



```
NAME
    UnlockLayer -- Unlock layer and allow graphics routines to use it.

SYNOPSIS
    UnlockLayer( l )
                 a0

    struct Layer *l;

FUNCTION
    When finished changing the ClipRects or whatever you were
    doing with this layer you must call UnlockLayer() to allow
    other tasks to proceed with graphic output to the layer.

INPUTS
    l - pointer to a layer

BUGS

SEE ALSO
    graphics/layers.h, graphics/clip.h
```

layers.library/UnlockLayerInfo

```
layers.library/UnlockLayerInfo                  layers.library/UnlockLayerInfo

    NAME
        UnlockLayerInfo -- Unlock the LayerInfo structure.

    SYNOPSIS
        UnlockLayerInfo( li )
                         a0

        struct Layer_Info *li;

    FUNCTION
        After the operation is complete that required a LockLayerInfo,
        unlock the LayerInfo structure so that  other tasks may
        affect the layers.

    INPUTS
        li - pointer to the Layer_Info structure

     BUGS

     SEE ALSO
        LockLayerInfo, graphics/layers.h
```

layers.library/UnlockLayers

```
layers.library/UnlockLayers                        layers.library/UnlockLayers

    NAME
        UnlockLayers -- Unlock all layers from graphics output.
                        Restart graphics output to layers that have been waiting

    SYNOPSIS
        UnlockLayers( li )
                      a0

        struct Layer_Info *li;

    FUNCTION
        Make all layers in this layer list unlocked.
        Then call UnlockLayerInfo

    INPUTS
        li - pointer to the Layer_Info structure

    BUGS

    SEE ALSO
        LockLayers, UnlockLayer, graphics/layers.h
```

```
NAME
    UpfrontLayer -- Put layer in front of all other layers.

SYNOPSIS
    result = UpfrontLayer( dummy, l )
    do                     a0  al

    BOOLEAN result;
    LONG dummy;
    struct Layer *l;

FUNCTION
    Move this layer to the most upfront position swapping bits
    in and out of the display with other layers.
    If this is a refresh layer then collect damage list and
    set the LAYERREFRESH bit in layer->Flags if redraw required.
    By clearing the BACKDROP bit in the layers Flags you may
    bring a Backdrop layer up to the front of all other layers.

    Note: this operation may generate refresh events in other layers
       associated with this layer's Layer_Info structure.

INPUTS
    dummy - unused
    l - pointer to a nonbackdrop layer

RESULTS
    result - TRUE   if operation successful
             FALSE  if operation unsuccessful (probably out of memory)

BUGS

SEE ALSO
    graphics/layers.h
```



```
NAME
    WhichLayer -- Which Layer is this point in?

SYNOPSIS
    layer = WhichLayer( li, x, y )
    d0                  a0  d0 d1

FUNCTION
    Starting at the topmost layer check to see if this point (x,y)
        occurs in this layer.  If it does return the pointer to this
        layer. Return NULL if there is no layer at this point.

INPUTS
    li  = pointer to LayerInfo structure
    (x,y)   = coordinate in the BitMap

RESULTS
    layer - pointer to the topmost layer that this point is in
            NULL if this point is not in a layer

SEE ALSO
    graphics/layers.h
```

TABLE OF CONTENTS

NAME

SPAbs - obtain the absolute value of the fast floating point number

C USAGE

```
fnum2 = SPAbs(fnum1);
                d0
```

FUNCTION

Accepts a floating point number and returns the absolute value of said number.

INPUTS

fnum1 - floating point number

RESULT

fnum2 - floating point absolute value of fnum1

BUGS

None

SEE ALSO

_LVOSPAbs, abs

NAME

SPAdd - add two floating point numbers

C USAGE

```
fnum3 = SPAdd(fnum1, fnum2);
                d1      d0
```

FUNCTION

Accepts two floating point numbers and returns the arithmetic sum of said numbers.

INPUTS

fnum1 - floating point number
fnum2 - floating point number

RESULT

fnum3 - floating point number

BUGS

None

SEE ALSO

_LVOSPAdd, faddi

NAME
SPCeil -- compute Ceil function of a number

SYNOPSIS
```
  x    = SPCeil(  y  );
 d0              d0

float   x,y;
```

FUNCTION
Calculate the least integer greater than or equal to x and return it. This identity is true. Ceil(x) = -Floor(-x).

INPUTS
y -- Motorola Fast Floating Point Format Number

RESULT
x -- Motorola Fast Floating Point Format Number

BUGS

SEE ALSO
SPFloor

NAME

```
SPCmp - compares two floating point numbers and sets
                appropriate condition codes
```

C USAGE

```
if (SPCmp(fnum1, fnum2)) {...}
            d1     d0
```

FUNCTION

Accepts two floating point numbers and returns the condition codes set to indicate the result of said comparison. Additionally, the integer functional result is returned to indicate the result of said comparison.

INPUTS

```
fnum1 - floating point number
fnum2 - floating point number
```

RESULT

Condition codes set to reflect the following branches:

```
GT - fnum2 >  fnum1
GE - fnum2 >= fnum1
EQ - fnum2 =  fnum1
NE - fnum2 != fnum1
LT - fnum2 <  fnum1
LE - fnum2 <= fnum1
```

Integer functional result as:

```
+1 => fnum1 > fnum2
-1 => fnum1 < fnum2
 0 => fnum1 = fnum2
```

BUGS

None

SEE ALSO

_LVOSPCmp, fcmpi

NAME

SPDiv - divide two floating point numbers

C USAGE

```
fnum3 = SPDiv(fnum1, fnum2);
                d1     d0
```

FUNCTION

Accepts two floating point numbers and returns the arithmetic division of said numbers.

INPUTS

```
fnum1 - floating point number
fnum2 - floating point number
```

RESULT

```
fnum3 - floating point number
```

BUGS

None

SEE ALSO

_LVOSPDiv, fdivi

```
mathffp.library/SPFix                                    mathffp.library/SPFix

NAME

        SPFix - convert fast floating point number to integer

C USAGE

        inum = SPFix(fnum);
                     d0

FUNCTION

        Accepts a floating point number and returns the truncated
        integer portion of said number.

INPUTS

        fnum - floating point number

RESULT

        inum - signed integer number

BUGS

        None

SEE ALSO

        _LVOSPFix, ffixi
```

```
mathffp.library/SPFloor                                mathffp.library/SPFloor

   NAME
        SPFloor -- compute Floor function of a number

   SYNOPSIS
        x    = SPFloor(  y  );
        d0               d0

        float   x,y;

   FUNCTION
        Calculate the largest integer less than or equal to x and return it.

   INPUTS
        y -- Motorola Fast Floating Point number

   RESULT
        x -- Motorola Fast Floating Point number

   BUGS

   SEE ALSO
        SPCeil
```

mathffp.library/SPFlt   mathffp.library/SPFlt

NAME

SPFlt - convert integer number to fast floating point

C USAGE

```
fnum = SPFlt(inum);
              d0
```

FUNCTION

Accepts an integer and returns the converted floating point result of said number.

INPUTS

inum - signed integer number

RESULT

fnum - floating point number

BUGS

None

SEE ALSO

_LVOSPFlt, fflti

mathffp.library/SPMul   mathffp.library/SPMul

NAME

SPMul - multiply two floating point numbers

C USAGE

```
fnum3 = SPMul(fnum1, fnum2);
              d1     d0
```

FUNCTION

Accepts two floating point numbers and returns the arithmetic multiplication of said numbers.

INPUTS

fnum1 - floating point number
fnum2 - floating point number

RESULT

fnum3 - floating point number

BUGS

None

SEE ALSO

_LVOSPMul, fmuli

NAME

SPNeg - negate the supplied floating point number

C USAGE

```
fnum2 = SPNeg(fnum1);
                d0
```

FUNCTION

Accepts a floating point number and returns the value of said number after having been subtracted from 0.0

INPUTS

fnum1 - floating point number

RESULT

fnum2 - floating point negation of fnum1

BUGS

None

SEE ALSO

_LVOSPNeg, fnegi

NAME

SPSub - subtract two floating point numbers

C USAGE

```
fnum3 = SPSub(fnum1, fnum2);
                d1     d0
```

FUNCTION

Accepts two floating point numbers and returns the arithmetic subtraction of said numbers.

INPUTS

fnum1 - floating point number
fnum2 - floating point number

RESULT

fnum3 - floating point number

BUGS

None

SEE ALSO

_LVOSPSub, fsubi

NAME

```
        SPTst - compares a fast floating point number against the
                value zero (0.0) and sets the appropriate
                condition codes
```

C USAGE

```
        if (!(SPTst(fnum))) {...}
                    d1
```

FUNCTION

```
        Accepts a floating point number and returns the condition
        codes set to indicate the result of a comparison against
        the value of zero (0.0).  Additionally, the integer functional
        result is returned.
```

INPUTS

```
        fnum - floating point number
```

RESULT

```
        Condition codes set to reflect the following branches:

                EQ - fnum =  0.0
                NE - fnum != 0.0
                PL - fnum >= 0.0
                MI - fnum <  0.0

        Integer functional result as:

                +1 => fnum > 0.0
                -1 => fnum < 0.0
                 0 => fnum = 0.0
```

BUGS

```
        None
```

SEE ALSO

```
        _LVOSPTst, ftsti
```

TABLE OF CONTENTS


```
NAME
     IEEEDPAbs -- compute absolute value of IEEE double precision argument

SYNOPSIS
       x    = IEEEDPAbs(  y  );
     d0/d1              d0/d1

     double  x,y;

FUNCTION
     Take the absolute value of argument y and return it to caller.

INPUTS
     y -- IEEE double precision floating point value

RESULT
     x -- IEEE double precision floating point value

BUGS

SEE ALSO
```

```
NAME
     IEEEDPAdd -- add one double precision IEEE number to another

SYNOPSIS
       x    = IEEEDPAdd(  y  ,  z  );
     d0/d1              d0/d1 d2/d3

     double  x,y,z;

FUNCTION
     Compute x = y + z in IEEE double precision.

INPUTS
     y -- IEEE double precision floating point value
     z -- IEEE double precision floating point value

RESULT
     x -- IEEE double precision floating point value

BUGS

SEE ALSO
     IEEEDPSub
```



```
NAME
     IEEEDPCeil -- compute Ceil function of IEEE double precision number

SYNOPSIS
       x    = IEEEDPCeil(  y  );
     d0/d1                d0/d1

     double  x,y;

FUNCTION
     Calculate the least integer greater than or equal to x and return it.
     This value may have more than 32 bits of significance.
     This identity is true.  Ceil(x) = -Floor(-x).

INPUTS
     y -- IEEE double precision floating point value

RESULT
     x -- IEEE double precision floating point value

BUGS

SEE ALSO
     IEEEDPFloor
```

```
NAME
     IEEEDPCmp -- compare two double precision floating point numbers

SYNOPSIS
       c    = IEEEDPCmp(  y   ,   z  );
       d0               d0/d1  d2/d3

     double  y,z;
     long    c;

FUNCTION
     Compare y with z. Set the condition codes for less, greater, or
     equal. Set return value c to -1 if y<z, or +1 if y>z, or 0 if
     y == z.

INPUTS
     y -- IEEE double precision floating point value
     z -- IEEE double precision floating point value

RESULT
    c = 1   cc = gt         for (y > z)
    c = 0   cc = eq         for (y == z)
    c = -1  cc = lt         for (y < z)

BUGS

SEE ALSO
```



```
NAME
     IEEEDPDiv -- divide one double precision IEEE by another

SYNOPSIS
       x    = IEEEDPDiv(  y   ,   z  );
     d0/d1              d0/d1  d2/d3

     double  x,y,z;

FUNCTION
     Compute x = y / z in IEEE double precision.

INPUTS
     y -- IEEE double precision floating point value
     z -- IEEE double precision floating point value

RESULT
     x -- IEEE double precision floating point value

BUGS

SEE ALSO
     IEEEDPMul
```

```
NAME
     IEEEDPFix -- convert IEEE double float to integer

SYNOPSIS
     x    = IEEEDPFix(  y  );
     d0                d0/d1

     long    x;
     double  y;

FUNCTION
     Convert IEEE double precision argument to a 32 bit signed integer
     and return result.

INPUTS
     y -- IEEE double precision floating point value

RESULT
     if no overflow occured then return
             x -- 32 bit signed integer
     if overflow return largest +- integer
             For round to zero

BUGS

SEE ALSO
     IEEEDPFlt
```



```
NAME
     IEEEDPFloor -- compute Floor function of IEEE double precision number

SYNOPSIS
      x    = IEEEDPFloor(  y  );
     d0/d1                d0/d1

     double  x,y;

FUNCTION
     Calculate the largest integer less than or equal to x and return it.
     This value may have more than 32 bits of significance.

INPUTS
     y -- IEEE double precision floating point value

RESULT
     x -- IEEE double precision floating point value

BUGS

SEE ALSO
     IEEEDPCeil
```

```
mathieeedoubbas.library/IEEEDPFlt          mathieeedoubbas.library/IEEEDPFlt

    NAME
        IEEEDPFlt -- convert integer to IEEE double precision number

    SYNOPSIS
          x    = IEEEDPFlt(  y  );
        d0/dl               d0

        double  x;
        long    y;

    FUNCTION
        Convert a signed 32 bit value to a double precision IEEE value
        and return it in d0/dl. No exceptions can occur with this
        function.

    INPUTS
        y -- 32 bit integer in d0

    RESULT
        x is a 64 bit double precision IEEE value

    BUGS

    SEE ALSO
        IEEEDPFix
```

```
mathieeedoubbas.library/IEEEDPMul          mathieeedoubbas.library/IEEEDPMul

    NAME
        IEEEDPMul -- multiply one double precision IEEE number by another

    SYNOPSIS
          x    = IEEEDPMul(  y  ,  z  );
        d0/dl              d0/dl d2/d3

        double  x,y,z;

    FUNCTION
        Compute x = y * z in IEEE double precision.

    INPUTS
        y -- IEEE double precision floating point value
        z -- IEEE double precision floating point value

    RESULT
        x -- IEEE double precision floating point value

    BUGS

    SEE ALSO
        IEEEDPDiv
```

mathieeedoubbas.library/IEEEDPNeg mathieeedoubbas.library/IEEEDPNeg

```
NAME
     IEEEDPNeg -- compute negative value of IEEE double precision number

SYNOPSIS
       x    = IEEEDPNeg(  y   );
     d0/d1              d0/d1

     double  x,y;

FUNCTION
     Invert the sign of argument y and return it to caller.

INPUTS
     y - IEEE double precision floating point value

RESULT
     x - IEEE double precision floating point value

BUGS

SEE ALSO
```

mathieeedoubbas.library/IEEEDPSub mathieeedoubbas.library/IEEEDPSub

```
NAME
     IEEEDPSub -- subtract one double precision IEEE number from another

SYNOPSIS
       x    = IEEEDPSub(  y   ,  z   );
     d0/d1              d0/d1 d2/d3

     double  x,y,z;

FUNCTION
     Compute x = y - z in IEEE double precision.

INPUTS
     y -- IEEE double precision floating point value
     z -- IEEE double precision floating point value

RESULT
     x -- IEEE double precision floating point value

BUGS

SEE ALSO
     IEEEDPAdd
```

```
NAME
     IEEEDPTst -- compare IEEE double precision value to 0.0

SYNOPSIS
       c    = IEEEDPTst(  y  );
       d0                d0/d1

     double  y;
     long    c;

FUNCTION
     Compare y to 0.0, set the condition codes for less than, greater
     than, or equal to 0.0.  Set the return value c to -1 if less than,
     to +1 if greater than, or 0 if equal to 0.0.

INPUTS
     y -- IEEE double precision floating point value

RESULT
     c = 1   cc = gt         for (y > 0.0)
     c = 0   cc = eq         for (y == 0.0)
     c = -1  cc = lt         for (y < 0.0)

BUGS

SEE ALSO
```

TABLE OF CONTENTS

mathieeedoubtrans.library/IEEEDPAcos

```
NAME
     IEEEDPAcos -- compute the arc cosine of a number

SYNOPSIS
      x    = IEEEDPAcos(  y  );
     d0/dl               d0/dl

     double  x,y;

FUNCTION
     Compute arc cosine of y in IEEE double precision

INPUTS
     y - IEEE double precision floating point value

RESULT
     x - IEEE double precision floating point value

BUGS

SEE ALSO
     IEEEDPCos(), IEEEDPAtan(), IEEEDPAsin()
```

```
mathieeedoubtrans.library/IEEEDPAsin

    NAME
        IEEEDPAsin -- compute the arcsine of a number

    SYNOPSIS
          x    = IEEEDPAsin(  y  );
        d0/d1                d0/d1

        double  x,y;

    FUNCTION
        Compute the arc sine of y in IEEE double precision

    INPUTS
        y - IEEE double precision floating point value

    RESULT
        x - IEEE double precision floating point value

    BUGS

    SEE ALSO
        IEEEDPSin(), IEEEDPAtan(), IEEEDPAcos()
```

```
mathieeedoubtrans.library/IEEEDPAtan

    NAME
        IEEEDPAtan -- compute the arctangent of a floating point number

    SYNOPSIS
          x    = IEEEDPAtan(  y  );
        d0/d1                d0/d1

        double  x,y;

    FUNCTION
        Compute arctangent of y in IEEE double precision

    INPUTS
        y - IEEE double precision floating point value

    RESULT
        x - IEEE double precision floating point value

    BUGS

    SEE ALSO
        IEEEDPTan(), IEEEDPAsin(), IEEEDPACos()
```

mathieeedoubtrans.library/IEEEDPCos

```
NAME
     IEEEDPCos -- compute the cosine of a floating point number

SYNOPSIS
       x    = IEEEDPCos(  y  );
     d0/d1               d0/d1

     double  x,y;

FUNCTION
     Compute cosine of y in IEEE double precision

INPUTS
     y - IEEE double precision floating point value

RESULT
     x - IEEE double precision floating point value

BUGS

SEE ALSO
     IEEEDPAcos(), IEEEDPSin(), IEEEDPTan()
```

mathieeedoubtrans.library/IEEEDPCosh

```
NAME
     IEEEDPCosh -- compute the hyperbolic cosine of a floating point number

SYNOPSIS
       x    = IEEEDPCosh(  y  );
     d0/d1                d0/d1

     double  x,y;

FUNCTION
     Compute hyperbolic cosine of y in IEEE double precision

INPUTS
     y - IEEE double precision floating point value

RESULT
     x - IEEE double precision floating point value

BUGS

SEE ALSO
     IEEEDPSinh(), IEEEDPTanh()
```

```
mathieeedoubtrans.library/IEEEDPExp

   NAME
        IEEEDPExp -- compute the exponential of e

   SYNOPSIS
          x    = IEEEDPExp(  y   );
        d0/d1              d0/d1

        double  x,y;

   FUNCTION
        Compute e^y in IEEE double precision

   INPUTS
        y - IEEE double precision floating point value

   RESULT
        x - IEEE double precision floating point value

   BUGS

   SEE ALSO
        IEEEDPLog()
```

```
mathieeedoubtrans.library/IEEEDPFieee

   NAME
        IEEEDPFieee -- convert IEEE single to IEEE double

   SYNOPSIS
          x    = IEEEDPFieee(  y  );
        d0/d1                  d0

        float   y;
        double  x;

   FUNCTION
        Convert IEEE single precision number to IEEE double precision.

   INPUTS
        y - IEEE single precision floating point value

   RESULT
        x - IEEE double precision floating point value

   BUGS

   SEE ALSO
        IEEEDPTieee()
```

mathieeedoubtrans.library/IEEEDPLog

```
NAME
     IEEEDPLog -- compute the natural logarithm of a floating point number

SYNOPSIS
       x    = IEEEDPLog(  y  );
     d0/dl              d0/dl

     double  x,y;

FUNCTION
     Compute ln(y) in IEEE double precision

INPUTS
     y - IEEE double precision floating point value

RESULT
     x - IEEE double precision floating point value

BUGS

SEE ALSO
     IEEEDPExp()
```

mathieeedoubtrans.library/IEEEDPLog10

```
NAME
     IEEEDPLog10 -- compute logarithm base 10 of a number

SYNOPSIS
       x    = IEEEDPLog10(  y  );
     d0/dl                d0/dl

     double  x,y;

FUNCTION
     Compute the logarithm base 10 of y in IEEE double precision

INPUTS
     y - IEEE double precision floating point value

RESULT
     x - IEEE double precision floating point value

BUGS

SEE ALSO
     IEEEDPLog()
```

mathieeedoubtrans.library/IEEEDPPow

```
NAME
     IEEEDPPow -- raise a number to another number power

SYNOPSIS
       z    = IEEEDPPow(  x   ,  y  );
     d0/d1             d2/d3 d0/d1

     double  x,y,z;

FUNCTION
     Compute y^x in IEEE double precision

INPUTS
     x - IEEE double precision floating point value
     y - IEEE double precision floating point value

RESULT
     z - IEEE double precision floating point value

BUGS

SEE ALSO
```

mathieeedoubtrans.library/IEEEDPSin

```
NAME
     IEEEDPSin -- compute the sine of a floating point number

SYNOPSIS
       x    = IEEEDPSin(  y  );
     d0/d1             d0/d1

     double  x,y;

FUNCTION
     Compute sine of y in IEEE double precision

INPUTS
     y - IEEE double precision floating point value

RESULT
     x - IEEE double precision floating point value

BUGS

SEE ALSO
     IEEEDPAsin(), IEEEDPTan(), IEEEDPCos()
```

mathieeedoubtrans.library/IEEEDPSincos

NAME
    IEEEDPSincos -- compute the arc tangent of a floating point number

SYNOPSIS
```
     x     = IEEEDPSincos( z ,  y  );
    d0/d1                  a0  d0/d1

    double  x,y,*z;
```

FUNCTION
    Compute sin and cosine of y in IEEE double precision.
    Store the cosine in *z. Return the sine of y.

INPUTS
    y - IEEE double precision floating point value
    z - pointer to IEEE double precision floating point number

RESULT
    x - IEEE double precision floating point value

BUGS

SEE ALSO
    IEEEDPSin(), IEEEDPCos()

mathieeedoubtrans.library/IEEEDPSinh

NAME
    IEEEDPSinh -- compute the hyperbolic sine of a floating point number

SYNOPSIS
```
     x     = IEEEDPSinh(  y  );
    d0/d1                d0/d1

    double  x,y;
```

FUNCTION
    Compute hyperbolic sine of y in IEEE double precision

INPUTS
    y - IEEE double precision floating point value

RESULT
    x - IEEE double precision floating point value

BUGS

SEE ALSO
    IEEEDPCosh, IEEEDPTanh

mathieeedoubtrans.library/IEEEDPSqrt

```
NAME
     IEEEDPSqrt -- compute the square root of a number

SYNOPSIS
       x    = IEEEDPSqrt(  y  );
     d0/dl               d0/dl

     double  x,y;

FUNCTION
     Compute square root of y in IEEE double precision

INPUTS
     y - IEEE double precision floating point value

RESULT
     x - IEEE double precision floating point value

BUGS

SEE ALSO
```

mathieeedoubtrans.library/IEEEDPTan

```
NAME
     IEEEDPTan -- compute the tangent of a floating point number

SYNOPSIS
       x    = IEEEDPTan(  y  );
     d0/dl              d0/dl

     double  x,y;

FUNCTION
     Compute tangent of y in IEEE double precision

INPUTS
     y - IEEE double precision floating point value

RESULT
     x - IEEE double precision floating point value

BUGS

SEE ALSO
     IEEEDPAtan(), IEEEDPSin(), IEEEDPCos()
```

mathieeedoubtrans.library/IEEEDPTanh

```
NAME
     IEEEDPTanh -- compute the hyperbolic tangent of a floating point number

SYNOPSIS
       x    = IEEEDPTanh(  y  );
     d0/d1                d0/d1

     double  x,y;

FUNCTION
     Compute hyperbolic tangent of y in IEEE double precision

INPUTS
     y - IEEE double precision floating point value

RESULT
     x - IEEE double precision floating point value

BUGS

SEE ALSO
     IEEEDPSinh(), IEEEDPCosh()
```

mathieeedoubtrans.library/IEEEDPTieee

```
NAME
     IEEEDPTieee -- convert IEEE double to IEEE single

SYNOPSIS
       x    = IEEEDPTieee(  y  );
      d0                   d0/d1

     double  y;
     float   x;

FUNCTION
     Convert IEEE double precision number to IEEE single precision.

INPUTS
     y - IEEE double precision floating point value

RESULT
     x - IEEE single precision floating point value

BUGS

SEE ALSO
     IEEEDPFieee()
```

TABLE OF CONTENTS

NAME

SPAcos - obtain the arccosine of the floating point number

SYNOPSIS

```
fnum2 = SPAcos(fnum1);
               d0.1
float fnum2;
float fnum1;
```

FUNCTION

Accepts a floating point number representing the cosine of an angle and returns the value of said angle in radians

INPUTS

fnum1 - Motorola fast floating point number

RESULT

fnum2 - Motorola fast floating point number

BUGS

None

SEE ALSO

SPSin

NAME

SPAsin - obtain the arcsine of the floating point number

SYNOPSIS

```
fnum2 = SPAsin(fnum1);
               d0.1
float fnum2;
float fnum1;
```

FUNCTION

Accepts a floating point number representing the sine of an angle and returns the value of said angle in radians

INPUTS

fnum1 - Motorola fast floating point number

RESULT

fnum2 - Motorola fast floating point number

BUGS

None

SEE ALSO

SPCos

NAME

SPAtan - obtain the arctangent of the floating point number

SYNOPSIS

```
fnum2 = SPAtan(fnum1);
               d0.1
float fnum2;
float fnum1;
```

FUNCTION

Accepts a floating point number representing the tangent of an angle and returns the value of said angle in radians

INPUTS

fnum1 - Motorola fast floating point number

RESULT

fnum2 - Motorola fast floating point number

BUGS

None

SEE ALSO

SPTan

NAME

SPCos - obtain the cosine of the floating point number

SYNOPSIS

```
fnum2 = SPCos(fnum1);
              d0.1
float fnum2;
float fnum1;
```

FUNCTION

Accepts a floating point number representing an angle
in radians and returns the cosine of said angle.

INPUTS

fnum1 - Motorola fast floating point number

RESULT

fnum2 - Motorola fast floating point number

BUGS

None

SEE ALSO

SPAcos

NAME

SPCosh - obtain the hyperbolic cosine of the floating point number

SYNOPSIS

```
fnum2 = SPCosh(fnum1);
               d0.1
float fnum2;
float fnum1;
```

FUNCTION

Accepts a floating point number representing an angle
in radians and returns the hyperbolic cosine of said angle.

INPUTS

fnum1 - Motorola fast floating point number

RESULT

fnum2 - Motorola fast floating point number

BUGS

None

SEE ALSO

SPSinh

NAME

SPExp - obtain the exponential (e**X) of the floating point number

SYNOPSIS

```
fnum2 = SPExp(fnum1);
                d0.1
float fnum2;
float fnum1;
```

FUNCTION

Accepts a floating point number and returns the value of e raised to the fnum1 power

INPUTS

fnum1 - Motorola fast floating point number

RESULT

fnum2 - Motorola fast floating point number

BUGS

None

SEE ALSO

SPLog

NAME

SPFieee - convert single precision ieee to FFP number

SYNOPSIS

```
fnum = SPFieee(ieeenum);
                d0.1
float fnum;
float ieeenum;
```

FUNCTION

Accepts a standard single precision format returns the same number, converted to Motorola fast floating point number

INPUTS

ieeenum - IEEE Single Precision Floating Point

RESULT

fnum - Motorola fast floating point number

BUGS

None

SEE ALSO

SPTieee

NAME

SPLog - obtain the natural logarithm of the floating point number

SYNOPSIS

```
fnum2 = SPLog(fnum1);
                d0.1
float fnum2;
float fnum1;
```

FUNCTION

Accepts a floating point number and returns the natural logarithem (base e) of said number

INPUTS

fnum1 - Motorola fast floating point number

RESULT

fnum2 - Motorola fast floating point number

BUGS

None

SEE ALSO

SPExp

NAME

SPLog10 - obtain the naperian logarithm(base 10) of the floating point number

SYNOPSIS

```
fnum2 = SPLog10(fnum1);
                d0.1
float fnum2;
float fnum1;
```

FUNCTION

Accepts a floating point number and returns the naperian logarithm (base 10) of said number

INPUTS

fnum1 - Motorola fast floating point number

RESULT

fnum2 - Motorola fast floating point number

BUGS

None

SEE ALSO

SPExp, SpLog

NAME

SPPow - raise a number to a power

SYNOPSIS

```
result = SPPow(fnum1, fnum2);
               d1.1    d0.1
float fnum1, fnum2;
float result;
```

FUNCTION

Accepts two floating point numbers and returns the result of fnum2 raised to the fnum1 power

INPUTS

fnum1 - Motorola fast floating point number
fnum2 - Motorola fast floating point number

RESULT

result - Motorola fast floating point number

BUGS

None

SEE ALSO

SPExp, SPLog

NAME

SPSin - obtain the sine of the floating point number

SYNOPSIS

```
fnum2 = SPSin(fnum1);
              d0.1
float fnum2;
float fnum1;
```

FUNCTION

Accepts a floating point number representing an angle in radians and returns the sine of said angle.

INPUTS

fnum1 - Motorola fast floating point number

RESULT

fnum2 - Motorola fast floating point number

BUGS

None

SEE ALSO

SPAsin

NAME

SPSincos - obtain the sine and cosine of a number

SYNOPSIS

```
fnum3 = SPSincos(pfnum2, fnum1);
                 d1.1,   d0.1
float *pfnum2;
float fnum1;
float fnum3;
```

FUNCTION

Accepts a floating point number (fnum1) representing an angle in radians and a pointer to another floating point number (pfnum2). It computes the cosine and places it in *pfnum2. It computes the sine and returns it as a result.

INPUTS

fnum1 - Motorola fast floating point number
pfnum2 - pointer to Motorola fast floating point number

RESULT

*pfnum2 - Motorola fast floating point number (cosine)
fnum3 - Motorola fast floating point number (sine)

BUGS

None

SEE ALSO

SPSin, SPCos

NAME

SPSinh - obtain the hyperbolic sine of the floating point number

SYNOPSIS

```
fnum2 = SPSinh(fnum1);
               d0.1
float fnum2;
float fnum1;
```

FUNCTION

Accepts a floating point number representing an angle in radians and returns the hyperbolic sine of said angle.

INPUTS

fnum1 - Motorola fast floating point number

RESULT

fnum2 - Motorola fast floating point number

BUGS

None

SEE ALSO

SPCosh

NAME

SPSqrt - obtain the square root of the floating point number

SYNOPSIS

```
fnum2 = SPSqrt(fnum1);
                d0.1
float fnum2;
float fnum1;
```

FUNCTION

Accepts a floating point number and returns the square toot of said number

INPUTS

fnum1 - Motorola fast floating point number

RESULT

fnum2 - Motorola fast floating point number

BUGS

None

SEE ALSO

SPPow, SPMul

NAME

SPTan - obtain the tangent of the floating point number

SYNOPSIS

```
fnum2 = SPTan(fnum1);
               d0.1
float fnum2;
float fnum1;
```

FUNCTION

Accepts a floating point number representing an angle in radians and returns the tangent of said angle.

INPUTS

fnum1 - Motorola fast floating point number

RESULT

fnum2 - Motorola fast floating point number

BUGS

None

SEE ALSO

SPAtan

NAME

SPTanh - obtain the hyperbolic tangent of the floating point number

SYNOPSIS

```
fnum2 = SPTanh(fnum1);
                d0.1
float fnum2;
float fnum1;
```

FUNCTION

Accepts a floating point number representing an angle
in radians and returns the hyperbolic tangent of said angle.

INPUTS

fnum1 - Motorola fast floating point number

RESULT

fnum2 - Motorola fast floating point number

BUGS

None

SEE ALSO

SPSinh, SPCosh

NAME

SPTieee - convert FFP number to single precision ieee

SYNOPSIS

```
ieeenum = SPTieee(fnum);
                   d0.1
float ieeenum;
float fnum;
```

FUNCTION

Accepts a Motorola fast floating point number and
returns the same number, converted into IEEE
standard single precision format

INPUTS

fnum - Motorola fast floating point number

RESULT

ieeenum - IEEE Single Precision Floating Point

BUGS

None

SEE ALSO

SPFieee

TABLE OF CONTENTS


```
NAME
    Translate - Converts an English string into phonemes

SYNOPSIS
    rtnCode = Translate(instring, inlen, outbuf, outlen)
    D0                  A0        D0     A1      D1

    LONG Translate(APTR,LONG,APTR,LONG);

FUNCTION
    The translate function converts an English string into
    a string of phonetic codes suitable as input to the
    narrator device.

INPUTS
    instring - pointer to English string
    inlen    - length of English string
    outbuf   - a char array which will hold the phonetic codes
    outlen   - the length of the output array

RESULTS
    rtnCode -
        Translate will return a zero if no error has occured.
        The only error that can occur is overflowing the output
        buffer.  If Translate determines that an overflow will
        occur, it will stop the translation at a word boundary
        before the overflow happens.  If this occurs, Translate
        will return a negative number whose absolute value
        indicates where in the INPUT string Translate stopped.
        The user can then use the offset -rtnCode from the
        beginning of the buffer in a subsequent Translate call
        to continue the translation where s/he left off.

BUGS

SEE ALSO
```

Section B

Device Summaries

This section contains summaries for the device calls that are built into the Amiga operating system software. These documents have been automatically extracted from the original source code and are often called **autodocs**.

Devices are based on the library concept mentioned in Section A. Libraries generally provide a set of usable functions. Devices usually are hardware independent mechanisms for talking to some sort of physical media (such as a disk drive or serial port). Devices often have their own independent tasks, and can perform asynchronous operations even when the task that called them is busy.

Devices are described fully in the *Amiga ROM Kernel Manual: Libraries and Devices.* Only a brief introduction will be given here.

The following is a partial list of the devices that are currently part of the Amiga software:

Device Names	
audio.device	narrator.device
clipboard.device	parallel.device
console.device	printer.device
gameport.device	serial.device
input.device	timer.device
keyboard.device	trackdisk.device

Devices are more complex to use than libraries. Opening a device requires:

- A message port (**MsgPort**). This structure is used for inter-task communication. Ports may be created with the amiga.lib/CreatePort() function (see Section F).

- An I/O Request (**IORequest**). This special structure, plus any extensions, is your sole source of communication with the device. Commands and data (or data pointers) are placed in this structure and sent off to the device. The exact format of this structure is defined in the "exec/io.h" include file in Section D. An IORequest is typically created with the amiga.lib/CreateExtIO() function (see Section F).

- The name of the device for the exec **OpenDevice()** call. The actual device may exist in ROM or on disk. This is transparent to the application programmer.

Opening the device prepares the **IORequest** for use. The request will be tied to the one and only device that initialized it. Commands may be placed in the **io_Command** field, then the request may be sent to the device. There are two primary options for starting I/O:

- **DoIO()** - An exec call that does the I/O, and returns after it has finished (this is "synchronous I/O"), and is the easiest option to use.

- **SendIO()** - An exec call that starts the I/O, but returns immediately ("asynchronous I/O"). The device will complete its job while the calling task continues to run. Before reusing the I/O Request, you must wait for the I/O to finish (multiple pending requests are possible with multiple **IORequest** structures).

When you have finished using a device, a call to **CloseDevice()** completes the transaction. For those programs using asynchronous I/O, any outstanding requests must have already been completed. This can be done by a **WaitIO()**, or by forcing termination with an **AbortIO()/WaitIO()** pair.

```
/*
 * A complete example of using the trackdisk.device.
 * This moves the heads from track 0 to 79 and back.
 *
 */
#include "exec/types.h"
#include "devices/trackdisk.h"
#include "libraries/dos.h"
/* #include "proto/exec.h" */
/* #include "functions.h" */

struct MsgPort   *CreatePort();   /* Declare return types */
struct IORequest *CreateExtIO();
void DeletePort();
void DeleteExtIO();

struct MsgPort *trackport;       /* Storage for pointers */
struct IOExtTD *trackIO;
short           openerror;       /* flag */

void cleanexit(returncode)
int returncode;
{
    printf("openerror =%d\n"  ,openerror);
    printf("trackIO   =$%lx\n",trackIO);
    printf("trackport =$%lx\n",trackport);
    printf("io_Error  =%d\n"  ,trackIO->iotd_Req.io_Error);

    if(!openerror) CloseDevice(trackIO);
    if(trackIO)    DeleteExtIO(trackIO,(long)sizeof(struct IOExtTD));
    if(trackport)  DeletePort(trackport);

    exit(returncode);
}


void main()
{
    trackport=CreatePort(0L,0L);
    if(!trackport)
        cleanexit(RETURN_FAIL);
    trackIO=(struct IOExtTD *)
            CreateExtIO(trackport,(long)sizeof(struct IOExtTD));
    if(!trackIO)
        cleanexit(RETURN_FAIL+1);
    if(openerror=OpenDevice("trackdisk.device",0L,trackIO,0L))
        cleanexit(RETURN_FAIL+2);

    trackIO->iotd_Req.io_Command=TD_SEEK;      /* command */

    trackIO->iotd_Req.io_Offset =0L;           /* out */
    printf("1\n");
    DoIO(trackIO);
    trackIO->iotd_Req.io_Offset =79*11*2*512L; /* in  */
    printf("2\n");
    DoIO(trackIO);
    trackIO->iotd_Req.io_Offset =0L;           /* out */
    printf("3\n");
    DoIO(trackIO);
    trackIO->iotd_Req.io_Offset =79*11*2*512L; /* in  */
    printf("4\n");
    DoIO(trackIO);

    cleanexit(RETURN_OK);
}
```

TABLE OF CONTENTS

TABLE OF CONTENTS

```
audio.device/CloseDevice

    NAME
        CloseDevice - terminate access to the audio device

    SYNOPSIS
        CloseDevice(iORequest);
                    Al

    FUNCTION
        The CloseDevice routine notifies the audio device that it will no
        longer be used.  It takes an I/O audio request block (IOAudio) and
        clears the device pointer (io_Device).  If there are any channels
        allocated with the same allocation key (ioa_AllocKey), CloseDevice
        frees (ADCMD_FREE) them. CloseDevice decrements the open count, if the
        count falls to zero, and the system needs memory, the device is expunged.

    INPUTS
        iORequest    - pointer to audio request block (struct IOAudio)
              io_Device    - pointer to device node, must be set by (or
                             copied from I/O block set by) open (OpenDevice)
              io_Unit      - bit map of channels to free (ADCMD_FREE) (bits 0
                             thru 3 correspond to channels 0 thru 3)
              ioa_AllocKey- allocation key, used to free channels

    OUTPUTS
        iORequest - pointer to audio request block (struct IOAudio)
              io_Device    - set to -1
              io_Unit      - set to zero
```

```
audio.device/ADCMD_ALLOCATE

    NAME
        ADCMD_ALLOCATE -- allocate a set of audio channels

    FUNCTION
        ADCMD_ALLOCATE is a command that allocates multiple audio channels.
        ADCMD_ALLOCATE takes an array of possible channel combinations
        (ioa_Data) and an allocation precedence (ln_Pri) and tries to allocate
        one of the combinations of channels.

        If the channel combination array is zero length (ioa_Length), the
        allocation succeeds; otherwise, ADCMD_ALLOCATE checks each
        combination, one at a time, in the specified order, to find one
        combination that does not require ADCMD_ALLOCATE to steal allocated
        channels.

        If it must steal allocated channels, it uses the channel combination
        that steals the lowest precedence channels.

        ADCMD_ALLOCATE cannot steal a channel of equal or greater precedence
        than the allocation precedence (ln_Pri).

        If it fails to allocate any channel combination and the no-wait flag
        (ADIOF_NOWAIT) is set ADCMD_ALLOCATE returns a zero in the unit field
        of the I/O request (io_Unit) and an error (IOERR_ALLOCFAILED).  If the
        no-wait flag is clear, it places the I/O request in a list that tries
        to allocate again whenever ADCMD_FREE frees channels or ADCMD_SETPREC
        lowers the channels' precedences.

        If the allocation is successful, ADCMD_ALLOCATE checks if any channels
        are locked (ADCMD_LOCK) and if so, replies (ReplyMsg) the lock I/O
        request with an error (ADIOERR_CHANNELSTOLEN). Then it places the
        allocation I/O request in a list waiting for the locked channels to be
        freed.  When all the allocated channels are un-locked, ADCMD_ALLOCATE:
          . resets (CMD_RESET) the allocated channels,
          . generates a new allocation key (ioa_AllocKey), if it is zero,
          . copies the allocation key into each of the allocated channels
          . copies the allocation precedence into each of the allocated
            channels, and
          . copies the channel bit map into the unit field of the I/O request.

        If channels are allocated with a non-zero allocation key,
        ADCMD_ALLOCATE allocates with that same key; otherwise, it generates a
        new and unique key.

        ADCMD_ALLOCATE is synchronous:
          . if the allocation succeeds and there are no locked channels to be
            stolen, or
          . if the allocation fails and the no-wait flag is set.
         . if the allocation fails and the no-wait flag is set.
        In either case, ADCMD_ALLOCATE only replies (mn_ReplyPort) if the
        quick flag (IOF_QUICK) is clear; otherwise, the allocation is
        asynchronous, so it clears the quick flag and replies the I/O request
        after the allocation is finished.  If channels are stolen, all audio
        device commands return an error (IOERR_NOALLOCATION) when the former
        user tries to use them again.  Do not use ADCMD_ALLOCATE in interrupt
        code.

        If you decide to store directly to the audio hardware registers, you
        must either lock the channels you've allocated, or set the precedence
        to maximum (ADALLOC_MAXPREC) to prevent the channels from being
        stolen.

        Under all circumstances, unless channels are stolen, you must free
        (ADCMD_FREE) all allocated channels when you are finished using them.

    INPUTS
        ln_Pri       - allocation precedence (-128 thru 127)
        mn_ReplyPort- pointer to message port that receives I/O request after
                      the allocation completes is asynchronous or quick flag
                      (ADIOF_QUICK) is set
```

```
    io_Device    - pointer to device node, must be set by (or copied from
                   I/O block set by) OpenDevice function
    io_Command   - command number for ADCMD_ALLOCATE
    io_Flags     - flags, must be cleared if not used:
                   IOF_QUICK    - (CLEAR) reply I/O request
                                  (SET) only reply I/O request only if
                                        asynchronous (see above text)
                   ADIOF_NOWAIT- (CLEAR) if allocation fails, wait till is
                                        succeeds
                                  (SET) if allocation fails, return error
                                        (ADIOERR_ALLOCFAILED)
    ioa_AllocKey- allocation key, zero to generate new key; otherwise,
                   it must be set by (or copied from I/O block set by)
                   OpenDevice function or previous ADCMD_ALLOCATE command
    ioa_Data     - pointer to channel combination options (byte array, bits
                   0 thru 3 correspond to channels 0 thru 3)
    ioa_Length   - length of the channel combination option array
                   (0 thru 16, 0 always succeeds)

OUTPUTS
    io_Unit      - bit map of successfully allocated channels (bits 0 thru
                   3 correspond to channels 0 thru 3)
    io_Flags     - IOF_QUICK flag cleared if asynchronous (see above text)
    io_Error     - error number:
                   0                   - no error
                   ADIOERR_ALLOCFAILED - allocation failed
    ioa_AllocKey- allocation key, set to a unique number if passed a zero
                   and command succeeds
```



```
NAME
    ADCMD_FINISH -- abort writes in progress to audio channels

FUNCTION
    ADCMD_FINISH is a command for multiple audio channels.  For each
    selected channel (io_Unit), if the allocation key (ioa_AllocKey) is
    correct and there is a write (CMD_WRITE)in progress, ADCMD_FINISH
    aborts the current write immediately or at the end of the current
    cycle depending on the sync flag (ADIOF_SYNCCYCLE).  If the allocation
    key is incorrect ADCMD_FINISH returns an error (ADIOERR_NOALLOCATION).
    ADCMD_FINISH is synchronous and only replies (mn_ReplyPort) if the
    quick flag (IOF_QUICK) is clear.  Do not use ADCMD_FINISH in interrupt
    code at interrupt level 5 or higher.

INPUTS
    mn_ReplyPort- pointer to message port that receives I/O request
                  if the quick flag (IOF_QUICK) is clear
    io_Device   - pointer to device node, must be set by (or copied from
                  I/O block set by) OpenDevice function
    io_Unit     - bit map of channels to finish (bits 0 thru 3 correspond
                  to channels 0 thru 3)
    io_Command  - command number for ADCMD_FINISH
    io_Flags    - flags, must be cleared if not used:
                  IOF_QUICK       - (CLEAR) reply I/O request
                  ADIOF_SYNCCYCLE- (CLEAR) finish immediately
                                    (SET) finish at the end of current
                                          cycle

    ioa_AllocKey- allocation key, must be set by (or copied from I/O block
                  set by) OpenDevice function or ADCMD_ALLOCATE command

OUTPUTS
    io_Unit     - bit map of channels successfully finished (bits 0 thru 3
                  correspond to channels 0 thru 3)
    io_Error    - error number:
                  0                    - no error
                  ADIOERR_NOALLOCATION - allocation key (ioa_AllocKey)
                                         does not match key for channel
```

```
NAME
     ADCMD_FREE -- free audio channels for allocation

FUNCTION
     ADCMD_FREE is a command for multiple audio channels.  For each
     selected channel (io_Unit), if the allocation key (ioa_AllocKey) is
     correct, ADCMD_FREE does the following:
        . restores the channel to a known state (CMD_RESET),
        . changes the channels allocation key, and
        . makes the channel available for re-allocation.
        . If the channel is locked (ADCMD_LOCK) ADCMD_FREE unlocks it and
          clears the bit for the channel (io_Unit) in the lock I/O request.
          If the lock I/O request has no channel bits set ADCMD_FREE replies
          the lock I/O request, and
        . checks if there are allocation requests (ADCMD_ALLOCATE) waiting
          for the channel.

     Otherwise, ADCMD_FREE returns an error (ADIOERR_NOALLOCATION).
     ADCMD_FREE is synchronous and only replies (mn_ReplyPort) if the quick
     flag (IOF_QUICK) is clear.  Do not use ADCMD_FREE in interrupt code.

INPUTS
     mn_ReplyPort- pointer to message port that receives I/O request
                   if the quick flag (IOF_QUICK) is clear
     io_Device   - pointer to device node, must be set by (or copied from
                   I/O block set by) OpenDevice function
     io_Unit     - bit map of channels to free (bits 0 thru 3 correspond to
                   channels 0 thru 3)
     io_Command  - command number for ADCMD_FREE
     io_Flags    - flags, must be cleared if not used:
                   IOF_QUICK - (CLEAR) reply I/O request
     ioa_AllocKey- allocation key, must be set by (or copied from I/O block
                   set by) OpenDevice function or ADCMD_ALLOCATE command

OUTPUTS
     io_Unit     - bit map of channels successfully freed (bits 0 thru 3
                   correspond to channels 0 thru 3)
     io_Error    - error number:
                   0                    - no error
                   ADIOERR_NOALLOCATION - allocation key (ioa_AllocKey)
                                          does not match key for channel
```



```
NAME
     ADCMD_LOCK -- prevent audio channels from being stolen

FUNCTION
     ADCMD_LOCK is a command for multiple audio channels.  For each
     selected channel (io_Unit), if the allocation key (ioa_AllocKey) is
     correct, ADCMD_LOCK locks the channel, preventing subsequent
     allocations (ADCMD_ALLOCATE or OpenDevice) from stealing the channel.
     Otherwise, ADCMD_LOCK returns an error (ADIOERR_NOALLOCATION) and will
     not lock any channels.

     Unlike setting the precedence (ADCMD_SETPREC, ADCMD_ALLOCATE or
     OpenDevice) to maximum (ADALLOC_MAXPREC) which would cause all
     subsequent allocations to fail, ADCMD_LOCK causes all higher
     precedence allocations, even no-wait (ADIOF_NOWAIT) allocations, to
     wait until the channels are un-locked.

     Locked channels can only be unlocked by freeing them (ADCMD_FREE),
     which clears the channel select bits (io_Unit).  ADCMD_LOCK does not
     reply the I/O request (mn_ReplyPort) until all the channels it locks
     are freed, unless a higher precedence allocation attempts to steal one
     the locked channels. If a steal occurs, ADCMD_LOCK replies and returns
     an error (ADIOERR_CHANNELSTOLEN).  If the lock is replied
     (mn_ReplyPort) with this error, the channels should be freed as soon
     as possible.  To avoid a possible deadlock, never make the freeing of
     stolen channels dependent on another allocations completion.

     ADCMD_LOCK is only asynchronous if the allocation key is correct, in
     which case it clears the quick flag (IOF_QUICK); otherwise, it is
     synchronous and only replies if the quick flag (IOF_QUICK) is clear.
     Do not use ADCMD_LOCK in interrupt code.

INPUTS
     mn_ReplyPort- pointer to message port that receives I/O request
                   if the quick flag (IOF_QUICK) is clear
     io_Device   - pointer to device node, must be set by (or copied from
                   I/O block set by) OpenDevice function
     io_Unit     - bit map of channels to lock (bits 0 thru 3 correspond to
                   channels 0 thru 3)
     io_Command  - command number for ADCMD_LOCK
     io_Flags    - flags, must be cleared
     ioa_AllocKey- allocation key. must be set by (or copied from I/O block
                   set by) OpenDevice function or ADCMD_ALLOCATE command

OUTPUTS
     io_Unit     - bit map of successfully locked channels (bits 0 thru 3
                   correspond to channels 0 thru 3) not freed (ADCMD_FREE)
     io_Flags    - IOF_QUICK flag cleared if the allocation key is correct
                   (no ADIOERR_NOALLOCATION error)
     io_Error    - error number:
                   0                     - no error
                   ADIOERR_NOALLOCATION  - allocation key (ioa_AllocKey)
                                           does not match key for channel
                   ADIOERR_CHANNELSTOLEN- allocation attempting to steal
                                           locked channel
```

```
NAME
    ADCMD_PERVOL -- change the period and volume for writes in progress to
                    audio channels

FUNCTION
    ADCMD_PERVOL is a command for multiple audio channels.  For each
    selected channel (io_Unit), if the allocation key (ioa_AllocKey) is
    correct and there is a write (CMD_WRITE) in progress, ADCMD_PERVOL
    loads a new volume and period immediately or at the end of the current
    cycle depending on the sync flag (ADIOF_SYNCCYCLE).  If the allocation
    key in incorrect, ADCMD_PERVOL returns an error
    (ADIOERR_NOALLOCATION).  ADCMD_PERVOL is synchronous and only replies
    (mn_ReplyPort) if the quick flag (IOF_QUICK) is clear.  Do not use
    ADCMD_PERVOL in interrupt code at interrupt level 5 or higher.

INPUTS
    mn_ReplyPort- pointer to message port that receives I/O request
                  if the quick flag (IOF_QUICK) is clear
    io_Device   - pointer to device node, must be set by (or copied from
                  I/O block set by) OpenDevice function
    io_Unit     - bit map of channels to load period and volume (bits 0
                  thru 3 correspond to channels 0 thru 3)
    io_Command  - command number for ADCMD_PERVOL
    io_Flags    - flags, must be cleared if not used:
                  IOF_QUICK       - (CLEAR) reply I/O request
                  ADIOF_SYNCCYCLE- (CLEAR) load period and volume
                                           immediately
                                   (SET) load period and volume at the end
                                         of the current cycle
    ioa_AllocKey- allocation key, must be set by (or copied from I/O block
                  set by) OpenDevice function or ADCMD_ALLOCATE command
    ioa_Period  - new sample period in 279.365 ns increments (124 thru
                  65536, anti-aliasing filter works below 300 to 500
                  depending on waveform)
    ioa_Volume  - new volume (0 thru 64, linear)

OUTPUTS
    io_Unit     - bit map of channels that successfully loaded period and
                  volume (bits 0 thru 3 correspond to channels 0 thru 3)
    io_Error    - error number:
                  0                    - no error
                  ADIOERR_NOALLOCATION - allocation key (ioa_AllocKey)
                                         does not match key for channel
```



```
NAME
    ADCMD_SETPREC -- set the allocation precedence for audio channels

FUNCTION
    ADCMD_SETPREC is a command for multiple audio channels.  For each
    selected channel (io_Unit), if the allocation key (ioa_AllocKey) is
    correct, ADCMD_SETPREC sets the allocation precedence to a new value
    (ln_Pri) and checks if there are allocation requests (ADCMD_ALLOCATE)
    waiting for the channel which now have higher precedence; otherwise,
    ADCMD_SETPREC returns an error (ADIOERR_NOALLOCATION).  ADCMD_SETPREC
    is synchronous and only replies (mn_ReplyPort) if the quick flag
    (IOF_QUICK) is clear.  Do not use ADCMD_SETPREC in interrupt code.

INPUTS
    ln_Pri      - new allocation precedence (-128 thru 127)
    mn_ReplyPort- pointer to message port that receives I/O request
                  if the quick flag (IOF_QUICK) is clear
    io_Device   - pointer to device node, must be set by (or copied from
                  I/O block set by) OpenDevice function
    io_Unit     - bit map of channels to set precedence (bits 0 thru 3
                  correspond to channels 0 thru 3)
    io_Command  - command number for ADCMD_SETPREC
    io_Flags    - flags, must be cleared if not used:
                  IOF_QUICK - (CLEAR) reply I/O request
    ioa_AllocKey- allocation key, must be set by (or copied from I/O block
                  set by) OpenDevice function or ADCMD_ALLOCATE command

OUTPUTS
    io_Unit     - bit map of channels that successfully set precedence
                  (bits 0 thru 3 correspond to channels 0 thru 3)
    io_Error    - error number:
                  0                    - no error
                  ADIOERR_NOALLOCATION - allocation key (ioa_AllocKey)
                                         does not match key for channel
```

```
NAME
    ADCMD_WAITCYCLE -- wait for an audio channel to complete the current
                       cycle of a write

FUNCTION
    ADCMD_WAITCYCLE is a command for a single audio channel (io_Unit).
    If the allocation key (ioa_AllocKey) is correct and there is a write
    (CMD_WRITE) in progress on selected channel, ADCMD_WAITCYCLE does not
    reply (mn_ReplyPort) until the end of the current cycle.  If there is
    no write is progress, ADCMD_WAITCYCLE replies immediately.  If the
    allocation key is incorrect, ADCMD_WAITCYCLE returns an error
    (ADIOERR_NOALLOCATION).  ADCMD_WAITCYCLE returns an error
    (IOERR_ABORTED) if it is canceled (AbortIO) or the channel is stolen
    (ADCMD_ALLOCATE).  ADCMD_WAITCYCLE is only asynchronous if it is
    waiting for a cycle to complete, in which case it clears the quick
    flag (IOF_QUICK); otherwise, it is synchronous and only replies if the
    quick flag (IOF_QUICK) is clear.  Do not use ADCMD_WAITCYCLE in
    interrupt code at interrupt level 5 or higher.

INPUTS
    mn_ReplyPort- pointer to message port that receives I/O request, if
                  the quick flag (IOF_QUICK) is clear, or if a write is in
                  progress on the selected channel and a cycle has
                  completed
    io_Device   - pointer to device node, must be set by (or copied from
                  I/O block set by) OpenDevice function
    io_Unit     - bit map of channel to wait for cycle (bits 0 thru 3
                  correspond to channels 0 thru 3), if more then one bit
                  is set lowest bit number channel is used
    io_Command  - command number for CMD_WAITCYCLE
    io_Flags    - flags, must be cleared if not used:
                  IOF_QUICK - (CLEAR) reply I/O request
                              (SET) only reply I/O request if a write is
                                    in progress on the selected channel
                                    and a cycle has completed
    ioa_AllocKey- allocation key, must be set by (or copied from I/O block
                  set by) OpenDevice function or ADCMD_ALLOCATE command

OUTPUTS
    io_Unit     - bit map of channel that successfully waited for cycle
                  (bits 0 thru 3 correspond to channels 0 thru 3)
    io_Flags    - IOF_QUICK flag cleared if a write is in progress on the
                  selected channel
    io_Error    - error number:
                  0                    - no error
                  IOERR_ABORTED        - canceled (AbortIO) or channel
                                         stolen
                  ADIOERR_NOALLOCATION - allocation key (ioa_AllocKey)
                                         does not match key for channel
```



```
NAME
    CMD_CLEAR -- throw away internal caches

FUNCTION
    CMD_CLEAR is a standard command for multiple audio channels.  For each
    selected channel (io_Unit), if the allocation key (ioa_AllocKey) is
    correct, CMD_CLEAR does nothing; otherwise, CMD_CLEAR returns an error
    (ADIOERR_NOALLOCATION).  CMD_CLEAR is synchronous and only replies
    (mn_ReplyPort) if the quick flag (IOF_QUICK) is clear.

INPUTS
    mn_ReplyPort- pointer to message port that receives I/O request after
                  if the quick flag (IOF_QUICK) is clear
    io_Device   - pointer to device node, must be set by (or copied from
                  I/O block set by) OpenDevice function
    io_Unit     - bit map of channels to clear (bits 0 thru 3 correspond
                  to channels 0 thru 3)
    io_Command  - command number for CMD_CLEAR
    io_Flags    - flags, must be cleared if not used:
                  IOF_QUICK - (CLEAR) reply I/O request
    ioa_AllocKey- allocation key, must be set by (or copied from I/O block
                  set by) OpenDevice function or ADCMD_ALLOCATE command

OUTPUTS
    io_Unit     - bit map of channels successfully cleared (bits 0 thru 3
                  correspond to channels 0 thru 3)
    io_Error    - error number:
                  0                    - no error
                  ADIOERR_NOALLOCATION - allocation key (ioa_AllocKey)
                                         does not match key for channel
```

```
audio.device/CMD_FLUSH                    audio.device/command/CMD_FLUSH

   NAME
       CMD_FLUSH -- cancel all pending I/O

   FUNCTION
       CMD_FLUSH is a standard command for multiple audio channels.  For each
       selected channel (io_Unit), if the allocation key (ioa_AllocKey) is
       correct, CMD_FLUSH aborts all writes (CMD_WRITE) in progress or queued
       and any I/O requests waiting to synchronize with the end of the cycle
       (ADCMD_WAITCYCLE); otherwise, CMD_FLUSH returns an error
       (ADIOERR_NOALLOCATION).  CMD_FLUSH is synchronous and only replies
       (mn_ReplyPort) if the quick flag (IOF_QUICK) is clear.  Do not use
       CMD_FLUSH in interrupt code at interrupt level 5 or higher.

   INPUTS
       mn_ReplyPort- pointer to message port that receives I/O request
                     if the quick flag (IOF_QUICK) is clear
       io_Device   - pointer to device node, must be set by (or copied from
                     I/O block set by) OpenDevice function
       io_Unit     - bit map of channels to flush (bits 0 thru 3 correspond
                     to channels 0 thru 3)
       io_Command  - command number for CMD_FLUSH
       io_Flags    - flags, must be cleared if not used:
                     IOF_QUICK - (CLEAR) reply I/O request
       ioa_AllocKey- allocation key, must be set by (or copied from I/O block
                     set by) OpenDevice function or ADCMD_ALLOCATE command

   OUTPUTS
       io_Unit     - bit map of channels successfully flushed (bits 0 thru 3
                     correspond to channels 0 thru 3)
       io_Error    - error number:
                     0                      - no error
                     ADIOERR_NOALLOCATION - allocation key (ioa_AllocKey)
                                            does not match key for channel
```

```
audio.device/CMD_READ                      audio.device/command/CMD_READ

   NAME
       CMD_READ -- normal I/O entry point

   FUNCTION
       CMD_READ is a standard command for a single audio channel (io_Unit).
       If the allocation key (ioa_AllocKey) is correct, CMD_READ returns a
       pointer (io_Data) to the I/O block currently writing (CMD_WRITE) on
       the selected channel; otherwise, CMD_READ returns an error
       (ADIOERR_NOALLOCATION).  If there is no write in progress, CMD_READ
       returns zero.  CMD_READ is synchronous and only replies (mn_ReplyPort)
       if the quick bit (IOF_QUICK) is clear.

   INPUTS
       mn_ReplyPort- pointer to message port that receives I/O request after
                     if the quick flag (IOF_QUICK) is clear
       io_Device   - pointer to device node, must be set by (or copied from
                     I/O block set by) OpenDevice function
       io_Unit     - bit map of channel to read (bit 0 thru 3 corresponds to
                     channel 0 thru 3), if more then one bit is set lowest
                     bit number channel read
       io_Command  - command number for CMD_READ
       io_Flags    - flags, must be cleared if not used:
                     IOF_QUICK - (CLEAR) reply I/O request
       ioa_AllocKey- allocation key, must be set by (or copied from I/O block
                     set by) OpenDevice function or ADCMD_ALLOCATE command

   OUTPUTS
       io_Unit     - bit map of channel successfully read (bit 0 thru 3
                     corresponds to channel 0 thru 3)
       io_Error    - error number:
                     0                      - no error
                     ADIOERR_NOALLOCATION - allocation key (ioa_AllocKey)
                                            does not match key for channel
       ioa_Data    - pointer to I/O block for current write, zero if none is
                     progress
```

```
NAME
    CMD_RESET -- restore device to a known state

FUNCTION
    CMD_RESET is a standard command for multiple audio channels.  For each
    selected channel (io_Unit), if the allocation key (ioa_AllocKey) is
    correct, CMD_RESET:
       . clears the hardware audio registers and attach bits,
       . sets the audio interrupt vector,
       . cancels all pending I/O (CMD_FLUSH), and
       . un-stops the channel if it is stopped (CMD_STOP),

    Otherwise, CMD_RESET returns an error (ADIOERR_NOALLOCATION).
    CMD_RESET is synchronous and only replies (mn_ReplyPort) if the quick
    flag (IOF_QUICK) is clear.  Do not use CMD_RESET in interrupt code at
    interrupt level 5 or higher.

INPUTS
    mn_ReplyPort- pointer to message port that receives I/O request
                  if the quick flag (IOF_QUICK) is clear
    io_Device   - pointer to device node, must be set by (or copied from
                  I/O block set by) OpenDevice function
    io_Unit     - bit map of channels to reset (bits 0 thru 3 correspond
                  to channels 0 thru 3)
    io_Command  - command number for CMD_RESET
    io_Flags    - flags, must be cleared if not used:
                  IOF_QUICK - (CLEAR) reply I/O request
    ioa_AllocKey- allocation key, must be set by (or copied from I/O block
                  set by) OpenDevice function or ADCMD_ALLOCATE command

OUTPUTS
    io_Unit     - bit map of channels to successfully reset (bits 0 thru 3
                  correspond to channels 0 thru 3)
    io_Error    - error number:
                  0                   - no error
                  ADIOERR_NOALLOCATION - allocation key (ioa_AllocKey)
                                        does not match key for channel
```



```
NAME
    CMD_START -- start device processing (like ^Q)

FUNCTION
    CMD_START is a standard command for multiple audio channels.  For each
    selected channel (io_Unit), if the allocation key (ioa_AllocKey) is
    correct and the channel was previously stopped (CMD_STOP), CMP_START
    immediately starts all writes (CMD_WRITE) to the channel.  If the
    allocation key is incorrect, CMD_START returns an error
    (ADIOERR_NOALLOCATION).  CMD_START starts multiple channels
    simultaneously to minimize distortion if the channels are playing the
    same waveform and their outputs are mixed. CMD_START is synchronous and

    only replies (mn_ReplyPort) if the quick flag (IOF_QUICK) is clear.  Do

    not use CMD_START in interrupt code at interrupt level 5 or higher.

INPUTS
    mn_ReplyPort- pointer to message port that receives I/O request after
                  if the quick flag (IOF_QUICK) is clear
    io_Device   - pointer to device node, must be set by (or copied from
                  I/O block set by) OpenDevice function
    io_Unit     - bit map of channels to start (bits 0 thru 3 correspond
                  to channels 0 thru 3)
    io_Command  - command number for CMD_START
    io_Flags    - flags, must be cleared if not used:
                  IOF_QUICK - (CLEAR) reply I/O request
    ioa_AllocKey- allocation key, must be set by (or copied from I/O block
                  set by) OpenDevice function or ADCMD_ALLOCATE command

OUTPUTS
    io_Unit     - bit map of channels successfully started (bits 0 thru 3
                  correspond to channels 0 thru 3)
    io_Error    - error number:
                  0                   - no error
                  ADIOERR_NOALLOCATION - allocation key (ioa_AllocKey)
                                        does not match key for channel
```

```
NAME
    CMD_STOP -- stop device processing (like ^S)

FUNCTION
    CMD_STOP is a standard command for multiple audio channels.  For each
    selected channel (io_Unit), if the allocation key (ioa_AllocKey) is
    correct, CMD_STOP immediately stops any writes (CMD_WRITE) in
    progress; otherwise, CMD_STOP returns an error (ADIOERR_NOALLOCATION).
    CMD_WRITE queues up writes to a stopped channel until CMD_START starts
    the channel or CMD_RESET resets the channel. CMD_STOP is synchronous
    and only replies (mn_ReplyPort) if the quick flag (IOF_QUICK) is
    clear.  Do not use CMD_STOP in interrupt code at interrupt level 5 or
    higher.

INPUTS
    mn_ReplyPort- pointer to message port that receives I/O request after
                  if the quick flag (IOF_QUICK) is clear
    io_Device   - pointer to device node, must be set by (or copied from
                  I/O block set by) OpenDevice function
    io_Unit     - bit map of channels to stop (bits 0 thru 3 correspond to
                  channels 0 thru 3)
    io_Command  - command number for CMD_STOP
    io_Flags    - flags, must be cleared if not used:
                  IOF_QUICK - (CLEAR) reply I/O request
    ioa_AllocKey- allocation key, must be set by (or copied from I/O block
                  set by) OpenDevice function or ADCMD_ALLOCATE command

OUTPUTS
    io_Unit     - bit map of channels successfully stopped (bits 0 thru 3
                  correspond to channels 0 thru 3)
    io_Error    - error number:
                  0                    - no error
                  ADIOERR_NOALLOCATION - allocation key (ioa_AllocKey)
                                         does not match key for channel
```



```
NAME
    CMD_UPDATE -- force dirty buffers out

FUNCTION
    CMD_UPDATE is a standard command for multiple audio channels.  For
    each selected channel (io_Unit), if the allocation key (ioa_AllocKey)
    is correct, CMD_UPDATE does nothing; otherwise, CMD_UPDATE returns an
    error (ADIOERR_NOALLOCATION).  CMD_UPDATE is synchronous and only
    replies (mn_ReplyPort) if the quick flag (IOF_QUICK) is clear.

INPUTS
    mn_ReplyPort- pointer to message port that receives I/O request after
                  if the quick flag (IOF_QUICK) is clear
    io_Device   - pointer to device node, must be set by (or copied from
                  I/O block set by) OpenDevice function
    io_Unit     - bit map of channels to update (bits 0 thru 3 correspond
                  to channels 0 thru 3)
    io_Command  - command number for CMD_UPDATE
    io_Flags    - flags, must be cleared if not used:
                  IOF_QUICK - (CLEAR) reply I/O request
    ioa_AllocKey- allocation key, must be set by (or copied from I/O block
                  set by) OpenDevice function or ADCMD_ALLOCATE command

OUTPUTS
    io_Unit     - bit map of channels successfully updated (bits 0 thru 3
                  correspond to channels 0 thru 3)
    io_Error    - error number:
                  0                    - no error
                  ADIOERR_NOALLOCATION - allocation key (ioa_AllocKey)
                                         does not match key for channel
```

```
NAME
     CMD_WRITE -- normal I/O entry point

FUNCTION
     CMD_WRITE is a standard command for a single audio channel (io_Unit).
     If the allocation key (ioa_AllocKey) is correct, CMD_WRITE plays a
     sound using the selected channel; otherwise, it returns an error
     (ADIOERR_NOALLOCATION).  CMD_WRITE queues up requests if there is
     another write in progress or if the channel is stopped (CMD_STOP).
     When the write actually starts; if the ADIOF_PERVOL flag is set,
     CMD_WRITE loads volume (ioa_Volume) and period (ioa_Period), and if
     the ADIOF_WRITEMESSAGE flag is set, CMD_WRITE replies the write
     message (ioa_WriteMsg).  CMD_WRITE returns an error (IOERR_ABORTED) if
     it is canceled (AbortIO) or the channel is stolen (ADCMD_ALLOCATE).
     CMD_WRITE is only asynchronous if there is no error, in which case it
     clears the quick flag (IOF_QUICK) and replies the I/O request
     (mn_ReplyPort) after it finishes writting; otherwise, it is synchronous

     and only replies if the quick flag (IOF_QUICK) is clear.  Do not use
     CMD_WRITE in interrupt code at interrupt level 5 or higher.

INPUTS
     mn_ReplyPort- pointer to message port that receives I/O request after
                   the write completes
     io_Device   - pointer to device node, must be set by (or copied from
                   I/O block set by) OpenDevice function
     io_Unit     - bit map of channel to write (bit 0 thru 3 corresponds to
                   channel 0 thru 3), if more then one bit is set lowest
                   bit number channel is written
     io_Command  - command number for CMD_WRITE
     io_Flags    - flags, must be cleared if not used:
                   ADIOF_PERVOL       - (SET) load volume and period
                   ADIOF_WRITEMESSAGE - (SET) reply message at write start
     ioa_AllocKey- allocation key, must be set by (or copied from I/O block
                   set by) OpenDevice function or ADCMD_ALLOCATE command
     ioa_Data    - pointer to waveform array (signed bytes (-128 thru 127)
                   in custom chip addressable ram and word aligned)
     ioa_Length  - length of the wave array in bytes (2 thru 131072, must
                   be even number)
     ioa_Period  - sample period in 279.365 ns increments (124 thru 65536,
                   anti-aliasing filter works below 300 to 500 depending on
                   waveform), if enabled by ADIOF_PERVOL
     ioa_Volume  - volume (0 thru 64, linear), if enabled by ADIOF_PERVOL
     ioa_Cycles  - number of times to repeat array (0 thru 65535, 0 for
                   infinite)
     ioa_WriteMsg- message replied at start of write,  if enabled by
                   ADIOF_WRITEMESSAGE

OUTPUTS
     io_Unit     - bit map of channel successfully written (bit 0 thru 3
                   corresponds to channel 0 thru 3)
     io_Flags    - IOF_QUICK flag cleared if there is no error
     io_Error    - error number:
                   0                    - no error
                   IOERR_ABORTED        - canceled (AbortIO) or channel
                                          stolen
                   ADIOERR_NOALLOCATION - allocation key (ioa_AllocKey)
                                          does not match key for channel

BUGS
     If CMD_WRITE starts the write immediately after stopping a previous
     write, you must set the ADIOF_PERVOL flag or else the new data pointer
     (ioa_Data) and length (ioa_Length) may not be loaded.
```



```
NAME
     OpenDevice - open the audio device

SYNOPSIS
     error = OpenDevice("audio.device", unitNumber, iORequest, flags);

FUNCTION
     The OpenDevice routine grants access to the audio device.  It takes an
     I/O audio request block (iORequest) and if it can successfully open
     the audio device, it loads the device pointer (io_Device) and the
     allocation key (ioa_AllocKey); otherwise, it returns an error
     (IOERR_OPENFAIL).  OpenDevice increments the open count keeping the
     device from being expunged (Expunge).  If the length (ioa_Length) is
     non-zero, OpenDevice tries to allocate (ADCMD_ALLOCATE) audio channels
     from a array of channel combination options (ioa_Data). If the
     allocation succeeds, the allocated channel combination is loaded into
     the unit field (ioa_Unit); otherwise, OpenDevice returns an error
     (ADIOERR_ALLOCFAILED).  OpenDevice does not wait for allocation to
     succeed and closes (CloseDevice) the audio device if it fails.  To
     allocate channels, OpenDevice also requires a properly initialized
     reply port (mn_ReplyPort) with an allocated signal bit.

INPUTS
     unitNumber- not used
     iORequest - pointer to audio request block (struct IOAudio)
             ln_Pri       - allocation precedence (-128 thru 127), only
                            necessary for allocation (non-zero length)
             mn_ReplyPort- pointer to message port for allocation, only
                            necessary for allocation (non-zero length)
             ioa_AllocKey- allocation key; zero to generate new key.
                            Otherwise, it must be set by (or copied from I/O
                            block that is set by) previous OpenDevice
                            function or ADCMD_ALLOCATE command (non-zero
                            length)
             ioa_Data     - pointer to channel combination options (byte
                            array, bits 0 thru 3 correspond to channels 0
                            thru 3), only necessary for allocation (non-zero
                            length)
             ioa_Length   - length of the channel combination option array
                            (0 thru 16), zero for no allocation
     flags      - not used

OUTPUTS
     iORequest - pointer to audio request block (struct IOAudio)
             io_Device    - pointer to device node if OpenDevice succeeds,
                            otherwise -1
             io_Unit      - bit map of successfully allocated channels (bits
                            0 thru 3 correspond to channels 0 thru 3)
             io_Error     - error number:
                            0                   - no error
                            IOERR_OPENFAIL      - open failed
                            ADIOERR_ALLOCFAILED - allocation failed, no open
             ioa_AllocKey- allocation key, set to a unique number if passed
                            a zero and OpenDevice succeeds
     error      - copy of io_Error
```

TABLE OF CONTENTS

NAME
CBD_POST - post clip to clipboard

FUNCTION
Indicate to the clipboard device that data is available for use by accessors of the clipboard. This is intended to be used when a cut is large, in a private data format, and/or changing frequently, and it thus makes sense to avoid converting it to an IFF form and writing it to the clipboard unless another application wants it. The post provides a message port to which the clipboard device will send a satisfy message if the data is required.

If the satisfy message is received, the write associated with the post must be performed. The act of writing the clip indicates that the message has been received: it may then be re-used by the clipboard device, and so must actually be removed from the satisfy message port so that the port is not corrupted.

If the application wishes to determine if a post it has performed is still the current clip, it should check the post's io_ClipID with that returned by the CBD_CLIPREADID command. If ClipID is greater, the clip is not still current.

If an application has a pending post and wishes to determine if it should satisfy it (e.g. before it exits), it should check the post's io_ClipID with that returned by the CBD_CLIPWRITEID command. If CurrentWriteID is greater, there is no need to satisfy the post.

IO REQUEST

io_Message	mn_ReplyPort set up
io_Device	preset by OpenDevice
io_Unit	preset by OpenDevice
io_Command	CBD_POST
io_Data	pointer to satisfy message port
io_ClipID	zero

RESULTS

io_Error	non-zero if an error occurred
io_ClipID	the clip ID assigned to this post, to be used in the write command if this is satisfied

```
NAME
     CBD_CLIPREADID - determine the current read identifier.

FUNCTION
     CBD_CLIPREADID fills the io_ClipID with a clip identifier that
     can be compared with that of a post command: if greater than
     the post identifier then the post data held privately by an
     application is not valid for its own pasting.

IO REQUEST
     io_Message      mn_ReplyPort set up
     io_Device       preset by OpenDevice
     io_Unit         preset by OpenDevice
     io_Command      CBD_CLIPREADID


     io_ClipID       the ClipID of the current write is set
```



```
NAME
     CBD_CLIPWRITEID - determine the current write identifier.

FUNCTION
     CBD_CLIPWRITEID fills the io_ClipID with a clip identifier that
     can be compared with that of a post command: if greater than
     the post identifier then the post is obsolete and need never
     be satisfied.

IO REQUEST
     io_Message      mn_ReplyPort set up
     io_Device       preset by OpenDevice
     io_Unit         preset by OpenDevice
     io_Command      CBD_CLIPWRITEID


     io_ClipID       the ClipID of the current write is set
```

NAME
CMD_READ - read clip from clipboard

FUNCTION
The read function serves two purposes.

When io_Offset is within the clip, this acts as a normal read request, and io_Data is filled with data from the clipboard. The first read request should have a zero io_ClipID, which will be filled with the ID assigned for this read. Normal sequential access from the beginning of the clip is achieved by setting io_Offset to zero for the first read, then leaving it untouched for subsequent reads. If io_Data is null, then io_Offset is incremented by io_Actual as if io_Length bytes had been read: this is useful to skip to the end of file by using a huge io_Length.

When io_Offset is beyond the end of the clip, this acts as a signal to the clipboard device that the application is through reading this clip. Realize that while an application is in the middle of reading a clip, any attempts to write new data to the clipboard are held off. This read past the end of file indicates that those operations may now be initiated.

```
IO REQUEST
    io_Message      mn_ReplyPort set up
    io_Device       preset by OpenDevice
    io_Unit         preset by OpenDevice
    io_Command      CMD_READ
    io_Length       number of bytes to put in data buffer
    io_Data         pointer to buffer of data to fill, or null to
                    skip over data
    io_Offset       byte offset of data to read
    io_ClipID       zero if this is the initial read

RESULTS
    io_Error        non-zero if an error occurred
    io_Actual       filled with the actual number of bytes read
    io_Data         (the buffer now has io_Actual bytes of data)
    io_Offset       updated to next read position, which is
                    beyond EOF if io_Actual != io_Length
    io_ClipID       the clip ID assigned to this read: do not
                    alter for subsequent reads
```


NAME
CMD_RESET - reset the clipboard

FUNCTION
CMD_RESET resets the clipboard device without destroying handles to the open device.

```
IO REQUEST
    io_Message      mn_ReplyPort set up
    io_Device       preset by OpenDevice
    io_Command      CMD_RESET
    io_Flags        IOB_QUICK set if quick I/O is possible
```

```
NAME
     CMD_UPDATE - terminate the writing of a cut to the clipboard

FUNCTION
     Indicate to the clipboard that the previous write commands are
     complete and can be used for any pending pastes (reads).  This
     command cannot be issued while any of the write commands are
     pending.

IO REQUEST
     io_Message      mn_ReplyPort set up
     io_Device       preset by OpenDevice
     io_Unit         preset by OpenDevice
     io_Command      CMD_UPDATE
     io_ClipID       the ClipID of the write

RESULTS
     io_Error        non-zero if an error occurred
```



```
NAME
     CMD_WRITE - write clip to clipboard

FUNCTION
     This command writes data to the clipboard.  This data can be
     provided sequentially by clearing io_Offset for the initial
     write, and using the incremented value unaltered for
     subsequent writes.  If io_Offset is ever beyond the current
     clip size, the clip is padded with zeros.

     If this write is in response to a SatisfyMsg for a pending
     post, then the io_ClipID returned by the Post command must
     be used.  Otherwise, a new ID is obtained by clearing the
     io_ClipID for the first write.  Subsequent writes must not
     alter the io_ClipID.

IO REQUEST
     io_Message      mn_ReplyPort set up
     io_Device       preset by OpenDevice
     io_Unit         preset by OpenDevice
     io_Command      CMD_WRITE
     io_Length       number of bytes from io_Data to write
     io_Data         pointer to block of data to write
     io_Offset       usually zero if this is the initial write
     io_ClipID       zero if this is the initial write, ClipID of
                     the Post if this is to satisfy a post

RESULTS
     io_Error        non-zero if an error occurred
     io_Actual       filled with the actual number of bytes written
     io_Offset       updated to next write position
     io_ClipID       the clip ID assigned to this write: do not
                     alter for subsequent writes
```

TABLE OF CONTENTS

console.device/CD_ASKDEFAULTKEYMAP

```
   NAME
       CD_ASKDEFAULTKEYMAP - get the current default keymap

   FUNCTION
       Fill the io_Data buffer with the current console device
       default keymap, which is used to initialize console unit
       keymaps when opened, and by RawKeyConvert with a null
       keyMap parameter.

   IO REQUEST
       io_Message      mn_ReplyPort set if quick I/O is not possible
       io_Device       preset by the call to OpenDevice
       io_Unit         preset by the call to OpenDevice
       io_Command      CD_ASKDEFAULTKEYMAP
       io_Flags        IOF_QUICK if quick I/O possible, else zero
       io_Length       sizeof(*keyMap)
       io_Data         struct KeyMap *keyMap
                       pointer to a structure that describes
                       the raw keycode to byte stream conversion.

   RESULTS
       This function sets the io_Error field in the IOStdReq, and fills
       the structure pointed to by io_Data with the current device
       default key map.

   BUGS

   SEE ALSO
       exec/io.h, devices/keymap.h, devices/console.h
```

```
console.device/CD_ASKKEYMAP          console.device/command/CD_ASKKEYMAP

    NAME
        CD_ASKKEYMAP - get the current key map structure for this console

    FUNCTION
        Fill the io_Data buffer with the current KeyMap structure in
        use by this console unit.

    IO REQUEST
        io_Message      mn_ReplyPort set if quick I/O is not possible
        io_Device       preset by the call to OpenDevice
        io_Unit         preset by the call to OpenDevice
        io_Command      CD_ASKKEYMAP
        io_Flags        IOF_QUICK if quick I/O possible, else zero
        io_Length       sizeof(*keyMap)
        io_Data         struct KeyMap *keyMap
                        pointer to a structure that describes
                        the raw keycode to byte stream conversion.

    RESULTS
        This function sets the io_Error field in the IOStdReq, and fills
        the structure the structure pointed to by io_Data with the current
         key map.

    BUGS

    SEE ALSO
        exec/io.h, devices/keymap.h, devices/console.h
```

```
console.device/CD_SETDEFAULTKEYMAP

    NAME
        CD_SETDEFAULTKEYMAP - set the current default keymap

    FUNCTION
        This console command copies the keyMap structure pointed to
        by io_Data to the console device default keymap, which is used
        to initialize console units when opened, and by RawKeyConvert
        with a null keyMap parameter.

    IO REQUEST
        io_Message      mn_ReplyPort set if quick I/O is not possible
        io_Device       preset by the call to OpenDevice
        io_Unit         preset by the call to OpenDevice
        io_Command      CD_SETDEFAULTKEYMAP
        io_Flags        IOF_QUICK if quick I/O possible, else zero
        io_Length       sizeof(*keyMap)
        io_Data         struct KeyMap *keyMap
                        pointer to a structure that describes
                        the raw keycode to byte stream conversion.

    RESULTS
        This function sets the io_Error field in the IOStdReq, and fills
        the current device default key map from the structure pointed to
        by io_Data.

    BUGS

    SEE ALSO
        exec/io.h, devices/keymap.h, devices/console.h
```

```
console.device/CD_SETKEYMAP          console.device/command/CD_SETKEYMAP

    NAME
        CD_SETKEYMAP - set the current key map structure for this console

    FUNCTION
        Set the current KeyMap structure used by this console unit to
        the structure pointed to by io_Data.

    IO REQUEST
        io_Message      mn_ReplyPort set if quick I/O is not possible
        io_Device       preset by the call to OpenDevice
        io_Unit         preset by the call to OpenDevice
        io_Command      CD_SETKEYMAP
        io_Flags        IOF_QUICK if quick I/O possible, else zero
        io_Length       sizeof(*keyMap)
        io_Data         struct KeyMap *keyMap
                        pointer to a structure that describes
                        the raw keycode to byte stream conversion.

    RESULTS
        This function sets the io_Error field in the IOStdReq, and fills
        the current key map from the structure pointed to by io_Data.

    BUGS

    SEE ALSO
        exec/io.h, devices/keymap.h, devices/console.h
```

```
console.device/CDInputHandler

    NAME
        CDInputHandler - handle an input event for the console device

    SYNOPSIS
        events = CDInputHandler(events, consoleDevice)
                                A0      A1

    FUNCTION
        Accept input events from the producer, which is usually the
        rom input.task.

    INPUTS
        events - a pointer to a list of input events.
        consoleDevice - a pointer to the library base address of the
            console device.  This has the same value as ConsoleDevice
            described below.

    RESULTS
        events - a pointer to a list of input events not used by this
            handler.

    NOTES
        This function is available for historical reasons.  It is
        preferred that input events be fed to the system via the
        WriteEvent command of the input.device.

        This function is different from standard device commands in
        that it is a function in the console device library vectors.
        In order to obtain a valid library base pointer for the
        console device (a.k.a. ConsoleDevice) call
        OpenDevice("console.device", -1, IOStdReq, 0),
        and then grab the io_Device pointer field out of the IOStdReq
        and use as ConsoleDevice.

    BUGS

    SEE ALSO
        input.device
```

console.device/CMD_CLEAR   console.device/command/CMD_CLEAR

NAME

CMD_CLEAR - clear console input buffer

FUNCTION

Remove from the input buffer any reports waiting to satisfy read requests.

IO REQUEST

io_Message	mn_ReplyPort set if quick I/O is not possible
io_Device	preset by the call to OpenDevice
io_Unit	preset by the call to OpenDevice
io_Command	CMD_CLEAR
io_Flags	IOB_QUICK set if quick I/O is possible, else 0

BUGS

SEE ALSO

exec/io.h, devices/console.h

console.device/CMD_READ   console.device/command/CMD_READ

NAME

CMD_READ - return the next input from the keyboard

FUNCTION

Read the next input, generally from the keyboard. The form of this input is as an ANSI byte stream: i.e. either ASCII text or control sequences. Raw input events received by the console device can be selectively filtered via the aSRE and aRRE control sequences (see the write command). Keys are converted via the keymap associated with the unit, which is modified with CD_AKSKEYMAP and CD_SETKEYMAP

If, for example, raw keycodes had been enabled by writing <CSI>1{ to the console (where <CSI> is $9B or Esc[), keys would return raw keycode reports with the information from the input event itself, in the form:
<CSI>1;0;<keycode>;<qualifiers>;0;0;<seconds>;<microseconds>q

If there is no pending input, this command will not be satisfied, but if there is some input, but not as much as can fill io_Length, the request will be satisfied with the input currently available.

IO REQUEST

io_Message	mn_ReplyPort set if quick I/O is not possible
io_Device	preset by the call to OpenDevice
io_Unit	preset by the call to OpenDevice
io_Command	CMD_READ
io_Flags	IOF_QUICK if quick I/O possible, else zero
io_Length	sizeof(*buffer)
io_Data	char buffer[] a pointer to the destination for the characters to read from the keyboard.

RESULTS

This function sets the error field in the IOStdReq, and fills in the io_Data area with the next input, and io_Actual with the number of bytes read.

BUGS

SEE ALSO

exec/io.h, devices/console.h

```
    NAME
        CMD_WRITE - write text to the display

    FUNCTION
        Write a text record to the display.  Note that the RPort of
        the console window is in use while this write command is
        pending.

    IO REQUEST
        io_Message      mn_ReplyPort set if quick I/O is not possible
        io_Device       preset by the call to OpenDevice
        io_Unit         preset by the call to OpenDevice
        io_Command      CMD_WRITE
        io_Flags        IOF_QUICK if quick I/O possible, else zero
        io_Length       sizeof(*buffer), or -1 if null terminated
        io_Data         char buffer[]
                        a pointer to a buffer containing the ANSI text
                        to write to the console device.

    ANSI CODES SUPPORTED

        Independent Control Functions (no introducer) --
        Code    Name    Definition
        -----   ---     ---------------------------------------------
        00/ 7   BEL     BELL (actually a DisplayBeep)
        00/ 8   BS      BACKSPACE
        00/ 9   HT      HORIZONTAL TAB
        00/10   LF      LINE FEED
        00/11   VT      VERTICAL TAB
        00/12   FF      FORM FEED
        00/13   CR      CARRIAGE RETURN
        00/14   SO      SHIFT OUT
        00/15   SI      SHIFT IN
        01/11   ESC     ESCAPE

        Code or Esc Name Definition
        -----   --- ---- ---------------------------------------------
        08/ 4   D   IND  INDEX: move the active position down one line
        08/ 5   E   NEL  NEXT LINE:
        08/ 8   H   HTS  HORIZONTAL TABULATION SET
        08/13   M   RI   REVERSE INDEX:
        09/11   [   CSI  CONTROL SEQUENCE INTRODUCER: see next list

        ISO Compatable Escape Sequences (introduced by Esc) --
        Esc   Name Definition
        ----- ---- ---------------------------------------------------
        c     RIS  RESET TO INITIAL STATE

        Control Sequences, with the number of indicated parameters.
        i.e. <CSI><parameters><control sequence letter(s)>.  Note the
        last entries consist of a space and a letter.  CSI is either
        9B or Esc[.  A minus after the number of parameters (#p)
        indicates less is valid.  Parameters are seperated by
        semicolins, e.g. Esc[14;80H sets the cursor position to row
        14, column 80.
        CSI #p  Name Definition
        --- --- ---- ---------------------------------------------------
        @   1-  ICH  INSERT CHARACTER
        A   1-  CUU  CURSOR UP
        B   1-  CUD  CURSOR DOWN
        C   1-  CUF  CURSOR FORWARD
        D   1-  CUB  CURSOR BACKWARD
        E   1-  CNL  CURSOR NEXT LINE
        F   1-  CPL  CURSOR PRECEEDING LINE
        H   2-  CUP  CURSOR POSITION
        I   1-  CHT  CURSOR HORIZONTAL TABULATION
        J   1-  ED   ERASE IN DISPLAY (only to end of display)
        K   1-  EL   ERASE IN LINE (only to end of line)
        L   1-  IL   INSERT LINE
        M   1-  DL   DELETE LINE
        P   1-  DCH  DELETE CHARACTER
        R   2   CPR  CURSOR POSITION REPORT (in Read stream only)
        S   1-  SU   SCROLL UP
        T   1-  SD   SCROLL DOWN
        W   n   CTC  CURSOR TABULATION CONTROL
        Z   1-  CBT  CURSOR BACKWARD TABULATION
        f   2-  HVP  HORIZONTAL AND VERTICAL POSITION
        g   1-  TBC  TABULATION CLEAR
        h   n   SM   SET MODE
        l   n   RM   RESET MODE
        m   n   SGR  SELECT GRAPHIC RENDITION
        n   1-  DSR  DEVICE STATUS REPORT
        t   1-  aSLPP SET PAGE LENGTH (private Amiga sequence)
        u   1-  aSLL SET LINE LENGTH (private Amiga sequence)
        x   1-  aSLO SET LEFT OFFSET (private Amiga sequence)
        y   1-  aSTO SET TOP OFFSET (private Amiga sequence)
        {   n   aSRE SET RAW EVENTS (private Amiga sequence)
        |   8   aIER INPUT EVENT REPORT (private Amiga Read sequence)
        }   n   aRRE RESET RAW EVENTS (private Amiga sequence)
        ~   1   aSKR SPECIAL KEY REPORT (private Amiga Read sequence)
         p  1-  aSCR SET CURSOR RENDITION (private Amiga sequence)
         q  0   aWSR WINDOW STATUS REQUEST (private Amiga sequence)
         r  4   aWBR WINDOW BOUNDS REPORT (private Amiga Read sequence)

        Modes, set with <CSI><mode-list>h, and cleared with
        <CSI><mode-list>l, where the mode-list is one or more of the
        following parameters, seperated by semicolins --
        Mode    Name Definition
        ------- ---- ----------------------------------------------------
        20      LNM  LINEFEED NEWLINE MODE: if a linefeed is a newline
        >1      ASM  AUTO SCROLL MODE: if scroll at bottom of window
        ?7      AWM  AUTO WRAP MODE: if wrap at right edge of window

    BUGS
        Does not display cursor in SuperBitMap layers.

    SEE ALSO
        ROM Kernal Manual: libraries and devices, exec/io.h
```

console.device/CloseDevice

```
NAME
   Close -- close the console device

SYNOPSIS
   CloseDevice(IOStdReq)

FUNCTION
    This function closes software access to the console device,
    and informs the system that access to this device/unit which was
    previously opened has been concluded.  The device may perform
    certain house-cleaning  operations.  The I/O request structure
    is now free to be recycled.

INPUTS
    IOStdReq - pointer to an IOStdReq structure, set by OpenDevice

BUGS

SEE ALSO
    console.device/OpenDevice, exec/io.h
```

console.device/OpenDevice   console.device/function/OpenDevice

```
NAME
    OpenDevice - a request to open a Console device

SYNOPSIS
    error = OpenDevice("console.device", unit, IOStdReq, 0 )
    D0                  A0               D0    A1        D1

FUNCTION
    The open routine grants access to a device.  There are two
    fields in the IOStdReq block that will be filled in: the
    io_Device field and possibly the io_Unit field.

    This open command differs from most other device open commands
    in that it requires some information to be supplied in the
    io_Data field of the IOStdReq block.  This initialization
    information supplies the window that is used by the console
    device for output.

    The unit number that is a standard parameter for an open call
    is used specially by this device.  A unit of -1 indicates that
    no actual console is to be opened, and is used to get a pointer
    to the device library vector ( which will be returned in the
    io_Device field of the IOStdReq block ).  A unit of zero binds
    the supplied window to a unique console.  Sharing a console
    must be done at a level higher than the device.  There are no
    other valid unit numbers.

IO REQUEST
    io_Data          struct Window *window
                     This is the window that will be used for this
                     console.  It must be supplied if the unit in
                     the OpenDevice call is 0 (see above).  The
                     RPort of this window is potentially in use by
                     the console whenever there is an outstanding
                     write command.
INPUTS
    "console.device" - a pointer to the name of the device to be opened.
    unit - the unit number to open on that device (0, or -1).
    IOStdReq - a pointer to a standard request block
    0 - a flag field of zero

RESULTS
    error - zero if successful, else an error is returned.

BUGS
    If a console.device is attached to a SUPERBITMAP window, the cursor
    will not be displayed.  In this case you are required to TURN OFF the
    console's cursor (with the standard escape sequence), and synthisize
    your own.  Memory loss and compatiblity problems are possible if the
    cursor is not turned off.

SEE ALSO
    console.device/CloseDevice, exec/io.h, intuition/intuition.h
```

```
console.device/RawKeyConvert

    NAME
        RawKeyConvert - decode raw input classes

    SYNOPSIS
        actual = RawKeyConvert(event, buffer, length, keyMap)
        D0                     A0     A1      D1      A2

        ConsoleDevice in A6 if called from Assembly Language.

    FUNCTION
        This console function converts input events of type
        IECLASS_RAWKEY to ANSI bytes, based on the keyMap, and
        places the result into the buffer.

    INPUTS
        event -  an InputEvent structure pointer.
        buffer - a byte buffer large enough to hold all anticipated
            characters generated by this conversion.
        length - maximum anticipation, i.e. the buffer size in bytes.
        keyMap - a KeyMap structure pointer, or null if the default
            console device key map is to be used.

    RESULTS
        actual - the number of characters in the buffer, or -1 if
            a buffer overflow was about to occur.

    ERRORS
        if actual is -1, a buffer overflow condition was detected.
        Not all of the characters in the buffer are valid.

    NOTES
        This function is different from standard device commands in
        that it is a function in the console device library vectors.
        In order to obtain a valid library base pointer for the
        console device (a.k.a. ConsoleDevice) call
        OpenDevice("console.device", -1, IOStdReq, 0),
        and then grab the io_Device pointer field out of the IOStdReq
        and use as ConsoleDevice.

    BUGS

    SEE ALSO
        console.device/OpenDevice, exec/io.h,
            devices/inputevent.h, devices/keymap.h
```

TABLE OF CONTENTS


```
NAME
     CMD_CLEAR - clear gameport input buffer

FUNCTION
     Remove from the input buffer any gameport reports waiting to
     satisfy read requests.

IO REQUEST
     io_Message      mn_ReplyPort set if quick I/O is not possible
     io_Device       preset by the call to OpenDevice
     io_Unit         preset by the call to OpenDevice
     io_Command      CMD_CLEAR
     io_Flags        IOB_QUICK set if quick I/O is possible
```

```
NAME
     GPD_ASKCTYPE - inquire the current game port controller type

FUNCTION
     This command identifies the type of controller at the game
     port, so that the signals at the port may be properly
     interpreted.  The controller type has been set by a previous
     GPD_SETCTYPE.

     This command always executes immediately.

IO REQUEST
     io_Message      mn_ReplyPort set if quick I/O is not possible
     io_Device       preset by the call to OpenDevice
     io_Unit         preset by the call to OpenDevice
     io_Command      GPD_ASKCTYPE
     io_Flags        IOB_QUICK set if quick I/O is possible
     io_Length       at least 1
     io_Data         the address of the byte variable for the
                     result
```



```
NAME
     GPD_ASKTRIGGER - inquire the conditions for a game port report

FUNCTION
     This command inquires what conditions must be met by a game
     port unit before a pending Read request will be satisfied.
     These conditions, called triggers, are independent -- that
     any one occurs is sufficient to queue a game port report to
     the Read queue.  These conditions are set by GPD_SETTRIGGER.

     This command always executes immediately.

IO REQUEST
     io_Message      mn_ReplyPort set if quick I/O is not possible
     io_Device       preset by the call to OpenDevice
     io_Unit         preset by the call to OpenDevice
     io_Command      GPD_ASKTRIGGER
     io_Flags        IOB_QUICK set if quick I/O is possible
     io_Length       sizeof(gameportTrigger)
     io_Data         a structure of type GameportTrigger, which
                     has the following elements
         gpt_Keys -
                 GPTB_DOWNKEYS set if button down transitions
                 trigger a report, and GPTB_UPKEYS set if button up
                 transitions trigger a report
         gpt_Timeout -
                 a time which, if exceeded, triggers a report;
                 measured in vertical blank units (60/sec)
         gpt_XDelta  -
                 a distance in x which, if exceeded, triggers a
                 report
         gpt_YDelta  -
                 a distance in x which, if exceeded, triggers a
                 report
```

```
NAME
     GPD_READEVENT - return the next game port event.

FUNCTION
     Read game port events from the game port and put them in the
     data area of the iORequest.  If there are no pending game port
     events, this command will not be satisfied, but if there are
     some events, but not as many as can fill IO_LENGTH, the
     request will be satisfied with those currently available.

IO REQUEST
     io_Message       mn_ReplyPort set if quick I/O is not possible
     io_Device        preset by the call to OpenDevice
     io_Unit          preset by the call to OpenDevice
     io_Command       GPD_READEVENT
     io_Flags         IOB_QUICK set if quick I/O is possible
     io_Length        the size of the io_Data area in bytes: there
                      are sizeof(inputEvent) bytes per input event.
     io_Data          a buffer area to fill with input events.  The
                      fields of the input event are:
         ie_NextEvent
                      links the events returned
         ie_Class
                      is IECLASS_RAWMOUSE
         ie_SubClass
                      is 0 for the left, 1 for the right game port
         ie_Code
                      contains any gameport button reports.  No
                      report is indicated by the value 0xff.
         ie_Qualifier
                      only the relative and button bits are set
         ie_X, ie_Y
                      the x and y values for this report, in either
                      relative or absolute device dependent units.
         ie_TimeStamp
                      the delta time since the last report, given
                      not as a standard timestamp, but as the frame
                      count in the TV_SECS field.

RESULTS
     This function sets the error field in the iORequest, and fills
     the iORequest with the next game port events (but not partial
     events).

SEE ALSO
     gameport.device/GPD_SETCTYPE, gameport.device/GPD_SETTRIGGER
```



```
NAME
     GPD_SETCTYPE - set the current game port controller type

FUNCTION
     This command sets the type of device at the game port, so that
     the signals at the port may be properly interpreted.  The port
     can also be turned off, so that no reports are generated.

     This command always executes immediately.

IO REQUEST
     io_Message       mn_ReplyPort set if quick I/O is not possible
     io_Device        preset by the call to OpenDevice
     io_Unit          preset by the call to OpenDevice
     io_Command       GPD_SETCTYPE
     io_Flags         IOB_QUICK set if quick I/O is possible
     io_Length        1
     io_Data          the address of the byte variable describing
                      the controller type, as per the equates in
                      the gameport include file
```

```
NAME
     GPD_SETTRIGGER - set the conditions for a game port report

FUNCTION
     This command sets what conditions must be met by a game
     port unit before a pending Read request will be satisfied.
     These conditions, called triggers, are independent -- that
     any one occurs is sufficient to queue a game port report to
     the Read queue.  These conditions are inquired with
     GPD_ASKTRIGGER.

     This command always executes immediately.

IO REQUEST
     io_Message      mn_ReplyPort set if quick I/O is not possible
     io_Device       preset by the call to OpenDevice
     io_Unit         preset by the call to OpenDevice
     io_Command      GPD_SETTRIGGER
     io_Flags        IOB_QUICK set if quick I/O is possible
     io_Length       sizeof(gameportTrigger)
     io_Data         a structure of type GameportTrigger, which
                     has the following elements
         gpt_Keys -
                 GPTB_DOWNKEYS set if button down transitions
                 trigger a report, and GPTB_UPKEYS set if button up
                 transitions trigger a report
         gpt_Timeout -
                 a time which, if exceeded, triggers a report;
                 measured in vertical blank units (60/sec)
         gpt_XDelta  -
                 a distance in x which, if exceeded, triggers a
                 report
         gpt_YDelta  -
                 a distance in x which, if exceeded, triggers a
                 report
```

TABLE OF CONTENTS


```
NAME
     AddHandler - add an input handler to the device

FUNCTION
     Add a function to the list of functions called to handle
     input events generated by this device.  The function is called
     as
         newInputEvents = Handler(inputEvents, handlerData);
         D0                       A0           A1

IO REQUEST
     io_Message       mn_ReplyPort set
     io_Device        preset by OpenDevice
     io_Unit          preset by OpenDevice
     io_Command       IND_ADDHANDLER
     io_Data          a pointer to an interrupt structure.
         is_Data      the handlerData pointer described above
         is_Code      the Handler function address

NOTES
     The interrupt structure is kept by the input device until a
     RemHandler command is satisfied for it.
```

```
NAME
     RemHandler - remove an input handler from the device

FUNCTION
     Remove a function previously added to the list of handler
     functions.

IO REQUEST
     io_Message      mn_ReplyPort set
     io_Device       preset by OpenDevice
     io_Unit         preset by OpenDevice
     io_Command      IND_REMHANDLER
     io_Data         a pointer to the interrupt structure.

NOTES
     This command is not immediate
```



```
NAME
     Reset - reset the input device

FUNCTION
     Reset resets the input device without destroying handles
     to the open device.

IO REQUEST
     io_Message      mn_ReplyPort set if quick I/O is not possible
     io_Device       preset by the call to OpenDevice
     io_Unit         preset by the call to OpenDevice
     io_Command      CMD_RESET
     io_Flags        IOB_QUICK set if quick I/O is possible
```

```
NAME
     SetMPort - set the current mouse port

FUNCTION
     This command sets the gameport port at which the mouse is
     connected.

IO REQUEST
     io_Message      mn_ReplyPort set if quick I/O is not possible
     io_Device       preset by the call to OpenDevice
     io_Unit         preset by the call to OpenDevice
     io_Command      IND_SETMPORT
     io_Flags        IOB_QUICK set if quick I/O is possible
     io_Length       1
     io_Data         a pointer to a byte that is either 0 or 1,
                     indicating that mouse input should be obtained
                     from either the left or right controller port,
                     respectively.
```



```
NAME
     SetMTrig - set the conditions for a mouse port report

FUNCTION
     This command sets what conditions must be met by a mouse
     before a pending Read request will be satisfied.  The trigger
     specification is that used by the gameport device.

IO REQUEST
     io_Message      mn_ReplyPort set if quick I/O is not possible
     io_Device       preset by the call to OpenDevice
     io_Unit         preset by the call to OpenDevice
     io_Command      IND_SETMTRIG
     io_Flags        IOB_QUICK set if quick I/O is possible
     io_Length       sizeof(gameportTrigger)
     io_Data         a structure of type GameportTrigger, which
                     has the following elements
         gpt_Keys -
                 GPTB_DOWNKEYS set if button down transitions
                 trigger a report, and GPTB_UPKEYS set if button up
                 transitions trigger a report
         gpt_Timeout -
                 a time which, if exceeded, triggers a report;
                 measured in vertical blank units (60/sec)
         gpt_XDelta  -
                 a distance in x which, if exceeded, triggers a
                 report
         gpt_YDelta  -
                 a distance in x which, if exceeded, triggers a
                 report
```

```
NAME
     SetMType - set the current mouse port controller type

FUNCTION
     This command sets the type of device at the mouse port, so
     the signals at the port may be properly interpreted.

IO REQUEST
     io_Message      mn_ReplyPort set if quick I/O is not possible
     io_Device       preset by the call to OpenDevice
     io_Unit         preset by the call to OpenDevice
     io_Command      IND_SETMTYPE
     io_Flags        IOB_QUICK set if quick I/O is possible
     io_Length       1
     io_Data         the address of the byte variable describing
                     the controller type, as per the equates in
                     the gameport include file
```



```
NAME
     SetPeriod - set the key repeat period

FUNCTION
     This command sets the period at which a repeating key repeats.

     This command always executes immediately.

IO REQUEST - a timerequest
     io_Message      mn_ReplyPort set if quick I/O is not possible
     io_Device       preset by the call to OpenDevice
     io_Unit         preset by the call to OpenDevice
     io_Command      IND_SETPERIOD
     io_Flags        IOB_QUICK set if quick I/O is possible
     io_tv_Secs      the repeat period seconds
     io_tv_Micro     the repeat period microseconds
```

```
NAME
     SetThresh - set the key repeat threshold

FUNCTION
     This command sets the time that a key must be held down before
     it can repeat.  The repeatability of a key may be restricted
     (as, for example, are the shift keys).

     This command always executes immediately.

IO REQUEST - a timerequest
     io_Message      mn_ReplyPort set if quick I/O is not possible
     io_Device       preset by the call to OpenDevice
     io_Unit         preset by the call to OpenDevice
     io_Command      IND_SETTHRESH
     io_Flags        IOB_QUICK set if quick I/O is possible
     io_tv_Secs      the threshold seconds
     io_tv_Micro     the threshold microseconds
```



```
NAME
     Start - restart after stop

FUNCTION
     Start restarts the unit after a stop command.

IO REQUEST
     io_Message      mn_ReplyPort set if quick I/O is not possible
     io_Device       preset by the call to OpenDevice
     io_Unit         preset by the call to OpenDevice
     io_Command      CMD_START
     io_Flags        IOB_QUICK set if quick I/O is possible
```

```
NAME
     WriteEvent - propagate input event(s) to all handlers

FUNCTION

IO REQUEST
     io_Message      mn_ReplyPort set if quick I/O is not possible
     io_Device       preset by the call to OpenDevice
     io_Unit         preset by the call to OpenDevice
     io_Command      IND_WRITEEVENT
     io_Flags        IOB_QUICK set if quick I/O is possible
     io_Length       the size of the io_Data area in bytes: there
                     are sizeof(inputEvent) bytes per input event.
     io_Data         a buffer area with input events(s).  The
                     fields of the input event are:
         ie_NextEvent
                     links the events together, the last event
                     has a zero ie_NextEvent.
         ie_Class
         ie_SubClass
         ie_Code
         ie_Qualifier
         ie_X, ie_Y
         ie_TimeStamp
                     as desired

NOTES
     The contents of the input event(s) are destroyed.
```

TABLE OF CONTENTS


```
   NAME
        CMD_CLEAR - clear keyboard input buffer

   FUNCTION
        Remove from the input buffer any keys transitions waiting to
        satisfy read requests.

   IO REQUEST
        io_Message      mn_ReplyPort set if quick I/O is not possible
        io_Device       preset by the call to OpenDevice
        io_Command      CMD_CLEAR
        io_Flags        IOB_QUICK set if quick I/O is possible
```

```
NAME
     CMD_RESET - reset the keyboard

FUNCTION
     CMD_RESET resets the keyboard device without destroying handles
     to the open device.

IO REQUEST
     io_Message      mn_ReplyPort set if quick I/O is not possible
     io_Device       preset by the call to OpenDevice
     io_Command      CMD_RESET
     io_Flags        IOB_QUICK set if quick I/O is possible
```



```
NAME
     KBD_ADDRESETHANDER - add a reset handler to the device

FUNCTION
     Add a function to the list of functions called to clean up
     before a hard reset:
         Handler(handlerData);
                 A1

     Note that the A500 does not support this.  CTRL-Amiga-Amiga
     on an A500 does an immediate hard processor reset.

IO REQUEST
     io_Message      mn_ReplyPort set
     io_Device       preset by OpenDevice
     io_Unit         preset by OpenDevice
     io_Command      KBD_ADDRESETHANDLER
     io_Data         a pointer to an interrupt structure.
         is_Data     the handlerData pointer described above
         is_Code     the Handler function address

NOTES
     The interrupt structure is kept by the keyboard device until a
     KBD_REMRESETHANDLER command is satisfied for it.
```

```
NAME
     KBD_READEVENT - return the next keyboard event.

FUNCTION
     Read raw keyboard events from the keyboard and put them in the
     data area of the iORequest.  If there are no pending keyboard
     events, this command will not be satisfied, but if there are
     some events, but not as many as can fill IO_LENGTH, the
     request will be satisfied with those currently available.

IO REQUEST
     io_Message      mn_ReplyPort set if quick I/O is not possible
     io_Device       preset by the call to OpenDevice
     io_Command      KBD_READEVENT
     io_Flags        IOB_QUICK set if quick I/O is possible
     io_Length       the size of the io_Data area in bytes: there
                     are sizeof(inputEvent) bytes per input event.
     io_Data         a buffer area to fill with input events.  The
                     fields of the input event are:
         ie_NextEvent
                     links the events returned
         ie_Class
                     is IECLASS_RAWKEY
         ie_Code
                     contains the next key up/down reports
         ie_Qualifier
                     only the shift and numeric pad bits are set
         ie_SubClass, ie_X, ie_Y, ie_TimeStamp
                     are not used, and set to zero

RESULTS
     This function sets the error field in the IORequest, and fills
     the IORequest with the next keyboard events (but not partial
     events).
```



```
NAME
     KBD_READMATRIX - read the current keyboard key matrix

FUNCTION
     This function reads the up/down state of every key in the
     key matrix.

IO REQUEST
     io_Message      mn_ReplyPort set if quick I/O is not possible
     io_Device       preset by the call to OpenDevice
     io_Command      KBD_READMATRIX
     io_Flags        IOB_QUICK set if quick I/O is possible
     io_Length       the size of the io_Data area in bytes: this
                     must be big enough to hold the key matrix.
     io_Data         a buffer area to fill with the key matrix:
                     an array of bytes whose component bits reflect
                     each keys state: the state of the key for
                     keycode n is at bit (n MOD 8) in byte
                     (n DIV 8) of this matrix.

NOTE
     For V1.2/V1.3 Kickstart, io_Length must be set to exactly 13 bytes.

RESULTS
     This function sets the error field in the IORequest, and sets
     matrix to the current key matrix.
```

keyboard.device/KBD_REMRESETHANDLER

```
NAME
     KBD_REMRESETHANDLER - remove a reset handler from the device

FUNCTION
     Remove a function previously added to the list of handler
     functions.

IO REQUEST
     io_Message      mn_ReplyPort set
     io_Device       preset by OpenDevice
     io_Unit         preset by OpenDevice
     io_Command      KBD_REMRESETHANDLER
     io_Data         a pointer to the handler interrupt structure.
```

keyboard.device/KBD_RESETHANDLERDONE

```
NAME
     KBD_RESETHANDLERDONE - indicate that reset can occur

FUNCTION
     Indicate that reset cleanup associated with the handler has
     completed.

IO REQUEST
     io_Message      mn_ReplyPort set
     io_Device       preset by OpenDevice
     io_Unit         preset by OpenDevice
     io_Command      KBD_RESETHANDLERDONE
     io_Data         a pointer to the handler interrupt structure.
```

TABLE OF CONTENTS


```
    NAME
        AbortIO - Abort an IO request

    SYNOPSIS
        AbortIO(iORequest)
                    A1

    FUNCTION
        Aborts a speech IO request.  The request may be in the queue
       or currently active.

    INPUTS
        iORequest - pointer to the IORequest block of request to abort.

    RESULTS
        io_Error field of IORequest set to IOERR_ABORTED

    BUGS

    SEE ALSO
        narrator.device/BeginIO, exec/io.h
```

```
narrator.device/CloseDevice

    NAME
        CloseDevice - terminates access to the narrator device

    SYNOPSIS
        CloseDevice(iORequest)
                    Al

    FUNCTION
        Close invalidates the io_Unit and io_Device fields in the
        IORequest, preventing subsequent IO until another OpenDevice.
        CloseDevice also reduces the open count.  If the count
        goes to 0 and the expunge bit is set, the device is
        expunged.  If the open count goes to zero and the delayed
        expunge bit is not set, CloseDevice sets the expunge bit.

    INPUTS
        iORequest- pointer to an IORequest block

    RESULTS
        The unit and device pointers of the IORequest block are invalidated.

    BUGS

    SEE ALSO
        narrator.device/OpenDevice, exec/io.h
```

```
narrator.device/CMD_FLUSH                    narrator.device/CMD_FLUSH

    NAME
        CMD_FLUSH - Aborts all inprogress and queued requests

    FUNCTION
        Aborts all in-progress and queued speech requests.

    IO REQUEST
        io_Device       set by OpenDevice
        io_Unit         set by OpenDevice
        io_Command      CMD_FLUSH

    RESULTS
        io_Error        always cleared

    BUGS

    SEE ALSO
        exec.library/SendIO, exec.library/DoIO, exec/io.h
```

```
NAME
    CMD_READ - Return the next different mouth shape from an
           associated write.

FUNCTION
    The read command of the narrator device returns mouth
    shapes to the user.  The shape returned is guaranteed
    to be differnt from the previously returned shape
    (allowing updating to be done only when something has
    changed).  Each read request is associated with a
    write request by the pseudo-unit number assigned by
    the OpenDevice call.  Since the first structure in
    the read-mouth IORequest block (IORB) is a narrator
    (write) IORB, this association is easily made by copying
    the narrator IORB into the narrate_rb field fo the read IORB.
    See the .h,i files.  If there is no write in progress
    or in the device input queue with the same pseudo-unit
    number as the read request, the read will be
    returned to the user with an error.  This is also
    how the user knows that the write request has
    finished and that s/he should not issue any more
    reads.  Note that in this case the mouth shapes may
    not be different from previously returned values.

IO REQUEST
    with the narrator_rb structure copied from the
    associated write request except for:
        io_Message  - message port for read request
        io_Command  - CMD_READ
        io_Error    - 0
        width       - 0
        height      - 0

RESULTS
    IORequest block fields set:
        width  - mouth width in millimeters/3.67
                 (division done for scaling)
        height - mouth height in millimeters
        shape  - compressed form of mouth shapes
                 (internal use only)

BUGS

SEE ALSO
    narrator.device/CMD_WRITE,
    exec.library/DoIO, exec.library/SendIO, exec/io.h
```



```
NAME
    CMD_RESET - Reset the device to a known state

FUNCTION
    Resets the device as though it has just be initialized.
    Aborts all read/write requests whether active of enqueued.
    Restarts device if it has been stopped.

IO REQUEST
    io_Device       set by OpenDevice
    io_Unit         set by OpenDevice
    io_Command      CMD_RESET

RESULTS
    io_Error        always cleared

BUGS

SEE ALSO
    exec.library/SendIO, exec.library/DoIO, exec/io.h
```

```
narrator.device/CMD_START                    narrator.device/CMD_START

    NAME
        CMD_START - Restarts the device after CMD_STOP

    FUNCTION
        CMD_START restarts the currently active speech (if any)
        and allows queued requests to start.

    IO REQUEST
        io_Device        set by OpenDevice
        io_Unit          set by OpenDevice
        io_Command       CMD_START

    RESULTS
        io_Error         always cleared

    BUGS

    SEE ALSO
        exec.library/DoIO, exec.library/SendIO, exec/io.h
```

```
narrator.device/CMD_STOP                      narrator.device/CMD_STOP

    NAME
        CMD_STOP  - Stops the device.

    FUNCTION
        CMD_STOP halts the currently active speech (if any) and
        prevents any queued requests from starting.

    IO REQUEST
        io_Device        set by OpenDevice
        io_Unit          set by OpenDevice
        io_Command       CMD_STOP

    RESULTS
        io_Error         always cleared

    BUGS

    SEE ALSO
        exec.library/DoIO, exec.library/SendIO, exec/io.h
```

```
NAME
    CMD_WRITE - Send speech request to the narrator device

FUNCTION
    Performs the speech request.  If there is an associated read
    request on the device input queue, write will remove it and
    return an initial mouth shape to the user.

    Note: if you are going to be doing reads,
          the mouths parameter must be set to 1.

IO REQUEST
    narrator_rb request block:
       ch_masks   - array of audio channel selection masks
                   (see audio device documentation for
                    description of this field)
       nm_masks   - number of audio channel selection masks
       mouths     - 0 if no mouths are desired
                    1 if mouths are to be read
       rate       - speaking rate
       pitch      - pitch
       mode       - pitch mode
                    0 if natural mode
                    1 if robotic mode
       sex        - 0 if male
                  - 1 if female
       io_Message - message port
       io_Command - CMD_WRITE
       io_Data    - input string
       io_Length  - length of input string

RESULTS
    The function sets the io_Error field of the IORB.  The
    io_Actual field is set to the length of the input string
    that was actually processed.  If the return code indicates
    a phoneme error (ND_PhonErr), io_Actual is the position in
    the input string where the error occured.

BUGS

SEE ALSO
    narrator.device/CMD_READ, devices/narrator.h
    exec.library/DoIO, exec.library/SendIO, exec/io.h
    Audio device documentation.
```



```
NAME
    OpenDevice - open the narrator device.

SYNOPSIS
    error = OpenDevice("narrator.device", 0 , iORequest , 0 );
    D0                 A0                 D0  A1          D1

FUNCTION
    The OpenDevice routine grants access to the narrator device.
    OpenDevice checks the unit number, and if non-zero, returns
    an error (ND_UnitErr).  If this is the first time the driver
    has been opened, OpenDevice will attempt to open the audio
    device and allocate the driver's static buffers.  If either
    of these operations fail, an error is returned (see the .h,i
    files for possible error return codes).  Next, OpenDevice
    (done for all opens, not just the first one) initializes the
    user's IORequest block (IORB).  Default values for sex, rate,
    pitch, pitch mode, sampling frequency, and mouths are set in
    the appropriate fields of the IORB.  Note that if users wish
    to use non-default values for these parms, the values must
    be set after the open is done.  OpenDevice then assigns a
    pseudo-unit number to the IORB for use in synchronizing read
    and write requests.  See the CMD_READ command for more details.
    Finally, OpenDevice stores the device node pointer in the
    IORB and clears the delayed expunge bit.

INPUTS
    deviceName - must be "narrator.device"
    unitNumber - must be 0
    iORequest  - a pointer to the user's IORequest block
                 ( need not be initialized )
    flags      - not used

RESULTS
    error - same as io_Error field of IORB

    IORequest block fields set:
       rate     - 150 words/minute
       pitch    - 110 Hz
       mode     - Natural
       sex      - Male
       mouths   - Off
       sampfreq - 22200
       volume   - 64 (max)

BUGS

SEE ALSO
    narrator.device/OpenDevice, narrator.device/CMD_READ,
    exec/io.h
```

TABLE OF CONTENTS


```
   NAME
       Clear -- clear the parallel port buffer

   FUNCTION
       This command just RTS's (no buffer to clear)

   IO REQUEST
       io_Message      mn_ReplyPort initialized
       io_Device       set by OpenDevice
       io_Unit         set by OpenDevice
       io_Command      CMD_CLEAR (05)
```

```
NAME
    Flush -- clear all queued I/O requests for the parallel port

FUNCTION
    This command purges the read and write request queues for the
    parallel device.

IO REQUEST
    io_Message      mn_ReplyPort initialized
    io_Device       set by OpenDevice
    io_Unit         set by OpenDevice
    io_Command      CMD_FLUSH (08)
```



```
NAME
    Read -- read input from parallel port

FUNCTION
    This command causes a stream of characters to be read from the
    parallel I/O register. The number of characters is specified in
    io_Length.
    The parallel.device has no internal buffer; if no read request has
    been made, pending input (i.e. handshake request) is not
    acknowledged.

IO REQUEST
    io_Message      mn_ReplyPort initialized
    io_Device       set by OpenDevice
    io_Unit         set by OpenDevice
    io_Command      CMD_READ (02)
    io_Flags        If IOF_QUICK is set, driver will attempt Quick IO
    io_Length       number of characters to receive.
    io_Data         pointer where to put the data.

RESULTS
    io_Error -- if the Read succeded, then io_Error will be null.
        If the Read failed, then io_Error will contain an error code.

SEE ALSO
    parallel.device/PDCMD_SETPARAMS
```

```
NAME
    Reset -- reinitializes the parallel device

FUNCTION
    This command resets the parallel device to its freshly initialized
    condition. It aborts all I/O requests both queued and current and
    sets the devices's flags and parameters to their boot-up time
    default values.

IO REQUEST
    io_Message      mn_ReplyPort initialized
    io_Device       set by OpenDevice
    io_Unit         set by OpenDevice
    io_Command      CMD_RESET (01)

RESULTS
    Error -- if the Reset succeded, then io_Error will be null.
        If the Reset failed, then the io_Error will be non-zero.
```



```
NAME
    Start -- restart paused I/O over the parallel port

FUNCTION
    This command restarts the current I/O activity on the parallel
    port by reactivating the handshaking sequence.

IO REQUEST
    io_Message      mn_ReplyPort initialized
    io_Device       set by OpenDevice
    io_Unit         set by OpenDevice
    io_Command      CMD_START (07)

SEE ALSO
    parallel.device/CMD_STOP
```

```
NAME
    Stop -- pause current activity on the parallel device

FUNCTION
    This command halts the current I/O activity on the parallel
    device by discontinuing the handshaking sequence.

IO REQUEST
    io_Message      mn_ReplyPort initialized
    io_Device       set by OpenDevice
    io_Unit         set by OpenDevice
    io_Command      CMD_STOP (06)

SEE ALSO
    parallel.device/CMD_START

BUGS
     Using any other parallel.device command will restart IO.
```



```
NAME
    Write -- send output to parallel port

FUNCTION
    This command causes a stream of characters to be written to the
    parallel output register. The number of characters is specified in
    io_Length, unless -1 is used, in which case output is sent until
    a zero byte in the data: note that this is independent of setting
    EOFMODE in io_ParFlags and using the PTermArray to terminate the
    write.

IO REQUEST
    io_Message      mn_ReplyPort initialized
    io_Device       set by OpenDevice
    io_Unit         set by OpenDevice
    io_Command      CMD_WRITE (03)
    io_Flags        If IOF_QUICK is set, driver will attempt Quick IO
    io_Length       number of characters to transmit, or if set
                    to -1 send until zero byte encountered
    io_Data         pointer to block of data to transmit

RESULTS
    io_Error -- If the Write succeded, then io_Error will be null.
         If the Write failed, then io_Error will contain an error code.

SEE ALSO
    parallel.device/PDCMD_SETPARAMS
```

```
NAME
    Open -- a request to open the parallel port

SYNOPSIS
    error = OpenDevice("parallel.device", unit, ioExtPar, flags)
    D0                  A0                 D0    A1        D1


FUNCTION
    This is an exec call that starts up the parallel.device.

    This function allows the requestor software access to the parallel
    device.  Unless the shared-access bit (bit 5 of io_ParFlags) is
    set, exclusive use is granted and no other access is allowed
    until the owner closes the device.  The PTermArray of the ioExtPar
    is initialized only if the EOFMODE bit is set in io_ParFlags.

INPUTS
    "parallel.device" - a pointer to literal string "parallel.device"
    unit - Must be zero for future compatibility
    ioExtPar - pointer to an IO Request block of structure IOExtPar
      to be initialized by the Open routine.  (see devices/parallel.h for
      definition)
      The io_ParFlags field must be set as desired (sce shared-access
      description, above).  Note that this is not a standard IO Request
      structure.
    flags - Must be zero for future compatibility

RESULTS
     d0 -- same as io_Error
    io_Error -- if the Open succeded, then io_Error will be null.
        If the Open failed, then io_Error will be non-zero.

SEE ALSO
    exec/CloseDevice
```



```
NAME
    Query -- query parallel port/line status

FUNCTION
    This command return the status of the parallel port lines and
    registers.

IO REQUEST
    io_Message      must have mn_ReplyPort initialized
    io_Device       set by OpenDevice
    io_Unit         set by OpenDevice
    io_Command      PDCMD_QUERY (09)

RESULTS
    io_Status         BIT  ACTIVE  FUNCTION

                       0    high   printer busy toggle (offline)
                       1    high   paper out
                       2    high   printer selected on the A1000
                                   printer selected & serial "Ring
                                   Indicator" on the A500/A2000
                                   Use care when making cables.
                       3     -     read=0,write=1
                     4-7           reserved

BUGS
     In a earlier version of this AutoDoc, BUSY and PSEL were reversed.
     The function has always been correct.
```

```
NAME
    SetParams -- change parameters for the parallel device

FUNCTION
    This command allows the caller to change parameters for the
    parallel port device. It will disallow changes if any reads or
    writes are active or queued.  The PARB_EOFMODE bit of io_ParFlags
    controlls whether the io_PTermArray is to be used as an additional
    termination criteria for reads and writes.  It may be set directly
    without a call to SetParams, setting it here performs the
    additional service of copying the PTermArray into the device
    default array which is used as the initial array for subsequent
    device opens. The Shared bit can be changed here, and overrides the
    current device access mode set at OpenDevice time.

IO REQUEST
    io_Message      mn_ReplyPort initialized
    io_Device       preset by OpenDevice
    io_Unit         preset by OpenDevice
    io_Command      PDCMD_SETPARAMS (0A)
                     NOTE that the following fields of your IORequest
                    are filled by Open to reflect the parallel device's
                    current configuration.
    io_PExtFlags    must be set to zero, unless used
    io_ParFlags     see definition in parallel.i or parallel.h
                     NOTE that x00 yields exclusive access, termarray
                    inactive.
    io_PTermArray   ASCII descending-ordered 8-byte array of
                    termination characters. If less than 8 chars
                    used, fill out array w/lowest valid value.
                    Terminators are used only if EOFMODE bit of
                    io_Parflags is set. (e.g. x512F040303030303 )
                    This field is filled on OpenDevice only if the
                    EOFMODE bit is set.

RESULTS
    io_Error -- if the SetParams succeded, then io_Error will be null.
        If the SetParams failed, then io_Error will be non-zero.
```

TABLE OF CONTENTS


```
NAME
     CMD_FLUSH - abort all I/O requests (immediate)

FUNCTION
     CMD_FLUSH aborts all stopped I/O at the unit.

IO REQUEST
     io_Message      mn_ReplyPort set if quick I/O is not possible
     io_Device       preset by the call to OpenDevice
     io_Command      CMD_FLUSH
     io_Flags        IOB_QUICK set if quick I/O is possible
```

```
NAME
     CMD_INVALID - invalid command

FUNCTION
     CMD_INVALID is always an invalid command, and sets the device
     error appropriately.

IO REQUEST
     io_Message      mn_ReplyPort set if quick I/O is not possible
     io_Command      CMD_INVALID
     io_Flags        IOB_QUICK set if quick I/O is possible
```



```
NAME
     CMD_RESET - reset the printer

FUNCTION
     CMD_RESET resets the printer device without destroying handles
     to the open device.

IO REQUEST
     io_Message      mn_ReplyPort set if quick I/O is not possible
     io_Device       preset by the call to OpenDevice
     io_Command      CMD_RESET
     io_Flags        IOB_QUICK set if quick I/O is possible
```

```
NAME
     CMD_START - restart after stop (immediate)

FUNCTION
     CMD_START restarts the unit after a stop command.

IO REQUEST
     io_Message      mn_ReplyPort set if quick I/O is not possible
     io_Device       preset by the call to OpenDevice
     io_Command      CMD_START
     io_Flags        IOB_QUICK set if quick I/O is possible
```



```
NAME
     CMD_STOP - pause current and queued I/O requests (immediate)

FUNCTION
     CMD_STOP pauses all queued requests for the unit, and tries to
     pause the current I/O request.  The only commands that will
     be subsequently allowed to be performed are immediate I/O
     requests, which include those to start, flush, and finish the
     I/O after the stop command.

IO REQUEST
     io_Message      mn_ReplyPort set if quick I/O is not possible
     io_Device       preset by the call to OpenDevice
     io_Command      CMD_STOP
     io_Flags        IOB_QUICK set if quick I/O is possible
```

```
   NAME
      CMD_WRITE -- send output to the printer

   FUNCTION
      This function causes a buffer of characters to be written to the
      current printer port (usually parallel or serial).  The number of
      characters is specified in io_Length, unless -1 is used, in which
      case output is sent until a 0x00 is encountered.

      The Printer device, like the Console device, maps ANSI X3.64 style
      7-bit printer control codes to the control code set of the current
      printer.  The ANSI codes supported can be found below.

   NOTES
      Not all printers will support all functions.  In particular you may
      not assume that the MARGINS or TABS can be set.  Close to half the
      supported printers don't fully implement one or the other.  If you
      want the features of margins or tabs you will need to fake it
      internally by sending out spaces.

      Note that the printer device may have already sent out a "set
      margins" command to the printer.  If you are faking your own
      margins, be sure to cancel the old ones first.  (use the "aCAM"
      command)

      Defaults are set up so that if a normal AmigaDOS text file
      is sent to PRT:, it has the greatest chance of working.
      (AmigaDOS text files are defined as follows:)
              tabs            - every 8
              CR (0x0D)       - moves to start of current line
              LF (0x0A)       - moves to start of next line

   IO REQUEST
       io_Message       mn_ReplyPort set
       io_Device        preset by OpenDevice
       io_Unit          preset by OpenDevice
       io_Command       CMD_WRITE
       io_Length        number of characters to process, or if -1,
                        process until 0x00 encountered
       io_Data          pointer to block of data to process

   RESULTS
       io_Error : if CMD_WRITE succeeded, then io_Error will be zero.
              Otherwise io_Error will be non-zero.

   SEE ALSO
       printer.h, parallel.device, serial.device, Preferences


   ANSI X3.64 style COMMANDS

aRIS         ESCc            hard reset
aRIN         ESC#1           initialize to defaults
aIND         ESCD            true linefeed (lf)
aNEL         ESCE            return,lf
aRI          ESCM            reverse lf                    *

aSGR0        ESC[0m          normal character set
aSGR3        ESC[3m          italics on
aSGR23       ESC[23m         italics off
aSGR4        ESC[4m          underline on
aSGR24       ESC[24m         underline off
aSGR1        ESC[1m          boldface on
aSGR22       ESC[22m         boldface off
aSFC         SGR30-39        set foreground color
aSBC         SGR40-49        set background color

aSHORP0      ESC[0w          normal pitch
aSHORP2      ESC[2w          elite on
aSHORP1      ESC[1w          elite off
aSHORP4      ESC[4w          condensed on
aSHORP3      ESC[3w          condensed off
aSHORP6      ESC[6w          enlarged on
aSHORP5      ESC[5w          enlarged off

aDEN6        ESC[6"z         shadow print on
aDEN5        ESC[5"z         shadow print off
aDEN4        ESC[4"z         doublestrike on
aDEN3        ESC[3"z         doublestrike off
aDEN2        ESC[2"z         Near Letter Quality (NLQ) on
aDEN1        ESC[1"z         NLQ off

aSUS2        ESC[2v          superscript on
aSUS1        ESC[1v          superscript off
aSUS4        ESC[4v          subscript on
aSUS3        ESC[3v          subscript off
aSUS0        ESC[0v          normalize the line       *
aPLU         ESCL            partial line up          *
aPLD         ESCK            partial line down        *

aFNT0        ESC(B           US char set (default)    or Font 0
aFNT1        ESC(R           French char set          or Font 1
aFNT2        ESC(K           German char set          or Font 2
aFNT3        ESC(A           UK char set              or Font 3
aFNT4        ESC(E           Danish I char set        or Font 4
aFNT5        ESC(H           Sweden char set          or Font 5
aFNT6        ESC(Y           Italian char set         or Font 6
aFNT7        ESC(Z           Spanish char set         or Font 7
aFNT8        ESC(J           Japanese char set        or Font 8
aFNT9        ESC(6           Norweign char set        or Font 9
aFNT10       ESC(C           Danish II char set       or Font 10

aPROP2       ESC[2p          proportional on          *
aPROP1       ESC[1p          proportional off         *
aPROP0       ESC[0p          proportional clear       *
aTSS         ESC[n E         set proportional offset  *
aJFY5        ESC[5 F         auto left justify        *
aJFY7        ESC[7 F         auto right justify       *
aJFY6        ESC[6 F         auto full justify        *
aJFY0        ESC[0 F         auto justify off         *
aJFY3        ESC[3 F         letter space (justify)   *
aJFY1        ESC[1 F         word fill(auto center)   *

aVERP0       ESC[0z          1/8" line spacing
aVERP1       ESC[1z          1/6" line spacing
aSLPP        ESC[nt          set form length n
aPERF        ESC[nq          set perforation skip to n lines (n>0)
aPERF0       ESC[0q          perforation skip off

aLMS         ESC#9           Left margin set          *
aRMS         ESC#0           Right margin set         *
aTMS         ESC#8           Top margin set           *
aBMS         ESC#2           Bottom margin set        *
aSTBM        ESC[Pn1;Pn2r    set T&B margins          *
aSLRM        ESC[Pn1;Pn2s    set L&R margin           *
aCAM         ESC#3           Clear margins

aHTS         ESCH            Set horiz tab            *
aVTS         ESCJ            Set vertical tabs        *
aTBC0        ESC[0g          Clr horiz tab            *
aTBC3        ESC[3g          Clear all h tab          *
aTBC1        ESC[1g          Clr vertical tabs        *
aTBC4        ESC[4g          Clr all v tabs           *
aTBCALL      ESC#4           Clr all h & v tabs       *
aTBSALL      ESC#5           Set default tabs (every 8)

aEXTEND      ESC[Pn"x        Extended commands
                             This is a mechanism for printer drivers to
                             support extra commands which can be called
                             by ANSI control sequences
aRAW         ESC[Pn"r        Next 'Pn' chars are raw (ie. they are not
                             parsed by the printer device, instead they
```

```
                    are sent directly to the printer.

(*) indicates that sending this command may cause unexpected results
    on a large number of printers.
```



```
   NAME
       PRD_DUMPRPORT - dump the specified RastPort to a graphics printer.

   FUNCTION
       Print a rendition of the supplied RastPort, using the supplied
       ColorMap, position and scaling information, as specified in
       the printer preferences.

   IO REQUEST
       io_Message      mn_ReplyPort set if quick I/O is not possible.
       io_Command      PRD_DUMPRPORT.
       io_Flags        IOB_QUICK set if quick I/O is possible.
       io_RastPort     ptr to a RastPort.
       io_ColorMap     ptr to a ColorMap.
       io_Modes        the 'modes' flag from a ViewPort structure,
                       (the upper word is reserved and should be zero).
       io_SrcX         x offset into the RastPort to start printing from.
       io_SrcY         y offset into the RastPort to start printing from.
       io_SrcWidth     width of the RastPort to print (from io_SrcX).
       io_SrcHeight    height of the RastPort to print (from io_SrcY).
       io_DestCols     width of the printout in printer pixels.
       io_DestRows     height of the printout in printer pixels.
       io_Special      flag bits
                       (some of which pertain to DestCols and DestRows).
                       -if SPECIAL_MIL is set, then the associated
                        parameter is specified in thousandths of
                        an inch on the printer.  ie. if DestCols = 8000,
                        DestRows = 10500 and SPECIAL_MILROWS and
                        SPECIAL_MILCOLS is set then the printout would be
                        8.000 x 10.500 inches.
                       -if SPECIAL_FULL is set, then the specific dimension
                        is set to the maximum possible as determined
                        by the printer limits or the configuration
                        limits; whichever is less.
                       -if SPECIAL_FRAC is set, the parameter is
                        taken to be a longword binary fraction
                        of the maximum for that dimension.
                       -if all bits for a dimension are clear,
                        (ie. SPECIAL MIL/FULL/FRAC and ASPECT are NOT set)
                        then the parameter is specified in printer pixels.
                       -if SPECIAL_CENTER is set then the image will be
                        put between the left and right edge of the paper.
                       -if SPECIAL_ASPECT is set, one of the dimensions
                        may be reduced/expanded to preserve the aspect
                        ratio of the print.
                       -SPECIAL_DENSITY(1-7) this allows for a maximum of 7
                        different print densities.  DENSITY1 is the lowest
                        density and the default.
                       -SPECIAL_NOFORMFEED - this allows for the mixing of
                        text and graphics or multiple graphic dumps on page
                        oriented printers (usually laser jet printers).
                        When this flag is set the page will not be ejected
                        after a graphic dump.  If you perform another
                        graphic dump without this flag set OR close the
                        printer after printing text after a graphic dump,
                        the page will be ejected.
                       -if SPECIAL_TRUSTME is set then the printer specific
                        driver is instructed to not issue a reset command
                        before and after the dump.  If this flag is NOT
                        checked by the printer specific driver then setting
                        this flag has no effect.  Since we now recommend
                        that printer driver writers no longer issue a reset
                        command it is probably a safe idea to always set
                        this flag when calling for a dump.
                       -if SPECIAL_NOPRINT is set then the following is done:
                        Compute print size, set 'io_DestCols' and
                        'io_DestRows' in the calling program's 'IODRPReq'
                        structure and exit, DON'T PRINT.  This allows the
                        calling program to see what the final print size
                        would be in printer pixels.  Note that it modifies
```

the 'io_DestCols' and 'io_DestRows' fields of your 'IODRPReq' structure. It also sets the print density and updates the 'MaxXDots', 'MaxYDots', 'XDotsInch', and 'YDotsInch' fields of the 'PrinterExtendedData' structure.

There following rules for the interpretation of io_DestRows and io_DestCols that may produce unexpected results when they are not greater than zero and io_Special is zero. They have been retained for compatability. The user will not trigger these other rules with well formed usage of io_Special.

When io_Special is equal to 0, the following rules (from the V1.1 printer.device, and retained for compatibility reasons) take effect. Remember, these special rules are for io_DestRows and io_DestCols and only take effect if io_Special is 0).

a) DestCols>0 & DestRows>0 - use as absolute values.
   ie. DestCols=320 & DestRows=200 means that the picture will appear on the printer as 320x200 dots.
b) DestCols=0 & DestRows>0 - use the printers maximum number of columns and print DestRows lines. ie. if DestCols=0 and DestRows=200 than the picture will appear on the printer as wide as it can be and 200 dots high.
c) DestCols=0 & DestRows=0 - same as above except the driver determines the proper number of lines to print based on the aspect ratio of the printer. ie. This results in the largest picture possible that is not distorted or inverted. Note: As of this writing, this is the call made by such program as DeluxePaint, GraphicCraft, and AegisImages.
d) DestCols>0 &DestRows=0 - use the specified width and the driver determines the proper number of lines to print based on the aspect ratio of the printer. ie. if you desire a picture that is 500 pixels wide and aspect ratio correct, use DestCols=500 and DestRows=0.
e) DestCols<0 or DestRows>0 - the final picture is either a reduction or expansion based on the fraction |DestCols| / DestRows in the proper aspect ratio.
   Some examples:
   1) if DestCols=-2 & DestRows=1 then the printed picture will be 2x the AMIGA picture and in the proper aspect ratio. (2x is derived from |-2| / 1 which gives 2.0)
   2) if DestCols=-1 & DestRows=2 then the printed picture will be 1/2x the AMIGA picture in the proper aspect ratio. (1/2x is derived from |-1| / 2 which gives 0.5)

NOTES

The printer selected in preferences must have graphics capability to use this command. The error 'PDERR_NOTGRAPHICS' is returned if the printer can not print graphics.

Color printers may not be able to print black and white or greyscale pictures -- specifically, the Okimate 20 cannot print these with a color ribbon: you must use a black ribbon instead. If the printer has an input buffer option, use it. If the printer can be uni or bi directional, select uni-directional; this produces a much cleaner picture. Most printer drivers will attempt to set unidirectional printing if it is possible under software control.

Please note that the width and height of the printable area on the printer is in terms of pixels and bounded by the folllowing:
 a) WIDTH = (RIGHT_MARGIN - LEFT_MARGIN + 1) / CHARACTERS_PER_INCH
 b) HEIGHT = LENGTH / LINES_PER_INCH
Margins are set by preferences.

For BGR printer support, the YMC values in the printer specific render.c functions equate to BGR respectively, ie. yellow is blue, magenta is green, and cyan is red.

The printer specific and non-specific data structures can be read ONCE you have opended the printer device. Here is a code fragment to illustrate how to do just that.

```
    #include <exec/types.h>
    #include <devices/printer.h>
    #include <devices/prtbase.h>
    #include <devices/prtgfx.h>

    struct IODRPReq PReq;
    struct PrinterData *PD;
    struct PrinterExtendedData *PED;

open the printer device / if it opended...
if (OpenDevice("printer.device", 0, &PReq, 0) == NULL) {
    get pointer to printer data
    PD = (struct PrinterData *)PReq.io_Device;
    get pointer to printer extended data
    PED = &PD->pd_SegmentData->ps_PED;
    let's see what's there
    printf("PrinterName = '%s', Version=%u, Revision=%u\n",
        PED->ped_PrinterName, PD->pd_SegmentData->ps_Version,
        PD->pd_SegmentData->ps_Revision,);
    printf("PrinterClass=%u, ColorClass=%u\n",
        PED->ped_PrinterClass, PED->ped_ColorClass);
    printf("MaxColumns=%u, NumCharSets=%u, NumRows=%u\n",
        PED->ped_MaxColumns, PED->ped_NumCharSets, PED->ped_NumRows);
    printf("MaxXDots=%lu, MaxYDots=%lu, XDotsInch=%u, YDotsInch=%u\n",
        PED->ped_MaxXDots, PED->ped_MaxYDots,
        PED->ped_XDotsInch, PED->ped_YDotsInch);
    CloseDevice(&PReq);
}
```

Preferences

If you want the user to be able to access the printer preferences items without having to run preferences (like DPAINT II's printer requestor), here is what you do. You can look at the printer's copy of preferences by referring to 'PD->pd_Preferences' (the printer device MUST already be opened at this point). After you have this you could put up a requestor and allow the user to change whatever parameters they wanted. BEAR IN MIND THAT YOU ARE RESPONSIBLE FOR RANGE CHECKING THESE SELECTIONS! Listed below are the printer preferences items and their valid values.

```
PrintPitch          - PICA, ELITE, FINE.
PrintQuality        - DRAFT, LETTER.
PrintSpacing        - SIX_LPI, EIGHT_LPI.
PrintLeftMargin     - 1 to PrintRightMargin.
PrintRightMargin    - PrintLeftMargin to 999.
PaperLength         - 1 to 999.
PrintImage          - IMAGE_POSITIVE, IMAGE_NEGATIVE.
PrintAspect         - ASPECT_HORIZ, ASPECT_VERT.
PrintShade          - SHADE_BW, SHADE_GREYSCALE, SHADE_COLOR.
PrintThreshold      - 1 to 15.
PrintFlags          - CORRECT_RED, CORRECT_GREEN, CORRECT_BLUE, CENTER_IMAGE,
                      IGNORE_DIMENSIONS, BOUNDED_DIMENSIONS,
                      ABSOLUTE_DIMENSIONS, PIXEL_DIMENSIONS,
                      MULTIPLY_DIMENSIONS, INTEGER_SCALING,
                      ORDERED_DITHERING, HALFTONE_DITHERING.
                      FLOYD_DITHERING, ANTI_ALIAS, GREY_SCALE2
PrintMaxWidth       - 0 to 65535.
PrintMaxHeight      - 0 to 65535.
PrintDensity        - 1 to 7.
PrintXOffset        - 0 to 255.
```

Asynchronous I/O

The recommended way to do asynchronous i/o is...

a) To send requests for i/o.

```
struct IORequest *ioreq;
struct MsgPort *port;
UBYTE signal;

port = ioreq->io_Message.mn_ReplyPort;
signal = port->mp_SigBit;

SendIO(ioreq);  send request
Wait(signal);  wait for completion (go to sleep)
while ((Msg = GetMsg(port)) != NULL) {  get ALL messages
}
```

b) To abort a previous request for i/o.

```
struct IORequest *ioreq;

AbortIO(ioreq);  abort request
WaitIO(ioreq);  wait for reply
```

at this point you can re-use 'ioreq'.

Note that in the above examples 'ioreq' could be any one of...
a) struct IOStdReq   a standard i/o request
b) struct IODRPReq   a dumprport i/o request
c) struct IOPrtCmdReq a printer command i/o request

It is recommend that you do asynchronous i/o in your programs and give the user a way of aborting all requests.

V1.3 Printer Driver Notes

In general densities which use more than one pass should only be used for B&W shade dumps. They can be used for Grey-Scale or Color Shade dumps BUT the output may tend to look muddy or dark. Also multiple pass Color dumps tend to dirty or smear the ribbon (ie. yellow will get contaminated with the other colors on the ribbon; you've been warned).

Alphacom_AlphaPro_101

1. Daisywheel printer (text only).

Brother_HR-15XL

1. Daisywheel printer (text only).

CalComp_ColorMaster

1. Thermal transfer b&w/color printer (text and graphics).
2. Use Black ribbon for non-color dumps; Color ribbon for color dumps.
3. Linefeeds # of vertical dots printed.
4. Densitie(s) supported are 203x200(1) dpi.
5. This is a dual printer driver. Select a PaperSize of 'Narrow Tractor' for use with the ColorMaster; 'Wide Tractor' for use with the ColorView-5912 (which uses 11 x 17 inch paper).

CalComp_ColorMaster2

1. Thermal transfer b&w/color printer (text and graphics).
2. Use Black ribbon for non-color dumps; Color ribbon for color dumps.
3. Linefeeds # of vertical dots printed.
4. Densitie(s) supported are 203x200(1) dpi.
5. This is a dual printer driver. Select a PaperSize of 'Narrow Tractor' for use with the ColorMaster; 'Wide Tractor' for use with the ColorView-5912 (which uses 11 x 17 inch paper).
6. This driver is the same as the Calcomp_ColorMaster driver EXCEPT it is approximately 2 times faster (during color dumps) and requires LOTS of memory (up to 1,272,003 bytes for a full 8 x 10 inch (1600 x 2000 dot) color dump). Typically full-size (color) dumps are 1600 x 1149 dots and require 730,767 bytes. Memory requirements for the ColorView-5912 are up to 2,572,803 bytes for a full 10 x 16 inch (2048 x 3200 dot) color dump. Typically full-size (color) dumps are 2048 x 2155 dots and require 1,732,623 bytes. The memory requirements are 1/3 when doing a non-color printout (on both the ColorMaster and ColorView).

Canon_PJ-1080A

1. Ink jet b&w/color printer (text and graphics).
2. Linefeeds # of vertical dots printed.
3. Densitie(s) supported are 83x84(1) dpi.

CBM_MPS1000

1. Dot matrix b&w printer (text and graphics).
2. Linefeeds # of vertical dots printed (-1/3 dot if PaperType = Single). *2
3. Density

Density	XDPI	YDPI	XYDPI	Comments	
1	120	72	8640		
2	120	144	17280	two pass	
3	240	72	17280		*1
4	120	216	25920	three pass	
5	240	144	34560	two pass	*1
6	240	216	51840	three pass	*1
7	same as 6				

Diablo_630

1. Daisywheel printer (text only).

Diablo_Advantage_D25

1. Daisywheel printer (text only).

Diablo_C-150

1. Ink jet b&w/color printer (text and graphics).
2. Always linefeeds 4 dots (limitation of printer).
3. A PaperSize of 'Wide Tractor' selects a maximum print width of 8.5 inches (for wide roll paper).
5. Densitie(s) supported are 120x120(1) dpi.

EpsonQ (24-pin Epson compatible)

1. Dot matrix b&w/color printer (text and graphics).
2. Drives all EpsonQ (LQ1500, LQ2500, etc.) compatible printers.
3. Linefeeds # of vertical dots printed.
4. Density

Density	XDPI	YDPI	XYDPI	Comments
1	90	180	16200	
2	120	180	21600	
3	180	180	32400	
4	360	180	64800	*1
5,6,7	same as 4			

5. A PaperSize of 'Wide Tractor' selects a maximum print width of 13.6 inches (for wide carriage printers).
6. A PaperType of 'Single' uses only 16 of the 24 pins, whereas a PaperType of 'Fanfold' uses all 24 pins. The 'Single' option is useful for those printers which have a weak power supply and cannot drive all 24 pins continuously. If during a single pass of the print head you notice that the top two thirds of the graphics are darker than the bottom one third then you'll probably need to drop down to 16 pins.

EpsonX[CBM_MPS-1250] (8/9-pin Epson compatible)

1. Dot matrix b&w/color printer (text and graphics).
2. Drives all EpsonX (EX/FX/JX/LX/MX/RX, etc.) compatible printers.
3. Linefeeds # of vertical dots printed (-1/3 dot if PaperType = Single). *2
4. Density

Density	XDPI	YDPI	XYDPI	Comments	
1	120	72	8640		
2	120	144	17280	two pass	
3	240	72	17280		*1
4	120	216	25920	three pass	

```
        5       240     144     34560   two pass        *1
        6       240     216     51840   three pass      *1
        7       same as 6

5. A PaperSize of 'Wide Tractor' selects a maximum print width of
   13.6 inches (for wide carriage printers).
6. Use this driver if you own a CBM_MPS-1250 (as it is EpsonX compatible).

EpsonXOld (8/9-pin Epson compatible)
---------
1. Dot matrix b&w printer (text and graphics).
2. Drives all very old EpsonX (EX/FX/JX/LX/MX/RX, etc.) compatible printers.
3. Linefeeds # of vertical dots printed.
4. Density      XDPI    YDPI    XYDPI   Comments
        1        60     72       4320
        2       120     72       8640   (double speed)                  *1
        3       120     72       8640
        4       240     72      17280                                   *1
        5       120     72       8640   (for use on old Star printers)
        6       240     72      17280   (for use on old Star printers)  *1
        7       240     72      17280   (same as density 4)             *1
5. A PaperSize of 'Wide Tractor' selects a maximum print width of
   13.6 inches (for wide carriage printers).
6. Use this driver if the EpsonX driver doesn't work properly in graphics
   or text mode on your EpsonX compatible printer.

generic
-------
1. Text only printer.

Howtek_Pixelmaster
------------------
1. Plastic ink jet b&w/color printer (text and graphics).
2. Linefeeds # of vertical dots printed.
3. Density      XDPI    YDPI    XYDPI   Comments
        1        80      80      6400
        2       120     120     14400
        3       160     160     25600
        4       240     240     57600
        5,6,7   same as 4
4. Maximum print area is 8.0 x 10.0 inches.

HP_DeskJet
----------
1. Ink jet non-color printer (text and graphics).
2. Linefeeds # of vertical dots printed.
3. Density      XDPI    YDPI    XYDPI   Comments
        1        75      75      5625
        2       100     100     10000
        3       150     150     22500
        4       300     300     90000
        5,6,7   same as 4
4. Maximum print area is 8.0 x 10.0 inches.

HP_LaserJet (LaserJet+/LaserJetII compatible)
-----------
1. Laser engine non-color printer (text and graphics).
2. Linefeeds # of vertical dots printed.
3. Density      XDPI    YDPI    XYDPI   Comments
        1        75      75      5625
        2       100     100     10000
        3       150     150     22500
        4       300     300     90000
        5,6,7   same as 4
4. Maximum print area is 8.0 x 10.0 inches.

HP_PaintJet
-----------
1. Ink jet b&w/color printer (text and graphics).
2. Linefeeds # of vertical dots printed.
3. Densitie(s) supported are 180x180(1) dpi.

HP_ThinkJet
-----------
1. Ink jet non-color printer (text and graphics).
2. Linefeeds # of vertical dots printed.
3. Density      XDPI    YDPI    XYDPI   Comments
        1        96     96       9216
        2       192     96      18432
        3,4,5,6,7       same as 4

Imagewriter II (Imagewriter compatible)
--------------
1. Dot matrix b&w/color printer (text and graphics).
2. Linefeeds # of vertical dots printed.
3. Density      XDPI    YDPI    XYDPI   Comments
        1        80     72       5760
        2       120     72       8640
        3       144     72      10368
        4       160     72      11520
        5       120     144     17280   two pass
        6       144     144     20736   two pass
        7       160     144     23040   two pass

Nec_Pinwriter (24-wire Pinwriter compatible (P5/P6/P7/P9/P2200))
-------------
1. Dot matrix b&w/color printer (text and graphics).
2. Drives all Nec 24-wire Pinwriter compatible printers.
3. Linefeeds # of vertical dots printed.
4. Density      XDPI    YDPI    XYDPI   Comments
        1        90     180      16200
        2       120     180      21600
        3       180     180      32400
        4       120     360      43200  two pass
        5       180     360      64800  two pass
        6       360     180      64800
        7       360     360     129600  two pass
5. A PaperSize of 'Wide Tractor' selects a maximum print width of
   13.6 inches (for wide carriage printers).

Okidata_92
----------
1. Dot matrix non-color printer (text and graphics).
2. Always linefeeds 7/72 inch (limitation of printer in graphics mode).
3. Densitie(s) supported are 72x72 dpi.

Okidata_293I
------------
1. Dot matrix b&w/color printer (text and graphics).
2. Drives 292 or 293 using the IBM interface module.
3. Linefeeds # of vertical dots printed (-1/2 dot if PaperType = Single) *3
4. Density      XDPI    YDPI    XYDPI   Comments
        1       120     144     17280
        2       240     144     34560
        3       120     288     34560   two pass
        4       240     288     69120   two pass
        5,6,7   same as 4
5. A PaperSize of 'Wide Tractor' selects a maximum print width of
   13.6 inches (for wide carriage printers).

Okimate-20
----------
1. Thermal transfer b&w/color printer (text and graphics).
2. Use Black ribbon for non-color dumps; Color ribbon for color dumps.
3. Linefeeds an even # of dots printed. (ie. if 3 printed, 4 advanced).
4. Densitie(s) supported are 120x144(1) dpi.

Quadram_QuadJet
---------------
1. Ink jet b&w/color printer (text and graphics).
2. Linefeeds # of vertical dots printed.
3. Densitie(s) supported are 83x84(1) dpi.

Qume_LetterPro_20
```

1. Daisywheel printer (text only).

Seiko_5300

1. Thermal transfer b&w/color printer (graphics only).
2. Use Black ribbon for non-color dumps; Color ribbon for color dumps.
3. Density

Density	XDPI	YDPI	XYDPI	Comments
1	152	152	23104	drives CH-5301 printer
2	203	203	41209	drives CH-5312 printer
3	240	240	57600	drives CH-5303 printer
4, 5,6,7		same as 3		

   You must select the proper density to drive the specific printer that you have.
4. This driver is not on the V1.3 Workbench or Extras disk. It is available on BIX and directly from Seiko.

Seiko_5300a

1. Thermal transfer b&w/color printer (graphics only).
2. Use Black ribbon for non-color dumps; Color ribbon for color dumps.
3. Density

Density	XDPI	YDPI	XYDPI	Comments
1	152	152	23104	drives CH-5301 printer
2	203	203	41209	drives CH-5312 printer
3	240	240	57600	drives CH-5303 printer
4, 5,6,7		same as 3		

   You must select the proper density to drive the specific printer that you have.
4. This driver is the same as the Seiko_5300 driver EXCEPT it is approximately 2 times faster (during color dumps) and requires LOTS of memory (up to 1,564,569 bytes for a full 8 x 10 inch (1927 x 2173 dot) color dump). Typically full-size (color) dumps are 1927 x 1248 dots and require 898,569 bytes. The memory requirements are 1/3 when doing a non-color printout.
5. This driver is not on the V1.3 Workbench or Extras disk. It is available on BIX and directly from Seiko.

Tektronix_4693D

1. Thermal transfer b&w/color printer (graphics only).
2. Densitie(s) supported are 300x300(1) dpi
3. Due to the way the printer images a picture none of the printer preferences options affect the printout with the following exceptions:
   a)Aspect - Horizontal, Vertical
   b)Shade - B&W, Grey_Scale, Color
   ...as a result of this only full size pictures can be printed.
4. Keypad menu option 3b COLOR ADJUSTMENT may be set from the keypad. For normal prints this option should be set to "do not adjust".
5. Keypad menu option 3d VIDEO COLOR CORRECTION may be set from the keypad. For normal prints this option should be set to "do not adjust".
6. Keypad menu option 5 BACKGROUND COLOR EXCHANGE may be set from the keypad. For normal prints this option should be set to "print colors as recieved".
7. Once a picture has been printed additional copies may be printed whithout resending by using the printers keypad.
8. This driver is not on the V1.3 Workbench or Extras disk. It is available on BIX and directly from Tektronix.

Tektronix_4696

1. Ink jet b&w/color printer (text and graphics).
2. Always linefeeds 4 dots (limitation of printer).
3. Densities supported are 121x120(1), 242x120(black)(2) and 242x120(color)(3).
   Selecting a density of 2 or higher really doesn't give you true 242 dpi resolution since the printer only has 121 x dots per inch.
   Instead this mode tells the printer to go into it's double pass mode. Here, it outputs a line of dots at 121 dpi; and outputs the line again (shifted to the right by 1/242 of an inch). This produces much more vibrate colors and gives the illusion of more resolution. One drawback is that large areas of solid colors (red, green, and blue specifically) tend to over-saturate the paper with ink. Density1 outputs all colors in one pass. Density 2 does a double pass on black. Density 3 does a double pass on all colors. Density 1 to 3 correspond to the printer's graphics printing modes 1 to 3 (respectively).
4. This driver is not on the V1.3 Workbench or Extras disk. It is available on BIX and directly from Tektronix.
5. A PaperSize of 'Wide Tractor' selects a maximum print width of 9.0 inches (for wide roll paper).

Toshiba_P351C (24-pin Toshiba compatible)

1. Dot matrix b&w/color printer (text and graphics).
2. Drives all Toshiba_P351C compatible printers.
3. Linefeeds # of vertical dots printed.
4. Density

Density	XDPI	YDPI	XYDPI	Comments
1	180	180	32400	
2	360	180	64800	
3,4,5,6,7		same as 2		

5. A PaperSize of 'Wide Tractor' selects a maximum print width of 13.5 inches (for wide carriage printers).

Toshiba_P351SX (24-pin Toshiba compatible)

1. Dot matrix b&w/color printer (text and graphics).
2. Drives all Toshiba_P351SX (321SL, 321SLC, 341SL) compatible printers.
3. Linefeeds # of vertical dots printed.
4. Density

Density	XDPI	YDPI	XYDPI	Comments
1	180	180	32400	
2	360	180	64800	
3	180	360	64800	two pass
4	360	360	129600	two pass
5,6,7	same as 4			

5. A PaperSize of 'Wide Tractor' selects a maximum print width of 13.5 inches (for wide carriage printers).

Xerox_4020

1. Ink jet b&w/color printer (text and graphics).
2. Always linefeeds 4 dots (limitation of printer).
3. This driver is IDENTICAL to the Diablo_C-150 driver EXCEPT it outputs all black dots TWICE. This is a special feature of this printer and produces much more solid, darker black shades. Please note that some printing time overhead results from this feature; if you don't want it use the Diablo_C-150 driver.
4. Densities supported are 121x120(1) and 242x240(2) dpi.
   Selecting a density of 2 or higher really doesn't give you true 240 dpi resolution since the Xerox_4020 only has 121 x dots per inch.
   Instead this mode tells the printer to go into it's pseudo 240 dpi mode. Here, it outputs a line of dots at 121 dpi; moves the paper up 1/240 of an inch and outputs the line again (shifted to the right by 1/240 of an inch). This produces much more vibrate colors and gives the illusion of more resolution. One drawback is that large areas of solid colors (red, green, and blue specifically) tend to over-saturate the paper with ink.
5. A PaperSize of 'Wide Tractor' selects a maximum print width of 9.0 inches (for wide roll paper).

Notes

*0 - on most printers friction fed paper tends to produce better looking (ie. less horizontal banding) graphic dumps than tractor fed paper.

*1 - in this mode the printer cannot print two consecutive dots in a row. It is recommended that you only use this density for B&W Shade dumps.

*2 - only when 72 YDPI is selected. This option is useful if you notice tiny white horizontal strips in your printout.

*3 - only when 144 YDPI is selected. This option is useful if you notice tiny white horizontal strips in your printout.

```
NAME
     PCPRD_PRTCOMMAND -- send a command to the printer

FUNCTION
   This function sends a command to either the parallel or serial
   device.  The printer device maps this command to the control
   code set of the current printer.  The commands supported can
   be found with the printer.device/Write command.  All printers
   may not support all functions.

IO REQUEST IOPrtCmdReq
     io_Message      mn_ReplyPort set
     io_Device       preset by OpenDevice
     io_Unit         preset by OpenDevice
     io_Command      PRD_PRTCOMMAND
     io_PrtCommand   the actual command number
     io_Parm0        parameter for the command
     io_Parm1        parameter for the command
     io_Parm2        parameter for the command
     io_Parm3        parameter for the command

RESULTS
     Errors: if the PRD_PRTCOMMAND succeeded, then io_Error will be zero.
     Otherwise io_Error will be non-zero.  An error of -1 indicates that
     the command is not supported by the current printer driver.  This
     could be used to check if the connected printer supports a particular
     command (italics for example).

SEE ALSO
     printer.device/Write printer.h, parallel.device, Preferences
```



```
NAME
     PRD_QUERY - query printer port/line status

FUNCTION
     This command returns the status of the printer port's lines and
     registers.  Since the printer port uses either the serial or
     parallel port for i/o, the actual status returned is either the
     serial or parallel port's status.

IO REQUEST
     io_Message      mn_ReplyPort set if quick I/O is not possible
     io_Device       preset by the call to OpenDevice
     io_Command      PRD_QUERY
     io_Data         ptr to 2 UBYTES where result will be stored.

RESULTS
  io_Data          BIT  ACTIVE  FUNCTION (SERIAL DEVICE)

          LSB        0   low    reserved
                     1   low    reserved
                     2   low    reserved
                     3   low    Data Set Ready
                     4   low    Clear To Send
                     5   low    Carrier Detect
                     6   low    Ready To Send
                     7   low    Data Terminal Ready
          MSB        8   high   read buffer overflow
                     9   high   break sent (most recent output)
                    10   high   break received (as latest input)
                    11   high   transmit x-OFFed
                    12   high   receive x-OFFed
                 13-15          reserved


  io_Data          BIT  ACTIVE  FUNCTION (PARALLEL DEVICE)

                     0   hi      printer busy (offline)
                     1   hi      paper out
                     2   hi      printer selected
                                  (WARNING: the bit 2 line is also connected
                                   to the serial port's ring indicator pin
                                   on the A500 and A2000)
                   3-7           reserved

  io_Actual        1-parallel, 2-serial
```

```
printer.device/PRD_RAWWRITE                          printer.device/PRD_RAWWRITE

    NAME
        PRD_RAWWRITE - transparent write command

    FUNCTION
        This is a non standard write command that performs no
        processing on the data passed to it.

    IO REQUEST
        io_Message      mn_ReplyPort set if quick I/O is not possible
        io_Command      PRD_RAWWRITE
        io_Flags        IOB_QUICK set if quick I/O is possible
        io_Length       the number of bytes in io_Data
        io_Data         the raw bytes to write to the printer
```

```
printer.device/PWrite                                      printer.device/PWrite

    NAME
        PWrite - internal write to printer port

    SYNOPSIS
        error = (*PrinterData->pd_PWrite)(buffer, length);
        D0                                 A0      D0

    FUNCTION
        PWrite writes 'length' bytes directly to the printer.  This
        function is generally called by printer drivers to send
        their buffer(s) to the printer.

        This function is accessed by referencing off the PrinterData (PD)
        structure.  Below is a code fragment to show how to do get access
        to a pointer to the PrinterData (PD) structure.

        #include <exec/types.h>
        #include <devices/printer.h>
        #include <devices/prtbase.h>

        struct IODRPReq PReq;
        struct PrinterData *PD;
        struct PrinterExtendedData *PED;

        /* open the printer device (any version); if it opened... */
        if (OpenDevice("printer.device", 0, &PReq, 0) == NULL) {

            /* get pointer to printer data strcuture */
            PD = (struct PrinterData *)PReq.io_Device;

            /* write something directly to the printer */
            (*PD->pd_PWrite)("Hello world\n", 12);

            CloseDevice(&PReq); /* close the printer device */
        }
```

TABLE OF CONTENTS


```
   NAME
       AbortIO(ioRequest) -- abort an I/O request
               A1
   FUNCTION
      This is an exec.library call.

      This function attempts to aborts a specified read or write request.
      If the request is active, it is stopped immediately. If the request is
      queued, it is painlessly removed.  The request will be returned
      in the same way any completed request it.

      After AbortIO(), you must generally do a WaitIO().

   INPUTS
      iORequest  -- pointer to the IORequest Block that is to be aborted.

   RESULTS
       io_Error -- if the Abort succeded, then io_Error will be #IOERR_ABORTED

           (-2) and the request will be flagged as aborted (bit 5 of
           io_Flags is set).  If the Abort failed, then the Error will be zero.
   BUGS
       Previous to version 34, the serial.device would often hang when
       aborting CTS/RTS handshake requests.  This was the cause of the
       incorrect assumption that AbortIO() does not need to be followed
       by a wait for a reply (or a WaitIO()).
```

```
NAME
    BeginIO(ioRequest),deviceNode -- start up an I/O process
            A1        A6
FUNCTION
    This is a direct function call to the device.  It is intended for
    more advanced programmers.  See exec's DoIO() and SendIO() for
    the normal method of calling devices.

    This function initiates a I/O request made to the serial
    device. Other than read or write, the functions are performed
    synchronously, and do not depend on any interrupt handling
    logic (or it's associated discontinuities), and hence should
    be performed as IO_QUICK.
    With some exceptions, reads and writes are merely initiated by
    BeginIO, and thusly return to the caller as begun, not completed.
    Completion is signalled via the standard ReplyMsg routine.
    Multiple requests are handled via FIFO queueing.
    One exception to this non-QUICK handling of reads and writes
    is for READS when:
      - IO_QUICK bit is set
      - There are no pending read requests
      - There is already enough data in the input buffer to satisfy
        this I/O Request immediately.
    In this case, the IO_QUICK flag is not cleared, and the request
    is completed by the time it returns to the caller. There is no
    ReplyMsg or signal bit activity in this case.

INPUTS
    ioRequest  -- pointer to an I/O Request Block of size
        io_ExtSerSize (see serial.i for size/definition),
        containing a valid command in io_Command to process,
        as well as the command's other required parameters.
    deviceNode -- pointer to the "serial.device", as found in
        the IO_DEVICE of the ioRequest.

RESULTS
    io_Error -- if the BeginIO succeded, then Error will be null.
        If the BeginIO failed, then the Error will be non-zero.
        I/O errors won't be reported until the io completes.

SEE ALSO
     devices/serial.h
```



```
NAME
    CloseDevice -- close the serial port

SYNOPSIS
    CloseDevice(deviceNode)
                A1
FUNCTION
    This is an exec call that terminates communication with the
    serial device.  Upon closing, the device's input buffer is freed.

    Note that all IORequests MUST be complete before closing.
     If any are pending, your program must AbortIO() then WaitIO()
    to complete them.

INPUTS
    deviceNode - pointer to the device node, set by Open

SEE ALSO
    serial.device/OpenDevice
```

```
NAME
    Break -- send a break signal over the serial line

FUNCTION
    This command sends a break signal (serial line held low
    for an extended period) out the serial port. This is accom-
    plished by setting the UARTBRK bit of reg ADKCON. After a
    duration (user specifiable via setparams, default 250000
    microseconds) the bit is reset and the signal discontinued.
    If the QUEUEDBRK bit of io_SerFlags is set in the io_Request
    block, the request is placed at the back of the write-request
    queue and executed in turn. If the QUEUEDBRK bit is not set,
    the break is started immediately, control returns to the
    caller, and the timer discontinues the signal after the
    duration is completed. Be aware that calling BREAK may
     affect other commands such as ABORT, FLUSH, STOP, START, etc...

IO REQUEST
    io_Message      mn_ReplyPort initialized
    io_Device       set by OpenDevice
    io_Unit         set by OpenDevice
    io_Command      SDCMD_BREAK
    io_Flags        set/reset IO_QUICK per above description

RESULTS
    Error -- if the Break succeded, then Error will be null.
        If the Break failed, then the Error will be non-zero.
```



```
NAME
    Clear -- clear the serial port buffers

FUNCTION
    This command resets the serial port's read buffer pointers.

IO REQUEST
    io_Message      mn_ReplyPort initialized
    io_Device       set by OpenDevice
    io_Unit         set by OpenDevice
    io_Command      CMD_CLEAR

RESULTS
    Error -- If the Clear succeded, then io_Error will be null.
             If the Clear failed, then the io_Error will be non-zero.
```

```
NAME
    Flush -- clear all queued I/O requests for the serial port

FUNCTION
    This command purges the read and write request queues for the
    serial device. Flush will not affect active requests.

IO REQUEST
    io_Message      mn_ReplyPort initialized
    io_Device       set by OpenDevice
    io_Unit         set by OpenDevice
    io_Command      CMD_FLUSH

RESULTS
    Error -- if the Flush succeded, then io_Error will be null.
             If the Flush failed, then the io_Error will be non-zero.
```



```
NAME
    Read -- read input from serial port

FUNCTION
    This command causes a stream of characters to be read in from
    the serial port buffer.  The number of characters is specified
    in io_Length.

    The Query function can be used to check how many characters
    are currently waiting in the serial port buffer.  If more characters
    are requested than are currently available, the ioRequest
    will be queued until it can be satisfied.


    The best way to handle reads is to first Query to get the number
    of characters currently in the buffer.  Then post a read request
    for that number of characters (or the maximum size of your buffer).

    If zero characters are in the buffer, post a request
    for 1 character.  When at least one is ready, the device will return
    it.  Now start over with another Query.

    Before the program exits, it must be sure to AbortIO() then WaitIO()
    any outstanding ioRequests.

IO REQUEST
    io_Message      A mn_ReplyPort is required
    io_Device       set by OpenDevice
    io_Unit         set by OpenDevice
    io_Command      CMD_READ
    io_Flags        If the IOB_QUICK bit is set, read will try
                     to complete the IO quickly
    io_Length       number of characters to receive.
    io_Data         pointer to buffer

RESULTS
    Error -- if the Read succeded, then io_Error will be null.
        If the Read failed, then io_Error will be non-zero.
          io_Error will indicate problems such as parity mismatch,
          break, and buffer overrun.

SEE ALSO
     serial.device/CMD_QUERY
     serial.device/SDCMD_SETPARAMS

BUGS
     Having multiple outstanding read IORequests at any one time will
     probably fail.

     Old documentation mentioned a mode where io_Length was set to -1.
     If you want a NULL terminated read, use the io_TermArray instead.
```

serial.device/CMD_RESET

```
serial.device/CMD_RESET                           serial.device/CMD_RESET

   NAME
       Reset -- reinitializes the serial port

   FUNCTION
       This command resets the serial port to its freshly initialized
       condition. It aborts all I/O requests both queued and current,
       relinquishes the current buffer, obtains a new default sized
       buffer, and sets the port's flags and parameters to their
       boot-up time default values. The functions places the reset
       parameter values in the ioRequest block.

   IO REQUEST
       io_Message      mn_ReplyPort initialized
       io_Device       set by OpenDevice
       io_Unit         set by OpenDevice
       io_Command      CMD_RESET

   RESULTS
       Error -- if the Reset succeded, then Error will be null.
           If the Reset failed, then the Error will be non-zero.
```

serial.device/CMD_START

```
serial.device/CMD_START                           serial.device/CMD_START

   NAME
       Start -- restart paused I/O over the serial port

   FUNCTION
       This function restarts all current I/O on the serial port by
       sending an xON to the "other side", and submitting a "logical
       xON" to "our side", if/when appropriate to current activity.

   IO REQUEST
       io_Message      mn_ReplyPort initialized
       io_Device       set by OpenDevice
       io_Unit         set by OpenDevice
       io_Command      CMD_START

   RESULTS

   SEE ALSO
       serial.device/CMD_STOP
```

```
NAME
    Stop -- pause all current I/O over the serial port

FUNCTION
    This command halts all current I/O on the serial port by
    sending an xOFF to the "other side", and submitting a "logical
    xOFF" to "our side", if/when appropriate to current activity.

IO REQUEST
    io_Message      mn_ReplyPort initialized
    io_Device       set by OpenDevice
    io_Unit         set by OpenDevice
    io_Command      CMD_STOP

RESULTS

SEE ALSO
    serial.device/CMD_START
```



```
NAME
    Write -- send output to serial port

FUNCTION
    This command causes a stream of characters to be written out
    the serial port. The number of characters is specified in
    io_Length, unless -1 is used, in which case output is sent until
    a null(0x00) is encountered.

IO REQUEST
    io_Message      must have mn_ReplyPort initialized
    io_Device       set by OpenDevice
    io_Unit         set by OpenDevice
    io_Command      CMD_WRITE
    io_Flags        Set IOF_QUICK to try quick I/O
    io_Length       number of characters to transmit, or if set
                    to -1 transmit until null encountered in buffer
    io_Data         pointer to block of data to transmit

RESULTS
    Error -- if the Write succeded, then io_Error will be null.
        If the Write failed, then the io_Error will be non-zero.

SEE ALSO
     serial.device/SDCMD_SETPARAMS
```

```
NAME
    OpenDevice -- Request an opening of the serial device.

SYNOPSIS
    error = OpenDevice(SERIALNAME, unit, ioRequest, flags)
    D0                 A0          D0    A1         D0

FUNCTION
    This is an exec call.  Exec will search for the serial.device, and
    if found, will pass this call on to the device.

    Unless the shared-access bit (bit 5 of io_SerFlags) is set,
    exclusive use is granted and no other access to that unit is
    allowed until the owner closes it.  All the serial-specific fields
    in the ioRequest are initialized to their most recent values (or
    the Preferences default, for the first time open).

    If support of 7-wire handshaking (i.e. RS232-C CTS/RTS protocol)
    is required, set the 7WIRE bit in io_SerFlags before opening
    the serial device.

INPUTS
    SERIALNAME      - pointer to literal string "serial.device"
    unit            - Must be zero, or a user setable unit number.
                       (This field is used by multiple port controllers)
                      Zero specifies the built-in serial port.
    ioRequest       - pointer to an ioRequest block of size io_ExtSerSize
                      to be initialized by the serial.device.
                       (see devices/serial.h for the definition)
                       NOTE use of io_SerFlags (see FUNCTION above)
             IMPORTANT: The ioRequest block MUST be of size io_ExtSerSize !
    flags           - Must be zero for future compatibility

RESULTS
    D0          - same as io_Error
    io_Error  - If the Open succeded, then io_Error will be null.
                  If the Open failed, then io_Error will be non-zero.
    io_Device - A pointer to whatever device will handle the calls
                for this unit.  This pointer may be different depending
                on what unit is requested.

BUGS
    If 7-wire handshaking is specified, this enables a timeout "feature".
    If the device holds off the computer for more than about 30-60
    seconds, the device will return the write request with the error
    SerErr_TimerErr.  Don't depend on this, however.  If you want a timeout,
    set up the timer.device and wait for either timer, or serial IO to
    complete.

    On open, the serial.device allocates the misc.resource for the
    serial port.  It does not return it until the serial.device is
    expunged from memory.  It should return it when no more openers
    exist.

SEE ALSO
    serial.device/CloseDevice
    devices/serial.h
```



```
NAME
    Query -- query serial port/line status

FUNCTION
    This command return the status of the serial port lines and
    registers. The number of unread bytes in the serial device's
    read buffer is shown in io_Actual.

     The break send & received flags are cleared by a query, and
     whenever a read IORequest is returned with a error
     in io_Error.

IO REQUEST
    io_Message      mn_ReplyPort initialized
    io_Device       preset by OpenDevice
    io_Unit         preset by OpenDevice
    io_Command      SDCMD_QUERY

RESULTS
    io_Status         BIT  ACTIVE  FUNCTION

              LSB      0    ---    reserved
                       1    ---    reserved
                       2    high   parallel "sel" on the A1000
                                   On the A500 & A2000, "sel" is also
                                   connected to the serial port's
                                   "Ring Indicator".  Be cautious when
                                   making cables.
                       3    low    Data Set Ready
                       4    low    Clear To Send
                       5    low    Carrier Detect
                       6    low    Ready To Send
                       7    low    Data Terminal Ready
              MSB      8    high   hardware overrun
                       9    high   break sent (most recent output)
                      10    high   break received (as latest input)
                      11    high   transmit x-OFFed
                      12    high   receive x-OFFed
                   13-15    ---    reserved

    io_Actual       set to count of unread input characters

    io_Error -- Query will always succeded.
```

```
NAME
    SetParams -- change parameters for the serial port

FUNCTION
    This command allows the caller to change parameters for the
    serial device. Except for xON-xOFF enable/disable, it will
    reject a setparams call if any reads or writes are active
    or pending.
       Note specifically:

 1. Valid input for io_Baud is between 112 and 292000 baud inclusive;
    asynchronous i/o above 32KB (especially on a busy system) may
    be ambitious.
 2. The EOFMODE and QUEUEDBRK bits of io_SerFlags can be set/reset
    in the io_Rqst block without a call to SetParams. The SHARED
    and 7WIRE bits of io_SerFlags can be used in OpenDevice calls.
    ALL OTHER PARAMETERS CAN ONLY BE CHANGED BY THE SetParams
    COMMAND.
 3. RBufLen must be at least 64.
 4. If not used, io_ExtFlags MUST be set to zero.
 5. xON-xOFF is by default enabled. The XDISABLED bit is the only
    parameter that can be changed via a SetParams call while the
    device is active. Note that this will return the value
    SerErr_DevBusy in the io_Error field.

     xON/xOFF handshaking is inappropriate for certain binary transfer
     protocalls, such as Xmodem.  The binary data might contain the
     xON (ASCII 17) and xOFF (ASCII 19) characters.

 6. If trying to run MIDI, you should set the RAD_BOOGIE bit of
    io_SerFlags to eliminate unneeded overhead. Specifically, this skips
    checks for parity, x-OFF handling, character lengths other than
    8 bits, and testing for a break signal. Setting RAD_BOOGIE will
    also set the XDISABLED bit.
    Note that writing data (that's already in MIDI format) at MIDI rates
    is easily accomplished. Using this driver alone for MIDI reads may,
    however, may not be reliable, due to MIDI timestamping requirements,
    and possibility of overruns in a busy multitasking and/or display
    intensive environment.
 7. If you select mark or space parity (see io_ExtFlags in serial.h),
    this will cause the SERB_PARTY_ON bit to be set, and the setting
    of SERB_PARTY_ODD to be ignored.
 8. For best results, set the RAD_BOOGIE flag whenever possible.  See
     #6 for details.
 9. Note that at this time parity is *not* calculated for the xON-xOFF
     characters.  If you have a system that is picky about the parity of
     these, you must set your own xON-xOFF characters in io_CtlChar.

IO REQUEST
    io_Message      mn_ReplyPort initialized
    io_Device       preset by OpenDevice
    io_Unit         preset by OpenDevice
    io_Command      SDCMD_SETPARAMS (0x0B)
                     NOTE that the following fields are filled in by Open
                    to reflect the serial device's current configuration.
    io_CtlChar      a longword containing byte values for the
                    xON,xOFF,INQ,ACK fields (respectively)
                    (INQ/ACK not used at this time)
    io_RBufLen      length in bytes of input buffer
                     NOTE that any change in buffer size causes the
                    current buffer to be deallocated and a new,
                    correctly sized one to be allocated. Thusly,
                    the CONTENTS OF THE OLD BUFFER ARE LOST.
    io_ExtFlags     additional serial flags (bitdefs in devices/serial.h)
                     mark & space parity may be specified here.
    io_Baud         baud rate for reads AND writes. (See 1 above)
    io_BrkTime      duration of break signal in MICROseconds
    io_TermArray    ASCII descending-ordered 8-byte array of
                    termination characters. If less than 8 chars
                    used, fill out array w/lowest valid value.
                    Terminators are checked only if EOFMODE bit of
                    io_Serflags is set. (e.g. x512F040303030303 )
    io_ReadLen      number of bits in read word (1-8) not including parity
    io_WriteLen     number of bits in write word (1-8) "      "       "
    io_StopBits     number of stop bits (0, 1 or 2)
    io_SerFlags     see devices/serial.h for bit equates, NOTE that x00
                    yields exclusive access, xON/OFF-enabled, no
                    parity checking, 3-wire protocol and TermArray
                    inactive.

RESULTS
    Error -- if the SetParams succeded, then Error will be null.
        If the SetParams failed, then the Error will be non-zero.

SEE ALSO
     exec/OpenDevice
```

TABLE OF CONTENTS


```
   TIMER REQUEST
        A time request is a non standard IO Request.  It has an IORequest
        followed by a timeval structure.

   TIMEVAL
        A timeval structure consists of two longwords.  The first is
        the number of seconds, the latter is the fractional number
        of microseconds.  The microseconds must always be 'normalized"
        e.g. the longword must be between 0 and one million.

   UNITS
        The timer contains two units -- one that is precise but
        inaccurate, the other that has little system overhead,
        is very stable over time, but only has limitied resolution.

   UNIT_MICROHZ
        This unit uses a programmable timer in the 8520 to keep
        track of its time.  It has precision down to about 2
        microseconds, but will drift as system load increases.
        The timer is typically accurate to within five percent.

   UNIT_VBLANK
        This unit is driven by the vertical blank interrupt.  It
        is very stable over time, but only has a resolution of
        16667 microseconds (or 20000 microseconds in PAL land).
        The timer is very cheap to use, and should be used by
        those who are waiting for long periods of time (typically
        1/2 second or more).

   LIBRARY
         In addition to the normal device calls, the timer also supports
         three direct, library like calls.  They are for manipulating
         timeval structures.  Addition, subtraction, and comparison
         are supported.

   BUGS
         In the V1.2/V1.3 release, the timer device has problems with
         very short time requests.  When one of these is made, other
         timer requests may be finished inaccurately.  A side effect
         is that AmigaDOS requests such as "Delay(0);" or
         "WaitForChar(x,0);" are unreliable.
```

```
NAME
     AddTime - add one time request to another

SYNOPSIS
     AddTime( Dest, Source ), timer.device
              A0    A1         A6

     void AddTime(struct *timeval, struct *timeval);

FUNCTION
     This routine adds one timeval structure to another.  The
     results are stored in the destination (Dest + Source -> Dest)

     A0 and A1 will be left unchanged

INPUTS
     Dest, Source -- pointers to timeval structures.

EXCEPTIONS

SEE ALSO

BUGS
```



```
NAME
     CmpTime - Compare two timeval structures

SYNOPSIS
     result = CmpTime( Dest, Source ), timer.device
     D0                A0    A1         A6

     BYTE CmpTime(struct *timeval, struct *timeval);

FUNCTION
     This routine compares two timeval structures.

     A0 and A1 will be left unchanged

INPUTS
     Dest, Source -- pointers to timeval structures.

RESULTS
     result = -1     if Dest has more time than Source
     result =  0     if Dest has the same time as Source
     result = +1     if Dest has less time than Source

EXCEPTIONS

SEE ALSO

BUGS
     Former versions of this AutoDoc had the sense of the result wrong.
```

```
NAME
     SubTime - subtract one time request from another

SYNOPSIS
     SubTime( Dest, Source ), timer.device
              A0    A1         A6

     void SubTime(struct *timeval, struct *timeval);

FUNCTION
     This routine subtracts one timeval structure from another.  The
     results are stored in the destination (Dest - Source -> Dest)

     A0 and A1 will be left unchanged

INPUTS
     Dest, Source -- pointers to timeval structures.

EXCEPTIONS

SEE ALSO

BUGS
```



```
NAME
    TR_ADDREQUEST -- submit a request to time time

FUNCTION
    Ask the timer to count off a specified amount of time.  The timer will
    chain this request with its other requests, and will reply the message
    back to the user when the timer counts down to zero.

    The message may be forced to finish early with an AbortIO()/WaitIO()
    pair.

TIMER REQUEST
    io_Message      mn_ReplyPort initialized
    io_Device       preset by timer in OpenDevice
    io_Unit         preset by timer in OpenDevice
    io_Command      TR_ADDREQUEST
    io_Flags        IOF_QUICK allowable
    tr_time         a timeval structure specifiy how long until
                        the driver will reply

RESULTS
    tr_time         will contain junk

SEE ALSO
    exec/AbortIO
    exec/WaitIO
```

```
NAME
    TR_GETSYSTIME -- get the system time

FUNCTION
    Ask the timer what time it is.  The system time starts
    off at zero at power on, but may be initialized via
    the TR_SETSYSTIME call.

    System time is monotonically increasing, and guaranteed
    to be unique (except of someone sets the time backwards).
    The time is incremented every vertical blank by the
    vertical blanking interval;  in addition it is changed
    every time someone asks what time it is.  This way
    the return value of the system time is unique
    and unrepeating.

TIMER REQUEST
    io_Message      mn_ReplyPort initialized
    io_Device       preset by timer in OpenDevice
    io_Unit         preset by timer in OpenDevice
    io_Command      TR_ADDREQUEST
    io_Flags        IOF_QUICK allowable

RESULTS
    tr_time         the timeval structure will be filled in with
                        the current system time
```



```
NAME
    TR_SETSYSTIME -- set the system time

FUNCTION
    Set the systems idea of what time it is.  The system
    starts out at time "zero" so it is safe to set it
    forward to the "real" time.  However care should be taken
    when setting the time backwards.  System time
    is speced as being monotonically increasing.

TIMER REQUEST
    io_Message      mn_ReplyPort initialized
    io_Device       preset by timer in OpenDevice
    io_Unit         preset by timer in OpenDevice
    io_Command      TR_ADDREQUEST
    io_Flags        IOF_QUICK allowable
    tr_time         a timeval structure with the current system
                       time

RESULTS
    none
```

TABLE OF CONTENTS


```
   NAME
       TD_ADDCHANGEINT - add a new change software int

   SYNOPSIS
       TDUAddChangeInt( IORequest ), UnitPtr
                        A1           A3

   FUNCTION
        Alas, the old TDURemove call was not robust enough.  This routine
        supports an extensible list of software interrupts for use by many
        different supporting drivers.

        The call does not "complete" (e.g. TermIO).  The request
        is stashed until TDURemChangeInt is called, when it is
        finally replied.

   INPUTS
        IORequest - a standard IO Request block (IO_DATA-> soft int struct).

   RESULTS

   EXCEPTIONS

   SEE ALSO

   BUGS
```

```
trackdisk.device/TD_CHANGENUM                    trackdisk.device/TD_CHANGENUM

   NAME
       TD_CHANGENUM - return the current disc change number

   SYNOPSIS
       TDUChangeNum( IORequest ), UnitPtr
                     A1           A3

   FUNCTION
       This routine checks to see if there is a disc in the drive
        of the specified unit.

   INPUTS
        IORequest - a standard IO Request block

   RESULTS

   EXCEPTIONS

   SEE ALSO

   BUGS
```

```
trackdisk.device/TD_CHANGESTATE                trackdisk.device/TD_CHANGESTATE

   NAME
       TD_CHANGESTATE - Return the current state of the disc

   SYNOPSIS
       TDUChangeState( IORequest ), UnitPtr
                       A1           A3

   FUNCTION
       This routine checks to see if there is a disc in the drive
        one the specified unit.

   INPUTS
        IORequest - a standard IO Request block

   RESULTS
        IO_ACTUAL -- nonzero if there is no diskette in the drive

   EXCEPTIONS

   SEE ALSO

   BUGS
```

```
NAME
     TD_FORMAT -- format the entire disc

SYNOPSIS
     TDUFormat( ioBlock ), DevNode
     D0         A1          A6

FUNCTION

     The function formats the entire disc, destroying all data.
     It fills all the sectors with the contents of the iOBlock.
     The iOBlock must point to (at least) one sector worth of
     information.  Any info greater than one sector is ignored.
     NO ERROR CHECKING is done

INPUTS


RESULTS


SEE ALSO
```



```
NAME
    TD_GETDRIVETYPE - return the type of the disk drive to the user

FUNCTION
     This routine returns the type of the disk to the user.
     This number will be a small integer.  It will come from
     the set of DRIVE... defines in trackdisk.h
     or trackdisk.i.

     The only way you can get to this call is if the trackdisk
     device understands the drive type of the hardware that is
     plugged in.  This is because the OpenDevice call will fail
     if the trackdisk device does not understand the drive type.
     To find raw drive identifiers see the disk resource's
     DR_GETUNITID entry point.

IO REQUEST
     io_Command      TD_GETDRIVETYPE

RESULTS
     io_Actual       the drive type connected to this unit.

SEE ALSO
     TD_GETNUMTRACKS
```

```
NAME
    TD_GETNUMTRACKS - return the number of tracks on this type of disk

FUNCTION
     This routine returns the number of tracks that are available
     on this disk unit.  This call obsoletes the older NUMTRACKS
     hard coded constant.

IO REQUEST
     io_Command      TD_GETNUMTRACKS

RESULTS
     io_Actual       number of tracks accessible on this unit

SEE ALSO
     TD_GETDRIVETYPE
```



```
NAME
     TD_MOTOR - user visible control for motor

SYNOPSIS
     TDUMotor( IOBlock ), UnitPtr, DevPtr
               A1         A3       A6

FUNCTION
     This routine allows the user to control the disc motor. He
     may turn it either on or off.  Note that the motor will be
     automatically turned on during an I/O request, but is never
     turned of except by this command.

INPUTS
     IOBlock - the command block for this IO operation.
         IO_ACTUAL -- returns the previous state of the motor
         IO_LENGTH -- the requested state of the motor
             0 ==> turn motor off
             1 ==> turn motor on

EXCEPTIONS

SEE ALSO

BUGS
```

```
NAME
     TD_PROTSTATUS -- return whether the current disk is write protected

SYNOPSIS
     TDUProtstatus( IOBlock ), UnitPtr, DevPtr
                     A1          A3       A6

FUNCTION
     This routine tells whether the current disk is write protected.

INPUTS
     IOBlock - the command block for this IO operation.
             IO_ACTUAL - nonzero if the disk is protected, 0 otherwise
             If there is no disk in the drive, then IO_ERROR is set
             to TDERR_DiskChanged

EXCEPTIONS

SEE ALSO

BUGS
```



```
NAME
     TD_RAWREAD - read a raw sector from the disk

FUNCTION
     This routine performs a raw read for the track disk.
     It seeks to the specified track and reads it in to the
     user's buffer.  This buffer MUST be in chip memory.

     NO PROCESSING OF THE TRACK IS DONE.  It will appear exactly
     as the bits come out off the disk -- hopefully in some legal MFM
     format (if you don't know what MFM is, you shouldn't be using
     this call...).  Caveat Programmer.

     This interface is intended for sophisticated programmers
     only.  Commodore-Amiga may make enhancements to the disk
     format in the future.  We will provide compatibility
     within the trackdisk device.  Anyone who uses this routine
     is bypassing this upwards compatibility.  If your application
     breaks, TOUGH!

     If this warning is not enough, then add suitable additional
     harrassment of your choice.


IO REQUEST
     io_Flags        if the IOTDB_INDEXSYNC bit is set then the driver
                       will make a best effort attempt to start reading
                       from the index mark.  Note that there
                       will be at least some delay, and perhaps a great
                       deal, of delay (if, for example, interrupts have
                       been Disabled()...).
     io_Command      TD_RAWREAD or ETD_RAWREAD.
     io_Length       Length of buffer (in bytes).  The maximum allowable
                       length is 32K bytes.
     io_Data         Pointer to buffer in chip memory where raw track
                       will be read into.
     io_Offset       The track number to read in (not this is different
                       from a normal trackdisk io call which is given
                       in terms of logical bytes from the beginning of
                       the disk.  This is because the trackdisk driver
                       has no idea what the format of the disk is).
     iotd_Count      (ETD_RAWREAD only) maximum allowable change counter
                       value

RESULTS
     io_Error        non-zero if there was an error

LIMITATIONS for synced reads and writes
     There is a delay between the index pulse and the start of bits
     coming in from the drive (e.g. dma started).  This delay
     is in the range of 135-200 micro seconds.  This delay breaks
     down as follows: 55 microsecs is software interrupt overhead
     (this is the time from interrupt to the write of the DSKLEN
     register).  66 microsecs is one horizontal line delay (remember
     that disk io is synchronized with agnus' display fetches).
     The last variable (0-65 microsecs) is an additional scan line
     since DSKLEN is poked anywhere in the horizontal line.  This leaves
     15 microsecs unaccounted for...  Sigh.

     In short, You will almost never get bits withing the first 135
     microseconds of the index pulse, and may not get it until 200
     microseconds.  At 4 microsecs/bit, this works out to be between
     4 and 7 bytes of user data of delay.

BUGS
     In V33/34 Kickstart, the length comparison depends on the
     value of a random memory location.  This makes the function
     unusable unless two drives are hooked up.

SEE ALSO
```

```
NAME
     TD_RAWWRITE - write a raw sector to the disk

FUNCTION
     NO PROCESSING OF THE TRACK IS DONE.  The disk will appear exactly
     as the bits come out of memory -- hopefully in some legal MFM
     format (if you don't know what MFM is, you shouldn't be using
     this call...).  Caveat Programmer.

     NO PROCESSING OF THE TRACK IS DONE.  It will exactly
     as the bits come out off the disk.  Caveat Programmer.

     This interface is intended for sophisticated programmers
     only.  Commodore-Amiga may make enhancements to the disk
     format in the future.  We will provide compatibility
     within the trackdisk device.  Anyone who uses this routine
     is bypassing this upwards compatibility.  If your application
     breaks, TOUGH!

     If this warning is not enough, then add suitable additional
     harrassment of your choice.


IO REQUEST
     io_Flags        if the IOTDB_INDEXSYNC bit is set then the driver
                       will make a best effort attempt to start writing
                       from the index mark.  Note that there
                       will be at least some delay, and perhaps a great
                       deal, of delay (if, for example, interrupts have
                       been Disabled()...).
     io_Command      TD_RAWWRITE or ETD_RAWWRITE.
     io_Length       Length of buffer (in bytes).  The maximum allowable
                       length is 32K bytes.
     io_Data         Pointer to buffer in chip memory where raw track
                       will be read into.
     io_Offset       The track number to read in (not this is different
                       from a normal trackdisk io call which is given
                       in terms of logical bytes from the beginning of
                       the disk.  This is because the trackdisk driver
                       has no idea what the format of the disk is).
     iotd_Count      (ETD_RAWWRITE only) maximum allowable change counter
                       value

RESULTS
     io_Error        non-zero if there was an error

LIMITATIONS for synced reads and writes
     There is a delay between the index pulse and the start of bits
     going out to the drive (e.g. write gate enabled).  This delay
     is in the range of 135-200 micro seconds.  This delay breaks
     down as follows: 55 microsecs is software interrupt overhead
     (this is the time from interrupt to the write of the DSKLEN
     register).  66 microsecs is one horizontal line delay (remember
     that disk io is synchronized with agnus' display fetches).
     The last variable (0-65 microsecs) is an additional scan line
     since DSKLEN is poked anywhere in the horizontal line.  This leaves
     15 microsecs unaccounted for...  Sigh.

     In short, You will almost never get bits withing the first 135
     microseconds of the index pulse, and may not get it until 200
     microseconds.  At 4 microsecs/bit, this works out to be between
     4 and 7 bytes of user data of delay.

BUGS
     In V33/34 Kickstart, the length comparison depends on the
     value of a random memory location.  This makes the function
     unusable unless two drives are hooked up.

SEE ALSO
     TD_RAWREAD
```

```
NAME
    TD_REMCHANGEINT - remove a change software int

SYNOPSIS
    TDURemChangeInt( IORequest ), UnitPtr
                     A1           A3

FUNCTION
     This function unlinks the IOReqest stashed by AddChangeInt.
     It also replies it to the user.

INPUTS
     IORequest - a standard IO Request block

RESULTS

EXCEPTIONS

SEE ALSO

BUGS
```



```
NAME
     TD_SEEK - user visible control for the heads

SYNOPSIS
     TDUSeek( IOBlock ), TDLib
              A1         A6

FUNCTION
     This routine allows the user to control the seek position.
     Note that the heads will be automatically seeked during an
     I/O request; this command allows the heads to be preseeked
     if the next position is known prior to the I/O being ready.

INPUTS
     IOBlock - the command block for this IO operation.
         IO_OFFSET -- the location to seek to

EXCEPTIONS

SEE ALSO

BUGS
```

Section C

Resource Summaries

This section contains summaries for system resource routines. These documents have been extracted from the original source code and are often called **autodocs**. Resources are low-level hardware control functions that, typically, are not used directly by programmers. Most of the resources only support access from assembly language.

> **WARNING**: *Under the multitasking operating system, user-level tasks are generally NOT allowed to directly use the hardware features. If your program requires direct hardware access, resources provide a way of asking for ownership of the involved hardware components. Indiscriminate hardware meddling will cause problems the next time the hardware or operating system is upgraded.*

There are currently four standard resources in the Amiga system:

disk — grants temporary exclusive access to the disk hardware. (For each of the four possible disk/MFM units)

cia — grants access to specific bits and individual interrupts from each of the 8520 CIA (Complex Interface Adapter) chips.

There are two cia resources: ciaa.resource and ciab.resource, which correspond to the odd and even 8520 chips.

potgo — manages the bits of the POTGO (write-only) and POTINP (read-only) registers. These custom chip registers control the proportional input pins on the controller ports. The pins may also be used for digital input and output. Intuition uses port 1 for reading the right and (optional) middle mouse buttons.

misc — grants exclusive access to functional blocks of chip registers. At this time definitions have been made for the serial and parallel hardware. When a task owns the misc resource for a port, it has control over that port's associated hardware.

See the *Amiga Hardware Reference Manual* for detailed information on the actual hardware involved. This section covers the proper arbitration under the multitasking system.

> **WARNING**: *Resources are just one step above direct hardware manipulation. You are advised to try the higher level device and library approach before resorting to the hardware.*

Examples:

```
*
* Assembly language fragment that grabs one of the two groups of serial
* port bits (using the misc.resource).  If it is successful at obtaining
* the resource, it will hang on to it forever, and never return.
*
* This example must be linked with "amiga.lib"
*
                INCLUDE "exec/types.i"
                INCLUDE "resources/misc.i"

_AbsExecBase    equ 4
JSRLIB  MACRO
        XREF    _LVO\1
        JSR     _LVO\1(A6)
        ENDM

                move.l  _AbsExecBase,a6
                lea.l   MiscName(pc),a1
                JSRLIB  OpenResource
                tst.l   d0
                beq.s   no_open
                move.l  d0,a6           ;resource base in A6
;
; We now have a pointer to a resource.
; Call one of its library-like vectors.
;
                move.l  #MR_SERIALBITS,d0   ;We want these bits
                lea.l   MyName(pc),a1       ;This is our name
                jsr     MR_ALLOCMISCRESOURCE(a6)
                tst.l   d0
                bne.s   no_get              ;Someone else got it
;
; We just stole the serial port registers.  Wait forever.
; Nobody else can use the serial port, including the serial.device!
;
                move.l  _AbsExecBase,a6
                moveq   #0,d0               ;Wait for nothing (forever)
                JSRLIB  Wait
no_get                                  ;Someone else has it, exit!
no_open         moveq   #21,d0
                rts

MiscName        dc.b    'misc.resource',0
MyName          dc.b    'Serial Port hog',0
                END
```

```
/* An example of using the potgo.resource to read pins 9 and 5 of
 * port 1 (the non-mouse port).  This bypasses the gameport.device.
 * When the right button on a mouse plugged into port 1 is pressed,
 * the read value will change.
 *
 * Use of port 0 (mouse) is unaffected.
 */
#include "exec/types.h"
#include "libraries/dos.h"

APTR  PotgoBase;
ULONG potbits;
UWORD value;

#define UNLESS(x) if(!(x))
#define UNTIL(x)  while(!(x))

#define OUTRY 1L<<15
#define DATRY 1L<<14
#define OUTRX 1L<<13
#define DATRX 1L<<12

void main()
{
        UNLESS(PotgoBase=(APTR)OpenResource("potgo.resource"))
            exit(RETURN_FAIL);
        printf("PotgoBase is at $%lx\n",PotgoBase);

        potbits=AllocPotBits(OUTRY|DATRY|OUTRX|DATRX);
        /* Get the bits for the right and middle mouse buttons
           on the alternate mouse port. */

        if(potbits != (OUTRY|DATRY|OUTRX|DATRX))
            {
            printf("Pot bits are already allocated! %lx\n",potbits);
            FreePotBits(potbits);
            exit(RETURN_FAIL+1);
            }

        WritePotgo(0xFFFFFFFFL,potbits);
        /* Set all ones in the register (masked by potbits) */

        UNTIL(SIGBREAKF_CTRL_C & SetSignal(0L,0L))
            /* until CTRL-C is pressed */
            {
            value=*(UWORD *)0x00DFF016;
            /* Read word at $DFF016 */
            printf("POTINP = $%lx\n",value & potbits);
            /* Show what was read (restricted to our allocated bits) */
            }

        FreePotBits(potbits);
}
```

TABLE OF CONTENTS

TABLE OF CONTENTS

```
NAME
    AbleICR -- enable/disable ICR interrupts

SYNOPSIS
    oldMask = AbleICR(mask),  Resource
    D0                 D0      A6

FUNCTION
    This function provides a means of enabling and disabling
    6526 CIA interrupt control registers.
    In addition it returns the previous enable mask.

INPUTS
    mask - a bit mask indicating which interrupts to be
        modified.  If bit 7 is clear the mask indicates
        interrupts to be disabled.  If bit 7 is set, the
        mask indicates interrupts to be enabled.
        Bit positions are identical to those in 6526 ICR.

RESULTS
    oldMask - the previous enable mask before the requested
        changes.  To get the current mask without making
        changes, call the function with a null parameter.

EXAMPLES
    Get the current mask:
        mask = AbleICR(0)
    Enable both timer interrupts:
        AbleICR(0x83)
    Disable serial port interrupt:
        AbleICR(0x08)

EXCEPTIONS
    Enabling the mask for a pending interrupt will cause
    an immediate processor interrupt (that is if everything
    else is enabled).  You may want to clear the pending
    interrupts with SetICRx prior to enabling them.

SEE ALSO
    SetICR
```



```
NAME
    AddICRVector -- attach an interrupt handler to a CIA bit

SYNOPSYS
    interrupt = AddICRVector(iCRBit, interrupt), resource
    D0                       D0      A1          A6

FUNCTION
    Assign interrupt processing code to a particular interrupt
    bit of the CIA ICR.  If the interrupt bit has already been
    assigned, this function will fail, and return a pointer
    to the owner interrupt.  If it succeeds, a null is returned.

    This function will also enable the CIA interrupt for the given
    ICR bit.

INPUTS
    iCRBit - bit number to set (0..4)
    interrupt - pointer to interrupt structure

RESULT
    interrupt - zero if successful, otherwise returns a pointer
            to the current owner interrupt structure.

SEE ALSO
    RemICRVector
```

```
NAME
     RemICRVector -- detach an interrupt handler from a CIA bit

SYNOPSYS
     RemICRVector(iCRBit, interrupt), resource
                  D0      A1          A6

FUNCTION
     Disconnect interrupt processing code for a particular interrupt
     bit of the CIA ICR.

     This function will also disable the CIA interrupt for the given
     ICR bit.

INPUTS
     iCRBit - bit number to set (0..4)
     interrupt - pointer to interrupt structure

RESULT

SEE ALSO
     AddICRVector
```



```
NAME
    SetICR -- cause, clear, and sample ICR interrupts

SYNOPSIS
    oldMask = SetICR(mask), Resource
    D0               D0     A6

FUNCTION
    This function provides a means of reseting, causing, and
    sampling 6526 CIA interrupt control registers.

INPUTS
    mask - a bit mask indicating which interrupts to be
        effected.  If bit 7 is clear the mask indicates
        interrupts to be reset.  If bit 7 is set, the
        mask indicates interrupts to be caused.
        Bit positions are identical to those in 6526 ICR.

RESULTS
    oldMask - the previous interrupt register status before
        making the requested changes.  To sample current
        status without making changes,  call the function
        with a null parameter.

EXAMPLES
    Get the interrupt mask:
        mask = SetICR(0)
    Clear serial port interrupt:
        SetICR(0x08)

EXCEPTIONS
    Setting an interrupt bit for an enabled interrupt will cause
     an immediate interrupt.

SEE ALSO
    AbleICR
```

TABLE OF CONTENTS


```
NAME
    AllocUnit - allocate a unit of the disk

SYNOPSIS
    Success = AllocUnit( unitNum ), DRResource
     D0                  D0         A6

FUNCTION
     This routine allocates one of the units of the disk.  It should
     be called before trying to use the disk (via GetUnit).

INPUTS
     unitNum -- a legal unit number (zero through three)

RESULTS
     Success -- nonzero if successful.  zero on failure.

EXCEPTIONS

SEE ALSO

BUGS
```

```
disk.resource/FreeUnit                              disk.resource/FreeUnit

   NAME
       FreeUnit - deallocate the disk

   SYNOPSIS
       FreeUnit( unitNum ), DRResource
                 D0         A6

   FUNCTION
       This routine deallocates one of the units of the disk.  It should
       be called when done with the disk.  Do not call it if you did
       no successfully allocate the disk (there is no protection -- you
       will probably crash the disk system).

   INPUTS
       unitNum -- a legal unit number (zero through three)

   RESULTS

   EXCEPTIONS

   SEE ALSO

   BUGS
```

```
disk.resource/GetUnit                                disk.resource/GetUnit

   NAME
       GetUnit - allocate the disk for a driver

   SYNOPSIS
       lastDriver = GetUnit( unitPointer ), DRResource
       D0                    A1             A6

   FUNCTION
       This routine allocates the disk to a driver.  It is either
       immediately available, or the request is saved until the disk
       is available.  When it is available, your unitPointer is
       sent back to you (via ReplyMsg).  You may then reattempt the
       GetUnit.

       Allocating the disk allows you to use the disk's resources.
       Remember however that there are four units to the disk; you are
       only one of them.  Please be polite to the other units (by never
       selecting them, and by not leaving interrupts enabled, etc.).

       When you are done, please leave the disk in the following state:
           dmacon dma bit ON
           dsklen dma bit OFF (write a #DSKDMAOFF to dsklen)
           adkcon disk bits -- any way you want
           entena:disk sync and disk block interrupts -- Both DISABLED
           CIA resource index interrupt -- DISABLED
           8520 outputs -- doesn't matter, because all bits will be
               set to inactive by the resource.
           8520 data direction regs -- restore to original state.

   INPUTS
       unitPtr - a pointer you your disk resource unit structure.
               Note that the message filed of the structure MUST
               be a valid message, ready to be replied to.

   RESULTS
       lastDriver - if the disk is not busy, then the last unit
               to use the disk is returned.  This may be used to
               see if a driver needs to reset device registers.
               (If you were the last user, then no one has changed
               any of the registers.  If someone else has used it,
               then any allowable changes may have been made).  If the
               disk is busy, then a null is returned.

   EXCEPTIONS

   SEE ALSO

   BUGS
```

```
NAME
    GetUnitID - find out what type of disk is out there

SYNOPSIS
    idtype = GetUnitID( unitNum ), DRResource
     D0                  D0          A6

FUNCTION

INPUTS

RESULTS
     idtype -- the type of the disk drive.  Standard types are
             defined in the resource include file.

EXCEPTIONS

SEE ALSO

BUGS
```



```
NAME
    GiveUnit - Free the disk back up

SYNOPSIS
    GiveUnit(), DRResource
                  A6

FUNCTION
     This routine frees the disk after a driver is done with it.
     If others are waiting, it will notify them.

INPUTS

RESULTS

EXCEPTIONS

SEE ALSO

BUGS
```

TABLE OF CONTENTS


```
NAME
    MR_ALLOCMISCRESOURCE - allocate one of the misc resources

SYNOPSIS
   CurrentUser = MR_ALLOCMISCRESOURCE( unitNum, name ), misc.resource
   D0                                  D0       A1      A6

    STRPTR CurrentUser;
    LONG unitNum;
    STRPTR name;

FUNCTION
    This routine allocates one of the miscellaneous resources.
    If the resource is currently allocated, an error is returned.
    If you do get it, your name is associated with the resource
    (so a user can see who has it allocated).

    This routine may not be called from an interrupt routine

DESCRIPTION
    There are certain parts of the hardware that a multitasking-
    friendly program may need to take over.  The serial port
    is a good example.  By grabbing the misc.resource for the
    serial port, the caller would "own" the hardware registers
    associated with that function.  Nobody else, including the
    system serial driver is allowed to interfere.

    The misc.resource must be accessed using assembly language.  The set
    of currently defined units and the function offsets from the resource
    base are listed in the resources/misc.i include file.

INPUTS
    unitNum - the number of the resource you want to allocate
            (eg.  MR_SERIALBITS).
    name - a mnenonic name that will help the user figure out
            what piece of software is hogging a resource.
            (havoc breaks out if a name of null is passed in...)

RESULTS
    CurrentUser - if the resource is busy, then the name of
            the current user is returned.  If the resource is
            free, then null is returned.

BUGS

SEE ALSO
    resources/misc.i
    misc.resource/MR_FREEMISCRESOURCE
```

```
NAME
    MR_FREEMISCRESOURCE - make a resource available for reallocation

SYNOPSIS
    MR_FREEMISCRESOURCE( unitNum ), misc.resource
                         D0          A6
    LONG unitNum;

FUNCTION
    This routine frees one of the resources allocated
    by MR_ALLOCMISCRESOURCE.  The resource is made available
    for reuse.

    This routine may not be called from an interrupt routine.

INPUTS
    unitNum - the number of the miscellaneous resource to be freed.

RESULTS
    Frees the appropriate resource.

BUGS

SEE ALSO
    misc.resource/MR_ALLOCMISCRESOURCE
```

TABLE OF CONTENTS


```
NAME
     AllocPotBits - allocate bits in the potgo register

SYNOPSIS
     allocated = AllocPotBits(bits), potgoResource
     D0                       D0     A6

FUNCTION
     The AllocPotBits routine allocates bits in the hardware potgo
     register that the application wishes to manipulate via
     WritePotgo.  The request may be for more than one bit.  A
     user trying to allocate bits may find that they are
     unavailable because they are already allocated, or because
     the start bit itself (bit 0) has been allocated, or if
     requesting the start bit, because input bits have been
     allocated.  A user can block itself from allocation: i.e.
     it should FreePotgoBits the bits it has and re-AllocPotBits if
     it is trying to change an allocation involving the start bit.

INPUTS
     bits - a description of the hardware bits that the application
             wishes to manipulate, loosely based on the register
             description itself:
         START (bit 0) - set if you wish to use start (i.e. start
                 thr proportional controller counters) with the
                 input ports you allocate (below).  You must
                 allocate all the DATxx ports you want to apply
                 START to in this same call, with the OUTxx bit
                 clear.
         DATLX (bit 8) - set if you wish to use the port associated
                 with the left (0) controller, pin 5.
         OUTLX (bit 9) - set if you promise to use the LX port in
                 output mode only.  The port is not set to output
                 for you at this time -- this bit set indicates
                 that you don't mind if STARTs are initiated at any
                 time by others, since ports that are enabled for
                 output are unaffected by START.
         DATLY (bit 10) - as DATLX but for the left (0) controller,
                 pin 9.
         OUTLY (bit 11) - as OUTLX but for LY.
         DATRX (bit 12) - the right (1) controller, pin 5.
         OUTRX (bit 13) - OUT for RX.
         DATRY (bit 14) - the right (1) controller, pin 9.
         OUTRY (bit 15) - OUT for RY.

RESULTS
     allocated - the START and DATxx bits of those requested that
             were granted.  The OUTxx bits are don't cares.
```

NAME
    FreePotBits - free allocated bits in the potgo register

SYNOPSIS

```
    FreePotBits(allocated), potgoResource
                D0          A6
```

FUNCTION
    The FreePotBits routine frees previously allocated bits in the hardware potgo register that the application had allocated via AllocPotBits and no longer wishes to use. It accepts the return value from AllocPotBits as its argument.

NAME
    WritePotgo - write to the hardware potgo register

SYNOPSIS

```
    WritePotgo(word, mask), potgoResource
               D0    D1     A6
```

FUNCTION
    The WritePotgo routine sets and clears bits in the hardware potgo register. Only those bits specified by the mask are affected -- it is improper to set bits in the mask that you have not successfully allocated. The bits in the high byte are saved to be maintained when other users write to the potgo register. The START bit is not saved, it is written only explicitly as the result of a call to this routine with the START bit set: other users will not restart it.

INPUTS
    word - the data to write to the hardware potgo register and save for further use, except the START bit, which is not saved.
    mask - those bits in word that are to be written. Other bits may have been provided by previous calls to this routine, and default to zero.

Section D

C Include Files—".h" Files

This section contains the C-language include files from the Amiga operating system source code. These include files define the data structures and constants used by the system software. Whenever the system requires that a certain structure or constant be passed, it will be defined in an include file. These include files are organized on a functional basis. For example, files pertinent to the graphics library are listed under "graphics/itemname.h."

This section is for easy reference only. Similar include files generally come on disk with whatever C compiler you may choose to use with the Amiga. A quick example of include file usage follows:

> WARNING: *Not all information in this section should be used in your programs. The include files contain definitions for some structure members and constants that are not supported for use by programs. In some cases these definitions are marked as private, in other cases they are not distinguished. Following the guidelines presented by Commodore-Amiga is the best way to insure compatibility with future system software releases.*

```
/*
 *  A quick example of using a C language include file.  The constant
 * "ID_KICKSTART_DISK" is not defined in this example; the value
 * is pulled from the "libraries/dos.h" include file.
 */
#include "libraries/dos.h"

void main()
{
        printf("ID_KICKSTART_DISK equals %lx\n",ID_KICKSTART_DISK);
        exit(RETURN_OK);
}
```

```
#ifndef DEVICES_AUDIO_H
#define DEVICES_AUDIO_H
/*
**      $Filename: devices/audio.h $
**      $Release: 1.3 $
**
**
**
**      (C) Copyright 1985,1986,1987,1988 Commodore-Amiga, Inc.
**          All Rights Reserved
*/

#ifndef EXEC_IO_H
#include "exec/io.h"
#endif

#define AUDIONAME                   "audio.device"

#define ADHARD_CHANNELS             4

#define ADALLOC_MINPREC             -128
#define ADALLOC_MAXPREC             127

#define ADCMD_FREE                  (CMD_NONSTD+0)
#define ADCMD_SETPREC               (CMD_NONSTD+1)
#define ADCMD_FINISH                (CMD_NONSTD+2)
#define ADCMD_PERVOL                (CMD_NONSTD+3)
#define ADCMD_LOCK                  (CMD_NONSTD+4)
#define ADCMD_WAITCYCLE             (CMD_NONSTD+5)
#define ADCMDB_NOUNIT               5
#define ADCMDF_NOUNIT               (1<<5)
#define ADCMD_ALLOCATE              (ADCMDF_NOUNIT+0)

#define ADIOB_PERVOL                4
#define ADIOF_PERVOL                (1<<4)
#define ADIOB_SYNCCYCLE             5
#define ADIOF_SYNCCYCLE             (1<<5)
#define ADIOB_NOWAIT                6
#define ADIOF_NOWAIT                (1<<6)
#define ADIOB_WRITEMESSAGE          7
#define ADIOF_WRITEMESSAGE          (1<<7)

#define ADIOERR_NOALLOCATION        -10
#define ADIOERR_ALLOCFAILED         -11
#define ADIOERR_CHANNELSTOLEN       -12

struct IOAudio {
    struct IORequest ioa_Request;
    WORD ioa_AllocKey;
    UBYTE *ioa_Data;
    ULONG ioa_Length;
    UWORD ioa_Period;
    UWORD ioa_Volume;
    UWORD ioa_Cycles;
    struct Message ioa_WriteMsg;
};

#endif  /* DEVICES_AUDIO_H */
```



```
#ifndef DEVICES_BOOTBLOCK_H
#define DEVICES_BOOTBLOCK_H
/*
**      $Filename: devices/bootblock.h $
**      $Release: 1.3 $
**
**      BootBlock definition:
**
**      (C) Copyright 1985,1986,1987,1988 Commodore-Amiga, Inc.
**          All Rights Reserved
*/

struct BootBlock {
        UBYTE   bb_id[4];               /* 4 character identifier */
        LONG    bb_chksum;      /* boot block checksum (balance) */
        LONG    bb_dosblock;    /* reserved for DOS patch */
};

#define         BOOTSECTS       2       /* 1K bootstrap */

#define BBID_DOS        { 'D', 'O', 'S', '\0' }
#define BBID_KICK       { 'K', 'I', 'C', 'K' }

#define BBNAME_DOS      (('D'<<24)|('O'<<16)|('S'<<8))
#define BBNAME_KICK     (('K'<<24)|('I'<<16)|('C'<<8)|('K'))

#endif  /* DEVICES_BOOTBLOCK_H */
```

```
#ifndef DEVICES_CLIPBOARD_H
#define DEVICES_CLIPBOARD_H
/*
**      $Filename: devices/clipboard.h $
**      $Release: 1.3 $
**
**      clipboard device command definitions
**
**      (C) Copyright 1985,1986,1987,1988 Commodore-Amiga, Inc.
**          All Rights Reserved
*/

#ifndef     EXEC_NODES_H
#include "exec/nodes.h"
#endif
#ifndef     EXEC_LISTS_H
#include "exec/lists.h"
#endif
#ifndef     EXEC_PORTS_H
#include "exec/ports.h"
#endif

#define  CBD_POST              (CMD_NONSTD+0)
#define  CBD_CURRENTREADID     (CMD_NONSTD+1)
#define  CBD_CURRENTWRITEID    (CMD_NONSTD+2)

#define  CBERR_OBSOLETEID      1


struct ClipboardUnitPartial {
    struct  Node cu_Node;       /* list of units */
    ULONG   cu_UnitNum;         /* unit number for this unit */
    /* the remaining unit data is private to the device */
};


struct IOClipReq {
    struct  Message io_Message;
    struct  Device  *io_Device; /* device node pointer  */
    struct  Unit    *io_Unit; /* unit (driver private)*/
    UWORD   io_Command;         /* device command */
    UBYTE   io_Flags;           /* including QUICK and SATISFY */
    BYTE    io_Error;           /* error or warning num */
    ULONG   io_Actual;          /* number of bytes transferred */
    ULONG   io_Length;          /* number of bytes requested */
    STRPTR  io_Data;            /* either clip stream or post port */
    ULONG   io_Offset;          /* offset in clip stream */
    LONG    io_ClipID;          /* ordinal clip identifier */
};

#define  PRIMARY_CLIP   0       /* primary clip unit */

struct SatisfyMsg {
    struct  Message sm_Msg;        /* the length will be 6 */
    UWORD   sm_Unit;            /* which clip unit this is */
    LONG    sm_ClipID;          /* the clip identifier of the post */
};

#endif  /* DEVICES_CLIPBOARD_H */
```



```
#ifndef DEVICES_CONSOLE_H
#define DEVICES_CONSOLE_H
/*
**      $Filename: devices/console.h $
**      $Release: 1.3 $
**
**      Console device command definitions
**
**      (C) Copyright 1985,1986,1987,1988 Commodore-Amiga, Inc.
**          All Rights Reserved
*/

#ifndef     EXEC_IO_H
#include "exec/io.h"
#endif

/****** Console commands ******/
#define  CD_ASKKEYMAP           (CMD_NONSTD+0)
#define  CD_SETKEYMAP           (CMD_NONSTD+1)
#define  CD_ASKDEFAULTKEYMAP    (CMD_NONSTD+2)
#define  CD_SETDEFAULTKEYMAP    (CMD_NONSTD+3)


/****** SGR parameters ******/

#define SGR_PRIMARY         0
#define SGR_BOLD            1
#define SGR_ITALIC          3
#define SGR_UNDERSCORE      4
#define SGR_NEGATIVE        7

/* these names refer to the ANSI standard, not the implementation */
#define SGR_BLACK           30
#define SGR_RED             31
#define SGR_GREEN           32
#define SGR_YELLOW          33
#define SGR_BLUE            34
#define SGR_MAGENTA         35
#define SGR_CYAN            36
#define SGR_WHITE           37
#define SGR_DEFAULT         39

#define SGR_BLACKBG         40
#define SGR_REDBG           41
#define SGR_GREENBG         42
#define SGR_YELLOWBG        43
#define SGR_BLUEBG          44
#define SGR_MAGENTABG       45
#define SGR_CYANBG          46
#define SGR_WHITEBG         47
#define SGR_DEFAULTBG       49

/* these names refer to the implementation, they are the preferred   */
/* names for use with the Amiga console device.       */
#define SGR_CLR0            30
#define SGR_CLR1            31
#define SGR_CLR2            32
#define SGR_CLR3            33
#define SGR_CLR4            34
#define SGR_CLR5            35
#define SGR_CLR6            36
#define SGR_CLR7            37

#define SGR_CLR0BG          40
#define SGR_CLR1BG          41
#define SGR_CLR2BG          42
#define SGR_CLR3BG          43
#define SGR_CLR4BG          44
#define SGR_CLR5BG          45
```

Sep 19 20:24 1988 devices/console.h Page 2

```
#define SGR_CLR6BG          46
#define SGR_CLR7BG          47


/****** DSR parameters ******/

#define DSR_CPR             6

/****** CTC parameters ******/
#define  CTC_HSETTAB       0
#define  CTC_HCLRTAB       2
#define  CTC_HCLRTABSALL   5

/******  TBC parameters ******/
#define  TBC_HCLRTAB       0
#define  TBC_HCLRTABSALL   3

/******  SM and RM parameters ******/
#define  M_LNM     20       /* linefeed newline mode */
#define  M_ASM     ">1"     /* auto scroll mode */
#define  M_AWM     "?7"     /* auto wrap mode */

#endif  /* DEVICES_CONSOLE_H */
```

Sep 19 20:24 1988 devices/conunit.h Page 1

```
#ifndef DEVICES_CONUNIT_H
#define DEVICES_CONUNIT_H
/*
**      $Filename: devices/conunit.h $
**      $Release: 1.3 $
**
**      Console device unit definitions
**
**      (C) Copyright 1986,1987,1988 Commodore-Amiga, Inc.
**          All Rights Reserved
*/

#ifndef  EXEC_PORTS_H
#include "exec/ports.h"
#endif

#ifndef  DEVICES_CONSOLE_H
#include "devices/console.h"
#endif

#ifndef  DEVICES_KEYMAP_H
#include "devices/keymap.h"
#endif

#ifndef  DEVICES_INPUTEVENT_H
#include "devices/inputevent.h"
#endif

#define  PMB_ASM      (M_LNM+1)   /* internal storage bit for AS flag */
#define  PMB_AWM      (PMB_ASM+1) /* internal storage bit for AW flag */
#define  MAXTABS      80


struct   ConUnit {
   struct   MsgPort cu_MP;
    /* ---- read only variables */
   struct   Window *cu_Window; /* intuition window bound to this unit */
   WORD  cu_XCP;               /* character position */
   WORD  cu_YCP;
   WORD  cu_XMax;              /* max character position */
   WORD  cu_YMax;
   WORD  cu_XRSize;            /* character raster size */
   WORD  cu_YRSize;
   WORD  cu_XROrigin;          /* raster origin */
   WORD  cu_YROrigin;
   WORD  cu_XRExtant;          /* raster maxima */
   WORD  cu_YRExtant;
   WORD  cu_XMinShrink;        /* smallest area intact from resize process */
   WORD  cu_YMinShrink;
   WORD  cu_XCCP;              /* cursor position */
   WORD  cu_YCCP;

   /* ---- read/write variables (writes must must be protected) */
   /* ---- storage for AskKeyMap and SetKeyMap */
   struct   KeyMap cu_KeyMapStruct;
   /* ---- tab stops */
   UWORD cu_TabStops[MAXTABS];   /* 0 at start, 0xffff at end of list */

   /* ---- console rastport attributes */
   BYTE     cu_Mask;
   BYTE     cu_FgPen;
   BYTE     cu_BgPen;
   BYTE     cu_AOLPen;
   BYTE     cu_DrawMode;
   BYTE     cu_AreaPtSz;
   APTR     cu_AreaPtrn;            /* cursor area pattern */
   UBYTE    cu_Minterms[8];         /* console minterms */
   struct   TextFont *cu_Font;
   UBYTE    cu_AlgoStyle;
```

```
    UBYTE    cu_TxFlags;
    UWORD    cu_TxHeight;
    UWORD    cu_TxWidth;
    UWORD    cu_TxBaseline;
    UWORD    cu_TxSpacing;

    /* ---- console MODES and RAW EVENTS switches */
    UBYTE    cu_Modes[(PMB_AWM+7)/8];   /* one bit per mode */
    UBYTE    cu_RawEvents[(IECLASS_MAX+7)/8];
};

#endif  /* DEVICES_CONUNIT_H */
```



```
#ifndef DEVICES_GAMEPORT_H
#define DEVICES_GAMEPORT_H
/*
**      $Filename: devices/gameport.h $
**      $Release: 1.3 $
**
**      GamePort device command definitions
**
**      (C) Copyright 1985,1986,1987,1988 Commodore-Amiga, Inc.
**          All Rights Reserved
*/

/******  GamePort commands ******/
#define  GPD_READEVENT      (CMD_NONSTD+0)
#define  GPD_ASKCTYPE       (CMD_NONSTD+1)
#define  GPD_SETCTYPE       (CMD_NONSTD+2)
#define  GPD_ASKTRIGGER     (CMD_NONSTD+3)
#define  GPD_SETTRIGGER     (CMD_NONSTD+4)

/******  GamePort structures ******/

/* gpt_Keys */
#define  GPTB_DOWNKEYS      0
#define  GPTF_DOWNKEYS      (1<<0)
#define  GPTB_UPKEYS        1
#define  GPTF_UPKEYS        (1<<1)

struct GamePortTrigger {
   UWORD gpt_Keys;          /* key transition triggers */
   UWORD gpt_Timeout;       /* time trigger (vertical blank units) */
   UWORD gpt_XDelta;        /* X distance trigger */
   UWORD gpt_YDelta;        /* Y distance trigger */
};

/****** Controller Types ******/
#define  GPCT_ALLOCATED    -1    /* allocated by another user */
#define  GPCT_NOCONTROLLER 0

#define  GPCT_MOUSE        1
#define  GPCT_RELJOYSTICK  2
#define  GPCT_ABSJOYSTICK  3


/****** Errors ******/
#define  GPDERR_SETCTYPE   1     /* this controller not valid at this time */

#endif  /* DEVICES_GAMEPORT_H */
```

```
#ifndef DEVICES_HARDBLOCKS_H
#define DEVICES_HARDBLOCKS_H
/*
**      $Filename: devices/hardblocks.h $
**      $Revision: 1.0 $
**      $Date: 88/07/11 15:32:49 $
**
**      File System identifier blocks for hard disks
**
**      (C) Copyright 1988 Commodore-Amiga, Inc.
**          All Rights Reserved
*/

/*------------------------------------------------------------------
 *
 *      This file describes blocks of data that exist on a hard disk
 *      to describe that disk.  They are not generically accessable to
 *      the user as they do not appear on any DOS drive.  The blocks
 *      are tagged with a unique identifier, checksummed, and linked
 *      together.  The root of these blocks is the RigidDiskBlock.
 *
 *      The RigidDiskBlock must exist on the disk within the first
 *      RDB_LOCATION_LIMIT blocks.  This inhibits the use of the zero
 *      cylinder in an AmigaDOS partition: although it is strictly
 *      possible to store the RigidDiskBlock data in the reserved
 *      area of a partition, this practice is discouraged since the
 *      reserved blocks of a partition are overwritten by "Format",
 *      "Install", "DiskCopy", etc.  The recommended disk layout,
 *      then, is to use the first cylinder(s) to store all the drive
 *      data specified by these blocks: i.e. partition descriptions,
 *      file system load images, drive bad block maps, spare blocks,
 *      etc.
 *
 *      Though only 512 byte blocks are currently supported by the
 *      file system, this proposal tries to be forward-looking by
 *      making the block size explicit, and by using only the first
 *      256 bytes for all blocks but the LoadSeg data.
 *
 *------------------------------------------------------------------*/

/*
 *  NOTE
 *      optional block addresses below contain $ffffffff to indicate
 *      a NULL address, as zero is a valid address
 */
struct RigidDiskBlock {
    ULONG   rdb_ID;                 /* 4 character identifier */
    ULONG   rdb_SummedLongs;        /* size of this checksummed structure */
    LONG    rdb_ChkSum;             /* block checksum (longword sum to zero) */
    ULONG   rdb_HostID;             /* SCSI Target ID of host */
    ULONG   rdb_BlockBytes;         /* size of disk blocks */
    ULONG   rdb_Flags;              /* see below for defines */
    /* block list heads */
    ULONG   rdb_BadBlockList;       /* optional bad block list */
    ULONG   rdb_PartitionList;      /* optional first partition block */
    ULONG   rdb_FileSysHeaderList;  /* optional file system header block */
    ULONG   rdb_DriveInit;          /* optional drive-specific init code */
                                    /* DriveInit(lun,rdb,ior): "C" stk & d0/a0/a1 */
    ULONG   rdb_Reserved1[6];       /* set to $ffffffff */
    /* physical drive characteristics */
    ULONG   rdb_Cylinders;          /* number of drive cylinders */
    ULONG   rdb_Sectors;            /* sectors per track */
    ULONG   rdb_Heads;              /* number of drive heads */
    ULONG   rdb_Interleave;         /* interleave */
    ULONG   rdb_Park;               /* landing zone cylinder */
    ULONG   rdb_Reserved2[3];
    ULONG   rdb_WritePreComp;       /* starting cylinder: write precompensation */
    ULONG   rdb_ReducedWrite;       /* starting cylinder: reduced write current */
    ULONG   rdb_StepRate;           /* drive step rate */
```



```
    ULONG   rdb_Reserved3[5];
    /* logical drive characteristics */
    ULONG   rdb_RDBBlocksLo;        /* low block of range reserved for hardblocks */
    ULONG   rdb_RDBBlocksHi;        /* high block of range for these hardblocks */
    ULONG   rdb_LoCylinder;         /* low cylinder of partitionable disk area */
    ULONG   rdb_HiCylinder;         /* high cylinder of partitionable data area */
    ULONG   rdb_CylBlocks;          /* number of blocks available per cylinder */
    ULONG   rdb_AutoParkSeconds; /* zero for no auto park */
    ULONG   rdb_Reserved4[2];
    /* drive identification */
    char    rdb_DiskVendor[8];
    char    rdb_DiskProduct[16];
    char    rdb_DiskRevision[4];
    char    rdb_ControllerVendor[8];
    char    rdb_ControllerProduct[16];
    char    rdb_ControllerRevision[4];
    ULONG   rdb_Reserved5[10];
};

#define IDNAME_RIGIDDISK        (('R'<<24)|('D'<<16)|('S'<<8)|('K'))

#define RDB_LOCATION_LIMIT      16

#define RDBFB_LAST      0       /* no disks exist to be configured after */
#define RDBFF_LAST      0x01L   /*   this one on this controller */
#define RDBFB_LASTLUN   1       /* no LUNs exist to be configured greater */
#define RDBFF_LASTLUN   0x02L   /*   than this one at this SCSI Target ID */
#define RDBFB_LASTTID   2       /* no Target IDs exist to be configured */
#define RDBFF_LASTTID   0x04L   /*   greater than this one on this SCSI bus */
#define RDBFB_NORESELECT 3      /* don't bother trying to perform reselection */
#define RDBFF_NORESELECT 0x08L  /*   when talking to this drive */
#define RDBFB_DISKID    4       /* rdb_Disk... identification valid */
#define RDBFF_DISKID    0x10L
#define RDBFB_CTRLRID   5       /* rdb_Controller... identification valid */
#define RDBFF_CTRLRID   0x20L

/*------------------------------------------------------------------*/
struct BadBlockEntry {
    ULONG   bbe_BadBlock;           /* block number of bad block */
    ULONG   bbe_GoodBlock;          /* block number of replacement block */
};

struct BadBlockBlock {
    ULONG   bbb_ID;                 /* 4 character identifier */
    ULONG   bbb_SummedLongs;        /* size of this checksummed structure */
    LONG    bbb_ChkSum;             /* block checksum (longword sum to zero) */
    ULONG   bbb_HostID;             /* SCSI Target ID of host */
    ULONG   bbb_Next;               /* block number of the next BadBlockBlock */
    ULONG   bbb_Reserved;
    struct BadBlockEntry bbb_BlockPairs[61]; /* bad block entry pairs */
    /* note [61] assumes 512 byte blocks */
};

#define IDNAME_BADBLOCK         (('B'<<24)|('A'<<16)|('D'<<8)|('B'))

/*------------------------------------------------------------------*/
struct PartitionBlock {
    ULONG   pb_ID;                  /* 4 character identifier */
    ULONG   pb_SummedLongs;         /* size of this checksummed structure */
    LONG    pb_ChkSum;              /* block checksum (longword sum to zero) */
    ULONG   pb_HostID;              /* SCSI Target ID of host */
    ULONG   pb_Next;                /* block number of the next PartitionBlock */
    ULONG   pb_Flags;               /* see below for defines */
    ULONG   pb_Reserved1[2];
    ULONG   pb_DevFlags;            /* preferred flags for OpenDevice */
    UBYTE   pb_DriveName[32];       /* preferred DOS device name: BSTR form */
                                    /* (not used if this name is in use) */
    ULONG   pb_Reserved2[15];       /* filler to 32 longwords */
    ULONG   pb_Environment[17]; /* environment vector for this partition */
```

```
    ULONG   pb_EReserved[15];   /* reserved for future environment vector */
};

#define IDNAME_PARTITION        (('P'<<24)|('A'<<16)|('R'<<8)|('T'))

#define PBFB_BOOTABLE   0       /* this partition is intended to be bootable */
#define PBFF_BOOTABLE   1L      /*   (expected directories and files exist) */
#define PBFB_NOMOUNT    1       /* do not mount this partition (e.g. manually */
#define PBFF_NOMOUNT    2L      /*   mounted, but space reserved here) */

/*------------------------------------------------------------------*/
struct FileSysHeaderBlock {
    ULONG   fhb_ID;             /* 4 character identifier */
    ULONG   fhb_SummedLongs;    /* size of this checksummed structure */
    LONG    fhb_ChkSum;         /* block checksum (longword sum to zero) */
    ULONG   fhb_HostID;         /* SCSI Target ID of host */
    ULONG   fhb_Next;           /* block number of next FileSysHeaderBlock */
    ULONG   fhb_Flags;          /* see below for defines */
    ULONG   fhb_Reserved1[2];
    ULONG   fhb_DosType;        /* file system description: match this with */
                                /* partition environment's DE_DOSTYPE entry */
    ULONG   fhb_Version;        /* release version of this code */
    ULONG   fhb_PatchFlags;     /* bits set for those of the following that */
                                /*   need to be substituted into a standard */
                                /*   device node for this file system: e.g. */
                                /*   0x180 to substitute SegList & GlobalVec */
    ULONG   fhb_Type;           /* device node type: zero */
    ULONG   fhb_Task;           /* standard dos "task" field: zero */
    ULONG   fhb_Lock;           /* not used for devices: zero */
    ULONG   fhb_Handler;        /* filename to loadseg: zero placeholder */
    ULONG   fhb_StackSize;      /* stacksize to use when starting task */
    LONG    fhb_Priority;       /* task priority when starting task */
    LONG    fhb_Startup;        /* startup msg: zero placeholder */
    LONG    fhb_SegListBlocks;  /* first of linked list of LoadSegBlocks: */
                                /*   note that this entry requires some */
                                /*   processing before substitution */
    LONG    fhb_GlobalVec;      /* BCPL global vector when starting task */
    ULONG   fhb_Reserved2[23];  /* (those reserved by PatchFlags) */
    ULONG   fhb_Reserved3[21];
};

#define IDNAME_FILESYSHEADER    (('F'<<24)|('S'<<16)|('H'<<8)|('D'))

/*------------------------------------------------------------------*/
struct LoadSegBlock {
    ULONG   lsb_ID;             /* 4 character identifier */
    ULONG   lsb_SummedLongs;    /* size of this checksummed structure */
    LONG    lsb_ChkSum;         /* block checksum (longword sum to zero) */
    ULONG   lsb_HostID;         /* SCSI Target ID of host */
    ULONG   lsb_Next;           /* block number of the next LoadSegBlock */
    ULONG   lsb_LoadData[123];  /* data for "loadseg" */
    /* note [123] assumes 512 byte blocks */
};

#define IDNAME_LOADSEG          (('L'<<24)|('S'<<16)|('E'<<8)|('G'))

#endif  /* DEVICES_HARDBLOCKS_H */
```



```
#ifndef DEVICES_INPUT_H
#define DEVICES_INPUT_H
/*
**      $Filename: devices/input.h $
**      $Release: 1.3 $
**
**      input device command definitions
**
**      (C) Copyright 1985,1986,1987,1988 Commodore-Amiga, Inc.
**          All Rights Reserved
*/

#ifndef     EXEC_IO_H
#include "exec/io.h"
#endif

#define  IND_ADDHANDLER     (CMD_NONSTD+0)
#define  IND_REMHANDLER     (CMD_NONSTD+1)
#define  IND_WRITEEVENT     (CMD_NONSTD+2)
#define  IND_SETTHRESH      (CMD_NONSTD+3)
#define  IND_SETPERIOD      (CMD_NONSTD+4)
#define  IND_SETMPORT       (CMD_NONSTD+5)
#define  IND_SETMTYPE       (CMD_NONSTD+6)
#define  IND_SETMTRIG       (CMD_NONSTD+7)

#endif  /* DEVICES_INPUT_H */
```

```
#ifndef DEVICES_INPUTEVENT_H
#define DEVICES_INPUTEVENT_H
/*
**      $Filename: devices/inputevent.h $
**      $Release: 1.3 $
**
**      input event definitions
**
**      (C) Copyright 1985,1986,1987,1988 Commodore-Amiga, Inc.
**          All Rights Reserved
*/

#ifndef     DEVICES_TIMER_H
#include "devices/timer.h"
#endif

/*------ constants ---------------------------------------------------*/

/*   --- InputEvent.ie_Class --- */
/* A NOP input event */
#define  IECLASS_NULL             0x00
/* A raw keycode from the keyboard device */
#define  IECLASS_RAWKEY           0x01
/* The raw mouse report from the game port device */
#define  IECLASS_RAWMOUSE         0x02
/* A private console event */
#define  IECLASS_EVENT            0x03
/* A Pointer Position report */
#define  IECLASS_POINTERPOS       0x04
/* A timer event */
#define  IECLASS_TIMER            0x06
/* select button pressed down over a Gadget (address in ie_EventAddress) */
#define  IECLASS_GADGETDOWN       0x07
/* select button released over the same Gadget (address in ie_EventAddress) */
#define  IECLASS_GADGETUP         0x08
/* some Requester activity has taken place.  See Codes REQCLEAR and REQSET */
#define  IECLASS_REQUESTER        0x09
/* this is a Menu Number transmission (Menu number is in ie_Code) */
#define  IECLASS_MENULIST         0x0A
/* User has selected the active Window's Close Gadget */
#define  IECLASS_CLOSEWINDOW      0x0B
/* this Window has a new size */
#define  IECLASS_SIZEWINDOW       0x0C
/* the Window pointed to by ie_EventAddress needs to be refreshed */
#define  IECLASS_REFRESHWINDOW    0x0D
/* new preferences are available */
#define  IECLASS_NEWPREFS         0x0E
/* the disk has been removed */
#define  IECLASS_DISKREMOVED      0x0F
/* the disk has been inserted */
#define  IECLASS_DISKINSERTED     0x10
/* the window is about to be been made active */
#define IECLASS_ACTIVEWINDOW      0x11
/* the window is about to be made inactive */
#define IECLASS_INACTIVEWINDOW    0x12


/* the last class */
#define  IECLASS_MAX              0x12



/*   --- InputEvent.ie_Code ---   */
/* IECLASS_RAWKEY */
#define  IECODE_UP_PREFIX         0x80
#define  IECODE_KEY_CODE_FIRST    0x00
#define  IECODE_KEY_CODE_LAST     0x77
#define  IECODE_COMM_CODE_FIRST   0x78
#define  IECODE_COMM_CODE_LAST    0x7F
```



```

/* IECLASS_ANSI */
#define  IECODE_C0_FIRST          0x00
#define  IECODE_C0_LAST           0x1F
#define  IECODE_ASCII_FIRST       0x20
#define  IECODE_ASCII_LAST        0x7E
#define  IECODE_ASCII_DEL         0x7F
#define  IECODE_C1_FIRST          0x80
#define  IECODE_C1_LAST           0x9F
#define  IECODE_LATIN1_FIRST      0xA0
#define  IECODE_LATIN1_LAST       0xFF

/* IECLASS_RAWMOUSE */
#define  IECODE_LBUTTON           0x68  /* also uses IECODE_UP_PREFIX */
#define  IECODE_RBUTTON           0x69
#define  IECODE_MBUTTON           0x6A
#define  IECODE_NOBUTTON          0xFF

/* IECLASS_EVENT */
#define  IECODE_NEWACTIVE         0x01  /* active input window changed */

/* IECLASS_REQUESTER Codes */
/* REQSET is broadcast when the first Requester (not subsequent ones) opens
 * in the Window
 */
#define  IECODE_REQSET            0x01
/* REQCLEAR is broadcast when the last Requester clears out of the Window */
#define  IECODE_REQCLEAR          0x00


/*   --- InputEvent.ie_Qualifier --- */
#define  IEQUALIFIER_LSHIFT       0x0001
#define  IEQUALIFIER_RSHIFT       0x0002
#define  IEQUALIFIER_CAPSLOCK     0x0004
#define  IEQUALIFIER_CONTROL      0x0008
#define  IEQUALIFIER_LALT         0x0010
#define  IEQUALIFIER_RALT         0x0020
#define  IEQUALIFIER_LCOMMAND     0x0040
#define  IEQUALIFIER_RCOMMAND     0x0080
#define  IEQUALIFIER_NUMERICPAD   0x0100
#define  IEQUALIFIER_REPEAT       0x0200
#define  IEQUALIFIER_INTERRUPT    0x0400
#define  IEQUALIFIER_MULTIBROADCAST 0x0800
#define  IEQUALIFIER_MIDBUTTON    0x1000
#define  IEQUALIFIER_RBUTTON      0x2000
#define  IEQUALIFIER_LEFTBUTTON   0x4000
#define  IEQUALIFIER_RELATIVEMOUSE  0x8000

#define  IEQUALIFIERB_LSHIFT            0
#define  IEQUALIFIERB_RSHIFT            1
#define  IEQUALIFIERB_CAPSLOCK          2
#define  IEQUALIFIERB_CONTROL           3
#define  IEQUALIFIERB_LALT              4
#define  IEQUALIFIERB_RALT              5
#define  IEQUALIFIERB_LCOMMAND          6
#define  IEQUALIFIERB_RCOMMAND          7
#define  IEQUALIFIERB_NUMERICPAD        8
#define  IEQUALIFIERB_REPEAT            9
#define  IEQUALIFIERB_INTERRUPT         10
#define  IEQUALIFIERB_MULTIBROADCAST    11
#define  IEQUALIFIERB_MIDBUTTON         12
#define  IEQUALIFIERB_RBUTTON           13
#define  IEQUALIFIERB_LEFTBUTTON        14
#define  IEQUALIFIERB_RELATIVEMOUSE     15

/*------ InputEvent ---------------------------------------------------*/

struct InputEvent {
    struct  InputEvent *ie_NextEvent;  /* the chronologically next event */
```

```
    UBYTE   ie_Class;                  /* the input event class */
    UBYTE   ie_SubClass;               /* optional subclass of the class */
    UWORD   ie_Code;                   /* the input event code */
    UWORD   ie_Qualifier;              /* qualifiers in effect for the event*/
    union {
   struct {
       WORD    ie_x;                   /* the pointer position for the event*/
       WORD    ie_y;
   } ie_xy;
   APTR    ie_addr;
    } ie_position;
    struct timeval ie_TimeStamp;       /* the system tick at the event */
};

#define  ie_X     ie_position.ie_xy.ie_x
#define  ie_Y     ie_position.ie_xy.ie_y
#define  ie_EventAddress   ie_position.ie_addr

#endif  /* DEVICES_INPUTEVENT_H */
```



```
#ifndef DEVICES_KEYBOARD_H
#define DEVICES_KEYBOARD_H
/*
**      $Filename: devices/keyboard.h $
**      $Release: 1.3 $
**
**      Keyboard device command definitions
**
**      (C) Copyright 1985,1986,1987,1988 Commodore-Amiga, Inc.
**          All Rights Reserved
*/

#ifndef  EXEC_IO_H
#include "exec/io.h"
#endif

#define  KBD_READEVENT        (CMD_NONSTD+0)
#define  KBD_READMATRIX       (CMD_NONSTD+1)
#define  KBD_ADDRESETHANDLER  (CMD_NONSTD+2)
#define  KBD_REMRESETHANDLER  (CMD_NONSTD+3)
#define  KBD_RESETHANDLERDONE (CMD_NONSTD+4)

#endif  /* DEVICES_KEYBOARD_H */
```

```
#ifndef DEVICES_KEYMAP_H
#define DEVICES_KEYMAP_H
/*
**      $Filename: devices/keymap.h $
**      $Release: 1.3 $
**
**      keymap.resource definitions and console.device key map definitions
**
**      (C) Copyright 1985,1986,1987,1988 Commodore-Amiga, Inc.
**          All Rights Reserved
*/

#ifndef EXEC_NODES_H
#include        "exec/nodes.h"
#endif
#ifndef EXEC_LISTS_H
#include        "exec/lists.h"
#endif

struct   KeyMap {
    UBYTE   *km_LoKeyMapTypes;
    ULONG   *km_LoKeyMap;
    UBYTE   *km_LoCapsable;
    UBYTE   *km_LoRepeatable;
    UBYTE   *km_HiKeyMapTypes;
    ULONG   *km_HiKeyMap;
    UBYTE   *km_HiCapsable;
    UBYTE   *km_HiRepeatable;
};

struct  KeyMapNode {
    struct Node kn_Node;        /* including name of keymap */
    struct KeyMap kn_KeyMap;
};

/* the structure of keymap.resource */
struct  KeyMapResource {
    struct Node kr_Node;
    struct List kr_List;        /* a list of KeyMapNodes */
};

/* Key Map Types */
#define  KC_NOQUAL   0
#define  KC_VANILLA  7          /* note that SHIFT+ALT+CTRL is VANILLA */
#define  KCB_SHIFT   0
#define  KCF_SHIFT   0x01
#define  KCB_ALT     1
#define  KCF_ALT     0x02
#define  KCB_CONTROL 2
#define  KCF_CONTROL 0x04
#define  KCB_DOWNUP  3
#define  KCF_DOWNUP  0x08

#define  KCB_DEAD    5          /* may be dead or modified by dead key: */
#define  KCF_DEAD    0x20       /*   use dead prefix bytes              */

#define  KCB_STRING  6
#define  KCF_STRING  0x40

#define  KCB_NOP     7
#define  KCF_NOP     0x80


/* Dead Prefix Bytes */
#define DPB_MOD         0
#define DPF_MOD         0x01
#define DPB_DEAD        3
#define DPF_DEAD        0x08

```



```
#define DP_2DINDEXMASK  0x0f    /* mask for index for 1st of two dead keys */
#define DP_2DFACSHIFT   4       /* shift for factor for 1st of two dead keys */

#endif  /* DEVICES_KEYMAP_H */
```

```
#ifndef DEVICES_NARRATOR_H
#define DEVICES_NARRATOR_H
/*
**      $Filename: devices/narrator.h $
**      $Release: 1.3 $
**
**
**
**      (C) Copyright 1985,1986,1987,1988 Commodore-Amiga, Inc.
**          All Rights Reserved
*/

#ifndef EXEC_IO_H
#include "exec/io.h"
#endif

                /*          Error Codes         */

#define ND_NoMem      -2         /* Can't allocate memory                  */
#define ND_NoAudLib   -3         /* Can't open audio device                */
#define ND_MakeBad    -4         /* Error in MakeLibrary call              */
#define ND_UnitErr    -5         /* Unit other than 0                      */
#define ND_CantAlloc  -6         /* Can't allocate audio channel(s)        */
#define ND_Unimpl     -7         /* Unimplemented command                  */
#define ND_NoWrite    -8         /* Read for mouth without write first     */
#define ND_Expunged   -9         /* Can't open, deferred expunge bit set   */
#define ND_PhonErr    -20        /* Phoneme code spelling error            */
#define ND_RateErr    -21        /* Rate out of bounds                     */
#define ND_PitchErr   -22        /* Pitch out of bounds                    */
#define ND_SexErr     -23        /* Sex not valid                          */
#define ND_ModeErr    -24        /* Mode not valid                         */
#define ND_FreqErr    -25        /* Sampling frequency out of bounds       */
#define ND_VolErr     -26        /* Volume out of bounds                   */



                /* Input parameters and defaults */

#define DEFPITCH     110         /* Default pitch                          */
#define DEFRATE      150         /* Default speaking rate (wpm)            */
#define DEFVOL       64          /* Default volume (full)                  */
#define DEFFREQ      22200       /* Default sampling frequency (Hz)        */
#define MALE         0           /* Male vocal tract                       */
#define FEMALE       1           /* Female vocal tract                     */
#define NATURALF0    0           /* Natural pitch contours                 */
#define ROBOTICF0    1           /* Monotone                               */
#define DEFSEX       MALE        /* Default sex                            */
#define DEFMODE      NATURALF0   /* Default mode                           */



                /*      Parameter bounds        */

#define MINRATE      40          /* Minimum speaking rate                  */
#define MAXRATE      400         /* Maximum speaking rate                  */
#define MINPITCH     65          /* Minimum pitch                          */
#define MAXPITCH     320         /* Maximum pitch                          */
#define MINFREQ      5000        /* Minimum sampling frequency             */
#define MAXFREQ      28000       /* Maximum sampling frequency             */
#define MINVOL       0           /* Minimum volume                         */
#define MAXVOL       64          /* Maximum volume                         */



                /*    Standard Write request    */

struct narrator_rb {
        struct IOStdReq  message;       /* Standard IORB                   */
        UWORD   rate;                   /* Speaking rate (words/minute)    */
```



```
        UWORD    pitch;                 /* Baseline pitch in Hertz         */
        UWORD    mode;                  /* Pitch mode                      */
        UWORD    sex;                   /* Sex of voice                    */
        UBYTE    *ch_masks;             /* Pointer to audio alloc maps     */
        UWORD    nm_masks;              /* Number of audio alloc maps      */
        UWORD    volume;                /* Volume. 0 (off) thru 64         */
        UWORD    sampfreq;              /* Audio sampling freq             */
        UBYTE    mouths;                /* If non-zero, generate mouths    */
        UBYTE    chanmask;              /* Which ch mask used (internal)*/
        UBYTE    numchan;               /* Num ch masks used (internal) */
        UBYTE    pad;                   /* For alignment                   */
    };



                /*    Standard Read request     */

struct mouth_rb {
        struct   narrator_rb voice;     /* Speech IORB                     */
        UBYTE    width;                 /* Width (returned value)          */
        UBYTE    height;                /* Height (returned value)         */
        UBYTE    shape;                 /* Internal use, do not modify     */
        UBYTE    pad;                   /* For alignment                   */
        };

#endif  /* DEVICES_NARRATOR_H */
```

```
#ifndef DEVICES_PARALLEL_H
#define DEVICES_PARALLEL_H
/*
**      $Filename: devices/parallel.h $
**      $Release: 1.3 $
**
**      external declarations for Serial Port Driver
**
**      (C) Copyright 1985,1986,1987,1988 Commodore-Amiga, Inc.
**          All Rights Reserved
*/

#ifndef   EXEC_IO_H
#include "exec/io.h"
#endif   !EXEC_IO_H

 struct  IOPArray {
        ULONG PTermArray0;
        ULONG PTermArray1;
};

/*****************************************************************/
/* CAUTION !!  IF YOU ACCESS the parallel.device, you MUST (!!!!) use
   an IOExtPar-sized structure or you may overlay innocent memory !! */
/*****************************************************************/

 struct   IOExtPar {
        struct   IOStdReq IOPar;

/*      STRUCT   MsgNode
*    0   APTR      Succ
*    4   APTR      Pred
*    8   UBYTE     Type
*    9   UBYTE     Pri
*    A   APTR      Name
*    E   APTR      ReplyPort
*   12   UWORD     MNLength
*       STRUCT   IOExt
*   14   APTR      io_Device
*   18   APTR      io_Unit
*   1C   UWORD     io_Command
*   1E   UBYTE     io_Flags
*   1F   UBYTE     io_Error
*       STRUCT   IOStdExt
*   20   ULONG     io_Actual
*   24   ULONG     io_Length
*   28   APTR      io_Data
*   2C   ULONG     io_Offset
*   30 */
        ULONG   io_PExtFlags;    /* (not used) flag extension area */
        UBYTE   io_Status;       /* status of parallel port and registers */
        UBYTE   io_ParFlags;     /* see PARFLAGS bit definitions below */
        struct  IOPArray io_PTermArray; /* termination character array */
};

#define PARB_SHARED     5           /* ParFlags non-exclusive access bit */
#define PARF_SHARED     (1<<5)      /*    "     non-exclusive access mask */
#define PARB_RAD_BOOGIE 3           /*    "     (not yet implemented) */
#define PARF_RAD_BOOGIE (1<<3)      /*    "     (not yet implemented) */
#define PARB_EOFMODE    1           /*    "     EOF mode enabled bit */
#define PARF_EOFMODE    (1<<1)      /*    "     EOF mode enabled mask */
#define IOPARB_QUEUED   6           /* IO_FLAGS rqst-queued bit */
#define IOPARF_QUEUED   (1<<6)      /*    "     rqst-queued mask */
#define IOPARB_ABORT    5           /*    "     rqst-aborted bit */
#define IOPARF_ABORT    (1<<5)      /*    "     rqst-aborted mask */
#define IOPARB_ACTIVE   4           /*    "     rqst-qued-or-current bit */
#define IOPARF_ACTIVE   (1<<4)      /*    "     rqst-qued-or-current mask */
#define IOPTB_RWDIR     3           /* IO_STATUS read=0,write=1 bit */
#define IOPTF_RWDIR     (1<<3)      /*    "     read=0,write=1 mask */
```



```
#define IOPTB_PARSEL    2           /*    "     printer selected on the A1000 */
#define IOPTF_PARSEL    (1<<2)      /* printer selected & serial "Ring Indicator"
                                       on the A500 & A2000.  Be careful when
                                       making cables */
#define IOPTB_PAPEROUT 1            /*    "     paper out bit */
#define IOPTF_PAPEROUT (1<<1)       /*    "     paper out mask */
#define IOPTB_PARBUSY  0            /*    "     printer in busy toggle bit */
#define IOPTF_PARBUSY  (1<<0)       /*    "     printer in busy toggle mask */
/* Note: previous versions of this include files had bits 0 and 2 swapped */

#define PARALLELNAME            "parallel.device"

#define PDCMD_QUERY             (CMD_NONSTD)
#define PDCMD_SETPARAMS         (CMD_NONSTD+1)

#define ParErr_DevBusy          1
#define ParErr_BufTooBig        2
#define ParErr_InvParam         3
#define ParErr_LineErr          4
#define ParErr_NotOpen          5
#define ParErr_PortReset        6
#define ParErr_InitErr          7

#endif  /* DEVICES_PARALLEL_H */
```

```
#ifndef DEVICES_PRINTER_H
#define DEVICES_PRINTER_H
/*
**      $Filename: devices/printer.h $
**      $Release: 1.3 $
**
**
**
**      (C) Copyright 1985,1986,1987,1988 Commodore-Amiga, Inc.
**          All Rights Reserved
*/

#ifndef  EXEC_NODES_H
#include "exec/nodes.h"
#endif

#ifndef  EXEC_LISTS_H
#include "exec/lists.h"
#endif

#ifndef  EXEC_PORTS_H
#include "exec/ports.h"
#endif

#define  PRD_RAWWRITE       (CMD_NONSTD+0)
#define  PRD_PRTCOMMAND     (CMD_NONSTD+1)
#define  PRD_DUMPRPORT      (CMD_NONSTD+2)
#define  PRD_QUERY          (CMD_NONSTD+3)

/* printer command definitions */

#define aRIS      0  /* ESCc  reset                        ISO */
#define aRIN      1  /* ESC#1 initialize                   +++ */
#define aIND      2  /* ESCD  lf                           ISO */
#define aNEL      3  /* ESCE  return,lf                    ISO */
#define aRI       4  /* ESCM  reverse lf                   ISO */

#define aSGR0     5  /* ESC[0m normal char set             ISO */
#define aSGR3     6  /* ESC[3m italics on                  ISO */
#define aSGR23    7  /* ESC[23m italics off                ISO */
#define aSGR4     8  /* ESC[4m underline on                ISO */
#define aSGR24    9  /* ESC[24m underline off              ISO */
#define aSGR1    10  /* ESC[1m boldface on                 ISO */
#define aSGR22   11  /* ESC[22m boldface off               ISO */
#define aSFC     12  /* SGR30-39  set foreground color ISO */
#define aSBC     13  /* SGR40-49  set background color ISO */

#define aSHORP0 14  /* ESC[0w normal pitch                DEC */
#define aSHORP2 15  /* ESC[2w elite on                    DEC */
#define aSHORP1 16  /* ESC[1w elite off                   DEC */
#define aSHORP4 17  /* ESC[4w condensed fine on           DEC */
#define aSHORP3 18  /* ESC[3w condensed off               DEC */
#define aSHORP6 19  /* ESC[6w enlarged on                 DEC */
#define aSHORP5 20  /* ESC[5w enlarged off                DEC */

#define aDEN6    21  /* ESC[6"z shadow print on           DEC (sort of) */
#define aDEN5    22  /* ESC[5"z shadow print off          DEC */
#define aDEN4    23  /* ESC[4"z doublestrike on           DEC */
#define aDEN3    24  /* ESC[3"z doublestrike off          DEC */
#define aDEN2    25  /* ESC[2"z  NLQ on                   DEC */
#define aDEN1    26  /* ESC[1"z  NLQ off                  DEC */

#define aSUS2    27  /* ESC[2v superscript on             +++ */
#define aSUS1    28  /* ESC[1v superscript off            +++ */
#define aSUS4    29  /* ESC[4v subscript on               +++ */
#define aSUS3    30  /* ESC[3v subscript off              +++ */
#define aSUS0    31  /* ESC[0v normalize the line         +++ */
#define aPLU     32  /* ESCL  partial line up             ISO */
#define aPLD     33  /* ESCK  partial line down           ISO */
```



```

#define aFNT0   34  /* ESC(B US char set        or Typeface  0 (default) */
#define aFNT1   35  /* ESC(R French char set    or Typeface  1 */
#define aFNT2   36  /* ESC(K German char set    or Typeface  2 */
#define aFNT3   37  /* ESC(A UK char set        or Typeface  3 */
#define aFNT4   38  /* ESC(E Danish I char set  or Typeface  4 */
#define aFNT5   39  /* ESC(H Sweden char set    or Typeface  5 */
#define aFNT6   40  /* ESC(Y Italian char set   or Typeface  6 */
#define aFNT7   41  /* ESC(Z Spanish char set   or Typeface  7 */
#define aFNT8   42  /* ESC(J Japanese char set  or Typeface  8 */
#define aFNT9   43  /* ESC(6 Norweign char set  or Typeface  9 */
#define aFNT10  44  /* ESC(C Danish II char set or Typeface 10 */

/*
        Suggested typefaces are:

         0 - default typeface.
         1 - Line Printer or equiv.
         2 - Pica or equiv.
         3 - Elite or equiv.
         4 - Helvetica or equiv.
         5 - Times Roman or equiv.
         6 - Gothic or equiv.
         7 - Script or equiv.
         8 - Prestige or equiv.
         9 - Caslon or equiv.
        10 - Orator or equiv.
*/

#define aPROP2  45  /* ESC[2p  proportional on         +++ */
#define aPROP1  46  /* ESC[1p  proportional off        +++ */
#define aPROP0  47  /* ESC[0p  proportional clear      +++ */
#define aTSS    48  /* ESC[n E set proportional offset ISO */
#define aJFY5   49  /* ESC[5 F auto left justify       ISO */
#define aJFY7   50  /* ESC[7 F auto right justify      ISO */
#define aJFY6   51  /* ESC[6 F auto full justify       ISO */
#define aJFY0   52  /* ESC[0 F auto justify off        ISO */
#define aJFY3   53  /* ESC[3 F letter space (justify) ISO (special) */
#define aJFY1   54  /* ESC[1 F word fill(auto center) ISO (special) */

#define aVERP0  55  /* ESC[0z  1/8" line spacing       +++ */
#define aVERP1  56  /* ESC[1z  1/6" line spacing       +++ */
#define aSLPP   57  /* ESC[nt  set form length n       DEC */
#define aPERF   58  /* ESC[nq  perf skip n (n>0)       +++ */
#define aPERF0  59  /* ESC[0q  perf skip off           +++ */

#define aLMS    60  /* ESC#9   Left margin set         +++ */
#define aRMS    61  /* ESC#0   Right margin set        +++ */
#define aTMS    62  /* ESC#8   Top margin set          +++ */
#define aBMS    63  /* ESC#2   Bottom marg set         +++ */
#define aSTBM   64  /* ESC[Pn1;Pn2r  T&B margins       DEC */
#define aSLRM   65  /* ESC[Pn1;Pn2s  L&R margin        DEC */
#define aCAM    66  /* ESC#3   Clear margins           +++ */

#define aHTS    67  /* ESCH    Set horiz tab           ISO */
#define aVTS    68  /* ESCJ    Set vertical tabs       ISO */
#define aTBC0   69  /* ESC[0g  Clr horiz tab           ISO */
#define aTBC3   70  /* ESC[3g  Clear all h tab         ISO */
#define aTBC1   71  /* ESC[1g  Clr vertical tabs       ISO */
#define aTBC4   72  /* ESC[4g  Clr all v tabs          ISO */
#define aTBCALL 73  /* ESC#4   Clr all h & v tabs      +++ */
#define aTBSALL 74  /* ESC#5   Set default tabs        +++ */
#define aEXTEND 75  /* ESC[Pn"x extended commands      +++ */

#define aRAW    76      /* ESC[Pn"r     Next 'Pn' chars are raw +++ */

struct IOPrtCmdReq {
    struct  Message io_Message;
    struct  Device  *io_Device;     /* device node pointer  */
```

```
    struct  Unit    *io_Unit;           /* unit (driver private)*/
    UWORD   io_Command;                 /* device command */
    UBYTE   io_Flags;
    BYTE    io_Error;                   /* error or warning num */
    UWORD   io_PrtCommand;              /* printer command */
    UBYTE   io_Parm0;                   /* first command parameter */
    UBYTE   io_Parm1;                   /* second command parameter */
    UBYTE   io_Parm2;                   /* third command parameter */
    UBYTE   io_Parm3;                   /* fourth command parameter */
};

struct IODRPReq {
    struct  Message io_Message;
    struct  Device  *io_Device;         /* device node pointer  */
    struct  Unit    *io_Unit;           /* unit (driver private)*/
    UWORD   io_Command;                 /* device command */
    UBYTE   io_Flags;
    BYTE    io_Error;                   /* error or warning num */
    struct  RastPort *io_RastPort;      /* raster port */
    struct  ColorMap *io_ColorMap;      /* color map */
    ULONG   io_Modes;                   /* graphics viewport modes */
    UWORD   io_SrcX;                    /* source x origin */
    UWORD   io_SrcY;                    /* source y origin */
    UWORD   io_SrcWidth;                /* source x width */
    UWORD   io_SrcHeight;               /* source x height */
    LONG    io_DestCols;                /* destination x width */
    LONG    io_DestRows;                /* destination y height */
    UWORD   io_Special;                 /* option flags */
};

#define SPECIAL_MILCOLS         0x0001  /* DestCols specified in 1/1000" */
#define SPECIAL_MILROWS         0x0002  /* DestRows specified in 1/1000" */
#define SPECIAL_FULLCOLS        0x0004  /* make DestCols maximum possible */
#define SPECIAL_FULLROWS        0x0008  /* make DestRows maximum possible */
#define SPECIAL_FRACCOLS        0x0010  /* DestCols is fraction of FULLCOLS */
#define SPECIAL_FRACROWS        0x0020  /* DestRows is fraction of FULLROWS */
#define SPECIAL_CENTER          0x0040  /* center image on paper */
#define SPECIAL_ASPECT          0x0080  /* ensure correct aspect ratio */
#define SPECIAL_DENSITY1        0x0100  /* lowest resolution (dpi) */
#define SPECIAL_DENSITY2        0x0200  /* next res */
#define SPECIAL_DENSITY3        0x0300  /* next res */
#define SPECIAL_DENSITY4        0x0400  /* next res */
#define SPECIAL_DENSITY5        0x0500  /* next res */
#define SPECIAL_DENSITY6        0x0600  /* next res */
#define SPECIAL_DENSITY7        0x0700  /* highest res */
#define SPECIAL_NOFORMFEED      0x0800  /* don't eject paper on gfx prints */
#define SPECIAL_TRUSTME         0x1000  /* don't reset on gfx prints */
/*
        Compute print size, set 'io_DestCols' and 'io_DestRows' in the calling
        program's 'IODRPReq' structure and exit, DON'T PRINT.  This allows the
        calling program to see what the final print size would be in printer
        pixels.  Note that it modifies the 'io_DestCols' and 'io_DestRows'
        fields of your 'IODRPReq' structure.  Also, set the print density and
        update the 'MaxXDots', 'MaxYDots', 'XDotsInch', and 'YDotsInch' fields
        of the 'PrinterExtendedData' structure.
*/
#define SPECIAL_NOPRINT         0x2000  /* see above */

#define PDERR_NOERR             0       /* clean exit, no errors */
#define PDERR_CANCEL            1       /* user cancelled print */
#define PDERR_NOTGRAPHICS       2       /* printer cannot output graphics */
#define PDERR_INVERTHAM         3       /* OBSOLETE */
#define PDERR_BADDIMENSION      4       /* print dimensions illegal */
#define PDERR_DIMENSIONOVFLOW   5       /* OBSOLETE */
#define PDERR_INTERNALMEMORY    6       /* no memory for internal variables */
#define PDERR_BUFFERMEMORY      7       /* no memory for print buffer */
/*
        Note : this is an internal error that can be returned from the render
        function to the printer device.  It is NEVER returned to the user.
```



```
        If the printer device sees this error it converts it 'PDERR_NOERR'
        and exits gracefully.  Refer to the document on
        'How to Write a Graphics Printer Driver' for more info.
*/
#define PDERR_TOOKCONTROL       8       /* Took control in case 0 of render */

/* internal use */
#define SPECIAL_DENSITYMASK     0x0700  /* masks out density values */
#define SPECIAL_DIMENSIONSMASK \
        (SPECIAL_MILCOLS|SPECIAL_MILROWS|SPECIAL_FULLCOLS|SPECIAL_FULLROWS\
        |SPECIAL_FRACCOLS|SPECIAL_FRACROWS|SPECIAL_ASPECT)

#endif  /* DEVICES_PRINTER_H */
```

```
#ifndef DEVICES_PRTBASE_H
#define DEVICES_PRTBASE_H
/*
**      $Filename: devices/prtbase.h $
**      $Release: 1.3 $
**
**      printer device data definition
**
**      (C) Copyright 1986,1987,1988 Commodore-Amiga, Inc.
**          All Rights Reserved
*/

#ifndef  EXEC_NODES_H
#include "exec/nodes.h"
#endif
#ifndef  EXEC_LISTS_H
#include "exec/lists.h"
#endif
#ifndef  EXEC_PORTS_H
#include "exec/ports.h"
#endif
#ifndef  EXEC_LIBRARIES_H
#include "exec/libraries.h"
#endif
#ifndef  EXEC_TASKS_H
#include "exec/tasks.h"
#endif

#ifndef  DEVICES_PARALLEL_H
#include "devices/parallel.h"
#endif
#ifndef  DEVICES_SERIAL_H
#include "devices/serial.h"
#endif
#ifndef  DEVICES_TIMER_H
#include "devices/timer.h"
#endif
#ifndef  LIBRARIES_DOSEXTENS_I
#include "libraries/dosextens.h"
#endif
#ifndef  INTUITION_INTUITION_H
#include "intuition/intuition.h"
#endif


struct DeviceData {
    struct Library dd_Device; /* standard library node */
    APTR dd_Segment;          /* A0 when initialized */
    APTR dd_ExecBase;         /* A6 for exec */
    APTR dd_CmdVectors;       /* command table for device commands */
    APTR dd_CmdBytes;         /* bytes describing which command queue */
    UWORD   dd_NumCommands;   /* the number of commands supported */
};

#define P_STKSIZE       0x0800  /* stack size for child task */
#define P_BUFSIZE       256     /* size of internal buffers for text i/o */
#define P_SAFESIZE      128     /* safety margin for text output buffer */

struct   PrinterData {
        struct DeviceData pd_Device;
        struct MsgPort pd_Unit; /* the one and only unit */
        BPTR pd_PrinterSegment; /* the printer specific segment */
        UWORD pd_PrinterType;   /* the segment printer type */
                                /* the segment data structure */
        struct PrinterSegment *pd_SegmentData;
        UBYTE *pd_PrintBuf;     /* the raster print buffer */
        int (*pd_PWrite)();     /* the write function */
        int (*pd_PBothReady)(); /* write function's done */
        union {                 /* port I/O request 0 */
                struct IOExtPar pd_p0;
                struct IOExtSer pd_s0;
        } pd_ior0;

#define  pd_PIOR0 pd_ior0.pd_p0
#define  pd_SIOR0 pd_ior0.pd_s0

        union {                     /*   and 1 for double buffering */
                struct IOExtPar pd_p1;
                struct IOExtSer pd_s1;
        } pd_ior1;

#define  pd_PIOR1 pd_ior1.pd_p1
#define  pd_SIOR1 pd_ior1.pd_s1

        struct timerequest pd_TIOR;     /* timer I/O request */
        struct MsgPort pd_IORPort;      /*   and message reply port */
        struct Task pd_TC;              /* write task */
        UBYTE pd_Stk[P_STKSIZE];        /*   and stack space */
        UBYTE pd_Flags;                 /* device flags */
        UBYTE pd_pad;
        struct Preferences pd_Preferences;      /* the latest preferences */
        UBYTE   pd_PWaitEnabled;        /* wait function switch */
};

/* Printer Class */
#define PPCB_GFX        0       /* graphics (bit position) */
#define PPCF_GFX        0x1     /* graphics (and/or flag) */
#define PPCB_COLOR      1       /* color (bit position) */
#define PPCF_COLOR      0x2     /* color (and/or flag) */

#define PPC_BWALPHA     0x00    /* black&white alphanumerics */
#define PPC_BWGFX       0x01    /* black&white graphics */
#define PPC_COLORALPHA  0x02    /* color alphanumerics */
#define PPC_COLORGFX    0x03    /* color graphics */

/* Color Class */
#define PCC_BW          0x01    /* black&white only */
#define PCC_YMC         0x02    /* yellow/magenta/cyan only */
#define PCC_YMC_BW      0x03    /* yellow/magenta/cyan or black&white */
#define PCC_YMCB        0x04    /* yellow/magenta/cyan/black */
#define PCC_4COLOR      0x04    /* a flag for YMCB and BGRW */
#define PCC_ADDITIVE    0x08    /* not ymcb but blue/green/red/white */
#define PCC_WB          0x09    /* black&white only, 0 == BLACK */
#define PCC_BGR         0x0A    /* blue/green/red */
#define PCC_BGR_WB      0x0B    /* blue/green/red or black&white */
#define PCC_BGRW        0x0C    /* blue/green/red/white */
/*
        The picture must be scanned once for each color component, as the
        printer can only define one color at a time.  ie. If 'PCC_YMC' then
        first pass sends all 'Y' info to printer, second pass sends all 'M'
        info, and third pass sends all C info to printer.  The CalComp
        PlotMaster is an example of this type of printer.
*/
#define PCC_MULTI_PASS  0x10    /* see explanation above */

struct PrinterExtendedData {
        char    *ped_PrinterName;    /* printer name, null terminated */
        VOID    (*ped_Init)();       /* called after LoadSeg */
        VOID    (*ped_Expunge)();    /* called before UnLoadSeg */
        int     (*ped_Open)();       /* called at OpenDevice */
        VOID    (*ped_Close)();      /* called at CloseDevice */
        UBYTE   ped_PrinterClass;    /* printer class */
        UBYTE   ped_ColorClass;      /* color class */
        UBYTE   ped_MaxColumns;      /* number of print columns available */
        UBYTE   ped_NumCharSets;     /* number of character sets */
        UWORD   ped_NumRows;         /* number of 'pins' in print head */
        ULONG   ped_MaxXDots;        /* number of dots max in a raster dump */
        ULONG   ped_MaxYDots;        /* number of dots max in a raster dump */
```

```
        UWORD   ped_XDotsInch;       /* horizontal dot density */
        UWORD   ped_YDotsInch;       /* vertical dot density */
        char    ***ped_Commands;     /* printer text command table */
        int     (*ped_DoSpecial)();  /* special command handler */
        int     (*ped_Render)();     /* raster render function */
        LONG    ped_TimeoutSecs;     /* good write timeout */
        /* the following only exists if the segment version is >= 33 */
        char    **ped_8BitChars;     /* conv. strings for the extended font */
        LONG    ped_PrintMode;       /* set if text printed, otherwise 0 */
        /* the following only exists if the segment version is >= 34 */
        /* ptr to conversion function for all chars */
        int     (*ped_ConvFunc)();
};

struct PrinterSegment {
    ULONG   ps_NextSegment;      /* (actually a BPTR) */
    ULONG   ps_runAlert;         /* MOVEQ #0,D0 : RTS */
    UWORD   ps_Version;          /* segment version */
    UWORD   ps_Revision;         /* segment revision */
    struct  PrinterExtendedData ps_PED;   /* printer extended data */
};

#endif  /* DEVICES_PRTBASE_H */
```



```
#ifndef DEVICES_PRTGFX_H
#define DEVICES_PRTGFX_H
/*
**      $Filename: devices/prtgfx.h $
**      $Release: 1.3 $
**
**
**
**      (C) Copyright 1987,1988 Commodore-Amiga, Inc.
**          All Rights Reserved
*/

#define PCMYELLOW       0               /* byte index for yellow */
#define PCMMAGENTA      1               /* byte index for magenta */
#define PCMCYAN         2               /* byte index for cyan */
#define PCMBLACK        3               /* byte index for black */
#define PCMBLUE         PCMYELLOW       /* byte index for blue */
#define PCMGREEN        PCMMAGENTA      /* byte index for green */
#define PCMRED          PCMCYAN         /* byte index for red */
#define PCMWHITE        PCMBLACK        /* byte index for white */

union colorEntry {
        ULONG colorLong;        /* quick access to all of YMCB */
        UBYTE colorByte[4];     /* 1 entry for each of YMCB */
        BYTE colorSByte[4];     /* ditto (except signed) */
};

struct PrtInfo { /* printer info */
        int (*pi_render)();             /* PRIVATE - DO NOT USE! */
        struct RastPort *pi_rp;         /* PRIVATE - DO NOT USE! */
        struct RastPort *pi_temprp;     /* PRIVATE - DO NOT USE! */
        UWORD *pi_RowBuf;               /* PRIVATE - DO NOT USE! */
        UWORD *pi_HamBuf;               /* PRIVATE - DO NOT USE! */
        union colorEntry *pi_ColorMap;  /* PRIVATE - DO NOT USE! */
        union colorEntry *pi_ColorInt;  /* color intensities for entire row */
        union colorEntry *pi_HamInt;    /* PRIVATE - DO NOT USE! */
        union colorEntry *pi_Dest1Int;  /* PRIVATE - DO NOT USE! */
        union colorEntry *pi_Dest2Int;  /* PRIVATE - DO NOT USE! */
        UWORD *pi_ScaleX;               /* array of scale values for X */
        UWORD *pi_ScaleXAlt;            /* PRIVATE - DO NOT USE! */
        UBYTE *pi_dmatrix;              /* pointer to dither matrix */
        UWORD *pi_TopBuf;               /* PRIVATE - DO NOT USE! */
        UWORD *pi_BotBuf;               /* PRIVATE - DO NOT USE! */

        UWORD pi_RowBufSize;            /* PRIVATE - DO NOT USE! */
        UWORD pi_HamBufSize;            /* PRIVATE - DO NOT USE! */
        UWORD pi_ColorMapSize;          /* PRIVATE - DO NOT USE! */
        UWORD pi_ColorIntSize;          /* PRIVATE - DO NOT USE! */
        UWORD pi_HamIntSize;            /* PRIVATE - DO NOT USE! */
        UWORD pi_Dest1IntSize;          /* PRIVATE - DO NOT USE! */
        UWORD pi_Dest2IntSize;          /* PRIVATE - DO NOT USE! */
        UWORD pi_ScaleXSize;            /* PRIVATE - DO NOT USE! */
        UWORD pi_ScaleXAltSize;         /* PRIVATE - DO NOT USE! */

        UWORD pi_PrefsFlags;            /* PRIVATE - DO NOT USE! */
        ULONG pi_special;               /* PRIVATE - DO NOT USE! */
        UWORD pi_xstart;                /* PRIVATE - DO NOT USE! */
        UWORD pi_ystart;                /* PRIVATE - DO NOT USE! */
        UWORD pi_width;                 /* source width (in pixels) */
        UWORD pi_height;                /* PRIVATE - DO NOT USE! */
        ULONG pi_pc;                    /* PRIVATE - DO NOT USE! */
        ULONG pi_pr;                    /* PRIVATE - DO NOT USE! */
        UWORD pi_ymult;                 /* PRIVATE - DO NOT USE! */
        UWORD pi_ymod;                  /* PRIVATE - DO NOT USE! */
        WORD pi_ety;                    /* PRIVATE - DO NOT USE! */
        UWORD pi_xpos;                  /* offset to start printing picture */
        UWORD pi_threshold;             /* threshold value (from prefs) */
        UWORD pi_tempwidth;             /* PRIVATE - DO NOT USE! */
        UWORD pi_flags;                 /* PRIVATE - DO NOT USE! */
```

```
};

#endif  /* DEVICES_PRTGFX_H */
```



```
#ifndef DEVICES_SCSIDISK_H
#define DEVICES_SCSIDISK_H
/*
**      $Filename: devices/scsidisk.h $
**      $Release: 1.3 $
**
**      SCSI exec-level device command
**
**      (C) Copyright 1988 Commodore-Amiga, Inc.
**          All Rights Reserved
*/

/*----------------------------------------------------------------------
 *
 *   SCSI Command
 *      Several Amiga SCSI controller manufacturers are converging on
 *      standard ways to talk to their controllers.  This include
 *      file describes an exec-device command (e.g. for hddisk.device)
 *      that can be used to issue SCSI commands
 *
 *   UNIT NUMBERS
 *      Unit numbers to the OpenDevice call have encoded in them which
 *      SCSI device is being referred to.  The three decimal digits of
 *      the unit number refer to the SCSI Target ID (bus address) in
 *      the 1's digit, the SCSI logical unit (LUN) in the 10's digit,
 *      and the controller board in the 100's digit.
 *
 *      Examples:
 *                0     drive at address 0
 *               12     LUN 1 on multiple drive controller at address 2
 *              104     second controller board, address 4
 *               88     not valid: both logical units and addresses
 *                      range from 0..7.
 *
 *   CAVEATS
 *      Original 2090 code did not support this command.
 *
 *      Commodore 2090/2090A unit numbers are different.  The SCSI
 *      logical unit is the 100's digit, and the SCSI Target ID
 *      is a permuted 1's digit: Target ID 0..6 maps to unit 3..9
 *      (7 is reserved for the controller).
 *
 *          Examples:
 *                3     drive at address 0
 *              109     drive at address 6, logical unit 1
 *                1     not valid: this is not a SCSI unit.  Perhaps
 *                      it's an ST506 unit.
 *
 *      Some controller boards generate a unique name (e.g. 2090A's
 *      iddisk.device) for the second controller board, instead of
 *      implementing the 100's digit.
 *
 *      There are optional restrictions on the alignment, bus
 *      accessability, and size of the data for the data phase.
 *      Be conservative to work with all manufacturer's controllers.
 *
 *----------------------------------------------------------------------*/

#define HD_SCSICMD      28      /* issue a SCSI command to the unit */
                                /* io_Data points to a SCSICmd */
                                /* io_Length is sizeof(struct SCSICmd) */
                                /* io_Actual and io_Offset are not used */

struct SCSICmd {
    UWORD  *scsi_Data;          /* word aligned data for SCSI Data Phase */
                                /* (optional) data need not be byte aligned */
                                /* (optional) data need not be bus accessable */
    ULONG   scsi_Length;        /* even length of Data area */
                                /* (optional) data can have odd length */
```

```
                                /* (optional) data length can be > 2**24 */
    ULONG   scsi_Actual;        /* actual Data used */
    UBYTE  *scsi_Command;       /* SCSI Command (same options as scsi_Data) */
    UWORD   scsi_CmdLength;     /* length of Command */
    UWORD   scsi_CmdActual;     /* actual Command used */
    UBYTE   scsi_Flags;         /* includes intended data direction */
    UBYTE   scsi_Status;        /* SCSI status of command */
};


/*----- scsi_Flags -----*/
#define SCSIF_WRITE             0       /* intended data direction is out */
#define SCSIF_READ              1       /* intended data direction is in */

/*----- SCSI io_Error values -----*/
#define HFERR_SelfUnit          40      /* cannot issue SCSI command to self */
#define HFERR_DMA               41      /* DMA error */
#define HFERR_Phase             42      /* illegal or unexpected SCSI phase */
#define HFERR_Parity            43      /* SCSI parity error */
#define HFERR_SelTimeout        44      /* Select timed out */
#define HFERR_BadStatus         45      /* status and/or sense error */

/*----- OpenDevice io_Error values -----*/
#define HFERR_NoBoard           50      /* Open failed for non-existant board */

#endif  /* DEVICES_SCSIDISK_H */
```



```
#ifndef DEVICES_SERIAL_H
#define DEVICES_SERIAL_H

/*
**      $Filename: devices/serial.h $
**      $Release: 1.3 $
**
**      external declarations for the serial device
**
**      (C) Copyright 1985,1986,1987,1988 Commodore-Amiga, Inc.
**          All Rights Reserved
*/

#ifndef EXEC_IO_H
#include        "exec/io.h"
#endif /* EXEC_IO_H */

                        /* array of termination char's */
                        /* to use,see serial.doc setparams */

 struct  IOTArray {
        ULONG TermArray0;
        ULONG TermArray1;
};


#define SER_DEFAULT_CTLCHAR 0x11130000  /* default chars for xON,xOFF */
/* You may change these via SETPARAMS.  At this time, parity is not
   calculated for xON/xOFF characters.  You must supply them with the
   desired parity. */

/*****************************************************************/
/* CAUTION !!  IF YOU ACCESS the serial.device, you MUST (!!!!) use an
   IOExtSer-sized structure or you may overlay innocent memory !! */
/*****************************************************************/

 struct  IOExtSer {
        struct   IOStdReq IOSer;

/*      STRUCT   MsgNode
*   0    APTR     Succ
*   4    APTR     Pred
*   8    UBYTE    Type
*   9    UBYTE    Pri
*   A    APTR     Name
*   E    APTR     ReplyPort
*  12    UWORD    MNLength
*      STRUCT   IOExt
*  14    APTR     io_Device
*  18    APTR     io_Unit
*  1C    UWORD    io_Command
*  1E    UBYTE    io_Flags
*  1F    UBYTE    io_Error
*      STRUCT   IOStdExt
*  20    ULONG    io_Actual
*  24    ULONG    io_Length
*  28    APTR     io_Data
*  2C    ULONG    io_Offset
*
*  30 */
   ULONG   io_CtlChar;     /* control char's (order = xON,xOFF,INQ,ACK) */
   ULONG   io_RBufLen;     /* length in bytes of serial port's read buffer */
   ULONG   io_ExtFlags;    /* additional serial flags (see bitdefs below) */
   ULONG   io_Baud;        /* baud rate requested (true baud) */
   ULONG   io_BrkTime;     /* duration of break signal in MICROseconds */
   struct  IOTArray io_TermArray; /* termination character array */
   UBYTE   io_ReadLen;     /* bits per read character (# of bits) */
   UBYTE   io_WriteLen;    /* bits per write character (# of bits) */
   UBYTE   io_StopBits;    /* stopbits for read (# of bits) */
```

```
   UBYTE   io_SerFlags;    /* see SerFlags bit definitions below  */
   UWORD   io_Status;
};
   /* status of serial port, as follows:
*                  BIT  ACTIVE  FUNCTION
*                   0    ---    reserved
*                   1    ---    reserved
*                   2    high   Connected to parallel "select" on the A1000.
*                               Connected to both the parallel "select" and
*                               serial "ring indicator" pins on the A500 &
*                               A2000.  Take care when making cables.
*                   3    low    Data Set Ready
*                   4    low    Clear To Send
*                   5    low    Carrier Detect
*                   6    low    Ready To Send
*                   7    low    Data Terminal Ready
*                   8    high   read overrun
*                   9    high   break sent
*                  10    high   break received
*                  11    high   transmit x-OFFed
*                  12    high   receive x-OFFed
*               13-15           reserved
*/

#define   SDCMD_QUERY            CMD_NONSTD
#define   SDCMD_BREAK           (CMD_NONSTD+1)
#define   SDCMD_SETPARAMS       (CMD_NONSTD+2)


#define SERB_XDISABLED  7       /* io_SerFlags xOn-xOff feature disabled bit */
#define SERF_XDISABLED  (1<<7)  /*    "       xOn-xOff feature disabled mask */
#define SERB_EOFMODE    6       /*    "       EOF mode enabled bit */
#define SERF_EOFMODE    (1<<6)  /*    "       EOF mode enabled mask */
#define SERB_SHARED     5       /*    "       non-exclusive access bit */
#define SERF_SHARED     (1<<5)  /*    "       non-exclusive access mask */
#define SERB_RAD_BOOGIE 4       /*    "       high-speed mode active bit */
#define SERF_RAD_BOOGIE (1<<4)  /*    "       high-speed mode active mask */
#define SERB_QUEUEDBRK  3       /*    "       queue this Break ioRqst */
#define SERF_QUEUEDBRK  (1<<3)  /*    "       queue this Break ioRqst */
#define SERB_7WIRE      2       /*    "       RS232 7-wire protocol */
#define SERF_7WIRE      (1<<2)  /*    "       RS232 7-wire protocol */
#define SERB_PARTY_ODD  1       /*    "       parity feature enabled bit */
#define SERF_PARTY_ODD  (1<<1)  /*    "       parity feature enabled mask */
#define SERB_PARTY_ON   0       /*    "       parity-enabled bit */
#define SERF_PARTY_ON   (1<<0)  /*    "       parity-enabled mask */

/* These now refect the actual bit positions in the io_Status UWORD */
#define IO_STATB_XOFFREAD 12       /* io_Status receive currently xOFF'ed bit */
#define IO_STATF_XOFFREAD (1<<12)  /*    "      receive currently xOFF'ed mask */
#define IO_STATB_XOFFWRITE 11      /*    "      transmit currently xOFF'ed bit */
#define IO_STATF_XOFFWRITE (1<<11) /*    "      transmit currently xOFF'ed mask *
#define IO_STATB_READBREAK 10      /*    "      break was latest input bit */
#define IO_STATF_READBREAK (1<<10) /*    "      break was latest input mask */
#define IO_STATB_WROTEBREAK 9      /*    "      break was latest output bit */
#define IO_STATF_WROTEBREAK (1<<9) /*    "      break was latest output mask */
#define IO_STATB_OVERRUN 8         /*    "      status word RBF overrun bit */
#define IO_STATF_OVERRUN (1<<8)    /*    "      status word RBF overrun mask */


#define SEXTB_MSPON     1       /* io_ExtFlags. Use mark-space parity, */
                                /*            instead of odd-even. */
#define SEXTF_MSPON     (1<<1)  /*    "       mark-space parity mask */
#define SEXTB_MARK      0       /*    "       if mark-space, use mark */
#define SEXTF_MARK      (1<<0)  /*    "       if mark-space, use mark mask */


#define SerErr_DevBusy         1
#define SerErr_BufErr          4        /* Failed to allocate new read buffer */
#define SerErr_InvParam        5
```



```
#define SerErr_LineErr         6
#define SerErr_ParityErr       9
#define SerErr_TimerErr       11        /*(See the serial/OpenDevice autodoc)*/
#define SerErr_BufOverflow    12
#define SerErr_NoDSR          13
#define SerErr_DetectedBreak  15


#ifdef  DEVICES_SERIAL_H_OBSOLETE
#define SerErr_BaudMismatch    2        /* unused */
#define SerErr_InvBaud         3        /* unused */
#define SerErr_NotOpen         7        /* unused */
#define SerErr_PortReset       8        /* unused */
#define SerErr_InitErr        10        /* unused */
#define SerErr_NoCTS          14        /* unused */
/* These defines refer to the HIGH ORDER byte of io_Status.  They have
   been replaced by the new, corrected ones above */
#define IOSTB_XOFFREAD  4        /* iost_hob receive currently xOFF'ed bit */
#define IOSTF_XOFFREAD  (1<<4)   /*    "     receive currently xOFF'ed mask */
#define IOSTB_XOFFWRITE 3        /*    "     transmit currently xOFF'ed bit */
#define IOSTF_XOFFWRITE (1<<3)   /*    "     transmit currently xOFF'ed mask */
#define IOSTB_READBREAK 2        /*    "     break was latest input bit */
#define IOSTF_READBREAK (1<<2)   /*    "     break was latest input mask */
#define IOSTB_WROTEBREAK 1       /*    "     break was latest output bit */
#define IOSTF_WROTEBREAK (1<<1)  /*    "     break was latest output mask */
#define IOSTB_OVERRUN   0        /*    "     status word RBF overrun bit */
#define IOSTF_OVERRUN   (1<<0)   /*    "     status word RBF overrun mask */

#define IOSERB_BUFRREAD 7        /* io_Flags from read buffer bit */
#define IOSERF_BUFRREAD (1<<7)   /*    "     from read buffer mask */
#define IOSERB_QUEUED   6        /*    "     rqst-queued bit */
#define IOSERF_QUEUED   (1<<6)   /*    "     rqst-queued mask */
#define IOSERB_ABORT    5        /*    "     rqst-aborted bit */
#define IOSERF_ABORT    (1<<5)   /*    "     rqst-aborted mask */
#define IOSERB_ACTIVE   4        /*    "     rqst-qued-or-current bit */
#define IOSERF_ACTIVE   (1<<4)   /*    "     rqst-qued-or-current mask */
#endif  /* DEVICES_SERIAL_H_OBSOLETE */


#define SERIALNAME     "serial.device"

#endif  /* DEVICES_SERIAL_H */
```

```
#ifndef DEVICES_TIMER_H
#define DEVICES_TIMER_H
/*
**      $Filename: devices/timer.h $
**      $Release: 1.3 $
**
**
**
**      (C) Copyright 1985,1986,1987,1988 Commodore-Amiga, Inc.
**          All Rights Reserved
*/

#ifndef EXEC_IO_H
#include "exec/io.h"
#endif EXEC_IO_H

/* unit defintions */
#define UNIT_MICROHZ    0
#define UNIT_VBLANK     1

#define TIMERNAME       "timer.device"

struct timeval {
    ULONG tv_secs;
    ULONG tv_micro;
};

struct timerequest {
    struct IORequest tr_node;
    struct timeval tr_time;
};

/* IO_COMMAND to use for adding a timer */
#define TR_ADDREQUEST   CMD_NONSTD
#define TR_GETSYSTIME   (CMD_NONSTD+1)
#define TR_SETSYSTIME   (CMD_NONSTD+2)

#endif  /* DEVICES_TIMER_H */
```



```
#ifndef DEVICES_TRACKDISK_H
#define DEVICES_TRACKDISK_H
/*
**      $Filename: devices/trackdisk.h $
**      $Release: 1.3 $
**
**
**
**      (C) Copyright 1985,1986,1987,1988 Commodore-Amiga, Inc.
**          All Rights Reserved
*/

#ifndef EXEC_IO_H
#include "exec/io.h"
#endif !EXEC_IO_H

#ifndef EXEC_DEVICES_H
#include "exec/devices.h"
#endif !EXEC_DEVICES_H

/*
 *--------------------------------------------------------------------
 *
 * Physical drive constants
 *
 *--------------------------------------------------------------------
 */

/* OBSOLETE -- use the TD_GETNUMTRACKS command! */
/*#define       NUMCYLS 80*/            /*  normal # of cylinders */
/*#define       MAXCYLS (NUMCYLS+20)*/  /* max # cyls to look for during cal */
/*#define       NUMHEADS 2*/
/*#define       NUMTRACKS (NUMCYLS*NUMHEADS)*/

#define NUMSECS 11
#define NUMUNITS 4

/*
 *--------------------------------------------------------------------
 *
 * Useful constants
 *
 *--------------------------------------------------------------------
 */

/*-- sizes before mfm encoding */
#define TD_SECTOR 512
#define TD_SECSHIFT 9           /* log TD_SECTOR */

/*
 *--------------------------------------------------------------------
 *
 * Driver Specific Commands
 *
 *--------------------------------------------------------------------
 */

/*
 *-- TD_NAME is a generic macro to get the name of the driver.  This
 *-- way if the name is ever changed you will pick up the change
 *-- automatically.
 *--
 *-- Normal usage would be:
 *--
 *-- char internalName[] = TD_NAME;
 *--
 */

#define TD_NAME "trackdisk.device"
```

```
#define TDF_EXTCOM (1<<15)              /* for internal use only! */


#define TD_MOTOR          (CMD_NONSTD+0)  /* control the disk's motor */
#define TD_SEEK           (CMD_NONSTD+1)  /* explicit seek (for testing) */
#define TD_FORMAT         (CMD_NONSTD+2)  /* format disk */
#define TD_REMOVE         (CMD_NONSTD+3)  /* notify when disk changes */
#define TD_CHANGENUM      (CMD_NONSTD+4)  /* number of disk changes */
#define TD_CHANGESTATE    (CMD_NONSTD+5)  /* is there a disk in the drive? */
#define TD_PROTSTATUS     (CMD_NONSTD+6)  /* is the disk write protected? */
#define TD_RAWREAD        (CMD_NONSTD+7)  /* read raw bits from the disk */
#define TD_RAWWRITE       (CMD_NONSTD+8)  /* write raw bits to the disk */
#define TD_GETDRIVETYPE   (CMD_NONSTD+9)  /* get the type of the disk drive */
#define TD_GETNUMTRACKS   (CMD_NONSTD+10) /* # of tracks for this type drive */
#define TD_ADDCHANGEINT   (CMD_NONSTD+11) /* TD_REMOVE done right */
#define TD_REMCHANGEINT   (CMD_NONSTD+12) /* remove softint set by ADDCHANGEINT */

#define TD_LASTCOMM       (CMD_NONSTD+13)

/*
 *
 * The disk driver has an "extended command" facility.  These commands
 * take a superset of the normal IO Request block.
 *
 */

#define ETD_WRITE         (CMD_WRITE|TDF_EXTCOM)
#define ETD_READ          (CMD_READ|TDF_EXTCOM)
#define ETD_MOTOR         (TD_MOTOR|TDF_EXTCOM)
#define ETD_SEEK          (TD_SEEK|TDF_EXTCOM)
#define ETD_FORMAT        (TD_FORMAT|TDF_EXTCOM)
#define ETD_UPDATE        (CMD_UPDATE|TDF_EXTCOM)
#define ETD_CLEAR         (CMD_CLEAR|TDF_EXTCOM)
#define ETD_RAWREAD       (TD_RAWREAD|TDF_EXTCOM)
#define ETD_RAWWRITE      (TD_RAWWRITE|TDF_EXTCOM)

/*
 *
 * extended IO has a larger than normal io request block.
 *
 */

struct IOExtTD {
        struct  IOStdReq iotd_Req;
        ULONG   iotd_Count;
        ULONG   iotd_SecLabel;
};

/*
** raw read and write can be synced with the index pulse.  This flag
** in io request's IO_FLAGS field tells the driver that you want this.
*/

#define IOTDB_INDEXSYNC 4
#define IOTDF_INDEXSYNC (1<<4)


/* labels are TD_LABELSIZE bytes per sector */

#define TD_LABELSIZE 16

/*
** This is a bit in the FLAGS field of OpenDevice.  If it is set, then
** the driver will allow you to open all the disks that the trackdisk
** driver understands.  Otherwise only 3.5" disks will succeed.
*/

#define TDB_ALLOW_NON_3_5       0
```



```
#define TDF_ALLOW_NON_3_5       (1<<0)

/*
**  If you set the TDB_ALLOW_NON_3_5 bit in OpenDevice, then you don't
**  know what type of disk you really got.  These defines are for the
**  TD_GETDRIVETYPE command.  In addition, you can find out how many
**  tracks are supported via the TD_GETNUMTRACKS command.
*/

#define DRIVE3_5        1
#define DRIVE5_25       2

/*
 *--------------------------------------------------------------------
 *
 * Driver error defines
 *
 *--------------------------------------------------------------------
 */

#define TDERR_NotSpecified      20      /* general catchall */
#define TDERR_NoSecHdr          21      /* couldn't even find a sector */
#define TDERR_BadSecPreamble    22      /* sector looked wrong */
#define TDERR_BadSecID          23      /* ditto */
#define TDERR_BadHdrSum         24      /* header had incorrect checksum */
#define TDERR_BadSecSum         25      /* data had incorrect checksum */
#define TDERR_TooFewSecs        26      /* couldn't find enough sectors */
#define TDERR_BadSecHdr         27      /* another "sector looked wrong" */
#define TDERR_WriteProt         28      /* can't write to a protected disk */
#define TDERR_DiskChanged       29      /* no disk in the drive */
#define TDERR_SeekError         30      /* couldn't find track 0 */
#define TDERR_NoMem             31      /* ran out of memory */
#define TDERR_BadUnitNum        32      /* asked for a unit > NUMUNITS */
#define TDERR_BadDriveType      33      /* not a drive that trackdisk groks */
#define TDERR_DriveInUse        34      /* someone else allocated the drive */
#define TDERR_PostReset         35      /* user hit reset; awaiting doom */

/*
 *--------------------------------------------------------------------
 *
 * public portion of the unit structure
 *
 *--------------------------------------------------------------------
 */

struct TDU_PublicUnit {
        struct  Unit tdu_Unit;          /* base message port */
        UWORD   tdu_Comp01Track;        /* track for first precomp */
        UWORD   tdu_Comp10Track;        /* track for second precomp */
        UWORD   tdu_Comp11Track;        /* track for third precomp */
        ULONG   tdu_StepDelay;          /* time to wait after stepping */
        ULONG   tdu_SettleDelay;        /* time to wait after seeking */
        UBYTE   tdu_RetryCnt;           /* # of times to retry */
};

#endif  /* DEVICES_TRACKDISK_H */
```

```
#ifndef EXEC_ALERTS_H
#define EXEC_ALERTS_H
/*
**      $Filename: exec/alerts.h $
**      $Release: 1.3 $
**
**
**
**      (C) Copyright 1985,1986,1987,1988 Commodore-Amiga, Inc.
**          All Rights Reserved
*/

#define SF_ALERTWACK    (1<<1)  /* in ExecBase.SysFlag */


/*********************************************************************
*
*  Format of the alert error number:
*
*    +-+-------------+----------------+--------------------------------+
*    |D|  SubSysId   |  General Error |    SubSystem Specific Error    |
*    +-+-------------+----------------+--------------------------------+
*
*                 D:  DeadEnd alert
*          SubSysId:  indicates ROM subsystem number.
*     General Error:  roughly indicates what the error was
*    Specific Error:  indicates more detail
**********************************************************************/

/*********************************************************************
*
*  General Dead-End Alerts
*
**********************************************************************/

/*------ alert types */
#define AT_DeadEnd      0x80000000
#define AT_Recovery     0x00000000

/*------ general purpose alert codes */
#define AG_NoMemory     0x00010000
#define AG_MakeLib      0x00020000
#define AG_OpenLib      0x00030000
#define AG_OpenDev      0x00040000
#define AG_OpenRes      0x00050000
#define AG_IOError      0x00060000
#define AG_NoSignal     0x00070000

/*------ alert objects: */
#define AO_ExecLib      0x00008001
#define AO_GraphicsLib  0x00008002
#define AO_LayersLib    0x00008003
#define AO_Intuition    0x00008004
#define AO_MathLib      0x00008005
#define AO_CListLib     0x00008006
#define AO_DOSLib       0x00008007
#define AO_RAMLib       0x00008008
#define AO_IconLib      0x00008009
#define AO_ExpansionLib 0x0000800A
#define AO_AudioDev     0x00008010
#define AO_ConsoleDev   0x00008011
#define AO_GamePortDev  0x00008012
#define AO_KeyboardDev  0x00008013
#define AO_TrackDiskDev 0x00008014
#define AO_TimerDev     0x00008015
#define AO_CIARsrc      0x00008020
#define AO_DiskRsrc     0x00008021
#define AO_MiscRsrc     0x00008022
#define AO_BootStrap    0x00008030
```



```
#define AO_Workbench    0x00008031


/*********************************************************************
*
*   Specific Dead-End Alerts:
*
**********************************************************************/

/*------ exec.library */
#define AN_ExecLib      0x01000000
#define AN_ExcptVect    0x81000001      /* 68000 exception vector checksum */
#define AN_BaseChkSum   0x81000002      /* execbase checksum */
#define AN_LibChkSum    0x81000003      /* library checksum failure */
#define AN_LibMem       0x81000004      /* no memory to make library */
#define AN_MemCorrupt   0x81000005      /* corrupted memory list */
#define AN_IntrMem      0x81000006      /* no memory for interrupt servers */
#define AN_InitAPtr     0x81000007      /* InitStruct() of an APTR source */
#define AN_SemCorrupt   0x81000008      /* a semaphore is in illegal state */
#define AN_FreeTwice    0x81000009      /* freeing memory already freed */
#define AN_BogusExcpt   0x8100000A      /* illegal 68k exception taken */

/*------ graphics.library */
#define AN_GraphicsLib  0x02000000
#define AN_GfxNoMem     0x82010000      /* graphics out of memory */
#define AN_LongFrame    0x82010006      /* long frame, no memory */
#define AN_ShortFrame   0x82010007      /* short frame, no memory */
#define AN_TextTmpRas   0x02010009      /* text, no memory for TmpRas */
#define AN_BltBitMap    0x8201000A      /* BltBitMap, no memory */
#define AN_RegionMemory 0x8201000B      /* regions, memory not available */
#define AN_MakeVPort    0x82010030      /* MakeVPort, no memory */
#define AN_GfxNoLCM     0x82011234      /* emergency memory not available */

/*------ layers.library */
#define AN_LayersLib    0x03000000
#define AN_LayersNoMem  0x83010000      /* layers out of memory */

/*------ intuition.library */
#define AN_Intuition    0x04000000
#define AN_GadgetType   0x84000001      /* unknown gadet type */
#define AN_BadGadget    0x04000001      /* Recovery form of AN_GadgetType */
#define AN_CreatePort   0x84010002      /* create port, no memory */
#define AN_ItemAlloc    0x04010003      /* item plane alloc, no memory */
#define AN_SubAlloc     0x04010004      /* sub alloc, no memory */
#define AN_PlaneAlloc   0x84010005      /* plane alloc, no memory */
#define AN_ItemBoxTop   0x84000006      /* item box top < RelZero */
#define AN_OpenScreen   0x84010007      /* open screen, no memory */
#define AN_OpenScrnRast 0x84010008      /* open screen, raster alloc, no memory
#define AN_SysScrnType  0x84000009      /* open sys screen, unknown type */
#define AN_AddSWGadget  0x8401000A      /* add SW gadgets, no memory */
#define AN_OpenWindow   0x8401000B      /* open window, no memory */
#define AN_BadState     0x8400000C      /* Bad State Return entering Intuition *
#define AN_BadMessage   0x8400000D      /* Bad Message received by IDCMP */
#define AN_WeirdEcho    0x8400000E      /* Weird echo causing incomprehension */
#define AN_NoConsole    0x8400000F      /* couldn't open the Console Device */


/*------ math.library */
#define AN_MathLib      0x05000000

/*------ clist.library */
#define AN_CListLib     0x06000000

/*------ dos.library */
#define AN_DOSLib       0x07000000
#define AN_StartMem     0x07010001      /* no memory at startup */
#define AN_EndTask      0x07000002      /* EndTask didn't */
#define AN_QPktFail     0x07000003      /* Qpkt failure */
#define AN_AsyncPkt     0x07000004      /* Unexpected packet received */
```

```
#define AN_FreeVec        0x07000005      /* Freevec failed */
#define AN_DiskBlkSeq     0x07000006      /* Disk block sequence error */
#define AN_BitMap         0x07000007      /* Bitmap corrupt */
#define AN_KeyFree        0x07000008      /* Key already free */
#define AN_BadChkSum      0x07000009      /* Invalid checksum */
#define AN_DiskError      0x0700000A      /* Disk Error */
#define AN_KeyRange       0x0700000B      /* Key out of range */
#define AN_BadOverlay     0x0700000C      /* Bad overlay */

/*------ ramlib.library */
#define AN_RAMLib         0x08000000
#define AN_BadSegList     0x08000001      /* no overlays in library seglists */

/*------ icon.library */
#define AN_IconLib        0x09000000

/*------ expansion.library */
#define AN_ExpansionLib 0x0A000000
#define AN_BadExpansionFree      0x0A000001

/*------ audio.device */
#define AN_AudioDev       0x10000000

/*------ console.device */
#define AN_ConsoleDev     0x11000000

/*------ gameport.device */
#define AN_GamePortDev    0x12000000

/*------ keyboard.device */
#define AN_KeyboardDev    0x13000000

/*------ trackdisk.device */
#define AN_TrackDiskDev 0x14000000
#define AN_TDCalibSeek    0x14000001      /* calibrate: seek error */
#define AN_TDDelay        0x14000002      /* delay: error on timer wait */

/*------ timer.device */
#define AN_TimerDev       0x15000000
#define AN_TMBadReq       0x15000001      /* bad request */
#define AN_TMBadSupply    0x15000002      /* power supply does not supply ticks */

/*------ cia.resource */
#define AN_CIARsrc        0x20000000

/*------ disk.resource */
#define AN_DiskRsrc       0x21000000
#define AN_DRHasDisk      0x21000001      /* get unit: already has disk */
#define AN_DRIntNoAct     0x21000002      /* interrupt: no active unit */

/*------ misc.resource */
#define AN_MiscRsrc       0x22000000

/*------ bootstrap */
#define AN_BootStrap      0x30000000
#define AN_BootError      0x30000001      /* boot code returned an error */

/*------ Workbench */
#define AN_Workbench      0x31000000

/*------ DiskCopy */
#define AN_DiskCopy       0x32000000

#endif  /* EXEC_ALERTS_H */
```



```
#ifndef EXEC_DEVICES_H
#define EXEC_DEVICES_H
/*
**      $Filename: exec/devices.h $
**      $Release: 1.3 $
**
**
**
**      (C) Copyright 1985,1986,1987,1988 Commodore-Amiga, Inc.
**          All Rights Reserved
*/

#ifndef EXEC_LIBRARIES_H
#include "exec/libraries.h"
#endif !EXEC_LIBRARIES_H

#ifndef EXEC_PORTS_H
#include "exec/ports.h"
#endif !EXEC_PORTS_H


/****** Device ******************************************************/

struct Device {
    struct  Library dd_Library;
};


/****** Unit ********************************************************/

struct Unit {
    struct  MsgPort unit_MsgPort;       /* queue for unprocessed messages */
                                        /* instance of msgport is recommended */
    UBYTE   unit_flags;
    UBYTE   unit_pad;
    UWORD   unit_OpenCnt;               /* number of active opens */
};


#define UNITF_ACTIVE    (1<<0)
#define UNITF_INTASK    (1<<1)

#endif  /* EXEC_DEVICES_H */
```

Sep 19 20:19 1988 exec/errors.h Page 1

```
#ifndef EXEC_ERRORS_H
#define EXEC_ERRORS_H
/*
**      $Filename: exec/errors.h $
**      $Release: 1.3 $
**
**      Standard IO Errors:
**
**      (C) Copyright 1985,1986,1987,1988 Commodore-Amiga, Inc.
**          All Rights Reserved
*/

#define IOERR_OPENFAIL  -1      /* device/unit failed to open */
#define IOERR_ABORTED   -2      /* request aborted */
#define IOERR_NOCMD     -3      /* command not supported */
#define IOERR_BADLENGTH -4      /* not a valid length */

#endif  /* EXEC_ERRORS_H */
```

Sep 19 20:19 1988 exec/exec.h Page 1

```
#ifndef EXEC_EXEC_H
#define EXEC_EXEC_H
/*
**      $Filename: exec/exec.h $
**      $Release: 1.3 $
**
**
**
**      (C) Copyright 1985,1986,1987,1988 Commodore-Amiga, Inc.
**          All Rights Reserved
*/

#include "exec/nodes.h"
#include "exec/lists.h"
#include "exec/interrupts.h"
#include "exec/memory.h"
#include "exec/ports.h"
#include "exec/tasks.h"
#include "exec/libraries.h"
#include "exec/devices.h"
#include "exec/io.h"

#endif  /* EXEC_EXEC_H */
```

```
#ifndef EXEC_EXECBASE_H
#define EXEC_EXECBASE_H
/*
**      $Filename: exec/execbase.h $
**      $Release: 1.3 $
**
**
**
**      (C) Copyright 1985,1986,1987,1988 Commodore-Amiga, Inc.
**          All Rights Reserved
*/

#ifndef EXEC_LISTS_H
#include "exec/lists.h"
#endif !EXEC_LISTS_H

#ifndef EXEC_INTERRUPTS_H
#include "exec/interrupts.h"
#endif !EXEC_INTERRUPTS_H

#ifndef EXEC_LIBRARIES_H
#include "exec/libraries.h"
#endif !EXEC_LIBRARIES_H

#ifndef EXEC_TASKS_H
#include "exec/tasks.h"
#endif !EXEC_TASKS_H


struct ExecBase {
        struct Library  LibNode;

        UWORD   SoftVer;        /* kickstart release number      */
        WORD    LowMemChkSum;
        ULONG   ChkBase;        /* system base pointer complement */
        APTR    ColdCapture;    /* coldstart soft vector         */
        APTR    CoolCapture;
        APTR    WarmCapture;
        APTR    SysStkUpper;    /* system stack base (upper bound) */
        APTR    SysStkLower;    /* top of system stack (lower bound) */
        ULONG   MaxLocMem;
        APTR    DebugEntry;
        APTR    DebugData;
        APTR    AlertData;
        APTR    MaxExtMem;      /* top of extended mem, or null if none */

        UWORD   ChkSum;

/****** Interrupt Related ***************************************/

        struct  IntVector IntVects[16];

/****** System Variables ****************************************/

        struct  Task *ThisTask; /* pointer to current task */
        ULONG   IdleCount;      /* idle counter */
        ULONG   DispCount;      /* dispatch counter */
        UWORD   Quantum;        /* time slice quantum */
        UWORD   Elapsed;        /* current quantum ticks */
        UWORD   SysFlags;       /* misc system flags */
        BYTE    IDNestCnt;      /* interrupt disable nesting count */
        BYTE    TDNestCnt;      /* task disable nesting count */

        UWORD   AttnFlags;      /* special attention flags */
        UWORD   AttnResched;    /* rescheduling attention */
        APTR    ResModules;     /* resident module array pointer */

        APTR    TaskTrapCode;
        APTR    TaskExceptCode;
```



```
        APTR    TaskExitCode;
        ULONG   TaskSigAlloc;
        UWORD   TaskTrapAlloc;


/****** System Lists ********************************************/

        struct  List MemList;
        struct  List ResourceList;
        struct  List DeviceList;
        struct  List IntrList;
        struct  List LibList;
        struct  List PortList;
        struct  List TaskReady;
        struct  List TaskWait;

        struct  SoftIntList SoftInts[5];

/****** Other Globals *******************************************/

        LONG    LastAlert[4];



        /* these next two variables are provided to allow
        ** system developers to have a rough idea of the
        ** period of two externally controlled signals --
        ** the time between vertical blank interrupts and the
        ** external line rate (which is counted by CIA A's
        ** "time of day" clock).  In general these values
        ** will be 50 or 60, and may or may not track each
        ** other.  These values replace the obsolete AFB_PAL
        ** and AFB_50HZ flags.
        */
        UBYTE   VBlankFrequency;
        UBYTE   PowerSupplyFrequency;

        struct  List SemaphoreList;

        /* these next two are to be able to kickstart into user ram.
        ** KickMemPtr holds a singly linked list of MemLists which
        ** will be removed from the memory list via AllocAbs.  If
        ** all the AllocAbs's succeeded, then the KickTagPtr will
        ** be added to the rom tag list.
        */
        APTR    KickMemPtr;     /* ptr to queue of mem lists */
        APTR    KickTagPtr;     /* ptr to rom tag queue */
        APTR    KickCheckSum;   /* checksum for mem and tags */

        UBYTE   ExecBaseReserved[10];
        UBYTE   ExecBaseNewReserved[20];
};

#define SYSBASESIZE  sizeof(struct ExecBase)

/******* AttnFlags */
/*  Processors and Co-processors: */
#define AFB_68010       0       /* also set for 68020 */
#define AFB_68020       1
#define AFB_68881       4

#define AFF_68010       (1<<0)
#define AFF_68020       (1<<1)
#define AFF_68881       (1<<4)

/* These two bits used to be AFB_PAL and AFB_50HZ.  After some soul
** searching we realized that they were misnomers, and the information
** is now kept in VBlankFrequency and PowerSupplyFrequency above.
** To find out what sort of video conversion is done, look in the
```

Sep 19 20:19 1988 exec/execbase.h Page 3

```
** graphics subsytem.
*/
#define AFB_RESERVED8   8
#define AFB_RESERVED9   9

#endif  /* EXEC_EXECBASE_H */
```

Sep 19 20:19 1988 exec/execname.h Page 1

```
#ifndef EXEC_EXECNAME_H
#define EXEC_EXECNAME_H
/*
**      $Filename: exec/execname.h $
**      $Release: 1.3 $
**
**
**
**      (C) Copyright 1985,1986,1987,1988 Commodore-Amiga, Inc.
**          All Rights Reserved
*/

#define EXECNAME "exec.library"

#endif  /* EXEC_EXECNAME_H */
```

```
#ifndef EXEC_INTERRUPTS_H
#define EXEC_INTERRUPTS_H
/*
**      $Filename: exec/interrupts.h $
**      $Release: 1.3 $
**
**
**
**      (C) Copyright 1985,1986,1987,1988 Commodore-Amiga, Inc.
**          All Rights Reserved
*/

#ifndef EXEC_NODES_H
#include "exec/nodes.h"
#endif !EXEC_NODES_H

#ifndef EXEC_LISTS_H
#include "exec/lists.h"
#endif !EXEC_LISTS_H


struct Interrupt {
    struct  Node is_Node;
    APTR    is_Data;                /* server data segment  */
    VOID    (*is_Code)();           /* server code entry    */
};


struct IntVector {              /* For EXEC use ONLY! */
    APTR    iv_Data;
    VOID    (*iv_Code)();
    struct  Node *iv_Node;
};


struct SoftIntList {            /* For EXEC use ONLY! */
    struct List sh_List;
    UWORD  sh_Pad;
};

#define SIH_PRIMASK (0xf0)

/* this is a fake INT definition, used only for AddIntServer and the like */
#define INTB_NMI        15
#define INTF_NMI        (1<<15)

#endif  /* EXEC_INTERRUPTS_H */
```



```
#ifndef EXEC_IO_H
#define EXEC_IO_H
/*
**      $Filename: exec/io.h $
**      $Release: 1.3 $
**
**
**
**      (C) Copyright 1985,1986,1987,1988 Commodore-Amiga, Inc.
**          All Rights Reserved
*/

#ifndef EXEC_PORTS_H
#include "exec/ports.h"
#endif !EXEC_PORTS_H


struct IORequest {
    struct  Message io_Message;
    struct  Device  *io_Device;     /* device node pointer  */
    struct  Unit    *io_Unit;       /* unit (driver private)*/
    UWORD   io_Command;             /* device command */
    UBYTE   io_Flags;
    BYTE    io_Error;               /* error or warning num */
};

struct IOStdReq {
    struct  Message io_Message;
    struct  Device  *io_Device;     /* device node pointer  */
    struct  Unit    *io_Unit;       /* unit (driver private)*/
    UWORD   io_Command;             /* device command */
    UBYTE   io_Flags;
    BYTE    io_Error;               /* error or warning num */
    ULONG   io_Actual;              /* actual number of bytes transferred */
    ULONG   io_Length;              /* requested number bytes transferred*/
    APTR    io_Data;                /* points to data area */
    ULONG   io_Offset;              /* offset for block structured devices */
};

/* library vector offsets for device reserved vectors */
#define DEV_BEGINIO     (-30)
#define DEV_ABORTIO     (-36)

/* io_Flags defined bits */
#define IOB_QUICK       0
#define IOF_QUICK       (1<<0)


#define CMD_INVALID     0
#define CMD_RESET       1
#define CMD_READ        2
#define CMD_WRITE       3
#define CMD_UPDATE      4
#define CMD_CLEAR       5
#define CMD_STOP        6
#define CMD_START       7
#define CMD_FLUSH       8

#define CMD_NONSTD      9

#endif  /* EXEC_IO_H */
```

Sep 19 20:19 1988 exec/libraries.h Page 1

```
#ifndef EXEC_LIBRARIES_H
#define EXEC_LIBRARIES_H
/*
**      $Filename: exec/libraries.h $
**      $Release: 1.3 $
**
**
**
**      (C) Copyright 1985,1986,1987,1988 Commodore-Amiga, Inc.
**          All Rights Reserved
*/

#ifndef EXEC_NODES_H
#include "exec/nodes.h"
#endif !EXEC_NODES_H


#define LIB_VECTSIZE    6
#define LIB_RESERVED    4
#define LIB_BASE        (-LIB_VECTSIZE)
#define LIB_USERDEF     (LIB_BASE-(LIB_RESERVED*LIB_VECTSIZE))
#define LIB_NONSTD      (LIB_USERDEF)

#define LIB_OPEN        (-6)
#define LIB_CLOSE       (-12)
#define LIB_EXPUNGE     (-18)
#define LIB_EXTFUNC     (-24)


struct Library {
    struct  Node lib_Node;
    UBYTE   lib_Flags;
    UBYTE   lib_pad;
    UWORD   lib_NegSize;            /* number of bytes before library */
    UWORD   lib_PosSize;            /* number of bytes after library */
    UWORD   lib_Version;
    UWORD   lib_Revision;
    APTR    lib_IdString;
    ULONG   lib_Sum;                /* the checksum itself */
    UWORD   lib_OpenCnt;            /* number of current opens */
};

#define LIBF_SUMMING    (1<<0)      /* we are currently checksumming */
#define LIBF_CHANGED    (1<<1)      /* we have just changed the lib */
#define LIBF_SUMUSED    (1<<2)      /* set if we should bother to sum */
#define LIBF_DELEXP     (1<<3)      /* delayed expunge */

/* Temporary Compatibility */
#define lh_Node         lib_Node
#define lh_Flags        lib_Flags
#define lh_pad          lib_pad
#define lh_NegSize      lib_NegSize
#define lh_PosSize      lib_PosSize
#define lh_Version      lib_Version
#define lh_Revision     lib_Revision
#define lh_IdString     lib_IdString
#define lh_Sum          lib_Sum
#define lh_OpenCnt      lib_OpenCnt

#endif  /* EXEC_LIBRARIES_H */
```

Sep 19 20:19 1988 exec/lists.h Page 1

```
#ifndef EXEC_LISTS_H
#define EXEC_LISTS_H
/*
**      $Filename: exec/lists.h $
**      $Release: 1.3 $
**
**
**
**      (C) Copyright 1985,1986,1987,1988 Commodore-Amiga, Inc.
**          All Rights Reserved
*/

#ifndef EXEC_NODES_H
#include "exec/nodes.h"
#endif !EXEC_NODES_H


/* normal, full featured list */
struct List {
    struct  Node *lh_Head;
    struct  Node *lh_Tail;
    struct  Node *lh_TailPred;
    UBYTE   lh_Type;
    UBYTE   l_pad;
};

/* minimum list -- no type checking possible */
struct MinList {
    struct MinNode *mlh_Head;
    struct MinNode *mlh_Tail;
    struct MinNode *mlh_TailPred;
};

#endif  /* EXEC_LISTS_H */
```

```
#ifndef EXEC_MEMORY_H
#define EXEC_MEMORY_H
/*
**      $Filename: exec/memory.h $
**      $Release: 1.3 $
**
**      definitions for use with the memory allocator
**
**      (C) Copyright 1985,1986,1987,1988 Commodore-Amiga, Inc.
**          All Rights Reserved
*/

#ifndef EXEC_NODES_H
#include "exec/nodes.h"
#endif !EXEC_NODES_H


/****** MemChunk ****************************************************/

struct  MemChunk {
    struct  MemChunk *mc_Next;  /* pointer to next chunk */
    ULONG   mc_Bytes;           /* chunk byte size      */
};


/****** MemHeader ***************************************************/

struct  MemHeader {
    struct  Node mh_Node;
    UWORD   mh_Attributes;      /* characteristics of this region */
    struct  MemChunk *mh_First; /* first free region            */
    APTR    mh_Lower;           /* lower memory bound           */
    APTR    mh_Upper;           /* upper memory bound+1         */
    ULONG   mh_Free;            /* total number of free bytes   */
};


/****** MemEntry ****************************************************/

struct  MemEntry {
union {
    ULONG   meu_Reqs;           /* the AllocMem requirements */
    APTR    meu_Addr;           /* the address of this memory region */
    } me_Un;
    ULONG   me_Length;          /* the length of this memory region */
};

#define me_un       me_Un       /* compatability */
#define me_Reqs     me_Un.meu_Reqs
#define me_Addr     me_Un.meu_Addr


/****** MemList *****************************************************/

struct  MemList {
    struct  Node ml_Node;
    UWORD   ml_NumEntries;      /* number of entries in this struct */
    struct  MemEntry ml_ME[1];  /* the first entry      */
};

#define ml_me   ml_ME           /* compatability */


/*----- Memory Requirement Types ---------------------------*/

#define MEMF_PUBLIC (1<<0)
#define MEMF_CHIP   (1<<1)
#define MEMF_FAST   (1<<2)

```



```
#define MEMF_CLEAR  (1<<16)
#define MEMF_LARGEST (1<<17)

#define MEM_BLOCKSIZE   8
#define MEM_BLOCKMASK   7

#endif  /* EXEC_MEMORY_H */
```

```
#ifndef EXEC_NODES_H
#define EXEC_NODES_H
/*
**      $Filename: exec/nodes.h $
**      $Release: 1.3 $
**
**
**
**      (C) Copyright 1985,1986,1987,1988 Commodore-Amiga, Inc.
**          All Rights Reserved
*/

/* normal node */
struct Node {
    struct  Node *ln_Succ;
    struct  Node *ln_Pred;
    UBYTE   ln_Type;
    BYTE    ln_Pri;
    char    *ln_Name;
};

/* stripped node -- no type checking is possible */
struct MinNode {
    struct MinNode *mln_Succ;
    struct MinNode *mln_Pred;
};


/*----- Node Types --------*/
#define NT_UNKNOWN      0
#define NT_TASK         1
#define NT_INTERRUPT    2       /* also for software interrupt node */
#define NT_DEVICE       3
#define NT_MSGPORT      4
#define NT_MESSAGE      5
#define NT_FREEMSG      6
#define NT_REPLYMSG     7
#define NT_RESOURCE     8
#define NT_LIBRARY      9
#define NT_MEMORY       10
#define NT_SOFTINT      11      /* exec private */
#define NT_FONT         12
#define NT_PROCESS      13
#define NT_SEMAPHORE    14
#define NT_SIGNALSEM    15      /* signal semaphores */
#define NT_BOOTNODE     16

#endif  /* EXEC_NODES_H */
```



```
#ifndef EXEC_PORTS_H
#define EXEC_PORTS_H
/*
**      $Filename: exec/ports.h $
**      $Release: 1.3 $
**
**
**
**      (C) Copyright 1985,1986,1987,1988 Commodore-Amiga, Inc.
**          All Rights Reserved
*/

#ifndef EXEC_NODES_H
#include "exec/nodes.h"
#endif !EXEC_NODES_H

#ifndef EXEC_LISTS_H
#include "exec/lists.h"
#endif !EXEC_LISTS_H

#ifndef EXEC_TASKS_H
#include "exec/tasks.h"
#endif !EXEC_TASKS_H


/****** MsgPort *****************************************************/

struct MsgPort {
    struct  Node mp_Node;
    UBYTE   mp_Flags;
    UBYTE   mp_SigBit;              /* signal bit number    */
    struct  Task *mp_SigTask;       /* task to be signalled */
    struct  List mp_MsgList;        /* message linked list  */
};

#define mp_SoftInt mp_SigTask

#define PF_ACTION       3

#define PA_SIGNAL       0
#define PA_SOFTINT      1
#define PA_IGNORE       2


/****** Message *****************************************************/

struct Message {
    struct  Node mn_Node;
    struct  MsgPort *mn_ReplyPort;  /* message reply port */
    UWORD   mn_Length;              /* message len in bytes */
};

#endif  /* EXEC_PORTS_H */
```

```
#ifndef EXEC_RESIDENT_H
#define EXEC_RESIDENT_H
/*
**      $Filename: exec/resident.h $
**      $Release: 1.3 $
**
**
**
**      (C) Copyright 1985,1986,1987,1988 Commodore-Amiga, Inc.
**          All Rights Reserved
*/

#ifndef EXEC_NODES_H
#include "exec/nodes.h"
#endif !EXEC_NODES_H

struct Resident {
    UWORD rt_MatchWord;            /* word to match on (ILLEGAL)   */
    struct Resident *rt_MatchTag; /* pointer to the above         */
    APTR  rt_EndSkip;              /* address to continue scan     */
    UBYTE rt_Flags;                /* various tag flags            */
    UBYTE rt_Version;              /* release version number       */
    UBYTE rt_Type;                 /* type of module (NT_mumble)   */
    BYTE  rt_Pri;                  /* initialization priority */
    char  *rt_Name;                /* pointer to node name         */
    char  *rt_IdString;            /* pointer to ident string      */
    APTR  rt_Init;                 /* pointer to init code         */
};

#define RTC_MATCHWORD   0x4AFC

#define RTF_AUTOINIT    (1<<7)
#define RTF_COLDSTART   (1<<0)

/* Compatibility: */
#define RTM_WHEN        3
#define RTW_NEVER       0
#define RTW_COLDSTART   1

#endif  /* EXEC_RESIDENT_H */
```



```
#ifndef EXEC_SEMAPHORES_H
#define EXEC_SEMAPHORES_H
/*
**      $Filename: exec/semaphores.h $
**      $Release: 1.3 $
**
**
**
**      (C) Copyright 1986,1987,1988 Commodore-Amiga, Inc.
**          All Rights Reserved
*/

#ifndef EXEC_NODES_H
#include "exec/nodes.h"
#endif !EXEC_NODES_H

#ifndef EXEC_LISTS_H
#include "exec/lists.h"
#endif !EXEC_LISTS_H

#ifndef EXEC_PORTS_H
#include "exec/ports.h"
#endif !EXEC_PORTS_H

#ifndef EXEC_TASKS_H
#include "exec/tasks.h"
#endif !EXEC_TASKS_H


/****** Semaphore ****************************************************/

struct Semaphore {
    struct MsgPort sm_MsgPort;
    WORD   sm_Bids;
};

#define sm_LockMsg      mp_SigTask


/****** SignalSemaphore **********************************************/

/* this is the structure used to request a signal semaphore */
struct SemaphoreRequest {
    struct  MinNode sr_Link;
    struct  Task *sr_Waiter;
};

/* this is the actual semaphore itself */
struct SignalSemaphore {
    struct  Node ss_Link;
    SHORT   ss_NestCount;
    struct  MinList ss_WaitQueue;
    struct  SemaphoreRequest ss_MultipleLink;
    struct  Task *ss_Owner;
    SHORT   ss_QueueCount;
};

#endif  /* EXEC_SEMAPHORES_H */
```

```
#ifndef EXEC_TASKS_H
#define EXEC_TASKS_H
/*
**      $Filename: exec/tasks.h $
**      $Release: 1.3 $
**
**
**
**      (C) Copyright 1985,1986,1987,1988 Commodore-Amiga, Inc.
**          All Rights Reserved
*/

#ifndef EXEC_NODES_H
#include "exec/nodes.h"
#endif !EXEC_NODES_H

#ifndef EXEC_LISTS_H
#include "exec/lists.h"
#endif !EXEC_LISTS_H


struct Task {
    struct  Node tc_Node;
    UBYTE   tc_Flags;
    UBYTE   tc_State;
    BYTE    tc_IDNestCnt;           /* intr disabled nesting*/
    BYTE    tc_TDNestCnt;           /* task disabled nesting*/
    ULONG   tc_SigAlloc;            /* sigs allocated */
    ULONG   tc_SigWait;             /* sigs we are waiting for */
    ULONG   tc_SigRecvd;            /* sigs we have received */
    ULONG   tc_SigExcept;           /* sigs we will take excepts for */
    UWORD   tc_TrapAlloc;           /* traps allocated */
    UWORD   tc_TrapAble;            /* traps enabled */
    APTR    tc_ExceptData;          /* points to except data */
    APTR    tc_ExceptCode;          /* points to except code */
    APTR    tc_TrapData;            /* points to trap code */
    APTR    tc_TrapCode;            /* points to trap data */
    APTR    tc_SPReg;               /* stack pointer        */
    APTR    tc_SPLower;             /* stack lower bound    */
    APTR    tc_SPUpper;             /* stack upper bound + 2*/
    VOID    (*tc_Switch)();         /* task losing CPU    */
    VOID    (*tc_Launch)();         /* task getting CPU  */
    struct  List tc_MemEntry;       /* allocated memory */
    APTR    tc_UserData;            /* per task data */
};

/*----- Flag Bits ------------------------------------------*/
#define TB_PROCTIME     0
#define TB_STACKCHK     4
#define TB_EXCEPT       5
#define TB_SWITCH       6
#define TB_LAUNCH       7

#define TF_PROCTIME     (1<<0)
#define TF_STACKCHK     (1<<4)
#define TF_EXCEPT       (1<<5)
#define TF_SWITCH       (1<<6)
#define TF_LAUNCH       (1<<7)

/*----- Task States ----------------------------------------*/
#define TS_INVALID      0
#define TS_ADDED        1
#define TS_RUN          2
#define TS_READY        3
#define TS_WAIT         4
#define TS_EXCEPT       5
#define TS_REMOVED      6

/*----- Predefined Signals ---------------------------------*/
```



```

#define SIGB_ABORT      0
#define SIGB_CHILD      1
#define SIGB_BLIT       4
#define SIGB_SINGLE     4
#define SIGB_DOS        8

#define SIGF_ABORT      (1<<0)
#define SIGF_CHILD      (1<<1)
#define SIGF_BLIT       (1<<4)
#define SIGF_SINGLE     (1<<4)
#define SIGF_DOS        (1<<8)

#endif  /* EXEC_TASKS_H */
```

```
#ifndef EXEC_TYPES_H
#define EXEC_TYPES_H
/*
**      $Filename: exec/types.h $
**      $Release: 1.3 $
**
**
**
**      (C) Copyright 1985,1986,1987,1988 Commodore-Amiga, Inc.
**          All Rights Reserved
*/

#define GLOBAL  extern      /* the declaratory use of an external */
#define IMPORT  extern      /* reference to an external */
#define STATIC  static      /* a local static variable */
#define REGISTER register   /* a (hopefully) register variable */

#define VOID            void    /* typedef does not seem to work here */

typedef long            LONG;       /* signed 32-bit quantity */
typedef unsigned long   ULONG;      /* unsigned 32-bit quantity */
typedef unsigned long   LONGBITS;   /* 32 bits manipulated individually */
typedef short           WORD;       /* signed 16-bit quantity */
typedef unsigned short  UWORD;      /* unsigned 16-bit quantity */
typedef unsigned short  WORDBITS;   /* 16 bits manipulated individually */
typedef char            BYTE;       /* signed 8-bit quantity */
typedef unsigned char   UBYTE;      /* unsigned 8-bit quantity */
typedef unsigned char   BYTEBITS;   /* 8 bits manipulated individually */
typedef unsigned char   *STRPTR;    /* string pointer */
typedef STRPTR          *APTR;      /* absolute memory pointer */

/* sigh.  APTR was misdefined, but compatibility rules.  Heres what it
 * should have been
 */
typedef ULONG           CPTR;       /* absolute memory pointer */

/* For compatability only: (don't use in new code) */
typedef short           SHORT;      /* signed 16-bit quantity (WORD) */
typedef unsigned short  USHORT;     /* unsigned 16-bit quantity (UWORD) */


/*      Types with specific semantics */
typedef float           FLOAT;
typedef double          DOUBLE;
typedef short           COUNT;
typedef unsigned short  UCOUNT;
typedef short           BOOL;
typedef unsigned char   TEXT;

#define TRUE            1
#define FALSE           0
#define NULL            0

#define BYTEMASK        0xFF

#define LIBRARY_VERSION 34

#endif  /* EXEC_TYPES_H */
```

```
#ifndef GRAPHICS_CLIP_H
#define GRAPHICS_CLIP_H
/*
**      $Filename: graphics/clip.h $
**      $Release: 1.3 $
**
**
**
**      (C) Copyright 1985,1986,1987,1988 Commodore-Amiga, Inc.
**          All Rights Reserved
*/

#ifndef GRAPHICS_GFX_H
#include <graphics/gfx.h>
#endif
#ifndef EXEC_SEMAPHORES_H
#include <exec/semaphores.h>
#endif

/* structures used by and constructed by windowlib.a */
/* understood by rom software */

#define NEWLOCKS

struct Layer
{
    struct  Layer *front,*back;     /* ignored by roms */
    struct  ClipRect    *ClipRect;  /* read by roms to find first cliprect */
    struct  RastPort    *rp;        /* ignored by roms, I hope */
    struct  Rectangle   bounds;     /* ignored by roms */
        UBYTE   reserved[4];
        UWORD   priority;                       /* system use only */
    UWORD   Flags;                  /* obscured ?, Virtual BitMap? */
    struct  BitMap *SuperBitMap;
    struct  ClipRect *SuperClipRect; /* super bitmap cliprects if
                                        VBitMap != 0*/
                                  /* else damage cliprect list for refresh */
    APTR    Window;                 /* reserved for user interface use */
    SHORT   Scroll_X,Scroll_Y;
        struct  ClipRect *cr,*cr2,*crnew;  /* used by dedice */
        struct  ClipRect *SuperSaveClipRects; /* preallocated cr's */
        struct  ClipRect *_cliprects;   /* system use during refresh */
        struct  Layer_Info  *LayerInfo; /* points to head of the list */
        struct  SignalSemaphore Lock;
        UBYTE   reserved3[8];
        struct Region *ClipRegion;
        struct Region *saveClipRects;   /* used to back out when in trouble*/
        UBYTE   reserved2[22];
        /* this must stay here */
    struct  Region  *DamageList;    /* list of rectangles to refresh
                                       through */
};

struct ClipRect
{
    struct  ClipRect *Next;         /* roms used to find next ClipRect */
    struct  ClipRect *prev;         /* ignored by roms, used by windowlib */
    struct  Layer   *lobs;          /* ignored by roms, used by windowlib */
    struct  BitMap  *BitMap;
    struct  Rectangle   bounds;     /* set up by windowlib, used by roms */
    struct  ClipRect *_p1,*_p2;     /* system reserved */
    LONG    reserved;               /* system use */
#ifdef NEWCLIPRECTS_1_1
    LONG    Flags;                  /* only exists in layer allocation */
#endif
};

/* internal cliprect flags */
#define CR_NEEDS_NO_CONCEALED_RASTERS  1
```



```

/* defines for code values for getcode */
#define ISLESSX 1
#define ISLESSY 2
#define ISGRTRX 4
#define ISGRTRY 8

#endif  /* GRAPHICS_CLIP_H */
```

```
#ifndef GRAPHICS_COLLIDE_H
#define GRAPHICS_COLLIDE_H
/*
**      $Filename: graphics/collide.h $
**      $Release: 1.3 $
**
**      include file for collision detection and control
**
**      (C) Copyright 1985,1986,1987,1988 Commodore-Amiga, Inc.
**          All Rights Reserved
*/

/* These bit descriptors are used by the GEL collide routines.
 *  These bits are set in the hitMask and meMask variables of
 *  a GEL to describe whether or not these types of collisions
 *  can affect the GEL.  BNDRY_HIT is described further below;
 *  this bit is permanently assigned as the boundary-hit flag.
 *  The other bit GEL_HIT is meant only as a default to cover
 *  any GEL hitting any other; the user may redefine this bit.
 */
#define BORDERHIT 0

/* These bit descriptors are used by the GEL boundry hit routines.
 *  When the user's boundry-hit routine is called (via the argument
 *  set by a call to SetCollision) the first argument passed to
 *  the user's routine is the address of the GEL involved in the
 *  boundry-hit, and the second argument has the appropriate bit(s)
 *  set to describe which boundry was surpassed
 */
#define TOPHIT    1
#define BOTTOMHIT 2
#define LEFTHIT   4
#define RIGHTHIT  8

#endif  /* GRAPHICS_COLLIDE_H */
```



```
#ifndef GRAPHICS_COPPER_H
#define GRAPHICS_COPPER_H
/*
**      $Filename: graphics/copper.h $
**      $Release: 1.3 $
**
**
**
**      (C) Copyright 1985,1986,1987,1988 Commodore-Amiga, Inc.
**          All Rights Reserved
*/

#define COPPER_MOVE 0       /* pseude opcode for move #XXXX,dir */
#define COPPER_WAIT 1       /* pseudo opcode for wait y,x */
#define CPRNXTBUF   2       /* continue processing with next buffer */
#define CPR_NT_LOF  0x8000  /* copper instruction only for short frames */
#define CPR_NT_SHT  0x4000  /* copper instruction only for long frames */
struct CopIns
{
    short   OpCode; /* 0 = move, 1 = wait */
    union
    {
    struct CopList *nxtlist;
    struct
    {
   union
   {
   SHORT   VWaitPos;         /* vertical beam wait */
   SHORT   DestAddr;         /* destination address of copper move */
   } u1;
   union
   {
   SHORT   HWaitPos;         /* horizontal beam wait position */
   SHORT   DestData;         /* destination immediate data to send */
   } u2;
    } u4;
    } u3;
};
/* shorthand for above */
#define NXTLIST     u3.nxtlist
#define VWAITPOS    u3.u4.u1.VWaitPos
#define DESTADDR    u3.u4.u1.DestAddr
#define HWAITPOS    u3.u4.u2.HWaitPos
#define DESTDATA    u3.u4.u2.DestData


/* structure of cprlist that points to list that hardware actually executes */
struct cprlist
{
    struct cprlist *Next;
    UWORD   *start;           /* start of copper list */
    SHORT   MaxCount;         /* number of long instructions */
};

struct CopList
{
    struct  CopList *Next;  /* next block for this copper list */
    struct  CopList *_CopList;  /* system use */
    struct  ViewPort *_ViewPort;    /* system use */
    struct  CopIns *CopIns; /* start of this block */
    struct  CopIns *CopPtr; /* intermediate ptr */
    UWORD   *CopLStart;       /* mrgcop fills this in for Long Frame*/
    UWORD   *CopSStart;       /* mrgcop fills this in for Short Frame*/
    SHORT   Count;            /* intermediate counter */
    SHORT   MaxCount;         /* max # of copins for this block */
    SHORT   DyOffset;         /* offset this copper list vertical waits */
};

struct UCopList
```

```
{
    struct UCopList *Next;
    struct CopList  *FirstCopList; /* head node of this copper list */
    struct CopList  *CopList;      /* node in use */
};

struct copinit
{
    UWORD diagstrt[4];      /* copper list for first bitplane */
    UWORD sprstrtup[(2*8*2)+2+(2*2)+2];
    UWORD   sprstop[2];
};

#endif  /* GRAPHICS_COPPER_H */
```



```
#ifndef GRAPHICS_DISPLAY_H
#define GRAPHICS_DISPLAY_H
/*
**      $Filename: graphics/display.h $
**      $Release: 1.3 $
**
**      include define file for display control registers
**
**      (C) Copyright 1985,1986,1987,1988 Commodore-Amiga, Inc.
**          All Rights Reserved
*/

/* bplcon0 defines */
#define MODE_640    0x8000
#define PLNCNTMSK   0x7             /* how many bit planes? */
                                    /* 0 = none, 1->6 = 1->6, 7 = reserved */
#define PLNCNTSHFT  12              /* bits to shift for bplcon0 */
#define PF2PRI      0x40            /* bplcon2 bit */
#define COLORON     0x0200          /* disable color burst */
#define DBLPF       0x400
#define HOLDNMODIFY 0x800
#define INTERLACE   4               /* interlace mode for 400 */

/* bplcon1 defines */
#define PFA_FINE_SCROLL       0xF
#define PFB_FINE_SCROLL_SHIFT 4
#define PF_FINE_SCROLL_MASK   0xF

/* display window start and stop defines */
#define DIW_HORIZ_POS   0x7F        /* horizontal start/stop */
#define DIW_VRTCL_POS   0x1FF       /* vertical start/stop */
#define DIW_VRTCL_POS_SHIFT 7

/* Data fetch start/stop horizontal position */
#define DFTCH_MASK      0xFF

/* vposr bits */
#define VPOSRLOF        0x8000

#endif  /* GRAPHICS_DISPLAY_H */
```

```
#ifndef GRAPHICS_GELS_H
#define GRAPHICS_GELS_H
/*
**      $Filename: graphics/gels.h $
**      $Release: 1.3 $
**
**      include file for AMIGA GELS (Graphics Elements)
**
**      (C) Copyright 1985,1986,1987,1988 Commodore-Amiga, Inc.
**          All Rights Reserved
*/

/* VSprite flags */
/* user-set VSprite flags: */
#define SUSERFLAGS  0x00FF    /* mask of all user-settable VSprite-flags */
#define VSPRITE     0x0001    /* set if VSprite, clear if Bob */
#define SAVEBACK    0x0002    /* set if background is to be saved/restored */
#define OVERLAY     0x0004    /* set to mask image of Bob onto background */
#define MUSTDRAW    0x0008    /* set if VSprite absolutely must be drawn */
/* system-set VSprite flags: */
#define BACKSAVED   0x0100    /* this Bob's background has been saved */
#define BOBUPDATE   0x0200    /* temporary flag, useless to outside world */
#define GELGONE     0x0400    /* set if gel is completely clipped (offscreen) */
#define VSOVERFLOW  0x0800    /* VSprite overflow (if MUSTDRAW set we draw!) */

/* Bob flags */
/* these are the user flag bits */
#define BUSERFLAGS  0x00FF    /* mask of all user-settable Bob-flags */
#define SAVEBOB     0x0001    /* set to not erase Bob */
#define BOBISCOMP   0x0002    /* set to identify Bob as AnimComp */
/* these are the system flag bits */
#define BWAITING    0x0100    /* set while Bob is waiting on 'after' */
#define BDRAWN      0x0200    /* set when Bob is drawn this DrawG pass*/
#define BOBSAWAY    0x0400    /* set to initiate removal of Bob */
#define BOBNIX      0x0800    /* set when Bob is completely removed */
#define SAVEPRESERVE 0x1000   /* for back-restore during double-buffer*/
#define OUTSTEP     0x2000    /* for double-clearing if double-buffer */

/* defines for the animation procedures */
#define ANFRACSIZE  6
#define ANIMHALF    0x0020
#define RINGTRIGGER 0x0001


/* UserStuff definitions
 *  the user can define these to be a single variable or a sub-structure
 *  if undefined by the user, the system turns these into innocuous variables
 *  see the manual for a thorough definition of the UserStuff definitions
 *
 */
#ifndef VUserStuff            /* VSprite user stuff */
#define VUserStuff SHORT
#endif

#ifndef BUserStuff            /* Bob user stuff */
#define BUserStuff SHORT
#endif

#ifndef AUserStuff            /* AnimOb user stuff */
#define AUserStuff SHORT
#endif




/*********************** GEL STRUCTURES ***********************************/

struct VSprite
{
```



```
/* -------------------- SYSTEM VARIABLES ------------------------------- */
/* GEL linked list forward/backward pointers sorted by y,x value */
    struct VSprite   *NextVSprite;
    struct VSprite   *PrevVSprite;

/* GEL draw list constructed in the order the Bobs are actually drawn, then
 *  list is copied to clear list
 *  must be here in VSprite for system boundary detection
 */
    struct VSprite   *DrawPath;     /* pointer of overlay drawing */
    struct VSprite   *ClearPath;    /* pointer for overlay clearing */

/* the VSprite positions are defined in (y,x) order to make sorting
 *  sorting easier, since (y,x) as a long integer
 */
    WORD OldY, OldX;            /* previous position */

/* -------------------- COMMON VARIABLES ------------------------------- */
    WORD Flags;                 /* VSprite flags */


/* -------------------- USER VARIABLES --------------------------------- */
/* the VSprite positions are defined in (y,x) order to make sorting
 *  sorting easier, since (y,x) as a long integer
 */
    WORD Y, X;                  /* screen position */

    WORD Height;
    WORD Width;                 /* number of words per row of image data */
    WORD Depth;                 /* number of planes of data */

    WORD MeMask;                /* which types can collide with this VSprite*/
    WORD HitMask;               /* which types this VSprite can collide with*/

    WORD *ImageData;            /* pointer to VSprite image */

/* borderLine is the one-dimensional logical OR of all
 *  the VSprite bits, used for fast collision detection of edge
 */
    WORD *BorderLine;           /* logical OR of all VSprite bits */
    WORD *CollMask;             /* similar to above except this is a matrix */

/* pointer to this VSprite's color definitions (not used by Bobs) */
    WORD *SprColors;

    struct Bob *VSBob;          /* points home if this VSprite is part of
                                       a Bob */

/* planePick flag:  set bit selects a plane from image, clear bit selects
 *  use of shadow mask for that plane
 * OnOff flag: if using shadow mask to fill plane, this bit (corresponding
 *  to bit in planePick) describes whether to fill with 0's or 1's
 * There are two uses for these flags:
 *      - if this is the VSprite of a Bob, these flags describe how the Bob
 *        is to be drawn into memory
 *      - if this is a simple VSprite and the user intends on setting the
 *        MUSTDRAW flag of the VSprite, these flags must be set too to describe
 *        which color registers the user wants for the image
 */
    BYTE PlanePick;
    BYTE PlaneOnOff;

    VUserStuff VUserExt;        /* user definable:  see note above */
};

struct Bob
/* blitter-objects */
{
/* -------------------- SYSTEM VARIABLES ------------------------------- */
```

```
/* --------------------- COMMON VARIABLES --------------------------------- */
    WORD Flags;          /* general purpose flags (see definitions below) */

/* --------------------- USER VARIABLES ----------------------------------- */
    WORD *SaveBuffer;    /* pointer to the buffer for background save */

/* used by Bobs for "cookie-cutting" and multi-plane masking */
    WORD *ImageShadow;

/* pointer to BOBs for sequenced drawing of Bobs
 *  for correct overlaying of multiple component animations
 */
    struct Bob *Before; /* draw this Bob before Bob pointed to by before */
    struct Bob *After;  /* draw this Bob after Bob pointed to by after */

    struct VSprite   *BobVSprite;   /* this Bob's VSprite definition */

    struct AnimComp  *BobComp;      /* pointer to this Bob's AnimComp def */

    struct DBufPacket *DBuffer;     /* pointer to this Bob's dBuf packet */

    BUserStuff BUserExt;            /* Bob user extension */
};

struct AnimComp
{
/* --------------------- SYSTEM VARIABLES --------------------------------- */

/* --------------------- COMMON VARIABLES --------------------------------- */
    WORD Flags;                     /* AnimComp flags for system & user */

/* timer defines how long to keep this component active:
 *  if set non-zero, timer decrements to zero then switches to nextSeq
 *  if set to zero, AnimComp never switches
 */
    WORD Timer;

/* --------------------- USER VARIABLES ----------------------------------- */
/* initial value for timer when the AnimComp is activated by the system */
    WORD TimeSet;

/* pointer to next and previous components of animation object */
    struct AnimComp  *NextComp;
    struct AnimComp  *PrevComp;

/* pointer to component component definition of next image in sequence */
    struct AnimComp  *NextSeq;
    struct AnimComp  *PrevSeq;

    WORD (*AnimCRoutine)(); /* address of special animation procedure */

    WORD YTrans;     /* initial y translation (if this is a component) */
    WORD XTrans;     /* initial x translation (if this is a component) */

    struct AnimOb    *HeadOb;

    struct Bob       *AnimBob;
};

struct AnimOb
{
/* --------------------- SYSTEM VARIABLES --------------------------------- */
    struct AnimOb    *NextOb, *PrevOb;

/* number of calls to Animate this AnimOb has endured */
    LONG Clock;

    WORD AnOldY, AnOldX;            /* old y,x coordinates */
```



```

/* --------------------- COMMON VARIABLES --------------------------------- */
    WORD AnY, AnX;                  /* y,x coordinates of the AnimOb */

/* --------------------- USER VARIABLES ----------------------------------- */
    WORD YVel, XVel;                /* velocities of this object */
    WORD YAccel, XAccel;            /* accelerations of this object */

    WORD RingYTrans, RingXTrans;    /* ring translation values */

    WORD (*AnimORoutine)();         /* address of special animation
                                       procedure */

    struct AnimComp  *HeadComp;     /* pointer to first component */

    AUserStuff AUserExt;            /* AnimOb user extension */
};

/* dBufPacket defines the values needed to be saved across buffer to buffer
 *  when in double-buffer mode
 */
struct DBufPacket
{
    WORD BufY, BufX;                /* save other buffers screen coordinates */
    struct VSprite   *BufPath;      /* carry the draw path over the gap */

/* these pointers must be filled in by the user */
/* pointer to other buffer's background save buffer */
    WORD *BufBuffer;
};



/* ************************************************************************ */

/* these are GEL functions that are currently simple enough to exist as a
 *  definition.  It should not be assumed that this will always be the case
 */
#define InitAnimate(animKey) {*(animKey) = NULL;}
#define RemBob(b) {(b)->Flags |= BOBSAWAY;}


/* ************************************************************************ */

#define B2NORM      0
#define B2SWAP      1
#define B2BOBBER    2

/* ************************************************************************ */

/* a structure to contain the 16 collision procedure addresses */
struct collTable
{
    int (*collPtrs[16])();
};

#endif  /* GRAPHICS_GELS_H */
```

```
#ifndef GRAPHICS_GFX_H
#define GRAPHICS_GFX_H
/*
**      $Filename: graphics/gfx.h $
**      $Release: 1.3 $
**
**      general include file for application programs
**
**      (C) Copyright 1985,1986,1987,1988 Commodore-Amiga, Inc.
**          All Rights Reserved
*/

#define BITSET  0x8000
#define BITCLR  0

#define AGNUS
#ifdef AGNUS
#define TOBB(a)      ((long)(a))
#else
#define TOBB(a)      ((long)(a)>>1)  /* convert Chip adr to Bread Board Adr */
#endif

struct Rectangle
{
    SHORT   MinX,MinY;
    SHORT   MaxX,MaxY;
};

typedef struct tPoint
{
    WORD x,y;
} Point;

typedef UBYTE *PLANEPTR;

struct BitMap
{
    UWORD   BytesPerRow;
    UWORD   Rows;
    UBYTE   Flags;
    UBYTE   Depth;
    UWORD   pad;
    PLANEPTR Planes[8];
};

#define RASSIZE(w,h)    ((h)*( (w+15)>>3&0xFFFE))

#endif  /* GRAPHICS_GFX_H */
```



```
#ifndef GRAPHICS_GFXBASE_H
#define GRAPHICS_GFXBASE_H
/*
**      $Filename: graphics/gfxbase.h $
**      $Release: 1.3 $
**
**
**
**      (C) Copyright 1985,1986,1987,1988 Commodore-Amiga, Inc.
**          All Rights Reserved
*/

#ifndef EXEC_LISTS_H
#include <exec/lists.h>
#endif
#ifndef EXEC_LIBRARIES_H
#include <exec/libraries.h>
#endif
#ifndef EXEC_INTERRUPTS_H
#include <exec/interrupts.h>
#endif

struct GfxBase
{
    struct Library  LibNode;
    struct View *ActiView;
    struct copinit *copinit;    /* ptr to copper start up list */
    long    *cia;       /* for 8520 resource use */
    long    *blitter;   /* for future blitter resource use */
    UWORD   *LOFlist;
    UWORD   *SHFlist;
    struct bltnode *blthd,*bltl;
    struct bltnode *bsblthd,*bsbltl;
    struct Interrupt vbsrv,timsrv,bltsrv;
    struct List     TextFonts;
    struct  TextFont *DefaultFont;
    UWORD  Modes;                /* copy of current first bplcon0 */
    BYTE VBlank;
    BYTE Debug;
    SHORT BeamSync;
    SHORT system_bplcon0; /* it is ored into each bplcon0 for display */
    UBYTE   SpriteReserved;
    UBYTE   bytereserved;
    USHORT   Flags;
    SHORT   BlitLock;
        short   BlitNest;

        struct  List    BlitWaitQ;
        struct  Task    *BlitOwner;
    struct  List    TOF_WaitQ;
        UWORD   DisplayFlags;   /* NTSC PAL GENLOC etc*/
                /* Display flags are determined at power on */
        struct SimpleSprite **SimpleSprites;
        UWORD   MaxDisplayRow;          /* hardware stuff, do not use */
        UWORD   MaxDisplayColumn;       /* hardware stuff, do not use */
        UWORD   NormalDisplayRows;
        UWORD   NormalDisplayColumns;
        /* the following are for standard non interlace, 1/2 wb width */
        UWORD   NormalDPMX;             /* Dots per meter on display */
        UWORD   NormalDPMY;             /* Dots per meter on display */
        struct  SignalSemaphore *LastChanceMemory;
        UWORD   *LCMptr;
        UWORD   MicrosPerLine;  /* 256 time usec/line */
        UWORD   MinDisplayColumn;
        ULONG   reserved[23];   /* for future use */
        };

#define NTSC    1
#define GENLOC  2
```

Sep 19 20:26 1988 graphics/gfxbase.h Page 2

```
#define PAL             4

#define BLITMSG_FAULT   4

#endif  /* GRAPHICS_GFXBASE_H */
```

Sep 19 20:26 1988 graphics/gfxmacros.h Page 1

```
#ifndef GRAPHICS_GFXMACROS_H
#define GRAPHICS_GFXMACROS_H
/*
**      $Filename: graphics/gfxmacros.h $
**      $Release: 1.3 $
**
**
**
**      (C) Copyright 1985,1986,1987,1988 Commodore-Amiga, Inc.
**          All Rights Reserved
*/

#ifndef  GRAPHICS_RASTPORT_H
#include <graphics/rastport.h>
#endif

#define ON_DISPLAY      custom.dmacon = BITSET|DMAF_RASTER;
#define OFF_DISPLAY     custom.dmacon = BITCLR|DMAF_RASTER;
#define ON_SPRITE       custom.dmacon = BITSET|DMAF_SPRITE;
#define OFF_SPRITE      custom.dmacon = BITCLR|DMAF_SPRITE;

#define ON_VBLANK       custom.intena = BITSET|INTF_VERTB;
#define OFF_VBLANK      custom.intena = BITCLR|INTF_VERTB;

#define SetOPen(w,c)    {(w)->AOlPen = c;(w)->Flags |= AREAOUTLINE;}
#define SetDrPt(w,p)    {(w)->LinePtrn = p;(w)->Flags |= FRST_DOT;(w)->linpatcnt
#define SetWrMsk(w,m)   {(w)->Mask = m;}
#define SetAfPt(w,p,n)  {(w)->AreaPtrn = p;(w)->AreaPtSz = n;}

#define BNDRYOFF(w)     {(w)->Flags &= ~AREAOUTLINE;}

#define CINIT(c,n)      { UCopperListInit(c,n); }
#define CMOVE(c,a,b)    { CMove(c,&a,b);CBump(c); }
#define CWAIT(c,a,b)    { CWait(c,a,b);CBump(c); }
#define CEND(c)         { CWAIT(c,10000,255); }

#define DrawCircle(rp,cx,cy,r)  DrawEllipse(rp,cx,cy,r,r);
#define AreaCircle(rp,cx,cy,r)  AreaEllipse(rp,cx,cy,r,r);

#endif  /* GRAPHICS_GFXMACROS_H */
```

Sep 19 20:26 1988 graphics/graphint.h Page 1

```
#ifndef GRAPHICS_GRAPHINT_H
#define GRAPHICS_GRAPHINT_H
/*
**      $Filename: graphics/graphint.h $
**      $Release: 1.3 $
**
**
**
**      (C) Copyright 1985,1986,1987,1988 Commodore-Amiga, Inc.
**          All Rights Reserved
*/

#ifndef EXEC_NODES_H
#include <exec/nodes.h>
#endif

/* structure used by AddTOFTask */
struct Isrvstr
{
    struct Node is_Node;
    struct Isrvstr *Iptr;   /* passed to srvr by os */
    int (*code)();
    int (*ccode)();
    int Carg;
};

#endif  /* GRAPHICS_GRAPHINT_H */
```

Sep 19 20:26 1988 graphics/layers.h Page 1

```
#ifndef GRAPHICS_LAYERS_H
#define GRAPHICS_LAYERS_H
/*
**      $Filename: graphics/layers.h $
**      $Release: 1.3 $
**
**
**
**      (C) Copyright 1985,1986,1987,1988 Commodore-Amiga, Inc.
**          All Rights Reserved
*/

#ifndef EXEC_LISTS_H
#include <exec/lists.h>
#endif

#ifndef EXEC_SEMAPHORES_H
#include <exec/semaphores.h>
#endif

#define LAYERSIMPLE     1
#define LAYERSMART      2
#define LAYERSUPER      4
#define LAYERUPDATING   0x10
#define LAYERBACKDROP   0x40
#define LAYERREFRESH    0x80
#define LAYER_CLIPRECTS_LOST    0x100   /* during BeginUpdate */
                                        /* or during layerop */
                                        /* this happens if out of memory */
#define LMN_REGION      -1

struct Layer_Info
{
    struct Layer *top_layer;
    struct Layer *check_lp;         /* system use */
    struct Layer *obs;              /* system use */
        struct MinList  FreeClipRects;
        struct SignalSemaphore Lock;
        struct List gs_Head;                    /* system use */
        LONG    longreserved;
        UWORD   Flags;
        BYTE    fatten_count;
        BYTE    LockLayersCount;
    UWORD  LayerInfo_extra_size;
    WORD        *blitbuff;
    struct LayerInfo_extra *LayerInfo_extra;
};

#define NEWLAYERINFO_CALLED 1
#define ALERTLAYERSNOMEM 0x83010000

#endif  /* GRAPHICS_LAYERS_H */
```

```
#ifndef GRAPHICS_RASTPORT_H
#define GRAPHICS_RASTPORT_H
/*
**      $Filename: graphics/rastport.h $
**      $Release: 1.3 $
**
**
**
**      (C) Copyright 1985,1986,1987,1988 Commodore-Amiga, Inc.
**          All Rights Reserved
*/

#ifndef GRAPHICS_GFX_H
#include <graphics/gfx.h>
#endif

struct AreaInfo
{
    SHORT   *VctrTbl;           /* ptr to start of vector table */
    SHORT   *VctrPtr;           /* ptr to current vertex */
    BYTE    *FlagTbl;           /* ptr to start of vector flag table */
    BYTE    *FlagPtr;           /* ptrs to areafill flags */
    SHORT   Count;              /* number of vertices in list */
    SHORT   MaxCount;           /* AreaMove/Draw will not allow Count>MaxCount*/
    SHORT   FirstX,FirstY;      /* first point for this polygon */
};

struct TmpRas
{
    BYTE *RasPtr;
    LONG Size;
};

/* unoptimized for 32bit alignment of pointers */
struct GelsInfo
{
    BYTE sprRsrvd;              /* flag of which sprites to reserve from
                                   vsprite system */
    UBYTE Flags;                /* system use */
    struct VSprite *gelHead, *gelTail; /* dummy vSprites for list management*/
    /* pointer to array of 8 WORDS for sprite available lines */
    WORD *nextLine;
    /* pointer to array of 8 pointers for color-last-assigned to vSprites */
    WORD **lastColor;
    struct collTable *collHandler;     /* addresses of collision routines */
    short leftmost, rightmost, topmost, bottommost;
   APTR firstBlissObj,lastBlissObj;    /* system use only */
};

struct RastPort
{
    struct  Layer *Layer;
    struct  BitMap   *BitMap;
    USHORT  *AreaPtrn;          /* ptr to areafill pattern */
    struct  TmpRas *TmpRas;
    struct  AreaInfo *AreaInfo;
    struct  GelsInfo *GelsInfo;
    UBYTE   Mask;               /* write mask for this raster */
    BYTE    FgPen;              /* foreground pen for this raster */
    BYTE    BgPen;              /* background pen  */
    BYTE    AOlPen;             /* areafill outline pen */
    BYTE    DrawMode;           /* drawing mode for fill, lines, and text */
    BYTE    AreaPtSz;           /* 2^n words for areafill pattern */
    BYTE    linpatcnt;          /* current line drawing pattern preshift */
    BYTE    dummy;
    USHORT  Flags;              /* miscellaneous control bits */
    USHORT  LinePtrn;           /* 16 bits for textured lines */
    SHORT   cp_x, cp_y;         /* current pen position */
    UBYTE   minterms[8];
```



```
    SHORT   PenWidth;
    SHORT   PenHeight;
    struct  TextFont *Font;     /* current font address */
    UBYTE   AlgoStyle;          /* the algorithmically generated style */
    UBYTE   TxFlags;            /* text specific flags */
    UWORD   TxHeight;           /* text height */
    UWORD   TxWidth;            /* text nominal width */
    UWORD   TxBaseline;         /* text baseline */
    WORD    TxSpacing;          /* text spacing (per character) */
    APTR    *RP_User;
    ULONG   longreserved[2];
#ifndef GFX_RASTPORT_1_2
    UWORD   wordreserved[7];    /* used to be a node */
    UBYTE   reserved[8];        /* for future use */
#endif
};

/* drawing modes */
#define JAM1        0           /* jam 1 color into raster */
#define JAM2        1           /* jam 2 colors into raster */
#define COMPLEMENT  2           /* XOR bits into raster */
#define INVERSVID   4           /* inverse video for drawing modes */

/* these are the flag bits for RastPort flags */
#define FRST_DOT    0x01        /* draw the first dot of this line ? */
#define ONE_DOT     0x02        /* use one dot mode for drawing lines */
#define DBUFFER     0x04        /* flag set when RastPorts
                                   are double-buffered */

            /* only used for bobs */

#define AREAOUTLINE 0x08        /* used by areafiller */
#define NOCROSSFILL 0x20        /* areafills have no crossovers */

/* there is only one style of clipping: raster clipping */
/* this preserves the continuity of jaggies regardless of clip window */
/* When drawing into a RastPort, if the ptr to ClipRect is nil then there */
/* is no clipping done, this is dangerous but useful for speed */

#endif  /* GRAPHICS_RASTPORT_H */
```

```
#ifndef GRAPHICS_REGIONS_H
#define GRAPHICS_REGIONS_H
/*
**      $Filename: graphics/regions.h $
**      $Release: 1.3 $
**
**
**
**      (C) Copyright 1985,1986,1987,1988 Commodore-Amiga, Inc.
**          All Rights Reserved
*/

#ifndef GRAPHICS_GFX_H
#include <graphics/gfx.h>
#endif

struct RegionRectangle
{
    struct RegionRectangle *Next,*Prev;
    struct Rectangle bounds;
};

struct Region
{
    struct Rectangle bounds;
    struct RegionRectangle *RegionRectangle;
};

#endif  /* GRAPHICS_REGIONS_H */
```



```
#ifndef GRAPHICS_SPRITE_H
#define GRAPHICS_SPRITE_H
/*
**      $Filename: graphics/sprite.h $
**      $Release: 1.3 $
**
**
**
**      (C) Copyright 1985,1986,1987,1988 Commodore-Amiga, Inc.
**          All Rights Reserved
*/

#define SPRITE_ATTACHED 0x80

struct SimpleSprite
{
    UWORD *posctldata;
    UWORD height;
    UWORD   x,y;    /* current position */
    UWORD   num;
};

#endif  /* GRAPHICS_SPRITE_H */
```

```
#ifndef GRAPHICS_TEXT_H
#define GRAPHICS_TEXT_H
/*
**      $Filename: graphics/text.h $
**      $Release: 1.3 $
**
**
**
**      (C) Copyright 1985,1986,1987,1988 Commodore-Amiga, Inc.
**          All Rights Reserved
*/

#ifndef     EXEC_PORTS_H
#include "exec/ports.h"
#endif

/*------ Font Styles ------------------------------------------------*/
#define FS_NORMAL    0         /* normal text (no style bits set) */
#define FSB_EXTENDED 3         /* extended face (wider than normal) */
#define FSF_EXTENDED (1<<3)
#define FSB_ITALIC   2         /* italic (slanted 1:2 right) */
#define FSF_ITALIC   (1<<2)
#define FSB_BOLD     1         /* bold face text (ORed w/ shifted) */
#define FSF_BOLD     (1<<1)
#define FSB_UNDERLINED  0      /* underlined (under baseline) */
#define FSF_UNDERLINED  (1<<0)

/*------ Font Flags ------------------------------------------------*/
#define FPB_ROMFONT  0         /* font is in rom */
#define FPF_ROMFONT  (1<<0)
#define FPB_DISKFONT 1         /* font is from diskfont.library */
#define FPF_DISKFONT (1<<1)
#define FPB_REVPATH  2         /* designed path is reversed (e.g. left) */
#define FPF_REVPATH  (1<<2)
#define  FPB_TALLDOT 3         /* designed for hires non-interlaced */
#define  FPF_TALLDOT (1<<3)
#define  FPB_WIDEDOT 4         /* designed for lores interlaced */
#define  FPF_WIDEDOT (1<<4)
#define FPB_PROPORTIONAL   5  /* character sizes can vary from nominal */
#define FPF_PROPORTIONAL   (1<<5)
#define FPB_DESIGNED 6         /* size is "designed", not constructed */
#define FPF_DESIGNED (1<<6)
#define FPB_REMOVED  7         /* the font has been removed */
#define FPF_REMOVED  (1<<7)

/****** TextAttr node, matches text attributes in RastPort **********/
struct TextAttr {
   STRPTR   ta_Name;           /* name of the font */
   UWORD    ta_YSize;          /* height of the font */
   UBYTE    ta_Style;          /* intrinsic font style */
   UBYTE    ta_Flags;          /* font preferences and flags */
};


/****** TextFonts node *********************************************/
struct TextFont {
   struct Message tf_Message;       /* reply message for font removal */
                               /* font name in LN        \    used in this */
   UWORD    tf_YSize;          /* font height            |    order to best */
   UBYTE    tf_Style;          /* font style             |    match a font */
   UBYTE    tf_Flags;          /* preferences and flags  /    request. */
   UWORD    tf_XSize;          /* nominal font width */
   UWORD    tf_Baseline;       /* distance from the top of char to baseline */
   UWORD    tf_BoldSmear;      /* smear to affect a bold enhancement */

   UWORD    tf_Accessors;      /* access count */

   UBYTE    tf_LoChar;         /* the first character described here */
   UBYTE    tf_HiChar;         /* the last character described here */
```



```
   APTR     tf_CharData;       /* the bit character data */

   UWORD    tf_Modulo;         /* the row modulo for the strike font data */
   APTR     tf_CharLoc;        /* ptr to location data for the strike font */
            /*    2 words: bit offset then size */
   APTR     tf_CharSpace;      /* ptr to words of proportional spacing data */
   APTR     tf_CharKern;       /* ptr to words of kerning data */
};

#endif  /* GRAPHICS_TEXT_H */
```

```
#ifndef GRAPHICS_VIEW_H
#define GRAPHICS_VIEW_H
/*
**      $Filename: graphics/view.h $
**      $Release: 1.3 $
**
**
**
**      (C) Copyright 1985,1986,1987,1988 Commodore-Amiga, Inc.
**          All Rights Reserved
*/

#ifndef GRAPHICS_GFX_H
#include <graphics/gfx.h>
#endif

#ifndef GRAPHICS_COPPER_H
#include <graphics/copper.h>
#endif

struct ColorMap
{
   UBYTE Flags;
   UBYTE Type;
   UWORD Count;
   APTR  ColorTable;
};
/* if Type == 0 then ColorTable is a table of UWORDS xRGB */

struct ViewPort
{
   struct   ViewPort *Next;
   struct   ColorMap  *ColorMap;    /* table of colors for this viewport */
                /* if this is nil, MakeVPort assumes default values */
   struct   CopList  *DspIns;       /* user by MakeView() */
   struct   CopList  *SprIns;       /* used by sprite stuff */
   struct   CopList  *ClrIns;       /* used by sprite stuff */
   struct   UCopList *UCopIns;      /* User copper list */
   SHORT    DWidth,DHeight;
   SHORT    DxOffset,DyOffset;
   UWORD    Modes;
   UBYTE        SpritePriorities;               /* used by makevp */
   UBYTE        reserved;
   struct   RasInfo *RasInfo;
};

struct View
{
   struct ViewPort *ViewPort;
   struct cprlist *LOFCprList;   /* used for interlaced and noninterlaced */
   struct cprlist *SHFCprList;   /* only used during interlace */
   short DyOffset,DxOffset;   /* for complete View positioning */
                              /* offsets are +- adjustments to standard #s */
   UWORD   Modes;             /* such as INTERLACE, GENLOC */
};

/* defines used for Modes in IVPargs */
#define PFBA            0x40
#define DUALPF          0x400
#define HIRES           0x8000
#define LACE            4
#define HAM             0x800
#define SPRITES         0x4000      /* reuse one of plane ctr bits */
#define VP_HIDE         0x2000      /* reuse another plane crt bit */
#define GENLOCK_AUDIO   0x100
#define GENLOCK_VIDEO   2
#define EXTRA_HALFBRITE 0x80

struct RasInfo  /* used by callers to and InitDspC() */
```



```
{
   struct   RasInfo *Next;          /* used for dualpf */
   struct   BitMap *BitMap;
   SHORT    RxOffset,RyOffset;      /* scroll offsets in this BitMap */
};

#endif  /* GRAPHICS_VIEW_H */
```

```
#ifndef HARDWARE_ADKBITS_H
#define HARDWARE_ADKBITS_H
/*
**      $Filename: hardware/adkbits.h $
**      $Release: 1.3 $
**
**      bit definitions for adkcon register
**
**      (C) Copyright 1985,1986,1987,1988 Commodore-Amiga, Inc.
**          All Rights Reserved
*/

#define  ADKB_SETCLR     15 /* standard set/clear bit */
#define  ADKB_PRECOMP1   14 /* two bits of precompensation */
#define  ADKB_PRECOMP0   13
#define  ADKB_MFMPREC    12 /* use mfm style precompensation */
#define  ADKB_UARTBRK    11 /* force uart output to zero */
#define  ADKB_WORDSYNC   10 /* enable DSKSYNC register matching */
#define  ADKB_MSBSYNC    9  /* (Apple GCR Only) sync on MSB for reading */
#define  ADKB_FAST       8  /* 1 -> 2 us/bit (mfm), 2 -> 4 us/bit (gcr) */
#define  ADKB_USE3PN     7  /* use aud chan 3 to modulate period of ?? */
#define  ADKB_USE2P3     6  /* use aud chan 2 to modulate period of 3 */
#define  ADKB_USE1P2     5  /* use aud chan 1 to modulate period of 2 */
#define  ADKB_USE0P1     4  /* use aud chan 0 to modulate period of 1 */
#define  ADKB_USE3VN     3  /* use aud chan 3 to modulate volume of ?? */
#define  ADKB_USE2V3     2  /* use aud chan 2 to modulate volume of 3 */
#define  ADKB_USE1V2     1  /* use aud chan 1 to modulate volume of 2 */
#define  ADKB_USE0V1     0  /* use aud chan 0 to modulate volume of 1 */

#define  ADKF_SETCLR     (1<<15)
#define  ADKF_PRECOMP1   (1<<14)
#define  ADKF_PRECOMP0   (1<<13)
#define  ADKF_MFMPREC    (1<<12)
#define  ADKF_UARTBRK    (1<<11)
#define  ADKF_WORDSYNC   (1<<10)
#define  ADKF_MSBSYNC    (1<<9)
#define  ADKF_FAST       (1<<8)
#define  ADKF_USE3PN     (1<<7)
#define  ADKF_USE2P3     (1<<6)
#define  ADKF_USE1P2     (1<<5)
#define  ADKF_USE0P1     (1<<4)
#define  ADKF_USE3VN     (1<<3)
#define  ADKF_USE2V3     (1<<2)
#define  ADKF_USE1V2     (1<<1)
#define  ADKF_USE0V1     (1<<0)

#define ADKF_PRE000NS    0                           /* 000 ns of precomp */
#define ADKF_PRE140NS    (ADKF_PRECOMP0)             /* 140 ns of precomp */
#define ADKF_PRE280NS    (ADKF_PRECOMP1)             /* 280 ns of precomp */
#define ADKF_PRE560NS    (ADKF_PRECOMP0|ADKF_PRECOMP1) /* 560 ns of precomp */

#endif  /* HARDWARE_ADKBITS_H */
```



```
#ifndef HARDWARE_BLIT_H
#define HARDWARE_BLIT_H
/*
**      $Filename: hardware/blit.h $
**      $Release: 1.3 $
**
**      include file for blitter
**
**      (C) Copyright 1985,1986,1987,1988 Commodore-Amiga, Inc.
**          All Rights Reserved
*/

#define  HSIZEBITS   6
#define VSIZEBITS 16-HSIZEBITS
#define HSIZEMASK 0x3f        /* 2^6 -- 1 */
#define VSIZEMASK 0x3FF       /* 2^10 - 1 */

#define  MAXBYTESPERROW 128

/* definitions for blitter control register 0 */

#define ABC    0x80
#define ABNC   0x40
#define ANBC   0x20
#define ANBNC  0x10
#define NABC   0x8
#define NABNC  0x4
#define NANBC  0x2
#define NANBNC 0x1

/* some commonly used operations */
#define A_OR_B    ABC|ANBC|NABC | ABNC|ANBNC|NABNC
#define A_OR_C    ABC|NABC|ABNC | ANBC|NANBC|ANBNC
#define A_XOR_C   NABC|ABNC   | NANBC|ANBNC
#define A_TO_D    ABC|ANBC|ABNC|ANBNC

#define BC0B_DEST 8
#define BC0B_SRCC 9
#define BC0B_SRCB   10
#define BC0B_SRCA 11
#define BC0F_DEST 0x100
#define BC0F_SRCC 0x200
#define BC0F_SRCB 0x400
#define BC0F_SRCA 0x800

#define BC1F_DESC   2         /* blitter descend direction */

#define DEST 0x100
#define SRCC 0x200
#define SRCB 0x400
#define SRCA 0x800

#define ASHIFTSHIFT  12       /* bits to right align ashift value */
#define BSHIFTSHIFT  12       /* bits to right align bshift value */

/* definations for blitter control register 1 */
#define LINEMODE      0x1
#define FILL_OR       0x8
#define FILL_XOR      0x10
#define FILL_CARRYIN 0x4
#define ONEDOT        0x2     /* one dot per horizontal line */
#define OVFLAG        0x20
#define SIGNFLAG      0x40
#define BLITREVERSE  0x2

#define SUD           0x10
#define SUL           0x8
#define AUL           0x4
```

```
#define OCTANT8   24
#define OCTANT7   4
#define OCTANT6   12
#define OCTANT5   28
#define OCTANT4   20
#define OCTANT3   8
#define OCTANT2   0
#define OCTANT1   16

/* stuff for blit qeuer */
struct bltnode
{
    struct  bltnode *n;
    int     (*function)();
    char    stat;
    short   blitsize;
    short   beamsync;
    int     (*cleanup)();
};

/* defined bits for bltstat */
#define CLEANUP 0x40
#define CLEANME CLEANUP

#endif  /* HARDWARE_BLIT_H */
```



```
#ifndef HARDWARE_CIA_H
#define HARDWARE_CIA_H
/*
**      $Filename: hardware/cia.h $
**      $Release: 1.3 $
**
**      registers and bits in the Complex Interface Adapter (CIA) chip
**
**      (C) Copyright 1985,1986,1987,1988 Commodore-Amiga, Inc.
**          All Rights Reserved
*/

/*
 * ciaa is on an ODD address (e.g. the low byte) -- $bfe001
 * ciab is on an EVEN address (e.g. the high byte) -- $bfd000
 *
 * do this to get the definitions:
 *    extern struct CIA ciaa, ciab;
 */


struct CIA {
    UBYTE   ciapra;
    UBYTE   pad0[0xff];
    UBYTE   ciaprb;
    UBYTE   pad1[0xff];
    UBYTE   ciaddra;
    UBYTE   pad2[0xff];
    UBYTE   ciaddrb;
    UBYTE   pad3[0xff];
    UBYTE   ciatalo;
    UBYTE   pad4[0xff];
    UBYTE   ciatahi;
    UBYTE   pad5[0xff];
    UBYTE   ciatblo;
    UBYTE   pad6[0xff];
    UBYTE   ciatbhi;
    UBYTE   pad7[0xff];
    UBYTE   ciatodlow;
    UBYTE   pad8[0xff];
    UBYTE   ciatodmid;
    UBYTE   pad9[0xff];
    UBYTE   ciatodhi;
    UBYTE   pad10[0xff];
    UBYTE   unusedreg;
    UBYTE   pad11[0xff];
    UBYTE   ciasdr;
    UBYTE   pad12[0xff];
    UBYTE   ciaicr;
    UBYTE   pad13[0xff];
    UBYTE   ciacra;
    UBYTE   pad14[0xff];
    UBYTE   ciacrb;
};


/* interrupt control register bit numbers */
#define CIAICRB_TA      0
#define CIAICRB_TB      1
#define CIAICRB_ALRM    2
#define CIAICRB_SP      3
#define CIAICRB_FLG     4
#define CIAICRB_IR      7
#define CIAICRB_SETCLR  7

/* control register A bit numbers */
#define CIACRAB_START   0
#define CIACRAB_PBON    1
#define CIACRAB_OUTMODE 2
```

```
#define CIACRAB_RUNMODE 3
#define CIACRAB_LOAD    4
#define CIACRAB_INMODE  5
#define CIACRAB_SPMODE  6
#define CIACRAB_TODIN   7

/* control register B bit numbers */
#define CIACRBB_START   0
#define CIACRBB_PBON    1
#define CIACRBB_OUTMODE 2
#define CIACRBB_RUNMODE 3
#define CIACRBB_LOAD    4
#define CIACRBB_INMODE0 5
#define CIACRBB_INMODE1 6
#define CIACRBB_ALARM   7

/* interrupt control register masks */
#define CIAICRF_TA      (1<<CIAICRB_TA)
#define CIAICRF_TB      (1<<CIAICRB_TB)
#define CIAICRF_ALRM    (1<<CIAICRB_ALRM)
#define CIAICRF_SP      (1<<CIAICRB_SP)
#define CIAICRF_FLG     (1<<CIAICRB_FLG)
#define CIAICRF_IR      (1<<CIAICRB_IR)
#define CIAICRF_SETCLR  (1<<CIAICRB_SETCLR)

/* control register A register masks */
#define CIACRAF_START   (1<<CIACRAB_START)
#define CIACRAF_PBON    (1<<CIACRAB_PBON)
#define CIACRAF_OUTMODE (1<<CIACRAB_OUTMODE)
#define CIACRAF_RUNMODE (1<<CIACRAB_RUNMODE)
#define CIACRAF_LOAD    (1<<CIACRAB_LOAD)
#define CIACRAF_INMODE  (1<<CIACRAB_INMODE)
#define CIACRAF_SPMODE  (1<<CIACRAB_SPMODE)
#define CIACRAF_TODIN   (1<<CIACRAB_TODIN)

/* control register B register masks */
#define CIACRBF_START   (1<<CIACRBB_START)
#define CIACRBF_PBON    (1<<CIACRBB_PBON)
#define CIACRBF_OUTMODE (1<<CIACRBB_OUTMODE)
#define CIACRBF_RUNMODE (1<<CIACRBB_RUNMODE)
#define CIACRBF_LOAD    (1<<CIACRBB_LOAD)
#define CIACRBF_INMODE0 (1<<CIACRBB_INMODE0)
#define CIACRBF_INMODE1 (1<<CIACRBB_INMODE1)
#define CIACRBF_ALARM   (1<<CIACRBB_ALARM)

/* control register B INMODE masks */
#define CIACRBF_IN_PHI2 0
#define CIACRBF_IN_CNT  (CIACRBF_INMODE0)
#define CIACRBF_IN_TA   (CIACRBF_INMODE1)
#define CIACRBF_IN_CNT_TA  (CIACRBF_INMODE0|CIACRBF_INMODE1)

/*
 * Port definitions -- what each bit in a cia peripheral register is tied to
 */

/* ciaa port A (0xbfe001) */
#define CIAB_GAMEPORT1  (7)   /* gameport 1, pin 6 (fire button*) */
#define CIAB_GAMEPORT0  (6)   /* gameport 0, pin 6 (fire button*) */
#define CIAB_DSKRDY     (5)   /* disk ready* */
#define CIAB_DSKTRACK0  (4)   /* disk on track 00* */
#define CIAB_DSKPROT    (3)   /* disk write protect* */
#define CIAB_DSKCHANGE  (2)   /* disk change* */
#define CIAB_LED        (1)   /* led light control (0==>bright) */
#define CIAB_OVERLAY    (0)   /* memory overlay bit */

/* ciaa port B (0xbfe101) -- parallel port */

/* ciab port A (0xbfd000) -- serial and printer control */
#define CIAB_COMDTR     (7)   /* serial Data Terminal Ready* */
```



```
#define CIAB_COMRTS     (6)   /* serial Request to Send* */
#define CIAB_COMCD      (5)   /* serial Carrier Detect* */
#define CIAB_COMCTS     (4)   /* serial Clear to Send* */
#define CIAB_COMDSR     (3)   /* serial Data Set Ready* */
#define CIAB_PRTRSEL    (2)   /* printer SELECT */
#define CIAB_PRTRPOUT   (1)   /* printer paper out */
#define CIAB_PRTRBUSY   (0)   /* printer busy */

/* ciab port B (0xbfd100) -- disk control */
#define CIAB_DSKMOTOR   (7)   /* disk motorr* */
#define CIAB_DSKSEL3    (6)   /* disk select unit 3* */
#define CIAB_DSKSEL2    (5)   /* disk select unit 2* */
#define CIAB_DSKSEL1    (4)   /* disk select unit 1* */
#define CIAB_DSKSEL0    (3)   /* disk select unit 0* */
#define CIAB_DSKSIDE    (2)   /* disk side select* */
#define CIAB_DSKDIREC   (1)   /* disk direction of seek* */
#define CIAB_DSKSTEP    (0)   /* disk step heads* */

/* ciaa port A (0xbfe001) */
#define CIAF_GAMEPORT1  (1<<7)
#define CIAF_GAMEPORT0  (1<<6)
#define CIAF_DSKRDY     (1<<5)
#define CIAF_DSKTRACK0  (1<<4)
#define CIAF_DSKPROT    (1<<3)
#define CIAF_DSKCHANGE  (1<<2)
#define CIAF_LED        (1<<1)
#define CIAF_OVERLAY    (1<<0)

/* ciaa port B (0xbfe101) -- parallel port */

/* ciab port A (0xbfd000) -- serial and printer control */
#define CIAF_COMDTR     (1<<7)
#define CIAF_COMRTS     (1<<6)
#define CIAF_COMCD      (1<<5)
#define CIAF_COMCTS     (1<<4)
#define CIAF_COMDSR     (1<<3)
#define CIAF_PRTRSEL    (1<<2)
#define CIAF_PRTRPOUT   (1<<1)
#define CIAF_PRTRBUSY   (1<<0)

/* ciab port B (0xbfd100) -- disk control */
#define CIAF_DSKMOTOR   (1<<7)
#define CIAF_DSKSEL3    (1<<6)
#define CIAF_DSKSEL2    (1<<5)
#define CIAF_DSKSEL1    (1<<4)
#define CIAF_DSKSEL0    (1<<3)
#define CIAF_DSKSIDE    (1<<2)
#define CIAF_DSKDIREC   (1<<1)
#define CIAF_DSKSTEP    (1<<0)

#endif  /* HARDWARE_CIA_H */
```

```
#ifndef HARDWARE_CUSTOM_H
#define HARDWARE_CUSTOM_H
/*
**      $Filename: hardware/custom.h $
**      $Release: 1.3 $
**
**
**
**      (C) Copyright 1985,1986,1987,1988 Commodore-Amiga, Inc.
**          All Rights Reserved
*/

/*
 * do this to get base of custom registers:
 * extern struct Custom custom;
 */


struct Custom {
    UWORD   bltddat;
    UWORD   dmaconr;
    UWORD   vposr;
    UWORD   vhposr;
    UWORD   dskdatr;
    UWORD   joy0dat;
    UWORD   joy1dat;
    UWORD   clxdat;
    UWORD   adkconr;
    UWORD   pot0dat;
    UWORD   pot1dat;
    UWORD   potinp;
    UWORD   serdatr;
    UWORD   dskbytr;
    UWORD   intenar;
    UWORD   intreqr;
    APTR    dskpt;
    UWORD   dsklen;
    UWORD   dskdat;
    UWORD   refptr;
    UWORD   vposw;
    UWORD   vhposw;
    UWORD   copcon;
    UWORD   serdat;
    UWORD   serper;
    UWORD   potgo;
    UWORD   joytest;
    UWORD   strequ;
    UWORD   strvbl;
    UWORD   strhor;
    UWORD   strlong;
    UWORD   bltcon0;
    UWORD   bltcon1;
    UWORD   bltafwm;
    UWORD   bltalwm;
    APTR    bltcpt;
    APTR    bltbpt;
    APTR    bltapt;
    APTR    bltdpt;
    UWORD   bltsize;
    UWORD   pad2d[3];
    UWORD   bltcmod;
    UWORD   bltbmod;
    UWORD   bltamod;
    UWORD   bltdmod;
    UWORD   pad34[4];
    UWORD   bltcdat;
    UWORD   bltbdat;
    UWORD   bltadat;
    UWORD   pad3b[4];
```



```
    UWORD   dsksync;
    ULONG   cop1lc;
    ULONG   cop2lc;
    UWORD   copjmp1;
    UWORD   copjmp2;
    UWORD   copins;
    UWORD   diwstrt;
    UWORD   diwstop;
    UWORD   ddfstrt;
    UWORD   ddfstop;
    UWORD   dmacon;
    UWORD   clxcon;
    UWORD   intena;
    UWORD   intreq;
    UWORD   adkcon;
    struct  AudChannel {
      UWORD *ac_ptr; /* ptr to start of waveform data */
      UWORD ac_len;     /* length of waveform in words */
      UWORD ac_per;     /* sample period */
      UWORD ac_vol;     /* volume */
      UWORD ac_dat;     /* sample pair */
      UWORD ac_pad[2];  /* unused */
    } aud[4];
    APTR    bplpt[6];
    UWORD   pad7c[4];
    UWORD   bplcon0;
    UWORD   bplcon1;
    UWORD   bplcon2;
    UWORD   pad83;
    UWORD   bpl1mod;
    UWORD   bpl2mod;
    UWORD   pad86[2];
    UWORD   bpl1dat[6];
    UWORD   pad8e[2];
    APTR    sprpt[8];
    struct  SpriteDef {
      UWORD pos;
      UWORD ctl;
      UWORD dataa;
      UWORD datab;
    } spr[8];
    UWORD   color[32];
};

#endif  /* HARDWARE_CUSTOM_H */
```

Sep 19 20:26 1988 hardware/dmabits.h Page 1

```
#ifndef HARDWARE_DMABITS_H
#define HARDWARE_DMABITS_H
/*
**      $Filename: hardware/dmabits.h $
**      $Release: 1.3 $
**
**      include file for defining dma control stuff
**
**      (C) Copyright 1985,1986,1987,1988 Commodore-Amiga, Inc.
**          All Rights Reserved
*/

/* write definitions for dmaconw */
#define DMAF_SETCLR  0x8000
#define DMAF_AUDIO   0x000F   /* 4 bit mask */
#define DMAF_AUD0    0x0001
#define DMAF_AUD1    0x0002
#define DMAF_AUD2    0x0004
#define DMAF_AUD3    0x0008
#define DMAF_DISK    0x0010
#define DMAF_SPRITE  0x0020
#define DMAF_BLITTER 0x0040
#define DMAF_COPPER  0x0080
#define DMAF_RASTER  0x0100
#define DMAF_MASTER  0x0200
#define DMAF_BLITHOG 0x0400
#define DMAF_ALL     0x01FF   /* all dma channels */

/* read definitions for dmaconr */
/* bits 0-8 correspnd to dmaconw definitions */
#define DMAF_BLTDONE 0x4000
#define DMAF_BLTNZERO   0x2000

#define DMAB_SETCLR  15
#define DMAB_AUD0    0
#define DMAB_AUD1    1
#define DMAB_AUD2    2
#define DMAB_AUD3    3
#define DMAB_DISK    4
#define DMAB_SPRITE  5
#define DMAB_BLITTER 6
#define DMAB_COPPER  7
#define DMAB_RASTER  8
#define DMAB_MASTER  9
#define DMAB_BLITHOG 10
#define DMAB_BLTDONE 14
#define DMAB_BLTNZERO   13

#endif  /* HARDWARE_DMABITS_H */
```

Sep 19 20:27 1988 hardware/intbits.h Page 1

```
#ifndef HARDWARE_INTBITS_H
#define HARDWARE_INTBITS_H
/*
**      $Filename: hardware/intbits.h $
**      $Release: 1.3 $
**
**      bits in the interrupt enable (and interrupt request) register
**
**      (C) Copyright 1985,1986,1987,1988 Commodore-Amiga, Inc.
**          All Rights Reserved
*/

#define  INTB_SETCLR    (15)  /* Set/Clear control bit. Determines if bits */
             /* written with a 1 get set or cleared. Bits */
             /* written with a zero are allways unchanged */
#define  INTB_INTEN     (14)  /* Master interrupt (enable only ) */
#define  INTB_EXTER     (13)  /* External interrupt */
#define  INTB_DSKSYNC   (12)  /* Disk re-SYNChronized */
#define  INTB_RBF       (11)  /* serial port Receive Buffer Full */
#define  INTB_AUD3      (10)  /* Audio channel 3 block finished */
#define  INTB_AUD2      (9)   /* Audio channel 2 block finished */
#define  INTB_AUD1      (8)   /* Audio channel 1 block finished */
#define  INTB_AUD0      (7)   /* Audio channel 0 block finished */
#define  INTB_BLIT      (6)   /* Blitter finished */
#define  INTB_VERTB     (5)   /* start of Vertical Blank */
#define  INTB_COPER     (4)   /* Coprocessor */
#define  INTB_PORTS     (3)   /* I/O Ports and timers */
#define  INTB_SOFTINT   (2)   /* software interrupt request */
#define  INTB_DSKBLK    (1)   /* Disk Block done */
#define  INTB_TBE       (0)   /* serial port Transmit Buffer Empty */



#define  INTF_SETCLR    (1<<15)
#define  INTF_INTEN     (1<<14)
#define  INTF_EXTER     (1<<13)
#define  INTF_DSKSYNC   (1<<12)
#define  INTF_RBF       (1<<11)
#define  INTF_AUD3      (1<<10)
#define  INTF_AUD2      (1<<9)
#define  INTF_AUD1      (1<<8)
#define  INTF_AUD0      (1<<7)
#define  INTF_BLIT      (1<<6)
#define  INTF_VERTB     (1<<5)
#define  INTF_COPER     (1<<4)
#define  INTF_PORTS     (1<<3)
#define  INTF_SOFTINT   (1<<2)
#define  INTF_DSKBLK    (1<<1)
#define  INTF_TBE       (1<<0)

#endif  /* HARDWARE_INTBITS_H */
```

```
#ifndef INTUITION_INTUITION_H
#define INTUITION_INTUITION_H
/*
**      $Filename: intuition/intuition.h $
**      $Release: 1.3 $
**
**      main intuition include
**
**      (C) Copyright 1985,1986,1987,1988 Commodore-Amiga, Inc.
**          All Rights Reserved
*/

#ifndef EXEC_TYPES_H
#include "exec/types.h"
#endif

#ifndef GRAPHICS_GFX_H
#include "graphics/gfx.h"
#endif

#ifndef GRAPHICS_CLIP_H
#include "graphics/clip.h"
#endif

#ifndef GRAPHICS_VIEW_H
#include "graphics/view.h"
#endif

#ifndef GRAPHICS_RASTPORT_H
#include "graphics/rastport.h"
#endif

#ifndef GRAPHICS_LAYERS_H
#include "graphics/layers.h"
#endif

#ifndef GRAPHICS_TEXT_H
#include "graphics/text.h"
#endif

#ifndef EXEC_PORTS_H
#include "exec/ports.h"
#endif

#ifndef DEVICES_TIMER_H
#include "devices/timer.h"
#endif

#ifndef DEVICES_INPUTEVENT_H
#include "devices/inputevent.h"
#endif


/* ======================================================================= */
/* === Menu ============================================================== */
/* ======================================================================= */
struct Menu
{
    struct Menu *NextMenu;      /* same level */
    SHORT LeftEdge, TopEdge;    /* position of the select box */
    SHORT Width, Height;        /* dimensions of the select box */
    USHORT Flags;               /* see flag definitions below */
    BYTE *MenuName;             /* text for this Menu Header */
    struct MenuItem *FirstItem; /* pointer to first in chain */

    /* these mysteriously-named variables are for internal use only */
    SHORT JazzX, JazzY, BeatX, BeatY;
};

```



```

/* FLAGS SET BY BOTH THE APPLIPROG AND INTUITION */
#define MENUENABLED 0x0001      /* whether or not this menu is enabled */

/* FLAGS SET BY INTUITION */
#define MIDRAWN 0x0100          /* this menu's items are currently drawn */






/* ======================================================================= */
/* === MenuItem ========================================================== */
/* ======================================================================= */
struct MenuItem
{
    struct MenuItem *NextItem;  /* pointer to next in chained list */
    SHORT LeftEdge, TopEdge;    /* position of the select box */
    SHORT Width, Height;        /* dimensions of the select box */
    USHORT Flags;               /* see the defines below */

    LONG MutualExclude;         /* set bits mean this item excludes that */

    APTR ItemFill;              /* points to Image, IntuiText, or NULL */

    /* when this item is pointed to by the cursor and the items highlight
     *  mode HIGHIMAGE is selected, this alternate image will be displayed
     */
    APTR SelectFill;            /* points to Image, IntuiText, or NULL */

    BYTE Command;               /* only if appliprog sets the COMMSEQ flag */

    struct MenuItem *SubItem;   /* if non-zero, DrawMenu shows "->" */

    /* The NextSelect field represents the menu number of next selected
     *  item (when user has drag-selected several items)
     */
    USHORT NextSelect;
};


/* FLAGS SET BY THE APPLIPROG */
#define CHECKIT         0x0001  /* whether to check this item if selected */
#define ITEMTEXT        0x0002  /* set if textual, clear if graphical item */
#define COMMSEQ         0x0004  /* set if there's an command sequence */
#define MENUTOGGLE      0x0008  /* set to toggle the check of a menu item */
#define ITEMENABLED     0x0010  /* set if this item is enabled */

/* these are the SPECIAL HIGHLIGHT FLAG state meanings */
#define HIGHFLAGS       0x00C0  /* see definitions below for these bits */
#define HIGHIMAGE       0x0000  /* use the user's "select image" */
#define HIGHCOMP        0x0040  /* highlight by complementing the selectbox */
#define HIGHBOX         0x0080  /* highlight by "boxing" the selectbox */
#define HIGHNONE        0x00C0  /* don't highlight */

/* FLAGS SET BY BOTH APPLIPROG AND INTUITION */
#define CHECKED         0x0100  /* if CHECKIT, then set this when selected */

/* FLAGS SET BY INTUITION */
#define ISDRAWN         0x1000  /* this item's subs are currently drawn */
#define HIGHITEM        0x2000  /* this item is currently highlighted */
#define MENUTOGGLED     0x4000  /* this item was already toggled */





/* ======================================================================= */
```

```
/* === Requester ============================================================ */
/* ========================================================================== */
struct Requester
{
    /* the ClipRect and BitMap and used for rendering the requester */
    struct Requester *OlderRequest;
    SHORT LeftEdge, TopEdge;            /* dimensions of the entire box */
    SHORT Width, Height;                /* dimensions of the entire box */
    SHORT RelLeft, RelTop;              /* for Pointer relativity offsets */

    struct Gadget *ReqGadget;           /* pointer to a list of Gadgets */
    struct Border *ReqBorder;           /* the box's border */
    struct IntuiText *ReqText;          /* the box's text */
    USHORT Flags;                       /* see definitions below */

    /* pen number for back-plane fill before draws */
    UBYTE BackFill;
    /* Layer in place of clip rect      */
    struct Layer *ReqLayer;

    UBYTE ReqPad1[32];

    /* If the BitMap plane pointers are non-zero, this tells the system
     * that the image comes pre-drawn (if the appliprog wants to define
     * it's own box, in any shape or size it wants!);  this is OK by
     * Intuition as long as there's a good correspondence between
     * the image and the specified Gadgets
     */
    struct BitMap *ImageBMap;   /* points to the BitMap of PREDRAWN imagery */
    struct Window *RWindow;     /* added.  points back to Window */
    UBYTE ReqPad2[36];
};


/* FLAGS SET BY THE APPLIPROG */
#define POINTREL 0x0001  /* if POINTREL set, TopLeft is relative to pointer*/
#define PREDRAWN 0x0002  /* if ReqBMap points to predrawn Requester imagery */
#define NOISYREQ 0x0004  /* if you don't want requester to filter input    */
/* FLAGS SET BY BOTH THE APPLIPROG AND INTUITION */

/* FLAGS SET BY INTUITION */
#define REQOFFWINDOW      0x1000  /* part of one of the Gadgets was offwindow */
#define REQACTIVE         0x2000  /* this requester is active */
#define SYSREQUEST        0x4000  /* this requester caused by system */
#define DEFERREFRESH      0x8000  /* this Requester stops a Refresh broadcast */





/* ========================================================================== */
/* === Gadget =============================================================== */
/* ========================================================================== */
struct Gadget
{
    struct Gadget *NextGadget;  /* next gadget in the list */

    SHORT LeftEdge, TopEdge;    /* "hit box" of gadget */
    SHORT Width, Height;        /* "hit box" of gadget */

    USHORT Flags;               /* see below for list of defines */

    USHORT Activation;          /* see below for list of defines */

    USHORT GadgetType;          /* see below for defines */

    /* appliprog can specify that the Gadget be rendered as either as Border
     * or an Image.  This variable points to which (or equals NULL if there's
```



```
     * nothing to be rendered about this Gadget)
     */
    APTR GadgetRender;

    /* appliprog can specify "highlighted" imagery rather than algorithmic
     * this can point to either Border or Image data
     */
    APTR SelectRender;

    struct IntuiText *GadgetText;   /* text for this gadget */

    /* by using the MutualExclude word, the appliprog can describe
     * which gadgets mutually-exclude which other ones.  The bits
     * in MutualExclude correspond to the gadgets in object containing
     * the gadget list.  If this gadget is selected and a bit is set
     * in this gadget's MutualExclude and the gadget corresponding to
     * that bit is currently selected (e.g. bit 2 set and gadget 2
     * is currently selected) that gadget must be unselected.
     * Intuition does the visual unselecting (with checkmarks) and
     * leaves it up to the program to unselect internally
     */
    LONG MutualExclude;  /* set bits mean this gadget excludes that gadget */

    /* pointer to a structure of special data required by Proportional,
     * String and Integer Gadgets
     */
    APTR SpecialInfo;

    USHORT GadgetID;        /* user-definable ID field */
    APTR UserData;          /* ptr to general purpose User data (ignored by In) */
};


/* --- FLAGS SET BY THE APPLIPROG ------------------------------------------ */
/* combinations in these bits describe the highlight technique to be used */
#define GADGHIGHBITS        0x0003
#define GADGHCOMP           0x0000  /* Complement the select box */
#define GADGHBOX            0x0001  /* Draw a box around the image */
#define GADGHIMAGE          0x0002  /* Blast in this alternate image */
#define GADGHNONE           0x0003  /* don't highlight */

/* set this flag if the GadgetRender and SelectRender point to Image imagery,
 * clear if it's a Border
 */
#define GADGIMAGE 0x0004

/* combinations in these next two bits specify to which corner the gadget's
 *  Left & Top coordinates are relative.  If relative to Top/Left,
 *  these are "normal" coordinates (everything is relative to something in
 *  this universe)
 */
#define GRELBOTTOM          0x0008  /* set if rel to bottom, clear if rel top */
#define GRELRIGHT           0x0010  /* set if rel to right, clear if to left */
/* set the RELWIDTH bit to spec that Width is relative to width of screen */
#define GRELWIDTH           0x0020
/* set the RELHEIGHT bit to spec that Height is rel to height of screen */
#define GRELHEIGHT          0x0040

/* the SELECTED flag is initialized by you and set by Intuition.  It
 * specifies whether or not this Gadget is currently selected/highlighted
 */
#define SELECTED            0x0080


/* the GADGDISABLED flag is initialized by you and later set by Intuition
 * according to your calls to On/OffGadget().  It specifies whether or not
 * this Gadget is currently disabled from being selected
 */
#define GADGDISABLED        0x0100
```

```


/* --- These are the Activation flag bits ------------------------------- */
/* RELVERIFY is set if you want to verify that the pointer was still over
 *  the gadget when the select button was released
 */
#define RELVERIFY       0x0001

/* the flag GADGIMMEDIATE, when set, informs the caller that the gadget
 *  was activated when it was activated.  this flag works in conjunction with
 *  the RELVERIFY flag
 */
#define GADGIMMEDIATE   0x0002

/* the flag ENDGADGET, when set, tells the system that this gadget, when
 * selected, causes the Requester or AbsMessage to be ended.  Requesters or
 *  AbsMessages that are ended are erased and unlinked from the system */
#define ENDGADGET       0x0004

/* the FOLLOWMOUSE flag, when set, specifies that you want to receive
 * reports on mouse movements (ie, you want the REPORTMOUSE function for
 * your Window).  When the Gadget is deselected (immediately if you have
 * no RELVERIFY) the previous state of the REPORTMOUSE flag is restored
 * You probably want to set the GADGIMMEDIATE flag when using FOLLOWMOUSE,
 * since that's the only reasonable way you have of learning why Intuition
 * is suddenly sending you a stream of mouse movement events.  If you don't
 * set RELVERIFY, you'll get at least one Mouse Position event.
 */
#define FOLLOWMOUSE     0x0008

/* if any of the BORDER flags are set in a Gadget that's included in the
 * Gadget list when a Window is opened, the corresponding Border will
 * be adjusted to make room for the Gadget
 */
#define RIGHTBORDER     0x0010
#define LEFTBORDER      0x0020
#define TOPBORDER       0x0040
#define BOTTOMBORDER    0x0080

#define TOGGLESELECT    0x0100  /* this bit for toggle-select mode */

#define STRINGCENTER    0x0200  /* should be a StringInfo flag, but it's OK */
#define STRINGRIGHT     0x0400  /* should be a StringInfo flag, but it's OK */

#define LONGINT         0x0800  /* this String Gadget is actually LONG Int */

#define ALTKEYMAP       0x1000  /* this String has an alternate keymap */

#define BOOLEXTEND      0x2000  /* this Boolean Gadget has a BoolInfo   */


/* --- GADGET TYPES ------------------------------------------------------- */
/* These are the Gadget Type definitions for the variable GadgetType
 * gadget number type MUST start from one.  NO TYPES OF ZERO ALLOWED.
 * first comes the mask for Gadget flags reserved for Gadget typing
 */
#define GADGETTYPE      0xFC00  /* all Gadget Global Type flags (padded) */
#define SYSGADGET       0x8000  /* 1 = SysGadget, 0 = AppliGadget */
#define SCRGADGET       0x4000  /* 1 = ScreenGadget, 0 = WindowGadget */
#define GZZGADGET       0x2000  /* 1 = Gadget for GIMMEZEROZERO borders */
#define REQGADGET       0x1000  /* 1 = this is a Requester Gadget */
/* system gadgets */
#define SIZING          0x0010
#define WDRAGGING       0x0020
#define SDRAGGING       0x0030
#define WUPFRONT        0x0040
#define SUPFRONT        0x0050
#define WDOWNBACK       0x0060
#define SDOWNBACK       0x0070
```



```
#define CLOSE           0x0080
/* application gadgets */
#define BOOLGADGET      0x0001
#define GADGET0002      0x0002
#define PROPGADGET      0x0003
#define STRGADGET       0x0004


/* ======================================================================= */
/* === BoolInfo======================================================== */
/* ======================================================================= */
/* This is the special data needed by an Extended Boolean Gadget
 * Typically this structure will be pointed to by the Gadget field SpecialInfo
 */
struct BoolInfo
{
    USHORT Flags;       /* defined below */
    UWORD  *Mask;       /* bit mask for highlighting and selecting
                         * mask must follow the same rules as an Image
                         * plane.  It's width and height are determined
                         * by the width and height of the gadget's
                         * select box. (i.e. Gadget.Width and .Height).
                         */
    ULONG  Reserved;    /* set to 0     */
};

/* set BoolInfo.Flags to this flag bit.
 * in the future, additional bits might mean more stuff hanging
 * off of BoolInfo.Reserved.
 */
#define BOOLMASK        0x0001  /* extension is for masked gadget */

/* ======================================================================= */
/* === PropInfo ========================================================== */
/* ======================================================================= */
/* this is the special data required by the proportional Gadget
 * typically, this data will be pointed to by the Gadget variable SpecialInfo
 */
struct PropInfo
{
    USHORT Flags;       /* general purpose flag bits (see defines below) */

    /* You initialize the Pot variables before the Gadget is added to
     * the system.  Then you can look here for the current settings
     * any time, even while User is playing with this Gadget.  To
     * adjust these after the Gadget is added to the System, use
     * ModifyProp();  The Pots are the actual proportional settings,
     * where a value of zero means zero and a value of MAXPOT means
     * that the Gadget is set to its maximum setting.
     */
    USHORT HorizPot;    /* 16-bit FixedPoint horizontal quantity percentage */
    USHORT VertPot;     /* 16-bit FixedPoint vertical quantity percentage */

    /* the 16-bit FixedPoint Body variables describe what percentage of
     * the entire body of stuff referred to by this Gadget is actually
     * shown at one time.  This is used with the AUTOKNOB routines,
     * to adjust the size of the AUTOKNOB according to how much of
     * the data can be seen.  This is also used to decide how far
     * to advance the Pots when User hits the Container of the Gadget.
     * For instance, if you were controlling the display of a 5-line
     * Window of text with this Gadget, and there was a total of 15
     * lines that could be displayed, you would set the VertBody value to
     *     (MAXBODY / (TotalLines / DisplayLines)) = MAXBODY / 3.
     * Therefore, the AUTOKNOB would fill 1/3 of the container, and
     * if User hits the Cotainer outside of the knob, the pot would
     * advance 1/3 (plus or minus) If there's no body to show, or
     * the total amount of displayable info is less than the display area,
     * set the Body variables to the MAX.  To adjust these after the
     * Gadget is added to the System, use ModifyProp();
```

```
     */
    USHORT HorizBody;           /* horizontal Body */
    USHORT VertBody;            /* vertical Body */

    /* these are the variables that Intuition sets and maintains */
    USHORT CWidth;      /* Container width (with any relativity absoluted) */
    USHORT CHeight;     /* Container height (with any relativity absoluted) */
    USHORT HPotRes, VPotRes; /* pot increments */
    USHORT LeftBorder;          /* Container borders */
    USHORT TopBorder;           /* Container borders */
};


/* --- FLAG BITS ---------------------------------------------------------- */
#define AUTOKNOB        0x0001  /* this flag sez:  gimme that old auto-knob */
#define FREEHORIZ       0x0002  /* if set, the knob can move horizontally */
#define FREEVERT        0x0004  /* if set, the knob can move vertically */
#define PROPBORDERLESS  0x0008  /* if set, no border will be rendered */
#define KNOBHIT         0x0100  /* set when this Knob is hit */

#define KNOBHMIN        6       /* minimum horizontal size of the Knob */
#define KNOBVMIN        4       /* minimum vertical size of the Knob */
#define MAXBODY         0xFFFF  /* maximum body value */
#define MAXPOT          0xFFFF  /* maximum pot value */






/* ====================================================================== */
/* === StringInfo ======================================================= */
/* ====================================================================== */
/* this is the special data required by the string Gadget
 * typically, this data will be pointed to by the Gadget variable SpecialInfo
 */
struct StringInfo
{
    /* you initialize these variables, and then Intuition maintains them */
    UBYTE *Buffer;      /* the buffer containing the start and final string */
    UBYTE *UndoBuffer;  /* optional buffer for undoing current entry */
    SHORT BufferPos;    /* character position in Buffer */
    SHORT MaxChars;     /* max number of chars in Buffer (including NULL) */
    SHORT DispPos;      /* Buffer position of first displayed character */

    /* Intuition initializes and maintains these variables for you */
    SHORT UndoPos;      /* character position in the undo buffer */
    SHORT NumChars;     /* number of characters currently in Buffer */
    SHORT DispCount;    /* number of whole characters visible in Container */
    SHORT CLeft, CTop;  /* topleft offset of the container */
    struct Layer *LayerPtr;     /* the RastPort containing this Gadget */

    /* you can initialize this variable before the gadget is submitted to
     * Intuition, and then examine it later to discover what integer
     * the user has entered (if the user never plays with the gadget,
     * the value will be unchanged from your initial setting)
     */
    LONG LongInt;

    /* If you want this Gadget to use your own Console keymapping, you
     * set the ALTKEYMAP bit in the Activation flags of the Gadget, and then
     * set this variable to point to your keymap.  If you don't set the
     * ALTKEYMAP, you'll get the standard ASCII keymapping.
     */
    struct KeyMap *AltKeyMap;
};
```



```
/* ====================================================================== */
/* === IntuiText ======================================================== */
/* ====================================================================== */
/* IntuiText is a series of strings that start with a screen location
 *  (always relative to the upper-left corner of something) and then the
 *  text of the string.  The text is null-terminated.
 */
struct IntuiText
{
    UBYTE FrontPen, BackPen;    /* the pen numbers for the rendering */
    UBYTE DrawMode;             /* the mode for rendering the text */
    SHORT LeftEdge;             /* relative start location for the text */
    SHORT TopEdge;              /* relative start location for the text */
    struct TextAttr *ITextFont; /* if NULL, you accept the default */
    UBYTE *IText;               /* pointer to null-terminated text */
    struct IntuiText *NextText; /* continuation to TxWrite another text */
};






/* ====================================================================== */
/* === Border =========================================================== */
/* ====================================================================== */
/* Data type Border, used for drawing a series of lines which is intended for
 *  use as a border drawing, but which may, in fact, be used to render any
 *  arbitrary vector shape.
 *  The routine DrawBorder sets up the RastPort with the appropriate
 *  variables, then does a Move to the first coordinate, then does Draws
 *  to the subsequent coordinates.
 *  After all the Draws are done, if NextBorder is non-zero we call DrawBorder
 *  recursively
 */
struct Border
{
    SHORT LeftEdge, TopEdge;    /* initial offsets from the origin */
    UBYTE FrontPen, BackPen;    /* pens numbers for rendering */
    UBYTE DrawMode;             /* mode for rendering */
    BYTE Count;                 /* number of XY pairs */
    SHORT *XY;                  /* vector coordinate pairs rel to LeftTop*/
    struct Border *NextBorder;  /* pointer to any other Border too */
};






/* ====================================================================== */
/* === Image ============================================================ */
/* ====================================================================== */
/* This is a brief image structure for very simple transfers of
 * image data to a RastPort
 */
struct Image
{
    SHORT LeftEdge;             /* starting offset relative to some origin */
    SHORT TopEdge;              /* starting offsets relative to some origin */
    SHORT Width;                /* pixel size (though data is word-aligned) */
    SHORT Height, Depth;        /* pixel sizes */
    USHORT *ImageData;          /* pointer to the actual word-aligned bits */

    /* the PlanePick and PlaneOnOff variables work much the same way as the
     * equivalent GELS Bob variables.  It's a space-saving
```

```
     * mechanism for image data.  Rather than defining the image data
     * for every plane of the RastPort, you need define data only
     * for the planes that are not entirely zero or one.  As you
     * define your Imagery, you will often find that most of the planes
     * ARE just as color selectors.  For instance, if you're designing
     * a two-color Gadget to use colors two and three, and the Gadget
     * will reside in a five-plane display, bit plane zero of your
     * imagery would be all ones, bit plane one would have data that
     * describes the imagery, and bit planes two through four would be
     * all zeroes.  Using these flags allows you to avoid wasting all
     * that memory in this way:  first, you specify which planes you
     * want your data to appear in using the PlanePick variable.  For
     * each bit set in the variable, the next "plane" of your image
     * data is blitted to the display.  For each bit clear in this
     * variable, the corresponding bit in PlaneOnOff is examined.
     * If that bit is clear, a "plane" of zeroes will be used.
     * If the bit is set, ones will go out instead.  So, for our example:
     *   Gadget.PlanePick = 0x02;
     *   Gadget.PlaneOnOff = 0x01;
     * Note that this also allows for generic Gadgets, like the
     * System Gadgets, which will work in any number of bit planes.
     * Note also that if you want an Image that is only a filled
     * rectangle, you can get this by setting PlanePick to zero
     * (pick no planes of data) and set PlaneOnOff to describe the pen
     * color of the rectangle.
     */
    UBYTE PlanePick, PlaneOnOff;

    /* if the NextImage variable is not NULL, Intuition presumes that
     * it points to another Image structure with another Image to be
     * rendered
     */
    struct Image *NextImage;
};






/* ====================================================================== */
/* === IntuiMessage ===================================================== */
/* ====================================================================== */
struct IntuiMessage
{
    struct Message ExecMessage;

    /* the Class bits correspond directly with the IDCMP Flags, except for the
     * special bit LONELYMESSAGE (defined below)
     */
    ULONG Class;

    /* the Code field is for special values like MENU number */
    USHORT Code;

    /* the Qualifier field is a copy of the current InputEvent's Qualifier */
    USHORT Qualifier;

    /* IAddress contains particular addresses for Intuition functions, like
     * the pointer to the Gadget or the Screen
     */
    APTR IAddress;

    /* when getting mouse movement reports, any event you get will have the
     * the mouse coordinates in these variables.  the coordinates are relative
     * to the upper-left corner of your Window (GIMMEZEROZERO notwithstanding)
     */
    SHORT MouseX, MouseY;

```



```
    /* the time values are copies of the current system clock time.  Micros
     * are in units of microseconds, Seconds in seconds.
     */
    ULONG Seconds, Micros;

    /* the IDCMPWindow variable will always have the address of the Window of
     * this IDCMP
     */
    struct Window *IDCMPWindow;

    /* system-use variable */
    struct IntuiMessage *SpecialLink;
};


/* --- IDCMP Classes ------------------------------------------------------ */
#define SIZEVERIFY          0x00000001  /*  See the Programmer's Guide  */
#define NEWSIZE             0x00000002  /*  See the Programmer's Guide  */
#define REFRESHWINDOW       0x00000004  /*  See the Programmer's Guide  */
#define MOUSEBUTTONS        0x00000008  /*  See the Programmer's Guide  */
#define MOUSEMOVE           0x00000010  /*  See the Programmer's Guide  */
#define GADGETDOWN          0x00000020  /*  See the Programmer's Guide  */
#define GADGETUP            0x00000040  /*  See the Programmer's Guide  */
#define REQSET              0x00000080  /*  See the Programmer's Guide  */
#define MENUPICK            0x00000100  /*  See the Programmer's Guide  */
#define CLOSEWINDOW         0x00000200  /*  See the Programmer's Guide  */
#define RAWKEY              0x00000400  /*  See the Programmer's Guide  */
#define REQVERIFY           0x00000800  /*  See the Programmer's Guide  */
#define REQCLEAR            0x00001000  /*  See the Programmer's Guide  */
#define MENUVERIFY          0x00002000  /*  See the Programmer's Guide  */
#define NEWPREFS            0x00004000  /*  See the Programmer's Guide  */
#define DISKINSERTED        0x00008000  /*  See the Programmer's Guide  */
#define DISKREMOVED         0x00010000  /*  See the Programmer's Guide  */
#define WBENCHMESSAGE       0x00020000  /*  See the Programmer's Guide  */
#define ACTIVEWINDOW        0x00040000  /*  See the Programmer's Guide  */
#define INACTIVEWINDOW      0x00080000  /*  See the Programmer's Guide  */
#define DELTAMOVE           0x00100000  /*  See the Programmer's Guide  */
#define VANILLAKEY          0x00200000  /*  See the Programmer's Guide  */
#define INTUITICKS          0x00400000  /*  See the Programmer's Guide  */
/* NOTEZ-BIEN:              0x80000000 is reserved for internal use   */

/* the IDCMP Flags do not use this special bit, which is cleared when
 * Intuition sends its special message to the Task, and set when Intuition
 * gets its Message back from the Task.  Therefore, I can check here to
 * find out fast whether or not this Message is available for me to send
 */
#define LONELYMESSAGE   0x80000000


/* --- IDCMP Codes -------------------------------------------------------- */
/* This group of codes is for the MENUVERIFY function */
#define MENUHOT         0x0001  /* IntuiWants verification or MENUCANCEL    */
#define MENUCANCEL      0x0002  /* HOT Reply of this cancels Menu operation */
#define MENUWAITING     0x0003  /* Intuition simply wants a ReplyMsg() ASAP */

/* These are internal tokens to represent state of verification attempts
 * shown here as a clue.
 */
#define OKOK            MENUHOT /* guy didn't care                      */
#define OKABORT         0x0004  /* window rendered question moot        */
#define OKCANCEL        MENUCANCEL /* window sent cancel reply          */

/* This group of codes is for the WBENCHMESSAGE messages */
#define WBENCHOPEN      0x0001
#define WBENCHCLOSE     0x0002



/* ====================================================================== */
```

```
/* === Window =========================================================== */
/* ====================================================================== */
struct Window
{
    struct Window *NextWindow;          /* for the linked list in a screen */

    SHORT LeftEdge, TopEdge;            /* screen dimensions of window */
    SHORT Width, Height;                /* screen dimensions of window */

    SHORT MouseY, MouseX;               /* relative to upper-left of window */

    SHORT MinWidth, MinHeight;          /* minimum sizes */
    USHORT MaxWidth, MaxHeight;         /* maximum sizes */

    ULONG Flags;                        /* see below for defines */

    struct Menu *MenuStrip;             /* the strip of Menu headers */

    UBYTE *Title;                       /* the title text for this window */

    struct Requester *FirstRequest;     /* all active Requesters */

    struct Requester *DMRequest;        /* double-click Requester */

    SHORT ReqCount;                     /* count of reqs blocking Window */

    struct Screen *WScreen;             /* this Window's Screen */
    struct RastPort *RPort;             /* this Window's very own RastPort */

    /* the border variables describe the window border.  If you specify
     * GIMMEZEROZERO when you open the window, then the upper-left of the
     * ClipRect for this window will be upper-left of the BitMap (with correct
     * offsets when in SuperBitMap mode; you MUST select GIMMEZEROZERO when
     * using SuperBitMap).  If you don't specify ZeroZero, then you save
     * memory (no allocation of RastPort, Layer, ClipRect and associated
     * Bitmaps), but you also must offset all your writes by BorderTop,
     * BorderLeft and do your own mini-clipping to prevent writing over the
     * system gadgets
     */
    BYTE BorderLeft, BorderTop, BorderRight, BorderBottom;
    struct RastPort *BorderRPort;


    /* You supply a linked-list of Gadgets for your Window.
     * This list DOES NOT include system gadgets.  You get the standard
     * window system gadgets by setting flag-bits in the variable Flags (see
     * the bit definitions below)
     */
    struct Gadget *FirstGadget;

    /* these are for opening/closing the windows */
    struct Window *Parent, *Descendant;

    /* sprite data information for your own Pointer
     * set these AFTER you Open the Window by calling SetPointer()
     */
    USHORT *Pointer;     /* sprite data */
    BYTE PtrHeight;      /* sprite height (not including sprite padding) */
    BYTE PtrWidth;       /* sprite width (must be less than or equal to 16) */
    BYTE XOffset, YOffset;      /* sprite offsets */

    /* the IDCMP Flags and User's and Intuition's Message Ports */
    ULONG IDCMPFlags;    /* User-selected flags */
    struct MsgPort *UserPort, *WindowPort;
    struct IntuiMessage *MessageKey;

    UBYTE DetailPen, BlockPen;  /* for bar/border/gadget rendering */

    /* the CheckMark is a pointer to the imagery that will be used when
```



```
     * rendering MenuItems of this Window that want to be checkmarked
     * if this is equal to NULL, you'll get the default imagery
     */
    struct Image *CheckMark;

    UBYTE *ScreenTitle; /* if non-null, Screen title when Window is active */

    /* These variables have the mouse coordinates relative to the
     * inner-Window of GIMMEZEROZERO Windows.  This is compared with the
     * MouseX and MouseY variables, which contain the mouse coordinates
     * relative to the upper-left corner of the Window, GIMMEZEROZERO
     * notwithstanding
     */
    SHORT GZZMouseX;
    SHORT GZZMouseY;
    /* these variables contain the width and height of the inner-Window of
     * GIMMEZEROZERO Windows
     */
    SHORT GZZWidth;
    SHORT GZZHeight;

    UBYTE *ExtData;

    BYTE *UserData;     /* general-purpose pointer to User data extension */

    /** jimm: NEW: 11/18/85: this pointer keeps a duplicate of what
     * Window.RPort->Layer is _supposed_ to be pointing at
     */
    struct Layer *WLayer;

    /* jimm: NEW 1.2: need to keep track of the font that
     * OpenWindow opened, in case user SetFont's into RastPort
     */
    struct TextFont *IFont;
};


/* --- FLAGS REQUESTED (NOT DIRECTLY SET THOUGH) BY THE APPLIPROG --------- */
#define WINDOWSIZING    0x0001    /* include sizing system-gadget? */
#define WINDOWDRAG      0x0002    /* include dragging system-gadget? */
#define WINDOWDEPTH     0x0004    /* include depth arrangement gadget? */
#define WINDOWCLOSE     0x0008    /* include close-box system-gadget? */

#define SIZEBRIGHT      0x0010  /* size gadget uses right border */
#define SIZEBBOTTOM     0x0020  /* size gadget uses bottom border */

/* --- refresh modes ------------------------------------------------------ */
/* combinations of the REFRESHBITS select the refresh type */
#define REFRESHBITS     0x00C0
#define SMART_REFRESH   0x0000
#define SIMPLE_REFRESH  0x0040
#define SUPER_BITMAP    0x0080
#define OTHER_REFRESH   0x00C0

#define BACKDROP        0x0100  /* this is an ever-popular BACKDROP window */

#define REPORTMOUSE     0x0200  /* set this to hear about every mouse move */

#define GIMMEZEROZERO   0x0400  /* make extra border stuff */

#define BORDERLESS      0x0800  /* set this to get a Window sans border */

#define ACTIVATE        0x1000  /* when Window opens, it's the Active one */

/* FLAGS SET BY INTUITION */
#define WINDOWACTIVE  0x2000    /* this window is the active one */
#define INREQUEST     0x4000    /* this window is in request mode */
#define MENUSTATE     0x8000    /* this Window is active with its Menus on */
```

```
/* --- Other User Flags ------------------------------------------------- */
#define RMBTRAP          0x00010000       /* Catch RMB events for your own */
#define NOCAREREFRESH    0x00020000       /* not to be bothered with REFRESH */


/* --- Other Intuition Flags -------------------------------------------- */
#define WINDOWREFRESH    0x01000000       /* Window is currently refreshing */
#define WBENCHWINDOW     0x02000000       /* WorkBench tool ONLY Window */
#define WINDOWTICKED     0x04000000       /* only one timer tick at a time */

#define SUPER_UNUSED     0xFCFC0000       /* bits of Flag unused yet */


/* --- see struct IntuiMessage for the IDCMP Flag definitions ------------- */




/* ======================================================================= */
/* === NewWindow ========================================================= */
/* ======================================================================= */
struct NewWindow
{
    SHORT LeftEdge, TopEdge;              /* screen dimensions of window */
    SHORT Width, Height;                  /* screen dimensions of window */

    UBYTE DetailPen, BlockPen;            /* for bar/border/gadget rendering */

    ULONG IDCMPFlags;                     /* User-selected IDCMP flags */

    ULONG Flags;                          /* see Window struct for defines */

    /* You supply a linked-list of Gadgets for your Window.
     *  This list DOES NOT include system Gadgets.  You get the standard
     *  system Window Gadgets by setting flag-bits in the variable Flags (see
     *  the bit definitions under the Window structure definition)
     */
    struct Gadget *FirstGadget;

    /* the CheckMark is a pointer to the imagery that will be used when
     * rendering MenuItems of this Window that want to be checkmarked
     * if this is equal to NULL, you'll get the default imagery
     */
    struct Image *CheckMark;

    UBYTE *Title;                           /* the title text for this window */

    /* the Screen pointer is used only if you've defined a CUSTOMSCREEN and
     * want this Window to open in it.  If so, you pass the address of the
     * Custom Screen structure in this variable.  Otherwise, this variable
     * is ignored and doesn't have to be initialized.
     */
    struct Screen *Screen;

    /* SUPER_BITMAP Window?  If so, put the address of your BitMap structure
     * in this variable.  If not, this variable is ignored and doesn't have
     * to be initialized
     */
    struct BitMap *BitMap;

    /* the values describe the minimum and maximum sizes of your Windows.
     * these matter only if you've chosen the WINDOWSIZING Gadget option,
     * which means that you want to let the User to change the size of
     * this Window.  You describe the minimum and maximum sizes that the
     * Window can grow by setting these variables.  You can initialize
     * any one these to zero, which will mean that you want to duplicate
     * the setting for that dimension (if MinWidth == 0, MinWidth will be
     * set to the opening Width of the Window).
     * You can change these settings later using SetWindowLimits().
```



```
     * If you haven't asked for a SIZING Gadget, you don't have to
     * initialize any of these variables.
     */
    SHORT MinWidth, MinHeight;        /* minimums */
    USHORT MaxWidth, MaxHeight;        /* maximums */

    /* the type variable describes the Screen in which you want this Window to
     * open.  The type value can either be CUSTOMSCREEN or one of the
     * system standard Screen Types such as WBENCHSCREEN.  See the
     * type definitions under the Screen structure
     */
    USHORT Type;
};


#ifndef INTUITION_SCREENS_H
#include "intuition/screens.h"
#endif

#ifndef INTUITION_PREFERENCES_H
#include "intuition/preferences.h"
#endif

/* ======================================================================= */
/* === Remember ========================================================== */
/* ======================================================================= */
/* this structure is used for remembering what memory has been allocated to
 * date by a given routine, so that a premature abort or systematic exit
 * can deallocate memory cleanly, easily, and completely
 */
struct Remember
{
    struct Remember *NextRemember;
    ULONG RememberSize;
    UBYTE *Memory;
};





/* ======================================================================= */
/* === Miscellaneous ===================================================== */
/* ======================================================================= */

/* = MACROS ============================================================== */
#define MENUNUM(n) (n & 0x1F)
#define ITEMNUM(n) ((n >> 5) & 0x003F)
#define SUBNUM(n) ((n >> 11) & 0x001F)

#define SHIFTMENU(n) (n & 0x1F)
#define SHIFTITEM(n) ((n & 0x3F) << 5)
#define SHIFTSUB(n) ((n & 0x1F) << 11)


#define SRBNUM(n)    (0x08 - (n >> 4))  /* SerRWBits -> read bits per char */
#define SWBNUM(n)    (0x08 - (n & 0x0F))/* SerRWBits -> write bits per chr */
#define SSBNUM(n)    (0x01 + (n >> 4))  /* SerStopBuf -> stop bits per chr */
#define SPARNUM(n)   (n >> 4)           /* SerParShk -> parity setting    */
#define SHAKNUM(n)   (n & 0x0F)         /* SerParShk -> handshake mode    */


/* = MENU STUFF ========================================================== */
#define NOMENU 0x001F
#define NOITEM 0x003F
#define NOSUB  0x001F
#define MENUNULL 0xFFFF
```

```
/* = =RJ='s peculiarities ================================================= */
#define FOREVER for(;;)
#define SIGN(x) ( ((x) > 0) - ((x) < 0) )
#define NOT !

/* these defines are for the COMMSEQ and CHECKIT menu stuff.  If CHECKIT,
 * I'll use a generic Width (for all resolutions) for the CheckMark.
 * If COMMSEQ, likewise I'll use this generic stuff
 */
#define CHECKWIDTH      19
#define COMMWIDTH       27
#define LOWCHECKWIDTH   13
#define LOWCOMMWIDTH    16


/* these are the AlertNumber defines.  if you are calling DisplayAlert()
 * the AlertNumber you supply must have the ALERT_TYPE bits set to one
 * of these patterns
 */
#define ALERT_TYPE      0x80000000
#define RECOVERY_ALERT  0x00000000      /* the system can recover from this */
#define DEADEND_ALERT   0x80000000      /* no recovery possible, this is it */


/* When you're defining IntuiText for the Positive and Negative Gadgets
 * created by a call to AutoRequest(), these defines will get you
 * reasonable-looking text.  The only field without a define is the IText
 * field; you decide what text goes with the Gadget
 */
#define AUTOFRONTPEN    0
#define AUTOBACKPEN     1
#define AUTODRAWMODE    JAM2
#define AUTOLEFTEDGE    6
#define AUTOTOPEDGE     3
#define AUTOITEXTFONT   NULL
#define AUTONEXTTEXT    NULL


/* --- RAWMOUSE Codes and Qualifiers (Console OR IDCMP) ------------------- */
#define SELECTUP        (IECODE_LBUTTON | IECODE_UP_PREFIX)
#define SELECTDOWN      (IECODE_LBUTTON)
#define MENUUP          (IECODE_RBUTTON | IECODE_UP_PREFIX)
#define MENUDOWN        (IECODE_RBUTTON)
#define ALTLEFT         (IEQUALIFIER_LALT)
#define ALTRIGHT        (IEQUALIFIER_RALT)
#define AMIGALEFT       (IEQUALIFIER_LCOMMAND)
#define AMIGARIGHT      (IEQUALIFIER_RCOMMAND)
#define AMIGAKEYS       (AMIGALEFT | AMIGARIGHT)

#define CURSORUP        0x4C
#define CURSORLEFT      0x4F
#define CURSORRIGHT     0x4E
#define CURSORDOWN      0x4D
#define KEYCODE_Q       0x10
#define KEYCODE_X       0x32
#define KEYCODE_N       0x36
#define KEYCODE_M       0x37
#define KEYCODE_V       0x34
#define KEYCODE_B       0x35

#endif  /* INTUITION_INTUITION_H */
```



```
#ifndef INTUITION_INTUITIONBASE_H
#define INTUITION_INTUITIONBASE_H
/*
**      $Filename: intuition/intuitionbase.h $
**      $Release: 1.3 $
**
**      the IntuitionBase structure and supporting structures
**
**      (C) Copyright 1985,1986,1987,1988 Commodore-Amiga, Inc.
**          All Rights Reserved
*/

#ifndef EXEC_TYPES_H
#include <exec/types.h>
#endif

#ifndef EXEC_LIBRARIES_H
#include <exec/libraries.h>
#endif

#ifndef INTUITION_INTUITION_H
#include <intuition/intuition.h>
#endif

#ifndef EXEC_INTERRUPTS_H
#include <exec/interrupts.h>
#endif

#ifdef INTUITIONPRIVATE
/* these types and constants are used in the forbidden part of IntuitionBase.
 * see below for an explanation that these are NOT supported for your use.
 * They will certainly change in subsequent releases, and are provided
 * for education, debugging, and information.
 */

/* these are the display modes for which we have corresponding parameter
 *  settings in the config arrays
 */
#define DMODECOUNT      0x0002  /* how many modes there are */
#define HIRESPICK       0x0000
#define LOWRESPICK      0x0001

#define EVENTMAX 10             /* size of event array */

/* these are the system Gadget defines */
#define RESCOUNT        2
#define HIRESGADGET     0
#define LOWRESGADGET    1

#define GADGETCOUNT     8
#define UPFRONTGADGET   0
#define DOWNBACKGADGET  1
#define SIZEGADGET      2
#define CLOSEGADGET     3
#define DRAGGADGET      4
#define SUPFRONTGADGET  5
#define SDOWNBACKGADGET 6
#define SDRAGGADGET     7

/* jimm: 1/10/86: Intuition Locking */
/* Let me say it again: don't even think about using this information
 * in a program.
 */
#define ISTATELOCK      0       /* Intuition() not re-entrant          */
#define LAYERINFOLOCK   1       /* dummy lock used to check protocol   */
#define GADGETSLOCK     2       /* gadget lists, refresh, flags        */
#define LAYERROMLOCK    3       /* (dummy) for lock layerrom           */
#define VIEWLOCK        4       /* access to ViewLord                  */
#define IBASELOCK       5       /* protexts IBase pointers and lists   */
```

```
#define RPLOCK          6       /* use of IBase->RP                       */
#define NUMILOCKS       7

/* ======================================================================= */
/* === Intuition Geometric Primitives ==================================== */
/* ======================================================================= */

struct FatIntuiMessage {
    struct IntuiMessage;
    ULONG  PrevKeys;
    };

struct IBox {
    SHORT Left;
    SHORT Top;
    SHORT Width;
    SHORT Height;
    };

struct Point {
    SHORT X;
    SHORT Y;
    };

struct PenPair {
    UBYTE DetailPen;
    UBYTE BlockPen;
    };

/* ======================================================================= */
/* === Gadget Environments =============================================== */
/* ======================================================================= */

/* environment for a whole list of gadgets. note that information for both
 * layers of a G00 window are included.
 */
struct GListEnv  {
    struct Screen       *ge_Screen;
    struct Window       *ge_Window;
    struct Requester    *ge_Requester;
    struct RastPort     *ge_RastPort;   /* rastport used to render gadget    */
    struct Layer        *ge_Layer;      /* layer for gadget (border, if G00)*/
    struct Layer        *ge_GZZLayer;   /* interior layer for G00 windows    */
    struct PenPair       ge_Pens;       /* pens for rendering gadget         */
    struct IBox          ge_Domain;
                        /* window, screen, requester, rel. to window/screen */
    struct IBox          ge_GZZdims;    /* interior window area              */
    };

/* information for a gadget in its environment. includes relatively
 * correct size, container for propgadgets, correct layer for this gadget,
 * and back pointers to the environment and gadget itself
 */
struct GadgetInfo  {
    struct GListEnv     *gi_Environ;    /* environment for this gadget      */
    struct Gadget       *gi_Gadget;     /* gadget this info is for          */
    struct IBox         gi_Box;         /* actual dimensions of gadget      */
    struct IBox         gi_Container;   /* inner container dimensions       */
    struct Layer        *gi_Layer;      /* correct layer for this gadget    */
    struct IBox         gi_NewKnob;     /* place to draw new slider knob    */
    };
#endif  /* PRIVATE VALUES */

/* ======================================================================= */
/* === IntuitionBase ===================================================== */
/* ======================================================================= */
/*
 * Be sure to protect yourself against someone modifying these data as
 * you look at them.  This is done by calling:
```



```
 *
 * lock = LockIBase(0), which returns a ULONG.  When done call
 * UnlockIBase(lock) where lock is what LockIBase() returned.
 */

struct IntuitionBase
/* IntuitionBase should never be directly modified by programs  */
/* even a little bit, guys/gals; do you hear me?        */
{
    struct Library LibNode;

    struct View ViewLord;

    struct Window *ActiveWindow;
    struct Screen *ActiveScreen;

    /* the FirstScreen variable points to the frontmost Screen.  Screens are
     * then maintained in a front to back order using Screen.NextScreen
     */
    struct Screen *FirstScreen; /* for linked list of all screens */

    ULONG Flags;        /* see definitions below */
    WORD MouseY, MouseX;        /* mouse position relative to View */

    ULONG Seconds;      /* timestamp of most current input event */
    ULONG Micros;       /* timestamp of most current input event */

#ifdef INTUITIONPRIVATE

    /* The following is a snapshot of the "private" part of
     * Intuition's library data.  It is included for educational
     * use and your debugging only.  It is absolutely guaranteed
     * that this structure will change from release to release.
     *
     * So: don't count on any of the values you find here
     *     don't even think about changing any of these fields
     *       (that goes for the "supported" fields above, too).
     *
     * Some work has been done to find the include files
     * that these fields depend on.
     *
     *                  jimm: 9/10/86.
     */

    WORD MinXMouse, MaxXMouse;  /* bounded X position for the mouse */
    WORD MinYMouse, MaxYMouse;  /* bounded Y position for the mouse */

    ULONG StartSecs, StartMicros;       /* measure double clicks */

    /* --------------- base vectors ----------------------------------- */
    /* DO MOVE THESE OFFSETS WITHOUT ADJUSTING EQUATES IN IWORK.ASM
     * this is automatically handled by standalone program offsets.c
     */
    APTR        SysBase;
    struct GfxBase *GfxBase;
    APTR        LayersBase;
    APTR        ConsoleDevice;

    /* --------------- Sprite Pointer --------------------------------- */
    USHORT *APointer;   /* the ActiveGroup pointer sprite definition    */
    BYTE APtrHeight;    /* height of the pointer */
    BYTE APtrWidth;     /* width in pixels of the pointer (<= 16!)      */
    BYTE AXOffset, AYOffset; /* sprite offsets */


    /* ---------------- Menu Rendering and Operation ------------------ */
    USHORT MenuDrawn;   /* menu/item/sub number of current display */
    USHORT MenuSelected;/* menu/item/sub number of selected (and highlights)*/
    USHORT OptionList;                  /* menu selection       */
```

```

    /* this is the work RastPort used for building item and subitem displays
     *  you can never count on it being stable, other than that it is
     *  mostly a copy of the active screen's RastPort.
     */
    struct RastPort MenuRPort;
    struct TmpRas       MenuTmpRas;
    struct ClipRect ItemCRect; /* for the item's screen display */
    struct ClipRect SubCRect; /* for the subitem's screen display */
    struct BitMap IBitMap; /* for the item's planes */
    struct BitMap SBitMap; /* for the subitem's planes */

    /* ---------------- Input Device Interface ------------------------ */
    struct IOStdReq InputRequest;
    struct Interrupt InputInterrupt;

    /* for dynamically allocated input events */
    struct Remember  *EventKey;
    struct InputEvent *IEvents;

    /* for statically "allocated" input events */
#define NUM_IEVENTS 4
    SHORT  EventCount;
    struct InputEvent IEBuffer[NUM_IEVENTS];

    /* ---------------- Active Gadget Information --------------------- */
    struct Gadget *ActiveGadget;
    struct PropInfo *ActivePInfo;
    struct Image *ActiveImage;
    struct GListEnv GadgetEnv;  /* environment of the active gadget     */
    struct GadgetInfo GadgetInfo;/* specific information for active gadget*/
    struct Point KnobOffset;    /* position in knob of mouse when selected*/

    /* ---------------- Verify Functions Support ---------------------- */
    /* hold information about getOK wait(), used for breakVerify() */
    struct Window *getOKWindow;
    struct IntuiMessage *getOKMessage;

    /* ---------------- State Machine --------------------------------- */
    USHORT setWExcept, GadgetReturn, StateReturn;

    /* ----------- Intuition's Rendering for Gadgets, Titles, ... ----- */
    /* This will be allocated on init */
    struct RastPort      *RP;
    struct TmpRas        ITmpRas;
    struct Region *OldClipRegion;       /* locks with RPort */
    struct Point    OldScroll;          /* user's Scroll_X/Y*/

    /* ----------- Frame Rendering for Window Size/Drag -------------- */
    struct IBox IFrame; /* window frame for sizing/dragging     */
    SHORT hthick, vthick;       /* IFrame thickness             */
    VOID   (*frameChange)();    /* function to change IFrame    */
    VOID   (*sizeDrag)();       /* either ISizeWindow or IMoveWindow */
    struct Point FirstPt;       /* point from which s/d started */
    struct Point OldPt;         /* previous point for s/d       */

    /* ---------------- System Gadget Templates ------------------------ */
    struct Gadget *SysGadgets[RESCOUNT][GADGETCOUNT];
    struct Image *CheckImage[RESCOUNT], *AmigaIcon[RESCOUNT];

    /* ---------------- Window Drag Rendering ------------------------- */
#ifdef OLDPATTERN
    USHORT apattern[3], bpattern[4];
#else
    USHORT apattern[8], bpattern[4];
#endif

    /* --- Preferences Section ----------------------------------------------- */
    USHORT *IPointer;   /* the INTUITION pointer default sprite definition */
```



```
    BYTE IPtrHeight;     /* height of the pointer */
    BYTE IPtrWidth;      /* width in pixels of the pointer (<= 16!) */
    BYTE IXOffset, IYOffset; /* sprite offsets */

    LONG DoubleSeconds, DoubleMicros; /* for testing double-click timeout */

    /* ---------------- Border Widths -------------------------------- */
    BYTE WBorLeft[DMODECOUNT];
    BYTE WBorTop[DMODECOUNT];
    BYTE WBorRight[DMODECOUNT];
    BYTE WBorBottom[DMODECOUNT];

    BYTE BarVBorder[DMODECOUNT];
    BYTE BarHBorder[DMODECOUNT];
    BYTE MenuVBorder[DMODECOUNT];
    BYTE MenuHBorder[DMODECOUNT];

    USHORT color0;
    USHORT color1;
    USHORT color2;
    USHORT color3;
    USHORT color17;
    USHORT color18;
    USHORT color19;

    struct TextAttr SysFont;

    /* WARNING:  you can easily wipe out Intuition by modifying this pointer
     * or the Preference data pointed to by this!
     */
    struct Preferences *Preferences;

    /* ----------------- Deferred action queue --------------------- */
    struct DistantEcho *Echoes;

    WORD ViewInitX, ViewInitY;  /* View initial offsets at startup   */

    SHORT CursorDX, CursorDY;   /* for accelerating pointer movement */

    struct KeyMap *KeyMap;      /* for the active String Gadget */

    SHORT MouseYMinimum;        /* magic        */

    SHORT ErrorX, ErrorY;       /* for retaining mouse movement round-off */

    struct timerequest IOExcess;

    SHORT HoldMinYMouse;

    struct MsgPort *WBPort, *iqd_FNKUHDPort;
    struct IntuiMessage WBMessage;
    struct Screen *HitScreen;   /* set by hitUpfront() routine */

    /** jimm:dale: 11/25/85, thought we'd take a chance for glory **/
    struct SimpleSprite *SimpleSprite;
    struct SimpleSprite *AttachedSSprite;
    BOOL        GotSprite1;

    /** jimm: 1/6/86: Intuition contention **/
    struct List                 SemaphoreList;  /* chain of the below */
    struct SignalSemaphore      ISemaphore[NUMILOCKS];

    WORD        MaxDisplayHeight;       /* in interlaced mode: 400 or 512 */
    WORD        MaxDisplayRow;          /* MaxDisplayHeight - 1           */
    WORD        MaxDisplayWidth;        /* copy of GfxBase's NormalDisplayCol */

    ULONG       Reserved[7];    /* cause one never know, do one? */
#endif  /* PRIVATE VALUES */
};
```

```
#endif  /* INTUITION_INTUITIONBASE_H */
```



```
#ifndef INTUITION_PREFERENCES_H
#define INTUITION_PREFERENCES_H
/*
**      $Filename: intuition/preferences.h $
**      $Release: 1.3 $
**
**
**
**      (C) Copyright 1987,1988 Commodore-Amiga, Inc.
**          All Rights Reserved
*/

#ifndef EXEC_TYPES_H
#include "exec/types.h"
#endif

#ifndef DEVICES_TIMER_H
#include "devices/timer.h"
#endif

/* ====================================================================== */
/* === Preferences ====================================================== */
/* ====================================================================== */

/* these are the definitions for the printer configurations */
#define FILENAME_SIZE   30          /* Filename size */

#define POINTERSIZE (1 + 16 + 1) * 2    /* Size of Pointer data buffer */

/* These defines are for the default font size.  These actually describe the
 * height of the defaults fonts.  The default font type is the topaz
 * font, which is a fixed width font that can be used in either
 * eighty-column or sixty-column mode.  The Preferences structure reflects
 * which is currently selected by the value found in the variable FontSize,
 * which may have either of the values defined below.  These values actually
 * are used to select the height of the default font.  By changing the
 * height, the resolution of the font changes as well.
 */
#define TOPAZ_EIGHTY 8
#define TOPAZ_SIXTY 9

struct Preferences
{
    /* the default font height */
    BYTE FontHeight;            /* height for system default font  */

    /* constant describing what's hooked up to the port */
    UBYTE PrinterPort;          /* printer port connection     */

    /* the baud rate of the port */
    USHORT BaudRate;            /* baud rate for the serial port   */

    /* various timing rates */
    struct timeval KeyRptSpeed;     /* repeat speed for keyboard       */
    struct timeval KeyRptDelay;     /* Delay before keys repeat        */
    struct timeval DoubleClick;     /* Interval allowed between clicks */

    /* Intuition Pointer data */
    USHORT PointerMatrix[POINTERSIZE];  /* Definition of pointer sprite    */
    BYTE XOffset;             /* X-Offset for active 'bit'      */
    BYTE YOffset;             /* Y-Offset for active 'bit'      */
    USHORT color17;           /***********************************/
    USHORT color18;           /* Colours for sprite pointer      */
    USHORT color19;           /***********************************/
    USHORT PointerTicks;        /* Sensitivity of the pointer      */

    /* Workbench Screen colors */
    USHORT color0;            /***********************************/
    USHORT color1;            /*  Standard default colours       */
```

```
    USHORT color2;           /*   Used in the Workbench         */
    USHORT color3;           /**********************************/

    /* positioning data for the Intuition View */
    BYTE ViewXOffset;            /* Offset for top lefthand corner  */
    BYTE ViewYOffset;            /* X and Y dimensions             */
    WORD ViewInitX, ViewInitY;       /* View initial offset values      */

    BOOL EnableCLI;          /* CLI availability switch */

    /* printer configurations */
    USHORT PrinterType;          /* printer type                    */
    UBYTE PrinterFilename[FILENAME_SIZE];/* file for printer        */

    /* print format and quality configurations */
    USHORT PrintPitch;           /* print pitch            */
    USHORT PrintQuality;         /* print quality          */
    USHORT PrintSpacing;         /* number of lines per inch    */
    UWORD PrintLeftMargin;       /* left margin in characters       */
    UWORD PrintRightMargin;      /* right margin in characters      */
    USHORT PrintImage;           /* positive or negative        */
    USHORT PrintAspect;          /* horizontal or vertical      */
    USHORT PrintShade;           /* b&w, half-tone, or color    */
    WORD PrintThreshold;         /* darkness ctrl for b/w dumps     */

    /* print paper descriptors */
    USHORT PaperSize;            /* paper size             */
    UWORD PaperLength;           /* paper length in number of lines */
    USHORT PaperType;            /* continuous or single sheet      */

    /* Serial device settings: These are six nibble-fields in three bytes */
    /* (these look a little strange so the defaults will map out to zero) */
    UBYTE   SerRWBits;        /* upper nibble = (8-number of read bits)     */
                              /* lower nibble = (8-number of write bits)    */
    UBYTE   SerStopBuf;       /* upper nibble = (number of stop bits - 1)   */
                              /* lower nibble = (table value for BufSize)   */
    UBYTE   SerParShk;        /* upper nibble = (value for Parity setting)  */
                              /* lower nibble = (value for Handshake mode)  */
    UBYTE   LaceWB;           /* if workbench is to be interlaced       */

    UBYTE   WorkName[FILENAME_SIZE];  /* temp file for printer          */

    BYTE    RowSizeChange;
    BYTE    ColumnSizeChange;

    UWORD   PrintFlags;     /* user preference flags */
    UWORD   PrintMaxWidth;  /* max width of printed picture in 10ths/inch */
    UWORD   PrintMaxHeight; /* max height of printed picture in 10ths/inch */
    UBYTE   PrintDensity;   /* print density */
    UBYTE   PrintXOffset;   /* offset of printed picture in 10ths/inch */

    UWORD   wb_Width;       /* override default workbench width  */
    UWORD   wb_Height;      /* override default workbench height */
    UBYTE   wb_Depth;       /* override default workbench depth  */

    UBYTE   ext_size;       /* extension information -- do not touch! */
                            /* extension size in blocks of 64 bytes */
};


/* Workbench Interlace (use one bit) */
#define LACEWB              0x01
#define LW_RESERVED         1        /* internal use only */

/* PrinterPort */
#define PARALLEL_PRINTER 0x00
#define SERIAL_PRINTER  0x01

/* BaudRate */
```



```
#define BAUD_110    0x00
#define BAUD_300    0x01
#define BAUD_1200   0x02
#define BAUD_2400   0x03
#define BAUD_4800   0x04
#define BAUD_9600   0x05
#define BAUD_19200  0x06
#define BAUD_MIDI   0x07

/* PaperType */
#define FANFOLD     0x00
#define SINGLE      0x80

/* PrintPitch */
#define PICA        0x000
#define ELITE       0x400
#define FINE        0x800

/* PrintQuality */
#define DRAFT       0x000
#define LETTER      0x100

/* PrintSpacing */
#define SIX_LPI     0x000
#define EIGHT_LPI   0x200

/* Print Image */
#define IMAGE_POSITIVE  0x00
#define IMAGE_NEGATIVE  0x01

/* PrintAspect */
#define ASPECT_HORIZ    0x00
#define ASPECT_VERT 0x01

/* PrintShade */
#define SHADE_BW    0x00
#define SHADE_GREYSCALE 0x01
#define SHADE_COLOR 0x02

/* PaperSize */
#define US_LETTER   0x00
#define US_LEGAL    0x10
#define N_TRACTOR   0x20
#define W_TRACTOR   0x30
#define CUSTOM      0x40

/* PrinterType */
#define CUSTOM_NAME     0x00
#define ALPHA_P_101     0x01
#define BROTHER_15XL        0x02
#define CBM_MPS1000     0x03
#define DIAB_630        0x04
#define DIAB_ADV_D25        0x05
#define DIAB_C_150      0x06
#define EPSON           0x07
#define EPSON_JX_80     0x08
#define OKIMATE_20      0x09
#define QUME_LP_20      0x0A
/* new printer entries, 3 October 1985 */
#define HP_LASERJET     0x0B
#define HP_LASERJET_PLUS    0x0C

/* Serial Input Buffer Sizes */
#define SBUF_512        0x00
#define SBUF_1024       0x01
#define SBUF_2048       0x02
#define SBUF_4096       0x03
#define SBUF_8000       0x04
#define SBUF_16000      0x05
```

```
/* Serial Bit Masks */
#define SREAD_BITS  0xF0 /* for SerRWBits   */
#define SWRITE_BITS 0x0F

#define SSTOP_BITS  0xF0 /* for SerStopBuf  */
#define SBUFSIZE_BITS   0x0F

#define SPARITY_BITS    0xF0 /* for SerParShk
#define SHSHAKE_BITS    0x0F

/* Serial Parity (upper nibble, after being shifted by
 * macro SPARNUM() )
 */
#define SPARITY_NONE     0
#define SPARITY_EVEN     1
#define SPARITY_ODD      2

/* Serial Handshake Mode (lower nibble, after masking using
 * macro SHANKNUM() )
 */
#define SHSHAKE_XON      0
#define SHSHAKE_RTS      1
#define SHSHAKE_NONE     2

/* new defines for PrintFlags */

#define CORRECT_RED          0x0001  /* color correct red shades */
#define CORRECT_GREEN        0x0002  /* color correct green shades */
#define CORRECT_BLUE         0x0004  /* color correct blue shades */

#define CENTER_IMAGE         0x0008  /* center image on paper */

#define IGNORE_DIMENSIONS    0x0000 /* ignore max width/height settings */
#define BOUNDED_DIMENSIONS   0x0010  /* use max width/height as boundaries */
#define ABSOLUTE_DIMENSIONS  0x0020  /* use max width/height as absolutes */
#define PIXEL_DIMENSIONS     0x0040  /* use max width/height as prt pixels */
#define MULTIPLY_DIMENSIONS  0x0080 /* use max width/height as multipliers */

#define INTEGER_SCALING      0x0100  /* force integer scaling */

#define ORDERED_DITHERING    0x0000 /* ordered dithering */
#define HALFTONE_DITHERING   0x0200  /* halftone dithering */
#define FLOYD_DITHERING      0x0400 /* Floyd-Steinberg dithering */

#define ANTI_ALIAS           0x0800 /* anti-alias image */
#define GREY_SCALE2          0x1000 /* for use with hi-res monitor */

/* masks used for checking bits */

#define CORRECT_RGB_MASK     (CORRECT_RED|CORRECT_GREEN|CORRECT_BLUE)
#define DIMENSIONS_MASK      (BOUNDED_DIMENSIONS|ABSOLUTE_DIMENSIONS|PIXEL_DIMENS
#define DITHERING_MASK       (HALFTONE_DITHERING|FLOYD_DITHERING)

#endif  /* INTUITION_PREFERENCES_H */
```



```
#ifndef INTUITION_SCREENS_H
#define INTUITION_SCREENS_H
/*
**      $Filename: intuition/screens.h $
**      $Release: 1.3 $
**
**
**
**      (C) Copyright 1987,1988 Commodore-Amiga, Inc.
**          All Rights Reserved
*/

#ifndef EXEC_TYPES_H
#include "exec/types.h"
#endif

#ifndef GRAPHICS_GFX_H
#include "graphics/gfx.h"
#endif

#ifndef GRAPHICS_CLIP_H
#include "graphics/clip.h"
#endif

#ifndef GRAPHICS_VIEW_H
#include "graphics/view.h"
#endif

#ifndef GRAPHICS_RASTPORT_H
#include "graphics/rastport.h"
#endif

#ifndef GRAPHICS_LAYERS_H
#include "graphics/layers.h"
#endif

/* ================================================================ */
/* === Screen ===================================================== */
/* ================================================================ */
struct Screen
{
    struct Screen *NextScreen;          /* linked list of screens */
    struct Window *FirstWindow;         /* linked list Screen's Windows */

    SHORT LeftEdge, TopEdge;            /* parameters of the screen */
    SHORT Width, Height;                /* parameters of the screen */

    SHORT MouseY, MouseX;               /* position relative to upper-left */

    USHORT Flags;                       /* see definitions below */

    UBYTE *Title;                       /* null-terminated Title text */
    UBYTE *DefaultTitle;                /* for Windows without ScreenTitle */

    /* Bar sizes for this Screen and all Window's in this Screen */
    BYTE BarHeight, BarVBorder, BarHBorder, MenuVBorder, MenuHBorder;
    BYTE WBorTop, WBorLeft, WBorRight, WBorBottom;

    struct TextAttr *Font;              /* this screen's default font      */

    /* the display data structures for this Screen */
    struct ViewPort ViewPort;           /* describing the Screen's display */
    struct RastPort RastPort;           /* describing Screen rendering     */
    struct BitMap BitMap;               /* extra copy of RastPort BitMap   */
    struct Layer_Info LayerInfo;        /* each screen gets a LayerInfo    */

    /* You supply a linked-list of Gadgets for your Screen.
     *  This list DOES NOT include system Gadgets.  You get the standard
     *  system Screen Gadgets by default
```

```
     */
    struct Gadget *FirstGadget;

    UBYTE DetailPen, BlockPen;          /* for bar/border/gadget rendering */

    /* the following variable(s) are maintained by Intuition to support the
     * DisplayBeep() color flashing technique
     */
    USHORT SaveColor0;

    /* This layer is for the Screen and Menu bars */
    struct Layer *BarLayer;

    UBYTE *ExtData;

    UBYTE *UserData;    /* general-purpose pointer to User data extension */
};


/* --- FLAGS SET BY INTUITION --------------------------------------------- */
/* The SCREENTYPE bits are reserved for describing various Screen types
 * available under Intuition.
 */
#define SCREENTYPE      0x000F  /* all the screens types available      */
/* --- the definitions for the Screen Type ------------------------------ */
#define WBENCHSCREEN    0x0001  /* Ta Da!  The Workbench                */
#define CUSTOMSCREEN    0x000F  /* for that special look                */

#define SHOWTITLE       0x0010  /* this gets set by a call to ShowTitle() */

#define BEEPING         0x0020  /* set when Screen is beeping           */

#define CUSTOMBITMAP    0x0040  /* if you are supplying your own BitMap */

#define SCREENBEHIND    0x0080  /* if you want your screen to open behind
                                 * already open screens
                                 */
#define SCREENQUIET     0x0100  /* if you do not want Intuition to render
                                 * into your screen (gadgets, title)
                                 */

#define STDSCREENHEIGHT -1      /* supply in NewScreen.Height           */


/* ==================================================================== */
/* === NewScreen ====================================================== */
/* ==================================================================== */
struct NewScreen
{
    SHORT LeftEdge, TopEdge, Width, Height, Depth;  /* screen dimensions */

    UBYTE DetailPen, BlockPen;          /* for bar/border/gadget rendering */

    USHORT ViewModes;               /* the Modes for the ViewPort (and View) */

    USHORT Type;                    /* the Screen type (see defines above) */

    struct TextAttr *Font;          /* this Screen's default text attributes */

    UBYTE *DefaultTitle;            /* the default title for this Screen */

    struct Gadget *Gadgets;         /* your own Gadgets for this Screen */

    /* if you are opening a CUSTOMSCREEN and already have a BitMap
     * that you want used for your Screen, you set the flags CUSTOMBITMAP in
     * the Type field and you set this variable to point to your BitMap
     * structure.  The structure will be copied into your Screen structure,
     * after which you may discard your own BitMap if you want
     */
```



```
    struct BitMap *CustomBitMap;
};

#endif  /* INTUITION_SCREENS_H */
```

```
#ifndef LIBRARIES_CONFIGREGS_H
#define LIBRARIES_CONFIGREGS_H
/*
**      $Filename: libraries/configregs.h $
**      $Release: 1.3 $
**
**      register and bit definitions for expansion boards
**
**      (C) Copyright 1986,1987,1988 Commodore-Amiga, Inc.
**          All Rights Reserved
*/

#ifndef EXEC_TYPES_H
#include "exec/types.h"
#endif  !EXEC_TYPES_H

/*
** Expansion boards are actually organized such that only one nibble per
** word (16 bits) are valid information.  This table is structured
** as LOGICAL information.  This means that it never corresponds
** exactly with a physical implementation.
**
** The expansion space is logically split into two regions:
** a rom portion and a control portion.  The rom portion is
** actually stored in one's complement form (except for the
** er_type field).
*/


struct ExpansionRom {
    UBYTE       er_Type;
    UBYTE       er_Product;
    UBYTE       er_Flags;
    UBYTE       er_Reserved03;
    UWORD       er_Manufacturer;
    ULONG       er_SerialNumber;
    UWORD       er_InitDiagVec;
    UBYTE       er_Reserved0c;
    UBYTE       er_Reserved0d;
    UBYTE       er_Reserved0e;
    UBYTE       er_Reserved0f;
};

struct ExpansionControl {
    UBYTE       ec_Interrupt;           /* interrupt control register */
    UBYTE       ec_Reserved11;
    UBYTE       ec_BaseAddress;         /* set new config address */
    UBYTE       ec_Shutup;              /* don't respond, pass config out */
    UBYTE       ec_Reserved14;
    UBYTE       ec_Reserved15;
    UBYTE       ec_Reserved16;
    UBYTE       ec_Reserved17;
    UBYTE       ec_Reserved18;
    UBYTE       ec_Reserved19;
    UBYTE       ec_Reserved1a;
    UBYTE       ec_Reserved1b;
    UBYTE       ec_Reserved1c;
    UBYTE       ec_Reserved1d;
    UBYTE       ec_Reserved1e;
    UBYTE       ec_Reserved1f;
};

/*
** many of the constants below consist of a triplet of equivalent
** definitions: xxMASK is a bit mask of those bits that matter.
** xxBIT is the starting bit number of the field.  xxSIZE is the
** number of bits that make up the definition.  This method is
** used when the field is larger than one bit.
**
```



```
** If the field is only one bit wide then the xxB_xx and xxF_xx convention
** is used (xxB_xx is the bit number, and xxF_xx is mask of the bit).
*/

/* manifest constants */
#define E_SLOTSIZE              0x10000
#define E_SLOTMASK              0xffff
#define E_SLOTSHIFT             16

/* these define the two free regions of Zorro memory space.
** THESE MAY WELL CHANGE FOR FUTURE PRODUCTS!
*/
#define E_EXPANSIONBASE         0xe80000
#define E_EXPANSIONSIZE         0x080000
#define E_EXPANSIONSLOTS        8

#define E_MEMORYBASE            0x200000
#define E_MEMORYSIZE            0x800000
#define E_MEMORYSLOTS           128



/****** ec_Type definitions */

/* board type -- ignore "old style" boards */
#define ERT_TYPEMASK            0xc0
#define ERT_TYPEBIT             6
#define ERT_TYPESIZE            2
#define ERT_NEWBOARD            0xc0


/* type field memory size */
#define ERT_MEMMASK             0x07
#define ERT_MEMBIT              0
#define ERT_MEMSIZE             3


/* other bits defined in type field */
#define ERTB_CHAINEDCONFIG      3
#define ERTB_DIAGVALID          4
#define ERTB_MEMLIST            5

#define ERTF_CHAINEDCONFIG      (1<<3)
#define ERTF_DIAGVALID          (1<<4)
#define ERTF_MEMLIST            (1<<5)


/* er_Flags byte -- for those things that didn't fit into the type byte */
#define ERFB_MEMSPACE           7       /* wants to be in 8 meg space.  Also
                                        ** implies that board is moveable
                                        */
#define ERFB_NOSHUTUP           6       /* board can't be shut up.  Must not
                                        ** be a board.  Must be a box that
                                        ** does not pass on the bus.
                                        */

#define ERFF_MEMSPACE           (1<<7)
#define ERFF_NOSHUTUP           (1<<6)


/* figure out amount of memory needed by this box/board */
#define ERT_MEMNEEDED(t)        \
        (((t)&ERT_MEMMASK)? 0x10000 << (((t)&ERT_MEMMASK) -1) : 0x800000 )

/* same as ERT_MEMNEEDED, but return number of slots */
#define ERT_SLOTSNEEDED(t)      \
        (((t)&ERT_MEMMASK)? 1 << (((t)&ERT_MEMMASK)-1) : 0x80 )

/* interrupt control register */
```

```
#define ECIB_INTENA             1
#define ECIB_RESET              3
#define ECIB_INT2PEND           4
#define ECIB_INT6PEND           5
#define ECIB_INT7PEND           6
#define ECIB_INTERRUPTING       7

#define ECIF_INTENA             (1<<1)
#define ECIF_RESET              (1<<3)
#define ECIF_INT2PEND           (1<<4)
#define ECIF_INT6PEND           (1<<5)
#define ECIF_INT7PEND           (1<<6)
#define ECIF_INTERRUPTING       (1<<7)


/* convert a expantion slot number into a memory address */
#define EC_MEMADDR(slot)                ((slot) << (E_SLOTSHIFT) )

/* a kludge to get the byte offset of a structure */
#define EROFFSET(er)    ((int)&((struct ExpansionRom *)0)->er)
#define ECOFFSET(ec)    \
 (sizeof(struct ExpansionRom)+((int)&((struct ExpansionControl *)0)->ec))


/***************************************************************************
**
** these are the specifications for the diagnostic area.  If the Diagnostic
** Address Valid bit is set in the Board Type byte (the first byte in
** expansion space) then the Diag Init vector contains a valid offset.
**
** The Diag Init vector is actually a word offset from the base of the
** board.  The resulting address points to the base of the DiagArea
** structure.  The structure may be physically implemented either four,
** eight, or sixteen bits wide.  The code will be copied out into
** ram first before being called.
**
** The da_Size field, and both code offsets (da_DiagPoint and da_BootPoint)
** are offsets from the diag area AFTER it has been copied into ram, and
** "de-nibbleized" (if needed).  Inotherwords, the size is the size of
** the actual information, not how much address space is required to
** store it.
**
** All bits are encoded with uninverted logic (e.g. 5 volts on the bus
** is a logic one).
**
** If your board is to make use of the boot facility then it must leave
** its config area available even after it has been configured.  Your
** boot vector will be called AFTER your board's final address has been
** set.
**
***************************************************************************/

struct DiagArea {
    UBYTE       da_Config;      /* see below for definitions */
    UBYTE       da_Flags;       /* see below for definitions */
    UWORD       da_Size;        /* the size (in bytes) of the total diag area */
    UWORD       da_DiagPoint;   /* where to start for diagnostics, or zero */
    UWORD       da_BootPoint;   /* where to start for booting */
    UWORD       da_Name;        /* offset in diag area where a string */
                                /*   identifier can be found (or zero if no */
                                /*   identifier is present). */

    UWORD       da_Reserved01;  /* two words of reserved data.  must be zero. */
    UWORD       da_Reserved02;
};

/* da_Config definitions */
#define DAC_BUSWIDTH    0xC0    /* two bits for bus width */
#define DAC_NIBBLEWIDE  0x00
```



```
#define DAC_BYTEWIDE    0x40
#define DAC_WORDWIDE    0x80

#define DAC_BOOTTIME    0x30    /* two bits for when to boot */
#define DAC_NEVER       0x00    /* obvious */
#define DAC_CONFIGTIME  0x10    /* call da_BootPoint when first configing the */
                                /*   the device */
#define DAC_BINDTIME    0x20    /* run when binding drivers to boards */

/*
** These are the calling conventions for Diag or Boot area
**
** A7 -- points to at least 2K of stack
** A6 -- ExecBase
** A5 -- ExpansionBase
** A3 -- your board's ConfigDev structure
** A2 -- Base of diag/init area that was copied
** A0 -- Base of your board
**
** Your board should return a value in D0.  If this value is NULL, then
** the diag/init area that was copied in will be returned to the free
** memory pool.
*/

#endif  /* LIBRARIES_CONFIGREGS_H */
```

```
#ifndef LIBRARIES_CONFIGVARS_H
#define LIBRARIES_CONFIGVARS_H
/*
**      $Filename: libraries/configvars.h $
**      $Release: 1.3 $
**
**      software structures for configuration subsystem
**
**      (C) Copyright 1986,1987,1988 Commodore-Amiga, Inc.
**          All Rights Reserved
*/

#ifndef EXEC_TYPES_H
#include "exec/types.h"
#endif  !EXEC_TYPES_H

#ifndef EXEC_NODES_H
#include "exec/nodes.h"
#endif !EXEC_NODES_H

#ifndef LIBRARIES_CONFIGREGS_H
#include "libraries/configregs.h"
#endif !LIBRARIES_CONFIGREGS_H


struct ConfigDev {
    struct Node          cd_Node;
    UBYTE                cd_Flags;
    UBYTE                cd_Pad;
    struct ExpansionRom  cd_Rom;         /* image of expansion rom area */
    APTR                 cd_BoardAddr;   /* where in memory the board is */
    APTR                 cd_BoardSize;   /* size in bytes */
    UWORD                cd_SlotAddr;    /* which slot number */
    UWORD                cd_SlotSize;    /* number of slots the board takes */
    APTR                 cd_Driver;      /* pointer to node of driver */
    struct ConfigDev *   cd_NextCD;      /* linked list of drivers to config */
    ULONG                cd_Unused[4];   /* for whatever the driver whats */
};

/* cd_Flags */
#define CDB_SHUTUP      0       /* this board has been shut up */
#define CDB_CONFIGME    1       /* this board needs a driver to claim it */

#define CDF_SHUTUP      0x01
#define CDF_CONFIGME    0x02

/* this structure is used by GetCurrentBinding() and SetCurrentBinding() */
struct CurrentBinding {
    struct ConfigDev *  cb_ConfigDev;         /* first configdev in chain */
    UBYTE *             cb_FileName;          /* file name of driver */
    UBYTE *             cb_ProductString;     /* product # string */
    UBYTE **            cb_ToolTypes;         /* tooltypes from disk object */
};


struct ConfigDev *AllocConfigDev(), *FindConfigDev();

#endif  /* LIBRARIES_CONFIGVARS_H */
```



```
#ifndef LIBRARIES_DISKFONT_H
#define LIBRARIES_DISKFONT_H
/*
**      $Filename: libraries/diskfont.h $
**      $Release: 1.3 $
**
**      diskfont library definitions
**
**      (C) Copyright 1985,1986,1987,1988 Commodore-Amiga, Inc.
**          All Rights Reserved
*/

#ifndef     EXEC_NODES_H
#include "exec/nodes.h"
#endif
#ifndef     EXEC_LISTS_H
#include "exec/lists.h"
#endif
#ifndef     GRAPHICS_TEXT_H
#include "graphics/text.h"
#endif

#define     MAXFONTPATH 256   /* including null terminator */

struct FontContents {
   char  fc_FileName[MAXFONTPATH];
   UWORD fc_YSize;
   UBYTE fc_Style;
   UBYTE fc_Flags;
};

#define     FCH_ID      0x0f00

struct FontContentsHeader {
   UWORD fch_FileID; /* FCH_ID */
   UWORD fch_NumEntries;   /* the number of FontContents elements */
    /*   struct FontContents fch_FC[]; */
};

#define     DFH_ID      0x0f80
#define     MAXFONTNAME 32 /* font name including ".font\0" */

struct DiskFontHeader {
    /* the following 8 bytes are not actually considered a part of the */
    /* DiskFontHeader, but immediately preceed it. The NextSegment is  */
    /* supplied by the linker/loader, and the ReturnCode is the code   */
    /* at the beginning of the font in case someone runs it...         */
    /*   ULONG dfh_NextSegment;/* actually a BPTR */
    /*   ULONG dfh_ReturnCode;   /* MOVEQ #0,D0 : RTS */
    /* here then is the official start of the DiskFontHeader...       */
   struct   Node dfh_DF;   /* node to link disk fonts */
   UWORD dfh_FileID; /* DFH_ID */
   UWORD dfh_Revision;  /* the font revision */
   LONG  dfh_Segment;   /* the segment address when loaded */
   char  dfh_Name[MAXFONTNAME];  /* the font name (null terminated) */
   struct   TextFont dfh_TF;/* loaded TextFont structure */
};


#define     AFB_MEMORY  0
#define     AFF_MEMORY  1
#define     AFB_DISK 1
#define     AFF_DISK 2

struct AvailFonts {
   UWORD af_Type;     /* MEMORY or DISK */
   struct   TextAttr af_Attr; /* text attributes for font */
};
```

```
struct AvailFontsHeader {
   UWORD afh_NumEntries;      /* number of AvailFonts elements */
   /*   struct   AvailFonts afh_AF[]; */
};

#endif  /* LIBRARIES_DISKFONT_H */
```



```
#ifndef LIBRARIES_DOS_H
#define LIBRARIES_DOS_H
/*
**      $Filename: libraries/dos.h $
**      $Release: 1.3 $
**
**      Standard C header for AmigaDOS
**
**      (C) Copyright 1985,1986,1987,1988 Commodore-Amiga, Inc.
**          All Rights Reserved
*/

#ifndef EXEC_TYPES_H
#include "exec/types.h"
#endif

#define  DOSNAME  "dos.library"

/* Predefined Amiga DOS global constants */

#define DOSTRUE (-1L)
#define DOSFALSE (0L)

/* Mode parameter to Open() */
#define MODE_OLDFILE          1005   /* Open existing file read/write
                                      * positioned at beginning of file. */
#define MODE_NEWFILE          1006   /* Open freshly created file (delete
                                      * old file) read/write            */
#define MODE_READWRITE        1004   /* Open old file w/exclusive lock */
/* Relative position to Seek() */
#define OFFSET_BEGINNING    -1       /* relative to Begining Of File */
#define OFFSET_CURRENT       0       /* relative to Current file position */
#define OFFSET_END           1       /* relative to End Of File    */

#define OFFSET_BEGINING     OFFSET_BEGINNING  /* ancient compatibility */

#define BITSPERBYTE          8
#define BYTESPERLONG         4
#define BITSPERLONG          32
#define MAXINT               0x7FFFFFFF
#define MININT               0x80000000

/* Passed as type to Lock() */
#define SHARED_LOCK          -2     /* File is readable by others */
#define ACCESS_READ          -2     /* Synonym */
#define EXCLUSIVE_LOCK       -1     /* No other access allowed    */
#define ACCESS_WRITE         -1     /* Synonym */

struct DateStamp {
   LONG  ds_Days;                /* Number of days since Jan. 1, 1978 */
   LONG  ds_Minute;              /* Number of minutes past midnight */
   LONG  ds_Tick;                /* Number of ticks past minute */
}; /* DateStamp */
#define TICKS_PER_SECOND      50   /* Number of ticks in one second */

/* Returned by Examine() and ExInfo(), must be on a 4 byte boundary */
struct FileInfoBlock {
   LONG   fib_DiskKey;
   LONG   fib_DirEntryType;  /* Type of Directory. If < 0, then a plain file.
                              * If > 0 a directory */
   char   fib_FileName[108]; /* Null terminated. Max 30 chars used for now */
   LONG   fib_Protection;    /* bit mask of protection, rwxd are 3-0.      */
   LONG   fib_EntryType;
   LONG   fib_Size;          /* Number of bytes in file */
   LONG   fib_NumBlocks;     /* Number of blocks in file */
   struct DateStamp fib_Date;/* Date file last changed */
   char   fib_Comment[80];  /* Null terminated comment associated with file */
   char   fib_Reserved[36];
}; /* FileInfoBlock */
```

```
/* FIB stands for FileInfoBlock */

/* FIBB are bit definitions, FIBF are field definitions */
#define FIBB_SCRIPT    6         /* program is a script (execute) file */
#define FIBB_PURE      5         /* program is reentrant and rexecutable*/
#define FIBB_ARCHIVE   4                 /* cleared whenever file is changed */
#define FIBB_READ      3                 /* ignored by old filesystem */
#define FIBB_WRITE     2                 /* ignored by old filesystem */
#define FIBB_EXECUTE   1                 /* ignored by system, used by Shell */
#define FIBB_DELETE    0                 /* prevent file from being deleted */
#define FIBF_SCRIPT    (1<<FIBB_SCRIPT)
#define FIBF_PURE      (1<<FIBB_PURE)
#define FIBF_ARCHIVE   (1<<FIBB_ARCHIVE)
#define FIBF_READ      (1<<FIBB_READ)
#define FIBF_WRITE     (1<<FIBB_WRITE)
#define FIBF_EXECUTE   (1<<FIBB_EXECUTE)
#define FIBF_DELETE    (1<<FIBB_DELETE)


/* All BCPL data must be long word aligned.  BCPL pointers are the long word
 *  address (i.e byte address divided by 4 (>>2)) */
typedef long  BPTR;                   /* Long word pointer */
typedef long  BSTR;                   /* Long word pointer to BCPL string  */

/* Convert BPTR to typical C pointer */
#ifdef OBSOLETE_LIBRARIES_DOS_H
#define BADDR( bptr )    (((ULONG)bptr) << 2)
#else
/* This one has no problems with CASTing */
#define BADDR(x)         ((APTR)((ULONG)x << 2))
#endif

/* BCPL strings have a length in the first byte and then the characters.
 * For example:  s[0]=3 s[1]=S s[2]=Y s[3]=S                          */

/* returned by Info(), must be on a 4 byte boundary */
struct InfoData {
   LONG   id_NumSoftErrors;     /* number of soft errors on disk */
   LONG   id_UnitNumber;        /* Which unit disk is (was) mounted on */
   LONG   id_DiskState;         /* See defines below */
   LONG   id_NumBlocks;         /* Number of blocks on disk */
   LONG   id_NumBlocksUsed;     /* Number of block in use */
   LONG   id_BytesPerBlock;
   LONG   id_DiskType;          /* Disk Type code */
   BPTR   id_VolumeNode;        /* BCPL pointer to volume node */
   LONG   id_InUse;             /* Flag, zero if not in use */
}; /* InfoData */

/* ID stands for InfoData */
        /* Disk states */
#define ID_WRITE_PROTECTED 80    /* Disk is write protected */
#define ID_VALIDATING      81    /* Disk is currently being validated */
#define ID_VALIDATED       82    /* Disk is consistent and writeable */

        /* Disk types */
#define ID_NO_DISK_PRESENT      (-1)
#define ID_UNREADABLE_DISK      (('B'<<24) | ('A'<<16) | ('D'<<8))
#define ID_DOS_DISK             (('D'<<24) | ('O'<<16) | ('S'<<8))
#define ID_NOT_REALLY_DOS       (('N'<<24) | ('D'<<16) | ('O'<<8) | ('S'))
#define ID_KICKSTART_DISK       (('K'<<24) | ('I'<<16) | ('C'<<8) | ('K'))

/* Errors from IoErr(), etc. */
#define ERROR_NO_FREE_STORE               103
#define ERROR_TASK_TABLE_FULL             105
#define ERROR_LINE_TOO_LONG               120
#define ERROR_FILE_NOT_OBJECT             121
#define ERROR_INVALID_RESIDENT_LIBRARY    122
#define ERROR_NO_DEFAULT_DIR              201
```



```
#define ERROR_OBJECT_IN_USE                 202
#define ERROR_OBJECT_EXISTS                 203
#define ERROR_DIR_NOT_FOUND                 204
#define ERROR_OBJECT_NOT_FOUND              205
#define ERROR_BAD_STREAM_NAME               206
#define ERROR_OBJECT_TOO_LARGE              207
#define ERROR_ACTION_NOT_KNOWN              209
#define ERROR_INVALID_COMPONENT_NAME        210
#define ERROR_INVALID_LOCK                  211
#define ERROR_OBJECT_WRONG_TYPE             212
#define ERROR_DISK_NOT_VALIDATED            213
#define ERROR_DISK_WRITE_PROTECTED          214
#define ERROR_RENAME_ACROSS_DEVICES         215
#define ERROR_DIRECTORY_NOT_EMPTY           216
#define ERROR_TOO_MANY_LEVELS               217
#define ERROR_DEVICE_NOT_MOUNTED            218
#define ERROR_SEEK_ERROR                    219
#define ERROR_COMMENT_TOO_BIG               220
#define ERROR_DISK_FULL                     221
#define ERROR_DELETE_PROTECTED              222
#define ERROR_WRITE_PROTECTED               223
#define ERROR_READ_PROTECTED                224
#define ERROR_NOT_A_DOS_DISK                225
#define ERROR_NO_DISK                       226
#define ERROR_NO_MORE_ENTRIES               232

/* These are the return codes used by convention by AmigaDOS commands */
/* See FAILAT and IF for relvance to EXECUTE files                    */
#define RETURN_OK                            0  /* No problems, success */
#define RETURN_WARN                          5  /* A warning only */
#define RETURN_ERROR                        10  /* Something wrong */
#define RETURN_FAIL                         20  /* Complete or severe failure*/

/* Bit numbers that signal you that a user has issued a break */
#define SIGBREAKB_CTRL_C   12
#define SIGBREAKB_CTRL_D   13
#define SIGBREAKB_CTRL_E   14
#define SIGBREAKB_CTRL_F   15

/* Bit fields that signal you that a user has issued a break */
/* for example:  if (SetSignal(0,0) & BREAK_CTRL_CF) cleanup_and_exit(); */
#define SIGBREAKF_CTRL_C   (1<<SIGBREAKB_CTRL_C)
#define SIGBREAKF_CTRL_D   (1<<SIGBREAKB_CTRL_D)
#define SIGBREAKF_CTRL_E   (1<<SIGBREAKB_CTRL_E)
#define SIGBREAKF_CTRL_F   (1<<SIGBREAKB_CTRL_F)

#endif  /* LIBRARIES_DOS_H */
```

```
#ifndef LIBRARIES_DOSEXTENS_H
#define LIBRARIES_DOSEXTENS_H
/*
**      $Filename: libraries/dosextens.h $
**      $Release: 1.3 $
**
**      DOS structures not needed for the casual AmigaDOS user
**
**      (C) Copyright 1985,1986,1987,1988 Commodore-Amiga, Inc.
**          All Rights Reserved
*/

#ifndef EXEC_TYPES_H
#include "exec/types.h"
#endif
#ifndef EXEC_TASKS_H
#include "exec/tasks.h"
#endif
#ifndef EXEC_PORTS_H
#include "exec/ports.h"
#endif
#ifndef EXEC_LIBRARIES_H
#include "exec/libraries.h"
#endif

#ifndef LIBRARIES_DOS_H
#include "libraries/dos.h"
#endif

/* All DOS processes have this structure */
/* Create and Device Proc returns pointer to the MsgPort in this structure */
/* dev_proc = (struct Process *) (DeviceProc(..) - sizeof(struct Task)); */

struct Process {
    struct  Task    pr_Task;
    struct  MsgPort pr_MsgPort; /* This is BPTR address from DOS functions  */
    WORD    pr_Pad;             /* Remaining variables on 4 byte boundaries */
    BPTR    pr_SegList;         /* Array of seg lists used by this process  */
    LONG    pr_StackSize;       /* Size of process stack in bytes           */
    APTR    pr_GlobVec;         /* Global vector for this process (BCPL)    */
    LONG    pr_TaskNum;         /* CLI task number of zero if not a CLI     */
    BPTR    pr_StackBase;       /* Ptr to high memory end of process stack  */
    LONG    pr_Result2;         /* Value of secondary result from last call */
    BPTR    pr_CurrentDir;      /* Lock associated with current directory   */
    BPTR    pr_CIS;             /* Current CLI Input Stream                 */
    BPTR    pr_COS;             /* Current CLI Output Stream                */
    APTR    pr_ConsoleTask;     /* Console handler process for current window*/
    APTR    pr_FileSystemTask;  /* File handler process for current drive   */
    BPTR    pr_CLI;             /* pointer to ConsoleLineInterpreter        */
    APTR    pr_ReturnAddr;      /* pointer to previous stack frame          */
    APTR    pr_PktWait;         /* Function to be called when awaiting msg  */
    APTR    pr_WindowPtr;       /* Window for error printing */
};  /* Process */

/* The long word address (BPTR) of this structure is returned by
 * Open() and other routines that return a file.  You need only worry
 * about this struct to do async io's via PutMsg() instead of
 * standard file system calls */

struct FileHandle {
   struct Message *fh_Link;      /* EXEC message              */
   struct MsgPort *fh_Port;      /* Reply port for the packet */
   struct MsgPort *fh_Type;      /* Port to do PutMsg() to
                                  * Address is negative if a plain file */
   LONG fh_Buf;
   LONG fh_Pos;
   LONG fh_End;
   LONG fh_Funcs;
#define fh_Func1 fh_Funcs
```



```
   LONG fh_Func2;
   LONG fh_Func3;
   LONG fh_Args;
#define fh_Arg1 fh_Args
   LONG fh_Arg2;
}; /* FileHandle */

/* This is the extension to EXEC Messages used by DOS */

struct DosPacket {
   struct Message *dp_Link;      /* EXEC message              */
   struct MsgPort *dp_Port;      /* Reply port for the packet */
                                 /* Must be filled in each send. */
   LONG dp_Type;                 /* See ACTION_... below and
                                  * 'R' means Read, 'W' means Write to the
                                  * file system */
   LONG dp_Res1;                 /* For file system calls this is the result
                                  * that would have been returned by the
                                  * function, e.g. Write ('W') returns actual
                                  * length written */
   LONG dp_Res2;                 /* For file system calls this is what would
                                  * have been returned by IoErr() */
/*  Device packets common equivalents */
#define dp_Action  dp_Type
#define dp_Status  dp_Res1
#define dp_Status2 dp_Res2
#define dp_BufAddr dp_Arg1
   LONG dp_Arg1;
   LONG dp_Arg2;
   LONG dp_Arg3;
   LONG dp_Arg4;
   LONG dp_Arg5;
   LONG dp_Arg6;
   LONG dp_Arg7;
}; /* DosPacket */

/* A Packet does not require the Message to be before it in memory, but
 * for convenience it is useful to associate the two.
 * Also see the function init_std_pkt for initializing this structure */

struct StandardPacket {
   struct Message   sp_Msg;
   struct DosPacket sp_Pkt;
}; /* StandardPacket */

/* Packet types */
#define ACTION_NIL              0
#define ACTION_GET_BLOCK        2       /* OBSOLETE */
#define ACTION_SET_MAP          4
#define ACTION_DIE              5
#define ACTION_EVENT            6
#define ACTION_CURRENT_VOLUME   7
#define ACTION_LOCATE_OBJECT    8
#define ACTION_RENAME_DISK      9
#define ACTION_WRITE            'W'
#define ACTION_READ             'R'
#define ACTION_FREE_LOCK        15
#define ACTION_DELETE_OBJECT    16
#define ACTION_RENAME_OBJECT    17
#define ACTION_MORE_CACHE       18
#define ACTION_COPY_DIR         19
#define ACTION_WAIT_CHAR        20
#define ACTION_SET_PROTECT      21
#define ACTION_CREATE_DIR       22
#define ACTION_EXAMINE_OBJECT   23
#define ACTION_EXAMINE_NEXT     24
#define ACTION_DISK_INFO        25
#define ACTION_INFO             26
#define ACTION_FLUSH            27
```

```
#define ACTION_SET_COMMENT      28
#define ACTION_PARENT           29
#define ACTION_TIMER            30
#define ACTION_INHIBIT          31
#define ACTION_DISK_TYPE        32
#define ACTION_DISK_CHANGE      33
#define ACTION_SET_DATE         34

#define ACTION_SCREEN_MODE      994

#define ACTION_READ_RETURN      1001
#define ACTION_WRITE_RETURN     1002
#define ACTION_SEEK             1008
#define ACTION_FINDUPDATE       1004
#define ACTION_FINDINPUT        1005
#define ACTION_FINDOUTPUT       1006
#define ACTION_END              1007
#define ACTION_TRUNCATE         1022    /* fast file system only */
#define ACTION_WRITE_PROTECT    1023    /* fast file system only */

/* DOS library node structure.
 * This is the data at positive offsets from the library node.
 * Negative offsets from the node is the jump table to DOS functions
 * node = (struct DosLibrary *) OpenLibrary( "dos.library" .. )      */

struct DosLibrary {
    struct  Library dl_lib;
    APTR    dl_Root;            /* Pointer to RootNode, described below */
    APTR    dl_GV;              /* Pointer to BCPL global vector        */
    LONG    dl_A2;              /* Private register dump of DOS         */
    LONG    dl_A5;
    LONG    dl_A6;
};  /*  DosLibrary */

/*                                  */

struct RootNode {
    BPTR    rn_TaskArray;               /* [0] is max number of CLI's
                                         * [1] is APTR to process id of CLI 1
                                         * [n] is APTR to process id of CLI n */
    BPTR    rn_ConsoleSegment; /* SegList for the CLI                          */
    struct  DateStamp rn_Time; /* Current time                                 */
    LONG    rn_RestartSeg;     /* SegList for the disk validator process       */
    BPTR    rn_Info;           /* Pointer ot the Info structure                */
    BPTR    rn_FileHandlerSegment; /* segment for a file handler               */
};  /* RootNode */

struct DosInfo {
    BPTR    di_McName;          /* Network name of this machine; currently 0 */
    BPTR    di_DevInfo;         /* Device List                               */
    BPTR    di_Devices;         /* Currently zero                            */
    BPTR    di_Handlers;        /* Currently zero                            */
    APTR    di_NetHand;         /* Network handler processid; currently zero */
};  /* DosInfo */

/* DOS Processes started from the CLI via RUN or NEWCLI have this additional
 * set to data associated with them */

struct CommandLineInterface {
    LONG    cli_Result2;        /* Value of IoErr from last command        */
    BSTR    cli_SetName;        /* Name of current directory               */
    BPTR    cli_CommandDir;     /* Lock associated with command directory  */
    LONG    cli_ReturnCode;     /* Return code from last command           */
    BSTR    cli_CommandName;    /* Name of current command                 */
    LONG    cli_FailLevel;      /* Fail level (set by FAILAT)              */
    BSTR    cli_Prompt;         /* Current prompt (set by PROMPT)          */
    BPTR    cli_StandardInput;  /* Default (terminal) CLI input            */
    BPTR    cli_CurrentInput;   /* Current CLI input                       */
    BSTR    cli_CommandFile;    /* Name of EXECUTE command file            */
```



```
    LONG    cli_Interactive;    /* Boolean; True if prompts required       */
    LONG    cli_Background;     /* Boolean; True if CLI created by RUN     */
    BPTR    cli_CurrentOutput;  /* Current CLI output                      */
    LONG    cli_DefaultStack;   /* Stack size to be obtained in long words */
    BPTR    cli_StandardOutput; /* Default (terminal) CLI output           */
    BPTR    cli_Module;         /* SegList of currently loaded command     */
};  /* CommandLineInterface */

/* This structure can take on different values depending on whether it is
 * a device, an assigned directory, or a volume.  Below is the structure
 * reflecting volumes only.  Following that is the structure representing
 * only devices. Following that is the unioned structure representing all
 * the values
 */

/* structure representing a volume */

struct DeviceList {
    BPTR                    dl_Next;        /* bptr to next device list */
    LONG                    dl_Type;        /* see DLT below */
    struct MsgPort *        dl_Task;        /* ptr to handler task */
    BPTR                    dl_Lock;        /* not for volumes */
    struct DateStamp        dl_VolumeDate;  /* creation date */
    BPTR                    dl_LockList;    /* outstanding locks */
    LONG                    dl_DiskType;    /* 'DOS', etc */
    LONG                    dl_unused;
    BSTR *                  dl_Name;        /* bptr to bcpl name */
};

/* device structure (same as the DeviceNode structure in filehandler.h) */

struct          DevInfo {
    BPTR  dvi_Next;
    LONG  dvi_Type;
    APTR  dvi_Task;
    BPTR  dvi_Lock;
    BSTR  dvi_Handler;
    LONG  dvi_StackSize;
    LONG  dvi_Priority;
    LONG  dvi_Startup;
    BPTR  dvi_SegList;
    BPTR  dvi_GlobVec;
    BSTR  dvi_Name;
};

/* combined structure for devices, assigned directories, volumes */

struct DosList {
    BPTR                    dol_Next;       /* bptr to next device on list */
    LONG                    dol_Type;       /* see DLT below */
    struct MsgPort         *dol_Task;       /* ptr to handler task */
    BPTR                    dol_Lock;
    union {
        struct {
        BSTR    dol_Handler;    /* file name to load if seglist is null */
        LONG    dol_StackSize;  /* stacksize to use when starting process */
        LONG    dol_Priority;   /* task priority when starting process */
        ULONG   dol_Startup;    /* startup msg: FileSysStartupMsg for disks */
        BPTR    dol_SegList;    /* already loaded code for new task */
        BPTR    dol_GlobVec;    /* BCPL global vector to use when starting
                                 * a process. -1 indicates a C/Assembler
                                 * program. */
        } dol_handler;

        struct {
        struct DateStamp        dol_VolumeDate;  /* creation date */
        BPTR                    dol_LockList;    /* outstanding locks */
        LONG                    dol_DiskType;    /* 'DOS', etc */
        } dol_volume;
```

```

    } dol_misc;

    BSTR                dol_Name;       /* bptr to bcpl name */
    };


/* definitions for dl_Type */
#define DLT_DEVICE      0
#define DLT_DIRECTORY   1
#define DLT_VOLUME      2

/* a lock structure, as returned by Lock() or DupLock() */
struct FileLock {
    BPTR                fl_Link;        /* bcpl pointer to next lock */
    LONG                fl_Key;         /* disk block number */
    LONG                fl_Access;      /* exclusive or shared */
    struct MsgPort *    fl_Task;        /* handler task's port */
    BPTR                fl_Volume;      /* bptr to a DeviceList */
};

#endif  /* LIBRARIES_DOSEXTENS_H */
```



```
#ifndef LIBRARIES_EXPANSION_H
#define LIBRARIES_EXPANSION_H
/*
**      $Filename: libraries/expansion.h $
**      $Release: 1.3 $
**
**      external definitions for expansion.library
**
**      (C) Copyright 1986,1987,1988 Commodore-Amiga, Inc.
**          All Rights Reserved
*/

#define EXPANSIONNAME   "expansion.library"

/* flags for the AddDosNode() call */
#define ADNB_STARTPROC  0

#define ADNF_STARTPROC  (1<<0)


/* correct types for C programs */

struct ConfigDev *AllocConfigDev();
CPTR AllocExpansionMem();
struct ConfigDev *FindConfigDev();
struct DeviceNode *MakeDosNode();

#endif  /* LIBRARIES_EXPANSION_H */
```

```
#ifndef LIBRARIES_EXPANSIONBASE_H
#define LIBRARIES_EXPANSIONBASE_H
/*
**      $Filename: libraries/expansionbase.h $
**      $Release: 1.3 $
**
**
**
**      (C) Copyright 1987,1988 Commodore-Amiga, Inc.
**          All Rights Reserved
*/

#ifndef EXEC_TYPES_H
#include "exec/types.h"
#endif  !EXEC_TYPES_H

#ifndef EXEC_LIBRARIES_H
#include "exec/libraries.h"
#endif  !EXEC_LIBRARIES_H

#ifndef EXEC_INTERRUPTS_H
#include "exec/interrupts.h"
#endif  !EXEC_INTERRUPTS_H

#ifndef EXEC_SEMAPHORES_H
#include "exec/semaphores.h"
#endif  !EXEC_SEMAPHORES_H

#ifndef LIBRARIES_CONFIGVARS_H
#include "libraries/configvars.h"
#endif  !LIBRARIES_CONFIGVARS_H

#define TOTALSLOTS 256

struct ExpansionInt
{
        UWORD   IntMask;
        UWORD   ArrayMax;
        UWORD   ArraySize;
};


struct  ExpansionBase
{
        struct Library  LibNode;
        UBYTE   Flags;
        UBYTE   pad;
        APTR    ExecBase;
        APTR    SegList;
        struct  CurrentBinding  CurrentBinding;
        struct  List    BoardList;
        struct  List    MountList;
        UBYTE   AllocTable[TOTALSLOTS];
        struct  SignalSemaphore BindSemaphore;
        struct  Interrupt       Int2List;
        struct  Interrupt       Int6List;
        struct  Interrupt       Int7List;
};

#endif  /* LIBRARIES_EXPANSIONBASE_H */
```



```
#ifndef LIBRARIES_FILEHANDLER_H
#define LIBRARIES_FILEHANDLER_H
/*
**      $Filename: libraries/filehandler.h $
**      $Release: 1.3 $
**
**      device and file handler specific code for AmigaDOS
**
**      (C) Copyright 1986,1987,1988 Commodore-Amiga, Inc.
**          All Rights Reserved
*/

#ifndef   EXEC_TYPES_H
#include "exec/types.h"
#endif   !EXEC_TYPES_H

#ifndef   EXEC_PORTS_H
#include "exec/ports.h"
#endif   !EXEC_PORTS_H

#ifndef   LIBRARIES_DOS_H
#include "libraries/dos.h"
#endif   !LIBRARIES_DOS_H


/* The disk "environment" is a longword array that describes the
 * disk geometry.  It is variable sized, with the length at the beginning.
 * Here are the constants for a standard geometry.
 */

struct DosEnvec {
    ULONG de_TableSize;       /* Size of Environment vector */
    ULONG de_SizeBlock;       /* in longwords: standard value is 128 */
    ULONG de_SecOrg;          /* not used; must be 0 */
    ULONG de_Surfaces;        /* # of heads (surfaces). drive specific */
    ULONG de_SectorPerBlock;  /* not used; must be 1 */
    ULONG de_BlocksPerTrack;  /* blocks per track. drive specific */
    ULONG de_Reserved;        /* DOS reserved blocks at start of partition. */
    ULONG de_PreAlloc;        /* DOS reserved blocks at end of partition */
    ULONG de_Interleave;      /* usually 0 */
    ULONG de_LowCyl;          /* starting cylinder. typically 0 */
    ULONG de_HighCyl;         /* max cylinder. drive specific */
    ULONG de_NumBuffers;      /* Initial # DOS of buffers.  */
    ULONG de_BufMemType;      /* type of mem to allocate for buffers */
    ULONG de_MaxTransfer;     /* Max number of bytes to transfer at a time */
    ULONG de_Mask;            /* Address Mask to block out certain memory */
    LONG  de_BootPri;         /* Boot priority for autoboot */
    ULONG de_DosType;         /* ASCII (HEX) string showing filesystem type;
                               * 0X444F5300 is old filesystem,
                               * 0X444F5301 is fast file system */
};

/* these are the offsets into the array */

#define DE_TABLESIZE    0       /* standard value is 11 */
#define DE_SIZEBLOCK    1       /* in longwords: standard value is 128 */
#define DE_SECORG       2       /* not used; must be 0 */
#define DE_NUMHEADS     3       /* # of heads (surfaces). drive specific */
#define DE_SECSPERBLK   4       /* not used; must be 1 */
#define DE_BLKSPERTRACK 5       /* blocks per track. drive specific */
#define DE_RESERVEDBLKS 6       /* unavailable blocks at start.  usually 2 */
#define DE_PREFAC       7       /* not used; must be 0 */
#define DE_INTERLEAVE   8       /* usually 0 */
#define DE_LOWCYL       9       /* starting cylinder. typically 0 */
#define DE_UPPERCYL     10      /* max cylinder.  drive specific */
#define DE_NUMBUFFERS   11      /* starting # of buffers.  typically 5 */
#define DE_MEMBUFTYPE   12      /* type of mem to allocate for buffers. */
#define DE_BUFMEMTYPE   12      /* same as above, better name
                                 * 1 is public, 3 is chip, 5 is fast */
```

```
#define DE_MAXTRANSFER  13      /* Max number bytes to transfer at a time */
#define DE_MASK         14      /* Address Mask to block out certain memory */
#define DE_BOOTPRI      15      /* Boot priority for autoboot */
#define DE_DOSTYPE      16      /* ASCII (HEX) string showing filesystem type;
                                 * 0X444F5300 is old filesystem,
                                 * 0X444F5301 is fast file system */

/* The file system startup message is linked into a device node's startup
** field.  It contains a pointer to the above environment, plus the
** information needed to do an exec OpenDevice().
*/
struct FileSysStartupMsg {
    ULONG       fssm_Unit;      /* exec unit number for this device */
    BSTR        fssm_Device;    /* null terminated bstring to the device name */
    BPTR        fssm_Environ;   /* ptr to environment table (see above) */
    ULONG       fssm_Flags;     /* flags for OpenDevice() */
};


/* The include file "libraries/dosextens.h" has a DeviceList structure.
 * The "device list" can have one of three different things linked onto
 * it.  Dosextens defines the structure for a volume.  DLT_DIRECTORY
 * is for an assigned directory.  The following structure is for
 * a dos "device" (DLT_DEVICE).
*/

struct DeviceNode {
    BPTR        dn_Next;        /* singly linked list */
    ULONG       dn_Type;        /* always 0 for dos "devices" */
    struct MsgPort *dn_Task;    /* standard dos "task" field.  If this is
                                 * null when the node is accesses, a task
                                 * will be started up */
    BPTR        dn_Lock;        /* not used for devices -- leave null */
    BSTR        dn_Handler;     /* filename to loadseg (if seglist is null) */
    ULONG       dn_StackSize;   /* stacksize to use when starting task */
    LONG        dn_Priority;    /* task priority when starting task */
    BPTR        dn_Startup;     /* startup msg: FileSysStartupMsg for disks */
    BPTR        dn_SegList;     /* code to run to start new task (if necessary).
                                 * if null then dn_Handler will be loaded. */
    BPTR        dn_GlobalVec;   /* BCPL global vector to use when starting
                                 * a task.  -1 means that dn_SegList is not
                                 * for a bcpl program, so the dos won't
                                 * try and construct one.  0 tell the
                                 * dos that you obey BCPL linkage rules,
                                 * and that it should construct a global
                                 * vector for you.
                                 */
    BSTR        dn_Name;        /* the node name, e.g. '\3','D','F','3' */
};

#endif  /* LIBRARIES_FILEHANDLER_H */
```



```
#ifndef LIBRARIES_MATHFFP_H
#define LIBRARIES_MATHFFP_H
/*
**      $Filename: libraries/mathffp.h $
**      $Release: 1.3 $
**
**      general floating point declarations
**
**      (C) Copyright 1985,1986,1987,1988 Commodore-Amiga, Inc.
**          All Rights Reserved
*/

#ifndef PI
#define PI          ((float) 3.141592653589793)
#endif
#define TWO_PI      (((float) 2) * PI)
#define PI2         (PI / ((float) 2))
#define PI4         (PI / ((float) 4))
#ifndef E
#define E           ((float) 2.718281828459045)
#endif
#define LOG10       ((float) 2.302585092994046)

#define FPTEN       ((float) 10.0)
#define FPONE       ((float) 1.0)
#define FPHALF      ((float) 0.5)
#define FPZERO      ((float) 0.0)

#define trunc(x)    ((int) (x))
#define round(x)    ((int) ((x) + 0.5))
#define itof(i)     ((float) (i))

#define fabs    SPAbs
#define floor   SPFloor
#define ceil    SPCeil

#define tan     SPTan
#define atan    SPAtan
#define cos     SPCos
#define acos    SPAcos
#define sin     SPSin
#define asin    SPAsin
#define exp     SPExp
#define pow(a,b)        SPPow((b),(a))
#define log     SPLog
#define log10   SPLog10
#define sqrt    SPSqrt

#define sinh    SPSinh
#define cosh    SPCosh
#define tanh    SPTanh


int     SPFix();                                        /* Basic math functions */
float   SPFlt();
int     SPCmp();
int     SPTst();
float   SPAbs();
float   SPFloor();
float   SPCeil();
#ifndef abs
float   abs();
#endif
float   SPNeg();
float   SPAdd();
float   SPSub();
float   SPMul();
float   SPDiv();

```

Sep 19 20:28 1988 libraries/mathffp.h Page 2

```
float    SPAsin(),  SPAcos(),  SPAtan();  /* Transcendental math functions */
float    SPSin(),   SPCos(),   SPTan(),   SPSincos();
float    SPSinh(),  SPCosh(),  SPTanh();
float    SPExp(),   SPLog(),   SPLog10(), SPPow();
float    SPSqrt(),  SPFieee();

float    afp(),    dbf();                 /* Math conversion functions */

#endif  /* LIBRARIES_MATHFFP_H */
```

Sep 19 20:28 1988 libraries/mathieeedp.h Page 1

```
#ifndef LIBRARIES_MATHIEEEDP_H
#define LIBRARIES_MATHIEEEDP_H
/*
**      $Filename: libraries/mathieeedp.h $
**      $Release: 1.3 $
**
**
**
**      (C) Copyright 1987,1988 Commodore-Amiga, Inc.
**          All Rights Reserved
*/

#ifndef PI
#define PI      ((double)       3.141592653589793))
#endif  PI

#define TWO_PI  (((double)      2)      * PI)
#define PI2     (PI/((double)2))
#define PI4     (PI/((double)4))

#ifndef E
#define E       ((double)       2.718281828459045)
#endif  E

#define LOG10   ((double)       2.302585092994046)
#define FPTEN   ((double)       10.0)
#define FPONE   ((double)       1.0)
#define FPHALF  ((double)       0.5)
#define FPZERO  ((double)       0.0)
#define trunc(x)        ((int)  (x))
#define round(x)        ((int)  ((x) + 0.5))
#define itof(i)         ((double) (i))

#define fabs    IEEEDPAbs
#define floor   IEEEDPFloor
#define ceil    IEEEDPCeil

#define tan     IEEEDPTan
#define atan    IEEEDPAtan
#define cos     IEEEDPCos
#define acos    IEEEDPAcos
#define sin     IEEEDPSin
#define asin    IEEEDPAsin
#define exp     IEEEDPExp
#define pow(a,b)        IEEEDPPow((b),(a))
#define log     IEEEDPLog
#define log10   IEEEDPLog10
#define sqrt    IEEEDPSqrt

#define sinh    IEEEDPSinh
#define cosh    IEEEDPCosh
#define tanh    IEEEDPTanh


double  IEEEDPTan(),IEEEDPAtan();
double  IEEEDPCos(),IEEEDPACos();
double  IEEEDPSin(),IEEEDPASin();
double  IEEEDPExp(),IEEEDPLog();
double  IEEEDPSqrt();
double  IEEEDPLog10(),IEEEDPPow();
double  IEEEDPSincos();
double  IEEEDPSinh(),IEEEDPCosh(),IEEEDPTanh();
float   IEEEDPTieee();
double  IEEEDPFieee();

int     IEEEDPFix();
int     IEEEDPCmp(),IEEEDPTst();
double  IEEEDPFlt();
double  IEEEDPAbs();
```

```
double  IEEEDPNeg();
double  IEEEDPAdd();
double  IEEEDPSub();
double  IEEEDPMul();
double  IEEEDPDiv();
double  IEEEDPFloor();
double  IEEEDPCeil();

#endif  /* LIBRARIES_MATHIEEEDP_H */
```



```
#ifndef LIBRARIES_MATHLIBRARY_H
#define LIBRARIES_MATHLIBRARY_H
/*
**      $Filename: libraries/mathlibrary.h $
**      $Release: 1.3 $
**
**
**
**      (C) Copyright 1987,1988 Commodore-Amiga, Inc.
**          All Rights Reserved
*/

#ifndef EXEC_TYPES_H
#include <exec/types.h>
#endif

#ifndef EXEC_LIBRARIES_H
#include <exec/libraries.h>
#endif

struct MathIEEEBase
{
        struct Library MathIEEEBase_LibNode;
        unsigned char   MathIEEEBase_Flags;
        unsigned char   MathIEEEBase_reserved1;
        unsigned short  *MathIEEEBase_68881;
        APTR    MathIEEEBase_SysLib;
        APTR    MathIEEEBase_SegList;
        struct  MathIEEEResource *MathIEEEBase_Resource;
        int     (*MathIEEEBase_TaskOpenLib)();
        int     (*MathIEEEBase_TaskCloseLib)();
        /*      This structure may be extended in the future */
};
/*
* Math resources may need to know when a program opens or closes this
* library. The functions TaskOpenLib and TaskCloseLib are called when
* a task opens or closes this library. They are initialized to point to
* local initialization pertaining to 68881 stuff if 68881 resources
* are found. To override the default the vendor must provide appropriate
* hooks in the MathIEEEResource. If specified, these will be called
* when the library initializes.
*/

#endif  /* LIBRARIES_MATHLIBRARY_H */
```

Sep 19 20:28 1988 libraries/romboot_base.h Page 1

```c
#ifndef LIBRARIES_ROMBOOT_BASE_H
#define LIBRARIES_ROMBOOT_BASE_H
/*
**      $Filename: libraries/romboot_base.h $
**      $Release: 1.3 $
**
**
**
**      (C) Copyright 1987,1988 Commodore-Amiga, Inc.
**          All Rights Reserved
*/

#ifndef EXEC_TYPES_H
#include <exec/types.h>
#endif
#ifndef EXEC_NODES_H
#include <exec/nodes.h>
#endif
#ifndef EXEC_LISTS_H
#include <exec/lists.h>
#endif
#ifndef EXEC_LIBRARIES_H
#include <exec/libraries.h>
#endif
#ifndef EXEC_EXECBASE_H
#include <exec/execbase.h>
#endif
#ifndef EXEC_EXECNAME_H
#include <exec/execname.h>
#endif

struct RomBootBase
{
    struct Library  LibNode;
        struct ExecBase *ExecBase;
        struct List             BootList;
        ULONG                   Reserved[4];    /* for future expansion */
};

struct BootNode
{
        struct Node bn_Node;
        UWORD   bn_Flags;
        CPTR    bn_DeviceNode;
};

#define ROMBOOT_NAME "romboot.library"

#endif  /* LIBRARIES_ROMBOOT_BASE_H */
```

Sep 19 20:28 1988 libraries/translator.h Page 1

```c
#ifndef LIBRARIES_TRANSLATOR_H
#define LIBRARIES_TRANSLATOR_H
/*
**      $Filename: libraries/translator.h $
**      $Release: 1.3 $
**
**      Translator error return codes
**
**      (C) Copyright 1985,1986,1987,1988 Commodore-Amiga, Inc.
**          All Rights Reserved
*/

#define TR_NotUsed      -1              /* This is an oft used system rc */
#define TR_NoMem        -2              /* Can't allocate memory */
#define TR_MakeBad      -4              /* Error in MakeLibrary call */

#endif  /* LIBRARIES_TRANSLATOR_H */
```

```
#ifndef RESOURCES_CIA_H
#define RESOURCES_CIA_H
/*
**      $Filename: resources/cia.h $
**      $Release: 1.3 $
**
**
**
**      (C) Copyright 1985,1986,1987,1988 Commodore-Amiga, Inc.
**          All Rights Reserved
*/

#define CIAANAME "ciaa.resource"
#define CIABNAME "ciab.resource"

#endif  /* RESOURCES_CIA_H */
```



```
#ifndef RESOURCES_DISK_H
#define RESOURCES_DISK_H
/*
**      $Filename: resources/disk.h $
**      $Release: 1.3 $
**
**      external declarations for disc resources
**
**      (C) Copyright 1985,1986,1987,1988 Commodore-Amiga, Inc.
**          All Rights Reserved
*/

#ifndef EXEC_TYPES_H
#include "exec/types.h"
#endif !EXEC_TYPES_H

#ifndef EXEC_LISTS_H
#include "exec/lists.h"
#endif !EXEC_LISTS_H

#ifndef EXEC_PORTS_H
#include "exec/ports.h"
#endif !EXEC_PORTS_H

#ifndef EXEC_INTERRUPTS_H
#include "exec/interrupts.h"
#endif !EXEC_INTERRUPTS_H

#ifndef EXEC_LIBRARIES_H
#include "exec/libraries.h"
#endif !EXEC_LIBRARIES_H


/**********************************************************************
*
* Resource structures
*
**********************************************************************/


struct DiscResourceUnit {
    struct Message dru_Message;
    struct Interrupt dru_DiscBlock;
    struct Interrupt dru_DiscSync;
    struct Interrupt dru_Index;
};

struct DiscResource {
    struct Library              dr_Library;
    struct DiscResourceUnit     *dr_Current;
    UBYTE                       dr_Flags;
    UBYTE                       dr_pad;
    struct Library              *dr_SysLib;
    struct Library              *dr_CiaResource;
    ULONG                       dr_UnitID[4];
    struct List                 dr_Waiting;
    struct Interrupt            dr_DiscBlock;
    struct Interrupt            dr_DiscSync;
    struct Interrupt            dr_Index;
};

/* dr_Flags entries */
#define DRB_ALLOC0      0       /* unit zero is allocated */
#define DRB_ALLOC1      1       /* unit one is allocated */
#define DRB_ALLOC2      2       /* unit two is allocated */
#define DRB_ALLOC3      3       /* unit three is allocated */
#define DRB_ACTIVE      7       /* is the disc currently busy? */

#define DRF_ALLOC0      (1<<0)  /* unit zero is allocated */
```

```
#define DRF_ALLOC1       (1<<1)  /* unit one is allocated */
#define DRF_ALLOC2       (1<<2)  /* unit two is allocated */
#define DRF_ALLOC3       (1<<3)  /* unit three is allocated */
#define DRF_ACTIVE       (1<<7)  /* is the disc currently busy? */



/*********************************************************************
*
* Hardware Magic
*
*********************************************************************/


#define DSKDMAOFF        0x4000  /* idle command for dsklen register */


/*********************************************************************
*
* Resource specific commands
*
*********************************************************************/

/*
 * DISKNAME is a generic macro to get the name of the resource.
 * This way if the name is ever changed you will pick up the
 *  change automatically.
 */

#define DISKNAME         "disk.resource"


#define DR_ALLOCUNIT     (LIB_BASE - 0*LIB_VECTSIZE)
#define DR_FREEUNIT      (LIB_BASE - 1*LIB_VECTSIZE)
#define DR_GETUNIT       (LIB_BASE - 2*LIB_VECTSIZE)
#define DR_GIVEUNIT      (LIB_BASE - 3*LIB_VECTSIZE)
#define DR_GETUNITID     (LIB_BASE - 4*LIB_VECTSIZE)


#define DR_LASTCOMM      (DR_GIVEUNIT)

/*********************************************************************
*
* drive types
*
*********************************************************************/

#define DRT_AMIGA        (0x00000000)
#define DRT_37422D2S     (0x55555555)
#define DRT_EMPTY        (0xFFFFFFFF)

#endif  /* RESOURCES_DISK_H */
```



```
#ifndef RESOURCES_FILESYSRES_H
#define RESOURCES_FILESYSRES_H
/*
**      $Filename: resources/filesysres.h $
**      $Revision: 1.0 $
**      $Date: 88/07/11 15:32:08 $
**
**      FileSystem.resource description
**
**      (C) Copyright 1988 Commodore-Amiga, Inc.
**          All Rights Reserved
*/

#ifndef EXEC_NODES_H
#include        "exec/nodes.h"
#endif
#ifndef EXEC_LISTS_H
#include        "exec/lists.h"
#endif
#ifndef LIBRARIES_DOS_H
#include        "libraries/dos.h"
#endif

#define FSRNAME "FileSystem.resource"

struct FileSysResource {
    struct Node fsr_Node;                /* on resource list */
    char   *fsr_Creator;                 /* name of creator of this resource */
    struct List fsr_FileSysEntries;      /* list of FileSysEntry structs */
};

struct FileSysEntry {
    struct Node fse_Node;       /* on fsr_FileSysEntries list */
                                /* ln_Name is of creator of this entry */
    ULONG   fse_DosType;        /* DosType of this FileSys */
    ULONG   fse_Version;        /* Version of this FileSys */
    ULONG   fse_PatchFlags;     /* bits set for those of the following that */
                                /*   need to be substituted into a standard */
                                /*   device node for this file system: e.g. */
                                /*   0x180 for substitute SegList & GlobalVec */
    ULONG   fse_Type;           /* device node type: zero */
    CPTR    fse_Task;           /* standard dos "task" field */
    BPTR    fse_Lock;           /* not used for devices: zero */
    BSTR    fse_Handler;        /* filename to loadseg (if SegList is null) */
    ULONG   fse_StackSize;      /* stacksize to use when starting task */
    LONG    fse_Priority;       /* task priority when starting task */
    BPTR    fse_Startup;        /* startup msg: FileSysStartupMsg for disks */
    BPTR    fse_SegList;        /* code to run to start new task */
    BPTR    fse_GlobalVec;      /* BCPL global vector when starting task */
    /* no more entries need exist than those implied by fse_PatchFlags */
};

#endif  /* RESOURCES_FILESYSRES_H */
```

Sep 19 20:28 1988 resources/mathresource.h Page 1

```
#ifndef RESOURCES_MATHRESOURCE_H
#define RESOURCES_MATHRESOURCE_H
/*
**      $Filename: resources/mathresource.h $
**      $Release: 1.3 $
**
**
**
**      (C) Copyright 1987,1988 Commodore-Amiga, Inc.
**          All Rights Reserved
*/

#ifndef EXEC_TYPES_H
#include <exec/types.h>
#endif

#ifndef EXEC_NODES_H
#include <exec/nodes.h>
#endif

/*
*       The 'Init' entries are only used if the corresponding
*       bit is set in the Flags field.
*
*       So if you are just a 68881, you do not need the Init stuff
*       just make sure you have cleared the Flags field.
*
*       This should allow us to add Extended Precision later.
*
*       For Init users, if you need to be called whenever a task
*       opens this library for use, you need to change the appropriate
*       entries in MathIEEELibrary.
*/

struct MathIEEEResource
{
        struct  Node    MathIEEEResource_Node;
        unsigned short  MathIEEEResource_Flags;
        unsigned short  *MathIEEEResource_BaseAddr; /* ptr to 881 if exists */
        void    (*MathIEEEResource_DblBasInit)();
        void    (*MathIEEEResource_DblTransInit)();
        void    (*MathIEEEResource_SglBasInit)();
        void    (*MathIEEEResource_SglTransInit)();
        void    (*MathIEEEResource_ExtBasInit)();
        void    (*MathIEEEResource_ExtTransInit)();
};

/* definations for MathIEEEResource_FLAGS */
#define MATHIEEERESOURCEF_DBLBAS        (1<<0)
#define MATHIEEERESOURCEF_DBLTRANS      (1<<1)
#define MATHIEEERESOURCEF_SGLBAS        (1<<2)
#define MATHIEEERESOURCEF_SGLTRANS      (1<<3)
#define MATHIEEERESOURCEF_EXTBAS        (1<<4)
#define MATHIEEERESOURCEF_EXTTRANS      (1<<5)

#endif  /* RESOURCES_MATHRESOURCE_H */
```

Sep 19 20:29 1988 resources/misc.h Page 1

```
#ifndef RESOURCES_MISC_H
#define RESOURCES_MISC_H
/*
**      $Filename: resources/misc.h $
**      $Release: 1.3 $
**
**      external declarations for misc system resources
**
**      (C) Copyright 1985,1986,1987,1988 Commodore-Amiga, Inc.
**          All Rights Reserved
*/

#ifndef EXEC_TYPES_H
#include "exec/types.h"
#endif  !EXEC_TYPES_H

#ifndef EXEC_LIBRARIES_H
#include "exec/libraries.h"
#endif  !EXEC_LIBRARIES_H


/*********************************************************************
*
* Resource structures
*
*********************************************************************/

#define MR_SERIALPORT   0
#define MR_SERIALBITS   1
#define MR_PARALLELPORT 2
#define MR_PARALLELBITS 3

#define NUMMRTYPES      4

struct MiscResource {
    struct Library mr_Library;
    ULONG mr_AllocArray[NUMMRTYPES];
};

#define MR_ALLOCMISCRESOURCE    (LIB_BASE)
#define MR_FREEMISCRESOURCE     (LIB_BASE + LIB_VECSIZE)


#define MISCNAME "misc.resource"

#endif  /* RESOURCES_MISC_H */
```

```
#ifndef RESOURCES_POTGO_H
#define RESOURCES_POTGO_H
/*
**      $Filename: resources/potgo.h $
**      $Release: 1.3 $
**
**
**
**      (C) Copyright 1985,1986,1987,1988 Commodore-Amiga, Inc.
**          All Rights Reserved
*/

#define  POTGONAME   "potgo.resource"

#endif  /* RESOURCES_POTGO_H */
```

```
#ifndef WORKBENCH_ICON_H
#define WORKBENCH_ICON_H
/*
**      $Filename: workbench/icon.h $
**      $Release: 1.3 $
**
**      external declarations for workbench support library
**
**      (C) Copyright 1985,1986,1987,1988 Commodore-Amiga, Inc.
**          All Rights Reserved
*/

/**********************************************************************
*
* library structures
*
**********************************************************************/


#define ICONNAME        "icon.library"

/**********************************************************************
*
* function types
*
**********************************************************************/

struct WBObject *GetWBObject(), *AllocWBObject();
struct DiskObject *GetDiskObject();
LONG PutWBObject(), PutIcon(), GetIcon(), MatchToolValue();
VOID FreeFreeList(), FreeWBObject(), AddFreeList();
char *FindToolType();

#endif  /* WORKBENCH_ICON_H */
```



```
#ifndef WORKBENCH_STARTUP_H
#define WORKBENCH_STARTUP_H
/*
**      $Filename: workbench/startup.h $
**      $Release: 1.3 $
**
**
**
**      (C) Copyright 1985,1986,1987,1988 Commodore-Amiga, Inc.
**          All Rights Reserved
*/

#ifndef EXEC_TYPES_H
#include "exec/types.h"
#endif !EXEC_TYPES_H

#ifndef EXEC_PORTS_H
#include "exec/ports.h"
#endif !EXEC_PORTS_H

#ifndef LIBRARIES_DOS_H
#include "libraries/dos.h"
#endif !LIBRARIES_DOS_H

struct WBStartup {
    struct Message      sm_Message;     /* a standard message structure */
    struct MsgPort *    sm_Process;     /* the process descriptor for you */
    BPTR                sm_Segment;     /* a descriptor for your code */
    LONG                sm_NumArgs;     /* the number of elements in ArgList */
    char *              sm_ToolWindow;  /* description of window */
    struct WBArg *      sm_ArgList;     /* the arguments themselves */
};

struct WBArg {
    BPTR                wa_Lock;        /* a lock descriptor */
    BYTE *              wa_Name;        /* a string relative to that lock */
};

#endif  /* WORKBENCH_STARTUP_H */
```

```
#ifndef WORKBENCH_WORKBENCH_H
#define WORKBENCH_WORKBENCH_H
/*
**      $Filename: workbench/workbench.h $
**      $Release: 1.3 $
**
**
**
**      (C) Copyright 1985,1986,1987,1988 Commodore-Amiga, Inc.
**          All Rights Reserved
*/

#ifndef EXEC_TYPES_H
#include "exec/types.h"
#endif !EXEC_TYPES_H

#ifndef EXEC_NODES_H
#include "exec/nodes.h"
#endif !EXEC_NODES_H

#ifndef EXEC_LISTS_H
#include "exec/lists.h"
#endif !EXEC_LISTS_H

#ifndef EXEC_TASKS_H
#include "exec/tasks.h"
#endif !EXEC_TASKS_H

#ifndef INTUITION_INTUITION_H
#include "intuition/intuition.h"
#endif !INTUITION_INTUITION_H

#define WBDISK          1
#define WBDRAWER        2
#define WBTOOL          3
#define WBPROJECT       4
#define WBGARBAGE       5
#define WBDEVICE        6
#define WBKICK          7

struct DrawerData {
    struct NewWindow    dd_NewWindow;   /* args to open window */
    LONG                dd_CurrentX;    /* current x coordinate of origin */
    LONG                dd_CurrentY;    /* current y coordinate of origin */
};

/* the amount of DrawerData actually written to disk */
#define DRAWERDATAFILESIZE      (sizeof( struct DrawerData ))


struct DiskObject {
    UWORD               do_Magic; /* a magic number at the start of the file */
    UWORD               do_Version; /* a version number, so we can change it */
    struct Gadget       do_Gadget;      /* a copy of in core gadget */
    UBYTE               do_Type;
    char *              do_DefaultTool;
    char **             do_ToolTypes;
    LONG                do_CurrentX;
    LONG                do_CurrentY;
    struct DrawerData * do_DrawerData;
    char *              do_ToolWindow;  /* only applies to tools */
    LONG                do_StackSize;   /* only applies to tools */

};

#define WB_DISKMAGIC    0xe310  /* a magic number, not easily impersonated */
#define WB_DISKVERSION  1       /* our current version number */

struct FreeList {
```



```
    WORD                fl_NumFree;
    struct List         fl_MemList;
};

/* each message that comes into the WorkBenchPort must have a type field
 * in the preceeding short.  These are the defines for this type
 */

#define MTYPE_PSTD              1       /* a "standard Potion" message */
#define MTYPE_TOOLEXIT          2       /* exit message from our tools */
#define MTYPE_DISKCHANGE        3       /* dos telling us of a disk change */
#define MTYPE_TIMER             4       /* we got a timer tick */
#define MTYPE_CLOSEDOWN         5       /* <unimplemented> */
#define MTYPE_IOPROC            6       /* <unimplemented> */

/* workbench does different complement modes for its gadgets.
 * It supports separate images, complement mode, and backfill mode.
 * The first two are identical to intuitions GADGIMAGE and GADGHCOMP.
 * backfill is similar to GADGHCOMP, but the region outside of the
 * image (which normally would be color three when complemented)
 * is flood-filled to color zero.
 */
#define GADGBACKFILL    0x0001

/* if an icon does not really live anywhere, set its current position
 * to here
 */
#define NO_ICON_POSITION        (0x80000000)

#endif  /* WORKBENCH_WORKBENCH_H */
```

Section E

Assembly Include Files—".i" Files

This section contains the 68000 assembly language include files from the operating system source code. Whenever the system software requires that a certain structure or constant be passed, it will be defined here. Each subsystem has its own include files. A quick example of include file usage is provided below.

This section is for reference only. Similar include files generally come on disk with whatever assembler you may choose to use with the Amiga.

WARNING: *Not all information in this section should be used in your programs. The include files contain definitions for some structure members and constants that are not supported for use by programs. In some cases these definitions are marked as private, in other cases they are not distinguished. Following the guidelines presented by Commodore-Amiga is the best way to insure compatibility with future system software releases.*

```
*
* A quick example of using an assembly language include file.  The
* constant "RETURN_FAIL" is not defined in this example, instead the
* value is pulled from the "libraries/dos.i" include file.  This is
* equivalent to:
*
*               moveq       #20,d0
*               rts
*
        INCLUDE "libraries/dos.i"

        moveq   #RETURN_FAIL,D0
        rts
```

TABLE OF CONTENTS

```
        IFND    DEVICES_AUDIO_I
DEVICES_AUDIO_I SET     1
**
**      $Filename: devices/audio.i $
**      $Release: 1.3 $
**
**
**
**      (C) Copyright 1985,1986,1987,1988 Commodore-Amiga, Inc.
**          All Rights Reserved
**

                        IFND    EXEC_IO_I
                        INCLUDE "exec/io.i"
                        ENDC

AUDIONAME               MACRO
                        DC.B    'audio.device',0
                        ENDM

ADHARD_CHANNELS         EQU     4

ADALLOC_MINPREC         EQU     -128
ADALLOC_MAXPREC         EQU     127

ADCMD_FREE              EQU     CMD_NONSTD+0
ADCMD_SETPREC           EQU     CMD_NONSTD+1
ADCMD_FINISH            EQU     CMD_NONSTD+2
ADCMD_PERVOL            EQU     CMD_NONSTD+3
ADCMD_LOCK              EQU     CMD_NONSTD+4
ADCMD_WAITCYCLE         EQU     CMD_NONSTD+5
ADCMDB_NOUNIT           EQU     5
ADCMDF_NOUNIT           EQU     1<<5
ADCMD_ALLOCATE          EQU     ADCMDF_NOUNIT+0

ADIOB_PERVOL            EQU     4
ADIOF_PERVOL            EQU     1<<4
ADIOB_SYNCCYCLE         EQU     5
ADIOF_SYNCCYCLE         EQU     1<<5
ADIOB_NOWAIT            EQU     6
ADIOF_NOWAIT            EQU     1<<6
ADIOB_WRITEMESSAGE      EQU     7
ADIOF_WRITEMESSAGE      EQU     1<<7

ADIOERR_NOALLOCATION    EQU     -10
ADIOERR_ALLOCFAILED     EQU     -11
ADIOERR_CHANNELSTOLEN   EQU     -12

                        STRUCTURE       IOAudio,IO_SIZE
                        WORD    ioa_AllocKey
                        APTR    ioa_Data
                        ULONG   ioa_Length
                        UWORD   ioa_Period
                        UWORD   ioa_Volume
                        UWORD   ioa_Cycles
                        STRUCT  ioa_WriteMsg,MN_SIZE
                        LABEL   ioa_SIZEOF

        ENDC    ; DEVICES_AUDIO_I
```



```
        IFND    DEVICES_BOOTBLOCK_I
DEVICES_BOOTBLOCK_I     SET     1
**
**      $Filename: devices/bootblock.i $
**      $Release: 1.3 $
**
**      BootBlock definition:
**
**      (C) Copyright 1985,1986,1987,1988 Commodore-Amiga, Inc.
**          All Rights Reserved
**

 STRUCTURE BB,0
        STRUCT  BB_ID,4         * 4 character identifier
        LONG    BB_CHKSUM       * boot block checksum (balance)
        LONG    BB_DOSBLOCK     * reserved for DOS patch
        LABEL   BB_ENTRY        * bootstrap entry point
        LABEL   BB_SIZE

BOOTSECTS       equ     2       * 1K bootstrap

BBID_DOS        macro           * something that is bootable
                dc.b    'DOS',0
                endm

BBID_KICK       macro           * firmware image disk
                dc.b    'KICK'
                endm


BBNAME_DOS      EQU     (('D'<<24)!('O'<<16)!('S'<<8))
BBNAME_KICK     EQU     (('K'<<24)!('I'<<16)!('C'<<8)!('K'))

        ENDC    ; DEVICES_BOOTBLOCK_I
```

```
        IFND    DEVICES_CLIPBOARD_I
DEVICES_CLIPBOARD_I     SET     1
**
**      $Filename: devices/clipboard.i $
**      $Release: 1.3 $
**
**      clipboard device command definitions
**
**      (C) Copyright 1985,1986,1987,1988 Commodore-Amiga, Inc.
**          All Rights Reserved
**

    IFND     EXEC_NODES_I
    INCLUDE     "exec/nodes.i"
    ENDC
    IFND     EXEC_LISTS_I
    INCLUDE     "exec/lists.i"
    ENDC
    IFND     EXEC_PORTS_I
    INCLUDE     "exec/ports.i"
    ENDC
    IFND     EXEC_IO_I
    INCLUDE     "exec/io.i"
    ENDC

    DEVINIT

    DEVCMD   CBD_POST
    DEVCMD   CBD_CURRENTREADID
    DEVCMD   CBD_CURRENTWRITEID

CBERR_OBSOLETEID  EQU   1


 STRUCTURE  ClipboardUnitPartial,0
    STRUCT  cu_Node,LN_SIZE;      ; list of units
    ULONG   cu_UnitNum;          ; unit number for this unit
    ; the remaining unit data is private to the device


 STRUCTURE  IOClipReq,0
    STRUCT  io_Message,MN_SIZE
    APTR    io_Device               ; device node pointer
    APTR    io_Unit                 ; unit (driver private)
    UWORD   io_Command              ; device command
    UBYTE   io_Flags                ; including QUICK and SATISFY
    BYTE    io_Error                ; error or warning num
    ULONG   io_Actual               ; number of bytes transferred
    ULONG   io_Length               ; number of bytes requested
    APTR    io_Data                 ; either clip stream or post port
    ULONG   io_Offset               ; offset in clip stream
    LONG    io_ClipID               ; ordinal clip identifier
    LABEL   iocr_SIZEOF


PRIMARY_CLIP   EQU   0          ; primary clip unit

 STRUCTURE  SatisfyMsg,0
    STRUCT  sm_Msg,MN_SIZE      ; the length will be 6
    UWORD   sm_Unit             ; which clip unit this is
    LONG    sm_ClipID           ; the clip identifier of the post
    LABEL   satisfyMsg_SIZEOF

        ENDC    ; DEVICES_CLIPBOARD_I
```



```
        IFND    DEVICES_CONSOLE_I
DEVICES_CONSOLE_I       SET     1
**
**      $Filename: devices/console.i $
**      $Release: 1.3 $
**
**      Console device command definitions
**
**      (C) Copyright 1985,1986,1987,1988 Commodore-Amiga, Inc.
**          All Rights Reserved
**

    IFND  EXEC_IO_I
    INCLUDE  "exec/io.i"
    ENDC

******* Console commands *******
    DEVINIT

    DEVCMD         CD_ASKKEYMAP
    DEVCMD         CD_SETKEYMAP
    DEVCMD         CD_ASKDEFAULTKEYMAP
    DEVCMD         CD_SETDEFAULTKEYMAP


******* SGR parameters

SGR_PRIMARY       EQU   0
SGR_BOLD          EQU   1
SGR_ITALIC        EQU   3
SGR_UNDERSCORE    EQU   4
SGR_NEGATIVE      EQU   7

*  these names refer to the ANSI standard, not the implementation
SGR_BLACK         EQU   30
SGR_RED           EQU   31
SGR_GREEN         EQU   32
SGR_YELLOW        EQU   33
SGR_BLUE          EQU   34
SGR_MAGENTA       EQU   35
SGR_CYAN          EQU   36
SGR_WHITE         EQU   37
SGR_DEFAULT       EQU   39

SGR_BLACKBG       EQU   40
SGR_REDBG         EQU   41
SGR_GREENBG       EQU   42
SGR_YELLOWBG      EQU   43
SGR_BLUEBG        EQU   44
SGR_MAGENTABG     EQU   45
SGR_CYANBG        EQU   46
SGR_WHITEBG       EQU   47
SGR_DEFAULTBG     EQU   49

*  these names refer to the implementation, they are the preferred
*  names for use with the Amiga console device.
SGR_CLR0          EQU   30
SGR_CLR1          EQU   31
SGR_CLR2          EQU   32
SGR_CLR3          EQU   33
SGR_CLR4          EQU   34
SGR_CLR5          EQU   35
SGR_CLR6          EQU   36
SGR_CLR7          EQU   37

SGR_CLR0BG        EQU   40
SGR_CLR1BG        EQU   41
SGR_CLR2BG        EQU   42
SGR_CLR3BG        EQU   43
```

```
SGR_CLR4BG        EQU   44
SGR_CLR5BG        EQU   45
SGR_CLR6BG        EQU   46
SGR_CLR7BG        EQU   47


******   DSR parameters

DSR_CPR           EQU   6

******   CTC parameters
CTC_HSETTAB       EQU   0
CTC_HCLRTAB       EQU   2
CTC_HCLRTABSALL   EQU   5

******   TBC parameters
TBC_HCLRTAB       EQU   0
TBC_HCLRTABSALL   EQU   3

******   SM and RM parameters
M_LNM             EQU   20     ; linefeed newline mode
M_ASM    MACRO
       DC.B  '>1'              ; auto scroll mode
       ENDM
M_AWM    MACRO
       DC.B  '?7'              ; auto wrap mode
       ENDM

         ENDC    ; DEVICES_CONSOLE_I
```



```
        IFND    DEVICES_CONUNIT_I
DEVICES_CONUNIT_I       SET     1
**
**      $Filename: devices/conunit.i $
**      $Release: 1.3 $
**
**      Console device unit definitions
**
**      (C) Copyright 1986,1987,1988 Commodore-Amiga, Inc.
**          All Rights Reserved
**

   IFND  EXEC_PORTS_I
   INCLUDE  "exec/ports.i"
   ENDC

   IFND  DEVICES_CONSOLE_I
   INCLUDE  "devices/console.i"
   ENDC

   IFND  DEVICES_KEYMAP_I
   INCLUDE  "devices/keymap.i"
   ENDC

   IFND  DEVICES_INPUTEVENT_I
   INCLUDE  "devices/inputevent.i"
   ENDC

PMB_ASM     EQU   M_LNM+1      ; internal storage bit for AS flag
PMB_AWM     EQU   PMB_ASM+1    ; internal storage bit for AW flag
MAXTABS     EQU   80


 STRUCTURE  ConUnit,MP_SIZE
    ;------ read only variables
   APTR  cu_Window             ; intuition window bound to this unit
   WORD  cu_XCP                ; character position
   WORD  cu_YCP
   WORD  cu_XMax               ; max character position
   WORD  cu_YMax
   WORD  cu_XRSize             ; character raster size
   WORD  cu_YRSize
   WORD  cu_XROrigin           ; raster origin
   WORD  cu_YROrigin
   WORD  cu_XRExtant           ; raster maxima
   WORD  cu_YRExtant
   WORD  cu_XMinShrink         ; smallest area intact from resize process
   WORD  cu_YMinShrink
   WORD  cu_XCCP               ; cursor position
   WORD  cu_YCCP

   ;------ read/write variables (writes must must be protected)
   ;------ storage for AskKeyMap and SetKeyMap
   STRUCT   cu_KeyMapStruct,km_SIZEOF
   ; ---- tab stops
   STRUCT   cu_TabStops,2*MAXTABS   ; 0 at start, 0xffff at end of list

   ;------ console rastport attributes
   BYTE  cu_Mask               ; these must appear as in RastPort
   BYTE  cu_FgPen              ;   |
   BYTE  cu_BgPen              ;   |
   BYTE  cu_AOLPen             ;   +
   BYTE  cu_DrawMode           ; these must appear as in RastPort
   BYTE  cu_AreaPtSz           ;   +
   APTR  cu_AreaPtrn           ; cursor area pattern
   STRUCT   cu_Minterms,8      ; console minterms
   APTR  cu_Font               ;
   UBYTE cu_AlgoStyle          ; these must appear as in RastPort
   UBYTE cu_TxFlags            ;   +
```

```
    UWORD cu_TxHeight          ; these must appear as in RastPort
    UWORD cu_TxWidth           ;  |
    UWORD cu_TxBaseline        ;  |
    UWORD cu_TxSpacing         ;  +

    ;------ console MODES and RAW EVENTS switches
    STRUCT   cu_Modes,<(PMB_AWM+7)/8>    ; one bit per mode
    STRUCT   cu_RawEvents,<(IECLASS_MAX+7)/8>

    ;------ ensure the ConsUnit structure is even
ODDEVEN  EQU   ((PMB_AWM+7)/8)+((IECLASS_MAX+7)/8)
    IFNE  ODDEVEN-((ODDEVEN/2)*2)
       UBYTE cu_pad
    ENDC

    LABEL ConUnit_SIZEOF

         ENDC    ; DEVICES_CONUNIT_I
```



```
        IFND    DEVICES_GAMEPORT_I
DEVICES_GAMEPORT_I      SET     1
**
**      $Filename: devices/gameport.i $
**      $Release: 1.3 $
**
**      Game Port device command definitions
**
**      (C) Copyright 1985,1986,1987,1988 Commodore-Amiga, Inc.
**          All Rights Reserved
**

   IFND  EXEC_IO_I
   INCLUDE  "exec/io.i"
   ENDC


******* GamePort commands *******
   DEVINIT

   DEVCMD   GPD_READEVENT
   DEVCMD   GPD_ASKCTYPE
   DEVCMD   GPD_SETCTYPE
   DEVCMD   GPD_ASKTRIGGER
   DEVCMD   GPD_SETTRIGGER

******* GamePort structures *******

*  gpt_Keys
   BITDEF       GPT,DOWNKEYS,0
   BITDEF       GPT,UPKEYS,1

 STRUCTURE  GamePortTrigger,0
       UWORD   gpt_Keys        ;key transition triggers
       UWORD   gpt_Timeout     ;time trigger (vertical blank units)
       UWORD   gpt_XDelta      ;X distance trigger
       UWORD   gpt_YDelta      ;Y distance trigger
       LABEL   gpt_SIZEOF

******* Controller Types ******
GPCT_ALLOCATED     EQU   -1     ; allocated by another user
GPCT_NOCONTROLLER EQU    0

GPCT_MOUSE         EQU   1
GPCT_RELJOYSTICK   EQU   2
GPCT_ABSJOYSTICK   EQU   3


******* Errors ******
GPDERR_SETCTYPE    EQU   1      ; this controller not valid at this time

        ENDC    ; DEVICES_GAMEPORT_I
```

```
        IFND    DEVICES_HARDBLOCKS_I
DEVICES_HARDBLOCKS_I    SET     1
**
**      $Filename: devices/hardblocks.i $
**      $Revision: 1.0 $
**      $Date: 88/07/11 15:32:58 $
**
**      File System identifier blocks for hard disks
**
**      (C) Copyright 1988 Commodore-Amiga, Inc.
**          All Rights Reserved
**

;-----------------------------------------------------------------------
;
;       This file describes blocks of data that exist on a hard disk
;       to describe that disk.  They are not generically accessable to
;       the user as they do not appear on any DOS drive.  The blocks
;       are tagged with a unique identifier, checksummed, and linked
;       together.  The root of these blocks is the RigidDiskBlock.
;
;       The RigidDiskBlock must exist on the disk within the first
;       RDB_LOCATION_LIMIT blocks.  This inhibits the use of the zero
;       cylinder in an AmigaDOS partition: although it is strictly
;       possible to store the RigidDiskBlock data in the reserved
;       area of a partition, this practice is discouraged since the
;       reserved blocks of a partition are overwritten by "Format",
;       "Install", "DiskCopy", etc.  The recommended disk layout,
;       then, is to use the first cylinder(s) to store all the drive
;       data specified by these blocks: i.e. partition descriptions,
;       file system load images, drive bad block maps, spare blocks,
;       etc.
;
;       Though only 512 byte blocks are currently supported by the
;       file system, this proposal tries to be forward-looking by
;       making the block size explicit, and by using only the first
;       256 bytes for all blocks but the LoadSeg data.
;
;-----------------------------------------------------------------------

;
;   NOTE
;       optional block addresses below contain $ffffffff to indicate
;       a NULL address
;
 STRUCTURE      RigidDiskBlock,0
    ULONG   rdb_ID                  ; 4 character identifier
    ULONG   rdb_SummedLongs         ; size of this checksummed structure
    LONG    rdb_ChkSum              ; block checksum (longword sum to zero)
    ULONG   rdb_HostID              ; SCSI Target ID of host
    ULONG   rdb_BlockBytes          ; size of disk blocks
    ULONG   rdb_Flags               ; see below for defines
    ; block list heads
    ULONG   rdb_BadBlockList        ; optional bad block list
    ULONG   rdb_PartitionList       ; optional first partition block
    ULONG   rdb_FileSysHeaderList ; optional fule system header block
    ULONG   rdb_DriveInit           ; optional drive-specific init code
                                    ; DriveInit(lun,rdb,ior): "C' stk & d0/a0/a1
    STRUCT  rdb_Reserved1,6*4       ; set to $ffffffff
    ; physical drive characteristics
    ULONG   rdb_Cylinders           ; number of drive cylinders
    ULONG   rdb_Sectors             ; sectors per track
    ULONG   rdb_Heads               ; number of drive heads
    ULONG   rdb_Interleave          ; interleave
    ULONG   rdb_Park                ; landing zone cylinder
    STRUCT  rdb_Reserved2,3*4
    ULONG   rdb_WritePreComp        ; starting cylinder: write precompensation
    ULONG   rdb_ReducedWrite        ; starting cylinder: reduced write current
    ULONG   rdb_StepRate            ; drive step rate
```



```
    STRUCT  rdb_Reserved3,5*4
    ; logical drive characteristics
    ULONG   rdb_RDBBlocksLo         ; low block of range reserved for hardblocks
    ULONG   rdb_RDBBlocksHi         ; high block of range for these hardblocks
    ULONG   rdb_LoCylinder          ; low cylinder of partitionable disk area
    ULONG   rdb_HiCylinder          ; high cylinder of partitionable data area
    ULONG   rdb_CylBlocks           ; number of blocks available per cylinder
    ULONG   rdb_AutoParkSeconds     ; zero for no auto park
    STRUCT  rdb_Reserved4,2*4
    ; drive identification
    STRUCT  rdb_DiskVendor,8
    STRUCT  rdb_DiskProduct,16
    STRUCT  rdb_DiskRevision,4
    STRUCT  rdb_ControllerVendor,8
    STRUCT  rdb_ControllerProduct,16
    STRUCT  rdb_ControllerRevision,4
    STRUCT  rdb_Reserved5,10*4

    LABEL   RigidDiskBlock_SIZEOF

IDNAME_RIGIDDISK        EQU     (('R'<<24)!('D'<<16)!('S'<<8)!('K'))

RDB_LOCATION_LIMIT      EQU     16

    BITDEF  RDBF,LAST,0             ; no disks exist to be configured after
                                    ;   this one on this controller
    BITDEF  RDBF,LASTLUN,1          ; no LUNs exist to be configured greater
                                    ;   than this one at this SCSI Target ID
    BITDEF  RDBF,LASTTID,2          ; no Target IDs exist to be configured
                                    ;   greater than this one on this SCSI bus
    BITDEF  RDBF,NORESELECT,3       ; don't bother trying to perform reselection
                                    ;   when talking to this drive
    BITDEF  RDBF,DISKID,4           ; rdb_Disk... identification valid
    BITDEF  RDBF,CTRLRID,5          ; rdb_Controller... identification valid


;-----------------------------------------------------------------------
 STRUCTURE      BadBlockEntry,0
    ULONG   bbe_BadBlock            ; block number of bad block
    ULONG   bbe_GoodBlock           ; block number of replacement block
    LABEL   BadBlockEntry_SIZEOF

 STRUCTURE      BadBlockBlock,0
    ULONG   bbb_ID                  ; 4 character identifier
    ULONG   bbb_SummedLongs         ; size of this checksummed structure
    LONG    bbb_ChkSum              ; block checksum (longword sum to zero)
    ULONG   bbb_HostID              ; SCSI Target ID of host
    ULONG   bbb_Next                ; block number of the next BadBlockBlock
    ULONG   bbb_Reserved
    STRUCT  bbb_BlockPairs,61*BadBlockEntry_SIZEOF ; bad block entry pairs
    ; note 61 assumes 512 byte blocks
    ; there is no BadBlockBlock_SIZEOF: try rdb_BlockBytes

IDNAME_BADBLOCK         EQU     (('B'<<24)!('A'<<16)!('D'<<8)!('B'))

;-----------------------------------------------------------------------
 STRUCTURE      PartitionBlock,0
    ULONG   pb_ID                   ; 4 character identifier
    ULONG   pb_SummedLongs          ; size of this checksummed structure
    LONG    pb_ChkSum               ; block checksum (longword sum to zero)
    ULONG   pb_HostID               ; SCSI Target ID of host
    ULONG   pb_Next                 ; block number of the next PartitionBlock
    ULONG   pb_Flags                ; see below for defines
    STRUCT  pb_Reserved1,2*4
    ULONG   pb_DevFlags             ; preferred flags for OpenDevice
    STRUCT  pb_DriveName,32         ; preferred DOS device name: BSTR form
                                    ; (not used if this name is in use)
    STRUCT  pb_Reserved2,15*4       ; filler to 32 longwords
    STRUCT  pb_Environment,17*4 ; environment vector for this partition
```

```
    STRUCT  pb_EReserved,15*4    ; reserved for future environment vector
    LABEL   PartitionBlock_SIZEOF

IDNAME_PARTITION        EQU      (('P'<<24)!('A'<<16)!('R'<<8)!('T'))

    BITDEF  PBF,BOOTABLE,0       ; this partition is intended to be bootable
                                 ;   (expected directories and files exist)
    BITDEF  PBF,NOMOUNT,1        ; do not mount this partition (e.g. manually
                                 ;   mounted, but space reserved here)

;----------------------------------------------------------------------
 STRUCTURE      FileSysHeaderBlock,0
    ULONG   fhb_ID               ; 4 character identifier
    ULONG   fhb_SummedLongs      ; size of this checksummed structure
    LONG    fhb_ChkSum           ; block checksum (longword sum to zero)
    ULONG   fhb_HostID           ; SCSI Target ID of host
    ULONG   fhb_Next             ; block number of the next FileSysHeaderBlock
    ULONG   fhb_Flags            ; see below for defines
    STRUCT  fhb_Reserved1,2*4
    ULONG   fhb_DosType          ; file system description: match this with
                                 ; partition environment's DE_DOSTYPE entry
    ULONG   fhb_Version          ; release version of this code
    ULONG   fhb_PatchFlags       ; bits set for those of the following that
                                 ;   need to be substituted into a standard
                                 ;   device node for this file system: e.g.
                                 ;   $180 to substitute SegList & GlobalVec
    ULONG   fhb_Type             ; device node type: zero
    ULONG   fhb_Task             ; standard dos "task" field: zero
    ULONG   fhb_Lock             ; not used for devices: zero
    ULONG   fhb_Handler          ; filename to loadseg: zero placeholder
    ULONG   fhb_StackSize        ; stacksize to use when starting task
    LONG    fhb_Priority         ; task priority when starting task
    LONG    fhb_Startup          ; startup msg: zero placeholder
    LONG    fhb_SegListBlocks    ; first of linked list of LoadSegBlocks:
                                 ;   note that this entry requires some
                                 ;   processing before substitution
    LONG    fhb_GlobalVec        ; BCPL global vector when starting task
    STRUCT  fhb_Reserved2,23*4   ; (those reserved by PatchFlags)
    STRUCT  fhb_Reserved3,21*4
    LABEL   FileSysHeader_SIZEOF

IDNAME_FILESYSHEADER    EQU      (('F'<<24)!('S'<<16)!('H'<<8)!('D'))

;----------------------------------------------------------------------
 STRUCTURE      LoadSegBlock,0
    ULONG   lsb_ID               ; 4 character identifier
    ULONG   lsb_SummedLongs      ; size of this checksummed structure
    LONG    lsb_ChkSum           ; block checksum (longword sum to zero)
    ULONG   lsb_HostID           ; SCSI Target ID of host
    ULONG   lsb_Next             ; block number of the next FileSysBlock
    STRUCT  lsb_LoadData,123*4   ; data for "loadseg"
    ; note 123 assumes 512 byte blocks
    ; there is no LoadSegBlock_SIZEOF: try rdb_BlockBytes

IDNAME_LOADSEG          EQU      (('L'<<24)!('S'<<16)!('E'<<8)!('G'))

        ENDC
```



```
        IFND    DEVICES_INPUT_I
DEVICES_INPUT_I SET     1
**
**      $Filename: devices/input.i $
**      $Release: 1.3 $
**
**      input device command definitions
**
**      (C) Copyright 1985,1986,1987,1988 Commodore-Amiga, Inc.
**          All Rights Reserved
**

    IFND     EXEC_IO_I
    INCLUDE      "exec/io.i"
    ENDC

    DEVINIT

    DEVCMD       IND_ADDHANDLER
    DEVCMD       IND_REMHANDLER
    DEVCMD       IND_WRITEEVENT
    DEVCMD       IND_SETTHRESH
    DEVCMD       IND_SETPERIOD
    DEVCMD       IND_SETMPORT
    DEVCMD       IND_SETMTYPE
    DEVCMD       IND_SETMTRIG

        ENDC    ; DEVICES_INPUT_I
```

```
        IFND    DEVICES_INPUTEVENT_I
DEVICES_INPUTEVENT_I    SET     1
**
**      $Filename: devices/inputevent.i $
**      $Release: 1.3 $
**
**      input event definitions
**
**      (C) Copyright 1985,1986,1987,1988 Commodore-Amiga, Inc.
**          All Rights Reserved
**

    IFND  DEVICES_TIMER_I
    INCLUDE  "devices/timer.i"
    ENDC

*------ constants -------------------------------------------------------

*   --- InputEvent.ie_Class ---
* A NOP input event
IECLASS_NULL            EQU   $00
* A raw keycode from the keyboard device
IECLASS_RAWKEY          EQU   $01
* A raw mouse report from the game port device
IECLASS_RAWMOUSE        EQU   $02
* A private console event
IECLASS_EVENT           EQU   $03
* A Pointer Position report
IECLASS_POINTERPOS      EQU   $04
* A timer event
IECLASS_TIMER           EQU   $06
* select button pressed down over a Gadget (address in ie_EventAddress)
IECLASS_GADGETDOWN      EQU $07
* select button released over the same Gadget (address in ie_EventAddress)
IECLASS_GADGETUP        EQU   $08
* some Requester activity has taken place.  See Codes REQCLEAR and REQSET
IECLASS_REQUESTER       EQU   $09
* this is a Menu Number transmission (Menu number is in ie_Code)
IECLASS_MENULIST        EQU   $0A
* User has selected the active Window's Close Gadget
IECLASS_CLOSEWINDOW     EQU   $0B
* this Window has a new size
IECLASS_SIZEWINDOW      EQU   $0C
* the Window pointed to by ie_EventAddress needs to be refreshed
IECLASS_REFRESHWINDOW   EQU   $0D
* new preferences are available
IECLASS_NEWPREFS        EQU   $0E
* the disk has been removed
IECLASS_DISKREMOVED     EQU   $0F
* the disk has been inserted
IECLASS_DISKINSERTED    EQU   $10
* the window is about to be been made active
IECLASS_ACTIVEWINDOW    EQU   $11
* the window is about to be made inactive
IECLASS_INACTIVEWINDOW  EQU   $12

* the last class
IECLASS_MAX             EQU   $12

*   --- InputEvent.ie_Code ---
*  IECLASS_RAWKEY
IECODE_UP_PREFIX        EQU   $80
IECODEB_UP_PREFIX       EQU   7
IECODE_KEY_CODE_FIRST   EQU   $00
IECODE_KEY_CODE_LAST    EQU   $77
IECODE_COMM_CODE_FIRST  EQU   $78
IECODE_COMM_CODE_LAST   EQU   $7F

*  IECLASS_ANSI
```



```
IECODE_C0_FIRST         EQU   $00
IECODE_C0_LAST          EQU   $1F
IECODE_ASCII_FIRST      EQU   $20
IECODE_ASCII_LAST       EQU   $7E
IECODE_ASCII_DEL        EQU   $7F
IECODE_C1_FIRST         EQU   $80
IECODE_C1_LAST          EQU   $9F
IECODE_LATIN1_FIRST     EQU   $A0
IECODE_LATIN1_LAST      EQU   $FF

*  IECLASS_RAWMOUSE
IECODE_LBUTTON          EQU   $68  ; also uses IECODE_UP_PREFIX
IECODE_RBUTTON          EQU   $69  ;
IECODE_MBUTTON          EQU   $6A  ;
IECODE_NOBUTTON         EQU   $FF

*  IECLASS_EVENT
IECODE_NEWACTIVE        EQU   $01  ; active input window changed

*  IECLASS_REQUESTER Codes
* REQSET is broadcast when the first Requester (not subsequent ones) opens
* in the Window
IECODE_REQSET           EQU   $01
* REQCLEAR is broadcast when the last Requester clears out of the Window
IECODE_REQCLEAR         EQU   $00


*   --- InputEvent.ie_Qualifier ---
IEQUALIFIER_LSHIFT          EQU   $0001
IEQUALIFIERB_LSHIFT         EQU   0
IEQUALIFIER_RSHIFT          EQU   $0002
IEQUALIFIERB_RSHIFT         EQU   1
IEQUALIFIER_CAPSLOCK        EQU   $0004
IEQUALIFIERB_CAPSLOCK       EQU   2
IEQUALIFIER_CONTROL         EQU   $0008
IEQUALIFIERB_CONTROL        EQU   3
IEQUALIFIER_LALT            EQU   $0010
IEQUALIFIERB_LALT           EQU   4
IEQUALIFIER_RALT            EQU   $0020
IEQUALIFIERB_RALT           EQU   5
IEQUALIFIER_LCOMMAND        EQU   $0040
IEQUALIFIERB_LCOMMAND       EQU   6
IEQUALIFIER_RCOMMAND        EQU   $0080
IEQUALIFIERB_RCOMMAND       EQU   7
IEQUALIFIER_NUMERICPAD      EQU   $0100
IEQUALIFIERB_NUMERICPAD     EQU   8
IEQUALIFIER_REPEAT          EQU   $0200
IEQUALIFIERB_REPEAT         EQU   9
IEQUALIFIER_INTERRUPT       EQU   $0400
IEQUALIFIERB_INTERRUPT      EQU   10
IEQUALIFIER_MULTIBROADCAST      EQU   $0800
IEQUALIFIERB_MULTIBROADCAST     EQU   11
IEQUALIFIER_MIDBUTTON       EQU   $1000
IEQUALIFIERB_MIDBUTTON      EQU   12
IEQUALIFIER_RBUTTON         EQU   $2000
IEQUALIFIERB_RBUTTON        EQU   13
IEQUALIFIER_LEFTBUTTON      EQU   $4000
IEQUALIFIERB_LEFTBUTTON     EQU   14
IEQUALIFIER_RELATIVEMOUSE       EQU   $8000
IEQUALIFIERB_RELATIVEMOUSE      EQU   15

*------ InputEvent ---------------------------------------------------

 STRUCTURE  InputEvent,0
   APTR  ie_NextEvent          ; the chronologically next event
   UBYTE   ie_Class            ; the input event class
   UBYTE   ie_SubClass         ; optional subclass of the class
   UWORD   ie_Code             ; the input event code
   UWORD   ie_Qualifier        ; qualifiers in effect for the event
```

```
        LABEL ie_EventAddress       ; a pointer parameter for an event
        WORD    ie_X                ; the pointer position for the event,
        WORD    ie_Y                ;   usually in canvas relative coords
        STRUCT  ie_TimeStamp,TV_SIZE  ; the system tick at the event
        LABEL   ie_SIZEOF

                ENDC    ; DEVICES_INPUTEVENT_I
```



```
        IFND    DEVICES_KEYBOARD_I
DEVICES_KEYBOARD_I      SET     1
**
**      $Filename: devices/keyboard.i $
**      $Release: 1.3 $
**
**      Keyboard device command definitions
**
**      (C) Copyright 1985,1986,1987,1988 Commodore-Amiga, Inc.
**          All Rights Reserved
**

    IFND     EXEC_IO_I
    INCLUDE     "exec/io.i"
    ENDC

    DEVINIT

    DEVCMD      KBD_READEVENT
    DEVCMD      KBD_READMATRIX
    DEVCMD      KBD_ADDRESETHANDLER
    DEVCMD      KBD_REMRESETHANDLER
    DEVCMD      KBD_RESETHANDLERDONE

        ENDC    ; DEVICES_KEYBOARD_I
```

```
        IFND    DEVICES_KEYMAP_I
DEVICES_KEYMAP_I        SET     1
**
**      $Filename: devices/keymap.i $
**      $Release: 1.3 $
**
**      keymap.resource definitions and console.device key map definitions
**
**      (C) Copyright 1985,1986,1987,1988 Commodore-Amiga, Inc.
**          All Rights Reserved
**

       IFND     EXEC_NODES_I
       INCLUDE  "exec/nodes.i"
       ENDC
       IFND     EXEC_LISTS_I
       INCLUDE  "exec/lists.i"
       ENDC

 STRUCTURE  KeyMap,0
   APTR  km_LoKeyMapTypes
   APTR  km_LoKeyMap
   APTR  km_LoCapsable
   APTR  km_LoRepeatable
   APTR  km_HiKeyMapTypes
   APTR  km_HiKeyMap
   APTR  km_HiCapsable
   APTR  km_HiRepeatable
   LABEL km_SIZEOF

 STRUCTURE      KeyMapNode,0
    STRUCT  kn_Node,LN_SIZE      ; including name of keymap
    STRUCT  kn_KeyMap,km_SIZEOF
    LABEL   kn_SIZEOF

;------ the structure of keymap.resource
 STRUCTURE      KeyMapResource,0
    STRUCT  kr_Node,LN_SIZE
    STRUCT  kr_List,LH_SIZE      ; a list of KeyMapNodes
    LABEL   kr_SIZEOF


KCB_NOP      EQU   7
KCF_NOP      EQU   $80

KC_NOQUAL    EQU   0
KC_VANILLA   EQU   7            ; note that SHIFT+ALT+CTRL is VANILLA
KCB_SHIFT    EQU   0
KCF_SHIFT    EQU   $01
KCB_ALT      EQU   1
KCF_ALT      EQU   $02
KCB_CONTROL EQU    2
KCF_CONTROL EQU    $04
KCB_DOWNUP   EQU   3
KCF_DOWNUP   EQU   $08
KCB_DEAD     EQU   5             ; may be dead or modified by dead key:
KCF_DEAD     EQU   $20           ;   use dead prefix bytes

KCB_STRING   EQU   6
KCF_STRING   EQU   $40

;------ Dead Prefix Bytes
DPB_MOD          EQU     0
DPF_MOD          EQU     $01
DPB_DEAD         EQU     3
DPF_DEAD         EQU     $08

DP_2DINDEXMASK   EQU     $0F     ; mask for index for 1st of two dead keys
DP_2DFACSHIFT    EQU     4       ; shift for factor for 1st of two dead keys
```



```

         ENDC    ; DEVICES_KEYMAP_I
```

```
        IFND    DEVICES_NARRATOR_I
DEVICES_NARRATOR_I      SET     1
**
**      $Filename: devices/narrator.i $
**      $Release: 1.3 $
**
**
**
**      (C) Copyright 1985,1986,1987,1988 Commodore-Amiga, Inc.
**          All Rights Reserved
**

        IFND    EXEC_IO_I
        INCLUDE "exec/io.i"
        ENDC

*-------- DEFAULT VALUES, USER PARMS, AND GENERAL CONSTANTS

DEFPITCH   EQU      110             ;DEFAULT PITCH
DEFRATE    EQU      150             ;DEFAULT RATE
DEFVOL     EQU      64              ;DEFAULT VOLUME (FULL)
DEFFREQ    EQU      22200           ;DEFAULT SAMPLING FREQUENCY
NATURALF0  EQU      0               ;NATURAL F0 CONTOURS
ROBOTICF0  EQU      1               ;MONOTONE F0
MALE       EQU      0               ;MALE SPEAKER
FEMALE     EQU      1               ;FEMALE SPEAKER
DEFSEX     EQU      MALE            ;DEFAULT SEX
DEFMODE    EQU      NATURALF0       ;DEFAULT MODE

*     Parameter bounds

MINRATE    EQU      40              ;MINIMUM SPEAKING RATE
MAXRATE    EQU      400             ;MAXIMUM SPEAKING RATE
MINPITCH   EQU      65              ;MINIMUM PITCH
MAXPITCH   EQU      320             ;MAXIMUM PITCH
MINFREQ    EQU      5000            ;MINIMUM SAMPLING FREQUENCY
MAXFREQ    EQU      28000           ;MAXIMUM SAMPLING FREQUENCY
MINVOL     EQU      0               ;MINIMUM VOLUME
MAXVOL     EQU      64              ;MAXIMUM VOLUME

*     Driver error codes

ND_NotUsed      EQU     -1          ;
ND_NoMem        EQU     -2          ;Can't allocate memory
ND_NoAudLib     EQU     -3          ;Can't open audio device
ND_MakeBad      EQU     -4          ;Error in MakeLibrary call
ND_UnitErr      EQU     -5          ;Unit other than 0
ND_CantAlloc    EQU     -6          ;Can't allocate the audio channel
ND_Unimpl       EQU     -7          ;Unimplemented command
ND_NoWrite      EQU     -8          ;Read for mouth shape without write
ND_Expunged     EQU     -9          ;Can't open, deferred expunge bit set
ND_PhonErr      EQU     -20         ;Phoneme code spelling error
ND_RateErr      EQU     -21         ;Rate out of bounds
ND_PitchErr     EQU     -22         ;Pitch out of bounds
ND_SexErr       EQU     -23         ;Sex not valid
ND_ModeErr      EQU     -24         ;Mode not valid
ND_FreqErr      EQU     -25         ;Sampling freq out of bounds
ND_VolErr       EQU     -26         ;Volume out of bounds



*               ;------ Write IORequest block
 STRUCTURE NDI,IOSTD_SIZE
        UWORD   NDI_RATE            ;Speaking rate in words/minute
        UWORD   NDI_PITCH           ;Baseline pitch in Hertz
        UWORD   NDI_MODE            ;F0 mode
        UWORD   NDI_SEX             ;Speaker sex
        APTR    NDI_CHMASKS         ;Pointer to audio channel masks
        UWORD   NDI_NUMMASKS        ;Size of channel masks array
```



```
        UWORD   NDI_VOLUME          ;Channel volume
        UWORD   NDI_SAMPFREQ        ;Sampling frequency
        UBYTE   NDI_MOUTHS          ;Generate mouths? (Boolean value)
        UBYTE   NDI_CHANMASK        ;Actual channel mask used (internal use)
        UBYTE   NDI_NUMCHAN         ;Number of channels used (internal use)
        UBYTE   NDI_PAD             ;For alignment
        LABEL   NDI_SIZE            ;Size of Narrator IORequest block


*               ;------ Mouth read IORB
 STRUCTURE MRB,NDI_SIZE
        UBYTE   MRB_WIDTH           ;Mouth width
        UBYTE   MRB_HEIGHT          ;Mouth height
        UBYTE   MRB_SHAPE           ;Compressed shape (height/width)
        UBYTE   MRB_PAD             ;Alignment
        LABEL   MRB_SIZE

        ENDC    ; DEVICES_NARRATOR_I
```

```
        IFND    DEVICES_PARALLEL_I
DEVICES_PARALLEL_I      SET     1
**
**      $Filename: devices/parallel.i $
**      $Release: 1.3 $
**
**      external declarations for Serial Port Driver
**
**      (C) Copyright 1985,1986,1987,1988 Commodore-Amiga, Inc.
**          All Rights Reserved
**

    IFND    EXEC_IO_I
    include "exec/io.i"
    ENDC        ; EXEC_IO_I

*------------------------------------------------------------------------
*
* Driver error definitions
*
*------------------------------------------------------------------------

ParErr_DevBusy          EQU     1
ParErr_BufTooBig        EQU     2
ParErr_InvParam         EQU     3
ParErr_LineErr          EQU     4
ParErr_NotOpen          EQU     5
ParErr_PortReset        EQU     6
ParErr_InitErr          EQU     7

*------------------------------------------------------------------------
*
* Useful constants
*
*------------------------------------------------------------------------
*
PDCMD_QUERY         EQU     CMD_NONSTD
PDCMD_SETPARAMS     EQU     CMD_NONSTD+1
Par_DEVFINISH       EQU     10          ; number of device comands
*
*------------------------------------------------------------------------
*
* Driver Specific Commands
*
*------------------------------------------------------------------------

PARALLELNAME:   MACRO
                dc.b    'parallel.device',0
                ds.w    0
                ENDM

        BITDEF  PAR,SHARED,5       ; PARFLAGS non-exclusive access
        BITDEF  PAR,RAD_BOOGIE,3   ;    "     (not yet implemented)
        BITDEF  PAR,EOFMODE,1      ;    "     EOF mode enabled bit
        BITDEF  IOPAR,QUEUED,6     ; IO_FLAGS rqst-queued bit
        BITDEF  IOPAR,ABORT,5      ;    "     rqst-aborted bit
        BITDEF  IOPAR,ACTIVE,4     ;    "     rqst-qued-or-current bit
        BITDEF  IOPT,RWDIR,3       ; IO_STATUS read=0,write=1
        BITDEF  IOPT,PARSEL,2      ;    "     printer selected on the A1000
                                   ; printer selected & serial "Ring Indicator"
                                   ; on the A500/A2000.  Be careful when making
                                   ; cables.
        BITDEF  IOPT,PAPEROUT,1    ;    "     paper out
        BITDEF  IOPT,PARBUSY,0     ;    "     printer in busy toggle
;Note: Previous versions of this include file had bits 0 and 2 swapped
*
**************************************************************************

 STRUCTURE PTERMARRAY,0
```



```
        ULONG   PTERMARRAY_0
        ULONG   PTERMARRAY_1
        LABEL   PTERMARRAY_SIZE

*****************************************************************
*  CAUTION !!!  IF YOU ACCESS the parallel.device, you MUST (!!!!) use an
*  IOEXTPAR-sized structure or you may overlay innocent memory, okay ?!
*****************************************************************

 STRUCTURE IOEXTPAR,IOSTD_SIZE

*     STRUCT   MsgNode
*   0   APTR     Succ
*   4   APTR     Pred
*   8   UBYTE    Type
*   9   UBYTE    Pri
*   A   APTR     Name
*   E   APTR     ReplyPort
*  12   UWORD    MNLength
*     STRUCT   IOExt
*  14   APTR     IO_DEVICE
*  18   APTR     IO_UNIT
*  1C   UWORD    IO_COMMAND
*  1E   UBYTE    IO_FLAGS
*  1F   UBYTE    IO_ERROR
*     STRUCT   IOStdExt
*  20   ULONG    IO_ACTUAL
*  24   ULONG    IO_LENGTH
*  28   APTR     IO_DATA
*  2C   ULONG    IO_OFFSET
*

*
*  30
        ULONG   IO_PEXTFLAGS    ; (not used) flag extension area
        UBYTE   IO_PARSTATUS    ; device status (see bit defs above)
        UBYTE   IO_PARFLAGS     ; see PARFLAGS bit definitions above
        STRUCT  IO_PTERMARRAY,PTERMARRAY_SIZE ; termination char array
        LABEL   IOEXTPar_SIZE

**************************************************************************

        ENDC    ; DEVICES_PARALLEL_I
```

```
        IFND    DEVICES_PRINTER_I
DEVICES_PRINTER_I       SET     1
**
**      $Filename: devices/printer.i $
**      $Release: 1.3 $
**
**      printer device command definitions
**
**      (C) Copyright 1985,1986,1987,1988 Commodore-Amiga, Inc.
**          All Rights Reserved
**

    IFND  EXEC_NODES_I
    INCLUDE  "exec/nodes.i"
    ENDC

    IFND  EXEC_LISTS_I
    INCLUDE  "exec/lists.i"
    ENDC

    IFND  EXEC_PORTS_I
    INCLUDE  "exec/ports.i"
    ENDC

    IFND  EXEC_IO_I
    INCLUDE  "exec/io.i"
    ENDC

    DEVINIT

    DEVCMD   PRD_RAWWRITE
    DEVCMD   PRD_PRTCOMMAND
    DEVCMD   PRD_DUMPRPORT
    DEVCMD   PRD_QUERY

;****** printer definitions
aRIS       EQU     0 ; ESCc  reset                      ISO
aRIN       EQU     1 ; ESC#1 initialize                 +++
aIND       EQU     2 ; ESCD  lf                         ISO
aNEL       EQU     3 ; ESCE  return,lf                  ISO
aRI        EQU     4 ; ESCM  reverse lf                 ISO

aSGR0      EQU     5 ; ESC[0m normal char set           ISO
aSGR3      EQU     6 ; ESC[3m italics on                ISO
aSGR23     EQU     7 ; ESC[23m italics off              ISO
aSGR4      EQU     8 ; ESC[4m underline on              ISO
aSGR24     EQU     9 ; ESC[24m underline off            ISO
aSGR1      EQU    10 ; ESC[1m boldface on               ISO
aSGR22     EQU    11 ; ESC[22m boldface off             ISO
aSFC       EQU    12 ; SGR30-39  set foreground color   ISO
aSBC       EQU    13 ; SGR40-49  set background color   ISO

aSHORP0    EQU    14 ; ESC[0w normal pitch              DEC
aSHORP2    EQU    15 ; ESC[2w elite on                  DEC
aSHORP1    EQU    16 ; ESC[1w elite off                 DEC
aSHORP4    EQU    17 ; ESC[4w condensed fine on         DEC
aSHORP3    EQU    18 ; ESC[3w condensed off             DEC
aSHORP6    EQU    19 ; ESC[6w enlarged on               DEC
aSHORP5    EQU    20 ; ESC[5w enlarged off              DEC

aDEN6      EQU    21 ; ESC[6"z shadow print on          DEC (sort of)
aDEN5      EQU    22 ; ESC[5"z shadow print off         DEC
aDEN4      EQU    23 ; ESC[4"z doublestrike on          DEC
aDEN3      EQU    24 ; ESC[3"z doublestrike off         DEC
aDEN2      EQU    25 ; ESC[2"z  NLQ on                  DEC
aDEN1      EQU    26 ; ESC[1"z  NLQ off                 DEC

aSUS2      EQU    27 ; ESC[2v superscript on            +++
aSUS1      EQU    28 ; ESC[1v superscript off           +++
```



```
aSUS4      EQU    29 ; ESC[4v subscript on              +++
aSUS3      EQU    30 ; ESC[3v subscript off             +++
aSUS0      EQU    31 ; ESC[0v normalize the line        +++
aPLU       EQU    32 ; ESCL  partial line up            ISO
aPLD       EQU    33 ; ESCK  partial line down          ISO

aFNT0      EQU    34 ; ESC(B US char set        or Typeface  0 (default)
aFNT1      EQU    35 ; ESC(R French char set    or Typeface  1
aFNT2      EQU    36 ; ESC(K German char set    or Typeface  2
aFNT3      EQU    37 ; ESC(A UK char set        or Typeface  3
aFNT4      EQU    38 ; ESC(E Danish I char set  or Typeface  4
aFNT5      EQU    39 ; ESC(H Sweden char set    or Typeface  5
aFNT6      EQU    40 ; ESC(Y Italian char set   or Typeface  6
aFNT7      EQU    41 ; ESC(Z Spanish char set   or Typeface  7
aFNT8      EQU    42 ; ESC(J Japanese char set  or Typeface  8
aFNT9      EQU    43 ; ESC(6 Norweign char set  or Typeface  9
aFNT10     EQU    44 ; ESC(C Danish II char set or Typeface 10

;        Suggested typefaces are:
;
;          0 - default typeface.
;          1 - Line Printer or equiv.
;          2 - Pica or equiv.
;          3 - Elite or equiv.
;          4 - Helvetica or equiv.
;          5 - Times Roman or equiv.
;          6 - Gothic or equiv.
;          7 - Script or equiv.
;          8 - Prestige or equiv.
;          9 - Caslon or equiv.
;         10 - Orator or equiv.
;

aPROP2     EQU    45 ; ESC[2p  proportional on          +++
aPROP1     EQU    46 ; ESC[1p  proportional off         +++
aPROP0     EQU    47 ; ESC[0p  proportional clear       +++
aTSS       EQU    48 ; ESC[n E set proportional offset  ISO
aJFY5      EQU    49 ; ESC[5 F auto left justify        ISO
aJFY7      EQU    50 ; ESC[7 F auto right justiy        ISO
aJFY6      EQU    51 ; ESC[6 F auto full justify        ISO
aJFY0      EQU    52 ; ESC[0 F auto justify off         ISO
aJFY2      EQU    53 ; ESC[2 F  word space(auto center) ISO (special)
aJFY3      EQU    54 ; ESC[3 F letter space (justify)   ISO (special)

aVERP0     EQU    55 ; ESC[0z  1/8" line spacing        +++
aVERP1     EQU    56 ; ESC[1z  1/6" line spacing        +++
aSLPP      EQU    57 ; ESC[nt  set form length n        DEC
aPERF      EQU    58 ; ESC[nq  perf skip n (n>0)        +++
aPERF0     EQU    59 ; ESC[0q  perf skip off            +++

aLMS       EQU    60 ; ESC#9  Left margin set           +++
aRMS       EQU    61 ; ESC#0  Right margin set          +++
aTMS       EQU    62 ; ESC#8  Top margin set            +++
aBMS       EQU    63 ; ESC#2  Bottom marg set           +++
aSTBM      EQU    64 ; ESC[Pn1;Pn2r  T&B margins        DEC
aSLRM      EQU    65 ; ESC[Pn1;Pn2s  L&R margin         DEC
aCAM       EQU    66 ; ESC#3  Clear margins             +++

aHTS       EQU    67 ; ESCH    Set horiz tab            ISO
aVTS       EQU    68 ; ESCJ    Set vertical tabs        ISO
aTBC0      EQU    69 ; ESC[0g  Clr horiz tab            ISO
aTBC3      EQU    70 ; ESC[3g  Clear all h tab          ISO
aTBC1      EQU    71 ; ESC[1g  Clr vertical tabs        ISO
aTBC4      EQU    72 ; ESC[4g  Clr all v tabs           ISO
aTBCALL    EQU    73 ; ESC#4   Clr all h & v tabs       +++
aTBSALL    EQU    74 ; ESC#5   Set default tabs         +++
aEXTEND    EQU    75 ; ESC[Pn"x extended commands       +++

aRAW       EQU    76 ; ESC[Pn"r Next 'Pn' chars are raw +++
```

```
   STRUCTURE IOPrtCmdReq,IO_SIZE
      UWORD    io_PrtCommand  ; printer command
      UBYTE    io_Parm0    ; first command parameter
      UBYTE    io_Parm1    ; second command parameter
      UBYTE    io_Parm2    ; third command parameter
      UBYTE    io_Parm3    ; fourth command parameter
      LABEL    iopcr_SIZEOF

   STRUCTURE  IODRPReq,IO_SIZE
      APTR     io_RastPort     ; raster port
      APTR     io_ColorMap     ; color map
      ULONG    io_Modes        ; graphics viewport modes
      UWORD    io_SrcX         ; source x origin
      UWORD    io_SrcY         ; source y origin
      UWORD    io_SrcWidth     ; source x width
      UWORD    io_SrcHeight    ; source x height
      LONG     io_DestCols     ; destination x width
      LONG     io_DestRows     ; destination y height
      UWORD    io_Special      ; option flags
      LABEL    iodrpr_SIZEOF

 SPECIAL_MILCOLS          EQU     $0001    ; DestCols specified in 1/1000"
 SPECIAL_MILROWS          EQU     $0002    ; DestRows specified in 1/1000"
 SPECIAL_FULLCOLS         EQU     $0004    ; make DestCols maximum possible
 SPECIAL_FULLROWS         EQU     $0008    ; make DestRows maximum possible
 SPECIAL_FRACCOLS         EQU     $0010    ; DestCols is fraction of FULLCOLS
 SPECIAL_FRACROWS         EQU     $0020    ; DestRows is fraction of FULLROWS
 SPECIAL_CENTER           EQU     $0040    ; center image on paper
 SPECIAL_ASPECT           EQU     $0080    ; ensure correct aspect ratio
 SPECIAL_DENSITY1         EQU     $0100    ; lowest resolution (dpi)
 SPECIAL_DENSITY2         EQU     $0200    ; next res
 SPECIAL_DENSITY3         EQU     $0300    ; next res
 SPECIAL_DENSITY4         EQU     $0400    ; next res
 SPECIAL_DENSITY5         EQU     $0500    ; next res
 SPECIAL_DENSITY6         EQU     $0600    ; next res
 SPECIAL_DENSITY7         EQU     $0700    ; highest res
 SPECIAL_NOFORMFEED       EQU     $0800    ; don't eject paper after gfx prints
 SPECIAL_TRUSTME          EQU     $1000    ; don't reset on gfx prints
;
;       Compute print size, set 'io_DestCols' and 'io_DestRows' in the calling
;       program's 'IODRPReq' structure and exit, don't print.  This allows the
;       calling program to see what the final print size would be in printer
;       pixels.  Note that it modifies the 'io_DestCols' and 'io_DestRows'
;       fields of your 'IODRPReq' structure.  Also, set the print density and
;       update the 'MaxXDots', 'MaxYDots', 'XDotsInch', and 'YDotsInch' fields
;       of the 'PrinterExtendedData' structure.
;
 SPECIAL_NOPRINT          EQU     $2000    ; see above

 PDERR_NOERR              EQU     0        ; clean exit, no errors
 PDERR_CANCEL             EQU     1        ; user cancelled print
 PDERR_NOTGRAPHICS        EQU     2        ; printer cannot output graphics
 PDERR_INVERTHAM          EQU     3        ; OBSOLETE
 PDERR_BADDIMENSION       EQU     4        ; print dimensions illegal
 PDERR_DIMENSIONOVFLOW    EQU     5        ; OBSOLETE
 PDERR_INTERNALMEMORY     EQU     6        ; no memory for internal variables
 PDERR_BUFFERMEMORY       EQU     7        ; no memory for print buffer
;
;       Note : this is an internal error that can be returned from the render
;       function to the printer device.  It is NEVER returned to the user.
;       If the printer device sees this error it converts it 'PDERR_NOERR'
;       and exits gracefully.  Refer to the document on
;       'How to Write a Graphics Printer Driver' for more info.
;
 PDERR_TOOKCONTROL        EQU     8        ; I took control in case 0 of render

; internal use
```



```
 SPECIAL_DENSITYMASK      EQU $0700        ;  masks out density values
 SPECIAL_DIMENSIONSMASK   EQU SPECIAL_MILCOLS!SPECIAL_MILROWS!SPECIAL_FULLCOLS!SPE

          ENDC     ; DEVICES_PRINTER_I
```

```
        IFND    DEVICES_PRTBASE_I
DEVICES_PRTBASE_I       SET     1
**
**      $Filename: devices/prtbase.i $
**      $Release: 1.3 $
**
**      printer device data definition
**
**      (C) Copyright 1986,1987,1988 Commodore-Amiga, Inc.
**          All Rights Reserved
**

   IFND  EXEC_NODES_I
   INCLUDE  "exec/nodes.i"
   ENDC
   IFND  EXEC_LISTS_I
   INCLUDE  "exec/lists.i"
   ENDC
   IFND  EXEC_PORTS_I
   INCLUDE  "exec/ports.i"
   ENDC
   IFND  EXEC_LIBRARIES_I
   INCLUDE  "exec/libraries.i"
   ENDC
   IFND  EXEC_TASKS_I
   INCLUDE  "exec/tasks.i"
   ENDC

   IFND  DEVICES_PARALLEL_I
   INCLUDE  "devices/parallel.i"
   ENDC
   IFND  DEVICES_SERIAL_I
   INCLUDE  "devices/serial.i"
   ENDC
   IFND  DEVICES_TIMER_I
   INCLUDE  "devices/timer.i"
   ENDC
   IFND  LIBRARIES_DOSEXTENS_I
   INCLUDE  "libraries/dosextens.i"
   ENDC
   IFND  INTUITION_INTUITION_I
   INCLUDE  "intuition/intuition.i"
   ENDC


 STRUCTURE  DeviceData,LIB_SIZE
    APTR dd_Segment             ; A0 when initialized
    APTR dd_ExecBase            ; A6 for exec
    APTR dd_CmdVectors          ; command table for device commands
    APTR dd_CmdBytes            ; bytes describing which command queue
    UWORD   dd_NumCommands      ; the number of commands supported
    LABEL   DeviceData_SIZEOF ; (was dd_SIZEOF)


*------
*------ device driver private variables -------------------------------
*------
du_Flags EQU   LN_PRI          ; various unit flags

;------ IO_FLAGS
    BITDEF  IO,QUEUED,4        ; command is queued to be performed
    BITDEF  IO,CURRENT,5       ; command is being performed
    BITDEF  IO,SERVICING,6     ; command is being actively performed
    BITDEF  IO,DONE,7          ; command is done

;------ du_Flags
    BITDEF  DU,STOPPED,0       ; commands are not to be performed

```



```
*------ Constants ---------------------------------------------------
P_PRIORITY      EQU     0
P_STKSIZE       EQU     $0800   ; stack size for child task
P_BUFSIZE       EQU     256     ; size of internal buffers for text i/o
P_SAFESIZE      EQU     128     ; safety margin for text output buffer

*------ pd_Flags ------
   BITDEF   P,IOR0,0            ; IOR0 is in use
   BITDEF   P,IOR1,1            ; IOR1 is in use
   BITDEF   P,EXPUNGED,7        ; device to be expunged when all closed

 STRUCTURE  PrinterData,DeviceData_SIZEOF
    STRUCT  pd_Unit,MP_SIZE    ; the one and only unit
    BPTR pd_PrinterSegment     ; the printer specific segment
    UWORD   pd_PrinterType     ; the segment printer type
    APTR pd_SegmentData        ; the segment data structure
    APTR pd_PrintBuf           ; the raster print buffer
    APTR pd_PWrite             ; the parallel write function
    APTR pd_PBothReady         ; the parallel write function's done

    IFGT IOEXTPar_SIZE-IOEXTSER_SIZE
    STRUCT  pd_IOR0,IOEXTPar_SIZE   ; port I/O request 0
    STRUCT  pd_IOR1,IOEXTPar_SIZE   ;   and 1 for double buffering
    ENDC

    IFLE IOEXTPar_SIZE-IOEXTSER_SIZE
    STRUCT  pd_IOR0,IOEXTSER_SIZE   ; port I/O request 0
    STRUCT  pd_IOR1,IOEXTSER_SIZE   ;   and 1 for double buffering
    ENDC

    STRUCT  pd_TIOR,IOTV_SIZE       ; timer I/O request
    STRUCT  pd_IORPort,MP_SIZE      ;   and message reply port
    STRUCT  pd_TC,TC_SIZE           ; write task
    STRUCT  pd_Stk,P_STKSIZE        ;   and stack space
    UBYTE   pd_Flags                ; device flags
    UBYTE   pd_pad
    STRUCT  pd_Preferences,pf_SIZEOF ; the latest preferences
    UBYTE      pd_PWaitEnabled      ; wait function switch
    LABEL   pd_SIZEOF               ; warning! this may be odd

    BITDEF  PPC,GFX,0             ;graphics (bit position)
    BITDEF  PPC,COLOR,1           ;color (bit position)

PPC_BWALPHA     EQU     $00     ;black&white alphanumerics
PPC_BWGFX       EQU     $01     ;black&white graphics
PPC_COLORALPHA  EQU     $02     ;color alphanumerics
PPC_COLORGFX    EQU     $03     ;color graphics

PCC_BW          EQU     1       ;black&white only
PCC_YMC         EQU     2       ;yellow/magenta/cyan only
PCC_YMC_BW      EQU     3       ;yellow/magenta/cyan or black&white
PCC_YMCB        EQU     4       ;yellow/magenta/cyan/black

PCC_4COLOR      EQU     $4      ;a flag for YMCB and BGRW
PCC_ADDITIVE    EQU     $8      ;not ymcb but blue/green/red/white
PCC_WB          EQU     $9      ;black&white only, 0 == BLACK
PCC_BGR         EQU     $a      ;blue/green/red
PCC_BGR_WB      EQU     $b      ;blue/green/red or black&white
PCC_BGRW        EQU     $c      ;blue/green/red/white
;       The picture must be scanned once for each color component, as the
;       printer can only define one color at a time.  ie. If 'PCC_YMC' then
;       first pass sends all 'Y' info to printer, second pass sends all 'M'
;       info, and third pass sends all C info to printer.  The CalComp
;       PlotMaster is an example of this type of printer.
PCC_MULTI_PASS  EQU     $10     ;see explanation above

 STRUCTURE  PrinterExtendedData,0
    APTR    ped_PrinterName     ; printer name, null terminated
    APTR    ped_Init            ; called after LoadSeg
```

Sep 28 17:08 1988 devices/prtbase.i Page 3

```
        APTR    ped_Expunge       ; called before UnLoadSeg
        APTR    ped_Open          ; called at OpenDevice
        APTR    ped_Close         ; called at CloseDevice
        UBYTE   ped_PrinterClass  ; printer class
        UBYTE   ped_ColorClass    ; color class
        UBYTE   ped_MaxColumns    ; number of print columns available
        UBYTE   ped_NumCharSets   ; number of character sets
        UWORD   ped_NumRows       ; number of 'pins' in print head
        ULONG   ped_MaxXDots      ; number of dots maximum in a raster dump
        ULONG   ped_MaxYDots      ; number of dots maximum in a raster dump
        UWORD   ped_XDotsInch     ; horizontal dot density
        UWORD   ped_YDotsInch     ; vertical dot density
        APTR    ped_Commands      ; printer text command table
        APTR    ped_DoSpecial     ; special command handler
        APTR    ped_Render        ; raster render function
        LONG    ped_TimeoutSecs   ; good write timeout
;------ the following only exists if the segment version is 33 or greater
            APTR    ped_8BitChars  ;conversion strings for the extended font
            LONG    ped_PrintMode  ;set if text printed, otherwise 0
;------ the following only exists if the segment version is 34 or greater
            APTR    ped_ConvFunv    ; ptr to conversion functior for all chars
            LABEL   ped_SIZEOF

 STRUCTURE  PrinterSegment,0
    ULONG   ps_NextSegment      ; (actually a BPTR)
    ULONG   ps_runAlert         ; MOVEQ #0,D0 : RTS
    UWORD   ps_Version          ; segment version
    UWORD   ps_Revision         ; segment revision
    LABEL   ps_PED              ; printer extended data

        ENDC    ; DEVICES_PRTBASE_I
```

Sep 28 20:33 1988 devices/prtgfx.i Page 1

```
        IFND    DEVICES_PRTGFX_I
DEVICES_PRTGFX_I        SET     1
**
**      $Filename: devices/prtgfx.i $
**      $Release: 1.3 $
**
**
**
**      (C) Copyright 1987,1988 Commodore-Amiga, Inc.
**          All Rights Reserved
**

PCMYELLOW       EQU     0               ; byte index for yellow
PCMMAGENTA      EQU     1               ; byte index for magenta
PCMCYAN         EQU     2               ; byte index for cyan
PCMBLACK        EQU     3               ; byte index for black
PCMBLUE         EQU     PCMYELLOW       ; byte index for blue
PCMGREEN        EQU     PCMMAGENTA      ; byte index for green
PCMRED          EQU     PCMCYAN         ; byte index for red
PCMWHITE        EQU     PCMBLACK        ; byte index for white

        STRUCTURE       colorEntry,0
                LABEL   colorLong       ; quick access to all of YMCB
                LABEL   colorSByte      ; 1 entry for each of YMCB
                STRUCT  colorByte,4     ; ditto (except signed)
                LABEL   ce_SIZEOF

        STRUCTURE       PrtInfo,0
                APTR    pi_render       ; PRIVATE - DO NOT USE!
                APTR    pi_rp           ; PRIVATE - DO NOT USE!
                APTR    pi_temprp       ; PRIVATE - DO NOT USE!
                APTR    pi_RowBuf       ; PRIVATE - DO NOT USE!
                APTR    pi_HamBuf       ; PRIVATE - DO NOT USE!
                APTR    pi_ColorMap     ; PRIVATE - DO NOT USE!
                APTR    pi_ColorInt     ; color intensities for entire row
                APTR    pi_HamInt       ; PRIVATE - DO NOT USE!
                APTR    pi_Dest1Int     ; PRIVATE - DO NOT USE!
                APTR    pi_Dest2Int     ; PRIVATE - DO NOT USE!
                APTR    pi_ScaleX       ; array of scale values for X
                APTR    pi_ScaleXAlt    ; PRIVATE - DO NOT USE!
                APTR    pi_dmatrix      ; pointer to dither matrix
                APTR    pi_TopBuf       ; PRIVATE - DO NOT USE!
                APTR    pi_BotBuf       ; PRIVATE - DO NOT USE!

                UWORD   pi_RowBufSize   ; PRIVATE - DO NOT USE!
                UWORD   pi_HamBufSize   ; PRIVATE - DO NOT USE!
                UWORD   pi_ColorMapSize ; PRIVATE - DO NOT USE!
                UWORD   pi_ColorIntSize ; PRIVATE - DO NOT USE!
                UWORD   pi_HamIntSize   ; PRIVATE - DO NOT USE!
                UWORD   pi_Dest1IntSize ; PRIVATE - DO NOT USE!
                UWORD   pi_Dest2IntSize ; PRIVATE - DO NOT USE!
                UWORD   pi_ScaleXSize   ; PRIVATE - DO NOT USE!
                UWORD   pi_ScaleXAltSize ; PRIVATE - DO NOT USE!

                UWORD   pi_PrefsFlags   ; PRIVATE - DO NOT USE!
                ULONG   pi_special      ; PRIVATE - DO NOT USE!
                UWORD   pi_xstart       ; PRIVATE - DO NOT USE!
                UWORD   pi_ystart       ; PRIVATE - DO NOT USE!
                UWORD   pi_width        ; source width (in pixels)
                UWORD   pi_height       ; PRIVATE - DO NOT USE!
                ULONG   pi_pc           ; PRIVATE - DO NOT USE!
                ULONG   pi_pr           ; PRIVATE - DO NOT USE!
                UWORD   pi_ymult        ; PRIVATE - DO NOT USE!
                UWORD   pi_ymod         ; PRIVATE - DO NOT USE!
                UWORD   pi_ety          ; PRIVATE - DO NOT USE!
                UWORD   pi_xpos         ; offset to start printing from
                UWORD   pi_threshold    ; copy of threshold value (from prefs)
                UWORD   pi_tempwidth    ; PRIVATE - DO NOT USE!
                UWORD   pi_flags        ; PRIVATE - DO NOT USE!
```

```
                LABEL   prtinfo_SIZEOF

        ENDC    ; DEVICES_PRTGFX_I
```



```
        IFND    DEVICES_SCSIDISK_I
DEVICES_SCSIDISK_I      EQU     1
**
**      $Filename: devices/scsidisk.i $
**      $Revision: 1.0 $
**      $Date: 88/07/11 15:33:14 $
**
**      SCSI exec-level device command
**
**      (C) Copyright 1988 Commodore-Amiga, Inc.
**          All Rights Reserved
**

;---------------------------------------------------------------------
;
;   SCSI Command
;       Several Amiga SCSI controller manufacturers are converging on
;       standard ways to talk to their controllers.  This include
;       file describes an exec-device command (e.g. for hddisk.device)
;       that can be used to issue SCSI commands
;
;   UNIT NUMBERS
;       Unit numbers to the OpenDevice call have encoded in them which
;       SCSI device is being referred to.  The three decimal digits of
;       the unit number refer to the SCSI Target ID (bus address) in
;       the 1's digit, the SCSI logical unit (LUN) in the 10's digit,
;       and the controller board in the 100's digit.
;
;       Examples:
;                 0     drive at address 0
;                12     LUN 1 on multiple drive controller at address 2
;               104     second controller board, address 4
;                88     not valid: both logical units and addresses
;                       range from 0..7.
;
;   CAVEATS
;       Original 2090 code did not support this command.
;
;       Commodore 2090/2090A unit numbers are different.  The SCSI
;       logical unit is the 100's digit, and the SCSI Target ID
;       is a permuted 1's digit: Target ID 0..6 maps to unit 3..9
;       (7 is reserved for the controller).
;
;           Examples:
;                 3     drive at address 0
;               109     drive at address 6, logical unit 1
;                 1     not valid: this is not a SCSI unit.  Perhaps
;                       it's an ST506 unit.
;
;       Some controller boards generate a unique name (e.g. 2090A's
;       iddisk.device) for the second controller board, instead of
;       implementing the 100's digit.
;
;       There are optional restrictions on the alignment, bus
;       accessability, and size of the data for the data phase.
;       Be conservative to work with all manufacturer's controllers.
;
;---------------------------------------------------------------------

HD_SCSICMD      EQU     28      ; issue a SCSI command to the unit
                                ; io_Data points to a SCSICmd
                                ; io_Length is sizeof(struct SCSICmd)
                                ; io_Actual and io_Offset are not used

 STRUCTURE      SCSICmd,0
    APTR    scsi_Data           ; word aligned data for SCSI Data Phase
                                ; (optional) data need not be byte aligned
                                ; (optional) data need not be bus accessable
    ULONG   scsi_Length         ; even length of Data area
```

Sep 28 17:08 1988 devices/scsidisk.i Page 2

```
                                        ; (optional) data can have odd length
                                        ; (optional) data length can be > 2**24
        ULONG   scsi_Actual             ; actual Data used
        APTR    scsi_Command            ; SCSI Command (same options as scsi_Data)
        UWORD   scsi_CmdLength          ; length of Command
        UWORD   scsi_CmdActual          ; actual Command used
        UBYTE   scsi_Flags              ; includes intended data direction
        UBYTE   scsi_Status             ; SCSI status of command
        LABEL   scsi_SIZEOF


;------ scsi_Flags ------
SCSIF_WRITE                 EQU     0       ; intended data direction is out
SCSIF_READ                  EQU     1       ; intended data direction is in

;------ SCSI io_Error values ------
HFERR_SelfUnit              EQU     40      ; cannot issue SCSI command to self
HFERR_DMA                   EQU     41      ; DMA error
HFERR_Phase                 EQU     42      ; illegal or unexpected SCSI phase
HFERR_Parity                EQU     43      ; SCSI parity error
HFERR_SelTimeout            EQU     44      ; Select timed out
HFERR_BadStatus             EQU     45      ; status and/or sense error

;------ OpenDevice io_Error values ------
HFERR_NoBoard               EQU     50      ; Open failed for non-existant board

        ENDC    ; DEVICES_SCSIDISK_I
```

Sep 28 17:08 1988 devices/serial.i Page 1

```
        IFND DEVICES_SERIAL_I
DEVICES_SERIAL_I SET 1
**
**      $Filename: devices/serial.i $
**      $Release: 1.3 $
**
**      external declarations for the serial device
**
**      (C) Copyright 1985,1986,1987,1988 Commodore-Amiga, Inc.
**          All Rights Reserved
**
    IFND     EXEC_IO_I
    include "exec/io.i"
    ENDC         ; EXEC_IO_I

*----------------------------------------------------------------------
*
* Useful constants
*
*----------------------------------------------------------------------
*
SER_DEFAULT_CTLCHAR EQU $11130000  ; default chars for xON,xOFF
; You may change these via SETPARAMS.  At this time, parity is not
; calculated for xON/xOFF characters.  You must supply them with the
; desired parity.

*
*----------------------------------------------------------------------
*
* Driver Specific Commands

SDCMD_QUERY     EQU     CMD_NONSTD
SDCMD_BREAK     EQU     CMD_NONSTD+1
SDCMD_SETPARAMS EQU     CMD_NONSTD+2

SER_DEVFINISH   EQU     CMD_NONSTD+2 ; number of device comands

*----------------------------------------------------------------------

SERIALNAME:     MACRO
                dc.b    'serial.device',0
                dc.w    0
                ENDM

        BITDEF  SER,XDISABLED,7   ; SERFLAGS xOn-xOff feature disabled bit
        BITDEF  SER,EOFMODE,6     ;    "     EOF mode enabled bit
        BITDEF  SER,SHARED,5      ;    "     non-exclusive access
        BITDEF  SER,RAD_BOOGIE,4  ;    "     high-speed mode active
        BITDEF  SER,QUEUEDBRK,3   ;    "     queue this Break ioRqst
        BITDEF  SER,7WIRE,2       ;    "     RS232 7-wire protocol
        BITDEF  SER,PARTY_ODD,1   ;    "     use-odd-parity bit
        BITDEF  SER,PARTY_ON,0    ;    "     parity-enabled bit
;
;WARNING: The next series of BITDEFs refer to the HIGH order BYTE of
;IO_STATUS.  Example usage: "BTST.B #IOST_XOFFWRITE,IO_STATUS+1(AX)"
;
        BITDEF  IOST,XOFFREAD,4   ; IOST_HOB receive currently xOFF'ed
        BITDEF  IOST,XOFFWRITE,3  ;    "     transmit currently xOFF'ed
        BITDEF  IOST,READBREAK,2  ;    "     break was latest input
        BITDEF  IOST,WROTEBREAK,1 ;    "     break was latest output
        BITDEF  IOST,OVERRUN,0    ;    "     status word RBF overrun
;
;       BITDEF's in a longword field)
;       Example usage: BSET.B #SEXTB_MSPON,IO_EXTFLAGS+3(AX)
                                  ;IO_EXTFLAGS (extended flag longword)
        BITDEF  SEXT,MSPON,1      ;     "    use mark-space parity,not odd-even
        BITDEF  SEXT,MARK,0       ;     "    if mark-space, use mark
*
**************************************************************************
```

```
 STRUCTURE TERMARRAY,0
        ULONG    TERMARRAY_0
        ULONG    TERMARRAY_1
        LABEL    TERMARRAY_SIZE

*******************************************************************
* CAUTION !!  IF YOU ACCESS the serial.device, you MUST (!!!!) use an
* IOEXTSER-sized structure or you may overlay innocent memory, okay ?!
*******************************************************************

 STRUCTURE IOEXTSER,IOSTD_SIZE

*      STRUCT   MsgNode
*   0   APTR     Succ
*   4   APTR     Pred
*   8   UBYTE    Type
*   9   UBYTE    Pri
*   A   APTR     Name
*   E   APTR     ReplyPort
*  12   UWORD    MNLength
*      STRUCT   IOExt
*  14   APTR     IO_DEVICE
*  18   APTR     IO_UNIT
*  1C   UWORD    IO_COMMAND
*  1E   UBYTE    IO_FLAGS
*  1F   UBYTE    IO_ERROR
*      STRUCT   IOStdExt
*  20   ULONG    IO_ACTUAL
*  24   ULONG    IO_LENGTH
*  28   APTR     IO_DATA
*  2C   ULONG    IO_OFFSET
*
*  30
        ULONG   IO_CTLCHAR      ; control char's (order = xON,xOFF,rsvd,rsvd)
        ULONG   IO_RBUFLEN      ; length in bytes of serial port's read buffer
        ULONG   IO_EXTFLAGS     ; additional serial flags (see bitdefs above)
        ULONG   IO_BAUD         ; baud rate requested (true baud)
        ULONG   IO_BRKTIME      ; duration of break signal in MICROseconds
        STRUCT  IO_TERMARRAY,TERMARRAY_SIZE ; termination character array
        UBYTE   IO_READLEN      ; bits per read char (bit count)
        UBYTE   IO_WRITELEN     ; bits per write char (bit count)
        UBYTE   IO_STOPBITS     ; stopbits for read (count)
        UBYTE   IO_SERFLAGS     ; see SERFLAGS bit definitions above
        UWORD   IO_STATUS       ; status of serial port, as follows:
*
*                BIT  ACTIVE  FUNCTION
*                 0    ---    reserved
*                 1    ---    reserved
*                 2    high   Connected to parallel "select" on the A1000.
*                             Connected to both the parallel "select" and
*                             serial "ring indicator" pins on the A500 &
*                             A2000.  Take care when making cables.
*                 3    low    Data Set Ready
*                 4    low    Clear To Send
*                 5    low    Carrier Detect
*                 6    low    Ready To Send
*                 7    low    Data Terminal Ready
*                 8    high   read overrun
*                 9    high   break sent
*                10    high   break received
*                11    high   transmit x-OFF'ed
*                12    high   receive x-OFF'ed
*             13-15           reserved
*
        LABEL   IOEXTSER_SIZE

*****************************************************************************

*---------------------------------------------------------------------
```



```
*
* Driver error definitions
*
*---------------------------------------------------------------------

SerErr_DevBusy          EQU     1
SerErr_BufErr           EQU     4       ;Failed to allocate new read buffer
SerErr_InvParam         EQU     5
SerErr_LineErr          EQU     6
SerErr_ParityErr        EQU     9
SerErr_TimerErr         EQU     11      ;(See the serial/OpenDevice autodoc)
SerErr_BufOverflow      EQU     12
SerErr_NoDSR            EQU     13
SerErr_DetectedBreak    EQU     15


 IFD    DEVICES_SERIAL_I_OBSOLETE
SER_DBAUD               EQU     9600    ;unused
SerErr_BaudMismatch     EQU     2       ;unused
SerErr_InvBaud          EQU     3       ;unused
SerErr_NotOpen          EQU     7       ;unused
SerErr_PortReset        EQU     8       ;unused
SerErr_InitErr          EQU     10      ;unused
SerErr_NoCTS            EQU     14      ;unused
        BITDEF  IOSER,QUEUED,6    ; IO_FLAGS rqst-queued bit
        BITDEF  IOSER,ABORT,5     ;     "    rqst-aborted bit
        BITDEF  IOSER,ACTIVE,4    ;     "    rqst-qued-or-current bit
 ENDC

        ENDC    ; DEVICES_SERIAL_I
```

```
        IFND    DEVICES_TIMER_I
DEVICES_TIMER_I SET     1
**
**      $Filename: devices/timer.i $
**      $Release: 1.3 $
**
**
**
**      (C) Copyright 1985,1986,1987,1988 Commodore-Amiga, Inc.
**          All Rights Reserved
**

        IFND    EXEC_IO_I
        INCLUDE "exec/io.i"
        ENDC    ; EXEC_IO_I

* unit defintions
UNIT_MICROHZ    EQU     0
UNIT_VBLANK     EQU     1

TIMERNAME       MACRO
                DC.B    'timer.device',0
                DS.W    0
                ENDM

 STRUCTURE TIMEVAL,0
        ULONG   TV_SECS
        ULONG   TV_MICRO
        LABEL   TV_SIZE

 STRUCTURE TIMEREQUEST,IO_SIZE
        STRUCT  IOTV_TIME,TV_SIZE
        LABEL   IOTV_SIZE

* IO_COMMAND to use for adding a timer
        DEVINIT
        DEVCMD  TR_ADDREQUEST
        DEVCMD  TR_GETSYSTIME
        DEVCMD  TR_SETSYSTIME

        ENDC    ; DEVICES_TIMER_I
```



```
        IFND    DEVICES_TRACKDISK_I
DEVICES_TRACKDISK_I     SET     1
**
**      $Filename: devices/trackdisk.i $
**      $Release: 1.3 $
**
**
**
**      (C) Copyright 1985,1986,1987,1988 Commodore-Amiga, Inc.
**          All Rights Reserved
**

        IFND    EXEC_IO_I
        INCLUDE "exec/io.i"
        ENDC    ; EXEC_IO_I

        IFND    EXEC_DEVICES_I
        INCLUDE "exec/devices.i"
        ENDC    ; EXEC_DEVICES_I

*----------------------------------------------------------------------
*
* Physical drive constants
*
*----------------------------------------------------------------------


* OBSOLETE -- only valid for 3 1/4" drives.  Use the TD_GETNUMTRACKS command!
*
*NUMCYLS                EQU     80              ; normal # of cylinders
*MAXCYLS                EQU     NUMCYLS+20      ; max # of cyls to look for
*                                               ;       during a calibrate
*NUMHEADS       EQU     2
*NUMTRACKS      EQU     NUMCYLS*NUMHEADS

NUMSECS         EQU     11
NUMUNITS        EQU     4

*----------------------------------------------------------------------
*
* Useful constants
*
*----------------------------------------------------------------------


*-- sizes before mfm encoding
TD_SECTOR       EQU     512
TD_SECSHIFT     EQU     9                       ; log TD_SECTOR
*                                               ;    2


*----------------------------------------------------------------------
*
* Driver Specific Commands
*
*----------------------------------------------------------------------

*-- TD_NAME is a generic macro to get the name of the driver.  This
*-- way if the name is ever changed you will pick up the change
*-- automatically.
*--
*-- Normal usage would be:
*--
*-- internalName:       TD_NAME
*--

TD_NAME:        MACRO
                DC.B    'trackdisk.device',0
                DS.W    0
```

```
                ENDM

        BITDEF  TD,EXTCOM,15

        DEVINIT
        DEVCMD  TD_MOTOR                ; control the disk's motor
        DEVCMD  TD_SEEK                 ; explicit seek (for testing)
        DEVCMD  TD_FORMAT               ; format disk
        DEVCMD  TD_REMOVE               ; notify when disk changes
        DEVCMD  TD_CHANGENUM            ; number of disk changes
        DEVCMD  TD_CHANGESTATE          ; is there a disk in the drive?
        DEVCMD  TD_PROTSTATUS           ; is the disk write protected?
        DEVCMD  TD_RAWREAD              ; read raw bits from the disk
        DEVCMD  TD_RAWWRITE             ; write raw bits to the disk
        DEVCMD  TD_GETDRIVETYPE         ; get the type of the disk drive
        DEVCMD  TD_GETNUMTRACKS         ; get the # of tracks on this disk
        DEVCMD  TD_ADDCHANGEINT         ; TD_REMOVE done right
        DEVCMD  TD_REMCHANGEINT         ; removes softint set by ADDCHANGEINT
        DEVCMD  TD_LASTCOMM             ; dummy placeholder for end of list


*
*
* The disk driver has an "extended command" facility.  These commands
* take a superset of the normal IO Request block.
*
ETD_WRITE       EQU     (CMD_WRITE!TDF_EXTCOM)
ETD_READ        EQU     (CMD_READ!TDF_EXTCOM)
ETD_MOTOR       EQU     (TD_MOTOR!TDF_EXTCOM)
ETD_SEEK        EQU     (TD_SEEK!TDF_EXTCOM)
ETD_FORMAT      EQU     (TD_FORMAT!TDF_EXTCOM)
ETD_UPDATE      EQU     (CMD_UPDATE!TDF_EXTCOM)
ETD_CLEAR       EQU     (CMD_CLEAR!TDF_EXTCOM)
ETD_RAWREAD     EQU     (TD_RAWREAD!TDF_EXTCOM)
ETD_RAWWRITE    EQU     (TD_RAWWRITE!TDF_EXTCOM)


*
* extended IO has a larger than normal io request block.
*

 STRUCTURE IOEXTTD,IOSTD_SIZE
        ULONG   IOTD_COUNT      ; removal/insertion count
        ULONG   IOTD_SECLABEL   ; sector label data region
        LABEL   IOTD_SIZE

*
* raw read and write can be synced with the index pulse.  This flag
* in io request's IO_FLAGS field tells the driver that you want this.
*
        BITDEF  IOTD,INDEXSYNC,4

* labels are TD_LABELSIZE bytes per sector

TD_LABELSIZE    EQU     16

*
* This is a bit in the FLAGS field of OpenDevice.  If it is set, then
* the driver will allow you to open all the disks that the trackdisk
* driver understands.  Otherwise only 3.5" disks will succeed.
*
*
        BITDEF  TD,ALLOW_NON_3_5,0

*
*  If you set the TDB_ALLOW_NON_3_5 bit in OpenDevice, then you don't
*  know what type of disk you really got.  These defines are for the
*  TD_GETDRIVETYPE command.  In addition, you can find out how many
*  tracks are supported via the TD_GETNUMTRACKS command.
```



```
*
DRIVE3_5        EQU     1
DRIVE5_25       EQU     2

*----------------------------------------------------------------------
*
* Driver error defines
*
*----------------------------------------------------------------------

TDERR_NotSpecified      EQU     20      ; general catchall
TDERR_NoSecHdr          EQU     21      ; couldn't even find a sector
TDERR_BadSecPreamble    EQU     22      ; sector looked wrong
TDERR_BadSecID          EQU     23      ; ditto
TDERR_BadHdrSum         EQU     24      ; header had incorrect checksum
TDERR_BadSecSum         EQU     25      ; data had incorrect checksum
TDERR_TooFewSecs        EQU     26      ; couldn't find enough sectors
TDERR_BadSecHdr         EQU     27      ; another "sector looked wrong"
TDERR_WriteProt         EQU     28      ; can't write to a protected disk
TDERR_DiskChanged       EQU     29      ; no disk in the drive
TDERR_SeekError         EQU     30      ; couldn't find track 0
TDERR_NoMem             EQU     31      ; ran out of memory
TDERR_BadUnitNum        EQU     32      ; asked for a unit > NUMUNITS
TDERR_BadDriveType      EQU     33      ; not a drive that trackdisk groks
TDERR_DriveInUse        EQU     34      ; someone else allocated the drive
TDERR_PostReset         EQU     35      ; user hit reset; awaiting doom

*----------------------------------------------------------------------
*
* Public portion of unit structure
*
*----------------------------------------------------------------------

 STRUCTURE TDU_PUBLICUNIT,UNIT_SIZE
        UWORD   TDU_COMP01TRACK         ; track for first precomp
        UWORD   TDU_COMP10TRACK         ; track for second precomp
        UWORD   TDU_COMP11TRACK         ; track for third precomp
        ULONG   TDU_STEPDELAY           ; time to wait after stepping
        ULONG   TDU_SETTLEDELAY         ; time to wait after seeking
        UBYTE   TDU_RETRYCNT            ; # of times to retry
        LABEL   TDU_PUBLICUNITSIZE

        ENDC    ; DEVICES_TRACKDISK_I
```

```
        IFND    EXEC_ABLES_I
EXEC_ABLES_I    SET     1
**
**      $Filename: exec/ables.i $
**      $Release: 1.3 $
**
**
**
**      (C) Copyright 1985,1986,1987,1988 Commodore-Amiga, Inc.
**          All Rights Reserved
**

    IFND EXEC_TYPES_I
    INCLUDE "exec/types.i"
    ENDC        ; EXEC_TYPES_I

    IFND EXEC_EXECBASE_I
    INCLUDE "exec/execbase.i"
    ENDC        ; EXEC_EXECBASE_I


*----------------------------------------------------------------
*
*   Interrupt Exclusion Macros
*
*----------------------------------------------------------------

INT_ABLES   MACRO                       * externals for dis/enable
            XREF    _intena
            ENDM


DISABLE     MACRO   * [scratchReg]
            IFC     '\1',''
            MOVE.W  #$04000,_intena     *(NOT IF_SETCLR)+IF_INTEN
            ADDQ.B  #1,IDNestCnt(A6)
            ENDC
            IFNC    '\1',''
            MOVE.L  4,\1
            MOVE.W  #$04000,_intena     *(NOT IF_SETCLR)+IF_INTEN
            ADDQ.B  #1,IDNestCnt(\1)
            ENDC
            ENDM


ENABLE      MACRO   * [scratchReg]
            IFC     '\1',''
            SUBQ.B  #1,IDNestCnt(A6)
            BGE.S   ENABLE\@
            MOVE.W  #$0C000,_intena     *IF_SETCLR+IF_INTEN
ENABLE\@:
            ENDC
            IFNC    '\1',''
            MOVE.L  4,\1
            SUBQ.B  #1,IDNestCnt(\1)
            BGE.S   ENABLE\@
            MOVE.W  #$0C000,_intena
ENABLE\@:
            ENDC
            ENDM


*----------------------------------------------------------------
*
*   Tasking Exclusion Macros
*
*----------------------------------------------------------------

TASK_ABLES  MACRO
```



```
*           INCLUDE "execbase.i" for TDNestCnt offset
            XREF    _LVOPermit
            ENDM


FORBID      MACRO
            IFC     '\1',''
            ADDQ.B  #1,TDNestCnt(A6)
            ENDC
            IFNC    '\1',''
            MOVE.L  4,\1
            ADDQ.B  #1,TDNestCnt(\1)
            ENDC
            ENDM


PERMIT      MACRO
            IFC     '\1',''
            JSR     _LVOPermit(A6)
            ENDC
            IFNC    '\1',''
            MOVE.L  A6,-(SP)
            MOVE.L  4,A6
            JSR     _LVOPermit(A6)
            MOVE.L  (SP)+,A6
            ENDC
            ENDM

        ENDC    ; EXEC_ABLES_I
```

```
        IFND    EXEC_ALERTS_I
EXEC_ALERTS_I   SET     1
**
**      $Filename: exec/alerts.i $
**      $Release: 1.3 $
**
**
**
**      (C) Copyright 1985,1986,1987,1988 Commodore-Amiga, Inc.
**          All Rights Reserved
**

    BITDEF  S,ALERTWACK,1       * in ExecBase.SysFlags


*********************************************************************
*
*  Format of the alert error number:
*
*    +-+-------------+----------------+--------------------------------+
*    |D|  SubSysId   |  General Error |    SubSystem Specific Error    |
*    +-+-------------+----------------+--------------------------------+
*
*                     D:  DeadEnd alert
*              SubSysId:  indicates ROM subsystem number.
*         General Error:  roughly indicates what the error was
*        Specific Error:  indicates more detail
**********************************************************************

*
*  Use this macro for causing an alert.  THIS MACRO MAY CHANGE!
*  It is very sensitive to memory corruption.... like stepping on
*  location 4!  But it should work for now.
*
ALERT           macro   (alertNumber, paramArray, scratch)
                movem.l d7/a5/a6,-(sp)
                move.l  #\1,d7
                IFNC    '\2',''
                lea     \2,a5
                ENDC
                move.l  4,a6            ; (use proper name!!!)
                jsr     _LVOAlert(a6)
                movem.l (sp)+,d7/a5/a6
                endm


*********************************************************************
*
*  General Dead-End Alerts
*
*  For example:  timer.device cannot open math.library:
*
*       ALERT  (AN_TimerDev!AG_OpenLib!AO_MathLib),(A0),A1
*
*********************************************************************

;------ alert types
AT_DeadEnd      equ $80000000
AT_Recovery     equ $00000000

;------ general purpose alert codes
AG_NoMemory     equ $00010000
AG_MakeLib      equ $00020000
AG_OpenLib      equ $00030000
AG_OpenDev      equ $00040000
AG_OpenRes      equ $00050000
AG_IOError      equ $00060000
AG_NoSignal     equ $00070000

```



```
;------ alert objects:
AO_ExecLib        equ $00008001
AO_GraphicsLib    equ $00008002
AO_LayersLib      equ $00008003
AO_Intuition      equ $00008004
AO_MathLib        equ $00008005
AO_CListLib       equ $00008006
AO_DOSLib         equ $00008007
AO_RAMLib         equ $00008008
AO_IconLib        equ $00008009
AO_ExpansionLib   equ $0000800A
AO_AudioDev       equ $00008010
AO_ConsoleDev     equ $00008011
AO_GamePortDev    equ $00008012
AO_KeyboardDev    equ $00008013
AO_TrackDiskDev   equ $00008014
AO_TimerDev       equ $00008015
AO_CIARsrc        equ $00008020
AO_DiskRsrc       equ $00008021
AO_MiscRsrc       equ $00008022
AO_BootStrap      equ $00008030
AO_Workbench      equ $00008031


*********************************************************************
*
*  Specific Dead-End Alerts:
*
*  For example:   exec.library -- corrupted memory list
*
*          ALERT  AN_MemCorrupt,(A0),A1
*
*********************************************************************

;------ exec.library
AN_ExecLib       equ $01000000
AN_ExcptVect     equ $81000001   ; 68000 exception vector checksum
AN_BaseChkSum    equ $81000002   ; execbase checksum
AN_LibChkSum     equ $81000003   ; library checksum failure
AN_LibMem        equ $81000004   ; no memory to make library
AN_MemCorrupt    equ $81000005   ; corrupted memory list
AN_IntrMem       equ $81000006   ; no memory for interrupt servers
AN_InitAPtr      equ $81000007   ; InitStruct() of an APTR source
AN_SemCorrupt    equ $81000008   ; a semaphore is in illegal state
AN_FreeTwice     equ $81000009   ; freeing memory that is already free
AN_BogusExcpt    equ $8100000A   ; illegal 68k exception taken

;------ graphics.library
AN_GraphicsLib   equ $02000000
AN_GfxNoMem      equ $82010000   ; graphics out of memory
AN_LongFrame     equ $82010006   ; long frame, no memory
AN_ShortFrame    equ $82010007   ; short frame, no memory
AN_TextTmpRas    equ $02010009   ; text, no memory for TmpRas
AN_BltBitMap     equ $8201000A   ; BltBitMap, no memory
AN_RegionMemory  equ $8201000B   ; regions, memory not available
AN_MakeVPort     equ $82010030   ; MakeVPort, no memory
AN_GfxNoLCM      equ $82011234   ; emergency memory not available

;------ layers.library
AN_LayersLib     equ $03000000
AN_LayersNoMem   equ $83010000   ; layers out of memory

;------ intuition.library
AN_Intuition     equ $04000000
AN_GadgetType    equ $84000001   ; unknown gadet type
AN_BadGadget     equ $04000001   ; Recovery form of AN_GadgetType
AN_CreatePort    equ $84010002   ; create port, no memory
AN_ItemAlloc     equ $04010003   ; item plane alloc, no memory
AN_SubAlloc      equ $04010004   ; sub alloc, no memory
```

```
AN_PlaneAlloc    equ $84010005   ; plane alloc, no memory
AN_ItemBoxTop    equ $84000006   ; item box top < RelZero
AN_OpenScreen    equ $84010007   ; open screen, no memory
AN_OpenScrnRast  equ $84010008   ; open screen, raster alloc, no memory
AN_SysScrnType   equ $84000009   ; open sys screen, unknown type
AN_AddSWGadget   equ $8401000A   ; add SW gadgets, no memory
AN_OpenWindow    equ $8401000B   ; open window, no memory
AN_BadState      equ $8400000C   ; Bad State Return entering Intuition
AN_BadMessage    equ $8400000D   ; Bad Message received by IDCMP
AN_WeirdEcho     equ $8400000E   ; Weird echo causing incomprehension
AN_NoConsole     equ $8400000F   ; couldn't open the Console Device

;------ math.library
AN_MathLib       equ $05000000

;------ clist.library
AN_CListLib      equ $06000000

;------ dos.library
AN_DOSLib        equ $07000000
AN_StartMem      equ $07010001   ; no memory at startup
AN_EndTask       equ $07000002   ; EndTask didn't
AN_QPktFail      equ $07000003   ; Qpkt failure
AN_AsyncPkt      equ $07000004   ; Unexpected packet received
AN_FreeVec       equ $07000005   ; Freevec failed
AN_DiskBlkSeq    equ $07000006   ; Disk block sequence error
AN_BitMap        equ $07000007   ; Bitmap corrupt
AN_KeyFree       equ $07000008   ; Key already free
AN_BadChkSum     equ $07000009   ; Invalid checksum
AN_DiskError     equ $0700000A   ; Disk Error
AN_KeyRange      equ $0700000B   ; Key out of range
AN_BadOverlay    equ $0700000C   ; Bad overlay

;------ ramlib.library
AN_RAMLib        equ $08000000
AN_BadSegList    equ $08000001   ; overlays are illegal for library segments

;------ icon.library
AN_IconLib       equ $09000000

;------ expansion.library
AN_ExpansionLib equ $0A000000
AN_BadExpansionFree      equ $0A000001

;------ audio.device
AN_AudioDev      equ $10000000

;------ console.device
AN_ConsoleDev    equ $11000000

;------ gameport.device
AN_GamePortDev   equ $12000000

;------ keyboard.device
AN_KeyboardDev   equ $13000000

;------ trackdisk.device
AN_TrackDiskDev equ $14000000
AN_TDCalibSeek   equ $14000001   ; calibrate: seek error
AN_TDDelay       equ $14000002   ; delay: error on timer wait

;------ timer.device
AN_TimerDev      equ $15000000
AN_TMBadReq      equ $15000001   ; bad request
AN_TMBadSupply   equ $15000002   ; power supply does not supply ticks

;------ cia.resource
AN_CIARsrc       equ $20000000

```



```
;------ disk.resource
AN_DiskRsrc      equ $21000000
AN_DRHasDisk     equ $21000001   : get unit: already has disk
AN_DRIntNoAct    equ $21000002   ; interrupt: no active unit

;------ misc.resource
AN_MiscRsrc      equ $22000000

;------ bootstrap
AN_BootStrap     equ $30000000
AN_BootError     equ $30000001   ; boot code returned an error

;------ workbench
AN_Workbench     equ $31000000

;------ DiskCopy
AN_DiskCopy      equ $32000000

        ENDC     ; EXEC_ALERTS_I
```

```
        IFND    EXEC_DEVICES_I
EXEC_DEVICES_I  SET     1
**
**      $Filename: exec/devices.i $
**      $Release: 1.3 $
**
**
**
**      (C) Copyright 1985,1986,1987,1988 Commodore-Amiga, Inc.
**          All Rights Reserved
**

    IFND EXEC_LIBRARIES_I
    INCLUDE "exec/libraries.i"
    ENDC          ; EXEC_LIBRARIES_I

    IFND EXEC_PORTS_I
    INCLUDE "exec/ports.i"
    ENDC          ; EXEC_PORTS_I


*----------------------------------------------------------------------
*
*   Device Data Structure
*
*----------------------------------------------------------------------

 STRUCTURE  DD,LIB_SIZE                    * identical to library
    LABEL   DD_SIZE


*----------------------------------------------------------------------
*
*   Suggested Unit Structure
*
*----------------------------------------------------------------------

 STRUCTURE  UNIT,MP_SIZE                   * queue for requests
    UBYTE   UNIT_FLAGS
    UBYTE   UNIT_pad
    UWORD   UNIT_OPENCNT
    LABEL   UNIT_SIZE


*------ UNIT_FLAG definitions:

    BITDEF  UNIT,ACTIVE,0                  * driver is active
    BITDEF  UNIT,INTASK,1                  * running in driver's task

        ENDC    ; EXEC_DEVICES_I
```



```
        IFND    EXEC_ERRORS_I
EXEC_ERRORS_I   SET     1
**
**      $Filename: exec/errors.i $
**      $Release: 1.3 $
**
**      Standard IO Errors:
**
**      (C) Copyright 1985,1986,1987,1988 Commodore-Amiga, Inc.
**          All Rights Reserved
**

IOERR_OPENFAIL   EQU    -1            * device/unit failed to open
IOERR_ABORTED    EQU    -2            * request aborted
IOERR_NOCMD      EQU    -3            * command not supported
IOERR_BADLENGTH  EQU    -4            * not a valid length


ERR_OPENDEVICE  EQU  IOERR_OPENFAIL   * REMOVE !!!

        ENDC    ; EXEC_ERRORS_I
```

```
        IFND    EXEC_EXEC_I
EXEC_EXEC_I     SET     1
**
**      $Filename: exec/exec.i $
**      $Release: 1.3 $
**
**
**
**      (C) Copyright 1985,1986,1987,1988 Commodore-Amiga, Inc.
**          All Rights Reserved
**

        INCLUDE "exec/nodes.i"
        INCLUDE "exec/lists.i"
        INCLUDE "exec/interrupts.i"
        INCLUDE "exec/memory.i"
        INCLUDE "exec/ports.i"
        INCLUDE "exec/tasks.i"
        INCLUDE "exec/libraries.i"
        INCLUDE "exec/devices.i"
        INCLUDE "exec/io.i"

        ENDC    ; EXEC_EXEC_I
```



```
        IFND    EXEC_EXEC_LIB_I
EXEC_EXEC_LIB_I SET     1
**
**      $Filename: exec/exec_lib.i $
**      $Release: 1.3 $
**
**
**
**      (C) Copyright 1985,1986,1987,1988 Commodore-Amiga, Inc.
**          All Rights Reserved
**

        FUNCDEF Supervisor
        FUNCDEF ExitIntr
        FUNCDEF Schedule
        FUNCDEF Reschedule
        FUNCDEF Switch
        FUNCDEF Dispatch
        FUNCDEF Exception
        FUNCDEF InitCode
        FUNCDEF InitStruct
        FUNCDEF MakeLibrary
        FUNCDEF MakeFunctions
        FUNCDEF FindResident
        FUNCDEF InitResident
        FUNCDEF Alert
        FUNCDEF Debug
        FUNCDEF Disable
        FUNCDEF Enable
        FUNCDEF Forbid
        FUNCDEF Permit
        FUNCDEF SetSR
        FUNCDEF SuperState
        FUNCDEF UserState
        FUNCDEF SetIntVector
        FUNCDEF AddIntServer
        FUNCDEF RemIntServer
        FUNCDEF Cause
        FUNCDEF Allocate
        FUNCDEF Deallocate
        FUNCDEF AllocMem
        FUNCDEF AllocAbs
        FUNCDEF FreeMem
        FUNCDEF AvailMem
        FUNCDEF AllocEntry
        FUNCDEF FreeEntry
        FUNCDEF Insert
        FUNCDEF AddHead
        FUNCDEF AddTail
        FUNCDEF Remove
        FUNCDEF RemHead
        FUNCDEF RemTail
        FUNCDEF Enqueue
        FUNCDEF FindName
        FUNCDEF AddTask
        FUNCDEF RemTask
        FUNCDEF FindTask
        FUNCDEF SetTaskPri
        FUNCDEF SetSignal
        FUNCDEF SetExcept
        FUNCDEF Wait
        FUNCDEF Signal
        FUNCDEF AllocSignal
        FUNCDEF FreeSignal
        FUNCDEF AllocTrap
        FUNCDEF FreeTrap
        FUNCDEF AddPort
        FUNCDEF RemPort
        FUNCDEF PutMsg
```

```
        FUNCDEF GetMsg
        FUNCDEF ReplyMsg
        FUNCDEF WaitPort
        FUNCDEF FindPort
        FUNCDEF AddLibrary
        FUNCDEF RemLibrary
        FUNCDEF OldOpenLibrary
        FUNCDEF CloseLibrary
        FUNCDEF SetFunction
        FUNCDEF SumLibrary
        FUNCDEF AddDevice
        FUNCDEF RemDevice
        FUNCDEF OpenDevice
        FUNCDEF CloseDevice
        FUNCDEF DoIO
        FUNCDEF SendIO
        FUNCDEF CheckIO
        FUNCDEF WaitIO
        FUNCDEF AbortIO
        FUNCDEF AddResource
        FUNCDEF RemResource
        FUNCDEF OpenResource
        FUNCDEF RawIOInit
        FUNCDEF RawMayGetChar
        FUNCDEF RawPutChar
        FUNCDEF RawDoFmt
        FUNCDEF GetCC
        FUNCDEF TypeOfMem
        FUNCDEF Procure
        FUNCDEF Vacate
        FUNCDEF OpenLibrary
        FUNCDEF InitSemaphore
        FUNCDEF ObtainSemaphore
        FUNCDEF ReleaseSemaphore
        FUNCDEF AttemptSemaphore
        FUNCDEF ObtainSemaphoreList
        FUNCDEF ReleaseSemaphoreList
        FUNCDEF FindSemaphore
        FUNCDEF AddSemaphore
        FUNCDEF RemSemaphore
        FUNCDEF SumKickData
        FUNCDEF AddMemList
        FUNCDEF CopyMem
        FUNCDEF CopyMemQuick

        ENDC    ; EXEC_EXEC_LIB_I
```



```
        IFND    EXEC_EXECBASE_I
EXEC_EXECBASE_I SET     1
**
**      $Filename: exec/execbase.i $
**      $Release: 1.3 $
**
**
**
**      (C) Copyright 1985,1986,1987,1988 Commodore-Amiga, Inc.
**          All Rights Reserved
**

    IFND EXEC_TYPES_I
    INCLUDE "exec/types.i"
    ENDC        ; EXEC_TYPES_I

    IFND EXEC_LISTS_I
    INCLUDE "exec/lists.i"
    ENDC        ; EXEC_LISTS_I

    IFND EXEC_INTERRUPTS_I
    INCLUDE "exec/interrupts.i"
    ENDC        ; EXEC_INTERRUPTS_I

    IFND EXEC_LIBRARIES_I
    INCLUDE "exec/libraries.i"
    ENDC        ; EXEC_LIBRARIES_I


******* Static System Variables **************************************

 STRUCTURE  ExecBase,LIB_SIZE          ; Standard library node

        UWORD       SoftVer         ; kickstart release number
        WORD        LowMemChkSum    ; checksum of 68000 trap vectors
        ULONG       ChkBase         ; system base pointer complement
        APTR        ColdCapture     ; cold soft capture vector
        APTR        CoolCapture     ; cool soft capture vector
        APTR        WarmCapture     ; warm soft capture vector
        APTR        SysStkUpper     ; system stack base   (upper bound)
        APTR        SysStkLower     ; top of system stack (lower bound)
        ULONG       MaxLocMem       ; last calculated local memory max
        APTR        DebugEntry      ; global debugger entry point
        APTR        DebugData       ; global debugger data segment
        APTR        AlertData       ; alert data segment
        APTR        MaxExtMem       ; top of extended mem, or null if none

        WORD        ChkSum          ; for all of the above


******* Interrupt Related ********************************************

        LABEL       IntVects
        STRUCT      IVTBE,IV_SIZE
        STRUCT      IVDSKBLK,IV_SIZE
        STRUCT      IVSOFTINT,IV_SIZE
        STRUCT      IVPORTS,IV_SIZE
        STRUCT      IVCOPER,IV_SIZE
        STRUCT      IVVERTB,IV_SIZE
        STRUCT      IVBLIT,IV_SIZE
        STRUCT      IVAUD0,IV_SIZE
        STRUCT      IVAUD1,IV_SIZE
        STRUCT      IVAUD2,IV_SIZE
        STRUCT      IVAUD3,IV_SIZE
        STRUCT      IVRBF,IV_SIZE
        STRUCT      IVDSKSYNC,IV_SIZE
        STRUCT      IVEXTER,IV_SIZE
        STRUCT      IVINTEN,IV_SIZE
        STRUCT      IVNMI,IV_SIZE
```

```


******* Dynamic System Variables *************************************

        APTR      ThisTask        ; pointer to current task
        ULONG     IdleCount       ; idle counter
        ULONG     DispCount       ; dispatch counter
        UWORD     Quantum         ; time slice quantum
        UWORD     Elapsed         ; current quantum ticks
        UWORD     SysFlags        ; misc system flags
        BYTE      IDNestCnt       ; interrupt disable nesting count
        BYTE      TDNestCnt       ; task disable nesting count

        UWORD     AttnFlags       ; special attention flags
        UWORD     AttnResched     ; rescheduling attention
        APTR      ResModules      ; pointer to resident module array

        APTR      TaskTrapCode    ; default task trap routine
        APTR      TaskExceptCode  ; default task exception code
        APTR      TaskExitCode    ; default task exit code
        ULONG     TaskSigAlloc    ; preallocated signal mask
        UWORD     TaskTrapAlloc   ; preallocated trap mask


******* System List Headers ******************************************

        STRUCT    MemList,LH_SIZE
        STRUCT    ResourceList,LH_SIZE
        STRUCT    DeviceList,LH_SIZE
        STRUCT    IntrList,LH_SIZE
        STRUCT    LibList,LH_SIZE
        STRUCT    PortList,LH_SIZE
        STRUCT    TaskReady,LH_SIZE
        STRUCT    TaskWait,LH_SIZE

        STRUCT    SoftInts,SH_SIZE*5

        STRUCT    LastAlert,4*4


        ;------ these next two variables are provided to allow
        ;------ system developers to have a rough idea of the
        ;------ period of two externally controlled signals --
        ;------ the time between vertical blank interrupts and the
        ;------ external line rate (which is counted by CIA A's
        ;------ "time of day" clock).  In general these values
        ;------ will be 50 or 60, and may or may not track each
        ;------ other.  These values replace the obsolete AFB_PAL
        ;------ and AFB_50HZ flags.
        UBYTE     VBlankFrequency
        UBYTE     PowerSupplyFrequency

        STRUCT    SemaphoreList,LH_SIZE

        ;------ these next two are to be able to kickstart into user ram.
        ;------ KickMemPtr holds a singly linked list of MemLists which
        ;------ will be removed from the memory list via AllocAbs.  If
        ;------ all the AllocAbs's succeeded, then the KickTagPtr will
        ;------ be added to the rom tag list.
        APTR      KickMemPtr      ; ptr to queue of mem lists
        APTR      KickTagPtr      ; ptr to rom tag queue
        APTR      KickCheckSum    ; checksum for mem and tags

        STRUCT    ExecBaseReserved,10
        STRUCT    ExecBaseNewReserved,20

        LABEL     SYSBASESIZE

******* AttnFlags
```



```

*  Processors and Co-processors:
        BITDEF  AF,68010,0      ; also set for 68020
        BITDEF  AF,68020,1
        BITDEF  AF,68881,4

; These two bits used to be AFB_PAL and AFB_50HZ.  After some soul
; searching we realized that they were misnomers, and the information
; is now kept in VBlankFrequency and PowerSupplyFrequency above.
; To find out what sort of video conversion is done, look in the
; graphics subsytem.
        BITDEF  AF,RESERVED8,8
        BITDEF  AF,RESERVED9,9

        ENDC    ; EXEC_EXECBASE_I
```

Sep 28 17:12 1988 exec/execname.i Page 1

```
        IFND    EXEC_EXECNAME_I
EXEC_EXECNAME_I SET     1
**
**      $Filename: exec/execname.i $
**      $Release: 1.3 $
**
**
**
**      (C) Copyright 1985,1986,1987,1988 Commodore-Amiga, Inc.
**          All Rights Reserved
**

EXECNAME        macro
                dc.b    'exec.library',0
                ds.w    0
                endm

        ENDC    ; EXEC_EXECNAME_I
```

Sep 28 17:12 1988 exec/initializers.i Page 1

```
        IFND    EXEC_INITIALIZERS_I
EXEC_INITIALIZERS_I     SET     1
**
**      $Filename: exec/initializers.i $
**      $Release: 1.3 $
**
**
**
**      (C) Copyright 1985,1986,1987,1988 Commodore-Amiga, Inc.
**          All Rights Reserved
**

INITBYTE        MACRO   * &offset,&value
                DC.B    $e0
                DC.B    0
                DC.W    \1
                DC.B    \2
                DC.B    0
                ENDM

INITWORD        MACRO   * &offset,&value
                DC.B    $d0
                DC.B    0
                DC.W    \1
                DC.W    \2
                ENDM

INITLONG        MACRO   * &offset,&value
                DC.B    $c0
                DC.B    0
                DC.W    \1
                DC.L    \2
                ENDM

INITSTRUCT  MACRO   * &size,&offset,&value,&count
            DS.W    0
            IFC     '\4',''
COUNT\@     SET     0
            ENDC
            IFNC    '\4',''
COUNT\@     SET     \4
            ENDC
CMD\@       SET     (((\1)<<4)!COUNT\@)
            IFLE    (\2)-255
            DC.B    (CMD\@)!$80
            DC.B    \2
            MEXIT
            ENDC
            DC.B    CMD\@!$0C0
            DC.B    (((\2)>>16)&$0FF)
            DC.W    ((\2)&$0FFFF)
            ENDM

        ENDC    ; EXEC_INITIALIZERS_I
```

```
        IFND    EXEC_INTERRUPTS_I
EXEC_INTERRUPTS_I       SET     1
**
**      $Filename: exec/interrupts.i $
**      $Release: 1.3 $
**
**
**
**      (C) Copyright 1985,1986,1987,1988 Commodore-Amiga, Inc.
**          All Rights Reserved
**

    IFND EXEC_NODES_I
    INCLUDE "exec/nodes.i"
    ENDC        ; EXEC_NODES_I

    IFND EXEC_LISTS_I
    INCLUDE "exec/lists.i"
    ENDC        ; EXEC_LISTS_I


*----------------------------------------------------------------
*
*   Interrupt Structure
*
*----------------------------------------------------------------

 STRUCTURE  IS,LN_SIZE
    APTR    IS_DATA
    APTR    IS_CODE
    LABEL   IS_SIZE


*----------------------------------------------------------------------
*
*   Exec Internal Interrupt Vectors
*
*----------------------------------------------------------------------

 STRUCTURE  IV,0
    APTR    IV_DATA
    APTR    IV_CODE
    APTR    IV_NODE
    LABEL   IV_SIZE


*------ System Flag bits (in SysBase.SysFlags )

    BITDEF  S,SAR,15        * scheduling attention required
    BITDEF  S,TQE,14        * time quantum expended -- time to resched
    BITDEF  S,SINT,13


*----------------------------------------------------------------------
*
*   Software Interrupt List Headers
*
*----------------------------------------------------------------------

 STRUCTURE  SH,LH_SIZE
    UWORD   SH_PAD
    LABEL   SH_SIZE

SIH_PRIMASK  EQU        $0F0
SIH_QUEUES   EQU        5

** this is a fake INT definition, used only for AddIntServer and the like
        BITDEF  INT,NMI,15

```



```
        ENDC    ; EXEC_INTERRUPTS_I
```

```
        IFND    EXEC_IO_I
EXEC_IO_I       SET     1
**
**      $Filename: exec/io.i $
**      $Release: 1.3 $
**
**
**
**      (C) Copyright 1985,1986,1987,1988 Commodore-Amiga, Inc.
**          All Rights Reserved
**

    IFND EXEC_PORTS_I
    INCLUDE "exec/ports.i"
    ENDC        ; EXEC_PORTS_I

    IFND EXEC_LIBRARIES_I
    INCLUDE "exec/libraries.i"
    ENDC        ; EXEC_LIBRARIES_I


*----------------------------------------------------------------
*
*   IO Request Structures
*
*----------------------------------------------------------------

*------ Required portion of IO request:

 STRUCTURE  IO,MN_SIZE
    APTR    IO_DEVICE                   * device node pointer
    APTR    IO_UNIT                     * unit (driver private)
    UWORD   IO_COMMAND                  * device command
    UBYTE   IO_FLAGS                    * special flags
    BYTE    IO_ERROR                    * error or warning code
    LABEL   IO_SIZE


*------ Standard IO request extension:

    ULONG   IO_ACTUAL                   * actual # of bytes transfered
    ULONG   IO_LENGTH                   * requested # of bytes transfered
    APTR    IO_DATA                     * pointer to data area
    ULONG   IO_OFFSET                   * offset for seeking devices
    LABEL   IOSTD_SIZE


*------ IO_FLAGS bit definitions:

    BITDEF  IO,QUICK,0                  * complete IO quickly


*----------------------------------------------------------------
*
*   Standard Device Library Functions
*
*----------------------------------------------------------------

            LIBINIT

            LIBDEF  DEV_BEGINIO         * process IO request
            LIBDEF  DEV_ABORTIO         * abort IO request


*----------------------------------------------------------------
*
*   IO Function Macros
*
*----------------------------------------------------------------
```



```

BEGINIO     MACRO
            LINKLIB DEV_BEGINIO,IO_DEVICE(A1)
            ENDM

ABORTIO     MACRO
            LINKLIB DEV_ABORTIO,IO_DEVICE(A1)
            ENDM


*----------------------------------------------------------------
*
*   Standard Device Command Definitions
*
*----------------------------------------------------------------

*------ Command definition macro:
DEVINIT     MACRO   * [baseOffset]
            IFC     '\1',''
CMD_COUNT   SET     CMD_NONSTD
            ENDC
            IFNC    '\1',''
CMD_COUNT   SET     \1
            ENDC
            ENDM

DEVCMD      MACRO   * cmdname
\1          EQU     CMD_COUNT
CMD_COUNT   SET     CMD_COUNT+1
            ENDM


*------ Standard device commands:

            DEVINIT 0

            DEVCMD  CMD_INVALID         * invalid command
            DEVCMD  CMD_RESET           * reset as if just inited
            DEVCMD  CMD_READ            * standard read
            DEVCMD  CMD_WRITE           * standard write
            DEVCMD  CMD_UPDATE          * write out all buffers
            DEVCMD  CMD_CLEAR           * clear all buffers
            DEVCMD  CMD_STOP            * hold current and queued
            DEVCMD  CMD_START           * restart after stop
            DEVCMD  CMD_FLUSH           * abort entire queue


*------ First non-standard device command value:

            DEVCMD  CMD_NONSTD

        ENDC    ; EXEC_IO_I
```

```
        IFND    EXEC_LIBRARIES_I
EXEC_LIBRARIES_I        SET     1
**
**      $Filename: exec/libraries.i $
**      $Release: 1.3 $
**
**
**
**      (C) Copyright 1985,1986,1987,1988 Commodore-Amiga, Inc.
**          All Rights Reserved
**

    IFND EXEC_NODES_I
    INCLUDE "exec/nodes.i"
    ENDC        ; EXEC_NODES_I


*------ Special Constants ---------------------------------------

LIB_VECTSIZE    EQU     6
LIB_RESERVED    EQU     4
LIB_BASE        EQU     $FFFFFFFA       * (-LIB_VECTSIZE)
LIB_USERDEF     EQU     LIB_BASE-(LIB_RESERVED*LIB_VECTSIZE)
LIB_NONSTD      EQU     LIB_USERDEF

*----------------------------------------------------------------
*
*   Library Definition Macros
*
*----------------------------------------------------------------

*------ LIBINIT sets base offset for library function definitions:

LIBINIT     MACRO   * [baseOffset]
            IFC     '\1',''
COUNT_LIB   SET     LIB_USERDEF
            ENDC
            IFNC    '\1',''
COUNT_LIB   SET     \1
            ENDC
            ENDM


*------ LIBDEF is used to define each library function entry:

LIBDEF      MACRO   * libraryFunctionSymbol
\1          EQU     COUNT_LIB
COUNT_LIB   SET     COUNT_LIB-LIB_VECTSIZE
            ENDM


*----------------------------------------------------------------
*
*   Standard Library Functions
*
*----------------------------------------------------------------

    LIBINIT LIB_BASE

    LIBDEF  LIB_OPEN
    LIBDEF  LIB_CLOSE
    LIBDEF  LIB_EXPUNGE
    LIBDEF  LIB_EXTFUNC                 * reserved *


*----------------------------------------------------------------
*
*   Standard Library Data Structure
*
```



```
*----------------------------------------------------------------

 STRUCTURE LIB,LN_SIZE
    UBYTE   LIB_FLAGS
    UBYTE   LIB_pad
    UWORD   LIB_NEGSIZE             * number of bytes before LIB
    UWORD   LIB_POSSIZE             * number of bytes after LIB
    UWORD   LIB_VERSION             * major
    UWORD   LIB_REVISION            * minor
    APTR    LIB_IDSTRING            * identification
    ULONG   LIB_SUM                 * the checksum itself
    UWORD   LIB_OPENCNT             * number of current opens
    LABEL   LIB_SIZE


*------ LIB_FLAGS bit definitions:

    BITDEF  LIB,SUMMING,0           * we are currently checksumming
    BITDEF  LIB,CHANGED,1           * we have just changed the lib
    BITDEF  LIB,SUMUSED,2           * set if we should bother to sum
    BITDEF  LIB,DELEXP,3            * delayed expunge


*----------------------------------------------------------------
*
*   Function Invocation Macros
*
*----------------------------------------------------------------

*------ CALLLIB for calling functions where A6 is already correct:

CALLLIB     MACRO   * functionOffset
        IFGT NARG-1
            FAIL    !!! CALLLIB MACRO - too many arguments !!!
        ENDC
            JSR     \1(A6)
            ENDM


*------ LINKLIB for calling functions where A6 is incorrect:

LINKLIB     MACRO   * functionOffset,libraryBase
        IFGT NARG-2
            FAIL    !!! LINKLIB MACRO - too many arguments !!!
        ENDC
            MOVE.L  A6,-(SP)
            MOVE.L  \2,A6
            CALLLIB \1
            MOVE.L  (SP)+,A6
            ENDM

        ENDC    ; EXEC_LIBRARIES_I
```

```
        IFND    EXEC_LISTS_I
EXEC_LISTS_I    SET     1
**
**      $Filename: exec/lists.i $
**      $Release: 1.3 $
**
**
**
**      (C) Copyright 1985,1986,1987,1988 Commodore-Amiga, Inc.
**          All Rights Reserved
**

    IFND EXEC_NODES_I
    INCLUDE "exec/nodes.i"
    ENDC        ; EXEC_NODES_I


*----------------------------------------------------------------------
*
*   List Structures
*
*----------------------------------------------------------------------

; normal, full featured list
 STRUCTURE  LH,0
    APTR    LH_HEAD
    APTR    LH_TAIL
    APTR    LH_TAILPRED
    UBYTE   LH_TYPE
    UBYTE   LH_pad
    LABEL   LH_SIZE

; minimal list, no type checking possible
 STRUCTURE  MLH,0
    APTR    MLH_HEAD
    APTR    MLH_TAIL
    APTR    MLH_TAILPRED
    LABEL   MLH_SIZE


NEWLIST         MACRO   * list
                MOVE.L  \1,(\1)
                ADDQ.L  #LH_TAIL,(\1)
                CLR.L   LH_TAIL(\1)
                MOVE.L  \1,(LH_TAIL+LN_PRED)(\1)
                ENDM

TSTLIST         MACRO   * [list]
                IFC     '\1',''
                CMP.L   LH_TAIL+LN_PRED(A0),A0
                ENDC
                IFNC    '\1',''
                CMP.L   LH_TAIL+LN_PRED(\1),\1
                ENDC
                ENDM

SUCC            MACRO   * node,succ
                MOVE.L  (\1),\2
                ENDM

PRED            MACRO   * node,pred
                MOVE.L  LN_PRED(\1),\2
                ENDM

IFEMPTY         MACRO   * list,label
                CMP.L   LH_TAIL+LN_PRED(\1),\1
                BEQ     \2
                ENDM

```



```
IFNOTEMPTY      MACRO   * list,label
                CMP.L   LH_TAIL+LN_PRED(\1),\1
                BNE     \2
                ENDM

TSTNODE         MACRO   * node,next
                MOVE.L  (\1),\2
                TST.L   (\2)
                ENDM

NEXTNODE        MACRO   * next,current,exit_label (DX,AX,DISP16)
                MOVE.L  \1,\2
                MOVE.L  (\2),\1
                IFC     '\0',''
                BEQ     \3
                ENDC
                IFNC    '\0',''
                BEQ.S   \3
                ENDC
                ENDM

ADDHEAD         MACRO
                MOVE.L  (A0),D0
                MOVE.L  A1,(A0)
                MOVEM.L D0/A0,(A1)
                MOVE.L  D0,A0
                MOVE.L  A1,LN_PRED(A0)
                ENDM

ADDTAIL         MACRO
                LEA     LH_TAIL(A0),A0
                MOVE.L  LN_PRED(A0),D0
                MOVE.L  A1,LN_PRED(A0)
                MOVE.L  A0,(A1)
                MOVE.L  D0,LN_PRED(A1)
                MOVE.L  D0,A0
                MOVE.L  A1,(A0)
                ENDM

REMOVE          MACRO
                MOVE.L  (A1),A0
                MOVE.L  LN_PRED(A1),A1
                MOVE.L  A0,(A1)
                MOVE.L  A1,LN_PRED(A0)
                ENDM

REMHEAD         MACRO
                MOVE.L  (A0),A1
                MOVE.L  (A1),D0
                BEQ.S   REMHEAD\@
                MOVE.L  D0,(A0)
                EXG.L   D0,A1
                MOVE.L  A0,LN_PRED(A1)
REMHEAD\@
                ENDM

*----------------------------------------------------------------------
*
*  REMHEADQ -- remove-head quickly
*
*       Useful when a scratch register is available, and
*       list is known to contain at least one node.
*
*----------------------------------------------------------------------

REMHEADQ        MACRO   * head,node,scratchReg
                MOVE.L  (\1),\2
                MOVE.L  (\2),\3
                MOVE.L  \3,(\1)
```

```
            MOVE.L  \1,LN_PRED(\3)
            ENDM

REMTAIL     MACRO
            MOVE.L  LH_TAIL+LN_PRED(A0),A1
            MOVE.L  LN_PRED(A1),D0
            BEQ.S   REMTAIL\@
            MOVE.L  D0,LH_TAIL+LN_PRED(A0)
            EXG.L   D0,A1
            MOVE.L  A0,(A1)
            ADDQ.L  #4,(A1)
REMTAIL\@
            ENDM

        ENDC    ; EXEC_LISTS_I
```



```
        IFND    EXEC_MEMORY_I
EXEC_MEMORY_I   SET     1
**
**      $Filename: exec/memory.i $
**      $Release: 1.3 $
**
**      definitions for use with the memory allocator
**
**      (C) Copyright 1985,1986,1987,1988 Commodore-Amiga, Inc.
**          All Rights Reserved
**

    IFND        EXEC_NODES_I
    INCLUDE     "exec/nodes.i"
    ENDC        ; EXEC_NODES_I


*----------------------------------------------------------------------
*
*   Memory List Structures
*
*----------------------------------------------------------------------
*
*   A memory list appears in two forms:  One is a requirements list*
*   the other is a list of already allocated memory.  The format is
*   the same, with the reqirements/address field occupying the same
*   position.
*
*   The format is a linked list of ML structures each of which has
*   an array of ME entries.
*
*----------------------------------------------------------------------

 STRUCTURE ML,LN_SIZE
    UWORD   ML_NUMENTRIES           * The number of ME structures that follow
    LABEL   ML_ME                   * where the ME structures begin
    LABEL   ML_SIZE


 STRUCTURE ME,0
    LABEL   ME_REQS                 * the AllocMem requirements
    APTR    ME_ADDR                 * the address of this block (an alias
*                                   *   for the same location as ME_REQS)
    ULONG   ME_LENGTH               * the length of this region
    LABEL   ME_SIZE


*------ memory options:

    BITDEF  MEM,PUBLIC,0
    BITDEF  MEM,CHIP,1
    BITDEF  MEM,FAST,2
    BITDEF  MEM,CLEAR,16
    BITDEF  MEM,LARGEST,17


*------ alignment rules for a memory block:

MEM_BLOCKSIZE   EQU 8
MEM_BLOCKMASK   EQU (MEM_BLOCKSIZE-1)


*----------------------------------------------------------------------
*
*   Memory Region Header
*
*----------------------------------------------------------------------

 STRUCTURE  MH,LN_SIZE
```

```
    UWORD   MH_ATTRIBUTES          * characteristics of this region
    APTR    MH_FIRST               * first free region
    APTR    MH_LOWER               * lower memory bound
    APTR    MH_UPPER               * upper memory bound+1
    ULONG   MH_FREE                * number of free bytes
    LABEL   MH_SIZE


*----------------------------------------------------------------------
*
*   Memory Chunk
*
*----------------------------------------------------------------------

 STRUCTURE  MC,0
    APTR    MC_NEXT                * ptr to next chunk
    ULONG   MC_BYTES               * chunk byte size
    LABEL   MC_SIZE

        ENDC    ; EXEC_MEMORY_I
```



```
        IFND    EXEC_NODES_I
EXEC_NODES_I    SET     1
**
**      $Filename: exec/nodes.i $
**      $Release: 1.3 $
**
**
**
**      (C) Copyright 1985,1986,1987,1988 Commodore-Amiga, Inc.
**          All Rights Reserved
**

*----------------------------------------------------------------------
*
*   List Node Structure
*
*----------------------------------------------------------------------

 STRUCTURE  LN,0
    APTR    LN_SUCC
    APTR    LN_PRED
    UBYTE   LN_TYPE
    BYTE    LN_PRI
    APTR    LN_NAME
    LABEL   LN_SIZE

; min node -- only has minimum necessary, no type checking possible
 STRUCTURE  MLN,0
    APTR    MLN_SUCC
    APTR    MLN_PRED
    LABEL   MLN_SIZE

*------ Node Types:

NT_UNKNOWN      EQU     0
NT_TASK         EQU     1
NT_INTERRUPT    EQU     2       ; also for software interrupt node
NT_DEVICE       EQU     3
NT_MSGPORT      EQU     4
NT_MESSAGE      EQU     5
NT_FREEMSG      EQU     6
NT_REPLYMSG     EQU     7
NT_RESOURCE     EQU     8
NT_LIBRARY      EQU     9
NT_MEMORY       EQU     10
NT_SOFTINT      EQU     11      ; exec private
NT_FONT         EQU     12
NT_PROCESS      EQU     13
NT_SEMAPHORE    EQU     14
NT_SIGNALSEM    EQU     15      ; signal semaphores
NT_BOOTNODE     EQU     16

        ENDC    ; EXEC_NODES_I
```

```
        IFND    EXEC_PORTS_I
EXEC_PORTS_I    SET     1
**
**      $Filename: exec/ports.i $
**      $Release: 1.3 $
**
**
**
**      (C) Copyright 1985,1986,1987,1988 Commodore-Amiga, Inc.
**          All Rights Reserved
**

    IFND EXEC_NODES_I
    INCLUDE "exec/nodes.i"
    ENDC            ; EXEC_NODES_I

    IFND EXEC_LISTS_I
    INCLUDE "exec/lists.i"
    ENDC            ; EXEC_LISTS_I


*----------------------------------------------------------------
*
*   Message Port Structure
*
*----------------------------------------------------------------

 STRUCTURE  MP,LN_SIZE
    UBYTE   MP_FLAGS
    UBYTE   MP_SIGBIT               * signal bit number
    APTR    MP_SIGTASK              * task to be signalled
    STRUCT  MP_MSGLIST,LH_SIZE      * message linked list
    LABEL   MP_SIZE


*------ unions:

MP_SOFTINT      EQU  MP_SIGTASK


*------ flags fields:

PF_ACTION       EQU  3


*------ PutMsg actions:

PA_SIGNAL       EQU  0
PA_SOFTINT      EQU  1
PA_IGNORE       EQU  2


*----------------------------------------------------------------
*
*   Message Structure
*
*----------------------------------------------------------------

 STRUCTURE  MN,LN_SIZE
    APTR    MN_REPLYPORT            * message reply port
    UWORD   MN_LENGTH               * message len in bytes
    LABEL   MN_SIZE

        ENDC    ; EXEC_PORTS_I
```



```
        IFND    EXEC_RESIDENT_I
EXEC_RESIDENT_I SET     1
**
**      $Filename: exec/resident.i $
**      $Release: 1.3 $
**
**
**
**      (C) Copyright 1985,1986,1987,1988 Commodore-Amiga, Inc.
**          All Rights Reserved
**

*----------------------------------------------------------------
*
*   Resident Module Tag
*
*----------------------------------------------------------------

 STRUCTURE RT,0
    UWORD RT_MATCHWORD                  * word to match
    APTR  RT_MATCHTAG                   * pointer to structure base
    APTR  RT_ENDSKIP                    * address to continue scan
    UBYTE RT_FLAGS                      * various tag flags
    UBYTE RT_VERSION                    * release version number
    UBYTE RT_TYPE                       * type of module
    BYTE  RT_PRI                        * initialization priority
    APTR  RT_NAME                       * pointer to node name
    APTR  RT_IDSTRING                   * pointer to id string
    APTR  RT_INIT                       * pointer to init code
    LABEL RT_SIZE


*------ Match word definition:

RTC_MATCHWORD   EQU     $4AFC           * (ILLEGAL instruction)


*------ RT_FLAGS bit and field definitions:

    BITDEF RT,COLDSTART,0
    BITDEF RT,AUTOINIT,7                * RT_INIT points to data

* Compatibility:
RTM_WHEN        EQU     1               * field position in RT_FLAGS
RTW_NEVER       EQU     0               * never ever init
RTW_COLDSTART   EQU     1               * init at coldstart time

        ENDC    ; EXEC_RESIDENT_I
```

```
        IFND    EXEC_SEMAPHORES_I
EXEC_SEMAPHORES_I       SET     1
**
**      $Filename: exec/semaphores.i $
**      $Release: 1.3 $
**
**
**
**      (C) Copyright 1986,1987,1988 Commodore-Amiga, Inc.
**          All Rights Reserved
**

    IFND EXEC_NODES_I
    INCLUDE "exec/nodes.i"
    ENDC        ; EXEC_NODES_I

    IFND EXEC_LISTS_I
    INCLUDE "exec/lists.i"
    ENDC        ; EXEC_LISTS_I

    IFND EXEC_PORTS_I
    INCLUDE "exec/ports.i"
    ENDC        ; EXEC_PORTS_I


*----------------------------------------------------------------
*
*   Semaphore Structure
*
*----------------------------------------------------------------


 STRUCTURE  SM,MP_SIZE
    WORD    SM_BIDS             * number of bids for lock
    LABEL   SM_SIZE


*------ unions:

SM_LOCKMSG    EQU  MP_SIGTASK


*----------------------------------------------------------------
*
*   Signal Semaphore Structure
*
*----------------------------------------------------------------

* this is the structure used to request a signal semaphore -- allocated
* on the fly by ObtainSemaphore()
 STRUCTURE  SSR,MLN_SIZE
    APTR    SSR_WAITER
    LABEL   SSR_SIZE


* this is the actual semaphore itself -- allocated statically
 STRUCTURE  SS,LN_SIZE
    SHORT   SS_NESTCOUNT
    STRUCT  SS_WAITQUEUE,MLH_SIZE
    STRUCT  SS_MULTIPLELINK,SSR_SIZE
    APTR    SS_OWNER
    SHORT   SS_QUEUECOUNT
    LABEL   SS_SIZE

        ENDC    ; EXEC_SEMAPHORES_I
```



```
        IFND    EXEC_STRINGS_I
EXEC_STRINGS_I  SET     1
**
**      $Filename: exec/strings.i $
**      $Release: 1.3 $
**
**
**
**      (C) Copyright 1985,1986,1987,1988 Commodore-Amiga, Inc.
**          All Rights Reserved
**

*------ Terminal Control:

EOS             EQU     0
BELL            EQU     7
LF              EQU     10
CR              EQU     13
BS              EQU     8
DEL             EQU     $7F
NL              EQU     LF


*----------------------------------------------------------------
*
*   String Support Macros
*
*----------------------------------------------------------------

STRING      MACRO
            DC.B    \1
            DC.B    0
            CNOP    0,2
            ENDM


STRINGL     MACRO
            DC.B    13,10
            DC.B    \1
            DC.B    0
            CNOP    0,2
            ENDM


STRINGR     MACRO
            DC.B    \1
            DC.B    13,10,0
            CNOP    0,2
            ENDM


STRINGLR    MACRO
            DC.B    13,10
            DC.B    \1
            DC.B    13,10,0
            CNOP    0,2
            ENDM

        ENDC    ; EXEC_STRINGS_I
```

```
        IFND    EXEC_TASKS_I
EXEC_TASKS_I    SET     1
**
**      $Filename: exec/tasks.i $
**      $Release: 1.3 $
**
**
**
**      (C) Copyright 1985,1986,1987,1988 Commodore-Amiga, Inc.
**          All Rights Reserved
**

    IFND EXEC_NODES_I
    INCLUDE "exec/nodes.i"
    ENDC            ; EXEC_NODES_I

    IFND EXEC_LISTS_I
    INCLUDE "exec/lists.i"
    ENDC            ; EXEC_LISTS_I


*----------------------------------------------------------------
*
*   Task Control Structure
*
*----------------------------------------------------------------

 STRUCTURE  TC,LN_SIZE
    UBYTE   TC_FLAGS
    UBYTE   TC_STATE
    BYTE    TC_IDNESTCNT            * intr disabled nesting
    BYTE    TC_TDNESTCNT            * task disabled nesting
    ULONG   TC_SIGALLOC             * sigs allocated
    ULONG   TC_SIGWAIT              * sigs we are waiting for
    ULONG   TC_SIGRECVD             * sigs we have received
    ULONG   TC_SIGEXCEPT            * sigs we take as exceptions
    UWORD   TC_TRAPALLOC            * traps allocated
    UWORD   TC_TRAPABLE             * traps enabled
    APTR    TC_EXCEPTDATA           * data for except proc
    APTR    TC_EXCEPTCODE           * exception procedure
    APTR    TC_TRAPDATA             * data for proc trap proc
    APTR    TC_TRAPCODE             * proc trap procedure
    APTR    TC_SPREG                * stack pointer
    APTR    TC_SPLOWER              * stack lower bound
    APTR    TC_SPUPPER              * stack upper bound + 2
    APTR    TC_SWITCH               * task losing CPU
    APTR    TC_LAUNCH               * task getting CPU
    STRUCT  TC_MEMENTRY,LH_SIZE     * allocated memory
    APTR    TC_Userdata
    LABEL   TC_SIZE


*------ Flag Bits:

    BITDEF  T,PROCTIME,0
    BITDEF  T,STACKCHK,4
    BITDEF  T,EXCEPT,5
    BITDEF  T,SWITCH,6
    BITDEF  T,LAUNCH,7


*------ Task States:
TS_INVALID  EQU     0
TS_ADDED    EQU     TS_INVALID+1
TS_RUN      EQU     TS_ADDED+1
TS_READY    EQU     TS_RUN+1
TS_WAIT     EQU     TS_READY+1
TS_EXCEPT   EQU     TS_WAIT+1
TS_REMOVED  EQU     TS_EXCEPT+1
```



```


*------ System Task Signals:

SIGF_ABORT      EQU     $0001
SIGF_CHILD      EQU     $0002
SIGF_BLIT       EQU     $0010
SIGF_SINGLE     EQU     $0010
SIGF_DOS        EQU     $0100

SIGB_ABORT      EQU     0
SIGB_CHILD      EQU     1
SIGB_BLIT       EQU     4
SIGB_SINGLE     EQU     4
SIGB_DOS        EQU     8


SYS_SIGALLOC    EQU     $0FFFF          ; pre-allocated signals
SYS_TRAPALLOC   EQU     $08000          ; pre-allocated traps

        ENDC    ; EXEC_TASKS_I
```

```
        IFND    EXEC_TYPES_I
EXEC_TYPES_I    SET     1
**
**      $Filename: exec/types.i $
**      $Release: 1.3 $
**
**
**
**      (C) Copyright 1985,1986,1987,1988 Commodore-Amiga, Inc.
**          All Rights Reserved
**

EXTERN_LIB  MACRO
            XREF    _LVO\1
            ENDM

STRUCTURE   MACRO
\1          EQU     0                   * for assembler's sake
SOFFSET     SET     \2
            ENDM

BOOL        MACRO
\1          EQU     SOFFSET
SOFFSET     SET     SOFFSET+2
            ENDM

BYTE        MACRO
\1          EQU     SOFFSET
SOFFSET     SET     SOFFSET+1
            ENDM

UBYTE       MACRO
\1          EQU     SOFFSET
SOFFSET     SET     SOFFSET+1
            ENDM

WORD        MACRO
\1          EQU     SOFFSET
SOFFSET     SET     SOFFSET+2
            ENDM

UWORD       MACRO
\1          EQU     SOFFSET
SOFFSET     SET     SOFFSET+2
            ENDM

SHORT        MACRO
\1          EQU     SOFFSET
SOFFSET     SET     SOFFSET+2
            ENDM

USHORT      MACRO
\1          EQU     SOFFSET
SOFFSET     SET     SOFFSET+2
            ENDM

LONG        MACRO
\1          EQU     SOFFSET
SOFFSET     SET     SOFFSET+4
            ENDM

ULONG       MACRO
\1          EQU     SOFFSET
SOFFSET     SET     SOFFSET+4
            ENDM

FLOAT       MACRO
\1          EQU     SOFFSET
SOFFSET     SET     SOFFSET+4
```



```
            ENDM

APTR        MACRO
\1          EQU     SOFFSET
SOFFSET     SET     SOFFSET+4
            ENDM

CPTR        MACRO
\1          EQU     SOFFSET
SOFFSET     SET     SOFFSET+4
            ENDM

RPTR        MACRO
\1          EQU     SOFFSET
SOFFSET     SET     SOFFSET+2
            ENDM

STRUCT      MACRO
\1          EQU     SOFFSET
SOFFSET     SET     SOFFSET+\2
            ENDM

LABEL       MACRO
\1          EQU     SOFFSET
            ENDM

*------ bit definition macro ----------------------------------
*
*   Given:
*
*       BITDEF  MEM,CLEAR,16
*
*  Yields:
*
*       MEMB_CLEAR  EQU 16
*       MEMF_CLEAR  EQU (1.SL.MEMB_CLEAR)
*

BITDEF      MACRO   * prefix,&name,&bitnum
            BITDEF0 \1,\2,B_,\3
\@BITDEF    SET     1<<\3
            BITDEF0 \1,\2,F_,\@BITDEF
            ENDM

BITDEF0     MACRO   * prefix,&name,&type,&value
\1\3\2      EQU     \4
            ENDM

LIBRARY_VERSION EQU     34

        ENDC    ; EXEC_TYPES_I
```

Sep 28 17:20 1988 graphics/clip.i Page 1

```
        IFND    GRAPHICS_CLIP_I
GRAPHICS_CLIP_I SET     1
**
**      $Filename: graphics/clip.i $
**      $Release: 1.3 $
**
**
**
**      (C) Copyright 1985,1986,1987,1988 Commodore-Amiga, Inc.
**          All Rights Reserved
**

    IFND    GRAPHICS_GFX_I
    include "graphics/gfx.i"
    ENDC
        IFND    EXEC_SEMAPHORES_I
        include "exec/semaphores.i"
        ENDC

NEWLOCKS        equ     1

 STRUCTURE  Layer,0
    LONG    lr_front
    LONG    lr_back
    LONG    lr_ClipRect
    LONG    lr_rp
    WORD    lr_MinX
    WORD    lr_MinY
    WORD    lr_MaxX
    WORD    lr_MaxY
        STRUCT  lr_reserved,4
        WORD    lr_priority
    WORD    lr_Flags
    LONG    lr_SuperBitMap
    LONG    lr_SuperClipRect
    APTR    lr_Window
    WORD    lr_Scroll_X
    WORD    lr_Scroll_Y
    APTR    lr_cr
    APTR    lr_cr2
    APTR    lr_crnew
    APTR    lr_SuperSaverClipRects
    APTR    lr__cliprects
    APTR    lr_LayerInfo
*                       just by lucky coincidence
*                       this is not confused with simplesprites
        STRUCT  lr_Lock,SS_SIZE
        STRUCT  lr_reserved3,8
        APTR    lr_ClipRegion
        APTR    lr_saveClipRects
        STRUCT  lr_reserved2,22
    APTR    lr_DamageList
    LABEL   lr_SIZEOF

 STRUCTURE  ClipRect,0
    LONG    cr_Next
    LONG    cr_prev
    LONG    cr_lobs
    LONG    cr_BitMap
    WORD    cr_MinX
    WORD    cr_MinY
    WORD    cr_MaxX
    WORD    cr_MaxY
    APTR    cr__p1
    APTR    cr__p2
    LONG    cr_reserved
    LONG    cr_Flags
 LABEL      cr_SIZEOF

```

Sep 28 17:20 1988 graphics/clip.i Page 2

```
* internal cliprect flags
CR_NEEDS_NO_CONCEALED_RASTERS   equ     1

* defines for clipping
ISLESSX equ 1
ISLESSY equ 2
ISGRTRX equ 4
ISGRTRY equ 8

* for ancient history reasons
        IFND    lr_Front
lr_Front        equ lr_front
lr_Back         equ lr_back
lr_RastPort     equ     lr_rp
cr_Prev         equ cr_prev
cr_LObs         equ     cr_lobs
        ENDC

        ENDC    ; GRAPHICS_CLIP_I
```

```
        IFND    GRAPHICS_COPPER_I
GRAPHICS_COPPER_I       SET     1
**
**      $Filename: graphics/copper.i $
**      $Release: 1.3 $
**
**
**
**      (C) Copyright 1985,1986,1987,1988 Commodore-Amiga, Inc.
**          All Rights Reserved
**

COPPER_MOVE equ 0       /* pseude opcode for move #XXXX,dir */
COPPER_WAIT equ 1        /* pseudo opcode for wait y,x */
CPRNXTBUF   equ 2       /* continue processing with next buffer */
CPR_NT_LOF  equ $8000  /* copper instruction only for short frames */
CPR_NT_SHT  equ $4000   /* copper instruction only for long frames */

   STRUCTURE   CopIns,0
      WORD  ci_OpCode      * 0 = move, 1 = wait */
      STRUCT   ci_nxtlist,0    * UNION
      STRUCT   ci_VWaitPos,0
      STRUCT   ci_DestAddr,2

      STRUCT   ci_HWaitPos,0
      STRUCT   ci_DestData,2

   LABEL ci_SIZEOF

* structure of cprlist that points to list that hardware actually executes */
   STRUCTURE   cprlist,0
      APTR  crl_Next
      APTR  crl_start
      WORD  crl_MaxCount
   LABEL crl_SIZEOF

   STRUCTURE   CopList,0
      APTR  cl_Next  /* next block for this copper list */
      APTR  cl__CopList  /* system use */
      APTR  cl__ViewPort /* system use */
      APTR  cl_CopIns /* start of this block */
      APTR  cl_CopPtr /* intermediate ptr */
      APTR  cl_CopLStart   /* mrgcop fills this in for Long Frame*/
      APTR  cl_CopSStart   /* mrgcop fills this in for Short Frame*/
      WORD  cl_Count       /* intermediate counter */
      WORD  cl_MaxCount   /* max # of copins for this block */
      WORD  cl_DyOffset    /* offset this copper list vertical waits */
   LABEL cl_SIZEOF

   STRUCTURE   UCopList,0
      APTR     ucl_Next
      APTR     ucl_FirstCopList /* head node of this copper list */
      APTR     ucl_CopList /* node in use */
   LABEL ucl_SIZEOF

*  private graphics data structure
   STRUCTURE   copinit,0
      STRUCT   copinit_diagstrt,8
      STRUCT   copinit_sprstrtup,2*((2*8*2)+2+(2*2)+2)
      STRUCT   copinit_sprstop,4
   LABEL copinit_SIZEOF

        ENDC    ; GRAPHICS_COPPER_I
```



```
        IFND    GRAPHICS_DISPLAY_I
GRAPHICS_DISPLAY_I      SET     1
**
**      $Filename: graphics/display.i $
**      $Release: 1.3 $
**
**      include define file for display control registers
**
**      (C) Copyright 1985,1986,1987,1988 Commodore-Amiga, Inc.
**          All Rights Reserved
**

* bplcon0 defines
MODE_640    equ   $8000
PLNCNTMSK   equ   $7                   * how many bit planes?
*                                      * 0 = none, 1->6 = 1->6, 7 = reserved
PLNCNTSHFT  equ   12                   * bits to shift for bplcon0
PF2PRI      equ   $40                  * bplcon2 bit
COLORON     equ   $0200                * disable color burst
DBLPF       equ   $400
HOLDNMODIFY equ   $800
INTERLACE   equ   4                    * interlace mode for 400

* bplcon1 defines
PFA_FINE_SCROLL        equ   $F
PFB_FINE_SCROLL_SHIFT equ   4
PF_FINE_SCROLL_MASK    equ   $F

* display window start and stop defines
DIW_HORIZ_POS          equ   $7F     * horizontal start/stop
DIW_VRTCL_POS          equ   $1FF    * vertical start/stop
DIW_VRTCL_POS_SHIFT    equ   7

* Data fetch start/stop horizontal position
DFTCH_MASK             equ   $FF

* vposr bits
VPOSRLOF               equ   $8000

        ENDC    ; GRAPHICS_DISPLAY_I
```

```
        IFND    GRAPHICS_GELS_I
GRAPHICS_GELS_I SET     1
**
**      $Filename: graphics/gels.i $
**      $Release: 1.3 $
**
**      include file for AMIGA GELS (Graphics Elements)
**
**      (C) Copyright 1985,1986,1987,1988 Commodore-Amiga, Inc.
**          All Rights Reserved
**

*------ VS_vSflags ---------------------------------------------------

*   ;-- user-set vSprite flags --
SUSERFLAGS  EQU $00FF           ; mask of all user-settable vSprite-flags
    BITDEF  VS,VSPRITE,0        ; set if vSprite, clear if bob
    BITDEF  VS,SAVEBACK,1       ; set if background is to be saved/restored
    BITDEF  VS,OVERLAY,2        ; set to mask image of bob onto background
    BITDEF  VS,MUSTDRAW,3       ; set if vSprite absolutely must be drawn
*   ;-- system-set vSprite flags --
    BITDEF  VS,BACKSAVED,8      ; this bob's background has been saved
    BITDEF  VS,BOBUPDATE,9      ; temporary flag, useless to outside world
    BITDEF  VS,GELGONE,10       ; set if gel is completely clipped (offscreen)
    BITDEF  VS,VSOVERFLOW,11    ; vSprite overflow (if MUSTDRAW set we draw!)


*------ B_flags -------------------------------------------------------
*   ;-- these are the user flag bits --
BUSERFLAGS  EQU $00FF           ; mask of all user-settable bob-flags
    BITDEF  B,SAVEBOB,0         ; set to not erase bob
    BITDEF  B,BOBISCOMP,1       ; set to identify bob as animComp
*   ;-- these are the system flag bits --
    BITDEF  B,BWAITING,8        ; set while bob is waiting on 'after'
    BITDEF  B,BDRAWN,9          ; set when bob is drawn this DrawG pass
    BITDEF  B,BOBSAWAY,10       ; set to initiate removal of bob
    BITDEF  B,BOBNIX,11         ; set when bob is completely removed
    BITDEF  B,SAVEPRESERVE,12   ; for back-restore during double-buffer
    BITDEF  B,OUTSTEP,13        ; for double-clearing if double-buffer


*------ defines for the animation procedures -------------------------

ANFRACSIZE  EQU 6
ANIMHALF    EQU $0020
RINGTRIGGER EQU $0001

*------ macros --------------------------------------------------------
* these are GEL functions that are currently simple enough to exist as a
* definition.  It should not be assumed that this will always be the case

InitAnimate MACRO   * &animKey
       CLR.L   \1
       ENDM


RemBob      MACRO   * &b
       OR.W    #BF_BOBSAWAY,b_BobFlags+\1
       ENDM

*------ VS : vSprite --------------------------------------------------
 STRUCTURE  VS,0    ; vSprite
*   -- SYSTEM VARIABLES --
*   GEL linked list forward/backward pointers sorted by y,x value
    APTR    vs_NextVSprite    ; struct *vSprite
    APTR    vs_PrevVSprite    ; struct *vSprite
*   GEL draw list constructed in the order the bobs are actually drawn, then
*   list is copied to clear list
*   must be here in vSprite for system boundary detection
```



```
    APTR    vs_DrawPath       ; struct *vSprite: pointer of overlay drawing
    APTR    vs_ClearPath      ; struct *vSprite: pointer for overlay clearing
*   the vSprite positions are defined in (y,x) order to make sorting
*   sorting easier, since (y,x) as a long integer
    WORD    vs_Oldy           ; previous position
    WORD    vs_Oldx           ;
*   -- COMMON VARIABLES --
    WORD    vs_VSFlags        ; vSprite flags
*   -- USER VARIABLES --
*    the vSprite positions are defined in (y,x) order to make sorting
*    easier, since (y,x) as a long integer
    WORD    vs_Y              ; screen position
    WORD    vs_X
    WORD    vs_Height
    WORD    vs_Width          ; number of words per row of image data
    WORD    vs_Depth          ; number of planes of data
    WORD    vs_MeMask         ; which types can collide with this vSprite
    WORD    vs_HitMask        ; which types this vSprite can collide with
    APTR    vs_ImageData      ; *WORD pointer to vSprite image
*    borderLine is the one-dimensional logical OR of all
*    the vSprite bits, used for fast collision detection of edge
    APTR    vs_BorderLine     ; *WORD: logical OR of all vSprite bits
    APTR    vs_CollMask       ; *WORD: similar to above except this is a
*    matrix pointer to this vSprite's color definitions (not used by bobs)
    APTR    vs_SprColors      ; *WORD
    APTR    vs_VSBob          ; struct *bob: points home if this vSprite is
                              ;  part of a bob
*    planePick flag:  set bit selects a plane from image, clear bit selects
*         use of shadow mask for that plane
*    OnOff flag: if using shadow mask to fill plane, this bit (corresponding
*         to bit in planePick) describes whether to fill with 0's or 1's
*    There are two uses for these flags:
*            - if this is the vSprite of a bob, these flags describe how
*              the bob is to be drawn into memory
*            - if this is a simple vSprite and the user intends on setting
*              the MUSTDRAW flag of the vSprite, these flags must be set
*              too to describe which color registers the user wants for
*              the image
    BYTE    vs_PlanePick
    BYTE    vs_PlaneOnOff
    LABEL   vs_SUserExt       ; user definable
    LABEL   vs_SIZEOF


*------ BOB : bob -----------------------------------------------------

 STRUCTURE  BOB,0     ; bob: blitter object
*   -- COMMON VARIABLES --
    WORD    bob_BobFlags      ; general purpose flags (see definitions below)
*   -- USER VARIABLES --
    APTR    bob_SaveBuffer    ; *WORD pointer to the buffer for background
*    save used by bobs for "cookie-cutting" and multi-plane masking
    APTR    bob_ImageShadow   ; *WORD
*    pointer to BOBs for sequenced drawing of bobs
*      for correct overlaying of multiple component animations
    APTR    bob_Before        ; struct *bob: draw this bob before bob pointed
                              ; to by before
    APTR    bob_After         ; struct *bob: draw this bob after bob pointed
                              ; to by after
    APTR    bob_BobVSprite    ; struct *vSprite: this bob's vSprite definition
    APTR    bob_BobComp       ; struct *animComp: pointer to this bob's
                              ; animComp def
    APTR    bob_DBuffer       ; struct dBufPacket: pointer to this bob's
                              ; dBuf packet
    LABEL   bob_BUserExt      ; bob user extension
    LABEL   bob_SIZEOF

*------ AC : animComp -------------------------------------------------
```

```
 STRUCTURE  AC,0    ; animComp
*   -- COMMON VARIABLES --
    WORD    ac_CompFlags        ; animComp flags for system & user
*    timer defines how long to keep this component active:
*      if set non-zero, timer decrements to zero then switches to nextSeq
*      if set to zero, animComp never switches
    WORD    ac_Timer
*   -- USER VARIABLES --
*    initial value for timer when the animComp is activated by the system
    WORD    ac_TimeSet
*    pointer to next and previous components of animation object
    APTR    ac_NextComp         ; struct *animComp
    APTR    ac_PrevComp         ; struct *animComp
*    pointer to component component definition of next image in sequence
    APTR    ac_NextSeq          ; struct *animComp
    APTR    ac_PrevSeq          ; struct *animComp
    APTR    ac_AnimCRoutine     ; address of special animation procedure
    WORD    ac_YTrans           ; initial y translation (if this is a component)
    WORD    ac_XTrans           ; initial x translation (if this is a component)
    APTR    ac_HeadOb           ; struct *animOb
    APTR    ac_AnimBob          ; struct *bob
    LABEL   ac_SIZE

*------ AO : animOb ---------------------------------------------

 STRUCTURE  AO,0    ; animOb
*   -- SYSTEM VARIABLES --
    APTR    ao_NextOb           ; struct *animOb
    APTR    ao_PrevOb           ; struct *animOb
*    number of calls to Animate this animOb has endured
    LONG    ao_Clock
    WORD    ao_AnOldY           ; old y,x coordinates
    WORD    ao_AnOldX           ;
*   -- COMMON VARIABLES --
    WORD    ao_AnY              ; y,x coordinates of the animOb
    WORD    ao_AnX              ;
*   -- USER VARIABLES --
    WORD    ao_YVel             ; velocities of this object
    WORD    ao_XVel             ;
    WORD    ao_XAccel           ; accelerations of this object
    WORD    ao_YAccel           ;   !!! backwards !!!
    WORD    ao_RingYTrans       ; ring translation values
    WORD    ao_RingXTrans       ;
    APTR    ao_AnimORoutine     ; address of special animation procedure
    APTR    ao_HeadComp         ; struct *animComp: pointer to first component
    LABEL   ao_AUserExt         ; animOb user extension
    LABEL   ao_SIZEOF


*------ DBP : dBufPacket ---------------------------------------------
* dBufPacket defines the values needed to be saved across buffer to buffer
*   when in double-buffer mode

 STRUCTURE  DBP,0               ; dBufPacket
    WORD    dbp_BufY            ; save the other buffers screen coordinates
    WORD    dbp_BufX            ;
    APTR    dbp_BufPath         ; struct *vSprite: carry the draw path over
                                ; the gap
*    these pointers must be filled in by the user
*    pointer to other buffer's background save buffer
    APTR    dbp_BufBuffer     ; *WORD
*    pointer to other buffer's background plane pointers
    APTR    dbp_BufPlanes     ; **WORD
    LABEL   dbp_SIZEOF

        ENDC    ; GRAPHICS_GELS_I
```



```
        IFND    GRAPHICS_GFX_I
GRAPHICS_GFX_I  SET     1
**
**      $Filename: graphics/gfx.i $
**      $Release: 1.3 $
**
**
**
**      (C) Copyright 1985,1986,1987,1988 Commodore-Amiga, Inc.
**          All Rights Reserved
**

BITSET      equ $8000
BITCLR      equ 0
AGNUS       equ 1
DENISE      equ 1

    STRUCTURE   BitMap,0
    WORD    bm_BytesPerRow
    WORD    bm_Rows
    BYTE    bm_Flags
    BYTE    bm_Depth
    WORD    bm_Pad
    STRUCT  bm_Planes,8*4
    LABEL   bm_SIZEOF

   STRUCTURE   Rectangle,0
      WORD  ra_MinX
      WORD  ra_MinY
      WORD  ra_MaxX
      WORD  ra_MaxY
   LABEL    ra_SIZEOF

        ENDC    ; GRAPHICS_GFX_I
```

```
        IFND    GRAPHICS_GFXBASE_I
GRAPHICS_GFXBASE_I      SET     1
**
**      $Filename: graphics/gfxbase.i $
**      $Release: 1.3 $
**
**
**
**      (C) Copyright 1985,1986,1987,1988 Commodore-Amiga, Inc.
**          All Rights Reserved
**

    IFND    EXEC_LISTS_I
    include "exec/lists.i"
    ENDC
    IFND    EXEC_LIBRARIES_I
    include "exec/libraries.i"
    ENDC
    IFND    EXEC_INTERRUPTS_I
    include "exec/interrupts.i"
    ENDC

 STRUCTURE  GfxBase,LIB_SIZE
    APTR    gb_ActiView     ; struct *View
    APTR    gb_copinit      ; struct *copinit; ptr to copper start up list
    APTR    gb_cia      ; for 6526 resource use
    APTR    gb_blitter      ; for blitter resource use
    APTR    gb_LOFlist      ; current copper list being run
    APTR    gb_SHFlist      ; current copper list being run
    APTR    gb_blthd        ; struct *bltnode
    APTR    gb_bltt1        ;
    APTR    gb_bsblthd      ;
    APTR    gb_bsbltt1      ;
    STRUCT  gb_vbsrv,IS_SIZE
    STRUCT  gb_timsrv,IS_SIZE
    STRUCT  gb_bltsrv,IS_SIZE
    STRUCT  gb_TextFonts,LH_SIZE
    APTR    gb_DefaultFont
    UWORD   gb_Modes        ; copy of bltcon0
    BYTE    gb_VBlank
    BYTE    gb_Debug
    UWORD   gb_BeamSync
    WORD    gb_system_bplcon0
    BYTE    gb_SpriteReserved
    BYTE    gb_bytereserved

    WORD    gb_Flags
    WORD    gb_BlitLock
        WORD    gb_BlitNest
        STRUCT  gb_BlitWaitQ,LH_SIZE
        APTR    gb_BlitOwner
        STRUCT  gb_TOF_WaitQ,LH_SIZE

        WORD    gb_DisplayFlags
        APTR    gb_SimpleSprites
        WORD    gb_MaxDisplayRow
        WORD    gb_MaxDisplayColumn
        WORD    gb_NormalDisplayRows
        WORD    gb_NormalDisplayColumns
        WORD    gb_NormalDPMX
        WORD    gb_NormalDPMY

        APTR    gb_LastChanceMemory
        APTR    gb_LCMptr

        WORD    gb_MicrosPerLine        ; usecs per line times 256
        WORD    gb_MinDisplayColumn

    STRUCT  gb_reserved,92    ; bytes reserved for future use
```



```
    LABEL   gb_SIZE

* bits for dalestuff, which may go away when blitter becomes a resource
OWNBLITTERn equ 0   * blitter owned bit
QBOWNERn    equ 1   * blitter owned by blit queuer

QBOWNER     equ 1<<QBOWNERn

        ENDC    ; GRAPHICS_GFXBASE_I
```

```
        IFND    GRAPHICS_LAYERS_I
GRAPHICS_LAYERS_I       SET     1
**
**      $Filename: graphics/layers.i $
**      $Release: 1.3 $
**
**
**
**      (C) Copyright 1985,1986,1987,1988 Commodore-Amiga, Inc.
**          All Rights Reserved
**

    IFND    EXEC_SEMAPHORES_I
       include "exec/semaphores.i"
    ENDC

    IFND  EXEC_LISTS_I
       include  "exec/lists.i"
    ENDC

* these should be clip.i/h but you know backwards compatibility etc.
LAYERSIMPLE             equ    1
LAYERSMART              equ    2
LAYERSUPER              equ    4
LAYERUPDATING           equ    $10
LAYERBACKDROP           equ    $40
LAYERREFRESH            equ    $80
LAYER_CLIPRECTS_LOST    equ    $100

LMN_REGION  equ -1

    STRUCTURE  Layer_Info,0
    APTR       li_top_layer
    APTR       li_check_lp
    APTR       li_obs
    STRUCT     li_FreeClipRects,MLH_SIZE
    STRUCT     li_Lock,SS_SIZE
        STRUCT     li_gs_Head,LH_SIZE
        LONG           li_long_reserved
        WORD       li_Flags
    BYTE       li_fatten_count
        BYTE       li_LockLayersCount
    WORD       li_LayerInfo_extra_size
        APTR           li_blitbuff
    APTR       li_LayerInfo_extra
    LABEL      li_SIZEOF

NEWLAYERINFO_CALLED     equ 1
ALERTLAYERSNOMEM        equ $83010000

        ENDC    ; GRAPHICS_LAYERS_I
```



```
        IFND    GRAPHICS_RASTPORT_I
GRAPHICS_RASTPORT_I     SET     1
**
**      $Filename: graphics/rastport.i $
**      $Release: 1.3 $
**
**
**
**      (C) Copyright 1985,1986,1987,1988 Commodore-Amiga, Inc.
**          All Rights Reserved
**

    IFND    GRAPHICS_GFX_I
       include "graphics/gfx.i"
    ENDC

*------ TR : TmpRas ------------------------------------------------

 STRUCTURE  TmpRas,0
   APTR     tr_RasPtr           ; *WORD
   LONG     tr_Size
   LABEL    tr_SIZEOF

*------ GelsInfo

   STRUCTURE   GelsInfo,0
   BYTE     gi_sprRsrvd         * flag of which sprites to reserve from
*                               * vsprite system
   BYTE     gi_Flags            * reserved for system use
   APTR     gi_gelHead
   APTR     gi_gelTail          * dummy vSprites for list management
* pointer to array of 8 WORDS for sprite available lines
   APTR     gi_nextLine
* pointer to array of 8 pointers for color-last-assigned to vSprites
   APTR     gi_lastColor
   APTR     gi_collHandler      * addresses of collision routines
   SHORT    gi_leftmost
   SHORT    gi_rightmost
   SHORT    gi_topmost
   SHORT    gi_bottommost
   APTR     gi_firstBlissObj
   APTR     gi_lastBlissObj     * system use only
   LABEL    gi_SIZEOF

*------ RP_Flags ------
   BITDEF   RP,FRST_DOT,0       ; draw the first dot of this line ?
   BITDEF   RP,ONE_DOT,1        ; use one dot mode for drawing lines
   BITDEF   RP,DBUFFER,2        ; flag set when RastPorts are double-buffered
*                               ;   (only used for bobs)
   BITDEF   RP,AREAOUTLINE,3    ; used by areafiller
   BITDEF   RP,NOCROSSFILL,5    ; used by areafiller

*------ RP_DrawMode ------
RP_JAM1         EQU 0
RP_JAM2         EQU 1
RP_COMPLEMENT   EQU 2
RP_INVERSVID    EQU 4           ; inverse video for drawing modes

*------ RP_TxFlags ------
   BITDEF  RP,TXSCALE,0

 STRUCTURE  RastPort,0
   LONG     rp_Layer
   LONG     rp_BitMap
   LONG     rp_AreaPtrn
   LONG     rp_TmpRas
   LONG     rp_AreaInfo
   LONG     rp_GelsInfo
   BYTE     rp_Mask
```

```
    BYTE      rp_FgPen
    BYTE      rp_BgPen
    BYTE      rp_AOLPen
    BYTE      rp_DrawMode
    BYTE      rp_AreaPtSz
    BYTE      rp_Dummy
    BYTE      rp_linpatcnt
    WORD      rp_Flags
    WORD      rp_LinePtrn
    WORD      rp_cp_x
    WORD      rp_cp_y
    STRUCT    rp_minterms,8
    WORD      rp_PenWidth
    WORD      rp_PenHeight
    LONG      rp_Font
    BYTE      rp_AlgoStyle
    BYTE      rp_TxFlags
    WORD      rp_TxHeight
    WORD      rp_TxWidth
    WORD      rp_TxBaseline
    WORD      rp_TxSpacing
    APTR      rp_RP_User
    STRUCT    rp_longreserved,8
         ifnd     GFX_RASTPORT_1_2
    STRUCT    rp_wordreserved,14
    STRUCT    rp_reserved,8
         endc
    LABEL     rp_SIZEOF

  STRUCTURE  AreaInfo,0
    LONG      ai_VctrTbl
    LONG      ai_VctrPtr
    LONG      ai_FlagTbl
    LONG      ai_FlagPtr
    WORD      ai_Count
    WORD      ai_MaxCount
    WORD      ai_FirstX
    WORD      ai_FirstY
    LABEL     ai_SIZEOF

ONE_DOTn     equu     1
ONE_DOT      equ      $2       * 1<<ONE_DOTn
FRST_DOTn    equ      0
FRST_DOT     equ      1        * 1<<FRST_DOTn

        ENDC    ; GRAPHICS_RASTPORT_I
```



```
        IFND    GRAPHICS_REGIONS_I
GRAPHICS_REGIONS_I      SET     1
**
**      $Filename: graphics/regions.i $
**      $Release: 1.3 $
**
**
**
**      (C) Copyright 1985,1986,1987,1988 Commodore-Amiga, Inc.
**          All Rights Reserved
**

   IFND  GRAPHICS_GFX_I
   include  "graphics/gfx.i"
   ENDC

    STRUCTURE   Region,0
      STRUCT   rg_bounds,ra_SIZEOF
      APTR  rg_RegionRectangle
   LABEL    rg_SIZEOF

   STRUCTURE   RegionRectangle,0
      APTR  rr_Next
      APTR  rr_Prev
      STRUCT   rr_bounds,ra_SIZEOF
   LABEL    rr_SIZEOF

        ENDC    ; GRAPHICS_REGIONS_I
```

```
        IFND    GRAPHICS_SPRITE_I
GRAPHICS_SPRITE_I       SET     1
**
**      $Filename: graphics/sprite.i $
**      $Release: 1.3 $
**
**
**
**      (C) Copyright 1985,1986,1987,1988 Commodore-Amiga, Inc.
**          All Rights Reserved
**

    STRUCTURE   SimpleSprite,0
    APTR        ss_posctldata
    WORD        ss_height
    WORD        ss_x
    WORD        ss_y
    WORD        ss_num
    LABEL       ss_SIZEOF

        ENDC    ; GRAPHICS_SPRITE_I
```



```
        IFND    GRAPHICS_TEXT_I
GRAPHICS_TEXT_I SET     1
**
**      $Filename: graphics/text.i $
**      $Release: 1.3 $
**
**      graphics library text structures
**
**      (C) Copyright 1985,1986,1987,1988 Commodore-Amiga, Inc.
**          All Rights Reserved
**

   IFND     EXEC_PORTS_I
   INCLUDE  "exec/ports.i"
   ENDC

*------ Font Styles ------------------------------------------------
FS_NORMAL    EQU 0                 ;normal text (no style attributes set)
   BITDEF    FS,EXTENDED,3         ;extended face (must be designed)
   BITDEF    FS,ITALIC,2           ;italic (slanted 1:2 right)
   BITDEF    FS,BOLD,1             ;bold face text (ORed w/ shifted right 1)
   BITDEF    FS,UNDERLINED,0       ;underlined (under baseline)

*------ Font Flags -------------------------------------------------
   BITDEF    FP,ROMFONT,0          ;font is in rom
   BITDEF    FP,DISKFONT,1         ;font is from diskfont.library
   BITDEF    FP,REVPATH,2          ;designed path is reversed (e.g. left)
   BITDEF    FP,TALLDOT,3          ;designed for hires non-interlaced
   BITDEF    FP,WIDEDOT,4          ;designed for lores interlaced
   BITDEF    FP,PROPORTIONAL,5     ;character sizes can vary from nominal
   BITDEF    FP,DESIGNED,6         ;size is "designed", not constructed
   BITDEF    FP,REMOVED,7          ; the font has been removed


******* TextAttr node **********************************************
 STRUCTURE  TextAttr,0
   APTR      ta_Name               ;name of the desired font
   UWORD     ta_YSize              ;size of the desired font
   UBYTE     ta_Style              ;desired font style
   UBYTE     ta_Flags              ;font preferences
   LABEL     ta_SIZEOF


******* TextFont node **********************************************
 STRUCTURE  TextFont,MN_SIZE
*                                  ;font name in LN        \ used in this
   UWORD     tf_YSize              ;font height            | order to best
   UBYTE     tf_Style              ;font style             | match a font
   UBYTE     tf_Flags              ;preference attributes  / request.
   UWORD     tf_XSize              ;nominal font width
   UWORD     tf_Baseline           ;distance from the top of char to baseline
   UWORD     tf_BoldSmear          ;smear to affect a bold enhancement

   UWORD     tf_Accessors          ;access count

   UBYTE     tf_LoChar             ;the first character described here
   UBYTE     tf_HiChar             ;the last character described here
   APTR      tf_CharData           ;the bit character data

   UWORD     tf_Modulo             ;the row modulo for the strike font data
   APTR      tf_CharLoc            ;ptr to location data for the strike font
*            ;  2 words: bit offset then size
   APTR      tf_CharSpace          ;ptr to words of proportional spacing data
   APTR      tf_CharKern           ;ptr to words of kerning data
   LABEL     tf_SIZEOF

        ENDC    ; GRAPHICS_TEXT_I
```

```
        IFND    GRAPHICS_VIEW_I
GRAPHICS_VIEW_I SET     1
**
**      $Filename: graphics/view.i $
**      $Release: 1.3 $
**
**
**
**      (C) Copyright 1985,1986,1987,1988 Commodore-Amiga, Inc.
**          All Rights Reserved
**

    IFND    GRAPHICS_GFX_I
    include "graphics/gfx.i"
    ENDC

    IFND    GRAPHICS_COPPER_I
    include "graphics/copper.i"
    ENDC

V_PFBA      EQU     $40
V_DUALPF    EQU     $400
V_HIRES     EQU     $8000
V_LACE      EQU     4
V_HAM       EQU     $800
V_SPRITES   EQU     $4000
GENLOCK_VIDEO   EQU 2

   STRUCTURE   ColorMap,0
      BYTE  cm_Flags
      BYTE  cm_Type
      WORD  cm_Count
      APTR  cm_ColorTable
   LABEL cm_SIZEOF


   STRUCTURE      ViewPort,0
   LONG    vp_Next
   LONG    vp_ColorMap
   LONG    vp_DspIns
   LONG    vp_SprIns
   LONG    vp_ClrIns
   LONG    vp_UCopIns
   WORD    vp_DWidth
   WORD    vp_DHeight
   WORD    vp_DxOffset
   WORD    vp_DyOffset
   WORD    vp_Modes
   BYTE    vp_SpritePriorities
   BYTE    vp_reserved
   APTR    vp_RasInfo
   LABEL   vp_SIZEOF


   STRUCTURE View,0
   LONG    v_ViewPort
   LONG    v_LOFCprList
   LONG    v_SHFCprList
   WORD    v_DyOffset
   WORD    v_DxOffset
   WORD    v_Modes
   LABEL   v_SIZEOF


   STRUCTURE  collTable,0
   LONG    cp_collPtrs,16
   LABEL   cp_SIZEOF


```



```
   STRUCTURE  RasInfo,0
   APTR    ri_Next
   LONG    ri_BitMap
   WORD    ri_RxOffset
   WORD    ri_RyOffset
   LABEL   ri_SIZEOF

        ENDC    ; GRAPHICS_VIEW_I
```

```
        IFND    HARDWARE_ADKBITS_I
HARDWARE_ADKBITS_I      SET     1
**
**      $Filename: hardware/adkbits.i $
**      $Release: 1.3 $
**
**      bit definitions for adkcon register
**
**      (C) Copyright 1985,1986,1987,1988 Commodore-Amiga, Inc.
**          All Rights Reserved
**

ADKB_SETCLR     EQU   15 ; standard set/clear bit
ADKB_PRECOMP1   EQU   14 ; two bits of precompensation
ADKB_PRECOMP0   EQU   13
ADKB_MFMPREC    EQU   12 ; use mfm style precompensation
ADKB_UARTBRK    EQU   11 ; force uart output to zero
ADKB_WORDSYNC   EQU   10 ; enable DSKSYNC register matching
ADKB_MSBSYNC    EQU   9  ; (Apple GCR Only) sync on MSB for reading
ADKB_FAST       EQU   8  ; 1 -> 2 us/bit (mfm), 2 -> 4 us/bit (gcr)
ADKB_USE3PN     EQU   7  ; use aud chan 3 to modulate period of ??
ADKB_USE2P3     EQU   6  ; use aud chan 2 to modulate period of 3
ADKB_USE1P2     EQU   5  ; use aud chan 1 to modulate period of 2
ADKB_USE0P1     EQU   4  ; use aud chan 0 to modulate period of 1
ADKB_USE3VN     EQU   3  ; use aud chan 3 to modulate volume of ??
ADKB_USE2V3     EQU   2  ; use aud chan 2 to modulate volume of 3
ADKB_USE1V2     EQU   1  ; use aud chan 1 to modulate volume of 2
ADKB_USE0V1     EQU   0  ; use aud chan 0 to modulate volume of 1

ADKF_SETCLR     EQU   (1<<15)
ADKF_PRECOMP1   EQU   (1<<14)
ADKF_PRECOMP0   EQU   (1<<13)
ADKF_MFMPREC    EQU   (1<<12)
ADKF_UARTBRK    EQU   (1<<11)
ADKF_WORDSYNC   EQU   (1<<10)
ADKF_MSBSYNC    EQU   (1<<9)
ADKF_FAST       EQU   (1<<8)
ADKF_USE3PN     EQU   (1<<7)
ADKF_USE2P3     EQU   (1<<6)
ADKF_USE1P2     EQU   (1<<5)
ADKF_USE0P1     EQU   (1<<4)
ADKF_USE3VN     EQU   (1<<3)
ADKF_USE2V3     EQU   (1<<2)
ADKF_USE1V2     EQU   (1<<1)
ADKF_USE0V1     EQU   (1<<0)

ADKF_PRE000NS   EQU   0                            ; 000 ns of precomp
ADKF_PRE140NS   EQU   (ADKF_PRECOMP0)              ; 140 ns of precomp
ADKF_PRE280NS   EQU   (ADKF_PRECOMP1)              ; 280 ns of precomp
ADKF_PRE560NS   EQU   (ADKF_PRECOMP0!ADKF_PRECOMP1) ; 560 ns of precomp

        ENDC    ; HARDWARE_ADKBITS_I
```



```
        IFND    HARDWARE_BLIT_I
HARDWARE_BLIT_I SET     1
**
**      $Filename: hardware/blit.i $
**      $Release: 1.3 $
**
**
**
**      (C) Copyright 1985,1986,1987,1988 Commodore-Amiga, Inc.
**          All Rights Reserved
**

   STRUCTURE bltnode,0
   LONG   bn_n
   LONG   bn_function
   BYTE   bn_stat
   BYTE   bn_dummy
   WORD   bn_blitsize
   WORD   bn_beamsync
   LONG   bn_cleanup
   LABEL  bn_SIZEOF

* bit defines used by blit queuer
CLEANMEn      equ 6
CLEANME       equ 1<<CLEANMEn

* include file for blitter */
HSIZEBITS     equu  6
VSIZEBITS     equ   16-HSIZEBITS
HSIZEMASK     equ   $3f        /* 2^6 -- 1 */
VSIZEMASK     equ   $3FF       /* 2^10 - 1 */

MAXBYTESPERROW EQU   128

* definitions for blitter control register 0 */

ABC           equ   $80
ABNC          equ   $40
ANBC          equ   $20
ANBNC         equ   $10
NABC          equ   $8
NABNC         equ   $4
NANBC         equ   $2
NANBNC        equ   $1

BC0B_DEST     equ     8
BC0B_SRCC     equ     9
BC0B_SRCB     equ    10
BC0B_SRCA     equ    11
BC0F_DEST     equ   $100
BC0F_SRCC     equ   $200
BC0F_SRCB     equ   $400
BC0F_SRCA     equ   $800

BC1F_DESC     equ 2

DEST          equ   $100
SRCC          equ   $200
SRCB          equ   $400
SRCA          equ   $800

ASHIFTSHIFT equu    12 /* bits to right align ashift value */
BSHIFTSHIFT equ     12 /* bits to right align bshift value */

* definations for blitter control register 1 */
LINEMODE      equ   $1
FILL_OR       equ   $8
FILL_XOR      equ   $10
FILL_CARRYIN     equ    $4
```

```
ONEDOT      equ   $2
OVFLAG      equ   $20
SIGNFLAG    equ   $40
BLITREVERSE equ   $2

SUD         equ   $10
SUL         equ   $8
AUL         equ   $4

OCTANT8     equ   24
OCTANT7     equ   4
OCTANT6     equ   12
OCTANT5     equ   28
OCTANT4     equ   20
OCTANT3     equ   8
OCTANT2     equ   0
OCTANT1     equ   16

        ENDC    ; HARDWARE_BLIT_I
```



```
        IFND    HARDWARE_CIA_I
HARDWARE_CIA_I  SET     1
**
**      $Filename: hardware/cia.i $
**      $Release: 1.3 $
**
**      registers and bits in the Complex Interface Adapter (CIA) chip
**
**      (C) Copyright 1985,1986,1987,1988 Commodore-Amiga, Inc.
**          All Rights Reserved
**

*
* _ciaa is on an ODD address (e.g. the low byte) -- $bfe001
* _ciab is on an EVEN address (e.g. the high byte) -- $bfd000
*
* do this to get the definitions:
*    XREF _ciaa
*    XREF _ciab
*


* cia register offsets
ciapra              EQU   $0000
ciaprb              EQU   $0100
ciaddra             EQU   $0200
ciaddrb             EQU   $0300
ciatalo             EQU   $0400
ciatahi             EQU   $0500
ciatblo             EQU   $0600
ciatbhi             EQU   $0700
ciatodlow           EQU   $0800
ciatodmid           EQU   $0900
ciatodhi            EQU   $0A00
ciasdr              EQU   $0C00
ciaicr              EQU   $0D00
ciacra              EQU   $0E00
ciacrb              EQU   $0F00

* interrupt control register bit numbers
CIAICRB_TA          EQU   0
CIAICRB_TB          EQU   1
CIAICRB_ALRM        EQU   2
CIAICRB_SP          EQU   3
CIAICRB_FLG         EQU   4
CIAICRB_IR          EQU   7
CIAICRB_SETCLR      EQU   7

* control register A bit numbers
CIACRAB_START       EQU   0
CIACRAB_PBON        EQU   1
CIACRAB_OUTMODE     EQU   2
CIACRAB_RUNMODE     EQU   3
CIACRAB_LOAD        EQU   4
CIACRAB_INMODE      EQU   5
CIACRAB_SPMODE      EQU   6
CIACRAB_TODIN       EQU   7

* control register B bit numbers
CIACRBB_START       EQU   0
CIACRBB_PBON        EQU   1
CIACRBB_OUTMODE     EQU   2
CIACRBB_RUNMODE     EQU   3
CIACRBB_LOAD        EQU   4
CIACRBB_INMODE0     EQU   5
CIACRBB_INMODE1     EQU   6
CIACRBB_ALARM       EQU   7

* interrupt control register bit masks
```

```
CIAICRF_TA         EQU   (1<<0)
CIAICRF_TB         EQU   (1<<1)
CIAICRF_ALRM       EQU   (1<<2)
CIAICRF_SP         EQU   (1<<3)
CIAICRF_FLG        EQU   (1<<4)
CIAICRF_IR         EQU   (1<<7)
CIAICRF_SETCLR     EQU   (1<<7)

* control register A bit masks
CIACRAF_START      EQU   (1<<0)
CIACRAF_PBON       EQU   (1<<1)
CIACRAF_OUTMODE    EQU   (1<<2)
CIACRAF_RUNMODE    EQU   (1<<3)
CIACRAF_LOAD       EQU   (1<<4)
CIACRAF_INMODE     EQU   (1<<5)
CIACRAF_SPMODE     EQU   (1<<6)
CIACRAF_TODIN      EQU   (1<<7)

* control register B bit masks
CIACRBF_START      EQU   (1<<0)
CIACRBF_PBON       EQU   (1<<1)
CIACRBF_OUTMODE    EQU   (1<<2)
CIACRBF_RUNMODE    EQU   (1<<3)
CIACRBF_LOAD       EQU   (1<<4)
CIACRBF_INMODE0    EQU   (1<<5)
CIACRBF_INMODE1    EQU   (1<<6)
CIACRBF_ALARM      EQU   (1<<7)

* control register B INMODE masks
CIACRBF_IN_PHI2    EQU   0
CIACRBF_IN_CNT     EQU   (CIACRBF_INMODE0)
CIACRBF_IN_TA      EQU   (CIACRBF_INMODE1)
CIACRBF_IN_CNT_TA EQU    (CIACRBF_INMODE0!CIACRBF_INMODE1)


*
* Port definitions -- what each bit in a cia peripheral register is tied to
*

* ciaa port A (0xbfe001)
CIAB_GAMEPORT1     EQU   (7)    * gameport 1, pin 6 (fire button*)
CIAB_GAMEPORT0     EQU   (6)    * gameport 0, pin 6 (fire button*)
CIAB_DSKRDY        EQU   (5)    * disk ready*
CIAB_DSKTRACK0     EQU   (4)    * disk on track 00*
CIAB_DSKPROT       EQU   (3)    * disk write protect*
CIAB_DSKCHANGE     EQU   (2)    * disk change*
CIAB_LED           EQU   (1)    * led light control (0==>bright)
CIAB_OVERLAY       EQU   (0)    * memory overlay bit

* ciaa port B (0xbfe101) -- parallel port

* ciab port A (0xbfd000) -- serial and printer control
CIAB_COMDTR        EQU   (7)    * serial Data Terminal Ready*
CIAB_COMRTS        EQU   (6)    * serial Request to Send*
CIAB_COMCD         EQU   (5)    * serial Carrier Detect*
CIAB_COMCTS        EQU   (4)    * serial Clear to Send*
CIAB_COMDSR        EQU   (3)    * serial Data Set Ready*
CIAB_PRTRSEL       EQU   (2)    * printer SELECT
CIAB_PRTRPOUT      EQU   (1)    * printer paper out
CIAB_PRTRBUSY      EQU   (0)    * printer busy

* ciab port B (0xbfd100) -- disk control
CIAB_DSKMOTOR      EQU   (7)    * disk motorr*
CIAB_DSKSEL3       EQU   (6)    * disk select unit 3*
CIAB_DSKSEL2       EQU   (5)    * disk select unit 2*
CIAB_DSKSEL1       EQU   (4)    * disk select unit 1*
CIAB_DSKSEL0       EQU   (3)    * disk select unit 0*
CIAB_DSKSIDE       EQU   (2)    * disk side select*
CIAB_DSKDIREC      EQU   (1)    * disk direction of seek*
```



```
CIAB_DSKSTEP       EQU   (0)    * disk step heads*

* ciaa port A (0xbfe001)
CIAF_GAMEPORT1     EQU   (1<<7)
CIAF_GAMEPORT0     EQU   (1<<6)
CIAF_DSKRDY        EQU   (1<<5)
CIAF_DSKTRACK0     EQU   (1<<4)
CIAF_DSKPROT       EQU   (1<<3)
CIAF_DSKCHANGE     EQU   (1<<2)
CIAF_LED           EQU   (1<<1)
CIAF_OVERLAY       EQU   (1<<0)

* ciaa port B (0xbfe101) -- parallel port

* ciab port A (0xbfd000) -- serial and printer control
CIAF_COMDTR        EQU   (1<<7)
CIAF_COMRTS        EQU   (1<<6)
CIAF_COMCD         EQU   (1<<5)
CIAF_COMCTS        EQU   (1<<4)
CIAF_COMDSR        EQU   (1<<3)
CIAF_PRTRSEL       EQU   (1<<2)
CIAF_PRTRPOUT      EQU   (1<<1)
CIAF_PRTRBUSY      EQU   (1<<0)

* ciab port B (0xbfd100) -- disk control
CIAF_DSKMOTOR      EQU   (1<<7)
CIAF_DSKSEL3       EQU   (1<<6)
CIAF_DSKSEL2       EQU   (1<<5)
CIAF_DSKSEL1       EQU   (1<<4)
CIAF_DSKSEL0       EQU   (1<<3)
CIAF_DSKSIDE       EQU   (1<<2)
CIAF_DSKDIREC      EQU   (1<<1)
CIAF_DSKSTEP       EQU   (1<<0)

        ENDC    ; HARDWARE_CIA_I
```

```
        IFND    HARDWARE_CUSTOM_I
HARDWARE_CUSTOM_I       SET     1
**
**      $Filename: hardware/custom.i $
**      $Release: 1.3 $
**
**
**
**      (C) Copyright 1985,1986,1987,1988 Commodore-Amiga, Inc.
**          All Rights Reserved
**

*
* do this to get base of custom registers:
*  XREF _custom;
*

bltddat     EQU   $000
dmaconr     EQU   $002
vposr       EQU   $004
vhposr      EQU   $006
dskdatr     EQU   $008
joy0dat     EQU   $00A
joy1dat     EQU   $00C
clxdat      EQU   $00E

adkconr     EQU   $010
pot0dat     EQU   $012
pot1dat     EQU   $014
potinp      EQU   $016
serdatr     EQU   $018
dskbytr     EQU   $01A
intenar     EQU   $01C
intreqr     EQU   $01E

dskpt       EQU   $020
dsklen      EQU   $024
dskdat      EQU   $026
refptr      EQU   $028
vposw       EQU   $02A
vhposw      EQU   $02C
copcon      EQU   $02E
serdat      EQU   $030
serper      EQU   $032
potgo       EQU   $034
joytest     EQU   $036
strequ      EQU   $038
strvbl      EQU   $03A
strhor      EQU   $03C
strlong     EQU   $03E

bltcon0     EQU   $040
bltcon1     EQU   $042
bltafwm     EQU   $044
bltalwm     EQU   $046
bltcpt      EQU   $048
bltbpt      EQU   $04C
bltapt      EQU   $050
bltdpt      EQU   $054
bltsize     EQU   $058

bltcmod     EQU   $060
bltbmod     EQU   $062
bltamod     EQU   $064
bltdmod     EQU   $066

bltcdat     EQU   $070
bltbdat     EQU   $072
bltadat     EQU   $074
```



```

dsksync     EQU   $07E

cop1lc      EQU   $080
cop2lc      EQU   $084
copjmp1     EQU   $088
copjmp2     EQU   $08A
copins      EQU   $08C
diwstrt     EQU   $08E
diwstop     EQU   $090
ddfstrt     EQU   $092
ddfstop     EQU   $094
dmacon      EQU   $096
clxcon      EQU   $098
intena      EQU   $09A
intreq      EQU   $09C
adkcon      EQU   $09E

aud         EQU   $0A0
aud0        EQU   $0A0
aud1        EQU   $0B0
aud2        EQU   $0C0
aud3        EQU   $0D0

* STRUCTURE AudChannel,0
ac_ptr      EQU   $00    ; ptr to start of waveform data
ac_len      EQU   $04    ; length of waveform in words
ac_per      EQU   $06    ; sample period
ac_vol      EQU   $08    ; volume
ac_dat      EQU   $0A    ; sample pair
ac_SIZEOF   EQU   $10

bplpt       EQU   $0E0

bplcon0     EQU   $100
bplcon1     EQU   $102
bplcon2     EQU   $104
bpl1mod     EQU   $108
bpl2mod     EQU   $10A

bpldat      EQU   $110

sprpt       EQU   $120

spr         EQU   $140
* STRUCTURE SpriteDef
sd_pos      EQU   $00
sd_ctl      EQU   $02
sd_dataa    EQU   $04
sd_datab    EQU   $08

color       EQU   $180

            ENDC    ; HARDWARE_CUSTOM_I
```

```
         IFND    HARDWARE_DMABITS_I
HARDWARE_DMABITS_I      SET     1
**
**       $Filename: hardware/dmabits.i $
**       $Release: 1.3 $
**
**       include file for defining dma control stuff
**
**       (C) Copyright 1985,1986,1987,1988 Commodore-Amiga, Inc.
**           All Rights Reserved
**

* write definitions for dmaconw
DMAF_SETCLR     EQU    $8000
DMAF_AUDIO      EQU    $000F   * 4 bit mask
DMAF_AUD0       EQU    $0001
DMAF_AUD1       EQU    $0002
DMAF_AUD2       EQU    $0004
DMAF_AUD3       EQU    $0008
DMAF_DISK       EQU    $0010
DMAF_SPRITE     EQU    $0020
DMAF_BLITTER    EQU    $0040
DMAF_COPPER     EQU    $0080
DMAF_RASTER     EQU    $0100
DMAF_MASTER     EQU    $0200
DMAF_BLITHOG    EQU    $0400
DMAF_ALL        EQU    $01FF   * all dma channels

* read definitions for dmaconr
* bits 0-8 correspnd to dmaconw definitions
DMAF_BLTDONE    EQU    $4000
DMAF_BLTNZERO   EQU    $2000

DMAB_SETCLR     EQU    15
DMAB_AUD0       EQU    0
DMAB_AUD1       EQU    1
DMAB_AUD2       EQU    2
DMAB_AUD3       EQU    3
DMAB_DISK       EQU    4
DMAB_SPRITE     EQU    5
DMAB_BLITTER    EQU    6
DMAB_COPPER     EQU    7
DMAB_RASTER     EQU    8
DMAB_MASTER     EQU    9
DMAB_BLITHOG    EQU    10
DMAB_BLTDONE    EQU    14
DMAB_BLTNZERO   EQU    13

         ENDC     ; HARDWARE_DMABITS_I
```



```
         IFND    HARDWARE_INTBITS_I
HARDWARE_INTBITS_I      SET     1
**
**       $Filename: hardware/intbits.i $
**       $Release: 1.3 $
**
**       bits in the interrupt enable (and interrupt request) register
**
**       (C) Copyright 1985,1986,1987,1988 Commodore-Amiga, Inc.
**           All Rights Reserved
**

INTB_SETCLR     EQU    (15)   ;Set/Clear control bit. Determines if bits
                              ;written with a 1 get set or cleared. Bits
                              ;written with a zero are allways unchanged.
INTB_INTEN      EQU    (14)   ;Master interrupt (enable only )
INTB_EXTER      EQU    (13)   ;External interrupt
INTB_DSKSYNC    EQU    (12)   ;Disk re-SYNChronized
INTB_RBF        EQU    (11)   ;serial port Receive Buffer Full
INTB_AUD3       EQU    (10)   ;Audio channel 3 block finished
INTB_AUD2       EQU    (9)    ;Audio channel 2 block finished
INTB_AUD1       EQU    (8)    ;Audio channel 1 block finished
INTB_AUD0       EQU    (7)    ;Audio channel 0 block finished
INTB_BLIT       EQU    (6)    ;Blitter finished
INTB_VERTB      EQU    (5)    ;start of Vertical Blank
INTB_COPER      EQU    (4)    ;Coprocessor
INTB_PORTS      EQU    (3)    ;I/O Ports and timers
INTB_SOFTINT    EQU    (2)    ;software interrupt request
INTB_DSKBLK     EQU    (1)    ;Disk Block done
INTB_TBE        EQU    (0)    ;serial port Transmit Buffer Empty



INTF_SETCLR     EQU    (1<<15)
INTF_INTEN      EQU    (1<<14)
INTF_EXTER      EQU    (1<<13)
INTF_DSKSYNC    EQU    (1<<12)
INTF_RBF        EQU    (1<<11)
INTF_AUD3       EQU    (1<<10)
INTF_AUD2       EQU    (1<<9)
INTF_AUD1       EQU    (1<<8)
INTF_AUD0       EQU    (1<<7)
INTF_BLIT       EQU    (1<<6)
INTF_VERTB      EQU    (1<<5)
INTF_COPER      EQU    (1<<4)
INTF_PORTS      EQU    (1<<3)
INTF_SOFTINT    EQU    (1<<2)
INTF_DSKBLK     EQU    (1<<1)
INTF_TBE        EQU    (1<<0)

         ENDC     ; HARDWARE_INTBITS_I
```

```
        IFND    INTUITION_INTUITION_I
INTUITION_INTUITION_I   SET     1
**
**      $Filename: intuition/intuition.i $
**      $Release: 1.3 $
**
**      main intuition include
**
**      (C) Copyright 1985,1986,1987,1988 Commodore-Amiga, Inc.
**          All Rights Reserved
**

        IFND EXEC_TYPES_I
        INCLUDE "exec/types.i"
        ENDC

        IFND    GRAPHICS_GFX_I
        include "graphics/gfx.i"
        ENDC

        IFND    GRAPHICS_CLIP_I
        include "graphics/clip.i"
        ENDC

        IFND    GRAPHICS_VIEW_I
        include "graphics/view.i"
        ENDC

        IFND    GRAPHICS_RASTPORT_I
        include "graphics/rastport.i"
        ENDC

        IFND    GRAPHICS_LAYERS_I
        include "graphics/layers.i"
        ENDC

        IFND    GRAPHICS_TEXT_I
        include "graphics/text.i"
        ENDC

        IFND EXEC_PORTS_I
        include "exec/ports.i"
        ENDC

        IFND    DEVICES_TIMER_I
        include "devices/timer.i"
        ENDC

        IFND    DEVICES_INPUTEVENT_I
        include "devices/inputevent.i"
        ENDC


; ====================================================================;
; === Menu ===========================================================;
; ====================================================================;
 STRUCTURE Menu,0

    APTR   mu_NextMenu   ; menu pointer, same level
    WORD mu_LeftEdge     ; position of the select box
    WORD mu_TopEdge      ; position of the select box
    WORD mu_Width        ; dimensions of the select box
    WORD mu_Height       ; dimensions of the select box
    WORD mu_Flags        ; see flag definitions below
    APTR mu_MenuName     ; text for this Menu Header
    APTR   mu_FirstItem  ; pointer to first in chain

    ; these mysteriously-named variables are for internal use only
    WORD mu_JazzX
```



```
    WORD mu_JazzY
    WORD mu_BeatX
    WORD mu_BeatY

    LABEL mu_SIZEOF

;*** FLAGS SET BY BOTH THE APPLIPROG AND INTUITION ***
MENUENABLED EQU $0001   ; whether or not this menu is enabled

;*** FLAGS SET BY INTUITION ***
MIDRAWN EQU $0100       ; this menu's items are currently drawn

; ====================================================================;
; === MenuItem =======================================================;
; ====================================================================;
 STRUCTURE MenuItem,0

    APTR mi_NextItem     ; pointer to next in chained list
    WORD mi_LeftEdge     ; position of the select box
    WORD mi_TopEdge      ; position of the select box
    WORD mi_Width        ; dimensions of the select box
    WORD mi_Height       ; dimensions of the select box
    WORD mi_Flags        ; see the defines below

    LONG mi_MutualExclude ; set bits mean this item excludes that item

    APTR mi_ItemFill     ; points to Image, IntuiText, or NULL

    ; when this item is pointed to by the cursor and the items highlight
    ; mode HIGHIMAGE is selected, this alternate image will be displayed
    APTR mi_SelectFill   ; points to Image, IntuiText, or NULL

    BYTE mi_Command      ; only if appliprog sets the COMMSEQ flag

    BYTE mi_KludgeFill00 ; This is strictly for word-alignment

    APTR mi_SubItem      ; if non-zero, DrawMenu shows "->"

   ; The NextSelect field represents the menu number of next selected
   ; item (when user has drag-selected several items)
    WORD mi_NextSelect

    LABEL  mi_SIZEOF

; --- FLAGS SET BY THE APPLIPROG ----------------------------------------
CHECKIT         EQU $0001       ; whether to check this item if selected
ITEMTEXT        EQU $0002       ; set if textual, clear if graphical item
COMMSEQ         EQU $0004       ; set if there's an command sequence
MENUTOGGLE      EQU $0008       ; set to toggle the check of a menu item
ITEMENABLED     EQU $0010       ; set if this item is enabled

; these are the SPECIAL HIGHLIGHT FLAG state meanings
HIGHFLAGS       EQU $00C0       ; see definitions below for these bits
HIGHIMAGE       EQU $0000       ; use the user's "select image"
HIGHCOMP        EQU $0040       ; highlight by complementing the select box
HIGHBOX         EQU $0080       ; highlight by drawing a box around the image
HIGHNONE        EQU $00C0       ; don't highlight

; --- FLAGS SET BY BOTH APPLIPROG AND INTUITION --------------------------
CHECKED         EQU $0100       ; if CHECKIT, then set this when selected


; --- FLAGS SET BY INTUITION ---------------------------------------------
ISDRAWN         EQU $1000       ; this item's subs are currently drawn
HIGHITEM        EQU $2000       ; this item is currently highlighted
MENUTOGGLED     EQU $4000       ; this item was already toggled
```

```



; ======================================================================
; === Requester ========================================================
; ======================================================================
 STRUCTURE Requester,0

    ; the ClipRect and BitMap and used for rendering the requester
    APTR  rq_OlderRequest
    WORD rq_LeftEdge              ; dimensions of the entire box
    WORD rq_TopEdge               ; dimensions of the entire box
    WORD rq_Width                 ; dimensions of the entire box
    WORD rq_Height                ; dimensions of the entire box

    WORD rq_RelLeft               ; get POINTREL Pointer relativity offsets
    WORD rq_RelTop                ; get POINTREL Pointer relativity offsets

    APTR  rq_ReqGadget            ; pointer to the first of a list of gadgets
    APTR  rq_ReqBorder            ; the box's border
    APTR  rq_ReqText              ; the box's text

    WORD  rq_Flags                ; see definitions below

    UBYTE rq_BackFill             ; pen number for back-plane fill before draws

    BYTE rq_KludgeFill00          ; This is strictly for word-alignment

    APTR rq_ReqLayer              ; layer in which requester rendered
    STRUCT rq_ReqPad1,32          ; for backwards compatibility (reserved)

    ; If the BitMap plane pointers are non-zero, this tells the system
    ; that the image comes pre-drawn (if the appliprog wants to define
    ; it's own box, in any shape or size it wants!); this is OK by
    ; Intuition as long as there's a good correspondence between the image
    ; and the specified Gadgets
    APTR  rq_ImageBMap            ; points to the BitMap of PREDRAWN imagery

    APTR  rq_RWindow              ; points back to requester's window
    STRUCT rq_ReqPad2,36          ; for backwards compatibility (reserved)

    LABEL rq_SIZEOF

; FLAGS SET BY THE APPLIPROG
POINTREL        EQU $0001  ; if POINTREL set, TopLeft is relative to pointer
PREDRAWN        EQU $0002  ; if ReqBMap points to predrawn Requester imagery
NOISYREQ        EQU $0004  ; if you don't want requester to filter input

; FLAGS SET BY INTUITION;
REQOFFWINDOW    EQU $1000         ; part of one of the Gadgets was offwindow
REQACTIVE       EQU $2000         ; this requester is active
SYSREQUEST      EQU $4000         ; this requester caused by system
DEFERREFRESH    EQU $8000         ; this Requester stops a Refresh broadcast





; ======================================================================
; === Gadget ===========================================================
; ======================================================================
 STRUCTURE Gadget,0

    APTR gg_NextGadget            ; next gadget in the list

    WORD gg_LeftEdge              ; "hit box" of gadget
    WORD gg_TopEdge               ; "hit box" of gadget
    WORD gg_Width                 ; "hit box" of gadget
    WORD gg_Height                ; "hit box" of gadget
```



```

    WORD gg_Flags                 ; see below for list of defines

    WORD gg_Activation            ; see below for list of defines

    WORD gg_GadgetType            ; see below for defines

    ; appliprog can specify that the Gadget be rendered as either as Border
    ; or an Image.  This variable points to which (or equals NULL if there's
    ; nothing to be rendered about this Gadget)
    APTR gg_GadgetRender

    ; appliprog can specify "highlighted" imagery rather than algorithmic
    ; this can point to either Border or Image data
    APTR gg_SelectRender

    APTR gg_GadgetText            ; text for this gadget;

    ; by using the MutualExclude word, the appliprog can describe
    ; which gadgets mutually-exclude which other ones.  The bits in
    ; MutualExclude correspond to the gadgets in object containing
    ; the gadget list.  If this gadget is selected and a bit is set
    ; in this gadget's MutualExclude and the gadget corresponding to
    ; that bit is currently selected (e.g. bit 2 set and gadget 2
    ; is currently selected) that gadget must be unselected.  Intuition
    ; does the visual unselecting (with checkmarks) and leaves it up
    ; to the program to unselect internally
    LONG gg_MutualExclude         ; set bits mean this gadget excludes that

    ; pointer to a structure of special data required by Proportional, String
    ; and Integer Gadgets
    APTR gg_SpecialInfo

    WORD gg_GadgetID     ; user-definable ID field
    APTR  gg_UserData    ; ptr to general purpose User data (ignored by Intuit)

    LABEL gg_SIZEOF

; --- FLAGS SET BY THE APPLIPROG -------------------------------------------
; combinations in these bits describe the highlight technique to be used
GADGHIGHBITS     EQU $0003
GADGHCOMP        EQU $0000        ; Complement the select box
GADGHBOX         EQU $0001        ; Draw a box around the image
GADGHIMAGE       EQU $0002        ; Blast in this alternate image
GADGHNONE        EQU $0003        ; don't highlight

; set this flag if the GadgetRender and SelectRender point to Image imagery,
; clear if it's a Border
GADGIMAGE        EQU $0004

; combinations in these next two bits specify to which corner the gadget's
; Left & Top coordinates are relative.  If relative to Top/Left,
; these are "normal" coordinates (everything is relative to something in
; this universe)
GRELBOTTOM       EQU $0008        ; set if rel to bottom, clear if rel top
GRELRIGHT        EQU $0010        ; set if rel to right, clear if to left
; set the RELWIDTH bit to spec that Width is relative to width of screen
GRELWIDTH        EQU $0020
; set the RELHEIGHT bit to spec that Height is rel to height of screen
GRELHEIGHT       EQU $0040

; the SELECTED flag is initialized by you and set by Intuition.  It
; specifies whether or not this Gadget is currently selected/highlighted
SELECTED         EQU $0080


; the GADGDISABLED flag is initialized by you and later set by Intuition
; according to your calls to On/OffGadget().  It specifies whether or not
; this Gadget is currently disabled from being selected
```

```
GADGDISABLED    EQU $0100


; --- These are the Activation flag bits ---------------------------------
; RELVERIFY is set if you want to verify that the pointer was still over
; the gadget when the select button was released
RELVERIFY       EQU $0001

; the flag GADGIMMEDIATE, when set, informs the caller that the gadget
; was activated when it was activated.  this flag works in conjunction with
; the RELVERIFY flag
GADGIMMEDIATE   EQU $0002

; the flag ENDGADGET, when set, tells the system that this gadget, when
; selected, causes the Requester or AbsMessage to be ended.  Requesters or
; AbsMessages that are ended are erased and unlinked from the system
ENDGADGET       EQU $0004

; the FOLLOWMOUSE flag, when set, specifies that you want to receive
; reports on mouse movements (ie, you want the REPORTMOUSE function for
; your Window).  When the Gadget is deselected (immediately if you have
; no RELVERIFY) the previous state of the REPORTMOUSE flag is restored
; You probably want to set the GADGIMMEDIATE flag when using FOLLOWMOUSE,
; since that's the only reasonable way you have of learning why Intuition
; is suddenly sending you a stream of mouse movement events.  If you don't
; set RELVERIFY, you'll get at least one Mouse Position event.
FOLLOWMOUSE     EQU $0008

; if any of the BORDER flags are set in a Gadget that"s included in the
; Gadget list when a Window is opened, the corresponding Border will
; be adjusted to make room for the Gadget
RIGHTBORDER     EQU $0010
LEFTBORDER      EQU $0020
TOPBORDER       EQU $0040
BOTTOMBORDER    EQU $0080

TOGGLESELECT    EQU $0100       ; this bit for toggle-select mode

STRINGCENTER    EQU $0200       ; center the String
STRINGRIGHT     EQU $0400       ; right-justify the String

LONGINT         EQU $0800       ; This String Gadget is a Long Integer

ALTKEYMAP       EQU $1000       ; This String has an alternate keymapping

BOOLEXTEND      EQU $2000       ; This Boolean Gadget has a BoolInfo

; --- GADGET TYPES ---------------------------------------------------------
; These are the Gaget Type definitions for the variable GadgetType.
; Gadget number type MUST start from one.  NO TYPES OF ZERO ALLOWED.
; first comes the mask for Gadget flags reserved for Gadget typing
GADGETTYPE      EQU $FC00       ; all Gadget Global Type flags (padded)
SYSGADGET       EQU $8000       ; 1 = SysGadget, 0 = AppliGadget
SCRGADGET       EQU $4000       ; 1 = ScreenGadget, 0 = WindowGadget
GZZGADGET       EQU $2000       ; 1 = Gadget for GIMMEZEROZERO borders
REQGADGET       EQU $1000       ; 1 = this is a Requester Gadget
; system gadgets
SIZING          EQU $0010
WDRAGGING       EQU $0020
SDRAGGING       EQU $0030
WUPFRONT        EQU $0040
SUPFRONT        EQU $0050
WDOWNBACK       EQU $0060
SDOWNBACK       EQU $0070
CLOSE           EQU $0080
; application gadgets
BOOLGADGET      EQU $0001
GADGET0002      EQU $0002
PROPGADGET      EQU $0003
```



```
STRGADGET       EQU $0004



; ==========================================================================
; === BoolInfo==============================================================
; ==========================================================================
; This is the special data needed by an Extended Boolean Gadget
; Typically this structure will be pointed to by the Gadget field SpecialInfo

 STRUCTURE BoolInfo,0

    WORD    bi_Flags    ; defined below
    APTR    bi_Mask     ; bit mask for highlighting and selecting
                        ; mask must follow the same rules as an Image
                        ; plane.  It's width and height are determined
                        ; by the width and height of the gadget's
                        ; select box. (i.e. Gadget.Width and .Height).
    LONG    bi_Reserved ; set to 0

    LABEL   bi_SIZEOF

; set BoolInfo.Flags to this flag bit.
; in the future, additional bits might mean more stuff hanging
; off of BoolInfo.Reserved.

BOOLMASK        EQU     $0001   ; extension is for masked gadget

; ==========================================================================
; === PropInfo =============================================================
; ==========================================================================
; this is the special data required by the proportional Gadget
; typically, this data will be pointed to by the Gadget variable SpecialInfo
 STRUCTURE PropInfo,0

    WORD pi_Flags       ; general purpose flag bits (see defines below)

    ; You initialize the Pot variables before the Gadget is added to
    ; the system.  Then you can look here for the current settings
    ; any time, even while User is playing with this Gadget.  To
    ; adjust these after the Gadget is added to the System, use
    ; ModifyProp(); The Pots are the actual proportional settings,
    ; where a value of zero means zero and a value of MAXPOT means
    ; that the Gadget is set to its maximum setting.
    WORD pi_HorizPot    ; 16-bit FixedPoint horizontal quantity percentage;
    WORD pi_VertPot     ; 16-bit FixedPoint vertical quantity percentage;

    ; the 16-bit FixedPoint Body variables describe what percentage
    ; of the entire body of stuff referred to by this Gadget is
    ; actually shown at one time.  This is used with the AUTOKNOB
    ; routines, to adjust the size of the AUTOKNOB according to how
    ; much of the data can be seen.  This is also used to decide how
    ; far to advance the Pots when User hits the Container of the Gadget.
    ; For instance, if you were controlling the display of a 5-line
    ; Window of text with this Gadget, and there was a total of 15
    ; lines that could be displayed, you would set the VertBody value to
    ;     (MAXBODY / (TotalLines / DisplayLines)) = MAXBODY / 3.
    ; Therefore, the AUTOKNOB would fill 1/3 of the container, and if
    ; User hits the Cotainer outside of the knob, the pot would advance
    ; 1/3 (plus or minus) If there's no body to show, or the total
    ; amount of displayable info is less than the display area, set the
    ; Body variables to the MAX.  To adjust these after the Gadget is
    ; added to the System, use ModifyProp().
    WORD pi_HorizBody   ; horizontal Body
    WORD pi_VertBody    ; vertical Body

    ; these are the variables that Intuition sets and maintains
    WORD pi_CWidth      ; Container width (with any relativity absoluted)
    WORD pi_CHeight     ; Container height (with any relativity absoluted)
```

```
    WORD pi_HPotRes      ; pot increments
    WORD pi_VPotRes      ; pot increments
    WORD pi_LeftBorder   ; Container borders
    WORD pi_TopBorder    ; Container borders
    LABEL  pi_SIZEOF

; --- FLAG BITS -------------------------------------------------------------
AUTOKNOB         EQU $0001       ; this flag sez:  gimme that old auto-knob
FREEHORIZ        EQU $0002       ; if set, the knob can move horizontally
FREEVERT         EQU $0004       ; if set, the knob can move vertically
PROPBORDERLESS   EQU $0008       ; if set, no border will be rendered
KNOBHIT          EQU $0100       ; set when this Knob is hit


KNOBHMIN         EQU 6           ; minimum horizontal size of the knob
KNOBVMIN         EQU 4           ; minimum vertical size of the knob
MAXBODY          EQU $FFFF       ; maximum body value
MAXPOT           EQU $FFFF       ; maximum pot value


; ===========================================================================
; === StringInfo ============================================================
; ===========================================================================
; this is the special data required by the string Gadget
; typically, this data will be pointed to by the Gadget variable SpecialInfo
 STRUCTURE StringInfo,0

    ; you initialize these variables, and then Intuition maintains them
    APTR  si_Buffer     ; the buffer containing the start and final string
    APTR  si_UndoBuffer ; optional buffer for undoing current entry
    WORD si_BufferPos   ; character position in Buffer
    WORD si_MaxChars    ; max number of chars in Buffer (including NULL)
    WORD si_DispPos     ; Buffer position of first displayed character

    ; Intuition initializes and maintains these variables for you
    WORD si_UndoPos     ; character position in the undo buffer
    WORD si_NumChars    ; number of characters currently in Buffer
    WORD si_DispCount   ; number of whole characters visible in Container
    WORD si_CLeft       ; topleft offset of the container
    WORD si_CTop        ; topleft offset of the container
    APTR  si_LayerPtr   ; the RastPort containing this Gadget

    ; you can initialize this variable before the gadget is submitted to
    ; Intuition, and then examine it later to discover what integer
    ; the user has entered (if the user never plays with the gadget,
    ; the value will be unchanged from your initial setting)
    LONG  si_LongInt    ; the LONG return value of a LONGINT String Gadget

    ; If you want this Gadget to use your own Console keymapping, you
    ; set the ALTKEYMAP bit in the Activation flags of the Gadget, and then
    ; set this variable to point to your keymap.  If you don't set the
    ; ALTKEYMAP, you'll get the standard ASCII keymapping.
    APTR si_AltKeyMap

    LABEL si_SIZEOF




; ===========================================================================
; === IntuiText =============================================================
; ===========================================================================
; IntuiText is a series of strings that start with a screen location
; (always relative to the upper-left corner of something) and then the
; text of the string.  The text is null-terminated.
 STRUCTURE IntuiText,0

    BYTE it_FrontPen            ; the pens for rendering the text
    BYTE it_BackPen             ; the pens for rendering the text
```



```

    BYTE it_DrawMode              ; the mode for rendering the text

    BYTE it_KludgeFill00          ; This is strictly for word-alignment

    WORD it_LeftEdge              ; relative start location for the text
    WORD it_TopEdge               ; relative start location for the text

    APTR  it_ITextFont            ; if NULL, you accept the defaults

    APTR it_IText                 ; pointer to null-terminated text

    APTR  it_NextText             ; continuation to TxWrite another text

    LABEL it_SIZEOF






; ===========================================================================
; === Border ================================================================
; ===========================================================================
; Data type Border, used for drawing a series of lines which is intended for
; use as a border drawing, but which may, in fact, be used to render any
; arbitrary vector shape.
; The routine DrawBorder sets up the RastPort with the appropriate
; variables, then does a Move to the first coordinate, then does Draws
; to the subsequent coordinates.
; After all the Draws are done, if NextBorder is non-zero we call DrawBorder
; recursively
 STRUCTURE Border,0

    WORD  bd_LeftEdge             ; initial offsets from the origin
    WORD  bd_TopEdge              ; initial offsets from the origin
    BYTE  bd_FrontPen             ; pen number for rendering
    BYTE  bd_BackPen              ; pen number for rendering
    BYTE  bd_DrawMode             ; mode for rendering
    BYTE  bd_Count                ; number of XY pairs
    APTR  bd_XY                   ; vector coordinate pairs rel to LeftTop
    APTR  bd_NextBorder           ; pointer to any other Border too

    LABEL bd_SIZEOF


; ===========================================================================
; === Image =================================================================
; ===========================================================================
; This is a brief image structure for very simple transfers of
; image data to a RastPort
 STRUCTURE Image,0

    WORD ig_LeftEdge              ; starting offset relative to something
    WORD ig_TopEdge               ; starting offset relative to something
    WORD ig_Width                 ; pixel size (though data is word-aligned)
    WORD ig_Height                ; pixel size
    WORD ig_Depth                 ; pixel size
    APTR ig_ImageData             ; pointer to the actual image bits

    ; the PlanePick and PlaneOnOff variables work much the same way as the
    ; equivalent GELS Bob variables.  It's a space-saving
    ; mechanism for image data.  Rather than defining the image data
    ; for every plane of the RastPort, you need define data only for planes
    ; that are not entirely zero or one.  As you define your Imagery, you will
    ; often find that most of the planes ARE just as color selectors.  For
    ; instance, if you're designing a two-color Gadget to use colors two and
    ; three, and the Gadget will reside in a five-plane display, plane zero
    ; of your imagery would be all ones, bit plane one would have data that
    ; describes the imagery, and bit planes two through four would be
```

```
    ; all zeroes.  Using these flags allows you to avoid wasting all that
    ; memory in this way:
    ; first, you specify which planes you want your data to appear
    ; in using the PlanePick variable.  For each bit set in the variable, the
    ; next "plane" of your image data is blitted to the display.  For each bit
    ; clear in this variable, the corresponding bit in PlaneOnOff is examined.
    ; If that bit is clear, a "plane" of zeroes will be used.  If the bit is
    ; set, ones will go out instead.  So, for our example:
    ;   Gadget.PlanePick = 0x02;
    ;   Gadget.PlaneOnOff = 0x01;
    ; Note that this also allows for generic Gadgets, like the System Gadgets,
    ; which will work in any number of bit planes
    ; Note also that if you want an Image that is only a filled rectangle,
    ; you can get this by setting PlanePick to zero (pick no planes of data)
    ; and set PlaneOnOff to describe the pen color of the rectangle.
    BYTE ig_PlanePick
    BYTE ig_PlaneOnOff

    ; if the NextImage variable is not NULL, Intuition presumes that
    ; it points to another Image structure with another Image to be
    ; rendered
    APTR ig_NextImage


    LABEL ig_SIZEOF




; ======================================================================
; === IntuiMessage =====================================================
; ======================================================================
 STRUCTURE IntuiMessage,0

    STRUCT im_ExecMessage,MN_SIZE

    ; the Class bits correspond directly with the IDCMP Flags, except for the
    ; special bit LONELYMESSAGE (defined below)
    LONG im_Class

    ; the Code field is for special values like MENU number
    WORD im_Code

    ; the Qualifier field is a copy of the current InputEvent's Qualifier
    WORD im_Qualifier

    ; IAddress contains particular addresses for Intuition functions, like
    ; the pointer to the Gadget or the Screen
    APTR im_IAddress

    ; when getting mouse movement reports, any event you get will have the
    ; the mouse coordinates in these variables.  the coordinates are relative
    ; to the upper-left corner of your Window (GIMMEZEROZERO notwithstanding)
    WORD im_MouseX
    WORD im_MouseY

    ; the time values are copies of the current system clock time.  Micros
    ; are in units of microseconds, Seconds in seconds.
    LONG im_Seconds
    LONG im_Micros

    ; the IDCMPWindow variable will always have the address of the Window of
    ; this IDCMP
    APTR im_IDCMPWindow

    ; system-use variable
    APTR im_SpecialLink

    LABEL  im_SIZEOF
```



```



; --- IDCMP Classes ------------------------------------------------------------
SIZEVERIFY      EQU     $00000001       ; See the Programmer's Guide
NEWSIZE         EQU     $00000002       ; See the Programmer's Guide
REFRESHWINDOW   EQU     $00000004       ; See the Programmer's Guide
MOUSEBUTTONS    EQU     $00000008       ; See the Programmer's Guide
MOUSEMOVE       EQU     $00000010       ; See the Programmer's Guide
GADGETDOWN      EQU     $00000020       ; See the Programmer's Guide
GADGETUP        EQU     $00000040       ; See the Programmer's Guide
REQSET          EQU     $00000080       ; See the Programmer's Guide
MENUPICK        EQU     $00000100       ; See the Programmer's Guide
CLOSEWINDOW     EQU     $00000200       ; See the Programmer's Guide
RAWKEY          EQU     $00000400       ; See the Programmer's Guide
REQVERIFY       EQU     $00000800       ; See the Programmer's Guide
REQCLEAR        EQU     $00001000       ; See the Programmer's Guide
MENUVERIFY      EQU     $00002000       ; See the Programmer's Guide
NEWPREFS        EQU     $00004000       ; See the Programmer's Guide
DISKINSERTED    EQU     $00008000       ; See the Programmer's Guide
DISKREMOVED     EQU     $00010000       ; See the Programmer's Guide
WBENCHMESSAGE   EQU     $00020000       ; See the Programmer's Guide
ACTIVEWINDOW    EQU     $00040000       ; See the Programmer's Guide
INACTIVEWINDOW  EQU     $00080000       ; See the Programmer's Guide
DELTAMOVE       EQU     $00100000       ; See the Programmer's Guide
VANILLAKEY      EQU     $00200000       ; See the Programmer's Guide
INTUITICKS      EQU     $00400000       ; See the Programmer's Guide
; NOTEZ-BIEN:           $80000000 is reserved for internal use by IDCMP

; the IDCMP Flags do not use this special bit, which is cleared when
; Intuition sends its special message to the Task, and set when Intuition
; gets its Message back from the Task.  Therefore, I can check here to
; find out fast whether or not this Message is available for me to send
LONELYMESSAGE   EQU     $80000000



; --- IDCMP Codes --------------------------------------------------------------
; This group of codes is for the MENUVERIFY function
MENUHOT         EQU     $0001   ; IntuiWants verification or MENUCANCEL
MENUCANCEL      EQU     $0002   ; HOT Reply of this cancels Menu operation
MENUWAITING     EQU     $0003   ; Intuition simply wants a ReplyMsg() ASAP

; These are internal tokens to represent state of verification attempts
; shown here as a clue.
OKOK            EQU     MENUHOT         ; guy didn't care
OKABORT         EQU     $0004           ; window rendered question moot
OKCANCEL        EQU     MENUCANCEL      ; window sent cancel reply

; This group of codes is for the WBENCHMESSAGE messages
WBENCHOPEN      EQU $0001
WBENCHCLOSE     EQU $0002




; ======================================================================
; === Window ===========================================================
; ======================================================================
 STRUCTURE Window,0

    APTR wd_NextWindow          ; for the linked list of a Screen

    WORD wd_LeftEdge            ; screen dimensions
    WORD wd_TopEdge             ; screen dimensions
    WORD wd_Width               ; screen dimensions
    WORD wd_Height              ; screen dimensions

    WORD wd_MouseY              ; relative top top-left corner
```

```
        WORD wd_MouseX                  ; relative top top-left corner

        WORD wd_MinWidth                ; minimum sizes
        WORD wd_MinHeight               ; minimum sizes
        WORD wd_MaxWidth                ; maximum sizes
        WORD wd_MaxHeight               ; maximum sizes

        LONG wd_Flags                   ; see below for definitions

        APTR wd_MenuStrip               ; first in a list of menu headers

        APTR wd_Title                   ; title text for the Window

        APTR wd_FirstRequest            ; first in linked list of active Requesters
        APTR wd_DMRequest               ; the double-menu Requester
        WORD wd_ReqCount                ; number of Requesters blocking this Window
        APTR wd_WScreen                 ; this Window's Screen
        APTR wd_RPort                   ; this Window's very own RastPort

        ; the border variables describe the window border.  If you specify
        ; GIMMEZEROZERO when you open the window, then the upper-left of the
        ; ClipRect for this window will be upper-left of the BitMap (with correct
        ; offsets when in SuperBitMap mode; you MUST select GIMMEZEROZERO when
        ; using SuperBitMap).  If you don't specify ZeroZero, then you save
        ; memory (no allocation of RastPort, Layer, ClipRect and associated
        ; Bitmaps), but you also must offset all your writes by BorderTop,
        ; BorderLeft and do your own mini-clipping to prevent writing over the
        ; system gadgets
        BYTE wd_BorderLeft
        BYTE wd_BorderTop
        BYTE wd_BorderRight
        BYTE wd_BorderBottom
        APTR wd_BorderRPort

        ; You supply a linked-list of gadget that you want for your Window.
        ; This list DOES NOT include system Gadgets.  You get the standard
        ; window system Gadgets by setting flag-bits in the variable Flags (see
        ; the bit definitions below)
        APTR wd_FirstGadget

        ; these are for opening/closing the windows
        APTR wd_Parent
        APTR wd_Descendant

        ; sprite data information for your own Pointer
        ; set these AFTER you Open the Window by calling SetPointer()
        APTR wd_Pointer
        BYTE wd_PtrHeight
        BYTE wd_PtrWidth
        BYTE wd_XOffset
        BYTE wd_YOffset

        ; the IDCMP Flags and User's and Intuition's Message Ports
        ULONG wd_IDCMPFlags
        APTR wd_UserPort
        APTR wd_WindowPort
        APTR wd_MessageKey

        BYTE wd_DetailPen
        BYTE wd_BlockPen

        ; the CheckMark is a pointer to the imagery that will be used when
        ; rendering MenuItems of this Window that want to be checkmarked
        ; if this is equal to NULL, you'll get the default imagery
        APTR wd_CheckMark

        ; if non-null, Screen title when Window is active
        APTR wd_ScreenTitle

```



```
        ; These variables have the mouse coordinates relative to the
        ; inner-Window of GIMMEZEROZERO Windows.  This is compared with the
        ; MouseX and MouseY variables, which contain the mouse coordinates
        ; relative to the upper-left corner of the Window, GIMMEZEROZERO
        ; notwithstanding
        WORD wd_GZZMouseX
        WORD wd_GZZMouseY
        ; these variables contain the width and height of the inner-Window of
        ; GIMMEZEROZERO Windows
        WORD wd_GZZWidth
        WORD wd_GZZHeight

        APTR wd_ExtData

        ; general-purpose pointer to User data extension
        APTR wd_UserData
        APTR wd_WLayer          ; stash of Window.RPort->Layer

        ; NEW 1.2: need to keep track of the font that OpenWindow opened,
        ; in case user SetFont's into RastPort
        APTR IFont

        LABEL wd_Size

; --- FLAGS REQUESTED (NOT DIRECTLY SET THOUGH) BY THE APPLIPROG ------------
WINDOWSIZING    EQU $0001       ; include sizing system-gadget?
WINDOWDRAG      EQU $0002       ; include dragging system-gadget?
WINDOWDEPTH     EQU $0004       ; include depth arrangement gadget?
WINDOWCLOSE     EQU $0008       ; include close-box system-gadget?

SIZEBRIGHT      EQU $0010       ; size gadget uses right border
SIZEBBOTTOM     EQU $0020       ; size gadget uses bottom border

; --- refresh modes --------------------------------------------------------
; combinations of the REFRESHBITS select the refresh type
REFRESHBITS     EQU $00C0
SMART_REFRESH   EQU $0000
SIMPLE_REFRESH  EQU $0040
SUPER_BITMAP    EQU $0080
OTHER_REFRESH   EQU $00C0

BACKDROP        EQU $0100       ; this is an ever-popular BACKDROP window

REPORTMOUSE     EQU $0200       ; set this to hear about every mouse move

GIMMEZEROZERO   EQU $0400       ; make extra border stuff

BORDERLESS      EQU $0800       ; set this to get a Window sans border

ACTIVATE        EQU $1000       ; when Window opens, it's the Active one

; FLAGS SET BY INTUITION
WINDOWACTIVE    EQU $2000       ; this window is the active one
INREQUEST       EQU $4000       ; this window is in request mode
MENUSTATE       EQU $8000       ; this Window is active with its Menus on

; --- Other User Flags -----------------------------------------------------
RMBTRAP         EQU $00010000   ; Catch RMB events for your own
NOCAREREFRESH   EQU $00020000   ; not to be bothered with REFRESH

; --- Other Intuition Flags -----------------------------------------------
WINDOWREFRESH   EQU $01000000   ; Window is currently refreshing
WBENCHWINDOW    EQU $02000000   ; WorkBench Window
WINDOWTICKED    EQU $04000000   ; only one timer tick at a time

SUPER_UNUSED    EQU $FCFC0000   ;bits of Flag unused yet


; --- see struct IntuiMessage for the IDCMP Flag definitions ---------------
```

```
; ==========================================================================
; === NewWindow ============================================================
; ==========================================================================
 STRUCTURE NewWindow,0

    WORD nw_LeftEdge             ; initial Window dimensions
    WORD nw_TopEdge              ; initial Window dimensions
    WORD nw_Width                ; initial Window dimensions
    WORD nw_Height               ; initial Window dimensions

    BYTE nw_DetailPen            ; for rendering the detail bits of the Window
    BYTE nw_BlockPen             ; for rendering the block-fill bits

    LONG nw_IDCMPFlags           ; initial IDCMP state

    LONG nw_Flags                ; see the Flag definition under Window

    ; You supply a linked-list of Gadgets for your Window.
    ; This list DOES NOT include system Gadgets.  You get the standard
    ; system Window Gadgets by setting flag-bits in the variable Flags (see
    ; the bit definitions under the Window structure definition)
    APTR        nw_FirstGadget

    ; the CheckMark is a pointer to the imagery that will be used when
    ; rendering MenuItems of this Window that want to be checkmarked
    ; if this is equal to NULL, you'll get the default imagery
    APTR nw_CheckMark

    APTR nw_Title                ; title text for the Window

    ; the Screen pointer is used only if you've defined a CUSTOMSCREEN and
    ; want this Window to open in it.  If so, you pass the address of the
    ; Custom Screen structure in this variable.  Otherwise, this variable
    ; is ignored and doesn't have to be initialized.
    APTR nw_Screen

    ; SUPER_BITMAP Window?  If so, put the address of your BitMap structure
    ; in this variable.  If not, this variable is ignored and doesn't have
    ; to be initialized
    APTR nw_BitMap

    ; the values describe the minimum and maximum sizes of your Windows.
    ; these matter only if you've chosen the WINDOWSIZING Gadget option,
    ; which means that you want to let the User to change the size of
    ; this Window.  You describe the minimum and maximum sizes that the
    ; Window can grow by setting these variables.  You can initialize
    ; any one these to zero, which will mean that you want to duplicate
    ; the setting for that dimension (if MinWidth == 0, MinWidth will be
    ; set to the opening Width of the Window).
    ; You can change these settings later using SetWindowLimits().
    ; If you haven't asked for a SIZING Gadget, you don't have to
    ; initialize any of these variables.
    WORD nw_MinWidth
    WORD nw_MinHeight
    WORD nw_MaxWidth
    WORD nw_MaxHeight

    ; the type variable describes the Screen in which you want this Window to
    ; open.  The type value can either be CUSTOMSCREEN or one of the
    ; system standard Screen Types such as WBENCHSCREEN.  See the
    ; type definitions under the Screen structure
    WORD nw_Type

    LABEL nw_SIZE


        IFND INTUITION_SCREENS_I
```



```
        INCLUDE "intuition/screens.i"
        ENDC

        IFND INTUITION_PREFERENCES_I
        INCLUDE "intuition/preferences.i"
        ENDC

; ==========================================================================
; === Remember =============================================================
; ==========================================================================
; this structure is used for remembering what memory has been allocated to
; date by a given routine, so that a premature abort or systematic exit
; can deallocate memory cleanly, easily, and completely
 STRUCTURE Remember,0

    APTR rm_NextRemember
    LONG rm_RememberSize
    APTR rm_Memory

 LABEL    rm_SIZEOF



; ==========================================================================
; === Miscellaneous ========================================================
; ==========================================================================

; = MACROS ================================================================
;#define MENUNUM(n) (n & 0x1F)
;#define ITEMNUM(n) ((n >> 5) & 0x003F)
;#define SUBNUM(n) ((n >> 11) & 0x001F)
;
;#define SHIFTMENU(n) (n & 0x1F)
;#define SHIFTITEM(n) ((n & 0x3F) << 5)
;#define SHIFTSUB(n) ((n & 0x1F) << 11)
;
;#define SRBNUM(n)   (0x08 - (n >> 4))  /* SerRWBits -> read bits per char */
;#define SWBNUM(n)   (0x08 - (n & 0x0F))/* SerRWBits -> write bits per chr */
;#define SSBNUM(n)   (0x01 + (n >> 4))  /* SerStopBuf -> stop bits per chr */
;#define SPARNUM(n)  (n >> 4)           /* SerParShk -> parity setting    */
;#define SHAKNUM(n)  (n & 0x0F)         /* SerParShk -> handshake mode    */
;
; = MENU STUFF =============================================================
NOMENU EQU      $001F
NOITEM EQU      $003F
NOSUB  EQU      $001F
MENUNULL EQU    $FFFF


; = =RJ='s peculiarities ===================================================
;#define FOREVER for(;;)
;#define SIGN(x) ( ((x) > 0) - ((x) < 0) )


; these defines are for the COMMSEQ and CHECKIT menu stuff.  If CHECKIT,
; I'll use a generic Width (for all resolutions) for the CheckMark.
; If COMMSEQ, likewise I'll use this generic stuff
CHECKWIDTH      EQU     19
COMMWIDTH       EQU     27
LOWCHECKWIDTH   EQU     13
LOWCOMMWIDTH    EQU     16


; these are the AlertNumber defines.  if you are calling DisplayAlert()
; the AlertNumber you supply must have the ALERT_TYPE bits set to one
; of these patterns
ALERT_TYPE      EQU     $80000000
RECOVERY_ALERT  EQU     $00000000       ; the system can recover from this
DEADEND_ALERT   EQU     $80000000       ; no recovery possible, this is it
```

```


; When you're defining IntuiText for the Positive and Negative Gadgets
; created by a call to AutoRequest(), these defines will get you
; reasonable-looking text.  The only field without a define is the IText
; field; you decide what text goes with the Gadget
AUTOFRONTPEN     EQU     0
AUTOBACKPEN      EQU     1
AUTODRAWMODE     EQU     RP_JAM2
AUTOLEFTEDGE     EQU     6
AUTOTOPEDGE      EQU     3
AUTOITEXTFONT    EQU     0
AUTONEXTTEXT     EQU     0



;* --- RAWMOUSE Codes and Qualifiers (Console OR IDCMP) -------------------
SELECTUP         EQU     (IECODE_LBUTTON+IECODE_UP_PREFIX)
SELECTDOWN       EQU     (IECODE_LBUTTON)
MENUUP           EQU     (IECODE_RBUTTON+IECODE_UP_PREFIX)
MENUDOWN         EQU     (IECODE_RBUTTON)
ALTLEFT          EQU     (IEQUALIFIER_LALT)
ALTRIGHT         EQU     (IEQUALIFIER_RALT)
AMIGALEFT        EQU     (IEQUALIFIER_LCOMMAND)
AMIGARIGHT       EQU     (IEQUALIFIER_RCOMMAND)
AMIGAKEYS        EQU     (AMIGALEFT+AMIGARIGHT)

CURSORUP         EQU     $4C
CURSORLEFT       EQU     $4F
CURSORRIGHT      EQU     $4E
CURSORDOWN       EQU     $4D
KEYCODE_Q        EQU     $10
KEYCODE_X        EQU     $32
KEYCODE_N        EQU     $36
KEYCODE_M        EQU     $37
KEYCODE_V        EQU     $34
KEYCODE_B        EQU     $35

         IFND    INTUITION_INTUITIONBASE_I
         include "intuition/intuitionbase.i"
         ENDC

         ENDC    ; INTUITION_INTUITION_I
```



```
        IFND    INTUITION_INTUITIONBASE_I
INTUITION_INTUITIONBASE_I       SET     1
**
**      $Filename: intuition/intuitionbase.i $
**      $Release: 1.3 $
**
**      the IntuitionBase structure and supporting structures
**
**      (C) Copyright 1985,1986,1987,1988 Commodore-Amiga, Inc.
**          All Rights Reserved
**

        IFND EXEC_TYPES_I
        INCLUDE "exec/types.i"
        ENDC

        IFND EXEC_LIBRARIES_I
        INCLUDE "exec/libraries.i"
        ENDC

        IFND    GRAPHICS_VIEW_I
        INCLUDE "graphics/view.i"
        ENDC

* Be sure to protect yourself against someone modifying these data as
* you look at them.  This is done by calling:
*
* lock = LockIBase(0), which returns a ULONG.  When done call
*  D0              D0
* UnlockIBase(lock) where lock is what LockIBase() returned.
*             A0
* NOTE: these library functions are simply stubs now, but should be called
* to be compatible with future releases.

* ======================================================================= *
* === IntuitionBase ===================================================== *
* ======================================================================= *
 STRUCTURE IntuitionBase,0

        STRUCT  ib_LibNode,LIB_SIZE
        STRUCT  ib_ViewLord,v_SIZEOF
        APTR    ib_ActiveWindow
        APTR    ib_ActiveScreen

* the FirstScreen variable points to the frontmost Screen.  Screens are
* then maintained in a front to back order using Screen.NextScreen

        APTR    ib_FirstScreen

* there is not size here because...
*
*

        ENDC    ; INTUITION_INTUITIONBASE_I
```

```
        IFND    INTUITION_PREFERENCES_I
INTUITION_PREFERENCES_I SET     1
**
**      $Filename: intuition/preferences.i $
**      $Release: 1.3 $
**
**
**
**      (C) Copyright 1987,1988 Commodore-Amiga, Inc.
**          All Rights Reserved
**

    IFND EXEC_TYPES_I
    INCLUDE "exec/types.i"
    ENDC

    IFND    DEVICES_TIMER_I
    include "devices/timer.i"
    ENDC

; ======================================================================
; === Preferences ======================================================
; ======================================================================

; these are the definitions for the printer configurations
FILENAME_SIZE EQU   30      ; Filename size

POINTERSIZE     EQU (1+16+1)*2  ; Size of Pointer data buffer

; These defines are for the default font size.  These actually describe the
; height of the defaults fonts.  The default font type is the topaz
; font, which is a fixed width font that can be used in either
; eighty-column or sixty-column mode.  The Preferences structure reflects
; which is currently selected by the value found in the variable FontSize,
; which may have either of the values defined below.  These values actually
; are used to select the height of the default font.  By changing the
; height, the resolution of the font changes as well.
TOPAZ_EIGHTY    EQU 8
TOPAZ_SIXTY     EQU 9

; ----------------------------------------------------------------------
 STRUCTURE Preferences,0

    ; the default font height
    BYTE pf_FontHeight      ; height for system default font

    ; constant describing what's hooked up to the port
    BYTE pf_PrinterPort ; printer port connection

    ; the baud rate of the port
    WORD pf_BaudRate        ; baud rate for the serial port

    ; various timing rates
    STRUCT pf_KeyRptSpeed,TV_SIZE ; repeat speed for keyboard
    STRUCT pf_KeyRptDelay,TV_SIZE ; Delay before keys repeat
    STRUCT pf_DoubleClick,TV_SIZE ; Interval allowed between clicks

    ; Intuition Pointer data
    STRUCT pf_PointerMatrix,POINTERSIZE*2 ; Definition of pointer sprite
    BYTE pf_XOffset     ; X-Offset for active 'bit'
    BYTE pf_YOffset     ; Y-Offset for active 'bit'
    WORD pf_color17     ;********************************
    WORD pf_color18     ; Colours for sprite pointer
    WORD pf_color19     ;********************************
    WORD pf_PointerTicks    ; Sensitivity of the pointer

    ; Workbench Screen colors
    WORD pf_color0      ;********************************
    WORD pf_color1      ;  Standard default colours
```



```
    WORD pf_color2      ;   Used in the Workbench
    WORD pf_color3      ;********************************

    ; positioning data for the Intuition View
    BYTE pf_ViewXOffset     ; Offset for top lefthand corner
    BYTE pf_ViewYOffset     ; X and Y dimensions
    WORD pf_ViewInitX       ; View initial offsets at startup
    WORD pf_ViewInitY       ; View initial offsets at startup

    BOOL EnableCLI      ; CLI availability switch

    ; printer configurations
    WORD pf_PrinterType     ; printer type
    STRUCT pf_PrinterFilename,FILENAME_SIZE ; file for printer

    ; print format and quality configurations
    WORD pf_PrintPitch      ; print pitch
    WORD pf_PrintQuality    ; print quality
    WORD pf_PrintSpacing    ; number of lines per inch
    WORD pf_PrintLeftMargin ; left margin in characters
    WORD pf_PrintRightMargin    ; right margin in characters
    WORD pf_PrintImage      ; positive or negative
    WORD pf_PrintAspect     ; horizontal or vertical
    WORD pf_PrintShade      ; b&w, half-tone, or color
    WORD pf_PrintThreshold  ; darkness ctrl for b/w dumps


    ; print paper description
    WORD pf_PaperSize       ; paper size
    WORD pf_PaperLength     ; paper length in lines
    WORD pf_PaperType       ; continuous or single sheet

    ; Serial device settings: These are six nibble-fields in three bytes
    ; (these look a little strange so the defaults will map out to zero)
    BYTE pf_SerRWBits               ; upper nibble = (8-number of read bits)
                                    ; lower nibble = (8-number of write bits)
    BYTE pf_SerStopBuf              ; upper nibble = (number of stop bits - 1)
                                    ; lower nibble = (table value for BufSize)
    BYTE pf_SerParShk               ; upper nibble = (value for Parity setting)
                                    ; lower nibble = (value for Handshake mode)

    BYTE pf_LaceWB      ; if workbench is to be interlaced

    STRUCT pf_WorkName,FILENAME_SIZE ; temp file for printer

    BYTE pf_RowSizeChange       ;
    BYTE pf_ColumnSizeChange        ;

    UWORD   pf_PrintFlags       ; user preference flags
    WORD    pf_PrintMaxWidth    ; max width of printed picture in 10ths/inch
    UWORD   pf_PrintMaxHeight   ; max height of printed picture in 10ths/inch
    UBYTE   pf_PrintDensity     ; print density
    UBYTE   pf_PrintXOffset     ; offset of printed picture in 10ths/inch

    UWORD   pf_wb_Width         ; override default workbench width
    UWORD   pf_wb_Height        ; override default workbench height
    UBYTE   pf_wb_Depth         ; override default workbench depth

    UBYTE   pf_ext_size         ; extension information -- do not touch!
                                ; extension size in blocks of 64 bytes
    LABEL pf_SIZEOF


; === Preferences definitions ==========================================

; Workbench Interlace (use one bit)
LACEWB      EQU $01

; PrinterPort
```

```
PARALLEL_PRINTER EQU     $00
SERIAL_PRINTER  EQU $01
; BaudRate
BAUD_110      EQU $00
BAUD_300      EQU $01
BAUD_1200     EQU $02
BAUD_2400     EQU $03
BAUD_4800     EQU $04
BAUD_9600     EQU $05
BAUD_19200    EQU $06
BAUD_MIDI     EQU $07
; PaperType
FANFOLD       EQU $00
SINGLE        EQU $80
; PrintPitch
PICA          EQU $000
ELITE         EQU $400
FINE          EQU $800
; PrintQuality
DRAFT         EQU $000
LETTER        EQU $100
; PrintSpacing
SIX_LPI       EQU $000
EIGHT_LPI     EQU $200
; Print Image
IMAGE_POSITIVE  EQU $00
IMAGE_NEGATIVE  EQU $01
; PrintAspect
ASPECT_HORIZ    EQU $00
ASPECT_VERT EQU $01
; PrintShade
SHADE_BW      EQU $00
SHADE_GREYSCALE EQU $01
SHADE_COLOR EQU $02
; PaperSize
US_LETTER     EQU $00
US_LEGAL      EQU $10
N_TRACTOR     EQU $20
W_TRACTOR     EQU $30
CUSTOM        EQU $40
; PrinterType
CUSTOM_NAME EQU $00
ALPHA_P_101 EQU $01
BROTHER_15XL     EQU $02
CBM_MPS1000 EQU $03
DIAB_630     EQU $04
DIAB_ADV_D25     EQU $05
DIAB_C_150   EQU $06
EPSON        EQU $07
EPSON_JX_80  EQU $08
OKIMATE_20   EQU $09
QUME_LP_20   EQU $0A
; new printer entries, 3 October 1985
HP_LASERJET EQU $0B
HP_LASERJET_PLUS EQU     $0C
; Serial Input Buffer Sizes
SBUF_512         EQU      $00
```



```
SBUF_1024        EQU      $01
SBUF_2048        EQU      $02
SBUF_4096        EQU      $03
SBUF_8000        EQU      $04
SBUF_16000       EQU      $05
; Serial Bit Masks
SREAD_BITS  EQU $F0 ; pf_SerRWBits
SWRITE_BITS EQU $0F
SSTOP_BITS  EQU $F0 ; pf_SerStopBuf
SBUFSIZE_BITS    EQU $0F
SPARITY_BITS     EQU $F0 ; pf_SerParShk
SHSHAKE_BITS     EQU $0F
; Serial Parity (high nibble, but here shifted right, as by C-macro SPARNUM)
SPARITY_NONE     EQU      $00
SPARITY_EVEN     EQU      $01
SPARITY_ODD      EQU      $02
; Serial Handshake Mode (low nibble, mask by SHSHAKE_BITS)
SHSHAKE_XON      EQU      $00
SHSHAKE_RTS      EQU      $01
SHSHAKE_NONE     EQU      $02
; new defines for PrintFlags
CORRECT_RED          EQU $0001    ; color correct red shades
CORRECT_GREEN        EQU $0002    ; color correct green shades
CORRECT_BLUE         EQU $0004    ; color correct blue shades
CENTER_IMAGE         EQU $0008      ; center image on paper
IGNORE_DIMENSIONS    EQU $0000    ; ignore max width/height settings
BOUNDED_DIMENSIONS   EQU $0010    ; use max width/height as boundaries
ABSOLUTE_DIMENSIONS  EQU $0020    ; use max width/height as absolutes
PIXEL_DIMENSIONS     EQU $0040    ; use max width/height as prt pixels
MULTIPLY_DIMENSIONS  EQU $0080    ; use max width/height as multipliers
INTEGER_SCALING      EQU $0100    ; force integer scaling
ORDERED_DITHERING    EQU $0000    ; ordered dithering
HALFTONE_DITHERING   EQU $0200    ; halftone dithering
FLOYD_DITHERING      EQU $0400    ; floyd-steinberg dithering
ANTI_ALIAS           EQU $0800    ; anti-alias image
GREY_SCALE2          EQU $1000    ; for use with hi-res monitor
CORRECT_RGB_MASK     EQU (CORRECT_RED+CORRECT_GREEN+CORRECT_BLUE)
DIMENSIONS_MASK      EQU (BOUNDED_DIMENSIONS+ABSOLUTE_DIMENSIONS+PIXEL_DIMENSIONS
DITHERING_MASK       EQU (HALFTONE_DITHERING+FLOYD_DITHERING)
        ENDC    ; INTUITION_PREFERENCES_I
```

```
        IFND    INTUITION_SCREENS_I
INTUITION_SCREENS_I     SET     1
**
**      $Filename: intuition/screens.i $
**      $Release: 1.3 $
**
**
**
**      (C) Copyright 1987,1988 Commodore-Amiga, Inc.
**          All Rights Reserved
**

        IFND EXEC_TYPES_I
        INCLUDE "exec/types.i"
        ENDC

        IFND GRAPHICS_GFX_I
        INCLUDE "graphics/gfx.i"
        ENDC

        IFND GRAPHICS_CLIP_I
        INCLUDE "graphics/clip.i"
        ENDC

        IFND GRAPHICS_VIEW_I
        INCLUDE "graphics/view.i"
        ENDC

        IFND GRAPHICS_RASTPORT_I
        INCLUDE "graphics/rastport.i"
        ENDC

        IFND GRAPHICS_LAYERS_I
        INCLUDE "graphics/layers.i"
        ENDC

; ======================================================================
; === Screen ===========================================================
; ======================================================================
 STRUCTURE Screen,0

    APTR sc_NextScreen          ; linked list of screens
    APTR sc_FirstWindow         ; linked list Screen's Windows

    WORD sc_LeftEdge            ; parameters of the screen
    WORD sc_TopEdge             ; parameters of the screen

    WORD sc_Width               ; null-terminated Title text
    WORD sc_Height              ; for Windows without ScreenTitle

    WORD sc_MouseY              ; position relative to upper-left
    WORD sc_MouseX              ; position relative to upper-left

    WORD sc_Flags               ; see definitions below

    APTR sc_Title
    APTR sc_DefaultTitle

    ; Bar sizes for this Screen and all Window's in this Screen
    BYTE sc_BarHeight
    BYTE sc_BarVBorder
    BYTE sc_BarHBorder
    BYTE sc_MenuVBorder
    BYTE sc_MenuHBorder
    BYTE sc_WBorTop
    BYTE sc_WBorLeft
    BYTE sc_WBorRight
    BYTE sc_WBorBottom

```



```
    BYTE sc_KludgeFill00        ; This is strictly for word-alignment

    ; the display data structures for this Screen
    APTR sc_Font                        ; this screen's default font
    STRUCT sc_ViewPort,vp_SIZEOF        ; describing the Screen's display
    STRUCT sc_RastPort,rp_SIZEOF        ; describing Screen rendering
    STRUCT sc_BitMap,bm_SIZEOF          ; auxiliary graphexcess baggage
    STRUCT sc_LayerInfo,li_SIZEOF       ; each screen gets a LayerInfo

    ; You supply a linked-list of Gadgets for your Screen.
    ; This list DOES NOT include system Gadgets.  You get the standard
    ; system Screen Gadgets by default
    APTR sc_FirstGadget

    BYTE sc_DetailPen           ; for bar/border/gadget rendering
    BYTE sc_BlockPen            ; for bar/border/gadget rendering

    ; the following variable(s) are maintained by Intuition to support the
    ; DisplayBeep() color flashing technique
    WORD sc_SaveColor0

    ; This layer is for the Screen and Menu bars
    APTR sc_BarLayer            ; was "BarLayer"

    APTR sc_ExtData

    APTR sc_UserData            ; general-purpose pointer to User data

    LABEL sc_SIZEOF


; --- FLAGS SET BY INTUITION -------------------------------------------
; The SCREENTYPE bits are reserved for describing various Screen types
; available under Intuition.
SCREENTYPE      EQU     $000F   ; all the screens types available
; --- the definitions for the Screen Type ------------------------------
WBENCHSCREEN    EQU     $0001   ; Ta Da!  The Workbench
CUSTOMSCREEN    EQU     $000F   ; for that special look

SHOWTITLE       EQU     $0010   ; this gets set by a call to ShowTitle()

BEEPING         EQU     $0020   ; set when Screen is beeping

CUSTOMBITMAP    EQU     $0040   ; if you are supplying your own BitMap

SCREENBEHIND    EQU     $0080   ; if you want your screen to open behind
                                ; already open screens

SCREENQUIET     EQU     $0100   ; if you do not want Intuition to render
                                ; into your screen (gadgets, title)

STDSCREENHEIGHT EQU     -1      ; supply in NewScreen.Height

; ======================================================================
; === NewScreen ========================================================
; ======================================================================
 STRUCTURE NewScreen,0

    WORD ns_LeftEdge            ; initial Screen dimensions
    WORD ns_TopEdge             ; initial Screen dimensions
    WORD ns_Width               ; initial Screen dimensions
    WORD ns_Height              ; initial Screen dimensions
    WORD ns_Depth               ; initial Screen dimensions

    BYTE ns_DetailPen           ; default rendering pens (for Windows too)
    BYTE ns_BlockPen            ; default rendering pens (for Windows too)

    WORD ns_ViewModes           ; display "modes" for this Screen

```

```
    WORD ns_Type                ; Intuition Screen Type specifier

    APTR ns_Font                ; default font for Screen and Windows

    APTR ns_DefaultTitle        ; Title when Window doesn't care

    APTR ns_Gadgets             ; Your own initial Screen Gadgets

    ; if you are opening a CUSTOMSCREEN and already have a BitMap
    ; that you want used for your Screen, you set the flags CUSTOMBITMAP in
    ; the Types variable and you set this variable to point to your BitMap
    ; structure.  The structure will be copied into your Screen structure,
    ; after which you may discard your own BitMap if you want
    APTR ns_CustomBitMap

 LABEL    ns_SIZEOF

        ENDC    ; INTUITION_SCREENS_I
```

```
        IFND    LIBRARIES_CONFIGREGS_I
LIBRARIES_CONFIGREGS_I  SET     1
**
**      $Filename: libraries/configregs.i $
**      $Release: 1.3 $
**
**      register and bit definitions for expansion boards
**
**      (C) Copyright 1986,1987,1988 Commodore-Amiga, Inc.
**          All Rights Reserved
**

** Expansion boards are actually organized such that only one nibble per
** word (16 bits) are valid information.  This table is structured
** as LOGICAL information.  This means that it never corresponds
** exactly with a physical implementation.
**
** The expansion space is logically split into two regions:
** a rom portion and a control portion.  The rom portion is
** actually stored in one's complement form (except for the
** er_type field).


 STRUCTURE ExpansionRom,0
    UBYTE       er_Type
    UBYTE       er_Product
    UBYTE       er_Flags
    UBYTE       er_Reserved03
    UWORD       er_Manufacturer
    ULONG       er_SerialNumber
    UWORD       er_InitDiagVec
    UBYTE       er_Reserved0c
    UBYTE       er_Reserved0d
    UBYTE       er_Reserved0e
    UBYTE       er_Reserved0f
    LABEL       ExpansionRom_SIZEOF

 STRUCTURE ExpansionControl,0
    UBYTE       ec_Interrupt            ; interrupt control register
    UBYTE       ec_Reserved11
    UBYTE       ec_BaseAddress          ; set new config address
    UBYTE       ec_Shutup               ; don't respond, pass config out
    UBYTE       ec_Reserved14
    UBYTE       ec_Reserved15
    UBYTE       ec_Reserved16
    UBYTE       ec_Reserved17
    UBYTE       ec_Reserved18
    UBYTE       ec_Reserved19
    UBYTE       ec_Reserved1a
    UBYTE       ec_Reserved1b
    UBYTE       ec_Reserved1c
    UBYTE       ec_Reserved1d
    UBYTE       ec_Reserved1e
    UBYTE       ec_Reserved1f
    LABEL       ExpansionControl_SIZEOF

**
** many of the constants below consist of a triplet of equivalent
** definitions: xxMASK is a bit mask of those bits that matter.
** xxBIT is the starting bit number of the field.  xxSIZE is the
** number of bits that make up the definition.  This method is
** used when the field is larger than one bit.
**
** If the field is only one bit wide then the xxB_xx and xxF_xx convention
** is used (xxB_xx is the bit number, and xxF_xx is mask of the bit).
**

** manifest constants */
E_SLOTSIZE              EQU     $10000
```



```
E_SLOTMASK              EQU     $ffff
E_SLOTSHIFT             EQU     16

** these define the two free regions of Zorro memory space.
** THESE MAY WELL CHANGE FOR FUTURE PRODUCTS!
E_EXPANSIONBASE         EQU     $e80000
E_EXPANSIONSIZE         EQU     $080000
E_EXPANSIONSLOTS        EQU     8

E_MEMORYBASE            EQU     $200000
E_MEMORYSIZE            EQU     $800000
E_MEMORYSLOTS           EQU     128



******* ec_Type definitions */

** board type -- ignore "old style" boards */
ERT_TYPEMASK            EQU     $c0
ERT_TYPEBIT             EQU     6
ERT_TYPESIZE            EQU     2
ERT_NEWBOARD            EQU     $c0


** type field memory size */
ERT_MEMMASK             EQU     $07
ERT_MEMBIT              EQU     0
ERT_MEMSIZE             EQU     3


** other bits defined in type field */
        BITDEF  ERT,CHAINEDCONFIG,3
        BITDEF  ERT,DIAGVALID,4
        BITDEF  ERT,MEMLIST,5


** er_Flags byte -- for those things that didn't fit into the type byte */
        BITDEF  ERF,MEMSPACE,7          ; wants to be in 8 meg space.  Also
                                        ;     implies that board is moveable
        BITDEF  ERF,NOSHUTUP,6          ; board can't be shut up.  Must not
                                        ;     be a board.  Must be a box that
                                        ;     does not pass on the bus.


** interrupt control register */
        BITDEF  ECI,INTENA,1
        BITDEF  ECI,RESET,3
        BITDEF  ECI,INT2PEND,4
        BITDEF  ECI,INT6PEND,5
        BITDEF  ECI,INT7PEND,6
        BITDEF  ECI,INTERRUPTING,7


***************************************************************************
**
** these are the specifications for the diagnostic area.  If the Diagnostic
** Address Valid bit is set in the Board Type byte (the first byte in
** expansion space) then the Diag Init vector contains a valid offset.
**
** The Diag Init vector is actually a word offset from the base of the
** board.  The resulting address points to the base of the DiagArea
** structure.  The structure may be physically implemented either four,
** eight, or sixteen bits wide.  The code will be copied out into
** ram first before being called.
**
** The da_Size field, and both code offsets (da_DiagPoint and da_BootPoint)
** are offsets from the diag area AFTER it has been copied into ram, and
** "de-nibbleized" (if needed).  Inotherwords, the size is the size of
** the actual information, not how much address space is required to
```

```
** store it.
**
** All bits are encoded with uninverted logic (e.g. 5 volts on the bus
** is a logic one).
**
** If your board is to make use of the boot facility then it must leave
** its config area available even after it has been configured.  Your
** boot vector will be called AFTER your board's final address has been
** set.
**
****************************************************************************

 STRUCTURE DiagArea,0
    UBYTE       da_Config         ; see below for definitions
    UBYTE       da_Flags          ; see below for definitions
    UWORD       da_Size           ; the size (in bytes) of the total diag area
    UWORD       da_DiagPoint      ; where to start for diagnostics, or zero
    UWORD       da_BootPoint      ; where to start for booting
    UWORD       da_Name           ; offset in diag area where a string
                                  ;   identifier can be found (or zero if no
                                  ;   identifier is present).

    UWORD       da_Reserved01     ; two words of reserved data.  must be zero.
    UWORD       da_Reserved02
    LABEL       DiagArea_SIZEOF

; da_Config definitions
DAC_BUSWIDTH    EQU     $C0       ; two bits for bus width
DAC_NIBBLEWIDE  EQU     $00
DAC_BYTEWIDE    EQU     $40
DAC_WORDWIDE    EQU     $80

DAC_BOOTTIME    EQU     $30       ; two bits for when to boot
DAC_NEVER       EQU     $00       ; obvious
DAC_CONFIGTIME  EQU     $10       ; call da_BootPoint when first configing the
                                  ;   the device
DAC_BINDTIME    EQU     $20       ; run when binding drivers to boards

**
** These are the calling conventions for Diag or Boot area
**
** A7 -- points to at least 2K of stack
** A6 -- ExecBase
** A5 -- ExpansionBase
** A3 -- your board's ConfigDev structure
** A2 -- Base of diag/init area that was copied
** A0 -- Base of your board
**
** Your board should return a value in D0.  If this value is NULL, then
** the diag/init area that was copied in will be returned to the free
** memory pool.
**

        ENDC    ; LIBRARIES_CONFIGREGS_I
```



```
        IFND    LIBRARIES_CONFIGVARS_I
LIBRARIES_CONFIGVARS_I  SET     1
**
**      $Filename: libraries/configvars.i $
**      $Release: 1.3 $
**
**      software structures for configuration subsystem
**
**      (C) Copyright 1986,1987,1988 Commodore-Amiga, Inc.
**          All Rights Reserved
**

        IFND    EXEC_NODES_I
        INCLUDE "exec/nodes.i"
        ENDC    ; EXEC_NODES_I

        IFND    LIBRARIES_CONFIGREGS_I
        INCLUDE "libraries/configregs.i"
        ENDC    ; LIBRARIES_CONFIGREGS_I


 STRUCTURE ConfigDev,0
    STRUCT      cd_Node,LN_SIZE
    UBYTE       cd_Flags
    UBYTE       cd_Pad
    STRUCT      cd_Rom,ExpansionRom_SIZEOF ; copy of boards config rom
    APTR        cd_BoardAddr    ; where in memory the board is
    APTR        cd_BoardSize    ; size in bytes
    UWORD       cd_SlotAddr     ; which slot number
    UWORD       cd_SlotSize     ; number of slots the board takes
    APTR        cd_Driver       ; pointer to node of driver
    APTR        cd_NextCD       ; linked list of drivers to config
    STRUCT      cd_Unused,4*4   ; for whatever the driver whats
    LABEL       ConfigDev_SIZEOF

; cd_Flags
        BITDEF  CD,SHUTUP,0     ; this board has been shut up
        BITDEF  CD,CONFIGME,1   ; this board needs a driver to claim it

; this structure is used by GetCurrentBinding() and SetCurrentBinding()
 STRUCTURE CurrentBinding,0
    APTR        cb_ConfigDev
    APTR        cb_FileName
    APTR        cb_ProductString
    APTR        cb_ToolTypes
    LABEL       CurrentBinding_SIZEOF

        ENDC    ; LIBRARIES_CONFIGVARS_I
```

```
        IFND    LIBRARIES_DISKFONT_I
LIBRARIES_DISKFONT_I    SET     1
**
**      $Filename: libraries/diskfont.i $
**      $Release: 1.3 $
**
**      diskfont library definitions
**
**      (C) Copyright 1985,1986,1987,1988 Commodore-Amiga, Inc.
**          All Rights Reserved
**

   IFND     EXEC_NODES_I
   INCLUDE     "exec/nodes.i"
   ENDC
   IFND     EXEC_LISTS_I
   INCLUDE     "exec/lists.i"
   ENDC
   IFND     GRAPHICS_TEXT_I
   INCLUDE     "graphics/text.i"
   ENDC

MAXFONTPATH EQU   256   ; including null terminator

 STRUCTURE  FC,0
   STRUCT   fc_FileName,MAXFONTPATH
   UWORD fc_YSize
   UBYTE fc_Style
   UBYTE fc_Flags
   LABEL fc_SIZEOF

FCH_ID      EQU   $0f00

 STRUCTURE  FCH,0
   UWORD fch_FileID  ; FCH_ID
   UWORD fch_NumEntries ; the number of FontContents elements
   LABEL fch_FC      ; the FontContents elements


DFH_ID      EQU   $0f80
MAXFONTNAME EQU   32 ; font name including ".font\0"

 STRUCTURE  DiskFontHeader,0
     ; the following 8 bytes are not actually considered a part of the
     ; DiskFontHeader, but immediately preceed it.  The NextSegment is supplied
     ; by the linker/loader, and the ReturnCode is the code at the beginning
     ; of the font in case someone runs it...
     ; ULONG dfh_NextSegment   ; actually a BPTR
     ; ULONG dfh_ReturnCode    ; MOVEQ #0,D0 : RTS
     ; here then is the official start of the DiskFontHeader...
   STRUCT   dfh_DF,LN_SIZE    ; node to link disk fonts
   UWORD dfh_FileID           ; DFH_ID
   UWORD dfh_Revision         ; the font revision in this version
   LONG  dfh_Segment          ; the segment address when loaded
   STRUCT   dfh_Name,MAXFONTNAME ; the font name (null terminated)
   STRUCT   dfh_TF,tf_SIZEOF  ; loaded TextFont structure
   LABEL dfh_SIZEOF


   BITDEF   AF,MEMORY,0
   BITDEF   AF,DISK,1

 STRUCTURE  AF,0
   UWORD af_Type        ; MEMORY or DISK
   STRUCT   af_Attr,ta_SIZEOF ; text attributes for font
   LABEL af_SIZEOF

 STRUCTURE  AFH,0
   UWORD afh_NumEntries    ; number of AvailFonts elements
```



```
   LABEL afh_AF         ; the AvailFonts elements

        ENDC    ; LIBRARIES_DISKFONT_I
```

Sep 28 20:25 1988 libraries/dos.i Page 1

```
        IFND    LIBRARIES_DOS_I
LIBRARIES_DOS_I SET     1
**
**      $Filename: libraries/dos.i $
**      $Release: 1.3 $
**
**      Standard assembler header for AmigaDOS
**
**      (C) Copyright 1985,1986,1987,1988 Commodore-Amiga, Inc.
**          All Rights Reserved
**

*       IFND EXEC_TYPES_I
*       INCLUDE "exec/types.i"
*       ENDC


DOSNAME     MACRO
      DC.B  'dos.library',0
      ENDM

* Predefined Amiga DOS global constants

DOSTRUE         EQU     -1
DOSFALSE        EQU      0

* Mode parameter to Open()
MODE_OLDFILE            EQU   1005   * Open existing file read/write
*                                    * positioned at beginning of file.
MODE_NEWFILE            EQU   1006   * Open freshly created file (delete
*                                    * old file) read/write
MODE_READWRITE          EQU   1004   * Open old file w/exclusive lock
* Relative position to Seek()
OFFSET_BEGINNING        EQU    -1    * relative to Beginning Of File
OFFSET_CURRENT          EQU     0    * relative to Current file position
OFFSET_END              EQU     1    * relative to End Of File

OFFSET_BEGINING      EQU   OFFSET_BEGINNING     * Ancient compatibility

BITSPERBYTE             EQU   8
BYTESPERLONG            EQU   4
BITSPERLONG             EQU   32
MAXINT                  EQU   $7FFFFFFF
MININT                  EQU   $80000000

* Passed as type to Lock()
SHARED_LOCK             EQU   -2   ; File is readable by others
ACCESS_READ             EQU   -2   ; Synonym
EXCLUSIVE_LOCK          EQU   -1   ; No other access allowed
ACCESS_WRITE            EQU   -1   ; Synonym


 STRUCTURE DateStamp,0
   LONG  ds_Days                   ; Number of days since Jan. 1, 1978
   LONG  ds_Minute                 ; Number of minutes past midnight
   LONG  ds_Tick                   ; Number of ticks past minute
   LABEL ds_SIZEOF                 ; DateStamp
TICKS_PER_SECOND EQU 50            ; Number of ticks in one second

* Returned by Examine() and ExInfo()
 STRUCTURE FileInfoBlock,0
   LONG   fib_DiskKey
   LONG   fib_DirEntryType         ; Type of Directory. If < 0, then a plain file.
                                   ; If > 0 a directory
   STRUCT fib_FileName,108         ; Null terminated. Max 30 chars used for now
   LONG   fib_Protection           ; bit mask of protection, rwxd are 3-0.
   LONG   fib_EntryType
   LONG   fib_Size                 ; Number of bytes in file
   LONG   fib_NumBlocks            ; Number of blocks in file
```

Sep 28 20:25 1988 libraries/dos.i Page 2

```
   STRUCT fib_DateStamp,ds_SIZEOF ; Date file last changed.
   STRUCT fib_Comment,80          ; Null terminated. Comment associated with file
   STRUCT fib_Reserved,36
   LABEL  fib_SIZEOF              ; FileInfoBlock

* FIB stands for FileInfoBlock
* FIBB are bit definitions, FIBF are field definitions
   BITDEF   FIB,SCRIPT,6          ; program is an execute script
   BITDEF   FIB,PURE,5            ; program is reentrant and reexecutable
   BITDEF   FIB,ARCHIVE,4         ; cleared whenever file is changed
   BITDEF   FIB,READ,3            ; ignored by the system
   BITDEF   FIB,WRITE,2           ; ignored by the system
   BITDEF   FIB,EXECUTE,1         ; ignored by the system
   BITDEF   FIB,DELETE,0          ; prevent file from being deleted


* All BCPL data must be long word aligned.  BCPL pointers are the long word
* address (i.e byte address divided by 4 (>>2))

* Macro to indicate BCPL pointers
BPTR     MACRO                          * Long word pointer
         LONG     \1
         ENDM
BSTR     MACRO                          * Long word pointer to BCPL string.
         LONG     \1
         ENDM

* #define BADDR( bptr ) (bptr << 2) * Convert BPTR to byte addressed pointer

* BCPL strings have a length in the first byte and then the characters.
* For example:  s[0]=3 s[1]=S s[2]=Y s[3]=S

* returned by Info()
 STRUCTURE InfoData,0
   LONG id_NumSoftErrors         * number of soft errors on disk
   LONG id_UnitNumber            * Which unit disk is (was) mounted on
   LONG id_DiskState             * See defines below
   LONG id_NumBlocks             * Number of blocks on disk
   LONG id_NumBlocksUsed         * Number of block in use
   LONG id_BytesPerBlock
   LONG id_DiskType              * Disk Type code
   BPTR id_VolumeNode            * BCPL pointer to volume node
   LONG id_InUse                 * Flag, zero if not in use
   LABEL id_SIZEOF               * InfoData

* ID stands for InfoData
*               Disk states
ID_WRITE_PROTECTED      EQU    80      * Disk is write protected
ID_VALIDATING           EQU    81      * Disk is currently being validated
ID_VALIDATED            EQU    82      * Disk is consistent and writeable
*              Disk types
ID_NO_DISK_PRESENT      EQU -1
ID_UNREADABLE_DISK      EQU   ('B'<<24)!('A'<<16)!('D'<<8)
ID_NOT_REALLY_DOS       EQU   ('N'<<24)!('D'<<16)!('O'<<8)!('S')
ID_DOS_DISK             EQU   ('D'<<24)!('O'<<16)!('S'<<8)
ID_KICKSTART_DISK       EQU   ('K'<<24)!('I'<<16)!('C'<<8)!('K')

* Errors from IoErr(), etc.
ERROR_NO_FREE_STORE                EQU  103
ERROR_TASK_TABLE_FULL              EQU  105
ERROR_LINE_TOO_LONG                EQU  120
ERROR_FILE_NOT_OBJECT              EQU  121
ERROR_INVALID_RESIDENT_LIBRARY     EQU  122
ERROR_OBJECT_IN_USE                EQU  202
ERROR_OBJECT_EXISTS                EQU  203
ERROR_OBJECT_NOT_FOUND             EQU  205
ERROR_ACTION_NOT_KNOWN             EQU  209
ERROR_INVALID_COMPONENT_NAME       EQU  210
ERROR_INVALID_LOCK                 EQU  211
```

```
ERROR_OBJECT_WRONG_TYPE           EQU  212
ERROR_DISK_NOT_VALIDATED          EQU  213
ERROR_DISK_WRITE_PROTECTED        EQU  214
ERROR_RENAME_ACROSS_DEVICES       EQU  215
ERROR_DIRECTORY_NOT_EMPTY         EQU  216
ERROR_DEVICE_NOT_MOUNTED          EQU  218
ERROR_SEEK_ERROR                  EQU  219
ERROR_COMMENT_TOO_BIG             EQU  220
ERROR_DISK_FULL                   EQU  221
ERROR_DELETE_PROTECTED            EQU  222
ERROR_WRITE_PROTECTED             EQU  223
ERROR_READ_PROTECTED              EQU  224
ERROR_NOT_A_DOS_DISK              EQU  225
ERROR_NO_DISK                     EQU  226
ERROR_NO_MORE_ENTRIES             EQU  232

* These are the return codes used by convention by AmigaDOS commands
* See FAILAT and IF for relvance to EXECUTE files
RETURN_OK                         EQU    0  * No problems, success
RETURN_WARN                       EQU    5  * A warning only
RETURN_ERROR                      EQU   10  * Something wrong
RETURN_FAIL                       EQU   20  * Complete or severe failure

* Bit numbers that signal you that a user has issued a break
        BITDEF  SIGBREAK,CTRL_C,12
        BITDEF  SIGBREAK,CTRL_D,13
        BITDEF  SIGBREAK,CTRL_E,14
        BITDEF  SIGBREAK,CTRL_F,15

        ENDC    ; LIBRARIES_DOS_I
```

Sep 28 17:22 1988 libraries/dos_lib.i Page 1

```
        IFND    LIBRARIES_DOS_LIB_I
LIBRARIES_DOS_LIB_I     SET     1
**
**      $Filename: libraries/dos_lib.i $
**      $Release: 1.3 $
**
**      Library interface offsets for DOS library
**
**      (C) Copyright 1985,1986,1987,1988 Commodore-Amiga, Inc.
**          All Rights Reserved
**

reserve EQU     4
vsize   EQU     6
count   SET     -vsize*(reserve+1)
LIBENT  MACRO
_LVO\1  EQU     count
count   SET     count-vsize
        ENDM
*
*
*
   LIBENT   Open
   LIBENT   Close
   LIBENT   Read
   LIBENT   Write
   LIBENT   Input
   LIBENT   Output
   LIBENT   Seek
   LIBENT   DeleteFile
   LIBENT   Rename
   LIBENT   Lock
   LIBENT   UnLock
   LIBENT   DupLock
   LIBENT   Examine
   LIBENT   ExNext
   LIBENT   Info
   LIBENT   CreateDir
   LIBENT   CurrentDir
   LIBENT   IoErr
   LIBENT   CreateProc
   LIBENT   Exit
   LIBENT   LoadSeg
   LIBENT   UnLoadSeg
   LIBENT   GetPacket
   LIBENT   QueuePacket
   LIBENT   DeviceProc
   LIBENT   SetComment
   LIBENT   SetProtection
   LIBENT   DateStamp
   LIBENT   Delay
   LIBENT   WaitForChar
   LIBENT   ParentDir
   LIBENT   IsInteractive
   LIBENT   Execute

        ENDC    ; LIBRARIES_DOS_LIB_I
```

Sep 28 17:23 1988 libraries/dosextens.i Page 1

```
        IFND    LIBRARIES_DOSEXTENS_I
LIBRARIES_DOSEXTENS_I   SET     1
**
**      $Filename: libraries/dosextens.i $
**      $Release: 1.3 $
**
**      DOS structures not needed for the casual AmigaDOS user
**
**      (C) Copyright 1985,1986,1987,1988 Commodore-Amiga, Inc.
**          All Rights Reserved
**

     IFND  EXEC_TYPES_I
     INCLUDE "exec/types.i"
     ENDC
     IFND  EXEC_TASKS_I
     INCLUDE "exec/tasks.i"
     ENDC
     IFND  EXEC_PORTS_I
     INCLUDE "exec/ports.i"
     ENDC
     IFND  EXEC_LIBRARIES_I
     INCLUDE "exec/libraries.i"
     ENDC

     IFND  LIBRARIES_DOS_I
     INCLUDE "libraries/dos.i"
     ENDC


* All DOS processes have this STRUCTure
* Create and DeviceProc returns pointer to the MsgPort in this STRUCTure
* Process_addr = DeviceProc(..) - TC_SIZE

 STRUCTURE Process,0
    STRUCT   pr_Task,TC_SIZE
    STRUCT   pr_MsgPort,MP_SIZE   * This is BPTR address from DOS functions
    WORD     pr_Pad               * Remaining variables on 4 byte boundaries
    BPTR     pr_SegList           * Array of seg lists used by this process
    LONG     pr_StackSize         * Size of process stack in bytes
    APTR     pr_GlobVec           * Global vector for this process (BCPL)
    LONG     pr_TaskNum           * CLI task number of zero if not a CLI
    BPTR     pr_StackBase         * Ptr to high memory end of process stack
    LONG     pr_Result2           * Value of secondary result from last call
    BPTR     pr_CurrentDir        * Lock associated with current directory
    BPTR     pr_CIS               * Current CLI Input Stream
    BPTR     pr_COS               * Current CLI Output Stream
    APTR     pr_ConsoleTask       * Console handler process for current window
    APTR     pr_FileSystemTask    * File handler process for current drive
    BPTR     pr_CLI               * pointer to ConsoleLineInterpreter
    APTR     pr_ReturnAddr        * pointer to previous stack frame
    APTR     pr_PktWait           * Function to be called when awaiting msg
    APTR     pr_WindowPtr         * Window pointer for errors
    LABEL    pr_SIZEOF            * Process

* The long word address (BPTR) of this STRUCTure is returned by
* Open() and other routines that return a file.  You need only worry
* about this STRUCT to do async io's via PutMsg() instead of
* standard file system calls

 STRUCTURE FileHandle,0
   APTR    fh_Link                * pointer to EXEC message
   APTR    fh_Interactive         * Boolean; TRUE if interactive handle
   APTR    fh_Type                * Port to do PutMsg() to
   LONG    fh_Buf
   LONG    fh_Pos
   LONG    fh_End
   LONG    fh_Funcs
fh_Func1 EQU fh_Funcs
```

```
    LONG    fh_Func2
    LONG    fh_Func3
    LONG    fh_Args
fh_Arg1 EQU fh_Args
    LONG    fh_Arg2
    LABEL   fh_SIZEOF * FileHandle

* This is the extension to EXEC Messages used by DOS
 STRUCTURE DosPacket,0
    APTR    dp_Link          * pointer to EXEC message
    APTR    dp_Port          * pointer to Reply port for the packet
*                            * Must be filled in each send.
    LONG    dp_Type          * See ACTION_... below and
*                            * 'R' means Read, 'W' means Write to the file system
    LONG    dp_Res1          * For file system calls this is the result
*                            * that would have been returned by the
*                            * function, e.g. Write ('W') returns actual
*                            * length written
    LONG    dp_Res2          * For file system calls this is what would
*                            * have been returned by IoErr()
    LONG    dp_Arg1
*   Device packets common equivalents
dp_Action  EQU  dp_Type
dp_Status  EQU  dp_Res1
dp_Status2 EQU  dp_Res2
dp_BufAddr EQU  dp_Arg1
    LONG    dp_Arg2
    LONG    dp_Arg3
    LONG    dp_Arg4
    LONG    dp_Arg5
    LONG    dp_Arg6
    LONG    dp_Arg7
    LABEL   dp_SIZEOF * DosPacket

* A Packet does not require the Message to before it in memory, but
* for convenience it is useful to associate the two.
* Also see the function init_std_pkt for initializing this STRUCTure

 STRUCTURE StandardPacket,0
    STRUCT sp_Msg,MN_SIZE
    STRUCT sp_Pkt,dp_SIZEOF
    LABEL  sp_SIZEOF * StandardPacket


* Packet types
ACTION_NIL                 EQU     0
ACTION_GET_BLOCK           EQU     2        ;OBSOLETE
ACTION_SET_MAP             EQU     4
ACTION_DIE                 EQU     5
ACTION_EVENT               EQU     6
ACTION_CURRENT_VOLUME      EQU     7
ACTION_LOCATE_OBJECT       EQU     8
ACTION_RENAME_DISK         EQU     9
ACTION_WRITE               EQU     'W'
ACTION_READ                EQU     'R'
ACTION_FREE_LOCK           EQU     15
ACTION_DELETE_OBJECT       EQU     16
ACTION_RENAME_OBJECT       EQU     17
ACTION_MORE_CACHE          EQU     18
ACTION_COPY_DIR            EQU     19
ACTION_WAIT_CHAR           EQU     20
ACTION_SET_PROTECT         EQU     21
ACTION_CREATE_DIR          EQU     22
ACTION_EXAMINE_OBJECT      EQU     23
ACTION_EXAMINE_NEXT        EQU     24
ACTION_DISK_INFO           EQU     25
ACTION_INFO                EQU     26
ACTION_FLUSH               EQU     27
ACTION_SET_COMMENT         EQU     28
```



```
ACTION_PARENT              EQU     29
ACTION_TIMER               EQU     30
ACTION_INHIBIT             EQU     31
ACTION_DISK_TYPE           EQU     32
ACTION_DISK_CHANGE         EQU     33
ACTION_SET_DATE            EQU     34

ACTION_SCREEN_MODE         EQU     994

ACTION_READ_RETURN         EQU     1001
ACTION_WRITE_RETURN        EQU     1002
ACTION_SEEK                EQU     1008
ACTION_FINDUPDATE          EQU     1004
ACTION_FINDINPUT           EQU     1005
ACTION_FINDOUTPUT          EQU     1006
ACTION_END                 EQU     1007
ACTION_TRUNCATE            EQU     1022     /* fast file system only */
ACTION_WRITE_PROTECT       EQU     1023     /* fast file system only */

* DOS library node structure.
* This is the data at positive offsets from the library node.
* Negative offsets from the node is the jump table to DOS functions
* node = (STRUCT DosLibrary *) OpenLibrary( "dos.library" .. )

 STRUCTURE DosLibrary,0
    STRUCT  dl_lib,LIB_SIZE
    APTR    dl_Root              * Pointer to RootNode, described below
    APTR    dl_GV                * Pointer to BCPL global vector
    LONG    dl_A2                * Private register dump of DOS
    LONG    dl_A5
    LONG    dl_A6
    LABEL   dl_SIZEOF *  DosLibrary

*

 STRUCTURE RootNode,0
    BPTR    rn_TaskArray         * [0] is max number of CLI's
*                                * [1] is APTR to process id of CLI 1
*                                * [n] is APTR to process id of CLI n
    BPTR    rn_ConsoleSegment    * SegList for the CLI
    STRUCT  rn_Time,ds_SIZEOF    * Current time
    LONG    rn_RestartSeg        * SegList for the disk validator process
    BPTR    rn_Info              * Pointer ot the Info structure
    BPTR    rn_FileHandlerSegment * code for file handler
    LABEL   rn_SIZEOF * RootNode

 STRUCTURE DosInfo,0
    BPTR    di_McName            * Network name of this machine currently 0
    BPTR    di_DevInfo           * Device List
    BPTR    di_Devices           * Currently zero
    BPTR    di_Handlers          * Currently zero
    APTR    di_NetHand           * Network handler processid currently zero
    LABEL   di_SIZEOF * DosInfo

* DOS Processes started from the CLI via RUN or NEWCLI have this additional
* set to data associated with them

 STRUCTURE CommandLineInterface,0
    LONG    cli_Result2          * Value of IoErr from last command
    BSTR    cli_SetName          * Name of current directory
    BPTR    cli_CommandDir       * Lock associated with command directory
    LONG    cli_ReturnCode       * Return code from last command
    BSTR    cli_CommandName      * Name of current command
    LONG    cli_FailLevel        * Fail level (set by FAILAT)
    BSTR    cli_Prompt           * Current prompt (set by PROMPT)
    BPTR    cli_StandardInput    * Default (terminal) CLI input
    BPTR    cli_CurrentInput     * Current CLI input
    BSTR    cli_CommandFile      * Name of EXECUTE command file
    LONG    cli_Interactive      * Boolean True if prompts required
```

```
    LONG   cli_Background      * Boolean True if CLI created by RUN
    BPTR   cli_CurrentOutput   * Current CLI output
    LONG   cli_DefaultStack    * Stack size to be obtained in long words
    BPTR   cli_StandardOutput  * Default (terminal) CLI output
    BPTR   cli_Module          * SegList of currently loaded command
    LABEL  cli_SIZEOF          * CommandLineInterface

* This structure can take on different values depending on whether it is
* a device, an assigned directory, or a volume.  Below is the structure
* reflecting volumes only.  Following that is the structure representing
* only devices. Following that is the unioned structure representing all
* the values

* structure representing a volume

 STRUCTURE DevList,0
    BPTR        dl_Next                   ; bptr to next device list
    LONG        dl_Type                   ; see DLT below
    APTR        dl_Task                   ; ptr to handler task
    BPTR        dl_Lock                   ; not for volumes
    STRUCT      dl_VolumeDate,ds_SIZEOF   ; creation date
    BPTR        dl_LockList               ; outstanding locks
    LONG        dl_DiskType               ; 'DOS', etc
    LONG        dl_unused
    BSTR        dl_Name                   ; bptr to bcpl name
    LABEL       DevList_SIZEOF

* device structure (same as the DeviceNode structure in filehandler.i

 STRUCTURE       DevInfo,0
    BPTR    dvi_Next
    LONG    dvi_Type
    APTR    dvi_Task
    BPTR    dvi_Lock
    BSTR    dvi_Handler
    LONG    dvi_Stacksize
    LONG    dvi_Priority
    LONG    dvi_Startup
    BPTR    dvi_SegList
    BPTR    dvi_GlobVec
    BSTR    dvi_Name
    LABEL   dvi_SIZEOF

* combined structure for devices, assigned directories, volumes

 STRUCTURE DosList,0
    BPTR     dol_Next        ; bptr to next device on lis
    LONG     dol_Type        ; see DLT below
    APTR     dol_Task        ; ptr to handler task
    BPTR     dol_Lock

    STRUCT      dol_VolumeDate,0          ; creation date (UNION)
    BSTR        dol_Handler               ; file name to load if seglist is null
    LONG        dol_StackSize             ; stacksize to use when starting process
    LONG        dol_Priority              ; task priority when starting process

    STRUCT      dol_LockList,0            ; outstanding locks (UNION)
    ULONG       dol_Startup               ; startup msg: FileSysStartupMsg
                                          ; for disks

    STRUCT      dol_DiskType,0            ; 'DOS', etc (UNION)
    BPTR        dol_SegList               ; already loaded code for new task

    BPTR        dol_GlobVec               ; BCPL global vector

    BSTR        dol_Name                  ; bptr to bcpl name
    LABEL       DosList_SIZEOF
```



```
* definitions for dl_Type
DLT_DEVICE       EQU     0
DLT_DIRECTORY    EQU     1
DLT_VOLUME       EQU     2


* a lock structure, as returned by Lock() or DupLock()
 STRUCTURE FileLock,0
    BPTR         fl_Link                  ; bcpl pointer to next lock
    LONG         fl_Key                   ; disk block number
    LONG         fl_Access                ; exclusive or shared
    APTR         fl_Task                  ; handler task's port
    BPTR         fl_Volume                ; bptr to a DeviceList
    LABEL        fl_SIZEOF

        ENDC    ; LIBRARIES_DOSEXTENS_I
```

Sep 28 17:23 1988 libraries/expansion.i Page 1

```
        IFND    LIBRARIES_EXPANSION_I
LIBRARIES_EXPANSION_I   SET     1
**
**      $Filename: libraries/expansion.i $
**      $Release: 1.3 $
**
**      external definitions for expansion.library
**
**      (C) Copyright 1986,1987,1988 Commodore-Amiga, Inc.
**          All Rights Reserved
**

EXPANSIONNAME   MACRO
                dc.b    'expansion.library',0
                ENDM


;* flags for the AddDosNode() call */
        BITDEF  ADN,STARTPROC,0

        ENDC    ; LIBRARIES_EXPANSION_I
```

Sep 28 17:23 1988 libraries/expansionbase.i Page 1

```
        IFND    LIBRARIES_EXPANSIONBASE_I
LIBRARIES_EXPANSIONBASE_I       SET     1
**
**      $Filename: libraries/expansionbase.i $
**      $Release: 1.3 $
**
**      library structure for expansion library
**
**      (C) Copyright 1987,1988 Commodore-Amiga, Inc.
**          All Rights Reserved
**

        IFND    EXEC_TYPES_I
        INCLUDE "exec/types.i"
        ENDC    ; EXEC_TYPES_I

        IFND    EXEC_LIBRARIES_I
        INCLUDE "exec/libraries.i"
        ENDC    ; EXEC_LIBRARIES_I

        IFND    EXEC_INTERRUPTS_I
        INCLUDE "exec/interrupts.i"
        ENDC    ; EXEC_INTERRUPTS_I

        IFND    EXEC_SEMAPHORES_I
        INCLUDE "exec/semaphores.i"
        ENDC    ; EXEC_SEMAPHORES_I

        IFND    LIBRARIES_CONFIGVARS_I
        INCLUDE "libraries/configvars.i"
        ENDC    ; LIBRARIES_CONFIGVARS_I


TOTALSLOTS      EQU     256

 STRUCTURE      ExpansionInt,0
    UWORD               ei_IntMask      ; mask for this list
    UWORD               ei_ArrayMax     ; current max valid index
    UWORD               ei_ArraySize    ; allocated size
    LABEL               ei_Array        ; actual data is after this
    LABEL               ExpansionInt_SIZEOF

 STRUCTURE      ExpansionBase,LIB_SIZE
    UBYTE               eb_Flags
    UBYTE               eb_pad
    ULONG               eb_ExecBase
    ULONG               eb_SegList
    STRUCT              eb_CurrentBinding,CurrentBinding_SIZEOF
    STRUCT              eb_BoardList,LH_SIZE
    STRUCT              eb_MountList,LH_SIZE
    STRUCT              eb_AllocTable,TOTALSLOTS
    STRUCT              eb_BindSemaphore,SS_SIZE
    STRUCT              eb_Int2List,IS_SIZE
    STRUCT              eb_Int6List,IS_SIZE
    STRUCT              eb_Int7List,IS_SIZE
    LABEL               ExpansionBase_SIZEOF


; error codes
EE_LASTBOARD    EQU     40      ; could not shut him up
EE_NOEXPANSION  EQU     41      ; not enough expansion mem; board shut up
EE_NOBOARD      EQU     42      ; no board at that address
EE_NOMEMORY     EQU     42      ; not enough normal memory

; flags
        BITDEF  EB,CLOGGED,0    ; someone could not be shutup
        BITDEF  EB,SHORTMEM,1   ; ran out of expansion mem

        ENDC    ; LIBRARIES_EXPANSIONBASE_I
```

```
        IFND    LIBRARIES_FILEHANDLER_I
LIBRARIES_FILEHANDLER_I SET     1
**
**      $Filename: libraries/filehandler.i $
**      $Release: 1.3 $
**
**      device and file handler specific code for AmigaDOS
**
**      (C) Copyright 1986,1987,1988 Commodore-Amiga, Inc.
**          All Rights Reserved
**

        IFND      EXEC_TYPES_I
        INCLUDE "exec/types.i"
        ENDC    ; EXEC_TYPES_I

        IFND      EXEC_PORTS_I
        INCLUDE "exec/ports.i"
        ENDC    ; EXEC_PORTS_I

        IFND      LIBRARIES_DOS_I
        INCLUDE "libraries/dos.i"
        ENDC    ; LIBRARIES_DOS_I


* The disk "environment" is a longword array that describes the
* disk geometry.  It is variable sized, with the length at the beginning.
* Here are the constants for a standard geometry.



 STRUCTURE DosEnvec,0
    ULONG de_TableSize        ; Size of Environment vector
    ULONG de_SizeBlock        ; in longwords: standard value is 128
    ULONG de_SecOrg           ; not used; must be 0
    ULONG de_Surfaces         ; # of heads (surfaces). drive specific
    ULONG de_SectorPerBlock   ; not used; must be 1
    ULONG de_BlocksPerTrack   ; blocks per track. drive specific
    ULONG de_Reserved         ; DOS reserved blocks at start of partition.
    ULONG de_PreAlloc         ; DOS reserved blocks at end of partition
    ULONG de_Interleave       ; usually 0
    ULONG de_LowCyl           ; starting cylinder. typically 0
    ULONG de_HighCyl          ; max cylinder. drive specific
    ULONG de_NumBuffers       ; Initial # DOS of buffers.
    ULONG de_BufMemType       ; type of mem to allocate for buffers
    ULONG de_MaxTransfer      ; Max number of bytes to transfer at a time
    ULONG de_Mask             ; Address Mask to block out certain memory
    LONG  de_BootPri          ; Boot priority for autoboot
    ULONG de_DosType          ; ASCII (HEX) string showing filesystem type;
                              ; 0X444F5300 is old filesystem,
                              ; 0X444F5301 is fast file system
    LABEL DosEnvec_SIZEOF

* these are the offsets into the array

DE_TABLESIZE    EQU     0       ; standard value is 11
DE_SIZEBLOCK    EQU     1       ; in longwords: standard value is 128
DE_SECORG       EQU     2       ; not used; must be 0
DE_NUMHEADS     EQU     3       ; # of heads (surfaces). drive specific
DE_SECSPERBLK   EQU     4       ; not used; must be 1
DE_BLKSPERTRACK EQU     5       ; blocks per track. drive specific
DE_RESERVEDBLKS EQU     6       ; unavailable blocks at start.  usually 2
DE_PREFAC       EQU     7       ; not used; must be 0
DE_INTERLEAVE   EQU     8       ; usually 0
DE_LOWCYL       EQU     9       ; starting cylinder. typically 0
DE_UPPERCYL     EQU     10      ; max cylinder.  drive specific
DE_NUMBUFFERS   EQU     11      ; starting # of buffers.  typically 5
DE_MEMBUFTYPE   EQU     12      ; type of mem to allocate for buffers.
DE_BUFMEMTYPE   EQU     12      ; same as above, better name
```

```
                                        ; 1 is public, 3 is chip, 5 is fast
DE_MAXTRANSFER      EQU     13          ; Maximum number of bytes to transfer at a time
DE_MASK             EQU     14          ; Address Mask to block out certain memory
DE_BOOTPRI          EQU     15          ; Boot priority for autoboot
DE_DOSTYPE          EQU     16          ; ASCII (HEX) string showing filesystem type
                                        ; 0X444F5300 is old filesystem,
                                        ; 0X444F5301 is fast file system



*
* The file system startup message is linked into a device node's startup
* field.  It contains a pointer to the above environment, plus the
* information needed to do an exec OpenDevice().
*

 STRUCTURE FileSysStartupMsg,0
    ULONG       fssm_Unit       ; exec unit number for this device
    BSTR        fssm_Device     ; null terminated bstring to the device name
    BPTR        fssm_Environ    ; ptr to environment table (see above)
    ULONG       fssm_Flags      ; flags for OpenDevice()
    LABEL       FileSysStartupMsg_SIZEOF


* The include file "libraries/dosextens.h" has a DeviceList structure.
* The "device list" can have one of three different things linked onto
* it.  Dosextens defines the structure for a volume.  DLT_DIRECTORY
* is for an assigned directory.  The following structure is for
* a dos "device" (DLT_DEVICE).

 STRUCTURE DeviceNode,0
    BPTR        dn_Next         ; singly linked list
    ULONG       dn_Type         ; always 0 for dos "devices"
    CPTR        dn_Task         ; standard dos "task" field.  If this is
                                ;     null when the node is accesses, a task
                                ;     will be started up
    BPTR        dn_Lock         ; not used for devices -- leave null
    BSTR        dn_Handler      ; filename to loadseg (if seglist is null)
    ULONG       dn_StackSize    ; stacksize to use when starting task
    LONG        dn_Priority     ; task priority when starting task
    BPTR        dn_Startup      ; startup msg: FileSysStartupMsg for disks
    BPTR        dn_SegList      ; code to run to start new task (if necessary).
                                ;     if null then dn_Handler will be loaded.
    BPTR        dn_GlobalVec    ; BCPL global vector to use when starting
                                ;     a task.  -1 means that dn_SegList is not
                                ;     for a bcpl program, so the dos won't
                                ;     try and construct one.  0 tell the
                                ;     dos that you obey BCPL linkage rules,
                                ;     and that it should construct a global
                                ;     vector for you.
    BSTR        dn_Name         ; the node name, e.g. '\3','D','F','3'
    LABEL       DeviceNode_SIZEOF

        ENDC    ; LIBRARIES_FILEHANDLER_I
```



```
        IFND    LIBRARIES_MATHLIBRARY_I
LIBRARIES_MATHLIBRARY_I SET     1
**
**      $Filename: libraries/mathlibrary.i $
**      $Release: 1.3 $
**
**
**
**      (C) Copyright 1987,1988 Commodore-Amiga, Inc.
**          All Rights Reserved
**

        ifnd    EXEC_TYPES_I
        include "exec/types.i"
        endc

        ifnd    EXEC_LIBRARIES_I
        include "exec/libraries.i"
        endc

        STRUCTURE MathIEEEBase,0
                STRUCT  MathIEEEBase_LibNode,LIB_SIZE
                UBYTE   MathIEEEBase_Flags
                UBYTE   MathIEEEBase_reserved1
                APTR    MathIEEEBase_68881      ; ptr to base of 68881 io
                APTR    MathIEEEBase_SysLib
                APTR    MathIEEEBase_SegList
                APTR    MathIEEEBase_Resource   ; ptr to math resource found
                APTR    MathIEEEBase_TaskOpenLib        ; hook
                APTR    MathIEEEBase_TaskCloseLib       ; hook
*       This structure may be extended in the future */
        LABEL   MathIEEEBase_SIZE

;       Math resources may need to know when a program opens or closes this
;       library. The functions TaskOpenLib and TaskCloseLib are called when
;       a task opens or closes this library. The yare initialized to point
;       local initialization pertaining to 68881 stuff if 68881 resources
;       are found. To override the default the vendor must provide appropriate
;       hooks in the MathIEEEResource. If specified, these will be called
;       when the library initializes.

        ENDC    ; LIBRARIES_MATHLIBRARY_I
```

Sep 28 17:23 1988 libraries/romboot_base.i Page 1

```
        IFND    LIBRARIES_ROMBOOT_BASE_I
LIBRARIES_ROMBOOT_BASE_I        SET     1
**
**      $Filename: libraries/romboot_base.i $
**      $Release: 1.3 $
**
**
**
**      (C) Copyright 1987,1988 Commodore-Amiga, Inc.
**          All Rights Reserved
**

    IFND    EXEC_TYPES_I
    include "exec/types.i"
    ENDC
    IFND    EXEC_NODES_I
    include "exec/nodes.i"
    ENDC
    IFND    EXEC_LISTS_I
    include "exec/lists.i"
    ENDC
    IFND    EXEC_LIBRARIES_I
    include "exec/libraries.i"
    ENDC
    IFND    EXEC_EXECBASE_I
    include "exec/execbase.i"
    ENDC
    IFND    EXEC_EXECNAME_I
    include "exec/execname.i"
    ENDC

 STRUCTURE  RomBootBase,LIB_SIZE
        APTR    rbb_ExecBase
        STRUCT  rbb_BootList,LH_SIZE
        STRUCT  rbb_Reserved,16                 ; for future expansion
    LABEL   rbb_SIZEOF

 STRUCTURE BootNode,LN_SIZE
        UWORD   bn_Flags
        CPTR    bn_DeviceNode
        LABEL   BootNode_SIZEOF

ROMBOOT_NAME:  MACRO
        DC.B    'romboot.library',0
        DS.W    0
        ENDM

        ENDC    ; LIBRARIES_ROMBOOT_BASE_I
```

Sep 28 17:23 1988 libraries/translator.i Page 1

```
        IFND    LIBRARIES_TRANSLATOR_I
LIBRARIES_TRANSLATOR_I  SET     1
**
**      $Filename: libraries/translator.i $
**      $Release: 1.3 $
**
**      Translator error codes
**
**      (C) Copyright 1985,1986,1987,1988 Commodore-Amiga, Inc.
**          All Rights Reserved
**

TR_NotUsed      EQU     -1              ;This is an often used system rc
TR_NoMem        EQU     -2              ;Can't allocate memory
TR_MakeBad      EQU     -4              ;Error in MakeLibrary call

        ENDC    ; LIBRARIES_TRANSLATOR_I
```

```
        IFND    RESOURCES_CIA_I
RESOURCES_CIA_I SET     1
**
**      $Filename: resources/cia.i $
**      $Release: 1.3 $
**
**
**
**      (C) Copyright 1985,1986,1987,1988 Commodore-Amiga, Inc.
**          All Rights Reserved
**

CIAANAME        MACRO
                DC.B    'ciaa.resource',0
                ENDM

CIABNAME        MACRO
                DC.B    'ciab.resource',0
                ENDM

        ENDC    ; RESOURCES_CIA_I
```



```
        IFND    RESOURCES_DISK_I
RESOURCES_DISK_I        SET     1
**
**      $Filename: resources/disk.i $
**      $Release: 1.3 $
**
**      external declarations for disc resources
**
**      (C) Copyright 1985,1986,1987,1988 Commodore-Amiga, Inc.
**          All Rights Reserved
**

        IFND    EXEC_TYPES_I
        INCLUDE "exec/types.i"
        ENDC    ; EXEC_TYPES_I

        IFND    EXEC_LISTS_I
        INCLUDE "exec/lists.i"
        ENDC    ; EXEC_LISTS_I

        IFND    EXEC_PORTS_I
        INCLUDE "exec/ports.i"
        ENDC    ; EXEC_PORTS_I

        IFND    EXEC_INTERRUPTS_I
        INCLUDE "exec/interrupts.i"
        ENDC    ; EXEC_INTERRUPTS_I

        IFND    EXEC_LIBRARIES_I
        INCLUDE "exec/libraries.i"
        ENDC    ; EXEC_LIBRARIES_I


**********************************************************************
*
* Resource structures
*
**********************************************************************

    STRUCTURE DISCRESOURCEUNIT,MN_SIZE
        STRUCT  DRU_DISCBLOCK,IS_SIZE
        STRUCT  DRU_DISCSYNC,IS_SIZE
        STRUCT  DRU_INDEX,IS_SIZE
        LABEL   DRU_SIZE



    STRUCTURE DISCRESOURCE,LIB_SIZE
        APTR    DR_CURRENT      ; pointer to current unit structure
        UBYTE   DR_FLAGS
        UBYTE   DR_pad
        APTR    DR_SYSLIB
        APTR    DR_CIARESOURCE
        STRUCT  DR_UNITID,4*4
        STRUCT  DR_WAITING,LH_SIZE
        STRUCT  DR_DISCBLOCK,IS_SIZE
        STRUCT  DR_DISCSYNC,IS_SIZE
        STRUCT  DR_INDEX,IS_SIZE
        LABEL   DR_SIZE

        BITDEF  DR,ALLOC0,0     ; unit zero is allocated
        BITDEF  DR,ALLOC1,1     ; unit one is allocated
        BITDEF  DR,ALLOC2,2     ; unit two is allocated
        BITDEF  DR,ALLOC3,3     ; unit three is allocated
        BITDEF  DR,ACTIVE,7     ; is the disc currently busy?


**********************************************************************
*
```

```
* Hardware Magic
*
*************************************************************************


DSKDMAOFF       EQU     $4000   ; idle command for dsklen register


*************************************************************************
*
* Resource specific commands
*
*************************************************************************

*-- DR_NAME is a generic macro to get the name of the resource.  This
*-- way if the name is ever changed you will pick up the change
*-- automatically.
*--
*-- Normal usage would be:
*--
*-- internalName:       DISKNAME
*--

DISKNAME:       MACRO
                DC.B    'disk.resource',0
                DS.W    0
                ENDM

        LIBINIT LIB_BASE
        LIBDEF  DR_ALLOCUNIT
        LIBDEF  DR_FREEUNIT
        LIBDEF  DR_GETUNIT
        LIBDEF  DR_GIVEUNIT
        LIBDEF  DR_GETUNITID

DR_LASTCOMM     EQU     DR_GIVEUNIT


*************************************************************************
*
* drive types
*
*************************************************************************

DRT_AMIGA       EQU     $00000000
DRT_37422D2S    EQU     $55555555
DRT_EMPTY       EQU     $FFFFFFFF

        ENDC    ; RESOURCES_DISK_I
```



```
        IFND    RESOURCES_FILESYSRES_I
RESOURCES_FILESYSRES_I  SET     1
**
**      $Filename: resources/filesysres.i $
**      $Revision: 1.0 $
**      $Date: 88/07/11 15:32:39 $
**
**      FileSystem.resource description
**
**      (C) Copyright 1988 Commodore-Amiga, Inc.
**          All Rights Reserved
**

        IFND    EXEC_NODES_I
        INCLUDE "exec/nodes.i"
        ENDC
        IFND    EXEC_LISTS_I
        INCLUDE "exec/lists.i"
        ENDC
        IFND    LIBRARIES_DOS_I
        INCLUDE "libraries/dos.i"
        ENDC

FSRNAME MACRO
                dc.b    'FileSystem.resource',0
        ENDM

 STRUCTURE  FileSysResource,LN_SIZE     ; on resource list
    CPTR    fsr_Creator                 ; name of creator of this resource
    STRUCT  fsr_FileSysEntries,LH_SIZE  ; list of FileSysEntry structs
    LABEL   FileSysResource_SIZEOF

 STRUCTURE  FileSysEntry,LN_SIZE        ; on fsr_FileSysEntries list
                                        ; LN_NAME is of creator of this entry
    ULONG   fse_DosType         ; DosType of this FileSys
    ULONG   fse_Version         ; Version of this FileSys
    ULONG   fse_PatchFlags      ; bits set for those of the following that need
                                ;   to be substituted into a standard device
                                ;   node for this file system: e.g. $180
                                ;   for substitute SegList & GlobalVec
    ULONG   fse_Type            ; device node type: zero
    CPTR    fse_Task            ; standard dos "task" field
    BPTR    fse_Lock            ; not used for devices: zero
    BSTR    fse_Handler         ; filename to loadseg (if SegList is null)
    ULONG   fse_StackSize       ; stacksize to use when starting task
    LONG    fse_Priority        ; task priority when starting task
    BPTR    fse_Startup         ; startup msg: FileSysStartupMsg for disks
    BPTR    fse_SegList         ; code to run to start new task
    BPTR    fse_GlobalVec       ; BCPL global vector when starting task
    ; no more entries need exist than those implied by fse_PatchFlags

        ENDC    ; RESOURCES_FILESYSRES_I
```

Sep 28 17:23 1988 resources/mathresource.i Page 1

```
        IFND    RESOURCES_MATHRESOURCE_I
RESOURCES_MATHRESOURCE_I        SET     1
**
**      $Filename: resources/mathresource.i $
**      $Release: 1.3 $
**
**
**
**      (C) Copyright 1987,1988 Commodore-Amiga, Inc.
**          All Rights Reserved
**

        IFND    EXEC_TYPES_I
        include "exec/types.i"
        ENDC

        IFND    EXEC_NODES_I
        include "exec/nodes.i"
        ENDC

*
*       The 'Init' entries are only used if the corresponding
*       bit is set in the Flags field.
*
*       So if you are just a 68881, you do not need the Init stuff
*       just make sure you have cleared the Flags field.
*
*       This should allow us to add Extended Precision later.
*
*       For Init users, if you need to be called whenever a task
*       opens this library for use, you need to change the appropriate
*       entries in MathIEEELibrary.
*

        STRUCTURE MathIEEEResourceResource,0
                STRUCT  MathIEEEResource_Node,LN_SIZE
                USHORT  MathIEEEResource_Flags
                APTR    MathIEEEResource_BaseAddr       * ptr to 881 if exists *
                APTR    MathIEEEResource_DblBasInit
                APTR    MathIEEEResource_DblTransInit
                APTR    MathIEEEResource_SglBasInit
                APTR    MathIEEEResource_SglTransInit
                APTR    MathIEEEResource_ExtBasInit
                APTR    MathIEEEResource_ExtTransInit
        LABEL   MathIEEEResourceResource_SIZE

* definations for MathIEEERESOURCE_FLAGS *
        BITDEF  MATHIEEERESOURCE,DBLBAS,0
        BITDEF  MATHIEEERESOURCE,DBLTRANS,1
        BITDEF  MATHIEEERESOURCE,SGLBAS,2
        BITDEF  MATHIEEERESOURCE,SGLTRANS,3
        BITDEF  MATHIEEERESOURCE,EXTBAS,4
        BITDEF  MATHIEEERESOURCE,EXTTRANS,5

        ENDC    ; RESOURCES_MATHRESOURCE_I
```

Sep 28 17:23 1988 resources/misc.i Page 1

```
        IFND    RESOURCES_MISC_I
RESOURCES_MISC_I        SET     1
**
**      $Filename: resources/misc.i $
**      $Release: 1.3 $
**
**      external declarations for misc system resources
**
**      (C) Copyright 1985,1986,1987,1988 Commodore-Amiga, Inc.
**          All Rights Reserved
**

        IFND    EXEC_TYPES_I
        INCLUDE "exec/types.i"
        ENDC    ; EXEC_TYPES_I

        IFND    EXEC_LIBRARIES_I
        INCLUDE "exec/libraries.i"
        ENDC    ; EXEC_LIBRARIES_I

**********************************************************************
*
* Resource structures
*
**********************************************************************

MR_SERIALPORT   EQU     0
MR_SERIALBITS   EQU     1
MR_PARALLELPORT EQU     2
MR_PARALLELBITS EQU     3

NUMMRTYPES      EQU     4

    STRUCTURE MiscResource,LIB_SIZE
        STRUCT  mr_AllocArray,4*NUMMRTYPES
        LABEL   mr_Sizeof

        LIBINIT LIB_BASE
        LIBDEF  MR_ALLOCMISCRESOURCE
        LIBDEF  MR_FREEMISCRESOURCE


MISCNAME        MACRO
                DC.B    'misc.resource',0
                ENDM

        ENDC    ; RESOURCES_MISC_I
```

```
        IFND    RESOURCES_POTGO_I
RESOURCES_POTGO_I       SET     1
**
**      $Filename: resources/potgo.i $
**      $Release: 1.3 $
**
**
**
**      (C) Copyright 1985,1986,1987,1988 Commodore-Amiga, Inc.
**          All Rights Reserved
**

POTGONAME   MACRO
      DC.B  'potgo.resource'
      DC.B  0
      DS.W  0
      ENDM

        ENDC    ; RESOURCES_POTGO_I
```

Sep 28 17:24 1988 workbench/icon.i Page 1

```
        IFND    WORKBENCH_ICON_I
WORKBENCH_ICON_I        SET     1
**
**      $Filename: workbench/icon.i $
**      $Release: 1.3 $
**
**      external declarations for workbench support library
**
**      (C) Copyright 1985,1986,1987,1988 Commodore-Amiga, Inc.
**          All Rights Reserved
**

**********************************************************************
*
* Library structures
*
**********************************************************************


ICONNAME        MACRO
                DC.B    'icon.library',0
                ENDM

        ENDC    ; WORKBENCH_ICON_I
```

Sep 28 17:24 1988 workbench/startup.i Page 1

```
        IFND    WORKBENCH_STARTUP_I
WORKBENCH_STARTUP_I     SET     1
**
**      $Filename: workbench/startup.i $
**      $Release: 1.3 $
**
**      Workbench startup definitions
**
**      (C) Copyright 1985,1986,1987,1988 Commodore-Amiga, Inc.
**          All Rights Reserved
**

        IFND    EXEC_TYPES_I
        INCLUDE "exec/types.i"
        ENDC    ; EXEC_TYPES_I

        IFND    EXEC_PORTS_I
        INCLUDE "exec/ports.i"
        ENDC    ; EXEC_PORTS_I

        IFND    LIBRARIES_DOS_I
        INCLUDE "libraries/dos.i"
        ENDC    ; LIBRARIES_DOS_I

 STRUCTURE WBStartup,0
    STRUCT      sm_Message,MN_SIZE      ; a standard message structure
    APTR        sm_Process              ; the process descriptor for you
    BPTR        sm_Segment              ; a descriptor for your code
    LONG        sm_NumArgs              ; the number of elements in ArgList
    APTR        sm_ToolWindow           ; description of window
    APTR        sm_ArgList              ; the arguments themselves
    LABEL       sm_SIZEOF

 STRUCTURE WBArg,0
    BPTR        wa_Lock                 ; a lock descriptor
    APTR        wa_Name                 ; a string relative to that lock
    LABEL       wa_SIZEOF

        ENDC    ; WORKBENCH_STARTUP_I
```

```
        IFND    WORKBENCH_WORKBENCH_I
WORKBENCH_WORKBENCH_I   SET     1
**
**      $Filename: workbench/workbench.i $
**      $Release: 1.3 $
**
**
**
**      (C) Copyright 1985,1986,1987,1988 Commodore-Amiga, Inc.
**          All Rights Reserved
**

        IFND    EXEC_TYPES_I
        INCLUDE "exec/types.i"
        ENDC    ; EXEC_TYPES_I

        IFND    EXEC_NODES_I
        INCLUDE "exec/nodes.i"
        ENDC    ; EXEC_NODES_I

        IFND    EXEC_LISTS_I
        INCLUDE "exec/lists.i"
        ENDC    ; EXEC_LISTS_I

        IFND    EXEC_TASKS_I
        INCLUDE "exec/tasks.i"
        ENDC    ; EXEC_TASKS_I

        IFND    INTUITION_INTUITION_I
        INCLUDE "intuition/intuition.i"
        ENDC    ; INTUITION_INTUITION_I


; the Workbench object types
WBDISK          EQU     1
WBDRAWER        EQU     2
WBTOOL          EQU     3
WBPROJECT       EQU     4
WBGARBAGE       EQU     5
WBDEVICE        EQU     6
WBKICK          EQU     7


; the main workbench object structure
 STRUCTURE DrawerData,0
    STRUCT      dd_NewWindow,nw_SIZE    ; args to open window
    LONG        dd_CurrentX             ; current x coordinate of origin
    LONG        dd_CurrentY             ; current y coordinate of origin
    LABEL       dd_SIZEOF

; the amount of DrawerData actually written to disk
DRAWERDATAFILESIZE      EQU (dd_SIZEOF)


 STRUCTURE DiskObject,0
    UWORD       do_Magic                ; a magic num at the start of the file
    UWORD       do_Version              ; a version number, so we can change it
    STRUCT      do_Gadget,gg_SIZEOF     ; a copy of in core gadget
    UWORD       do_Type
    APTR        do_DefaultTool
    APTR        do_ToolTypes
    LONG        do_CurrentX
    LONG        do_CurrentY
    APTR        do_DrawerData
    APTR        do_ToolWindow           ; only applies to tools
    LONG        do_StackSize            ; only applies to tools
    LABEL       do_SIZEOF

WB_DISKMAGIC    EQU     $e310   ; a magic number, not easily impersonated
```



```
WB_DISKVERSION  EQU     1       ; our current version number

 STRUCTURE FreeList,0
    WORD        fl_NumFree
    STRUCT      fl_MemList,LH_SIZE
    ; weird name to avoid conflicts with FileLocks
    LABEL       FreeList_SIZEOF



* each message that comes into the WorkBenchPort must have a type field
* in the preceeding short.  These are the defines for this type
*

MTYPE_PSTD              EQU     1       ; a "standard Potion" message
MTYPE_TOOLEXIT          EQU     2       ; exit message from our tools
MTYPE_DISKCHANGE        EQU     3       ; dos telling us of a disk change
MTYPE_TIMER             EQU     4       ; we got a timer tick
MTYPE_CLOSEDOWN         EQU     5       ; <unimplemented>
MTYPE_IOPROC            EQU     6       ; <unimplemented>


* workbench does different complement modes for its gadgets.
* It supports separate images, complement mode, and backfill mode.
* The first two are identical to intuitions GADGIMAGE and GADGHCOMP.
* backfill is similar to GADGHCOMP, but the region outside of the
* image (which normally would be color three when complemented)
* is flood-filled to color zero.
*
GADGBACKFILL            EQU     $0001

* if an icon does not really live anywhere, set its current position
* to here
*
NO_ICON_POSITION        EQU     ($80000000)

        ENDC    ; WORKBENCH_WORKBENCH_I
```

Section F

Linker Libraries

This section contains autodoc summaries for the "amiga.lib" and "debug.lib" linker libraries, and reference source code listings for exec support functions in amiga.lib. Unlike the libraries described in Section A, these are not shared run-time libraries. Instead, they are concatenated Amiga format object modules which are linked with your code as library files. The linker scans specified library files and inserts a copy of each referenced library function into your program code.

The libraries described here are:

debug.lib

Contains "stdio"-like functions for communicating with a serial terminal connected to the Amiga via its built-in serial port. Typically this terminal will be a 9600 baud, 8 data bits, one stop bit connection to an external terminal or an Amiga running a terminal package. The debug.lib functions allow you to output messages and prompt for input, even from within low level task or interrupt code, without disturbing the Amiga's display and or current state (other than the state of the serial hardware itself). No matter how badly the system may have crashed, these functions can usually get a message out. A similar debugging library currently called ddebug.lib is available for sending debugging output to the parallel port. This is useful for debugging serial applications. Ddebug.lib is not documented here. It contains functions similar to debug.lib but with names starting with 'd' instead 'k'.

amiga.lib

This is the main Amiga scanned linker library, generally linked with every program for the Amiga. The major components of amiga.lib are:

stubs	- Individual interface stubs for each Amiga ROM routine that enable stack based C compilers to call register based Amiga ROM routines.
offsets	- The negative Library Vector Offset (_LVO) for each Amiga function.
exec_support	- C functions which simplify many exec procedures such as the creation and deletion of tasks, ports, and IO request structures. Source code is provided for these functions.
clib	- C support functions including pseudo-random number generation and a limited set of file and stdio functions designed to work directly with AmigaDOS file handles.
other	- Miscellaneous handy functions, callable from any language.

```
*
*  Demonstrates assembler use of the compiled C exec support
*  routines (CreatePort, etc.) in Amiga.lib, and also the use of
*  Amiga.lib csupport functions such as _printf for simple formatted
*  output and debugging.  Creates port, outputs address, deletes port.
*
*  LINK INSTRUCTIONS: Alink with Astartup.obj ... LIBRARY Amiga.lib
*   Astartup sets up DOSBase and the stdout needed for Amiga.lib _printf.
*   If you do not link with Astartup.obj, you must add the following
*   variables, XDEF them, and initialize them as commented:
*   DC.L  _DOSBase   0  ;needs base returned from OpenLibrary of dos.library
*   DC.L  _stdout    0  ;needs an AmigaDOS file handle from a dos Open call
*   DC.L  _SysBase   0  ;needs the address stored at location 4

   INCLUDE "exec/types.i"
   INCLUDE "exec/io.i"
   INCLUDE "libraries/dos.i"

*------ Imported labels:  C interface Amiga.lib routines
   XREF     _CreatePort
   XREF     _DeletePort
   XREF     _printf

*------ Exported labels:  Where Astartup.obj JSR's to our code
   XDEF     _main

            CODE

;use startup code (_main + link with Astartup.obj)
_main:
            movem.l   d2-d7/a2-a6,-(sp)  ;Save registers

*----- Exec Support function:  msgPort = CreatePort(name,pri)

            move.l    #0,-(sp)         ;push priority 0 on stack as long
            pea       portname         ;push addr of null-termed portname
            jsr       _CreatePort      ;call CreatePort
            addq.l    #8,sp            ;add 4 to stack for each long pushed
            jsr       mydebug0         ;rtn to print d0 (preserves d0)
            tst.l     d0               ;test result
            beq.s     failure          ;if zero, CreatePort failed

*----- Exec Support function:  DeletePort(port)
            move.l    d0,-(sp)            ;else push d0 (now our msgPort)
            jsr       _DeletePort         ;call DeletePort
            addq.l    #4,sp               ;add 4 to stack for pushed long

            move.l    #RETURN_OK,d0           ;set up success return code
            bra.s     endcode                 ;and skip to exit code

*----- Failure to CreatePort branches here
failure:
            move.l    #RETURN_FAIL,d0         ;set up failure return code

endcode:
            movem.l   (sp)+,d2-d7/a2-a6          ;Restore registers
            rts                                  ;rts with d0 = return code


*----- mydebug0 - Subroutine uses Amiga.lib _printf to print the contents
*                 of d0.  Preserves all registers.
mydebug0:
            movem.l   d0-d7/a0-a6,-(sp)       ;save registers

*----- C Support function printf(): here  printf("$%lx\n",contents_of_d0)
*      Note that the fstrl DC.B below specifies '\n' and null as 10,0
```

```
            move.l    d0,-(sp)                      ;push d0 on the stack
            pea       fstrl                         ;push addr of format string
            jsr       _printf                       ;call printf
            addq.l    #8,sp                         ;add 4 to stack for each long
            movem.l   (sp)+,d0-d7/a0-a6             ;restore saved registers
            rts                                     ;rts


            DATA

portname    DC.B  'sample_msgport',0
fstrl       DC.B  '$%lx',10,0
            END
```

```
;-----------------------------------------------------------------------
;
; Example C Callable function that adds two numbers.  From C, the
; call would look like this:
;               result=AddThemUp(first,second);
;
                XDEF     _AddThemUp          ;Make an External Definition
_AddThemUp
                move.l   4(sp),D0            ;Get FIRST number
                move.l   8(sp),D1            ;Get SECOND number
                add.l    D1,D0               ;Add them
                rts                          ;Return result
```

TABLE OF CONTENTS


```
NAME
    AddTOF - add a task to the TopOfFrame Interrupt server chain.

SYNOPSIS
    AddTOF(i,p,a);
     void AddTOF(struct Isrvstr *, APTR, APTR);

FUNCTION
    Adds a task to the vertical-blanking interval interrupt server
    chain.  This prevents C programmers from needing to write an
    assembly language stub to do this function.

INPUTS
    i - pointer to structure Isrvstr.
    p - pointer to the C-code routine that this server is to call each
        time TOF happens.
    a - pointer to the first longword in an array of longwords that
        is to be used as the arguments passed to your routine
        pointed to by p.

SEE ALSO
    RemTOF, graphics/graphint.h
```

```
NAME
     BeginIO -- initiate asynchronous I/O

SYNOPSIS
     BeginIO(ioRequest)
     void BeginIO(struct IORequest *);

FUNCTION
     This function takes an IORequest, and passes it directly to the
     BEGINIO vector of the proper device.  This works exactly like
     SendIO, but does not clear the io_Flags field first.

     This function does not wait for the I/O to complete.

INPUTS
     ioRequest - Pointer to an initialized, open IORequest structure
                 with the io_Flags field set to a reasonable value
                 (use zero if you do not require io_Flags).

SEE ALSO
     exec/DoIO, exec/SendIO, exec/WaitIO
```



```
NAME
     CreateExtIO() -- create an IORequest structure

SYNOPSIS
     ioReq = CreateExtIO( ioReplyPort, size );
     struct IORequest *CreateExtIO(struct MsgPort *, ULONG);

FUNCTION
     Allocates memory for and initializes a new IO request block
     of a user-specified number of bytes.  The number of bytes
     MUST be the size of a legal IORequest (or extended IORequest)
     or very nasty things will happen.

INPUTS
     ioReplyPort - a pointer to an already initialized
             message port to be used for this IO request's reply port.
             (usually created by CreatePort()).
     size - the size of the IO request to be created.

RESULT
     Returns a pointer to the new IO Request block, or NULL if
             the request failed.

SEE ALSO
     CreatePort, DeleteExtIO
     CreateIORequest
```

```
NAME
     CreatePort - Allocate and initialize a new message port

SYNOPSIS
     CreatePort(name,pri)
     struct MsgPort *CreatePort(char *,LONG);

FUNCTION
     Allocates and initializes a new message port.  The message list
     of the new port will be prepared for use (via NewList).  The port
     will be set to signal your task when a message arrives (PA_SIGNAL).

INPUTS
     name - NULL if other tasks will not search for this port
             via the FindPort() call.  If non-null, this must be
             a null-terminated string; the port will be added to
             the system public port list.  The name is not copied.
     pri  - Priority used for insertion into the public port list.

RESULT
     A new MsgPort structure ready for use.

SEE ALSO
     DeletePort, exec/FindPort, exec/ports.h
```



```
NAME
     CreateTask -- Create task with given name, priority, stacksize

SYNOPSIS
     CreateTask( name, pri, initPC, stackSize)
     task=(struct Task *)CreateTask(char *, LONG, funcEntry, ULONG);

FUNCTION
     This function simplifies program creation of subtasks by
     dynamically allocating and initializing required structures
     and stack space, and adding the task to Exec's task list
     with the given name and priority.  A tc_MemEntry list is provided
     so that all stack and structure memory allocated by CreateTask
     is automatically deallocated when the task is removed.

     An Exec task may not call dos.library functions or any function
     which might cause the loading of a disk-resident library, device,
     or file (since such functions are indirectly calls to dos.library).
     Only AmigaDOS Processes may call AmigaDOS; see the DOS CreateProc()
     call for more information.

     If other tasks or processes will need to find this task by name,
     provide a complex and unique name to avoid conflicts.

     If your compiler provides automatic insertion of stack-checking
     code, you may need to disable this feature when compiling subtask
     code since the stack for the subtask is at a dynamically allocated
     location.  If your compiler requires 68000 registers to contain
     particular values for base relative addressing, you may need to
     save these registers from your main process, and restore them
     in your initial subtask code.

     The function entry initPC is generally provided as follows:

     In C:
     extern void functionName();
     char *tname = "unique name";
     task = CreateTask(tname, 0L, functionName, 4000L);

     In assembler:
             PEA     startLabel

INPUTS

     name - a null terminated string.
     pri - an Exec task priority between -128 and 127 (commonly 0)
     funcEntry - the address of the first executable instruction
                 of the subtask code.
     stackSize - size in bytes of stack for the subtask.  Don't cut it
                 too close - system function stack usage may change.

SEE ALSO
     DeleteTask, exec/FindTask
```

```
NAME
     DeleteExtIO() - return memory allocated for extended IO request

SYNOPSIS
     DeleteExtIO( ioReq );
     void DeleteExtIO(struct IORequest *);

FUNCTION
     Frees up an IO request as allocated by CreateExtIO().  By
     looking at the mn_Length field, it knows how much memory
     to deallocate.

INPUTS
     ioReq - A pointer to the IORequest block to be freed.

SEE ALSO
     CreateExtIO
```



```
NAME
     DeletePort - Free a message port created by CreatePort

SYNOPSIS
     DeletePort(msgPort)
     void DeletePort(struct MsgPort *);

FUNCTION
     Frees a message port created by CreatePort.  All messages that
     may have been attached to this port must have already been
     replied to.

INPUTS
     msgPort - A message port

SEE ALSO
     CreatePort
```

```
amiga.lib/DeleteTask                                    amiga.lib/DeleteTask

   NAME
        DeleteTask -- Delete a task created with CreateTask

   SYNOPSIS
        DeleteTask( task )
        void DeleteTask(struct Task *);

   FUNCTION
        This function simply calls exec/RemTask, deleting a task from the
        Exec task lists and automatically freeing any stack and
        structure memory allocated for it by CreateTask.

        Before deleting a task, you must first make sure that the task is
        not currently executing any system code which might try to signal
        the task after it is gone.

        This can be accomplished by stopping all sources that might reference
        the doomed task, then causing the subtask execute a Wait(0L).  Another
        option is to have have the task DeleteTask()/RemTask() itself.

   INPUTS
        task - pointer to a Task

   SEE ALSO
        CreateTask, exec/RemTask
```

```
amiga.lib/FastRand                                        amiga.lib/FastRand

   NAME
        FastRand - quickly generate a somewhat random integer

   SYNOPSIS
        number = FastRand(seed);
         ULONG FastRand(ULONG);

   FUNCTION
        C-implementation only.   Seed value is taken from stack, shifted
        left one position, exclusive-or'ed with hex value $1D872B41 and
        returned (D0).

   INPUTS
        seed - a 32-bit integer

   RESULT
        number - new random seed, a 32-bit value

   SEE ALSO
        RangeRand
```

```
NAME
     afp - Convert ASCII string variable into fast floating point

USAGE
    ffp_value = afp(string);

 FUNCTION
     Accepts the address of the ASCII string in C format that is
     converted into an FFP floating point number.

     The string is expected in this Format:
     {S}{digits}{'.'}{digits}{'E'}{S}{digits}
     <*******MANTISSA*******><***EXPONENT***>


     Syntax rules:
     Both signs are optional and are '+' or '-'. The mantissa must be
     present. The exponent need not be present. The mantissa may lead
     with a decimal point. The mantissa need not have a decimal point.
     Examples: All of these values represent the number fourty-two.
                  42            .042e3
                  42.          +.042e+03
                 +42.          0.000042e6
             0000042.00       420000e-4
                            420000.00e-0004

     Floating point range:
     Fast floating point supports the value zero and non-zero values
     within the following bounds -
                    18                        20
      9.22337177 x 10   > +number >  5.42101070 x 10
                    18                        -20
     -9.22337177 x 10   > -number > -2.71050535 x 10

     Precision:
     This conversion results in a 24 bit precision with guaranteed
     error less than or equal to one-half least significant bit.

     INPUTS
     string - Pointer to the ASCII string to be converted.


     OUTPUTS
     string - points to the character which terminated the scan
     equ - fast floating point equivalent
```



```
NAME
     arnd - ASCII round of the provided floating point string

USAGE
     arnd(place, exp, &string[0]);

FUNCTION
     Accepts an ASCII string representing an FFP floating point
     number, the binary representation of the exponent of said
     floating point number and the number of places to round to.
     A rounding process is initiated, either to the left or right
     of the decimal place and the result placed back at the
     input address defined by &string[0].

INPUTS
     place - integer representing number of decimal places to round to
     exp - integer representing exponent value of the ASCII string
     &string[0] - address where rounded ASCII string is to be placed
                  (16 bytes)

RESULT
     &string[0] - rounded ASCII string

BUGS
     None
```

```
NAME
     dbf - convert FFP dual-binary number to FFP format

USAGE
     fnum = dbf(exp, mant);

FUNCTION
     Accepts a dual-binary format (described below) floating point
     number and converts it to an FFP format floating point number.
     The dual-binary format is defined as:

             exp bit  16     = sign (0=>positive, 1=>negative)
             exp bits 15-0   = binary integer representing the base
                                    ten (10) exponent
             man             = binary integer mantissa

INPUTS
     exp - binary integer representing sign and exponent
     mant - binary integer representing the mantissa

RESULT
     fnum - converted FFP floating point format number

BUGS
     None
```



```
NAME
     fpa - convert fast floating point into ASCII string equivalent

USAGE
     exp = fpa(fnum, &string[0]);

FUNCTION
     Accepts an FFP number and the address of the ASCII string where it's
     onverted output is to be stored.  The number is converted to a NULL
     terminated ASCII string in and stored at the address provided.
     Additionally, the base ten (10) exponent in binary form is returned.

INPUTS
     fnum        - Motorola Fast Floating Point number
     &string[0]  - address for output of converted ASCII character string
                   (16 bytes)

RESULT
     &string[0]  - converted ASCII character string
     exp         - integer exponent value in binary form

BUGS
     None
```

```
NAME
     fpbcd - convert FFP floating point number to BCD format

USAGE
     fpbcd(fnum, &string[0]);

FUNCTION
     Accepts a floating point number and the address where the
     converted BCD data is to be stored.  The FFP number is
     converted and stored at the specified address in an ASCII
     form in accordance with the following format:

             MMMM S E S B

     Where:  M = Four bytes of BCD, each with two (2) digits of
                 the mantissa (8 digits)
             S = Sign of mantissa (0x00 = positive, 0xFF = negative)
             E = BCD byte for two (2) digit exponent
             S = Sign of exponent (0x00 = positive, 0xFF = negative)
             B = One (1) byte binary two's compliment representation
                     of the exponent

INPUTS
     fnum - floating point number
     &string[0] - address where converted BCD data is to be placed

RESULT
     &string[0] - converted BCD data
```



```
NAME
     NewList -- prepare a list structure for use

SYNOPSIS
     NewList(list*)
     void NewList(struct List *);

FUNCTION
     Prepare a List structure for use; the list will be empty and
     ready to use.

     This function prepares the lh_Head, lh_Tail and lh_TailPred fields.
     You are responsible for initializing lh_Type.  Assembly programmers
     will want to use the NEWLIST macro instead.

INPUTS
     list - Pointer to a List

SEE ALSO
     exec/lists.h
```

```
NAME
     printf - print a formatted output line to the standard output.

SYNOPSIS
     printf( formatstring [,value [,values] ] );

FUNCTION
     Format the output in accordance with specifications in the format
     string:

INPUTS
     formatstring - a pointer to a null-terminated string describing the
                    output data, and locations for parameter substitutions.
     value(s) - numeric variables or addresses of null-terminated strings
                to be added to the format information.

     The function printf can handle the following format conversions, in
     common with the normal C language call to printf:

     %c  - the next long word in the array is to be formatted
           as a character (8-bit) value
     %d  - the next long word in the array is to be formatted
           as a decimal number
     %x  - the next long word in the array is to be formatted
           as a hexadecimal number
     %s  - the next long word is the starting address of a
           null-terminated string of characters

 And "l" (small-L) character must be added between the % and the letter
 if the value is a long (32 bits) or if the compiler in use forces
 passed paramters to 32 bits.

 Floating point output is not supported.

 Following the %, you may also specify:

 o       an optional minus (-) sign that tells the formatter
         to left-justify the formatted item within the field
         width

 o       an optional field-width specifier... that is, how
         many spaces to allot for the full width of this
         item.  If the field width specifier begins with
         a zero (0), it means that leading spaces, ahead of
         the formatted item (usually a number) are to be
         zero-filled instead of blank-filled

 o       an optional period (.) that separates the width
         specifier from a maximum number of characters
         specifier

 o       an optional digit string (for %ls specifications
         only) that specifies the maximum number of characters
         to print from a string.

 See other books on C language programming for examples of the use
 of these formatting options (see "printf" in other books).

NOTE
     The global "_stdout" must be defined, and contain a pointer to
     a legal AmigaDOS file handle.  Using the standard Amiga startup
     module sets this up.  In other cases you will need to define
     stdout, and assign it to some reasonable value (like what the
     AmigaDOS Output() call returns).  This code would set it up:

     ULONG stdout;
             stdout=Output();
```



```
NAME
     RangeRand - To obtain a random number within a specific integer range
                 of 0 to value.

SYNOPSIS
     number = RangeRand(value);

FUNCTION
     RangeRand accepts a value from 1 to 65535, and returns a value
     within that range. (16-bit integer).  Note:  C-language implementation.

     Value is passed on stack as a 32-bit integer but used as though
     it is only a 16-bit integer.  Variable named RangeSeed is available
     beginning with V1.2 that contains the global seed value passed from
     call to call and thus can be changed by a program by declaring::

             extern ULONG RangeSeed;

INPUTS
     value - integer in the range of 1 to 65535.

RESULT
     number - pseudo random integer in the range of 1 to <value>.

SEE ALSO
     FastRand
```

amiga.lib/RemTOF


```
NAME
    RemTOF - Remove a task from the TopOfFrame interrupt server chain.

SYNOPSIS
    RemTOF(i);
    void RemTOF(struct Isrvstr *);

FUNCTION
    To remove a task from the vertical-blanking interval interrupt server
    chain.

INPUTS
    i - pointer to structure Isrvstr.

SEE ALSO
    AddTOF,graphics/graphinit.h
```

amiga.lib/sprintf


```
NAME
    sprintf - format a C-like string into a string buffer

SYNOPSIS
    sprintf( destination, formatstring [,value [, values] ] );

FUNCTION
    perform string formatting identical to printf, but direct the output
    into a specific destination in memory.  This uses the ROM version
     of printf, so it is very small.

     Assembly programmers can call this by placing values on the
     stack, followed by a pointer to the formatstring, followed
     by a pointer to the destination string.

INPUTS
    destination - the address of an area in memory into which the
                  formatted output is to be placed.
    formatstring - pointer to a null terminated string describing the
                   desired output formatting.
    value(s) - numeric information to be formatted into the output
               stream.

SEE ALSO
    printf, exec/RawDoFmt
```

```
NAMES
     fclose  - close file
     fgetc   - get a character from a file
     fprintf - format data to file (see exec.library/RawDoFmt)
     fputc   - put character to file
     fputs   - write string to file
     getchar - get a character from stdin
     printf  - put format data to stdout (see exec.library/RawDoFmt)
     putchar - put character to stdout
     puts    - put string to stdout, followed by newline
     sprintf - format data into string (see exec.library/RawDoFmt)

FUNCTION
     These functions work much like the standard C functions of the same
     names.  The file I/O functions all use non-buffered AmigaDOS
     filehandles, and must not be mixed with the file I/O of any C
     compiler.  The names of these function match those found in many
     standard C libraries, when a name conflict occurs, the function is
     generally taken from the FIRST library that was specified on the
     linker's command line.  Thus to use these functions, specify
     the amiga.lib library first.

     To get a suitable AmigaDOS filehandle, the AmigaDOS Open()
     function must be used.

     All of the functions that write to stdout expect an appropriate
     filehandle to have been set up ahead of time.  Depending on
     your C compiler and options, this may have been done by the
     startup code.  Or it can be done manually:

FROM C:
     extern ULONG stdout;
     /* Remove the extern if startup code did not define stdout */
             stdout=Output();

FROM ASSEMBLY:
             XDEF     _stdout
             DC.L     _stdout ;<- Place result of dos.library Output() here.
```

TABLE OF CONTENTS

NAME
    KCmpStr - compare two null terminated strings

SYNOPSIS
```
    mismatch = KCmpStr(string1, string2)
    D0                 A0       A1
```

FUNCTION
    string1 is compared to string2 using the ASCII coalating sequence. 0 indicates the strings are identical.

debug.lib/KGetChar

```
NAME
     KGetChar - get a character from the console
                (defaults to the serial port at 9600 baud)

SYNOPSIS
     char = KGetChar()
     D0

FUNCTION
     busy wait until a character arrives from the console.
     KGetChar is the assembly interface, _KGetChar and _kgetc
     are the C interfaces.
```

debug.lib/KGetNum

```
NAME
     KGetNum - get a number from the console

SYNOPSIS
     number = KGetNum()
     D0

FUNCTION
     get a signed decimal integer from the console.  This will busy
     wait until the number arrives.
```

```
debug.lib/KMayGetChar                                    debug.lib/KMayGetChar

   NAME
        KMayGetChar - return a character if present, but don't wait
                      (defaults to the serial port at 9600 baud)

   SYNOPSIS
        flagChar = KMayGetChar()
        D0

   FUNCTION
        return either a -1, saying that there is no character present, or
        whatever character was waiting.  KMayGetChar is the assembly
        interface,  _KMayGetChar is the C interface.
```

```
debug.lib/KPrintF                                            debug.lib/KPrintF

   NAME
        KPrintF - print formatted data to the console
                  (defaults to the serial port at 9600 baud)

   SYNOPSIS
        KPrintF("format string",values)
                 A0              A1

   FUNCTION
        print a formatted C-type string to the console.  See the
        exec RawDoFmt() call for the supported % formatting commands.

   INPUTS
        "format string" - A C style string with % commands to indicate
                          where paramters are to be inserted.
        values - A pointer to an array of paramters, to be inserted into
                 specified places in the string.

        KPrintf is the assembly interface that wants the two pointers
        in registers.  _KPrintF and _kprintf are the C interfaces that
        expect the format string on the stack, and the paramters on
        the stack above that.

   SEE ALSO
        exec.library/RawDoFmt, any C compiler's "printf" call.
```

```
NAME
     KPutChar - put a character to the console
                (defaults to the serial port at 9600 baud)

SYNOPSIS
     char = KPutChar(char)
     D0             D0

FUNCTION
     put a character to the console.  This function will not return
     until the character has been completely transmitted.

INPUTS
     KPutChar is the assembly interface, the character must be in D0.
     _KPutchar and _kputc are the C interfaces, the character must be
     a longword on the stack.
```



```
NAME
     KPutStr - put a string to the console
                (defaults to the serial port at 9600 baud)

SYNOPSIS
     KPutStr(string)
             A0

FUNCTION
     put a null terminated string to the console.  This function will
     not return until the string has been completely transmitted.

INPUTS
     KPutStr is the assembly interface, a string pointer must be in A0.
     _KPutStr and _kputs are the C interfaces, the string pointer must
     be on the stack.
```

```
/****** amiga.lib/CreateExtIO ***************************************/

#include "exec/types.h"
#include "exec/memory.h"
#include "exec/io.h"
/*
#include "proto/exec.h"
#include "functions.h"
*/


struct IORequest *CreateExtIO( ioReplyPort, size )
struct MsgPort *ioReplyPort;
ULONG  size;
{
struct IORequest *ioReq;

    if(! ioReplyPort )
        return(NULL);

    ioReq =
         (struct IORequest *)AllocMem( size, (ULONG)MEMF_CLEAR|MEMF_PUBLIC );

    if(!ioReq)
        return(NULL);

    ioReq->io_Message.mn_Node.ln_Type = NT_MESSAGE;
    ioReq->io_Message.mn_Length       = size;   /* save for later */
    ioReq->io_Message.mn_ReplyPort    = ioReplyPort;

    return( ioReq );
}

/****** amiga.lib/DeleteExtIO ***************************************/

void DeleteExtIO( ioExt )
struct IORequest *ioExt;
{
    /* try to make it hard to reuse the request by accident */
    ioExt->io_Message.mn_Node.ln_Type = -1;
    ioExt->io_Message.mn_ReplyPort    = (struct MsgPort *)-1;
    ioExt->io_Device                  = (struct Device *) -1;

    FreeMem( ioExt, (ULONG)ioExt->io_Message.mn_Length );
}
```



```
/****** amiga.lib/CreatePort ************************************/

#include "exec/types.h"
#include "exec/ports.h"
#include "exec/memory.h"
/*
#include "proto/exec.h"
#include "functions.h"
*/


/* Example only, please use the amiga.lib version where possible */

struct MsgPort *CreatePort(name, pri)
char *name;
LONG  pri;
{
int sigBit;
struct MsgPort *port;

    if ((sigBit = AllocSignal(-1L)) == -1)
        return(NULL);

    port = (struct MsgPort *)
      AllocMem((ULONG)sizeof(struct MsgPort),(ULONG)MEMF_CLEAR|MEMF_PUBLIC);

    if (!port)
        {
        FreeSignal(sigBit);
        return(NULL);
        }

    port-> mp_Node.ln_Name = name;
    port-> mp_Node.ln_Pri  = pri;
    port-> mp_Node.ln_Type = NT_MSGPORT;

    port-> mp_Flags   = PA_SIGNAL;
    port-> mp_SigBit  = sigBit;
    port-> mp_SigTask = (struct Task *)FindTask(0L); /* find THIS task */

    if (name)
        AddPort(port);
    else
        NewList(&(port-> mp_MsgList)); /* init message list */

    return(port);
}


/****** amiga.lib/DeletePort ************************************/

void DeletePort(port)
struct MsgPort *port;
{
    if ( port-> mp_Node.ln_Name ) /* if it was public... */
        RemPort(port);

    /* Make it difficult to re-use the port */
    port-> mp_SigTask        = (struct Task *) -1;
    port-> mp_MsgList.lh_Head = (struct Node *) -1;

    FreeSignal( port-> mp_SigBit );

    FreeMem( port, (ULONG)sizeof(struct MsgPort) );
}
```

```
/****** amiga.lib/CreateTask ***************************/

#include "exec/types.h"
#include "exec/tasks.h"
#include "exec/memory.h"

#include "proto/exec.h"
/*
#include "functions.h"
*/

/* the template for the mementries.  Unfortunately, this is hard to
 * do from C; mementries have unions, and they cannot be statically
 * initialized...
 *
 * In the interest of simplicity I recreate the mem entry structures
 * here with appropriate sizes.  We will copy this to a local
 * variable and set the stack size to what the user specified,
 * then attempt to actually allocate the memory.
 */
#define ME_TASK         0
#define ME_STACK        1
#define NUMENTRIES      2

struct FakeMemEntry {
    ULONG fme_Reqs;
    ULONG fme_Length;
};

struct FakeMemList {
    struct Node fml_Node;
    UWORD       fml_NumEntries;
    struct FakeMemEntry fml_ME[NUMENTRIES];
} TaskMemTemplate = {
    { 0 },                                          /* Node */
    NUMENTRIES,                                     /* num entries */
    {                                               /* actual entries: */
        { MEMF_PUBLIC | MEMF_CLEAR, sizeof( struct Task ) },    /* task */
        { MEMF_CLEAR,   0 }                                     /* stack */
    }
};



struct Task * CreateTask( name, pri, initPC, stackSize )
char  *name;
ULONG pri;
APTR  initPC;
ULONG stackSize;
{
struct Task *newTask;
struct FakeMemList fakememlist;
struct MemList *ml;

    /* round the stack up to longwords... */
    stackSize = (stackSize +3) & ~3;

    /*
     * This will allocate two chunks of memory: task of PUBLIC
     * and stack of PRIVATE
     */
    fakememlist = TaskMemTemplate;
    fakememlist.fml_ME[ME_STACK].fme_Length = stackSize;

    ml = (struct MemList *)AllocEntry( (struct MemList *)&fakememlist );

    if(! ml )
        return( NULL );
```



```

    /* set the stack accounting stuff */
    newTask = (struct Task *) ml->ml_ME[ME_TASK].me_Addr;

    newTask->tc_SPLower = ml->ml_ME[ME_STACK].me_Addr;
    newTask->tc_SPUpper = (APTR)((ULONG)(newTask->tc_SPLower) + stackSize);
    newTask->tc_SPReg   = newTask->tc_SPUpper;

    /* misc task data structures */
    newTask->tc_Node.ln_Type = NT_TASK;
    newTask->tc_Node.ln_Pri  = pri;
    newTask->tc_Node.ln_Name = name;

    /* add it to the tasks memory list */
    NewList( &newTask->tc_MemEntry );
    AddHead( &newTask->tc_MemEntry, (struct Node *)ml );

    /* add the task to the system -- use the default final PC */
    AddTask( newTask, initPC, 0L );
    return( newTask );
}


/****** amiga.lib/DeleteTask **********************************/

void DeleteTask( tc )
struct Task *tc;
{
    /* because we added a MemList structure to the tasks's TC_MEMENTRY
     * structure, all the memory will be freed up for us! */
    RemTask( tc );
}
```

```
****** amiga.lib/BeginIO ************************

        INCLUDE "exec/types.i"
        INCLUDE "exec/lists.i"
        INCLUDE "exec/io.i"

;Call the BeginIO vector of a device directly.  Much like exec/SendIO, but
;does not touch IO_FLAGS.
                SECTION _BeginIO
                XDEF    _BeginIO

_BeginIO:       move.l  4(sp),a1          ;Get IORequest pointer
                move.l  a6,-(a7)
                move.l  IO_DEVICE(a1),a6 ;Pointer to device
                jsr     DEV_BEGINIO(a6)  ;Jump to device's BEGINIO vector
                move.l  (a7)+,a6
                rts

                END

****** amiga.lib/NewList ************************

        INCLUDE "exec/types.i"
        INCLUDE "exec/lists.i"

                SECTION _NewList
                XDEF    _NewList

_NewList:       move.l  4(sp),a0         ;Get pointer from C's stack
                move.l  a0,d0            :pass the list back in D0

;This next code is equavalent to the NEWLIST macro
                clr.l   LH_TAIL(a0)
                move.l  a0,LH_TAILPRED(a0)
                addq.l  #LH_TAIL,a0      ;pointer plus 4...
                move.l  a0,-(a0)         ;...back down to LH_HEAD
                rts

                END
```

Section G

Sample Device, Sample Library

This section contains source code for a sample library and sample device. These examples can provide an excellent starting point in the creation of a custom device or library.

The library has two functions: one that adds two numbers together and one that doubles a number. Supporting interface code source is provided. The device is a complete 4 unit, static-sized RAM disk that works under the old (standard) filing system, the new V1.3 FastFileSystem, and has optional code to bind it to an AutoConfig device.

The examples have been assembled under the Metacomco assembler, V11.0 and under the CAPE assembler, V2.0.

```
*************************************************************************
*
*       Copyright (C) 1985, Commodore Amiga Inc.  All rights reserved.
*       Permission granted for non-commercial use
*
* asmsupp.i -- random low level assembly support routines
*              used by the Commodore sample Library & Device
*
*************************************************************************

CLEAR   MACRO           ;quick way to clear a D register on 68000
        MOVEQ   #0,\1
        ENDM

;BHS     MACRO
;        BCC.\0  \1 ;\0 is the extension used on the macro (such as ".s")
;        ENDM
;BLO     MACRO
;        BCS.\0  \1
;        ENDM

EVEN    MACRO           ; word align code stream
        DS.W    0
        ENDM

LINKSYS MACRO           ; link to a library without having to see a _LVO
        MOVE.L  A6,-(SP)
        MOVE.L  \2,A6
        JSR     _LVO\1(A6)
        MOVE.L  (SP)+,A6
        ENDM

CALLSYS MACRO           ; call a library via A6 without having to see _LVO
        JSR     _LVO\1(A6)
        ENDM

XLIB    MACRO           ; define a library reference without the _LVO
        XREF    _LVO\1
        ENDM
;
; Put a message to the serial port at 9600 baud.  Used as so:
;
;     PUTMSG   30,<'%s/Init: called'>
;
; Parameters can be printed out by pushing them on the stack and
; adding the appropriate C printf-style % formatting commands.
;
                XREF    KPutFmt
PUTMSG:         MACRO   * level,msg

                IFGE    INFO_LEVEL-\1

                PEA     subSysName(PC)
                MOVEM.L A0/A1/D0/D1,-(SP)
                LEA     msg\@(pc),A0    ;Point to static format string
                LEA     4*4(SP),A1      ;Point to args
                JSR     KPutFmt
                MOVEM.L (SP)+,D0/D1/A0/A1
                ADDQ.L  #4,SP
                BRA.S   end\@

msg\@           DC.B    \2
                DC.B    10
                DC.B    0
                DS.W    0
end\@
                ENDC
                ENDM
```



```
/*
 * Mountlist for manually mounting the sample ramdisk driver.
 *
 * F0: and F1: are set up for the V1.3 fast file system (FFS).
 * S2: and S3: are setup for the old file system (OFS).
 *
 *
 * After mounting, the drives must be formatted.  Be sure to
 * use the FFS flag when formatting the Fast File System
 * ramdrives:
 *
 *     ;make sure "ramdev.device" is in DEVS:
 *
 *     mount f0: from mydev-mountlist
 *     format drive f0: name "Zippy" FFS
 *
 */
F0:        Device = ramdev.device
           Unit   = 0
           LowCyl = 0 ; HighCyl = 14
           Surfaces  = 1
           Buffers = 1
           BlocksPerTrack = 10
           Flags  = 0
           Reserved = 2
           GlobVec = -1
           BufMemType = 0
           DosType = 0x444F5301
           StackSize = 4000
           FileSystem = l:fastfilesystem
#
F1:        Device = ramdev.device
           Unit   = 1
           LowCyl = 0 ; HighCyl = 14
           Surfaces  = 1
           Buffers = 1
           BlocksPerTrack = 10
           Flags  = 0
           Reserved = 2
           GlobVec = -1
           BufMemType = 0
           DosType = 0x444F5301
           StackSize = 4000
           FileSystem = l:fastfilesystem
#
S2:        Device = ramdev.device
           Unit   = 2
           Flags  = 0
           Surfaces  = 1
           BlocksPerTrack = 10
           Reserved = 1
           Interleave = 0
           LowCyl = 0  ;  HighCyl = 14
           Buffers = 1
           BufMemType = 0
#
S3:        Device = ramdev.device
           Unit   = 3
           Flags  = 0
           Surfaces  = 1
           BlocksPerTrack = 10
           Reserved = 1
           Interleave = 0
           LowCyl = 0  ;  HighCyl = 14
           Buffers = 1
           BufMemType = 0
#
```

```
**************************************************************************
*
*   Copyright (C) 1986,1988 Commodore Amiga Inc.  All rights reserved.
*   Permission granted for non-commercial use.
*
**************************************************************************
*
* ramdev.asm -- Skeleton device code.
*
* A sample 4 unit ramdisk that can be bound to an expansion slot device,
* or used without.  Works with the Fast File System.
* This code is required reading for device driver writers.  It contains
* information not found elsewhere.
*
* This example includes a task, though a task is not actually needed for
* a simple ram disk.  Unlike a single set of hardware registers that
* may need to be shared by multiple tasks, ram can be freely shared.
* This example does not show arbitration of hardware resources.
*
* Tested with CAPE and Metacomco
*
*           Based on mydev.asm
*           10/07/86 Modified by Lee Erickson to be a simple disk device
*                    using RAM to simulate a disk.
*           02/02/88 Modified by C. Scheppner, renamed ramdev
*           09/28/88 Repaired by Bryce Nesbitt for new release
*           11/01/88 More clarifications
**************************************************************************

   SECTION firstsection

   NOLIST
   include "exec/types.i"
   include "exec/devices.i"
   include "exec/initializers.i"
   include "exec/memory.i"
   include "exec/resident.i"
   include "exec/io.i"
   include "exec/ables.i"
   include "exec/errors.i"
   include "exec/tasks.i"
   include "hardware/intbits.i"
   IFNE AUTOMOUNT
   include "libraries/expansion.i"
   include "libraries/configvars.i"
   include "libraries/configregs.i"
   ENDC

   include "asmsupp.i"  ;standard asmsupp.i, same as used for library
   LIST
   include "ramdev.i"


ABSEXECBASE equ 4   ;Absolute location of the pointer to exec.library base


   ;------ These don't have to be external, but it helps some
   ;------ debuggers to have them globally visible
   XDEF   Init
   XDEF   Open
   XDEF   Close
   XDEF   Expunge
   XDEF   Null
   XDEF   myName
   XDEF   BeginIO
   XDEF   AbortIO

   ;Pull these _LVOs in from amiga.lib
   XLIB   AddIntServer
```



```
   XLIB   RemIntServer
   XLIB   Debug
   XLIB   InitStruct
   XLIB   OpenLibrary
   XLIB   CloseLibrary
   XLIB   Alert
   XLIB   FreeMem
   XLIB   Remove
   XLIB   AddPort
   XLIB   AllocMem
   XLIB   AddTask
   XLIB   PutMsg
   XLIB   RemTask
   XLIB   ReplyMsg
   XLIB   Signal
   XLIB   GetMsg
   XLIB   Wait
   XLIB   WaitPort
   XLIB   AllocSignal
   XLIB   SetTaskPri
   XLIB   GetCurrentBinding     ;Use to get list of boards for this driver
   XLIB   MakeDosNode
   XLIB   AddDosNode
   XLIB   CopyMemQuick  ;Highly optimized copy function from exec.library

   INT_ABLES        ;Macro from exec/ables.i


;-----------------------------------------------------------------------
; The first executable location.  This should return an error
; in case someone tried to run you as a program (instead of
; loading you as a device).

FirstAddress:
        moveq   #-1,d0
        rts

;-----------------------------------------------------------------------
; A romtag structure.  You load module will be scanned for
; this structure to discover magic constants about you
; (such as where to start running you from...).
;-----------------------------------------------------------------------

   ; Most people will not need a priority and should leave it at zero.
   ; the RT_PRI field is used for configuring the roms.  Use "mods" from
   ; wack to look at the other romtags in the system
MYPRI   EQU   0


initDDescrip:
               ;STRUCTURE RT,0
     DC.W    RTC_MATCHWORD      ; UWORD RT_MATCHWORD (Magic cookie)
     DC.L    initDDescrip       ; APTR  RT_MATCHTAG  (Back pointer)
     DC.L    EndCode            ; APTR  RT_ENDSKIP   (To end of this hunk)
     DC.B    RTF_AUTOINIT       ; UBYTE RT_FLAGS     (magic-see "Init:")
     DC.B    VERSION            ; UBYTE RT_VERSION
     DC.B    NT_DEVICE          ; UBYTE RT_TYPE
     DC.B    MYPRI              ; BYTE  RT_PRI
     DC.L    myName             ; APTR  RT_NAME
     DC.L    idString           ; APTR  RT_IDSTRING
     DC.L    Init               ; APTR  RT_INIT
               ; LABEL RT_SIZE


   ;This name for debugging use
   IFNE INFO_LEVEL  ;If any debugging enabled at all
subSysName:
    dc.b    "ramdev",0
   ENDC
```

```
    ; this is the name that the device will have
myName:       MYDEVNAME

 IFNE  AUTOMOUNT
ExLibName     dc.b 'expansion.library',0    ; Expansion Library Name
 ENDC

    ; a major version number.
VERSION:     EQU    1

    ; A particular revision.  This should uniquely identify the bits in the
    ; device.  I use a script that advances the revision number each time
    ; I recompile.  That way there is never a question of which device
    ; that really is.
REVISION:    EQU    30

    ; this is an identifier tag to help in supporting the device
    ; format is 'name version.revision (dd MON yyyy)',<cr>,<lf>,<null>
idString:    dc.b    'ramdev 1.30 (1 Nov 1988)',13,10,0

    ; force word alignment
    ds.w    0


    ; The romtag specified that we were "RTF_AUTOINIT".  This means
    ; that the RT_INIT structure member points to one of these
    ; tables below.  If the AUTOINIT bit was not set then RT_INIT
    ; would point to a routine to run.

Init:
    DC.L    MyDev_Sizeof        ; data space size
    DC.L    funcTable           ; pointer to function initializers
    DC.L    dataTable           ; pointer to data initializers
    DC.L    initRoutine         ; routine to run


funcTable:

    ;------ standard system routines
    dc.l    Open
    dc.l    Close
    dc.l    Expunge
    dc.l    Null        ;Reserved for future use!

    ;------ my device definitions
    dc.l    BeginIO
    dc.l    AbortIO

    ;------ custom extended functions
    dc.l    FunctionA
    dc.l    FunctionB

    ;------ function table end marker
    dc.l    -1


    ;The data table initializes static data structures. The format is
    ;specified in exec/InitStruct routine's manual pages.  The
    ;INITBYTE/INITWORD/INITLONG macros are in the file "exec/initializers.i".
    ;The first argument is the offset from the device base for this
    ;byte/word/long. The second argument is the value to put in that cell.
    ;The table is null terminated
    ;
dataTable:
    INITBYTE    LN_TYPE,NT_DEVICE         ;Must be LN_TYPE!
    INITLONG    LN_NAME,myName
    INITBYTE    LIB_FLAGS,LIBF_SUMUSED!LIBF_CHANGED
    INITWORD    LIB_VERSION,VERSION
```



```
   INITWORD    LIB_REVISION,REVISION
   INITLONG    LIB_IDSTRING,idString
   DC.L    0


;----------------------------------------------------------------------
; FOR RTF_AUTOINIT:
;   This routine gets called after the device has been allocated.
;   The device pointer is in D0.  The AmigaDOS segment list is in a0.
;   If it returns it's device pointer, then the device will be linked
;   into the device list.  If it returns NULL, then the device
;   will be unloaded.
;
; IMPORTANT:
;   If you don't use the "RTF_AUTOINIT" feature, there is an additional
;   caveat.  If you allocate memory in your Open function, remember that
;   allocating memory can cause an Expunge... including an expunge of your
;   device.  This must not be fatal.  The easy solution is don't add your
;   device to the list until after it is ready for action.
;
; This call is single-threaded; please read the description for
; "Open" below.
;
initRoutine:

; Register Usage
; ==============
; a3 -- Points to temporary RAM
; a4 -- Expansion library base
; a5 -- device pointer
; a6 -- Exec base
;
;----------------------------------------------------------------------
   ;------ get the device pointer into a convenient A register
   PUTMSG   5,<'%s/Init: called'>
   movem.l  d1-d7/a0-a5,-(sp)    ; Preserve ALL modified registers
   move.l   d0,a5

   ;------ save a pointer to exec
   move.l   a6,md_SysLib(a5)

   ;------ save a pointer to our loaded code
   move.l   a0,md_SegList(a5)

**************************************************************************
*
* Here starts the AutoConfig stuff.  Normally you would put this driver
* in the expansion drawer, and be called when binddrivers finds a board
* that matches your driver (the "PRODUCT=" in TOOLTYPES).
* GetCurrentBinding() would return your board.
*
 IFNE  AUTOMOUNT

   lea.l     ExLibName,A1        ; Get expansion lib. name
   moveq.l   #0,D0
   CALLSYS   OpenLibrary         ; Open the expansion library
   tst.l     D0
   beq       Init_Error

   ;------ init_OpSuccess:
   move.l    D0,A4             ;[expansionbase to A4]
   moveq     #0,D3
   lea       md_Base(A5),A0    ; Get the Current Bindings
   moveq     #4,D0             ; Just get address (length = 4 bytes)
   LINKLIB   _LVOGetCurrentBinding,A4
   move.l    md_Base(A5),D0       ; Get start of list
   tst.l     D0           ; If controller not found
   beq       Init_End       ; Exit and unload driver
```

```
   PUTMSG     10,<'%s/Init: GetCurrentBinding returned non-zero'>
   move.l     D0,A0           ; Get config structure address
   move.l     cd_BoardAddr(A0),md_Base(A5); Save board base address
   bclr.b     #CDB_CONFIGME,cd_Flags(A0); Mark board as configured

;----------------------------------------------------------------------
;
; Here we build a packet describing the characteristics of our disk to
; pass to AmigaDOS.  This serves the same purpose as a "mount" command
; of this device would.  For disks, it might be useful to actually
; get this information right from the disk itself.  Just as mount,
; it could be for multiple partitions on the single physical device.
; For this example, we will simply hard code the appropriate parameters.
;
; The AddDosNode call adds things to dos's list without needing to
; use mount.  We'll mount all 4 of our units whenever we are
; started.
;
;----------------------------------------------------------------------

;!!! If your card was successfully configured, you can mount the
;!!! units as DOS nodes

   ;------    Allocate temporary RAM to build MakeDosNode parameter packet
   move.l     #MEMF_CLEAR!MEMF_PUBLIC,dl
   move.l     #mdn_Sizeof,d0    ; Enough room for our parameter packet
   CALLSYS    AllocMem
   move.l     d0,a3

   ;-----   Use InitStruct to initialize the constant portion of packet
   move.l     d0,a2           ; Point to memory to initialize
   moveq.l    #0,d0           ; Don't need to re-zero it
   lea.l      mdn_Init(pc),Al
   CALLSYS    InitStruct

   lea        mdn_dName(a3),a0      ; Get addr of Device name
   move.l     a0,mdn_dosName(a3)    ;   and save in environment

   moveq      #0,d6              ; Now tell AmigaDOS about all units UNITNUM
Uloop:
   move.b     d6,d0             ; Get unit number
   add.b      #$30,d0           ; Make ASCII, minus 1
   move.b     d0,mdn_dName+2(a3)    ;   and store in name
   move.l     d6,mdn_unit(a3)       ;  Store unit # in environment

;
;! Before adding to the dos list, you should really check if you
;! are about to cause a name collision.  This example does not.
;

   move.l     a3,a0
   LINKLIB    _LVOMakeDosNode,a4    ; Build AmigaDOS structures
   ;This can fail, but so what?
   move.l     d0,a0                 ; Get deviceNode address
   moveq.l    #0,d0                 ; Set device priority to 0
   moveq.l    #0,dl
*  moveq.l    #ADNF_STARTPROC,dl      ; See note below
   ;It's ok to pass a zero in here
   LINKLIB    _LVOAddDosNode,a4


; ADNF_STARTPROC will work, but only if dn_SegList is filled in
; in the SegPtr of the handler task.


   addq       #1,d6             ; Bump unit number
   cmp.b      #MD_NUMUNITS,d6
   bls.s      Uloop             ; Loop until all units installed
```



```
   move.l   a3,al        ; Return RAM to system
   move.l   #mdn_Sizeof,d0
   CALLSYS  FreeMem

Init_End:

   move.l   a4,al        ; Now close expansion library
   CALLSYS  CloseLibrary
   ;
   ; You would normally set d0 to a NULL if your initialization failed,
   ; but I'm not doing that for this demo, since it is unlikely
   ; you actually have a board with any particular manufacturer ID
   ; installed when running this demo.
   ;
*************************************************************************
  ENDC

   move.l   a5,d0
Init_Error:
   movem.l  (sp)+,dl-d7/a0-a5
   rts


;----------------------------------------------------------------------
;
; Here begins the system interface commands.  When the user calls
; OpenDevice/CloseDevice/RemDevice, this eventually gets translated
; into a call to the following routines (Open/Close/Expunge).
; Exec has already put our device pointer in a6 for us.
;
; IMPORTANT:
;   These calls are guaranteed to be single-threaded; only one task
;   will execute your Open/Close/Expunge at a time.
;
;   For Kickstart V33/34, the single-threading method involves "Forbid".
;   There is a good chance this will change.  Anything inside your
;   Open/Close/Expunge that causes a direct or indirect Wait() will break
;   the Forbid().  If the Forbid() is broken, some other task might
;   manage to enter your Open/Close/Expunge code at the same time.
;   Take care!
;
; Since exec has turned off task switching while in these routines
; (via Forbid/Permit), we should not take too long in them.
;
;----------------------------------------------------------------------

   ; Open sets the IO_ERROR field on an error.  If it was successfull,
   ; we should also set up the IO_UNIT field.

Open:       ; ( device:a6, iob:al, unitnum:d0, flags:dl )
   PUTMSG   20,<'%s/Open: called'>
   movem.l  d2/a2/a3/a4,-(sp)

   move.l   al,a2        ; save the iob

   ;------ see if the unit number is in range   *!* UNIT 0 to 3 *!*
;  subq     #1,d0       ; Unit ZERO IS allowed!
   cmp.l    #MD_NUMUNITS,d0
   bcc.s    Open_Range_Error    ; unit number out of range (BHS)

   ;------ see if the unit is already initialized
   move.l   d0,d2        ; save unit number
   lsl.l    #2,d0
   lea.l    md_Units(a6,d0.l),a4
   move.l   (a4),d0
   bne.s    Open_UnitOK

   ;------ try and conjure up a unit
   bsr      InitUnit    ;scratch:a3 unitnum:d2 devpoint:a6
```

```
   ;------ see if it initialized OK
   move.l   (a4),d0
   beq.s    Open_Error

Open_UnitOK:
   move.l   d0,a3       ; unit pointer in a3
   move.l   d0,IO_UNIT(a2)

   ;------ mark us as having another opener
   addq.w   #1,LIB_OPENCNT(a6)
   addq.w   #1,UNIT_OPENCNT(a3)      ;Internal bookkeeping

   ;------ prevent delayed expunges
   bclr     #LIBB_DELEXP,md_Flags(a6)

   moveq.l  #0,d0
   clr.b    IO_ERROR(a2)

Open_End:

   movem.l  (sp)+,d2/a2/a3/a4
   rts

Open_Range_Error:
Open_Error:
   moveq    #IOERR_OPENFAIL,d0
   move.b   d0,IO_ERROR(a2)
   PUTMSG   2,<'%s/Open: failed'>
   bra.s    Open_End


   ; There are two different things that might be returned from the Close
   ; routine.  If the device wishes to be unloaded, then Close should return
   ; the segment list (as given to Init).  Otherwise close MUST return NULL.

Close:       ; ( device:a6, iob:a1 )
   movem.l  d1/a2-a3,-(sp)
   PUTMSG   20,<'%s/Close: called'>

   move.l   a1,a2

   move.l   IO_UNIT(a2),a3

   ;------ make sure the iob is not used again
   ;------ with a -1 in IO_DEVICE, any BeginIO() attempt will
   ;------ immediatly crash (which is better than a subtle corruption
   ;------ that will lead to hard-to-trace crashes.
   moveq.l  #-1,d0
   move.l   d0,IO_UNIT(a2)       ;We're closed...
   move.l   d0,IO_DEVICE(a2)     ;customers not welcome at this IORequest!!

   ;------ see if the unit is still in use
   subq.w   #1,UNIT_OPENCNT(a3)

;!!!!!! Since this example is a RAM disk (and we don't want the contents to
;!!!!!! disappear between opens, ExpungeUnit will be skipped here.  It would
;!!!!!! be used for drivers of "real" devices
;!!!!!!   bne.s   Close_Device
;!!!!!!   bsr     ExpungeUnit

Close_Device:
   ;------ mark us as having one fewer openers
   moveq.l #0,d0
   subq.w  #1,LIB_OPENCNT(a6)

   ;------ see if there is anyone left with us open
   bne.s   Close_End
```



```
   ;------ see if we have a delayed expunge pending
   btst     #LIBB_DELEXP,md_Flags(a6)
   beq.s    Close_End

   ;------ do the expunge
   bsr      Expunge

Close_End:
   movem.l   (sp)+,d1/a2-a3
   rts                            ;MUST return either zero or the SegList!!!


   ; There are two different things that might be returned from the Expunge
   ; routine.  If the device is no longer open then Expunge should return the
   ; segment list (as given to Init).  Otherwise Expunge should set the
   ; delayed expunge flag and return NULL.
   ;
   ; One other important note: because Expunge is called from the memory
   ; allocator, it may NEVER Wait() or otherwise take long time to complete.

Expunge:    ; ( device: a6 )
   PUTMSG   10,<'%s/Expunge: called'>

   movem.l  d1/d2/a5/a6,-(sp)    ; Save ALL modified registers
   move.l   a6,a5
   move.l   md_SysLib(a5),a6

   ;------ see if anyone has us open
   tst.w    LIB_OPENCNT(a5)
;!!!!!  The following line is commented out for this RAM disk demo, since
;!!!!!  we don't want the RAM to be freed after FORMAT, for example.
;   beq     1$

   ;------ it is still open.  set the delayed expunge flag
   bset     #LIBB_DELEXP,md_Flags(a5)
   CLEAR    d0
   bra.s    Expunge_End

1$:
   ;------ go ahead and get rid of us.  Store our seglist in d2
   move.l    md_SegList(a5),d2

   ;------ unlink from device list
   move.l     a5,a1
   CALLSYS    Remove               ;Remove first (before FreeMem)

   ;
   ; device specific closings here...
   ;

   ;------ free our memory
   CLEAR     d0
   CLEAR     d1
   move.l    a5,a1
   move.w    LIB_NEGSIZE(a5),d1
   sub.w     d1,a1                 ;Calculate base of functions
   add.w     LIB_POSSIZE(a5),d0
   add.l     d1,d0                 ;Calculate size of functions + data area

   CALLSYS  FreeMem

   ;------ set up our return value
   move.l   d2,d0

Expunge_End:
   movem.l  (sp)+,d1/d2/a5/a6
   rts
```

```
Null:
   PUTMSG  1,<'%s/Null: called'>
   CLEAR   d0
   rts      ;The Null function MUST return NULL.


;
;Two "do nothing" device-specific functions
;
FunctionA:
    add.l   d1,d0   ;Add
    rts
FunctionB:
    add.l   d0,d0   ;Double
    rts



InitUnit:   ; ( d2:unit number, a3:scratch, a6:devptr )
   PUTMSG   30,<'%s/InitUnit: called'>
   movem.l  d2-d4/a2,-(sp)

   ;------ allocate unit memory
   move.l   #MyDevUnit_Sizeof,d0
   move.l   #MEMF_PUBLIC!MEMF_CLEAR,d1
   LINKSYS  AllocMem,md_SysLib(a6)
   tst.l    d0
   beq      InitUnit_End
   move.l   d0,a3

   moveq.l  #0,d0          ; Don't need to re-zero it
   move.l   a3,a2          ; InitStruct is initializing the UNIT
   lea.l    mdu_Init(pc),A1
   LINKSYS  InitStruct,md_SysLib(a6)

   ;!! IMPORTANT !!
   move.l   #42414400,mdu_RAM(a3)   ;Mark offset zero as ASCII "BAD "
   ;!! IMPORTANT !!

   move.b   d2,mdu_UnitNum(a3)      ;initialize unit number
   move.l   a6,mdu_Device(a3)       ;initialize device pointer

   ;------ start up the unit task.  We do a trick here --
   ;------ we set his message port to PA_IGNORE until the
   ;------ new task has a change to set it up.
   ;------ We cannot go to sleep here: it would be very nasty
   ;------ if someone else tried to open the unit
   ;------ (exec's OpenDevice has done a Forbid() for us --
   ;------ we depend on this to become single threaded).

   ;------ Initialize the stack information
   lea      mdu_stack(a3),a0          ; Low end of stack
   move.l   a0,mdu_tcb+TC_SPLOWER(a3)
   lea      MYPROCSTACKSIZE(a0),a0    ; High end of stack
   move.l   a0,mdu_tcb+TC_SPUPPER(a3)
   move.l   a3,-(A0)                  ; argument -- unit ptr (send on stack)
   move.l   a0,mdu_tcb+TC_SPREG(a3)
   lea      mdu_tcb(a3),a0
   move.l   a0,MP_SIGTASK(a3)

   IFGE INFO_LEVEL-30
       move.l   a0,-(SP)
       move.l   a3,-(SP)
       PUTMSG   30,<'%s/InitUnit, unit= %lx, task=%lx'>
       addq.l   #8,sp
   ENDC

   ;------ initialize the unit's message port's list
   lea      MP_MSGLIST(a3),a0
```



```
   NEWLIST  a0                    ;<- IMPORTANT! Lists MUST! have NEWLIST
                                  ;work magic on them before use.  (AddPort()
                                  ;can do this for you)

   IFD   INTRRUPT
   move.l   a3,mdu_is+IS_DATA(a3)   ; Pass unit addr to interrupt server
   ENDC

;   Startup the task
   lea      mdu_tcb(a3),a1
   lea      Task_Begin(PC),a2
   move.l   a3,-(sp)        ; Preserve UNIT pointer
   lea      -1,a3           ; generate address error
                            ; if task ever "returns" (we RemTask() it
                            ; to get rid of it...)
   CLEAR    d0
   PUTMSG   30,<'%s/About to add task'>
   LINKSYS AddTask,md_SysLib(a6)
   move.l   (sp)+,a3        ; restore UNIT pointer

   ;------ mark us as ready to go
   move.l   d2,d0           ; unit number
   lsl.l    #2,d0
   move.l   a3,md_Units(a6,d0.l)   ; set unit table
   PUTMSG   30,<'%s/InitUnit: ok'>

InitUnit_End:
   movem.l   (sp)+,d2-d4/a2
   rts



FreeUnit:   ; ( a3:unitptr, a6:deviceptr )
   move.l   a3,a1
   move.l   #MyDevUnit_Sizeof,d0
   LINKSYS  FreeMem,md_SysLib(a6)
   rts



ExpungeUnit:   ; ( a3:unitptr, a6:deviceptr )
   PUTMSG   10,<'%s/ExpungeUnit: called'>
   move.l   d2,-(sp)

;
; If you can expunge you unit, and each unit has it's own interrupts,
; you must remember to remove its interrupt server
;

   IFD   INTRRUPT
   lea.l    mdu_is(a3),a1              ; Point to interrupt structure
   moveq    #INTB_PORTS,d0             ; Portia interrupt bit 3
   LINKSYS RemIntServer,md_SysLib(a6) ;Now remove the interrupt server
   ENDC

   ;------ get rid of the unit's task.  We know this is safe
   ;------ because the unit has an open count of zero, so it
   ;------ is 'guaranteed' not in use.
   lea    mdu_tcb(a3),a1
   LINKSYS RemTask,md_SysLib(a6)

   ;------ save the unit number
   CLEAR    d2
   move.b   mdu_UnitNum(a3),d2

   ;------ free the unit structure.
   bsr      FreeUnit

   ;------ clear out the unit vector in the device
```

```
    lsl.l   #2,d2
    clr.l   md_Units(a6,d2.l)

    move.l  (sp)+,d2
    rts



;------------------------------------------------------------------------
;
; here begins the device specific functions
;
;------------------------------------------------------------------------
; cmdtable is used to look up the address of a routine that will
; implement the device command.
;
; NOTE: the "extended" commands (ETD_READ/ETD_WRITE) have bit 15 set!
; We deliberately refuse to operate on such commands.  However a driver
; that supports removable media may want to implement this.  One
; open issue is the handling of the "seclabel" area. It is probably
; best to reject any command with a non-null "seclabel" pointer.
;
cmdtable:
    DC.L   Invalid         ;$00000001  ;0  CMD_INVALID
    DC.L   MyReset         ;$00000002  ;1  CMD_RESET
    DC.L   RdWrt           ;$00000004  ;2  CMD_READ        (\/common)
    DC.L   RdWrt           ;$00000008  ;3  CMD_WRITE       (/\common)  ETD_
    DC.L   Update          ;$00000010  ;4  CMD_UPDATE      (NO-OP)     ETD_
    DC.L   Clear           ;$00000020  ;5  CMD_CLEAR       (NO-OP)     ETD_
    DC.L   MyStop          ;$00000040  ;6  CMD_STOP                    ETD_
    DC.L   Start           ;$00000080  ;7  CMD_START
    DC.L   Flush           ;$00000100  ;8  CMD_FLUSH
    DC.L   Motor           ;$00000200  ;9  TD_MOTOR        (NO-OP)     ETD_
    DC.L   Seek            ;$00000400  ;A  TD_SEEK         (NO-OP)     ETD_
    DC.L   RdWrt           ;$00000800  ;B  TD_FORMAT       (Same as write)
    DC.L   MyRemove        ;$00001000  ;C  TD_REMOVE       (NO-OP)
    DC.L   ChangeNum       ;$00002000  ;D  TD_CHANGENUM    (returns 0)
    DC.L   ChangeState     ;$00004000  ;E  TD_CHANGESTATE  (returns 0)
    DC.L   ProtStatus      ;$00008000  ;F  TD_PROTSTATUS   (returns 0)
    DC.L   RawRead         ;$00010000  ;10 TD_RAWREAD      (INVALID)
    DC.L   RawWrite        ;$00020000  ;11 TD_RAWWRITE     (INVALID)
    DC.L   GetDriveType    ;$00040000  ;12 TD_GETDRIVETYPE (Returns 1)
    DC.L   GetNumTracks    ;$00080000  ;13 TD_GETNUMTRACKS (Returns NUMTRKS)
    DC.L   AddChangeInt    ;$00100000  ;14 TD_ADDCHANGEINT (NO-OP)
    DC.L   RemChangeInt    ;$00200000  ;15 TD_REMCHANGEINT (NO-OP)
cmdtable_end:

; this define is used to tell which commands should be handled
; immediately (on the caller's schedule).
;
; The immediate commands are Invalid, Reset, Stop, Start, Flush
;
; Note that this method limits you to just 32 device specific commands,
; which may not be enough.
;IMMEDIATES    EQU   %00000000000000000000000111000011
;;                    --------========--------========
;;                    FEDCBA9876543210FEDCBA9876543210

;;An alternate version.  All commands that are trivially short
;;and %100 reentrant are included.  This way you won't get the
;;task switch overhead for these commands.
;;
IMMEDIATES    EQU   %11111111111111111111011111110011
;                   --------========--------========
;                   FEDCBA9876543210FEDCBA9876543210

    IFD    INTRRUPT    ; if using interrupts,
; These commands can NEVER be done "immediately" if using interrupts,
; since they would "wait" for the interrupt forever!
```



```
; Read, Write, Format
NEVERIMMED    EQU    $0000080C
    ENDC


;--------------------------------
; BeginIO starts all incoming io.  The IO is either queued up for the
; unit task or processed immediately.
;
;
; BeginIO often is given the responsibility of making devices single
; threaded... so two tasks sending commands at the same time don't cause
; a problem.  Once this has been done, the command is dispatched via
; PerformIO.
;
; There are many ways to do the threading.  This example uses the
; UNITB_ACTIVE bit.  Be sure this is good enough for your device before
; using!  Any method is ok.  If immediate access can not be obtained, the
; request is queued for later processing.
;
; Some IO requests do not need single threading, these can be performed
; immediatley.
;
; IMPORTANT:
;   The exec WaitIO() function uses the IORequest node type (LN_TYPE)
;   as a flag.  If set to NT_MESSAGE, it assumes the request is
;   still pending and will wait.  If set to NT_REPLYMSG, it assumes the
;   request is finished.  It's the responsibility of the device driver
;   to set the node type to NT_MESSAGE before returning to the user.
;
BeginIO:    ; ( iob: a1, device:a6 )

    IFGE INFO_LEVEL-1
        bchg.b  #1,$bfe001  ;Blink the power LED
    ENDC
    IFGE INFO_LEVEL-3
     clr.l     -(sp)
     move.w    IO_COMMAND(a1),2(sp)  ;Get entire word
     PUTMSG    3,<'%s/BeginIO  --  %ld'>
     addq.l    #4,sp
    ENDC

    movem.l   d1/a0/a3,-(sp)

    move.b   #NT_MESSAGE,LN_TYPE(a1) ;So WaitIO() is guaranteed to work
    move.l   IO_UNIT(a1),a3          ;bookkeeping -> what unit to play with
    move.w   IO_COMMAND(a1),d0

    ;Do a range check & make sure ETD_XXX type requests are rejected
    cmp.w    #MYDEV_END,d0         ;Compare all 16 bits
    bcc      BeginIO_NoCmd         ;no, reject it.  (bcc=bhs - unsigned)

    ;------ process all immediate commands no matter what
    move.l   #IMMEDIATES,d1
    DISABLE  a0                    ;<-- Ick, nasty stuff, but needed here.
    btst.l   d0,d1
    bne      BeginIO_Immediate

    IFD   INTRRUPT    ; if using interrupts,
     ;------ queue all NEVERIMMED commands no matter what
     move.w   #NEVERIMMED,d1
     btst     d0,d1
     bne.s    BeginIO_QueueMsg
    ENDC


    ;------ see if the unit is STOPPED.  If so, queue the msg.
    btst     #MDUB_STOPPED,UNIT_FLAGS(a3)
    bne      BeginIO_QueueMsg
```

```
    ;------ This is not an immediate command.  See if the device is
    ;------ busy.  If the device is not, do the command on the
    ;------ user schedule.  Else fire up the task.
    ;------ This type of arbitration is not really needed for a ram
    ;------ disk, but is essential for a device to reliably work
    ;------ with shared hardware
    ;------
    ;------ When the lines below are ";" commented out, the task gets
    ;------ a better workout.  When the lines are active, the calling
    ;------ process is usually used for the operation.
    ;------
    ;------ REMEMBER:::: Never Wait() on the user's schedule in BeginIO()!
    ;------ The only exception is when the user has indicated it is ok
    ;------ by setting the "quick" bit.  Since this device copies from
    ;------ ram that never needs to be waited for, this subtlely may not
    ;------ be clear.
    ;------
    bset    #UNITB_ACTIVE,UNIT_FLAGS(a3)    ;<---- comment out these
    beq.s   BeginIO_Immediate               ;<---- lines to test task.


    ;------ we need to queue the device.  mark us as needing
    ;------ task attention.  Clear the quick flag
BeginIO_QueueMsg:
    bset    #UNITB_INTASK,UNIT_FLAGS(a3)
    bclr    #IOB_QUICK,IO_FLAGS(al)    ;We did NOT complete this quickly
    ENABLE  a0


    IFGE INFO_LEVEL-250
     move.l  al,-(sp)
     move.l  a3,-(sp)
     PUTMSG  250,<'%s/PutMsg: Port=%lx Message=%lx'>
     addq.l  #8,sp
    ENDC

    move.l  a3,a0
    LINKSYS  PutMsg,md_SysLib(a6)    ;Port=a0, Message=al
    bra.s   BeginIO_End
    ;----- return to caller before completing


    ;------ Do it on the schedule of the calling process
    ;------
BeginIO_Immediate:
    ENABLE  a0
    bsr.s   PerformIO

BeginIO_End:
    PUTMSG  200,<'%s/BeginIO_End'>
    movem.l (sp)+,dl/a0/a3
    rts

BeginIO_NoCmd:
    move.b  #IOERR_NOCMD,IO_ERROR(al)
    bra.s   BeginIO_End


;
; PerformIO actually dispatches an io request.  It might be called from
; the task, or directly from BeginIO (thus on the callers's schedule)
;
; It expects a3 to already
; have the unit pointer in it.  a6 has the device pointer (as always).
; al has the io request.  Bounds checking has already been done on
; the I/O Request.
;
```



```
PerformIO:    ; ( iob:al, unitptr:a3, devptr:a6 )
    IFGE INFO_LEVEL-150
     clr.l    -(sp)
     move.w   IO_COMMAND(al),2(sp)  ;Get entire word
     PUTMSG   150,<'%s/PerformIO -- %ld'>
     addq.l   #4,sp
    ENDC

    moveq   #0,d0
    move.b  d0,IO_ERROR(Al)       ; No error so far
    move.b  IO_COMMAND+l(al),d0  ;Look only at low byte
    lsl.w   #2,d0                 ; Multiply by 4 to get table offset
    lea.l   cmdtable(pc),a0
    move.l  0(a0,d0.w),a0

    jmp     (a0)    ;iob:al  unit:a3  devprt:a6



;
; TermIO sends the IO request back to the user.  It knows not to mark
; the device as inactive if this was an immediate request or if the
; request was started from the server task.
;

TermIO:       ; ( iob:al, unitptr:a3, devptr:a6 )
    PUTMSG  160,<'%s/TermIO'>
    move.w  IO_COMMAND(al),d0

    move.w  #IMMEDIATES,dl
    btst    d0,dl
    bne.s   TermIO_Immediate    ;IO was immediate, don't do task stuff...

    ;------ we may need to turn the active bit off.
    btst    #UNITB_INTASK,UNIT_FLAGS(a3)
    bne.s   TermIO_Immediate    ;IO was came from task, don't clear ACTIVE...

    ;------ the task does not have more work to do
    bclr    #UNITB_ACTIVE,UNIT_FLAGS(a3)

TermIO_Immediate:
    ;------ if the quick bit is still set then we don't need to reply
    ;------ msg -- just return to the user.
    btst    #IOB_QUICK,IO_FLAGS(al)
    bne.s   TermIO_End
    LINKSYS ReplyMsg,md_SysLib(a6)      ;al-message
    ;(ReplyMsg sets the LN_TYPE to NT_REPLYMSG)

TermIO_End:
    rts


;-----------------------------------------------------------------------
; Here begins the functions that implement the device commands
; all functions are called with:
;   al -- a pointer to the io request block
;   a3 -- a pointer to the unit
;   a6 -- a pointer to the device
;
; Commands that conflict with 68000 instructions have a "My" prepended
; to them.
;-----------------------------------------------------------------------

;We can't AbortIO anything, so don't touch the IORequest!
AbortIO:         ; ( iob: al, device:a6 )
    moveq   #IOERR_NOCMD,d0
    rts
```

```
RawRead:        ; 10 Not supported   (INVALID)
RawWrite:       ; 11 Not supported   (INVALID)
Invalid:
    move.b  #IOERR_NOCMD,IO_ERROR(a1)
    bra.s   TermIO

;
; Update and Clear are internal buffering commands.  Update forces all
; io out to its final resting spot, and does not return until this is
; totally done.  Since this is automatic in a ramdisk, we simply return "Ok".
;
; Clear invalidates all internal buffers.  Since this device
; has no internal buffers, these commands do not apply.
;
Update:
Clear:
MyReset:                        ;Do nothing (nothing reasonable to do)
AddChangeInt:                   ;Do nothing
RemChangeInt:                   ;Do nothing
MyRemove:                       ;Do nothing
Seek:                           ;Do nothing
Motor:                          ;Do nothing
ChangeNum:                      ;Zero ok
ChangeState:                    ;Zero indicates disk inserted
ProtStatus:                     ;Zero indicates unprotected
    clr.l   IO_ACTUAL(a1)
    bra.s   TermIO


GetDriveType:                   ;make it look like 3.5" (90mm) drive
    moveq   #DRIVE3_5,d0
    move.l  d0,IO_ACTUAL(a1)
    bra.s   TermIO


GetNumTracks:
    move.l  #RAMSIZE/BYTESPERTRACK,IO_ACTUAL(a1) ;Number of tracks
    bra.s   TermIO

;
; Foo and Bar are two device specific commands that are provided just
; to show you how to add your own commands.  They currently return that
; no work was done.
;

Foo:
Bar:
    clr.l   IO_ACTUAL(a1)
    bra.s   TermIO


;---------------------------------
; This device is designed so that no combination of bad
; inputs can ever cause the device driver to crash.
;---------------------------------
RdWrt:
    IFGE INFO_LEVEL-200
        move.l  IO_LENGTH(a1),-(sp)
        PUTMSG  200,<'%s/RdWrt len %ld'>
        addq.l  #4,sp
    ENDC

    movem.l a2/a3,-(sp)
    move.l  a1,a2               ;Copy iob
    move.l  IO_UNIT(a2),a3      ;Get unit pointer

*       check operation for legality
    btst.b  #0,IO_DATA(a2)      ;check if user's pointer is ODD
    bne.s   IO_LenErr           ;bad...
```



```
    ;[D0=offset]

    move.l  IO_OFFSET(a2),d0
    move.l  d0,d1
    and.l   #SECTOR-1,d1        ;Bad sector boundary or alignment?
    bne.s   IO_LenErr           ;bad...
    ;[D0=offset]

*       check for IO within disc range
    ;[D0=offset]
    add.l   IO_LENGTH(a2),d0    ;Add length to offset
    bcs.s   IO_LenErr           ;overflow... (important test)
    cmp.l   #RAMSIZE,d0         ;Last byte is highest acceptable total
    bhi.s   IO_LenErr           ;bad... (unsigned compare)
    and.l   #SECTOR-1,d0        ;Even sector boundary?
    bne.s   IO_LenErr           ;bad...

*       We've gotten this far, it must be a valid request.

    IFD   INTRRUPT
     move.l   mdu_SigMask(a3),d0  ; Get signals to wait for
     LINKSYS  Wait,md_SysLib(a6)  ; Wait for interrupt before proceeding
    ENDC


    lea.l   mdu_RAM(a3),a0      ; Point to RAMDISK "sector" for I/O
    add.l   IO_OFFSET(a2),a0    ; Add offset to ram base
    move.l  IO_LENGTH(a2),d0
    move.l  d0,IO_ACTUAL(a2)    ; Indicate we've moved all bytes
    beq.s   RdWrt_end           ;---deal with zero length I/O
    move.l  IO_DATA(a2),a1      ; Point to data buffer
;
;A0=ramdisk index
;A1=user buffer
;D0=length
;
    cmp.b   #CMD_READ,IO_COMMAND+1(a2)  ; Decide on direction
    BEQ.S   CopyTheBlock
    EXG     A0,A1               ; For Write and Format, swap source & dest
CopyTheBlock:
    LINKSYS CopyMemQuick,md_SysLib(a6)  ;A0=source A1=dest D0=size
    ;CopyMemQuick is very fast


RdWrt_end:
    move.l  a2,a1
    movem.l (sp)+,a2/a3
    bra     TermIO      ;END
IO_LenErr:
    move.b  #IOERR_BADLENGTH,IO_ERROR(a2)
IO_End:
    clr.l   IO_ACTUAL(a2)       ;Initially, no data moved
    bra.s   RdWrt_end


;
; the Stop command stop all future io requests from being
; processed until a Start command is received.  The Stop
; command is NOT stackable: e.g. no matter how many stops
; have been issued, it only takes one Start to restart
; processing.
;
;Stop is rather silly for a ramdisk
MyStop:
   PUTMSG   30,<'%s/MyStop: called'>
   bset   #MDUB_STOPPED,UNIT_FLAGS(a3)
   bra   TermIO
```

```
Start:
    PUTMSG   30,<'%s/Start: called'>
    bsr    InternalStart
    bra    TermIO


InternalStart:
     move.l  a1,-(sp)
    ;------ turn processing back on
    bclr    #MDUB_STOPPED,UNIT_FLAGS(a3)

    ;------ kick the task to start it moving
    move.b   MP_SIGBIT(a3),d1
    CLEAR    d0
    bset      d1,d0
    LINKSYS   Signal,md_SysLib(a3)
     move.l  (sp)+,a1
    rts


;
; Flush pulls all I/O requests off the queue and sends them back.
; We must be careful not to destroy work in progress, and also
; that we do not let some io requests slip by.
;
; Some funny magic goes on with the STOPPED bit in here.  Stop is
; defined as not being reentrant.  We therefore save the old state
; of the bit and then restore it later.  This keeps us from
; needing to DISABLE in flush.  It also fails miserably if someone
; does a start in the middle of a flush. (A semaphore might help...)
;

Flush:
    PUTMSG   30,<'%s/Flush: called'>
    movem.l   d2/a1/a6,-(sp)

    move.l   md_SysLib(a6),a6

    bset    #MDUB_STOPPED,UNIT_FLAGS(a3)
    sne     d2

Flush_Loop:
    move.l   a3,a0
    CALLSYS   GetMsg     ;Steal messages from task's port

    tst.l   d0
    beq.s   Flush_End

    move.l   d0,a1
    move.b   #IOERR_ABORTED,IO_ERROR(a1)
    CALLSYS   ReplyMsg

    bra.s   Flush_Loop

Flush_End:
    move.l   d2,d0
    movem.l   (sp)+,d2/a1/a6

    tst.b   d0
    beq.s   1$

    bsr   InternalStart
1$:

    bra     TermIO


;-----------------------------------------------------------------------
; Here begins the task related routines
```



```
;
; A Task is provided so that queued requests may be processed at
; a later time.  This is not very justifiable for a ram disk, but
; is very useful for "real" hardware devices.  Take care with
; your arbitration of shared hardware with all the multitasking
; programs that might call you at once.
;
; Register Usage
; ==============
; a3 -- unit pointer
; a6 -- syslib pointer
; a5 -- device pointer
; a4 -- task (NOT process) pointer
; d7 -- wait mask
;-----------------------------------------------------------------------

; some dos magic, useful for Processes (not us).  A process is started at
; the first  executable address  after a segment list.  We hand craft a
; segment list here.  See the the DOS technical reference if you really
; need to know more about this.
; The next instruction after the segment list is the first executable address

    cnop    0,4      ; long word align
    DC.L    16       ; segment length -- any number will do (this is 4
                     ; bytes back from the segment pointer)
myproc_seglist:
    DC.L    0        ; pointer to next segment

Task_Begin:
    PUTMSG  35,<'%s/Task_Begin'>
    move.l  ABSEXECBASE,a6

    ;------ Grab the argument passed down from our parent
    move.l  4(sp),a3           ; Unit pointer
    move.l  mdu_Device(a3),a5  ; Point to device structure

    IFD   INTRRUPT
     ;------ Allocate a signal for "I/O Complete" interrupts
     moveq   #-1,d0           ; -1 is any signal at all
     CALLSYS   AllocSignal
     move.b   d0,mdu_SigBit(A3)    ; Save in unit structure
     moveq   #0,d7           ; Convert bit number signal mask
     bset   d0,d7
     move.l   d7,mdu_SigMask(A3)    ; Save in unit structure
     lea.l   mdu_is(a3),a1       ; Point to interrupt structure
     moveq   #INTB_PORTS,d0      ; Portia interrupt bit 3
     CALLSYS AddIntServer        ; Now install the server
     move.l   md_Base(a5),a0       ; Get board base address
*    bset.b   #INTENABLE,INTCTRL2(a0)    ; Enable interrupts
    ENDC

    ;------ Allocate a signal
    moveq   #-1,d0           ; -1 is any signal at all
    CALLSYS AllocSignal
    move.b  d0,MP_SIGBIT(a3)
    move.b  #PA_SIGNAL,MP_FLAGS(a3) ;Make message port "live"
    ;------ change the bit number into a mask, and save in d7
    moveq   #0,d7        ;Clear D7
    bset    d0,d7

    IFGE INFO_LEVEL-40
     move.l  $114(a6),-(sp)
     move.l  a5,-(sp)
     move.l  a3,-(sp)
     move.l  d0,-(sp)
     PUTMSG  40,<'%s/Signal=%ld, Unit=%lx Device=%lx Task=%lx'>
     add.l   #4*4,sp
    ENDC
```

```
    bra.s   Task_StartHere

; OK, kids, we are done with initialization.  We now can start the main loop
; of the driver.  It goes like this.  Because we had the port marked
; PA_IGNORE for a while (in InitUnit) we jump to the getmsg code on entry.
; (The first message will probably be posted BEFORE our task gets a chance
; to run)
;------     wait for a message
;------     lock the device
;------     get a message.  If no message, unlock device and loop
;------     dispatch the message
;------     loop back to get a message

    ;------ no more messages.  back ourselves out.
Task_Unlock:
    and.b   #$ff&(~(UNITF_ACTIVE!UNITF_INTASK)),UNIT_FLAGS(a3)
    ;------ main loop: wait for a new message

Task_MainLoop:
    PUTMSG   75,<'%s/++Sleep'>
    move.l  d7,d0
    CALLSYS Wait
    IFGE INFO_LEVEL-5
        bchg.b  #1,$bfe001  ;Blink the power LED
    ENDC
Task_StartHere:
    PUTMSG   75,<'%s/++Wakeup'>
    ;------ see if we are stopped
    btst    #MDUB_STOPPED,UNIT_FLAGS(a3)
    bne.s   Task_MainLoop       ; device is stopped, ignore messages
    ;------ lock the device
    bset    #UNITB_ACTIVE,UNIT_FLAGS(a3)
    bne     Task_MainLoop       ; device in use (immediate command?)


   ;------ get the next request
Task_NextMessage:
    move.l  a3,a0
    CALLSYS GetMsg
    PUTMSG  1,<'%s/GotMsg'>
    tst.l   d0
    beq     Task_Unlock ; no message?

    ;------ do this request
    move.l  d0,a1
    exg     a5,a6       ; put device ptr in right place
    bsr     PerformIO
    exg     a5,a6       ; get syslib back in a6

    bra.s   Task_NextMessage

;
; Here is a dummy interrupt handler, with some crucial components commented
; out.  If the IFD INTRRUPT is enabled, this code will cause the device to
; wait for a level two interrupt before it will process each request
; (pressing a key on the keyboard will do it).  This code is normally
; disabled, and must fake or omit certain operations since there  isn't
; really any hardware for this driver.  Similar code has been used
; successfully in other, "REAL" device drivers.
;

  IFD   INTRRUPT
;   A1 should be pointing to the unit structure upon entry!

myintr:     move.l   mdu_Device(a1),a0   ; Get device pointer
      move.l   md_Base(a0),a0       ; point to board base address
*      btst.b   #IAMPULLING,INTCTRL1(a0);See if I'm interrupting
*      beq.s   myexnm          ; if not set, exit, not mine
*      move.b   #0,INTACK(a0)       ; toggle controller's int2 bit
```



```
;      ------ signal the task that an interrupt has occurred

       move.l   mdu_SigMask(a1),d0
      lea   mdu_tcb(a1),a1
      move.l   md_SysLib(a0),a6   ; Get pointer to system
      CALLSYS   Signal

;       now clear the zero condition code so that
;       the interrupt handler doesn't call the next
;       interrupt server.
;
*       moveq   #1,d0         clear zero flag
*       bra.s   myexit         now exit
;
;       this exit point sets the zero condition code
;       so the interrupt handler will try the next server
;       in the interrupt chain
;
myexnm      moveq   #0,d0         set zero condition code
;
myexit      rts
   ENDC

mdu_Init:
;   ------ Initialize the device

    INITBYTE    MP_FLAGS,PA_IGNORE  ;Unit starts with a message port
    INITBYTE    LN_TYPE,NT_MSGPORT  ;
    INITLONG    LN_NAME,myName      ;
    INITLONG    mdu_tcb+LN_NAME,myName
    INITBYTE    mdu_tcb+LN_TYPE,NT_TASK
    INITBYTE    mdu_tcb+LN_PRI,5
    IFD   INTRRUPT
     INITBYTE    mdu_is+LN_PRI,4       ; Int priority 4
     INITLONG    mdu_is+IS_CODE,myintr  ; Interrupt routine addr
     INITLONG    mdu_is+LN_NAME,myName
    ENDC
    DC.L   0

 IFNE  AUTOMOUNT
mdn_Init:
*    ;------ Initialize packet for MakeDosNode

    INITLONG    mdn_execName,myName      ; Address of driver name
    INITLONG    mdn_tableSize,11         ; # long words in AmigaDOS env.
    INITLONG    mdn_dName,$524d0000      ; Store 'RM' in name
    INITLONG    mdn_sizeBlock,SECTOR/4   ; # longwords in a block
    INITLONG    mdn_numHeads,1           ; RAM disk has only one "head"
    INITLONG    mdn_secsPerBlk,1         ; secs/logical block, must = "1"
    INITLONG    mdn_blkTrack,SECTORSPER  ; secs/track (must be reasonable)
    INITLONG    mdn_resBlks,1            ; reserved blocks, MUST > 0!
    INITLONG    mdn_upperCyl,(RAMSIZE/BYTESPERTRACK)-1 ; upper cylinder
    INITLONG    mdn_numBuffers,1         ; # AmigaDOS buffers to start
    DC.L   0
 ENDC

;----------------------------------------------------------------------
; EndCode is a marker that shows the end of your code.  Make sure it does not
; span hunks, and is not before the rom tag!  It is ok to put it right after
; the rom tag -- that way you are always safe.  I put it here because it
; happens to be the "right" thing to do, and I know that it is safe in this
; case (this program has only a single code hunk).
;----------------------------------------------------------------------
EndCode:    END
```

```
*******************************************************************
*
*
* Copyright (C) 1986, Commodore Amiga Inc.  All rights reserved.
* Permission granted for non-commercial use
*
******************************************************************
*
* ramdev.i -- external declarations for skeleton ramdisk device
*
******************************************************************


;--- Assemble-time options
INFO_LEVEL  EQU 0      ; Specify amount of debugging info desired
                       ; If > 0 you must link with debug.lib!
                       ; You will need to run a terminal program to
                       ; set the baud rate.
*INTRRUPT    SET 1     ; Remove "*" to enable fake interrupt code
AUTOMOUNT   EQU 0      ; Work with the "mount" command if 0
                       ; Do it automatically if 1

;--- stack size and priority for the process we will create
MYPROCSTACKSIZE   EQU   $900
MYPROCPRI         EQU   0   ;Devices are often 5, NOT higher

;--- Base constants
NUMBEROFTRACKS EQU  40  ;<<<< Change THIS to change size of ramdisk <<<<
SECTOR         EQU  512 ;# bytes per sector
SECSHIFT       EQU  9   ;Shift count to convert byte # to sector #
SECTORSPER     EQU  10  ;# Sectors per "track"

RAMSIZE        EQU   SECTOR*NUMBEROFTRACKS*SECTORSPER
                     ; Use this much RAM per unit
BYTESPERTRACK EQU    SECTORSPER*SECTOR

IAMPULLING     EQU   7      ; "I am pulling the interrupt" bit of INTCRL1
INTENABLE      EQU   4      ; "Interrupt Enable" bit of INTCRL2
INTCTRL1       EQU   $40    ; Interrupt control register offset on board
INTCTRL2       EQU   $42    ; Interrupt control register offset on board
INTACK         EQU   $50    ; My board's interrupt reset address
;-----------------------------------------------------------------------
;
; device command definitions (copied from devices/trackdisk.i)
;
;-----------------------------------------------------------------------
   BITDEF  TD,EXTCOM,15       ; for "extended" commands !!!

   DEVINIT
   DEVCMD   CMD_MOTOR         ; control the disk's motor (NO-OP)
   DEVCMD   CMD_SEEK          ; explicit seek (NO-OP)
   DEVCMD   CMD_FORMAT        ; format disk - equated to WRITE for RAMDISK
   DEVCMD   CMD_REMOVE        ; notify when disk changes (NO-OP)
   DEVCMD   CMD_CHANGENUM     ; number of disk changes (always 0)
   DEVCMD   CMD_CHANGESTATE   ; is there a disk in the drive? (always TRUE)
   DEVCMD   CMD_PROTSTATUS    ; is the disk write protected? (always FALSE)
   DEVCMD   CMD_RAWREAD       ; Not supported
   DEVCMD   CMD_RAWWRITE      ; Not supported
   DEVCMD   CMD_GETDRIVETYPE  ; Get drive type
   DEVCMD   CMD_GETNUMTRACKS  ; Get number of tracks
   DEVCMD   CMD_ADDCHANGEINT  ; Add disk change interrupt (NO-OP)
   DEVCMD   CMD_REMCHANGEINT  ; Remove disk change interrupt ( NO-OP)
   DEVCMD   MYDEV_END         ; place marker -- first illegal command #

DRIVE3_5        EQU     1
DRIVE5_25       EQU     2
;-----------------------------------------------------------------------
;
; Layout of parameter packet for MakeDosNode
```



```
;
;-----------------------------------------------------------------------


    STRUCTURE MkDosNodePkt,0
   APTR     mdn_dosName    ; Pointer to DOS file handler name
   APTR     mdn_execName    ; Pointer to device driver name
   ULONG    mdn_unit    ; Unit number
   ULONG    mdn_flags    ; OpenDevice flags
   ULONG    mdn_tableSize    ; Environment size
   ULONG    mdn_sizeBlock    ; # longwords in a block
   ULONG    mdn_secOrg    ; sector origin -- unused
   ULONG    mdn_numHeads    ; number of surfaces
   ULONG    mdn_secsPerBlk    ; secs per logical block -- unused
   ULONG    mdn_blkTrack    ; secs per track
   ULONG    mdn_resBlks    ; reserved blocks -- MUST be at least 1!
   ULONG    mdn_prefac    ; unused
   ULONG    mdn_interleave    ; interleave
   ULONG    mdn_lowCyl    ; lower cylinder
   ULONG    mdn_upperCyl    ; upper cylinder
   ULONG    mdn_numBuffers    ; number of buffers
   ULONG    mdn_memBufType    ; Type of memory for AmigaDOS buffers
   STRUCT   mdn_dName,5    ; DOS file handler name "RAM0"
   LABEL    mdn_Sizeof    ; Size of this structure

;-----------------------------------------------------------------------
;
; device data structures
;
;-----------------------------------------------------------------------

; maximum number of units in this device
MD_NUMUNITS    EQU    4

    STRUCTURE MyDev,LIB_SIZE
   UBYTE    md_Flags
   UBYTE    md_Pad1
   ;now longword aligned
   ULONG    md_SysLib
   ULONG    md_SegList
   ULONG    md_Base       ; Base address of this device's expansion board
   STRUCT   md_Units,MD_NUMUNITS*4
   LABEL    MyDev_Sizeof


   STRUCTURE MyDevUnit,UNIT_SIZE    ;Odd # longwords
   UBYTE     mdu_UnitNum
   UBYTE     mdu_SigBit        ; Signal bit allocated for interrupts
   ;Now longword aligned!
   APTR      mdu_Device
   STRUCT    mdu_stack,MYPROCSTACKSIZE
   STRUCT    mdu_tcb,TC_SIZE       ; Task Control Block (TCB) for disk task
   ULONG     mdu_SigMask           ; Signal these bits on interrupt
   IFD   INTRRUPT
    STRUCT   mdu_is,IS_SIZE        ; Interrupt structure
    UWORD    mdu_pad1             ;Longword align
   ENDC
   STRUCT    mdu_RAM,RAMSIZE       ; RAM used to simulate disk
   LABEL     MyDevUnit_Sizeof

   ;------ state bit for unit stopped
   BITDEF   MDU,STOPPED,2

MYDEVNAME   MACRO
      DC.B   'ramdev.device',0
      ENDM
```

```
/*
 *
 * samplebase.h -- C include file defining sample.library base
 *
 * Copyright (C) 1985, 1988 Commodore Amiga Inc.  All rights reserved.
 *
 */

#ifndef SAMPLE_BASE_H
#define SAMPLE_BASE_H

#ifndef  EXEC_TYPES_H
#include  <exec/types.h>
#endif   EXEC_TYPES_H

#ifndef  EXEC_LISTS_H
#include  <exec/lists.h>
#endif   EXEC_LISTS_H

#ifndef  EXEC_LIBRARIES_H
#include <exec/libraries.h>
#endif   EXEC_LIBRARIES_H

/* library data structures
 *
 *  Note that the library base begins with a library node
 */

struct SampleBase {
   struct Library LibNode;
   UBYTE  Flags;
   UBYTE  pad;
   /* We are now longword aligned */
   ULONG  SysLib;
   ULONG  DosLib;
   ULONG  SegList;
   };


#define SAMPLENAME   "sample.library"

#endif EXEC_SAMPLEBASE_H
```



```
*********************************************************************
*                                                                   *
* samplebase.i -- definition of sample.library base                 *
*                                                                   *
* Copyright (C) 1985, 1988 Commodore Amiga Inc.  All rights reserved. *
*                                                                   *
*********************************************************************

   IFND  SAMPLE_BASE_I
SAMPLE_BASE_I SET 1


   IFND  EXEC_TYPES_I
   INCLUDE  "exec/types.i"
   ENDC   ; EXEC_TYPES_I

   IFND  EXEC_LISTS_I
   INCLUDE  "exec/lists.i"
   ENDC   ; EXEC_LISTS_I

   IFND  EXEC_LIBRARIES_I
   INCLUDE  "exec/libraries.i"
   ENDC   ; EXEC_LIBRARIES_I


;-----------------------------------------------------------------------
;
; library data structures
;
;-----------------------------------------------------------------------

;  Note that the library base begins with a library node

   STRUCTURE SampleBase,LIB_SIZE
   UBYTE   sb_Flags
   UBYTE   sb_pad
   ;We are now longword aligned
   ULONG   sb_SysLib
   ULONG   sb_DosLib
   ULONG   sb_SegList
   LABEL   SampleBase_SIZEOF


SAMPLENAME   MACRO
      DC.B   'sample.library',0
      ENDM

   ENDC  ;EXEC_SAMPLEBASE_I
```

Oct 7 20:31 1988 SampleLibrary/lib/samplelib_lvos.asm Page 1

```
*************************************************************************
* samplelib_stubs.asm
*
* Copyright 1988 Commodore-Amiga, Inc.
*
* _LVO definitions that match this .fd file:
*
*       ##base _SampleBase
*       ##bias 30
*       ##public
*       Double(n1)(D0)
*       AddThese(n1,n2)(D0,D1)
*       ##end
*
* After assembling,
*   JOIN samplelib_stubs.o samplelib_lvos.o AS sample.lib
*
* LINK with LIBRARY sample.lib when calling sample.library functions
*
*************************************************************************

   INCLUDE   "exec/types.i"
   INCLUDE   "exec/libraries.i"

          SECTION _LVO

             DATA

*----- LIBINIT initializes an LVO value to -30 to skip the first four
*----- 6-byte required library vectors (Open, Expunge, etc)

             LIBINIT

*----- LIBDEF assigns the current LVO value to a label, and then
*----- bumps the LVO value by -6 in preparation for next LVO label

*----- This assigns the value -30 to our first _LVO label

             LIBDEF       _LVODouble      ;-30
             XDEF         _LVODouble

*----- The value -30-6 is asigned to our second _LVO label

             LIBDEF       _LVOAddThese    ;-36
             XDEF         _LVOAddThese

             END
```

Oct 7 20:31 1988 SampleLibrary/lib/samplelib_stubs.asm Page 1

```
*************************************************************************
* samplelib_stubs.asm
*
* Copyright 1988 Commodore-Amiga, Inc.
*
* Stubs that match this .fd file:
*
*       ##base _SampleBase
*       ##bias 30
*       ##public
*       Double(n1)(D0)
*       AddThese(n1,n2)(D0,D1)
*       ##end
*
* After assembling,
*   JOIN samplelib_stubs.o samplelib_lvos.o AS sample.lib
*
* LINK with LIBRARY sample.lib when calling sample.library functions
*
*************************************************************************
   INCLUDE   "exec/types.i"
   INCLUDE   "exec/libraries.i"

          SECTION CSTUB

            CODE

*------ Caller declares and initializes SampleBase in their C code

            XREF         _SampleBase

*------ Must externally reference the _LVO labels defined in samplelib_lvos

            XREF         _LVODouble
            XREF         _LVOAddThese

*------ Make C function stubs available to caller

            XDEF         _Double
            XDEF         _AddThese

*------- These stubs move C args from stack to appropriate registers,
*------- call the library function, and return result in d0

_Double:
            MOVE.L       A6,-(SP)            ;Save register(s)
            MOVE.L       8(SP),D0            ;Copy param to register
            MOVE.L       _SampleBase,A6      ;Library base to A6
            JSR          _LVODouble(A6)      ;Go to real routine
            MOVE.L       (SP)+,A6            ;Restore register(s)
            RTS

_AddThese:
            MOVE.L       A6,-(SP)            ;Save register(s)
            MOVEM.L      8(SP),D0/D1         ;Copy params to registers
                                             ;8(SP)  goes into D0
                                             ;12(SP) goes into D1
            MOVE.L       _SampleBase,A6      ;Library base to A6
            JSR          _LVOAddThese(A6)    ;Go to real routine
            MOVE.L       (SP)+,A6            ;Restore register(s)
            RTS

          END
```

```
**********************************************************************
*                                                                    *
*   sample.library.asm -- Example run-time library source code      *
*                                                                    *
*   Copyright (C) 1985, 1988 Commodore Amiga Inc.  All rights reserved. *
*                                                                    *
*   Assemble and link, without startup code, to create Sample.library, *
*     a LIBS: drawer run-time shared library                        *
*                                                                    *
*  Linkage Info:                                                     *
*  FROM     sample.library.o                                         *
*  LIBRARY  LIB:Amiga.lib                                            *
*  TO       sample.library                                           *
*                                                                    *
**********************************************************************

   SECTION   section

   NOLIST
   INCLUDE "exec/types.i"
   INCLUDE "exec/libraries.i"
   INCLUDE "exec/lists.i"
   INCLUDE "exec/alerts.i"
   INCLUDE "exec/initializers.i"
   INCLUDE "exec/resident.i"
   INCLUDE "libraries/dos.i"

   INCLUDE "asmsupp.i"
   INCLUDE "samplebase.i"

   LIST

   ;------ These don't have to be external, but it helps some
   ;------ debuggers to have them globally visible
   XDEF   Init
   XDEF   Open
   XDEF   Close
   XDEF   Expunge
   XDEF   Null
   XDEF   sampleName
   XDEF   Double
   XDEF   AddThese

   XREF   _AbsExecBase

   XLIB   OpenLibrary
   XLIB   CloseLibrary
   XLIB   Alert
   XLIB   FreeMem
   XLIB   Remove


   ; The first executable location.  This should return an error
   ; in case someone tried to run you as a program (instead of
   ; loading you as a library).
Start:
   MOVEQ   #-1,d0
   rts

;-----------------------------------------------------------------------
; A romtag structure.  Both "exec" and "ramlib" look for
; this structure to discover magic constants about you
; (such as where to start running you from...).
;-----------------------------------------------------------------------

   ; Most people will not need a priority and should leave it at zero.
   ; the RT_PRI field is used for configuring the roms.  Use "mods" from
   ; wack to look at the other romtags in the system
```



```
MYPRI   EQU   0

initDDescrip:
                ;STRUCTURE RT,0
     DC.W    RTC_MATCHWORD        ; UWORD RT_MATCHWORD
     DC.L    initDDescrip         ; APTR  RT_MATCHTAG
     DC.L    EndCode              ; APTR  RT_ENDSKIP
     DC.B    RTF_AUTOINIT         ; UBYTE RT_FLAGS
     DC.B    VERSION              ; UBYTE RT_VERSION
     DC.B    NT_LIBRARY           ; UBYTE RT_TYPE
     DC.B    MYPRI                ; BYTE  RT_PRI
     DC.L    sampleName           ; APTR  RT_NAME
     DC.L    idString             ; APTR  RT_IDSTRING
     DC.L    Init                 ; APTR  RT_INIT


   ; this is the name that the library will have
sampleName:    SAMPLENAME

   ; a major version number.
VERSION:   EQU   34

   ; A particular revision.  This should uniquely identify the bits in the
   ; library.  I use a script that advances the revision number each time
   ; I recompile.  That way there is never a question of which library
   ; that really is.
REVISION:   EQU  1

   ; this is an identifier tag to help in supporting the library
   ; format is 'name version.revision (dd MON yyyy)',<cr>,<lf>,<null>
idString:   dc.b   'samplelib 1.3 (03 Oct 1988)',13,10,0

dosName:   DOSNAME

   ; force word allignment
   ds.w   0


   ; The romtag specified that we were "RTF_AUTOINIT".  This means
   ; that the RT_INIT structure member points to one of these
   ; tables below.  If the AUTOINIT bit was not set then RT_INIT
   ; would point to a routine to run.

Init:
   DC.L   SampleBase_SIZEOF ; size of library base data space
   DC.L   funcTable         ; pointer to function initializers
   DC.L   dataTable         ; pointer to data initializers
   DC.L   initRoutine       ; routine to run


funcTable:

   ;------ standard system routines
   dc.l   Open
   dc.l   Close
   dc.l   Expunge
   dc.l   Null

   ;------ my libraries definitions
   dc.l   Double
   dc.l   AddThese

   ;------ function table end marker
   dc.l   -1


   ; The data table initializes static data structures.
   ; The format is specified in exec/InitStruct routine's
   ; manual pages.  The INITBYTE/INITWORD/INITLONG routines
```

```
    ; are in the file 'exec/initializers.i".  The first argument
    ; is the offset from the library base for this byte/word/long.
    ; The second argument is the value to put in that cell.
    ; The table is null terminated
    ; NOTE - LN_TYPE below is a correction - old example had LH_TYPE

dataTable:
   INITBYTE   LN_TYPE,NT_LIBRARY
   INITLONG   LN_NAME,sampleName
   INITBYTE   LIB_FLAGS,LIBF_SUMUSED!LIBF_CHANGED
   INITWORD   LIB_VERSION,VERSION
   INITWORD   LIB_REVISION,REVISION
   INITLONG   LIB_IDSTRING,idString
   DC.L   0


    ; This routine gets called after the library has been allocated.
    ; The library pointer is in D0.  The segment list is in A0.
    ; If it returns non-zero then the library will be linked into
    ; the library list.
initRoutine:

   ;------ get the library pointer into a convenient A register
   move.l   a5,-(sp)
   move.l   d0,a5

   ;------ save a pointer to exec
   move.l   a6,sb_SysLib(a5)

   ;------ save a pointer to our loaded code
   move.l   a0,sb_SegList(a5)

   ;------ open the dos library
   lea   dosName(pc),a1
   CLEAR   d0
   CALLSYS   OpenLibrary

   move.l   d0,sb_DosLib(a5)
   bne.s   1$

   ;------ can't open the dos!  what gives
   ALERT   AG_OpenLib!AO_DOSLib

1$:
   ;------ now build the static data that we need

   ;
   ; put your initialization here...
   ;

   move.l   a5,d0
   move.l   (sp)+,a5
   rts

;----------------------------------------------------------------------
;
; here begins the system interface commands.  When the user calls
; OpenLibrary/CloseLibrary/RemoveLibrary, this eventually gets translated
; into a call to the following routines (Open/Close/Expunge).  Exec
; has already put our library pointer in A6 for us.  Exec has turned
; off task switching while in these routines (via Forbid/Permit), so
; we should not take too long in them.
;
;----------------------------------------------------------------------


   ; Open returns the library pointer in d0 if the open
   ; was successful.  If the open failed then null is returned.
   ; It might fail if we allocated memory on each open, or
```



```
    ; if only open application could have the library open
    ; at a time...

Open:      ; ( libptr:a6, version:d0 )

   ;------ mark us as having another opener
   addq.w   #1,LIB_OPENCNT(a6)

   ;------ prevent delayed expunges
   bclr   #LIBB_DELEXP,sb_Flags(a6)

   move.l   a6,d0
   rts

   ; There are two different things that might be returned from
   ; the Close routine.  If the library is no longer open and
   ; there is a delayed expunge then Close should return the
   ; segment list (as given to Init).  Otherwise close should
   ; return NULL.

Close:      ; ( libptr:a6 )

   ;------ set the return value
   CLEAR   d0

   ;------ mark us as having one fewer openers
   subq.w   #1,LIB_OPENCNT(a6)

   ;------ see if there is anyone left with us open
   bne.s   1$

   ;------ see if we have a delayed expunge pending
   btst   #LIBB_DELEXP,sb_Flags(a6)
   beq.s   1$

   ;------ do the expunge
   bsr   Expunge
1$:
   rts


   ; There are two different things that might be returned from
   ; the Expunge routine.  If the library is no longer open
   ; then Expunge should return the segment list (as given to
   ; Init).  Otherwise Expunge should set the delayed expunge
   ; flag and return NULL.
   ;
   ; One other important note: because Expunge is called from
   ; the memory allocator, it may NEVER Wait() or otherwise
   ; take long time to complete.

Expunge:   ; ( libptr: a6 )

   movem.l   d2/a5/a6,-(sp)
   move.l   a6,a5
   move.l   sb_SysLib(a5),a6

   ;------ see if anyone has us open
   tst.w   LIB_OPENCNT(a5)
   beq   1$

   ;------ it is still open.  set the delayed expunge flag
   bset   #LIBB_DELEXP,sb_Flags(a5)
   CLEAR   d0
   bra.s   Expunge_End

1$:
   ;------ go ahead and get rid of us.  Store our seglist in d2
   move.l   sb_SegList(a5),d2
```

```
   ;------ unlink from library list
   move.l    a5,a1
   CALLSYS   Remove

   ;
   ; device specific closings here...
   ;

   ;------ close the dos library
   move.l    sb_DosLib(a5),a1
   CALLSYS   CloseLibrary

   ;------ free our memory
   CLEAR     d0
   move.l    a5,a1
   move.w    LIB_NEGSIZE(a5),d0

   sub.l     d0,a1
   add.w     LIB_POSSIZE(a5),d0

   CALLSYS   FreeMem

   ;------ set up our return value
   move.l    d2,d0

Expunge_End:
   movem.l   (sp)+,d2/a5/a6
   rts


Null:
   CLEAR     d0
   rts

;----------------------------------------------------------------------
;
; Here begins the library specific functions.
;
; Both of these simple functions are entirely in assembler, but you
; can write your functions in C if you wish and interface to them here.
; If, for instance, the bulk of the AddThese function was written
; in C, you could interface to it as follows:
;
;   - write a C function  addTheseC(n1,n2) and compile it
;   - XDEF _addThese C  in this library code
;   - change the AddThese function code below to:
;       move.l d1,-(sp)      ;push rightmost C arg first
;       move.l d0,-(sp)      ;push other C arg(s), right to left
;       jsr    _addTheseC    ;call the C code
;       addq   #8,sp         ;fix stack
;       rts                  ;return with result in d0
;
;----------------------------------------------------------------------


*----- Double(d0)
Double:
   lsl      #1,d0
   rts

*----- AddThese(d0,d1)
AddThese:
   add.l    d1,d0
   rts


   ; EndCode is a marker that show the end of your code.
   ; Make sure it does not span sections nor is before the
   ; rom tag in memory!  It is ok to put it right after
```



```
   ; the rom tag -- that way you are always safe.  I put
   ; it here because it happens to be the "right" thing
   ; to do, and I know that it is safe in this case.
EndCode:

   END
```

Oct 7 20:32 1988 SampleLibrary/test/alibtest.asm Page 1

```
************************************************************************
*                                                                      *
*  alibtest.asm -- Asm example that calls the Sample.library functions *
*                                                                      *
*  Copyright 1988 Commodore Amiga Inc.  All rights reserved.           *
*                                                                      *
*  Linkage Info:                                                       *
*  FROM     Astartup.obj, alibtest.o                                   *
*  LIBRARY  LIB:amiga.lib, LIB:sample.lib                              *
*  TO       ALibTest                                                   *
*                                                                      *
************************************************************************


   INCLUDE   "exec/types.i"
   INCLUDE   "exec/libraries.i"

   INCLUDE   "asmsupp.i"
   INCLUDE   "samplebase.i"

ABSEXECBASE   EQU   4

   XDEF   _main

   XREF   _printf
   XREF   _LVODouble
   XREF   _LVOAddThese

   XLIB   OpenLibrary
   XLIB   CloseLibrary


_main:
   ;------ open the test library: this will bring it in from disk
   move.l   ABSEXECBASE,a6
   lea      sampleName(pc),a1
   moveq    #0,d0
   jsr      _LVOOpenLibrary(a6)

   tst.l    d0
   bne.s    1$

   ;------ couldn't find the library
   pea      sampleName(pc)
   pea      nolibmsg(pc)
   jsr      _printf
   addq.l   #8,sp

   bra      main_end

1$:
   move.l   d0,a6    ;sample.library base to a6

   ;------ print the library name, version, and revision
   clr.l    d0
   move.w   LIB_REVISION(a6),d0
   move.l   d0,-(sp)
   move.w   LIB_VERSION(a6),d0
   move.l   d0,-(sp)
   move.l   LN_NAME(a6),-(sp)
   pea      verRevMsg(pc)
   jsr      _printf            ;call Amiga.lib printf
   adda.l   #16,sp             ;fix 4 long stack pushes

   ;------ call the first test function
   moveq    #-7,d0
   jsr      _LVODouble(a6)
   move.l   d0,-(sp)
   pea      doubleMsg(pc)
```

Oct 7 20:32 1988 SampleLibrary/test/alibtest.asm Page 2

```
   jsr      _printf
   lea      8(sp),sp          ;fix 2 long stack pushes

   ;------ call the second test function
   moveq    #21,d0
   moveq    #4,d1
   jsr      _LVOAddThese(a6)
   move.l   d0,-(sp)
   pea      addTheseMsg(pc)
   jsr      _printf
   lea      8(sp),sp

   ;------ close the library
   move.l   a6,a1
   move.l   ABSEXECBASE,a6
   jsr      _LVOCloseLibrary(a6)

main_end:
            rts

sampleName:  SAMPLENAME
nolibmsg:     dc.b   'can not open library "%s"',10,0
doubleMsg:    dc.b   'Function Double(-7) returned %ld',10,0
addTheseMsg:  dc.b   'Function AddThese(21,4) returned %ld',10,0
verRevMsg:    dc.b   '%s   Version %ld   Revision %ld',10,0
   END
```

```
/*
 *  clibtest.c -- C example that calls the Sample.library functions
 *
 *  Copyright 1988 Commodore Amiga Inc.  All rights reserved.
 *
 *  Linkage Info:
 *  FROM     Astartup.obj, clibtest.o
 *  LIBRARY  LIB:amiga.lib, LIB:sample.lib
 *  TO       CLibTest
 */


#include <exec/types.h>
#include <exec/libraries.h>
#include <libraries/dos.h>

#include "samplebase.h"

struct SampleBase *SampleBase;

void main()
   {
   LONG n;
   struct Library *slib;

   /* Open sample.library */
   if(!(SampleBase=(struct SampleBase *)OpenLibrary("sample.library",0)))
      {
      printf("Can't open sample.library\n");
      exit(RETURN_FAIL);
      }

   /* Print library name, version, revision */
   slib = &SampleBase->LibNode;
   printf("%s   Version %ld   Revision %ld\n",
            slib->lib_Node.ln_Name, slib->lib_Version, slib->lib_Revision);

   /* Call the two functions */
   n = Double(-7);
   printf("Function Double(-7) returned %ld\n", n);

   n = AddThese(21,4);
   printf("Function AddThese(21,4) returned %ld\n", n);

   CloseLibrary(SampleBase);
   exit(RETURN_OK);
   }
```

Section H

Reference Charts

This section contains several handy reference charts. These are often useful when searching memory or scanning structures during debugging. The charts are:

- o 1.3 Function Offsets - The Amiga libraries are listed, with a separate entry for each library function. The chart lists the function's negative offset from the library base and a short summary of register usage.
- o Assembly Prefix Reference - Structure members in the assembly language include files often have a prefix associated with them. This chart lists the name of the include file that each prefix is associated with.
- o Structure Offset Reference - Lists the Amiga structures individually by name, followed by the structure size and offset of each member. This chart is typically used

when you know the base address of a structure and wish to examine its members.

- Hardware Register Map - A short reference listing of each chip register in the system, for those developers that must access the hardware directly. For more detail see the *Amiga Hardware Manual.*

- C Language Cross-Reference - Each element from the Amiga include files is listed along with its resolved value, the location where it was defined, and each place that references it. Since the elements have similar names, this chart is also useful for assembly language users.

```
**************************** cia.resource ************************************
##bias 6
  6 $fffa -$0006 AddICRVector(bit,interrupt)(d0,a1)
 12 $fff4 -$000c RemICRVector(bit)(d0)
 18 $ffee -$0012 AbleICR(mask)(d0)
 24 $ffe8 -$0018 SetICR(mask)(d0)


**************************** console.device **********************************
##base _ConsoleDevice
##bias 42
 42 $ffd6 -$002a CDInputHandler(events,device)(A0/A1)
 48 $ffd0 -$0030 RawKeyConvert(events,buffer,length,keyMap)(A0/A1,D1/A2)


**************************** diskfont.library ********************************
##base _DiskfontBase
##bias 30
 30 $ffe2 -$001e OpenDiskFont(textAttr)(A0)
 36 $ffdc -$0024 AvailFonts(buffer,bufBytes,flags)(A0,D0/D1)
*--- Added as of version 34 (distributed on V1.3 Workbench) ---
 42 $ffd6 -$002a NewFontContents(fontsLock,fontName)(A0/A1)
 48 $ffd0 -$0030 DisposeFontContents(fontContentsHeader)(A1)


**************************** dos.library *************************************
##base _DOSBase
##bias 30
 30 $ffe2 -$001e Open(name,accessMode)(D1/D2)
 36 $ffdc -$0024 Close(file)(D1)
 42 $ffd6 -$002a Read(file,buffer,length)(D1/D2/D3)
 48 $ffd0 -$0030 Write(file,buffer,length)(D1/D2/D3)
 54 $ffca -$0036 Input()
 60 $ffc4 -$003c Output()
 66 $ffbe -$0042 Seek(file,position,offset)(D1/D2/D3)
 72 $ffb8 -$0048 DeleteFile(name)(D1)
 78 $ffb2 -$004e Rename(oldName,newName)(D1/D2)
 84 $ffac -$0054 Lock(name,type)(D1/D2)
 90 $ffa6 -$005a UnLock(lock)(D1)
 96 $ffa0 -$0060 DupLock(lock)(D1)
102 $ff9a -$0066 Examine(lock,fileInfoBlock)(D1/D2)
108 $ff94 -$006c ExNext(lock,fileInfoBlock)(D1/D2)
114 $ff8e -$0072 Info(lock,parameterBlock)(D1/D2)
120 $ff88 -$0078 CreateDir(name)(D1)
126 $ff82 -$007e CurrentDir(lock)(D1)
132 $ff7c -$0084 IoErr()
138 $ff76 -$008a CreateProc(name,pri,segList,stackSize)(D1/D2/D3/D4)
144 $ff70 -$0090 Exit(returnCode)(D1)
150 $ff6a -$0096 LoadSeg(fileName)(D1)
156 $ff64 -$009c UnLoadSeg(segment)(D1)
##private
162 $ff5e -$00a2 GetPacket(wait)(D1)
168 $ff58 -$00a8 QueuePacket(packet)(D1)
##public
174 $ff52 -$00ae DeviceProc(name)(D1)
180 $ff4c -$00b4 SetComment(name,comment)(D1/D2)
186 $ff46 -$00ba SetProtection(name,mask)(D1/D2)
192 $ff40 -$00c0 DateStamp(date)(D1)
198 $ff3a -$00c6 Delay(timeout)(D1)
204 $ff34 -$00cc WaitForChar(file,timeout)(D1/D2)
210 $ff2e -$00d2 ParentDir(lock)(D1)
216 $ff28 -$00d8 IsInteractive(file)(D1)
222 $ff22 -$00de Execute(string,file,file)(D1/D2/D3)


**************************** exec.library ************************************
##base _SysBase
##bias 30
##private
```



```
*------ special functions ---------------------------------------------
 30 $ffe2 -$001e Supervisor()
 36 $ffdc -$0024 ExitIntr()
 42 $ffd6 -$002a Schedule()
 48 $ffd0 -$0030 Reschedule()
 54 $ffca -$0036 Switch()
 60 $ffc4 -$003c Dispatch()
 66 $ffbe -$0042 Exception()
##public
 72 $ffb8 -$0048 InitCode(startClass,version)(D0/D1)
 78 $ffb2 -$004e InitStruct(initTable,memory,size)(A1/A2,D0)
 84 $ffac -$0054 MakeLibrary(funcInit,structInit,libInit,dataSize,codeSize)
                 (A0/A1/A2,D0/D1)
 90 $ffa6 -$005a MakeFunctions(target,functionArray,funcDispBase)(A0,A1,A2)
 96 $ffa0 -$0060 FindResident(name)(A1)
102 $ff9a -$0066 InitResident(resident,segList)(A1,D1)
108 $ff94 -$006c Alert(alertNum,parameters)(D7,A5)
114 $ff8e -$0072 Debug()
*------ interrupts -----------------------------------------------------
120 $ff88 -$0078 Disable()
126 $ff82 -$007e Enable()
132 $ff7c -$0084 Forbid()
138 $ff76 -$008a Permit()
144 $ff70 -$0090 SetSR(newSR,mask)(D0/D1)
150 $ff6a -$0096 SuperState()
156 $ff64 -$009c UserState(sysStack)(D0)
162 $ff5e -$00a2 SetIntVector(intNumber,interrupt)(D0/A1)
168 $ff58 -$00a8 AddIntServer(intNumber,interrupt)(D0/A1)
174 $ff52 -$00ae RemIntServer(intNumber,interrupt)(D0/A1)
180 $ff4c -$00b4 Cause(interrupt)(A1)
*------ memory allocation: ---------------------------------------------
186 $ff46 -$00ba Allocate(freeList,byteSize)(A0,D0)
192 $ff40 -$00c0 Deallocate(freeList,memoryBlock,byteSize)(A0/A1,D0)
198 $ff3a -$00c6 AllocMem(byteSize,requirements)(D0/D1)
204 $ff34 -$00cc AllocAbs(byteSize,location)(D0/A1)
210 $ff2e -$00d2 FreeMem(memoryBlock,byteSize)(A1,D0)
216 $ff28 -$00d8 AvailMem(requirements)(D1)
222 $ff22 -$00de AllocEntry(entry)(A0)
228 $ff1c -$00e4 FreeEntry(entry)(A0)
*------ lists: ---------------------------------------------------------
234 $ff16 -$00ea Insert(list,node,pred)(A0/A1/A2)
240 $ff10 -$00f0 AddHead(list,node)(A0/A1)
246 $ff0a -$00f6 AddTail(list,node)(A0/A1)
252 $ff04 -$00fc Remove(node)(A1)
258 $fefe -$0102 RemHead(list)(A0)
264 $fef8 -$0108 RemTail(list)(A0)
270 $fef2 -$010e Enqueue(list,node)(A0/A1)
276 $feec -$0114 FindName(list,name)(A0/A1)
*------ tasks: ---------------------------------------------------------
282 $fee6 -$011a AddTask(task,initPC,finalPC)(A1/A2/A3)
288 $fee0 -$0120 RemTask(task)(A1)
294 $feda -$0126 FindTask(name)(A1)
300 $fed4 -$012c SetTaskPri(task,priority)(A1,D0)
306 $fece -$0132 SetSignal(newSignals,signalSet)(D0/D1)
312 $fec8 -$0138 SetExcept(newSignals,signalSet)(D0/D1)
318 $fec2 -$013e Wait(signalSet)(D0)
324 $febc -$0144 Signal(task,signalSet)(A1,D0)
330 $feb6 -$014a AllocSignal(signalNum)(D0)
336 $feb0 -$0150 FreeSignal(signalNum)(D0)
342 $feaa -$0156 AllocTrap(trapNum)(D0)
348 $fea4 -$015c FreeTrap(trapNum)(D0)
*------ messages: ------------------------------------------------------
354 $fe9e -$0162 AddPort(port)(A1)
360 $fe98 -$0168 RemPort(port)(A1)
366 $fe92 -$016e PutMsg(port,message)(A0/A1)
372 $fe8c -$0174 GetMsg(port)(A0)
378 $fe86 -$017a ReplyMsg(message)(A1)
384 $fe80 -$0180 WaitPort(port)(A0)
390 $fe7a -$0186 FindPort(name)(A1)
```

```
*------ libraries: ----------------------------------------------------
396 $fe74 -$018c AddLibrary(library)(A1)
402 $fe6e -$0192 RemLibrary(library)(A1)
408 $fe68 -$0198 OldOpenLibrary(libName)(A1)
414 $fe62 -$019e CloseLibrary(library)(A1)
420 $fe5c -$01a4 SetFunction(library,funcOffset,funcEntry)(A1,A0,D0)
426 $fe56 -$01aa SumLibrary(library)(A1)
*------ devices: ------------------------------------------------------
432 $fe50 -$01b0 AddDevice(device)(A1)
438 $fe4a -$01b6 RemDevice(device)(A1)
444 $fe44 -$01bc OpenDevice(devName,unit,ioRequest,flags)(A0,D0/A1,D1)
450 $fe3e -$01c2 CloseDevice(ioRequest)(A1)
456 $fe38 -$01c8 DoIO(ioRequest)(A1)
462 $fe32 -$01ce SendIO(ioRequest)(A1)
468 $fe2c -$01d4 CheckIO(ioRequest)(A1)
474 $fe26 -$01da WaitIO(ioRequest)(A1)
480 $fe20 -$01e0 AbortIO(ioRequest)(A1)
*------ resources: ---------------------------------------------------
486 $fe1a -$01e6 AddResource(resource)(A1)
492 $fe14 -$01ec RemResource(resource)(A1)
498 $fe0e -$01f2 OpenResource(resName,version)(A1,D0)
*------ new functions:
##private
504 $fe08 -$01f8 RawIOInit()
510 $fe02 -$01fe RawMayGetChar()
516 $fdfc -$0204 RawPutChar(char)(d0)
##public
522 $fdf6 -$020a RawDoFmt()(A0/A1/A2/A3)
528 $fdf0 -$0210 GetCC()
534 $fdea -$0216 TypeOfMem(address)(A1);
540 $fde4 -$021c Procure(semaport,bidMsg)(A0/A1)
546 $fdde -$0222 Vacate(semaport)(A0)
552 $fdd8 -$0228 OpenLibrary(libName,version)(A1,D0)
*------ 1.2 new semaphore support
558 $fdd2 -$022e InitSemaphore(sigSem)(A0)
564 $fdcc -$0234 ObtainSemaphore(sigSem)(A0)
570 $fdc6 -$023a ReleaseSemaphore(sigSem)(A0)
576 $fdc0 -$0240 AttemptSemaphore(sigSem)(A0)
582 $fdba -$0246 ObtainSemaphoreList(sigSem)(A0)
588 $fdb4 -$024c ReleaseSemaphoreList(sigSem)(A0)
594 $fdae -$0252 FindSemaphore(sigSem)(A1)
600 $fda8 -$0258 AddSemaphore(sigSem)(A1)
606 $fda2 -$025e RemSemaphore(sigSem)(A1)
*------ 1.2 rom "kickstart" support + memory support
612 $fd9c -$0264 SumKickData()
618 $fd96 -$026a AddMemList(size,attributes,pri,base,name)(D0/D1/D2/A0/A1)
624 $fd90 -$0270 CopyMem(source,dest,size)(A0/A1,D0)
630 $fd8a -$0276 CopyMemQuick(source,dest,size)(A0/A1,D0)


**************************** expansion.library ******************************
##base _ExpansionBase
##bias 30
 30 $ffe2 -$001e AddConfigDev(configDev)(A0)
##private
 36 $ffdc -$0024 expansionUnused()
##public
 42 $ffd6 -$002a AllocBoardMem(slotSpec)(D0)
 48 $ffd0 -$0030 AllocConfigDev()
 54 $ffca -$0036 AllocExpansionMem(numSlots,SlotAlign,SlotOffset)(D0/D1/D2)
 60 $ffc4 -$003c ConfigBoard(board,configDev)(A0/A1)
 66 $ffbe -$0042 ConfigChain(baseAddr)(A0)
 72 $ffb8 -$0048 FindConfigDev(oldConfigDev,manufacturer,product)(A0,D0/D1)
 78 $ffb2 -$004e FreeBoardMem(startSlot,slotSpec)(D0/D1)
 84 $ffac -$0054 FreeConfigDev(configDev)(A0)
 90 $ffa6 -$005a FreeExpansionMem(startSlot,numSlots)(D0/D1)
 96 $ffa0 -$0060 ReadExpansionByte(board,offset)(A0,D0)
102 $ff9a -$0066 ReadExpansionRom(board,configDev)(A0/A1)
108 $ff94 -$006c RemConfigDev(configDev)(A0)
```



```
114 $ff8e -$0072 WriteExpansionByte(board,offset,byte)(A0,D0/D1)
120 $ff88 -$0078 ObtainConfigBinding()
126 $ff82 -$007e ReleaseConfigBinding()
132 $ff7c -$0084 SetCurrentBinding(currentBinding,bindingSize)(A0,D0)
138 $ff76 -$008a GetCurrentBinding(currentBinding,bindingSize)(A0,D0)
144 $ff70 -$0090 MakeDosNode(parmPacket)(A0)
150 $ff6a -$0096 AddDosNode(bootPri,flags,dosNode)(D0/D1/A0)


**************************** graphics.library ******************************
##base _GfxBase
##bias 30
*------ Text routines
 30 $ffe2 -$001e BltBitMap(srcBitMap,srcX,srcY,destBitMap,destX,destY,sizeX,
                   sizeY,minterm,mask,tempA)(A0,D0/D1,A1,D2/D3/D4/D5/D6/D7/A2)
 36 $ffdc -$0024 BltTemplate(source,srcX,srcMod,destRastPort,destX,destY,
                   sizeX,sizeY)(A0,D0/D1/A1,D2/D3/D4/D5)
 42 $ffd6 -$002a ClearEOL(rastPort)(A1)
 48 $ffd0 -$0030 ClearScreen(rastPort)(A1)
 54 $ffca -$0036 TextLength(RastPort,string,count)(A1,A0,D0)
 60 $ffc4 -$003c Text(RastPort,string,count)(A1,A0,D0)
 66 $ffbe -$0042 SetFont(RastPortID,textFont)(A1,A0)
 72 $ffb8 -$0048 OpenFont(textAttr)(A0)
 78 $ffb2 -$004e CloseFont(textFont)(A1)
 84 $ffac -$0054 AskSoftStyle(rastPort)(A1)
 90 $ffa6 -$005a SetSoftStyle(rastPort,style,enable)(A1,D0/D1)
*------ Gels routines ------
 96 $ffa0 -$0060 AddBob(bob,rastPort)(A0,A1)
102 $ff9a -$0066 AddVSprite(vSprite,rastPort)(A0/A1)
108 $ff94 -$006c DoCollision(rasPort)(A1)
114 $ff8e -$0072 DrawGList(rastPort,viewPort)(A1,A0)
120 $ff88 -$0078 InitGels(dummyHead,dummyTail,GelsInfo)(A0/A1/A2)
126 $ff82 -$007e InitMasks(vSprite)(A0)
132 $ff7c -$0084 RemIBob(bob,rastPort,viewPort)(A0/A1/A2)
138 $ff76 -$008a RemVSprite(vSprite)(A0)
144 $ff70 -$0090 SetCollision(type,routine,gelsInfo)(D0/A0/A1)
150 $ff6a -$0096 SortGList(rastPort)(A1)
156 $ff64 -$009c AddAnimOb(obj,animationKey,rastPort)(A0/A1/A2)
162 $ff5e -$00a2 Animate(animationKey,rastPort)(A0/A1)
168 $ff58 -$00a8 GetGBuffers(animationObj,rastPort,doubleBuffer)(A0/A1,D0)
174 $ff52 -$00ae InitGMasks(animationObj)(A0)
180 $ff4c -$00b4 DrawEllipse(rastPort,cx,cy,a,b)(A1,D0/D1/D2/D3)
186 $ff46 -$00ba AreaEllipse(rastPort,cx,cy,a,b)(A1,D0/D1/D2/D3)
*------ Remaining graphics routines ------
192 $ff40 -$00c0 LoadRGB4(viewPort,colors,count)(A0/A1,D0)
198 $ff3a -$00c6 InitRastPort(rastPort)(A1)
204 $ff34 -$00cc InitVPort(viewPort)(A0)
210 $ff2e -$00d2 MrgCop(view)(A1)
216 $ff28 -$00d8 MakeVPort(view,viewPort)(A0/A1)
222 $ff22 -$00de LoadView(view)(A1)
228 $ff1c -$00e4 WaitBlit()
234 $ff16 -$00ea SetRast(rastPort,color)(A1,D0)
240 $ff10 -$00f0 Move(rastPort,x,y)(A1,D0/D1)
246 $ff0a -$00f6 Draw(rastPort,x,y)(A1,D0/D1)
252 $ff04 -$00fc AreaMove(rastPort,x,y)(A1,D0/D1)
258 $fefe -$0102 AreaDraw(rastPort,x,y)(A1,D0/D1)
264 $fef8 -$0108 AreaEnd(rastPort)(A1)
270 $fef2 -$010e WaitTOF()
276 $feec -$0114 QBlit(blit)(A1)
282 $fee6 -$011a InitArea(areaInfo,vectorTable,vectorTableSize)(A0/A1,D0)
288 $fee0 -$0120 SetRGB4(viewPort,index,r,g,b)(A0,D0/D1/D2/D3)
294 $feda -$0126 QBSBlit(blit)(A1)
300 $fed4 -$012c BltClear(memory,size,flags)(A1,D0/D1)
306 $fece -$0132 RectFill(rastPort,xl,yl,xu,yu)(A1,D0/D1/D2/D3)
312 $fec8 -$0138 BltPattern(rastPort,ras,xl,yl,maxX,maxY,fillBytes)
                   (a1,a0,D0/D1/D2/D3/D4)
318 $fec2 -$013e ReadPixel(rastPort,x,y)(A1,D0/D1)
324 $febc -$0144 WritePixel(rastPort,x,y)(A1,D0/D1)
330 $feb6 -$014a Flood(rastPort,mode,x,y)(A1,D2,D0/D1)
```

```
336 $feb0 -$0150 PolyDraw(rastPort,count,polyTable)(A1,D0,A0)
342 $feaa -$0156 SetAPen(rastPort,pen)(A1,D0)
348 $fea4 -$015c SetBPen(rastPort,pen)(A1,D0)
354 $fe9e -$0162 SetDrMd(rastPort,drawMode)(A1,D0)
360 $fe98 -$0168 InitView(view)(A1)
366 $fe92 -$016e CBump(copperList)(A1)
372 $fe8c -$0174 CMove(copperList,destination,data)(A1,D0/D1)
378 $fe86 -$017a CWait(copperList,x,y)(A1,D0/D1)
384 $fe80 -$0180 VBeamPos()
390 $fe7a -$0186 InitBitMap(bitMap,depth,width,height)(A0,D0/D1/D2)
396 $fe74 -$018c ScrollRaster(rastPort,dX,dY,minx,miny,maxx,maxy)
                 (A1,D0/D1/D2/D3/D4/D5)
402 $fe6e -$0192 WaitBOVP(viewport)(a0)
408 $fe68 -$0198 GetSprite(simplesprite,num)(a0,d0)
414 $fe62 -$019e FreeSprite(num)(d0)
420 $fe5c -$01a4 ChangeSprite(vp,simplesprite,data)(a0/a1/a2)
426 $fe56 -$01aa MoveSprite(viewport,simplesprite,x,y)(a0/a1,d0/d1)
432 $fe50 -$01b0 LockLayerRom(layer)(a5)
438 $fe4a -$01b6 UnlockLayerRom(layer)(a5)
444 $fe44 -$01bc SyncSBitMap(l)(a0)
450 $fe3e -$01c2 CopySBitMap(l)(a0)
456 $fe38 -$01c8 OwnBlitter()()
462 $fe32 -$01ce DisownBlitter()()
468 $fe2c -$01d4 InitTmpRas(tmpras,buff,size)(a0/a1,d0)
474 $fe26 -$01da AskFont(rastPort,textAttr)(A1,A0)
480 $fe20 -$01e0 AddFont(textFont)(A1)
486 $fe1a -$01e6 RemFont(textFont)(A1)
492 $fe14 -$01ec AllocRaster(width,height)(D0/D1)
498 $fe0e -$01f2 FreeRaster(planeptr,width,height)(A0,D0/D1)
504 $fe08 -$01f8 AndRectRegion(rgn,rect)(A0/A1)
510 $fe02 -$01fe OrRectRegion(rgn,rect)(A0/A1)
516 $fdfc -$0204 NewRegion()()
522 $fdf6 -$020a ClearRectRegion(rgn)(A0/A1)
528 $fdf0 -$0210 ClearRegion(rgn)(A0)
534 $fdea -$0216 DisposeRegion(rgn)(A0)
540 $fde4 -$021c FreeVPortCopLists(viewport)(a0)
546 $fdde -$0222 FreeCopList(coplist)(a0)
552 $fdd8 -$0228 ClipBlit(srcrp,srcX,srcY,destrp,destX,destY,sizeX,sizeY,
                  minterm)(A0,D0/D1,A1,D2/D3/D4/D5/D6)
558 $fdd2 -$022e XorRectRegion(rgn,rect)(a0/a1)
564 $fdcc -$0234 FreeCprList(cprlist)(a0)
570 $fdc6 -$023a GetColorMap(entries)(d0)
576 $fdc0 -$0240 FreeColorMap(colormap)(a0)
582 $fdba -$0246 GetRGB4(colormap,entry)(a0,d0)
588 $fdb4 -$024c ScrollVPort(vp)(a0)
594 $fdae -$0252 UCopperListInit(copperlist,num)(a0,d0)
600 $fda8 -$0258 FreeGBuffers(animationObj,rastPort,doubleBuffer)(A0/A1,D0)
606 $fda2 -$025e BltBitMapRastPort(srcbm,srcx,srcy,destrp,destX,destY,sizeX,
                  sizeY,minterm)(A0,D0/D1,A1,D2/D3/D4/D5/D6)
612 $fd9c -$0264 OrRegionRegion(src,dst)(a0/a1)
618 $fd96 -$026a XorRegionRegion(src,dst)(a0/a1)
624 $fd90 -$0270 AndRegionRegion(src,dst)(a0/a1)
630 $fd8a -$0276 SetRGB4CM(cm,i,r,g,b)(a0,d0/d1/d2/d3)
636 $fd84 -$027c BltMaskBitMapRastPort(srcbm,srcx,srcy,destrp,destX,destY,
                  sizeX,sizeY,minterm,bltmask)(A0,D0/D1,A1,D2/D3/D4/D5/D6,A2)
##private
642 $fd7e -$0282 GraphicsReserved1()()
648 $fd78 -$0288 GraphicsReserved2()()
##public
654 $fd72 -$028e AttemptLockLayerRom(layer)(a5)


**************************** icon.library ***********************************
##base _IconBase
##bias 30
 30 $ffe2 -$001e GetWBObject()()
 36 $ffdc -$0024 PutWBObject()()
 42 $ffd6 -$002a GetIcon()()
 48 $ffd0 -$0030 PutIcon()()
```



```
##public
 54 $ffca -$0036 FreeFreeList(freelist)(A0)
##private
 60 $ffc4 -$003c FreeWBObject(WBObject)(A0)
 66 $ffbe -$0042 AllocWBObject()()
##public
 72 $ffb8 -$0048 AddFreeList(freelist,mem,size)(A0/A1/A2)
*------ normal functions -----------------------------------------------
 78 $ffb2 -$004e GetDiskObject(name)(A0)
 84 $ffac -$0054 PutDiskObject(name,diskobj)(A0,A1)
 90 $ffa6 -$005a FreeDiskObject(diskobj)(A0)
 96 $ffa0 -$0060 FindToolType(toolTypeArray,typeName)(A0/A1)
102 $ff9a -$0066 MatchToolValue(typeString,value)(A0/A1)
108 $ff94 -$006c BumpRevision(newname,oldname)(A0/A1)


**************************** intuition.library ******************************
##base _IntuitionBase
##bias 30
 30 $ffe2 -$001e OpenIntuition()()
 36 $ffdc -$0024 Intuition(ievent)(A0)
 42 $ffd6 -$002a AddGadget(AddPtr,Gadget,Position)(A0/A1,D0)
 48 $ffd0 -$0030 ClearDMRequest(Window)(A0)
 54 $ffca -$0036 ClearMenuStrip(Window)(A0)
 60 $ffc4 -$003c ClearPointer(Window)(A0)
 66 $ffbe -$0042 CloseScreen(Screen)(A0)
 72 $ffb8 -$0048 CloseWindow(Window)(A0)
 78 $ffb2 -$004e CloseWorkBench()()
 84 $ffac -$0054 CurrentTime(Seconds,Micros)(A0/A1)
 90 $ffa6 -$005a DisplayAlert(AlertNumber,String,Height)(D0/A0,D1)
 96 $ffa0 -$0060 DisplayBeep(Screen)(A0)
102 $ff9a -$0066 DoubleClick(sseconds,smicros,cseconds,cmicros)(D0/D1/D2/D3)
108 $ff94 -$006c DrawBorder(RPort,Border,LeftOffset,TopOffset)(A0/A1,D0/D1)
114 $ff8e -$0072 DrawImage(RPort,Image,LeftOffset,TopOffset)(A0/A1,D0/D1)
120 $ff88 -$0078 EndRequest(requester,window)(A0/A1)
126 $ff82 -$007e GetDefPrefs(preferences,size)(A0,D0)
132 $ff7c -$0084 GetPrefs(preferences,size)(A0,D0)
138 $ff76 -$008a InitRequester(req)(A0)
144 $ff70 -$0090 ItemAddress(MenuStrip,MenuNumber)(A0,D0)
150 $ff6a -$0096 ModifyIDCMP(Window,Flags)(A0,D0)
156 $ff64 -$009c ModifyProp(Gadget,Ptr,Req,Flags,HPos,VPos,HBody,VBody)
                  (A0/A1/A2,D0/D1/D2/D3/D4)
162 $ff5e -$00a2 MoveScreen(Screen,dx,dy)(A0,D0/D1)
168 $ff58 -$00a8 MoveWindow(window,dx,dy)(A0,D0/D1)
174 $ff52 -$00ae OffGadget(Gadget,Ptr,Req)(A0/A1/A2)
180 $ff4c -$00b4 OffMenu(Window,MenuNumber)(A0,D0)
186 $ff46 -$00ba OnGadget(Gadget,Ptr,Req)(A0/A1/A2)
192 $ff40 -$00c0 OnMenu(Window,MenuNumber)(A0,D0)
198 $ff3a -$00c6 OpenScreen(OSargs)(A0)
204 $ff34 -$00cc OpenWindow(OWargs)(A0)
210 $ff2e -$00d2 OpenWorkBench()()
216 $ff28 -$00d8 PrintIText(rp,itext,left,top)(A0/A1,D0/D1)
222 $ff22 -$00de RefreshGadgets(Gadgets,Ptr,Req)(A0/A1/A2)
228 $ff1c -$00e4 RemoveGadget(RemPtr,Gadget)(A0/A1)
* The official calling sequence for ReportMouse is given below.  Note the
* register order. For the complete story, read the ReportMouse AutoDoc.
234 $ff16 -$00ea ReportMouse(Boolean,Window)(D0/A0)
240 $ff10 -$00f0 Request(Requester,Window)(A0/A1)
246 $ff0a -$00f6 ScreenToBack(Screen)(A0)
252 $ff04 -$00fc ScreenToFront(Screen)(A0)
258 $fefe -$0102 SetDMRequest(Window,req)(A0/A1)
264 $fef8 -$0108 SetMenuStrip(Window,Menu)(A0/A1)
270 $fef2 -$010e SetPointer(Window,Pointer,Height,Width,Xoffset,Yoffset)
                  (A0/A1,D0/D1/D2/D3)
276 $feec -$0114 SetWindowTitles(window,windowtitle,screentitle)(A0/A1/A2)
282 $fee6 -$011a ShowTitle(Screen,ShowIt)(A0,D0)
288 $fee0 -$0120 SizeWindow(window,dx,dy)(A0,D0/D1)
294 $feda -$0126 ViewAddress()()
300 $fed4 -$012c ViewPortAddress(window)(A0)
```

```
306 $fece -$0132 WindowToBack(window)(A0)
312 $fec8 -$0138 WindowToFront(window)(A0)
318 $fec2 -$013e WindowLimits(window,minwidth,minheight,maxwidth,maxheight)
                 (A0,D0/D1/D2/D3)
*--- start of next generation of names -----------------------------------
324 $febc -$0144 SetPrefs(preferences,size,flag)(A0,D0/D1)
*--- start of next next generation of names ------------------------------
330 $feb6 -$014a IntuiTextLength(itext)(A0)
336 $feb0 -$0150 WBenchToBack()()
342 $feaa -$0156 WBenchToFront()()
*--- start of next next next generation of names -------------------------
348 $fea4 -$015c AutoRequest(Window,Body,PText,NText,PFlag,NFlag,W,H)
                 (A0,A1,A2,A3,D0,D1,D2,D3)
354 $fe9e -$0162 BeginRefresh(Window)(A0)
360 $fe98 -$0168 BuildSysRequest(Window,Body,PosText,NegText,Flags,W,H)
                 (A0,A1,A2,A3,D0,D1,D2)
366 $fe92 -$016e EndRefresh(Window,Complete)(A0,D0)
372 $fe8c -$0174 FreeSysRequest(Window)(A0)
378 $fe86 -$017a MakeScreen(Screen)(A0)
384 $fe80 -$0180 RemakeDisplay()()
390 $fe7a -$0186 RethinkDisplay()()
*--- start of next next next generation of names -------------------------
396 $fe74 -$018c AllocRemember(RememberKey,Size,Flags)(A0,D0,D1)
402 $fe6e -$0192 AlohaWorkbench(wbport)(A0)
408 $fe68 -$0198 FreeRemember(RememberKey,ReallyForget)(A0,D0)
* PointerColors(Screen,Red,Gren,Blue)(A0,D0,D1,D2)
*--- start of 15 Nov 85 names -----------------------
414 $fe62 -$019e LockIBase(dontknow)(D0)
420 $fe5c -$01a4 UnlockIBase(IBLock)(A0)
*--- start of post-1.1 names ----
426 $fe56 -$01aa GetScreenData(buffer,size,type,screen)(A0,D0,D1,A1)
432 $fe50 -$01b0 RefreshGList(Gadgets,Ptr,Req,NumGad)(A0/A1/A2,D0)
438 $fe4a -$01b6 AddGList(AddPtr,Gadget,Position,NumGad,Requester)
                 (A0/A1,D0/D1/A2)
444 $fe44 -$01bc RemoveGList(RemPtr,Gadget,NumGad)(A0/A1,D0)
450 $fe3e -$01c2 ActivateWindow(Window)(A0)
456 $fe38 -$01c8 RefreshWindowFrame(Window)(A0)
462 $fe32 -$01ce ActivateGadget(Gadgets,Window,Req)(A0/A1/A2)
468 $fe2c -$01d4 NewModifyProp(Gadget,Ptr,Req,Flags,HPos,VPos,HBody,VBody,
                 NumGad)(A0/A1/A2,D0/D1/D2/D3/D4/D5)


**************************** layers.library *********************************
##base _LayersBase
##bias 30
 30 $ffe2 -$001e InitLayers(li)(A0)
 36 $ffdc -$0024 CreateUpfrontLayer(li,bm,x0,y0,x1,y1,flags,bm2)
                 (A0/A1,D0/D1/D2/D3/D4,A2)
 42 $ffd6 -$002a CreateBehindLayer(li,bm,x0,y0,x1,y1,flags,bm2)
                 (A0/A1,D0/D1/D2/D3/D4,A2)
 48 $ffd0 -$0030 UpfrontLayer(li,layer)(A0/A1)
 54 $ffca -$0036 BehindLayer(li,layer)(A0/A1)
 60 $ffc4 -$003c MoveLayer(li,layer,dx,dy)(A0/A1,D0/D1)
 66 $ffbe -$0042 SizeLayer(li,layer,dx,dy)(A0/A1,D0/D1)
 72 $ffb8 -$0048 ScrollLayer(li,layer,dx,dy)(A0/A1,D0/D1)
 78 $ffb2 -$004e BeginUpdate(layer)(A0)
 84 $ffac -$0054 EndUpdate(layer,flag)(A0,d0)
 90 $ffa6 -$005a DeleteLayer(li,layer)(A0/A1)
 96 $ffa0 -$0060 LockLayer(li,layer)(A0/A1)
102 $ff9a -$0066 UnlockLayer(layer)(A0)
108 $ff94 -$006c LockLayers(li)(A0)
114 $ff8e -$0072 UnlockLayers(li)(A0)
120 $ff88 -$0078 LockLayerInfo(li)(A0)
126 $ff82 -$007e SwapBitsRastPortClipRect(rp,cr)(A0/A1)
132 $ff7c -$0084 WhichLayer(li,x,y)(a0,d0/d1)
138 $ff76 -$008a UnlockLayerInfo(li)(A0)
144 $ff70 -$0090 NewLayerInfo()()
150 $ff6a -$0096 DisposeLayerInfo(li)(a0)
156 $ff64 -$009c FattenLayerInfo(li)(a0)
```



```
162 $ff5e -$00a2 ThinLayerInfo(li)(a0)
168 $ff58 -$00a8 MoveLayerInFrontOf(layer_to_move,layer_to_be_infront_of)
                 (a0/a1)
174 $ff52 -$00ae InstallClipRegion(layer,region)(a0/a1)


***************************** mathffp.library *********************************
##base _MathBase
##bias 30
 30 $ffe2 -$001e SPFix(float)(D0)
 36 $ffdc -$0024 SPFlt(integer)(D0)
 42 $ffd6 -$002a SPCmp(leftFloat,rightFloat)(D1,D0)
 48 $ffd0 -$0030 SPTst(float)(D1)
 54 $ffca -$0036 SPAbs(float)(D0)
 60 $ffc4 -$003c SPNeg(float)(D0)
 66 $ffbe -$0042 SPAdd(leftFloat,rightFloat)(D1,D0)
 72 $ffb8 -$0048 SPSub(leftFloat,rightFloat)(D1,D0)
 78 $ffb2 -$004e SPMul(leftFloat,rightFloat)(D1,D0)
 84 $ffac -$0054 SPDiv(leftFloat,rightFloat)(D1,D0)
*  New functions added for release 1.2
 90 $ffa6 -$005a SPFloor(float)(D0)
 96 $ffa0 -$0060 SPCeil(float)(D0)


***************************** mathieeedoubbas.library ***********************
##base _MathIeeeDoubBasBase
##bias 30
 30 $ffe2 -$001e IEEEDPFix(double)(D0/D1)
 36 $ffdc -$0024 IEEEDPFlt(integer)(D0)
 42 $ffd6 -$002a IEEEDPCmp(double,double)(D0/D1/D2/D3)
 48 $ffd0 -$0030 IEEEDPTst(double)(D0/D1)
 54 $ffca -$0036 IEEEDPAbs(double)(D0/D1)
 60 $ffc4 -$003c IEEEDPNeg(double)(D0/D1)
 66 $ffbe -$0042 IEEEDPAdd(double,double)(D0/D1/D2/D3)
 72 $ffb8 -$0048 IEEEDPSub(double,double)(D0/D1/D2/D3)
 78 $ffb2 -$004e IEEEDPMul(double,double)(D0/D1/D2/D3)
 84 $ffac -$0054 IEEEDPDiv(double,double)(D0/D1/D2/D3)
*  New functions added for release 1.2
 90 $ffa6 -$005a IEEEDPFloor(double)(D0/D1)
 96 $ffa0 -$0060 IEEEDPCeil(double)(D0/D1)


***************************** mathieeedoubtrans.library *********************
##base _MathIeeeDoubTransBase
##bias 30
 30 $ffe2 -$001e IEEEDPAtan(double)(D0/D1)
 36 $ffdc -$0024 IEEEDPSin(double)(D0/D1)
 42 $ffd6 -$002a IEEEDPCos(double)(D0/D1)
 48 $ffd0 -$0030 IEEEDPTan(double)(D0/D1)
 54 $ffca -$0036 IEEEDPSincos(double,pf2)(A0,D0/D1)
 60 $ffc4 -$003c IEEEDPSinh(double)(D0/D1)
 66 $ffbe -$0042 IEEEDPCosh(double)(D0/D1)
 72 $ffb8 -$0048 IEEEDPTanh(double)(D0/D1)
 78 $ffb2 -$004e IEEEDPExp(double)(D0/D1)
 84 $ffac -$0054 IEEEDPLog(double)(D0/D1)
 90 $ffa6 -$005a IEEEDPPow(exp,arg)(D2/D3,D0/D1)
 96 $ffa0 -$0060 IEEEDPSqrt(double)(D0/D1)
102 $ff9a -$0066 IEEEDPTieee(double)(D0/D1)
108 $ff94 -$006c IEEEDPFieee(single)(D0)
114 $ff8e -$0072 IEEEDPAsin(double)(D0/D1)
120 $ff88 -$0078 IEEEDPAcos(double)(D0/D1)
126 $ff82 -$007e IEEEDPLog10(double)(D0/D1)


***************************** mathtrans.library *****************************
##base _MathTransBase
##bias 30
 30 $ffe2 -$001e SPAtan(float)(D0)
 36 $ffdc -$0024 SPSin(float)(D0)
```

```
 42 $ffd6 -$002a SPCos(float)(D0)
 48 $ffd0 -$0030 SPTan(float)(D0)
 54 $ffca -$0036 SPSincos(leftFloat,rightFloat)(D1,D0)
 60 $ffc4 -$003c SPSinh(float)(D0)
 66 $ffbe -$0042 SPCosh(float)(D0)
 72 $ffb8 -$0048 SPTanh(float)(D0)
 78 $ffb2 -$004e SPExp(float)(D0)
 84 $ffac -$0054 SPLog(float)(D0)
 90 $ffa6 -$005a SPPow(leftFloat,rightFloat)(D1,D0)
 96 $ffa0 -$0060 SPSqrt(float)(D0)
102 $ff9a -$0066 SPTieee(float)(D0)
108 $ff94 -$006c SPFieee(integer)(D0)
*  New functions added for Release 1.1
114 $ff8e -$0072 SPAsin(float)(D0)
120 $ff88 -$0078 SPAcos(float)(D0)
126 $ff82 -$007e SPLog10(float)(D0)


**************************** potgo.resource ********************************
##base _PotgoBase
##bias 6
  6 $fffa -$0006 AllocPotBits(bits)(D0)
 12 $fff4 -$000c FreePotBits(bits)(D0)
 18 $ffee -$0012 WritePotgo(word,mask)(D0,D1)


**************************** timer.device **********************************
##base _TimerBase
##bias 42
 42 $ffd6 -$002a AddTime(dest,src)(A0/A1)
 48 $ffd0 -$0030 SubTime(dest,src)(A0/A1)
 54 $ffca -$0036 CmpTime(dest,src)(A0/A1)


**************************** translator.library ****************************
##base _TranslatorBase
##bias 30
 30 $ffe2 -$001e Translate(inputString,inputLength,outputBuffer,bufferSize)
                  (A0,D0/A1,D1)
```

Sep 20 14:00 1988 Assembly_Prefix_Reference Page 1

```
ac_         graphics/gels.i
af_         libraries/diskfont.i
ahf_        libraries/diskfont.i
ai_         graphics/rastport.i
ao_         graphics/gels.i
BB_         devices/bootblock.i
bd_         intuition/intuition.i
bi_         intuition/intuition.i
bm_         graphics/gfx.i
bn_         hardware/blit.i
bob_        graphics/gels.i
cb_         libraries/configvars.i
cd_         libraries/configvars.i
ci_         graphics/copper.i
cli_        libraries/dosextens.i
cl_         graphics/copper.i
cm_         graphics/view.i
copinit_    graphics/copper.i
cp_         graphics/view.i
crl_        graphics/copper.i
cr_         graphics/clip.i
cu_         devices/clipboard.i
cu_         devices/conunit.i
da_         libraries/configregs.i
dbp_        graphics/gels.i
dd_         devices/prtbase.i
DD_         exec/devices.i
dd_         workbench/workbench.i
dfh_        libraries/diskfont.i
di_         libraries/dosextens.i
dl_         libraries/dosextens.i
dl_         libraries/dosextens.i
dn_         libraries/filehandler.i
do_         workbench/workbench.i
dp_         libraries/dosextens.i
DRU_        resources/disk.i
DR_         resources/disk.i
ds_         libraries/dos.i
ec_         libraries/configregs.i
er_         libraries/configregs.i
fch_        libraries/diskfont.i
fc_         libraries/diskfont.i
fh_         libraries/dosextens.i
fib_        libraries/dos.i
fl_         libraries/dosextens.i
fl_         workbench/workbench.i
fssm_       libraries/filehandler.i
gb_         graphics/gfxbase.i
gg_         intuition/intuition.i
gi_         graphics/rastport.i
gpt_        devices/gameport.i
ib_         intuition/intuitionbase.i
id_         libraries/dos.i
ie_         devices/inputevent.i
ig_         intuition/intuition.i
im_         intuition/intuition.i
ioa_        devices/audio.i
iocpr_      devices/printer.i
iocr_       devices/clipboard.i
iodrpr_     devices/printer.i
IOEXPar_    devices/parallel.i
IOEXTSER_   devices/serial.i
IOSTD_      exec/io.i
IOTD_       devices/trackdisk.i
IOTV_       devices/timer.i
IO_         devices/parallel.i
IO_         exec/io.i
io_         devices/clipboard.i
io_         devices/printer.i
```

Sep 20 14:00 1988 Assembly_Prefix_Reference Page 2

```
IS_         exec/interrupts.i
it_         intuition/intuition.i
IV_         exec/interrupts.i
km_         devices/keymap.i
kn_         devices/keymap.i
kr_         devices/keymap.i
LH_         exec/lists.i
LIB_        exec/libraries.i
lie_        graphics/layers.i
li_         graphics/layers.i
LN_         exec/nodes.i
lpd_        devices/prtbase.i
lr_         graphics/clip.i
MC_         exec/memory.i
ME_         exec/memory.i
MH_         exec/memory.i
mi_         intuition/intuition.i
MLH_        exec/lists.i
MLN_        exec/nodes.i
ML_         exec/memory.i
MN_         exec/ports.i
MP_         exec/ports.i
MRB_        devices/narrator.i
mr_         resources/misc.i
mu_         intuition/intuition.i
NDI_        devices/narrator.i
ns_         intuition/intuition.i
nw_         intuition/intuition.i
ped_        devices/prtbase.i
pf_         intuition/intuition.i
pi_         intuition/intuition.i
pr_         libraries/dosextens.i
ps_         devices/prtbase.i
PTERMARRAY_ devices/parallel.i
ra_         graphics/gfx.i
rg_         graphics/regions.i
ri_         graphics/view.i
rm_         intuition/intuition.i
rn_         libraries/dosextens.i
rp_         graphics/rastport.i
rq_         intuition/intuition.i
rr_         graphics/regions.i
RT_         exec/resident.i
sc_         intuition/intuition.i
SH_         exec/interrupts.i
si_         intuition/intuition.i
sm_         devices/clipboard.i
SM_         exec/semaphores.i
sm_         workbench/startup.i
sp_         libraries/dosextens.i
SSR_        exec/semaphores.i
SS_         exec/semaphores.i
ss_         graphics/sprite.i
ta_         graphics/text.i
TC_         exec/tasks.i
TDU_        devices/trackdisk.i
TERMARRAY_  devices/serial.i
tf_         graphics/text.i
tr_         graphics/rastport.i
TV_         devices/timer.i
ucl_        graphics/copper.i
UNIT_       exec/devices.i
vp_         graphics/view.i
vs_         graphics/gels.i
v_          graphics/view.i
wa_         workbench/startup.i
wd_         intuition/intuition.i
```

```
_cliprects         pointer to struct ClipRect in struct Layer
        +0x0040    graphics/clip.h: *42
_CopList           pointer to struct CopList in struct CopList
        +0x0004    graphics/copper.h: *58
_pl                pointer to struct ClipRect in struct ClipRect
        +0x0018    graphics/clip.h: *61
_p2                pointer to struct ClipRect in struct ClipRect
        +0x001c    graphics/clip.h: *61
_ViewPort          pointer to struct ViewPort in struct CopList
        +0x0008    graphics/copper.h: *59
ABC                #define 0x80 =0x00000080 hardware/blit.h: *22
aBMS               #define 63 =0x0000003f devices/printer.h: *119
ABNC               #define 0x40 =0x00000040 hardware/blit.h: *23
abs                extern function returning float libraries/mathffp.h: *62
ABSOLUTE_DIMENSIONS #define 0x0020 =0x00000020 intuition/preferences.h: *243
aCAM               #define 66 =0x00000042 devices/printer.h: *122
ACCESS_READ        #define -2 =0xfffffffe libraries/dos.h: *45
ACCESS_WRITE       #define -1 =0xffffffff libraries/dos.h: *47
acos               #define SPAcos =0x00000000 libraries/mathffp.h: *40
acos               #define IEEEDPAcos =0x00000000 libraries/mathieeedp.h: *41
ACTION_COPY_DIR    #define 19 =0x00000013 libraries/dosextens.h: *130
ACTION_CREATE_DIR #define 22 =0x00000016 libraries/dosextens.h: *133
ACTION_CURRENT_VOLUME #define 7 =0x00000007 libraries/dosextens.h: *121
ACTION_DELETE_OBJECT #define 16 =0x00000010 libraries/dosextens.h: *127
ACTION_DIE         #define 5 =0x00000005 libraries/dosextens.h: *119
ACTION_DISK_CHANGE #define 33 =0x00000021 libraries/dosextens.h: *144
ACTION_DISK_INFO #define 25 =0x00000019 libraries/dosextens.h: *136
ACTION_DISK_TYPE #define 32 =0x00000020 libraries/dosextens.h: *143
ACTION_END         #define 1007 =0x000003ef libraries/dosextens.h: *155
ACTION_EVENT       #define 6 =0x00000006 libraries/dosextens.h: *120
ACTION_EXAMINE_NEXT #define 24 =0x00000018 libraries/dosextens.h: *135
ACTION_EXAMINE_OBJECT #define 23 =0x00000017 libraries/dosextens.h: *134
ACTION_FINDINPUT #define 1005 =0x000003ed libraries/dosextens.h: *153
ACTION_FINDOUTPUT #define 1006 =0x000003ee libraries/dosextens.h: *154
ACTION_FINDUPDATE #define 1004 =0x000003ec libraries/dosextens.h: *152
ACTION_FLUSH       #define 27 =0x0000001b libraries/dosextens.h: *138
ACTION_FREE_LOCK #define 15 =0x0000000f libraries/dosextens.h: *126
ACTION_GET_BLOCK #define 2 =0x00000002 libraries/dosextens.h: *117
ACTION_INFO        #define 26 =0x0000001a libraries/dosextens.h: *137
ACTION_INHIBIT     #define 31 =0x0000001f libraries/dosextens.h: *142
ACTION_LOCATE_OBJECT #define 8 =0x00000008 libraries/dosextens.h: *122
ACTION_MORE_CACHE #define 18 =0x00000012 libraries/dosextens.h: *129
ACTION_NIL         #define 0 =0x00000000 libraries/dosextens.h: *116
ACTION_PARENT      #define 29 =0x0000001d libraries/dosextens.h: *140
ACTION_READ        #define 'R' =0x00000052 libraries/dosextens.h: *125
ACTION_READ_RETURN #define 1001 =0x000003e9 libraries/dosextens.h: *149
ACTION_RENAME_DISK #define 9 =0x00000009 libraries/dosextens.h: *123
ACTION_RENAME_OBJECT #define 17 =0x00000011 libraries/dosextens.h: *128
ACTION_SCREEN_MODE #define 994 =0x000003e2 libraries/dosextens.h: *147
ACTION_SEEK        #define 1008 =0x000003f0 libraries/dosextens.h: *151
ACTION_SET_COMMENT #define 28 =0x0000001c libraries/dosextens.h: *139
ACTION_SET_DATE  #define 34 =0x00000022 libraries/dosextens.h: *145
ACTION_SET_MAP   #define 4 =0x00000004 libraries/dosextens.h: *118
ACTION_SET_PROTECT #define 21 =0x00000015 libraries/dosextens.h: *132
ACTION_TIMER       #define 30 =0x0000001e libraries/dosextens.h: *141
ACTION_TRUNCATE  #define 1022 =0x000003fe libraries/dosextens.h: *156
ACTION_WAIT_CHAR #define 20 =0x00000014 libraries/dosextens.h: *131
ACTION_WRITE       #define 'W' =0x00000057 libraries/dosextens.h: *124
ACTION_WRITE_PROTECT #define 1023 =0x000003ff libraries/dosextens.h: *157
ACTION_WRITE_RETURN #define 1002 =0x000003ea libraries/dosextens.h: *150
ACTIVATE           #define 0x1000 =0x00001000 intuition/intuition.h: *822
Activation         unsigned short int in struct Gadget
        +0x000e    intuition/intuition.h: *202
ActiveScreen       pointer to struct Screen in struct IntuitionBase
        +0x0038    intuition/intuitionbase.h: *153
ACTIVEWINDOW       #define 0x00040000 =0x00040000 intuition/intuition.h: *656
ActiveWindow       pointer to struct Window in struct IntuitionBase
        +0x0034    intuition/intuitionbase.h: *152
ActiView           pointer to struct View in struct GfxBase
```



```
        +0x0022    graphics/gfxbase.h: *26
ac_dat             unsigned short int in struct AudChannel
        +0x000a    hardware/custom.h: *90
ac_len             unsigned short int in struct AudChannel
        +0x0004    hardware/custom.h: *87
ac_pad             array [2] of unsigned short int in struct AudChannel
        +0x000c    hardware/custom.h: *91
ac_per             unsigned short int in struct AudChannel
        +0x0006    hardware/custom.h: *88
ac_ptr             pointer to unsigned short int in struct AudChannel
        +0x0000    hardware/custom.h: *86
ac_vol             unsigned short int in struct AudChannel
        +0x0008    hardware/custom.h: *89
ADALLOC_MAXPREC    #define 127 =0x0000007f devices/audio.h: *22
ADALLOC_MINPREC    #define -128 =0xffffff80 devices/audio.h: *21
ADCMDB_NOUNIT      #define 5 =0x00000005 devices/audio.h: *30
ADCMDF_NOUNIT      #define (1<<5) =0x00000020 devices/audio.h: *31
ADCMD_ALLOCATE     #define (ADCMDF_NOUNIT+0) =0x00000020 devices/audio.h: *32
ADCMD_FINISH       #define (CMD_NONSTD+2) =0x0000000b devices/audio.h: *26
ADCMD_FREE         #define (CMD_NONSTD+0) =0x00000009 devices/audio.h: *24
ADCMD_LOCK         #define (CMD_NONSTD+4) =0x0000000d devices/audio.h: *28
ADCMD_PERVOL       #define (CMD_NONSTD+3) =0x0000000c devices/audio.h: *27
ADCMD_SETPREC      #define (CMD_NONSTD+1) =0x0000000a devices/audio.h: *25
ADCMD_WAITCYCLE    #define (CMD_NONSTD+5) =0x0000000e devices/audio.h: *29
AddFreeList        extern function returning void workbench/icon.h: *31
aDEN1              #define 26 =0x0000001a devices/printer.h: *61
aDEN2              #define 25 =0x00000019 devices/printer.h: *60
aDEN3              #define 24 =0x00000018 devices/printer.h: *59
aDEN4              #define 23 =0x00000017 devices/printer.h: *58
aDEN5              #define 22 =0x00000016 devices/printer.h: *57
aDEN6              #define 21 =0x00000015 devices/printer.h: *56
ADHARD_CHANNELS    #define 4 =0x00000004 devices/audio.h: *19
ADIOB_NOWAIT       #define 6 =0x00000006 devices/audio.h: *38
ADIOB_PERVOL       #define 4 =0x00000004 devices/audio.h: *34
ADIOB_SYNCCYCLE    #define 5 =0x00000005 devices/audio.h: *36
ADIOB_WRITEMESSAGE #define 7 =0x00000007 devices/audio.h: *40
ADIOERR_ALLOCFAILED #define -11 =0xfffffff5 devices/audio.h: *44
ADIOERR_CHANNELSTOLEN #define -12 =0xfffffff4 devices/audio.h: *45
ADIOERR_NOALLOCATION #define -10 =0xfffffff6 devices/audio.h: *43
ADIOF_NOWAIT       #define (1<<6) =0x00000040 devices/audio.h: *39
ADIOF_PERVOL       #define (1<<4) =0x00000010 devices/audio.h: *35
ADIOF_SYNCCYCLE    #define (1<<5) =0x00000020 devices/audio.h: *37
ADIOF_WRITEMESSAGE #define (1<<7) =0x00000080 devices/audio.h: *41
ADKB_FAST          #define 8 =0x00000008 hardware/adkbits.h: *20
ADKB_MFMPREC       #define 12 =0x0000000c hardware/adkbits.h: *16
ADKB_MSBSYNC       #define 9 =0x00000009 hardware/adkbits.h: *19
ADKB_PRECOMP0      #define 13 =0x0000000d hardware/adkbits.h: *15
ADKB_PRECOMP1      #define 14 =0x0000000e hardware/adkbits.h: *14
ADKB_SETCLR        #define 15 =0x0000000f hardware/adkbits.h: *13
ADKB_UARTBRK       #define 11 =0x0000000b hardware/adkbits.h: *17
ADKB_USE0P1        #define 4 =0x00000004 hardware/adkbits.h: *24
ADKB_USE0V1        #define 0 =0x00000000 hardware/adkbits.h: *28
ADKB_USE1P2        #define 5 =0x00000005 hardware/adkbits.h: *23
ADKB_USE1V2        #define 1 =0x00000001 hardware/adkbits.h: *27
ADKB_USE2P3        #define 6 =0x00000006 hardware/adkbits.h: *22
ADKB_USE2V3        #define 2 =0x00000002 hardware/adkbits.h: *26
ADKB_USE3PN        #define 7 =0x00000007 hardware/adkbits.h: *21
ADKB_USE3VN        #define 3 =0x00000003 hardware/adkbits.h: *25
ADKB_WORDSYNC      #define 10 =0x0000000a hardware/adkbits.h: *18
adkcon             unsigned short int in struct Custom
        +0x009e    hardware/custom.h: *84
adkconr            unsigned short int in struct Custom
        +0x0010    hardware/custom.h: *28
ADKF_FAST          #define (1<<8) =0x00000100 hardware/adkbits.h: *37
ADKF_MFMPREC       #define (1<<12) =0x00001000 hardware/adkbits.h: *33
ADKF_MSBSYNC       #define (1<<9) =0x00000200 hardware/adkbits.h: *36
ADKF_PRE000NS      #define 0 =0x00000000 hardware/adkbits.h: *47
ADKF_PRE140NS      #define (ADKF_PRECOMP0) =0x00002000 hardware/adkbits.h: *48
ADKF_PRE280NS      #define (ADKF_PRECOMP1) =0x00004000 hardware/adkbits.h: *49
```

```
ADKF_PRE560NS      #define (ADKF_PRECOMP0|ADKF_PRECOMP1) =0x00006000
                   hardware/adkbits.h: *50
ADKF_PRECOMP0      #define (1<<13) =0x00002000 hardware/adkbits.h: *32
ADKF_PRECOMP1      #define (1<<14) =0x00004000 hardware/adkbits.h: *31
ADKF_SETCLR        #define (1<<15) =0x00008000 hardware/adkbits.h: *30
ADKF_UARTBRK       #define (1<<11) =0x00000800 hardware/adkbits.h: *34
ADKF_USE0P1        #define (1<<4) =0x00000010 hardware/adkbits.h: *41
ADKF_USE0V1        #define (1<<0) =0x00000001 hardware/adkbits.h: *45
ADKF_USE1P2        #define (1<<5) =0x00000020 hardware/adkbits.h: *40
ADKF_USE1V2        #define (1<<1) =0x00000002 hardware/adkbits.h: *44
ADKF_USE2P3        #define (1<<6) =0x00000040 hardware/adkbits.h: *39
ADKF_USE2V3        #define (1<<2) =0x00000004 hardware/adkbits.h: *43
ADKF_USE3PN        #define (1<<7) =0x00000080 hardware/adkbits.h: *38
ADKF_USE3VN        #define (1<<3) =0x00000008 hardware/adkbits.h: *42
ADKF_WORDSYNC      #define (1<<10) =0x00000400 hardware/adkbits.h: *35
ADNB_STARTPROC     #define 0 =0x00000000 libraries/expansion.h: *16
ADNF_STARTPROC     #define (1<<0) =0x00000001 libraries/expansion.h: *18
aEXTEND            #define 75 =0x0000004b devices/printer.h: *132
AFB_68010          #define 0 =0x00000000 exec/execbase.h: *127
AFB_68020          #define 1 =0x00000001 exec/execbase.h: *128
AFB_68881          #define 4 =0x00000004 exec/execbase.h: *129
AFB_DISK           #define 1 =0x00000001 libraries/diskfont.h: *62
AFB_MEMORY         #define 0 =0x00000000 libraries/diskfont.h: *60
AFB_RESERVED8      #define 8 =0x00000008 exec/execbase.h: *141
AFB_RESERVED9      #define 9 =0x00000009 exec/execbase.h: *142
AFF_68010          #define (1<<0) =0x00000001 exec/execbase.h: *131
AFF_68020          #define (1<<1) =0x00000002 exec/execbase.h: *132
AFF_68881          #define (1<<4) =0x00000010 exec/execbase.h: *133
AFF_DISK           #define 2 =0x00000002 libraries/diskfont.h: *63
AFF_MEMORY         #define 1 =0x00000001 libraries/diskfont.h: *61
afh_NumEntries     unsigned short int in struct AvailFontsHeader
        +0x0000    libraries/diskfont.h: *71
aFNT0              #define 34 =0x00000022 devices/printer.h: *71
aFNT1              #define 35 =0x00000023 devices/printer.h: *72
aFNT10             #define 44 =0x0000002c devices/printer.h: *81
aFNT2              #define 36 =0x00000024 devices/printer.h: *73
aFNT3              #define 37 =0x00000025 devices/printer.h: *74
aFNT4              #define 38 =0x00000026 devices/printer.h: *75
aFNT5              #define 39 =0x00000027 devices/printer.h: *76
aFNT6              #define 40 =0x00000028 devices/printer.h: *77
aFNT7              #define 41 =0x00000029 devices/printer.h: *78
aFNT8              #define 42 =0x0000002a devices/printer.h: *79
aFNT9              #define 43 =0x0000002b devices/printer.h: *80
afp                extern function returning float libraries/mathffp.h: *76
After              pointer to struct Bob in struct Bob
        +0x000e    graphics/gels.h: *153
af_Attr            struct TextAttr (size 0x0008) in struct AvailFonts
        +0x0002    libraries/diskfont.h: *67
af_Type            unsigned short int in struct AvailFonts
        +0x0000    libraries/diskfont.h: *66
AGNUS              #define =0x00000000 graphics/gfx.h: *16
AG_IOError         #define 0x00060000 =0x00060000 exec/alerts.h: *46
AG_MakeLib         #define 0x00020000 =0x00020000 exec/alerts.h: *42
AG_NoMemory        #define 0x00010000 =0x00010000 exec/alerts.h: *41
AG_NoSignal        #define 0x00070000 =0x00070000 exec/alerts.h: *47
AG_OpenDev         #define 0x00040000 =0x00040000 exec/alerts.h: *44
AG_OpenLib         #define 0x00030000 =0x00030000 exec/alerts.h: *43
AG_OpenRes         #define 0x00050000 =0x00050000 exec/alerts.h: *45
aHTS               #define 67 =0x00000043 devices/printer.h: *124
aIND               #define 2 =0x00000002 devices/printer.h: *34
aJFY0              #define 52 =0x00000034 devices/printer.h: *106
aJFY1              #define 54 =0x00000036 devices/printer.h: *108
aJFY3              #define 53 =0x00000035 devices/printer.h: *107
aJFY5              #define 49 =0x00000031 devices/printer.h: *103
aJFY6              #define 51 =0x00000033 devices/printer.h: *105
aJFY7              #define 50 =0x00000032 devices/printer.h: *104
AlertData          pointer to pointer to char in struct ExecBase
        +0x004a    exec/execbase.h: *44
ALERTLAYERSNOMEM #define 0x83010000 =0x83010000 graphics/layers.h: *50
```



```
ALERT_TYPE         #define 0x80000000 =0x80000000 intuition/intuition.h: *986
AlgoStyle          char in struct RastPort
        +0x0038    graphics/rastport.h: *73
AllocConfigDev     extern function returning pointer to struct ConfigDev (size 0x44)
                   libraries/configvars.h: *56
                   libraries/expansion.h: *23
AllocExpansionMem extern function returning "CPTR" libraries/expansion.h: *24
AllocTable         array [256] of char in struct ExpansionBase
        +0x0058    libraries/expansionbase.h: *53
AllocWBObject      extern function returning pointer to struct WBObject (size 0x000)
                   workbench/icon.h: *28
aLMS               #define 60 =0x0000003c devices/printer.h: *116
ALPHA_P_101        #define 0x01 =0x00000001 intuition/preferences.h: *187
ALTKEYMAP          #define 0x1000 =0x00001000 intuition/intuition.h: *323
AltKeyMap          pointer to struct KeyMap in struct StringInfo
        +0x0020    intuition/intuition.h: *479
ALTLEFT            #define (IEQUALIFIER_LALT) =0x00000010
                   intuition/intuition.h: *1010
ALTRIGHT           #define (IEQUALIFIER_RALT) =0x00000020
                   intuition/intuition.h: *1011
AMIGAKEYS          #define (AMIGALEFT | AMIGARIGHT) =0x000000c0
                   intuition/intuition.h: *1014
AMIGALEFT          #define (IEQUALIFIER_LCOMMAND) =0x00000040
                   intuition/intuition.h: *1012
AMIGARIGHT         #define (IEQUALIFIER_RCOMMAND) =0x00000080
                   intuition/intuition.h: *1013
ANBC               #define 0x20 =0x00000020 hardware/blit.h: *24
ANBNC              #define 0x10 =0x00000010 hardware/blit.h: *25
aNEL               #define 3 =0x00000003 devices/printer.h: *35
ANFRACSIZE         #define 6 =0x00000006 graphics/gels.h: *40
AnimBob            pointer to struct Bob in struct AnimComp
        +0x0022    graphics/gels.h: *196
AnimComp           structure tag
    size 0x0026    graphics/gels.h: 157, *164, 182, 183, 186, 187, 221
AnimCRoutine       pointer to function returning short int in struct AnimComp
        +0x0016    graphics/gels.h: *189
ANIMHALF           #define 0x0020 =0x00000020 graphics/gels.h: *41
AnimOb             structure tag
    size 0x002a    graphics/gels.h: 194, *199, 202
AnimORoutine       pointer to function returning short int in struct AnimOb
        +0x0020    graphics/gels.h: *218
AnOldX             short int in struct AnimOb
        +0x000e    graphics/gels.h: *207
AnOldY             short int in struct AnimOb
        +0x000c    graphics/gels.h: *207
ANTI_ALIAS         #define 0x0800 =0x00000800 intuition/preferences.h: *253
AnX                short int in struct AnimOb
        +0x0012    graphics/gels.h: *210
AnY                short int in struct AnimOb
        +0x0010    graphics/gels.h: *210
AN_AddSWGadget     #define 0x8401000A =0x8401000a exec/alerts.h: *119
AN_AsyncPkt        #define 0x07000004 =0x07000004 exec/alerts.h: *138
AN_AudioDev        #define 0x10000000 =0x10000000 exec/alerts.h: *160
AN_BadChkSum       #define 0x07000009 =0x07000009 exec/alerts.h: *143
AN_BadExpansionFree #define 0x0A000001 =0x0a000001 exec/alerts.h: *157
AN_BadGadget       #define 0x04000001 =0x04000001 exec/alerts.h: *110
AN_BadMessage      #define 0x8400000D =0x8400000d exec/alerts.h: *122
AN_BadOverlay      #define 0x0700000C =0x0700000c exec/alerts.h: *146
AN_BadSegList      #define 0x08000001 =0x08000001 exec/alerts.h: *150
AN_BadState        #define 0x8400000C =0x8400000c exec/alerts.h: *121
AN_BaseChkSum      #define 0x81000002 =0x81000002 exec/alerts.h: *82
AN_BitMap          #define 0x07000007 =0x07000007 exec/alerts.h: *141
AN_BltBitMap       #define 0x8201000A =0x8201000a exec/alerts.h: *98
AN_BogusExcpt      #define 0x8100000A =0x8100000a exec/alerts.h: *90
AN_BootError       #define 0x30000001 =0x30000001 exec/alerts.h: *194
AN_BootStrap       #define 0x30000000 =0x30000000 exec/alerts.h: *193
AN_CIARsrc         #define 0x20000000 =0x20000000 exec/alerts.h: *182
AN_CListLib        #define 0x06000000 =0x06000000 exec/alerts.h: *131
AN_ConsoleDev      #define 0x11000000 =0x11000000 exec/alerts.h: *163
```

```
AN_CreatePort     #define 0x84010002 =0x84010002 exec/alerts.h: *111
AN_DiskBlkSeq     #define 0x07000006 =0x07000006 exec/alerts.h: *140
AN_DiskCopy       #define 0x32000000 =0x32000000 exec/alerts.h: *200
AN_DiskError      #define 0x0700000A =0x0700000a exec/alerts.h: *144
AN_DiskRsrc       #define 0x21000000 =0x21000000 exec/alerts.h: *185
AN_DOSLib         #define 0x07000000 =0x07000000 exec/alerts.h: *134
AN_DRHasDisk      #define 0x21000001 =0x21000001 exec/alerts.h: *186
AN_DRIntNoAct     #define 0x21000002 =0x21000002 exec/alerts.h: *187
AN_EndTask        #define 0x07000002 =0x07000002 exec/alerts.h: *136
AN_ExcptVect      #define 0x81000001 =0x81000001 exec/alerts.h: *81
AN_ExecLib        #define 0x01000000 =0x01000000 exec/alerts.h: *80
AN_ExpansionLib   #define 0x0A000000 =0x0a000000 exec/alerts.h: *156
AN_FreeTwice      #define 0x81000009 =0x81000009 exec/alerts.h: *89
AN_FreeVec        #define 0x07000005 =0x07000005 exec/alerts.h: *139
AN_GadgetType     #define 0x84000001 =0x84000001 exec/alerts.h: *109
AN_GamePortDev    #define 0x12000000 =0x12000000 exec/alerts.h: *166
AN_GfxNoLCM       #define 0x82011234 =0x82011234 exec/alerts.h: *101
AN_GfxNoMem       #define 0x82010000 =0x82010000 exec/alerts.h: *94
AN_GraphicsLib    #define 0x02000000 =0x02000000 exec/alerts.h: *93
AN_IconLib        #define 0x09000000 =0x09000000 exec/alerts.h: *153
AN_InitAPtr       #define 0x81000007 =0x81000007 exec/alerts.h: *87
AN_IntrMem        #define 0x81000006 =0x81000006 exec/alerts.h: *86
AN_Intuition      #define 0x04000000 =0x04000000 exec/alerts.h: *108
AN_ItemAlloc      #define 0x04010003 =0x04010003 exec/alerts.h: *112
AN_ItemBoxTop     #define 0x84000006 =0x84000006 exec/alerts.h: *115
AN_KeyboardDev    #define 0x13000000 =0x13000000 exec/alerts.h: *169
AN_KeyFree        #define 0x07000008 =0x07000008 exec/alerts.h: *142
AN_KeyRange       #define 0x0700000B =0x0700000b exec/alerts.h: *145
AN_LayersLib      #define 0x03000000 =0x03000000 exec/alerts.h: *104
AN_LayersNoMem    #define 0x83010000 =0x83010000 exec/alerts.h: *105
AN_LibChkSum      #define 0x81000003 =0x81000003 exec/alerts.h: *83
AN_LibMem         #define 0x81000004 =0x81000004 exec/alerts.h: *84
AN_LongFrame      #define 0x82010006 =0x82010006 exec/alerts.h: *95
AN_MakeVPort      #define 0x82010030 =0x82010030 exec/alerts.h: *100
AN_MathLib        #define 0x05000000 =0x05000000 exec/alerts.h: *128
AN_MemCorrupt     #define 0x81000005 =0x81000005 exec/alerts.h: *85
AN_MiscRsrc       #define 0x22000000 =0x22000000 exec/alerts.h: *190
AN_NoConsole      #define 0x8400000F =0x8400000f exec/alerts.h: *124
AN_OpenScreen     #define 0x84010007 =0x84010007 exec/alerts.h: *116
AN_OpenScrnRast   #define 0x84010008 =0x84010008 exec/alerts.h: *117
AN_OpenWindow     #define 0x8401000B =0x8401000b exec/alerts.h: *120
AN_PlaneAlloc     #define 0x84010005 =0x84010005 exec/alerts.h: *114
AN_QPktFail       #define 0x07000003 =0x07000003 exec/alerts.h: *137
AN_RAMLib         #define 0x08000000 =0x08000000 exec/alerts.h: *149
AN_RegionMemory   #define 0x8201000B =0x8201000b exec/alerts.h: *99
AN_SemCorrupt     #define 0x81000008 =0x81000008 exec/alerts.h: *88
AN_ShortFrame     #define 0x82010007 =0x82010007 exec/alerts.h: *96
AN_StartMem       #define 0x07010001 =0x07010001 exec/alerts.h: *135
AN_SubAlloc       #define 0x04010004 =0x04010004 exec/alerts.h: *113
AN_SysScrnType    #define 0x84000009 =0x84000009 exec/alerts.h: *118
AN_TDCalibSeek    #define 0x14000001 =0x14000001 exec/alerts.h: *173
AN_TDDelay        #define 0x14000002 =0x14000002 exec/alerts.h: *174
AN_TextTmpRas     #define 0x02010009 =0x02010009 exec/alerts.h: *97
AN_TimerDev       #define 0x15000000 =0x15000000 exec/alerts.h: *177
AN_TMBadReq       #define 0x15000001 =0x15000001 exec/alerts.h: *178
AN_TMBadSupply    #define 0x15000002 =0x15000002 exec/alerts.h: *179
AN_TrackDiskDev   #define 0x14000000 =0x14000000 exec/alerts.h: *172
AN_WeirdEcho      #define 0x8400000E =0x8400000e exec/alerts.h: *123
AN_Workbench      #define 0x31000000 =0x31000000 exec/alerts.h: *197
AOlPen            char in struct RastPort
        +0x001b   graphics/rastport.h: *61
AO_AudioDev       #define 0x00008010 =0x00008010 exec/alerts.h: *60
AO_BootStrap      #define 0x00008030 =0x00008030 exec/alerts.h: *69
AO_CIARsrc        #define 0x00008020 =0x00008020 exec/alerts.h: *66
AO_CListLib       #define 0x00008006 =0x00008006 exec/alerts.h: *55
AO_ConsoleDev     #define 0x00008011 =0x00008011 exec/alerts.h: *61
AO_DiskRsrc       #define 0x00008021 =0x00008021 exec/alerts.h: *67
AO_DOSLib         #define 0x00008007 =0x00008007 exec/alerts.h: *56
AO_ExecLib        #define 0x00008001 =0x00008001 exec/alerts.h: *50
```



```
AO_ExpansionLib   #define 0x0000800A =0x0000800a exec/alerts.h: *59
AO_GamePortDev    #define 0x00008012 =0x00008012 exec/alerts.h: *62
AO_GraphicsLib    #define 0x00008002 =0x00008002 exec/alerts.h: *51
AO_IconLib        #define 0x00008009 =0x00008009 exec/alerts.h: *58
AO_Intuition      #define 0x00008004 =0x00008004 exec/alerts.h: *53
AO_KeyboardDev    #define 0x00008013 =0x00008013 exec/alerts.h: *63
AO_LayersLib      #define 0x00008003 =0x00008003 exec/alerts.h: *52
AO_MathLib        #define 0x00008005 =0x00008005 exec/alerts.h: *54
AO_MiscRsrc       #define 0x00008022 =0x00008022 exec/alerts.h: *68
AO_RAMLib         #define 0x00008008 =0x00008008 exec/alerts.h: *57
AO_TimerDev       #define 0x00008015 =0x00008015 exec/alerts.h: *65
AO_TrackDiskDev   #define 0x00008014 =0x00008014 exec/alerts.h: *64
AO_Workbench      #define 0x00008031 =0x00008031 exec/alerts.h: *70
aPERF             #define 58 =0x0000003a devices/printer.h: *113
aPERF0            #define 59 =0x0000003b devices/printer.h: *114
aPLD              #define 33 =0x00000021 devices/printer.h: *69
aPLU              #define 32 =0x00000020 devices/printer.h: *68
aPROP0            #define 47 =0x0000002f devices/printer.h: *101
aPROP1            #define 46 =0x0000002e devices/printer.h: *100
aPROP2            #define 45 =0x0000002d devices/printer.h: *99
APTR              typedef pointer to "STRPTR"
                  many references; defined in exec/types.h: *30
aRAW              #define 76 =0x0000004c devices/printer.h: *134
AreaCircle        Macro (4 arguments) graphics/gfxmacros.h: *38
AreaInfo          structure tag
     size 0x0018  graphics/rastport.h: *17, 56
AreaInfo          pointer to struct AreaInfo in struct RastPort
         +0x0010  graphics/rastport.h: *56
AREAOUTLINE       #define 0x08 =0x00000008 graphics/rastport.h: *101
AreaPtrn          pointer to unsigned short int in struct RastPort
         +0x0008  graphics/rastport.h: *54
AreaPtSz          char in struct RastPort
         +0x001d  graphics/rastport.h: *63
aRI               #define 4 =0x00000004 devices/printer.h: *36
aRIN              #define 1 =0x00000001 devices/printer.h: *33
aRIS              #define 0 =0x00000000 devices/printer.h: *32
aRMS              #define 61 =0x0000003d devices/printer.h: *117
ArrayMax          unsigned short int in struct ExpansionInt
         +0x0002  libraries/expansionbase.h: *38
ArraySize         unsigned short int in struct ExpansionInt
         +0x0004  libraries/expansionbase.h: *39
aSBC              #define 13 =0x0000000d devices/printer.h: *46
aSFC              #define 12 =0x0000000c devices/printer.h: *45
aSGR0             #define 5 =0x00000005 devices/printer.h: *38
aSGR1             #define 10 =0x0000000a devices/printer.h: *43
aSGR22            #define 11 =0x0000000b devices/printer.h: *44
aSGR23            #define 7 =0x00000007 devices/printer.h: *40
aSGR24            #define 9 =0x00000009 devices/printer.h: *42
aSGR3             #define 6 =0x00000006 devices/printer.h: *39
aSGR4             #define 8 =0x00000008 devices/printer.h: *41
ASHIFTSHIFT       #define 12 =0x0000000c hardware/blit.h: *53
aSHORP0           #define 14 =0x0000000e devices/printer.h: *48
aSHORP1           #define 16 =0x00000010 devices/printer.h: *50
aSHORP2           #define 15 =0x0000000f devices/printer.h: *49
aSHORP3           #define 18 =0x00000012 devices/printer.h: *52
aSHORP4           #define 17 =0x00000011 devices/printer.h: *51
aSHORP5           #define 20 =0x00000014 devices/printer.h: *54
aSHORP6           #define 19 =0x00000013 devices/printer.h: *53
asin              #define SPAsin =0x00000000 libraries/mathffp.h: *42
asin              #define IEEEDPAsin =0x00000000 libraries/mathieeedp.h: *43
aSLPP             #define 57 =0x00000039 devices/printer.h: *112
aSLRM             #define 65 =0x00000041 devices/printer.h: *121
ASPECT_HORIZ      #define 0x00 =0x00000000 intuition/preferences.h: *170
ASPECT_VERT       #define 0x01 =0x00000001 intuition/preferences.h: *171
aSTBM             #define 64 =0x00000040 devices/printer.h: *120
aSUS0             #define 31 =0x0000001f devices/printer.h: *67
aSUS1             #define 28 =0x0000001c devices/printer.h: *64
aSUS2             #define 27 =0x0000001b devices/printer.h: *63
aSUS3             #define 30 =0x0000001e devices/printer.h: *66
```

```
aSUS4              #define 29 =0x0000001d devices/printer.h: *65
atan               #define SPAtan =0x00000000 libraries/mathffp.h: *38
atan               #define IEEEDPAtan =0x00000000 libraries/mathieeedp.h: *39
aTBC0              #define 69 =0x00000045 devices/printer.h: *126
aTBC1              #define 71 =0x00000047 devices/printer.h: *128
aTBC3              #define 70 =0x00000046 devices/printer.h: *127
aTBC4              #define 72 =0x00000048 devices/printer.h: *129
aTBCALL            #define 73 =0x00000049 devices/printer.h: *130
aTBSALL            #define 74 =0x0000004a devices/printer.h: *131
aTMS               #define 62 =0x0000003e devices/printer.h: *118
aTSS               #define 48 =0x00000030 devices/printer.h: *102
AttnFlags          unsigned short int in struct ExecBase
        +0x0128    exec/execbase.h: *64
AttnResched        unsigned short int in struct ExecBase
        +0x012a    exec/execbase.h: *65
AT_DeadEnd         #define 0x80000000 =0x80000000 exec/alerts.h: *37
AT_Recovery        #define 0x00000000 =0x00000000 exec/alerts.h: *38
aud                array [4] of struct AudChannel (size 0x0010) in struct Custom
        +0x00a0    hardware/custom.h: *92
AudChannel         structure tag in struct Custom
    size 0x0010    hardware/custom.h: *85
AUDIONAME          #define "audio.device" devices/audio.h: *17
AUL                #define 0x4 =0x00000004 hardware/blit.h: *68
AUserExt           short int in struct AnimOb
        +0x0028    graphics/gels.h: *223
AUserStuff         #define SHORT =0x00000000 graphics/gels.h: *60, 223
AUTOBACKPEN        #define 1 =0x00000001 intuition/intuition.h: *997
AUTODRAWMODE       #define JAM2 =0x00000001 intuition/intuition.h: *998
AUTOFRONTPEN       #define 0 =0x00000000 intuition/intuition.h: *996
AUTOITEXTFONT      #define NULL =0x00000000 intuition/intuition.h: *1001
AUTOKNOB           #define 0x0001 =0x00000001 intuition/intuition.h: *429
AUTOLEFTEDGE       #define 6 =0x00000006 intuition/intuition.h: *999
AUTONEXTTEXT       #define NULL =0x00000000 intuition/intuition.h: *1002
AUTOTOPEDGE        #define 3 =0x00000003 intuition/intuition.h: *1000
AvailFonts         structure tag
    size 0x000a    libraries/diskfont.h: *65
AvailFontsHeader   structure tag
    size 0x0002    libraries/diskfont.h: *70
aVERP0             #define 55 =0x00000037 devices/printer.h: *110
aVERP1             #define 56 =0x00000038 devices/printer.h: *111
aVTS               #define 68 =0x00000044 devices/printer.h: *125
A_OR_B             #define ABC|ANBC|NABC | ABNC|ANBNC|NABNC =0x000000fc
                   hardware/blit.h: *32
A_OR_C             #define ABC|NABC|ABNC | ANBC|NANBC|ANBNC =0x000000fa
                   hardware/blit.h: *33
A_TO_D             #define ABC|ANBC|ABNC|ANBNC =0x000000f0 hardware/blit.h: *35
A_XOR_C            #define NABC|ABNC | NANBC|ANBNC =0x0000005a
                   hardware/blit.h: *34
B2BOBBER           #define 2 =0x00000002 graphics/gels.h: *254
B2NORM             #define 0 =0x00000000 graphics/gels.h: *252
B2SWAP             #define 1 =0x00000001 graphics/gels.h: *253
back               pointer to struct Layer in struct Layer
        +0x0004    graphics/clip.h: *27
BACKDROP           #define 0x0100 =0x00000100 intuition/intuition.h: *814
BackFill           char in struct Requester
        +0x001e    intuition/intuition.h: *155
BackPen            char in struct IntuiText
        +0x0001    intuition/intuition.h: *496
BackPen            char in struct Border
        +0x0005    intuition/intuition.h: *525
BACKSAVED          #define 0x0100 =0x00000100 graphics/gels.h: *21
BadBlockBlock      structure tag size 0x0200   devices/hardblocks.h: *112
BadBlockEntry      structure tag size 0x0008   devices/hardblocks.h: *107, 119
BADDR              Macro (1 argument) libraries/dos.h: *100
BarHBorder         char in struct Screen
        +0x0020    intuition/screens.h: *56
BarHeight          char in struct Screen
        +0x001e    intuition/screens.h: *56
BarLayer           pointer to struct Layer in struct Screen
```



```
        +0x014e    intuition/screens.h: *81
BarVBorder         char in struct Screen
        +0x001f    intuition/screens.h: *56
BaudRate           unsigned short int in struct Preferences
        +0x0002    intuition/preferences.h: *51
BAUD_110           #define 0x00 =0x00000000 intuition/preferences.h: *139
BAUD_1200          #define 0x02 =0x00000002 intuition/preferences.h: *141
BAUD_19200         #define 0x06 =0x00000006 intuition/preferences.h: *145
BAUD_2400          #define 0x03 =0x00000003 intuition/preferences.h: *142
BAUD_300           #define 0x01 =0x00000001 intuition/preferences.h: *140
BAUD_4800          #define 0x04 =0x00000004 intuition/preferences.h: *143
BAUD_9600          #define 0x05 =0x00000005 intuition/preferences.h: *144
BAUD_MIDI          #define 0x07 =0x00000007 intuition/preferences.h: *146
bbb_BlockPairs     array [61] of struct BadBlockEntry (size 0x0008) in struct
                   BadBlockBlock
        +0x0018    devices/hardblocks.h: *119
bbb_ChkSum         int in struct BadBlockBlock
        +0x0008    devices/hardblocks.h: *115
bbb_HostID         unsigned int in struct BadBlockBlock
        +0x000c    devices/hardblocks.h: *116
bbb_ID             unsigned int in struct BadBlockBlock
        +0x0000    devices/hardblocks.h: *113
bbb_Next           unsigned int in struct BadBlockBlock
        +0x0010    devices/hardblocks.h: *117
bbb_Reserved       unsigned int in struct BadBlockBlock
        +0x0014    devices/hardblocks.h: *118
bbb_SummedLongs    unsigned int in struct BadBlockBlock
        +0x0004    devices/hardblocks.h: *114
bbe_BadBlock       unsigned int in struct BadBlockEntry
        +0x0000    devices/hardblocks.h: *108
bbe_GoodBlock      unsigned int in struct BadBlockEntry
        +0x0004    devices/hardblocks.h: *109
BBID_DOS           #define { 'D', 'O', 'S', '\0' } devices/bootblock.h: *21
BBID_KICK          #define { 'K', 'I', 'C', 'K' } devices/bootblock.h: *22
BBNAME_DOS         #define (('D'<<24)|('O'<<16)|('S'<<8)) =0x444f5300
                   devices/bootblock.h: *24
BBNAME_KICK        #define (('K'<<24)|('I'<<16)|('C'<<8)|('K')) =0x4b49434b
                   devices/bootblock.h: *25
bb_chksum          int in struct BootBlock
        +0x0004    devices/bootblock.h: *15
bb_dosblock        int in struct BootBlock
        +0x0008    devices/bootblock.h: *16
bb_id              array [4] of char in struct BootBlock
        +0x0000    devices/bootblock.h: *14
BC0B_DEST          #define 8 =0x00000008 hardware/blit.h: *37
BC0B_SRCA          #define 11 =0x0000000b hardware/blit.h: *40
BC0B_SRCB          #define 10 =0x0000000a hardware/blit.h: *39
BC0B_SRCC          #define 9 =0x00000009 hardware/blit.h: *38
BC0F_DEST          #define 0x100 =0x00000100 hardware/blit.h: *41
BC0F_SRCA          #define 0x800 =0x00000800 hardware/blit.h: *44
BC0F_SRCB          #define 0x400 =0x00000400 hardware/blit.h: *43
BC0F_SRCC          #define 0x200 =0x00000200 hardware/blit.h: *42
BC1F_DESC          #define 2 =0x00000002 hardware/blit.h: *46
BDRAWN             #define 0x0200 =0x00000200 graphics/gels.h: *33
BeamSync           short int in struct GfxBase
        +0x00a2    graphics/gfxbase.h: *40
beamsync           short int in struct bltnode
        +0x000c    hardware/blit.h: *86
BeatX              short int in struct Menu
        +0x001a    intuition/intuition.h: *67
BeatY              short int in struct Menu
        +0x001c    intuition/intuition.h: *67
BEEPING            #define 0x0020 =0x00000020 intuition/screens.h: *100
Before             pointer to struct Bob in struct Bob
        +0x000a    graphics/gels.h: *152
BgPen              char in struct RastPort
        +0x001a    graphics/rastport.h: *60
BindSemaphore      struct SignalSemaphore (size 0x002e) in struct ExpansionBase
        +0x0158    libraries/expansionbase.h: *54
```

```
BITCLR             #define 0 =0x00000000 graphics/gfx.h: *14
BitMap             structure tag
    size 0x0028    graphics/gfx.h: *36
                   graphics/clip.h: 34, 59
                   graphics/view.h: 72
                   graphics/rastport.h: 53
                   intuition/intuition.h: 167, 887
                   intuition/screens.h: 64, 139
BitMap             pointer to struct BitMap in struct ClipRect
         +0x000c   graphics/clip.h: *59
BitMap             pointer to struct BitMap in struct RasInfo
         +0x0004   graphics/view.h: *72
BitMap             pointer to struct BitMap in struct RastPort
         +0x0004   graphics/rastport.h: *53
BitMap             pointer to struct BitMap in struct NewWindow
         +0x0022   intuition/intuition.h: *887
BitMap             struct BitMap (size 0x0028) in struct Screen
         +0x00b8   intuition/screens.h: *64
BITSET             #define 0x8000 =0x00008000 graphics/gfx.h: *13
BITSPERBYTE        #define 8 =0x00000008 libraries/dos.h: *37
BITSPERLONG        #define 32 =0x00000020 libraries/dos.h: *39
blitbuff           pointer to short int in struct Layer_Info
         +0x005e   graphics/layers.h: *45
BlitLock           short int in struct GfxBase
         +0x00aa   graphics/gfxbase.h: *45
BLITMSG_FAULT      #define 4 =0x00000004 graphics/gfxbase.h: *72
BlitNest           short int in struct GfxBase
         +0x00ac   graphics/gfxbase.h: *46
BlitOwner          pointer to struct Task in struct GfxBase
         +0x00bc   graphics/gfxbase.h: *49
BLITREVERSE        #define 0x2 =0x00000002 hardware/blit.h: *64
blitsize           short int in struct bltnode
         +0x000a   hardware/blit.h: *85
blitter            pointer to long int in struct GfxBase
         +0x002e   graphics/gfxbase.h: *29
BlitWaitQ          struct List (size 0x000e) in struct GfxBase
         +0x00ae   graphics/gfxbase.h: *48
BlockPen           char in struct Window
         +0x0063   intuition/intuition.h: *757
BlockPen           char in struct NewWindow
         +0x0009   intuition/intuition.h: *855
BlockPen           char in struct Screen
         +0x014b   intuition/screens.h: *73
BlockPen           char in struct NewScreen
         +0x000b   intuition/screens.h: *121
bltadat            unsigned short int in struct Custom
         +0x0074   hardware/custom.h: *68
bltafwm            unsigned short int in struct Custom
         +0x0044   hardware/custom.h: *53
bltalwm            unsigned short int in struct Custom
         +0x0046   hardware/custom.h: *54
bltamod            unsigned short int in struct Custom
         +0x0064   hardware/custom.h: *63
bltapt             pointer to pointer to char in struct Custom
         +0x0050   hardware/custom.h: *57
bltbdat            unsigned short int in struct Custom
         +0x0072   hardware/custom.h: *67
bltbmod            unsigned short int in struct Custom
         +0x0062   hardware/custom.h: *62
bltbpt             pointer to pointer to char in struct Custom
         +0x004c   hardware/custom.h: *56
bltcdat            unsigned short int in struct Custom
         +0x0070   hardware/custom.h: *66
bltcmod            unsigned short int in struct Custom
         +0x0060   hardware/custom.h: *61
bltcon0            unsigned short int in struct Custom
         +0x0040   hardware/custom.h: *51
bltcon1            unsigned short int in struct Custom
         +0x0042   hardware/custom.h: *52
```



```
bltcpt             pointer to pointer to char in struct Custom
         +0x0048   hardware/custom.h: *55
bltddat            unsigned short int in struct Custom
         +0x0000   hardware/custom.h: *20
bltdmod            unsigned short int in struct Custom
         +0x0066   hardware/custom.h: *64
bltdpt             pointer to pointer to char in struct Custom
         +0x0054   hardware/custom.h: *58
blthd              pointer to struct bltnode in struct GfxBase
         +0x003a   graphics/gfxbase.h: *32
bltnode            structure tag
    size 0x0012    graphics/gfxbase.h: 32, 33
                   hardware/blit.h: *80, 82
bltsize            unsigned short int in struct Custom
         +0x0058   hardware/custom.h: *59
bltsrv             struct Interrupt (size 0x0016) in struct GfxBase
         +0x0076   graphics/gfxbase.h: *34
blttl              pointer to struct bltnode in struct GfxBase
         +0x003e   graphics/gfxbase.h: *32
BNDRYOFF           Macro (1 argument) graphics/gfxmacros.h: *30
bn_DeviceNode      unsigned int in struct BootNode
         +0x0010   libraries/romboot_base.h: *44
bn_Flags           unsigned short int in struct BootNode
         +0x000e   libraries/romboot_base.h: *43
bn_Node            struct Node (size 0x000e) in struct BootNode
         +0x0000   libraries/romboot_base.h: *42
BoardList          struct List (size 0x000e) in struct ExpansionBase
         +0x003c   libraries/expansionbase.h: *51
Bob                structure tag
    size 0x0020    graphics/gels.h: 115, *135, 152, 153, 196
BobComp            pointer to struct AnimComp in struct Bob
         +0x0016   graphics/gels.h: *157
BOBISCOMP          #define 0x0002 =0x00000002 graphics/gels.h: *30
BOBNIX             #define 0x0800 =0x00000800 graphics/gels.h: *35
BOBSAWAY           #define 0x0400 =0x00000400 graphics/gels.h: *34
BOBUPDATE          #define 0x0200 =0x00000200 graphics/gels.h: *22
BobVSprite         pointer to struct VSprite in struct Bob
         +0x0012   graphics/gels.h: *155
BOOL               typedef short int
                   exec/types.h: *47
                   intuition/preferences.h: 78
BOOLEXTEND         #define 0x2000 =0x00002000 intuition/intuition.h: *325
BOOLGADGET         #define 0x0001 =0x00000001 intuition/intuition.h: *348
BoolInfo           structure tag
    size 0x000a    intuition/intuition.h: *360
BOOLMASK           #define 0x0001 =0x00000001 intuition/intuition.h: *376
BootBlock          structure tag
    size 0x000c    devices/bootblock.h: *13
BootList           struct List (size 0x000e) in struct RomBootBase
         +0x0026   libraries/romboot_base.h: *36
BootNode           structure tag
    size 0x0014    libraries/romboot_base.h: *40
BOOTSECTS          #define 2 =0x00000002 devices/bootblock.h: *19
Border             structure tag
    size 0x0010    intuition/intuition.h: 150, *522, 529
BorderBottom       char in struct Window
         +0x0039   intuition/intuition.h: *730
BORDERHIT          #define 0 =0x00000000 graphics/collide.h: *21
BorderLeft         char in struct Window
         +0x0036   intuition/intuition.h: *730
BORDERLESS         #define 0x0800 =0x00000800 intuition/intuition.h: *820
BorderLine         pointer to short int in struct VSprite
         +0x0028   graphics/gels.h: *109
BorderRight        char in struct Window
         +0x0038   intuition/intuition.h: *730
BorderRPort        pointer to struct RastPort in struct Window
         +0x003a   intuition/intuition.h: *731
BorderTop          char in struct Window
         +0x0037   intuition/intuition.h: *730
```

```
BOTTOMBORDER        #define 0x0080 =0x00000080 intuition/intuition.h: *314
BOTTOMHIT           #define 2 =0x00000002 graphics/collide.h: *31
bottommost          short int in struct GelsInfo
        +0x001c     graphics/rastport.h: *46
BOUNDED_DIMENSIONS #define 0x0010 =0x00000010 intuition/preferences.h: *242
bounds              struct Rectangle (size 0x0008) in struct Layer
        +0x0010     graphics/clip.h: *30
bounds              struct Rectangle (size 0x0008) in struct ClipRect
        +0x0010     graphics/clip.h: *60
bounds              struct Rectangle (size 0x0008) in struct RegionRectangle
        +0x0008     graphics/regions.h: *20
bounds              struct Rectangle (size 0x0008) in struct Region
        +0x0000     graphics/regions.h: *25
bpl1mod             unsigned short int in struct Custom
        +0x0108     hardware/custom.h: *99
bpl2mod             unsigned short int in struct Custom
        +0x010a     hardware/custom.h: *100
bplcon0             unsigned short int in struct Custom
        +0x0100     hardware/custom.h: *95
bplcon1             unsigned short int in struct Custom
        +0x0102     hardware/custom.h: *96
bplcon2             unsigned short int in struct Custom
        +0x0104     hardware/custom.h: *97
bpldat              array [6] of unsigned short int in struct Custom
        +0x0110     hardware/custom.h: *102
bplpt               array [6] of pointer to pointer to char in struct Custom
        +0x00e0     hardware/custom.h: *93
BPTR                typedef long int
                    many references; defined in libraries/dos.h: *92
BROTHER_15XL        #define 0x02 =0x00000002 intuition/preferences.h: *188
bsblthd             pointer to struct bltnode in struct GfxBase
        +0x0042     graphics/gfxbase.h: *33
bsbltt1             pointer to struct bltnode in struct GfxBase
        +0x0046     graphics/gfxbase.h: *33
BSHIFTSHIFT         #define 12 =0x0000000c hardware/blit.h: *54
BSTR                typedef long int
                    many references; defined in libraries/dos.h: *93
BufBuffer           pointer to short int in struct DBufPacket
        +0x0008     graphics/gels.h: *236
Buffer              pointer to char in struct StringInfo
        +0x0000     intuition/intuition.h: *454
BufferPos           short int in struct StringInfo
        +0x0008     intuition/intuition.h: *456
BufPath             pointer to struct VSprite in struct DBufPacket
        +0x0004     graphics/gels.h: *232
BufX                short int in struct DBufPacket
        +0x0002     graphics/gels.h: *231
BufY                short int in struct DBufPacket
        +0x0000     graphics/gels.h: *231
BUserExt            short int in struct Bob
        +0x001e     graphics/gels.h: *161
BUSERFLAGS          #define 0x00FF =0x000000ff graphics/gels.h: *28
BUserStuff          #define SHORT =0x00000000 graphics/gels.h: *56, 161
BWAITING            #define 0x0100 =0x00000100 graphics/gels.h: *32
BYTE                typedef char
                    many references; defined in exec/types.h: *26
BYTEBITS            typedef unsigned char
                    exec/types.h: *28
BYTEMASK            #define 0xFF =0x000000ff exec/types.h: *54
bytereserved        char in struct GfxBase
        +0x00a7     graphics/gfxbase.h: *43
BYTESPERLONG        #define 4 =0x00000004 libraries/dos.h: *38
BytesPerRow         unsigned short int in struct BitMap
        +0x0000     graphics/gfx.h: *38
Carg                int in struct Isrvstr
        +0x001a     graphics/graphint.h: *24
CBD_CURRENTREADID #define (CMD_NONSTD+1) =0x0000000a devices/clipboard.h: *24
CBD_CURRENTWRITEID #define (CMD_NONSTD+2) =0x0000000b devices/clipboard.h: *25
CBD_POST            #define (CMD_NONSTD+0) =0x00000009 devices/clipboard.h: *23
```



```
CBERR_OBSOLETEID  #define 1 =0x00000001 devices/clipboard.h: *27
CBM_MPS1000       #define 0x03 =0x00000003 intuition/preferences.h: *189
cb_ConfigDev      pointer to struct ConfigDev in struct CurrentBinding
          +0x0000 libraries/configvars.h: *49
cb_FileName       pointer to char in struct CurrentBinding
          +0x0004 libraries/configvars.h: *50
cb_ProductString  pointer to char in struct CurrentBinding
          +0x0008 libraries/configvars.h: *51
cb_ToolTypes      pointer to pointer to char in struct CurrentBinding
          +0x000c libraries/configvars.h: *52
ccode             pointer to function returning int in struct Isrvstr
          +0x0016 graphics/graphint.h: *23
CDB_CONFIGME      #define 1 =0x00000001 libraries/configvars.h: *42
CDB_SHUTUP        #define 0 =0x00000000 libraries/configvars.h: *41
CDF_CONFIGME      #define 0x02 =0x00000002 libraries/configvars.h: *45
CDF_SHUTUP        #define 0x01 =0x00000001 libraries/configvars.h: *44
CD_ASKDEFAULTKEYMAP #define (CMD_NONSTD+2) =0x0000000b devices/console.h: *20
CD_ASKKEYMAP      #define (CMD_NONSTD+0) =0x00000009 devices/console.h: *18
cd_BoardAddr      pointer to pointer to char in struct ConfigDev
          +0x0020 libraries/configvars.h: *31
cd_BoardSize      pointer to pointer to char in struct ConfigDev
          +0x0024 libraries/configvars.h: *32
cd_Driver         pointer to pointer to char in struct ConfigDev
          +0x002c libraries/configvars.h: *35
cd_Flags          char in struct ConfigDev
          +0x000e libraries/configvars.h: *28
cd_NextCD         pointer to struct ConfigDev in struct ConfigDev
          +0x0030 libraries/configvars.h: *36
cd_Node           struct Node (size 0x000e) in struct ConfigDev
          +0x0000 libraries/configvars.h: *27
cd_Pad            char in struct ConfigDev
          +0x000f libraries/configvars.h: *29
cd_Rom            struct ExpansionRom (size 0x0010) in struct ConfigDev
          +0x0010 libraries/configvars.h: *30
CD_SETDEFAULTKEYMAP #define (CMD_NONSTD+3) =0x0000000c devices/console.h: *21
CD_SETKEYMAP      #define (CMD_NONSTD+1) =0x0000000a devices/console.h: *19
cd_SlotAddr       unsigned short int in struct ConfigDev
          +0x0028 libraries/configvars.h: *33
cd_SlotSize       unsigned short int in struct ConfigDev
          +0x002a libraries/configvars.h: *34
cd_Unused         array [4] of unsigned int in struct ConfigDev
          +0x0034 libraries/configvars.h: *37
ceil              #define SPCeil =0x00000000 libraries/mathffp.h: *35
ceil              #define IEEEDPCeil =0x00000000 libraries/mathieeedp.h: *36
CEND              Macro (1 argument) graphics/gfxmacros.h: *35
CENTER_IMAGE      #define 0x0008 =0x00000008 intuition/preferences.h: *239
chanmask          char in struct narrator_rb
          +0x0043 devices/narrator.h: *78
CHECKED           #define 0x0100 =0x00000100 intuition/intuition.h: *127
CHECKIT           #define 0x0001 =0x00000001 intuition/intuition.h: *113
CheckMark         pointer to struct Image in struct Window
          +0x0064 intuition/intuition.h: *763
CheckMark         pointer to struct Image in struct NewWindow
          +0x0016 intuition/intuition.h: *872
CHECKWIDTH        #define 19 =0x00000013 intuition/intuition.h: *976
check_lp          pointer to struct Layer in struct Layer_Info
          +0x0004 graphics/layers.h: *35
CHeight           unsigned short int in struct PropInfo
          +0x000c intuition/intuition.h: *421
ChkBase           unsigned int in struct ExecBase
          +0x0026 exec/execbase.h: *35
ChkSum            unsigned short int in struct ExecBase
          +0x0052 exec/execbase.h: *47
ch_masks          pointer to char in struct narrator_rb
          +0x0038 devices/narrator.h: *73
cia               pointer to long int in struct GfxBase
          +0x002a graphics/gfxbase.h: *28
CIA               structure tag
     size 0x0f01  hardware/cia.h: *22
```

```
CIAANAME          #define "ciaa.resource" resources/cia.h: *13
CIABNAME          #define "ciab.resource" resources/cia.h: *14
CIAB_COMCD        #define (5) =0x00000005 hardware/cia.h: *140
CIAB_COMCTS       #define (4) =0x00000004 hardware/cia.h: *141
CIAB_COMDSR       #define (3) =0x00000003 hardware/cia.h: *142
CIAB_COMDTR       #define (7) =0x00000007 hardware/cia.h: *138
CIAB_COMRTS       #define (6) =0x00000006 hardware/cia.h: *139
CIAB_DSKCHANGE    #define (2) =0x00000002 hardware/cia.h: *131
CIAB_DSKDIREC     #define (1) =0x00000001 hardware/cia.h: *154
CIAB_DSKMOTOR     #define (7) =0x00000007 hardware/cia.h: *148
CIAB_DSKPROT      #define (3) =0x00000003 hardware/cia.h: *130
CIAB_DSKRDY       #define (5) =0x00000005 hardware/cia.h: *128
CIAB_DSKSEL0      #define (3) =0x00000003 hardware/cia.h: *152
CIAB_DSKSEL1      #define (4) =0x00000004 hardware/cia.h: *151
CIAB_DSKSEL2      #define (5) =0x00000005 hardware/cia.h: *150
CIAB_DSKSEL3      #define (6) =0x00000006 hardware/cia.h: *149
CIAB_DSKSIDE      #define (2) =0x00000002 hardware/cia.h: *153
CIAB_DSKSTEP      #define (0) =0x00000000 hardware/cia.h: *155
CIAB_DSKTRACK0    #define (4) =0x00000004 hardware/cia.h: *129
CIAB_GAMEPORT0    #define (6) =0x00000006 hardware/cia.h: *127
CIAB_GAMEPORT1    #define (7) =0x00000007 hardware/cia.h: *126
CIAB_LED          #define (1) =0x00000001 hardware/cia.h: *132
CIAB_OVERLAY      #define (0) =0x00000000 hardware/cia.h: *133
CIAB_PRTRBUSY     #define (0) =0x00000000 hardware/cia.h: *145
CIAB_PRTRPOUT     #define (1) =0x00000001 hardware/cia.h: *144
CIAB_PRTRSEL      #define (2) =0x00000002 hardware/cia.h: *143
ciacra            char in struct CIA
        +0x0e00   hardware/cia.h: *51
CIACRAB_INMODE    #define 5 =0x00000005 hardware/cia.h: *72
CIACRAB_LOAD      #define 4 =0x00000004 hardware/cia.h: *71
CIACRAB_OUTMODE   #define 2 =0x00000002 hardware/cia.h: *69
CIACRAB_PBON      #define 1 =0x00000001 hardware/cia.h: *68
CIACRAB_RUNMODE   #define 3 =0x00000003 hardware/cia.h: *70
CIACRAB_SPMODE    #define 6 =0x00000006 hardware/cia.h: *73
CIACRAB_START     #define 0 =0x00000000 hardware/cia.h: *67
CIACRAB_TODIN     #define 7 =0x00000007 hardware/cia.h: *74
CIACRAF_INMODE    #define (1<<CIACRAB_INMODE) =0x00000020 hardware/cia.h: *101
CIACRAF_LOAD      #define (1<<CIACRAB_LOAD) =0x00000010 hardware/cia.h: *100
CIACRAF_OUTMODE   #define (1<<CIACRAB_OUTMODE) =0x00000004 hardware/cia.h: *98
CIACRAF_PBON      #define (1<<CIACRAB_PBON) =0x00000002 hardware/cia.h: *97
CIACRAF_RUNMODE   #define (1<<CIACRAB_RUNMODE) =0x00000008 hardware/cia.h: *99
CIACRAF_SPMODE    #define (1<<CIACRAB_SPMODE) =0x00000040 hardware/cia.h: *102
CIACRAF_START     #define (1<<CIACRAB_START) =0x00000001 hardware/cia.h: *96
CIACRAF_TODIN     #define (1<<CIACRAB_TODIN) =0x00000080 hardware/cia.h: *103
ciacrb            char in struct CIA
        +0x0f00   hardware/cia.h: *53
CIACRBB_ALARM     #define 7 =0x00000007 hardware/cia.h: *84
CIACRBB_INMODE0   #define 5 =0x00000005 hardware/cia.h: *82
CIACRBB_INMODE1   #define 6 =0x00000006 hardware/cia.h: *83
CIACRBB_LOAD      #define 4 =0x00000004 hardware/cia.h: *81
CIACRBB_OUTMODE   #define 2 =0x00000002 hardware/cia.h: *79
CIACRBB_PBON      #define 1 =0x00000001 hardware/cia.h: *78
CIACRBB_RUNMODE   #define 3 =0x00000003 hardware/cia.h: *80
CIACRBB_START     #define 0 =0x00000000 hardware/cia.h: *77
CIACRBF_ALARM     #define (1<<CIACRBB_ALARM) =0x00000080 hardware/cia.h: *113
CIACRBF_INMODE0   #define (1<<CIACRBB_INMODE0) =0x00000020 hardware/cia.h: *111
CIACRBF_INMODE1   #define (1<<CIACRBB_INMODE1) =0x00000040 hardware/cia.h: *112
CIACRBF_IN_CNT    #define (CIACRBF_INMODE0) =0x00000020 hardware/cia.h: *117
CIACRBF_IN_CNT_TA #define (CIACRBF_INMODE0|CIACRBF_INMODE1) =0x00000060
                  hardware/cia.h: *119
CIACRBF_IN_PHI2   #define 0 =0x00000000 hardware/cia.h: *116
CIACRBF_IN_TA     #define (CIACRBF_INMODE1) =0x00000040 hardware/cia.h: *118
CIACRBF_LOAD      #define (1<<CIACRBB_LOAD) =0x00000010 hardware/cia.h: *110
CIACRBF_OUTMODE   #define (1<<CIACRBB_OUTMODE) =0x00000004 hardware/cia.h: *108
CIACRBF_PBON      #define (1<<CIACRBB_PBON) =0x00000002 hardware/cia.h: *107
CIACRBF_RUNMODE   #define (1<<CIACRBB_RUNMODE) =0x00000008 hardware/cia.h: *109
CIACRBF_START     #define (1<<CIACRBB_START) =0x00000001 hardware/cia.h: *106
ciaddra           char in struct CIA
        +0x0200   hardware/cia.h: *27
```



```
ciaddrb           char in struct CIA
        +0x0300   hardware/cia.h: *29
CIAF_COMCD        #define (1<<5) =0x00000020 hardware/cia.h: *172
CIAF_COMCTS       #define (1<<4) =0x00000010 hardware/cia.h: *173
CIAF_COMDSR       #define (1<<3) =0x00000008 hardware/cia.h: *174
CIAF_COMDTR       #define (1<<7) =0x00000080 hardware/cia.h: *170
CIAF_COMRTS       #define (1<<6) =0x00000040 hardware/cia.h: *171
CIAF_DSKCHANGE    #define (1<<2) =0x00000004 hardware/cia.h: *163
CIAF_DSKDIREC     #define (1<<1) =0x00000002 hardware/cia.h: *186
CIAF_DSKMOTOR     #define (1<<7) =0x00000080 hardware/cia.h: *180
CIAF_DSKPROT      #define (1<<3) =0x00000008 hardware/cia.h: *162
CIAF_DSKRDY       #define (1<<5) =0x00000020 hardware/cia.h: *160
CIAF_DSKSEL0      #define (1<<3) =0x00000008 hardware/cia.h: *184
CIAF_DSKSEL1      #define (1<<4) =0x00000010 hardware/cia.h: *183
CIAF_DSKSEL2      #define (1<<5) =0x00000020 hardware/cia.h: *182
CIAF_DSKSEL3      #define (1<<6) =0x00000040 hardware/cia.h: *181
CIAF_DSKSIDE      #define (1<<2) =0x00000004 hardware/cia.h: *185
CIAF_DSKSTEP      #define (1<<0) =0x00000001 hardware/cia.h: *187
CIAF_DSKTRACK0    #define (1<<4) =0x00000010 hardware/cia.h: *161
CIAF_GAMEPORT0    #define (1<<6) =0x00000040 hardware/cia.h: *159
CIAF_GAMEPORT1    #define (1<<7) =0x00000080 hardware/cia.h: *158
CIAF_LED          #define (1<<1) =0x00000002 hardware/cia.h: *164
CIAF_OVERLAY      #define (1<<0) =0x00000001 hardware/cia.h: *165
CIAF_PRTRBUSY     #define (1<<0) =0x00000001 hardware/cia.h: *177
CIAF_PRTRPOUT     #define (1<<1) =0x00000002 hardware/cia.h: *176
CIAF_PRTRSEL      #define (1<<2) =0x00000004 hardware/cia.h: *175
ciaicr            char in struct CIA
        +0x0d00   hardware/cia.h: *49
CIAICRB_ALRM      #define 2 =0x00000002 hardware/cia.h: *60
CIAICRB_FLG       #define 4 =0x00000004 hardware/cia.h: *62
CIAICRB_IR        #define 7 =0x00000007 hardware/cia.h: *63
CIAICRB_SETCLR    #define 7 =0x00000007 hardware/cia.h: *64
CIAICRB_SP        #define 3 =0x00000003 hardware/cia.h: *61
CIAICRB_TA        #define 0 =0x00000000 hardware/cia.h: *58
CIAICRB_TB        #define 1 =0x00000001 hardware/cia.h: *59
CIAICRF_ALRM      #define (1<<CIAICRB_ALRM) =0x00000004 hardware/cia.h: *89
CIAICRF_FLG       #define (1<<CIAICRB_FLG) =0x00000010 hardware/cia.h: *91
CIAICRF_IR        #define (1<<CIAICRB_IR) =0x00000080 hardware/cia.h: *92
CIAICRF_SETCLR    #define (1<<CIAICRB_SETCLR) =0x00000080 hardware/cia.h: *93
CIAICRF_SP        #define (1<<CIAICRB_SP) =0x00000008 hardware/cia.h: *90
CIAICRF_TA        #define (1<<CIAICRB_TA) =0x00000001 hardware/cia.h: *87
CIAICRF_TB        #define (1<<CIAICRB_TB) =0x00000002 hardware/cia.h: *88
ciapra            char in struct CIA
        +0x0000   hardware/cia.h: *23
ciaprb            char in struct CIA
        +0x0100   hardware/cia.h: *25
ciasdr            char in struct CIA
        +0x0c00   hardware/cia.h: *47
ciatahi           char in struct CIA
        +0x0500   hardware/cia.h: *33
ciatalo           char in struct CIA
        +0x0400   hardware/cia.h: *31
ciatbhi           char in struct CIA
        +0x0700   hardware/cia.h: *37
ciatblo           char in struct CIA
        +0x0600   hardware/cia.h: *35
ciatodhi          char in struct CIA
        +0x0a00   hardware/cia.h: *43
ciatodlow         char in struct CIA
        +0x0800   hardware/cia.h: *39
ciatodmid         char in struct CIA
        +0x0900   hardware/cia.h: *41
CINIT             Macro (2 arguments) graphics/gfxmacros.h: *32
Class             unsigned int in struct IntuiMessage
        +0x0014   intuition/intuition.h: *603
CLEANME           #define CLEANUP =0x00000040 hardware/blit.h: *92
cleanup           pointer to function returning int in struct bltnode
        +0x000e   hardware/blit.h: *87
CLEANUP           #define 0x40 =0x00000040 hardware/blit.h: *91
```

```
ClearPath         pointer to struct VSprite in struct VSprite
       +0x000c    graphics/gels.h: *80
CLeft             short int in struct StringInfo
       +0x0014    intuition/intuition.h: *464
ClipboardUnitPartial structure tag
    size 0x0012   devices/clipboard.h: *30
ClipRect          structure tag
    size 0x0024   graphics/clip.h: 28, 35, 40, 41, 42, *54, 56, 57, 61
ClipRect          pointer to struct ClipRect in struct Layer
       +0x0008    graphics/clip.h: *28
ClipRegion        pointer to struct Region in struct Layer
       +0x007e    graphics/clip.h: *46
cli_Background    int in struct CommandLineInterface
       +0x002c    libraries/dosextens.h: *209
cli_CommandDir    int in struct CommandLineInterface
       +0x0008    libraries/dosextens.h: *200
cli_CommandFile   int in struct CommandLineInterface
       +0x0024    libraries/dosextens.h: *207
cli_CommandName   int in struct CommandLineInterface
       +0x0010    libraries/dosextens.h: *202
cli_CurrentInput  int in struct CommandLineInterface
       +0x0020    libraries/dosextens.h: *206
cli_CurrentOutput int in struct CommandLineInterface
       +0x0030    libraries/dosextens.h: *210
cli_DefaultStack  int in struct CommandLineInterface
       +0x0034    libraries/dosextens.h: *211
cli_FailLevel     int in struct CommandLineInterface
       +0x0014    libraries/dosextens.h: *203
cli_Interactive   int in struct CommandLineInterface
       +0x0028    libraries/dosextens.h: *208
cli_Module        int in struct CommandLineInterface
       +0x003c    libraries/dosextens.h: *213
cli_Prompt        int in struct CommandLineInterface
       +0x0018    libraries/dosextens.h: *204
cli_Result2       int in struct CommandLineInterface
       +0x0000    libraries/dosextens.h: *198
cli_ReturnCode    int in struct CommandLineInterface
       +0x000c    libraries/dosextens.h: *201
cli_SetName       int in struct CommandLineInterface
       +0x0004    libraries/dosextens.h: *199
cli_StandardInput int in struct CommandLineInterface
       +0x001c    libraries/dosextens.h: *205
cli_StandardOutput int in struct CommandLineInterface
       +0x0038    libraries/dosextens.h: *212
Clock             int in struct AnimOb
       +0x0008    graphics/gels.h: *205
CLOSE             #define 0x0080 =0x00000080 intuition/intuition.h: *346
CLOSEWINDOW       #define 0x00000200 =0x00000200 intuition/intuition.h: *647
ClrIns            pointer to struct CopList in struct ViewPort
       +0x0010    graphics/view.h: *37
clxcon            unsigned short int in struct Custom
       +0x0098    hardware/custom.h: *81
clxdat            unsigned short int in struct Custom
       +0x000e    hardware/custom.h: *27
CMD_CLEAR         #define 5 =0x00000005 exec/io.h:  *54
CMD_FLUSH         #define 8 =0x00000008 exec/io.h:  *57
CMD_INVALID       #define 0 =0x00000000 exec/io.h:  *49
CMD_NONSTD        #define 9 =0x00000009 exec/io.h:  *59
CMD_READ          #define 2 =0x00000002 exec/io.h:  *51
CMD_RESET         #define 1 =0x00000001 exec/io.h:  *50
CMD_START         #define 7 =0x00000007 exec/io.h:  *56
CMD_STOP          #define 6 =0x00000006 exec/io.h:  *55
CMD_UPDATE        #define 4 =0x00000004 exec/io.h:  *53
CMD_WRITE         #define 3 =0x00000003 exec/io.h:  *52
CMOVE             Macro (3 arguments) graphics/gfxmacros.h: *33
Code              unsigned short int in struct IntuiMessage
       +0x0018    intuition/intuition.h: *606
code              pointer to function returning int in struct Isrvstr
       +0x0012    graphics/graphint.h: *22
```



```
ColdCapture       pointer to pointer to char in struct ExecBase
       +0x002a    exec/execbase.h: *36
collHandler       pointer to struct collTable in struct GelsInfo
       +0x0012    graphics/rastport.h: *45
CollMask          pointer to short int in struct VSprite
       +0x002c    graphics/gels.h: *110
collPtrs          array [16] of pointer to function returning int in struct
                  collTable
       +0x0000    graphics/gels.h: *261
collTable         structure tag
    size 0x0040   graphics/rastport.h: 45
                  graphics/gels.h: *259
color             array [32] of unsigned short int in struct Custom
       +0x0180    hardware/custom.h: *111
color0            unsigned short int in struct Preferences
       +0x006e    intuition/preferences.h: *68
color1            unsigned short int in struct Preferences
       +0x0070    intuition/preferences.h: *69
color17           unsigned short int in struct Preferences
       +0x0066    intuition/preferences.h: *62
color18           unsigned short int in struct Preferences
       +0x0068    intuition/preferences.h: *63
color19           unsigned short int in struct Preferences
       +0x006a    intuition/preferences.h: *64
color2            unsigned short int in struct Preferences
       +0x0072    intuition/preferences.h: *70
color3            unsigned short int in struct Preferences
       +0x0074    intuition/preferences.h: *71
colorByte         array [4] of char in union colorEntry
       +0x0000    devices/prtgfx.h: *24
colorEntry        union tag
    size 0x0004   devices/prtgfx.h: *22, 34, 35, 36, 37, 38
colorLong         unsigned int in union colorEntry
       +0x0000    devices/prtgfx.h: *23
ColorMap          structure tag
    size 0x0008   devices/printer.h: 158
                  graphics/view.h: *21, 33
ColorMap          pointer to struct ColorMap in struct ViewPort
       +0x0004    graphics/view.h: *33
COLORON           #define 0x0200 =0x00000200 graphics/display.h: *19
colorSByte        array [4] of char in union colorEntry
       +0x0000    devices/prtgfx.h: *25
ColorTable        pointer to pointer to char in struct ColorMap
       +0x0004    graphics/view.h: *26
ColumnSizeChange  char in struct Preferences
       +0x00d9    intuition/preferences.h: *113
Command           char in struct MenuItem
       +0x001a    intuition/intuition.h: *101
CommandLineInterface structure tag
    size 0x0040   libraries/dosextens.h: *197
COMMSEQ           #define 0x0004 =0x00000004 intuition/intuition.h: *115
COMMWIDTH         #define 27 =0x0000001b intuition/intuition.h: *977
COMPLEMENT        #define 2 =0x00000002 graphics/rastport.h: *90
ConfigDev         structure tag
    size 0x0044   libraries/configvars.h: *26, 36, 49, 56
                  libraries/expansion.h: 23, 25
ConUnit           structure tag
    size 0x0128   devices/conunit.h: *34
CoolCapture       pointer to pointer to char in struct ExecBase
       +0x002e    exec/execbase.h: *37
cop1lc            unsigned int in struct Custom
       +0x0080    hardware/custom.h: *71
cop2lc            unsigned int in struct Custom
       +0x0084    hardware/custom.h: *72
copcon            unsigned short int in struct Custom
       +0x002e    hardware/custom.h: *42
copinit           structure tag
    size 0x005c   graphics/copper.h: *76
                  graphics/gfxbase.h: 27
```

```
copinit            pointer to struct copinit in struct GfxBase
        +0x0026    graphics/gfxbase.h: *27
CopIns             structure tag
    size 0x0006    graphics/copper.h: *18, 60, 61
CopIns             pointer to struct CopIns in struct CopList
        +0x000c    graphics/copper.h: *60
copins             unsigned short int in struct Custom
        +0x008c    hardware/custom.h: *75
copjmpl            unsigned short int in struct Custom
        +0x0088    hardware/custom.h: *73
copjmp2            unsigned short int in struct Custom
        +0x008a    hardware/custom.h: *74
CopList            structure tag
    size 0x0022    graphics/view.h: 35, 36, 37
                   graphics/copper.h: 23, *55, 57, 58, 72, 73
CopList            pointer to struct CopList in struct UCopList
        +0x0008    graphics/copper.h: *73
CopLStart          pointer to unsigned short int in struct CopList
        +0x0014    graphics/copper.h: *62
COPPER_MOVE        #define 0 =0x00000000 graphics/copper.h: *13
COPPER_WAIT        #define 1 =0x00000001 graphics/copper.h: *14
CopPtr             pointer to struct CopIns in struct CopList
        +0x0010    graphics/copper.h: *61
CopSStart          pointer to unsigned short int in struct CopList
        +0x0018    graphics/copper.h: *63
CORRECT_BLUE       #define 0x0004 =0x00000004 intuition/preferences.h: *237
CORRECT_GREEN      #define 0x0002 =0x00000002 intuition/preferences.h: *236
CORRECT_RED        #define 0x0001 =0x00000001 intuition/preferences.h: *235
CORRECT_RGB_MASK #define (CORRECT_RED|CORRECT_GREEN|CORRECT_BLUE) =0x00000007
                   intuition/preferences.h: *258
cos                #define SPCos =0x00000000 libraries/mathffp.h: *39
ccs                #define IEEEDPCos =0x00000000 libraries/mathieeedp.h: *40
cosh               #define SPCosh =0x00000000 libraries/mathffp.h: *50
cosh               #define IEEEDPCosh =0x00000000 libraries/mathieeedp.h: *51
COUNT              typedef short int
                   exec/types.h: *45
Count              unsigned short int in struct ColorMap
        +0x0002    graphics/view.h: *25
Count              short int in struct AreaInfo
        +0x0010    graphics/rastport.h: *23
Count              char in struct Border
        +0x0007    intuition/intuition.h: *527
Count              short int in struct CopList
        +0x001c    graphics/copper.h: *64
cprlist            structure tag
    size 0x000a    graphics/view.h: 50, 51
                   graphics/copper.h: *48, 50
CPRNXTBUF          #define 2 =0x00000002 graphics/copper.h: *15
CPR_NT_LOF         #define 0x8000 =0x00008000 graphics/copper.h: *16
CPR_NT_SHT         #define 0x4000 =0x00004000 graphics/copper.h: *17
CPTR               typedef ULONG
                   exec/types.h: *35
                   libraries/expansion.h: 24
                   libraries/romboot_base.h: 44
                   resources/filesysres.h: 42
cp_x               short int in struct RastPort
        +0x0024    graphics/rastport.h: *68
cp_y               short int in struct RastPort
        +0x0026    graphics/rastport.h: *68
cr                 pointer to struct ClipRect in struct Layer
        +0x0030    graphics/clip.h: *40
cr2                pointer to struct ClipRect in struct Layer
        +0x0034    graphics/clip.h: *40
crnew              pointer to struct ClipRect in struct Layer
        +0x0038    graphics/clip.h: *40
CR_NEEDS_NO_CONCEALED_RASTERS #define 1 =0x00000001 graphics/clip.h: *69
CTC_HCLRTAB        #define 2 =0x00000002 devices/console.h: *80
CTC_HCLRTABSALL    #define 5 =0x00000005 devices/console.h: *81
CTC_HSETTAB        #define 0 =0x00000000 devices/console.h: *79
```



```
ctl                unsigned short int in struct SpriteDef
        +0x0002    hardware/custom.h: *107
CTop               short int in struct StringInfo
        +0x0016    intuition/intuition.h: *464
CurrentBinding     structure tag
    size 0x0010    libraries/configvars.h: *48
                   libraries/expansionbase.h: 50
CurrentBinding     struct CurrentBinding (size 0x0010) in struct ExpansionBase
        +0x002c    libraries/expansionbase.h: *50
CURSORDOWN         #define 0x4D =0x0000004d intuition/intuition.h: *1019
CURSORLEFT         #define 0x4F =0x0000004f intuition/intuition.h: *1017
CURSORRIGHT        #define 0x4E =0x0000004e intuition/intuition.h: *1018
CURSORUP           #define 0x4C =0x0000004c intuition/intuition.h: *1016
CUSTOM             #define 0x40 =0x00000040 intuition/preferences.h: *183
Custom             structure tag
    size 0x01c0    hardware/custom.h: *19
CUSTOMBITMAP       #define 0x0040 =0x00000040 intuition/screens.h: *102
CustomBitMap       pointer to struct BitMap in struct NewScreen
        +0x001c    intuition/screens.h: *139
CUSTOMSCREEN       #define 0x000F =0x0000000f intuition/screens.h: *96
CUSTOM_NAME        #define 0x00 =0x00000000 intuition/preferences.h: *186
cu_AlgoStyle       char in struct ConUnit
        +0x0118    devices/conunit.h: *69
cu_AOLPen          char in struct ConUnit
        +0x0105    devices/conunit.h: *63
cu_AreaPtrn        pointer to pointer to char in struct ConUnit
        +0x0108    devices/conunit.h: *66
cu_AreaPtSz        char in struct ConUnit
        +0x0107    devices/conunit.h: *65
cu_BgPen           char in struct ConUnit
        +0x0104    devices/conunit.h: *62
cu_DrawMode        char in struct ConUnit
        +0x0106    devices/conunit.h: *64
cu_FgPen           char in struct ConUnit
        +0x0103    devices/conunit.h: *61
cu_Font            pointer to struct TextFont in struct ConUnit
        +0x0114    devices/conunit.h: *68
cu_KeyMapStruct    struct KeyMap (size 0x0020) in struct ConUnit
        +0x0042    devices/conunit.h: *55
cu_Mask            char in struct ConUnit
        +0x0102    devices/conunit.h: *60
cu_Minterms        array [8] of char in struct ConUnit
        +0x010c    devices/conunit.h: *67
cu_Modes           array [3] of char in struct ConUnit
        +0x0122    devices/conunit.h: *77
cu_MP              struct MsgPort (size 0x0022) in struct ConUnit
        +0x0000    devices/conunit.h: *35
cu_Node            struct Node (size 0x000e) in struct ClipboardUnitPartial
        +0x0000    devices/clipboard.h: *31
cu_RawEvents       array [3] of char in struct ConUnit
        +0x0125    devices/conunit.h: *78
cu_TabStops        array [80] of unsigned short int in struct ConUnit
        +0x0062    devices/conunit.h: *57
cu_TxBaseline      unsigned short int in struct ConUnit
        +0x011e    devices/conunit.h: *73
cu_TxFlags         char in struct ConUnit
        +0x0119    devices/conunit.h: *70
cu_TxHeight        unsigned short int in struct ConUnit
        +0x011a    devices/conunit.h: *71
cu_TxSpacing       unsigned short int in struct ConUnit
        +0x0120    devices/conunit.h: *74
cu_TxWidth         unsigned short int in struct ConUnit
        +0x011c    devices/conunit.h: *72
cu_UnitNum         unsigned int in struct ClipboardUnitPartial
        +0x000e    devices/clipboard.h: *32
cu_Window          pointer to struct Window in struct ConUnit
        +0x0022    devices/conunit.h: *37
cu_XCCP            short int in struct ConUnit
        +0x003e    devices/conunit.h: *50
```

```
cu_XCP           short int in struct ConUnit
        +0x0026  devices/conunit.h: *38
cu_XMax          short int in struct ConUnit
        +0x002a  devices/conunit.h: *40
cu_XMinShrink    short int in struct ConUnit
        +0x003a  devices/conunit.h: *48
cu_XRExtant      short int in struct ConUnit
        +0x0036  devices/conunit.h: *46
cu_XROrigin      short int in struct ConUnit
        +0x0032  devices/conunit.h: *44
cu_XRSize        short int in struct ConUnit
        +0x002e  devices/conunit.h: *42
cu_YCCP          short int in struct ConUnit
        +0x0040  devices/conunit.h: *51
cu_YCP           short int in struct ConUnit
        +0x0028  devices/conunit.h: *39
cu_YMax          short int in struct ConUnit
        +0x002c  devices/conunit.h: *41
cu_YMinShrink    short int in struct ConUnit
        +0x003c  devices/conunit.h: *49
cu_YRExtant      short int in struct ConUnit
        +0x0038  devices/conunit.h: *47
cu_YROrigin      short int in struct ConUnit
        +0x0034  devices/conunit.h: *45
cu_YRSize        short int in struct ConUnit
        +0x0030  devices/conunit.h: *43
CWAIT            Macro (3 arguments) graphics/gfxmacros.h: *34
CWidth           unsigned short int in struct PropInfo
        +0x000a  intuition/intuition.h: *420
DAC_BINDTIME     #define 0x20 =0x00000020 libraries/configregs.h: *215
DAC_BOOTTIME     #define 0x30 =0x00000030 libraries/configregs.h: *211
DAC_BUSWIDTH     #define 0xC0 =0x000000c0 libraries/configregs.h: *206
DAC_BYTEWIDE     #define 0x40 =0x00000040 libraries/configregs.h: *208
DAC_CONFIGTIME   #define 0x10 =0x00000010 libraries/configregs.h: *213
DAC_NEVER        #define 0x00 =0x00000000 libraries/configregs.h: *212
DAC_NIBBLEWIDE   #define 0x00 =0x00000000 libraries/configregs.h: *207
DAC_WORDWIDE     #define 0x80 =0x00000080 libraries/configregs.h: *209
DamageList       pointer to struct Region in struct Layer
        +0x009c  graphics/clip.h: *50
dataa            unsigned short int in struct SpriteDef
        +0x0004  hardware/custom.h: *108
datab            unsigned short int in struct SpriteDef
        +0x0006  hardware/custom.h: *109
DateStamp        structure tag
    size 0x000c  libraries/dos.h: *49, 66
                 libraries/dosextens.h: 180, 230, 273
da_BootPoint     unsigned short int in struct DiagArea
        +0x0006  libraries/configregs.h: *196
da_Config        char in struct DiagArea
        +0x0000  libraries/configregs.h: *192
da_DiagPoint     unsigned short int in struct DiagArea
        +0x0004  libraries/configregs.h: *195
da_Flags         char in struct DiagArea
        +0x0001  libraries/configregs.h: *193
da_Name          unsigned short int in struct DiagArea
        +0x0008  libraries/configregs.h: *197
da_Reserved01    unsigned short int in struct DiagArea
        +0x000a  libraries/configregs.h: *201
da_Reserved02    unsigned short int in struct DiagArea
        +0x000c  libraries/configregs.h: *202
da_Size          unsigned short int in struct DiagArea
        +0x0002  libraries/configregs.h: *194
dbf              extern function returning float libraries/mathffp.h: *76
DBLPF            #define 0x400 =0x00000400 graphics/display.h: *20
DBUFFER          #define 0x04 =0x00000004 graphics/rastport.h: *97
DBuffer          pointer to struct DBufPacket in struct Bob
        +0x001a  graphics/gels.h: *159
DBufPacket       structure tag
    size 0x000c  graphics/gels.h: 159, *229
```



```
ddfstop          unsigned short int in struct Custom
        +0x0094  hardware/custom.h: *79
ddfstrt          unsigned short int in struct Custom
        +0x0092  hardware/custom.h: *78
dd_CmdBytes      pointer to pointer to char in struct DeviceData
        +0x002e  devices/prtbase.h: *51
dd_CmdVectors    pointer to pointer to char in struct DeviceData
        +0x002a  devices/prtbase.h: *50
dd_CurrentX      int in struct DrawerData
        +0x0030  workbench/workbench.h: *43
dd_CurrentY      int in struct DrawerData
        +0x0034  workbench/workbench.h: *44
dd_Device        struct Library (size 0x0022) in struct DeviceData
        +0x0000  devices/prtbase.h: *47
dd_ExecBase      pointer to pointer to char in struct DeviceData
        +0x0026  devices/prtbase.h: *49
dd_Library       struct Library (size 0x0022) in struct Device
        +0x0000  exec/devices.h: *25
dd_NewWindow     struct NewWindow (size 0x0030) in struct DrawerData
        +0x0000  workbench/workbench.h: *42
dd_NumCommands   unsigned short int in struct DeviceData
        +0x0032  devices/prtbase.h: *52
dd_Segment       pointer to pointer to char in struct DeviceData
        +0x0022  devices/prtbase.h: *48
DEADEND_ALERT    #define 0x80000000 =0x80000000 intuition/intuition.h: *988
Debug            char in struct GfxBase
        +0x00a1  graphics/gfxbase.h: *39
DebugData        pointer to pointer to char in struct ExecBase
        +0x0046  exec/execbase.h: *43
DebugEntry       pointer to pointer to char in struct ExecBase
        +0x0042  exec/execbase.h: *42
DefaultFont      pointer to struct TextFont in struct GfxBase
        +0x009a  graphics/gfxbase.h: *36
DefaultTitle     pointer to char in struct Screen
        +0x001a  intuition/screens.h: *53
DefaultTitle     pointer to char in struct NewScreen
        +0x0014  intuition/screens.h: *129
DEFERREFRESH     #define 0x8000 =0x00008000 intuition/intuition.h: *183
DEFFREQ          #define 22200 =0x000056b8 devices/narrator.h: *42
DEFMODE          #define NATURALF0 =0x00000000 devices/narrator.h: *48
DEFPITCH         #define 110 =0x0000006e devices/narrator.h: *39
DEFRATE          #define 150 =0x00000096 devices/narrator.h: *40
DEFSEX           #define MALE =0x00000000 devices/narrator.h: *47
DEFVOL           #define 64 =0x00000040 devices/narrator.h: *41
DELTAMOVE        #define 0x00100000 =0x00100000 intuition/intuition.h: *658
Depth            char in struct BitMap
        +0x0005  graphics/gfx.h: *41
Depth            short int in struct Image
        +0x0008  intuition/intuition.h: *548
Depth            short int in struct NewScreen
        +0x0008  intuition/screens.h: *119
Depth            short int in struct VSprite
        +0x001e  graphics/gels.h: *99
Descendant       pointer to struct Window in struct Window
        +0x0046  intuition/intuition.h: *742
DEST             #define 0x100 =0x00000100 hardware/blit.h: *48
DestAddr         short int in union (no tag)
        +0x0000  graphics/copper.h: *29
DESTADDR         #define u3.u4.u1.DestAddr
                 graphics/copper.h: *42
DestData         short int in union (no tag)
        +0x0000  graphics/copper.h: *34
DESTDATA         #define u3.u4.u2.DestData
                 graphics/copper.h: *44
DetailPen        char in struct Window
        +0x0062  intuition/intuition.h: *757
DetailPen        char in struct NewWindow
        +0x0008  intuition/intuition.h: *855
DetailPen        char in struct Screen
```

```
        +0x014a  intuition/screens.h: *73
DetailPen        char in struct NewScreen
        +0x000a  intuition/screens.h: *121
Device           structure tag
    size 0x0022  exec/devices.h: *24
                 exec/io.h:  20, 29
                 devices/clipboard.h: 39
                 devices/printer.h: 138, 152
DeviceData       structure tag
    size 0x0034  devices/prtbase.h: *46, 60
DeviceList       struct List (size 0x000e) in struct ExecBase
        +0x015e  exec/execbase.h: *79
DeviceList       structure tag
    size 0x002c  libraries/dosextens.h: *225
DeviceNode       structure tag
    size 0x002c  libraries/expansion.h: 26
                 libraries/filehandler.h: *96
DEVICES_AUDIO_H  #define =0x00000000 devices/audio.h: *2
DEVICES_BOOTBLOCK_H #define =0x00000000 devices/bootblock.h: *2
DEVICES_CLIPBOARD_H #define =0x00000000 devices/clipboard.h: *2
DEVICES_CONSOLE_H #define =0x00000000 devices/console.h: *2
DEVICES_CONUNIT_H #define =0x00000000 devices/conunit.h: *2
DEVICES_GAMEPORT_H #define =0x00000000 devices/gameport.h: *2
DEVICES_HARDBLOCKS_H #define =0x00000000 devices/hardblocks.h: *2
DEVICES_INPUTEVENT_H #define =0x00000000 devices/inputevent.h: *2
DEVICES_INPUT_H  #define =0x00000000 devices/input.h: *2
DEVICES_KEYBOARD_H #define =0x00000000 devices/keyboard.h: *2
DEVICES_KEYMAP_H #define =0x00000000 devices/keymap.h: *2
DEVICES_NARRATOR_H #define =0x00000000 devices/narrator.h: *2
DEVICES_PARALLEL_H #define =0x00000000 devices/parallel.h: *2
DEVICES_PRINTER_H #define =0x00000000 devices/printer.h: *2
DEVICES_PRTBASE_H #define =0x00000000 devices/prtbase.h: *2
DEVICES_PRTGFX_H #define =0x00000000 devices/prtgfx.h: *2
DEVICES_SCSIDISK_H #define =0x00000000 devices/scsidisk.h: *2
DEVICES_SERIAL_H #define =0x00000000 devices/serial.h: *2
DEVICES_TIMER_H  #define =0x00000000 devices/timer.h: *2
DEVICES_TRACKDISK_H #define =0x00000000 devices/trackdisk.h: *2
DevInfo          structure tag
    size 0x002c  libraries/dosextens.h: *239
DEV_ABORTIO      #define (-36) =0xffffffdc exec/io.h:  *42
DEV_BEGINIO      #define (-30) =0xffffffe2 exec/io.h:  *41
DE_BLKSPERTRACK  #define 5 =0x00000005 libraries/filehandler.h: *60
de_BlocksPerTrack unsigned int in struct DosEnvec
        +0x0014  libraries/filehandler.h: *37
de_BootPri       int in struct DosEnvec
        +0x003c  libraries/filehandler.h: *47
DE_BOOTPRI       #define 15 =0x0000000f libraries/filehandler.h: *72
de_BufMemType    unsigned int in struct DosEnvec
        +0x0030  libraries/filehandler.h: *44
DE_BUFMEMTYPE    #define 12 =0x0000000c libraries/filehandler.h: *69
de_DosType       unsigned int in struct DosEnvec
        +0x0040  libraries/filehandler.h: *48
DE_DOSTYPE       #define 16 =0x00000010 libraries/filehandler.h: *75
de_HighCyl       unsigned int in struct DosEnvec
        +0x0028  libraries/filehandler.h: *42
de_Interleave    unsigned int in struct DosEnvec
        +0x0020  libraries/filehandler.h: *40
DE_INTERLEAVE    #define 8 =0x00000008 libraries/filehandler.h: *63
de_LowCyl        unsigned int in struct DosEnvec
        +0x0024  libraries/filehandler.h: *41
DE_LOWCYL        #define 9 =0x00000009 libraries/filehandler.h: *64
de_Mask          unsigned int in struct DosEnvec
        +0x0038  libraries/filehandler.h: *46
DE_MASK          #define 14 =0x0000000e libraries/filehandler.h: *71
de_MaxTransfer   unsigned int in struct DosEnvec
        +0x0034  libraries/filehandler.h: *45
DE_MAXTRANSFER   #define 13 =0x0000000d libraries/filehandler.h: *70
DE_MEMBUFTYPE    #define 12 =0x0000000c libraries/filehandler.h: *67
de_NumBuffers    unsigned int in struct DosEnvec
```



```
        +0x002c  libraries/filehandler.h: *43
DE_NUMBUFFERS    #define 11 =0x0000000b libraries/filehandler.h: *66
DE_NUMHEADS      #define 3 =0x00000003 libraries/filehandler.h: *58
de_PreAlloc      unsigned int in struct DosEnvec
        +0x001c  libraries/filehandler.h: *39
DE_PREFAC        #define 7 =0x00000007 libraries/filehandler.h: *62
de_Reserved      unsigned int in struct DosEnvec
        +0x0018  libraries/filehandler.h: *38
DE_RESERVEDBLKS  #define 6 =0x00000006 libraries/filehandler.h: *61
de_SecOrg        unsigned int in struct DosEnvec
        +0x0008  libraries/filehandler.h: *34
DE_SECORG        #define 2 =0x00000002 libraries/filehandler.h: *57
DE_SECSPERBLK    #define 4 =0x00000004 libraries/filehandler.h: *59
de_SectorPerBlock unsigned int in struct DosEnvec
        +0x0010  libraries/filehandler.h: *36
de_SizeBlock     unsigned int in struct DosEnvec
        +0x0004  libraries/filehandler.h: *33
DE_SIZEBLOCK     #define 1 =0x00000001 libraries/filehandler.h: *56
de_Surfaces      unsigned int in struct DosEnvec
        +0x000c  libraries/filehandler.h: *35
de_TableSize     unsigned int in struct DosEnvec
        +0x0000  libraries/filehandler.h: *32
DE_TABLESIZE     #define 0 =0x00000000 libraries/filehandler.h: *55
DE_UPPERCYL      #define 10 =0x0000000a libraries/filehandler.h: *65
dfh_DF           struct Node (size 0x000e) in struct DiskFontHeader
        +0x0000  libraries/diskfont.h: *51
dfh_FileID       unsigned short int in struct DiskFontHeader
        +0x000e  libraries/diskfont.h: *52
DFH_ID           #define 0x0f80 =0x00000f80 libraries/diskfont.h: *40
dfh_Name         array [32] of char in struct DiskFontHeader
        +0x0016  libraries/diskfont.h: *55
dfh_Revision     unsigned short int in struct DiskFontHeader
        +0x0010  libraries/diskfont.h: *53
dfh_Segment      int in struct DiskFontHeader
        +0x0012  libraries/diskfont.h: *54
dfh_TF           struct TextFont (size 0x0034) in struct DiskFontHeader
        +0x0036  libraries/diskfont.h: *56
DFTCH_MASK       #define 0xFF =0x000000ff graphics/display.h: *35
DHeight          short int in struct ViewPort
        +0x001a  graphics/view.h: *39
DIAB_630         #define 0x04 =0x00000004 intuition/preferences.h: *190
DIAB_ADV_D25     #define 0x05 =0x00000005 intuition/preferences.h: *191
DIAB_C_150       #define 0x06 =0x00000006 intuition/preferences.h: *192
DiagArea         structure tag
    size 0x000e  libraries/configregs.h: *191
diagstrt         array [4] of unsigned short int in struct copinit
        +0x0000  graphics/copper.h: *78
DIMENSIONS_MASK  #define (BOUNDED_DIMENSIONS|ABSOLUTE_DIMENSIONS|
                      PIXEL_DIMENSIONS|MULTIPLY_DIMENSIONS) =0x000000f0
                 intuition/preferences.h: *259
DiscResource     structure tag
    size 0x0090  resources/disk.h: *48
DiscResourceUnit structure tag
    size 0x0056  resources/disk.h: *41, 50
DiskFontHeader   structure tag
    size 0x006a  libraries/diskfont.h: *43
DISKINSERTED     #define 0x00008000 =0x00008000 intuition/intuition.h: *653
DISKNAME         #define "disk.resource" resources/disk.h: *99
DiskObject       structure tag
    size 0x004e  workbench/icon.h: 29
                 workbench/workbench.h: *51
DISKREMOVED      #define 0x00010000 =0x00010000 intuition/intuition.h: *654
DispCount        unsigned int in struct ExecBase
        +0x011c  exec/execbase.h: *57
DispCount        short int in struct StringInfo
        +0x0012  intuition/intuition.h: *463
DisplayFlags     unsigned short int in struct GfxBase
        +0x00ce  graphics/gfxbase.h: *51
DispPos          short int in struct StringInfo
```

```
        +0x000c  intuition/intuition.h: *458
DITHERING_MASK   #define (HALFTONE_DITHERING|FLOYD_DITHERING) =0x00000600
                 intuition/preferences.h: *260
diwstop          unsigned short int in struct Custom
        +0x0090  hardware/custom.h: *77
diwstrt          unsigned short int in struct Custom
        +0x008e  hardware/custom.h: *76
DIW_HORIZ_POS    #define 0x7F =0x0000007f graphics/display.h: *30
DIW_VRTCL_POS    #define 0x1FF =0x000001ff graphics/display.h: *31
DIW_VRTCL_POS_SHIFT #define 7 =0x00000007 graphics/display.h: *32
di_Devices       int in struct DosInfo
        +0x0008  libraries/dosextens.h: *189
di_DevInfo       int in struct DosInfo
        +0x0004  libraries/dosextens.h: *188
di_Handlers      int in struct DosInfo
        +0x000c  libraries/dosextens.h: *190
di_McName        int in struct DosInfo
        +0x0000  libraries/dosextens.h: *187
di_NetHand       pointer to pointer to char in struct DosInfo
        +0x0010  libraries/dosextens.h: *191
DLT_DEVICE       #define 0 =0x00000000 libraries/dosextens.h: *285
DLT_DIRECTORY    #define 1 =0x00000001 libraries/dosextens.h: *286
DLT_VOLUME       #define 2 =0x00000002 libraries/dosextens.h: *287
dl_A2            int in struct DosLibrary
        +0x002a  libraries/dosextens.h: *168
dl_A5            int in struct DosLibrary
        +0x002e  libraries/dosextens.h: *169
dl_A6            int in struct DosLibrary
        +0x0032  libraries/dosextens.h: *170
dl_DiskType      int in struct DeviceList
        +0x0020  libraries/dosextens.h: *232
dl_GV            pointer to pointer to char in struct DosLibrary
        +0x0026  libraries/dosextens.h: *167
dl_lib           struct Library (size 0x0022) in struct DosLibrary
        +0x0000  libraries/dosextens.h: *165
dl_Lock          int in struct DeviceList
        +0x000c  libraries/dosextens.h: *229
dl_LockList      int in struct DeviceList
        +0x001c  libraries/dosextens.h: *231
dl_Name          pointer to int in struct DeviceList
        +0x0028  libraries/dosextens.h: *234
dl_Next          int in struct DeviceList
        +0x0000  libraries/dosextens.h: *226
dl_Root          pointer to pointer to char in struct DosLibrary
        +0x0022  libraries/dosextens.h: *166
dl_Task          pointer to struct MsgPort in struct DeviceList
        +0x0008  libraries/dosextens.h: *228
dl_Type          int in struct DeviceList
        +0x0004  libraries/dosextens.h: *227
dl_unused        int in struct DeviceList
        +0x0024  libraries/dosextens.h: *233
dl_VolumeDate    struct DateStamp (size 0x000c) in struct DeviceList
        +0x0010  libraries/dosextens.h: *230
DMAB_AUD0        #define 0 =0x00000000 hardware/dmabits.h: *35
DMAB_AUD1        #define 1 =0x00000001 hardware/dmabits.h: *36
DMAB_AUD2        #define 2 =0x00000002 hardware/dmabits.h: *37
DMAB_AUD3        #define 3 =0x00000003 hardware/dmabits.h: *38
DMAB_BLITHOG     #define 10 =0x0000000a hardware/dmabits.h: *45
DMAB_BLITTER     #define 6 =0x00000006 hardware/dmabits.h: *41
DMAB_BLTDONE     #define 14 =0x0000000e hardware/dmabits.h: *46
DMAB_BLTNZERO    #define 13 =0x0000000d hardware/dmabits.h: *47
DMAB_COPPER      #define 7 =0x00000007 hardware/dmabits.h: *42
DMAB_DISK        #define 4 =0x00000004 hardware/dmabits.h: *39
DMAB_MASTER      #define 9 =0x00000009 hardware/dmabits.h: *44
DMAB_RASTER      #define 8 =0x00000008 hardware/dmabits.h: *43
DMAB_SETCLR      #define 15 =0x0000000f hardware/dmabits.h: *34
DMAB_SPRITE      #define 5 =0x00000005 hardware/dmabits.h: *40
dmacon           unsigned short int in struct Custom
        +0x0096  hardware/custom.h: *80
```



```
dmaconr          unsigned short int in struct Custom
        +0x0002  hardware/custom.h: *21
DMAF_ALL         #define 0x01FF =0x000001ff hardware/dmabits.h: *27
DMAF_AUD0        #define 0x0001 =0x00000001 hardware/dmabits.h: *16
DMAF_AUD1        #define 0x0002 =0x00000002 hardware/dmabits.h: *17
DMAF_AUD2        #define 0x0004 =0x00000004 hardware/dmabits.h: *18
DMAF_AUD3        #define 0x0008 =0x00000008 hardware/dmabits.h: *19
DMAF_AUDIO       #define 0x000F =0x0000000f hardware/dmabits.h: *15
DMAF_BLITHOG     #define 0x0400 =0x00000400 hardware/dmabits.h: *26
DMAF_BLITTER     #define 0x0040 =0x00000040 hardware/dmabits.h: *22
DMAF_BLTDONE     #define 0x4000 =0x00004000 hardware/dmabits.h: *31
DMAF_BLTNZERO    #define 0x2000 =0x00002000 hardware/dmabits.h: *32
DMAF_COPPER      #define 0x0080 =0x00000080 hardware/dmabits.h: *23
DMAF_DISK        #define 0x0010 =0x00000010 hardware/dmabits.h: *20
DMAF_MASTER      #define 0x0200 =0x00000200 hardware/dmabits.h: *25
DMAF_RASTER      #define 0x0100 =0x00000100 hardware/dmabits.h: *24
DMAF_SETCLR      #define 0x8000 =0x00008000 hardware/dmabits.h: *14
DMAF_SPRITE      #define 0x0020 =0x00000020 hardware/dmabits.h: *21
DMRequest        pointer to struct Requester in struct Window
        +0x0028  intuition/intuition.h: *713
dn_GlobalVec     int in struct DeviceNode
        +0x0024  libraries/filehandler.h: *109
dn_Handler       int in struct DeviceNode
        +0x0010  libraries/filehandler.h: *103
dn_Lock          int in struct DeviceNode
        +0x000c  libraries/filehandler.h: *102
dn_Name          int in struct DeviceNode
        +0x0028  libraries/filehandler.h: *117
dn_Next          int in struct DeviceNode
        +0x0000  libraries/filehandler.h: *97
dn_Priority      int in struct DeviceNode
        +0x0018  libraries/filehandler.h: *105
dn_SegList       int in struct DeviceNode
        +0x0020  libraries/filehandler.h: *107
dn_StackSize     unsigned int in struct DeviceNode
        +0x0014  libraries/filehandler.h: *104
dn_Startup       int in struct DeviceNode
        +0x001c  libraries/filehandler.h: *106
dn_Task          pointer to struct MsgPort in struct DeviceNode
        +0x0008  libraries/filehandler.h: *99
dn_Type          unsigned int in struct DeviceNode
        +0x0004  libraries/filehandler.h: *98
dol_DiskType     int in struct (no tag)
        +0x0010  libraries/dosextens.h: *275
dol_GlobVec      int in struct (no tag)
        +0x0014  libraries/dosextens.h: *267
dol_Handler      int in struct (no tag)
        +0x0000  libraries/dosextens.h: *262
dol_handler      struct (no tag) (size 0x0018) in union (no tag)
        +0x0000  libraries/dosextens.h: *270
dol_Lock         int in struct DosList
        +0x000c  libraries/dosextens.h: *259
dol_LockList     int in struct (no tag)
        +0x000c  libraries/dosextens.h: *274
dol_misc         union (no tag) (size 0x0018) in struct DosList
        +0x0010  libraries/dosextens.h: *278
dol_Name         int in struct DosList
        +0x0028  libraries/dosextens.h: *280
dol_Next         int in struct DosList
        +0x0000  libraries/dosextens.h: *256
dol_Priority     int in struct (no tag)
        +0x0008  libraries/dosextens.h: *264
dol_SegList      int in struct (no tag)
        +0x0010  libraries/dosextens.h: *266
dol_StackSize    int in struct (no tag)
        +0x0004  libraries/dosextens.h: *263
dol_Startup      unsigned int in struct (no tag)
        +0x000c  libraries/dosextens.h: *265
dol_Task         pointer to struct MsgPort in struct DosList
```

```
        +0x0008  libraries/dosextens.h: *258
dol_Type         int in struct DosList
        +0x0004  libraries/dosextens.h: *257
dol_volume       struct (no tag) (size 0x0014) in union (no tag)
        +0x0000  libraries/dosextens.h: *276
dol_VolumeDate   struct DateStamp (size 0x000c) in struct (no tag)
        +0x0000  libraries/dosextens.h: *273
DosEnvec         structure tag
    size 0x0044  libraries/filehandler.h: *31
DOSFALSE         #define (0L) libraries/dos.h: *22
DosInfo          structure tag
    size 0x0014  libraries/dosextens.h: *186
DosLibrary       structure tag
    size 0x0036  libraries/dosextens.h: *164
DosList          structure tag
    size 0x002c  libraries/dosextens.h: *255
DOSNAME          #define "dos.library" libraries/dos.h: *17
DosPacket        structure tag
    size 0x0030  libraries/dosextens.h: *79, 112
DOSTRUE          #define (-1L) libraries/dos.h: *21
DOUBLE           typedef double exec/types.h: *44
DoubleClick      struct timeval (size 0x0008) in struct Preferences
        +0x0014  intuition/preferences.h: *56
do_CurrentX      int in struct DiskObject
        +0x003a  workbench/workbench.h: *58
do_CurrentY      int in struct DiskObject
        +0x003e  workbench/workbench.h: *59
do_DefaultTool   pointer to char in struct DiskObject
        +0x0032  workbench/workbench.h: *56
do_DrawerData    pointer to struct DrawerData in struct DiskObject
        +0x0042  workbench/workbench.h: *60
do_Gadget        struct Gadget (size 0x002c) in struct DiskObject
        +0x0004  workbench/workbench.h: *54
do_Magic         unsigned short int in struct DiskObject
        +0x0000  workbench/workbench.h: *52
do_StackSize     int in struct DiskObject
        +0x004a  workbench/workbench.h: *62
do_ToolTypes     pointer to pointer to char in struct DiskObject
        +0x0036  workbench/workbench.h: *57
do_ToolWindow    pointer to char in struct DiskObject
        +0x0046  workbench/workbench.h: *61
do_Type          char in struct DiskObject
        +0x0030  workbench/workbench.h: *55
do_Version       unsigned short int in struct DiskObject
        +0x0002  workbench/workbench.h: *53
DPB_DEAD         #define 3 =0x00000003 devices/keymap.h: *67
DPB_MOD          #define 0 =0x00000000 devices/keymap.h: *65
DPF_DEAD         #define 0x08 =0x00000008 devices/keymap.h: *68
DPF_MOD          #define 0x01 =0x00000001 devices/keymap.h: *66
DP_2DFACSHIFT    #define 4 =0x00000004 devices/keymap.h: *71
DP_2DINDEXMASK   #define 0x0f =0x0000000f devices/keymap.h: *70
dp_Action        #define dp_Type =0x00000000 libraries/dosextens.h: *93
dp_Arg1          int in struct DosPacket
        +0x0014  libraries/dosextens.h: *97
dp_Arg2          int in struct DosPacket
        +0x0018  libraries/dosextens.h: *98
dp_Arg3          int in struct DosPacket
        +0x001c  libraries/dosextens.h: *99
dp_Arg4          int in struct DosPacket
        +0x0020  libraries/dosextens.h: *100
dp_Arg5          int in struct DosPacket
        +0x0024  libraries/dosextens.h: *101
dp_Arg6          int in struct DosPacket
        +0x0028  libraries/dosextens.h: *102
dp_Arg7          int in struct DosPacket
        +0x002c  libraries/dosextens.h: *103
dp_BufAddr       #define dp_Arg1 =0x00000000 libraries/dosextens.h: *96
dp_Link          pointer to struct Message in struct DosPacket
        +0x0000  libraries/dosextens.h: *80
```



```
dp_Port          pointer to struct MsgPort in struct DosPacket
        +0x0004  libraries/dosextens.h: *81
dp_Res1          int in struct DosPacket
        +0x000c  libraries/dosextens.h: *86
dp_Res2          int in struct DosPacket
        +0x0010  libraries/dosextens.h: *90
dp_Status        #define dp_Res1 =0x00000000 libraries/dosextens.h: *94
dp_Status2       #define dp_Res2 =0x00000000 libraries/dosextens.h: *95
dp_Type          int in struct DosPacket
        +0x0008  libraries/dosextens.h: *83
DRAFT            #define 0x000 =0x00000000 intuition/preferences.h: *158
DrawCircle       Macro (4 arguments) graphics/gfxmacros.h: *37
DrawerData       structure tag
    size 0x0038  workbench/workbench.h: *41, 60
DRAWERDATAFILESIZE #define (sizeof( struct DrawerData ))
                 workbench/workbench.h: *48
DrawMode         char in struct RastPort
        +0x001c  graphics/rastport.h: *62
DrawMode         char in struct IntuiText
        +0x0002  intuition/intuition.h: *497
DrawMode         char in struct Border
        +0x0006  intuition/intuition.h: *526
DrawPath         pointer to struct VSprite in struct VSprite
        +0x0008  graphics/gels.h: *79
DRB_ACTIVE       #define 7 =0x00000007 resources/disk.h: *67
DRB_ALLOC0       #define 0 =0x00000000 resources/disk.h: *63
DRB_ALLOC1       #define 1 =0x00000001 resources/disk.h: *64
DRB_ALLOC2       #define 2 =0x00000002 resources/disk.h: *65
DRB_ALLOC3       #define 3 =0x00000003 resources/disk.h: *66
DRF_ACTIVE       #define (1<<7) =0x00000080 resources/disk.h: *73
DRF_ALLOC0       #define (1<<0) =0x00000001 resources/disk.h: *69
DRF_ALLOC1       #define (1<<1) =0x00000002 resources/disk.h: *70
DRF_ALLOC2       #define (1<<2) =0x00000004 resources/disk.h: *71
DRF_ALLOC3       #define (1<<3) =0x00000008 resources/disk.h: *72
DRIVE3_5         #define 1 =0x00000001 devices/trackdisk.h: *148
DRIVE5_25        #define 2 =0x00000002 devices/trackdisk.h: *149
DRT_37422D2S     #define (0x55555555) =0x55555555 resources/disk.h: *118
DRT_AMIGA        #define (0x00000000) =0x00000000 resources/disk.h: *117
DRT_EMPTY        #define (0xFFFFFFFF) =0xffffffff resources/disk.h: *119
dru_DiscBlock    struct Interrupt (size 0x0016) in struct DiscResourceUnit
        +0x0014  resources/disk.h: *43
dru_DiscSync     struct Interrupt (size 0x0016) in struct DiscResourceUnit
        +0x002a  resources/disk.h: *44
dru_Index        struct Interrupt (size 0x0016) in struct DiscResourceUnit
        +0x0040  resources/disk.h: *45
dru_Message      struct Message (size 0x0014) in struct DiscResourceUnit
        +0x0000  resources/disk.h: *42
DR_ALLOCUNIT     #define (LIB_BASE - 0*LIB_VECTSIZE) =0xfffffffa
                 resources/disk.h: *102
dr_CiaResource   pointer to struct Library in struct DiscResource
        +0x002c  resources/disk.h: *54
dr_Current       pointer to struct DiscResourceUnit in struct DiscResource
        +0x0022  resources/disk.h: *50
dr_DiscBlock     struct Interrupt (size 0x0016) in struct DiscResource
        +0x004e  resources/disk.h: *57
dr_DiscSync      struct Interrupt (size 0x0016) in struct DiscResource
        +0x0064  resources/disk.h: *58
dr_Flags         char in struct DiscResource
        +0x0026  resources/disk.h: *51
DR_FREEUNIT      #define (LIB_BASE - 1*LIB_VECTSIZE) =0xfffffff4
                 resources/disk.h: *103
DR_GETUNIT       #define (LIB_BASE - 2*LIB_VECTSIZE) =0xffffffee
                 resources/disk.h: *104
DR_GETUNITID     #define (LIB_BASE - 4*LIB_VECTSIZE) =0xffffffe2
                 resources/disk.h: *106
DR_GIVEUNIT      #define (LIB_BASE - 3*LIB_VECTSIZE) =0xffffffe8
                 resources/disk.h: *105
dr_Index         struct Interrupt (size 0x0016) in struct DiscResource
        +0x007a  resources/disk.h: *59
```

```
DR_LASTCOMM      #define (DR_GIVEUNIT) =0xffffffe8 resources/disk.h: *109
dr_Library       struct Library (size 0x0022) in struct DiscResource
         +0x0000 resources/disk.h: *49
dr_pad           char in struct DiscResource
         +0x0027 resources/disk.h: *52
dr_SysLib        pointer to struct Library in struct DiscResource
         +0x0028 resources/disk.h: *53
dr_UnitID        array [4] of unsigned int in struct DiscResource
         +0x0030 resources/disk.h: *55
dr_Waiting       struct List (size 0x000e) in struct DiscResource
         +0x0040 resources/disk.h: *56
dskbytr          unsigned short int in struct Custom
         +0x001a hardware/custom.h: *33
dskdat           unsigned short int in struct Custom
         +0x0026 hardware/custom.h: *38
dskdatr          unsigned short int in struct Custom
         +0x0008 hardware/custom.h: *24
DSKDMAOFF        #define 0x4000 =0x00004000 resources/disk.h: *84
dsklen           unsigned short int in struct Custom
         +0x0024 hardware/custom.h: *37
dskpt            pointer to pointer to char in struct Custom
         +0x0020 hardware/custom.h: *36
dsksync          unsigned short int in struct Custom
         +0x007e hardware/custom.h: *70
DspIns           pointer to struct CopList in struct ViewPort
         +0x0008 graphics/view.h: *35
DSR_CPR          #define 6 =0x00000006 devices/console.h: *76
ds_Days          int in struct DateStamp
         +0x0000 libraries/dos.h: *50
ds_Minute        int in struct DateStamp
         +0x0004 libraries/dos.h: *51
ds_Tick          int in struct DateStamp
         +0x0008 libraries/dos.h: *52
DUALPF           #define 0x400 =0x00000400 graphics/view.h: *59
dummy            char in struct RastPort
         +0x001f graphics/rastport.h: *65
dvi_GlobVec      int in struct DevInfo
         +0x0024 libraries/dosextens.h: *249
dvi_Handler      int in struct DevInfo
         +0x0010 libraries/dosextens.h: *244
dvi_Lock         int in struct DevInfo
         +0x000c libraries/dosextens.h: *243
dvi_Name         int in struct DevInfo
         +0x0028 libraries/dosextens.h: *250
dvi_Next         int in struct DevInfo
         +0x0000 libraries/dosextens.h: *240
dvi_Priority     int in struct DevInfo
         +0x0018 libraries/dosextens.h: *246
dvi_SegList      int in struct DevInfo
         +0x0020 libraries/dosextens.h: *248
dvi_StackSize    int in struct DevInfo
         +0x0014 libraries/dosextens.h: *245
dvi_Startup      int in struct DevInfo
         +0x001c libraries/dosextens.h: *247
dvi_Task         pointer to pointer to char in struct DevInfo
         +0x0008 libraries/dosextens.h: *242
dvi_Type         int in struct DevInfo
         +0x0004 libraries/dosextens.h: *241
DWidth           short int in struct ViewPort
         +0x0018 graphics/view.h: *39
DxOffset         short int in struct ViewPort
         +0x001c graphics/view.h: *40
DxOffset         short int in struct View
         +0x000e graphics/view.h: *52
DyOffset         short int in struct ViewPort
         +0x001e graphics/view.h: *40
DyOffset         short int in struct View
         +0x000c graphics/view.h: *52
DyOffset         short int in struct CopList
```



```
         +0x0020 graphics/copper.h: *66
E                #define ((float) 2.718281828459045) libraries/mathffp.h: *20
ECIB_INT2PEND    #define 4 =0x00000004 libraries/configregs.h: *141
ECIB_INT6PEND    #define 5 =0x00000005 libraries/configregs.h: *142
ECIB_INT7PEND    #define 6 =0x00000006 libraries/configregs.h: *143
ECIB_INTENA      #define 1 =0x00000001 libraries/configregs.h: *139
ECIB_INTERRUPTING #define 7 =0x00000007 libraries/configregs.h: *144
ECIB_RESET       #define 3 =0x00000003 libraries/configregs.h: *140
ECIF_INT2PEND    #define (1<<4) =0x00000010 libraries/configregs.h: *148
ECIF_INT6PEND    #define (1<<5) =0x00000020 libraries/configregs.h: *149
ECIF_INT7PEND    #define (1<<6) =0x00000040 libraries/configregs.h: *150
ECIF_INTENA      #define (1<<1) =0x00000002 libraries/configregs.h: *146
ECIF_INTERRUPTING #define (1<<7) =0x00000080 libraries/configregs.h: *151
ECIF_RESET       #define (1<<3) =0x00000008 libraries/configregs.h: *147
ECOFFSET         Macro (1 argument) libraries/configregs.h: *160
ec_BaseAddress   char in struct ExpansionControl
         +0x0002 libraries/configregs.h: *47
ec_Interrupt     char in struct ExpansionControl
         +0x0000 libraries/configregs.h: *45
EC_MEMADDR       Macro (1 argument) libraries/configregs.h: *155
ec_Reserved11    char in struct ExpansionControl
         +0x0001 libraries/configregs.h: *46
ec_Reserved14    char in struct ExpansionControl
         +0x0004 libraries/configregs.h: *49
ec_Reserved15    char in struct ExpansionControl
         +0x0005 libraries/configregs.h: *50
ec_Reserved16    char in struct ExpansionControl
         +0x0006 libraries/configregs.h: *51
ec_Reserved17    char in struct ExpansionControl
         +0x0007 libraries/configregs.h: *52
ec_Reserved18    char in struct ExpansionControl
         +0x0008 libraries/configregs.h: *53
ec_Reserved19    char in struct ExpansionControl
         +0x0009 libraries/configregs.h: *54
ec_Reserved1a    char in struct ExpansionControl
         +0x000a libraries/configregs.h: *55
ec_Reserved1b    char in struct ExpansionControl
         +0x000b libraries/configregs.h: *56
ec_Reserved1c    char in struct ExpansionControl
         +0x000c libraries/configregs.h: *57
ec_Reserved1d    char in struct ExpansionControl
         +0x000d libraries/configregs.h: *58
ec_Reserved1e    char in struct ExpansionControl
         +0x000e libraries/configregs.h: *59
ec_Reserved1f    char in struct ExpansionControl
         +0x000f libraries/configregs.h: *60
ec_Shutup        char in struct ExpansionControl
         +0x0003 libraries/configregs.h: *48
EIGHT_LPI        #define 0x200 =0x00000200 intuition/preferences.h: *163
Elapsed          unsigned short int in struct ExecBase
         +0x0122 exec/execbase.h: *59
ELITE            #define 0x400 =0x00000400 intuition/preferences.h: *154
EnableCLI        short int in struct Preferences
         +0x007c intuition/preferences.h: *78
ENDGADGET        #define 0x0004 =0x00000004 intuition/intuition.h: *294
EPSON            #define 0x07 =0x00000007 intuition/preferences.h: *193
EPSON_JX_80      #define 0x08 =0x00000008 intuition/preferences.h: *194
ERFB_MEMSPACE    #define 7 =0x00000007 libraries/configregs.h: *120
ERFB_NOSHUTUP    #define 6 =0x00000006 libraries/configregs.h: *124
ERFF_MEMSPACE    #define (1<<7) =0x00000080 libraries/configregs.h: *126
ERFF_NOSHUTUP    #define (1<<6) =0x00000040 libraries/configregs.h: *127
EROFFSET         Macro (1 argument) libraries/configregs.h: *158
ERROR_ACTION_NOT_KNOWN #define 209 =0x000000d1 libraries/dos.h: *145
ERROR_BAD_STREAM_NAME #define 206 =0x000000ce libraries/dos.h: *143
ERROR_COMMENT_TOO_BIG #define 220 =0x000000dc libraries/dos.h: *156
ERROR_DELETE_PROTECTED #define 222 =0x000000de libraries/dos.h: *158
ERROR_DEVICE_NOT_MOUNTED #define 218 =0x000000da libraries/dos.h: *154
ERROR_DIRECTORY_NOT_EMPTY #define 216 =0x000000d8 libraries/dos.h: *152
ERROR_DIR_NOT_FOUND #define 204 =0x000000cc libraries/dos.h: *141
```

```
ERROR_DISK_FULL  #define 221 =0x000000dd libraries/dos.h: *157
ERROR_DISK_NOT_VALIDATED #define 213 =0x000000d5 libraries/dos.h: *149
ERROR_DISK_WRITE_PROTECTED #define 214 =0x000000d6 libraries/dos.h: *150
ERROR_FILE_NOT_OBJECT #define 121 =0x00000079 libraries/dos.h: *136
ERROR_INVALID_COMPONENT_NAME #define 210 =0x000000d2 libraries/dos.h: *146
ERROR_INVALID_LOCK #define 211 =0x000000d3 libraries/dos.h: *147
ERROR_INVALID_RESIDENT_LIBRARY #define 122 =0x0000007a libraries/dos.h: *137
ERROR_LINE_TOO_LONG #define 120 =0x00000078 libraries/dos.h: *135
ERROR_NOT_A_DOS_DISK #define 225 =0x000000e1 libraries/dos.h: *161
ERROR_NO_DEFAULT_DIR #define 201 =0x000000c9 libraries/dos.h: *138
ERROR_NO_DISK    #define 226 =0x000000e2 libraries/dos.h: *162
ERROR_NO_FREE_STORE #define 103 =0x00000067 libraries/dos.h: *133
ERROR_NO_MORE_ENTRIES #define 232 =0x000000e8 libraries/dos.h: *163
ERROR_OBJECT_EXISTS #define 203 =0x000000cb libraries/dos.h: *140
ERROR_OBJECT_IN_USE #define 202 =0x000000ca libraries/dos.h: *139
ERROR_OBJECT_NOT_FOUND #define 205 =0x000000cd libraries/dos.h: *142
ERROR_OBJECT_TOO_LARGE #define 207 =0x000000cf libraries/dos.h: *144
ERROR_OBJECT_WRONG_TYPE #define 212 =0x000000d4 libraries/dos.h: *148
ERROR_READ_PROTECTED #define 224 =0x000000e0 libraries/dos.h: *160
ERROR_RENAME_ACROSS_DEVICES #define 215 =0x000000d7 libraries/dos.h: *151
ERROR_SEEK_ERROR #define 219 =0x000000db libraries/dos.h: *155
ERROR_TASK_TABLE_FULL #define 105 =0x00000069 libraries/dos.h: *134
ERROR_TOO_MANY_LEVELS #define 217 =0x000000d9 libraries/dos.h: *153
ERROR_WRITE_PROTECTED #define 223 =0x000000df libraries/dos.h: *159
ERTB_CHAINEDCONFIG #define 3 =0x00000003 libraries/configregs.h: *108
ERTB_DIAGVALID    #define 4 =0x00000004 libraries/configregs.h: *109
ERTB_MEMLIST      #define 5 =0x00000005 libraries/configregs.h: *110
ERTF_CHAINEDCONFIG #define (1<<3) =0x00000008 libraries/configregs.h: *112
ERTF_DIAGVALID    #define (1<<4) =0x00000010 libraries/configregs.h: *113
ERTF_MEMLIST      #define (1<<5) =0x00000020 libraries/configregs.h: *114
ERT_MEMBIT        #define 0 =0x00000000 libraries/configregs.h: *103
ERT_MEMMASK       #define 0x07 =0x00000007 libraries/configregs.h: *102
ERT_MEMNEEDED     Macro (1 argument) libraries/configregs.h: *132
ERT_MEMSIZE       #define 3 =0x00000003 libraries/configregs.h: *104
ERT_NEWBOARD      #define 0xc0 =0x000000c0 libraries/configregs.h: *98
ERT_SLOTSNEEDED   Macro (1 argument) libraries/configregs.h: *136
ERT_TYPEBIT       #define 6 =0x00000006 libraries/configregs.h: *96
ERT_TYPEMASK      #define 0xc0 =0x000000c0 libraries/configregs.h: *95
ERT_TYPESIZE      #define 2 =0x00000002 libraries/configregs.h: *97
er_Flags          char in struct ExpansionRom
         +0x0002  libraries/configregs.h: *33
er_InitDiagVec    unsigned short int in struct ExpansionRom
         +0x000a  libraries/configregs.h: *37
er_Manufacturer   unsigned short int in struct ExpansionRom
         +0x0004  libraries/configregs.h: *35
er_Product        char in struct ExpansionRom
         +0x0001  libraries/configregs.h: *32
er_Reserved03     char in struct ExpansionRom
         +0x0003  libraries/configregs.h: *34
er_Reserved0c     char in struct ExpansionRom
         +0x000c  libraries/configregs.h: *38
er_Reserved0d     char in struct ExpansionRom
         +0x000d  libraries/configregs.h: *39
er_Reserved0e     char in struct ExpansionRom
         +0x000e  libraries/configregs.h: *40
er_Reserved0f     char in struct ExpansionRom
         +0x000f  libraries/configregs.h: *41
er_SerialNumber   unsigned int in struct ExpansionRom
         +0x0006  libraries/configregs.h: *36
er_Type           char in struct ExpansionRom
         +0x0000  libraries/configregs.h: *31
ETD_CLEAR         #define (CMD_CLEAR|TDF_EXTCOM) =0x00008005
                  devices/trackdisk.h: *103
ETD_FORMAT        #define (TD_FORMAT|TDF_EXTCOM) =0x0000800b
                  devices/trackdisk.h: *101
ETD_MOTOR         #define (TD_MOTOR|TDF_EXTCOM) =0x00008009
                  devices/trackdisk.h: *99
ETD_RAWREAD       #define (TD_RAWREAD|TDF_EXTCOM) =0x00008010
                  devices/trackdisk.h: *104
```



```
ETD_RAWWRITE      #define (TD_RAWWRITE|TDF_EXTCOM) =0x00008011
                  devices/trackdisk.h: *105
ETD_READ          #define (CMD_READ|TDF_EXTCOM) =0x00008002
                  devices/trackdisk.h: *98
ETD_SEEK          #define (TD_SEEK|TDF_EXTCOM) =0x0000800a
                  devices/trackdisk.h: *100
ETD_UPDATE        #define (CMD_UPDATE|TDF_EXTCOM) =0x00008004
                  devices/trackdisk.h: *102
ETD_WRITE         #define (CMD_WRITE|TDF_EXTCOM) =0x00008003
                  devices/trackdisk.h: *97
EXCLUSIVE_LOCK    #define -1 =0xffffffff libraries/dos.h: *46
ExecBase          structure tag
    size 0x024c   exec/execbase.h: *30
                  libraries/romboot_base.h: 35
ExecBase          pointer to pointer to char in struct ExpansionBase
         +0x0024  libraries/expansionbase.h: *48
ExecBase          pointer to struct ExecBase in struct RomBootBase
         +0x0022  libraries/romboot_base.h: *35
ExecBaseNewReserved array [20] of char in struct ExecBase
         +0x0238  exec/execbase.h: *120
ExecBaseReserved  array [10] of char in struct ExecBase
         +0x022e  exec/execbase.h: *119
ExecMessage       struct Message (size 0x0014) in struct IntuiMessage
         +0x0000  intuition/intuition.h: *598
EXECNAME          #define "exec.library" exec/execname.h: *13
EXEC_ALERTS_H     #define =0x00000000 exec/alerts.h: *2
EXEC_DEVICES_H    #define =0x00000000 exec/devices.h: *2
EXEC_ERRORS_H     #define =0x00000000 exec/errors.h: *2
EXEC_EXECBASE_H   #define =0x00000000 exec/execbase.h: *2
EXEC_EXECNAME_H   #define =0x00000000 exec/execname.h: *2
EXEC_EXEC_H       #define =0x00000000 exec/exec.h: *2
EXEC_INTERRUPTS_H #define =0x00000000 exec/interrupts.h: *2
EXEC_IO_H         #define =0x00000000 exec/io.h:  *2
EXEC_LIBRARIES_H  #define =0x00000000 exec/libraries.h: *2
EXEC_LISTS_H      #define =0x00000000 exec/lists.h: *2
EXEC_MEMORY_H     #define =0x00000000 exec/memory.h: *2
EXEC_NODES_H      #define =0x00000000 exec/nodes.h: *2
EXEC_PORTS_H      #define =0x00000000 exec/ports.h: *2
EXEC_RESIDENT_H   #define =0x00000000 exec/resident.h: *2
EXEC_SEMAPHORES_H #define =0x00000000 exec/semaphores.h: *2
EXEC_TASKS_H      #define =0x00000000 exec/tasks.h: *2
EXEC_TYPES_H      #define =0x00000000 exec/types.h: *2
exp               #define SPExp =0x00000000 libraries/mathffp.h: *43
exp               #define IEEEDPExp =0x00000000 libraries/mathieeedp.h: *44
ExpansionBase     structure tag
    size 0x01c8   libraries/expansionbase.h: *43
ExpansionControl  structure tag
    size 0x0010   libraries/configregs.h: *44
ExpansionInt      structure tag
    size 0x0006   libraries/expansionbase.h: *35
EXPANSIONNAME     #define "expansion.library" libraries/expansion.h: *13
ExpansionRom      structure tag
    size 0x0010   libraries/configregs.h: *30
                  libraries/configvars.h: 30
ExtData           pointer to char in struct Window
         +0x0074  intuition/intuition.h: *781
ExtData           pointer to char in struct Screen
         +0x0152  intuition/screens.h: *83
EXTRA_HALFBRITE   #define 0x80 =0x00000080 graphics/view.h: *67
ext_size          char in struct Preferences
         +0x00e7  intuition/preferences.h: *125
E_EXPANSIONBASE   #define 0xe80000 =0x00e80000 libraries/configregs.h: *82
E_EXPANSIONSIZE   #define 0x080000 =0x00080000 libraries/configregs.h: *83
E_EXPANSIONSLOTS  #define 8 =0x00000008 libraries/configregs.h: *84
E_MEMORYBASE      #define 0x200000 =0x00200000 libraries/configregs.h: *86
E_MEMORYSIZE      #define 0x800000 =0x00800000 libraries/configregs.h: *87
E_MEMORYSLOTS     #define 128 =0x00000080 libraries/configregs.h: *88
E_SLOTMASK        #define 0xffff =0x0000ffff libraries/configregs.h: *76
E_SLOTSHIFT       #define 16 =0x00000010 libraries/configregs.h: *77
```

```
E_SLOTSIZE          #define 0x10000 =0x00010000 libraries/configregs.h: *75
fabs                #define SPAbs =0x00000000 libraries/mathffp.h: *33
fabs                #define IEEEDPAbs =0x00000000 libraries/mathieeedp.h: *34
FALSE               #define 0 =0x00000000 exec/types.h: *51
FANFOLD             #define 0x00 =0x00000000 intuition/preferences.h: *149
fatten_count        char in struct Layer_Info
         +0x005a    graphics/layers.h: *42
fch_FileID          unsigned short int in struct FontContentsHeader
         +0x0000    libraries/diskfont.h: *35
FCH_ID              #define 0x0f00 =0x00000f00 libraries/diskfont.h: *32
fch_NumEntries      unsigned short int in struct FontContentsHeader
         +0x0002    libraries/diskfont.h: *36
fc_FileName         array [256] of char in struct FontContents
         +0x0000    libraries/diskfont.h: *26
fc_Flags            char in struct FontContents
         +0x0103    libraries/diskfont.h: *29
fc_Style            char in struct FontContents
         +0x0102    libraries/diskfont.h: *28
fc_YSize            unsigned short int in struct FontContents
         +0x0100    libraries/diskfont.h: *27
FEMALE              #define 1 =0x00000001 devices/narrator.h: *44
FgPen               char in struct RastPort
         +0x0019    graphics/rastport.h: *59
fhb_ChkSum          int in struct FileSysHeaderBlock
         +0x0008    devices/hardblocks.h: *153
fhb_DosType         unsigned int in struct FileSysHeaderBlock
         +0x0020    devices/hardblocks.h: *158
fhb_Flags           unsigned int in struct FileSysHeaderBlock
         +0x0014    devices/hardblocks.h: *156
fhb_GlobalVec       int in struct FileSysHeaderBlock
         +0x004c    devices/hardblocks.h: *175
fhb_Handler         unsigned int in struct FileSysHeaderBlock
         +0x0038    devices/hardblocks.h: *168
fhb_HostID          unsigned int in struct FileSysHeaderBlock
         +0x000c    devices/hardblocks.h: *154
fhb_ID              unsigned int in struct FileSysHeaderBlock
         +0x0000    devices/hardblocks.h: *151
fhb_Lock            unsigned int in struct FileSysHeaderBlock
         +0x0034    devices/hardblocks.h: *167
fhb_Next            unsigned int in struct FileSysHeaderBlock
         +0x0010    devices/hardblocks.h: *155
fhb_PatchFlags      unsigned int in struct FileSysHeaderBlock
         +0x0028    devices/hardblocks.h: *161
fhb_Priority        int in struct FileSysHeaderBlock
         +0x0040    devices/hardblocks.h: *170
fhb_Reserved1       array [2] of unsigned int in struct FileSysHeaderBlock
         +0x0018    devices/hardblocks.h: *157
fhb_Reserved2       array [23] of unsigned int in struct FileSysHeaderBlock
         +0x0050    devices/hardblocks.h: *176
fhb_Reserved3       array [21] of unsigned int in struct FileSysHeaderBlock
         +0x00ac    devices/hardblocks.h: *177
fhb_SegListBlocks int in struct FileSysHeaderBlock
         +0x0048    devices/hardblocks.h: *172
fhb_StackSize       unsigned int in struct FileSysHeaderBlock
         +0x003c    devices/hardblocks.h: *169
fhb_Startup         int in struct FileSysHeaderBlock
         +0x0044    devices/hardblocks.h: *171
fhb_SummedLongs     unsigned int in struct FileSysHeaderBlock
         +0x0004    devices/hardblocks.h: *152
fhb_Task            unsigned int in struct FileSysHeaderBlock
         +0x0030    devices/hardblocks.h: *166
fhb_Type            unsigned int in struct FileSysHeaderBlock
         +0x002c    devices/hardblocks.h: *165
fhb_Version         unsigned int in struct FileSysHeaderBlock
         +0x0024    devices/hardblocks.h: *160
fh_Arg1             #define fh_Args =0x00000000 libraries/dosextens.h: *73
fh_Arg2             int in struct FileHandle
         +0x0028    libraries/dosextens.h: *74
fh_Args             int in struct FileHandle
```



```
         +0x0024    libraries/dosextens.h: *72
fh_Buf              int in struct FileHandle
         +0x000c    libraries/dosextens.h: *65
fh_End              int in struct FileHandle
         +0x0014    libraries/dosextens.h: *67
fh_Func1            #define fh_Funcs =0x00000000 libraries/dosextens.h: *69
fh_Func2            int in struct FileHandle
         +0x001c    libraries/dosextens.h: *70
fh_Func3            int in struct FileHandle
         +0x0020    libraries/dosextens.h: *71
fh_Funcs            int in struct FileHandle
         +0x0018    libraries/dosextens.h: *68
fh_Link             pointer to struct Message in struct FileHandle
         +0x0000    libraries/dosextens.h: *61
fh_Port             pointer to struct MsgPort in struct FileHandle
         +0x0004    libraries/dosextens.h: *62
fh_Pos              int in struct FileHandle
         +0x0010    libraries/dosextens.h: *66
fh_Type             pointer to struct MsgPort in struct FileHandle
         +0x0008    libraries/dosextens.h: *63
FIBB_ARCHIVE        #define 4 =0x00000004 libraries/dos.h: *76
FIBB_DELETE         #define 0 =0x00000000 libraries/dos.h: *80
FIBB_EXECUTE        #define 1 =0x00000001 libraries/dos.h: *79
FIBB_PURE           #define 5 =0x00000005 libraries/dos.h: *75
FIBB_READ           #define 3 =0x00000003 libraries/dos.h: *77
FIBB_SCRIPT         #define 6 =0x00000006 libraries/dos.h: *74
FIBB_WRITE          #define 2 =0x00000002 libraries/dos.h: *78
FIBF_ARCHIVE        #define (1<<FIBB_ARCHIVE) =0x00000010 libraries/dos.h: *83
FIBF_DELETE         #define (1<<FIBB_DELETE) =0x00000001 libraries/dos.h: *87
FIBF_EXECUTE        #define (1<<FIBB_EXECUTE) =0x00000002 libraries/dos.h: *86
FIBF_PURE           #define (1<<FIBB_PURE) =0x00000020 libraries/dos.h: *82
FIBF_READ           #define (1<<FIBB_READ) =0x00000008 libraries/dos.h: *84
FIBF_SCRIPT         #define (1<<FIBB_SCRIPT) =0x00000040 libraries/dos.h: *81
FIBF_WRITE          #define (1<<FIBB_WRITE) =0x00000004 libraries/dos.h: *85
fib_Comment         array [80] of char in struct FileInfoBlock
         +0x0090    libraries/dos.h: *67
fib_Date            struct DateStamp (size 0x000c) in struct FileInfoBlock
         +0x0084    libraries/dos.h: *66
fib_DirEntryType int in struct FileInfoBlock
         +0x0004    libraries/dos.h: *59
fib_DiskKey         int in struct FileInfoBlock
         +0x0000    libraries/dos.h: *58
fib_EntryType       int in struct FileInfoBlock
         +0x0078    libraries/dos.h: *63
fib_FileName        array [108] of char in struct FileInfoBlock
         +0x0008    libraries/dos.h: *61
fib_NumBlocks       int in struct FileInfoBlock
         +0x0080    libraries/dos.h: *65
fib_Protection      int in struct FileInfoBlock
         +0x0074    libraries/dos.h: *62
fib_Reserved        array [36] of char in struct FileInfoBlock
         +0x00e0    libraries/dos.h: *68
fib_Size            int in struct FileInfoBlock
         +0x007c    libraries/dos.h: *64
FileHandle          structure tag
    size 0x002c     libraries/dosextens.h: *60
FileInfoBlock       structure tag
    size 0x0104     libraries/dos.h: *57
FileLock            structure tag
    size 0x0014     libraries/dosextens.h: *290
FILENAME_SIZE       #define 30 =0x0000001e intuition/preferences.h: *26, 82, 110
FileSysEntry        structure tag
    size 0x003e     resources/filesysres.h: *32
FileSysHeaderBlock structure tag
    size 0x0100     devices/hardblocks.h: *150
FileSysResource     structure tag
    size 0x0020     resources/filesysres.h: *26
FileSysStartupMsg structure tag
    size 0x0010     libraries/filehandler.h: *81
```

```
FILL_CARRYIN      #define 0x4 =0x00000004 hardware/blit.h: *60
FILL_OR           #define 0x8 =0x00000008 hardware/blit.h: *58
FILL_XOR          #define 0x10 =0x00000010 hardware/blit.h: *59
FindConfigDev     extern function returning pointer to struct ConfigDev (size 0x44)
                  libraries/configvars.h: *56
                  libraries/expansion.h: *25
FindToolType      extern function returning pointer to char workbench/icon.h: *32
FINE              #define 0x800 =0x00000800 intuition/preferences.h: *155
firstBlissObj     pointer to pointer to char in struct GelsInfo
         +0x001e  graphics/rastport.h: *47
FirstCopList      pointer to struct CopList in struct UCopList
         +0x0004  graphics/copper.h: *72
FirstGadget       pointer to struct Gadget in struct Window
         +0x003e  intuition/intuition.h: *739
FirstGadget       pointer to struct Gadget in struct NewWindow
         +0x0012  intuition/intuition.h: *866
FirstGadget       pointer to struct Gadget in struct Screen
         +0x0146  intuition/screens.h: *71
FirstItem         pointer to struct MenuItem in struct Menu
         +0x0012  intuition/intuition.h: *64
FirstRequest      pointer to struct Requester in struct Window
         +0x0024  intuition/intuition.h: *711
FirstScreen       pointer to struct Screen in struct IntuitionBase
         +0x003c  intuition/intuitionbase.h: *158
FirstWindow       pointer to struct Window in struct Screen
         +0x0004  intuition/screens.h: *43
FirstX            short int in struct AreaInfo
         +0x0014  graphics/rastport.h: *25
FirstY            short int in struct AreaInfo
         +0x0016  graphics/rastport.h: *25
FlagPtr           pointer to char in struct AreaInfo
         +0x000c  graphics/rastport.h: *22
Flags             char in struct BitMap
         +0x0004  graphics/gfx.h: *40
Flags             unsigned short int in struct Layer
         +0x001e  graphics/clip.h: *33
Flags             char in struct ColorMap
         +0x0000  graphics/view.h: *23
Flags             char in struct GelsInfo
         +0x0001  graphics/rastport.h: *39
Flags             unsigned short int in struct RastPort
         +0x0020  graphics/rastport.h: *66
Flags             unsigned short int in struct Layer_Info
         +0x0058  graphics/layers.h: *41
Flags             unsigned short int in struct Menu
         +0x000c  intuition/intuition.h: *62
Flags             unsigned short int in struct MenuItem
         +0x000c  intuition/intuition.h: *90
Flags             unsigned short int in struct Requester
         +0x001c  intuition/intuition.h: *152
Flags             unsigned short int in struct Gadget
         +0x000c  intuition/intuition.h: *200
Flags             unsigned short int in struct BoolInfo
         +0x0000  intuition/intuition.h: *362
Flags             unsigned short int in struct PropInfo
         +0x0000  intuition/intuition.h: *386
Flags             unsigned int in struct Window
         +0x0018  intuition/intuition.h: *705
Flags             unsigned int in struct NewWindow
         +0x000e  intuition/intuition.h: *859
Flags             unsigned short int in struct Screen
         +0x0014  intuition/screens.h: *50
Flags             short int in struct VSprite
         +0x0014  graphics/gels.h: *88
Flags             short int in struct Bob
         +0x0000  graphics/gels.h: *141
Flags             short int in struct AnimComp
         +0x0000  graphics/gels.h: *169
Flags             unsigned short int in struct GfxBase
```



```
         +0x00a8  graphics/gfxbase.h: *44
Flags             unsigned int in struct IntuitionBase
         +0x0040  intuition/intuitionbase.h: *160
Flags             char in struct ExpansionBase
         +0x0022  libraries/expansionbase.h: *46
FlagTbl           pointer to char in struct AreaInfo
         +0x0008  graphics/rastport.h: *21
FLOAT             typedef float
                  exec/types.h: *43
floor             #define SPFloor =0x00000000 libraries/mathffp.h: *34
floor             #define IEEEDPFloor =0x00000000 libraries/mathieeedp.h: *35
FLOYD_DITHERING   #define 0x0400 =0x00000400 intuition/preferences.h: *251
fl_Access         int in struct FileLock
         +0x0008  libraries/dosextens.h: *293
fl_Key            int in struct FileLock
         +0x0004  libraries/dosextens.h: *292
fl_Link           int in struct FileLock
         +0x0000  libraries/dosextens.h: *291
fl_MemList        struct List (size 0x000e) in struct FreeList
         +0x0002  workbench/workbench.h: *71
fl_NumFree        short int in struct FreeList
         +0x0000  workbench/workbench.h: *70
fl_Task           pointer to struct MsgPort in struct FileLock
         +0x000c  libraries/dosextens.h: *294
fl_Volume         int in struct FileLock
         +0x0010  libraries/dosextens.h: *295
FOLLOWMOUSE       #define 0x0008 =0x00000008 intuition/intuition.h: *305
Font              pointer to struct TextFont in struct RastPort
         +0x0034  graphics/rastport.h: *72
Font              pointer to struct TextAttr in struct Screen
         +0x0028  intuition/screens.h: *59
Font              pointer to struct TextAttr in struct NewScreen
         +0x0010  intuition/screens.h: *127
FontContents      structure tag
     size 0x0104  libraries/diskfont.h: *25
FontContentsHeader structure tag
     size 0x0004  libraries/diskfont.h: *34
FontHeight        char in struct Preferences
         +0x0000  intuition/preferences.h: *45
FOREVER           #define for(;;) intuition/intuition.h: *968
FPB_DESIGNED      #define 6 =0x00000006 graphics/text.h: *41
FPB_DISKFONT      #define 1 =0x00000001 graphics/text.h: *31
FPB_PROPORTIONAL  #define 5 =0x00000005 graphics/text.h: *39
FPB_REMOVED       #define 7 =0x00000007 graphics/text.h: *43
FPB_REVPATH       #define 2 =0x00000002 graphics/text.h: *33
FPB_ROMFONT       #define 0 =0x00000000 graphics/text.h: *29
FPB_TALLDOT       #define 3 =0x00000003 graphics/text.h: *35
FPB_WIDEDOT       #define 4 =0x00000004 graphics/text.h: *37
FPF_DESIGNED      #define (1<<6) =0x00000040 graphics/text.h: *42
FPF_DISKFONT      #define (1<<1) =0x00000002 graphics/text.h: *32
FPF_PROPORTIONAL  #define (1<<5) =0x00000020 graphics/text.h: *40
FPF_REMOVED       #define (1<<7) =0x00000080 graphics/text.h: *44
FPF_REVPATH       #define (1<<2) =0x00000004 graphics/text.h: *34
FPF_ROMFONT       #define (1<<0) =0x00000001 graphics/text.h: *30
FPF_TALLDOT       #define (1<<3) =0x00000008 graphics/text.h: *36
FPF_WIDEDOT       #define (1<<4) =0x00000010 graphics/text.h: *38
FPHALF            #define ((float) 0.5) libraries/mathffp.h: *26
FPHALF            #define ((double) 0.5) libraries/mathieeedp.h: *28
FPONE             #define ((float) 1.0) libraries/mathffp.h: *25
FPONE             #define ((double) 1.0) libraries/mathieeedp.h: *27
FPTEN             #define ((float) 10.0) libraries/mathffp.h: *24
FPTEN             #define ((double) 10.0) libraries/mathieeedp.h: *26
FPZERO            #define ((float) 0.0) libraries/mathffp.h: *27
FPZERO            #define ((double) 0.0) libraries/mathieeedp.h: *29
FreeClipRects     struct MinList (size 0x000c) in struct Layer_Info
         +0x000c  graphics/layers.h: *37
FreeFreeList      extern function returning void workbench/icon.h: *31
FREEHORIZ         #define 0x0002 =0x00000002 intuition/intuition.h: *430
FreeList          structure tag
```

```
    size 0x0010  workbench/workbench.h: *69
FREEVERT         #define 0x0004 =0x00000004 intuition/intuition.h: *431
FreeWBObject     extern function returning void workbench/icon.h: *31
front            pointer to struct Layer in struct Layer
         +0x0000 graphics/clip.h: *27
FrontPen         char in struct IntuiText
         +0x0000 intuition/intuition.h: *496
FrontPen         char in struct Border
         +0x0004 intuition/intuition.h: *525
FRST_DOT         #define 0x01 =0x00000001 graphics/rastport.h: *94
FSB_BOLD         #define 1 =0x00000001 graphics/text.h: *23
FSB_EXTENDED     #define 3 =0x00000003 graphics/text.h: *19
FSB_ITALIC       #define 2 =0x00000002 graphics/text.h: *21
FSB_UNDERLINED   #define 0 =0x00000000 graphics/text.h: *25
fse_DosType      unsigned int in struct FileSysEntry
         +0x000e resources/filesysres.h: *35
fse_GlobalVec    int in struct FileSysEntry
         +0x003a resources/filesysres.h: *49
fse_Handler      int in struct FileSysEntry
         +0x0026 resources/filesysres.h: *44
fse_Lock         int in struct FileSysEntry
         +0x0022 resources/filesysres.h: *43
fse_Node         struct Node (size 0x000e) in struct FileSysEntry
         +0x0000 resources/filesysres.h: *33
fse_PatchFlags   unsigned int in struct FileSysEntry
         +0x0016 resources/filesysres.h: *37
fse_Priority     int in struct FileSysEntry
         +0x002e resources/filesysres.h: *46
fse_SegList      int in struct FileSysEntry
         +0x0036 resources/filesysres.h: *48
fse_StackSize    unsigned int in struct FileSysEntry
         +0x002a resources/filesysres.h: *45
fse_Startup      int in struct FileSysEntry
         +0x0032 resources/filesysres.h: *47
fse_Task         unsigned int in struct FileSysEntry
         +0x001e resources/filesysres.h: *42
fse_Type         unsigned int in struct FileSysEntry
         +0x001a resources/filesysres.h: *41
fse_Version      unsigned int in struct FileSysEntry
         +0x0012 resources/filesysres.h: *36
FSF_BOLD         #define (1<<1) =0x00000002 graphics/text.h: *24
FSF_EXTENDED     #define (1<<3) =0x00000008 graphics/text.h: *20
FSF_ITALIC       #define (1<<2) =0x00000004 graphics/text.h: *22
FSF_UNDERLINED   #define (1<<0) =0x00000001 graphics/text.h: *26
FSRNAME          #define "FileSystem.resource" resources/filesysres.h: *24
fsr_Creator      pointer to char in struct FileSysResource
         +0x000e resources/filesysres.h: *28
fsr_FileSysEntries struct List (size 0x000e) in struct FileSysResource
         +0x0012 resources/filesysres.h: *29
fsr_Node         struct Node (size 0x000e) in struct FileSysResource
         +0x0000 resources/filesysres.h: *27
fssm_Device      int in struct FileSysStartupMsg
         +0x0004 libraries/filehandler.h: *83
fssm_Environ     int in struct FileSysStartupMsg
         +0x0008 libraries/filehandler.h: *84
fssm_Flags       unsigned int in struct FileSysStartupMsg
         +0x000c libraries/filehandler.h: *85
fssm_Unit        unsigned int in struct FileSysStartupMsg
         +0x0000 libraries/filehandler.h: *82
FS_NORMAL        #define 0 =0x00000000 graphics/text.h: *18
function         pointer to function returning int in struct bltnode
         +0x0004 hardware/blit.h: *83
GADGBACKFILL     #define 0x0001 =0x00000001 workbench/workbench.h: *92
GADGDISABLED     #define 0x0100 =0x00000100 intuition/intuition.h: *276
Gadget           structure tag
    size 0x002c  intuition/intuition.h: 149, *193, 195, 739, 866
                 intuition/screens.h: 71, 131
                 workbench/workbench.h: 54
GADGET0002       #define 0x0002 =0x00000002 intuition/intuition.h: *349
```



```
GADGETDOWN       #define 0x00000020 =0x00000020 intuition/intuition.h: *643
GadgetID         unsigned short int in struct Gadget
         +0x0026 intuition/intuition.h: *236
GadgetRender     pointer to pointer to char in struct Gadget
         +0x0012 intuition/intuition.h: *210
Gadgets          pointer to struct Gadget in struct NewScreen
         +0x0018 intuition/screens.h: *131
GadgetText       pointer to struct IntuiText in struct Gadget
         +0x001a intuition/intuition.h: *217
GadgetType       unsigned short int in struct Gadget
         +0x0010 intuition/intuition.h: *204
GADGETTYPE       #define 0xFC00 =0x0000fc00 intuition/intuition.h: *333
GADGETUP         #define 0x00000040 =0x00000040 intuition/intuition.h: *644
GADGHBOX         #define 0x0001 =0x00000001 intuition/intuition.h: *245
GADGHCOMP        #define 0x0000 =0x00000000 intuition/intuition.h: *244
GADGHIGHBITS     #define 0x0003 =0x00000003 intuition/intuition.h: *243
GADGHIMAGE       #define 0x0002 =0x00000002 intuition/intuition.h: *246
GADGHNONE        #define 0x0003 =0x00000003 intuition/intuition.h: *247
GADGIMAGE        #define 0x0004 =0x00000004 intuition/intuition.h: *252
GADGIMMEDIATE    #define 0x0002 =0x00000002 intuition/intuition.h: *289
GamePortTrigger  structure tag
    size 0x0008  devices/gameport.h: *28
GELGONE          #define 0x0400 =0x00000400 graphics/gels.h: *23
gelHead          pointer to struct VSprite in struct GelsInfo
         +0x0002 graphics/rastport.h: *40
GelsInfo         structure tag
    size 0x0026  graphics/rastport.h: *35, 57
GelsInfo         pointer to struct GelsInfo in struct RastPort
         +0x0014 graphics/rastport.h: *57
gelTail          pointer to struct VSprite in struct GelsInfo
         +0x0006 graphics/rastport.h: *40
GENLOC           #define 2 =0x00000002 graphics/gfxbase.h: *69
GENLOCK_AUDIO    #define 0x100 =0x00000100 graphics/view.h: *65
GENLOCK_VIDEO    #define 2 =0x00000002 graphics/view.h: *66
GetDiskObject    extern function returning pointer to struct DiskObject
                 (size 0x004e) workbench/icon.h: *29
GetIcon          extern function returning "LONG" workbench/icon.h: *30
GetWBObject      extern function returning pointer to struct WBObject (size
                 0x0000) workbench/icon.h: *28
GfxBase          structure tag
    size 0x0148  graphics/gfxbase.h: *23
GIMMEZEROZERO    #define 0x0400 =0x00000400 intuition/intuition.h: *818
GLOBAL           #define extern =0x00000000 exec/types.h: *13
GPCT_ABSJOYSTICK #define 3 =0x00000003 devices/gameport.h: *41
GPCT_ALLOCATED   #define -1 =0xffffffff devices/gameport.h: *36
GPCT_MOUSE       #define 1 =0x00000001 devices/gameport.h: *39
GPCT_NOCONTROLLER #define 0 =0x00000000 devices/gameport.h: *37
GPCT_RELJOYSTICK #define 2 =0x00000002 devices/gameport.h: *40
GPDERR_SETCTYPE  #define 1 =0x00000001 devices/gameport.h: *45
GPD_ASKCTYPE     #define (CMD_NONSTD+1) =0x0000000a devices/gameport.h: *15
GPD_ASKTRIGGER   #define (CMD_NONSTD+3) =0x0000000c devices/gameport.h: *17
GPD_READEVENT    #define (CMD_NONSTD+0) =0x00000009 devices/gameport.h: *14
GPD_SETCTYPE     #define (CMD_NONSTD+2) =0x0000000b devices/gameport.h: *16
GPD_SETTRIGGER   #define (CMD_NONSTD+4) =0x0000000d devices/gameport.h: *18
GPTB_DOWNKEYS    #define 0 =0x00000000 devices/gameport.h: *23
GPTB_UPKEYS      #define 1 =0x00000001 devices/gameport.h: *25
GPTF_DOWNKEYS    #define (1<<0) =0x00000001 devices/gameport.h: *24
GPTF_UPKEYS      #define (1<<1) =0x00000002 devices/gameport.h: *26
gpt_Keys         unsigned short int in struct GamePortTrigger
         +0x0000 devices/gameport.h: *29
gpt_Timeout      unsigned short int in struct GamePortTrigger
         +0x0002 devices/gameport.h: *30
gpt_XDelta       unsigned short int in struct GamePortTrigger
         +0x0004 devices/gameport.h: *31
gpt_YDelta       unsigned short int in struct GamePortTrigger
         +0x0006 devices/gameport.h: *32
GRAPHICS_CLIP_H  #define =0x00000000 graphics/clip.h: *2
GRAPHICS_COLLIDE_H #define =0x00000000 graphics/collide.h: *2
GRAPHICS_COPPER_H #define =0x00000000 graphics/copper.h: *2
```

```
GRAPHICS_DISPLAY_H #define =0x00000000 graphics/display.h: *2
GRAPHICS_GELS_H   #define =0x00000000 graphics/gels.h: *2
GRAPHICS_GFXBASE_H #define =0x00000000 graphics/gfxbase.h: *2
GRAPHICS_GFXMACROS_H #define =0x00000000 graphics/gfxmacros.h: *2
GRAPHICS_GFX_H    #define =0x00000000 graphics/gfx.h: *2
GRAPHICS_GRAPHINT_H #define =0x00000000 graphics/graphint.h: *2
GRAPHICS_LAYERS_H #define =0x00000000 graphics/layers.h: *2
GRAPHICS_RASTPORT_H #define =0x00000000 graphics/rastport.h: *2
GRAPHICS_REGIONS_H #define =0x00000000 graphics/regions.h: *2
GRAPHICS_SPRITE_H #define =0x00000000 graphics/sprite.h: *2
GRAPHICS_TEXT_H   #define =0x00000000 graphics/text.h: *2
GRAPHICS_VIEW_H   #define =0x00000000 graphics/view.h: *2
GRELBOTTOM        #define 0x0008 =0x00000008 intuition/intuition.h: *259
GRELHEIGHT        #define 0x0040 =0x00000040 intuition/intuition.h: *264
GRELRIGHT         #define 0x0010 =0x00000010 intuition/intuition.h: *260
GRELWIDTH         #define 0x0020 =0x00000020 intuition/intuition.h: *262
GREY_SCALE2       #define 0x1000 =0x00001000 intuition/preferences.h: *254
gs_Head           struct List (size 0x000e) in struct Layer_Info
        +0x0046   graphics/layers.h: *39
GZZGADGET         #define 0x2000 =0x00002000 intuition/intuition.h: *336
GZZHeight         short int in struct Window
        +0x0072   intuition/intuition.h: *779
GZZMouseX         short int in struct Window
        +0x006c   intuition/intuition.h: *773
GZZMouseY         short int in struct Window
        +0x006e   intuition/intuition.h: *774
GZZWidth          short int in struct Window
        +0x0070   intuition/intuition.h: *778
HALFTONE_DITHERING #define 0x0200 =0x00000200 intuition/preferences.h: *250
HAM               #define 0x800 =0x00000800 graphics/view.h: *62
HARDWARE_ADKBITS_H #define =0x00000000 hardware/adkbits.h: *2
HARDWARE_BLIT_H   #define =0x00000000 hardware/blit.h: *2
HARDWARE_CIA_H    #define =0x00000000 hardware/cia.h: *2
HARDWARE_CUSTOM_H #define =0x00000000 hardware/custom.h: *2
HARDWARE_DMABITS_H #define =0x00000000 hardware/dmabits.h: *2
HARDWARE_INTBITS_H #define =0x00000000 hardware/intbits.h: *2
HD_SCSICMD        #define 28 =0x0000001c devices/scsidisk.h: *59
HeadComp          pointer to struct AnimComp in struct AnimOb
        +0x0024   graphics/gels.h: *221
HeadOb            pointer to struct AnimOb in struct AnimComp
        +0x001e   graphics/gels.h: *194
height            char in struct mouth_rb
        +0x0047   devices/narrator.h: *90
Height            short int in struct Menu
        +0x000a   intuition/intuition.h: *61
Height            short int in struct MenuItem
        +0x000a   intuition/intuition.h: *89
Height            short int in struct Requester
        +0x000a   intuition/intuition.h: *146
Height            short int in struct Gadget
        +0x000a   intuition/intuition.h: *198
Height            short int in struct Image
        +0x0006   intuition/intuition.h: *548
Height            short int in struct Window
        +0x000a   intuition/intuition.h: *698
Height            short int in struct NewWindow
        +0x0006   intuition/intuition.h: *853
Height            short int in struct Screen
        +0x000e   intuition/screens.h: *46
Height            short int in struct NewScreen
        +0x0006   intuition/screens.h: *119
Height            short int in struct VSprite
        +0x001a   graphics/gels.h: *97
height            unsigned short int in struct SimpleSprite
        +0x0004   graphics/sprite.h: *18
HFERR_BadStatus   #define 45 =0x0000002d devices/scsidisk.h: *90
HFERR_DMA         #define 41 =0x00000029 devices/scsidisk.h: *86
HFERR_NoBoard     #define 50 =0x00000032 devices/scsidisk.h: *93
HFERR_Parity      #define 43 =0x0000002b devices/scsidisk.h: *88
```



```
HFERR_Phase       #define 42 =0x0000002a devices/scsidisk.h: *87
HFERR_SelfUnit    #define 40 =0x00000028 devices/scsidisk.h: *85
HFERR_SelTimeout  #define 44 =0x0000002c devices/scsidisk.h: *89
HIGHBOX           #define 0x0080 =0x00000080 intuition/intuition.h: *123
HIGHCOMP          #define 0x0040 =0x00000040 intuition/intuition.h: *122
HIGHFLAGS         #define 0x00C0 =0x000000c0 intuition/intuition.h: *120
HIGHIMAGE         #define 0x0000 =0x00000000 intuition/intuition.h: *121
HIGHITEM          #define 0x2000 =0x00002000 intuition/intuition.h: *131
HIGHNONE          #define 0x00C0 =0x000000c0 intuition/intuition.h: *124
HIRES             #define 0x8000 =0x00008000 graphics/view.h: *60
HitMask           short int in struct VSprite
        +0x0022   graphics/gels.h: *102
HOLDNMODIFY       #define 0x800 =0x00000800 graphics/display.h: *21
HorizBody         unsigned short int in struct PropInfo
        +0x0006   intuition/intuition.h: *416
HorizPot          unsigned short int in struct PropInfo
        +0x0002   intuition/intuition.h: *396
HPotRes           unsigned short int in struct PropInfo
        +0x000e   intuition/intuition.h: *422
HP_LASERJET       #define 0x0B =0x0000000b intuition/preferences.h: *198
HP_LASERJET_PLUS  #define 0x0C =0x0000000c intuition/preferences.h: *199
HSIZEBITS         #define 6 =0x00000006 hardware/blit.h: *13
HSIZEMASK         #define 0x3f =0x0000003f hardware/blit.h: *15
HWaitPos          short int in union (no tag)
        +0x0000   graphics/copper.h: *33
HWAITPOS          #define u3.u4.u2.HWaitPos graphics/copper.h: *43
IAddress          pointer to pointer to char in struct IntuiMessage
        +0x001c   intuition/intuition.h: *614
ICONNAME          #define "icon.library" workbench/icon.h: *20
IDCMPFlags        unsigned int in struct Window
        +0x0052   intuition/intuition.h: *753
IDCMPFlags        unsigned int in struct NewWindow
        +0x000a   intuition/intuition.h: *857
IDCMPWindow       pointer to struct Window in struct IntuiMessage
        +0x002c   intuition/intuition.h: *630
IdleCount         unsigned int in struct ExecBase
        +0x0118   exec/execbase.h: *56
IDNAME_BADBLOCK   #define (('B'<<24)|('A'<<16)|('D'<<8)|('B')) =0x42414442
                  devices/hardblocks.h: *123
IDNAME_FILESYSHEADER #define (('F'<<24)|('S'<<16)|('H'<<8)|('D')) =0x46534844
                  devices/hardblocks.h: *180
IDNAME_LOADSEG    #define (('L'<<24)|('S'<<16)|('E'<<8)|('G')) =0x4c534547
                  devices/hardblocks.h: *193
IDNAME_PARTITION  #define (('P'<<24)|('A'<<16)|('R'<<8)|('T')) =0x50415254
                  devices/hardblocks.h: *142
IDNAME_RIGIDDISK  #define (('R'<<24)|('D'<<16)|('S'<<8)|('K')) =0x5244534b
                  devices/hardblocks.h: *89
IDNestCnt         char in struct ExecBase
        +0x0126   exec/execbase.h: *61
id_BytesPerBlock  int in struct InfoData
        +0x0014   libraries/dos.h: *113
id_DiskState      int in struct InfoData
        +0x0008   libraries/dos.h: *110
id_DiskType       int in struct InfoData
        +0x0018   libraries/dos.h: *114
ID_DOS_DISK       #define (('D'<<24) | ('O'<<16) | ('S'<<8)) =0x444f5300
                  libraries/dos.h: *128
id_InUse          int in struct InfoData
        +0x0020   libraries/dos.h: *116
ID_KICKSTART_DISK #define (('K'<<24) | ('I'<<16) | ('C'<<8) | ('K')) =0x4b49434b
                  libraries/dos.h: *130
ID_NOT_REALLY_DOS #define (('N'<<24) | ('D'<<16) | ('O'<<8) | ('S')) =0x4e444f53
                  libraries/dos.h: *129
ID_NO_DISK_PRESENT #define (-1) =0xffffffff libraries/dos.h: *126
id_NumBlocks      int in struct InfoData
        +0x000c   libraries/dos.h: *111
id_NumBlocksUsed  int in struct InfoData
        +0x0010   libraries/dos.h: *112
id_NumSoftErrors  int in struct InfoData
```

```
        +0x0000  libraries/dos.h: *108
id_UnitNumber    int in struct InfoData
        +0x0004  libraries/dos.h: *109
ID_UNREADABLE_DISK #define (('B'<<24) | ('A'<<16) | ('D'<<8)) =0x42414400
                 libraries/dos.h: *127
ID_VALIDATED     #define 82 =0x00000052 libraries/dos.h: *123
ID_VALIDATING    #define 81 =0x00000051 libraries/dos.h: *122
id_VolumeNode    int in struct InfoData
        +0x001c  libraries/dos.h: *115
ID_WRITE_PROTECTED #define 80 =0x00000050 libraries/dos.h: *121
IECLASS_ACTIVEWINDOW #define 0x11 =0x00000011 devices/inputevent.h: *53
IECLASS_CLOSEWINDOW #define 0x0B =0x0000000b devices/inputevent.h: *41
IECLASS_DISKINSERTED #define 0x10 =0x00000010 devices/inputevent.h: *51
IECLASS_DISKREMOVED #define 0x0F =0x0000000f devices/inputevent.h: *49
IECLASS_EVENT    #define 0x03 =0x00000003 devices/inputevent.h: *27
IECLASS_GADGETDOWN #define 0x07 =0x00000007 devices/inputevent.h: *33
IECLASS_GADGETUP #define 0x08 =0x00000008 devices/inputevent.h: *35
IECLASS_INACTIVEWINDOW #define 0x12 =0x00000012 devices/inputevent.h: *55
IECLASS_MAX      #define 0x12 =0x00000012 devices/inputevent.h: *59
                 devices/conunit.h: 78
IECLASS_MENULIST #define 0x0A =0x0000000a devices/inputevent.h: *39
IECLASS_NEWPREFS #define 0x0E =0x0000000e devices/inputevent.h: *47
IECLASS_NULL     #define 0x00 =0x00000000 devices/inputevent.h: *21
IECLASS_POINTERPOS #define 0x04 =0x00000004 devices/inputevent.h: *29
IECLASS_RAWKEY   #define 0x01 =0x00000001 devices/inputevent.h: *23
IECLASS_RAWMOUSE #define 0x02 =0x00000002 devices/inputevent.h: *25
IECLASS_REFRESHWINDOW #define 0x0D =0x0000000d devices/inputevent.h: *45
IECLASS_REQUESTER #define 0x09 =0x00000009 devices/inputevent.h: *37
IECLASS_SIZEWINDOW #define 0x0C =0x0000000c devices/inputevent.h: *43
IECLASS_TIMER    #define 0x06 =0x00000006 devices/inputevent.h: *31
IECODE_ASCII_DEL #define 0x7F =0x0000007f devices/inputevent.h: *76
IECODE_ASCII_FIRST #define 0x20 =0x00000020 devices/inputevent.h: *74
IECODE_ASCII_LAST #define 0x7E =0x0000007e devices/inputevent.h: *75
IECODE_C0_FIRST  #define 0x00 =0x00000000 devices/inputevent.h: *72
IECODE_C0_LAST   #define 0x1F =0x0000001f devices/inputevent.h: *73
IECODE_C1_FIRST  #define 0x80 =0x00000080 devices/inputevent.h: *77
IECODE_C1_LAST   #define 0x9F =0x0000009f devices/inputevent.h: *78
IECODE_COMM_CODE_FIRST #define 0x78 =0x00000078 devices/inputevent.h: *68
IECODE_COMM_CODE_LAST #define 0x7F =0x0000007f devices/inputevent.h: *69
IECODE_KEY_CODE_FIRST #define 0x00 =0x00000000 devices/inputevent.h: *66
IECODE_KEY_CODE_LAST #define 0x77 =0x00000077 devices/inputevent.h: *67
IECODE_LATIN1_FIRST #define 0xA0 =0x000000a0 devices/inputevent.h: *79
IECODE_LATIN1_LAST #define 0xFF =0x000000ff devices/inputevent.h: *80
IECODE_LBUTTON   #define 0x68 =0x00000068 devices/inputevent.h: *83
IECODE_MBUTTON   #define 0x6A =0x0000006a devices/inputevent.h: *85
IECODE_NEWACTIVE #define 0x01 =0x00000001 devices/inputevent.h: *89
IECODE_NOBUTTON  #define 0xFF =0x000000ff devices/inputevent.h: *86
IECODE_RBUTTON   #define 0x69 =0x00000069 devices/inputevent.h: *84
IECODE_REQCLEAR  #define 0x00 =0x00000000 devices/inputevent.h: *97
IECODE_REQSET    #define 0x01 =0x00000001 devices/inputevent.h: *95
IECODE_UP_PREFIX #define 0x80 =0x00000080 devices/inputevent.h: *65
IEEEDPAbs        extern function returning double libraries/mathieeedp.h: *69
IEEEDPACos       extern function returning double libraries/mathieeedp.h: *56
IEEEDPAdd        extern function returning double libraries/mathieeedp.h: *71
IEEEDPASin       extern function returning double libraries/mathieeedp.h: *57
IEEEDPAtan       extern function returning double libraries/mathieeedp.h: *55
IEEEDPCeil       extern function returning double libraries/mathieeedp.h: *76
IEEEDPCmp        extern function returning int    libraries/mathieeedp.h: *67
IEEEDPCos        extern function returning double libraries/mathieeedp.h: *56
IEEEDPCosh       extern function returning double libraries/mathieeedp.h: *62
IEEEDPDiv        extern function returning double libraries/mathieeedp.h: *74
IEEEDPExp        extern function returning double libraries/mathieeedp.h: *58
IEEEDPFieee      extern function returning double libraries/mathieeedp.h: *64
IEEEDPFix        extern function returning int    libraries/mathieeedp.h: *66
IEEEDPFloor      extern function returning double libraries/mathieeedp.h: *75
IEEEDPFlt        extern function returning double libraries/mathieeedp.h: *68
IEEEDPLog        extern function returning double libraries/mathieeedp.h: *58
IEEEDPLog10      extern function returning double libraries/mathieeedp.h: *60
IEEEDPMul        extern function returning double libraries/mathieeedp.h: *73
```



```
IEEEDPNeg        extern function returning double libraries/mathieeedp.h: *70
IEEEDPPow        extern function returning double libraries/mathieeedp.h: *60
IEEEDPSin        extern function returning double libraries/mathieeedp.h: *57
IEEEDPSincos     extern function returning double libraries/mathieeedp.h: *61
IEEEDPSinh       extern function returning double libraries/mathieeedp.h: *62
IEEEDPSqrt       extern function returning double libraries/mathieeedp.h: *59
IEEEDPSub        extern function returning double libraries/mathieeedp.h: *72
IEEEDPTan        extern function returning double libraries/mathieeedp.h: *55
IEEEDPTanh       extern function returning double libraries/mathieeedp.h: *62
IEEEDPTieee      extern function returning float libraries/mathieeedp.h: *63
IEEEDPTst        extern function returning int libraries/mathieeedp.h: *67
IEQUALIFIERB_CAPSLOCK #define 2 =0x00000002 devices/inputevent.h: *120
IEQUALIFIERB_CONTROL #define 3 =0x00000003 devices/inputevent.h: *121
IEQUALIFIERB_INTERRUPT #define 10 =0x0000000a devices/inputevent.h: *128
IEQUALIFIERB_LALT #define 4 =0x00000004 devices/inputevent.h: *122
IEQUALIFIERB_LCOMMAND #define 6 =0x00000006 devices/inputevent.h: *124
IEQUALIFIERB_LEFTBUTTON #define 14 =0x0000000e devices/inputevent.h: *132
IEQUALIFIERB_LSHIFT #define 0 =0x00000000 devices/inputevent.h: *118
IEQUALIFIERB_MIDBUTTON #define 12 =0x0000000c devices/inputevent.h: *130
IEQUALIFIERB_MULTIBROADCAST #define 11 =0x0000000b devices/inputevent.h: *129
IEQUALIFIERB_NUMERICPAD #define 8 =0x00000008 devices/inputevent.h: *126
IEQUALIFIERB_RALT #define 5 =0x00000005 devices/inputevent.h: *123
IEQUALIFIERB_RBUTTON #define 13 =0x0000000d devices/inputevent.h: *131
IEQUALIFIERB_RCOMMAND #define 7 =0x00000007 devices/inputevent.h: *125
IEQUALIFIERB_RELATIVEMOUSE #define 15 =0x0000000f devices/inputevent.h: *133
IEQUALIFIERB_REPEAT #define 9 =0x00000009 devices/inputevent.h: *127
IEQUALIFIERB_RSHIFT #define 1 =0x00000001 devices/inputevent.h: *119
IEQUALIFIER_CAPSLOCK #define 0x0004 =0x00000004 devices/inputevent.h: *103
IEQUALIFIER_CONTROL #define 0x0008 =0x00000008 devices/inputevent.h: *104
IEQUALIFIER_INTERRUPT #define 0x0400 =0x00000400 devices/inputevent.h: *111
IEQUALIFIER_LALT #define 0x0010 =0x00000010 devices/inputevent.h: *105
IEQUALIFIER_LCOMMAND #define 0x0040 =0x00000040 devices/inputevent.h: *107
IEQUALIFIER_LEFTBUTTON #define 0x4000 =0x00004000 devices/inputevent.h: *115
IEQUALIFIER_LSHIFT #define 0x0001 =0x00000001 devices/inputevent.h: *101
IEQUALIFIER_MIDBUTTON #define 0x1000 =0x00001000 devices/inputevent.h: *113
IEQUALIFIER_MULTIBROADCAST #define 0x0800 =0x00000800 devices/inputevent.h: *112
IEQUALIFIER_NUMERICPAD #define 0x0100 =0x00000100 devices/inputevent.h: *109
IEQUALIFIER_RALT #define 0x0020 =0x00000020 devices/inputevent.h: *106
IEQUALIFIER_RBUTTON #define 0x2000 =0x00002000 devices/inputevent.h: *114
IEQUALIFIER_RCOMMAND #define 0x0080 =0x00000080 devices/inputevent.h: *108
IEQUALIFIER_RELATIVEMOUSE #define 0x8000 =0x00008000 devices/inputevent.h: *116
IEQUALIFIER_REPEAT #define 0x0200 =0x00000200 devices/inputevent.h: *110
IEQUALIFIER_RSHIFT #define 0x0002 =0x00000002 devices/inputevent.h: *102
ie_addr          pointer to pointer to char in union (no tag)
         +0x0000 devices/inputevent.h: *148
ie_Class         char in struct InputEvent
         +0x0004 devices/inputevent.h: *139
ie_Code          unsigned short int in struct InputEvent
         +0x0006 devices/inputevent.h: *141
ie_EventAddress  #define ie_position.ie_addr devices/inputevent.h: *155
ie_NextEvent     pointer to struct InputEvent in struct InputEvent
         +0x0000 devices/inputevent.h: *138
ie_position      union (no tag) (size 0x0004) in struct InputEvent
         +0x000a devices/inputevent.h: *149
ie_Qualifier     unsigned short int in struct InputEvent
         +0x0008 devices/inputevent.h: *142
ie_SubClass      char in struct InputEvent
         +0x0005 devices/inputevent.h: *140
ie_TimeStamp     struct timeval (size 0x0008) in struct InputEvent
         +0x000e devices/inputevent.h: *150
ie_x             short int in struct (no tag)
         +0x0000 devices/inputevent.h: *145
ie_X             #define ie_position.ie_xy.ie_x devices/inputevent.h: *153
ie_xy            struct (no tag) (size 0x0004) in union (no tag)
         +0x0000 devices/inputevent.h: *147
ie_y             short int in struct (no tag)
         +0x0002 devices/inputevent.h: *146
ie_Y             #define ie_position.ie_xy.ie_y devices/inputevent.h: *154
IFont            pointer to struct TextFont in struct Window
```

```
        +0x0080  intuition/intuition.h: *793
IGNORE_DIMENSIONS #define 0x0000 =0x00000000 intuition/preferences.h: *241
Image            structure tag
    size 0x0014  intuition/intuition.h: *543, 585, 763, 872
ImageBMap        pointer to struct BitMap in struct Requester
        +0x0044  intuition/intuition.h: *167
ImageData        pointer to unsigned short int in struct Image
        +0x000a  intuition/intuition.h: *549
ImageData        pointer to short int in struct VSprite
        +0x0024  graphics/gels.h: *104
ImageShadow      pointer to short int in struct Bob
        +0x0006  graphics/gels.h: *147
IMAGE_NEGATIVE   #define 0x01 =0x00000001 intuition/preferences.h: *167
IMAGE_POSITIVE   #define 0x00 =0x00000000 intuition/preferences.h: *166
IMPORT           #define extern =0x00000000 exec/types.h: *14
INACTIVEWINDOW   #define 0x00080000 =0x00080000 intuition/intuition.h: *657
IND_ADDHANDLER   #define (CMD_NONSTD+0) =0x00000009 devices/input.h: *17
IND_REMHANDLER   #define (CMD_NONSTD+1) =0x0000000a devices/input.h: *18
IND_SETMPORT     #define (CMD_NONSTD+5) =0x0000000e devices/input.h: *22
IND_SETMTRIG     #define (CMD_NONSTD+7) =0x00000010 devices/input.h: *24
IND_SETMTYPE     #define (CMD_NONSTD+6) =0x0000000f devices/input.h: *23
IND_SETPERIOD    #define (CMD_NONSTD+4) =0x0000000d devices/input.h: *21
IND_SETTHRESH    #define (CMD_NONSTD+3) =0x0000000c devices/input.h: *20
IND_WRITEEVENT   #define (CMD_NONSTD+2) =0x0000000b devices/input.h: *19
InfoData         structure tag
    size 0x0024  libraries/dos.h: *107
InitAnimate      Macro (1 argument) graphics/gels.h: *246
InputEvent       structure tag in struct InputEvent
    size 0x0016  devices/inputevent.h: *137, 138
INREQUEST        #define 0x4000 =0x00004000 intuition/intuition.h: *826
Int2List         struct Interrupt (size 0x0016) in struct ExpansionBase
        +0x0186  libraries/expansionbase.h: *55
Int6List         struct Interrupt (size 0x0016) in struct ExpansionBase
        +0x019c  libraries/expansionbase.h: *56
Int7List         struct Interrupt (size 0x0016) in struct ExpansionBase
        +0x01b2  libraries/expansionbase.h: *57
INTB_AUD0        #define (7) =0x00000007 hardware/intbits.h: *23
INTB_AUD1        #define (8) =0x00000008 hardware/intbits.h: *22
INTB_AUD2        #define (9) =0x00000009 hardware/intbits.h: *21
INTB_AUD3        #define (10) =0x0000000a hardware/intbits.h: *20
INTB_BLIT        #define (6) =0x00000006 hardware/intbits.h: *24
INTB_COPER       #define (4) =0x00000004 hardware/intbits.h: *26
INTB_DSKBLK      #define (1) =0x00000001 hardware/intbits.h: *29
INTB_DSKSYNC     #define (12) =0x0000000c hardware/intbits.h: *18
INTB_EXTER       #define (13) =0x0000000d hardware/intbits.h: *17
INTB_INTEN       #define (14) =0x0000000e hardware/intbits.h: *16
INTB_NMI         #define 15 =0x0000000f exec/interrupts.h: *44
INTB_PORTS       #define (3) =0x00000003 hardware/intbits.h: *27
INTB_RBF         #define (11) =0x0000000b hardware/intbits.h: *19
INTB_SETCLR      #define (15) =0x0000000f hardware/intbits.h: *13
INTB_SOFTINT     #define (2) =0x00000002 hardware/intbits.h: *28
INTB_TBE         #define (0) =0x00000000 hardware/intbits.h: *30
INTB_VERTB       #define (5) =0x00000005 hardware/intbits.h: *25
INTEGER_SCALING  #define 0x0100 =0x00000100 intuition/preferences.h: *247
intena           unsigned short int in struct Custom
        +0x009a  hardware/custom.h: *82
intenar          unsigned short int in struct Custom
        +0x001c  hardware/custom.h: *34
INTERLACE        #define 4 =0x00000004 graphics/display.h: *22
Interrupt        structure tag
    size 0x0016  exec/interrupts.h: *22
                 graphics/gfxbase.h: 34
                 libraries/expansionbase.h: 55, 56, 57
                 resources/disk.h: 43, 44, 45, 57, 58, 59
INTF_AUD0        #define (1<<7) =0x00000080 hardware/intbits.h: *42
INTF_AUD1        #define (1<<8) =0x00000100 hardware/intbits.h: *41
INTF_AUD2        #define (1<<9) =0x00000200 hardware/intbits.h: *40
INTF_AUD3        #define (1<<10) =0x00000400 hardware/intbits.h: *39
INTF_BLIT        #define (1<<6) =0x00000040 hardware/intbits.h: *43
```



```
INTF_COPER       #define (1<<4) =0x00000010 hardware/intbits.h: *45
INTF_DSKBLK      #define (1<<1) =0x00000002 hardware/intbits.h: *48
INTF_DSKSYNC     #define (1<<12) =0x00001000 hardware/intbits.h: *37
INTF_EXTER       #define (1<<13) =0x00002000 hardware/intbits.h: *36
INTF_INTEN       #define (1<<14) =0x00004000 hardware/intbits.h: *35
INTF_NMI         #define (1<<15) =0x00008000 exec/interrupts.h: *45
INTF_PORTS       #define (1<<3) =0x00000008 hardware/intbits.h: *46
INTF_RBF         #define (1<<11) =0x00000800 hardware/intbits.h: *38
INTF_SETCLR      #define (1<<15) =0x00008000 hardware/intbits.h: *34
INTF_SOFTINT     #define (1<<2) =0x00000004 hardware/intbits.h: *47
INTF_TBE         #define (1<<0) =0x00000001 hardware/intbits.h: *49
INTF_VERTB       #define (1<<5) =0x00000020 hardware/intbits.h: *44
IntMask          unsigned short int in struct ExpansionInt
        +0x0000  libraries/expansionbase.h: *37
intreq           unsigned short int in struct Custom
        +0x009c  hardware/custom.h: *83
intreqr          unsigned short int in struct Custom
        +0x001e  hardware/custom.h: *35
IntrList         struct List (size 0x000e) in struct ExecBase
        +0x016c  exec/execbase.h: *80
IntuiMessage     structure tag
    size 0x0034  intuition/intuition.h: *596, 633, 755
IntuiText        structure tag
    size 0x0014  intuition/intuition.h: 151, 217, *494, 502
INTUITICKS       #define 0x00400000 =0x00400000 intuition/intuition.h: *660
IntuitionBase    structure tag
    size 0x0050  intuition/intuitionbase.h: *144
INTUITION_INTUITIONBASE_H #define =0x00000000 intuition/intuitionbase.h: *2
INTUITION_INTUITION_H #define =0x00000000 intuition/intuition.h: *2
INTUITION_PREFERENCES_H #define =0x00000000 intuition/preferences.h: *2
INTUITION_SCREENS_H #define =0x00000000 intuition/screens.h: *2
IntVector        structure tag
    size 0x000c  exec/interrupts.h: *29
                 exec/execbase.h: 51
IntVects         array [16] of struct IntVector (size 0x000c) in struct
                 ExecBase
        +0x0054  exec/execbase.h: *51
INVERSVID        #define 4 =0x00000004 graphics/rastport.h: *91
IOAudio          structure tag
    size 0x0044  devices/audio.h: *47
ioa_AllocKey     short int in struct IOAudio
        +0x0020  devices/audio.h: *49
ioa_Cycles       unsigned short int in struct IOAudio
        +0x002e  devices/audio.h: *54
ioa_Data         pointer to char in struct IOAudio
        +0x0022  devices/audio.h: *50
ioa_Length       unsigned int in struct IOAudio
        +0x0026  devices/audio.h: *51
ioa_Period       unsigned short int in struct IOAudio
        +0x002a  devices/audio.h: *52
ioa_Request      struct IORequest (size 0x0020) in struct IOAudio
        +0x0000  devices/audio.h: *48
ioa_Volume       unsigned short int in struct IOAudio
        +0x002c  devices/audio.h: *53
ioa_WriteMsg     struct Message (size 0x0014) in struct IOAudio
        +0x0030  devices/audio.h: *55
IOB_QUICK        #define 0 =0x00000000 exec/io.h:  *45
IOClipReq        structure tag
    size 0x0034  devices/clipboard.h: *37
IODRPReq         structure tag
    size 0x003e  devices/printer.h: *150
IOERR_ABORTED    #define -2 =0xfffffffe exec/errors.h: *14
IOERR_BADLENGTH  #define -4 =0xfffffffc exec/errors.h: *16
IOERR_NOCMD      #define -3 =0xfffffffd exec/errors.h: *15
IOERR_OPENFAIL   #define -1 =0xffffffff exec/errors.h: *13
IOExtPar         structure tag
    size 0x003e  devices/parallel.h: *27
                 devices/prtbase.h: 70, 78
IOExtSer         structure tag
```

```
    size 0x0052  devices/serial.h: *37
                 devices/prtbase.h: 71, 79
IOExtTD          structure tag
    size 0x0038  devices/trackdisk.h: *113
IOF_QUICK        #define (1<<0) =0x00000001 exec/io.h:  *46
IOPar            struct IOStdReq (size 0x0030) in struct IOExtPar
         +0x0000 devices/parallel.h: *28
IOPARB_ABORT     #define 5 =0x00000005 devices/parallel.h: *64
IOPARB_ACTIVE    #define 4 =0x00000004 devices/parallel.h: *66
IOPARB_QUEUED    #define 6 =0x00000006 devices/parallel.h: *62
IOPARF_ABORT     #define (1<<5) =0x00000020 devices/parallel.h: *65
IOPARF_ACTIVE    #define (1<<4) =0x00000010 devices/parallel.h: *67
IOPARF_QUEUED    #define (1<<6) =0x00000040 devices/parallel.h: *63
IOPArray         structure tag
    size 0x0008  devices/parallel.h: *17, 53
IOPrtCmdReq      structure tag
    size 0x0026  devices/printer.h: *136
IOPTB_PAPEROUT   #define 1 =0x00000001 devices/parallel.h: *74
IOPTB_PARBUSY    #define 0 =0x00000000 devices/parallel.h: *76
IOPTB_PARSEL     #define 2 =0x00000002 devices/parallel.h: *70
IOPTB_RWDIR      #define 3 =0x00000003 devices/parallel.h: *68
IOPTF_PAPEROUT   #define (1<<1) =0x00000002 devices/parallel.h: *75
IOPTF_PARBUSY    #define (1<<0) =0x00000001 devices/parallel.h: *77
IOPTF_PARSEL     #define (1<<2) =0x00000004 devices/parallel.h: *73
IOPTF_RWDIR      #define (1<<3) =0x00000008 devices/parallel.h: *69
IORequest        structure tag
    size 0x0020  exec/io.h:  *18
                 devices/audio.h: 48
                 devices/timer.h: 29
IOSer            struct IOStdReq (size 0x0030) in struct IOExtSer
         +0x0000 devices/serial.h: *38
IOStdReq         structure tag
    size 0x0030  exec/io.h:  *27
                 devices/narrator.h: 68
                 devices/parallel.h: 28
                 devices/serial.h: 38
                 devices/trackdisk.h: 114
IOTArray         structure tag
    size 0x0008  devices/serial.h: *21, 66
IOTDB_INDEXSYNC  #define 4 =0x00000004 devices/trackdisk.h: *124
IOTDF_INDEXSYNC  #define (1<<4) =0x00000010 devices/trackdisk.h: *125
iotd_Count       unsigned int in struct IOExtTD
         +0x0030 devices/trackdisk.h: *115
iotd_Req         struct IOStdReq (size 0x0030) in struct IOExtTD
         +0x0000 devices/trackdisk.h: *114
iotd_SecLabel    unsigned int in struct IOExtTD
         +0x0034 devices/trackdisk.h: *116
io_Actual        unsigned int in struct IOStdReq
         +0x0020 exec/ic.h:  *34
io_Actual        unsigned int in struct IOClipReq
         +0x0020 devices/clipboard.h: *44
io_Baud          unsigned int in struct IOExtSer
         +0x003c devices/serial.h: *64
io_BrkTime       unsigned int in struct IOExtSer
         +0x0040 devices/serial.h: *65
io_ClipID        int in struct IOClipReq
         +0x0030 devices/clipboard.h: *48
io_ColorMap      pointer to struct ColorMap in struct IODRPReq
         +0x0024 devices/printer.h: *158
io_Command       unsigned short int in struct IORequest
         +0x001c exec/io.h:  *22
io_Command       unsigned short int in struct IOStdReq
         +0x001c exec/io.h:  *31
io_Command       unsigned short int in struct IOClipReq
         +0x001c devices/clipboard.h: *41
io_Command       unsigned short int in struct IOPrtCmdReq
         +0x001c devices/printer.h: *140
io_Command       unsigned short int in struct IODRPReq
         +0x001c devices/printer.h: *154
```



```
io_CtlChar       unsigned int in struct IOExtSer
         +0x0030 devices/serial.h: *61
io_Data          pointer to pointer to char in struct IOStdReq
         +0x0028 exec/io.h:  *36
io_Data          pointer to char in struct IOClipReq
         +0x0028 devices/clipboard.h: *46
io_DestCols      int in struct IODRPReq
         +0x0034 devices/printer.h: *164
io_DestRows      int in struct IODRPReq
         +0x0038 devices/printer.h: *165
io_Device        pointer to struct Device in struct IORequest
         +0x0014 exec/io.h:  *20
io_Device        pointer to struct Device in struct IOStdReq
         +0x0014 exec/io.h:  *29
io_Device        pointer to struct Device in struct IOClipReq
         +0x0014 devices/clipboard.h: *39
io_Device        pointer to struct Device in struct IOPrtCmdReq
         +0x0014 devices/printer.h: *138
io_Device        pointer to struct Device in struct IODRPReq
         +0x0014 devices/printer.h: *152
io_Error         char in struct IORequest
         +0x001f exec/io.h:  *24
io_Error         char in struct IOStdReq
         +0x001f exec/io.h:  *33
io_Error         char in struct IOClipReq
         +0x001f devices/clipboard.h: *43
io_Error         char in struct IOPrtCmdReq
         +0x001f devices/printer.h: *142
io_Error         char in struct IODRPReq
         +0x001f devices/printer.h: *156
io_ExtFlags      unsigned int in struct IOExtSer
         +0x0038 devices/serial.h: *63
io_Flags         char in struct IORequest
         +0x001e exec/io.h:  *23
io_Flags         char in struct IOStdReq
         +0x001e exec/io.h:  *32
io_Flags         char in struct IOClipReq
         +0x001e devices/clipboard.h: *42
io_Flags         char in struct IOPrtCmdReq
         +0x001e devices/printer.h: *141
io_Flags         char in struct IODRPReq
         +0x001e devices/printer.h: *155
io_Length        unsigned int in struct IOStdReq
         +0x0024 exec/io.h:  *35
io_Length        unsigned int in struct IOClipReq
         +0x0024 devices/clipboard.h: *45
io_Message       struct Message (size 0x0014) in struct IORequest
         +0x0000 exec/io.h:  *19
io_Message       struct Message (size 0x0014) in struct IOStdReq
         +0x0000 exec/io.h:  *28
io_Message       struct Message (size 0x0014) in struct IOClipReq
         +0x0000 devices/clipboard.h: *38
io_Message       struct Message (size 0x0014) in struct IOPrtCmdReq
         +0x0000 devices/printer.h: *137
io_Message       struct Message (size 0x0014) in struct IODRPReq
         +0x0000 devices/printer.h: *151
io_Modes         unsigned int in struct IODRPReq
         +0x0028 devices/printer.h: *159
io_Offset        unsigned int in struct IOStdReq
         +0x002c exec/io.h:  *37
io_Offset        unsigned int in struct IOClipReq
         +0x002c devices/clipboard.h: *47
io_ParFlags      char in struct IOExtPar
         +0x0035 devices/parallel.h: *52
io_Parm0         char in struct IOPrtCmdReq
         +0x0022 devices/printer.h: *144
io_Parm1         char in struct IOPrtCmdReq
         +0x0023 devices/printer.h: *145
io_Parm2         char in struct IOPrtCmdReq
```

```
        +0x0024  devices/printer.h: *146
io_Parm3         char in struct IOPrtCmdReq
        +0x0025  devices/printer.h: *147
io_PExtFlags     unsigned int in struct IOExtPar
        +0x0030  devices/parallel.h: *50
io_PrtCommand    unsigned short int in struct IOPrtCmdReq
        +0x0020  devices/printer.h: *143
io_PTermArray    struct IOPArray (size 0x0008) in struct IOExtPar
        +0x0036  devices/parallel.h: *53
io_RastPort      pointer to struct RastPort in struct IODRPReq
        +0x0020  devices/printer.h: *157
io_RBufLen       unsigned int in struct IOExtSer
        +0x0034  devices/serial.h: *62
io_ReadLen       char in struct IOExtSer
        +0x004c  devices/serial.h: *67
io_SerFlags      char in struct IOExtSer
        +0x004f  devices/serial.h: *70
io_Special       unsigned short int in struct IODRPReq
        +0x003c  devices/printer.h: *166
io_SrcHeight     unsigned short int in struct IODRPReq
        +0x0032  devices/printer.h: *163
io_SrcWidth      unsigned short int in struct IODRPReq
        +0x0030  devices/printer.h: *162
io_SrcX          unsigned short int in struct IODRPReq
        +0x002c  devices/printer.h: *160
io_SrcY          unsigned short int in struct IODRPReq
        +0x002e  devices/printer.h: *161
IO_STATB_OVERRUN #define 8 =0x00000008 devices/serial.h: *125
IO_STATB_READBREAK #define 10 =0x0000000a devices/serial.h: *121
IO_STATB_WROTEBREAK #define 9 =0x00000009 devices/serial.h: *123
IO_STATB_XOFFREAD #define 12 =0x0000000c devices/serial.h: *117
IO_STATB_XOFFWRITE #define 11 =0x0000000b devices/serial.h: *119
IO_STATF_OVERRUN #define (1<<8) =0x00000100 devices/serial.h: *126
IO_STATF_READBREAK #define (1<<10) =0x00000400 devices/serial.h: *122
IO_STATF_WROTEBREAK #define (1<<9) =0x00000200 devices/serial.h: *124
IO_STATF_XOFFREAD #define (1<<12) =0x00001000 devices/serial.h: *118
IO_STATF_XOFFWRITE #define (1<<11) =0x00000800 devices/serial.h: *120
io_Status        char in struct IOExtPar
        +0x0034  devices/parallel.h: *51
io_Status        unsigned short int in struct IOExtSer
        +0x0050  devices/serial.h: *71
io_StopBits      char in struct IOExtSer
        +0x004e  devices/serial.h: *69
io_TermArray     struct IOTArray (size 0x0008) in struct IOExtSer
        +0x0044  devices/serial.h: *66
io_Unit          pointer to struct Unit in struct IORequest
        +0x0018  exec/io.h:  *21
io_Unit          pointer to struct Unit in struct IOStdReq
        +0x0018  exec/io.h:  *30
io_Unit          pointer to struct Unit in struct IOClipReq
        +0x0018  devices/clipboard.h: *40
io_Unit          pointer to struct Unit in struct IOPrtCmdReq
        +0x0018  devices/printer.h: *139
io_Unit          pointer to struct Unit in struct IODRPReq
        +0x0018  devices/printer.h: *153
io_WriteLen      char in struct IOExtSer
        +0x004d  devices/serial.h: *68
Iptr             pointer to struct Isrvstr in struct Isrvstr
        +0x000e  graphics/graphint.h: *21
ISDRAWN          #define 0x1000 =0x00001000 intuition/intuition.h: *130
ISGRTRX          #define 4 =0x00000004 graphics/clip.h: *74
ISGRTRY          #define 8 =0x00000008 graphics/clip.h: *75
ISLESSX          #define 1 =0x00000001 graphics/clip.h: *72
ISLESSY          #define 2 =0x00000002 graphics/clip.h: *73
Isrvstr          structure tag
     size 0x001e graphics/graphint.h: *18, 21
is_Code          pointer to function returning void in struct Interrupt
        +0x0012  exec/interrupts.h: *25
is_Data          pointer to pointer to char in struct Interrupt
```



```
        +0x000e  exec/interrupts.h: *24
is_Node          struct Node (size 0x000e) in struct Interrupt
        +0x0000  exec/interrupts.h: *23
is_Node          struct Node (size 0x000e) in struct Isrvstr
        +0x0000  graphics/graphint.h: *20
ITEMENABLED      #define 0x0010 =0x00000010 intuition/intuition.h: *117
ItemFill         pointer to pointer to char in struct MenuItem
        +0x0012  intuition/intuition.h: *94
ITEMNUM          Macro (1 argument) intuition/intuition.h: *945
ITEMTEXT         #define 0x0002 =0x00000002 intuition/intuition.h: *114
IText            pointer to char in struct IntuiText
        +0x000c  intuition/intuition.h: *501
ITextFont        pointer to struct TextAttr in struct IntuiText
        +0x0008  intuition/intuition.h: *500
itof             Macro (1 argument) libraries/mathffp.h: *31
itof             Macro (1 argument) libraries/mathieeedp.h: *32
iv_Code          pointer to function returning void in struct IntVector
        +0x0004  exec/interrupts.h: *31
iv_Data          pointer to pointer to char in struct IntVector
        +0x0000  exec/interrupts.h: *30
iv_Node          pointer to struct Node in struct IntVector
        +0x0008  exec/interrupts.h: *32
JAM1             #define 0 =0x00000000 graphics/rastport.h: *88
JAM2             #define 1 =0x00000001 graphics/rastport.h: *89
JazzX            short int in struct Menu
        +0x0016  intuition/intuition.h: *67
JazzY            short int in struct Menu
        +0x0018  intuition/intuition.h: *67
joy0dat          unsigned short int in struct Custom
        +0x000a  hardware/custom.h: *25
joy1dat          unsigned short int in struct Custom
        +0x000c  hardware/custom.h: *26
joytest          unsigned short int in struct Custom
        +0x0036  hardware/custom.h: *46
KBD_ADDRESETHANDLER #define (CMD_NONSTD+2) =0x0000000b devices/keyboard.h: *19
KBD_READEVENT    #define (CMD_NONSTD+0) =0x00000009 devices/keyboard.h: *17
KBD_READMATRIX   #define (CMD_NONSTD+1) =0x0000000a devices/keyboard.h: *18
KBD_REMRESETHANDLER #define (CMD_NONSTD+3) =0x0000000c devices/keyboard.h: *20
KBD_RESETHANDLERDONE #define (CMD_NONSTD+4) =0x0000000d devices/keyboard.h: *21
KCB_ALT          #define 1 =0x00000001 devices/keymap.h: *47
KCB_CONTROL      #define 2 =0x00000002 devices/keymap.h: *49
KCB_DEAD         #define 5 =0x00000005 devices/keymap.h: *54
KCB_DOWNUP       #define 3 =0x00000003 devices/keymap.h: *51
KCB_NOP          #define 7 =0x00000007 devices/keymap.h: *60
KCB_SHIFT        #define 0 =0x00000000 devices/keymap.h: *45
KCB_STRING       #define 6 =0x00000006 devices/keymap.h: *57
KCF_ALT          #define 0x02 =0x00000002 devices/keymap.h: *48
KCF_CONTROL      #define 0x04 =0x00000004 devices/keymap.h: *50
KCF_DEAD         #define 0x20 =0x00000020 devices/keymap.h: *55
KCF_DOWNUP       #define 0x08 =0x00000008 devices/keymap.h: *52
KCF_NOP          #define 0x80 =0x00000080 devices/keymap.h: *61
KCF_SHIFT        #define 0x01 =0x00000001 devices/keymap.h: *46
KCF_STRING       #define 0x40 =0x00000040 devices/keymap.h: *58
KC_NOQUAL        #define 0 =0x00000000 devices/keymap.h: *43
KC_VANILLA       #define 7 =0x00000007 devices/keymap.h: *44
KEYCODE_B        #define 0x35 =0x00000035 intuition/intuition.h: *1025
KEYCODE_M        #define 0x37 =0x00000037 intuition/intuition.h: *1023
KEYCODE_N        #define 0x36 =0x00000036 intuition/intuition.h: *1022
KEYCODE_Q        #define 0x10 =0x00000010 intuition/intuition.h: *1020
KEYCODE_V        #define 0x34 =0x00000034 intuition/intuition.h: *1024
KEYCODE_X        #define 0x32 =0x00000032 intuition/intuition.h: *1021
KeyMap           structure tag
     size 0x0020 devices/keymap.h: *20, 33
                 devices/conunit.h: 55
                 intuition/intuition.h: 479
KeyMapNode       structure tag
     size 0x002e devices/keymap.h: *31
KeyMapResource   structure tag
     size 0x001c devices/keymap.h: *37
```

```
KeyRptDelay        struct timeval (size 0x0008) in struct Preferences
        +0x000c    intuition/preferences.h: *55
KeyRptSpeed        struct timeval (size 0x0008) in struct Preferences
        +0x0004    intuition/preferences.h: *54
KickCheckSum       pointer to pointer to char in struct ExecBase
        +0x022a    exec/execbase.h: *117
KickMemPtr         pointer to pointer to char in struct ExecBase
        +0x0222    exec/execbase.h: *115
KickTagPtr         pointer to pointer to char in struct ExecBase
        +0x0226    exec/execbase.h: *116
km_HiCapsable      pointer to char in struct KeyMap
        +0x0018    devices/keymap.h: *27
km_HiKeyMap        pointer to unsigned int in struct KeyMap
        +0x0014    devices/keymap.h: *26
km_HiKeyMapTypes   pointer to char in struct KeyMap
        +0x0010    devices/keymap.h: *25
km_HiRepeatable    pointer to char in struct KeyMap
        +0x001c    devices/keymap.h: *28
km_LoCapsable      pointer to char in struct KeyMap
        +0x0008    devices/keymap.h: *23
km_LoKeyMap        pointer to unsigned int in struct KeyMap
        +0x0004    devices/keymap.h: *22
km_LoKeyMapTypes   pointer to char in struct KeyMap
        +0x0000    devices/keymap.h: *21
km_LoRepeatable    pointer to char in struct KeyMap
        +0x000c    devices/keymap.h: *24
KNOBHIT            #define 0x0100 =0x00000100 intuition/intuition.h: *433
KNOBHMIN           #define 6 =0x00000006 intuition/intuition.h: *435
KNOBVMIN           #define 4 =0x00000004 intuition/intuition.h: *436
kn_KeyMap          struct KeyMap (size 0x0020) in struct KeyMapNode
        +0x000e    devices/keymap.h: *33
kn_Node            struct Node (size 0x000e) in struct KeyMapNode
        +0x0000    devices/keymap.h: *32
kr_List            struct List (size 0x000e) in struct KeyMapResource
        +0x000e    devices/keymap.h: *39
kr_Node            struct Node (size 0x000e) in struct KeyMapResource
        +0x0000    devices/keymap.h: *38
LACE               #define 4 =0x00000004 graphics/view.h: *61
LaceWB             char in struct Preferences
        +0x00b9    intuition/preferences.h: *108
LACEWB             #define 0x01 =0x00000001 intuition/preferences.h: *131
LastAlert          array [4] of int in struct ExecBase
        +0x0202    exec/execbase.h: *90
lastBlissObj       pointer to pointer to char in struct GelsInfo
        +0x0022    graphics/rastport.h: *47
LastChanceMemory   pointer to struct SignalSemaphore in struct GfxBase
        +0x00e0    graphics/gfxbase.h: *61
lastColor          pointer to pointer to short int in struct GelsInfo
        +0x000e    graphics/rastport.h: *44
Layer              structure tag
    size 0x00a0    graphics/clip.h: *25, 27, 58
                   graphics/rastport.h: 52
                   graphics/layers.h: 34, 35, 36
                   intuition/intuition.h: 157, 465, 788
                   intuition/screens.h: 81
Layer              pointer to struct Layer in struct RastPort
        +0x0000    graphics/rastport.h: *52
LAYERBACKDROP      #define 0x40 =0x00000040 graphics/layers.h: *25
LayerInfo          pointer to struct Layer_Info in struct Layer
        +0x0044    graphics/clip.h: *43
LayerInfo          struct Layer_Info (size 0x0066) in struct Screen
        +0x00e0    intuition/screens.h: *65
LayerInfo_extra    structure tag
    size 0x0000    graphics/layers.h: 46
LayerInfo_extra    pointer to struct LayerInfo_extra in struct Layer_Info
        +0x0062    graphics/layers.h: *46
LayerInfo_extra_size unsigned short int in struct Layer_Info
        +0x005c    graphics/layers.h: *44
LayerPtr           pointer to struct Layer in struct StringInfo
```



```
        +0x0018    intuition/intuition.h: *465
LAYERREFRESH       #define 0x80 =0x00000080 graphics/layers.h: *26
LAYERSIMPLE        #define 1 =0x00000001 graphics/layers.h: *21
LAYERSMART         #define 2 =0x00000002 graphics/layers.h: *22
LAYERSUPER         #define 4 =0x00000004 graphics/layers.h: *23
LAYERUPDATING      #define 0x10 =0x00000010 graphics/layers.h: *24
LAYER_CLIPRECTS_LOST #define 0x100 =0x00000100 graphics/layers.h: *27
Layer_Info         structure tag
    size 0x0066    graphics/clip.h: 43
                   graphics/layers.h: *32
                   intuition/screens.h: 65
LCMptr             pointer to unsigned short int in struct GfxBase
        +0x00e4    graphics/gfxbase.h: *62
LEFTBORDER         #define 0x0020 =0x00000020 intuition/intuition.h: *312
LeftBorder         unsigned short int in struct PropInfo
        +0x0012    intuition/intuition.h: *423
LeftEdge           short int in struct Menu
        +0x0004    intuition/intuition.h: *60
LeftEdge           short int in struct MenuItem
        +0x0004    intuition/intuition.h: *88
LeftEdge           short int in struct Requester
        +0x0004    intuition/intuition.h: *145
LeftEdge           short int in struct Gadget
        +0x0004    intuition/intuition.h: *197
LeftEdge           short int in struct IntuiText
        +0x0004    intuition/intuition.h: *498
LeftEdge           short int in struct Border
        +0x0000    intuition/intuition.h: *524
LeftEdge           short int in struct Image
        +0x0000    intuition/intuition.h: *545
LeftEdge           short int in struct Window
        +0x0004    intuition/intuition.h: *697
LeftEdge           short int in struct NewWindow
        +0x0000    intuition/intuition.h: *852
LeftEdge           short int in struct Screen
        +0x0008    intuition/screens.h: *45
LeftEdge           short int in struct NewScreen
        +0x0000    intuition/screens.h: *119
LEFTHIT            #define 4 =0x00000004 graphics/collide.h: *32
leftmost           short int in struct GelsInfo
        +0x0016    graphics/rastport.h: *46
LETTER             #define 0x100 =0x00000100 intuition/preferences.h: *159
lh_Flags           #define lib_Flags =0x00000000 exec/libraries.h: *50
lh_Head            pointer to struct Node in struct List
        +0x0000    exec/lists.h: *20
lh_IdString        #define lib_IdString =0x00000000 exec/libraries.h: *56
lh_NegSize         #define lib_NegSize =0x00000000 exec/libraries.h: *52
lh_Node            #define lib_Node =0x00000000 exec/libraries.h: *49
lh_OpenCnt         #define lib_OpenCnt =0x00000000 exec/libraries.h: *58
lh_pad             #define lib_pad =0x00000000 exec/libraries.h: *51
lh_PosSize         #define lib_PosSize =0x00000000 exec/libraries.h: *53
lh_Revision        #define lib_Revision =0x00000000 exec/libraries.h: *55
lh_Sum             #define lib_Sum =0x00000000 exec/libraries.h: *57
lh_Tail            pointer to struct Node in struct List
        +0x0004    exec/lists.h: *21
lh_TailPred        pointer to struct Node in struct List
        +0x0008    exec/lists.h: *22
lh_Type            char in struct List
        +0x000c    exec/lists.h: *23
lh_Version         #define lib_Version =0x00000000 exec/libraries.h: *54
LIBF_CHANGED       #define (1<<1) =0x00000002 exec/libraries.h: *44
LIBF_DELEXP        #define (1<<3) =0x00000008 exec/libraries.h: *46
LIBF_SUMMING       #define (1<<0) =0x00000001 exec/libraries.h: *43
LIBF_SUMUSED       #define (1<<2) =0x00000004 exec/libraries.h: *45
LibList            struct List (size 0x000e) in struct ExecBase
        +0x017a    exec/execbase.h: *81
LibNode            struct Library (size 0x0022) in struct ExecBase
        +0x0000    exec/execbase.h: *31
LibNode            struct Library (size 0x0022) in struct GfxBase
```

```
        +0x0000  graphics/gfxbase.h: *25
LibNode          struct Library (size 0x0022) in struct IntuitionBase
        +0x0000  intuition/intuitionbase.h: *148
LibNode          struct Library (size 0x0022) in struct ExpansionBase
        +0x0000  libraries/expansionbase.h: *45
LibNode          struct Library (size 0x0022) in struct RomBootBase
        +0x0000  libraries/romboot_base.h: *34
LIBRARIES_CONFIGREGS_H #define =0x00000000 libraries/configregs.h: *2
LIBRARIES_CONFIGVARS_H #define =0x00000000 libraries/configvars.h: *2
LIBRARIES_DISKFONT_H #define =0x00000000 libraries/diskfont.h: *2
LIBRARIES_DOSEXTENS_H #define =0x00000000 libraries/dosextens.h: *2
LIBRARIES_DOS_H  #define =0x00000000 libraries/dos.h: *2
LIBRARIES_EXPANSIONBASE_H #define =0x00000000 libraries/expansionbase.h: *2
LIBRARIES_EXPANSION_H #define =0x00000000 libraries/expansion.h: *2
LIBRARIES_FILEHANDLER_H #define =0x00000000 libraries/filehandler.h: *2
LIBRARIES_MATHFFP_H #define =0x00000000 libraries/mathffp.h: *2
LIBRARIES_MATHIEEEDP_H #define =0x00000000 libraries/mathieeedp.h: *2
LIBRARIES_MATHLIBRARY_H #define =0x00000000 libraries/mathlibrary.h: *2
LIBRARIES_ROMBOOT_BASE_H #define =0x00000000 libraries/romboot_base.h: *2
LIBRARIES_TRANSLATOR_H #define =0x00000000 libraries/translator.h: *2
Library          structure tag
    size 0x0022  exec/libraries.h: *30
                 exec/devices.h: 25
                 exec/execbase.h: 31
                 libraries/dosextens.h: 165
                 devices/prtbase.h: 47
                 graphics/gfxbase.h: 25
                 intuition/intuitionbase.h: 148
                 libraries/expansionbase.h: 45
                 libraries/mathlibrary.h: 23
                 libraries/romboot_base.h: 34
                 resources/disk.h: 49, 53, 54
                 resources/misc.h: 36
LIBRARY_VERSION  #define 34 =0x00000022 exec/types.h: *56
LIB_BASE         #define (-LIB_VECTSIZE) =0xfffffffa exec/libraries.h: *20
LIB_CLOSE        #define (-12) =0xfffffff4 exec/libraries.h: *25
LIB_EXPUNGE      #define (-18) =0xffffffee exec/libraries.h: *26
LIB_EXTFUNC      #define (-24) =0xffffffe8 exec/libraries.h: *27
lib_Flags        char in struct Library
        +0x000e  exec/libraries.h: *32
lib_IdString     pointer to pointer to char in struct Library
        +0x0018  exec/libraries.h: *38
lib_NegSize      unsigned short int in struct Library
        +0x0010  exec/libraries.h: *34
lib_Node         struct Node (size 0x000e) in struct Library
        +0x0000  exec/libraries.h: *31
LIB_NONSTD       #define (LIB_USERDEF) =0xffffffe2 exec/libraries.h: *22
LIB_OPEN         #define (-6) =0xfffffffa exec/libraries.h: *24
lib_OpenCnt      unsigned short int in struct Library
        +0x0020  exec/libraries.h: *40
lib_pad          char in struct Library
        +0x000f  exec/libraries.h: *33
lib_PosSize      unsigned short int in struct Library
        +0x0012  exec/libraries.h: *35
LIB_RESERVED     #define 4 =0x00000004 exec/libraries.h: *19
lib_Revision     unsigned short int in struct Library
        +0x0016  exec/libraries.h: *37
lib_Sum          unsigned int in struct Library
        +0x001c  exec/libraries.h: *39
LIB_USERDEF      #define (LIB_BASE-(LIB_RESERVED*LIB_VECTSIZE)) =0xffffffe2
                 exec/libraries.h: *21
LIB_VECTSIZE     #define 6 =0x00000006 exec/libraries.h: *18
lib_Version      unsigned short int in struct Library
        +0x0014  exec/libraries.h: *36
LINEMODE         #define 0x1 =0x00000001 hardware/blit.h: *57
LinePtrn         unsigned short int in struct RastPort
        +0x0022  graphics/rastport.h: *67
linpatcnt        char in struct RastPort
        +0x001e  graphics/rastport.h: *64
```



```
List             structure tag
    size 0x000e  exec/lists.h: *19
                 exec/tasks.h: 43
                 exec/ports.h: 33
                 exec/interrupts.h: 37
                 exec/execbase.h: 77, 78, 79, 80, 81, 82, 83, 84, 107
                 devices/keymap.h: 39
                 graphics/layers.h: 39
                 graphics/gfxbase.h: 35, 48, 50
                 libraries/expansionbase.h: 51, 52
                 libraries/romboot_base.h: 36
                 resources/disk.h: 56
                 resources/filesysres.h: 29
                 workbench/workbench.h: 71
LMN_REGION       #define -1 =0xffffffff graphics/layers.h: *30
ln_Name          pointer to char in struct Node
        +0x000a  exec/nodes.h: *19
ln_Pred          pointer to struct Node in struct Node
        +0x0004  exec/nodes.h: *16
ln_Pri           char in struct Node
        +0x0009  exec/nodes.h: *18
ln_Succ          pointer to struct Node in struct Node
        +0x0000  exec/nodes.h: *15
ln_Type          char in struct Node
        +0x0008  exec/nodes.h: *17
LoadSegBlock     structure tag
    size 0x0200  devices/hardblocks.h: *183
lobs             pointer to struct Layer in struct ClipRect
        +0x0008  graphics/clip.h: *58
Lock             struct SignalSemaphore (size 0x002e) in struct Layer
        +0x0048  graphics/clip.h: *44
Lock             struct SignalSemaphore (size 0x002e) in struct Layer_Info
        +0x0018  graphics/layers.h: *38
LockLayersCount  char in struct Layer_Info
        +0x005b  graphics/layers.h: *43
LOFCprList       pointer to struct cprlist in struct View
        +0x0004  graphics/view.h: *50
LOFlist          pointer to unsigned short int in struct GfxBase
        +0x0032  graphics/gfxbase.h: *30
log              #define SPLog =0x00000000 libraries/mathffp.h: *45
log              #define IEEEDPLog =0x00000000 libraries/mathieeedp.h: *46
LOG10            #define ((float) 2.302585092994046) libraries/mathffp.h: *22
log10            #define SPLog10 =0x00000000 libraries/mathffp.h: *46
LOG10            #define ((double) 2.302585092994046) libraries/mathieeedp.h: *25
log10            #define IEEEDPLog10 =0x00000000 libraries/mathieeedp.h: *47
LONELYMESSAGE    #define 0x80000000 =0x80000000 intuition/intuition.h: *668
LONG             typedef long int
                 many references; defined in exec/types.h: *20
LONGBITS         typedef unsigned long int
                 exec/types.h: *22
LONGINT          #define 0x0800 =0x00000800 intuition/intuition.h: *321
LongInt          int in struct StringInfo
        +0x001c  intuition/intuition.h: *472
longreserved     array [2] of unsigned int in struct RastPort
        +0x0046  graphics/rastport.h: *80
longreserved     int in struct Layer_Info
        +0x0054  graphics/layers.h: *40
LOWCHECKWIDTH    #define 13 =0x0000000d intuition/intuition.h: *978
LOWCOMMWIDTH     #define 16 =0x00000010 intuition/intuition.h: *979
LowMemChkSum     short int in struct ExecBase
        +0x0024  exec/execbase.h: *34
lsb_ChkSum       int in struct LoadSegBlock
        +0x0008  devices/hardblocks.h: *186
lsb_HostID       unsigned int in struct LoadSegBlock
        +0x000c  devices/hardblocks.h: *187
lsb_ID           unsigned int in struct LoadSegBlock
        +0x0000  devices/hardblocks.h: *184
lsb_LoadData     array [123] of unsigned int in struct LoadSegBlock
        +0x0014  devices/hardblocks.h: *189
```

```
lsb_Next           unsigned int in struct LoadSegBlock
        +0x0010    devices/hardblocks.h: *188
lsb_SummedLongs    unsigned int in struct LoadSegBlock
        +0x0004    devices/hardblocks.h: *185
LW_RESERVED        #define 1 =0x00000001 intuition/preferences.h: *132
l_pad              char in struct List
        +0x000d    exec/lists.h: *24
MakeDosNode        extern function returning pointer to struct DeviceNode
                   (size 0x002c)
                   libraries/expansion.h: *26
MALE               #define 0 =0x00000000 devices/narrator.h: *43
Mask               char in struct RastPort
        +0x0018    graphics/rastport.h: *58
Mask               pointer to unsigned short int in struct BoolInfo
        +0x0002    intuition/intuition.h: *363
MatchToolValue     extern function returning "LONG" workbench/icon.h: *30
MathIEEEBase       structure tag
    size 0x003c    libraries/mathlibrary.h: *21
MathIEEEBase_68881 pointer to unsigned short int in struct MathIEEEBase
        +0x0024    libraries/mathlibrary.h: *26
MathIEEEBase_Flags unsigned char in struct MathIEEEBase
        +0x0022    libraries/mathlibrary.h: *24
MathIEEEBase_LibNode struct Library (size 0x0022) in struct MathIEEEBase
        +0x0000    libraries/mathlibrary.h: *23
MathIEEEBase_reserved1 unsigned char in struct MathIEEEBase
        +0x0023    libraries/mathlibrary.h: *25
MathIEEEBase_Resource pointer to struct MathIEEEResource in struct
                   MathIEEEBase
        +0x0030    libraries/mathlibrary.h: *29
MathIEEEBase_SegList pointer to pointer to char in struct MathIEEEBase
        +0x002c    libraries/mathlibrary.h: *28
MathIEEEBase_SysLib pointer to pointer to char in struct MathIEEEBase
        +0x0028    libraries/mathlibrary.h: *27
MathIEEEBase_TaskCloseLib pointer to function returning int in struct
                   MathIEEEBase
        +0x0038    libraries/mathlibrary.h: *31
MathIEEEBase_TaskOpenLib pointer to function returning int in struct
                   MathIEEEBase
        +0x0034    libraries/mathlibrary.h: *30
MathIEEEResource   structure tag
    size 0x002c    libraries/mathlibrary.h: 29
                   resources/mathresource.h: *35
MATHIEEERESOURCEF_DBLBAS #define (1<<0) =0x00000001
                   resources/mathresource.h: *49
MATHIEEERESOURCEF_DBLTRANS #define (1<<1) =0x00000002
                   resources/mathresource.h: *50
MATHIEEERESOURCEF_EXTBAS #define (1<<4) =0x00000010
                   resources/mathresource.h: *53
MATHIEEERESOURCEF_EXTTRANS #define (1<<5) =0x00000020
                   resources/mathresource.h: *54
MATHIEEERESOURCEF_SGLBAS #define (1<<2) =0x00000004
                   resources/mathresource.h: *51
MATHIEEERESOURCEF_SGLTRANS #define (1<<3) =0x00000008
                   resources/mathresource.h: *52
MathIEEEResource_BaseAddr pointer to unsigned short int in struct
                   MathIEEEResource
        +0x0010    resources/mathresource.h: *39
MathIEEEResource_DblBasInit pointer to function returning void in struct
                   MathIEEEResource
        +0x0014    resources/mathresource.h: *40
MathIEEEResource_DblTransInit pointer to function returning void in struct
                   MathIEEEResource
        +0x0018    resources/mathresource.h: *41
MathIEEEResource_ExtBasInit pointer to function returning void in struct
                   MathIEEEResource
        +0x0024    resources/mathresource.h: *44
MathIEEEResource_ExtTransInit pointer to function returning void in struct
                   MathIEEEResource
        +0x0028    resources/mathresource.h: *45
```



```
MathIEEEResource_Flags unsigned short int in struct MathIEEEResource
        +0x000e    resources/mathresource.h: *38
MathIEEEResource_Node struct Node (size 0x000e) in struct MathIEEEResource
        +0x0000    resources/mathresource.h: *37
MathIEEEResource_SglBasInit pointer to function returning void in struct
                   MathIEEEResource
        +0x001c    resources/mathresource.h: *42
MathIEEEResource_SglTransInit pointer to function returning void in struct
                   MathIEEEResource
        +0x0020    resources/mathresource.h: *43
MAXBODY            #define 0xFFFF =0x0000ffff intuition/intuition.h: *437
MAXBYTESPERROW     #define 128 =0x00000080 hardware/blit.h: *18
MaxChars           short int in struct StringInfo
        +0x000a    intuition/intuition.h: *457
MaxCount           short int in struct AreaInfo
        +0x0012    graphics/rastport.h: *24
MaxCount           short int in struct cprlist
        +0x0008    graphics/copper.h: *52
MaxCount           short int in struct CopList
        +0x001e    graphics/copper.h: *65
MaxDisplayColumn   unsigned short int in struct GfxBase
        +0x00d6    graphics/gfxbase.h: *55
MaxDisplayRow      unsigned short int in struct GfxBase
        +0x00d4    graphics/gfxbase.h: *54
MaxExtMem          pointer to pointer to char in struct ExecBase
        +0x004e    exec/execbase.h: *45
MAXFONTNAME        #define 32 =0x00000020 libraries/diskfont.h: *41, 55
MAXFONTPATH        #define 256 =0x00000100 libraries/diskfont.h: *23, 26
MAXFREQ            #define 28000 =0x00006d60 devices/narrator.h: *59
MaxHeight          unsigned short int in struct Window
        +0x0016    intuition/intuition.h: *703
MaxHeight          unsigned short int in struct NewWindow
        +0x002c    intuition/intuition.h: *902
MAXINT             #define 0x7FFFFFFF =0x7fffffff libraries/dos.h: *40
MaxLocMem          unsigned int in struct ExecBase
        +0x003e    exec/execbase.h: *41
MAXPITCH           #define 320 =0x00000140 devices/narrator.h: *57
MAXPOT             #define 0xFFFF =0x0000ffff intuition/intuition.h: *438
MAXRATE            #define 400 =0x00000190 devices/narrator.h: *55
MAXTABS            #define 80 =0x00000050 devices/conunit.h: *31, 57
MAXVOL             #define 64 =0x00000040 devices/narrator.h: *61
MaxWidth           unsigned short int in struct Window
        +0x0014    intuition/intuition.h: *703
MaxWidth           unsigned short int in struct NewWindow
        +0x002a    intuition/intuition.h: *902
MaxX               short int in struct Rectangle
        +0x0004    graphics/gfx.h: *26
MaxY               short int in struct Rectangle
        +0x0006    graphics/gfx.h: *26
mc_Bytes           unsigned int in struct MemChunk
        +0x0004    exec/memory.h: *22
mc_Next            pointer to struct MemChunk in struct MemChunk
        +0x0000    exec/memory.h: *21
MeMask             short int in struct VSprite
        +0x0020    graphics/gels.h: *101
MemChunk           structure tag
    size 0x0008    exec/memory.h: *20, 21, 31
MemEntry           structure tag
    size 0x0008    exec/memory.h: *40, 58
MEMF_CHIP          #define (1<<1) =0x00000002 exec/memory.h: *67
MEMF_CLEAR         #define (1<<16) =0x00010000 exec/memory.h: *70
MEMF_FAST          #define (1<<2) =0x00000004 exec/memory.h: *68
MEMF_LARGEST       #define (1<<17) =0x00020000 exec/memory.h: *71
MEMF_PUBLIC        #define (1<<0) =0x00000001 exec/memory.h: *66
MemHeader          structure tag
    size 0x0020    exec/memory.h: *28
MemList            structure tag
    size 0x0018    exec/memory.h: *55
MemList            struct List (size 0x000e) in struct ExecBase
```

```
        +0x0142  exec/execbase.h: *77
Memory           pointer to char in struct Remember
        +0x0008  intuition/intuition.h: *932
MEM_BLOCKMASK    #define 7 =0x00000007 exec/memory.h: *74
MEM_BLOCKSIZE    #define 8 =0x00000008 exec/memory.h: *73
Menu             structure tag
    size 0x001e  intuition/intuition.h: *57, 59, 707
MENUCANCEL       #define 0x0002 =0x00000002 intuition/intuition.h: *674
MENUDOWN         #define (IECODE_RBUTTON) =0x00000069
                 intuition/intuition.h: *1009
MENUENABLED      #define 0x0001 =0x00000001 intuition/intuition.h: *72
MenuHBorder      char in struct Screen
        +0x0022  intuition/screens.h: *56
MENUHOT          #define 0x0001 =0x00000001 intuition/intuition.h: *673
MenuItem         structure tag
    size 0x0022  intuition/intuition.h: 64, *85, 87, 103
MenuName         pointer to char in struct Menu
        +0x000e  intuition/intuition.h: *63
MENUNULL         #define 0xFFFF =0x0000ffff intuition/intuition.h: *964
MENUNUM          Macro (1 argument) intuition/intuition.h: *944
MENUPICK         #define 0x00000100 =0x00000100 intuition/intuition.h: *646
MENUSTATE        #define 0x8000 =0x00008000 intuition/intuition.h: *827
MenuStrip        pointer to struct Menu in struct Window
        +0x001c  intuition/intuition.h: *707
MENUTOGGLE       #define 0x0008 =0x00000008 intuition/intuition.h: *116
MENUTOGGLED      #define 0x4000 =0x00004000 intuition/intuition.h: *132
MENUUP           #define (IECODE_RBUTTON | IECODE_UP_PREFIX) =0x000000e9
                 intuition/intuition.h: *1008
MenuVBorder      char in struct Screen
        +0x0021  intuition/screens.h: *56
MENUVERIFY       #define 0x00002000 =0x00002000 intuition/intuition.h: *651
MENUWAITING      #define 0x0003 =0x00000003 intuition/intuition.h: *675
Message          structure tag
    size 0x0014  exec/ports.h: *47
                 exec/io.h:  19, 28
                 devices/audio.h: 55
                 devices/clipboard.h: 38, 54
                 devices/printer.h: 137, 151
                 libraries/dosextens.h: 61, 80, 111
                 graphics/text.h: 57
                 intuition/intuition.h: 598
                 resources/disk.h: 42
                 workbench/startup.h: 26
message          struct IOStdReq (size 0x0030) in struct narrator_rb
        +0x0000  devices/narrator.h: *68
MessageKey       pointer to struct IntuiMessage in struct Window
        +0x005e  intuition/intuition.h: *755
meu_Addr         pointer to pointer to char in union (no tag)
        +0x0000  exec/memory.h: *43
meu_Reqs         unsigned int in union (no tag)
        +0x0000  exec/memory.h: *42
me_Addr          #define me_Un.meu_Addr exec/memory.h: *50
me_Length        unsigned int in struct MemEntry
        +0x0004  exec/memory.h: *45
me_Reqs          #define me_Un.meu_Reqs exec/memory.h: *49
me_Un            union (no tag) (size 0x0004) in struct MemEntry
        +0x0000  exec/memory.h: *44
me_un            #define me_Un =0x00000000 exec/memory.h: *48
mh_Attributes    unsigned short int in struct MemHeader
        +0x000e  exec/memory.h: *30
mh_First         pointer to struct MemChunk in struct MemHeader
        +0x0010  exec/memory.h: *31
mh_Free          unsigned int in struct MemHeader
        +0x001c  exec/memory.h: *34
mh_Lower         pointer to pointer to char in struct MemHeader
        +0x0014  exec/memory.h: *32
mh_Node          struct Node (size 0x000e) in struct MemHeader
        +0x0000  exec/memory.h: *29
mh_Upper         pointer to pointer to char in struct MemHeader
```



```
        +0x0018  exec/memory.h: *33
Micros           unsigned int in struct IntuiMessage
        +0x0028  intuition/intuition.h: *625
Micros           unsigned int in struct IntuitionBase
        +0x004c  intuition/intuitionbase.h: *164
MicrosPerLine    unsigned short int in struct GfxBase
        +0x00e8  graphics/gfxbase.h: *63
MIDRAWN          #define 0x0100 =0x00000100 intuition/intuition.h: *75
MinDisplayColumn unsigned short int in struct GfxBase
        +0x00ea  graphics/gfxbase.h: *64
MINFREQ          #define 5000 =0x00001388 devices/narrator.h: *58
MinHeight        short int in struct Window
        +0x0012  intuition/intuition.h: *702
MinHeight        short int in struct NewWindow
        +0x0028  intuition/intuition.h: *901
MININT           #define 0x80000000 =0x80000000 libraries/dos.h: *41
MinList          structure tag
    size 0x000c  exec/lists.h: *28
                 exec/semaphores.h: 52
                 graphics/layers.h: 37
MinNode          structure tag
    size 0x0008  exec/nodes.h: *23, 24, 25
                 exec/lists.h: 29, 30, 31
                 exec/semaphores.h: 44
MINPITCH         #define 65 =0x00000041 devices/narrator.h: *56
MINRATE          #define 40 =0x00000028 devices/narrator.h: *54
minterms         array [8] of char in struct RastPort
        +0x0028  graphics/rastport.h: *69
MINVOL           #define 0 =0x00000000 devices/narrator.h: *60
MinWidth         short int in struct Window
        +0x0010  intuition/intuition.h: *702
MinWidth         short int in struct NewWindow
        +0x0026  intuition/intuition.h: *901
MinX             short int in struct Rectangle
        +0x0000  graphics/gfx.h: *25
MinY             short int in struct Rectangle
        +0x0002  graphics/gfx.h: *25
MISCNAME         #define "misc.resource" resources/misc.h: *44
MiscResource     structure tag
    size 0x0032  resources/misc.h: *35
mlh_Head         pointer to struct MinNode in struct MinList
        +0x0000  exec/lists.h: *29
mlh_Tail         pointer to struct MinNode in struct MinList
        +0x0004  exec/lists.h: *30
mlh_TailPred     pointer to struct MinNode in struct MinList
        +0x0008  exec/lists.h: *31
mln_Pred         pointer to struct MinNode in struct MinNode
        +0x0004  exec/nodes.h: *25
mln_Succ         pointer to struct MinNode in struct MinNode
        +0x0000  exec/nodes.h: *24
ml_ME            array [1] of struct MemEntry (size 0x0008) in struct MemList
        +0x0010  exec/memory.h: *58
ml_me            #define ml_ME =0x00000000 exec/memory.h: *61
ml_Node          struct Node (size 0x000e) in struct MemList
        +0x0000  exec/memory.h: *56
ml_NumEntries    unsigned short int in struct MemList
        +0x000e  exec/memory.h: *57
mn_Length        unsigned short int in struct Message
        +0x0012  exec/ports.h: *50
mn_Node          struct Node (size 0x000e) in struct Message
        +0x0000  exec/ports.h: *48
mn_ReplyPort     pointer to struct MsgPort in struct Message
        +0x000e  exec/ports.h: *49
mode             unsigned short int in struct narrator_rb
        +0x0034  devices/narrator.h: *71
Modes            unsigned short int in struct ViewPort
        +0x0020  graphics/view.h: *41
Modes            unsigned short int in struct View
        +0x0010  graphics/view.h: *54
```

```
Modes               unsigned short int in struct GfxBase
         +0x009e    graphics/gfxbase.h: *37
MODE_640            #define 0x8000 =0x00008000 graphics/display.h: *14
MODE_NEWFILE        #define 1006 =0x000003ee libraries/dos.h: *28
MODE_OLDFILE        #define 1005 =0x000003ed libraries/dos.h: *26
MODE_READWRITE      #define 1004 =0x000003ec libraries/dos.h: *30
MountList           struct List (size 0x000e) in struct ExpansionBase
         +0x004a    libraries/expansionbase.h: *52
MOUSEBUTTONS        #define 0x00000008 =0x00000008 intuition/intuition.h: *641
MOUSEMOVE           #define 0x00000010 =0x00000010 intuition/intuition.h: *642
MouseX              short int in struct IntuiMessage
         +0x0020    intuition/intuition.h: *620
MouseX              short int in struct Window
         +0x000e    intuition/intuition.h: *700
MouseX              short int in struct Screen
         +0x0012    intuition/screens.h: *48
MouseX              short int in struct IntuitionBase
         +0x0046    intuition/intuitionbase.h: *161
MouseY              short int in struct IntuiMessage
         +0x0022    intuition/intuition.h: *620
MouseY              short int in struct Window
         +0x000c    intuition/intuition.h: *700
MouseY              short int in struct Screen
         +0x0010    intuition/screens.h: *48
MouseY              short int in struct IntuitionBase
         +0x0044    intuition/intuitionbase.h: *161
mouths              char in struct narrator_rb
         +0x0042    devices/narrator.h: *77
mouth_rb            structure tag
     size 0x004a    devices/narrator.h: *87
mp_Flags            char in struct MsgPort
         +0x000e    exec/ports.h: *30
mp_MsgList          struct List (size 0x000e) in struct MsgPort
         +0x0014    exec/ports.h: *33
mp_Node             struct Node (size 0x000e) in struct MsgPort
         +0x0000    exec/ports.h: *29
mp_SigBit           char in struct MsgPort
         +0x000f    exec/ports.h: *31
mp_SigTask          pointer to struct Task in struct MsgPort
         +0x0010    exec/ports.h: *32
mp_SoftInt          #define mp_SigTask =0x00000000 exec/ports.h: *36
mr_AllocArray       array [4] of unsigned int in struct MiscResource
         +0x0022    resources/misc.h: *37
MR_ALLOCMISCRESOURCE #define (LIB_BASE) =0xfffffffa resources/misc.h: *40
MR_FREEMISCRESOURCE #define (LIB_BASE + LIB_VECSIZE) =0xfffffffa
                    resources/misc.h: *41
mr_Library          struct Library (size 0x0022) in struct MiscResource
         +0x0000    resources/misc.h: *36
MR_PARALLELBITS     #define 3 =0x00000003 resources/misc.h: *31
MR_PARALLELPORT     #define 2 =0x00000002 resources/misc.h: *30
MR_SERIALBITS       #define 1 =0x00000001 resources/misc.h: *29
MR_SERIALPORT       #define 0 =0x00000000 resources/misc.h: *28
MsgPort             structure tag
     size 0x0022    exec/ports.h: *28, 49
                    exec/devices.h: 32
                    exec/semaphores.h: 33
                    devices/conunit.h: 35
                    libraries/dosextens.h: 36, 62, 63, 81, 228, 258, 294
                    intuition/intuition.h: 754
                    devices/prtbase.h: 61, 86
                    libraries/filehandler.h: 99
                    workbench/startup.h: 27
MTYPE_CLOSEDOWN     #define 5 =0x00000005 workbench/workbench.h: *82
MTYPE_DISKCHANGE    #define 3 =0x00000003 workbench/workbench.h: *80
MTYPE_IOPROC        #define 6 =0x00000006 workbench/workbench.h: *83
MTYPE_PSTD          #define 1 =0x00000001 workbench/workbench.h: *78
MTYPE_TIMER         #define 4 =0x00000004 workbench/workbench.h: *81
MTYPE_TOOLEXIT      #define 2 =0x00000002 workbench/workbench.h: *79
MULTIPLY_DIMENSIONS #define 0x0080 =0x00000080 intuition/preferences.h: *245
```



```
MUSTDRAW            #define 0x0008 =0x00000008 graphics/gels.h: *19
MutualExclude       int in struct MenuItem
         +0x000e    intuition/intuition.h: *92
MutualExclude       int in struct Gadget
         +0x001e    intuition/intuition.h: *229
M_ASM               #define ">1" devices/console.h: *89
M_AWM               #define "?7" devices/console.h: *90
M_LNM               #define 20 =0x00000014 devices/console.h: *88
                    devices/conunit.h: 77
n                   pointer to struct bltnode in struct bltnode
         +0x0000    hardware/blit.h: *82
NABC                #define 0x8 =0x00000008 hardware/blit.h: *26
NABNC               #define 0x4 =0x00000004 hardware/blit.h: *27
NANBC               #define 0x2 =0x00000002 hardware/blit.h: *28
NANBNC              #define 0x1 =0x00000001 hardware/blit.h: *29
narrator_rb         structure tag
     size 0x0046    devices/narrator.h: *67, 88
NATURALF0           #define 0 =0x00000000 devices/narrator.h: *45
ND_CantAlloc        #define -6 =0xfffffffa devices/narrator.h: *23
ND_Expunged         #define -9 =0xfffffff7 devices/narrator.h: *26
ND_FreqErr          #define -25 =0xffffffe7 devices/narrator.h: *32
ND_MakeBad          #define -4 =0xfffffffc devices/narrator.h: *21
ND_ModeErr          #define -24 =0xffffffe8 devices/narrator.h: *31
ND_NoAudLib         #define -3 =0xfffffffd devices/narrator.h: *20
ND_NoMem            #define -2 =0xfffffffe devices/narrator.h: *19
ND_NoWrite          #define -8 =0xfffffff8 devices/narrator.h: *25
ND_PhonErr          #define -20 =0xffffffec devices/narrator.h: *27
ND_PitchErr         #define -22 =0xffffffea devices/narrator.h: *29
ND_RateErr          #define -21 =0xffffffeb devices/narrator.h: *28
ND_SexErr           #define -23 =0xffffffe9 devices/narrator.h: *30
ND_Unimpl           #define -7 =0xfffffff9 devices/narrator.h: *24
ND_UnitErr          #define -5 =0xfffffffb devices/narrator.h: *22
ND_VolErr           #define -26 =0xffffffe6 devices/narrator.h: *33
NEWLAYERINFO_CALLED #define 1 =0x00000001 graphics/layers.h: *49
NEWLOCKS            #define =0x00000000 graphics/clip.h: *23
NEWPREFS            #define 0x00004000 =0x00004000 intuition/intuition.h: *652
NewScreen           structure tag
     size 0x0020    intuition/screens.h: *117
NEWSIZE             #define 0x00000002 =0x00000002 intuition/intuition.h: *639
NewWindow           structure tag
     size 0x0030    intuition/intuition.h: *850
                    workbench/workbench.h: 42
Next                pointer to struct ClipRect in struct ClipRect
         +0x0000    graphics/clip.h: *56
Next                pointer to struct ViewPort in struct ViewPort
         +0x0000    graphics/view.h: *32
Next                pointer to struct RasInfo in struct RasInfo
         +0x0000    graphics/view.h: *71
Next                pointer to struct cprlist in struct cprlist
         +0x0000    graphics/copper.h: *50
Next                pointer to struct CopList in struct CopList
         +0x0000    graphics/copper.h: *57
Next                pointer to struct UCopList in struct UCopList
         +0x0000    graphics/copper.h: *71
Next                pointer to struct RegionRectangle in struct RegionRectangle
         +0x0000    graphics/regions.h: *19
NextBorder          pointer to struct Border in struct Border
         +0x000c    intuition/intuition.h: *529
NextComp            pointer to struct AnimComp in struct AnimComp
         +0x0006    graphics/gels.h: *182
NextGadget          pointer to struct Gadget in struct Gadget
         +0x0000    intuition/intuition.h: *195
NextImage           pointer to struct Image in struct Image
         +0x0010    intuition/intuition.h: *585
NextItem            pointer to struct MenuItem in struct MenuItem
         +0x0000    intuition/intuition.h: *87
nextLine            pointer to short int in struct GelsInfo
         +0x000a    graphics/rastport.h: *42
NextMenu            pointer to struct Menu in struct Menu
```

```
        +0x0000  intuition/intuition.h: *59
NextOb           pointer to struct AnimOb in struct AnimOb
        +0x0000  graphics/gels.h: *202
NextRemember     pointer to struct Remember in struct Remember
        +0x0000  intuition/intuition.h: *930
NextScreen       pointer to struct Screen in struct Screen
        +0x0000  intuition/screens.h: *42
NextSelect       unsigned short int in struct MenuItem
        +0x0020  intuition/intuition.h: *108
NextSeq          pointer to struct AnimComp in struct AnimComp
        +0x000e  graphics/gels.h: *186
NextText         pointer to struct IntuiText in struct IntuiText
        +0x0010  intuition/intuition.h: *502
NextVSprite      pointer to struct VSprite in struct VSprite
        +0x0000  graphics/gels.h: *72
NextWindow       pointer to struct Window in struct Window
        +0x0000  intuition/intuition.h: *695
nm_masks         unsigned short int in struct narrator_rb
        +0x003c  devices/narrator.h: *74
NOCAREREFRESH    #define 0x00020000 =0x00020000 intuition/intuition.h: *831
NOCROSSFILL      #define 0x20 =0x00000020 graphics/rastport.h: *102
Node             structure tag
    size 0x000e  exec/nodes.h: *14, 15, 16
                 exec/libraries.h: 31
                 exec/lists.h: 20, 21, 22
                 exec/tasks.h: 23
                 exec/ports.h: 29, 48
                 exec/interrupts.h: 23, 32
                 exec/memory.h: 29, 56
                 exec/semaphores.h: 50
                 devices/clipboard.h: 31
                 devices/keymap.h: 32, 38
                 graphics/graphint.h: 20
                 libraries/configvars.h: 27
                 libraries/diskfont.h: 51
                 libraries/romboot_base.h: 42
                 resources/filesysres.h: 27, 33
                 resources/mathresource.h: 37
NOISYREQ         #define 0x0004 =0x00000004 intuition/intuition.h: *176
NOITEM           #define 0x003F =0x0000003f intuition/intuition.h: *962
NOMENU           #define 0x001F =0x0000001f intuition/intuition.h: *961
NormalDisplayColumns unsigned short int in struct GfxBase
        +0x00da  graphics/gfxbase.h: *57
NormalDisplayRows unsigned short int in struct GfxBase
        +0x00d8  graphics/gfxbase.h: *56
NormalDPMX       unsigned short int in struct GfxBase
        +0x00dc  graphics/gfxbase.h: *59
NormalDPMY       unsigned short int in struct GfxBase
        +0x00de  graphics/gfxbase.h: *60
NOSUB            #define 0x001F =0x0000001f intuition/intuition.h: *963
NOT              #define !
                 intuition/intuition.h: *970
NO_ICON_POSITION #define (0x80000000) =0x80000000 workbench/workbench.h: *97
NTSC             #define 1 =0x00000001 graphics/gfxbase.h: *68
NT_BOOTNODE      #define 16 =0x00000010 exec/nodes.h: *46
NT_DEVICE        #define 3 =0x00000003 exec/nodes.h: *33
NT_FONT          #define 12 =0x0000000c exec/nodes.h: *42
NT_FREEMSG       #define 6 =0x00000006 exec/nodes.h: *36
NT_INTERRUPT     #define 2 =0x00000002 exec/nodes.h: *32
NT_LIBRARY       #define 9 =0x00000009 exec/nodes.h: *39
NT_MEMORY        #define 10 =0x0000000a exec/nodes.h: *40
NT_MESSAGE       #define 5 =0x00000005 exec/nodes.h: *35
NT_MSGPORT       #define 4 =0x00000004 exec/nodes.h: *34
NT_PROCESS       #define 13 =0x0000000d exec/nodes.h: *43
NT_REPLYMSG      #define 7 =0x00000007 exec/nodes.h: *37
NT_RESOURCE      #define 8 =0x00000008 exec/nodes.h: *38
NT_SEMAPHORE     #define 14 =0x0000000e exec/nodes.h: *44
NT_SIGNALSEM     #define 15 =0x0000000f exec/nodes.h: *45
NT_SOFTINT       #define 11 =0x0000000b exec/nodes.h: *41
```



```
NT_TASK          #define 1 =0x00000001 exec/nodes.h: *31
NT_UNKNOWN       #define 0 =0x00000000 exec/nodes.h: *30
NULL             #define 0 =0x00000000 exec/types.h: *52
num              unsigned short int in struct SimpleSprite
         +0x000a graphics/sprite.h: *20
numchan          char in struct narrator_rb
         +0x0044 devices/narrator.h: *79
NumChars         short int in struct StringInfo
         +0x0010 intuition/intuition.h: *462
NUMMRTYPES       #define 4 =0x00000004 resources/misc.h: *33, 37
NUMSECS          #define 11 =0x0000000b devices/trackdisk.h: *35
NUMUNITS         #define 4 =0x00000004 devices/trackdisk.h: *36
nxtlist          pointer to struct CopList in union (no tag)
         +0x0000 graphics/copper.h: *23
NXTLIST          #define u3.nxtlist
                 graphics/copper.h: *40
N_TRACTOR        #define 0x20 =0x00000020 intuition/preferences.h: *181
obs              pointer to struct Layer in struct Layer_Info
         +0x0008 graphics/layers.h: *36
OCTANT1          #define 16 =0x00000010 hardware/blit.h: *77
OCTANT2          #define 0 =0x00000000 hardware/blit.h: *76
OCTANT3          #define 8 =0x00000008 hardware/blit.h: *75
OCTANT4          #define 20 =0x00000014 hardware/blit.h: *74
OCTANT5          #define 28 =0x0000001c hardware/blit.h: *73
OCTANT6          #define 12 =0x0000000c hardware/blit.h: *72
OCTANT7          #define 4 =0x00000004 hardware/blit.h: *71
OCTANT8          #define 24 =0x00000018 hardware/blit.h: *70
OFFSET_BEGINING  #define OFFSET_BEGINNING =0xffffffff libraries/dos.h: *35
OFFSET_BEGINNING #define -1 =0xffffffff libraries/dos.h: *31
OFFSET_CURRENT   #define 0 =0x00000000 libraries/dos.h: *32
OFFSET_END       #define 1 =0x00000001 libraries/dos.h: *33
OFF_DISPLAY      #define custom.dmacon = BITCLR|DMAF_RASTER;
                 graphics/gfxmacros.h: *18
OFF_SPRITE       #define custom.dmacon = BITCLR|DMAF_SPRITE;
                 graphics/gfxmacros.h: *20
OFF_VBLANK       #define custom.intena = BITCLR|INTF_VERTB;
                 graphics/gfxmacros.h: *23
OKABORT          #define 0x0004 =0x00000004 intuition/intuition.h: *681
OKCANCEL         #define MENUCANCEL =0x00000002 intuition/intuition.h: *682
OKIMATE_20       #define 0x09 =0x00000009 intuition/preferences.h: *195
OKOK             #define MENUHOT =0x00000001 intuition/intuition.h: *680
OlderRequest     pointer to struct Requester in struct Requester
         +0x0000 intuition/intuition.h: *144
OldX             short int in struct VSprite
         +0x0012 graphics/gels.h: *85
OldY             short int in struct VSprite
         +0x0010 graphics/gels.h: *85
ONEDOT           #define 0x2 =0x00000002 hardware/blit.h: *61
ONE_DOT          #define 0x02 =0x00000002 graphics/rastport.h: *95
ON_DISPLAY       #define custom.dmacon = BITSET|DMAF_RASTER;
                 graphics/gfxmacros.h: *17
ON_SPRITE        #define custom.dmacon = BITSET|DMAF_SPRITE;
                 graphics/gfxmacros.h: *19
ON_VBLANK        #define custom.intena = BITSET|INTF_VERTB;
                 graphics/gfxmacros.h: *22
OpCode           short int in struct CopIns
         +0x0000 graphics/copper.h: *20
ORDERED_DITHERING #define 0x0000 =0x00000000 intuition/preferences.h: *249
OTHER_REFRESH    #define 0x00C0 =0x000000c0 intuition/intuition.h: *812
OUTSTEP          #define 0x2000 =0x00002000 graphics/gels.h: *37
OVERLAY          #define 0x0004 =0x00000004 graphics/gels.h: *18
OVFLAG           #define 0x20 =0x00000020 hardware/blit.h: *62
pad              char in struct narrator_rb
         +0x0045 devices/narrator.h: *80
pad              char in struct mouth_rb
         +0x0049 devices/narrator.h: *92
pad              unsigned short int in struct BitMap
         +0x0006 graphics/gfx.h: *42
pad              char in struct ExpansionBase
```

```
        +0x0023  libraries/expansionbase.h: *47
pad0             array [255] of char in struct CIA
        +0x0001  hardware/cia.h: *24
pad1             array [255] of char in struct CIA
        +0x0101  hardware/cia.h: *26
pad10            array [255] of char in struct CIA
        +0x0a01  hardware/cia.h: *44
pad11            array [255] of char in struct CIA
        +0x0b01  hardware/cia.h: *46
pad12            array [255] of char in struct CIA
        +0x0c01  hardware/cia.h: *48
pad13            array [255] of char in struct CIA
        +0x0d01  hardware/cia.h: *50
pad14            array [255] of char in struct CIA
        +0x0e01  hardware/cia.h: *52
pad2             array [255] of char in struct CIA
        +0x0201  hardware/cia.h: *28
pad2d            array [3] of unsigned short int in struct Custom
        +0x005a  hardware/custom.h: *60
pad3             array [255] of char in struct CIA
        +0x0301  hardware/cia.h: *30
pad34            array [4] of unsigned short int in struct Custom
        +0x0068  hardware/custom.h: *65
pad3b            array [4] of unsigned short int in struct Custom
        +0x0076  hardware/custom.h: *69
pad4             array [255] of char in struct CIA
        +0x0401  hardware/cia.h: *32
pad5             array [255] of char in struct CIA
        +0x0501  hardware/cia.h: *34
pad6             array [255] of char in struct CIA
        +0x0601  hardware/cia.h: *36
pad7             array [255] of char in struct CIA
        +0x0701  hardware/cia.h: *38
pad7c            array [4] of unsigned short int in struct Custom
        +0x00f8  hardware/custom.h: *94
pad8             array [255] of char in struct CIA
        +0x0801  hardware/cia.h: *40
pad83            unsigned short int in struct Custom
        +0x0106  hardware/custom.h: *98
pad86            array [2] of unsigned short int in struct Custom
        +0x010c  hardware/custom.h: *101
pad8e            array [2] of unsigned short int in struct Custom
        +0x011c  hardware/custom.h: *103
pad9             array [255] of char in struct CIA
        +0x0901  hardware/cia.h: *42
PAL              #define 4 =0x00000004 graphics/gfxbase.h: *70
PaperLength      unsigned short int in struct Preferences
        +0x00b2  intuition/preferences.h: *97
PaperSize        unsigned short int in struct Preferences
        +0x00b0  intuition/preferences.h: *96
PaperType        unsigned short int in struct Preferences
        +0x00b4  intuition/preferences.h: *98
PARALLELNAME     #define "parallel.device" devices/parallel.h: *80
PARALLEL_PRINTER #define 0x00 =0x00000000 intuition/preferences.h: *135
PARB_EOFMODE     #define 1 =0x00000001 devices/parallel.h: *60
PARB_RAD_BOOGIE  #define 3 =0x00000003 devices/parallel.h: *58
PARB_SHARED      #define 5 =0x00000005 devices/parallel.h: *56
Parent           pointer to struct Window in struct Window
        +0x0042  intuition/intuition.h: *742
ParErr_BufTooBig #define 2 =0x00000002 devices/parallel.h: *86
ParErr_DevBusy   #define 1 =0x00000001 devices/parallel.h: *85
ParErr_InitErr   #define 7 =0x00000007 devices/parallel.h: *91
ParErr_InvParam  #define 3 =0x00000003 devices/parallel.h: *87
ParErr_LineErr   #define 4 =0x00000004 devices/parallel.h: *88
ParErr_NotOpen   #define 5 =0x00000005 devices/parallel.h: *89
ParErr_PortReset #define 6 =0x00000006 devices/parallel.h: *90
PARF_EOFMODE     #define (1<<1) =0x00000002 devices/parallel.h: *61
PARF_RAD_BOOGIE  #define (1<<3) =0x00000008 devices/parallel.h: *59
PARF_SHARED      #define (1<<5) =0x00000020 devices/parallel.h: *57
```



```
PartitionBlock     structure tag
    size 0x0100    devices/hardblocks.h: *126
PA_IGNORE          #define 2 =0x00000002 exec/ports.h: *42
PA_SIGNAL          #define 0 =0x00000000 exec/ports.h: *40
PA_SOFTINT         #define 1 =0x00000001 exec/ports.h: *41
PBFB_BOOTABLE      #define 0 =0x00000000 devices/hardblocks.h: *144
PBFB_NOMOUNT       #define 1 =0x00000001 devices/hardblocks.h: *146
PBFF_BOOTABLE      #define 1L devices/hardblocks.h: *145
PBFF_NOMOUNT       #define 2L devices/hardblocks.h: *147
pb_ChkSum          int in struct PartitionBlock
          +0x0008  devices/hardblocks.h: *129
pb_DevFlags        unsigned int in struct PartitionBlock
          +0x0020  devices/hardblocks.h: *134
pb_DriveName       array [32] of char in struct PartitionBlock
          +0x0024  devices/hardblocks.h: *135
pb_Environment     array [17] of unsigned int in struct PartitionBlock
          +0x0080  devices/hardblocks.h: *138
pb_EReserved       array [15] of unsigned int in struct PartitionBlock
          +0x00c4  devices/hardblocks.h: *139
pb_Flags           unsigned int in struct PartitionBlock
          +0x0014  devices/hardblocks.h: *132
pb_HostID          unsigned int in struct PartitionBlock
          +0x000c  devices/hardblocks.h: *130
pb_ID              unsigned int in struct PartitionBlock
          +0x0000  devices/hardblocks.h: *127
pb_Next            unsigned int in struct PartitionBlock
          +0x0010  devices/hardblocks.h: *131
pb_Reserved1       array [2] of unsigned int in struct PartitionBlock
          +0x0018  devices/hardblocks.h: *133
pb_Reserved2       array [15] of unsigned int in struct PartitionBlock
          +0x0044  devices/hardblocks.h: *137
pb_SummedLongs     unsigned int in struct PartitionBlock
          +0x0004  devices/hardblocks.h: *128
PCC_4COLOR         #define 0x04 =0x00000004 devices/prtbase.h: *111
PCC_ADDITIVE       #define 0x08 =0x00000008 devices/prtbase.h: *112
PCC_BGR            #define 0x0A =0x0000000a devices/prtbase.h: *114
PCC_BGRW           #define 0x0C =0x0000000c devices/prtbase.h: *116
PCC_BGR_WB         #define 0x0B =0x0000000b devices/prtbase.h: *115
PCC_BW             #define 0x01 =0x00000001 devices/prtbase.h: *107
PCC_MULTI_PASS     #define 0x10 =0x00000010 devices/prtbase.h: *124
PCC_WB             #define 0x09 =0x00000009 devices/prtbase.h: *113
PCC_YMC            #define 0x02 =0x00000002 devices/prtbase.h: *108
PCC_YMCB           #define 0x04 =0x00000004 devices/prtbase.h: *110
PCC_YMC_BW         #define 0x03 =0x00000003 devices/prtbase.h: *109
PCMBLACK           #define 3 =0x00000003 devices/prtgfx.h: *16
PCMBLUE            #define PCMYELLOW =0x00000000 devices/prtgfx.h: *17
PCMCYAN            #define 2 =0x00000002 devices/prtgfx.h: *15
PCMGREEN           #define PCMMAGENTA =0x00000001 devices/prtgfx.h: *18
PCMMAGENTA         #define 1 =0x00000001 devices/prtgfx.h: *14
PCMRED             #define PCMCYAN =0x00000002 devices/prtgfx.h: *19
PCMWHITE           #define PCMBLACK =0x00000003 devices/prtgfx.h: *20
PCMYELLOW          #define 0 =0x00000000 devices/prtgfx.h: *13
PDCMD_QUERY        #define (CMD_NONSTD) =0x00000009 devices/parallel.h: *82
PDCMD_SETPARAMS    #define (CMD_NONSTD+1) =0x0000000a devices/parallel.h: *83
PDERR_BADDIMENSION #define 4 =0x00000004 devices/printer.h: *201
PDERR_BUFFERMEMORY #define 7 =0x00000007 devices/printer.h: *204
PDERR_CANCEL       #define 1 =0x00000001 devices/printer.h: *198
PDERR_DIMENSIONOVFLOW #define 5 =0x00000005 devices/printer.h: *202
PDERR_INTERNALMEMORY #define 6 =0x00000006 devices/printer.h: *203
PDERR_INVERTHAM    #define 3 =0x00000003 devices/printer.h: *200
PDERR_NOERR        #define 0 =0x00000000 devices/printer.h: *197
PDERR_NOTGRAPHICS  #define 2 =0x00000002 devices/printer.h: *199
PDERR_TOOKCONTROL  #define 8 =0x00000008 devices/printer.h: *212
pd_Device          struct DeviceData (size 0x0034) in struct PrinterData
          +0x0000  devices/prtbase.h: *60
pd_Flags           char in struct PrinterData
          +0x09b6  devices/prtbase.h: *89
pd_ior0            union (no tag) (size 0x0052) in struct PrinterData
          +0x006c  devices/prtbase.h: *72
```

```
pd_iorl             union (no tag) (size 0x0052) in struct PrinterData
          +0x00be   devices/prtbase.h: *80
pd_IORPort          struct MsgPort (size 0x0022) in struct PrinterData
          +0x0138   devices/prtbase.h: *86
pd_p0               struct IOExtPar (size 0x003e) in union (no tag)
          +0x0000   devices/prtbase.h: *70
pd_pl               struct IOExtPar (size 0x003e) in union (no tag)
          +0x0000   devices/prtbase.h: *78
pd_pad              char in struct PrinterData
          +0x09b7   devices/prtbase.h: *90
pd_PBothReady       pointer to function returning int in struct PrinterData
          +0x0068   devices/prtbase.h: *68
pd_PIOR0            #define pd_ior0.pd_p0 devices/prtbase.h: *74
pd_PIORl            #define pd_iorl.pd_pl devices/prtbase.h: *82
pd_Preferences      struct Preferences (size 0x00e8) in struct PrinterData
          +0x09b8   devices/prtbase.h: *91
pd_PrintBuf         pointer to char in struct PrinterData
          +0x0060   devices/prtbase.h: *66
pd_PrinterSegment int in struct PrinterData
          +0x0056   devices/prtbase.h: *62
pd_PrinterType      unsigned short int in struct PrinterData
          +0x005a   devices/prtbase.h: *63
pd_PWaitEnabled     char in struct PrinterData
          +0x0aa0   devices/prtbase.h: *92
pd_PWrite           pointer to function returning int in struct PrinterData
          +0x0064   devices/prtbase.h: *67
pd_s0               struct IOExtSer (size 0x0052) in union (no tag)
          +0x0000   devices/prtbase.h: *71
pd_sl               struct IOExtSer (size 0x0052) in union (no tag)
          +0x0000   devices/prtbase.h: *79
pd_SegmentData      pointer to struct PrinterSegment in struct PrinterData
          +0x005c   devices/prtbase.h: *65
pd_SIOR0            #define pd_ior0.pd_s0 devices/prtbase.h: *75
pd_SIORl            #define pd_iorl.pd_sl devices/prtbase.h: *83
pd_Stk              array [2048] of char in struct PrinterData
          +0x01b6   devices/prtbase.h: *88
pd_TC               struct Task (size 0x005c) in struct PrinterData
          +0x015a   devices/prtbase.h: *87
pd_TIOR             struct timerequest (size 0x0028) in struct PrinterData
          +0x0110   devices/prtbase.h: *85
pd_Unit             struct MsgPort (size 0x0022) in struct PrinterData
          +0x0034   devices/prtbase.h: *61
ped_8BitChars       pointer to pointer to char in struct PrinterExtendedData
          +0x0036   devices/prtbase.h: *146
ped_Close           pointer to function returning void in struct PrinterExtendedData
          +0x0010   devices/prtbase.h: *131
ped_ColorClass      char in struct PrinterExtendedData
          +0x0015   devices/prtbase.h: *133
ped_Commands        pointer to pointer to pointer to char in struct
                    PrinterExtendedData
          +0x0026   devices/prtbase.h: *141
ped_ConvFunc        pointer to function returning int in struct PrinterExtendedData
          +0x003e   devices/prtbase.h: *150
ped_DoSpecial       pointer to function returning int in struct PrinterExtendedData
          +0x002a   devices/prtbase.h: *142
ped_Expunge         pointer to function returning void in struct PrinterExtendedData
          +0x0008   devices/prtbase.h: *129
ped_Init            pointer to function returning void in struct PrinterExtendedData
          +0x0004   devices/prtbase.h: *128
ped_MaxColumns      char in struct PrinterExtendedData
          +0x0016   devices/prtbase.h: *134
ped_MaxXDots        unsigned int in struct PrinterExtendedData
          +0x001a   devices/prtbase.h: *137
ped_MaxYDots        unsigned int in struct PrinterExtendedData
          +0x001e   devices/prtbase.h: *138
ped_NumCharSets     char in struct PrinterExtendedData
          +0x0017   devices/prtbase.h: *135
ped_NumRows         unsigned short int in struct PrinterExtendedData
          +0x0018   devices/prtbase.h: *136
```



```
ped_Open            pointer to function returning int in struct PrinterExtendedData
          +0x000c   devices/prtbase.h: *130
ped_PrinterClass char in struct PrinterExtendedData
          +0x0014   devices/prtbase.h: *132
ped_PrinterName     pointer to char in struct PrinterExtendedData
          +0x0000   devices/prtbase.h: *127
ped_PrintMode       int in struct PrinterExtendedData
          +0x003a   devices/prtbase.h: *147
ped_Render          pointer to function returning int in struct PrinterExtendedData
          +0x002e   devices/prtbase.h: *143
ped_TimeoutSecs     int in struct PrinterExtendedData
          +0x0032   devices/prtbase.h: *144
ped_XDotsInch       unsigned short int in struct PrinterExtendedData
          +0x0022   devices/prtbase.h: *139
ped_YDotsInch       unsigned short int in struct PrinterExtendedData
          +0x0024   devices/prtbase.h: *140
PenHeight           short int in struct RastPort
          +0x0032   graphics/rastport.h: *71
PenWidth            short int in struct RastPort
          +0x0030   graphics/rastport.h: *70
PF2PRI              #define 0x40 =0x00000040 graphics/display.h: *18
PFA_FINE_SCROLL     #define 0xF =0x0000000f graphics/display.h: *25
PFBA                #define 0x40 =0x00000040 graphics/view.h: *58
PFB_FINE_SCROLL_SHIFT #define 4 =0x00000004 graphics/display.h: *26
PF_ACTION           #define 3 =0x00000003 exec/ports.h: *38
PF_FINE_SCROLL_MASK #define 0xF =0x0000000f graphics/display.h: *27
PI                  #define ((float) 3.141592653589793) libraries/mathffp.h: *14
PI2                 #define (PI / ((float) 2)) libraries/mathffp.h: *17
PI2                 #define (PI/((double)2)) libraries/mathieeedp.h: *18
PI4                 #define (PI / ((float) 4)) libraries/mathffp.h: *18
PI4                 #define (PI/((double)4)) libraries/mathieeedp.h: *19
PICA                #define 0x000 =0x00000000 intuition/preferences.h: *153
pitch               unsigned short int in struct narrator_rb
          +0x0032   devices/narrator.h: *70
PIXEL_DIMENSIONS #define 0x0040 =0x00000040 intuition/preferences.h: *244
pi_ColorInt         pointer to union colorEntry in struct PrtInfo
          +0x0018   devices/prtgfx.h: *32
pi_dmatrix          pointer to char in struct PrtInfo
          +0x0030   devices/prtgfx.h: *38
pi_ScaleX           pointer to unsigned short int in struct PrtInfo
          +0x0028   devices/prtgfx.h: *36
pi_height           unsigned short int in struct PrtInfo
          +0x005a   devices/prtgfx.h: *57
pi_threshold        unsigned short int in struct PrtInfo
          +0x006c   devices/prtgfx.h: *64
pi_width            unsigned short int in struct PrtInfo
          +0x0058   devices/prtgfx.h: *56
pi_xpos             unsigned short int in struct PrtInfo
          +0x006a   devices/prtgfx.h: *63
PlaneOnOff          char in struct Image
          +0x000f   intuition/intuition.h: *579
PlaneOnOff          char in struct VSprite
          +0x0039   graphics/gels.h: *130
PlanePick           char in struct Image
          +0x000e   intuition/intuition.h: *579
PlanePick           char in struct VSprite
          +0x0038   graphics/gels.h: *129
PLANEPTR            typedef pointer to "UBYTE"
                    graphics/gfx.h: *34, 43
Planes              array [8] of pointer to char in struct BitMap
          +0x0008   graphics/gfx.h: *43
PLNCNTMSK           #define 0x7 =0x00000007 graphics/display.h: *15
PLNCNTSHFT          #define 12 =0x0000000c graphics/display.h: *17
PMB_ASM             #define (M_LNM+1) =0x00000015 devices/conunit.h: *29, 77
PMB_AWM             #define (PMB_ASM+1) =0x00000016 devices/conunit.h: *30, 77
Point               typedef struct tPoint (size 0x0004)
                    graphics/gfx.h: *32
Pointer             pointer to unsigned short int in struct Window
          +0x004a   intuition/intuition.h: *747
```

```
PointerMatrix       array [36] of unsigned short int in struct Preferences
        +0x001c     intuition/preferences.h: *59
POINTERSIZE         #define (1 + 16 + 1) * 2 =0x00000024
                    intuition/preferences.h: *28, 59
PointerTicks        unsigned short int in struct Preferences
        +0x006c     intuition/preferences.h: *65
POINTREL            #define 0x0001 =0x00000001 intuition/intuition.h: *174
PortList            struct List (size 0x000e) in struct ExecBase
        +0x0188     exec/execbase.h: *82
pos                 unsigned short int in struct SpriteDef
        +0x0000     hardware/custom.h: *106
posctldata          pointer to unsigned short int in struct SimpleSprite
        +0x0000     graphics/sprite.h: *17
pot0dat             unsigned short int in struct Custom
        +0x0012     hardware/custom.h: *29
pot1dat             unsigned short int in struct Custom
        +0x0014     hardware/custom.h: *30
potgo               unsigned short int in struct Custom
        +0x0034     hardware/custom.h: *45
POTGONAME           #define "potgo.resource" resources/potgo.h: *13
potinp              unsigned short int in struct Custom
        +0x0016     hardware/custom.h: *31
pow                 Macro (2 arguments) libraries/mathffp.h: *44
pow                 Macro (2 arguments) libraries/mathieeedp.h: *45
PowerSupplyFrequency char in struct ExecBase
        +0x0213     exec/execbase.h: *105
PPCB_COLOR          #define 1 =0x00000001 devices/prtbase.h: *98
PPCB_GFX            #define 0 =0x00000000 devices/prtbase.h: *96
PPCF_COLOR          #define 0x2 =0x00000002 devices/prtbase.h: *99
PPCF_GFX            #define 0x1 =0x00000001 devices/prtbase.h: *97
PPC_BWALPHA         #define 0x00 =0x00000000 devices/prtbase.h: *101
PPC_BWGFX           #define 0x01 =0x00000001 devices/prtbase.h: *102
PPC_COLORALPHA      #define 0x02 =0x00000002 devices/prtbase.h: *103
PPC_COLORGFX        #define 0x03 =0x00000003 devices/prtbase.h: *104
PRD_DUMPRPORT       #define (CMD_NONSTD+2) =0x0000000b devices/printer.h: *27
PRD_PRTCOMMAND      #define (CMD_NONSTD+1) =0x0000000a devices/printer.h: *26
PRD_QUERY           #define (CMD_NONSTD+3) =0x0000000c devices/printer.h: *28
PRD_RAWWRITE        #define (CMD_NONSTD+0) =0x00000009 devices/printer.h: *25
PREDRAWN            #define 0x0002 =0x00000002 intuition/intuition.h: *175
Preferences         structure tag
    size 0x00e8     intuition/preferences.h: *42
                    devices/prtbase.h: 91
prev                pointer to struct ClipRect in struct ClipRect
        +0x0004     graphics/clip.h: *57
Prev                pointer to struct RegionRectangle in struct RegionRectangle
        +0x0004     graphics/regions.h: *19
PrevComp            pointer to struct AnimComp in struct AnimComp
        +0x000a     graphics/gels.h: *183
PrevOb              pointer to struct AnimOb in struct AnimOb
        +0x0004     graphics/gels.h: *202
PrevSeq             pointer to struct AnimComp in struct AnimComp
        +0x0012     graphics/gels.h: *187
PrevVSprite         pointer to struct VSprite in struct VSprite
        +0x0004     graphics/gels.h: *73
PRIMARY_CLIP        #define 0 =0x00000000 devices/clipboard.h: *51
PrintAspect         unsigned short int in struct Preferences
        +0x00aa     intuition/preferences.h: *91
PrintDensity        char in struct Preferences
        +0x00e0     intuition/preferences.h: *118
PrinterData         structure tag in struct PrinterData
    size 0x0aa1     devices/prtbase.h: *59
PrinterExtendedData structure tag
    size 0x0042     devices/prtbase.h: *126, 158
PrinterFilename     array [30] of char in struct Preferences
        +0x0080     intuition/preferences.h: *82
PrinterPort         char in struct Preferences
        +0x0001     intuition/preferences.h: *48
PrinterSegment      structure tag
    size 0x004e     devices/prtbase.h: 65, *153
```



```
PrinterType         unsigned short int in struct Preferences
        +0x007e     intuition/preferences.h: *81
PrintFlags          unsigned short int in struct Preferences
        +0x00da     intuition/preferences.h: *115
PrintImage          unsigned short int in struct Preferences
        +0x00a8     intuition/preferences.h: *90
PrintLeftMargin     unsigned short int in struct Preferences
        +0x00a4     intuition/preferences.h: *88
PrintMaxHeight      unsigned short int in struct Preferences
        +0x00de     intuition/preferences.h: *117
PrintMaxWidth       unsigned short int in struct Preferences
        +0x00dc     intuition/preferences.h: *116
PrintPitch          unsigned short int in struct Preferences
        +0x009e     intuition/preferences.h: *85
PrintQuality        unsigned short int in struct Preferences
        +0x00a0     intuition/preferences.h: *86
PrintRightMargin    unsigned short int in struct Preferences
        +0x00a6     intuition/preferences.h: *89
PrintShade          unsigned short int in struct Preferences
        +0x00ac     intuition/preferences.h: *92
PrintSpacing        unsigned short int in struct Preferences
        +0x00a2     intuition/preferences.h: *87
PrintThreshold      short int in struct Preferences
        +0x00ae     intuition/preferences.h: *93
PrintXOffset        char in struct Preferences
        +0x00e1     intuition/preferences.h: *119
priority            unsigned short int in struct Layer
        +0x001c     graphics/clip.h: *32
Process             structure tag
    size 0x00bc     libraries/dosextens.h: *34
PROPBORDERLESS      #define 0x0008 =0x00000008 intuition/intuition.h: *432
PROPGADGET          #define 0x0003 =0x00000003 intuition/intuition.h: *350
PropInfo            structure tag
    size 0x0016     intuition/intuition.h: *384
PrtInfo             structure tag
    size 0x0072     devices/prtgfx.h: *28
pr_CIS              int in struct Process
        +0x009c     libraries/dosextens.h: *45
pr_CLI              int in struct Process
        +0x00ac     libraries/dosextens.h: *49
pr_ConsoleTask      pointer to pointer to char in struct Process
        +0x00a4     libraries/dosextens.h: *47
pr_COS              int in struct Process
        +0x00a0     libraries/dosextens.h: *46
pr_CurrentDir       int in struct Process
        +0x0098     libraries/dosextens.h: *44
pr_FileSystemTask pointer to pointer to char in struct Process
        +0x00a8     libraries/dosextens.h: *48
pr_GlobVec          pointer to pointer to char in struct Process
        +0x0088     libraries/dosextens.h: *40
pr_MsgPort          struct MsgPort (size 0x0022) in struct Process
        +0x005c     libraries/dosextens.h: *36
pr_Pad              short int in struct Process
        +0x007e     libraries/dosextens.h: *37
pr_PktWait          pointer to pointer to char in struct Process
        +0x00b4     libraries/dosextens.h: *51
pr_Result2          int in struct Process
        +0x0094     libraries/dosextens.h: *43
pr_ReturnAddr       pointer to pointer to char in struct Process
        +0x00b0     libraries/dosextens.h: *50
pr_SegList          int in struct Process
        +0x0080     libraries/dosextens.h: *38
pr_StackBase        int in struct Process
        +0x0090     libraries/dosextens.h: *42
pr_StackSize        int in struct Process
        +0x0084     libraries/dosextens.h: *39
pr_Task             struct Task (size 0x005c) in struct Process
        +0x0000     libraries/dosextens.h: *35
pr_TaskNum          int in struct Process
```

```
        +0x008c  libraries/dosextens.h: *41
pr_WindowPtr     pointer to pointer to char in struct Process
        +0x00b8  libraries/dosextens.h: *52
ps_NextSegment   unsigned int in struct PrinterSegment
        +0x0000  devices/prtbase.h: *154
ps_PED           struct PrinterExtendedData (size 0x0042) in struct
                 PrinterSegment
        +0x000c  devices/prtbase.h: *158
ps_Revision      unsigned short int in struct PrinterSegment
        +0x000a  devices/prtbase.h: *157
ps_runAlert      unsigned int in struct PrinterSegment
        +0x0004  devices/prtbase.h: *155
ps_Version       unsigned short int in struct PrinterSegment
        +0x0008  devices/prtbase.h: *156
PTermArray0      unsigned int in struct IOPArray
        +0x0000  devices/parallel.h: *18
PTermArray1      unsigned int in struct IOPArray
        +0x0004  devices/parallel.h: *19
PtrHeight        char in struct Window
        +0x004e  intuition/intuition.h: *748
PtrWidth         char in struct Window
        +0x004f  intuition/intuition.h: *749
PutIcon          extern function returning "LONG" workbench/icon.h: *30
PutWBObject      extern function returning "LONG" workbench/icon.h: *30
P_BUFSIZE        #define 256 =0x00000100 devices/prtbase.h: *56
P_SAFESIZE       #define 128 =0x00000080 devices/prtbase.h: *57
P_STKSIZE        #define 0x0800 =0x00000800 devices/prtbase.h: *55, 88
Qualifier        unsigned short int in struct IntuiMessage
        +0x001a  intuition/intuition.h: *609
Quantum          unsigned short int in struct ExecBase
        +0x0120  exec/execbase.h: *58
QUME_LP_20       #define 0x0A =0x0000000a intuition/preferences.h: *196
RasInfo          structure tag
    size 0x000c  graphics/view.h: 44, *69, 71
RasInfo          pointer to struct RasInfo in struct ViewPort
        +0x0024  graphics/view.h: *44
RasPtr           pointer to char in struct TmpRas
        +0x0000  graphics/rastport.h: *30
RASSIZE          Macro (2 arguments) graphics/gfx.h: *46
RastPort         structure tag
    size 0x0064  devices/printer.h: 157
                 graphics/clip.h: 29
                 graphics/rastport.h: *50
                 intuition/intuition.h: 718, 731
                 intuition/screens.h: 63
                 devices/prtgfx.h: 30, 31
RastPort         struct RastPort (size 0x0064) in struct Screen
        +0x0054  intuition/screens.h: *63
rate             unsigned short int in struct narrator_rb
        +0x0030  devices/narrator.h: *69
RAWKEY           #define 0x00000400 =0x00000400 intuition/intuition.h: *648
RDBFB_CTRLRID    #define 5 =0x00000005 devices/hardblocks.h: *103
RDBFB_DISKID     #define 4 =0x00000004 devices/hardblocks.h: *101
RDBFB_LAST       #define 0 =0x00000000 devices/hardblocks.h: *93
RDBFB_LASTLUN    #define 1 =0x00000001 devices/hardblocks.h: *95
RDBFB_LASTTID    #define 2 =0x00000002 devices/hardblocks.h: *97
RDBFB_NORESELECT #define 3 =0x00000003 devices/hardblocks.h: *99
RDBFF_CTRLRID    #define 0x20L devices/hardblocks.h: *104
RDBFF_DISKID     #define 0x10L devices/hardblocks.h: *102
RDBFF_LAST       #define 0x01L devices/hardblocks.h: *94
RDBFF_LASTLUN    #define 0x02L devices/hardblocks.h: *96
RDBFF_LASTTID    #define 0x04L devices/hardblocks.h: *98
RDBFF_NORESELECT #define 0x08L devices/hardblocks.h: *100
rdb_AutoParkSeconds unsigned int in struct RigidDiskBlock
        +0x0094  devices/hardblocks.h: *77
rdb_BadBlockList unsigned int in struct RigidDiskBlock
        +0x0018  devices/hardblocks.h: *54
rdb_BlockBytes   unsigned int in struct RigidDiskBlock
        +0x0010  devices/hardblocks.h: *51
```



```
rdb_ChkSum       int in struct RigidDiskBlock
        +0x0008  devices/hardblocks.h: *49
rdb_ControllerProduct array [16] of char in struct RigidDiskBlock
        +0x00c4  devices/hardblocks.h: *84
rdb_ControllerRevision array [4] of char in struct RigidDiskBlock
        +0x00d4  devices/hardblocks.h: *85
rdb_ControllerVendor array [8] of char in struct RigidDiskBlock
        +0x00bc  devices/hardblocks.h: *83
rdb_CylBlocks    unsigned int in struct RigidDiskBlock
        +0x0090  devices/hardblocks.h: *76
rdb_Cylinders    unsigned int in struct RigidDiskBlock
        +0x0040  devices/hardblocks.h: *61
rdb_DiskProduct  array [16] of char in struct RigidDiskBlock
        +0x00a8  devices/hardblocks.h: *81
rdb_DiskRevision array [4] of char in struct RigidDiskBlock
        +0x00b8  devices/hardblocks.h: *82
rdb_DiskVendor   array [8] of char in struct RigidDiskBlock
        +0x00a0  devices/hardblocks.h: *80
rdb_DriveInit    unsigned int in struct RigidDiskBlock
        +0x0024  devices/hardblocks.h: *57
rdb_FileSysHeaderList unsigned int in struct RigidDiskBlock
        +0x0020  devices/hardblocks.h: *56
rdb_Flags        unsigned int in struct RigidDiskBlock
        +0x0014  devices/hardblocks.h: *52
rdb_Heads        unsigned int in struct RigidDiskBlock
        +0x0048  devices/hardblocks.h: *63
rdb_HiCylinder   unsigned int in struct RigidDiskBlock
        +0x008c  devices/hardblocks.h: *75
rdb_HostID       unsigned int in struct RigidDiskBlock
        +0x000c  devices/hardblocks.h: *50
rdb_ID           unsigned int in struct RigidDiskBlock
        +0x0000  devices/hardblocks.h: *47
rdb_Interleave   unsigned int in struct RigidDiskBlock
        +0x004c  devices/hardblocks.h: *64
RDB_LOCATION_LIMIT #define 16 =0x00000010 devices/hardblocks.h: *91
rdb_LoCylinder   unsigned int in struct RigidDiskBlock
        +0x0088  devices/hardblocks.h: *74
rdb_Park         unsigned int in struct RigidDiskBlock
        +0x0050  devices/hardblocks.h: *65
rdb_PartitionList unsigned int in struct RigidDiskBlock
        +0x001c  devices/hardblocks.h: *55
rdb_RDBBlocksHi  unsigned int in struct RigidDiskBlock
        +0x0084  devices/hardblocks.h: *73
rdb_RDBBlocksLo  unsigned int in struct RigidDiskBlock
        +0x0080  devices/hardblocks.h: *72
rdb_ReducedWrite unsigned int in struct RigidDiskBlock
        +0x0064  devices/hardblocks.h: *68
rdb_Reserved1    array [6] of unsigned int in struct RigidDiskBlock
        +0x0028  devices/hardblocks.h: *59
rdb_Reserved2    array [3] of unsigned int in struct RigidDiskBlock
        +0x0054  devices/hardblocks.h: *66
rdb_Reserved3    array [5] of unsigned int in struct RigidDiskBlock
        +0x006c  devices/hardblocks.h: *70
rdb_Reserved4    array [2] of unsigned int in struct RigidDiskBlock
        +0x0098  devices/hardblocks.h: *78
rdb_Reserved5    array [10] of unsigned int in struct RigidDiskBlock
        +0x00d8  devices/hardblocks.h: *86
rdb_Sectors      unsigned int in struct RigidDiskBlock
        +0x0044  devices/hardblocks.h: *62
rdb_StepRate     unsigned int in struct RigidDiskBlock
        +0x0068  devices/hardblocks.h: *69
rdb_SummedLongs  unsigned int in struct RigidDiskBlock
        +0x0004  devices/hardblocks.h: *48
rdb_WritePreComp unsigned int in struct RigidDiskBlock
        +0x0060  devices/hardblocks.h: *67
RECOVERY_ALERT   #define 0x00000000 =0x00000000 intuition/intuition.h: *987
Rectangle        structure tag
    size 0x0008  graphics/gfx.h: *23
                 graphics/clip.h: 30, 60
```

```
                 graphics/regions.h: 20, 25
refptr           unsigned short int in struct Custom
         +0x0028 hardware/custom.h: *39
REFRESHBITS      #define 0x00C0 =0x000000c0 intuition/intuition.h: *808
REFRESHWINDOW    #define 0x00000004 =0x00000004 intuition/intuition.h: *640
Region           structure tag
    size 0x000c  graphics/clip.h: 46, 47, 50
                 graphics/regions.h: *23
RegionRectangle  structure tag
    size 0x0010  graphics/regions.h: *17, 19, 26
RegionRectangle  pointer to struct RegionRectangle in struct Region
         +0x0008 graphics/regions.h: *26
REGISTER         #define register =0x00000000 exec/types.h: *16
RelLeft          short int in struct Requester
         +0x000c intuition/intuition.h: *147
RelTop           short int in struct Requester
         +0x000e intuition/intuition.h: *147
RELVERIFY        #define 0x0001 =0x00000001 intuition/intuition.h: *283
RemBob           Macro (1 argument) graphics/gels.h: *247
Remember         structure tag
    size 0x000c  intuition/intuition.h: *928, 930
RememberSize     unsigned int in struct Remember
         +0x0004 intuition/intuition.h: *931
REPORTMOUSE      #define 0x0200 =0x00000200 intuition/intuition.h: *816
REQACTIVE        #define 0x2000 =0x00002000 intuition/intuition.h: *181
ReqBorder        pointer to struct Border in struct Requester
         +0x0014 intuition/intuition.h: *150
REQCLEAR         #define 0x00001000 =0x00001000 intuition/intuition.h: *650
ReqCount         short int in struct Window
         +0x002c intuition/intuition.h: *715
ReqGadget        pointer to struct Gadget in struct Requester
         +0x0010 intuition/intuition.h: *149
REQGADGET        #define 0x1000 =0x00001000 intuition/intuition.h: *337
ReqLayer         pointer to struct Layer in struct Requester
         +0x0020 intuition/intuition.h: *157
REQOFFWINDOW     #define 0x1000 =0x00001000 intuition/intuition.h: *180
ReqPad1          array [32] of char in struct Requester
         +0x0024 intuition/intuition.h: *159
ReqPad2          array [36] of char in struct Requester
         +0x004c intuition/intuition.h: *169
REQSET           #define 0x00000080 =0x00000080 intuition/intuition.h: *645
ReqText          pointer to struct IntuiText in struct Requester
         +0x0018 intuition/intuition.h: *151
Requester        structure tag
    size 0x0070  intuition/intuition.h: *141, 144, 711, 713
REQVERIFY        #define 0x00000800 =0x00000800 intuition/intuition.h: *649
reserved         array [4] of char in struct Layer
         +0x0018 graphics/clip.h: *31
reserved         int in struct ClipRect
         +0x0020 graphics/clip.h: *62
reserved         char in struct ViewPort
         +0x0023 graphics/view.h: *43
reserved         array [8] of char in struct RastPort
         +0x005c graphics/rastport.h: *83
Reserved         unsigned int in struct BoolInfo
         +0x0006 intuition/intuition.h: *369
reserved         array [23] of unsigned int in struct GfxBase
         +0x00ec graphics/gfxbase.h: *65
Reserved         array [4] of unsigned int in struct RomBootBase
         +0x0034 libraries/romboot_base.h: *37
reserved2        array [22] of char in struct Layer
         +0x0086 graphics/clip.h: *48
reserved3        array [8] of char in struct Layer
         +0x0076 graphics/clip.h: *45
Resident         structure tag
    size 0x001a  exec/resident.h: *17, 19
ResModules       pointer to pointer to char in struct ExecBase
         +0x012c exec/execbase.h: *66
ResourceList     struct List (size 0x000e) in struct ExecBase
```



```
         +0x0150 exec/execbase.h: *78
RESOURCES_CIA_H  #define =0x00000000 resources/cia.h: *2
RESOURCES_DISK_H #define =0x00000000 resources/disk.h: *2
RESOURCES_FILESYSRES_H #define =0x00000000 resources/filesysres.h: *2
RESOURCES_MATHRESOURCE_H #define =0x00000000 resources/mathresource.h: *2
RESOURCES_MISC_H #define =0x00000000 resources/misc.h: *2
RESOURCES_POTGO_H #define =0x00000000 resources/potgo.h: *2
RETURN_ERROR     #define 10 =0x0000000a libraries/dos.h: *169
RETURN_FAIL      #define 20 =0x00000014 libraries/dos.h: *170
RETURN_OK        #define 0 =0x00000000 libraries/dos.h: *167
RETURN_WARN      #define 5 =0x00000005 libraries/dos.h: *168
RIGHTBORDER      #define 0x0010 =0x00000010 intuition/intuition.h: *311
RIGHTHIT         #define 8 =0x00000008 graphics/collide.h: *33
rightmost        short int in struct GelsInfo
         +0x0018 graphics/rastport.h: *46
RigidDiskBlock   structure tag
    size 0x0100  devices/hardblocks.h: *46
RINGTRIGGER      #define 0x0001 =0x00000001 graphics/gels.h: *42
RingXTrans       short int in struct AnimOb
         +0x001e graphics/gels.h: *216
RingYTrans       short int in struct AnimOb
         +0x001c graphics/gels.h: *216
RMBTRAP          #define 0x00010000 =0x00010000 intuition/intuition.h: *830
rn_ConsoleSegment int in struct RootNode
         +0x0004 libraries/dosextens.h: *179
rn_FileHandlerSegment int in struct RootNode
         +0x001c libraries/dosextens.h: *183
rn_Info          int in struct RootNode
         +0x0018 libraries/dosextens.h: *182
rn_RestartSeg    int in struct RootNode
         +0x0014 libraries/dosextens.h: *181
rn_TaskArray     int in struct RootNode
         +0x0000 libraries/dosextens.h: *176
rn_Time          struct DateStamp (size 0x000c) in struct RootNode
         +0x0008 libraries/dosextens.h: *180
ROBOTICF0        #define 1 =0x00000001 devices/narrator.h: *46
RomBootBase      structure tag
    size 0x0044  libraries/romboot_base.h: *32
ROMBOOT_NAME     #define "romboot.library" libraries/romboot_base.h: *47
RootNode         structure tag
    size 0x0020  libraries/dosextens.h: *175
round            Macro (1 argument) libraries/mathffp.h: *30
round            Macro (1 argument) libraries/mathieeedp.h: *31
Rows             unsigned short int in struct BitMap
         +0x0002 graphics/gfx.h: *39
RowSizeChange    char in struct Preferences
         +0x00d8 intuition/preferences.h: *112
rp               pointer to struct RastPort in struct Layer
         +0x000c graphics/clip.h: *29
RPort            pointer to struct RastPort in struct Window
         +0x0032 intuition/intuition.h: *718
RP_User          pointer to pointer to pointer to char in struct RastPort
         +0x0042 graphics/rastport.h: *79
RTC_MATCHWORD    #define 0x4AFC =0x00004afc exec/resident.h: *30
RTF_AUTOINIT     #define (1<<7) =0x00000080 exec/resident.h: *32
RTF_COLDSTART    #define (1<<0) =0x00000001 exec/resident.h: *33
RTM_WHEN         #define 3 =0x00000003 exec/resident.h: *36
RTW_COLDSTART    #define 1 =0x00000001 exec/resident.h: *38
RTW_NEVER        #define 0 =0x00000000 exec/resident.h: *37
rt_EndSkip       pointer to pointer to char in struct Resident
         +0x0006 exec/resident.h: *20
rt_Flags         char in struct Resident
         +0x000a exec/resident.h: *21
rt_IdString      pointer to char in struct Resident
         +0x0012 exec/resident.h: *26
rt_Init          pointer to pointer to char in struct Resident
         +0x0016 exec/resident.h: *27
rt_MatchTag      pointer to struct Resident in struct Resident
         +0x0002 exec/resident.h: *19
```

```
rt_MatchWord       unsigned short int in struct Resident
        +0x0000    exec/resident.h: *18
rt_Name            pointer to char in struct Resident
        +0x000e    exec/resident.h: *25
rt_Pri             char in struct Resident
        +0x000d    exec/resident.h: *24
rt_Type            char in struct Resident
        +0x000c    exec/resident.h: *23
rt_Version         char in struct Resident
        +0x000b    exec/resident.h: *22
RWindow            pointer to struct Window in struct Requester
        +0x0048    intuition/intuition.h: *168
RxOffset           short int in struct RasInfo
        +0x0008    graphics/view.h: *73
RyOffset           short int in struct RasInfo
        +0x000a    graphics/view.h: *73
sampfreq           unsigned short int in struct narrator_rb
        +0x0040    devices/narrator.h: *76
SatisfyMsg         structure tag
    size 0x001a    devices/clipboard.h: *53
SAVEBACK           #define 0x0002 =0x00000002 graphics/gels.h: *17
SAVEBOB            #define 0x0001 =0x00000001 graphics/gels.h: *29
SaveBuffer         pointer to short int in struct Bob
        +0x0002    graphics/gels.h: *144
saveClipRects      pointer to struct Region in struct Layer
        +0x0082    graphics/clip.h: *47
SaveColor0         unsigned short int in struct Screen
        +0x014c    intuition/screens.h: *78
SAVEPRESERVE       #define 0x1000 =0x00001000 graphics/gels.h: *36
SBUFSIZE_BITS      #define 0x0F =0x0000000f intuition/preferences.h: *214
SBUF_1024          #define 0x01 =0x00000001 intuition/preferences.h: *203
SBUF_16000         #define 0x05 =0x00000005 intuition/preferences.h: *207
SBUF_2048          #define 0x02 =0x00000002 intuition/preferences.h: *204
SBUF_4096          #define 0x03 =0x00000003 intuition/preferences.h: *205
SBUF_512           #define 0x00 =0x00000000 intuition/preferences.h: *202
SBUF_8000          #define 0x04 =0x00000004 intuition/preferences.h: *206
Screen             structure tag
    size 0x015a    intuition/intuition.h: 717, 881
                   intuition/screens.h: *40, 42
                   intuition/intuitionbase.h: 153, 158
Screen             pointer to struct Screen in struct NewWindow
        +0x001e    intuition/intuition.h: *881
SCREENBEHIND       #define 0x0080 =0x00000080 intuition/screens.h: *106
SCREENQUIET        #define 0x0100 =0x00000100 intuition/screens.h: *109
ScreenTitle        pointer to char in struct Window
        +0x0068    intuition/intuition.h: *765
SCREENTYPE         #define 0x000F =0x0000000f intuition/screens.h: *93
SCRGADGET          #define 0x4000 =0x00004000 intuition/intuition.h: *335
Scroll_X           short int in struct Layer
        +0x002c    graphics/clip.h: *39
Scroll_Y           short int in struct Layer
        +0x002e    graphics/clip.h: *39
SCSICmd            structure tag
    size 0x0016    devices/scsidisk.h: *64
SCSIF_READ         #define 1 =0x00000001 devices/scsidisk.h: *82
SCSIF_WRITE        #define 0 =0x00000000 devices/scsidisk.h: *81
scsi_Actual        unsigned int in struct SCSICmd
        +0x0008    devices/scsidisk.h: *71
scsi_CmdActual     unsigned short int in struct SCSICmd
        +0x0012    devices/scsidisk.h: *74
scsi_CmdLength     unsigned short int in struct SCSICmd
        +0x0010    devices/scsidisk.h: *73
scsi_Command       pointer to char in struct SCSICmd
        +0x000c    devices/scsidisk.h: *72
scsi_Data          pointer to unsigned short int in struct SCSICmd
        +0x0000    devices/scsidisk.h: *65
scsi_Flags         char in struct SCSICmd
        +0x0014    devices/scsidisk.h: *75
scsi_Length        unsigned int in struct SCSICmd
```



```
        +0x0004    devices/scsidisk.h: *68
scsi_Status        char in struct SCSICmd
        +0x0015    devices/scsidisk.h: *76
SDCMD_BREAK        #define (CMD_NONSTD+1) =0x0000000a devices/serial.h: *95
SDCMD_QUERY        #define CMD_NONSTD =0x00000009 devices/serial.h: *94
SDCMD_SETPARAMS    #define (CMD_NONSTD+2) =0x0000000b devices/serial.h: *96
SDOWNBACK          #define 0x0070 =0x00000070 intuition/intuition.h: *345
SDRAGGING          #define 0x0030 =0x00000030 intuition/intuition.h: *341
Seconds            unsigned int in struct IntuiMessage
        +0x0024    intuition/intuition.h: *625
Seconds            unsigned int in struct IntuitionBase
        +0x0048    intuition/intuitionbase.h: *163
SegList            pointer to pointer to char in struct ExpansionBase
        +0x0028    libraries/expansionbase.h: *49
SELECTDOWN         #define (IECODE_LBUTTON) =0x00000068
                   intuition/intuition.h: *1007
SELECTED           #define 0x0080 =0x00000080 intuition/intuition.h: *269
SelectFill         pointer to pointer to char in struct MenuItem
        +0x0016    intuition/intuition.h: *99
SelectRender       pointer to pointer to char in struct Gadget
        +0x0016    intuition/intuition.h: *215
SELECTUP           #define (IECODE_LBUTTON | IECODE_UP_PREFIX) =0x000000e8
                   intuition/intuition.h: *1006
Semaphore          structure tag
    size 0x0024    exec/semaphores.h: *32
SemaphoreList      struct List (size 0x000e) in struct ExecBase
        +0x0214    exec/execbase.h: *107
SemaphoreRequest   structure tag
    size 0x000c    exec/semaphores.h: *43, 53
SERB_7WIRE         #define 2 =0x00000002 devices/serial.h: *109
SERB_EOFMODE       #define 6 =0x00000006 devices/serial.h: *101
SERB_PARTY_ODD     #define 1 =0x00000001 devices/serial.h: *111
SERB_PARTY_ON      #define 0 =0x00000000 devices/serial.h: *113
SERB_QUEUEDBRK     #define 3 =0x00000003 devices/serial.h: *107
SERB_RAD_BOOGIE    #define 4 =0x00000004 devices/serial.h: *105
SERB_SHARED        #define 5 =0x00000005 devices/serial.h: *103
SERB_XDISABLED     #define 7 =0x00000007 devices/serial.h: *99
serdat             unsigned short int in struct Custom
        +0x0030    hardware/custom.h: *43
serdatr            unsigned short int in struct Custom
        +0x0018    hardware/custom.h: *32
SerErr_BufErr      #define 4 =0x00000004 devices/serial.h: *137
SerErr_BufOverflow #define 12 =0x0000000c devices/serial.h: *142
SerErr_DetectedBreak #define 15 =0x0000000f devices/serial.h: *144
SerErr_DevBusy     #define 1 =0x00000001 devices/serial.h: *136
SerErr_InvParam    #define 5 =0x00000005 devices/serial.h: *138
SerErr_LineErr     #define 6 =0x00000006 devices/serial.h: *139
SerErr_NoDSR       #define 13 =0x0000000d devices/serial.h: *143
SerErr_ParityErr   #define 9 =0x00000009 devices/serial.h: *140
SerErr_TimerErr    #define 11 =0x0000000b devices/serial.h: *141
SERF_7WIRE         #define (1<<2) =0x00000004 devices/serial.h: *110
SERF_EOFMODE       #define (1<<6) =0x00000040 devices/serial.h: *102
SERF_PARTY_ODD     #define (1<<1) =0x00000002 devices/serial.h: *112
SERF_PARTY_ON      #define (1<<0) =0x00000001 devices/serial.h: *114
SERF_QUEUEDBRK     #define (1<<3) =0x00000008 devices/serial.h: *108
SERF_RAD_BOOGIE    #define (1<<4) =0x00000010 devices/serial.h: *106
SERF_SHARED        #define (1<<5) =0x00000020 devices/serial.h: *104
SERF_XDISABLED     #define (1<<7) =0x00000080 devices/serial.h: *100
SERIALNAME         #define "serial.device" devices/serial.h: *178
SERIAL_PRINTER     #define 0x01 =0x00000001 intuition/preferences.h: *136
SerParShk          char in struct Preferences
        +0x00b8    intuition/preferences.h: *106
serper             unsigned short int in struct Custom
        +0x0032    hardware/custom.h: *44
SerRWBits          char in struct Preferences
        +0x00b6    intuition/preferences.h: *102
SerStopBuf         char in struct Preferences
        +0x00b7    intuition/preferences.h: *104
SER_DEFAULT_CTLCHAR #define 0x11130000 =0x11130000 devices/serial.h: *27
```

```
SetAfPt           Macro (3 arguments) graphics/gfxmacros.h: *28
SetDrPt           Macro (2 arguments) graphics/gfxmacros.h: *26
SetOPen           Macro (2 arguments) graphics/gfxmacros.h: *25
SetWrMsk          Macro (2 arguments) graphics/gfxmacros.h: *27
sex               unsigned short int in struct narrator_rb
         +0x0036  devices/narrator.h: *72
SEXTB_MARK        #define 0 =0x00000000 devices/serial.h: *132
SEXTB_MSPON       #define 1 =0x00000001 devices/serial.h: *129
SEXTF_MARK        #define (1<<0) =0x00000001 devices/serial.h: *133
SEXTF_MSPON       #define (1<<1) =0x00000002 devices/serial.h: *131
SF_ALERTWACK      #define (1<<1) =0x00000002 exec/alerts.h: *13
SGR_BLACK         #define 30 =0x0000001e devices/console.h: *33
SGR_BLACKBG       #define 40 =0x00000028 devices/console.h: *43
SGR_BLUE          #define 34 =0x00000022 devices/console.h: *37
SGR_BLUEBG        #define 44 =0x0000002c devices/console.h: *47
SGR_BOLD          #define 1 =0x00000001 devices/console.h: *27
SGR_CLR0          #define 30 =0x0000001e devices/console.h: *55
SGR_CLR0BG        #define 40 =0x00000028 devices/console.h: *64
SGR_CLR1          #define 31 =0x0000001f devices/console.h: *56
SGR_CLR1BG        #define 41 =0x00000029 devices/console.h: *65
SGR_CLR2          #define 32 =0x00000020 devices/console.h: *57
SGR_CLR2BG        #define 42 =0x0000002a devices/console.h: *66
SGR_CLR3          #define 33 =0x00000021 devices/console.h: *58
SGR_CLR3BG        #define 43 =0x0000002b devices/console.h: *67
SGR_CLR4          #define 34 =0x00000022 devices/console.h: *59
SGR_CLR4BG        #define 44 =0x0000002c devices/console.h: *68
SGR_CLR5          #define 35 =0x00000023 devices/console.h: *60
SGR_CLR5BG        #define 45 =0x0000002d devices/console.h: *69
SGR_CLR6          #define 36 =0x00000024 devices/console.h: *61
SGR_CLR6BG        #define 46 =0x0000002e devices/console.h: *70
SGR_CLR7          #define 37 =0x00000025 devices/console.h: *62
SGR_CLR7BG        #define 47 =0x0000002f devices/console.h: *71
SGR_CYAN          #define 36 =0x00000024 devices/console.h: *39
SGR_CYANBG        #define 46 =0x0000002e devices/console.h: *49
SGR_DEFAULT       #define 39 =0x00000027 devices/console.h: *41
SGR_DEFAULTBG     #define 49 =0x00000031 devices/console.h: *51
SGR_GREEN         #define 32 =0x00000020 devices/console.h: *35
SGR_GREENBG       #define 42 =0x0000002a devices/console.h: *45
SGR_ITALIC        #define 3 =0x00000003 devices/console.h: *28
SGR_MAGENTA       #define 35 =0x00000023 devices/console.h: *38
SGR_MAGENTABG     #define 45 =0x0000002d devices/console.h: *48
SGR_NEGATIVE      #define 7 =0x00000007 devices/console.h: *30
SGR_PRIMARY       #define 0 =0x00000000 devices/console.h: *26
SGR_RED           #define 31 =0x0000001f devices/console.h: *34
SGR_REDBG         #define 41 =0x00000029 devices/console.h: *44
SGR_UNDERSCORE    #define 4 =0x00000004 devices/console.h: *29
SGR_WHITE         #define 37 =0x00000025 devices/console.h: *40
SGR_WHITEBG       #define 47 =0x0000002f devices/console.h: *50
SGR_YELLOW        #define 33 =0x00000021 devices/console.h: *36
SGR_YELLOWBG      #define 43 =0x0000002b devices/console.h: *46
SHADE_BW          #define 0x00 =0x00000000 intuition/preferences.h: *174
SHADE_COLOR       #define 0x02 =0x00000002 intuition/preferences.h: *176
SHADE_GREYSCALE   #define 0x01 =0x00000001 intuition/preferences.h: *175
SHAKNUM           Macro (1 argument) intuition/intuition.h: *957
shape             char in struct mouth_rb
         +0x0048  devices/narrator.h: *91
SHARED_LOCK       #define -2 =0xfffffffe libraries/dos.h: *44
SHFCprList        pointer to struct cprlist in struct View
         +0x0008  graphics/view.h: *51
SHFlist           pointer to unsigned short int in struct GfxBase
         +0x0036  graphics/gfxbase.h: *31
SHIFTITEM         Macro (1 argument) intuition/intuition.h: *949
SHIFTMENU         Macro (1 argument) intuition/intuition.h: *948
SHIFTSUB          Macro (1 argument) intuition/intuition.h: *950
SHORT             typedef short int
                  many references; defined in exec/types.h: *38
SHOWTITLE         #define 0x0010 =0x00000010 intuition/screens.h: *98
SHSHAKE_NONE      #define 2 =0x00000002 intuition/preferences.h: *231
SHSHAKE_RTS       #define 1 =0x00000001 intuition/preferences.h: *230
```



```
SHSHAKE_XON       #define 0 =0x00000000 intuition/preferences.h: *229
sh_List           struct List (size 0x000e) in struct SoftIntList
         +0x0000  exec/interrupts.h: *37
sh_Pad            unsigned short int in struct SoftIntList
         +0x000e  exec/interrupts.h: *38
SIGBREAKB_CTRL_C  #define 12 =0x0000000c libraries/dos.h: *173
SIGBREAKB_CTRL_D  #define 13 =0x0000000d libraries/dos.h: *174
SIGBREAKB_CTRL_E  #define 14 =0x0000000e libraries/dos.h: *175
SIGBREAKB_CTRL_F  #define 15 =0x0000000f libraries/dos.h: *176
SIGBREAKF_CTRL_C  #define (1<<SIGBREAKB_CTRL_C) =0x00001000 libraries/dos.h: *180
SIGBREAKF_CTRL_D  #define (1<<SIGBREAKB_CTRL_D) =0x00002000 libraries/dos.h: *181
SIGBREAKF_CTRL_E  #define (1<<SIGBREAKB_CTRL_E) =0x00004000 libraries/dos.h: *182
SIGBREAKF_CTRL_F  #define (1<<SIGBREAKB_CTRL_F) =0x00008000 libraries/dos.h: *183
SIGB_ABORT        #define 0 =0x00000000 exec/tasks.h: *71
SIGB_BLIT         #define 4 =0x00000004 exec/tasks.h: *73
SIGB_CHILD        #define 1 =0x00000001 exec/tasks.h: *72
SIGB_DOS          #define 8 =0x00000008 exec/tasks.h: *75
SIGB_SINGLE       #define 4 =0x00000004 exec/tasks.h: *74
SIGF_ABORT        #define (1<<0) =0x00000001 exec/tasks.h: *77
SIGF_BLIT         #define (1<<4) =0x00000010 exec/tasks.h: *79
SIGF_CHILD        #define (1<<1) =0x00000002 exec/tasks.h: *78
SIGF_DOS          #define (1<<8) =0x00000100 exec/tasks.h: *81
SIGF_SINGLE       #define (1<<4) =0x00000010 exec/tasks.h: *80
SIGN              Macro (1 argument) intuition/intuition.h: *969
SignalSemaphore   structure tag
    size 0x002e   exec/semaphores.h: *49
                  graphics/clip.h: 44
                  graphics/layers.h: 38
                  graphics/gfxbase.h: 61
                  libraries/expansionbase.h: 54
SIGNFLAG          #define 0x40 =0x00000040 hardware/blit.h: *63
SIH_PRIMASK       #define (0xf0) =0x000000f0 exec/interrupts.h: *41
SimpleSprite      structure tag
    size 0x000c   graphics/gfxbase.h: 53
                  graphics/sprite.h: *15
SimpleSprites     pointer to pointer to struct SimpleSprite in struct GfxBase
         +0x00d0  graphics/gfxbase.h: *53
SIMPLE_REFRESH    #define 0x0040 =0x00000040 intuition/intuition.h: *810
sin               #define SPSin =0x00000000 libraries/mathffp.h: *41
sin               #define IEEEDPSin =0x00000000 libraries/mathieeedp.h: *42
SINGLE            #define 0x80 =0x00000080 intuition/preferences.h: *150
sinh              #define SPSinh =0x00000000 libraries/mathffp.h: *49
sinh              #define IEEEDPSinh =0x00000000 libraries/mathieeedp.h: *50
SIX_LPI           #define 0x000 =0x00000000 intuition/preferences.h: *162
Size              int in struct TmpRas
         +0x0004  graphics/rastport.h: *31
SIZEBBOTTOM       #define 0x0020 =0x00000020 intuition/intuition.h: *804
SIZEBRIGHT        #define 0x0010 =0x00000010 intuition/intuition.h: *803
SIZEVERIFY        #define 0x00000001 =0x00000001 intuition/intuition.h: *638
SIZING            #define 0x0010 =0x00000010 intuition/intuition.h: *339
SMART_REFRESH     #define 0x0000 =0x00000000 intuition/intuition.h: *809
sm_ArgList        pointer to struct WBArg in struct WBStartup
         +0x0024  workbench/startup.h: *31
sm_Bids           short int in struct Semaphore
         +0x0022  exec/semaphores.h: *34
sm_ClipID         int in struct SatisfyMsg
         +0x0016  devices/clipboard.h: *56
sm_LockMsg        #define mp_SigTask =0x00000000 exec/semaphores.h: *37
sm_Message        struct Message (size 0x0014) in struct WBStartup
         +0x0000  workbench/startup.h: *26
sm_Msg            struct Message (size 0x0014) in struct SatisfyMsg
         +0x0000  devices/clipboard.h: *54
sm_MsgPort        struct MsgPort (size 0x0022) in struct Semaphore
         +0x0000  exec/semaphores.h: *33
sm_NumArgs        int in struct WBStartup
         +0x001c  workbench/startup.h: *29
sm_Process        pointer to struct MsgPort in struct WBStartup
         +0x0014  workbench/startup.h: *27
sm_Segment        int in struct WBStartup
```

```
          +0x0018  workbench/startup.h: *28
sm_ToolWindow      pointer to char in struct WBStartup
          +0x0020  workbench/startup.h: *30
sm_Unit            unsigned short int in struct SatisfyMsg
          +0x0014  devices/clipboard.h: *55
SoftIntList        structure tag
     size 0x0010   exec/interrupts.h: *36
                   exec/execbase.h: 86
SoftInts           array [5] of struct SoftIntList (size 0x0010) in struct
                   ExecBase
          +0x01b2  exec/execbase.h: *86
SoftVer            unsigned short int in struct ExecBase
          +0x0022  exec/execbase.h: *33
SPAbs              extern function returning float libraries/mathffp.h: *58
SPAcos             extern function returning float libraries/mathffp.h: *70
SPAdd              extern function returning float libraries/mathffp.h: *65
SPARITY_BITS       #define 0xF0 =0x000000f0 intuition/preferences.h: *221
SPARITY_EVEN       #define 1 =0x00000001 intuition/preferences.h: *223
SPARITY_NONE       #define 0 =0x00000000 intuition/preferences.h: *222
SPARITY_ODD        #define 2 =0x00000002 intuition/preferences.h: *224
SPARNUM            Macro (1 argument) intuition/intuition.h: *956
SPAsin             extern function returning float libraries/mathffp.h: *70
SPAtan             extern function returning float libraries/mathffp.h: *70
SPCeil             extern function returning float libraries/mathffp.h: *60
SPCmp              extern function returning int libraries/mathffp.h: *56
SPCos              extern function returning float libraries/mathffp.h: *71
SPCosh             extern function returning float libraries/mathffp.h: *72
SPDiv              extern function returning float libraries/mathffp.h: *68
SpecialInfo        pointer to pointer to char in struct Gadget
          +0x0022  intuition/intuition.h: *234
SpecialLink        pointer to struct IntuiMessage in struct IntuiMessage
          +0x0030  intuition/intuition.h: *633
SPECIAL_ASPECT     #define 0x0080 =0x00000080 devices/printer.h: *176
SPECIAL_CENTER     #define 0x0040 =0x00000040 devices/printer.h: *175
SPECIAL_DENSITY1   #define 0x0100 =0x00000100 devices/printer.h: *177
SPECIAL_DENSITY2   #define 0x0200 =0x00000200 devices/printer.h: *178
SPECIAL_DENSITY3   #define 0x0300 =0x00000300 devices/printer.h: *179
SPECIAL_DENSITY4   #define 0x0400 =0x00000400 devices/printer.h: *180
SPECIAL_DENSITY5   #define 0x0500 =0x00000500 devices/printer.h: *181
SPECIAL_DENSITY6   #define 0x0600 =0x00000600 devices/printer.h: *182
SPECIAL_DENSITY7   #define 0x0700 =0x00000700 devices/printer.h: *183
SPECIAL_DENSITYMASK #define 0x0700 =0x00000700 devices/printer.h: *215
SPECIAL_DIMENSIONSMASK #define (SPECIAL_MILCOLS|SPECIAL_MILROWS|
                   SPECIAL_FULLCOLS|SPECIAL_FULLROWS |SPECIAL_FRACCOLS|
                   SPECIAL_FRACROWS|SPECIAL_ASPECT) =0x000000bf
                   devices/printer.h: *218
SPECIAL_FRACCOLS   #define 0x0010 =0x00000010 devices/printer.h: *173
SPECIAL_FRACROWS   #define 0x0020 =0x00000020 devices/printer.h: *174
SPECIAL_FULLCOLS   #define 0x0004 =0x00000004 devices/printer.h: *171
SPECIAL_FULLROWS   #define 0x0008 =0x00000008 devices/printer.h: *172
SPECIAL_MILCOLS    #define 0x0001 =0x00000001 devices/printer.h: *169
SPECIAL_MILROWS    #define 0x0002 =0x00000002 devices/printer.h: *170
SPECIAL_NOFORMFEED #define 0x0800 =0x00000800 devices/printer.h: *184
SPECIAL_NOPRINT    #define 0x2000 =0x00002000 devices/printer.h: *195
SPECIAL_TRUSTME    #define 0x1000 =0x00001000 devices/printer.h: *185
SPExp              extern function returning float libraries/mathffp.h: *73
SPFieee            extern function returning float libraries/mathffp.h: *74
SPFix              extern function returning int   libraries/mathffp.h: *54
SPFloor            extern function returning float libraries/mathffp.h: *59
SPFlt              extern function returning float libraries/mathffp.h: *55
SPLog              extern function returning float libraries/mathffp.h: *73
SPLog10            extern function returning float libraries/mathffp.h: *73
SPMul              extern function returning float libraries/mathffp.h: *67
SPNeg              extern function returning float libraries/mathffp.h: *64
SPPow              extern function returning float libraries/mathffp.h: *73
spr                array [8] of struct SpriteDef (size 0x0008) in struct Custom
          +0x0140  hardware/custom.h: *110
SprColors          pointer to short int in struct VSprite
          +0x0030  graphics/gels.h: *113
```



```
SprIns             pointer to struct CopList in struct ViewPort
          +0x000c  graphics/view.h: *36
SpriteDef          structure tag in struct Custom
     size 0x0008   hardware/custom.h: *105
SpritePriorities   char in struct ViewPort
          +0x0022  graphics/view.h: *42
SpriteReserved     char in struct GfxBase
          +0x00a6  graphics/gfxbase.h: *42
SPRITES            #define 0x4000 =0x00004000 graphics/view.h: *63
SPRITE_ATTACHED    #define 0x80 =0x00000080 graphics/sprite.h: *13
sprpt              array [8] of pointer to pointer to char in struct Custom
          +0x0120  hardware/custom.h: *104
sprRsrvd           char in struct GelsInfo
          +0x0000  graphics/rastport.h: *37
sprstop            array [2] of unsigned short int in struct copinit
          +0x0058  graphics/copper.h: *80
sprstrtup          array [40] of unsigned short int in struct copinit
          +0x0008  graphics/copper.h: *79
SPSin              extern function returning float libraries/mathffp.h: *71
SPSincos           extern function returning float libraries/mathffp.h: *71
SPSinh             extern function returning float libraries/mathffp.h: *72
SPSqrt             extern function returning float libraries/mathffp.h: *74
SPSub              extern function returning float libraries/mathffp.h: *66
SPTan              extern function returning float libraries/mathffp.h: *71
SPTanh             extern function returning float libraries/mathffp.h: *72
SPTst              extern function returning int libraries/mathffp.h: *57
sp_Msg             struct Message (size 0x0014) in struct StandardPacket
          +0x0000  libraries/dosextens.h: *111
sp_Pkt             struct DosPacket (size 0x0030) in struct StandardPacket
          +0x0014  libraries/dosextens.h: *112
sqrt               #define SPSqrt =0x00000000 libraries/mathffp.h: *47
sqrt               #define IEEEDPSqrt =0x00000000 libraries/mathieeedp.h: *48
SRBNUM             Macro (1 argument) intuition/intuition.h: *953
SRCA               #define 0x800 =0x00000800 hardware/blit.h: *51
SRCB               #define 0x400 =0x00000400 hardware/blit.h: *50
SRCC               #define 0x200 =0x00000200 hardware/blit.h: *49
SREAD_BITS         #define 0xF0 =0x000000f0 intuition/preferences.h: *210
sr_Link            struct MinNode (size 0x0008) in struct SemaphoreRequest
          +0x0000  exec/semaphores.h: *44
sr_Waiter          pointer to struct Task in struct SemaphoreRequest
          +0x0008  exec/semaphores.h: *45
SSBNUM             Macro (1 argument) intuition/intuition.h: *955
SSTOP_BITS         #define 0xF0 =0x000000f0 intuition/preferences.h: *213
ss_Link            struct Node (size 0x000e) in struct SignalSemaphore
          +0x0000  exec/semaphores.h: *50
ss_MultipleLink    struct SemaphoreRequest (size 0x000c) in struct
                   SignalSemaphore
          +0x001c  exec/semaphores.h: *53
ss_NestCount       short int in struct SignalSemaphore
          +0x000e  exec/semaphores.h: *51
ss_Owner           pointer to struct Task in struct SignalSemaphore
          +0x0028  exec/semaphores.h: *54
ss_QueueCount      short int in struct SignalSemaphore
          +0x002c  exec/semaphores.h: *55
ss_WaitQueue       struct MinList (size 0x000c) in struct SignalSemaphore
          +0x0010  exec/semaphores.h: *52
StandardPacket     structure tag
     size 0x0044   libraries/dosextens.h: *110
start              pointer to unsigned short int in struct cprlist
          +0x0004  graphics/copper.h: *51
stat               char in struct bltnode
          +0x0008  hardware/blit.h: *84
STATIC             #define static =0x00000000 exec/types.h: *15
STDSCREENHEIGHT    #define -1 =0xffffffff intuition/screens.h: *111
strequ             unsigned short int in struct Custom
          +0x0038  hardware/custom.h: *47
STRGADGET          #define 0x0004 =0x00000004 intuition/intuition.h: *351
strhor             unsigned short int in struct Custom
          +0x003c  hardware/custom.h: *49
```

```
STRINGCENTER      #define 0x0200 =0x00000200 intuition/intuition.h: *318
StringInfo        structure tag
    size 0x0024   intuition/intuition.h: *451
STRINGRIGHT       #define 0x0400 =0x00000400 intuition/intuition.h: *319
strlong           unsigned short int in struct Custom
        +0x003e   hardware/custom.h: *50
STRPTR            typedef pointer to unsigned char
                  exec/types.h: *29, 30
                  devices/clipboard.h: 46
                  graphics/text.h: 48
strvbl            unsigned short int in struct Custom
        +0x003a   hardware/custom.h: *48
SubItem           pointer to struct MenuItem in struct MenuItem
        +0x001c   intuition/intuition.h: *103
SUBNUM            Macro (1 argument) intuition/intuition.h: *946
SUD               #define 0x10 =0x00000010 hardware/blit.h: *66
SUL               #define 0x8 =0x00000008 hardware/blit.h: *67
SuperBitMap       pointer to struct BitMap in struct Layer
        +0x0020   graphics/clip.h: *34
SuperClipRect     pointer to struct ClipRect in struct Layer
        +0x0024   graphics/clip.h: *35
SuperSaveClipRects pointer to struct ClipRect in struct Layer
        +0x003c   graphics/clip.h: *41
SUPER_BITMAP      #define 0x0080 =0x00000080 intuition/intuition.h: *811
SUPER_UNUSED      #define 0xFCFC0000 =0xfcfc0000 intuition/intuition.h: *839
SUPFRONT          #define 0x0050 =0x00000050 intuition/intuition.h: *343
SUSERFLAGS        #define 0x00FF =0x000000ff graphics/gels.h: *15
SWBNUM            Macro (1 argument) intuition/intuition.h: *954
SWRITE_BITS       #define 0x0F =0x0000000f intuition/preferences.h: *211
SYSBASESIZE       #define sizeof(struct ExecBase)
                  exec/execbase.h: *123
SysFlags          unsigned short int in struct ExecBase
        +0x0124   exec/execbase.h: *60
SYSGADGET         #define 0x8000 =0x00008000 intuition/intuition.h: *334
SYSREQUEST        #define 0x4000 =0x00004000 intuition/intuition.h: *182
SysStkLower       pointer to pointer to char in struct ExecBase
        +0x003a   exec/execbase.h: *40
SysStkUpper       pointer to pointer to char in struct ExecBase
        +0x0036   exec/execbase.h: *39
system_bplcon0    short int in struct GfxBase
        +0x00a4   graphics/gfxbase.h: *41
tan               #define SPTan =0x00000000 libraries/mathffp.h: *37
tan               #define IEEEDPTan =0x00000000 libraries/mathieeedp.h: *38
tanh              #define SPTanh =0x00000000 libraries/mathffp.h: *51
tanh              #define IEEEDPTanh =0x00000000 libraries/mathieeedp.h: *52
Task              structure tag
   size 0x005c    exec/tasks.h: *22
                  exec/ports.h: 32
                  exec/execbase.h: 55
                  exec/semaphores.h: 45, 54
                  libraries/dosextens.h: 35
                  devices/prtbase.h: 87
                  graphics/gfxbase.h: 49
TaskExceptCode    pointer to pointer to char in struct ExecBase
        +0x0134   exec/execbase.h: *69
TaskExitCode      pointer to pointer to char in struct ExecBase
        +0x0138   exec/execbase.h: *70
TaskReady         struct List (size 0x000e) in struct ExecBase
        +0x0196   exec/execbase.h: *83
TaskSigAlloc      unsigned int in struct ExecBase
        +0x013c   exec/execbase.h: *71
TaskTrapAlloc     unsigned short int in struct ExecBase
        +0x0140   exec/execbase.h: *72
TaskTrapCode      pointer to pointer to char in struct ExecBase
        +0x0130   exec/execbase.h: *68
TaskWait          struct List (size 0x000e) in struct ExecBase
        +0x01a4   exec/execbase.h: *84
ta_Flags          char in struct TextAttr
        +0x0007   graphics/text.h: *51
```



```
ta_Name           pointer to char in struct TextAttr
        +0x0000   graphics/text.h: *48
ta_Style          char in struct TextAttr
        +0x0006   graphics/text.h: *50
ta_YSize          unsigned short int in struct TextAttr
        +0x0004   graphics/text.h: *49
TBC_HCLRTAB       #define 0 =0x00000000 devices/console.h: *84
TBC_HCLRTABSALL   #define 3 =0x00000003 devices/console.h: *85
TB_EXCEPT         #define 5 =0x00000005 exec/tasks.h: *50
TB_LAUNCH         #define 7 =0x00000007 exec/tasks.h: *52
TB_PROCTIME       #define 0 =0x00000000 exec/tasks.h: *48
TB_STACKCHK       #define 4 =0x00000004 exec/tasks.h: *49
TB_SWITCH         #define 6 =0x00000006 exec/tasks.h: *51
tc_ExceptCode     pointer to pointer to char in struct Task
        +0x002a   exec/tasks.h: *35
tc_ExceptData     pointer to pointer to char in struct Task
        +0x0026   exec/tasks.h: *34
tc_Flags          char in struct Task
        +0x000e   exec/tasks.h: *24
tc_IDNestCnt      char in struct Task
        +0x0010   exec/tasks.h: *26
tc_Launch         pointer to function returning void in struct Task
        +0x0046   exec/tasks.h: *42
tc_MemEntry       struct List (size 0x000e) in struct Task
        +0x004a   exec/tasks.h: *43
tc_Node           struct Node (size 0x000e) in struct Task
        +0x0000   exec/tasks.h: *23
tc_SigAlloc       unsigned int in struct Task
        +0x0012   exec/tasks.h: *28
tc_SigExcept      unsigned int in struct Task
        +0x001e   exec/tasks.h: *31
tc_SigRecvd       unsigned int in struct Task
        +0x001a   exec/tasks.h: *30
tc_SigWait        unsigned int in struct Task
        +0x0016   exec/tasks.h: *29
tc_SPLower        pointer to pointer to char in struct Task
        +0x003a   exec/tasks.h: *39
tc_SPReg          pointer to pointer to char in struct Task
        +0x0036   exec/tasks.h: *38
tc_SPUpper        pointer to pointer to char in struct Task
        +0x003e   exec/tasks.h: *40
tc_State          char in struct Task
        +0x000f   exec/tasks.h: *25
tc_Switch         pointer to function returning void in struct Task
        +0x0042   exec/tasks.h: *41
tc_TDNestCnt      char in struct Task
        +0x0011   exec/tasks.h: *27
tc_TrapAble       unsigned short int in struct Task
        +0x0024   exec/tasks.h: *33
tc_TrapAlloc      unsigned short int in struct Task
        +0x0022   exec/tasks.h: *32
tc_TrapCode       pointer to pointer to char in struct Task
        +0x0032   exec/tasks.h: *37
tc_TrapData       pointer to pointer to char in struct Task
        +0x002e   exec/tasks.h: *36
tc_UserData       pointer to pointer to char in struct Task
        +0x0058   exec/tasks.h: *44
TDB_ALLOW_NON_3_5 #define 0 =0x00000000 devices/trackdisk.h: *138
TDERR_BadDriveType #define 33 =0x00000021 devices/trackdisk.h: *172
TDERR_BadHdrSum   #define 24 =0x00000018 devices/trackdisk.h: *163
TDERR_BadSecHdr   #define 27 =0x0000001b devices/trackdisk.h: *166
TDERR_BadSecID    #define 23 =0x00000017 devices/trackdisk.h: *162
TDERR_BadSecPreamble #define 22 =0x00000016 devices/trackdisk.h: *161
TDERR_BadSecSum   #define 25 =0x00000019 devices/trackdisk.h: *164
TDERR_BadUnitNum  #define 32 =0x00000020 devices/trackdisk.h: *171
TDERR_DiskChanged #define 29 =0x0000001d devices/trackdisk.h: *168
TDERR_DriveInUse  #define 34 =0x00000022 devices/trackdisk.h: *173
TDERR_NoMem       #define 31 =0x0000001f devices/trackdisk.h: *170
TDERR_NoSecHdr    #define 21 =0x00000015 devices/trackdisk.h: *160
```

```
TDERR_NotSpecified #define 20 =0x00000014 devices/trackdisk.h: *159
TDERR_PostReset    #define 35 =0x00000023 devices/trackdisk.h: *174
TDERR_SeekError    #define 30 =0x0000001e devices/trackdisk.h: *169
TDERR_TooFewSecs   #define 26 =0x0000001a devices/trackdisk.h: *165
TDERR_WriteProt    #define 28 =0x0000001c devices/trackdisk.h: *167
TDF_ALLOW_NON_3_5  #define (1<<0) =0x00000001 devices/trackdisk.h: *139
TDF_EXTCOM         #define (1<<15) =0x00008000 devices/trackdisk.h: *71
TDNestCnt          char in struct ExecBase
        +0x0127    exec/execbase.h: *62
tdu_Comp01Track    unsigned short int in struct TDU_PublicUnit
        +0x0026    devices/trackdisk.h: *186
tdu_Comp10Track    unsigned short int in struct TDU_PublicUnit
        +0x0028    devices/trackdisk.h: *187
tdu_Comp11Track    unsigned short int in struct TDU_PublicUnit
        +0x002a    devices/trackdisk.h: *188
TDU_PublicUnit     structure tag
    size 0x0035    devices/trackdisk.h: *184
tdu_RetryCnt       char in struct TDU_PublicUnit
        +0x0034    devices/trackdisk.h: *191
tdu_SettleDelay    unsigned int in struct TDU_PublicUnit
        +0x0030    devices/trackdisk.h: *190
tdu_StepDelay      unsigned int in struct TDU_PublicUnit
        +0x002c    devices/trackdisk.h: *189
tdu_Unit           struct Unit (size 0x0026) in struct TDU_PublicUnit
        +0x0000    devices/trackdisk.h: *185
TD_ADDCHANGEINT    #define (CMD_NONSTD+11) =0x00000014 devices/trackdisk.h: *85
TD_CHANGENUM       #define (CMD_NONSTD+4) =0x0000000d devices/trackdisk.h: *78
TD_CHANGESTATE     #define (CMD_NONSTD+5) =0x0000000e devices/trackdisk.h: *79
TD_FORMAT          #define (CMD_NONSTD+2) =0x0000000b devices/trackdisk.h: *76
TD_GETDRIVETYPE    #define (CMD_NONSTD+9) =0x00000012 devices/trackdisk.h: *83
TD_GETNUMTRACKS    #define (CMD_NONSTD+10) =0x00000013 devices/trackdisk.h: *84
TD_LABELSIZE       #define 16 =0x00000010 devices/trackdisk.h: *130
TD_LASTCOMM        #define (CMD_NONSTD+13) =0x00000016 devices/trackdisk.h: *88
TD_MOTOR           #define (CMD_NONSTD+0) =0x00000009 devices/trackdisk.h: *74
TD_NAME            #define "trackdisk.device" devices/trackdisk.h: *69
TD_PROTSTATUS      #define (CMD_NONSTD+6) =0x0000000f devices/trackdisk.h: *80
TD_RAWREAD         #define (CMD_NONSTD+7) =0x00000010 devices/trackdisk.h: *81
TD_RAWWRITE        #define (CMD_NONSTD+8) =0x00000011 devices/trackdisk.h: *82
TD_REMCHANGEINT    #define (CMD_NONSTD+12) =0x00000015 devices/trackdisk.h: *86
TD_REMOVE          #define (CMD_NONSTD+3) =0x0000000c devices/trackdisk.h: *77
TD_SECSHIFT        #define 9 =0x00000009 devices/trackdisk.h: *48
TD_SECTOR          #define 512 =0x00000200 devices/trackdisk.h: *47
TD_SEEK            #define (CMD_NONSTD+1) =0x0000000a devices/trackdisk.h: *75
TermArray0         unsigned int in struct IOTArray
        +0x0000    devices/serial.h: *22
TermArray1         unsigned int in struct IOTArray
        +0x0004    devices/serial.h: *23
TEXT               typedef unsigned char
                   exec/types.h: *48
TextAttr           structure tag
    size 0x0008    graphics/text.h: *47
                   intuition/intuition.h: 500
                   intuition/screens.h: 59, 127
                   libraries/diskfont.h: 67
TextFont           structure tag
    size 0x0034    devices/conunit.h: 68
                   graphics/rastport.h: 72
                   graphics/text.h: *56
                   intuition/intuition.h: 793
                   graphics/gfxbase.h: 36
                   libraries/diskfont.h: 56
TextFonts          struct List (size 0x000e) in struct GfxBase
        +0x008c    graphics/gfxbase.h: *35
tf_Accessors       unsigned short int in struct TextFont
        +0x001e    graphics/text.h: *66
tf_Baseline        unsigned short int in struct TextFont
        +0x001a    graphics/text.h: *63
tf_BoldSmear       unsigned short int in struct TextFont
        +0x001c    graphics/text.h: *64
```



```
tf_CharData        pointer to pointer to char in struct TextFont
        +0x0022    graphics/text.h: *70
tf_CharKern        pointer to pointer to char in struct TextFont
        +0x0030    graphics/text.h: *76
tf_CharLoc         pointer to pointer to char in struct TextFont
        +0x0028    graphics/text.h: *73
tf_CharSpace       pointer to pointer to char in struct TextFont
        +0x002c    graphics/text.h: *75
TF_EXCEPT          #define (1<<5) =0x00000020 exec/tasks.h: *56
tf_Flags           char in struct TextFont
        +0x0017    graphics/text.h: *61
tf_HiChar          char in struct TextFont
        +0x0021    graphics/text.h: *69
TF_LAUNCH          #define (1<<7) =0x00000080 exec/tasks.h: *58
tf_LoChar          char in struct TextFont
        +0x0020    graphics/text.h: *68
tf_Message         struct Message (size 0x0014) in struct TextFont
        +0x0000    graphics/text.h: *57
tf_Modulo          unsigned short int in struct TextFont
        +0x0026    graphics/text.h: *72
TF_PROCTIME        #define (1<<0) =0x00000001 exec/tasks.h: *54
TF_STACKCHK        #define (1<<4) =0x00000010 exec/tasks.h: *55
tf_Style           char in struct TextFont
        +0x0016    graphics/text.h: *60
TF_SWITCH          #define (1<<6) =0x00000040 exec/tasks.h: *57
tf_XSize           unsigned short int in struct TextFont
        +0x0018    graphics/text.h: *62
tf_YSize           unsigned short int in struct TextFont
        +0x0014    graphics/text.h: *59
ThisTask           pointer to struct Task in struct ExecBase
        +0x0114    exec/execbase.h: *55
TICKS_PER_SECOND   #define 50 =0x00000032 libraries/dos.h: *54
Timer              short int in struct AnimComp
        +0x0002    graphics/gels.h: *175
timerequest        structure tag
    size 0x0028    devices/timer.h: *28
                   devices/prtbase.h: 85
TIMERNAME          #define "timer.device" devices/timer.h: *21
TimeSet            short int in struct AnimComp
        +0x0004    graphics/gels.h: *179
timeval            structure tag
    size 0x0008    devices/timer.h: *23, 30
                   devices/inputevent.h: 150
                   intuition/preferences.h: 54, 55, 56
timsrv             struct Interrupt (size 0x0016) in struct GfxBase
        +0x0060    graphics/gfxbase.h: *34
Title              pointer to char in struct Window
        +0x0020    intuition/intuition.h: *709
Title              pointer to char in struct NewWindow
        +0x001a    intuition/intuition.h: *874
Title              pointer to char in struct Screen
        +0x0016    intuition/screens.h: *52
TmpRas             structure tag
    size 0x0008    graphics/rastport.h: *28, 55
TmpRas             pointer to struct TmpRas in struct RastPort
        +0x000c    graphics/rastport.h: *55
TOBB               Macro (1 argument) graphics/gfx.h: *18
TOF_WaitQ          struct List (size 0x000e) in struct GfxBase
        +0x00c0    graphics/gfxbase.h: *50
TOGGLESELECT       #define 0x0100 =0x00000100 intuition/intuition.h: *316
TOPAZ_EIGHTY       #define 8 =0x00000008 intuition/preferences.h: *39
TOPAZ_SIXTY        #define 9 =0x00000009 intuition/preferences.h: *40
TOPBORDER          #define 0x0040 =0x00000040 intuition/intuition.h: *313
TopBorder          unsigned short int in struct PropInfo
        +0x0014    intuition/intuition.h: *424
TopEdge            short int in struct Menu
        +0x0006    intuition/intuition.h: *60
TopEdge            short int in struct MenuItem
        +0x0006    intuition/intuition.h: *88
```

```
TopEdge             short int in struct Requester
        +0x0006     intuition/intuition.h: *145
TopEdge             short int in struct Gadget
        +0x0006     intuition/intuition.h: *197
TopEdge             short int in struct IntuiText
        +0x0006     intuition/intuition.h: *499
TopEdge             short int in struct Border
        +0x0002     intuition/intuition.h: *524
TopEdge             short int in struct Image
        +0x0002     intuition/intuition.h: *546
TopEdge             short int in struct Window
        +0x0006     intuition/intuition.h: *697
TopEdge             short int in struct NewWindow
        +0x0002     intuition/intuition.h: *852
TopEdge             short int in struct Screen
        +0x000a     intuition/screens.h: *45
TopEdge             short int in struct NewScreen
        +0x0002     intuition/screens.h: *119
TOPHIT              #define 1 =0x00000001 graphics/collide.h: *30
topmost             short int in struct GelsInfo
        +0x001a     graphics/rastport.h: *46
top_layer           pointer to struct Layer in struct Layer_Info
        +0x0000     graphics/layers.h: *34
TOTALSLOTS          #define 256 =0x00000100 libraries/expansionbase.h: *33, 53
tPoint              structure tag
    size 0x0004     graphics/gfx.h: *29
TRUE                #define 1 =0x00000001 exec/types.h: *50
trunc               Macro (1 argument) libraries/mathffp.h: *29
trunc               Macro (1 argument) libraries/mathieeedp.h: *30
TR_ADDREQUEST       #define CMD_NONSTD =0x00000009 devices/timer.h: *34
TR_GETSYSTIME       #define (CMD_NONSTD+1) =0x0000000a devices/timer.h: *35
TR_MakeBad          #define -4 =0xfffffffc libraries/translator.h: *15
tr_node             struct IORequest (size 0x0020) in struct timerequest
        +0x0000     devices/timer.h: *29
TR_NoMem            #define -2 =0xfffffffe libraries/translator.h: *14
TR_NotUsed          #define -1 =0xffffffff libraries/translator.h: *13
TR_SETSYSTIME       #define (CMD_NONSTD+2) =0x0000000b devices/timer.h: *36
tr_time             struct timeval (size 0x0008) in struct timerequest
        +0x0020     devices/timer.h: *30
TS_ADDED            #define 1 =0x00000001 exec/tasks.h: *62
TS_EXCEPT           #define 5 =0x00000005 exec/tasks.h: *66
TS_INVALID          #define 0 =0x00000000 exec/tasks.h: *61
TS_READY            #define 3 =0x00000003 exec/tasks.h: *64
TS_REMOVED          #define 6 =0x00000006 exec/tasks.h: *67
TS_RUN              #define 2 =0x00000002 exec/tasks.h: *63
TS_WAIT             #define 4 =0x00000004 exec/tasks.h: *65
tv_micro            unsigned int in struct timeval
        +0x0004     devices/timer.h: *25
tv_secs             unsigned int in struct timeval
        +0x0000     devices/timer.h: *24
TWO_PI              #define (((float) 2) * PI) libraries/mathffp.h: *16
TWO_PI              #define (((double) 2) * PI) libraries/mathieeedp.h: *17
TxBaseline          unsigned short int in struct RastPort
        +0x003e     graphics/rastport.h: *77
TxFlags             char in struct RastPort
        +0x0039     graphics/rastport.h: *74
TxHeight            unsigned short int in struct RastPort
        +0x003a     graphics/rastport.h: *75
TxSpacing           short int in struct RastPort
        +0x0040     graphics/rastport.h: *78
TxWidth             unsigned short int in struct RastPort
        +0x003c     graphics/rastport.h: *76
Type                char in struct ColorMap
        +0x0001     graphics/view.h: *24
Type                unsigned short int in struct NewWindow
        +0x002e     intuition/intuition.h: *909
Type                unsigned short int in struct NewScreen
        +0x000e     intuition/screens.h: *125
u1                  union (no tag) (size 0x0002) in struct (no tag)
```



```
        +0x0000     graphics/copper.h: *30
u2                  union (no tag) (size 0x0002) in struct (no tag)
        +0x0002     graphics/copper.h: *35
u3                  union (no tag) (size 0x0004) in struct CopIns
        +0x0002     graphics/copper.h: *37
u4                  struct (no tag) (size 0x0004) in union (no tag)
        +0x0000     graphics/copper.h: *36
UBYTE               typedef unsigned char
                    many references; defined in exec/types.h: *27
UCopIns             pointer to struct UCopList in struct ViewPort
        +0x0014     graphics/view.h: *38
UCopList            structure tag
    size 0x000c     graphics/view.h: 38
                    graphics/copper.h: *69, 71
UCOUNT              typedef unsigned short int exec/types.h: *46
ULONG               typedef unsigned long int
                    many references; defined in exec/types.h: *21
UndoBuffer          pointer to char in struct StringInfo
        +0x0004     intuition/intuition.h: *455
UndoPos             short int in struct StringInfo
        +0x000e     intuition/intuition.h: *461
Unit                structure tag
    size 0x0026     exec/devices.h: *31
                    exec/io.h:  21, 30
                    devices/clipboard.h: 40
                    devices/printer.h: 139, 153
                    devices/trackdisk.h: 185
UNITF_ACTIVE        #define (1<<0) =0x00000001 exec/devices.h: *40
UNITF_INTASK        #define (1<<1) =0x00000002 exec/devices.h: *41
unit_flags          char in struct Unit
        +0x0022     exec/devices.h: *34
UNIT_MICROHZ        #define 0 =0x00000000 devices/timer.h: *18
unit_MsgPort        struct MsgPort (size 0x0022) in struct Unit
        +0x0000     exec/devices.h: *32
unit_OpenCnt        unsigned short int in struct Unit
        +0x0024     exec/devices.h: *36
unit_pad            char in struct Unit
        +0x0023     exec/devices.h: *35
UNIT_VBLANK         #define 1 =0x00000001 devices/timer.h: *19
unusedreg           char in struct CIA
        +0x0b00     hardware/cia.h: *45
UserData            pointer to pointer to char in struct Gadget
        +0x0028     intuition/intuition.h: *237
UserData            pointer to char in struct Window
        +0x0078     intuition/intuition.h: *783
UserData            pointer to char in struct Screen
        +0x0156     intuition/screens.h: *85
UserPort            pointer to struct MsgPort in struct Window
        +0x0056     intuition/intuition.h: *754
USHORT              typedef unsigned short int
                    many references; defined in exec/types.h: *39
US_LEGAL            #define 0x10 =0x00000010 intuition/preferences.h: *180
US_LETTER           #define 0x00 =0x00000000 intuition/preferences.h: *179
UWORD               typedef unsigned short int
                    many references; defined in exec/types.h: *24
VANILLAKEY          #define 0x00200000 =0x00200000 intuition/intuition.h: *659
VBlank              char in struct GfxBase
        +0x00a0     graphics/gfxbase.h: *38
VBlankFrequency     char in struct ExecBase
        +0x0212     exec/execbase.h: *104
vbsrv               struct Interrupt (size 0x0016) in struct GfxBase
        +0x004a     graphics/gfxbase.h: *34
VctrPtr             pointer to short int in struct AreaInfo
        +0x0004     graphics/rastport.h: *20
VctrTbl             pointer to short int in struct AreaInfo
        +0x0000     graphics/rastport.h: *19
VertBody            unsigned short int in struct PropInfo
        +0x0008     intuition/intuition.h: *417
VertPot             unsigned short int in struct PropInfo
```

```
        +0x0004  intuition/intuition.h: *397
vhposr           unsigned short int in struct Custom
        +0x0006  hardware/custom.h: *23
vhposw           unsigned short int in struct Custom
        +0x002c  hardware/custom.h: *41
View             structure tag
    size 0x0012  graphics/view.h: *47
                 graphics/gfxbase.h: 26
                 intuition/intuitionbase.h: 150
ViewInitX        short int in struct Preferences
        +0x0078  intuition/preferences.h: *76
ViewInitY        short int in struct Preferences
        +0x007a  intuition/preferences.h: *76
ViewLord         struct View (size 0x0012) in struct IntuitionBase
        +0x0022  intuition/intuitionbase.h: *150
ViewModes        unsigned short int in struct NewScreen
        +0x000c  intuition/screens.h: *123
ViewPort         structure tag
    size 0x0028  graphics/view.h: *30, 32, 49
                 intuition/screens.h: 62
                 graphics/copper.h: 59
ViewPort         pointer to struct ViewPort in struct View
        +0x0000  graphics/view.h: *49
ViewPort         struct ViewPort (size 0x0028) in struct Screen
        +0x002c  intuition/screens.h: *62
ViewXOffset      char in struct Preferences
        +0x0076  intuition/preferences.h: *74
ViewYOffset      char in struct Preferences
        +0x0077  intuition/preferences.h: *75
voice            struct narrator_rb (size 0x0046) in struct mouth_rb
        +0x0000  devices/narrator.h: *88
VOID             #define void =0x00000000 exec/types.h: *18
                 exec/tasks.h: 41, 42
                 exec/interrupts.h: 25, 31
                 devices/prtbase.h: 128, 129, 131
                 workbench/icon.h: 31
volume           unsigned short int in struct narrator_rb
        +0x003e  devices/narrator.h: *75
vposr            unsigned short int in struct Custom
        +0x0004  hardware/custom.h: *22
VPOSRLOF         #define 0x8000 =0x00008000 graphics/display.h: *38
vposw            unsigned short int in struct Custom
        +0x002a  hardware/custom.h: *40
VPotRes          unsigned short int in struct PropInfo
        +0x0010  intuition/intuition.h: *422
VP_HIDE          #define 0x2000 =0x00002000 graphics/view.h: *64
VSBob            pointer to struct Bob in struct VSprite
        +0x0034  graphics/gels.h: *115
VSIZEBITS        #define 16-HSIZEBITS =0x0000000a hardware/blit.h: *14
VSIZEMASK        #define 0x3FF =0x000003ff hardware/blit.h: *16
VSOVERFLOW       #define 0x0800 =0x00000800 graphics/gels.h: *24
VSprite          structure tag
    size 0x003c  graphics/rastport.h: 40
                 graphics/gels.h: *68, 72, 73, 79, 80, 155, 232
VSPRITE          #define 0x0001 =0x00000001 graphics/gels.h: *16
VUserExt         short int in struct VSprite
        +0x003a  graphics/gels.h: *132
VUserStuff       #define SHORT =0x00000000 graphics/gels.h: *52, 132
VWaitPos         short int in union (no tag)
        +0x0000  graphics/copper.h: *28
VWAITPOS         #define u3.u4.ul.VWaitPos
                 graphics/copper.h: *41
WarmCapture      pointer to pointer to char in struct ExecBase
        +0x0032  exec/execbase.h: *38
wa_Lock          int in struct WBArg
        +0x0000  workbench/startup.h: *35
wa_Name          pointer to char in struct WBArg
        +0x0004  workbench/startup.h: *36
WBArg            structure tag
```



```
    size 0x0008  workbench/startup.h: 31, *34
WBDEVICE         #define 6 =0x00000006 workbench/workbench.h: *38
WBDISK           #define 1 =0x00000001 workbench/workbench.h: *33
WBDRAWER         #define 2 =0x00000002 workbench/workbench.h: *34
WBENCHCLOSE      #define 0x0002 =0x00000002 intuition/intuition.h: *686
WBENCHMESSAGE    #define 0x00020000 =0x00020000 intuition/intuition.h: *655
WBENCHOPEN       #define 0x0001 =0x00000001 intuition/intuition.h: *685
WBENCHSCREEN     #define 0x0001 =0x00000001 intuition/screens.h: *95
WBENCHWINDOW     #define 0x02000000 =0x02000000 intuition/intuition.h: *836
WBGARBAGE        #define 5 =0x00000005 workbench/workbench.h: *37
WBKICK           #define 7 =0x00000007 workbench/workbench.h: *39
WBObject         structure tag
    size 0x0000  workbench/icon.h: 28
WBorBottom       char in struct Screen
        +0x0026  intuition/screens.h: *57
WBorLeft         char in struct Screen
        +0x0024  intuition/screens.h: *57
WBorRight        char in struct Screen
        +0x0025  intuition/screens.h: *57
WBorTop          char in struct Screen
        +0x0023  intuition/screens.h: *57
WBPROJECT        #define 4 =0x00000004 workbench/workbench.h: *36
WBStartup        structure tag
    size 0x0028  workbench/startup.h: *25
WBTOOL           #define 3 =0x00000003 workbench/workbench.h: *35
wb_Depth         char in struct Preferences
        +0x00e6  intuition/preferences.h: *123
WB_DISKMAGIC     #define 0xe310 =0x0000e310 workbench/workbench.h: *66
WB_DISKVERSION   #define 1 =0x00000001 workbench/workbench.h: *67
wb_Height        unsigned short int in struct Preferences
        +0x00e4  intuition/preferences.h: *122
wb_Width         unsigned short int in struct Preferences
        +0x00e2  intuition/preferences.h: *121
WDOWNBACK        #define 0x0060 =0x00000060 intuition/intuition.h: *344
WDRAGGING        #define 0x0020 =0x00000020 intuition/intuition.h: *340
width            char in struct mouth_rb
        +0x0046  devices/narrator.h: *89
Width            short int in struct Menu
        +0x0008  intuition/intuition.h: *61
Width            short int in struct MenuItem
        +0x0008  intuition/intuition.h: *89
Width            short int in struct Requester
        +0x0008  intuition/intuition.h: *146
Width            short int in struct Gadget
        +0x0008  intuition/intuition.h: *198
Width            short int in struct Image
        +0x0004  intuition/intuition.h: *547
Width            short int in struct Window
        +0x0008  intuition/intuition.h: *698
Width            short int in struct NewWindow
        +0x0004  intuition/intuition.h: *853
Width            short int in struct Screen
        +0x000c  intuition/screens.h: *46
Width            short int in struct NewScreen
        +0x0004  intuition/screens.h: *119
Width            short int in struct VSprite
        +0x001c  graphics/gels.h: *98
Window           structure tag
    size 0x0084  devices/conunit.h: 37
                 intuition/intuition.h: 168, 630, *693, 695, 742
                 intuition/screens.h: 43
                 intuition/intuitionbase.h: 152
Window           pointer to pointer to char in struct Layer
        +0x0028  graphics/clip.h: *38
WINDOWACTIVE     #define 0x2000 =0x00002000 intuition/intuition.h: *825
WINDOWCLOSE      #define 0x0008 =0x00000008 intuition/intuition.h: *801
WINDOWDEPTH      #define 0x0004 =0x00000004 intuition/intuition.h: *800
WINDOWDRAG       #define 0x0002 =0x00000002 intuition/intuition.h: *799
WindowPort       pointer to struct MsgPort in struct Window
```

```
        +0x005a  intuition/intuition.h: *754
WINDOWREFRESH    #define 0x01000000 =0x01000000 intuition/intuition.h: *835
WINDOWSIZING     #define 0x0001 =0x00000001 intuition/intuition.h: *798
WINDOWTICKED     #define 0x04000000 =0x04000000 intuition/intuition.h: *837
WLayer           pointer to struct Layer in struct Window
        +0x007c  intuition/intuition.h: *788
WORD             typedef short int
                 many references; defined in exec/types.h: *23
WORDBITS         typedef unsigned short int
                 exec/types.h: *25
wordreserved     array [7] of unsigned short int in struct RastPort
        +0x004e  graphics/rastport.h: *82
WORKBENCH_ICON_H #define =0x00000000 workbench/icon.h: *2
WORKBENCH_STARTUP_H #define =0x00000000 workbench/startup.h: *2
WORKBENCH_WORKBENCH_H #define =0x00000000 workbench/workbench.h: *2
WorkName         array [30] of char in struct Preferences
        +0x00ba  intuition/preferences.h: *110
WScreen          pointer to struct Screen in struct Window
        +0x002e  intuition/intuition.h: *717
WUPFRONT         #define 0x0040 =0x00000040 intuition/intuition.h: *342
W_TRACTOR        #define 0x30 =0x00000030 intuition/preferences.h: *182
x                short int in struct tPoint
        +0x0000  graphics/gfx.h: *31
X                short int in struct VSprite
        +0x0018  graphics/gels.h: *95
x                unsigned short int in struct SimpleSprite
        +0x0006  graphics/sprite.h: *19
XAccel           short int in struct AnimOb
        +0x001a  graphics/gels.h: *214
XOffset          char in struct Window
        +0x0050  intuition/intuition.h: *750
XOffset          char in struct Preferences
        +0x0064  intuition/preferences.h: *60
XTrans           short int in struct AnimComp
        +0x001c  graphics/gels.h: *192
XVel             short int in struct AnimOb
        +0x0016  graphics/gels.h: *213
XY               pointer to short int in struct Border
        +0x0008  intuition/intuition.h: *528
y                short int in struct tPoint
        +0x0002  graphics/gfx.h: *31
Y                short int in struct VSprite
        +0x0016  graphics/gels.h: *95
y                unsigned short int in struct SimpleSprite
        +0x0008  graphics/sprite.h: *19
YAccel           short int in struct AnimOb
        +0x0018  graphics/gels.h: *214
YOffset          char in struct Window
        +0x0051  intuition/intuition.h: *750
YOffset          char in struct Preferences
        +0x0065  intuition/preferences.h: *61
YTrans           short int in struct AnimComp
        +0x001a  graphics/gels.h: *191
YVel             short int in struct AnimOb
```

A true software memory map, showing system utilization of the various sections of RAM and free space is not provided, or possible with the Amiga. All memory is dynamically allocated by the memory manager, and the actual locations may change from release-to-release, machine-to-machine or boot-to-boot (see the exec/AllocMem function for details). To find the locations of system structures software must use the defined access procedures, starting by fetching the address of the exec.library from location 4; the only absolute memory location in the system. All software is written so that it can be loaded and relocated anywhere in memory by the loader. What follows are maps that show the relative locations of all custom chip registers. This is provided for the convenience of the few developers that may need to directly access them.

BRIEF CHIP REGISTER MAPS

When dealing directly with the hardware, all unused bits must be written as zeros. The value of any unused read bit must not be trusted.

The register names for the two 8520 Complex Interface Adapters are listed below. Under the multitasking Operating System, access is controlled by the cia.resource. The 8520's are byte-oriented; writing them as a word is NOT allowed (it affects both chips in strange ways). The address at which each register is to be accessed is given in this list:

Address for:

8520-A	8520-B	NAME	EXPLANATION
BFE001	BFD000	PRA	Peripheral data register A
BFE101	BFD100	PRB	Peripheral data register B
BFE201	BFD200	DDRB	Data direction register A
BFE301	BFD300	DDRA	Data direction register B
BFE401	BFD400	TALO	TIMER A low register (.715909 Mhz under)
BFE501	BFD500	TAHI	TIMER A high register (NTSC. Under PAL)
BFE601	BFD600	TBLO	TIMER B low register (these run at)
BFE701	BFD700	TBHI	TIMER B high register (.709379 Mhz)
BFE801	BFD800		Event LSB (A=VBlank B=HSync)
BFE901	BFD900		Event 8 - 15
BFEA01	BFDA00		Event MSB
BFEB01	BFDB00		No connect
BFEC01	BFDC00	SDR	Serial data register
BFED01	BFDD00	ICR	Interrupt control register
BFEE01	BFDE00	CRA	Control register A
BFEF01	BFDF00	CRB	Control register B

```
;---------Amiga Custom Chips-----------
;The custom chips must be addressed starting at $DFF000, and no other address.
;All registers are Write-only or Read-only; violating this restriction in any
;way will cause subtle problems.  Unused registers must not be accessed.
;Custom chip registers must be addressed as words or longs, never bytes.
;
; Key:
;       &        = register used by DMA only
;       %        = register used by DMA usually, processor sometimes
;       +        = register pair - always write as one 32 bit write
;       *        = Not writable by the Copper
;       ~        = Not writable unless the Copper danger bit is set.
;       A,D,P    = Agnus, Denise or Paula
;       W,R,ER   = Write-Only, Read-Only or DMA-related Early Read
;       S        - Strobe, writing 0's to the address causes an effect
```

NAME		ADD	R/W	CHIP			FUNCTION
BLTDDAT	&	*000	ER	A			Blitter destination early read (dummy address)
DMACONR		*002	R	A		P	DMA control (and Blitter status) read
VPOSR		*004	R	A			Read vert most significant bit (and frame flop)

NAME		ADD	R/W	A	D	P	FUNCTION
VHPOSR		*006	R	A			Read vert and horiz. position of beam
DSKDATR	&	*008	ER			P	Disk data early read (dummy address)
JOY0DAT		*00A	R		D		Joystick-mouse 0 data (vert,horiz)
JOY1DAT		*00C	R		D		Joystick-mouse 1 data (vert,horiz)
CLXDAT		*00E	R		D		Collision data register (read and clear)
ADKCONR		*010	R			P	Audio, disk control register read
POT0DAT		*012	R			P	Pot counter pair 0 data (vert,horiz)
POT1DAT		*014	R			P	Pot counter pair 1 data (vert,horiz)
POTINP		*016	R			P	Pot port data read (was POTGOR)(see potgo.resource)
SERDATR		*018	R			P	Serial port data and status read
DSKBYTR		*01A	R			P	Disk data byte and status read
INTENAR		*01C	R			P	Interrupt enable bits read
INTREQR		*01E	R			P	Interrupt request bits read
DSKPT	+	*020	W	A			Disk pointer (register pair)
DSKLEN		*024	W			P	Disk length
DSKDAT	&	*026	W			P	Disk DMA data write
REFPTR	&	*028	W	A			Refresh pointer
VPOSW		*02A	W	A			Write vert most significant bit (and frame flop)
VHPOSW		*02C	W	A			Write vert and horiz position of beam
COPCON		*02E	W	A			Coprocessor control register (CDANG)
SERDAT		*030	W			P	Serial port data and stop bits write
SERPER		*032	W			P	Serial port period and control
POTGO		*034	W			P	Pot port data write and start
JOYTEST		*036	W		D		Write to all four joystick-mouse counters at once
STREQU	&	*038	S		D		Strobe for horiz sync with VB and EQU
STRVBL	&	*03A	S		D		Strobe for horiz sync with VB (vert. blank)
STRHOR	&	*03C	S		D	P	Strobe for horiz sync
STRLONG	&	*03E	S		D		Strobe for identification of long horiz. line.
BLTCON0		~040	W	A			Blitter control register 0
BLTCON1		~042	W	A			Blitter control register 1
BLTAFWM		~044	W	A			Blitter first word mask for source A
BLTALWM		~046	W	A			Blitter last word mask for source A
BLTCPT	+	~048	W	A			Blitter pointer to source C (register pair)
BLTBPT	+	~04C	W	A			Blitter pointer to source B (register pair)
BLTAPT	+	~050	W	A			Blitter pointer to source A (register pair)
BLTDPT	+	~054	W	A			Blitter pointer to destination D (register pair))
BLTSIZE		~058	W	A			Blitter start and size (window width, height)
BLTCMOD		~060	W	A			Blitter modulo for source C
BLTBMOD		~062	W	A			Blitter modulo for source B
BLTAMOD		~064	W	A			Blitter modulo for source A
BLTDMOD		~066	W	A			Blitter modulo for destination D
BLTCDAT	%	~070	W	A			Blitter source C data register
BLTBDAT	%	~072	W	A			Blitter source B data register
BLTADAT	%	~074	W	A			Blitter source A data register
DSKSYNC		~07E	R			P	Disk sync pattern register for disk read
COP1LC	+	080	W	A			Coprocessor first location register (pair)
COP2LC	+	084	W	A			Coprocessor second location register (pair)
COPJMP1		088	S	A			Coprocessor restart at first location
COPJMP2		08A	S	A			Coprocessor restart at second location
COPINS		08C	W	A			Coprocessor instruction fetch identify
DIWSTRT		08E	W	A			Display window start (upper left vert-horiz position)
DIWSTOP		090	W	A			Display window stop (lower right vert.-horiz. position)
DDFSTRT		092	W	A			Display bit plane data fetch start (horiz. position)
DDFSTOP		094	W	A			Display bit plane data fetch stop (horiz. position)
DMACON		096	W	A	D	P	DMA control write (clear or set)
CLXCON		098	W		D		Collision control
INTENA		09A	W			P	Interrupt enable bits (clear or set bits)
INTREQ		09C	W			P	Interrupt request bits (clear or set bits)
ADKCON		09E	W			P	Audio, disk, UART control
AUD0LC	+	0A0	W	A			Audio channel 0 location (pair)
AUD0LEN		0A4	W			P	Audio channel 0 length
AUD0PER		0A6	W			P	Audio channel 0 period
AUD0VOL		0A8	W			P	Audio channel 0 volume
AUD0DAT	&	0AA	W			P	Audio channel 0 data

```
            0AC
            0AE
AUD1LC    + 0B0  W  A       Audio channel 1 location (pair)
AUD1LEN     0B4  W      P   Audio channel 1 length
AUD1PER     0B6  W      P   Audio channel 1 period
AUD1VOL     0B8  W      P   Audio channel 1 volume
AUD1DAT   & 0BA  W      P   Audio channel 1 data
            0BC
            0BE
AUD2LC    + 0C0  W  A       Audio channel 2 location (pair)
AUD2LEN     0C4  W      P   Audio channel 2 length
AUD2PER     0C6  W      P   Audio channel 2 period
AUD2VOL     0C8  W      P   Audio channel 2 volume
AUD2DAT   & 0CA  W      P   Audio channel 2 data
            0CC
            0CE
AUD3LC    + 0D0  W  A       Audio channel 3 location (pair)
AUD3LEN     0D4  W      P   Audio channel 3 length
AUD3PER     0D6  W      P   Audio channel 3 period
AUD3VOL     0D8  W      P   Audio channel 3 volume
AUD3DAT   & 0DA  W      P   Audio channel 3 data
            0DC
            0DE

BPL1PT    + 0E0  W  A       Bit plane 1 pointer (register pair)
BPL2PT    + 0E4  W  A       Bit plane 2 pointer (register pair)
BPL3PT    + 0E8  W  A       Bit plane 3 pointer (register pair)
BPL4PT    + 0EC  W  A       Bit plane 4 pointer (register pair)
BPL5PT    + 0F0  W  A       Bit plane 5 pointer (register pair)
BPL6PT    + 0F4  W  A       Bit plane 6 pointer (register pair)
            0F8
            0FA
            0FC
            0FE
BPLCON0     100  W  A D     Bit plane control register (misc. control bits)
BPLCON1     102  W    D     Bit plane control reg. (scroll value PF1, PF2)
BPLCON2     104  W    D     Bit plane control reg. (priority control)
            106
BPL1MOD     108  W  A       Bit plane modulo (odd planes)
BPL2MOD     10A  W  A       Bit Plane modulo (even planes)
            10C
            10E
BPL1DAT   & 110  W    D     Bit plane 1 data (parallel-to-serial convert)
BPL2DAT   & 112  W    D     Bit plane 2 data (parallel-to-serial convert)
BPL3DAT   & 114  W    D     Bit plane 3 data (parallel-to-serial convert)
BPL4DAT   & 116  W    D     Bit plane 4 data (parallel-to-serial convert)
BPL5DAT   & 118  W    D     Bit plane 5 data (parallel-to-serial convert)
BPL6DAT   & 11A  W    D     Bit plane 6 data (parallel-to-serial convert)
            11C
            11E

SPR0PT    + 120  W  A       Sprite 0 pointer (register pair)
SPR1PT    + 124  W  A       Sprite 1 pointer (register pair)
SPR2PT    + 128  W  A       Sprite 2 pointer (register pair)
SPR3PT    + 12C  W  A       Sprite 3 pointer (register pair)
SPR4PT    + 130  W  A       Sprite 4 pointer (register pair)
SPR5PT    + 134  W  A       Sprite 5 pointer (register pair)
SPR6PT    + 138  W  A       Sprite 6 pointer (register pair)
SPR7PT    + 13C  W  A       Sprite 7 pointer (register pair)
SPR0POS   % 140  W  A D     Sprite 0 vert-horiz start position data
SPR0CTL   % 142  W  A D     Sprite 0 vert stop position and control data
SPR0DATA  % 144  W    D     Sprite 0 image data register A
SPR0DATB  % 146  W    D     Sprite 0 image data register B
SPR1POS   % 148  W  A D     Sprite 1 vert-horiz start position data
SPR1CTL   % 14A  W  A D     Sprite 1 vert stop position and control data
SPR1DATA  % 14C  W    D     Sprite 1 image data register A
SPR1DATB  % 14E  W    D     Sprite 1 image data register B
SPR2POS   % 150  W  A D     Sprite 2 vert-horiz start position data
SPR2CTL   % 152  W  A D     Sprite 2 vert stop position and control data
```



```
SPR2DATA  % 154  W    D     Sprite 2 image data register A
SPR2DATB  % 156  W    D     Sprite 2 image data register B
SPR3POS   % 158  W  A D     Sprite 3 vert-horiz start position data
SPR3CTL   % 15A  W  A D     Sprite 3 vert stop position and control data
SPR3DATA  % 15C  W    D     Sprite 3 image data register A
SPR3DATB  % 15E  W    D     Sprite 3 image data register B
SPR4POS   % 160  W  A D     Sprite 4 vert-horiz start position data
SPR4CTL   % 162  W  A D     Sprite 4 vert stop position and control data
SPR4DATA  % 164  W    D     Sprite 4 image data register A
SPR4DATB  % 166  W    D     Sprite 4 image data register B
SPR5POS   % 168  W  A D     Sprite 5 vert-horiz start position data
SPR5CTL   % 16A  W  A D     Sprite 5 vert stop position and control data
SPR5DATA  % 16C  W    D     Sprite 5 image data register A
SPR5DATB  % 16E  W    D     Sprite 5 image data register B
SPR6POS   % 170  W  A D     Sprite 6 vert-horiz start position data
SPR6CTL   % 172  W  A D     Sprite 6 vert stop position and control data
SPR6DATA  % 174  W    D     Sprite 6 image data register A
SPR6DATB  % 176  W    D     Sprite 6 image data register B
SPR7POS   % 178  W  A D     Sprite 7 vert-horiz start position data
SPR7CTL   % 17A  W  A D     Sprite 7 vert stop position and control data
SPR7DATA  % 17C  W    D     Sprite 7 image data register A
SPR7DATB  % 17E  W    D     Sprite 7 image data register B

COLOR00     180  W    D     Color table 00
  ...                            ...
COLOR31     1BE  W    D     Color table 31
RESERVED    1110X
RESERVED    1111X
NO-OP(NULL) 1FE
```

```
Struct.doc   by Kodiak
==========

AnimComp:
  $0026   38  sizeof(AnimComp)
  $0000    0  Flags
  $0002    2  Timer
  $0004    4  TimeSet
  $0006    6  NextComp
  $000a   10  PrevComp
  $000e   14  NextSeq
  $0012   18  PrevSeq
  $0016   22  AnimCRoutine
  $001a   26  YTrans
  $001c   28  XTrans
  $001e   30  HeadOb
  $0022   34  AnimBob
AnimOb:
  $002a   42  sizeof(AnimOb)
  $0000    0  NextOb
  $0004    4  PrevOb
  $0008    8  Clock
  $000c   12  AnOldY
  $000e   14  AnOldX
  $0010   16  AnY
  $0012   18  AnX
  $0014   20  YVel
  $0016   22  XVel
  $0018   24  YAccel
  $001a   26  XAccel
  $001c   28  RingYTrans
  $001e   30  RingXTrans
  $0020   32  AnimORoutine
  $0024   36  HeadComp
  $0028   40  AUserExt
AreaInfo:
  $0018   24  sizeof(AreaInfo)
  $0000    0  VctrTbl
  $0004    4  VctrPtr
  $0008    8  FlagTbl
  $000c   12  FlagPtr
  $0010   16  Count
  $0012   18  MaxCount
  $0014   20  FirstX
  $0016   22  FirstY
AudChannel:
  $0010   16  sizeof(AudChannel)
  $0000    0  ac_ptr
  $0004    4  ac_len
  $0006    6  ac_per
  $0008    8  ac_vol
  $000a   10  ac_dat
  $000c   12  ac_pad[0]
AvailFonts:
  $000a   10  sizeof(AvailFonts)
  $0000    0  af_Type
  $0002    2  af_Attr
AvailFontsHeader:
  $0002    2  sizeof(AvailFontsHeader)
  $0000    0  afh_NumEntries
BitMap:
  $0028   40  sizeof(BitMap)
  $0000    0  BytesPerRow
  $0002    2  Rows
  $0004    4  Flags
  $0005    5  Depth
  $0006    6  pad
  $0008    8  Planes[0]
Bob:
  $0020   32  sizeof(Bob)
  $0000    0  Flags
  $0002    2  SaveBuffer
  $0006    6  ImageShadow
  $000a   10  Before
  $000e   14  After
  $0012   18  BobVSprite
  $0016   22  BobComp
  $001a   26  DBuffer
  $001e   30  BUserExt
BoolInfo:
  $000a   10  sizeof(BoolInfo)
  $0000    0  Flags
  $0002    2  Mask
  $0006    6  Reserved
BootBlock:
  $000c   12  sizeof(BootBlock)
  $0000    0  bb_id[0]
  $0004    4  bb_chksum
  $0008    8  bb_dosblock
BootNode:
  $0014   20  sizeof(BootNode)
  $0000    0  bn_Node
  $000e   14  bn_Flags
  $0010   16  bn_DeviceNode
Border:
  $0010   16  sizeof(Border)
  $0000    0  LeftEdge
  $0002    2  TopEdge
  $0004    4  FrontPen
  $0005    5  BackPen
  $0006    6  DrawMode
  $0007    7  Count
  $0008    8  XY
  $000c   12  NextBorder
CIA:
  $0f02 3842  sizeof(CIA)
  $0000    0  ciapra
  $0001    1  pad0[0]
  $0100  256  ciaprb
  $0101  257  pad1[0]
  $0200  512  ciaddra
  $0201  513  pad2[0]
  $0300  768  ciaddrb
  $0301  769  pad3[0]
  $0400 1024  ciatalo
  $0401 1025  pad4[0]
  $0500 1280  ciatahi
  $0501 1281  pad5[0]
  $0600 1536  ciatblo
  $0601 1537  pad6[0]
  $0700 1792  ciatbhi
  $0701 1793  pad7[0]
  $0800 2048  ciatodlow
  $0801 2049  pad8[0]
  $0900 2304  ciatodmid
  $0901 2305  pad9[0]
  $0a00 2560  ciatodhi
  $0a01 2561  pad10[0]
  $0b00 2816  unusedreg
  $0b01 2817  pad11[0]
  $0c00 3072  ciasdr
  $0c01 3073  pad12[0]
  $0d00 3328  ciaicr
  $0d01 3329  pad13[0]
  $0e00 3584  ciacra
  $0e01 3585  pad14[0]
  $0f00 3840  ciacrb
ClipRect:
```



```
  $0024   36  sizeof(ClipRect)
  $0000    0  Next
  $0004    4  prev
  $0008    8  lobs
  $000c   12  BitMap
  $0010   16  bounds
  $0018   24  _p1
  $001c   28  _p2
  $0020   32  reserved
ClipboardUnitPartial:
  $0012   18  sizeof(ClipboardUnitPartial
  $0000    0  cu_Node
  $000e   14  cu_UnitNum
ColorMap:
  $0008    8  sizeof(ColorMap)
  $0000    0  Flags
  $0001    1  Type
  $0002    2  Count
  $0004    4  ColorTable
CommandLineInterface:
  $0040   64  sizeof(CommandLineInterface
  $0000    0  cli_Result2
  $0004    4  cli_SetName
  $0008    8  cli_CommandDir
  $000c   12  cli_ReturnCode
  $0010   16  cli_CommandName
  $0014   20  cli_FailLevel
  $0018   24  cli_Prompt
  $001c   28  cli_StandardInput
  $0020   32  cli_CurrentInput
  $0024   36  cli_CommandFile
  $0028   40  cli_Interactive
  $002c   44  cli_Background
  $0030   48  cli_CurrentOutput
  $0034   52  cli_DefaultStack
  $0038   56  cli_StandardOutput
  $003c   60  cli_Module
ConUnit:
  $0128  296  sizeof(ConUnit)
  $0000    0  cu_MP
  $0022   34  cu_Window
  $0026   38  cu_XCP
  $0028   40  cu_YCP
  $002a   42  cu_XMax
  $002c   44  cu_YMax
  $002e   46  cu_XRSize
  $0030   48  cu_YRSize
  $0032   50  cu_XROrigin
  $0034   52  cu_YROrigin
  $0036   54  cu_XRExtant
  $0038   56  cu_YRExtant
  $003a   58  cu_XMinShrink
  $003c   60  cu_YMinShrink
  $003e   62  cu_XCCP
  $0040   64  cu_YCCP
  $0042   66  cu_KeyMapStruct
  $0062   98  cu_TabStops[0]
  $0102  258  cu_Mask
  $0103  259  cu_FgPen
  $0104  260  cu_BgPen
  $0105  261  cu_AOLPen
  $0106  262  cu_DrawMode
  $0107  263  cu_AreaPtSz
  $0108  264  cu_AreaPtrn
  $010c  268  cu_Minterms[0]
  $0114  276  cu_Font
  $0118  280  cu_AlgoStyle
  $0119  281  cu_TxFlags
  $011a  282  cu_TxHeight
  $011c  284  cu_TxWidth
  $011e  286  cu_TxBaseline
  $0120  288  cu_TxSpacing
  $0122  290  cu_Modes[0]
  $0125  293  cu_RawEvents[0]
ConfigDev:
  $0044   68  sizeof(ConfigDev)
  $0000    0  cd_Node
  $000e   14  cd_Flags
  $000f   15  cd_Pad
  $0010   16  cd_Rom
  $0020   32  cd_BoardAddr
  $0024   36  cd_BoardSize
  $0028   40  cd_SlotAddr
  $002a   42  cd_SlotSize
  $002c   44  cd_Driver
  $0030   48  cd_NextCD
  $0034   52  cd_Unused[0]
CopIns:
  $0006    6  sizeof(CopIns)
  $0000    0  OpCode
  $0002    2  u3
  $0002    2  u3.nxtlist
  $0002    2  u3.u4
  $0002    2  u3.u4.u1
  $0002    2  u3.u4.u1.VWaitPos
  $0002    2  u3.u4.u1.DestAddr
  $0004    4  u3.u4.u2
  $0004    4  u3.u4.u2.HWaitPos
  $0004    4  u3.u4.u2.DestData
CopList:
  $0022   34  sizeof(CopList)
  $0000    0  Next
  $0004    4  _CopList
  $0008    8  _ViewPort
  $000c   12  CopIns
  $0010   16  CopPtr
  $0014   20  CopLStart
  $0018   24  CopSStart
  $001c   28  Count
  $001e   30  MaxCount
  $0020   32  DyOffset
CurrentBinding:
  $0010   16  sizeof(CurrentBinding)
  $0000    0  cb_ConfigDev
  $0004    4  cb_FileName
  $0008    8  cb_ProductString
  $000c   12  cb_ToolTypes
Custom:
  $01c0  448  sizeof(Custom)
  $0000    0  bltddat
  $0002    2  dmaconr
  $0004    4  vposr
  $0006    6  vhposr
  $0008    8  dskdatr
  $000a   10  joy0dat
  $000c   12  joy1dat
  $000e   14  clxdat
  $0010   16  adkconr
  $0012   18  pot0dat
  $0014   20  pot1dat
  $0016   22  potinp
  $0018   24  serdatr
  $001a   26  dskbytr
  $001c   28  intenar
  $001e   30  intreqr
  $0020   32  dskpt
  $0024   36  dsklen
  $0026   38  dskdat
```

```
 $0028    40  refptr
 $002a    42  vposw
 $002c    44  vhposw
 $002e    46  copcon
 $0030    48  serdat
 $0032    50  serper
 $0034    52  potgo
 $0036    54  joytest
 $0038    56  strequ
 $003a    58  strvbl
 $003c    60  strhor
 $003e    62  strlong
 $0040    64  bltcon0
 $0042    66  bltcon1
 $0044    68  bltafwm
 $0046    70  bltalwm
 $0048    72  bltcpt
 $004c    76  bltbpt
 $0050    80  bltapt
 $0054    84  bltdpt
 $0058    88  bltsize
 $005a    90  pad2d[0]
 $0060    96  bltcmod
 $0062    98  bltbmod
 $0064   100  bltamod
 $0066   102  bltdmod
 $0068   104  pad34[0]
 $0070   112  bltcdat
 $0072   114  bltbdat
 $0074   116  bltadat
 $0076   118  pad3b[0]
 $007e   126  dsksync
 $0080   128  cop1lc
 $0084   132  cop2lc
 $0088   136  copjmp1
 $008a   138  copjmp2
 $008c   140  copins
 $008e   142  diwstrt
 $0090   144  diwstop
 $0092   146  ddfstrt
 $0094   148  ddfstop
 $0096   150  dmacon
 $0098   152  clxcon
 $009a   154  intena
 $009c   156  intreq
 $009e   158  adkcon
 $00a0   160  aud[0]
 $00a0   160  aud[0].ac_ptr
 $00a4   164  aud[0].ac_len
 $00a6   166  aud[0].ac_per
 $00a8   168  aud[0].ac_vol
 $00aa   170  aud[0].ac_dat
 $00ac   172  aud[0].ac_pad[0]
 $00e0   224  bplpt[0]
 $00f8   248  pad7c[0]
 $0100   256  bplcon0
 $0102   258  bplcon1
 $0104   260  bplcon2
 $0106   262  pad83
 $0108   264  bpl1mod
 $010a   266  bpl2mod
 $010c   268  pad86[0]
 $0110   272  bpldat[0]
 $011c   284  pad8e[0]
 $0120   288  sprpt[0]
 $0140   320  spr[0]
 $0140   320  spr[0].pos
 $0142   322  spr[0].ctl
 $0144   324  spr[0].dataa
```

```
 $0146   326  spr[0].datab
 $0180   384  color[0]
DBufPacket:
 $000c    12  sizeof(DBufPacket)
 $0000     0  BufY
 $0002     2  BufX
 $0004     4  BufPath
 $0008     8  BufBuffer
DateStamp:
 $000c    12  sizeof(DateStamp)
 $0000     0  ds_Days
 $0004     4  ds_Minute
 $0008     8  ds_Tick
DevInfo:
 $002c    44  sizeof(DevInfo)
 $0000     0  dvi_Next
 $0004     4  dvi_Type
 $0008     8  dvi_Task
 $000c    12  dvi_Lock
 $0010    16  dvi_Handler
 $0014    20  dvi_StackSize
 $0018    24  dvi_Priority
 $001c    28  dvi_Startup
 $0020    32  dvi_SegList
 $0024    36  dvi_GlobVec
 $0028    40  dvi_Name
Device:
 $0022    34  sizeof(Device)
 $0000     0  dd_Library
DeviceData:
 $0034    52  sizeof(DeviceData)
 $0000     0  dd_Device
 $0022    34  dd_Segment
 $0026    38  dd_ExecBase
 $002a    42  dd_CmdVectors
 $002e    46  dd_CmdBytes
 $0032    50  dd_NumCommands
DeviceList:
 $002c    44  sizeof(DeviceList)
 $0000     0  dl_Next
 $0004     4  dl_Type
 $0008     8  dl_Task
 $000c    12  dl_Lock
 $0010    16  dl_VolumeDate
 $001c    28  dl_LockList
 $0020    32  dl_DiskType
 $0024    36  dl_unused
 $0028    40  dl_Name
DeviceNode:
 $002c    44  sizeof(DeviceNode)
 $0000     0  dn_Next
 $0004     4  dn_Type
 $0008     8  dn_Task
 $000c    12  dn_Lock
 $0010    16  dn_Handler
 $0014    20  dn_StackSize
 $0018    24  dn_Priority
 $001c    28  dn_Startup
 $0020    32  dn_SegList
 $0024    36  dn_GlobalVec
 $0028    40  dn_Name
DiagArea:
 $000e    14  sizeof(DiagArea)
 $0000     0  da_Config
 $0001     1  da_Flags
 $0002     2  da_Size
 $0004     4  da_DiagPoint
 $0006     6  da_BootPoint
 $0008     8  da_Name
```



```
 $000a    10  da_Reserved01
 $000c    12  da_Reserved02
DiscResource:
 $0090   144  sizeof(DiscResource)
 $0000     0  dr_Library
 $0022    34  dr_Current
 $0026    38  dr_Flags
 $0027    39  dr_pad
 $0028    40  dr_SysLib
 $002c    44  dr_CiaResource
 $0030    48  dr_UnitID[0]
 $0040    64  dr_Waiting
 $004e    78  dr_DiscBlock
 $0064   100  dr_DiscSync
 $007a   122  dr_Index
DiscResourceUnit:
 $0056    86  sizeof(DiscResourceUnit)
 $0000     0  dru_Message
 $0014    20  dru_DiscBlock
 $002a    42  dru_DiscSync
 $0040    64  dru_Index
DiskFontHeader:
 $006a   106  sizeof(DiskFontHeader)
 $0000     0  dfh_DF
 $000e    14  dfh_FileID
 $0010    16  dfh_Revision
 $0012    18  dfh_Segment
 $0016    22  dfh_Name[0]
 $0036    54  dfh_TF
DiskObject:
 $004e    78  sizeof(DiskObject)
 $0000     0  do_Magic
 $0002     2  do_Version
 $0004     4  do_Gadget
 $0030    48  do_Type
 $0032    50  do_DefaultTool
 $0036    54  do_ToolTypes
 $003a    58  do_CurrentX
 $003e    62  do_CurrentY
 $0042    66  do_DrawerData
 $0046    70  do_ToolWindow
 $004a    74  do_StackSize
DosEnvec:
 $0044    68  sizeof(DosEnvec)
 $0000     0  de_TableSize
 $0004     4  de_SizeBlock
 $0008     8  de_SecOrg
 $000c    12  de_Surfaces
 $0010    16  de_SectorPerBlock
 $0014    20  de_BlocksPerTrack
 $0018    24  de_Reserved
 $001c    28  de_PreAlloc
 $0020    32  de_Interleave
 $0024    36  de_LowCyl
 $0028    40  de_HighCyl
 $002c    44  de_NumBuffers
 $0030    48  de_BufMemType
 $0034    52  de_MaxTransfer
 $0038    56  de_Mask
 $003c    60  de_BootPri
 $0040    64  de_DosType
DosInfo:
 $0014    20  sizeof(DosInfo)
 $0000     0  di_McName
 $0004     4  di_DevInfo
 $0008     8  di_Devices
 $000c    12  di_Handlers
 $0010    16  di_NetHand
DosLibrary:
```

```
 $0036    54  sizeof(DosLibrary)
 $0000     0  dl_lib
 $0022    34  dl_Root
 $0026    38  dl_GV
 $002a    42  dl_A2
 $002e    46  dl_A5
 $0032    50  dl_A6
DosList:
 $002c    44  sizeof(DosList)
 $0000     0  dol_Next
 $0004     4  dol_Type
 $0008     8  dol_Task
 $000c    12  dol_Lock
 $0010    16  dol_misc
 $0010    16  dol_misc.dol_handler
 $0010    16  dol_misc.dol_handler.dol_Ha
 $0014    20  dol_misc.dol_handler.dol_St
 $0018    24  dol_misc.dol_handler.dol_Pr
 $001c    28  dol_misc.dol_handler.dol_St
 $0020    32  dol_misc.dol_handler.dol_Se
 $0024    36  dol_misc.dol_handler.dol_Gl
 $0010    16  dol_misc.dol_volume
 $0010    16  dol_misc.dol_volume.dol_Vol
 $001c    28  dol_misc.dol_volume.dol_Loc
 $0020    32  dol_misc.dol_volume.dol_Dis
 $0028    40  dol_Name
DosPacket:
 $0030    48  sizeof(DosPacket)
 $0000     0  dp_Link
 $0004     4  dp_Port
 $0008     8  dp_Type
 $000c    12  dp_Res1
 $0010    16  dp_Res2
 $0014    20  dp_Arg1
 $0018    24  dp_Arg2
 $001c    28  dp_Arg3
 $0020    32  dp_Arg4
 $0024    36  dp_Arg5
 $0028    40  dp_Arg6
 $002c    44  dp_Arg7
DrawerData:
 $0038    56  sizeof(DrawerData)
 $0000     0  dd_NewWindow
 $0030    48  dd_CurrentX
 $0034    52  dd_CurrentY
ExecBase:
 $024c   588  sizeof(ExecBase)
 $0000     0  LibNode
 $0022    34  SoftVer
 $0024    36  LowMemChkSum
 $0026    38  ChkBase
 $002a    42  ColdCapture
 $002e    46  CoolCapture
 $0032    50  WarmCapture
 $0036    54  SysStkUpper
 $003a    58  SysStkLower
 $003e    62  MaxLocMem
 $0042    66  DebugEntry
 $0046    70  DebugData
 $004a    74  AlertData
 $004e    78  MaxExtMem
 $0052    82  ChkSum
 $0054    84  IntVects[0]
 $0114   276  ThisTask
 $0118   280  IdleCount
 $011c   284  DispCount
 $0120   288  Quantum
 $0122   290  Elapsed
 $0124   292  SysFlags
```

```
  $0126   294  IDNestCnt
  $0127   295  TDNestCnt
  $0128   296  AttnFlags
  $012a   298  AttnResched
  $012c   300  ResModules
  $0130   304  TaskTrapCode
  $0134   308  TaskExceptCode
  $0138   312  TaskExitCode
  $013c   316  TaskSigAlloc
  $0140   320  TaskTrapAlloc
  $0142   322  MemList
  $0150   336  ResourceList
  $015e   350  DeviceList
  $016c   364  IntrList
  $017a   378  LibList
  $0188   392  PortList
  $0196   406  TaskReady
  $01a4   420  TaskWait
  $01b2   434  SoftInts[0]
  $0202   514  LastAlert[0]
  $0212   530  VBlankFrequency
  $0213   531  PowerSupplyFrequency
  $0214   532  SemaphoreList
  $0222   546  KickMemPtr
  $0226   550  KickTagPtr
  $022a   554  KickCheckSum
  $022e   558  ExecBaseReserved[0]
  $0238   568  ExecBaseNewReserved[0]
ExpansionBase:
  $01c8   456  sizeof(ExpansionBase)
  $0000     0  LibNode
  $0022    34  Flags
  $0023    35  pad
  $0024    36  ExecBase
  $0028    40  SegList
  $002c    44  CurrentBinding
  $003c    60  BoardList
  $004a    74  MountList
  $0058    88  AllocTable[0]
  $0158   344  BindSemaphore
  $0186   390  Int2List
  $019c   412  Int6List
  $01b2   434  Int7List
ExpansionControl:
  $0010    16  sizeof(ExpansionControl)
  $0000     0  ec_Interrupt
  $0001     1  ec_Reserved11
  $0002     2  ec_BaseAddress
  $0003     3  ec_Shutup
  $0004     4  ec_Reserved14
  $0005     5  ec_Reserved15
  $0006     6  ec_Reserved16
  $0007     7  ec_Reserved17
  $0008     8  ec_Reserved18
  $0009     9  ec_Reserved19
  $000a    10  ec_Reserved1a
  $000b    11  ec_Reserved1b
  $000c    12  ec_Reserved1c
  $000d    13  ec_Reserved1d
  $000e    14  ec_Reserved1e
  $000f    15  ec_Reserved1f
ExpansionInt:
  $0006     6  sizeof(ExpansionInt)
  $0000     0  IntMask
  $0002     2  ArrayMax
  $0004     4  ArraySize
ExpansionRom:
  $0010    16  sizeof(ExpansionRom)
  $0000     0  er_Type
  $0001     1  er_Product
  $0002     2  er_Flags
  $0003     3  er_Reserved03
  $0004     4  er_Manufacturer
  $0006     6  er_SerialNumber
  $000a    10  er_InitDiagVec
  $000c    12  er_Reserved0c
  $000d    13  er_Reserved0d
  $000e    14  er_Reserved0e
  $000f    15  er_Reserved0f
FileHandle:
  $002c    44  sizeof(FileHandle)
  $0000     0  fh_Link
  $0004     4  fh_Port
  $0008     8  fh_Type
  $000c    12  fh_Buf
  $0010    16  fh_Pos
  $0014    20  fh_End
  $0018    24  fh_Funcs
  $001c    28  fh_Func2
  $0020    32  fh_Func3
  $0024    36  fh_Args
  $0028    40  fh_Arg2
FileInfoBlock:
  $0104   260  sizeof(FileInfoBlock)
  $0000     0  fib_DiskKey
  $0004     4  fib_DirEntryType
  $0008     8  fib_FileName[0]
  $0074   116  fib_Protection
  $0078   120  fib_EntryType
  $007c   124  fib_Size
  $0080   128  fib_NumBlocks
  $0084   132  fib_Date
  $0090   144  fib_Comment[0]
  $00e0   224  fib_Reserved[0]
FileLock:
  $0014    20  sizeof(FileLock)
  $0000     0  fl_Link
  $0004     4  fl_Key
  $0008     8  fl_Access
  $000c    12  fl_Task
  $0010    16  fl_Volume
FileSysStartupMsg:
  $0010    16  sizeof(FileSysStartupMsg)
  $0000     0  fssm_Unit
  $0004     4  fssm_Device
  $0008     8  fssm_Environ
  $000c    12  fssm_Flags
FontContents:
  $0104   260  sizeof(FontContents)
  $0000     0  fc_FileName[0]
  $0100   256  fc_YSize
  $0102   258  fc_Style
  $0103   259  fc_Flags
FontContentsHeader:
  $0004     4  sizeof(FontContentsHeader)
  $0000     0  fch_FileID
  $0002     2  fch_NumEntries
FreeList:
  $0010    16  sizeof(FreeList)
  $0000     0  fl_NumFree
  $0002     2  fl_MemList
Gadget:
  $002c    44  sizeof(Gadget)
  $0000     0  NextGadget
  $0004     4  LeftEdge
  $0006     6  TopEdge
  $0008     8  Width
  $000a    10  Height
```



```
  $000c    12  Flags
  $000e    14  Activation
  $0010    16  GadgetType
  $0012    18  GadgetRender
  $0016    22  SelectRender
  $001a    26  GadgetText
  $001e    30  MutualExclude
  $0022    34  SpecialInfo
  $0026    38  GadgetID
  $0028    40  UserData
GamePortTrigger:
  $0008     8  sizeof(GamePortTrigger)
  $0000     0  gpt_Keys
  $0002     2  gpt_Timeout
  $0004     4  gpt_XDelta
  $0006     6  gpt_YDelta
GelsInfo:
  $0026    38  sizeof(GelsInfo)
  $0000     0  sprRsrvd
  $0001     1  Flags
  $0002     2  gelHead
  $0006     6  gelTail
  $000a    10  nextLine
  $000e    14  lastColor
  $0012    18  collHandler
  $0016    22  leftmost
  $0018    24  rightmost
  $001a    26  topmost
  $001c    28  bottommost
  $001e    30  firstBlissObj
  $0022    34  lastBlissObj
GfxBase:
  $0148   328  sizeof(GfxBase)
  $0000     0  LibNode
  $0022    34  ActiView
  $0026    38  copinit
  $002a    42  cia
  $002e    46  blitter
  $0032    50  LOFlist
  $0036    54  SHFlist
  $003a    58  blthd
  $003e    62  blttl
  $0042    66  bsblthd
  $0046    70  bsbltl
  $004a    74  vbsrv
  $0060    96  timsrv
  $0076   118  bltsrv
  $008c   140  TextFonts
  $009a   154  DefaultFont
  $009e   158  Modes
  $00a0   160  VBlank
  $00a1   161  Debug
  $00a2   162  BeamSync
  $00a4   164  system_bplcon0
  $00a6   166  SpriteReserved
  $00a7   167  bytereserved
  $00a8   168  Flags
  $00aa   170  BlitLock
  $00ac   172  BlitNest
  $00ae   174  BlitWaitQ
  $00bc   188  BlitOwner
  $00c0   192  TOF_WaitQ
  $00ce   206  DisplayFlags
  $00d0   208  SimpleSprites
  $00d4   212  MaxDisplayRow
  $00d6   214  MaxDisplayColumn
  $00d8   216  NormalDisplayRows
  $00da   218  NormalDisplayColumns
  $00dc   220  NormalDPMX
  $00de   222  NormalDPMY
  $00e0   224  LastChanceMemory
  $00e4   228  LCMptr
  $00e8   232  MicrosPerLine
  $00ea   234  MinDisplayColumn
  $00ec   236  reserved[0]
IOAudio:
  $0044    68  sizeof(IOAudio)
  $0000     0  ioa_Request
  $0020    32  ioa_AllocKey
  $0022    34  ioa_Data
  $0026    38  ioa_Length
  $002a    42  ioa_Period
  $002c    44  ioa_Volume
  $002e    46  ioa_Cycles
  $0030    48  ioa_WriteMsg
IOClipReq:
  $0034    52  sizeof(IOClipReq)
  $0000     0  io_Message
  $0014    20  io_Device
  $0018    24  io_Unit
  $001c    28  io_Command
  $001e    30  io_Flags
  $001f    31  io_Error
  $0020    32  io_Actual
  $0024    36  io_Length
  $0028    40  io_Data
  $002c    44  io_Offset
  $0030    48  io_ClipID
IODRPReq:
  $003e    62  sizeof(IODRPReq)
  $0000     0  io_Message
  $0014    20  io_Device
  $0018    24  io_Unit
  $001c    28  io_Command
  $001e    30  io_Flags
  $001f    31  io_Error
  $0020    32  io_RastPort
  $0024    36  io_ColorMap
  $0028    40  io_Modes
  $002c    44  io_SrcX
  $002e    46  io_SrcY
  $0030    48  io_SrcWidth
  $0032    50  io_SrcHeight
  $0034    52  io_DestCols
  $0038    56  io_DestRows
  $003c    60  io_Special
IOExtPar:
  $003e    62  sizeof(IOExtPar)
  $0000     0  IOPar
  $0030    48  io_PExtFlags
  $0034    52  io_Status
  $0035    53  io_ParFlags
  $0036    54  io_PTermArray
IOExtSer:
  $0052    82  sizeof(IOExtSer)
  $0000     0  IOSer
  $0030    48  io_CtlChar
  $0034    52  io_RBufLen
  $0038    56  io_ExtFlags
  $003c    60  io_Baud
  $0040    64  io_BrkTime
  $0044    68  io_TermArray
  $004c    76  io_ReadLen
  $004d    77  io_WriteLen
  $004e    78  io_StopBits
  $004f    79  io_SerFlags
  $0050    80  io_Status
IOExtTD:
```

```
  $0038   56  sizeof(IOExtTD)
  $0000    0  iotd_Req
  $0030   48  iotd_Count
  $0034   52  iotd_SecLabel
IOPArray:
  $0008    8  sizeof(IOPArray)
  $0000    0  PTermArray0
  $0004    4  PTermArray1
IOPrtCmdReq:
  $0026   38  sizeof(IOPrtCmdReq)
  $0000    0  io_Message
  $0014   20  io_Device
  $0018   24  io_Unit
  $001c   28  io_Command
  $001e   30  io_Flags
  $001f   31  io_Error
  $0020   32  io_PrtCommand
  $0022   34  io_Parm0
  $0023   35  io_Parm1
  $0024   36  io_Parm2
  $0025   37  io_Parm3
IORequest:
  $0020   32  sizeof(IORequest)
  $0000    0  io_Message
  $0014   20  io_Device
  $0018   24  io_Unit
  $001c   28  io_Command
  $001e   30  io_Flags
  $001f   31  io_Error
IOStdReq:
  $0030   48  sizeof(IOStdReq)
  $0000    0  io_Message
  $0014   20  io_Device
  $0018   24  io_Unit
  $001c   28  io_Command
  $001e   30  io_Flags
  $001f   31  io_Error
  $0020   32  io_Actual
  $0024   36  io_Length
  $0028   40  io_Data
  $002c   44  io_Offset
IOTArray:
  $0008    8  sizeof(IOTArray)
  $0000    0  TermArray0
  $0004    4  TermArray1
Image:
  $0014   20  sizeof(Image)
  $0000    0  LeftEdge
  $0002    2  TopEdge
  $0004    4  Width
  $0006    6  Height
  $0008    8  Depth
  $000a   10  ImageData
  $000e   14  PlanePick
  $000f   15  PlaneOnOff
  $0010   16  NextImage
InfoData:
  $0024   36  sizeof(InfoData)
  $0000    0  id_NumSoftErrors
  $0004    4  id_UnitNumber
  $0008    8  id_DiskState
  $000c   12  id_NumBlocks
  $0010   16  id_NumBlocksUsed
  $0014   20  id_BytesPerBlock
  $0018   24  id_DiskType
  $001c   28  id_VolumeNode
  $0020   32  id_InUse
InputEvent:
  $0016   22  sizeof(InputEvent)
  $0000    0  ie_NextEvent
  $0004    4  ie_Class
  $0005    5  ie_SubClass
  $0006    6  ie_Code
  $0008    8  ie_Qualifier
  $000a   10  ie_position
  $000a   10  ie_position.ie_xy
  $000a   10  ie_position.ie_xy.ie_x
  $000c   12  ie_position.ie_xy.ie_y
  $000a   10  ie_position.ie_addr
  $000e   14  ie_TimeStamp
IntVector:
  $000c   12  sizeof(IntVector)
  $0000    0  iv_Data
  $0004    4  iv_Code
  $0008    8  iv_Node
Interrupt:
  $0016   22  sizeof(Interrupt)
  $0000    0  is_Node
  $000e   14  is_Data
  $0012   18  is_Code
IntuiMessage:
  $0034   52  sizeof(IntuiMessage)
  $0000    0  ExecMessage
  $0014   20  Class
  $0018   24  Code
  $001a   26  Qualifier
  $001c   28  IAddress
  $0020   32  MouseX
  $0022   34  MouseY
  $0024   36  Seconds
  $0028   40  Micros
  $002c   44  IDCMPWindow
  $0030   48  SpecialLink
IntuiText:
  $0014   20  sizeof(IntuiText)
  $0000    0  FrontPen
  $0001    1  BackPen
  $0002    2  DrawMode
  $0004    4  LeftEdge
  $0006    6  TopEdge
  $0008    8  ITextFont
  $000c   12  IText
  $0010   16  NextText
IntuitionBase:
  $0050   80  sizeof(IntuitionBase)
  $0000    0  LibNode
  $0022   34  ViewLord
  $0034   52  ActiveWindow
  $0038   56  ActiveScreen
  $003c   60  FirstScreen
  $0040   64  Flags
  $0044   68  MouseY
  $0046   70  MouseX
  $0048   72  Seconds
  $004c   76  Micros
Isrvstr:
  $001e   30  sizeof(Isrvstr)
  $0000    0  is_Node
  $000e   14  Iptr
  $0012   18  code
  $0016   22  ccode
  $001a   26  Carg
KeyMap:
  $0020   32  sizeof(KeyMap)
  $0000    0  km_LoKeyMapTypes
  $0004    4  km_LoKeyMap
  $0008    8  km_LoCapsable
  $000c   12  km_LoRepeatable
```



```
  $0010   16  km_HiKeyMapTypes
  $0014   20  km_HiKeyMap
  $0018   24  km_HiCapsable
  $001c   28  km_HiRepeatable
KeyMapNode:
  $002e   46  sizeof(KeyMapNode)
  $0000    0  kn_Node
  $000e   14  kn_KeyMap
KeyMapResource:
  $001c   28  sizeof(KeyMapResource)
  $0000    0  kr_Node
  $000e   14  kr_List
Layer:
  $00a0  160  sizeof(Layer)
  $0000    0  front
  $0004    4  back
  $0008    8  ClipRect
  $000c   12  rp
  $0010   16  bounds
  $0018   24  reserved[0]
  $001c   28  priority
  $001e   30  Flags
  $0020   32  SuperBitMap
  $0024   36  SuperClipRect
  $0028   40  Window
  $002c   44  Scroll_X
  $002e   46  Scroll_Y
  $0030   48  cr
  $0034   52  cr2
  $0038   56  crnew
  $003c   60  SuperSaveClipRects
  $0040   64  _cliprects
  $0044   68  LayerInfo
  $0048   72  Lock
  $0076  118  reserved3[0]
  $007e  126  ClipRegion
  $0082  130  saveClipRects
  $0086  134  reserved2[0]
  $009c  156  DamageList
Layer_Info:
  $0066  102  sizeof(Layer_Info)
  $0000    0  top_layer
  $0004    4  check_lp
  $0008    8  obs
  $000c   12  FreeClipRects
  $0018   24  Lock
  $0046   70  gs_Head
  $0054   84  longreserved
  $0058   88  Flags
  $005a   90  fatten_count
  $005b   91  LockLayersCount
  $005c   92  LayerInfo_extra_size
  $005e   94  blitbuff
  $0062   98  LayerInfo_extra
Library:
  $0022   34  sizeof(Library)
  $0000    0  lib_Node
  $000e   14  lib_Flags
  $000f   15  lib_pad
  $0010   16  lib_NegSize
  $0012   18  lib_PosSize
  $0014   20  lib_Version
  $0016   22  lib_Revision
  $0018   24  lib_IdString
  $001c   28  lib_Sum
  $0020   32  lib_OpenCnt
List:
  $000e   14  sizeof(List)
  $0000    0  lh_Head
  $0004    4  lh_Tail
  $0008    8  lh_TailPred
  $000c   12  lh_Type
  $000d   13  l_pad
MathIEEEBase:
  $003c   60  sizeof(MathIEEEBase)
  $0000    0  MathIEEEBase_LibNode
  $0022   34  MathIEEEBase_Flags
  $0023   35  MathIEEEBase_reserved1
  $0024   36  MathIEEEBase_68881
  $0028   40  MathIEEEBase_SysLib
  $002c   44  MathIEEEBase_SegList
  $0030   48  MathIEEEBase_Resource
  $0034   52  MathIEEEBase_TaskOpenLib
  $0038   56  MathIEEEBase_TaskCloseLib
MathIEEEResource:
  $002c   44  sizeof(MathIEEEResource)
  $0000    0  MathIEEEResource_Node
  $000e   14  MathIEEEResource_Flags
  $0010   16  MathIEEEResource_BaseAddr
  $0014   20  MathIEEEResource_DblBasInit
  $0018   24  MathIEEEResource_DblTransIn
  $001c   28  MathIEEEResource_SglBasInit
  $0020   32  MathIEEEResource_SglTransIn
  $0024   36  MathIEEEResource_ExtBasInit
  $0028   40  MathIEEEResource_ExtTransIn
MemChunk:
  $0008    8  sizeof(MemChunk)
  $0000    0  mc_Next
  $0004    4  mc_Bytes
MemEntry:
  $0008    8  sizeof(MemEntry)
  $0000    0  me_Un
  $0000    0  me_Un.meu_Reqs
  $0000    0  me_Un.meu_Addr
  $0004    4  me_Length
MemHeader:
  $0020   32  sizeof(MemHeader)
  $0000    0  mh_Node
  $000e   14  mh_Attributes
  $0010   16  mh_First
  $0014   20  mh_Lower
  $0018   24  mh_Upper
  $001c   28  mh_Free
MemList:
  $0018   24  sizeof(MemList)
  $0000    0  ml_Node
  $000e   14  ml_NumEntries
  $0010   16  ml_ME[0]
Menu:
  $001e   30  sizeof(Menu)
  $0000    0  NextMenu
  $0004    4  LeftEdge
  $0006    6  TopEdge
  $0008    8  Width
  $000a   10  Height
  $000c   12  Flags
  $000e   14  MenuName
  $0012   18  FirstItem
  $0016   22  JazzX
  $0018   24  JazzY
  $001a   26  BeatX
  $001c   28  BeatY
MenuItem:
  $0022   34  sizeof(MenuItem)
  $0000    0  NextItem
  $0004    4  LeftEdge
  $0006    6  TopEdge
  $0008    8  Width
```

```
  $000a    10  Height
  $000c    12  Flags
  $000e    14  MutualExclude
  $0012    18  ItemFill
  $0016    22  SelectFill
  $001a    26  Command
  $001c    28  SubItem
  $0020    32  NextSelect
Message:
  $0014    20  sizeof(Message)
  $0000     0  mn_Node
  $000e    14  mn_ReplyPort
  $0012    18  mn_Length
MinList:
  $000c    12  sizeof(MinList)
  $0000     0  mlh_Head
  $0004     4  mlh_Tail
  $0008     8  mlh_TailPred
MinNode:
  $0008     8  sizeof(MinNode)
  $0000     0  mln_Succ
  $0004     4  mln_Pred
MiscResource:
  $0032    50  sizeof(MiscResource)
  $0000     0  mr_Library
  $0022    34  mr_AllocArray[0]
MsgPort:
  $0022    34  sizeof(MsgPort)
  $0000     0  mp_Node
  $000e    14  mp_Flags
  $000f    15  mp_SigBit
  $0010    16  mp_SigTask
  $0014    20  mp_MsgList
NewScreen:
  $0020    32  sizeof(NewScreen)
  $0000     0  LeftEdge
  $0002     2  TopEdge
  $0004     4  Width
  $0006     6  Height
  $0008     8  Depth
  $000a    10  DetailPen
  $000b    11  BlockPen
  $000c    12  ViewModes
  $000e    14  Type
  $0010    16  Font
  $0014    20  DefaultTitle
  $0018    24  Gadgets
  $001c    28  CustomBitMap
NewWindow:
  $0030    48  sizeof(NewWindow)
  $0000     0  LeftEdge
  $0002     2  TopEdge
  $0004     4  Width
  $0006     6  Height
  $0008     8  DetailPen
  $0009     9  BlockPen
  $000a    10  IDCMPFlags
  $000e    14  Flags
  $0012    18  FirstGadget
  $0016    22  CheckMark
  $001a    26  Title
  $001e    30  Screen
  $0022    34  BitMap
  $0026    38  MinWidth
  $0028    40  MinHeight
  $002a    42  MaxWidth
  $002c    44  MaxHeight
  $002e    46  Type
Node:
  $000e    14  sizeof(Node)
  $0000     0  ln_Succ
  $0004     4  ln_Pred
  $0008     8  ln_Type
  $0009     9  ln_Pri
  $000a    10  ln_Name
Preferences:
  $00e8   232  sizeof(Preferences)
  $0000     0  FontHeight
  $0001     1  PrinterPort
  $0002     2  BaudRate
  $0004     4  KeyRptSpeed
  $000c    12  KeyRptDelay
  $0014    20  DoubleClick
  $001c    28  PointerMatrix[0]
  $0064   100  XOffset
  $0065   101  YOffset
  $0066   102  color17
  $0068   104  color18
  $006a   106  color19
  $006c   108  PointerTicks
  $006e   110  color0
  $0070   112  color1
  $0072   114  color2
  $0074   116  color3
  $0076   118  ViewXOffset
  $0077   119  ViewYOffset
  $0078   120  ViewInitX
  $007a   122  ViewInitY
  $007c   124  EnableCLI
  $007e   126  PrinterType
  $0080   128  PrinterFilename[0]
  $009e   158  PrintPitch
  $00a0   160  PrintQuality
  $00a2   162  PrintSpacing
  $00a4   164  PrintLeftMargin
  $00a6   166  PrintRightMargin
  $00a8   168  PrintImage
  $00aa   170  PrintAspect
  $00ac   172  PrintShade
  $00ae   174  PrintThreshold
  $00b0   176  PaperSize
  $00b2   178  PaperLength
  $00b4   180  PaperType
  $00b6   182  SerRWBits
  $00b7   183  SerStopBuf
  $00b8   184  SerParShk
  $00b9   185  LaceWB
  $00ba   186  WorkName[0]
  $00d8   216  RowSizeChange
  $00d9   217  ColumnSizeChange
  $00da   218  PrintFlags
  $00dc   220  PrintMaxWidth
  $00de   222  PrintMaxHeight
  $00e0   224  PrintDensity
  $00e1   225  PrintXOffset
  $00e2   226  wb_Width
  $00e4   228  wb_Height
  $00e6   230  wb_Depth
  $00e7   231  ext_size
PrinterData:
  $0aa2  2722  sizeof(PrinterData)
  $0000     0  pd_Device
  $0034    52  pd_Unit
  $0056    86  pd_PrinterSegment
  $005a    90  pd_PrinterType
  $005c    92  pd_SegmentData
  $0060    96  pd_PrintBuf
  $0064   100  pd_PWrite
```



```
  $0068   104  pd_PBothReady
  $006c   108  pd_ior0
  $006c   108  pd_ior0.pd_p0
  $006c   108  pd_ior0.pd_s0
  $00be   190  pd_iorl
  $00be   190  pd_iorl.pd_pl
  $00be   190  pd_iorl.pd_sl
  $0110   272  pd_TIOR
  $0138   312  pd_IORPort
  $015a   346  pd_TC
  $01b6   438  pd_Stk[0]
  $09b6  2486  pd_Flags
  $09b7  2487  pd_pad
  $09b8  2488  pd_Preferences
  $0aa0  2720  pd_PWaitEnabled
PrinterExtendedData:
  $0042    66  sizeof(PrinterExtendedData)
  $0000     0  ped_PrinterName
  $0004     4  ped_Init
  $0008     8  ped_Expunge
  $000c    12  ped_Open
  $0010    16  ped_Close
  $0014    20  ped_PrinterClass
  $0015    21  ped_ColorClass
  $0016    22  ped_MaxColumns
  $0017    23  ped_NumCharSets
  $0018    24  ped_NumRows
  $001a    26  ped_MaxXDots
  $001e    30  ped_MaxYDots
  $0022    34  ped_XDotsInch
  $0024    36  ped_YDotsInch
  $0026    38  ped_Commands
  $002a    42  ped_DoSpecial
  $002e    46  ped_Render
  $0032    50  ped_TimeoutSecs
  $0036    54  ped_8BitChars
  $003a    58  ped_PrintMode
  $003e    62  ped_ConvFunc
PrinterSegment:
  $004e    78  sizeof(PrinterSegment)
  $0000     0  ps_NextSegment
  $0004     4  ps_runAlert
  $0008     8  ps_Version
  $000a    10  ps_Revision
  $000c    12  ps_PED
Process:
  $00bc   188  sizeof(Process)
  $0000     0  pr_Task
  $005c    92  pr_MsgPort
  $007e   126  pr_Pad
  $0080   128  pr_SegList
  $0084   132  pr_StackSize
  $0088   136  pr_GlobVec
  $008c   140  pr_TaskNum
  $0090   144  pr_StackBase
  $0094   148  pr_Result2
  $0098   152  pr_CurrentDir
  $009c   156  pr_CIS
  $00a0   160  pr_COS
  $00a4   164  pr_ConsoleTask
  $00a8   168  pr_FileSystemTask
  $00ac   172  pr_CLI
  $00b0   176  pr_ReturnAddr
  $00b4   180  pr_PktWait
  $00b8   184  pr_WindowPtr
PropInfo:
  $0016    22  sizeof(PropInfo)
  $0000     0  Flags
  $0002     2  HorizPot
  $0004     4  VertPot
  $0006     6  HorizBody
  $0008     8  VertBody
  $000a    10  CWidth
  $000c    12  CHeight
  $000e    14  HPotRes
  $0010    16  VPotRes
  $0012    18  LeftBorder
  $0014    20  TopBorder
PrtInfo:
  $0072   114  sizeof(PrtInfo)
  $0000     0  pi_render
  $0004     4  pi_rp
  $0008     8  pi_temprp
  $000c    12  pi_RowBuf
  $0010    16  pi_HamBuf
  $0014    20  pi_ColorMap
  $0018    24  pi_ColorInt
  $001c    28  pi_HamInt
  $0020    32  pi_Dest1Int
  $0024    36  pi_Dest2Int
  $0028    40  pi_ScaleX
  $002c    44  pi_ScaleXAlt
  $0030    48  pi_dmatrix
  $0034    52  pi_TopBuf
  $0038    56  pi_BotBuf
  $003c    60  pi_RowBufSize
  $003e    62  pi_HamBufSize
  $0040    64  pi_ColorMapSize
  $0042    66  pi_ColorIntSize
  $0044    68  pi_HamIntSize
  $0046    70  pi_Dest1IntSize
  $0048    72  pi_Dest2IntSize
  $004a    74  pi_ScaleXSize
  $004c    76  pi_ScaleXAltSize
  $004e    78  pi_PrefsFlags
  $0050    80  pi_special
  $0054    84  pi_xstart
  $0056    86  pi_ystart
  $0058    88  pi_width
  $005a    90  pi_height
  $005c    92  pi_pc
  $0060    96  pi_pr
  $0064   100  pi_ymult
  $0066   102  pi_ymod
  $0068   104  pi_ety
  $006a   106  pi_xpos
  $006c   108  pi_threshold
  $006e   110  pi_tempwidth
  $0070   112  pi_flags
RasInfo:
  $000c    12  sizeof(RasInfo)
  $0000     0  Next
  $0004     4  BitMap
  $0008     8  RxOffset
  $000a    10  RyOffset
RastPort:
  $0064   100  sizeof(RastPort)
  $0000     0  Layer
  $0004     4  BitMap
  $0008     8  AreaPtrn
  $000c    12  TmpRas
  $0010    16  AreaInfo
  $0014    20  GelsInfo
  $0018    24  Mask
  $0019    25  FgPen
  $001a    26  BgPen
  $001b    27  AOlPen
  $001c    28  DrawMode
```

```
  $001d    29  AreaPtSz
  $001e    30  linpatcnt
  $001f    31  dummy
  $0020    32  Flags
  $0022    34  LinePtrn
  $0024    36  cp_x
  $0026    38  cp_y
  $0028    40  minterms[0]
  $0030    48  PenWidth
  $0032    50  PenHeight
  $0034    52  Font
  $0038    56  AlgoStyle
  $0039    57  TxFlags
  $003a    58  TxHeight
  $003c    60  TxWidth
  $003e    62  TxBaseline
  $0040    64  TxSpacing
  $0042    66  RP_User
  $0046    70  longreserved[0]
  $004e    78  wordreserved[0]
  $005c    92  reserved[0]
Rectangle:
  $0008     8  sizeof(Rectangle)
  $0000     0  MinX
  $0002     2  MinY
  $0004     4  MaxX
  $0006     6  MaxY
Region:
  $000c    12  sizeof(Region)
  $0000     0  bounds
  $0008     8  RegionRectangle
RegionRectangle:
  $0010    16  sizeof(RegionRectangle)
  $0000     0  Next
  $0004     4  Prev
  $0008     8  bounds
Remember:
  $000c    12  sizeof(Remember)
  $0000     0  NextRemember
  $0004     4  RememberSize
  $0008     8  Memory
Requester:
  $0070   112  sizeof(Requester)
  $0000     0  OlderRequest
  $0004     4  LeftEdge
  $0006     6  TopEdge
  $0008     8  Width
  $000a    10  Height
  $000c    12  RelLeft
  $000e    14  RelTop
  $0010    16  ReqGadget
  $0014    20  ReqBorder
  $0018    24  ReqText
  $001c    28  Flags
  $001e    30  BackFill
  $0020    32  ReqLayer
  $0024    36  ReqPad1[0]
  $0044    68  ImageBMap
  $0048    72  RWindow
  $004c    76  ReqPad2[0]
Resident:
  $001a    26  sizeof(Resident)
  $0000     0  rt_MatchWord
  $0002     2  rt_MatchTag
  $0006     6  rt_EndSkip
  $000a    10  rt_Flags
  $000b    11  rt_Version
  $000c    12  rt_Type
  $000d    13  rt_Pri
  $000e    14  rt_Name
  $0012    18  rt_IdString
  $0016    22  rt_Init
RomBootBase:
  $0044    68  sizeof(RomBootBase)
  $0000     0  LibNode
  $0022    34  ExecBase
  $0026    38  BootList
  $0034    52  Reserved[0]
RootNode:
  $0020    32  sizeof(RootNode)
  $0000     0  rn_TaskArray
  $0004     4  rn_ConsoleSegment
  $0008     8  rn_Time
  $0014    20  rn_RestartSeg
  $0018    24  rn_Info
  $001c    28  rn_FileHandlerSegment
SatisfyMsg:
  $001a    26  sizeof(SatisfyMsg)
  $0000     0  sm_Msg
  $0014    20  sm_Unit
  $0016    22  sm_ClipID
Screen:
  $015a   346  sizeof(Screen)
  $0000     0  NextScreen
  $0004     4  FirstWindow
  $0008     8  LeftEdge
  $000a    10  TopEdge
  $000c    12  Width
  $000e    14  Height
  $0010    16  MouseY
  $0012    18  MouseX
  $0014    20  Flags
  $0016    22  Title
  $001a    26  DefaultTitle
  $001e    30  BarHeight
  $001f    31  BarVBorder
  $0020    32  BarHBorder
  $0021    33  MenuVBorder
  $0022    34  MenuHBorder
  $0023    35  WBorTop
  $0024    36  WBorLeft
  $0025    37  WBorRight
  $0026    38  WBorBottom
  $0028    40  Font
  $002c    44  ViewPort
  $0054    84  RastPort
  $00b8   184  BitMap
  $00e0   224  LayerInfo
  $0146   326  FirstGadget
  $014a   330  DetailPen
  $014b   331  BlockPen
  $014c   332  SaveColor0
  $014e   334  BarLayer
  $0152   338  ExtData
  $0156   342  UserData
Semaphore:
  $0024    36  sizeof(Semaphore)
  $0000     0  sm_MsgPort
  $0022    34  sm_Bids
SemaphoreRequest:
  $000c    12  sizeof(SemaphoreRequest)
  $0000     0  sr_Link
  $0008     8  sr_Waiter
SignalSemaphore:
  $002e    46  sizeof(SignalSemaphore)
  $0000     0  ss_Link
  $000e    14  ss_NestCount
  $0010    16  ss_WaitQueue
```



```
  $001c    28  ss_MultipleLink
  $0028    40  ss_Owner
  $002c    44  ss_QueueCount
SimpleSprite:
  $000c    12  sizeof(SimpleSprite)
  $0000     0  posctldata
  $0004     4  height
  $0006     6  x
  $0008     8  y
  $000a    10  num
SoftIntList:
  $0010    16  sizeof(SoftIntList)
  $0000     0  sh_List
  $000e    14  sh_Pad
SpriteDef:
  $0008     8  sizeof(SpriteDef)
  $0000     0  pos
  $0002     2  ctl
  $0004     4  dataa
  $0006     6  datab
StandardPacket:
  $0044    68  sizeof(StandardPacket)
  $0000     0  sp_Msg
  $0014    20  sp_Pkt
StringInfo:
  $0024    36  sizeof(StringInfo)
  $0000     0  Buffer
  $0004     4  UndoBuffer
  $0008     8  BufferPos
  $000a    10  MaxChars
  $000c    12  DispPos
  $000e    14  UndoPos
  $0010    16  NumChars
  $0012    18  DispCount
  $0014    20  CLeft
  $0016    22  CTop
  $0018    24  LayerPtr
  $001c    28  LongInt
  $0020    32  AltKeyMap
TDU_PublicUnit:
  $0036    54  sizeof(TDU_PublicUnit)
  $0000     0  tdu_Unit
  $0026    38  tdu_Comp01Track
  $0028    40  tdu_Comp10Track
  $002a    42  tdu_Comp11Track
  $002c    44  tdu_StepDelay
  $0030    48  tdu_SettleDelay
  $0034    52  tdu_RetryCnt
Task:
  $005c    92  sizeof(Task)
  $0000     0  tc_Node
  $000e    14  tc_Flags
  $000f    15  tc_State
  $0010    16  tc_IDNestCnt
  $0011    17  tc_TDNestCnt
  $0012    18  tc_SigAlloc
  $0016    22  tc_SigWait
  $001a    26  tc_SigRecvd
  $001e    30  tc_SigExcept
  $0022    34  tc_TrapAlloc
  $0024    36  tc_TrapAble
  $0026    38  tc_ExceptData
  $002a    42  tc_ExceptCode
  $002e    46  tc_TrapData
  $0032    50  tc_TrapCode
  $0036    54  tc_SPReg
  $003a    58  tc_SPLower
  $003e    62  tc_SPUpper
  $0042    66  tc_Switch
  $0046    70  tc_Launch
  $004a    74  tc_MemEntry
  $0058    88  tc_UserData
TextAttr:
  $0008     8  sizeof(TextAttr)
  $0000     0  ta_Name
  $0004     4  ta_YSize
  $0006     6  ta_Style
  $0007     7  ta_Flags
TextFont:
  $0034    52  sizeof(TextFont)
  $0000     0  tf_Message
  $0014    20  tf_YSize
  $0016    22  tf_Style
  $0017    23  tf_Flags
  $0018    24  tf_XSize
  $001a    26  tf_Baseline
  $001c    28  tf_BoldSmear
  $001e    30  tf_Accessors
  $0020    32  tf_LoChar
  $0021    33  tf_HiChar
  $0022    34  tf_CharData
  $0026    38  tf_Modulo
  $0028    40  tf_CharLoc
  $002c    44  tf_CharSpace
  $0030    48  tf_CharKern
TmpRas:
  $0008     8  sizeof(TmpRas)
  $0000     0  RasPtr
  $0004     4  Size
UCopList:
  $000c    12  sizeof(UCopList)
  $0000     0  Next
  $0004     4  FirstCopList
  $0008     8  CopList
Unit:
  $0026    38  sizeof(Unit)
  $0000     0  unit_MsgPort
  $0022    34  unit_flags
  $0023    35  unit_pad
  $0024    36  unit_OpenCnt
VSprite:
  $003c    60  sizeof(VSprite)
  $0000     0  NextVSprite
  $0004     4  PrevVSprite
  $0008     8  DrawPath
  $000c    12  ClearPath
  $0010    16  OldY
  $0012    18  OldX
  $0014    20  Flags
  $0016    22  Y
  $0018    24  X
  $001a    26  Height
  $001c    28  Width
  $001e    30  Depth
  $0020    32  MeMask
  $0022    34  HitMask
  $0024    36  ImageData
  $0028    40  BorderLine
  $002c    44  CollMask
  $0030    48  SprColors
  $0034    52  VSBob
  $0038    56  PlanePick
  $0039    57  PlaneOnOff
  $003a    58  VUserExt
View:
  $0012    18  sizeof(View)
  $0000     0  ViewPort
  $0004     4  LOFCprList
```

```
  $0008     8  SHFCprList
  $000c    12  DyOffset
  $000e    14  DxOffset
  $0010    16  Modes
ViewPort:
  $0028    40  sizeof(ViewPort)
  $0000     0  Next
  $0004     4  ColorMap
  $0008     8  DspIns
  $000c    12  SprIns
  $0010    16  ClrIns
  $0014    20  UCopIns
  $0018    24  DWidth
  $001a    26  DHeight
  $001c    28  DxOffset
  $001e    30  DyOffset
  $0020    32  Modes
  $0022    34  SpritePriorities
  $0023    35  reserved
  $0024    36  RasInfo
WBArg:
  $0008     8  sizeof(WBArg)
  $0000     0  wa_Lock
  $0004     4  wa_Name
WBStartup:
  $0028    40  sizeof(WBStartup)
  $0000     0  sm_Message
  $0014    20  sm_Process
  $0018    24  sm_Segment
  $001c    28  sm_NumArgs
  $0020    32  sm_ToolWindow
  $0024    36  sm_ArgList
Window:
  $0084   132  sizeof(Window)
  $0000     0  NextWindow
  $0004     4  LeftEdge
  $0006     6  TopEdge
  $0008     8  Width
  $000a    10  Height
  $000c    12  MouseY
  $000e    14  MouseX
  $0010    16  MinWidth
  $0012    18  MinHeight
  $0014    20  MaxWidth
  $0016    22  MaxHeight
  $0018    24  Flags
  $001c    28  MenuStrip
  $0020    32  Title
  $0024    36  FirstRequest
  $0028    40  DMRequest
  $002c    44  ReqCount
  $002e    46  WScreen
  $0032    50  RPort
  $0036    54  BorderLeft
  $0037    55  BorderTop
  $0038    56  BorderRight
  $0039    57  BorderBottom
  $003a    58  BorderRPort
  $003e    62  FirstGadget
  $0042    66  Parent
  $0046    70  Descendant
  $004a    74  Pointer
  $004e    78  PtrHeight
  $004f    79  PtrWidth
  $0050    80  XOffset
  $0051    81  YOffset
  $0052    82  IDCMPFlags
  $0056    86  UserPort
  $005a    90  WindowPort
  $005e    94  MessageKey
  $0062    98  DetailPen
  $0063    99  BlockPen
  $0064   100  CheckMark
  $0068   104  ScreenTitle
  $006c   108  GZZMouseX
  $006e   110  GZZMouseY
  $0070   112  GZZWidth
  $0072   114  GZZHeight
  $0074   116  ExtData
  $0078   120  UserData
  $007c   124  WLayer
  $0080   128  IFont
bltnode:
  $0012    18  sizeof(bltnode)
  $0000     0  n
  $0004     4  function
  $0008     8  stat
  $000a    10  blitsize
  $000c    12  beamsync
  $000e    14  cleanup
collTable:
  $0040    64  sizeof(collTable)
  $0000     0  collPtrs[0]
copinit:
  $005c    92  sizeof(copinit)
  $0000     0  diagstrt[0]
  $0008     8  sprstrtup[0]
  $0058    88  sprstop[0]
cprlist:
  $000a    10  sizeof(cprlist)
  $0000     0  Next
  $0004     4  start
  $0008     8  MaxCount
mouth_rb:
  $004a    74  sizeof(mouth_rb)
  $0000     0  voice
  $0046    70  width
  $0047    71  height
  $0048    72  shape
  $0049    73  pad
narrator_rb:
  $0046    70  sizeof(narrator_rb)
  $0000     0  message
  $0030    48  rate
  $0032    50  pitch
  $0034    52  mode
  $0036    54  sex
  $0038    56  ch_masks
  $003c    60  nm_masks
  $003e    62  volume
  $0040    64  sampfreq
  $0042    66  mouths
  $0043    67  chanmask
  $0044    68  numchan
  $0045    69  pad
tPoint:
  $0004     4  sizeof(tPoint)
timerequest:
  $0028    40  sizeof(timerequest)
  $0000     0  tr_node
  $0020    32  tr_time
timeval:
  $0008     8  sizeof(timeval)
  $0000     0  tv_secs
  $0004     4  tv_micro
tPoint:
  $0004     4  sizeof(tPoint)
colorEntry:
```



```
  $0004     4  sizeof(colorEntry)
  $0000     0  colorLong
  $0000     0  colorByte[0]
  $0000     0  colorSByte[0]
```

Section I

IFF - Interchange File Format

This section contains the specification for the Interchange File Format. IFF is a standard for creating data files specifically designed for easy transfer between programs and machines. The text of these documents and the standard itself are in the public domain.

One of the Amiga's assets is the wide acceptance of several IFF specifications. Most notable is the ease with which IFF graphic files (of form "ILBM") can be transferred among dozens of paint, animation, and special effects packages. The user can pick and choose among the strengths of several programs, rather than fighting the restrictions of just one. Developers can market specialized applications that are good at a certain limited set of operations, and with help of the multitasking operating system, create the effect of a large integrated system.

We encourage all developers who wish to write out data files to adopt or expand an existing IFF specification. Or, if no current IFF form is suitable, to contact other developers and users with similar goals and work out a new specification. To prevent conflicts, new FORM identifications must be registered with Commodore before use. No additional restrictions are placed on the design of IFF FORMs, aside from the general IFF syntax rules.

Contents of the IFF Section

A Quick Introduction to IFF

Jerry Morrison, Electronic Arts
10-17-88

IFF is the Amiga-standard "Interchange File Format", designed to work across many machines.

Why IFF?

Did you ever have this happen to your picture file?

You can't load it into another paint program.
You need a converter to adopt to "ZooPaint" release 2.0 or a new hardware feature.
You must "export" and "import" to use it in a page layout program.
You can't move it to another brand of computer.

What about interchanging musical scores, digitized audio, and other data? It seems the only thing that *does* interchange well is plain ASCII text files.

It's inexcusable. And yet this is "normal" in MS-DOS.

What is IFF?

IFF, the "Interchange File Format" standard, encourages multimedia interchange between different programs and different computers. It supports long-lived, extensible data. It's great for composite files like a page layout file that includes photos, an animation file that includes music, and a library of sound effects.

IFF is a 2-level standard. The first layer is the "wrapper" or "envelope" structure for all IFF files. Technically, it's the syntax. The second layer defines particular IFF file types such as ILBM (standard raster pictures), ANIM (animation), SMUS (simple musical score), and 8SVX (8-bit sampled audio voice).

IFF is also a design idea:

programs should use interchange formats for their everyday storage

This way, users rarely need converters and import/export commands to change software releases, application programs, or hardware.

What's the trick?

File compatibility is easy to achieve if programmers let go of one notion—dumping internal data structures to disk. A program's internal data structures should really be suited to what the program does and how it works. What's "best" changes as the program evolves new functions and methods. But a disk format should be suited to storage and interchange.

Once we design internal formats and disk formats for their own separate purposes, the rest is easy. Reading and writing become behind-the-scenes conversions. But two conversions hidden in each program is much better than a pile of conversion programs.

Does this seem strange? It's what ASCII text programs do! Text editors use line tables, piece tables, gaps, and other structures for fast editing and searching. Text generators and consumers construct and parse files. That's why the ASCII standard works so well.

Also, every file must be self-sufficient. E.g. a picture file has to include its size and number of bits/pixel.

What's an IFF file look like?

IFF is based on data blocks called "chunks". Here's an example color map chunk:

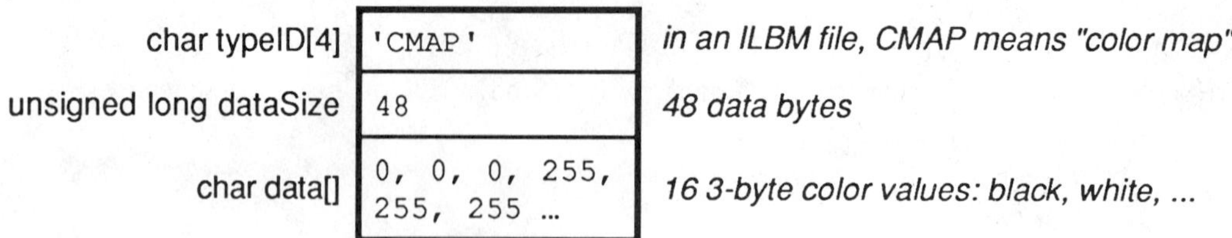

A chunk is made of a 4-character type identifier, a 32 bit data byte count, and the data bytes. It's like a Macintosh "resource" with a 32-bit size.

Fine points:

- Every 16- and 32-bit number is stored in 68000 byte order—highest byte first.
  An Intel CPU must reverse the 2- or 4-byte sequence of each number. This applies to chunk `dataSize` fields and to numbers inside chunk data. It does not affect character strings and byte data because you can't reverse a 1-byte sequence. But it does affect the 32-bit math used in IFF's MakeID macro. The standard does allow CPU specific byte ordering hidden within a chunk itself, but the practice is discouraged.
- Every 16- and 32-bit number is stored on an even address.
- Every odd-length chunk must be followed by a 0 pad byte. This pad byte is not counted in `dataSize`.
- An ID is made of 4 ASCII characters in the range " " (space, hex 20) through "~" (tilde, hex 7E). Leading spaces are not permitted.
- IDs are compared using a quick 32-bit equality test. Case matters.

A chunk typically holds a C structure, Pascal record, or an array. For example, an 'ILBM' picture has a 'BMHD' bitmap header chunk (a structure) and a 'BODY' raster body chunk (an array).

To construct an IFF file, just put a file type ID (like 'ILBM') into a wrapper chunk called a 'FORM' (Think "FILE"). Inside that wrapper place chunks one after another (with pad bytes as needed) . The chunk size always tells you how many more bytes you need to skip over to get to the next chunk.

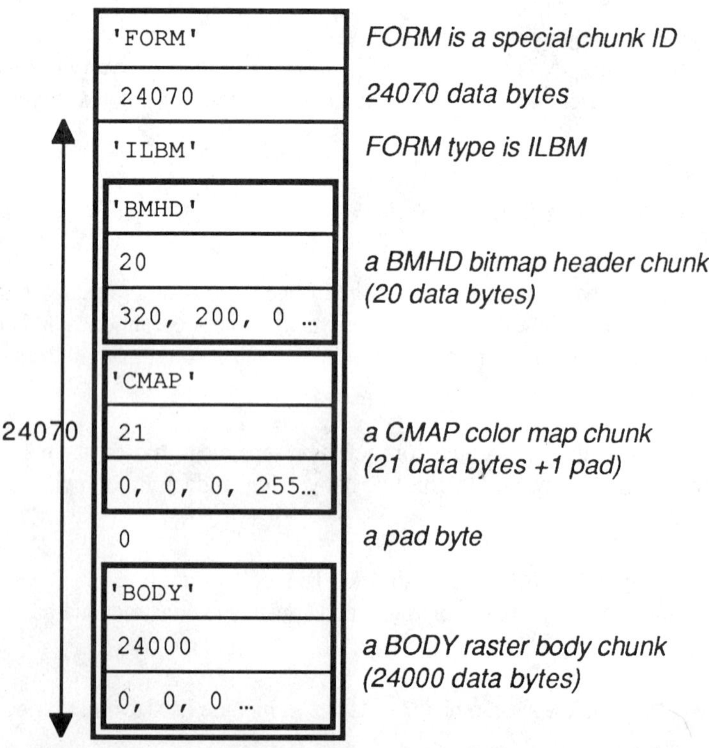

A FORM always contains one 4-character FORM type ID (a file type, in this case 'ILBM') followed by any number of data chunks. In this example, the FORM type is 'ILBM', which stands for "InterLeaved BitMap". (ILBM is an IFF standard for bitplane raster pictures.) This example has 3 chunks. Note the pad byte after the odd length chunk.

Within FORMs ILBM, 'BMHD' identifies a bitmap header chunk, 'CMAP' a color map, and 'BODY' a raster body. In general, the chunk IDs in a FORM are local to the FORM type ID. The exceptions are the 4 global chunk IDs 'FORM', 'LIST', 'CAT ', and 'PROP'. (A FORM may contain other FORM chunks. E.g. an animation FORM might contain picture FORMs and sound FORMs.)

How to read an IFF file?

Given the C subroutine "GetChunkHeader()":

```
/* Skip any remaining bytes of the current chunk, skip any pad byte, and
   read the next chunk header. Returns the chunk ID or END_MARK. */
ID GetChunkHeader();
```

we read the chunks in a FORM ILBM with a loop like this:

```
do
   switch (id = GetChunkHeader())
      {
      case 'CMAP': ProcessCMAP(); break;
      case 'BMHD': ProcessBMHD(); break;
      case 'BODY': ProcessBODY(); break;
      /* default: just ignore the chunk */
      }
   until (id == END_MARK);
```

This loop processes each chunk by dispatching to a routine that reads the specific type of chunk data. We don't assume a particular order of chunks. This is a simple parser. Note that even if you have fully processed a chunk, you should respect it's chunk size, even if the size is larger than you expected.

This sample ignores important details like I/O errors. There are also higher-level errors to check, e.g. if we hit END_MARK without reading a BODY, we didn't get a picture.

Every IFF file is a 'FORM', 'LIST', or 'CAT ' chunk. You can recognize an IFF file by those first 4 bytes. ('FORM' is far and away the most common. We'll get to LIST and CAT below.) If the file contains a FORM, dispatch on the FORM type ID to a chunk-reader loop like the one above.

File extensibility

IFF files are extensible and forward/backward compatible:

- Chunk contents should be designed for compatibility across environments and for longevity. Every chunk should have a path for future expansion; at minimum this will be an unused bit or two.
- The standards team for a FORM type can extend one of the chunks that contains a structure by appending new, optional structure fields.
- Anyone can define new FORM types as well as new chunk types within a FORM type. Storing private chunks within a FORM is ok, but be sure to register your activities with Commodore-Amiga Technical Support.
- A chunk can be superseded by a new chunk type, e.g. to store more bits per RGB color register. New programs can output the old chunk (for backward compatibility) along with the new chunk.
- If you must change data in an incompatible way, change the chunk ID or the FORM type ID.

Advanced Topics: CAT, LIST, and PROP (not all that important)

Sometimes you want to put several "files" into one, such as a picture library. This is what CAT is for. It "concatenates" FORM and LIST chunks.

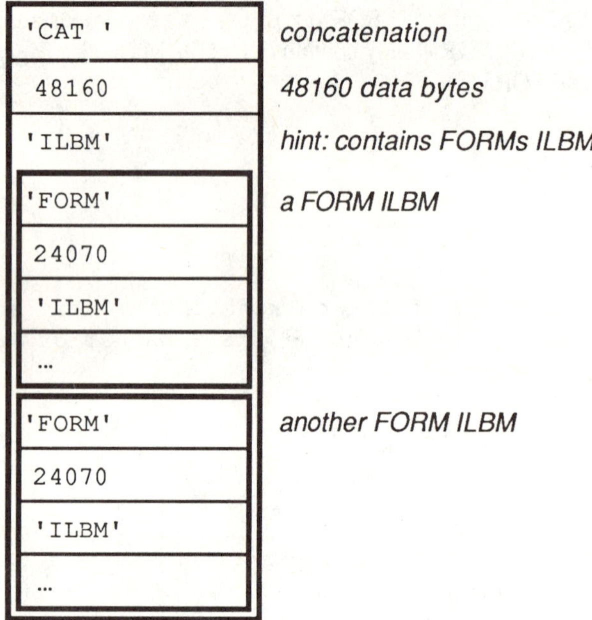

This example CAT holds two ILBMs. It can be shown outline-style:

```
CAT ILBM
..FORM ILBM          \
....BMHD             |  a complete FORM ILBM picture
....CMAP             |
....BODY             /
..FORM ILBM
....BMHD
....CMAP
....BODY
```

Sometimes you want to share the same color map across many pictures. LIST and PROP do this:

```
LIST ILBM
..PROP ILBM          default properties for FORMs ILBM
....CMAP             an ILBM CMAP chunk (there could be a BMHD chunk here, too)
..FORM ILBM
....BMHD             (there could be a CMAP here to override the default)
....BODY
..FORM ILBM
....BMHD             (there could be a CMAP here to override the default)
....BODY
```

A LIST holds PROPs and FORMs (and occasionally LISTs and CATs). A PROP ILBM contains default data (in the above example, just one CMAP chunk) for all FORMs ILBM in the LIST. Any FORM may override the PROP-defined default with its own CMAP. All PROPs must appear at the beginning of a LIST. Each FORM type standardizes (among other things) which of its chunks are "property chunks" (may appear in PROPs) and which are "data chunks" (may not appear in PROPs).

"EA IFF 85" Standard for Interchange Format Files

Document Date: January 14, 1985 (Re-typeset Oct, 1988 Commodore-Amiga, Inc.)
From: Jerry Morrison, Electronic Arts
Status of Standard: Released to the public domain, and in use

1. Introduction

Standards are Good for Software Developers

As home computer hardware evolves into better and better media machines, the demand increases for higher quality, more detailed data. Data development gets more expensive, requires more expertise and better tools, and has to be shared across projects. Think about several ports of a product on one CD-ROM with 500M Bytes of common data!

Development tools need standard interchange file formats. Imagine scanning in images of "player" shapes, transferring them to an image enhancement package, moving them to a paint program for touch up, then incorporating them into a game. Or writing a theme song with a Macintosh score editor and incorporating it into an Amiga game. The data must at times be transformed, clipped, filled out, and moved across machine kinds. Media projects will depend on data transfer from graphic, music, sound effect, animation, and script tools.

Standards are Good for Software Users

Customers should be able to move their own data between independently developed software products. And they should be able to buy data libraries usable across many such products. The types of data objects to exchange are open-ended and include plain and formatted text, raster and structured graphics, fonts, music, sound effects, musical instrument descriptions, and animation.

The problem with expedient file formats—typically memory dumps—is that they're too provincial. By designing data for one particular use (such as a screen snapshot), they preclude future expansion (would you like a full page picture? a multi-page document?). In neglecting the possibility that other programs might read their data, they fail to save contextual information (how many bit planes? what resolution?). Ignoring that other programs might create such files, they're intolerant of extra data (a different picture editor may want to save a texture palette with the image), missing data (such as no color map), or minor variations (perhaps a smaller image). In practice, a filed representation should rarely mirror an in-memory representation. The former should be designed for longevity; the latter to optimize the manipulations of a particular program. The same filed data will be read into different memory formats by different programs.

The IFF philosophy: "A little behind-the-scenes conversion when programs read and write files is far better than NxM explicit conversion utilities for highly specialized formats".

So we need some standardization for data interchange among development tools and products. The more developers that adopt a standard, the better for all of us and our customers.

Here is "EA IFF 1985"

Here is our offering: Electronic Arts' IFF standard for Interchange File Format. The full name is "EA IFF 1985". Alternatives and justifications are included for certain choices. Public domain subroutine packages and utility programs are available to make it easy to write and use IFF-compatible programs.

Part 1 introduces the standard. Part 2 presents its requirements and background. Parts 3, 4, and 5 define the primitive data types, FORMs, and LISTs, respectively, and how to define new high level types. Part 6 specifies the top level file structure. Section 7 lists names of the group responsible for this standard. Appendix A is included for quick reference and Appendix B.

References

American National Standard Additional Control Codes for Use with ASCII, ANSI standard 3.64-1979 for an 8-bit character set. See also ISO standard 2022 and ISO/DIS standard 6429.2.

The C Programming Language, Brian W. Kernighan and Dennis M. Ritchie, Bell Laboratories. Prentice-Hall, Englewood Cliffs, NJ, 1978.

C, A Reference Manual, Samuel P. Harbison and Guy L. Steele Jr., Tartan Laboratories. Prentice-Hall, Englewood Cliffs, NJ, 1984.

Compiler Construction, An Advanced Course, edited by F. L. Bauer and J. Eickel (Springer-Verlag, 1976). This book is one of many sources for information on recursive descent parsing.

DIF Technical Specification © 1981 by Software Arts, Inc. DIF™ is the format for spreadsheet data interchange developed by Software Arts, Inc. DIF™ is a trademark of Software Arts, Inc.

"FTXT" IFF Formatted Text, from Electronic Arts. IFF supplement document for a text format.

"ILBM" IFF Interleaved Bitmap, from Electronic Arts. IFF supplement document for a raster image format.

M68000 16/32-Bit Microprocessor Programmer's Reference Manual © 1984, 1982, 1980, 1979 by Motorola, Inc.

PostScript Language Manual © 1984 Adobe Systems Incorporated.
PostScript™ is a trademark of Adobe Systems, Inc.
Times and Helvetica® are registered trademarks of Allied Corporation.

Inside Macintosh © 1982, 1983, 1984, 1985 Apple Computer, Inc., a programmer's reference manual.
Apple® is a trademark of Apple Computer, Inc.
MacPaint™ is a trademark of Apple Computer, Inc.
Macintosh™ is a trademark licensed to Apple Computer, Inc.

InterScript: A Proposal for a Standard for the Interchange of Editable Documents © 1984 Xerox Corporation.
Introduction to InterScript © 1985 Xerox Corporation.

Amiga® is a registered trademark of Commodore-Amiga, Inc.

Electronics Arts™ is a trademark of Electronic Arts.

2. Background for Designers

Part 2 is about the background, requirements, and goals for the standard. It's geared for people who want to design new types of IFF objects. People just interested in using the standard may wish to quickly scan this section.

What Do We Need?

A standard should be long on prescription and short on overhead. It should give lots of rules for designing programs and data files for synergy. But neither the programs nor the files should cost too much more than the expedient variety. Although we are looking to a future with CD-ROMs and perpendicular recording, the standard must work well on floppy disks.

For program portability, simplicity, and efficiency, formats should be designed with more than one implementation style in mind. It ought to be possible to read one of many objects in a file without scanning all the preceding data. (In practice, pure stream I/O is adequate although random access makes it easier to write files.) Some programs need to read and play out their data in real time, so we need good compromises between generality and efficiency.

As much as we need standards, they can't hold up product schedules. So we also need a kind of decentralized extensibility where any software developer can define and refine new object types without some "standards authority" in the loop. Developers must be able to extend existing formats in a forward- and backward-compatible way. A central repository for design information and example programs can help us take full advantage of the standard.

For convenience, data formats should heed the restrictions of various processors and environments. For example, word-alignment greatly helps 68000 access at insignificant cost to 8088 programs.

Other goals include the ability to share common elements over a list of objects and the ability to construct composite objects.

And finally, "Simple things should be simple and complex things should be possible".—Alan Kay.

Think Ahead

Let's think ahead and build programs that read and write files for each other and for programs yet to be designed. Build data formats to last for future computers so long as the overhead is acceptable. This extends the usefulness and life of today's programs and data.

To maximize interconnectivity, the standard file structure and the specific object formats must all be general and extensible. Think ahead when designing an object. File formats should serve many purposes and allow many programs to store and read back all the information they need; even squeeze in custom data. Then a programmer can store the available data and is encouraged to include fixed contextual details. Recipient programs can read the needed parts, skip unrecognized stuff, default missing data, and use the stored context to help transform the data as needed.

Scope

IFF addresses these needs by defining a standard file structure, some initial data object types, ways to define new types, and rules for accessing these files. We can accomplish a great deal by writing programs according to this standard, but do not expect direct compatibility with existing software. We'll need conversion programs to bridge the gap from the old world.

IFF is geared for computers that readily process information in 8-bit bytes. It assumes a "physical layer" of data storage and transmission that reliably maintains "files" as sequences of 8-bit bytes. The standard treats a "file" as a container of data bytes and is independent of how to find a file and whether it has a byte count.

This standard does not by itself implement a clipboard for cutting and pasting data between programs. A clipboard needs software to mediate access, and provide a notification mechanism so updates and requests for data can be detected.

Data Abstraction

The basic problem is *how to represent information* in a way that's program-independent, compiler- independent, machine-independent, and device-independent.

The computer science approach is "data abstraction", also known as "objects", "actors", and "abstract data types". A data abstraction has a "concrete representation" (its storage format), an "abstract representation" (its capabilities and uses), and access procedures that isolate all the calling software from the concrete representation. Only the access procedures touch the data storage. Hiding mutable details behind an interface is called "information hiding". What is hidden are the non-portable details of implementing the object, namely the selected storage representation and algorithms for manipulating it.

The power of this approach is modularity. By adjusting the access procedures we can extend and restructure the data without impacting the interface or its callers. Conversely, we can extend and restructure the interface and callers without making existing data obsolete. It's great for interchange!

But we seem to need the opposite: fixed file formats for all programs to access. Actually, we could file data abstractions ("filed objects") by storing the data and access procedures together. We'd have to encode the access procedures in a standard machine-independent programming language á la PostScript. Even with this, the interface can't evolve freely since we can't update all copies of the access procedures. So we'll have to design our abstract representations for limited evolution and occasional revolution (conversion).

In any case, today's microcomputers can't practically store true data abstractions. They <u>can</u> do the next best thing: store arbitrary types of data in "data chunks", each with a type identifier and a length count. The type identifier is a reference by name to the access procedures (any local implementation). The length count enables storage-level object operations like "copy" and "skip to next" independent of object type or contents.

Chunk writing is straightforward. Chunk reading requires a trivial parser to scan each chunk and dispatch to the proper access/conversion procedure. Reading chunks nested inside other chunks may require recursion, but no look ahead or backup.

That's the main idea of IFF. There are, of course, a few other details...

Previous Work

Where our needs are similar, we borrow from existing standards.

Our basic need to move data between independently developed programs is similar to that addressed by the Apple Macintosh desk scrap or "clipboard" [<u>Inside Macintosh</u> chapter "Scrap Manager"]. The Scrap Manager works closely with the Resource Manager, a handy filer and swapper for data objects (text strings, dialog window templates, pictures, fonts...) including types yet to be designed [<u>Inside Macintosh</u> chapter "Resource Manager"]. The Resource Manager is akin to Smalltalk's object swapper.

We will probably write a Macintosh desk accessory that converts IFF files to and from the Macintosh clipboard for quick and easy interchange with programs like MacPaint and Resource Mover.

Macintosh uses a simple and elegant scheme of four-character "identifiers" to identify resource types, clipboard format types, file types, and file creator programs. Alternatives are unique ID numbers assigned by a central authority or by hierarchical authorities, unique ID numbers generated by algorithm, other fixed length character strings, and variable length strings. Character string identifiers double as readable signposts in data files and programs. The choice of 4 characters is a good tradeoff between storage space, fetch/compare/store time, and name space size. We'll honor Apple's designers by adopting this scheme.

"PICT" is a good example of a standard structured graphics format (including raster images) and its many uses [Inside Macintosh chapter "QuickDraw"]. Macintosh provides QuickDraw routines in ROM to create, manipulate, and display PICTs. Any application can create a PICT by simply asking QuickDraw to record a sequence of drawing commands. Since it's just as easy to ask QuickDraw to render a PICT to a screen or a printer, it's very effective to pass them between programs, say from an illustrator to a word processor. An important feature is the ability to store "comments" in a PICT which QuickDraw will ignore. (Actually, it passes them to your optional custom "comment handler".)

PostScript, Adobe System's print file standard, is a more general way to represent any print image (which is a specification for putting marks on paper) [PostScript Language Manual]. In fact, PostScript is a full-fledged programming language. To interpret a PostScript program is to render a document on a raster output device. The language is defined in layers: a lexical layer of identifiers, constants, and operators; a layer of reverse polish semantics including scope rules and a way to define new subroutines; and a printing-specific layer of built-in identifiers and operators for rendering graphic images. It is clearly a powerful (Turing equivalent) image definition language. PICT and a subset of PostScript are candidates for structured graphics standards.

A PostScript document can be printed on any raster output device (including a display) but cannot generally be edited. That's because the original flexibility and constraints have been discarded. Besides, a PostScript program may use arbitrary computation to supply parameters like placement and size to each operator. A QuickDraw PICT, in comparison, is a more restricted format of graphic primitives parameterized by constants. So a PICT can be edited at the level of the primitives, e.g. move or thicken a line. It cannot be edited at the higher level of, say, the bar chart data which generated the picture.

PostScript has another limitation: Not all kinds of data amount to marks on paper. A musical instrument description is one example. PostScript is just not geared for such uses.

"DIF" is another example of data being stored in a general format usable by future programs [DIF Technical Specification]. DIF is a format for spreadsheet data interchange. DIF and PostScript are both expressed in plain ASCII text files. This is very handy for printing, debugging, experimenting, and transmitting across modems. It can have substantial cost in compaction and read/write work, depending on use. We won't store IFF files this way but we could define an ASCII alternate representation with a converter program.

InterScript is Xerox' standard for interchange of editable documents [Introduction to InterScript]. It approaches a harder problem: How to represent editable word processor documents that may contain formatted text, pictures, cross-references like figure numbers, and even highly specialized objects like mathematical equations? InterScript aims to define one standard representation for each kind of information. Each InterScript-compatible editor is supposed to preserve the objects it doesn't understand and even maintain nested cross-references. So a simple word processor would let you edit the text of a fancy document without discarding the equations or disrupting the equation numbers.

Our task is similarly to store high level information and preserve as much content as practical while moving it between programs. But we need to span a larger universe of data types and cannot expect to centrally define them all. Fortunately, we don't need to make programs preserve information that they don't understand. And for better or worse, we don't have to tackle general-purpose cross-references yet.

3. Primitive Data Types

Atomic components such as integers and characters that are interpretable directly by the CPU are specified in one format for all processors. We chose a format that's the same as used by the Motorola MC68000 processor [M68000 16/32-Bit Microprocessor Programmer's Reference Manual]. The high byte and high word of a number are stored *first*.

N.B.: Part 3 dictates the format for "primitive" data types where—and only where—used in the overall file structure. The number of such occurrences of dictated formats will be small enough that the costs of conversion, storage, and management of processor-specific files would far exceed the costs of conversion during I/O by "foreign" programs. A particular data chunk may be specified with a different format for its internal primitive types or with processor or environment specific variants if necessary to optimize local usage. Since that hurts data interchange, it's not recommended. (Cf. Designing New Data Sections, in Part 4.).

Alignment

All data objects larger than a byte are aligned on even byte addresses relative to the start of the file. This may require padding. Pad bytes are to be written as zeros, but don't count on that when reading.

This means that every odd-length "chunk" must be padded so that the next one will fall on an even boundary. Also, designers of structures to be stored in chunks should include pad fields where needed to align every field larger than a byte. For best efficiency, long word data should be arranged on long word (4 byte) boundaries. Zeros should be stored in all the pad bytes.

Justification: Even-alignment causes a little extra work for files that are used only on certain processors but allows 68000 programs to construct and scan the data in memory and do block I/O. Any 16 bit or greater CPU will have faster access to aligned data. You just add an occasional pad field to data structures that you're going to block read/write or else stream read/write an extra byte. And the same source code works on all processors. Unspecified alignment, on the other hand, would force 68000 programs to (dis)assemble word and long word data one byte at a time. Pretty cumbersome in a high level language. And if you don't conditionally compile that step out for other processors, you won't gain anything.

Numbers

Numeric types supported are two's complement binary integers in the format used by the MC68000 processor—high byte first, high word first—the reverse of 8088 and 6502 format.

```
UBYTE            8 bits unsigned
WORD            16 bits signed
UWORD           16 bits unsigned
LONG            32 bits signed
```

The actual type definitions depend on the CPU and the compiler. In this document, we'll express data type definitions in the C programming language. [See C, A Reference Manual.] In 68000 Lattice C:

```
typedef unsigned char  UBYTE;     /*  8 bits unsigned */
typedef short          WORD;      /* 16 bits signed   */
typedef unsigned short UWORD;     /* 16 bits unsigned */
typedef long           LONG;      /* 32 bits signed   */
```

Characters

The following character set is assumed wherever characters are used, e.g. in text strings, IDs, and TEXT chunks (see below). Characters are encoded in 8-bit ASCII. Characters in the range NUL (hex 0) through DEL (hex 7F) are well defined by the 7-bit ASCII standard. IFF uses the graphic group " " (SP, hex 20) through "~" (hex 7E).

Most of the control character group hex 01 through hex 1F have no standard meaning in IFF. The control character LF (hex 0A) is defined as a "newline" character. It denotes an intentional line break, that is, a paragraph or line terminator. (There is no way to store an automatic line break. That is strictly a function of the margins in the environment the text is placed.) The control character ESC (hex 1B) is a reserved escape character under the rules of ANSI standard 3.64-1979 American National Standard Additional Control Codes for Use with ASCII, ISO standard 2022, and ISO/DIS standard 6429.2.

Characters in the range hex 7F through hex FF are not globally defined in IFF. They are best left reserved for future standardization. (Note that the FORM type FTXT (formatted text) defines the meaning of these characters within FTXT forms.) In particular, character values hex 7F through hex 9F are control codes while characters hex A0 through hex FF are extended graphic characters like Å, as per the ISO and ANSI standards cited above. [See the supplementary document "FTXT" IFF Formatted Text.]

Dates

A "creation date" is defined as the date and time a stream of data bytes was created. (Some systems call this a "last modified date".) Editing some data changes its creation date. Moving the data between volumes or machines does not.

The IFF standard date format will be one of those used in MS-DOS, Macintosh, or AmigaDOS (probably a 32-bit unsigned number of seconds since a reference point). Issue: Investigate these three.

Type IDs

A "type ID", "property name", "FORM type", or any other IFF identifier is a 32-bit value: the concatenation of four ASCII characters in the range " " (SP, hex 20) through "~" (hex 7E). Spaces (hex 20) should not precede printing characters; trailing spaces are ok. Control characters are forbidden.

```
typedef CHAR ID[4];
```

IDs are compared using a simple 32-bit case-dependent equality test. FORM type IDs are restricted. Since they may be stored in filename extensions lower case letters and punctuation marks are forbidden. Trailing spaces are ok.

Carefully choose those four characters when you pick a new ID. Make them mnemonic so programmers can look at an interchange format file and figure out what kind of data it contains. The name space makes it possible for developers scattered around the globe to generate ID values with minimal collisions so long as they choose specific names like "MUS4" instead of general ones like "TYPE" and "FILE".

Commodore-Amiga Technical Support has undertaken the task of maintaining the registry of FORM type IDs and format descriptions. See the IFF registry document for more information.

Sometimes it's necessary to make data format changes that aren't backward compatible. As much as we work for compatibility, unintended interactions can develop. Since IDs are used to denote data formats in IFF, new IDs are chosen to denote revised formats. Since programs won't read chunks whose IDs they don't recognize (see Chunks, below), the new IDs keep old programs from stumbling over new data. The conventional way to chose a "revision"

ID is to increment the last character if it's a digit or else change the last character to a digit. E.g. first and second revisions of the ID "XY" would be "XY1" and "XY2". Revisions of "CMAP" would be "CMA1" and "CMA2".

Chunks

Chunks are the building blocks in the IFF structure. The form expressed as a C typedef is:

```
typedef struct {
  ID      ckID;                      /* 4 character ID */
  LONG    ckSize;                    /* sizeof(ckData) */
  UBYTE   ckData[/* ckSize */];
  } Chunk;
```

We can diagram an example chunk—a "CMAP" chunk containing 12 data bytes—like this:

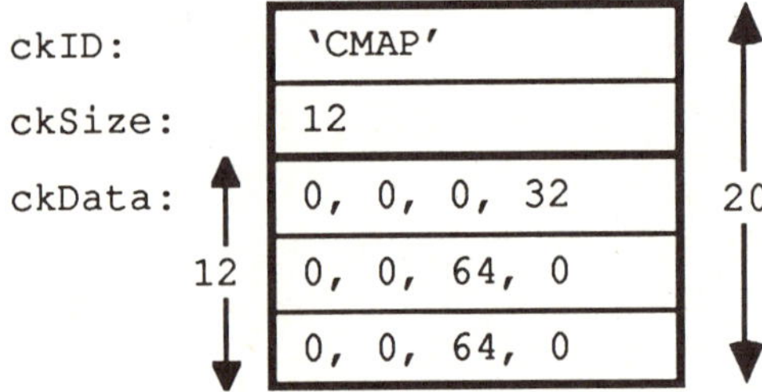

That's 4 bytes of `ckID`, 4 bytes of `ckSize` and 12 data bytes. The total space used is 20 bytes.

The `ckID` identifies the format and purpose of the chunk. As a rule, a program must recognize `ckID` to interpret `ckData`. It should skip over all unrecognized chunks. The `ckID` also serves as a format version number as long as we pick new IDs to identify new formats of `ckData` (see above).

The following `ckID`s are universally reserved to identify chunks with particular IFF meanings: "LIST", "FORM", "PROP", "CAT ", and "   ". The special ID "   " (4 spaces) is a `ckID` for "filler" chunks, that is, chunks that fill space but have no meaningful contents. The IDs "LIS1" through "LIS9", "FOR1" through "FOR9", and "CAT1" through "CAT9" are reserved for future "version number" variations. All IFF-compatible software must account for these chunk IDs.

The ckSize is a logical block size—how many data bytes are in ckData. If `ckData` is an odd number of bytes long, a 0 pad byte follows which is <u>not</u> included in `ckSize`. (Cf. Alignment.) A chunk's total physical size is `ckSize` rounded up to an even number plus the size of the header. So the smallest chunk is 8 bytes long with `ckSize = 0`. For the sake of following chunks, programs must respect every chunk's ckSize as a virtual end-of-file for reading its `ckData` even if that data is malformed, e.g. if nested contents are truncated.

We can describe the syntax of a chunk as a regular expression with "#" representing the `ckSize`, the length of the following {braced} bytes. The "`[0]`" represents a sometimes needed pad byte. (The regular expressions in this document are collected in Appendix A along with an explanation of notation.)

```
Chunk          ::= ID #{ UBYTE* } [0]
```

One chunk output technique is to stream write a chunk header, stream write the chunk contents, then random access back to the header to fill in the size. Another technique is to make a preliminary pass over the data to compute the size, then write it out all at once.

Strings, String Chunks, and String Properties

In a string of ASCII text, linefeed (0x0A) denotes a forced line break (paragraph or line terminator). Other control characters are not used. (Cf. Characters.) For maximum compatibility with line editors, two linefeed characters are often used to indicate a paragraph boundary.

The `ckID` for a chunk that contains a string of plain, unformatted text is "TEXT". As a practical matter, a text string should probably not be longer than 32767 bytes. The standard allows up to $2^{31} - 1$ bytes. The `ckID` "TEXT" is globally reserved for this use.

When used as a data property (see below), a text string chunk may be 0 to 255 characters long. Such a string is readily converted to a C string or a Pascal `STRING[255]`. The `ckID` of a property must have a unique property name, *not* "TEXT".

When used as a part of a chunk or data property, restricted C string format is normally used. That means 0 to 255 characters followed by a NULL byte (ASCII value 0).

Data Properties (advanced topic)

Data properties specify attributes for following (non-property) chunks. A data property essentially says "identifier = value", for example "XY = (10, 200)", telling something about following chunks. Properties may only appear inside data sections ("FORM" chunks, cf. Data Sections) and property sections ("PROP" chunks, cf. Group PROP).

The form of a data property is a type of Chunk. The `ckID` is a property name as well as a property type. The `ckSize` should be small since data properties are intended to be accumulated in RAM when reading a file. (256 bytes is a reasonable upper bound.) Syntactically:

```
Property    ::= Chunk
```

When designing a data object, use properties to describe context information like the size of an image, even if they don't vary in your program. Other programs will need this information.

Think of property settings as assignments to variables in a programming language. Multiple assignments are redundant and local assignments temporarily override global assignments. The order of assignments doesn't matter as long as they precede the affected chunks. (Cf. LISTs, CATs, and Shared Properties.)

Each object type (FORM type) is a local name space for property IDs. Think of a "CMAP" property in a "FORM ILBM" as the qualified ID "ILBM.CMAP". A "CMAP" inside some other type of FORM may not have the same meaning. Property IDs specified when an object type is designed (and therefore known to all clients) are called "standard" while specialized ones added later are "nonstandard".

Links

Issue: A standard mechanism for "links" or "cross references" is very desirable for things like combining images and sounds into animations. Perhaps we'll define "link" chunks within FORMs that refer to other FORMs or to specific chunks within the same and other FORMs. This needs further work. EA IFF 1985 has no standard link mechanism.

For now, it may suffice to read a list of, say, musical instruments, and then just refer to them within a musical score by sequence number.

File References

Issue: We may need a standard form for references to other files. A "file ref" could name a directory and a file in the same type of operating system as the reference's originator. Following the reference would expect the file to be on some mounted volume, or perhaps the same directory as the file that made the reference. In a network environment, a file reference could name a server, too.

Issue: How can we express operating-system independent file references?
Issue: What about a means to reference a portion of another file? Would this be a "file ref" plus a reference to a "link" within the target file?

4. Data Sections

The first thing we need of a file is to check: Does it contain IFF data and, if so, does it contain the kind of data we're looking for? So we come to the notion of a "data section".

A "data section" or IFF "FORM" is one self-contained "data object" that might be stored in a file by itself. It is one high level data object such as a picture or a sound effect, and generally contains a grouping of chunks. The IFF structure "FORM" makes it self- identifying. It could be a composite object like a musical score with nested musical instrument descriptions.

Group FORM

A data section is a chunk with `ckID` "FORM" and this arrangement:

```
FORM          ::= "FORM" #{ FormType (LocalChunk | FORM | LIST | CAT)* }
FormType      ::= ID
LocalChunk    ::= Property | Chunk
```

The ID "FORM" is a syntactic keyword like "struct" in C. Think of a "struct ILBM" containing a field "CMAP". If you see "FORM" you will know to expect a FORM type ID (the structure name, "ILBM" in this example) and a particular contents arrangement or "syntax" (local chunks, FORMs, LISTs, and CATs). A "FORM ILBM", in particular, might contain a local chunk "CMAP", an "ILBM.CMAP" (to use a qualified name).

So the chunk ID "FORM" indicates a data section. It implies that the chunk contains an ID and some number of nested chunks. In reading a FORM, like any other chunk, programs must respect its `ckSize` as a virtual end-of-file for reading its contents, even if they're truncated.

The FORM type is a restricted ID that may not contain lower case letters or punctuation characters. (Cf. Type IDs. Cf. Single Purpose Files.)

The type-specific information in a FORM is composed of its "local chunks": data properties and other chunks. Each FORM type is a local name space for local chunk IDs. So "CMAP" local chunks in other FORM types may be unrelated to "ILBM.CMAP". More than that, each FORM type defines semantic scope. If you know what a FORM ILBM is, you will know what an ILBM.CMAP is.

Local chunks defined when the FORM type is designed (and therefore known to all clients of this type) are called "standard" while specialized ones added later are "nonstandard".

Among the local chunks, property chunks give settings for various details like text font while the other chunks supply the essential information. This distinction is not clear cut. A property setting can be cancelled by a later setting of the same property. E.g. in the sequence:

```
prop1 = x  (Data A)  prop1 = z  prop1 = y (Data B)
```

`prop1 is = x` for Data A, and `y` for Data B. The setting `prop1 = z` has no effect.

For clarity, the universally reserved chunk IDs "LIST", "FORM", "PROP", "CAT ", "   ", "LIS1" through "LIS9", "FOR1" through "FOR9", and "CAT1" through "CAT9" may not be FORM type IDs.

Part 5, below, talks about grouping FORMs into LISTs and CATs. They let you group a bunch of FORMs but don't impose any particular meaning or constraints on the grouping. Read on.

Composite FORMs

A FORM chunk inside a FORM is a full-fledged data section. This means you can build a composite object such as a multi-frame animation sequence by nesting available picture FORMs and sound effect FORMs. You can insert additional chunks with information like frame rate and frame count.

Using composite FORMs, you leverage on existing programs that create and edit the component FORMs. Those editors may even look into your composite object to copy out its type of component. Such editors are not allowed to replace their component objects within your composite object. That's because the IFF standard lets you specify consistency requirements for the composite FORM such as maintaining a count or a directory of the components. Only programs that are written to uphold the rules of your FORM type may create or modify such FORMs.

Therefore, in designing a program that creates composite objects, you are strongly requested to provide a facility for your users to import and export the nested FORMs. Import and export could move the data through a clipboard or a file.

Here are several existing FORM types and rules for defining new ones:

FTXT

An FTXT data section contains text with character formatting information like fonts and faces. It has no paragraph or document formatting information like margins and page headers. FORM FTXT is well matched to the text representation in Amiga's Intuition environment. See the supplemental document "FTXT" IFF Formatted Text.

ILBM

"ILBM" is an InterLeaved BitMap image with color map; a machine-independent format for raster images. FORM ILBM is the standard image file format for the Commodore-Amiga computer and is useful in other environments, too. See the supplemental document "ILBM" IFF Interleaved Bitmap.

PICS

The data chunk inside a "PICS" data section has ID "PICT" and holds a QuickDraw picture. Issue: Allow more than one PICT in a PICS? See Inside Macintosh chapter "QuickDraw" for details on PICTs and how to create and display them on the Macintosh computer.

The only standard property for PICS is "XY", an optional property that indicates the position of the PICT relative to "the big picture". The contents of an XY is a QuickDraw Point.

Note: PICT may be limited to Macintosh use, in which case there'll be another format for structured graphics in other environments.

Other Macintosh Resource Types

Some other Macintosh resource types could be adopted for use within IFF files; perhaps MWRT, ICN, ICN#, and STR#.

Issue: Consider the candidates and reserve some more IDs.

Designing New Data Sections

Supplemental documents will define additional object types. A supplement needs to specify the object's purpose, its FORM type ID, the IDs and formats of standard local chunks, and rules for generating and interpreting the data. It's a good idea to supply typedefs and an example source program that accesses the new object. See "ILBM" IFF Interleaved Bitmap for such an example.

Anyone can pick a new FORM type ID but should reserve it with Commodore-Amiga Technical Support (CATS) at their earliest convenience. While decentralized format definitions and extensions are possible in IFF, our preference is to get design consensus by committee, implement a program to read and write it, perhaps tune the format before it becomes locked in stone, and then publish the format with example code. Some organization should remain in charge of answering questions and coordinating extensions to the format.

If it becomes necessary to incompatibly revise the design of some data section, its FORM type ID will serve as a version number (Cf. Type IDs). E.g. a revised "VDEO" data section could be called "VDE1". But try to get by with compatible revisions within the existing FORM type.

In a new FORM type, the rules for primitive data types and word-alignment (Cf. Primitive Data Types) may be overridden for the contents of its local chunks—but not for the chunk structure itself—if your documentation spells out the deviations. If machine-specific type variants are needed, e.g. to store vast numbers of integers in reverse bit order, then outline the conversion algorithm and indicate the variant inside each file, perhaps via different FORM types. Needless to say, variations should be minimized.

In designing a FORM type, encapsulate all the data that other programs will need to interpret your files. E.g. a raster graphics image should specify the image size even if your program always uses 320 x 200 pixels x 3 bitplanes. Receiving programs are then empowered to append or clip the image rectangle, to add or drop bitplanes, etc. This enables a lot more compatibility.

Separate the central data (like musical notes) from more specialized information (like note beams) so simpler programs can extract the central parts during read-in. Leave room for expansion so other programs can squeeze in new kinds of information (like lyrics). And remember to keep the property chunks manageably short—let's say ≤ 256 bytes.

When designing a data object, try to strike a good tradeoff between a super-general format and a highly-specialized one. Fit the details to at least one particular need, for example a raster image might as well store pixels in the current machine's scan order. But add the kind of generality that makes the format usable with foreseeable hardware and software. E.g. use a whole byte for each red, green, and blue color value even if this year's computer has only 4-bit video DACs. Think ahead and help other programs so long as the overhead is acceptable. E.g. run compress a raster by scan line rather than as a unit so future programs can swap images by scan line to and from secondary storage.

Try to design a general purpose "least common multiple" format that encompasses the needs of many programs without getting too complicated. Be sure to leave provisions for future expansion. Let's coalesce our uses around a few such formats widely separated in the vast design space. Two factors make this flexibility and simplicity practical. First, file storage space is getting very plentiful, so compaction is not always a priority. Second, nearly any locally-performed data conversion work during file reading and writing will be cheap compared to the I/O time.

It must be ok to copy a LIST or FORM or CAT intact, e.g. to incorporate it into a composite FORM. So any kind of internal references within a FORM must be relative references. They could be relative to the start of the containing FORM, relative from the referencing chunk, or a sequence number into a collection.

With composite FORMs, you leverage on existing programs that create and edit the components. If you write a program that creates composite objects, please provide a facility for users to import and export the nested FORMs.

Finally, don't forget to specify all implied rules in detail.

5. LISTs, CATs, and Shared Properties (Advanced topics)

Data often needs to be grouped together, for example, consider a list of icons. Sometimes a trick like arranging little images into a big raster works, but generally they'll need to be structured as a first class group. The objects "LIST" and "CAT" are IFF-universal mechanisms for this purpose. Note: LIST and CAT are advanced topics the first time reader will want to skip.

Property settings sometimes need to be shared over a list of similar objects. E.g. a list of icons may share one color map. LIST provides a means called "PROP" to do this. One purpose of a LIST is to define the scope of a PROP. A "CAT", on the other hand, is simply a concatenation of objects.

Simpler programs may skip LISTs and PROPs altogether and just handle FORMs and CATs. All "fully-conforming" IFF programs also know about "CAT ", "LIST", and "PROP". Any program that reads a FORM inside a LIST must process shared PROPs to correctly interpret that FORM.

Group CAT

A CAT is just an untyped group of data objects.

Structurally, a CAT is a chunk with chunk ID "CAT " containing a "contents type" ID followed by the nested objects. The `ckSize` of each contained chunk is essentially a relative pointer to the next one.

```
CAT           ::= "CAT " #{ ContentsType (FORM | LIST | CAT)* }
ContentsType  ::= ID                  -- a hint or an "abstract data type" ID
```

In reading a CAT, like any other chunk, programs must respect it's `ckSize` as a virtual end-of-file for reading the nested objects even if they're malformed or truncated.

The "contents type" following the CAT's `ckSize` indicates what kind of FORMs are inside. So a CAT of ILBMs would store "ILBM" there. It's just a hint. It may be used to store an "abstract data type". A CAT could just have blank contents ID ("   ") if it contains more than one kind of FORM.

CAT defines only the format of the group. The group's meaning is open to interpretation. This is like a list in LISP: the structure of cells is predefined but the meaning of the contents as, say, an association list depends on use. If you need a group with an enforced meaning (an "abstract data type" or Smalltalk "subclass"), some consistency constraints, or additional data chunks, use a composite FORM instead (Cf. Composite FORMs).

Since a CAT just means a concatenation of objects, CATs are rarely nested. Programs should really merge CATs rather than nest them.

Group LIST

A LIST defines a group very much like CAT but it also gives a scope for PROPs (see below). And unlike CATs, LISTs should not be merged without understanding their contents.

Structurally, a LIST is a chunk with `ckID` "LIST" containing a "contents type" ID, optional shared properties, and the nested contents (FORMs, LISTs, and CATs), in that order. The `ckSize` of each contained chunk is a relative pointer to the next one. A LIST is not an arbitrary linked list—the cells are simply concatenated.

```
LIST          ::= "LIST" #{ ContentsType PROP* (FORM | LIST | CAT)* }
ContentsType  ::= ID
```

Group PROP

PROP chunks may appear in LISTs (not in FORMs or CATs). They supply shared properties for the FORMs in that LIST. This ability to elevate some property settings to shared status for a list of forms is useful for both indirection and compaction. E.g. a list of images with the same size and colors can share one "size" property and one "color map" property. Individual FORMs can override the shared settings.

The contents of a PROP is like a FORM with no data chunks:

```
PROP          ::= "PROP" #{ FormType Property* }
```

It means, "Here are the shared properties for FORM type <FormType>".

A LIST may have at most one PROP of a FORM type, and all the PROPs must appear before any of the FORMs or nested LISTs and CATs. You can have subsequences of FORMs sharing properties by making each subsequence a LIST.

Scoping: Think of property settings as variable bindings in nested blocks of a programming language. In C this would look like:

```
#define Roman              0
#define Helvetica          1

void main()
  {
  int font=Roman;          /* The global default */
    {
    printf("The font number is %d\n",font);
    }
    {
    int font=Helvetica;  /* local setting */
    printf("The font number is %d\n",font);
    }
    {
    printf("The font number is %d\n",font);
    }
  }
/*
 * Sample output:          The font number is 0
 *                         The font number is 1
 *                         The font number is 0
 */
```

An IFF file could contain:

```
LIST {
  PROP TEXT {
    FONT {TimesRoman}                   /* shared setting            */
    }

  FORM TEXT {
    FONT {Helvetica}                    /* local setting             */
    CHRS {Hello }                       /* uses font Helvetica       */
    }

  FORM TEXT {
    CHRS {there.}                       /* uses font TimesRoman      */
    }
}
```

The shared property assignments selectively override the reader's global defaults, but only for FORMs within the group. A FORM's own property assignments selectively override the global and group-supplied values. So when reading an IFF file, keep property settings on a stack. They are designed to be small enough to hold in main memory.

Shared properties are semantically equivalent to copying those properties into each of the nested FORMs right after their FORM type IDs.

Properties for LIST

Optional "properties for LIST" store the origin of the list's contents in a PROP chunk for the pseudo FORM type "LIST". They are the properties originating program "OPGM", processor family "OCPU", computer type "OCMP", computer serial number or network address "OSN ", and user name "UNAM". In our imperfect world, these could be called upon to distinguish between unintended variations of a data format or to work around bugs in particular originating/receiving program pairs. Issue: Specify the format of these properties.

A creation date could also be stored in a property, but let's ask that file creating, editing, and transporting programs maintain the correct date in the local file system. Programs that move files between machine types are expected to copy across the creation dates.

6. Standard File Structure

File Structure Overview

An IFF file is just a single chunk of type FORM, LIST, or CAT. Therefore an IFF file can be recognized by its first 4 bytes: "FORM", "LIST", or "CAT ". Any file contents after the chunk's end are to be ignored. (Some file transfer programs add garbage to the end of transferred files. This specification protects against such common damage).

The simplest IFF file would be one that does no more than encapsulate some binary data (perhaps even an old-fashioned single-purpose binary file). Here is a binary dump of such a minimal IFF example:

```
0000: 464F524D 0000001A 534E4150 43524143    FORM....SNAPCRAC
0010: 0000000D 68656C6C 6F2C776F 726C6421    ....hello,world!
0020: 0A00                                   ..
```

The first 4 bytes indicate this is a "FORM"; the most common IFF top level structure. The following 4 bytes indicate that the contents totals 26 bytes. The form type is listed as "SNAP".

Our form "SNAP" contains only one chunk at the moment; a chunk of type "CRAC". From the size ($0000000D) the amount of data must be 13 bytes. In this case, the data happens to correspond to the ASCII string "`hello, world!`<lf>". Since the number 13 is odd, a zero pad byte is added to the file. At any time new chunks could be added to form SNAP without affecting any other aspect of the file (other than the form size). It's that simple.

Since an IFF file can be a group of objects, programs that read/write single objects can communicate to an extent with programs that read/write groups. You're encouraged to write programs that handle all the objects in a LIST or CAT. A graphics editor, for example, could process a list of pictures as a multiple page document, one page at a time.

Programs should enforce IFF's syntactic rules when reading and writing files. Users should be told when a file is corrupt. This ensures robust data transfer. For minor damage, you may wish to give the user the option of using the suspect data, or cancelling. Presumably a user could read in a damaged file, then save whatever was salvaged to a valid file. The public domain IFF reader/writer subroutine package does some syntatic checks for you. A utility program "IFFCheck" is available that scans an IFF file and checks it for conformance to IFF's syntactic rules. IFFCheck also prints an outline of the chunks in the file, showing the `ckID` and `ckSize` of each. This is quite handy when building IFF programs. Example programs are also available to show details of reading and writing IFF files.

A merge program "IFFJoin" will be available that logically appends IFF files into a single CAT group. It "unwraps" each input file that is a CAT so that the combined file isn't nested CATs.

If we need to revise the IFF standard, the three anchoring IDs will be used as "version numbers". That's why IDs "FOR1" through "FOR9", "LIS1" through "LIS9", and "CAT1" through "CAT9" are reserved.

IFF formats are designed for reasonable performance with floppy disks. We achieve considerable simplicity in the formats and programs by relying on the host file system rather than defining universal grouping structures like directories for LIST contents. On huge storage systems, IFF files could be leaf nodes in a file structure like a B-tree. Let's hope the host file system implements that for us!

There are two kinds of IFF files: single purpose files and scrap files. They differ in the interpretation of multiple data objects and in the file's external type.

Single Purpose Files

A single purpose IFF file is for normal "document" and "archive" storage. This is in contrast with "scrap files" (see below) and temporary backing storage (non-interchange files).

The external file type (or filename extension, depending on the host file system) indicates the file's contents. It's generally the FORM type of the data contained, hence the restrictions on FORM type IDs.

Programmers and users may pick an "intended use" type as the filename extension to make it easy to filter for the relevant files in a filename requester. This is actually a "subclass" or "subtype" that conveniently separates files of the same FORM type that have different uses. Programs cannot demand conformity to its expected subtypes without overly restricting data interchange since they cannot know about the subtypes to be used by future programs that users will want to exchange data with.

Issue: How to generate 3-letter MS-DOS extensions from 4-letter FORM type IDs?

Most single purpose files will be a single FORM (perhaps a composite FORM like a musical score containing nested FORMs like musical instrument descriptions). If it's a LIST or a CAT, programs should skip over unrecognized objects to read the recognized ones or the first recognized one. Then a program that can read a single purpose file can read something out of a "scrap file", too.

Scrap Files (not currently used)

A "scrap file" is for maximum interconnectivity in getting data between programs; the core of a clipboard function. Scrap files may have type "IFF " or filename extension ".IFF".

A scrap file is typically a CAT containing alternate representations of the same basic information. Include as many alternatives as you can readily generate. This redundancy improves interconnectivity in situations where we can't make all programs read and write super-general formats. [Inside Macintosh chapter "Scrap Manager".] E.g. a graphically-annotated musical score might be supplemented by a stripped down 4-voice melody and by a text (the lyrics).

The originating program should write the alternate representations in order of "preference": most preferred (most comprehensive) type to least preferred (least comprehensive) type. A receiving program should either use the first appearing type that it understands or search for its own "preferred" type.

A scrap file should have at most one alternative of any type. (A LIST of same type objects is ok as one of the alternatives.) But don't count on this when reading; ignore extra sections of a type. Then a program that reads scrap files can read something out of single purpose files.

Rules for Reader Programs

Here are some notes on building programs that read IFF files. If you use the standard IFF reader module "IFFR.C", many of these rules and details will be automatically handled. (See "Support Software" in Appendix A.) We recommend that you start from the example program "ShowILBM.C". For LIST and PROP work, you should also read up on recursive descent parsers. [See, for example, Compiler Construction, An Advanced Course.]

- The standard is very flexible so many programs can exchange data. This implies a program has to scan the file and react to what's actually there in whatever order it appears. An IFF reader program is a parser.

- For interchange to really work, programs must be willing to do some conversion during read-in. If the data isn't exactly what you expect, say, the raster is smaller than those created by your program, then adjust it. Similarly, your program could crop a large picture, add or drop bitplanes, or create/discard a mask plane. The program should give up gracefully on data that it can't convert.

- If it doesn't start with "FORM", "LIST", or "CAT ", it's not an IFF-85 file.

- For any chunk you encounter, you must recognize its type ID to understand its contents.

- For any FORM chunk you encounter, you must recognize its FORM type ID to understand the contained "local chunks". Even if you don't recognize the FORM type, you can still scan it for nested FORMs, LISTs, and CATs of interest.

- Don't forget to skip the implied pad byte after every odd-length chunk, this is *not* included in the chunk count!

- Chunk types LIST, FORM, PROP, and CAT are generic groups. They always contain a subtype ID followed by chunks.

- Readers ought to handle a CAT of FORMs in a file. You may treat the FORMs like document pages to sequence through, or just use the first FORM.

- Many IFF readers completely skip LISTs. "Fully IFF-conforming" readers are those that handle LISTs, even if just to read the first FORM from a file. If you do look into a LIST, you must process shared properties (in PROP chunks) properly. The idea is to get the correct data or none at all.

- The nicest readers are willing to look into unrecognized FORMs for nested FORM types that they do recognize. For example, a musical score may contain nested instrument descriptions and and animation or desktop publishing files may contain still pictures. This extra step is highly recommended.

Note to programmers: Processing PROP chunks is not simple! You'll need some background in interpreters with stack frames. If this is foreign to you, build programs that read/write only one FORM per file. For the more intrepid programmers, the next paragraph summarizes how to process LISTs and PROPs. See the general IFF reader module "IFFR.C" and the example program "ShowILBM.C" for details.

Allocate a stack frame for every LIST and FORM you encounter and initialize it by copying the stack frame of the parent LIST or FORM. At the top level, you'll need a stack frame initialized to your program's global defaults. While reading each LIST or FORM, store all encountered properties into the current stack frame. In the example ShowILBM, each stack frame has a place for a bitmap header property ILBM.BMHD and a color map property ILBM.CMAP. When you finally get to the ILBM's BODY chunk, use the property settings accumulated in the current stack frame.

An alternate implementation would just remember PROPs encountered, forgetting each on reaching the end of its scope (the end of the containing LIST). When a FORM XXXX is encountered, scan the chunks in all remembered PROPs XXXX, in order, as if they appeared before the chunks actually in the FORM XXXX. This gets trickier if you read FORMs inside of FORMs.

Rules for Writer Programs

Here are some notes on building programs that write IFF files, which is much easier than reading them. If you use the standard IFF writer module "IFFW.C", many of these rules and details will automatically be enforced. See the example program "Raw2ILBM.C".

- An IFF file is a single FORM, LIST, or CAT chunk.

- Any IFF-85 file must start with the 4 characters "FORM", "LIST", or "CAT ", followed by a LONG `ckSize`. There should be no data after the chunk end.

- Chunk types LIST, FORM, PROP, and CAT are generic. They always contain a subtype ID followed by chunks. These three IDs are universally reserved, as are "LIS1" through "LIS9", "FOR1" through "FOR9", "CAT1" through "CAT9", and "   ".

- Don't forget to write a 0 pad byte after each odd-length chunk.

- Do not try to edit a file that you don't know how to create. Programs may look into a file and copy out nested FORMs of types that they recognize, but they should not edit and replace the nested FORMs and not add or remove them. Breaking these rules could make the containing structure inconsistent. You may write a new file containing items you copied, or copied and modified, but don't copy structural parts you don't understand.

- You must adhere to the syntax descriptions in Appendix A. E.g. PROPs may only appear inside LISTs.

There are at least four common techniques for writing an IFF group:

(1) build the data in a file mapped into virtual memory.
(2) build the data in memory blocks and use block I/O.
(3) stream write the data piecemeal and (don't forget!) random access back to set the group (or FORM) length count.
(4) make a preliminary pass to compute the length count then stream write the data.

Issue: The standard disallows "blind" chunk copying for consistency reasons. Perhaps we can define a ckID convention for chunks that are ok to replicate without knowledge of the contents. Any such chunks would need to be internally consistent, and not be bothered by changed external references. This is a proposal, and has not been adopted.

Issue: Stream-writing an IFF FORM can be inconvenient. With random access files one can write all the chunks then go back to fix up the FORM size. With stream access, the FORM size must be calculated before the file is written. When compression is involved, this can be slow or inconvenient. Perhaps we can define an "END " chunk. The stream writer would use -1 ($FFFFFFFF) as the FORM size. The reader would follow each chunk; when the reader reaches an "END ", it would terminate the last -1 sized chunk. Certain new IFF FORMs could require that readers understand "END ". This is a proposal, and has not been adopted; current reader software would consider a file with an incorrect FORM size to be corrupt.

7. Standards Committee

The following people contributed to the design of this IFF standard:

Bob "Kodiak" Burns, Commodore-Amiga
R. J. Mical, Commodore-Amiga
Jerry Morrison, Electronic Arts
Greg Riker, Electronic Arts
Steve Shaw, Electronic Arts
Barry Walsh, Commodore-Amiga
Oct, 1988 revision by Bryce Nesbitt, and Carolyn Scheppner, Commodore-Amiga

Appendix A. Reference

Type Definitions

The following C typedefs describe standard IFF structures. Declarations to use in practice will vary with the CPU and compiler. For example, 68000 Lattice C produces efficient comparison code if we define ID as a "LONG". A macro "MakeID" builds these IDs at compile time.

```
/* Standard IFF types, expressed in 68000 Lattice C.              */

typedef unsigned char UBYTE;       /*  8 bits unsigned             */
typedef short WORD;                /* 16 bits signed               */
typedef unsigned short UWORD;      /* 16 bits unsigned             */
typedef long LONG;                 /* 32 bits signed               */

typedef char ID[4];                /* 4 chars in ' ' through '~' */

typedef struct {
  ID    ckID;
  LONG  ckSize;                    /* sizeof(ckData)               */
  UBYTE ckData[/* ckSize */];
  } Chunk;

/* ID typedef and builder for 68000 Lattice C. */
typedef LONG ID;                   /* 4 chars in ' ' through '~' */
#define MakeID(a,b,c,d)  ( (a)<<24 | (b)<<16 | (c)<<8 | (d) )

/* Globally reserved IDs. */
#define ID_FORM   MakeID('F','O','R','M')
#define ID_LIST   MakeID('L','I','S','T')
#define ID_PROP   MakeID('P','R','O','P')
#define ID_CAT    MakeID('C','A','T',' ')
#define ID_FILLER MakeID(' ',' ',' ',' ')
```

Syntax Definitions

Here's a collection of the syntax definitions in this document.

```
Chunk         ::= ID #{ UBYTE* } [0]

Property      ::= Chunk

FORM          ::= "FORM" #{ FormType (LocalChunk | FORM | LIST | CAT)* }
FormType      ::= ID
LocalChunk    ::= Property | Chunk

CAT           ::= "CAT " #{ ContentsType (FORM | LIST | CAT)* }
ContentsType  ::= ID                 -- a hint or an "abstract data type" ID

LIST          ::= "LIST" #{ ContentsType PROP* (FORM | LIST | CAT)* }
PROP          ::= "PROP" #{ FormType Property* }
```

In this extended regular expression notation, the token "#" represents a count of the following {braced} data bytes. Literal items are shown in "quotes", [square bracketed items] are optional, and "*" means 0 or more instances. A sometimes-needed pad byte is shown as "[0]".

Example Diagrams

Here's a box diagram for an example IFF file, a raster image FORM ILBM. This FORM contains a bitmap header property chunk BMHD, a color map property chunk CMAP, and a raster data chunk BODY. This particular raster is 320 x 200 pixels x 3 bit planes uncompressed. The "0" after the CMAP chunk represents a zero pad byte; included since the CMAP chunk has an odd length. The text to the right of the diagram shows the outline that would be printed by the IFFCheck utility program for this particular file.

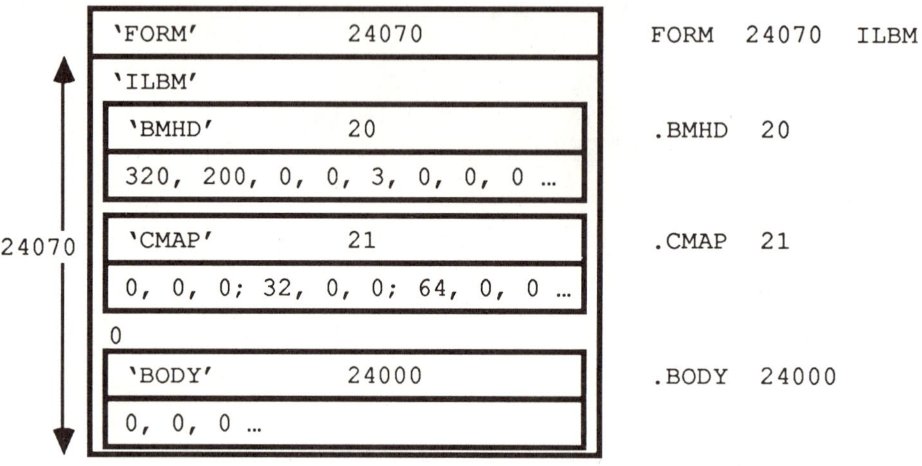

This second diagram shows a LIST of two FORMs ILBM sharing a common BMHD property and a common CMAP property. Again, the text on the right is an outline á la IFFCheck.

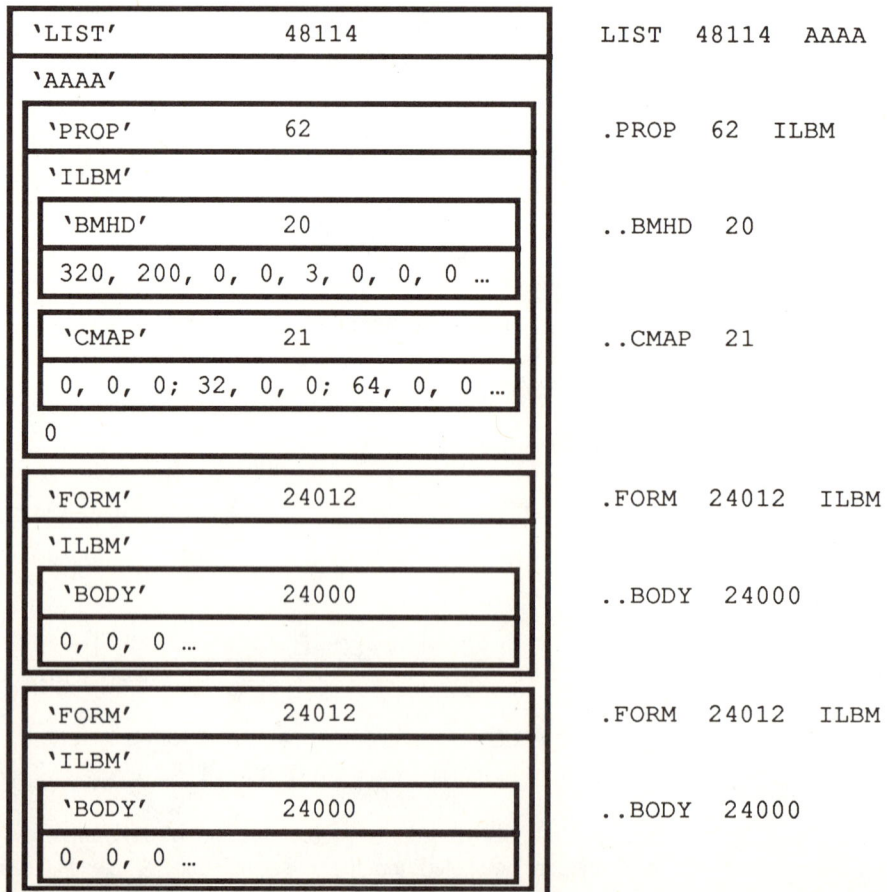

```
'LIST'          48114                        LIST  48114  AAAA
'AAAA'
  'PROP'        62                           .PROP  62  ILBM
  'ILBM'
    'BMHD'      20                           ..BMHD  20
    320, 200, 0, 0, 3, 0, 0, 0 ...
    'CMAP'      21                           ..CMAP  21
    0, 0, 0; 32, 0, 0; 64, 0, 0 ...
  0
  'FORM'        24012                        .FORM  24012  ILBM
  'ILBM'
    'BODY'      24000                        ..BODY  24000
    0, 0, 0 ...
  'FORM'        24012                        .FORM  24012  ILBM
  'ILBM'
    'BODY'      24000                        ..BODY  24000
    0, 0, 0 ...
```

"ILBM" IFF Interleaved Bitmap

Date: January 17, 1986 (CRNG data updated Oct, 1988 by Jerry Morrison)
(Appendix E added and CAMG data updated Oct, 1988 by Commodore-Amiga, Inc.)
From: Jerry Morrison, Electronic Arts
Status: Released and in use

1. Introduction

"EA IFF 85" is Electronic Arts' standard for interchange format files. "ILBM" is a format for a 2 dimensional raster graphics image, specifically an InterLeaved bitplane BitMap image with color map. An ILBM is an IFF "data section" or "FORM type", which can be an IFF file or a part of one. ILBM allows simple, highly portable raster graphic storage.

An ILBM is an archival representation designed for three uses. First, a stand-alone image that specifies exactly how to display itself (resolution, size, color map, etc.). Second, an image intended to be merged into a bigger picture which has its own depth, color map, and so on. And third, an empty image with a color map selection or "palette" for a paint program. ILBM is also intended as a building block for composite IFF FORMs like "animation sequences" and "structured graphics". Some uses of ILBM will be to preserve as much information as possible across disparate environments. Other uses will be to store data for a single program or highly cooperative programs while maintaining subtle details. So we're trying to accomplish a lot with this one format.

This memo is the IFF supplement for FORM ILBM. Section 2 defines the purpose and format of property chunks bitmap header "BMHD", color map "CMAP", hotspot "GRAB", destination merge data "DEST", sprite information "SPRT", and Commodore Amiga viewport mode "CAMG". Section 3 defines the standard data chunk "BODY". These are the "standard" chunks. Section 4 defines the nonstandard data chunks. Additional specialized chunks like texture pattern can be added later. The ILBM syntax is summarized in Appendix A as a regular expression and in Appendix B as a box diagram. Appendix C explains the optional run encoding scheme. Appendix D names the committee responsible for this FORM ILBM standard.

Details of the raster layout are given in part 3, "Standard Data Chunk". Some elements are based on the Commodore Amiga hardware but generalized for use on other computers. An alternative to ILBM would be appropriate for computers with true color data in each pixel, though the wealth of available ILBM images makes import and export important.

Reference:

"EA IFF 85" Standard for Interchange Format Files describes the underlying conventions for all IFF files.
Amiga® is a registered trademark of Commodore-Amiga, Inc.
Electronic Arts™ is a trademark of Electronic Arts.
Macintosh™ is a trademark licensed to Apple Computer, Inc.
MacPaint™ is a trademark of Apple Computer, Inc.

2. Standard Properties

ILBM has several defined property chunks that act on the main data chunks. The required property "BMHD" and any optional properties must appear before any "BODY" chunk. (Since an ILBM has only one BODY chunk, any following properties would be superfluous.) Any of these properties may be shared over a LIST of several IBLMs by putting them in a PROP ILBM (See the EA IFF 85 document).

BMHD

The required property "BMHD" holds a BitMapHeader as defined in the following documentation. It describes the dimensions of the image, the encoding used, and other data necessary to understand the BODY chunk to follow.

```
typedef UBYTE Masking;          /* Choice of masking technique. */
#define mskNone                 0
#define mskHasMask              1
#define mskHasTransparentColor 2
#define mskLasso                3

typedef UBYTE Compression;      /* Choice of compression algorithm applied to
  the rows of all source and mask planes. "cmpByteRun1" is the byte run
  encoding described in Appendix C. Do not compress across rows! */
#define cmpNone                 0
#define cmpByteRun1             1

typedef struct {
  UWORD w, h;                   /* raster width & height in pixels       */
  WORD  x, y;                   /* pixel position for this image          */
  UBYTE nPlanes;                /* # source bitplanes                     */
  Masking     masking;
  Compression compression;
  UBYTE pad1;                   /* unused; ignore on read, write as 0    */
  UWORD transparentColor;       /* transparent "color number" (sort of)  */
  UBYTE xAspect, yAspect;       /* pixel aspect, a ratio width : height  */
  WORD  pageWidth, pageHeight;  /* source "page" size in pixels          */
  } BitMapHeader;
```

Fields are filed in the order shown. The UBYTE fields are byte-packed (the C compiler must not add pad bytes to the structure).

The fields `w` and `h` indicate the size of the image rectangle in pixels. Each row of the image is stored in an integral number of 16 bit words. The number of words per row is `words=((w+15)/16)` or `Ceiling(w/16)`. The fields `x` and `y` indicate the desired position of this image within the destination picture. Some reader programs may ignore `x` and `y`. A safe default for writing an ILBM is (`x`, `y`) = (0, 0).

The number of source bitplanes in the BODY chunk is stored in `nPlanes`. An ILBM with a CMAP but no BODY and `nPlanes` = 0 is the recommended way to store a color map.

Note: Color numbers are color map index values formed by pixels in the destination bitmap, which may be deeper than `nPlanes` if a DEST chunk calls for merging the image into a deeper image.

The field `masking` indicates what kind of masking is to be used for this image. The value `mskNone` designates an opaque rectangular image. The value `mskHasMask` means that a mask plane is interleaved with the bitplanes in the BODY chunk (see below). The value `mskHasTransparentColor` indicates that pixels in the source planes matching `transparentColor` are to be considered "transparent". (Actually, `transparentColor` isn't a "color number" since it's matched with numbers formed by the source bitmap rather than the possibly deeper destination bitmap. Note that having a transparent color implies ignoring one of the color registers. The value mskLasso indicates the reader may construct a mask by lassoing the image as in MacPaint™. To do this, put a 1 pixel border of transparentColor around the image rectangle. Then do a seed fill from this border. Filled pixels are to be transparent.

Issue: Include in an appendix an algorithm for converting a transparent color to a mask plane, and maybe a lasso algorithm.

A code indicating the kind of data compression used is stored in compression. Beware that using data compression makes your data unreadable by programs that don't implement the matching decompression algorithm. So we'll employ as few compression encodings as possible. The run encoding byteRun1 is documented in Appendix C.

The field pad1 is a pad byte reserved for future use. It must be set to 0 for consistency.

The transparentColor specifies which bit pattern means "transparent". This only applies if masking is mskHasTransparentColor or mskLasso. Otherwise, transparentColor should be 0. (see above)

The pixel aspect ratio is stored as a ratio in the two fields xAspect and yAspect. This may be used by programs to compensate for different aspects or to help interpret the fields w, h, x, y, pageWidth, and pageHeight, which are in units of pixels. The fraction xAspect/yAspect represents a pixel's width/height. It's recommended that your programs store proper fractions in the BitMapHeader, but aspect ratios can always be correctly compared with the test:

```
xAspect•yDesiredAspect = yAspect•xDesiredAspect
```

Typical values for aspect ratio are width : height = 10 : 11 for an Amiga 320 x 200 display and 1 : 1 for a Macintosh™ display.

The size in pixels of the source "page" (any raster device) is stored in pageWidth and pageHeight, e.g. (320, 200) for a low resolution Amiga display. This information might be used to scale an image or to automatically set the display format to suit the image. Note that the image can be larger than the page.

CMAP

The optional (but encouraged) property "CMAP" stores color map data as triplets of red, green, and blue intensity values. The n color map entries ("color registers") are stored in the order 0 through n-1, totaling 3n bytes. Thus n is the ckSize/3. Normally, n would equal $2^{nPlanes}$.

A CMAP chunk contains a ColorMap array as defined below. Note that these typedefs assume a C compiler that implements packed arrays of 3-byte elements.

```
typedef struct {
  UBYTE red, green, blue;          /* color intensities 0..255 */
  } ColorRegister;                 /* size = 3 bytes */

typedef ColorRegister ColorMap[n]; /* size = 3n bytes */
```

The color components red, green, and blue represent fractional intensity values in the range 0 through 255 256ths. White is (255, 255, 255) and black is (0, 0, 0). If your machine has less color resolution, use the <u>high order</u> bits. Shift each field right on reading (or left on writing) and assign it to (from) a field in a local packed format like Color4, below. This achieves automatic conversion of images across environments with different color resolutions. On reading an ILBM, use defaults if the color map is absent or has fewer color registers than you need. Ignore any extra color registers. (See Appendix E for a better way to write colors)

The example type `Color4` represents the format of a color register in working memory of an Amiga computer, which has 4 bit video DACs. (The ": 4" tells smarter C compilers to pack the field into 4 bits.)

```
typedef struct {
  unsigned pad1 :4, red :4, green :4, blue :4;
  } Color4;                                  /* Amiga RAM format. Not filed. */
```

Remember that every chunk must be padded to an even length, so a color map with an odd number of entries would be followed by a 0 byte, not included in the `ckSize`.

GRAB

The optional property "GRAB" locates a "handle" or "hotspot" of the image relative to its upper left corner, e.g. when used as a mouse cursor or a "paint brush". A GRAB chunk contains a Point2D.

```
typedef struct {
  WORD x, y;            /* relative coordinates (pixels) */
  } Point2D;
```

DEST

The optional property "DEST" is a way to say how to scatter zero or more source bitplanes into a deeper destination image. Some readers may ignore DEST.

The contents of a DEST chunk is DestMerge structure:

```
typedef struct {
  UBYTE depth;       /* # bitplanes in the original source              */
  UBYTE pad1;        /* unused; for consistency put 0 here              */
  UWORD planePick;   /* how to scatter source bitplanes into destination */
  UWORD planeOnOff;  /* default bitplane data for planePick             */
  UWORD planeMask;   /* selects which bitplanes to store into           */
  } DestMerge;
```

The low order `depth` number of bits in `planePick`, `planeOnOff`, and `planeMask` correspond one-to-one with destination bitplanes. Bit 0 with bitplane 0, etc. (Any higher order bits should be ignored.) "1" bits in `planePick` mean "put the next source bitplane into this bitplane", so the number of "1" bits should equal `nPlanes`. "0" bits mean "put the corresponding bit from `planeOnOff` into this bitplane". Bits in planeMask gate writing to the destination bitplane: "1" bits mean "write to this bitplane" while "0" bits mean "leave this bitplane alone". The normal case (with no DEST property) is equivalent to `planePick = planeMask =` $2^{nPlanes} - 1$.

Remember that color numbers are formed by pixels in the destination bitmap (`depth` planes deep) not in the source bitmap (`nPlanes` planes deep).

SPRT

The presence of an "SPRT" chunk indicates that this image is intended as a sprite. It's up to the reader program to actually make it a sprite, if even possible, and to use or overrule the sprite precedence data inside the SPRT chunk:

```
typedef UWORD SpritePrecedence; /* relative precedence, 0 is the highest */
```

Precedence 0 is the highest, denoting a sprite that is foremost.

Creating a sprite may imply other setup. E.g. a 2 plane Amiga sprite would have `transparentColor` = 0. Color registers 1, 2, and 3 in the CMAP would be stored into the correct hardware color registers for the hardware sprite number used, while CMAP color register 0 would be ignored.

CAMG

A "CAMG" chunk is specifically for the Commodore Amiga computer, readers on other computers may ignore CAMG. All Amiga-based reader and writer software should deal with CAMG. The Amiga supports many different video display modes including interlace, extra half-bright, and hold & modify. At this time a CAMG chunk contains a single long word (length=4). The high 16 bits are currently reserved by Commodore; they must be written as zeros and ignored when read. The low 16 bits of the CAMG will contain a ViewModes word. This value can be used to determine the ViewModes information in effect when the ILBM was saved. In the future CAMG may be extended to specify other information or video modes.

Some of the `ViewModes` flags are not appropriate to use in a CAMG, these should be masked out when writing or reading. Here are definitions for the bits to be removed:

```
#include <graphics/view.h>

#define BADFLAGS     (SPRITES|VP_HIDE|GENLOCK_AUDIO|GENLOCK_VIDEO)
#define FLAGMASK     (~BADFLAGS)
#define CAMGMASK     (FLAGMASK & 0000FFFFL)
  ...
camg.ViewModes       = myScreen->ViewPort.Modes & CAMGMASK; /* Writing */
NewScreen.ViewModes  = camg.ViewModes & CAMGMASK;           /* Reading */
```

3. Standard "BODY" Data Chunk

Raster Layout

Raster scan proceeds left-to-right (increasing X) across scan lines, then top-to-bottom (increasing Y) down columns of scan lines. The coordinate system is in units of pixels, where (0,0) is the upper left corner.

The raster is typically organized as bitplanes in memory. The corresponding bits from each plane, taken together, make up an index into the color map which gives a color value for that pixel. The first bitplane, plane 0, is the low order bit of these color indexes.

A scan line is made of one "row" from each bitplane. A row is one planes' bits for one scan line, but padded out to a word (2 byte) boundary (not necessarily the first word boundary). Within each row, successive bytes are displayed in order and the most significant bit of each byte is displayed first.

A "mask" is an optional "plane" of data the same size (`w, h`) as a bitplane. It tells how to "cut out" part of the image when painting it onto another image. "One" bits in the mask mean "copy the corresponding pixel to the destination". "Zero" mask bits mean "leave this destination pixel alone". In other words, "zero" bits designate transparent pixels.

The rows of the different bitplanes and mask are interleaved in the file (see below). This localizes all the information pertinent to each scan line. It makes it much easier to transform the data while reading it to adjust the image size or depth. It also makes it possible to scroll a big image by swapping rows directly from the file without the need for random-access to all the bitplanes.

BODY

The source raster is stored in a "BODY" chunk. This one chunk holds all bitplanes and the optional mask, interleaved by row.

The BitMapHeader, in a BMHD property chunk, specifies the raster's dimensions `w`, `h`, and `nPlanes`. It also holds the `masking` field which indicates if there is a mask plane and the `compression` field which indicates the compression algorithm used. This information is needed to interpret the BODY chunk, so the BMHD chunk must appear first. While reading an ILBM's BODY, a program may convert the image to another size by filling (with `transparentColor`) or clipping.

The BODY's content is a concatenation of scan lines. Each scan line is a concatenation of one row of data from each plane in order 0 through `nPlanes-1` followed by one row from the mask (if `masking = hasMask`). If the BitMapHeader field `compression` is `cmpNone`, all `h` rows are exactly `(w+15)/16` words wide. Otherwise, every row is compressed according to the specified algorithm and the stored widths depend on the data compression.

Reader programs that require fewer bitplanes than appear in a particular ILBM file can combine planes or drop the high-order (later) planes. Similarly, they may add bitplanes and/or discard the mask plane.

Do not compress across rows, and don't forget to compress the mask just like the bitplanes. Remember to pad any BODY chunk that contains an odd number of bytes and skip the pad when reading.

4. Nonstandard Data Chunks

The following data chunks were defined after various programs began using FORM ILBM so they are "nonstandard" chunks. See the registry document for the latest information on additional nonstandard chunks.

CRNG

A "CRNG" chunk contains "color register range" information. It's used by Electronic Arts' Deluxe Paint program to identify a contiguous range of color registers for a "shade range" and color cycling. There can be zero or more CRNG chunks in an ILBM, but all should appear before the BODY chunk. Deluxe Paint normally writes 4 CRNG chunks in an ILBM when the user asks it to "Save Picture".

```
typedef struct {
  WORD  pad1;          /* reserved for future use; store 0 here      */
  WORD  rate;          /* color cycle rate                           */
  WORD  flags;         /* see below                                  */
  UBYTE low, high;     /* lower and upper color registers selected   */
  } CRange;
```

The bits of the `flags` word are interpreted as follows: if the low bit is set then the cycle is "active", and if this bit is clear it is not active. Normally, color cycling is done so that colors move to the next higher position in the cycle, with the color in the high slot moving around to the low slot. If the second bit of the flags word is set, the cycle moves in the opposite direction. As usual, the other bits of the flags word are reserved for future expansion. Here are the masks to test these bits:

```
#define RNG_ACTIVE  1
#define RNG_REVERSE 2
```

The fields `low` and `high` indicate the range of color registers (color numbers) selected by this CRange.

The field `active` indicates whether color cycling is on or off. Zero means off.

The field `rate` determines the speed at which the colors will step when color cycling is on. The units are such that a rate of 60 steps per second is represented as 2^{14} = 16384. Slower rates can be obtained by linear scaling: for 30 steps/second, rate = 8192; for 1 step/second, rate = 16384/60 ≈ 273.

CCRT

Commodore's Graphicraft program uses a similar chunk "CCRT" (for Color Cycling Range and Timing). This chunk contains a CycleInfo structure.

```
typedef struct {
  WORD  direction;     /* 0 = don't cycle. 1 = cycle forwards (1, 2, 3).
                        * -1 = cycle backwards (3, 2, 1)               */
  UBYTE start, end;    /* lower and upper color registers selected     */
  LONG  seconds;       /* # seconds between changing colors plus...    */
  LONG  microseconds;  /* # microseconds between changing colors       */
  WORD  pad;           /* reserved for future use; store 0 here        */
  } CycleInfo;
```

This is very similar to a CRNG chunk. A program would probably only use one of these two methods of expressing color cycle data, new programs should use CRNG. You could write out both if you want to communicate this information to both Deluxe Paint and Graphicraft.

Appendix A. ILBM Regular Expression

Here's a regular expression summary of the FORM ILBM syntax. This could be an IFF file or a part of one.

```
ILBM ::= "FORM" #{  "ILBM" BMHD [CMAP] [GRAB] [DEST] [SPRT] [CAMG]
                    CRNG* CCRT* [BODY]                           }

BMHD ::= "BMHD" #{  BitMapHeader        }
CMAP ::= "CMAP" #{  (red green blue)*   } [0]
GRAB ::= "GRAB" #{  Point2D             }
DEST ::= "DEST" #{  DestMerge           }
SPRT ::= "SPRT" #{  SpritePrecedence    }
CAMG ::= "CAMG" #{  LONG                }

CRNG ::= "CRNG" #{  CRange              }
CCRT ::= "CCRT" #{  CycleInfo           }
BODY ::= "BODY" #{  UBYTE*              } [0]
```

The token "#" represents a `ckSize` LONG count of the following {braced} data bytes. E.g. a BMHD's "#" should equal `sizeof(BitMapHeader)`. Literal strings are shown in "quotes", [square bracket items] are optional, and "*" means 0 or more repetitions. A sometimes-needed pad byte is shown as "[0]".

The property chunks BMHD, CMAP, GRAB, DEST, SPRT, CAMG and any CRNG and CCRT data chunks may actually be in any order but all must appear before the BODY chunk since ILBM readers usually stop as soon as they read the BODY. If any of the 6 property chunks are missing, default values are inherited from any shared properties (if the ILBM appears inside an IFF LIST with PROPs) or from the reader program's defaults. If any property appears more than once, the last occurrence before the BODY is the one that counts since that's the one that modifies the BODY.

Appendix B. ILBM Box Diagram

Here's a box diagram for a simple example: an uncompressed image 320 x 200 pixels x 3 bitplanes. The text to the right of the diagram shows the outline that would be printed by the IFFCheck utility program for this particular file.

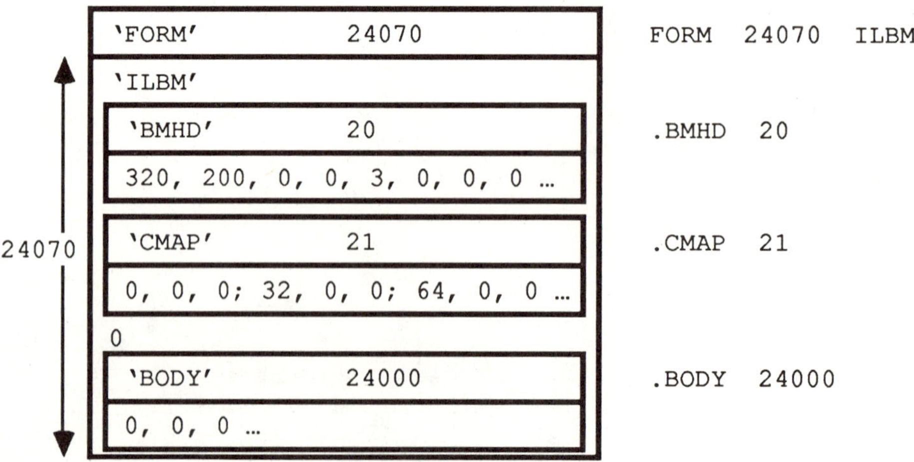

The "0" after the CMAP chunk is a pad byte.

Appendix C. ByteRun1 Run Encoding

The run encoding scheme `byteRun1` is best described by pseudo code for the decoder Unpacker (called UnPackBits in the Macintosh™ toolbox):

```
UnPacker:
  LOOP until produced the desired number of bytes
    Read the next source byte into n
    SELECT n FROM
      [0..127]    => copy the next n+1 bytes literally
      [-1..-127]  => replicate the next byte -n+1 times
      -128        => no operation
      ENDCASE;
    ENDLOOP;
```

In the inverse routine Packer, it's best to encode a 2 byte repeat run as a replicate run except when preceded and followed by a literal run, in which case it's best to merge the three into one literal run. Always encode 3 byte repeats as replicate runs.

Remember that each row of each scan line of a raster is separately packed.

Appendix D. Standards Committee

The following people contributed to the design of this FORM ILBM standard:

Bob "Kodiak" Burns, Commodore-Amiga
R. J. Mical, Commodore-Amiga
Jerry Morrison, Electronic Arts
Greg Riker, Electronic Arts
Steve Shaw, Electronic Arts
Dan Silva, Electronic Arts
Barry Walsh, Commodore-Amiga

Appendix E. IFF Hints

Hints on ILBM files from Jerry Morrison, Oct 1988. How to avoid some pitfalls when reading ILBM files:

- Don't ignore the BitMapHeader.masking field. A bitmap with a mask (such as a partially-transparent DPaint brush or a DPaint picture with a stencil) will read as garbage if you don't de-interleave the mask.
- Don't assume all images are compressed. Narrow images aren't usually run-compressed since that would actually make them longer.
- Don't assume a particular image size. You may encounter overscan pictures and PAL pictures.

There's a better way to read a BODY than the example IFF code. The GetBODY routine should call a GetScanline routine once per scan line, which calls a GetRow routine for each bitplane in the file. This in turn calls a GetUnpackedBytes routine, which calls a GetBytes routine as needed and unpacks the result. (If the picture is uncompressed, GetRow calls GetBytes directly.) Since the unpacker knows how many packed bytes to read, this avoids juggling buffers for a memory-to-memory UnPackBytes routine.

Caution: If you make many AmigaDOS calls to read or write a few bytes at a time, performance will be mud! AmigaDOS has a high overhead per call, even with RAM disk. So use buffered read/write routines.

Different hardware display devices have different color resolutions:

Device	R:G:B bits	maxColor
Mac SE	1	1
IBM EGA	2:2:2	3
Atari ST	3:3:3	7
Amiga	4:4:4	15
CD-I	5:5:5	31
IBM VGA	6:6:6	63
Mac II	8:8:8	255

An ILBM CMAP defines 8 bits of Red, Green and Blue (ie. 8:8:8 bits of R:G:B). When displaying on hardware which has less color resolution, just take the high order bits. For example, to convert ILBM's 8-bit Red to the Amiga's 4-bit Red, right shift the data by 4 bits (R4 := R8 >> 4).

To convert hardware colors to ILBM colors, the ILBM specification says just set the high bits (R8 := R4 << 4). But you can transmit higher contrast to foreign display devices by scaling the data [0..maxColor] to the full range [0..255]. In other words, R8 := (Rn x 255) ÷ maxColor. (Example #1: EGA color 1:2:3 scales to 85:170:255. Example #2: Amiga 15:7:0 scales to 255:119:0) This makes a big difference where maxColor is less than 15. In the extreme case, Mac SE white (1) should be converted to ILBM white (255), not to ILBM gray (128).

CGA and EGA subtleties

IBM EGA colors in 350 scan line mode are 2:2:2 bits of R:G:B, stored in memory as xxR'G'B'RBG. That's 3 low-order bits followed by 3 high-order bits.

IBM CGA colors are 4 bits stored in a byte as xxxxIRGB. (EGA colors in 200 scan line modes are the same as CGA colors, but stored in memory as xxxIxRGB.) That's 3 high-order bits (one for each of R, G, and B) plus one low-order "Intensity" bit for all 3 components R, G, and B. Exception: IBM monitors show IRGB = 0110 as brown, which is really the EGA color R:G:B = 2:1:0, not dark yellow 2:2:0.

"FTXT" IFF Formatted Text

Date: November 15, 1985 (Updated Oct, 1988 Commodore-Amiga, Inc.)
From: Steve Shaw and Jerry Morrison, Electronic Arts and Bob "Kodiak" Burns, Commodore-Amiga
Status: Adopted

1. Introduction

This memo is the IFF supplement for FORM FTXT. An FTXT is an IFF "data section" or "FORM type"—which can be an IFF file or a part of one—containing a stream of text plus optional formatting information."EA IFF 85" is Electronic Arts' standard for interchange format files. (See the IFF reference.)

An FTXT is an archival and interchange representation designed for three uses. The simplest use is for a "console device" or "glass teletype" (the minimal 2-D text layout means): a stream of "graphic" ("printable") characters plus positioning characters "space" ("SP") and line terminator ("LF"). This is not intended for cursor movements on a screen although it does not conflict with standard cursor-moving characters. The second use is text that has explicit formatting information (or "looks") such as font family and size, typeface, etc. The third use is as the lowest layer of a structured document that also has "inherited" styles to implicitly control character looks. For that use, FORMs FTXT would be embedded within a future document FORM type. The beauty of FTXT is that these three uses are interchangeable, that is, a program written for one purpose can read and write the others' files. So a word processor does not have to write a separate plain text file to communicate with other programs.

Text is stored in one or more "CHRS" chunks inside an FTXT. Each CHRS contains a stream of 8-bit text compatible with ISO and ANSI data interchange standards. FTXT uses just the central character set from the ISO/ANSI standards. (These two standards are henceforth called "ISO/ANSI" as in "see the ISO/ANSI reference".)

Since it's possible to extract just the text portions from future document FORM types, programs can exchange data without having to save both plain text and formatted text representations.

Character looks are stored as embedded control sequences within CHRS chunks. This document specifies which class of control sequences to use: the CSI group. This document does not yet specify their meanings, e.g. which one means "turn on italic face". Consult ISO/ANSI.

Section 2 defines the chunk types character stream "CHRS" and font specifier "FONS". These are the "standard" chunks. Specialized chunks for private or future needs can be added later. Section 3 outlines an FTXT reader program that strips a document down to plain unformatted text. Appendix A is a code table for the 8-bit ISO/ANSI character set used here. Appendix B is an example FTXT shown as a box diagram. Appendix C is a racetrack diagram of the syntax of ISO/ANSI control sequences.

Reference:

Amiga® is a registered trademark of Commodore-Amiga, Inc.
Electronic Arts™ is a trademark of Electronic Arts.

IFF: "EA IFF 85" Standard for Interchange Format Files describes the underlying conventions for all IFF files.

ISO/ANSI: ISO/DIS 6429.2 and ANSI X3.64-1979. International Organization for Standardization (ISO) and American National Standards Institute (ANSI) data-interchange standards. The relevant parts of these two standards documents are identical. ISO standard 2022 is also relevant.

2. Standard Data and Property Chunks

The main contents of a FORM FTXT is in its character stream "CHRS" chunks. Formatting property chunks may also appear. The only formatting property yet defined is "FONS", a font specifier. A FORM FTXT with no CHRS represents an empty text stream. A FORM FTXT may contain nested IFF FORMs, LISTs, or CATs, although a "stripping" reader (see section 3) will ignore them.

Character Set

FORM FTXT uses the core of the 8-bit character set defined by the ISO/ANSI standards cited at the start of this document. (See Appendix A for a character code table.) This character set is divided into two "graphic" groups plus two "control" groups. Eight of the control characters begin ISO/ANSI standard control sequences. (See "Control Sequences", below.) Most control sequences and control characters are reserved for future use and for compatibility with ISO/ANSI. Current reader programs should skip them.

- C0 is the group of control characters in the range NUL (hex 0) through hex 1F. Of these, only LF (hex 0A) and ESC (hex 1B) are significant. ESC begins a control sequence. LF is the line terminator, meaning "go to the first horizontal position of the next line". All other C0 characters are not used. In particular, CR (hex 0D) is not recognized as a line terminator.
- G0 is the group of graphic characters in the range hex 20 through hex 7F. SP (hex 20) is the space character. DEL (hex 7F) is the delete character which is not used. The rest are the standard ASCII printable characters "!" (hex 21) through "~" (hex 7E).
- C1 is the group of extended control characters in the range hex 80 through hex 9F. Some of these begin control sequences. The control sequence starting with CSI (hex 9B) is used for FTXT formatting. All other control sequences and C1 control characters are unused.
- G1 is the group of extended graphic characters in the range NBSP (hex A0) through "ÿ" (hex FF). It is one of the alternate graphic groups proposed for ISO/ANSI standardization.

Control Sequences

Eight of the control characters begin ISO/ANSI standard "control sequences" (or "escape sequences"). These sequences are described below and diagramed in Appendix C.

```
G0          ::= (SP through DEL)
G1          ::= (NBSP through "ÿ")

ESC-Seq     ::= ESC (SP through "/")* ("0" through "~")
ShiftToG2   ::= SS2 G0
ShiftToG3   ::= SS3 G0
CSI-Seq     ::= CSI (SP through "?")* ("@" through "~")
DCS-Seq     ::= (DCS | OSC | PM | APC) (SP through "~" | G1)* ST
```

"ESC-Seq" is the control sequence ESC (hex 1B), followed by zero or more characters in the range SP through "/" (hex 20 through hex 2F), followed by a character in the range "0" through "~" (hex 30 through hex 7E). These sequences are reserved for future use and should be skipped by current FTXT reader programs.

SS2 (hex 8E) and SS3 (hex 8F) shift the single following G0 character into yet-to-be-defined graphic sets G2 and G3, respectively. These sequences should not be used until the character sets G2 and G3 are standardized. A reader may simply skip the SS2 or SS3 (taking the following character as a corresponding G0 character) or replace the two-character sequence with a character like "?" to mean "absent".

FTXT uses "CSI-Seq" control sequences to store character formatting (font selection by number, type face, and text size) and perhaps layout information (position and rotation). "CSI-Seq" control sequences start with CSI (the "control sequence introducer", hex 9B). Syntactically, the sequence includes zero or more characters in the range SP through

"?" (hex 20 through hex 3F) and a concluding character in the range "@" through "~" (hex 40 through hex 7E). These sequences may be skipped by a minimal FTXT reader, i.e. one that ignores formatting information.

Note: A future FTXT standardization document will explain the uses of CSI-Seq sequences for setting character face (light weight vs. medium vs. bold, italic vs. upright, height, pitch, position, and rotation). For now, consult the ISO/ANSI references.

"DCS-Seq" is the control sequences starting with DCS (hex 90), OSC (hex 9D), PM (hex 9E), or APC (hex 9F), followed by zero or more characters each of which is in the range SP through "~" (hex 20 through hex 7E) or else a G1 character, and terminated by an ST (hex 9C). These sequences are reserved for future use and should be skipped by current FTXT reader programs.

Data Chunk CHRS

A CHRS chunk contains a sequence of 8-bit characters abiding by the ISO/ANSI standards cited at the start of this document. This includes the character set and control sequences as described above and summarized in Appendix A and C.

A FORM FTXT may contain any number of CHRS chunks. Taken together, they represent a single stream of textual information. That is, the contents of CHRS chunks are effectively concatenated except that (1) each control sequence must be completely within a single CHRS chunk, and (2) any formatting property chunks appearing between two CHRS chunks affects the formatting of the latter chunk's text. Any formatting settings set by control sequences inside a CHRS carry over to the next CHRS in the same FORM FTXT. All formatting properties stop at the end of the FORM since IFF specifies that adjacent FORMs are independent of each other (although not independent of any properties inherited from an enclosing LIST or FORM).

Property Chunk FONS

The optional property "FONS" holds a FontSpecifier as defined in the C declaration below. It assigns a font to a numbered "font register" so it can be referenced by number within subsequent CHRS chunks. (This function is not provided within the ISO and ANSI standards.) The font specifier gives both a name and a description for the font so the recipient program can do font substitution.

By default, CHRS text uses font 1 until it selects another font. A minimal text reader always uses font 1. If font 1 hasn't been specified, the reader may use the local system font as font 1.

```
typedef struct {
  UBYTE id;       /* 0 through 9 is a font id number referenced by an SGR
                  control sequence selective parameter of 10 through 19.
                  Other values are reserved for future standardization.  */
  UBYTE pad1;     /* reserved for future use; store 0 here               */
  UBYTE proportional; /* proportional font? 0 = unknown, 1 = no, 2 = yes*/
  UBYTE serif;        /* serif font? 0 = unknown, 1 = no, 2 = yes        */
  char name[];    /* A NUL-terminated string naming the preferred font.  */
  } FontSpecifier;
```

Fields are filed in the order shown. The UBYTE fields are byte-packed (2 per 16-bit word). The field `pad1` is reserved for future standardization. Programs should store 0 there for now.

The field `proportional` indicates if the desired font is proportional width as opposed to fixed width. The field `serif` indicates if the desired font is serif as opposed to sans serif. [Issue: Discuss font substitution!]

Future Properties

New optional property chunks may be defined in the future to store additional formatting information. They will be used to represent formatting not encoded in standard ISO/ANSI control sequences and for "inherited" formatting in structured documents. Text orientation might be one example.

Positioning Units

Unless otherwise specified, position and size units used in FTXT formatting properties and control sequences are in decipoints (720 decipoints/inch). This is ANSI/ISO Positioning Unit Mode (PUM) 2. While a metric standard might be nice, decipoints allow the existing U.S.A. typographic units to be encoded easily, e.g. "12 points" is "120 decipoints".

3. FTXT Stripper

An FTXT reader program can read the text and ignore all formatting and structural information in a document FORM that uses FORMs FTXT for the leaf nodes. This amounts to stripping a document down to a stream of plain text. It would do this by skipping over all chunks except FTXT.CHRS (CHRS chunks found inside a FORM FTXT) and within the FTXT.CHRS chunks skipping all control characters and control sequences. (Appendix C diagrams this text scanner.) It may also read FTXT.FONS chunks to find a description for font 1.

Here's a Pascal-ish program for an FTXT stripper. Given a FORM (a document of some kind), it scans for all FTXT.CHRS chunks. This would likely be applied to the first FORM in an IFF file.

```
PROCEDURE ReadFORM4CHRS();      {Read an IFF FORM for FTXT.CHRS chunks.}
  BEGIN
  IF the FORM's subtype = "FTXT"
    THEN ReadFTXT4CHRS()
    ELSE WHILE something left to read in the FORM DO BEGIN
         read the next chunk header;
         CASE the chunk's ID OF
           "LIST", "CAT ": ReadCAT4CHRS();
           "FORM": ReadFORM4CHRS();
           OTHERWISE skip the chunk's body;
           END
         END
  END;

{Read a LIST or CAT for all FTXT.CHRS chunks.}
PROCEDURE ReadCAT4CHRS();
  BEGIN
  WHILE something left to read in the LIST or CAT DO BEGIN
    read the next chunk header;
    CASE the chunk's ID OF
       "LIST", "CAT ": ReadCAT4CHRS();
       "FORM": ReadFORM4CHRS();
       "PROP": IF we're reading a LIST AND the PROP's subtype = "FTXT"
              THEN read the PROP for "FONS" chunks;
       OTHERWISE error--malformed IFF file;
       END
    END
  END;
```

```
PROCEDURE ReadFTXT4CHRS();    {Read a FORM FTXT for CHRS chunks.}
  BEGIN
  WHILE something left to read in the FORM FTXT DO BEGIN
    read the next chunk header;
    CASE the chunk's ID OF
      "CHRS": ReadCHRS();
      "FONS": BEGIN
        read the chunk's contents into a FontSpecifier variable;
        IF the font specifier's id = 1 THEN use this font;
        END;
      OTHERWISE skip the chunk's body;
      END
    END
  END;

{Read an FTXT.CHRS. Skip all control sequences and unused control chars.}
PROCEDURE ReadCHRS();
  BEGIN
  WHILE something left to read in the CHRS chunk DO
    CASE read the next character OF
      LF:  start a new output line;
      ESC: SkipControl([' '..'/'], ['0'..'~']);
      IN [' '..'~'], IN [NBSP..'ÿ']: output the character;
      SS2, SS3: ;  {Just handle the following G0 character directly,
                    ignoring the shift to G2 or G3.}
      CSI: SkipControl([' '..'?'], ['@'..'~']);
      DCS, OSC, PM, APC: SkipControl([' '..'~'] + [NBSP..'ÿ'], [ST]);
      END
  END;

{Skip a control sequence of the format (rSet)* (tSet), i.e. any number of
  characters in the set rSet followed by a character in the set tSet.}
PROCEDURE SkipControl(rSet, tSet);
  VAR c: CHAR;
  BEGIN
  REPEAT c := read the next character
    UNTIL c NCT IN rSet;
  IF c NOT IN tSet
    THEN put character c back into the input stream;
  END
```

The following program is an optimized version of the above routines `ReadFORM4CHRS` and `ReadCAT4CHRS` for the case where you're ignoring fonts as well as formatting. It takes advantage of certain facts of the IFF format to read a document FORM and its nested FORMs, LISTs, and CATs without a stack. In other words, it's a hack that ignores all fonts and faces to cheaply get to the plain text of the document.

```
{Cheap scan of an IFF FORM for FTXT.CHRS chunks.}
PROCEDURE ScanFORM4CHRS();
  BEGIN
  IF the document FORM's subtype = "FTXT"
    THEN ReadFTXT4CHRS()
    ELSE WHILE something left to read in the FORM DO BEGIN
         read the next chunk header;
         IF it's a group chunk (LIST, FORM, PROP, or CAT)
```

```
            THEN read its subtype ID;
          CASE the chunk's ID OF
            "LIST", "CAT ":;        {NOTE: See explanation below.*}
            "FORM": IF this FORM's subtype = "FTXT" THEN ReadFTXT4CHRS()
               ELSE;                {NOTE: See explanation below.*}
            OTHERWISE skip the chunk's body;
            END
          END
    END;
```

*Note: This implementation is subtle. After reading a group header other than FORM FTXT it just continues reading. This amounts to reading all the chunks inside that group as if they weren't nested in a group.

Appendix A: Character Code Table

This table corresponds to the ISO/DIS 6429.2 and ANSI X3.64-1979 8-bit character set standards. Only the core character set of those standards is used in FTXT.

Two G1 characters aren't defined in the standards and are shown as dark gray entries in this table. Light gray shading denotes control characters. (DEL is a control character although it belongs to the graphic group G0.)

ISO/DIS 6429.2 and ANSI X3.64-1979 Character Code Table

Most Significant Nibble (hex digit)

LSN	0	1	2	3	4	5	6	7	8	9	A	B	C	D	E	F
0	NUL		SP	0	@	P	`	p		DCS	NBSP	°	À	Ð	à	ð
1			!	1	A	Q	a	q			¡	±	Á	Ñ	á	ñ
2			"	2	B	R	b	r			¢	²	Â	Ò	â	ò
3			#	3	C	S	c	s			£	³	Ã	Ó	ã	ó
4			$	4	D	T	d	t			¤	´	Ä	Ô	ä	ô
5			%	5	E	U	e	u			¥	µ	Å	Õ	å	õ
6			&	6	F	V	f	v			¦	¶	Æ	Ö	æ	ö
7			'	7	G	W	g	w			§	•	Ç	×	ç	÷
8			(	8	H	X	h	x			¨	¸	È	Ø	è	ø
9			)	9	I	Y	i	y			©	¹	É	Ù	é	ù
A	LF		*	:	J	Z	j	z			ª	º	Ê	Ú	ê	ú
B		ESC	+	;	K	[	k	{		CSI	«	»	Ë	Û	ë	û
C			,	<	L	\	l	|		ST	¬	1/4	Ì	Ü	ì	ü
D	CR		-	=	M	]	m	}		OSC	SHY	1/2	Í	Ý	í	ý
E			.	>	N	^	n	~	SS2	PM	®	3/4	Î	Þ	î	þ
F			/	?	O	_	o	DEL	SS3	APC	¯	¿	Ï	ß	ï	ÿ

Control group C0 (columns 0–1); Graphic group G0 (columns 2–7); Control group C1 (columns 8–9); Graphic group G1 (columns A–F)

"NBSP" is a "non-breaking space"
"SHY" is a "soft hyphen"

Appendix B. FTXT Example

Here's a box diagram for a simple example: "The quick brown fox jumped.Four score and seven", written in a proportional serif font named "Roman".

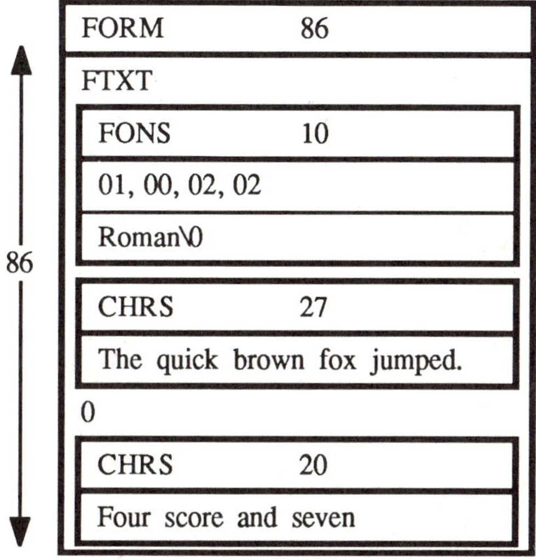

The "0" after the first CHRS chunk is a pad byte.

Appendix C. ISO/ANSI Control Sequences

This is a racetrack diagram of the ISO/ANSI characters and control sequences as used in FTXT CHRS chunks.

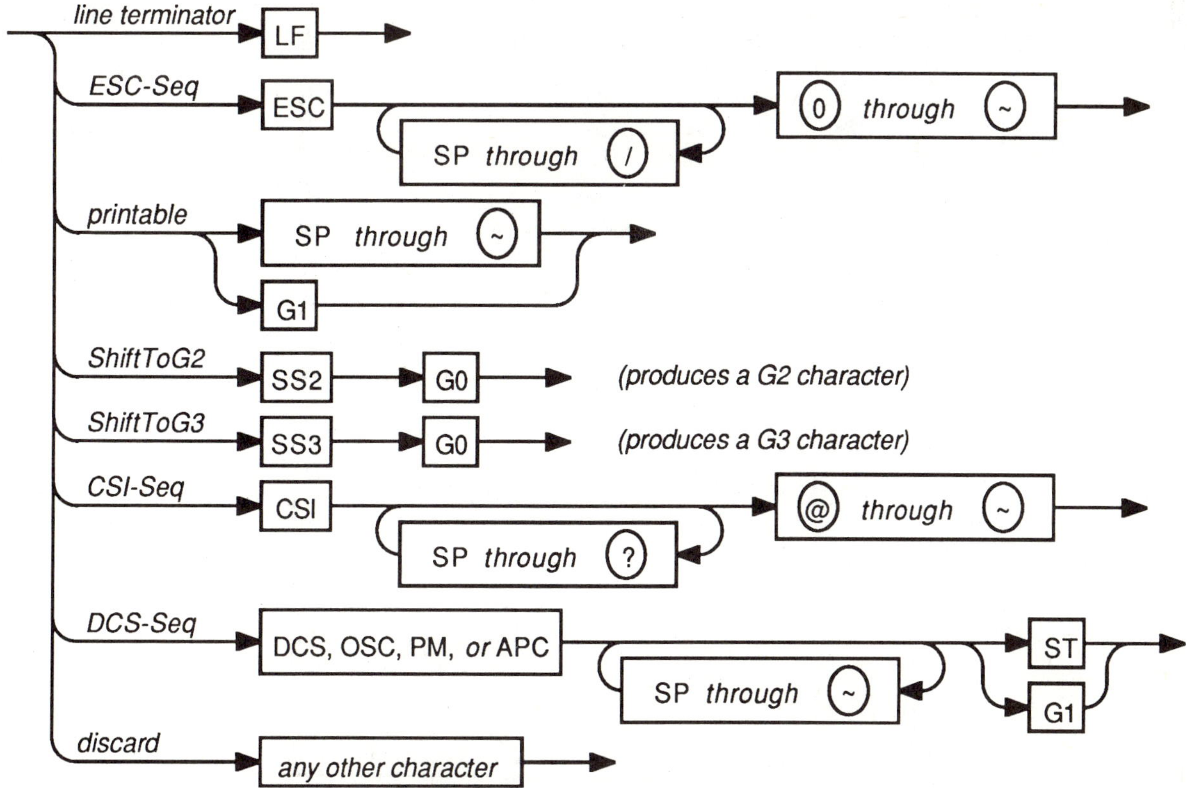

Of the various control sequences, only CSI-Seq is used for FTXT character formatting information. The others are reserved for future use and for compatibility with ISO/ANSI standards. Certain character sequences are syntactically malformed, e.g. CSI followed by a C0, C1, or G1 character. Writer programs should not generate reserved or malformed sequences and reader programs should skip them.

Consult the ISO/ANSI standards for the meaning of the CSI-Seq control sequences.

The two character set shifts SS2 and SS3 may be used when the graphic character groups G2 and G3 become standardized.

"SMUS" IFF Simple Musical Score

Date: February 20, 1987 (SID _Clef and SID_Tempo added Oct, 1988)
From: Jerry Morrison, Electronic Arts
Status: Adopted

1. Introduction

This is a reference manual for the data interchange format "SMUS", which stands for Simple MUsical Score. "EA IFF 85" is Electronic Arts' standard for interchange format files. A FORM (or "data section") such as FORM SMUS can be an IFF file or a part of one. [See "EA IFF 85" Electronic Arts Interchange File Format.]

SMUS is a practical data format for uses like moving limited scores between programs and storing theme songs for game programs. The format should be geared for easy read-in and playback. So FORM SMUS uses the compact time encoding of Common Music Notation (half notes, dotted quarter rests, etc.). The SMUS format should also be structurally simple. So it has no provisions for fancy notational information needed by graphical score editors or the more general timing (overlapping notes, etc.) and continuous data (pitch bends, etc.) needed by performance-oriented MIDI recorders and sequencers. Complex music programs may wish to save in a more complete format, but still import and export SMUS when requested.

A SMUS score can say which "instruments" are supposed play which notes. But the score is independent of whatever output device and driver software is used to perform the notes. The score can contain device- and driver-dependent instrument data, but this is just a cache. As long as a SMUS file stays in one environment, the embedded instrument data is very convenient. When you move a SMUS file between programs or hardware configurations, the contents of this cache usually become useless.

Like all IFF formats, SMUS is a filed or "archive" format. It is completely independent of score representations in working memory, editing operations, user interface, display graphics, computation hardware, and sound hardware. Like all IFF formats, SMUS is extensible.

SMUS is not an end-all musical score format. Other formats may be more appropriate for certain uses. (We'd like to design an general-use IFF score format "GSCR". FORM GSCR would encode fancy notational data and performance data. There would be a SMUS to/from GSCR converter.)

Section 2 gives important background information. Section 3 details the SMUS components by defining the required property score header "SHDR", the optional text properties name "NAME", copyright "(c) ", and author "AUTH", optional text annotation "ANNO", the optional instrument specifier "INS1", and the track data chunk "TRAK". Section 4 defines some chunks for particular programs to store private information. These are "standard" chunks; specialized chunks for future needs can be added later. Appendix A is a quick-reference summary. Appendix B is an example box diagram. Appendix C names the committee responsible for this standard.

References:

"EA IFF 85" Standard for Interchange Format Files describes the underlying conventions for all IFF files.
"8SVX" IFF 8-Bit Sampled Voice documents a data format for sampled instruments.
MIDI: Musical Instrument Digital Interface Specification 1.0, International MIDI Association, 1983.
SSSP: See various articles on Structured Sound Synthesis Project in Foundations of Computer Music.

2. Background

Here's some background information on score representation in general and design choices for SMUS.

First, we'll borrow some terminology from the Structured Sound Synthesis Project. [See the SSSP reference.] A "musical note" is one kind of *scheduled event*. It's properties include an *event duration*, an *event delay*, and a *timbre object*. The *event duration* tells the scheduler how long the note should last. The *event delay* tells how long after starting this note to wait before starting the next event. The *timbre object* selects sound driver data for the note; an "instrument" or "timbre". A "rest" is a sort of a null event. Its only property is an event delay.

Classical Event Durations

SMUS is geared for "classical" scores, not free-form performances. So its event durations are classical (whole note, dotted quarter rest, etc.). SMUS can tie notes together to build a "note event" with an unusual event duration. The set of useful classical durations is very small. So SMUS needs only a handful of bits to encode an event duration. This is very compact. It's also very easy to display in Common Music Notation (CMN).

Tracks

The events in a SMUS score are grouped into parallel "tracks". Each track is a linear stream of events.

Why use tracks? Tracks serve 4 functions:

1. Tracks make it possible to encode event delays very compactly. A "classical" score has chorded notes and sequential notes; no overlapping notes. That is, each event begins either simultaneous with or immediately following the previous event <u>in that track</u>. So each event delay is either 0 or the same as the event's duration. This binary distinction requires only one bit of storage.

2. Tracks represent the "voice tracks" in Common Music Notation. CMN organizes a score in parallel staves, with one or two "voice tracks" per staff. So one or two SMUS tracks represents a CMN staff.

3. Tracks are a good match to available sound hardware. We can use "instrument settings" in a track to store the timbre assignments for that track's notes. The instrument setting may change over the track.

   Furthermore, tracks can help to allocate notes among available output channels or performance devices or tape recorder "tracks". Tracks can also help to adapt polyphonic data to monophonic output channels.

4. Tracks are a good match to simple sound software. Each track is a place to hold state settings like "dynamic mark *pp* ", "time signature 3/4", "mute this track", etc., just as it's a context for instrument settings. This is a lot like a text stream with running "font" and "face" properties (attributes). Running state is usually more compact than, say, storing an instrument setting in every note event. It's also a useful way to organize "attributes" of notes. With "running track state" we can define new note attributes in an upward- and backward-compatible way.

   Running track state can be expanded (run decoded) while loading a track into memory or while playing the track. The runtime track state must be reinitialized every time the score is played.

Separated vs. interleaved tracks. Multi-track data could be stored either as separate event streams or interleaved into one stream. To interleave the streams, each event has to carry a "track number" attribute.

If we were designing an editable score format, we might interleave the streams so that nearby events are stored nearby. This helps when searching the data, especially if you can't fit the entire score into memory at once. But it takes extra storage for the track numbers and may take extra work to manipulate the interleaved tracks.

The musical score format FORM SMUS is intended for simple loading and playback of small scores that fit entirely in main memory. So we chose to store its tracks separately.

There can be up to 255 tracks in a FORM SMUS. Each track is stored as a TRAK chunk. The count of tracks (the number of TRAK chunks) is recorded in the SHDR chunk at the beginning of the FORM SMUS. The TRAK chunks appear in numerical order 1, 2, 3, ... This is also priority order, most important track first. A player program that can handle up to N parallel tracks should read the first N tracks and ignore any others.

The different tracks in a score may have different lengths. This is true both of storage length and of playback duration.

Instrument Registers

Instrument reference. In SSSP, each note event points to a "timbre object" which supplies the "instrument" (the sound driver data) for that note. FORM SMUS stores these pointers as a "current instrument setting" for each track. It's just a run encoded version of the same information. SSSP uses a symbol table to hold all the pointers to "timbre object". SMUS uses INS1 chunks for the same purpose. They name the score's instruments.

The actual instrument data to use depends on the playback environment, but we want the score to be independent of environment. Different playback environments have different audio output hardware and different sound driver software. And there are channel allocation issues like how many output channels there are, which ones are polyphonic, and which I/O ports they're connected to. If you use MIDI to control the instruments, you get into issues of what kind of device is listening to each MIDI channel and what each of its presets sounds like. If you use computer-based instruments, you need driver-specific data like waveform tables and oscillator parameters.

We just want some orchestration. If the score wants a "piano", we let the playback program find a "piano".

Instrument reference by name. A reference from a SMUS score to actual instrument data is normally by name. The score simply names the instrument, for instance "tubular bells". It's up to the player program to find suitable instrument data for its output devices. (More on locating instruments below.)

Instrument reference by MIDI channel and preset. A SMUS score can also ask for a specific MIDI channel number and preset number. MIDI programs may honor these specific requests. But these channel allocations can become obsolete or the score may be played without MIDI hardware. In such cases, the player program should fall back to instrument reference by name.

Instrument reference via instrument register. Each reference from a SMUS track to an instrument is via an "instrument register". Each track selects an instrument register which in turn points to the specific instrument data.

Each score has an array of instrument registers. Each track has a "current instrument setting", which is simply an index number into this array. This is like setting a raster image's pixel to a specific color number (a reference to a color value through a "color register") or setting a text character to a specific font number (a reference to a font through a "font register"). This is diagramed below:

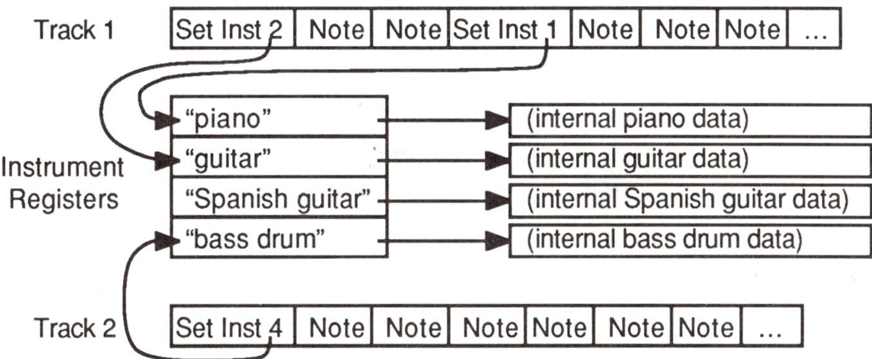

Locating instrument data by name. "INS1" chunks in a SMUS score name the instruments to use for that score. The player program uses these names to locate instrument data.

To locate instrument data, the player performs these steps:

For each instrument register, check for a suitable instrument with the right name...
{"Suitable" means usable with an available output device and driver.}
{Use case independent name comparisons.}

1. Initialize the instrument register to point to a built-in default instrument.
   {Every player program must have default instruments. Simple programs stop here. For fancier programs, the default instruments are a backstop in case the search fails.}

2. Check any instrument FORMs embedded in the FORM SMUS. (This is an "instrument cache".)

3. Else check the default instruments.

4. Else search the local "instrument library". (The library might simply be a disk directory.)

5. If all else fails, display the desired instrument name and ask the user to pick an available one.

This algorithm can be implemented to varying degrees of fanciness. It's ok to stop searching after step 1, 2, 3, or 4. If exact instrument name matches fail, it's ok to try approximate matches. E.g. search for any kind of "guitar" if you can't find a "Spanish guitar". In any case, a player only has to search for instruments while loading a score.

When the embedded instruments are suitable, they save the program from asking the user to insert the "right" disk in a drive and searching that disk for the "right" instrument. But it's just a cache. In practice, we rarely move scores between environments so the cache often works. When the score is moved, embedded instruments must be discarded (a cache miss) and other instrument data used.

Be careful to distinguish an instrument's name from its filename—the contents name vs. container name. A musical instrument FORM should contain a NAME chunk that says what instrument it really is. Its filename, on the other hand, is a handle used to locate the FORM. Filenames are affected by external factors like drives, directories, and filename character and length limits. Instrument names are not.

Issue: Consider instrument naming conventions for consistency. Consider a naming convention that aids approximate matches. E.g. we could accept "guitar, bass1" if we didn't find "guitar, bass". Failing that, we could accept "guitar" or any name starting with "guitar".

Set instrument events. If the player implements the set-instrument score event, each track can change instrument numbers while playing. That is, it can switch between the loaded instruments.

Initial instrument settings. Each time a score is played, every track's running state information must be initialized. Specifically, each track's instrument number should be initialized to its track number. Track 1 to instrument 1, etc. It's as if each track began with a set-instrument event.

In this way, programs that don't implement the set-instrument event still assign an instrument to each track. The INS1 chunks imply these initial instrument settings.

MIDI Instruments

As mentioned above, A SMUS score can also ask for MIDI instruments. This is done by putting the MIDI channel and preset numbers in an INS1 chunk with the instrument name. Some programs will honor these requests while others will just find instruments by name.

MIDI Recorder and sequencer programs may simply transcribe the MIDI channel and preset commands in a recording session. For this purpose, set-MIDI-channel and set-MIDI-preset events can be embedded in a SMUS score's tracks. Most programs should ignore these events. An editor program that wants to exchange scores with such programs should recognize these events. It should let the user change them to the more general set-instrument events.

3. Standard Data and Property Chunks

A FORM SMUS contains a required property "SHDR" followed by any number of parallel "track" data chunks "TRAK". Optional property chunks such as "NAME", copyright "(c) ", and instrument reference "INS1" may also appear. Any of the properties may be shared over a LIST of FORMs SMUS by putting them in a PROP SMUS. [See the IFF reference.]

Required Property SHDR

The required property "SHDR" holds an SScoreHeader as defined in these C declarations and following documentation. An SHDR specifies global information for the score. It must appear before the TRAKs in a FORM SMUS.

```
#define ID_SMUS MakeID('S', 'M', 'U', 'S')
#define ID_SHDR MakeID('S', 'H', 'D', 'R')

typedef struct {
   UWORD tempo;                 /* tempo, 128ths quarter note/minute       */
   UBYTE volume;                /* overall playback volume 0 through 127   */
   UBYTE ctTrack;               /* count of tracks in the score            */
   } SScoreHeader;
```

[Implementation details. In the C struct definitions in this memo, fields are filed in the order shown. A UBYTE field is packed into an 8-bit byte. Programs should set all "pad" fields to 0. MakeID is a C macro defined in the main IFF document and in the source file IFF.h.]

The field `tempo` gives the nominal tempo for all tracks in the score. It is expressed in 128ths of a quarter note per minute, i.e. 1 represents 1 quarter note per 128 minutes while 12800 represents 100 quarter notes per minute. You may think of this as a fixed point fraction with a 9-bit integer part and a 7-bit fractional part (to the right of the point). A coarse-tempoed program may simply shift `tempo` right by 7 bits to get a whole number of quarter notes per minute. The `tempo` field can store tempi in the range 0 up to 512. The playback program may adjust this tempo, perhaps under user control.

Actually, this global `tempo` could actually be just an initial tempo if there are any "set tempo" SEvents inside the score (see TRAK, below). Or the global tempo could be scaled by "scale tempo" SEvents inside the score. These are potential extensions that can safely be ignored by current programs. [See More SEvents To Be Defined, below.]

The field `volume` gives an overall nominal playback volume for all tracks in the score. The range of `volume` values 0 through 127 is like a MIDI key velocity value. The playback program may adjust this volume, perhaps under direction of a user "volume control".

Actually, this global volume level could be scaled by dynamic-mark SEvents inside the score (see TRAK, below).

The field `ctTrack` holds the count of tracks, i.e. the number of TRAK chunks in the FORM SMUS (see below). This information helps the reader prepare for the following data.

A playback program will typically load the score and call a driver routine `PlayScore(tracks, tempo, volume)`, supplying the `tempo` and `volume` from the SHDR chunk.

Optional Text Chunks NAME, (c), AUTH, ANNO

Several text chunks may be included in a FORM SMUS to keep ancillary information.

The optional property "NAME" names the musical score, for instance "Fugue in C".

The optional property "(c) " holds a copyright notice for the score. The chunk ID "(c) " serves the function of the copyright characters "© ". E.g. a "(c) " chunk containing "1986 Electronic Arts" means "© 1986 Electronic Arts".

The optional property "AUTH" holds the name of the score's author.

The chunk types "NAME", "(c) ", and "AUTH" are property chunks. Putting more than one NAME (or other) property in a FORM is redundant. Just the last NAME counts. A property should be shorter than 256 characters. Properties can appear in a PROP SMUS to share them over a LIST of FORMs SMUS.

The optional data chunk "ANNO" holds any text annotations typed in by the author.

An ANNO chunk is not a property chunk, so you can put more than one in a FORM SMUS. You can make ANNO chunks any length up to $2^{31} - 1$ characters, but 32767 is a practical limit. Since they're not properties, ANNO chunks don't belong in a PROP SMUS. That means they can't be shared over a LIST of FORMs SMUS.

Syntactically, each of these chunks contains an array of 8-bit ASCII characters in the range " " (SP, hex 20) through "~" (tilde, hex 7F), just like a standard "TEXT" chunk. [See "Strings, String Chunks, and String Properties" in "EA IFF 85" Electronic Arts Interchange File Format.] The chunk's `ckSize` field holds the count of characters.

```
#define ID_NAME MakeID('N', 'A', 'M', 'E')
/* NAME chunk contains a CHAR[], the musical score's name.        */

#define ID_Copyright MakeID('(', 'c', ')', ' ')
/* "(c) " chunk contains a CHAR[], the FORM's copyright notice.   */

#define ID_AUTH MakeID('A', 'U', 'T', 'H')
/* AUTH chunk contains a CHAR[], the name of the score's author.  */

#define ID_ANNO MakeID('A', 'N', 'N', 'O')
/* ANNO chunk contains a CHAR[], author's text annotations.       */
```

Remember to store a 0 pad byte after any odd-length chunk.

Optional Property INS1

The "INS1" chunks in a FORM SMUS identify the instruments to use for this score. A program can ignore INS1 chunks and stick with its built-in default instrument assignments. Or it can use them to locate instrument data. [See "Instrument Registers" in section 2, above.]

```
#define ID_INS1 MakeID('I', 'N', 'S', '1')

/* Values for the RefInstrument field "type".                          */
#define INS1_Name  0          /* just use the name; ignore data1, data2  */
```

```
#define INS1_MIDI  1          /* <data1, data2> = MIDI <channel, preset> */

typedef struct {
   UBYTE register;            /* set this instrument register number     */
   UBYTE type;                /* instrument reference type               */
   UBYTE data1, data2;        /* depends on the "type" field             */
   CHAR  name[];              /* instrument name                         */
   } RefInstrument;
```

An INS1 chunk names the instrument for instrument register number `register`. The `register` field can range from 0 through 255. In practice, most scores will need only a few instrument registers.

The `name` field gives a text name for the instrument. The string length can be determined from the `ckSize` of the INS1 chunk. The string is simply an array of 8-bit ASCII characters in the range " " (SP, hex 20) through "~" (tilde, hex 7F).

Besides the instrument name, an INS1 chunk has two data numbers to help locate an instrument. The use of these data numbers is controlled by the `type` field. A value `type` = `INS1_Name` means just find an instrument by name. In this case, `data1` and `data2` should just be set to 0. A value `type` = `INS1_MIDI` means look for an instrument on MIDI channel # `data1`, preset # `data2`. Programs and computers without MIDI outputs will just ignore the MIDI data. They'll always look for the named instrument. Other values of the `type` field are reserved for future standardization.

See section 2, above, for the algorithm for locating instrument data by name.

Obsolete Property INST

The chunk type "INST" is obsolete in SMUS. It was revised to form the "INS1" chunk.

Data Chunk TRAK

The main contents of a score is stored in one or more TRAK chunks representing parallel "tracks". One TRAK chunk per track.

The contents of a TRAK chunk is an array of 16-bit "events" such as "note", "rest", and "set instrument". Events are really commands to a simple scheduler, stored in time order. The tracks can be polyphonic, that is, they can contain chorded "note" events.

Each event is stored as an "SEvent" record. ("SEvent" means "simple musical event".) Each SEvent has an 8-bit type field called an "sID" and 8 bits of type-dependent data. This is like a machine language instruction with an 8-bit opcode and an 8-bit operand.

This format is extensible since new event types can be defined in the future. The "note" and "rest" events are the only ones that every program must understand. *We will carefully design any new event types so that programs can safely skip over unrecognized events in a score.*

Caution: ID codes must be allocated by a central clearinghouse to avoid conflicts. Commodore-Amiga Technical Support provides this clearinghouse service.

Here are the C type definitions for TRAK and SEvent and the currently defined sID values. Afterward are details on each SEvent.

```
#define ID_TRAK MakeID('T', 'R', 'A', 'K')
```

```
/* TRAK chunk contains an SEvent[].                                 */

/* SEvent: Simple musical event.                                    */
typedef struct {
   UBYTE sID;                  /* SEvent type code                  */
   UBYTE data;                 /* sID-dependent data                */
   } SEvent;

/* SEvent type codes "sID".                                         */
#define SID_FirstNote      0
#define SID_LastNote     127   /* sIDs in the range SID_FirstNote through
                                * SID_LastNote (sign bit = 0) are notes. The
                                * sID is the MIDI tone number (pitch).   */
#define SID_Rest         128   /* a rest (same data format as a note).   */

#define SID_Instrument   129   /* set instrument number for this track.  */
#define SID_TimeSig      130   /* set time signature for this track.     */
#define SID_KeySig       131   /* set key signature for this track.      */
#define SID_Dynamic      132   /* set volume for this track.             */
#define SID_MIDI_Chnl    133   /* set MIDI channel number (sequencers)   */
#define SID_MIDI_Preset  134   /* set MIDI preset number (sequencers)    */
#define SID_Clef         135   /* inline clef change.
                                * 0=Treble, 1=Bass, 2=Alto, 3=Tenor.(new) */
#define SID_Tempo        136   /* Inline tempo in beats per minute.(new)  */

/* SID values 144 through 159: reserved for Instant Music SEvents.  */

/* Remaining sID values up through 254: reserved for future
 * standardization.                                                 */

#define SID_Mark         255   /* sID reserved for an end-mark in RAM.   */
```

Note and Rest SEvents

The note and rest SEvents `SID_FirstNote` through `SID_Rest` have the following structure overlaid onto the SEvent structure:

```
typedef struct {
   UBYTE    tone;              /* MIDI tone number 0 to 127; 128 = rest  */
   unsigned chord     :1,      /* 1 = a chorded note                     */
            tieOut    :1,      /* 1 = tied to the next note or chord     */
            nTuplet   :2,      /* 0 = none, 1 = triplet, 2 = quintuplet,
                                * 3 = septuplet                          */
            dot       :1,      /* dotted note; multiply duration by 3/2  */
            division  :3;      /* basic note duration is 2^-division: 0 = whole
                                * note, 1 = half note, 2 = quarter note, ...
                                * 7 = 128th note                         */
   } SNote;
```

[Implementation details. Unsigned ":n" fields are packed into n bits in the order shown, most significant bit to least significant bit. An SNote fits into 16 bits like any other SEvent. Warning: Some compilers don't implement bit-packed fields properly. E.g. Lattice 68000 C pads a group of bit fields out to a LONG, which would make SNote take 5-bytes! In that situation, use the bit-field constants defined below.]

The SNote structure describes one "note" or "rest" in a track. The field `SNote.tone`, which is overlaid with the `SEvent.sID` field, indicates the MIDI tone number (pitch) in the range 0 through 127. A value of 128 indicates a rest.

The fields `nTuplet`, `dot`, and `division` together give the duration of the note or rest. The `division` gives the basic duration: whole note, half note, etc. The `dot` indicates if the note or rest is dotted. A dotted note is 3/2 as long as an undotted note. The value `nTuplet` (0 through 3) tells if this note or rest is part of an N-tuplet of order 1 (normal), 3, 5, or 7; an N-tuplet of order `(2 * nTuplet + 1)`. A triplet note is 2/3 as long as a normal note, while a quintuplet is 4/5 as long and a septuplet is 6/7 as long.

Putting these three fields together, the duration of the note or rest is

$$2^{-\text{division}} * \{1,\ 3/2\} * \{1,\ 2/3,\ 4/5,\ 6/7\}$$

These three fields are contiguous so you can easily convert to your local duration encoding by using the combined 6 bits as an index into a mapping table.

The field `chord` indicates if the note is chorded with the following note (which is supposed to have the same duration). A group of notes may be chorded together by setting the `chord` bit of all but the last one. (In the terminology of SSSP and GSCR, setting the chord bit to 1 makes the "entry delay" 0.) A monophonic-track player can simply ignore any SNote event whose `chord` bit is set, either by discarding it when reading the track or by skipping it when playing the track.

Programs that create polyphonic tracks are expected to store the most important note of each chord last, which is the note with the 0 `chord` bit. This way, monophonic programs will play the most important note of the chord. The most important note might be the chord's root note or its melody note.

If the field `tieOut` is set, the note is tied to the following note in the track <u>if</u> the following note has the same pitch. A group of tied notes is played as a single note whose duration is the sum of the component durations. Actually, the tie mechanism ties a group of one or more chorded notes to another group of one or more chorded notes. Every note in a tied chord should have its `tieOut` bit set.

Of course, the `chord` and `tieOut` fields don't apply to `SID_Rest` SEvents.

Programs should be robust enough to ignore an unresolved tie, i.e. a note whose `tieOut` bit is set but isn't followed by a note of the same pitch. If that's true, monophonic-track programs can simply ignore chorded notes even in the presense of ties. That is, tied chords pose no extra problems.

The following diagram shows some combinations of notes and chords tied to notes and chords. The text below the staff has a column for each SNote SEvent to show the pitch, `chord` bit, and `tieOut` bit.

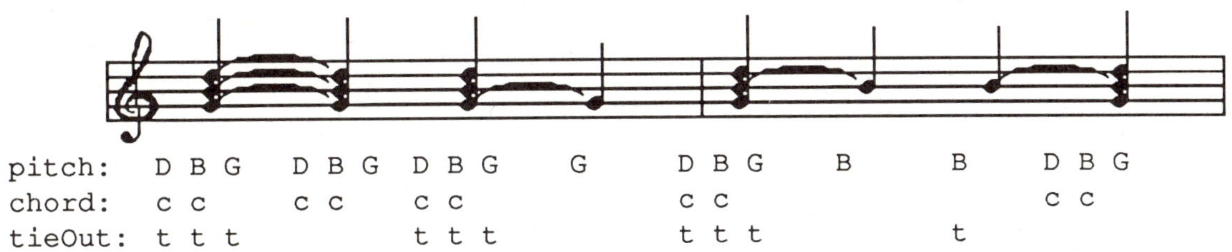

If you read the above track into a monophonic-track program, it'll strip out the chorded notes and ignore unresolved ties. You'll end up with:

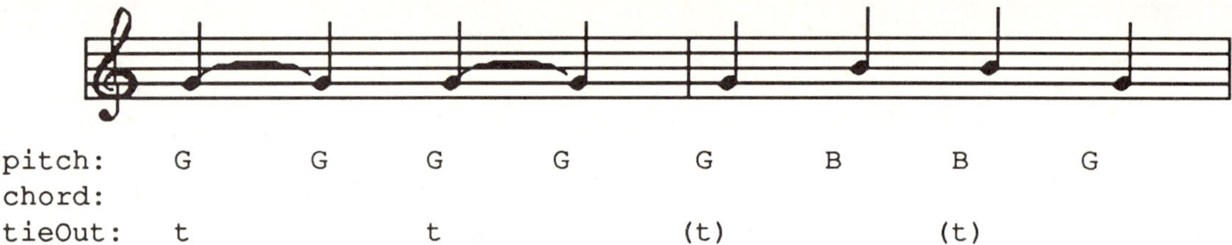

```
pitch:    G       G      G      G       G      B      B      G
chord:
tieOut:   t              t             (t)           (t)
```

A rest event (`sID = SID_Rest`) has the same `SEvent.data` field as a note. It tells the duration of the rest. The `chord` and `tieOut` fields of rest events are ignored.

Within a TRAK chunk, note and rest events appear in time order.

Instead of the bit-packed structure SNote, it might be easier to assemble `data` values by or-ing constants and to disassemble them by masking and shifting. In that case, use the following definitions.

```
#define noteChord  (1<<7)           /* note is chorded to next note       */
#define noteTieOut (1<<6)           /* tied to next note/chord            */

#define noteNShift 4                /* shift count for nTuplet field      */
#define noteN3     (1<<noteNShift)  /* note is a triplet                  */
#define noteN5     (2<<noteNShift)  /* note is a quintuplet               */
#define noteN7     (3<<noteNShift)  /* note is a septuplet                */
#define noteNMask  noteN7           /* bit mask for the nTuplet field     */

#define noteDot    (1<<3)           /* note is dotted                     */

#define noteD1     0                /* whole note division                */
#define noteD2     1                /* half note division                 */
#define noteD4     2                /* quarter note division              */
#define noteD8     3                /* eighth note division               */
#define noteD16    4                /* sixteenth note division            */
#define noteD32    5                /* thirty-second'th note division     */
#define noteD64    6                /* sixty-fourth note division         */
#define noteD128   7                /* 1/128 note division                */
#define noteDMask  noteD128         /* bit mask for the division field    */

#define noteDurMask 0x3F            /* mask for combined duration fields */
```

Note: The remaining SEvent types are optional. A writer program doesn't have to generate them. A reader program can safely ignore them.

Set Instrument SEvent

One of the running state variables of every track is an instrument number. An instrument number is the array index of an "instrument register", which in turn points to an instrument. (See "Instrument Registers", in section 2.) This is like a color number in a bitmap; a reference to a color through a "color register".

The initial setting for each track's instrument number is the track number. Track 1 is set to instrument 1, etc. Each time the score is played, every track's instrument number should be reset to the track number.

The SEvent `SID_Instrument` changes the instrument number for a track, that is, which instrument plays the following notes. Its `SEvent.data` field is an instrument register number in the range 0 through 255. If a program doesn't implement the `SID_Instrument` event, each track is fixed to one instrument.

Set Time Signature SEvent

The SEvent `SID_TimeSig` sets the time signature for the track. A "time signature" SEvent has the following structure overlaid on the SEvent structure:

```
typedef struct {
    UBYTE    type;              /* = SID_TimeSig                        */
    unsigned timeNSig :5,       /* time sig. "numerator" is timeNSig + 1    */
             timeDSig :3;       /* time sig. "denominator" is 2^timeDSig:
                                 * 0 = whole note, 1 = half note, 2 = quarter
                                 * note, ... 7 = 128th note             */
    } STimeSig;
```

[Implementation details. Unsigned ":n" fields are packed into n bits in the order shown, most significant bit to least significant bit. An STimeSig fits into 16 bits like any other SEvent. Warning: Some compilers don't implement bit-packed fields properly. E.g. Lattice C pads a group of bit fields out to a LONG, which would make an STimeSig take 5-bytes! In that situation, use the bit-field constants defined below.]

The field `type` contains the value `SID_TimeSig`, indicating that this SEvent is a "time signature" event. The field `timeNSig` indicates the time signature "numerator" is `timeNSig + 1`, that is, 1 through 32 beats per measure. The field `timeDSig` indicates the time signature "denominator" is $2^{\texttt{timeDSig}}$, that is each "beat" is a $2^{-\texttt{timeDSig}}$ note (see SNote `division`, above). So 4/4 time is expressed as `timeNSig` = 3, `timeDSig` = 2.

The default time signature is 4/4 time. Be aware that the time signature has no effect on the score's playback. Tempo is uniformly expressed in quarter notes per minute, independent of time signature. (Quarter notes per minute would equal beats per minute only if `timeDSig` = 2, n/4 time). Nonetheless, any program that has time signatures should put them at the beginning of each TRAK when creating a FORM SMUS because music editors need them.

Instead of the bit-packed structure STimeSig, it might be easier to assemble `data` values by or-ing constants and to disassemble them by masking and shifting. In that case, use the following definitions.

```
#define timeNMask  0xF8            /* bit mask for the timeNSig field   */
#define timeNShift 3               /* shift count for  timeNSig field   */

#define timeDMask  0x07            /* bit mask for the timeDSig field   */
```

Key Signature SEvent

An SEvent `SID_KeySig` sets the key signature for the track. Its `data` field is a UBYTE number encoding a major key:

data	key	music notation	data	key	music notation
0	C maj				
1	G	#	8	F	b
2	D	##	9	Bb	bb
3	A	###	10	Eb	bbb
4	E	####	11	Ab	bbbb
5	B	#####	12	Db	bbbbb
6	F#	######	13	Gb	bbbbbb
7	C#	#######	14	Cb	bbbbbbb

A `SID_KeySig` SEvent changes the key for the following notes in that track. C major is the default key in every track before the first `SID_KeySig` SEvent.

Dynamic Mark SEvent

An SEvent `SID_Dynamic` represents a dynamic mark like *ppp* and *fff* in Common Music Notation. Its `data` field is a MIDI key velocity number 0 through 127. This sets a "volume control" for following notes in the track. This "track volume control" is scaled by the overall score `volume` in the SHDR chunk. The default dynamic level is 127 (full volume).

Set MIDI Channel SEvent

The SEvent `SID_MIDI_Chnl` is for recorder programs to record the set-MIDI-channel low level event. The `data` byte contains a MIDI channel number. Other programs should use instrument registers instead.

Set MIDI Preset SEvent

The SEvent `SID_MIDI_Preset` is for recorder programs to record the set-MIDI-preset low level event. The `data` byte contains a MIDI preset number. Other programs should use instrument registers instead.

Instant Music Private SEvents

Sixteen SEvents are used for private data for the Instant Music program. SID values 144 through 159 are reserved for this purpose. Other programs should skip over these SEvents.

End-Mark SEvent

The SEvent type `SID_Mark` is reserved for an end marker in working memory. *This event is never stored in a file.* It may be useful if you decide to use the filed TRAK format intact in working memory.

More SEvents To Be Defined

More SEvents can be defined in the future. The sID codes 133 through 143 and 160 through 254 are reserved for future needs. Caution: sID codes must be allocated by a central "clearinghouse" to avoid conflicts.

The following SEvent types are under consideration and should not yet be used.

Issue: A "change tempo" SEvent changes tempo during a score. Changing the tempo affects all tracks, not just the track containing the change tempo event.

One possibility is a "scale tempo" SEvent `SID_ScaleTempo` that rescales the global tempo:

```
currentTempo := globalTempo * (data + 1) / 128
```

This can scale the global tempo (in the SHDR) anywhere from x1/128 to x2 in roughly 1% increments.

An alternative is two events `SID_SetHTempo` and `SID_SetLTempo`. `SID_SetHTempo` gives the high byte and `SID_SetLTempo` gives the low byte of a new tempo setting, in 128ths quarter note/minute. `SetHTempo` automatically sets the low byte to 0, so the `SetLTempo` event isn't needed for coarse settings. In this scheme, the SHDR's `tempo` is simply a starting tempo.

An advantage of SID_ScaleTempo is that the playback program can just alter the global tempo to adjust the overall performance time and still easily implement tempo variations during the score. But the "set tempo" SEvent may be simpler to generate.

Issue: The events SID_BeginRepeat and SID_EndRepeat define a repeat span for one track. The span of events between a BeginRepeat and an EndRepeat is played twice. The SEvent.data field in the BeginRepeat event could give an iteration count, 1 through 255 times or 0 for "repeat forever".

Repeat spans can be nested. All repeat spans automatically end at the end of the track.

An event SID_Ending begins a section like "first ending" or "second ending". The SEvent.data field gives the ending number. This SID_Ending event only applies to the innermost repeat group. (Consider generalizing it.)

A more general alternative is a "subtrack" or "subscore" event. A "subtrack" event is essentially a "subroutine call" to another series of SEvents. This is a nice way to encode all the possible variations of repeats, first endings, codas, and such.

To define a subtrack, we must demark its start and end. One possibility is to define a relative branch-to-subtrack event SID_BSR and a return-from-subtrack event SID_RTS. The 8-bit data field in the SID_BSR event can reach as far as 512 SEvents. A second possibility is to call a subtrack by index number, with an IFF chunk outside the TRAK defining the start and end of all subtracks. This is very general since a portion of one subtrack can be used as another subtrack. It also models the tape recording practice of first "laying down a track" and then selecting portions of it to play and repeat. To embody the music theory idea of playing a sequence like "ABBA", just compose the "main" track entirely of subtrack events. A third possibility is to use a numbered subtrack chunk "STRK" for each subroutine.

4. Private Chunks

As in any IFF FORM, there can be private chunks in a FORM SMUS that are designed for one particular program to store its private information. All IFF reader programs skip over unrecognized chunks, so the presense of private chunks can't hurt.

Instant Music stores some global score information in a chunk of ID "IRev" and some other information in a chunk of ID "BIAS".

Appendix A. Quick Reference

Type Definitions

Here's a collection of the C type definitions in this memo. In the "struct" type definitions, fields are filed in the order shown. A UBYTE field is packed into an 8-bit byte. Programs should set all "pad" fields to 0.

```
#define ID_SMUS MakeID('S', 'M', 'U', 'S')
#define ID_SHDR MakeID('S', 'H', 'D', 'R')

typedef struct {
   UWORD tempo;              /* tempo, 128ths quarter note/minute       */
   UBYTE volume;             /* overall playback volume 0 through 127   */
   UBYTE ctTrack;            /* count of tracks in the score            */
   } SScoreHeader;


#define ID_NAME MakeID('N', 'A', 'M', 'E')
/* NAME chunk contains a CHAR[], the musical score's name.              */


#define ID_Copyright MakeID('(', 'c', ')', ' ')
/* "(c) " chunk contains a CHAR[], the FORM's copyright notice.         */


#define ID_AUTH MakeID('A', 'U', 'T', 'H')
/* AUTH chunk contains a CHAR[], the name of the score's author.        */


#define ID_ANNO MakeID('A', 'N', 'N', 'O')
/* ANNO chunk contains a CHAR[], author's text annotations.             */


#define ID_INS1 MakeID('I', 'N', 'S', '1')

/* Values for the RefInstrument field "type".                           */
#define INS1_Name 0          /* just use the name; ignore data1, data2  */
#define INS1_MIDI 1          /* <data1, data2> = MIDI <channel, preset> */

typedef struct {
   UBYTE register;           /* set this instrument register number     */
   UBYTE type;               /* instrument reference type               */
   UBYTE data1, data2;       /* depends on the "type" field             */
   CHAR  name[];             /* instrument name                         */
   } RefInstrument;


#define ID_TRAK MakeID('T', 'R', 'A', 'K')
/* TRAK chunk contains an SEvent[].                                     */

/* SEvent: Simple musical event.                                        */
typedef struct {
   UBYTE sID;                /* SEvent type code                        */
   UBYTE data;               /* sID-dependent data                      */
   } SEvent;
```

```
/* SEvent type codes "sID".                                                */
#define SID_FirstNote     0
#define SID_LastNote    127    /* sIDs in the range SID_FirstNote through
                                * SID_LastNote (sign bit = 0) are notes. The
                                * sID is the MIDI tone number (pitch).     */
#define SID_Rest        128    /* a rest (same data format as a note).     */

#define SID_Instrument  129    /* set instrument number for this track.    */
#define SID_TimeSig     130    /* set time signature for this track.       */
#define SID_KeySig      131    /* set key signature for this track.        */
#define SID_Dynamic     132    /* set volume for this track.               */
#define SID_MIDI_Chnl   133    /* set MIDI channel number (sequencers)     */
#define SID_MIDI_Preset 134    /* set MIDI preset number (sequencers)      */
#define SID_Clef        135    /* inline clef change.
                                * 0=Treble, 1=Bass, 2=Alto, 3=Tenor.       */
#define SID_Tempo       136    /* Inline tempo in beats per minute.        */

/* SID values 144 through 159: reserved for Instant Music SEvents.         */

/* Remaining sID values up through 254: reserved for future
 * standardization.                                                        */

#define SID_Mark        255    /* sID reserved for an end-mark in RAM.     */


/* SID_FirstNote..SID_LastNote, SID_Rest SEvents                           */
typedef struct {
   UBYTE    tone;              /* MIDI tone number 0 to 127; 128 = rest    */
   unsigned chord    :1,       /* 1 = a chorded note                       */
            tieOut   :1,       /* 1 = tied to the next note or chord       */
            nTuplet  :2,       /* 0 = none, 1 = triplet, 2 = quintuplet,
                                * 3 = septuplet                            */
            dot      :1,       /* dotted note; multiply duration by 3/2    */
            division :3;       /* basic note duration is 2^-division: 0 = whole
                                * note, 1 = half note, 2 = quarter note, …
                                * 7 = 128th note                           */
   } SNote;

#define noteChord  (1<<7)            /* note is chorded to next note      */

#define noteTieOut (1<<6)            /* tied to next note/chord           */

#define noteNShift 4                 /* shift count for nTuplet field     */
#define noteN3     (1<<noteNShift)   /* note is a triplet                 */
#define noteN5     (2<<noteNShift)   /* note is a quintuplet              */
#define noteN7     (3<<noteNShift)   /* note is a septuplet               */
#define noteNMask  noteN7            /* bit mask for the nTuplet field    */

#define noteDot    (1<<3)            /* note is dotted                    */

#define noteD1     0                 /* whole note division               */
#define noteD2     1                 /* half note division                */
#define noteD4     2                 /* quarter note division             */
#define noteD8     3                 /* eighth note division              */
```

```
#define noteD16     4               /* sixteenth note division            */
#define noteD32     5               /* thirty-secondth note division      */
#define noteD64     6               /* sixty-fourth note division         */
#define noteD128    7               /* 1/128 note division                */
#define noteDMask   noteD128        /* bit mask for the division field    */

#define noteDurMask 0x3F            /* mask for combined duration fields */


/* SID_Instrument SEvent                                                  */
/* "data" value is an instrument register number 0 through 255.          */


/* SID_TimeSig SEvent                                                     */
typedef struct {
   UBYTE    type;             /* = SID_TimeSig                            */
   unsigned timeNSig :5,      /* time sig. "numerator" is timeNSig + 1    */
            timeDSig :3;      /* time sig. "denominator" is 2^timeDSig:
                               * 0 = whole note, 1 = half note, 2 = quarter
                               * note, ... 7 = 128th note                 */
   } STimeSig;

#define timeNMask  0xF8       /* bit mask for the timeNSig field          */
#define timeNShift 3          /* shift count for  timeNSig field          */

#define timeDMask  0x07       /* bit mask for the timeDSig field          */


/* SID_KeySig SEvent                                                      */
/* "data" value 0 = Cmaj; 1 through 7 = G,D,A,E,B,F#,C#;
 * 8 through 14 = F,Bb,Eb,Ab,Db,Gb,Cb.                                    */


/* SID_Dynamic SEvent                                                     */
/* "data" value is a MIDI key velocity 0..127.                            */
```

SMUS Regular Expression

Here's a regular expression summary of the FORM SMUS syntax. This could be an IFF file or part of one.

```
SMUS       ::= "FORM" #{  "SMUS" SHDR [NAME] [Copyright] [AUTH] [IRev]
                          ANNO* INS1*  TRAK*  InstrForm* }

SHDR       ::= "SHDR" #{  SScoreHeader  }
NAME       ::= "NAME" #{  CHAR*         } [0]
Copyright  ::= "(c) " #{  CHAR*         } [0]
AUTH       ::= "AUTH" #{  CHAR*         } [0]
IRev       ::= "IRev" #{  ...           }

ANNO       ::= "ANNO" #{  CHAR*         } [0]
INS1       ::= "INS1" #{  RefInstrument } [0]

TRAK       ::= "TRAK" #{  SEvent*       }
InstrForm  ::= "FORM" #{  ...           }
```

The token "#" represents a `ckSize` LONG count of the following {braced} data bytes. Literal items are shown in "quotes", [square bracket items] are optional, and "*" means 0 or more replications. A sometimes-needed pad byte is shown as "[0]".

Actually, the order of chunks in a FORM SMUS is not as strict as this regular expression indicates. The SHDR, NAME, Copyright, AUTH, IRev, ANNO, and INS1 chunks may appear in any order, as long as they precede the TRAK chunks.

The chunk "`InstrForm`" represents any kind of instrument data FORM embedded in the FORM SMUS. For example, see the document "8SVX" IFF 8-Bit Sampled Voice. Of course, a recipient program will ignore an instrument FORM if it doesn't recognize that FORM type.

Appendix B. SMUS Example

Here's a box diagram for a simple example, a SMUS with two instruments and two tracks. Each track contains 1 note event and 1 rest event.

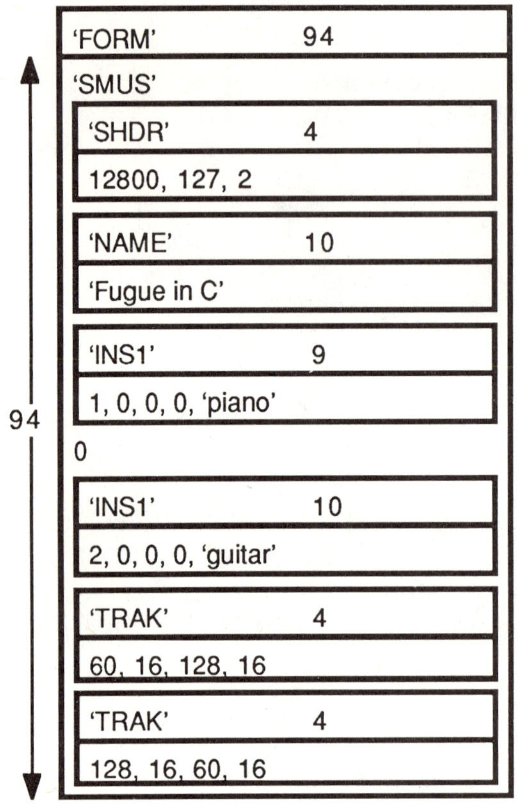

The "0" after the first INS1 chunk is a pad byte.

Appendix C. Standards Committee

The following people contributed to the design of this SMUS standard:

Ralph Bellafatto, Cherry Lane Technologies
Geoff Brown, Uhuru Sound Software
Steve Hayes, Electronic Arts
Jerry Morrison, Electronic Arts

"8SVX" IFF 8-Bit Sampled Voice

Date: February 7, 1985 (Re-Typeset Oct, 1988 Commodore-Amiga, Inc.)
From: Steve Hayes and Jerry Morrison, Electronic Arts
Status: Adopted

1. Introduction

This is the IFF supplement for FORM "8SVX". An 8SVX is an IFF "data section" or "FORM" (which can be an IFF file or a part of one) containing a digitally sampled audio voice consisting of 8-bit samples. A voice can be a one-shot sound or—with repetition and pitch scaling—a musical instrument. "EA IFF 85" is Electronic Arts' standard interchange file format. [See "EA IFF 85" Standard for Interchange Format Files.]

The 8SVX format is designed for playback hardware that uses 8-bit samples attenuated by a volume control for good overall signal-to-noise ratio. So a FORM 8SVX stores 8-bit samples and a volume level.

A similar data format (or two) will be needed for higher resolution samples (typically 12 or 16 bits). Properly converting a high resolution sample down to 8 bits requires one pass over the data to find the minimum and maximum values and a second pass to scale each sample into the range -128 through 127. So it's reasonable to store higher resolution data in a different FORM type and convert between them.

For instruments, FORM 8SVX can record a repeating waveform optionally preceded by a startup transient waveform. These two recorded signals can be pre-synthesized or sampled from an acoustic instrument. For many instruments, this representation is compact. FORM 8SVX is less practical for an instrument whose waveform changes from cycle to cycle like a plucked string, where a long sample is needed for accurate results.

FORM 8SVX can store an "envelope" or "amplitude contour" to enrich musical notes. A future voice FORM could also store amplitude, frequency, and filter modulations.

FORM 8SVX is geared for relatively simple musical voices, where one waveform per octave is sufficient, the waveforms for the different octaves follow a factor-of-two size rule, and one envelope is adequate for all octaves. You could store a more general voice as a LIST containing one or more FORMs 8SVX per octave. A future voice FORM could go beyond one "one-shot" waveform and one "repeat" waveform per octave.

Section 2 defines the required property sound header "VHDR", optional properties name "NAME", copyright "(c) ", and author "AUTH", the optional annotation data chunk "ANNO", the required data chunk "BODY", and optional envelope chunks "ATAK" and "RLSE". These are the "standard" chunks. Specialized chunks for private or future needs can be added later, e.g. to hold a frequency contour or Fourier series coefficients. The 8SVX syntax is summarized in Appendix A as a regular expression and in Appendix B as an example box diagram. Appendix C explains the optional Fibonacci-delta compression algorithm.

Reference:

"EA IFF 85" Standard for Interchange Format Files describes the underlying conventions for all IFF files.

2. Standard Data and Property Chunks

FORM 8SVX stores all the waveform data in one body chunk "BODY". It stores playback parameters in the required header chunk "VHDR". "VHDR" and any optional property chunks "NAME", "(c) ", and "AUTH" must all appear before the BODY chunk. Any of these properties may be shared over a LIST of FORMs 8SVX by putting them in a PROP 8SVX. [See "EA IFF 85" Standard for Interchange Format Files.]

Background

There are two ways to use FORM 8SVX: as a one-shot sampled sound or as a sampled musical instrument that plays "notes". Storing both kinds of sounds in the same kind of FORM makes it easy to play a one-shot sound as an instrument or an instrument as a one-note sound.

A one-shot sound is a series of audio data samples with a nominal playback rate and amplitude. The recipient program can optionally adjust or modulate the amplitude and playback data rate.

For musical instruments, the idea is to store a sampled (or pre-synthesized) waveform that will be parameterized by pitch, duration, and amplitude to play each "note". The creator of the FORM 8SVX can supply a waveform per octave over a range of octaves for this purpose. The intent is to perform a pitch by selecting the closest octave's waveform and scaling the playback data rate. An optional "one-shot" waveform supplies an arbitrary startup transient, then a "repeat" waveform is iterated as long as necessary to sustain the note.

A FORM 8SVX can also store an envelope to modulate the waveform. Envelopes are mostly useful for variable-duration notes but could be used for one-shot sounds, too.

The FORM 8SVX standard has some restrictions. For example, each octave of data must be twice as long as the next higher octave. Most sound driver software and hardware imposes additional restrictions. E.g. the Amiga sound hardware requires an even number of samples in each one-shot and repeat waveform.

Required Property VHDR

The required property "VHDR" holds a Voice8Header structure as defined in these C declarations and following documentation. This structure holds the playback parameters for the sampled waveforms in the BODY chunk. (See "Data Chunk BODY", below, for the storage layout of these waveforms.)

```
#define ID_8SVX MakeID('8', 'S', 'V', 'X')
#define ID_VHDR MakeID('V', 'H', 'D', 'R')

typedef LONG Fixed;           /* A fixed-point value, 16 bits to the left of
                              the point and 16 to the right. A Fixed is a
                              number of 2^16ths, i.e. 65536ths.          */
#define Unity 0x10000L        /* Unity = Fixed 1.0 = maximum volume      */

/* sCompression: Choice of compression algorithm applied to the samples.
                                                                         */
#define sCmpNone        0     /* not compressed                          */
#define sCmpFibDelta    1     /* Fibonacci-delta encoding (Appendix C)   */
                              /* Can be more kinds in the future.        */

typedef struct {
  ULONG oneShotHiSamples,     /* # samples in the high octave 1-shot part
                                                                         */
        repeatHiSamples,      /* # samples in the high octave repeat part
```

```
                                                                   */
        samplesPerHiCycle;    /* # samples/cycle in high octave, else 0  */
  UWORD samplesPerSec;        /* data sampling rate                      */
  UBYTE ctOctave,             /* # octaves of waveforms                  */
        sCompression;         /* data compression technique used         */
  Fixed volume;               /* playback volume from 0 to Unity (full
                               * volume). Map this value into the output
                               * hardware's dynamic range.               */
  } Voice8Header;
```

[Implementation details. Fields are filed in the order shown. The UBYTE fields are byte-packed (2 per 16-bit word). MakeID is a C macro defined in the main IFF document and in the source file IFF.h.]

A FORM 8SVX holds waveform data for one or more octaves, each containing a one-shot part and a repeat part. The fields `oneShotHiSamples` and `repeatHiSamples` tell the number of audio samples in the two parts of the highest frequency octave. Each successive (lower frequency) octave contains twice as many data samples in both its one-shot and repeat parts. One of these two parts can be empty across all octaves.

Note: Most audio output hardware and software has limitations. For example the Amiga computer has sound hardware that requires that all one-shot and repeat parts have even numbers of samples. Amiga sound driver software should adjust an odd-sized waveform, ignore an odd-sized lowest octave, or ignore odd 8SVX FORMs altogether. Some other output devices require all sample sizes to be powers of two.

The field `samplesPerHiCycle` tells the number of samples/cycle in the highest frequency octave of data, or else 0 for "unknown". Each successive (lower frequency) octave contains twice as many samples/cycle. The `samplesPerHiCycle` value is needed to compute the data rate for a desired playback pitch.

Actually, `samplesPerHiCycle` is an average number of samples/cycle. If the one-shot part contains pitch bends, store the samples/cycle of the repeat part in `samplesPerHiCycle`. The division `repeatHiSamples/samplesPerHiCycle` should yield an integer number of cycles. (When the repeat waveform is repeated, a partial cycle would come out as a higher-frequency cycle with a "click".)

More limitations: some Amiga music drivers require `samplesPerHiCycle` to be a power of two in order to play the FORM 8SVX as a musical instrument in tune. They may even assume `samplesPerHiCycle` is a particular power of two without checking. (If `samplesPerHiCycle` is different by a factor of two, the instrument will just be played an octave too low or high.)

The field `samplesPerSec` gives the sound sampling rate. A program may adjust this to achieve frequency shifts or vary it dynamically to achieve pitch bends and vibrato. A program that plays a FORM 8SVX as a musical instrument would ignore `samplesPerSec` and select a playback rate for each musical pitch.

The field `ctOctave` tells how many octaves of data are stored in the BODY chunk. See "Data Chunk BODY", below, for the layout of the octaves.

The field `sCompression` indicates the compression scheme, if any, that was applied to the entire set of data samples stored in the BODY chunk. This field should contain one of the values defined above. Of course, the matching decompression algorithm must be applied to the BODY data before the sound can be played. (The Fibonacci-delta encoding scheme `sCmpFibDelta` is described in Appendix C.) Note that the whole series of data samples is compressed as a unit.

The field `volume` gives an overall playback volume for the waveforms (all octaves). It lets the 8-bit data samples use the full range -128 through 127 for good signal-to-noise ratio. The playback program should multiply this value by a "volume control" and perhaps by a playback envelope (see ATAK and RLSE, below).

Recording a one-shot sound. To store a one-shot sound in a FORM 8SVX, set `oneShotHiSamples` = number of samples, `repeatHiSamples` = 0 , `samplesPerHiCycle` = 0, `samplesPerSec` = sampling rate, and `ctOctave` = 1. Scale the signal amplitude to the full sampling range -128 through 127. Set `volume` so the sound will playback at the desired volume level. If you set the `samplesPerHiCycle` field properly, the data can also be used as a musical instrument.

Experiment with data compression. If the decompressed signal sounds okay, store the compressed data in the BODY chunk and set `sCompression` to the compression code number.

Recording a musical instrument. To store a musical instrument in a FORM 8SVX, first record or synthesize as many octaves of data as you want to make available for playback. Set `ctOctaves` to the count of octaves. From the recorded data, excerpt an integral number of steady state cycles for the repeat part and set `repeatHiSamples` and `samplesPerHiCycle`. Either excerpt a startup transient waveform and set `oneShotHiSamples`, or else set `oneShotHiSamples` to 0. Remember, the one-shot and repeat parts of each octave must be twice as long as those of the next higher octave. Scale the signal amplitude to the full sampling range and set `volume` to adjust the instrument playback volume. If you set the `samplesPerSec` field properly, the data can also be used as a one-shot sound.

A distortion-introducing compressor like `sCmpFibDelta` is not recommended for musical instruments, but you might try it anyway.

Typically, creators of FORM 8SVX record an acoustic instrument at just one frequency. Decimate (down- sample with filtering) to compute higher octaves. Interpolate to compute lower octaves.

If you sample an acoustic instrument at different octaves, you may find it hard to make the one-shot and repeat waveforms follow the factor-of-two rule for octaves. To compensate, lengthen an octave's one-shot part by appending replications of the repeating cycle or prepending zeros. (This will have minimal impact on the sound's start time.) You may be able to equalize the ratio of one-shot-samples to repeat-samples across all octaves.

Note that a "one-shot sound" may be played as a "musical instrument" and vice versa. However, an instrument player depends on `samplesPerHiCycle`, and a one-shot player depends on `samplesPerSec`.

Playing a one-shot sound. To play any FORM 8SVX data as a one-shot sound, first select an octave if `ctOctave` > 1. (The lowest-frequency octave has the greatest resolution.) Play the one-shot samples then the repeat samples, scaled by `volume`, at a data rate of `samplesPerSec`. Of course, you may adjust the playback rate and volume. You can play out an envelope, too. (See ATAK and RLSE, below.)

Playing a musical note. To play a musical note using any FORM 8SVX, first select the nearest octave of data from those available. Play the one-shot waveform then cycle on the repeat waveform as long as needed to sustain the note. Scale the signal by `volume`, perhaps also by an envelope, and by a desired note volume. Select a playback data rate s samples/second to achieve the desired frequency (in Hz):

```
frequency = s / samplesPerHiCycle
```

for the highest frequency octave.

The idea is to select an octave and one of 12 sampling rates (assuming a 12-tone scale). If the FORM 8SVX doesn't have the right octave, you can decimate or interpolate from the available data.

When it comes to musical instruments, FORM 8SVX is geared for a simple sound driver. Such a driver uses a single table of 12 data rates to reach all notes in all octaves. That's why 8SVX requires each octave of data to have twice as many samples as the next higher octave. If you restrict `samplesPerHiCycle` to a power of two, you can use a predetermined table of data rates.

Optional Text Chunks NAME, (c), AUTH, ANNO

Several text chunks may be included in a FORM 8SVX to keep ancillary information.

The optional property "NAME" names the voice, for instance "tubular bells".

The optional property "(c) " holds a copyright notice for the voice. The chunk ID "(c) " serves as the copyright characters "© ". E.g. a "(c) " chunk containing "1986 Electronic Arts" means "© 1986 Electronic Arts".

The optional property "AUTH" holds the name of the instrument's "author" or "creator".

The chunk types "NAME", "(c) ", and "AUTH" are property chunks. Putting more than one NAME (or other) property in a FORM is redundant. Just the last NAME counts. A property should be shorter than 256 characters. Properties can appear in a PROP 8SVX to share them over a LIST of FORMs 8SVX.

The optional data chunk "ANNO" holds any text annotations typed in by the author.

An ANNO chunk is not a property chunk, so you can put more than one in a FORM 8SVX. You can make ANNO chunks any length up to 2^{31} - 1 characters, but 32767 is a practical limit. Since they're not properties, ANNO chunks don't belong in a PROP 8SVX. That means they can't be shared over a LIST of FORMs 8SVX.

Syntactically, each of these chunks contains an array of 8-bit ASCII characters in the range " " (SP, hex 20) through "~" (tilde, hex 7F), just like a standard "TEXT" chunk. [See "Strings, String Chunks, and String Properties" in "EA IFF 85" Electronic Arts Interchange File Format.] The chunk's `ckSize` field holds the count of characters.

```
#define ID_NAME MakeID('N', 'A', 'M', 'E')
/* NAME chunk contains a CHAR[], the voice's name.              */

#define ID_Copyright MakeID('(', 'c', ')', ' ')
/* "(c) " chunk contains a CHAR[], the FORM's copyright notice.
                                                                */

#define ID_AUTH MakeID('A', 'U', 'T', 'H')
/* AUTH chunk contains a CHAR[], the author's name.             */

#define ID_ANNO MakeID('A', 'N', 'N', 'O')
/* ANNO chunk contains a CHAR[], author's text annotations.     */
```

Remember to store a 0 pad byte after any odd-length chunk.

Optional Data Chunks ATAK and RLSE

The optional data chunks ATAK and RLSE together give a piecewise-linear "envelope" or "amplitude contour". This contour may be used to modulate the sound during playback. It's especially useful for playing musical notes of variable durations. Playback programs may ignore the supplied envelope or substitute another.

```
#define ID_ATAK MakeID('A', 'T', 'A', 'K')
#define ID_RLSE MakeID('R', 'L', 'S', 'E')

typedef struct {
  UWORD duration;          /* segment duration in milliseconds, > 0  */
  Fixed dest;              /* destination volume factor              */
  } EGPoint;
```

```
/* ATAK and RLSE chunks contain an EGPoint[], piecewise-linear envelope.
                                                                        */

/* The envelope defines a function of time returning Fixed values. It's
 * used to scale the nominal volume specified in the Voice8Header.      */
```

To explain the meaning of the ATAK and RLSE chunks, we'll overview the envelope generation algorithm. Start at 0 volume, step through the ATAK contour, then hold at the sustain level (the last ATAK EGPoint's `dest`), and then step through the RLSE contour. Begin the release at the desired note stop time minus the total duration of the release contour (the sum of the RLSE EGPoints' `durations`). The attack contour should be cut short if the note is shorter than the release contour.

The envelope is a piecewise-linear function. The envelope generator interpolates between the EGPoints.

Remember to multiply the envelope function by the nominal voice header `volume` and by any desired note volume.

Figure 1 shows an example envelope. The attack period is described by 4 EGPoints in an ATAK chunk. The release period is described by 4 EGPoints in a RLSE chunk. The sustain period in the middle just holds the final ATAK level until it's time for the release.

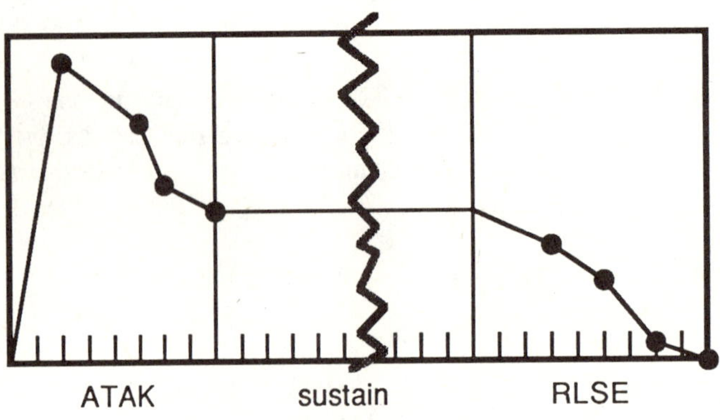

Figure 1. Amplitude contour.

Note: The number of EGPoints in an ATAK or RLSE chunk is its `ckSize / sizeof(EGPoint)`. In RAM, the playback program may terminate the array with a 0 `duration` EGPoint.

Issue: Synthesizers also provide frequency contour (pitch bend), filtering contour (wah-wah), amplitude oscillation (tremolo), frequency oscillation (vibrato), and filtering oscillation (leslie). In the future, we may define optional chunks to encode these modulations. The contours can be encoded in linear segments. The oscillations can be stored as segments with rate and depth parameters.

Data Chunk BODY

The BODY chunk contains the audio data samples.

```
#define ID_BODY MakeID('B', 'O', 'D', 'Y')

typedef character BYTE;        /* 8 bit signed number, -128 through 127. */

/* BODY chunk contains a BYTE[], array of audio data samples.             */
```

The BODY contains data samples grouped by octave. Within each octave are one-shot and repeat portions. Figure 2 depicts this arrangement of samples for an 8SVX where `oneShotHiSamples` = 24, `repeatHiSamples` = 16, `samplesPerHiCycle` = 8, and `ctOctave` = 3. The major divisions are octaves, the intermediate divisions separate the one-shot and repeat portions, and the minor divisions are cycles.

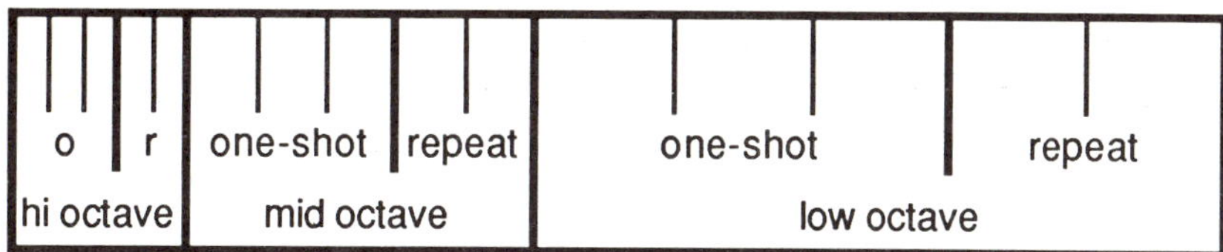

Figure 2. BODY subdivisions.

In general, the BODY has `ctOctave` octaves of data. The highest frequency octave comes first, comprising the fewest samples: `oneShotHiSamples + repeatHiSamples`. Each successive octave contains twice as many samples as the next higher octave but the same number of cycles. The lowest frequency octave comes last with the most samples: $2^{\mathtt{ctOctave-1}}$ `* (oneShotHiSamples + repeatHiSamples).`

The number of samples in the BODY chunk is

$$(2^0 + \ldots + 2^{\mathtt{ctOctave-1}}) * (\mathtt{oneShotHiSamples} + \mathtt{repeatHiSamples})$$

Figure 3, below, looks closer at an example waveform within one octave of a different BODY chunk. In this example, `oneShotHiSamples / samplesPerHiCycle` = 2 cycles and `repeatHiSamples / samplesPerHiCycle` = 1 cycle.

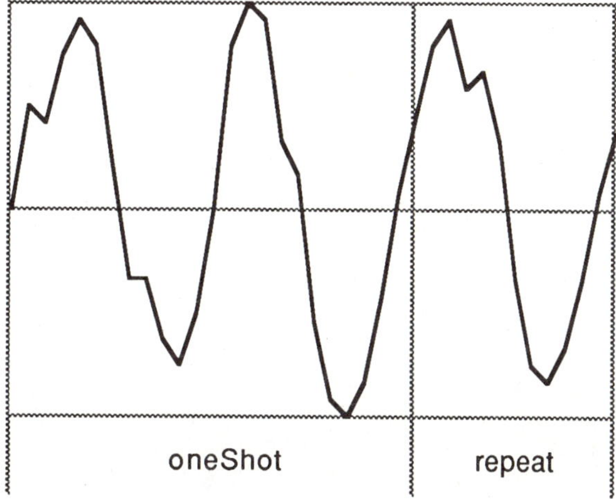

Figure 3. Example waveform.

To avoid playback "clicks" the one-shot part should begin with a small sample value, and flow smoothly into the repeat part. The end of the repeat part should flow smoothly into the beginning of the next repeat part.

If the VHDR field `sCompression` ≠ `sCmpNone`, the BODY chunk is just an array of data bytes to feed through the specified decompresser function. All this stuff about sample sizes, octaves, and repeat parts applies to the decompressed data.

Be sure to follow an odd-length BODY chunk with a 0 pad byte.

Other Chunks

Issue: In the future, we may define an optional chunk containing Fourier series coefficients for a repeating waveform. An editor for this kind of synthesized voice could modify the coefficients and regenerate the waveform.

See the registry document for the latest information.

Appendix A. Quick Reference

Type Definitions

```
#define ID_8SVX MakeID('8', 'S', 'V', 'X')
#define ID_VHDR MakeID('V', 'H', 'D', 'R')

typedef LONG Fixed;           /* A fixed-point value, 16 bits to the left of
                                 the point and 16 to the right. A Fixed is a
                                 number of 2^16ths, i.e. 65536ths.          */
#define Unity 0x10000L        /* Unity = Fixed 1.0 = maximum volume         */

/* sCompression: Choice of compression algorithm.                          */
#define sCmpNone         0    /* not compressed                             */
#define sCmpFibDelta     1    /* Fibonacci-delta encoding (Appendix C)      */
                              /* Can be more kinds in the future.           */

typedef struct {
  ULONG oneShotHiSamples,     /* # samples in the high octave 1-shot part
                                                                            */
        repeatHiSamples,      /* # samples in the high octave repeat part
                                                                            */
        samplesPerHiCycle;    /* # samples/cycle in high octave, else 0    */
  UWORD samplesPerSec;        /* data sampling rate                         */
  UBYTE ctOctave,             /* # octaves of waveforms                     */
        sCompression;         /* data compression technique used            */
  Fixed volume;               /* playback volume from 0 to Unity (full
                               * volume). Map this value into the output
                               * hardware's dynamic range.                  */
  } Voice8Header;

#define ID_NAME MakeID('N', 'A', 'M', 'E')
/* NAME chunk contains a CHAR[], the voice's name.                          */
#define ID_Copyright MakeID('(', 'c', ')', ' ')
/* "(c) " chunk contains a CHAR[], the FORM's copyright notice.             */
#define ID_AUTH MakeID('A', 'U', 'T', 'H')
/* AUTH chunk contains a CHAR[], the author's name.                         */
#define ID_ANNO MakeID('A', 'N', 'N', 'O')
/* ANNO chunk contains a CHAR[], author's text annotations.                 */

#define ID_ATAK MakeID('A', 'T', 'A', 'K')
#define ID_RLSE MakeID('R', 'L', 'S', 'E')

typedef struct {
  UWORD duration;               /* segment duration in milliseconds, > 0   */
  Fixed dest;                   /* destination volume factor                */
  } EGPoint;

/* ATAK and RLSE chunks contain an EGPoint[],piecewise-linear envelope.  */
/* The envelope defines a function of time returning Fixed values. It's
 * used to scale the nominal volume specified in the Voice8Header.         */

#define ID_BODY MakeID('B', 'O', 'D', 'Y')
typedef character BYTE;        /* 8 bit signed number, -128 through 127.  */
/* BODY chunk contains a BYTE[], array of audio data samples.               */
```

8SVX Regular Expression

Here's a regular expression summary of the FORM 8SVX syntax. This could be an IFF file or part of one.

```
8SVX      ::= "FORM" #{  "8SVX" VHDR [NAME] [Copyright] [AUTH] ANNO*
                         [ATAK] [RLSE] BODY }

VHDR      ::= "VHDR" #{ Voice8Header   }
NAME      ::= "NAME" #{ CHAR*          } [0]
Copyright ::= "(c) " #{ CHAR*          } [0]
AUTH      ::= "AUTH" #{ CHAR*          } [0]
ANNO      ::= "ANNO" #{ CHAR*          } [0]

ATAK      ::= "ATAK" #{ EGPoint*       }
RLSE      ::= "RLSE" #{ EGPoint*       }
BODY      ::= "FORM" #{ BYTE*          } [0]
```

The token "#" represents a `ckSize` LONG count of the following {braced} data bytes. E.g. a VHDR's "#" should equal `sizeof(Voice8Header)`. Literal items are shown in "quotes", [square bracket items] are optional, and "*" means 0 or more replications. A sometimes-needed pad byte is shown as "[0]".

Actually, the order of chunks in a FORM 8SVX is not as strict as this regular expression indicates. The property chunks VHDR, NAME, Copyright, and AUTH may actually appear in any order as long as they all precede the BODY chunk. The optional data chunks ANNO, ATAK, and RLSE don't have to precede the BODY chunk. And of course, new kinds of chunks may appear inside a FORM 8SVX in the future.

Appendix B. 8SVX Example

Here's a box diagram for a simple example containing the three octave BODY shown earlier in Figure 2.

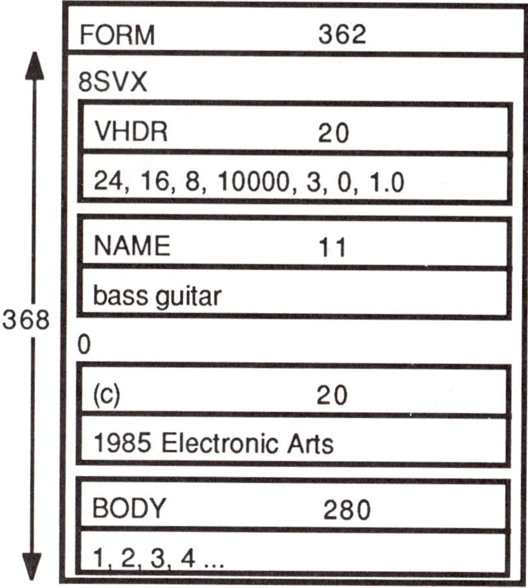

The "0" after the NAME chunk is a pad byte.

Appendix C. Fibonacci Delta Compression

This is Steve Hayes' Fibonacci Delta sound compression technique. It's like the traditional delta encoding but encodes each delta in a mere 4 bits. The compressed data is half the size of the original data plus a 2-byte overhead for the initial value. This much compression introduces some distortion, so try it out and use it with discretion.

To achieve a reasonable slew rate, this algorithm looks up each stored 4-bit value in a table of Fibonacci numbers. So very small deltas are encoded precisely while larger deltas are approximated. When it has to make approximations, the compressor should adjust all the values (forwards and backwards in time) for minimum overall distortion.

Here is the decompressor written in the C programming language.

```
/* Fibonacci delta encoding for sound data. */

BYTE codeToDelta[16] = {-34,-21,-13,-8,-5,-3,-2,-1,0,1,2,3,5,8,13,21};

/* Unpack Fibonacci-delta encoded data from n byte source buffer into 2*n byte
 * dest buffer, given initial data value x. It returns the last data value x
 * so you can call it several times to incrementally decompress the data. */
short D1Unpack(source, n, dest, x)
   BYTE source[], dest[];
   LONG n;
   BYTE x;
   {
   BYTE d;
   LONG i, lim;

   lim = n << 1;
   for (i = 0; i < lim; ++i)
     { /* Decode a data nybble; high nybble then low nybble. */
     d = source[i >> 1];         /* get a pair of nybbles */
     if (i & 1)                  /* select low or high nybble? */
       d &= 0xf;                 /* mask to get the low nybble */
     else
       d >>= 4;                  /* shift to get the high nybble */
     x += codeToDelta[d];        /* add in the decoded delta */
     dest[i] = x;                /* store a 1-byte sample */
     }
   return(x);
   }

/* Unpack Fibonacci-delta encoded data from n byte source buffer into 2*(n-2)
 * byte dest buffer. Source buffer has a pad byte, an 8-bit initial value,
 * followed by n-2 bytes comprising 2*(n-2) 4-bit encoded samples. */
void DUnpack(source, n, dest)
   BYTE source[], dest[];
   LONG n;
   {
   D1Unpack(source + 2, n - 2, dest, source[1]);
   }
```

Additional IFF Documents

These documents include the lattest IFF News, FORM and CHUNK registration, an introduction to ILBM and Amiga ViewModes, design theory of IFF, and descriptions of the EA code modules.

IFF News 11/88

Carolyn Scheppner - CBM

FORMS and Chunks not in the original EA IFF specs

A "Registry" document has been added to the IFF specs. The Registry contains lists of all registered chunks and forms, and notes on additions and changes to the specs of the original EA forms and their chunks.

Form specifications for registered public third-party forms will appear in the Third-Party section of the IFF manual. However, due to the proliferation of application-specific forms, future IFF manuals might only contain forms in use by more than one company's products.

Creating and Registering New FORMs and Chunks

Authors who wish to create new forms or chunks are strongly urged to

- Collaborate with other software authors and CBM on their design
- Choose unique names and reserve them with CBM to avoid conflicts
- Register all new forms and chunks with CBM

Authors should remember special-purpose chunks are usually lost when an IFF FORM is loaded into another application and saved back out. The IFF spec states that IFF writers must not write back chunks that they don't understand because inconsistencies could be created in the FORM.

The current CBM contact for registration of IFF FORMs and chunks is:

Carolyn Scheppner - CATS/IFF
CBM
1200 Wilson Drive
West Chester, PA. 19380 U.S.A.

UUCP: {allegra|rutgers|uunet}!cbmvax!carolyn
BIX: cscheppner (proposals may be posted/discussed in amiga.dev/iff)

3. The embedded ILBM forms in an ANIM do not adhere to the ILBM spec and technically should have had a different chunk ID. They do not contain the required ILBM property BMHD, and instead contain an ANHD and delta information for changing the previous image. This inconsistency occurred because the original ANIM concept of sequential ILBMs was slowly modified, for speed and compactness, into a single ILBM followed by frames containing encoded animation changes. After much discussion with the authors and third parties supporting the ANIM form, it was decided that this inconsistency must remain for now to avoid breaking existing products.

ILBM Problem Areas

Thanks to John Bittner of the Zuma Group for organizing much of this information in our amiga.dev/iff conference on BIX.

1. PageWidth and PageHeight - Overscan or Not ?

   There are two sets of variables in an ILBM which describe the size of the picture. The image dimensions are stored in w and h. The other two variables, pageWidth and pageHeight, have been interpreted in different ways by the various applications which create ILBMs.

   The ILBM spec describes them as follows:

   "The size in pixels of the source "page" (any raster device) is stored in pageWidth and pageHeight, e.g. (320,200) for a low resolution Amiga display. This information might be used to scale an image or to automatically set the display format to suit the image. (The image can be larger than the page.)"

   DPaintII stores the normal Amiga screen size in pageWidth and pageHeight, and the image size (which may be larger) in w and h. Up until now, we have maintained that this is the correct use of these variables because it preserves the normal screen dimensions for programs which wish to clip or scroll larger images in a normal size display. In addition, storage of the normal screen size makes it possible for the correct ViewModes to be determined in the absence of an Amiga ViewModes CAMG chunk.

   However, a number of other applications which save overscan images store the full size of their display ViewPort in the pageWidth and pageHeight variables, and there seems to be a growing consensus that this is the correct use of these variables. This approach is non-Amiga-specific and preserves the artist's intent of the size raster in which the image was meant to be displayed.

   For now, flexible ILBM readers should be prepared to deal with with either alternative, and must parse CAMG chunks for the correct Amiga ViewModes. If a CAMG chunk is not present, ViewModes must be guessed based on the pageWidth and pageHeight. For 1.3 viewmodes, width greater than or equal to 640 can be assumed HIRES, and height greater than or equal to 400 assumed LACE. These assumptions may be incorrect for future viewmodes.

2. The Use and Misuse of the CAMG chunk

   The "optional" ILBM chunk CAMG holds the Amiga ViewModes for displaying the image contained in an ILBM.

   With the current variety of overscan storage methods, and the introduction of HAM and HALFBRITE paint packages, it is extremely important that all Amiga ILBM readers and writers save and parse this chunk. I have actually seen HALFBRITE ILBMs with NO CAMG chunk! I guess the reader programs are supposed to see that it's 6 bitplanes and toss a coin to decide if it's HAM or HALFBRITE. Please store CAMG chunks in all ILBMs and parse them when reading ILBMs.

   When saving and parsing the CAMG chunk, you should be aware that certain ViewMode bits can cause problems for display programs which use the CAMG contents directly for Screen or View modes. The following Amiga Viewmode bits should be masked out when reading or writing a CAMG chunk: SPRITES, VP_HIDE, GENLOCK_AUDIO, and GENLOCK_VIDEO. The reserved high word of the CAMG must currently be written as zero but not assumed to be zero when read.

3. CRNG Color Cycling chunks - Active or Not ?

   DPaintII, by default, usually saves CRNG chunks which contain cycle ranges and are marked as active, regardless of whether a picture is meant to be cycled. This makes it impossible for a cycling display program to reliably identify ILBMs which should not be cycled. Internally, DPaintII interprets a cycle rate <= 36 (RNG_NORATE) to mark a cycle range as non-active.

4. How many colors should a CMAP contain ?

   There seems to be a great deal of variation in the size of the CMAP stored in HAM ILBMs by various applications. Some store only the number of absolute colors used in that particular HAM ILBM. Programs that do this must be really careful about following the IFF spec rules regarding the padding between odd-sized chunks. Some store the maximum number of absolute colors in a HAM display (16). Some store a full palette of 32, and many may store a palette of 64 because the supplied IFF example code generically uses 1<<bitmap->depth when calculating the size CMAP to write. ILBM display programs must be careful to not blindly accept and set the number of color registers provided in a CMAP.

A Word about Compatibility

There have been several incidences of new ILBM graphic products going to market and then being found incompatible with major existing ILBM graphic software. Before releasing any product which saves IFF files of any type, please test the compatibility of your files by loading them into the major existing software products which read and write files of the same type, and try loading the files created by other applications. If you do not have access to a large number of these other products, try to find people who do and arrange file exchanges and compatibility tests. If your product adapts to PAL screen sizes or clock rate (important in audio period calculations), arrange for your product to also be tested on a PAL system.

Be especially careful if you are not using the EA supplied IFF reading, writing, and compression routines. This can sometimes lead to the creation of subtly out-of-spec IFF files which are rejected by products which use the IFF code supplied by EA. Some examples would be odd length chunks not followed by a pad byte or a reader not designed to handle pad bytes. Another would be a badly compressed ILBM. The EA compresser is smart and does not encode a scan line if encoding would result in more bytes. The EA decompressor expects a smartly compressed file, and will return an error if handed an encoded line more than one control byte larger than destination scan line. If you are not using the EA IFF code, please make sure that your code follows all of the rules.

Future IFF

We hope to see a shared run-time iff.library sometime this year, through a coordinated effort between CBM and third-parties. Core IFF reading and writing routines will probably be in an IFF.library, with form-specific routines in separate modules or libraries. An IFF.library would take a lot of the code burden off of applications and would be especially useful for programmers using languages other than C.

```
IFF Registry 10/88
==================

   ( Note - If anyone notices any omissions, please let me know.
     If anyone is writing unregistered FORMs or chunks, please
     register them.    C. Scheppner CBM )

========================================================================
Original EA Filetypes and FORMs
========================================================================

Filetypes:   FORM,PROP,LIST,CAT

------------------------------------------------------------------------
Chunks found in more than one type of FORM:

AUTH, CHRS, (c), ANNO, NAME, TEXT
                        - Described in EA spec, may be found in some ILBMs
                          and other forms.
                          AUTH and (c) should be preserved by read/writers

------------------------------------------------------------------------
FORM ILBM
=========

BMHD - Bitmap header
CMAP - rgb color map
GRAB - Hot spot
DEST - Planepick
SPRT - Sprite info
CAMG - Amiga Viewmodes
CCRT - Cycle info (Graphicraft)
CRNG - Cycle info (DPaint)
BODY - Interleaved bitplane data

DPPV - DPaintII Perspective chunk  (see Third Party Specs)
DGVW - DigiView private chunk in 21-bit SaveRGB ILBMs
BHSM - Photon Paint private (see their manual) (appears first in ILBM)
BHCP - Photon Paint private (see their manual) (in full images)
BHBA - Photon Paint private (see their manual) (in brushes)

also AUTH, (c), CHRS, etc.


ADDENDA

1. CRNG bit 1 defined as Reverse cycling flag

   In DPaintII, Dan Silva has defined bit 1 (next to lowest bit) of
   the CRNG cycling chunk "active" variable as a flag for reverse
   color cycling.  If this bit is set, cycle direction is reversed.
   Unfortunately, DPaintII internally uses rate <= RNG_NORATE (36)
   to mean that a cycle range is inactive, and is not too careful
   about the value saved in the CRNG.active variable.  This makes
   it impossible to determine programatically whether or not a DPaint
   pic should be cycled.

2. CAMG bits require masking

   Under certain circumstances, unwanted application-specific ViewMode
   bits are saved to or loaded from a CAMG chunk.  The SPRITES, VP_HIDE,
   GENLOCK_AUDIO, and GENLOCK_VIDEO flags should be masked out of the
   camg.ViewModes when saving or loading a CAMG chunk.  The UWORD
   of masked Amiga viewmodes is stored in the low word of CAMG.Viewmodes.
   The high word of CAMG.Viewmodes is reserved by Commodore and must
   currently be written as zeros, but not assumed to be zeros when read.
```



```
   #include <graphics/view.h>
   #define BADFLAGS  (SPRITES|VP_HIDE|GENLOCK_AUDIO|GENLOCK_VIDEO)
   #define FLAGMASK  (~BADFLAGS)
   #define CAMGMASK  (FLAGMASK & 0x0000FFFFL)

   camg.ViewModes = viewport->Modes & CAMGMASK;


3. ILBMs in ANIM are non-standard

   The embedded ILBM forms in an ANIM do not adhere to the ILBM spec
   and technically should have had a different chunk ID.  They do
   not contain the required ILBM property BMHD, and instead contain
   an ANHD and delta information for changing the previous image.
   This inconsistency occurred because the original ANIM concept of
   sequential ILBMs was slowly modified, for speed and compactness,
   into a single ILBM followed by frames containing encoded animation
   changes.  After much discussion with the authors and third parties
   supporting the ANIM form, it was decided that this inconsistency
   must remain for now to avoid breaking existing products.


------------------------------------------------------------------------
FORM FTXT
=========
FONS - Font specification
CHRS - Ascii characters and ISO/ANSII standard control sequences

also AUTH, (c), CHRS, etc.

------------------------------------------------------------------------
FORM SMUS
=========

SHDR - Score header
NAME - Name of score
INS1 - Instrument
TRAK - Data chunk for one track

also AUTH, (c), NAME, ANNO, CHRS, etc.

ADDENDA

   EA has reserved two new sEvents for SMUS since the IFF release which
   appears in the Addison-Wesley manuals:

         SID Value                    Next Data Byte
         =========                    ==============
   #define SID_Clef    135          0=treble, 1=bass, 2=alto, 3=tenor
   #define SID_Tempo   136          beats per second (0-255)


------------------------------------------------------------------------
FORM 8SVX
=========

VHDR - Voice header
ATAK - Attack info
RLSE - Release info
BODY - Data samples grouped by octave (may be Fibonacci-delta encoded)

CHAN - Stereo channel chunk (Gold Disk - see third party specs)
PAN  - Stereo pan chunk (Gold Disk - see third party specs)

also AUTH, (c), NAME, ANNO, etc.


========================================================================
Public Registered Third Party FORMs
```

```
==========================================================================
FORM ACBM
=========
Amiga Contiguous Bitmap (used in AmigaBasic Demos)
Contains normal ILBM chunks except:

ABIT replaces BODY (ABIT is uncompressed contiguous bitplane data)

--------------------------------------------------------------------------
FORM AIFF
=========
Apple Audio IFF Form for 1 to 32-bit audio samples.  By Steve Milne, Apple
I posted a general description in BIX amiga.dev/iff.
I don't plan to add it to our Amiga IFF manual.

--------------------------------------------------------------------------
FORM ANBM
=========
Animated bitmap FORM, used in Deluxe Video by Posehn & Case for EA
Should appear in 1988 IFF manual.

--------------------------------------------------------------------------
FORM ANIM
=========
Cel Animation FORM used by Videoscape-3D (Aegis)

ANHD
DLTA

ANIM contains embedded "ILBM"'s, all but first not true ILBM's but rather
containing ANHD (Anim header) and DLTA (changes to create next cell).

Latest ANIM spec is in the May/June 88 AmigaMail, and is also posted on
BIX in amiga.dev/docs.  Spec in August 87 IFF manual is outdated.
The new spec will appear in 1988 IFF manual.

--------------------------------------------------------------------------
FORM BANK
=========
SoundQuest Editor/Librarian format for MIDI system-exclusive data dump.
Form spec has not yet been provided.

--------------------------------------------------------------------------
FORM HEAD
=========
Idea processor FORM used by Flow (New Horizons Software)
Described in current IFF manual.

NEST
TEXT
FSCC

--------------------------------------------------------------------------
FORM MIDI
=========
Expecting spec soon - watch BIX amiga.dev/iff
Circum Design

--------------------------------------------------------------------------
FORM PGTB
=========
ProGram TraceBack diagnostic dump image - John Toebes, S.A.S.
Presented at Devcon.  Should appear in 1988 IFF manual.

--------------------------------------------------------------------------
FORM SYTH
=========
SoundQuest Master Librarian format for MIDI system-exclusive driver.
```



```
Form spec has not yet been provided.

--------------------------------------------------------------------------
FORM WORD
=========
Word processing FORM used by Prowrite (New Horizons Software)
See spec in current IFF manual.

FONT
COLR
DOC
HEAD
FOOT
PCTS
PARA
TABS
PAGE
TEXT
FSCC
PINF

==========================================================================
Private Registered Third Party FORMs
==========================================================================
FORM C100
=========
Cloanto Italia (private word processing form)
          Chunks C1C0, C1K0, C1F0, C1U0, C1K1
          C1C0 and C1K0 used in C100 forms
          C1F0 and C1U0 used in C100 and FTXT forms
          Also SGR9    SGR29  (label start and end)

--------------------------------------------------------------------------
FORM PDEF
=========
Deluxe Print page definition (EA)

--------------------------------------------------------------------------
FORM RGB4
=========
For 4 bit R G B pixel information

   COMP (chunk containing compression table for the FORM)

   The RGB4 FORM contains a BMHD which will specify 2 as its Compression.
   BMHD compression value 2 has been reserved for this algorithm
   which is a modified Huffman encoding.

--------------------------------------------------------------------------
FORM SHAK
=========
Used by Shakespeare, Infinity Software (private)
Contains embedded ILBMs

--------------------------------------------------------------------------
FORM VDEO
=========
Deluxe Video (EA)

==========================================================================
Proposed Third Party FORMs
==========================================================================
FORM SAMP
```

```
=========
Sound sample FORM proposed by "dissidents" (BIX: jfiore)
Will be posted there if I get author's permission.
Designed to work cohesively with the MIDI standard.

-------------------------------------------------------------------------

FORM TDDD
=========
For ray-tracing program Turbo Silver by Impulse
Will probably be posted on BIX when finalized.


=========================================================================
Unregistered Third Party FORMs
=========================================================================
FORM SC3D
=========
Sculpt-3D


=========================================================================
Additional Reserved Names
=========================================================================

Other IDs reserved in original EA IFF 85 spec:

1. TEXT - a chunk containing plain unformatted ASCII text
2. FNTR - raster font
3. FNTV - vector font
4. GSCR - general-use musical score
5. PICS - Macintosh picture
6. PLBM - obsolete
7. USCR - Uhuru Sound Software musical score
8. UVOX - Uhuru Sound Software Macintosh voice
9. Property IDs: OPGM, OCPU, OCMP, OSN, UNAM


Temporarily reserved by CBM or third parties:

1. CAT  CLIP - to hold various representations of data clipped to clipboard
2. FORM ARC  - possible archiving form discussed on Usenet a while back
3. ATXT, PTXT - temporarily reserved
4. ILBM chunks 3DCM, 3DPA  - temporarily reserved
5. RGBX, CDAT - temporarily reserved
6. FORM MSMP, chunks MSHD, SSHD, SSLP - temporarily reserved
7. FORM FIGR - temporarily reserved
8. LIST MOVI - reserved
9. Chunk name END  - reserved by CBM for future stream end indication
```

Intro to IFF Amiga ILBM Files and Amiga Viewmodes

The IFF (Interchange File Format) for graphic images on the Amiga is called FORM ILBM (InterLeaved BitMap). It follows a standard parsable IFF format.

Sample hex dump of beginning of an ILBM:

Important note! You can NOT ever depend on any particular ILBM chunk being at any particular offset into the file! IFF files are composed, in their simplest form, of chunks within a FORM. Each chunk starts starts with a 4-letter chunkID, followed by a 32-bit length of the rest of the chunk. You PARSE IFF files, skipping past unneeded or unknown chunks by seeking their length (+1 if odd length) to the next 4-letter chunkID.

```
0000: 464F524D 00016418 494C424D 424D4844    FORM..d.ILBMBMHD
0010: 00000014 01400190 00000000 06000100    .....@..........
0020: 00000A0B 01400190 43414D47 00000004    .....@..CAMG....
0030: 00000804 434D4150 00000030 001000E0    ....CMAP...0....
0040: E0E00000 20000050 30303050 50500030    .... ..P000PPP.0
0050: 90805040 70707010 60E02060 E06080D0    ..P@ppp.`. `.`..
0060: A0A0A0A0 90E0C0C0 C0D0A0E0 424F4459    ............BODY
0070: 000163AC F8000F80 148A5544 2ABDEFFF    ..c.......UD*...   etc.
```

Interpretation:

```
       'F O R M' length  'I L B M''B M H D'<-start of BitMapHeader chunk
0000: 464F524D 00016418 494C424D 424D4844    FORM..d.ILBMBMHD
        length  WideHigh XorgYorg PlMkCoPd <- Planes Mask Compressior Pad

0010: 00000014 01400190 00000000 06000100    .....@..........
      TranAspt PagwPagh 'C A M G' length   <- start of C-AMiGa View modes chunk

0020: 00000A0B 01400190 43414D47 00000004    .....@..CAMG....
      Viewmode 'C M A P' length    R g b R <- Viewmode 800=HAM | 4=LACE

0030: 00000804 434D4150 00000030 001000E0    ....CMAP...0....

        g b R g  b R g b  R g b R  g b R g <- Rgb's are for reg0 thru regN
0040: E0E00000 20000050 30303050 50500030    .... ..P000PPP.0

        b R g b  R g b R  g b R g  b R g b
0050: 90805040 70707010 60E02060 E06080D0    ..P@ppp.`. `.`..

        R g b R  g b R g  b R g b 'B O D Y'
0060: A0A0A0A0 90E0C0C0 C0D0A000 424F4459    ............BODY

        length   start of body data        <- Compacted (Compression=1 above)
0070: 000163AC F8000F80 148A5544 2ABDEFFF    ..c.......UD*...
0080: FFBFF800 0F7FF7FC FF04F85A 77AD5DFE    ..........Zw.].  etc.
```

Notes on CAMG Viewmodes: HIRES=0x8000 LACE=0x4 HAM=0x800 HALFBRITE=0x80

Interpreting ILBMs

ILBM is a fairly simple IFF FORM. All you really need to deal with to extract the image are the following chunks:

(Note - Also watch for AUTH Author chunks and (c) Copyright chunks and preserve any copyright information if you rewrite the ILBM)

```
   BMHD - info about the size, depth, compaction method
          (See interpreted hex dump above)
```



```
   CAMG - optional Amiga viewmodes chunk
          Most HAM and HALFBRITE ILBMs should have this chunk.  If no
          CAMG chunk is present, and image is 6 planes deep, assume
          HAM and you'll probably be right.  Some Amiga viewmodes
          flags are HIRES=0x8000, LACE=0x4, HAM=0x800, HALFBRITE=0x80.

   CMAP - RGB values for color registers 0 to n
          (each component left justified in a byte)

   BODY - The pixel data, stored in an interleaved fashion as follows:
          (each line individually compacted if BMHD Compression = 1)
             plane 0 scan line 0
             plane 1 scan line 0
             plane 2 scan line 0
             ...
             plane n scan line 0
             plane 0 scan line 1
             plane 1 scan line 1
             etc.
```

Body Compression

The BODY contains pixel data for the image. Width, Height, and depth (Planes) is specified in the BMHD.

If the BMHD Compression byte is 0, then the scan line data is not compressed.
If Compression=1, then each scan line is individually compressed as follows:

More than 2 bytes the same stored as BYTE code value n from -1 to -127 followed by byte to be repeated (-n) + 1 times.
Varied bytes stored as BYTE code n from 0 to 127 followed by n+1 bytes of data.
The byte code -128 is a NOP.

Interpreting the Scan Line Data:

If the ILBM is not HAM or HALFBRITE, then after parsing and uncompacting if necessary, you will have N planes of pixel data. Color register used for each pixel is specified by looking at each pixel thru the planes. IE - if you have 5 planes, and the bit for a particular pixel is set in planes 0 and 3:

```
      PLANE     4 3 2 1 0
      PIXEL     0 1 0 0 1
```

then that pixel uses color register binary 01001 = 9

The RGB value for each color register is stored in the CMAP chunk of the ILBM, starting with register 0, with each register's RGB value stored as one byte of R, one byte G, and one byte of B, with each component left justified in the byte. (ie. Amiga R, G, and B components are each stored in the high nibble of a byte)

BUT - if the picture is HAM or HALFBRITE, it is interpreted differently.

Hopefully, if the picture is HAM or HALFBRITE, the package that saved it properly saved a CAMG chunk (look at a hex dump of your file with ascii interpretation - you will see the chunks - they all start with a 4-ascii-char chunk ID). If the picture is 6 planes deep and has no CAMG chunk, it is probably HAM. If you see a CAMG chunk, the "CAMG" is followed by the 32-bit chunk length, and then the 32-bit Amiga Viewmode flags.

HAM pics will have the 0x800 bit set in CAMG chunk ViewModes.
HALBRITE pics will have the 0x80 bit set.

To transport a HAM or HALFBRITE picture to another machine, you must understand how HAM and HALFBRITE work on the Amiga.

How Amiga HAM mode works:
=========================

Amiga HAM (Hold and Modify) mode lets the Amiga display all 4096 RGB values. In HAM mode, the bits in the two last planes describe an R G or B modification to the color of the previous pixel on the line to create the color of the current pixel. So a 6-plane HAM picture has 4 planes for specifying absolute color pixels giving up to 16 absolute colors which would be specified in the ILBM CMAP chunk. The bits in the last two planes are color modification bits which cause the Amiga, in HAM mode, to take the RGB value of the previous pixel (Hold and), substitute the 4 bits in planes 0-3 for the previous color's R G or B component (Modify) and display the result for the current pixel. If the first pixel of a scan line is a modification pixel, it modifies the RGB value of the border color (register 0). The color modification bits in the last two planes (planes 4 and 5) are interpreted as follows:

```
   00 - no modification.  Use planes 0-3 as normal color register index
   10 - hold previous, replacing Blue component with bits from planes 0-3
   01 - hold previous, replacing Red component with bits from planes 0-3
   11 - hold previous. replacing Green component with bits from planes 0-3
```

How Amiga HALFBRITE mode works:
===============================

This one is simpler. In HALFBRITE mode, the Amiga interprets the bit in the last plane as HALFBRITE modification. The bits in the other planes are treated as normal color register numbers (RGB values for each color register is specified in the CMAP chunk). If the bit in the last plane is set (1), then that pixel is displayed at half brightness. This can provide up to 64 absolute colors.

Other Notes:
============

Amiga ILBMs images must be a even number of bytes wide. Smaller images (such as brushes) are padded to an even byte width.

ILBMs created with Electronic Arts IBM and Amiga "DPaintII" packages are compatible (though you may have to use a '.lbm' filename extension on an IBM). The ILBM graphic files may be transferred between the machines (or between the Amiga and IBM sides your Amiga if you have a CBM Bridgeboard card installed) and loaded into either package.

BACKGROUND ON THE EXAMPLE IFF SOURCE CODE

Jerry Morrison, 1/30/86

The example IFF code is written using a programming style and techniques that may be unfamiliar to you. So here's a tutorial on "call-back procedures","enumerators", "interfaces", and "sub-classed structures". I recommend these programming practices independently of IFF software.

DEFINITIONS: "CLIENT" VS. "USER"

First, some definitions. The word "user" is reserved for a human user of a software package. That's you and me.

A "client" of a software package, on the other hand, is a piece of software that uses that software package. A program that calls operating system routines such as "OpenFile" is a client of that operating system.

CALL-BACK PROCEDURES

Consider an operating system subroutine "ListDir" that lists the files in a disk directory. It might allow you to list just the filenames matching a pattern like "a*.text". Maybe you can ask it to list just the files created since yesterday ... or those longer than 2000 bytes. ListDir is a fancy, general-purpose directory subroutine that lets you pass in a number of arguments to filter the listing.

A C definition might look like:

```
   void ListDir(directory, namePattern, minSize, maxSize, minDate ...); ... {
      for (each file in the directory)
         if ( PatternMatch(namePattern, filename)
              &&  fileSize >= minSize
              &&  fileSize <= maxSize
              &&  fileDate >= minDate
              && ... )
            printf("%s\n", filename);  /* probably fancier than this... */
      }
```

and your call to it:

```
   ListDir(myDir, "a*.text", 0, maxFileSize, date1_1_1900, ...);
```

When you think about it, these filtering arguments make up a special-purpose "file filtering language". The person who designed this subroutine "ListDir" might be pretty pleased with his accomplishment. But in practice he can never put in enough features into this special-purpose language to satisfy everyone. (You say you need to list just the files currently open?) And he may have provided a lot of functionality that is rarely needed. Is this filtering language what he should spending his time designing, writing, and debugging?

A much better technique is to use a "call-back procedure". The concept is simple: instead of all those filter arguments to ListDir, you pass it a pointer to a "filter procedure". ListDir simply calls your procedure (via the pointer) to do the filtering, once per file. It passes each filename to your "filter proc", which returns "TRUE" to include that file in the listing or "FALSE" to skip it.

```
   typedef BOOL FilterProc();  /* FilterProc: a BOOL procedure */

   void ListDir(directory, filterProc);
         Directory directory;  FilterProc *filterProc;  {
      for (each file in the directory)
         if ( (*filterProc)(filename) )  printf("%s\n", filename);
      }
```

and your code:

```
   BOOL MyFilterProc(filename)  STRING filename;  {
      return(PatternMatch("a*.text", filename));
      }

      ...
      ListDir(myDir, MyFilterProc);
```

This technique has many advantages. It gives unlimited flexibility to ListProc. It means you can use a general-purpose programming language instead of learning a special-purpose filtering language. It's more efficient to call a compiled subroutine than to "interpret" the filtering parameters. And it means you can do anything you want in a filter proc, from selecting files on the basis of numerology to copying files to backup tape.

In practice, ListDir would have data about each file readily available. So it should pass this data to the filter proc to save time.

As Alan Kay once said, "Simple things should be simple and complex things should be possible."

STANDARD CALL-BACK PROCEDURE

I could extend ListDir to accept a NULL FilterProc pointer to mean "list all files". More likely, I'd supply a standard call-back procedure "FilterTRUE" that always returns TRUE. Then ListDir(directory, FilterTRUE) will list all files with no special test for filterProc == NULL.

```
   BOOL FilterTRUE(filename)  STRING filename;  {
      return(TRUE);
      }
```

ENUMERATORS

Let's take our ListDir example one step further. Rather than have ListDir print the selected filenames, have it JUST call your custom proc for every file. Let your custom proc print the filenames, maybe in your own personal format. Or maybe have it quietly backup new files, or ask the user which ones to delete, or ...

```
   typedef CallBackProc(/* filename */);

   void ListDir(directory, callBackProc);
         Directory directory;  CallBackProc *callBackProc;  {
      for (each file in the directory)
         (*callBackProc)(filename);
      }
```

and your code:

```
   void MyProc(filename)  STRING filename;  {
      if ( PatternMatch("a*.text", filename) )
         printf("%s\n", filename);
      }

      ...
      ListDir(myDir, MyProc);
```

Now we're talking about a full-blown "enumerator". The procedure "ListDir" is said to "enumerate" all the files in a directory. It "applies" your call-back procedure to each file. The enumerator scans the directory and your call-back procedure processes the files. It deals with the internal directory details and you deal with the printout. A nice separation of concerns.

ListDir should come with a standard call-back procedure "PrintFilename" that lists the filename. By simply passing PrintFilename to ListDir, you can print a directory. By writing a call-back procedure that selectively calls the PrintFilename, you can filter the listing.

```
   void PrintFilename(filename)  STRING filename;  {
      printf("%s\n", filename);
      }
```

ENUMERATION CONTROL

A simple enhancement is to empower the call-back procedure to stop the enumeration early. That's easy. Have it return "TRUE" to stop. This is very handy, for example, to quit when you find what you're looking for. Let's expand this boolean "continue/stop" result into an integer error code.

```
   #define OKAY   0
   #define DONE  -1
   typedef int CallBackProc(/* filename */);

   int ListDir(directory, callBackProc);
         Directory directory;  CallBackProc *callBackProc;  {
      int result = OKAY;
      for (each file in the directory) while (result == OKAY)
         result = (*callBackProc)(filename);
      return(result);
      }
```

IFF FILE ENUMERATOR

Now we'll relate these techniques to the example IFF code. I'm assuming that you've read "EA IFF 85" Standard for Interchange Format Files. That memo is available from Commodore as part of their Amiga documentation. Also ask Commodore for "ILBM" IFF Interleaved Bitmap and the example IFF source code.

Two things make IFF files very flexible for lots of interchange between programs. First, file formats are independent of RAM formats. That means you have to do some conversion when you read and write IFF files. Second, the contents are stored in chunks according to global rules. That means you have to parse the file, i.e. scan it and react to what's actually there.

In the example IFF files IFF.H and IFFR.C, the routines ReadIFF, ReadIList, & ReadICat are enumeration procedures. ReadIFF scans an IFF file, enumerating all the "FORM", "LIST", "PROP", and "CAT" chunks encountered. ReadIList & ReadICat enumerate all the chunks in a LIST and CAT, respectively.

A ClientFrame record is a bundle of pointers to 4 "call-back procedures" getList, getProp, getForm, and getCat. These 4 procedures are called by ReadIFF, ReadIList, and ReadICat when the 4 kinds of IFF "groups" are encountered: "LIST", "PROP", "FORM", or "CAT".

These 3 enumerator procedures and 4 client procedures together make up a reader for IFF files--a very simple recursive descent parser. If you want to learn more about parsing, a real good place to look is the new edition "dragon book" by Aho, Ullman, and Sethi.

The procedure "SkipGroup" is just a default call-back procedure.

The "IFFP" values IFF_OKAY through BAD_IFF are the error codes used by the IFF enumerators. We use the type "IFFP" to declare variables (and procedure results) that hold such values. The code "IFF_OKAY" means "AOK; keep enumerating". The other values mean "stop" for one reason or other. "IFF_DONE" means "we're all done", while "END_MARK" means "we hit the end at this nesting level".

CALL-BACK PROCEDURE STATE

ListDir is an enumerator with some internal state--it internally remembers its place in the directory. It loops over the directory, calling the client proc once per file. That's fine for some cases and less convenient for others. Consider this example that just lists the first 10 files:

```
   int count;

   int PrintFirst10(filename)  STRING filename;  {
      if (++count > 10)  return(DONE);
      printf("%s\n", filename);
      return(OKAY);
      }

   void DoIt();  {
      ...
      count = 0;
      ListDir(myDir, PrintFirst10);
      ...
      }
```

Inherently, the client's code has to be split into code that calls the enumerator and a call-back procedure. Thus any communication between the two must be via global variables. In this trivial example, the global "count" saves state data between calls to PrintFirst10. Often, it's much more complex. But globals won't work if you need reenterent or recursive code. We really want "count" to be a local variable of DoIt.

Fixing this in Pascal is easy: Define PrintFirst10 as a nested procedure within DoIt so it can access DoIt's local variables. The manual analog in C is to redefine the enumerator to pass a raw "client data pointer" straight through to the call-back procedure. The two client procedures then communicate through the "client data pointer". DoIt would call ListDir(myDir, PrintFirst10, &count) which calls PrintFirst10(filename, &count).

```
   #define OKAY   0
   #define DONE  -1
   typedef int CallBackProc(/* filename, clientData */);

   int ListDir(directory, callBackProc, clientData);
         Directory directory; CallBackProc *callBackProc; BYTE *clientData; {
      int result = OKAY;
      for (each file in the directory) while (result == OKAY)
         result = (*callBackProc)(filename, clientData);
      return(result);
      }
```

In general, an enumerator is sometimes inconvenient because it takes over control. Think about this: How could you enumerate two directories in parallel and copy the newer files from one directory to the other?

STATELESS ENUMERATOR

An alternate form without this disadvantage is the "stateless enumerator".

In a stateless enumerator, it's up to the client to keep its place in the enumeration. Call a procedure like GetNextFilename each time around the loop.

```
      STRING curFilename = NULL;
      int count = 0;
```



```
      do {
         if (++count > 10)  break;  /* stop after 10 files */
         curFilename = GetNextFilename(directory, curFilename);
         if (curFilename == NULL)  break;  /* stop at end of directory */
         printf("%s\n", filename);
         }
```

The stateless enumerator is sometimes better because it puts the client in control. The above example shows how easy it is to keep state information between iterations and to stop the enumeration easy. It's also easy to do things like list two directories in parallel.

IFF CHUNK ENUMERATOR

The following IFFR.C routines make up a stateless IFF chunk enumerator: OpenRIFF, OpenRGroup, GetChunkHdr and CloseRGroup. Together with IFFReadBytes, we have a complete layer of "chunk reader" subroutines. These subroutines are built upon the file stream package in the local system library.

GetChunkHdr is the "get next" procedure you call to get the next IFF chunk. (GetFChunkHdr, GetF1ChunkHdr, and GetPChunkHdr are subroutines that call GetChunkHdr and do a little extra work.) OpenRIFF and OpenRGroup do the initialization needed before you can call GetChunkHdr. CloseRGroup does the cleanup work.

You supply a "GroupContext" pointer each time you call one of these "chunk reader" procedures. The enumeration state is kept in a GroupContext record which the *client* must allocate but the *enumerator* routines initialize and maintain. (The client may peek into a GroupContext but should never modify it directly.) The two procedures OpenRIFF and OpenRGroup initialize the GroupContext record. This "opens a context" for reading chunks. The procedure CloseRGroup cleans up when you're done with a GroupContext.

Here's the essense of an IFF scanner program. It handles whatever it finds, unlike inflexible file readers that demand conformance to a rigid file format. [Note: This code doesn't check for errors or end-of-context.]

```
   OpenRGroup(..., context);  /* initialize */
   do {
      id = GetChunkHdr(context);  /* get the next chunk's ID */
      switch (id)  {
         case AAAA: {read in an AAAA chunk; break};
         case BBBB: {read in a BBBB chunk; break};
         ...
         default: {};  /* just ignore unrecognized chunks */
         }
   CloseRGroup(context);  /* cleanup */
```

GetChunkHdr reads the next chunk header and returns its chunk ID. You then dispatch on the chunk ID, that is, switch to a different piece of code for each type of chunk. If you don't recognize the chunk ID, just keep looping.

In each "case:" statement, call IFFReadBytes one or more times to read the chunk's contents. The readin work you do here depends on the chunk type and what you need in RAM. Since GetChunkHdr automatically skips to the start of the next chunk, it doesn't matter if you don't read all the data bytes.

GetChunkHdr does some other things for you automatically. When it reads a "group" chunk header (a chunk of type "FORM", "LIST", "CAT ", or "PROP") it automatically reads the subtype ID. That makes it very convenient to just open the contents of the group chunk as a group context and read the nested chunks. See the example source program ShowILBM for more about the relationship between a "GroupContext" and a "ClientFrame".

Like all the example IFF code, GetChunkHdr checks for errors. To handle GetChunkHdr errors, we just add cases to the switch statment. To stop at end-of-context or an error in a switch case, we add a "while" clause at the end of the "do" statement.

CLIENTS, INTERFACES, AND IMPLEMENTORS

In the ListDir example, you can see that a lot of flexibility comes from decoupling the task of tracing through the directory's data structures from the task of filtering files and printing filenames. This is called modularity, or simply, dividing a program into parts.

Choosing good module boundaries is an art. It has a big impact on a programmer's ability to coope with lrge programs. Good modularity makes programs much easier to understand and modify. But this topic would be another whole tutorial in itself.

Just be aware that the example IFF program is divided into various "modules", each of which implements a different part of the bigger picture. One such module is the low level IFF reader/writer. It's split into two files IFFR.C and IFFW.C. Other such modules are the run encoder/decoder Packer.C and UnPacker.C, and ILBM read/write subroutines ILBMR.C and ILBMW.C.

You'll notice that all three of these "modules" are split into a pair of files. That's because most linkers aren't fancy enough to automatically eliminate unused subroutines, e.g. for a program like ShowILBM that reads but doesn't need the writer code. Also, a program like DeluxePaint wants read and write code in separate overlays. So think of each pair as a single module.

What I want to point out is the basic structure. Each "module" has an "interface" file (a .H file) that separates the "implementor" .C file(s) from the "client" programs. This interface is very important, in fact, more important than the code details inside the .C files. The interfaces for the above-mentioned modules are called IFF.H, Packer.H, and ILBM.H.

Everything about a layer of software that the clients need to know belongs in its interface: constant and type definitions, extern declarations for the procedures, and comments. The comments detail the purpose of the module and each procedure, the procedure arguments, side effects, results, and error codes, etc. Nothing the clients don't need to know belongs in its interface: internal implementation details that might change.

Thus, the modularization and other important design information is collected and documented in these interface files. So if you want to understand what a module does and how to use it, READ ITS INTERFACE. Don't dive headfirst into the implementation.

Two of the original articles on modular programming are

D.L. Parnas, "On the Criteria To Be Used in Decomposing Systems into Modules". Communications of the ACM 15, 12 (Dec. '72), pp 1053-1058.

B. Liskov and S. Zilles, "Programming with Abstract Data Types". Proceedings ACM SIGPLAN Conference on Very High-Level Languages. SIGPLAN Notices 9, 4 (April '74), pp 50-59.

SUBCLASSED STRUCTURES

One more technique. In programming, a general-purpose module may define a structure like ClientFrame. Along comes a more special-purpose program that needs a structure like it but with specialized fields added on. The answer is to build a larger structure whose first field is the earlier structure. This is called "subclassing" a structure, a term that comes from subclassing in Smalltalk.

In the Macintosh(tm) toolbox, the record GrafPort is subclassed to produce the record WindowRecord, which is subclassed again to produce a DialogWindow record.

Similarly in the example IFF program ShowILBM, the structure ClientFrame is subclassed to produce the more specialized structure ILBMFrame.

```
typedef struct {
   ClientFrame clientFrame;
   UBYTE foundBMHD;
   ...
   } ILBMFrame;
```

Since the first field of an ILBMFrame is a ClientFrame, the ShowILBM procedure ReadPicture can coerce a *ClientFrame pointer to an *ILBMFrame pointer to pass it to ReadIFF (which knows nothing about ILBMFrame). When ReadIFF calls back ShowILBM's getForm procedure, we can coerce it back to an *ILBMFrame pointer. Take a look at ShowILBM to see how this works.

Overview of EA IFF example source files

This source code is distributed as public domain software. Use it to help write robust IFF-compatible programs.

Caveat: Electronic Arts developed this code, and is releasing it to promote the success of the Amiga. EA does not have the resources to supply support for this code. For support, Amiga software developers contact Commodore directly.

1. Description of the EA-provided sources and include files

```
        COMPILER.H      Portability file to isolate compiler idiosyncrasies.

        INTUALL .H      A super-include file for Amiga include files.

        REMALLOC.H      Header for RemAlloc subroutines.
        REMALLOC.C      Memory ALLOCators which REMember the size allocated,
                        for simpler freeing.

        GIO     .H      Header file for Generic I/O speed up package.
        GIO     .C      Generic I/O speed up routines (a disk cache).
        GIOCALL .C      Outline of example GIO client.
                        To turn on the GIO package, change a switch in GIO.H,
                        add GIO.O to the linker control file, and recompile.

        IFF     .H      Header file for general IFF read/write support.
        IFFR    .C      IFF reader support routines.
        IFFW    .C      IFF writer support routines.
                        These routines do a lot of the work for reading and
                        writing IFF files robustly. The reader and writer are
                        separate since some programs don't need both.

        IFFCHECK.C      IFF checker utility source (very handy for debugging).
                        The IFF checker scans an IFF file, checks it for
                        syntax errors, and prints an outline of its contents.

        PACKER  .H      Header for byte run encoder (compressor) subroutines.
        PACKER  .C      Run encoder subroutines.
        UNPACKER.C      Run decoder subroutines. This run encoder/decoder is
                        used for ILBM raster images.

        ILBM    .H      Header for ILBM (raster image file) subroutines.
        ILBMR   .C      ILBM reader support routines. Uses IFFR.
        ILBMW   .C      ILBM writer support routines. Uses IFFW.

        READPICT.H      Header for ReadPicture subroutines.
        READPICT.C      ReadPicture subroutines read an ILBM file into an
                        Amiga BitMap in RAM. Uses ILBMR and IFFR.

        SHOWILBM.C      Example program that reads and displays an ILBM file.

        PUTPICT .H      Header for PutPict subroutines.
        PUTPICT .C      PutPict subroutines write an Amiga BitMap from RAM
                        to an ILBM file. Uses ILBMW and IFFW.

        RAW2ILBM.C      Example program that reads a "raw" raster image file
                        and writes the image as an ILBM file.

        ILBM2Raw.C      Example program that reads an image as an ILBM file
                        and writes the image as a "raw" raster image file.

        BMPrintC.C      Subroutine that actually does the text dump.
        ILBMDump.C      Example program that reads an image as an ILBM file
                        and writes the image as a text file containing C data
                        initialization statements for either a BOB or a
                        Sprite.
```


2. Compiler idiosyncracies.

This source code was built for the Lattice 68000 Amiga C cross-compiler, and the Metacomco ALink linker. Some of the IFF source code assumes that the compiler will support function protyping: the ability to typecheck procedure arguments (templates). Believe me, typechecking is useful! The more bugs I find at compile time, the less I have to find at run time.

The programmer asks for this typechecking via an "extern" statement like this:

```
        extern IFFP Seek(BPTR, LONG, LONG);
        typedef IFFP ClientProc(struct _GroupContext *);
```

Unfortunately, this chokes some C compilers. If you have such a compiler, you have to comment out the stuff in parentheses. The above two examples become:

```
        extern IFFP Seek(/* BPTR, LONG, LONG */);
        typedef IFFP ClientProc(/* struct _GroupContext * */);
```

Don't remove the parentheses!

The header file COMPILER.H defines macros to isolate the compiler dependencies. The macro FDwAT ("function definitions with argument types") switches on/off the argument type declarations in the header files in this directory.

3. RemAlloc subroutines.

The "REMembering ALLOCator" is a useful little subroutine package included here. It saves you from having to remember the size of each node you allocate. (Why doesn't the Amiga allocator do this?)

4. Optional buffered file I/O package GIO.

Amiga file I/O can be greatly sped up by use of a RAM buffer. So we now have a layer of software that provides optional buffering. Some compilers may also have such a layer, in which case ignore this one. The "option" is controlled by changing a "#define" inside the header file GIO.H, adding GIO.O to your link file, recompiling, and recompiling. When turned off, this layer becomes just a layer of macro calls between the IFFR and IFFW modules and the AmigaDOS routines they call.

This RAM buffer speeds things up when you're doing numerous small Writes and/or Seeks while writing. The general IFF writer IFFW.C tends to do this. It should be extended to optimize reading, too. If you are not using IFF, and already Write in chunks of 256 bytes or more, don't bother using GIO.

Third Party Public Registered FORM and Chunk Specifications

This section contains the specifications of many public registered third party IFF FORMs and Chunks currently used in Amiga software products. As noted in the Registry, there are additional forms for which final specs are not yet available, most notably the SAMP, SYTH, and BANK midi-related formats. Check for availability of these form specs in the CATS IFF topic on BIX (amiga.dev/iff).

SMUS.CHAN and SMUS.PAN Chunks
Stereo imaging in the "8SVX" IFF 8-bit Sample Voice

Registered by David Jones, Gold Disk Inc.

There are two ways to create stereo imaging when playing back a digitized sound. The first relies on the original sound being created with a stereo sampler: two different samples are digitized simultaneously, using right and left inputs. To play back this type of sample while maintaining the stereo imaging, both channels must be set to the same volume. The second type of stereo sound plays the identical information on two different channels at different volumes. This gives the sample an absolute position in the stereo field. Unfortunately, there are currently a number of methods for doing this currently implemented on the Amiga, none truly adhering to any type of standard. What I have tried to to is provide a way of doing this consistently, while retaining compatibility with existing (non-standard) systems. Introduced below are two optional data chunks, CHAN and PAN. CHAN deals with sounds sampled in stereo, and PAN with samples given stereo characteristics after the fact.

Optional Data Chunk CHAN

This chunk is already written by the software for a popular stereo sampler. To maintain the ability read these samples, its implementation here is therefore limited to maintain compatability.

The optional data chunk CHAN gives the information neccessary to play a sample on a specified channel, or combination of channels. This chunk would be useful for programs employing stereo recording or playback of sampled sounds.

```
#define RIGHT           4L
#define LEFT            2L
#define STEREO          6L

#define ID_CHAN MakeID('C','H','A','N')

typedef sampletype LONG;
```

If "sampletype" is RIGHT, the program reading the sample knows that it was originally intended to play on a channel routed to the right speaker, (channels 1 and 2 on the Amiga). If "sampletype" is LEFT, the left speaker was intended (Amiga channels 0 and 3). It is left to the discretion of the programmer to decide whether or not to play a sample when a channel on the side designated by "sampletype" cannot be allocated.

If "sampletype" is STEREO, then the sample requires a pair of channels routed to both speakers (Amiga pairs [0,1] and [2,3]). The BODY chunk for stereo pairs contains both left and right information. To adhere to existing conventions, sampling software should write first the LEFT information, followed by the RIGHT. The LEFT and RIGHT information should be equal in length.

Again, it is left to the programmer to decide what to do if a channel for a stereo pair can't be allocated; wether to play the available channel only, or to allocate another channels routed to the wrong speaker.

Optional Data Chunk PAN

The optional data chunk PAN provides the neccessary information to create a stereo sound using a single array of data. It is neccessary to replay the sample simultaneously on two channels, at different volumes.


```
#define ID_PAN MakeID('P','A','N',' ')

typedef sposition Fixed; /* 0 <= sposition <= Unity */
                                                /* Unity is elsewhere #defi
                                                 * refers to the maximum po
                                                 * /

/* Please note that 'Fixed' (elsewhere #defined as LONG) is used to
 * allow for compatabilty between audio hardware of different resolutions.
 */
```

The 'sposition' variable describes a position in the stereo field. The numbers of discrete stereo positions available is equal to 1/2 the number of discrete volumes for a single channel.

The sample must be played on both the right and left channels. The overall volume of the sample is determined by the "volume" field in the Voice8Header structure in the VHDR chunk.

```
The left channel volume = overall volume / (Unity / sposition).
 "  right   "       "   = overall volume - left channel volume.
```

For example:

```
If sposition = Unity, the sample is panned all the way to the left.
If sposition = 0, the sample is panned all the way to the right.
If sposition = Unity/2, the sample is centered in the stereo field.
```

IFF FORM / CHUNK DESCRIPTION
============================

Form/Chunk ID: FORM ACBM (Amiga Contiguous BitMap)
                 Chunk ABIT (Amiga BITplanes)

Date Submitted: 05/29/86
Submitted by: Carolyn Scheppner   CBM

FORM
====

FORM ID: ACBM (Amiga Contiguous BitMap)

FORM Description:

FORM ACBM has the same format as FORM ILBM except the normal BODY chunk (InterLeaved BitMap) is replaced by an ABIT chunk (Amiga BITplanes).

FORM Purpose:

To enable faster loading/saving of screens, especially from Basic, while retaining the flexibility and portability of IFF format files.

CHUNKS
======

Chunk ID: ABIT (Amiga BITplanes)

Chunk Description:

The ABIT chunk contains contiguous bitplane data. The chunk contains sequential data for bitplane 0 through bitplane n.

Chunk Purpose:

To enable loading/storing of bitmaps with one DOS Read/Write per bitplane. Significant speed increases are realized when loading/saving screens from Basic.

SUPPORTING SOFTWARE
===================

(Public Domain, available soon via Fish PD disk, various networks)

LoadILBM-SaveACBM (AmigaBasic)
   Loads and displays an IFF ILBM pic file (Graphicraft, DPaint, Images).
   Optionally saves the screen in ACBM format.

LoadACBM (AmigaBasic)
   Loads and display an ACBM format pic file.

SaveILBM (AmigaBasic)
   Saves a demo screen as an ILBM pic file which can be loaded into
   Graphicraft, DPaint, Images.

TITLE: Form ANBM (animated bitmap form used by Framer, Deluxe Video)

(note from the author)

The format was designed for simplicity at a time when the IFF standard was very new and strange to us all. It was not designed to be a general purpose animation format. It was intended to be a private format for use by DVideo, with the hope that a more powerful format would emerge as the Amiga became more popular.

I hope you will publish this format so that other formats will not inadvertantly conflict with it.

PURPOSE: To define simple animated bitmaps for use in DeluxeVideo.

In Deluxe Video objects appear and move in the foreground with a picture in the background. Objects are "small" bitmaps usually saved as brushes from DeluxePaint and pictures are large full screen bitmaps saved as files from DeluxePaint.

Two new chunk headers are defined: ANBM and FSQN.

An animated bitmap (ANBM) is a series of bitmaps of the same size and depth. Each bitmap in the series is called a frame and is labeled by a character, 'a b c ...' in the order they appear in the file.

The frame sequence chunk (FSQN) specifies the playback sequence of the individual bitmaps to achieve animation. FSQN_CYCLE and FSQN_TOFRO specify two algorithmic sequences. If neither of these bits is set, an arbitrary sequence can be used instead.

```
ANBM          - identifies this file as an animated bitmap
.FSQN         - playback sequence information
.LIST ILBM    - LIST allows following ILBMs to share properties
..PROP ILBM   - properties follow
...BMHD       - bitmap header defines common size and depth
...CMAP       - colormap defines common colors
..FORM ILBM   - first frame follows
..BODY        - the first frame
   .          - FORM ILBM and BODY for each remaining frame
   .
   .
```

Chunk Description:

The ANBM chunk identifes this file as an animated bitmap

Chunk Spec:

```
#define ANBM    MakeID('A','N','B','M')
```

Disk record:

none

Chunk Description:

The FSQN chunk specifies the frame playback sequence

Chunk Spec:

```
#define FSQN    MakeID('F','S','Q','N')

/* Flags */
#define FSQN_CYCLE  0x0001  /* Ignore sequence, cycle a,b,..y,z,a,b,.. */
#define FSQN_TOFRO  0x0002  /* Ignore sequence, cycle a,b,..y,z,y,..a,b, */
```

```
/* Disk record */
typedef struct {
    WORD numframes;       /* Number of frames in the sequence */
    LONG dt;              /* Nominal time between frames in jiffies */
    WORDBITS flags;       /* Bits modify behavior of the animation */
    UBYTE sequence[30];   /* string of 'a'..'z' specifying sequence */
    } FrameSeqn;
```

Supporting Software:

DeluxeVideo by Mike Posehn and Tom Case for Electronic Arts

Thanks,
Mike Posehn

TITLE: New ANIM spec (with typos corrected)

A N I M
An IFF Format For CEL Animations

Revision date: 4 May 1988

prepared by:
SPARTA Inc.
23041 de la Carlota
Laguna Hills, Calif 92653
(714) 768-8161
contact: Gary Bonham

also by:
Aegis Development Co.
2115 Pico Blvd.
Santa Monica, Calif 90405
213) 392-9972

1.0 Introduction

The ANIM IFF format was developed at Sparta originally for the production of animated video sequences on the Amiga computer. The intent was to be able to store, and play back, sequences of frames and to minimize both the storage space on disk (through compression) and playback time (through efficient de-compression algorithms). It was desired to maintain maximum compatibility with existing IFF formats and to be able to display the initial frame as a normal still IFF picture.

Several compression schemes have been introduced in the ANIM format. Most of these are strictly of historical interest as the only one currently being placed in new code is the vertical run length encoded byte encoding developed by Jim Kent.

1.1 ANIM Format Overview

The general philosophy of ANIMs is to present the initial frame as a normal, run-length-encoded, IFF picture. Subsequent frames are then described by listing only their differences from a previous frame. Normally, the "previous" frame is two frames back as that is the frame remaining in the hidden screen buffer when double-buffering is used. To better understand this, suppose one has two screens, called A and B, and the ability to instantly switch the display from one to the other. The normal playback mode is to load the initial frame into A and duplicate it into B. Then frame A is displayed on the screen. Then the differences for frame 2 are used to alter screen B and it is displayed. Then the differences for frame 3 are used to alter screen A and it is displayed, and so on. Note that frame 2 is stored as differences from frame 1, but all other frames are stored as differences from two frames back.

ANIM is an IFF FORM and its basic format is as follows (this assumes the reader has a basic understanding of IFF format files):

```
                FORM ANIM
                . FORM ILBM         first frame
                . . BMHD                normal type IFF data
                . . ANHD                optional animation header
                                        chunk for timing of 1st frame.
                . . CMAP
                . . BODY
                . FORM ILBM         frame 2
                . . ANHD                animation header chunk
                . . DLTA                delta mode data
```

```
. FORM ILBM         frame 3
. . ANHD
. . DLTA
     ...
```

The initial FORM ILBM can contain all the normal ILBM chunks, such as CRNG, etc. The BODY will normally be a standard run-length-encoded data chunk (but may be any other legal compression mode as indicated by the BMHD). If desired, an ANHD chunk can appear here to provide timing data for the first frame. If it is here, the operation field should be =0.

The subsequent FORMs ILBM contain an ANHD, instead of a BMHD, which duplicates some of BMHD and has additional parameters pertaining to the animation frame. The DLTA chunk contains the data for the delta compression modes. If the older XOR compression mode is used, then a BODY chunk will be here. In addition, other chunks may be placed in each of these as deemed necessary (and as code is placed in player programs to utilize them). A good example would be CMAP chunks to alter the color palette. A basic assumption in ANIMs is that the size of the bitmap, and the display mode (e.g. HAM) will not change through the animation. Take care when playing an ANIM that if a CMAP occurs with a frame, then the change must be applied to both buffers.

Note that the DLTA chunks are not interleaved bitmap representations, thus the use of the ILBM form is inappropriate for these frames. However, this inconsistency was not noted until there were a number of commercial products either released or close to release which generated/played this format. Therefore, this is probably an inconsistency which will have to stay with us.

1.2 Recording ANIMs

To record an ANIM will require three bitmaps - one for creation of the next frame, and two more for a "history" of the previous two frames for performing the compression calculations (e.g. the delta mode calculations).

There are five frame-to-frame compression methods currently defined. The first three are mainly for historical interest. The product Aegis VideoScape 3D utilizes the third method in version 1.0, but switched to method 5 on 2.0. This is the only instance known of a commercial product generating ANIMs of any of the first three methods. The fourth method is a general short or long word compression scheme which has several options including whether the compression is horizontal or vertical, and whether or not it is XOR format. This offers a choice to the user for the optimization of file size and/or playback speed. The fifth method is the byte vertical run length encoding as designed by Jim Kent. Do not confuse this with Jim's RIFF file format which is different than ANIM. Here we utilized his compression/decompression routines within the ANIM file structure.

The following paragraphs give a general outline of each of the methods of compression currently included in this spec.

1.2.1 XOR mode

This mode is the original and is included here for historical interest. In general, the delta modes are far superior. The creation of XOR mode is quite simple. One simply performs an exclusive-or (XOR) between all corresponding bytes of the new frame and two frames back. This results in a new bitmap with 0 bits wherever the two frames were identical, and 1 bits where they are different. Then this new bitmap is saved using run-length-encoding. A major

obstacle of this mode is in the time consumed in performing the XOR upon reconstructing the image.

1.2.2 Long Delta mode

This mode stores the actual new frame long-words which are different, along with the offset in the bitmap. The exact format is shown and discussed in section 2 below. Each plane is handled separately, with no data being saved if no changes take place in a given plane. Strings of 2 or more long-words in a row which change can be run together so offsets do not have to be saved for each one.

Constructing this data chunk usually consists of having a buffer to hold the data, and calculating the data as one compares the new frame, long-word by long-word, with two frames back.

1.2.3 Short Delta mode

This mode is identical to the Long Delta mode except that short-words are saved instead of long-words. In most instances, this mode results in a smaller DLTA chunk. The Long Delta mode is mainly of interest in improving the playback speed when used on a 32-bit 68020 Turbo Amiga.

1.2.4 General Delta mode

The above two delta compression modes were hastily put together. This mode was an attempt to provide a well-thought-out delta compression scheme. Options provide for both short and long word compression, either vertical or horizontal compression, XOR mode (which permits reverse playback), etc. About the time this was being finalized, the fifth mode, below, was developed by Jim Kent. In practice the short-vertical-run-length-encoded deltas in this mode play back faster than the fifth mode (which is in essence a byte-vertical-run-length-encoded delta mode) but does not compress as well - especially for very noisy data such as digitized images. In most cases, playback speed not being terrifically slower, the better compression (sometimes 2x) is preferable due to limited storage media in most machines.

Details on this method are contained in section 2.2.2 below.

1.2.5 Byte Vertical Compression

This method does not offer the many options that method 4 offers, but is very successful at producing decent compression even for very noisy data such as digitized images. The method was devised by Jim Kent and is utilized in his RIFF file format which is different than the ANIM format. The description of this method in this document is taken from Jim's writings. Further, he has released both compression and decompression code to public domain.

Details on this method are contained in section 2.2.3 below.

1.3 Playing ANIMs

Playback of ANIMs will usually require two buffers, as mentioned above, and double-buffering between them. The frame data from the ANIM file is used to modify the hidden frame to the next frame to be shown. When using the XOR mode, the usual run-length-decoding routine can be easily modified to do the exclusive-or operation required. Note that runs of zero bytes, which will be very common, can be ignored, as an exclusive or of any byte value to a byte of zero will not alter the original byte value.

The general procedure, for all compression techniques, is to first decode the initial ILBM picture into the hidden buffer and double-buffer it into view. Then this picture is copied to the other (now hidden) buffer. At this point each frame is displayed with the same procedure. The next frame is formed in the hidden buffer by applying the DLTA data (or the XOR data from the BODY chunk in the case of the first XOR method) and the new frame is double-buffered into view. This process continues to the end of the file.

A master colormap should be kept for the entire ANIM which would be initially set from the CMAP chunk in the initial ILBM. This colormap should be used for each frame. If a CMAP chunk appears in one of the frames, then this master colormap is updated and the new colormap applies to all frames until the occurrance of another CMAP chunk.

Looping ANIMs may be constructed by simply making the last two frames identical to the first two. Since the first two frames are special cases (the first being a normal ILBM and the second being a delta from the first) one can continually loop the anim by repeating from frame three. In this case the delta for creating frame three will modify the next to the last frame which is in the hidden buffer (which is identical to the first frame), and the delta for creating frame four will modify the last frame which is identical to the second frame.

Multi-File ANIMs are also supported so long as the first two frames of a subsequent file are identical to the last two frames of the preceeding file. Upon reading subsequent files, the ILBMs for the first two frames are simply ignored, and the remaining frames are simply appended to the preceeding frames. This permits splitting ANIMs across multiple floppies and also permits playing each section independently and/or editing it independent of the rest of the ANIM.

Timing of ANIM playback is easily achieved using the vertical blank interrupt of the Amiga. There is an example of setting up such a timer in the ROM Kernel Manual. Be sure to remember the timer value when a frame is flipped up, so the next frame can be flipped up relative to that time. This will make the playback independent of how long it takes to decompress a frame (so long as there is enough time between frames to accomplish this decompression).

2.0 Chunk Formats

2.1 ANHD Chunk

The ANHD chunk consists of the following data structure:

```
UBYTE operation  The compression method:
                 =0 set directly (normal ILBM BODY),
                 =1 XOR ILBM mode,
                 =2 Long Delta mode,
                 =3 Short Delta mode,
                 =4 Generalized short/long Delta mode,
                 =5 Byte Vertical Delta mode
                 =74 (ascii 'J') reserved for Eric Graham's
                    compression technique (details to be
                    released later).

UBYTE mask      (XOR mode only - plane mask where each
                 bit is set =1 if there is data and =0
                 if not.)
UWORD w,h       (XOR mode only - width and height of the
                 area represented by the BODY to eliminate
                 unnecessary un-changed data)
WORD  x,y       (XOR mode only - position of rectangular
                 area representd by the BODY)
ULONG abstime   (currently unused - timing for a frame
                 relative to the time the first frame
                 was displayed - in jiffies (1/60 sec))
ULONG reltime   (timing for frame relative to time
                 previous frame was displayed - in
                 jiffies (1/60 sec))
```



```
UBYTE interleave (unused so far - indicates how may frames
                 back this data is to modify.  =0 defaults
                 to indicate two frames back (for double
                 buffering). =n indicates n frames back.
                 The main intent here is to allow values
                 of =1 for special applications where
                 frame data would modify the immediately
                 previous frame)
UBYTE pad0       Pad byte, not used at present.
ULONG bits       32 option bits used by options=4 and 5.
                 At present only 6 are identified, but the
                 rest are set =0 so they can be used to
                 implement future ideas.  These are defined
                 for option 4 only at this point.  It is
                 recommended that all bits be set =0 for
                 option 5 and that any bit settings
                 used in the future (such as for XOR mode)
                 be compatible with the option 4
                 bit settings.   Player code should check
                 undefined bits in options 4 and 5 to assure
                 they are zero.

                 The six bits for current use are:

                 bit #          set =0             set =1
                 ===============================================
                 0            short data          long data
                 1               set                 XOR
                 2           separate info       one info list
                             for each plane      for all planes
                 3              not RLC         RLC (run length coded)
                 4            horizontal           vertical
                 5          short info offsets  long info offsets

UBYTE pad[16]    This is a pad for future use for future
                 compression modes.
```

2.2 DLTA Chunk

This chunk is the basic data chunk used to hold delta compression data. The format of the data will be dependent upon the exact compression format selected. At present there are two basic formats for the overall structure of this chunk.

2.2.1 Format for methods 2 & 3

This chunk is a basic data chunk used to hold the delta compression data. The minimum size of this chunk is 32 bytes as the first 8 long-words are byte pointers into the chunk for the data for each of up to 8 bitplanes. The pointer for the plane data starting immediately following these 8 pointers will have a value of 32 as the data starts in the 33-rd byte of the chunk (index value of 32 due to zero-base indexing).

The data for a given plane consists of groups of data words. In Long Delta mode, these groups consist of both short and long words - short words for offsets and numbers, and long words for the actual data. In Short Delta mode, the groups are identical except data words are also shorts so all data is short words. Each group consists of a starting word which is an offset. If the offset is positive then it indicates the increment in long or short words (whichever is appropriate) through the bitplane. In other words, if you were reconstructing the plane, you would start a pointer (to shorts or longs depending on the mode) to point to the first word of the bitplane. Then the offset would be added to it and the following data word would be placed at that position. Then the next offset would be added to the pointer and the following data word would be placed at that position. And so on... The data terminates with an offset equal to 0xFFFF.

A second interpretation is given if the offset is negative. In that case, the absolute value is the offset+2. Then the following short-word indicates the number of data words that follow. Following that is the indicated number of contiguous data words (longs or shorts depending on mode) which are to be placed in contiguous locations of the bitplane.

If there are no changed words in a given plane, then the pointer in the first 32 bytes of the chunk is =0.

2.2.2 Format for method 4

The DLTA chunk is modified slightly to have 16 long pointers at the start. The first 8 are as before - pointers to the start of the data for each of the bitplanes (up to a theoretical max of 8 planes). The next 8 are pointers to the start of the offset/numbers data list. If there is only one list of offset/numbers for all planes, then the pointer to that list is repeated in all positions so the playback code need not even be aware of it. In fact, one could get fancy and have some bitplanes share lists while others have different lists, or no lists (the problems in these schemes lie in the generation, not in the playback).

The best way to show the use of this format is in a sample playback routine.

```
SetDLTAshort(bm,deltaword)
struct BitMap *bm;
WORD *deltaword;
{
   int i;
   LONG *deltadata;
   WORD *ptr,*planeptr;
   register int s,size,nw;
   register WORD *data,*dest;

   deltadata = (LONG *)deltaword;
   nw = bm->BytesPerRow >>1;

   for (i=0;i<bm->Depth;i++) {
      planeptr = (WORD *)(bm->Planes[i]);
      data = deltaword + deltadata[i];
      ptr  = deltaword + deltadata[i+8];
      while (*ptr != 0xFFFF) {
         dest = planeptr + *ptr++;
         size = *ptr++;
         if (size < 0) {
            for (s=size;s<0;s++) {
               *dest = *data;
               dest += nw;
            }
            data++;
         }
         else {
            for (s=0;s<size;s++) {
               *dest = *data++;
               dest += nw;
            }
         }
      }
   }
   return(0);
}
```

The above routine is for short word vertical compression with run length compression. The most efficient way to support the various options is to replicate this routine and make

alterations for, say, long word or XOR. The variable nw indicates the number of words to skip to go down the vertical column. This one routine could easily handle horizontal compression by simply setting nw=1. For ultimate playback speed, the core, at least, of this routine should be coded in assembly language.

2.2.2 Format for method 5

In this method the same 16 pointers are used as in option 4. The first 8 are pointers to the data for up to 8 planes. The second set of 8 are not used but were retained for several reasons. First to be somewhat compatible with code for option 4 (although this has not proven to be of any benefit) and second, to allow extending the format for more bitplanes (code has been written for up to 12 planes).

Compression/decompression is performed on a plane-by-plane basis. For each plane, compression can be handled by the skip.c code (provided Public Domain by Jim Kent) and decompression can be handled by unvscomp.asm (also provided Public Domain by Jim Kent).

Compression/decompression is performed on a plane-by-plane basis. The following description of the method is taken directly from Jim Kent's code with minor re-wording. Please refer to Jim's code (skip.c and unvscomp.asm) for more details:

Each column of the bitplane is compressed separately. A 320x200 bitplane would have 40 columns of 200 bytes each. Each column starts with an op-count followed by a number of ops. If the op-count is zero, that's ok, it just means there's no change in this column from the last frame. The ops are of three classes, and followed by a varying amount of data depending on which class:

1. Skip ops - this is a byte with the hi bit clear that says how many rows to move the "dest" pointer forward, ie to skip. It is non-zero.
2. Uniq ops - this is a byte with the hi bit set. The hi bit is masked down and the remainder is a count of the number of bytes of data to copy literally. It's of course followed by the data to copy.
3. Same ops - this is a 0 byte followed by a count byte, followed by a byte value to repeat count times.

Do bear in mind that the data is compressed vertically rather than horizontally, so to get to the next byte in the destination we add the number of bytes per row instead of one!

TITLE: HEAD (FORM used by Flow - New Horizons Software, Inc.)

IFF FORM / CHUNK DESCRIPTION
============================

Form/Chunk ID: FORM HEAD, Chunks NEST, TEXT, FSCC

Date Submitted: 03/87
Submitted by: James Bayless - New Horizons Software, Inc.

FORM
====

FORM ID: HEAD

FORM Description:

FORM HEAD is the file storage format of the Flow idea processor by New Horizons Software, Inc. Currently only the TEXT and NEST chunks are used. There are plans to incorporate FSCC and some additional chunks for headers and footers.

CHUNKS
======

CHUNK ID: NEST

This chunk consists of only of a word (two byte) value that gives the new current nesting level of the outline. The initial nesting level (outermost level) is zero. It is necessary to include a NEST chunk only when the nesting level changes. Valid changes to the nesting level are either to decrease the current value by any amount (with a minimum of 0) or to increase it by one (and not more than one).

CHUNK ID: TEXT

This chunk is the actual text of a heading. Each heading has a TEXT chunk (even if empty). The text is not NULL terminated - the chunk size gives the length of the heading text.

CHUNK ID: FSCC

This chunk gives the Font/Style/Color changes in the heading from the most recent TEXT chunk. It should occur immediately after the TEXT chunk it modifies. The format is identical to the FSCC chunk for the IFF form type 'WORD' (for compatibility), except that only the 'Location' and 'Style' values are used (i.e., there can be currently only be style changes in an outline heading). The structure definition is:

```
typedef struct {
   UWORD  Location;   /* Char location of change */
   UBYTE  FontNum;    /* Ignored */
   UBYTE  Style;      /* Amiga style bits */
   UBYTE  MiscStyle;  /* Ignored */
   UBYTE  Color;      /* Ignored */
   UWORD  pad;        /* Ignored */
} FSCChange;
```

The actual chunk consists of an array of these structures, one entry for each Style change in the heading text.

IFF FORM / CHUNK DESCRIPTION
============================

Form/Chunk ID: Chunk DPPV (DPaint II ILBM perspective chunk)
Date Submitted: 12/86
Submitted by: Dan Silva

Chunk Description:

The DPPV chunk describes the perspective state in a DPaintII ILBM.

Chunk Spec:

```
/* The chunk identifier DPPV */
#define ID_DPPV    MakeID('D','P','P','V')

typedef LONG LongFrac;
typedef struct ( LongFrac x,y,z; )  LFPoint;
typedef LongFrac  APoint[3];

typedef union {
   LFPoint l;
   APoint  a;
   } UPoint;

/* values taken by variable rotType */
#define ROT_EULER  0
#define ROT_INCR   1

/* Disk record describing Perspective state */

typedef struct {
   WORD      rotType;            /* rotation type */
   WORD      iA, iB, iC;         /* rotation angles (in degrees) */
   LongFrac  Depth;              /* perspective depth */
   WORD      uCenter, vCenter;   /* coords of center perspective,
                                  * relative to backing bitmap,
                                  * in Virtual coords
                                  */
   WORD      fixCoord;           /* which coordinate is fixed */
   WORD      angleStep;          /* large angle stepping amount */
   UPoint    grid;               /* gridding spacing in X,Y,Z */
   UPoint    gridReset;          /* where the grid goes on Reset */
   UPoint    gridBrCenter;       /* Brush center when grid was last on,
                                  * as reference point
                                  */
   UPoint    permBrCenter;       /* Brush center the last time the mouse
                                  * button was clicked, a rotation performed,
                                  * or motion along "fixed" axis
                                  */
   LongFrac rot[3][3];           /* rotation matrix */
   } PerspState;
```

SUPPORTING SOFTWARE
===================

DPaint II   by Dan Silva for Electronic Arts

```
FORM PGTB

Proposal:
        New IFF chunk type, to be named PGTB, meaning ProGram TraceBack.

Format:

        'PGTB'          - chunk identifier
        length          - longword for length of chunk

        'FAIL'          - subfield giving environment at time of crash
        length          - longword length of subfield
        NameLen         - length of program name in longwords (BSTR)
        Name            - program name packed in longwords
        Environment     - copy of AttnFlags field from ExecBase,
                          gives type of processor, and existence of
                          math chip
        VBlankFreq      - copy of VBlankFrequency field from ExecBase
        PowerSupFreq    - copy of PowerSupplyFrequency field from ExecBase
                          above fields may be used to determine whether
                          machine was PAL or NTSC
        Starter         - non-zero = CLI, zero = WorkBench
        GURUNum         - exception number of crash
        SegCount        - number of segments for program
        SegList         - copy of seglist for program
                          (Includes all seglist pointers, paired with
                           sizes of the segments)

        'REGS'          - register dump subfield
        length          - length of subfield in longwords
        GURUAddr        - PC at time of crash
        Flags           - copy of Condition Code Register
        DDump           - dump of data registers
        ADump           - dump of address registers

        'VERS'          - revision of program which created this file
        length          - length of subfield in longwords
        version         - main version of writing program
        revision        - minor revision level of writing program
        TBNameLen       - length of name of writing program
        TBName          - name of writing program packed in longwords (BSTR)

        'STAK'          - stack dump subfield
        length          - length of subfield in longwords
        (type)          - tells type of stack subfield, which can be any of
                          the following:
                ----------------------------------------------------------
                Info            - value 0
                StackTop        - address of top of stack
                StackPtr        - stack pointer at time of crash
                StackLen        - number of longwords on stack

                ----------------------------------------------------------
                Whole stack     - value 1
                                  only used if total stack to be dumped is 8k
                                  or less in size
                Stack           - dump of stack from current to top

                ----------------------------------------------------------
                Top 4k          - value 2
                                  if stack used larger than 8k, this part
                                  is a dump of the top 4k
                Stack           - dump of stack from top - 4k to top

                ----------------------------------------------------------
                Bottom 4k       - value 3
                                  if stack used larger than 8k, this part
                                  is a dump of the bottom 4k
```



```
                Stack           - dump of stack from current to current + 4k

        In other words, we will dump a maximum of 8k of stack data.  This
        does NOT mean the stack must be less than 8k in size to dump the
        entire stack, just that the amount of stack USED be less than 8k.

        'UDAT'          - Optional User DATa chunk.  If the user assigns
                          a function pointer to the label "_ONGURU", the
                          catcher will call this routine prior to closing
                          the SnapShot file, passing one parameter on the
                          stack - an AmigaDOS file pointer to the SnapShot
                          file.  Spec for the _ONGURU routine:

                                void <function name>(fp)
                                long fp;

                          In other words, your routine must be of type 'void'
                          and must take one parameter, an AmigaDOS file
                          handle (which AmigaDOS wants to see as a LONG).
        length          - length of the UserDATa chunk, calculated after the
                          user routine terminates.
```

```
TITLE:  WORD  (word processing FORM used by ProWrite)

IFF FORM / CHUNK DESCRIPTION
============================

Form/Chunk IDs:
   FORM    WORD
   Chunks FONT,COLR,DOC,HEAD,FOOT,PCTS,PARA,TABS,PAGE,TEXT,FSCC,PINF

Date Submitted: 03/87
Submitted by:   James Bayless - New Horizons Software, Inc.


FORM
====

FORM ID:  WORD

FORM Purpose:  Document storage (supports color, fonts, pictures)

FORM Description:

This include file describes FORM WORD and its Chunks

/*
 *      IFF Form WORD structures and defines
 *      Copyright (c) 1987 New Horizons Software, Inc.
 *
 *      Permission is hereby granted to use this file in any and all
 *      applications.  Modifying the structures or defines included
 *      in this file is not permitted without written consent of
 *      New Horizons Software, Inc.
 */

#include ":IFF/ILBM.h"        /* Makes use of ILBM defines */

#define ID_WORD      MakeID('W','O','R','D')      /* Form type */

#define ID_FONT      MakeID('F','O','N','T')      /* Chunks */
#define ID_COLR      MakeID('C','O','L','R')
#define ID_DOC       MakeID('D','O','C',' ')
#define ID_HEAD      MakeID('H','E','A','D')
#define ID_FOOT      MakeID('F','O','O','T')
#define ID_PCTS      MakeID('P','C','T','S')
#define ID_PARA      MakeID('P','A','R','A')
#define ID_TABS      MakeID('T','A','B','S')
#define ID_PAGE      MakeID('P','A','G','E')
#define ID_TEXT      MakeID('T','E','X','T')
#define ID_FSCC      MakeID('F','S','C','C')
#define ID_PINF      MakeID('P','I','N','F')

/*
 *   Special text characters for page number, date, and time
 *   Note:  ProWrite currently supports only PAGENUM_CHAR, and only in
 *      headers and footers
 */

#define PAGENUM_CHAR    0x80
#define DATE_CHAR       0x81
#define TIME_CHAR       0x82

/*
 *   Chunk structures follow
 */

/*
 *   FONT - Font name/number table
 *   There are one of these for each font/size combination
 *   These chunks should appear at the top of the file (before document data)
```



```
 */

typedef struct {
   UBYTE    Num;            /* 0 .. 255 */
   UWORD    Size;
/* UBYTE    Name[];         */   /* NULL terminated, without ".font" */
} FontID;

/*
 *    COLR - Color translation table
 *    Translates from color numbers used in file to ISO color numbers
 *    Should be at top of file (before document data)
 *    Note:  Currently ProWrite only checks these values to be its current map,
 *       it does no translation as it does for FONT chunks
 */

typedef struct {
   UBYTE    ISOColors[8];
} ISOColors;

/*
 *    DOC - Begin document section
 *    All text and paragraph formatting following this chunk and up to a
 *    HEAD, FOOT, or PICT chunk belong to the document section
 */

#define PAGESTYLE_1    0       /* 1, 2, 3 */
#define PAGESTYLE_I    1       /* I, II, III */
#define PAGESTYLE_i    2       /* i, ii, iii */
#define PAGESTYLE_A    3       /* A, B, C */
#define PAGESTYLE_a    4       /* a, b, c */

typedef struct {
   UWORD    StartPage;       /* Starting page number */
   UBYTE    PageNumStyle;    /* From defines above */
   UBYTE    pad1;
   LONG     pad2;
} DocHdr;

/*
 *    HEAD/FOOT - Begin header/footer section
 *    All text and paragraph formatting following this chunk and up to a
 *    DOC, HEAD, FOOT, or PICT chunk belong to this header/footer
 *    Note:  This format supports multiple headers and footers, but currently
 *       ProWrite only allows a single header and footer per document
 */

#define PAGES_NONE   0
#define PAGES_LEFT   1
#define PAGES_RIGHT  2
#define PAGES_BOTH   3

typedef struct {
   UBYTE    PageType;        /* From defines above */
   UBYTE    FirstPage;       /* 0 = Not on first page */
   LONG     pad;
} HeadHdr;

/*
 *    PCTS - Begin picture section
 *    Note:  ProWrite currently requires NPlanes to be three (3)
 */

typedef struct {
   UBYTE    NPlanes;       /* Number of planes used in picture bitmaps */
   UBYTE    pad;
} PictHdr;

/*
```

```
 *   PARA - New paragraph format
 *   This chunk should be inserted first when a new section is started (DOC,
 *      HEAD, or FOOT), and again whenever the paragraph format changes
 */

#define SPACE_SINGLE   0
#define SPACE_DOUBLE   0x10

#define JUSTIFY_LEFT    0
#define JUSTIFY_CENTER  1
#define JUSTIFY_RIGHT   2
#define JUSTIFY_FULL    3

#define MISCSTYLE_NONE   0
#define MISCSTYLE_SUPER  1      /* Superscript */
#define MISCSTYLE_SUB    2      /* Subscript */

typedef struct {
   UWORD   LeftIndent;     /* In decipoints (720 dpi) */
   UWORD   LeftMargin;
   UWORD   RightMargin;
   UBYTE   Spacing;        /* From defines above */
   UBYTE   Justify;        /* From defines above */
   UBYTE   FontNum;        /* FontNum, Style, etc. for first char in para*/
   UBYTE   Style;          /* Standard Amiga style bits */
   UBYTE   MiscStyle;      /* From defines above */
   UBYTE   Color;          /* Internal number, use COLR to translate */
   LONG    pad;
} ParaFormat;

/*
 *   TABS - New tab stop types/locations
 *   Use an array of values in each chunk
 *   Like the PARA chunk, this should be inserted whenever the tab settings
 *      for a paragraph change
 *   Note:  ProWrite currently does not support TAB_CENTER
 */

#define TAB_LEFT     0
#define TAB_CENTER   1
#define TAB_RIGHT    2
#define TAB_DECIMAL  3

typedef struct {
   UWORD   Position;       /* In decipoints */
   UBYTE   Type;
   UBYTE   pad;
} TabStop;

/*
 *   PAGE - Page break
 *   Just a marker -- this chunk has no data
 */

/*
 *   TEXT - Paragraph text (one block per paragraph)
 *   Block is actual text, no need for separate structure
 *   If the paragraph is empty, this is an empty chunk -- there MUST be
 *   a TEXT block for every paragraph
 *   Note:  The only ctrl characters ProWrite can currently handle in TEXT
 *   chunks are Tab and PAGENUM_CHAR, ie no Return's, etc.
 */

/*
 *   FSCC - Font/Style/Color changes in previous TEXT block
 *   Use an array of values in each chunk
 *   Only include this chunk if the previous TEXT block did not have
 *      the same Font/Style/Color for all its characters
 */
```



```
typedef struct {
   UWORD   Location;       /* Character location in TEXT chunk of change */
   UBYTE   FontNum;
   UBYTE   Style;
   UBYTE   MiscStyle;
   UBYTE   Color;
   UWORD   pad;
} FSCChange;

/*
 *    PINF - Picture info
 *    This chunk must only be in a PCTS section
 *    Must be followed by ILBM BODY chunk
 *    Pictures are treated independently of the document text (like a
 *       page-layout system), this chunk includes information about what
 *       page and location on the page the picture is at
 *    Note:  ProWrite currently only supports mskTransparentColor and
 *       mskHasMask masking
 */

typedef struct {
   UWORD          Width, Height;    /* In pixels */
   UWORD          Page;         /* Which page picture is on (0..max) */
   UWORD          XPos, YPos;       /* Location on page in decipoints */
   Masking        Masking;      /* Like ILBM format */
   Compression    Compression;   /* Like ILBM format */
   UBYTE          TransparentColor;   /* Like ILBM format */
   UBYTE          pad;
} PictInfo;

/* end */
```

EA IFF Source Code Listings

This section contains source code listings of the EA IFF include files, reader and writer modules, and the IFF examples provided by EA.

```
/*----------------------------------------------------------------------*
 * 8SVX.H  Definitions for 8-bit sampled voice (VOX).   2/10/86
 *
 * By Jerry Morrison and Steve Hayes, Electronic Arts.
 * This software is in the public domain.
 *
 * This version for the Commodore-Amiga computer.
 *----------------------------------------------------------------------*/
#ifndef EIGHTSVX_H
#define EIGHTSVX_H

#ifndef COMPILER_H
#include "iff/compiler.h"
#endif

#include "iff/iff.h"

#define ID_8SVX      MakeID('8', 'S', 'V', 'X')
#define ID_VHDR      MakeID('V', 'H', 'D', 'R')
#define ID_NAME      MakeID('N', 'A', 'M', 'E')
#define ID_Copyright MakeID('(', 'c', ')', ' ')

#define ID_AUTH      MakeID('A', 'U', 'T', 'H')
#define ID_ANNO      MakeID('A', 'N', 'N', 'O')

#define ID_BODY      MakeID('B', 'O', 'D', 'Y')

#define ID_ATAK      MakeID('A', 'T', 'A', 'K')
#define ID_RLSE      MakeID('R', 'L', 'S', 'E')

/* ---------- Voice8Header ---------------------------------------------*/
typedef LONG Fixed;     /* A fixed-point value, 16 bits to the left of
                         * the point and 16 to the right. A Fixed is a
                         * number of 2**16ths, i.e. 65536ths. */
#define Unity 0x10000L  /* Unity = Fixed 1.0 = maximum volume */

/* sCompression: Choice of compression algorithm applied to the samples. */
#define sCmpNone       0        /* not compressed */
#define sCmpFibDelta   1        /* Fibonacci-delta encoding (Appendix C) */
                                /* Could be more kinds in the future. */
typedef struct {
    ULONG oneShotHiSamples,     /* # samples in the high octave 1-shot part */
          repeatHiSamples,      /* # samples in the high octave repeat part */
          samplesPerHiCycle;    /* # samples/cycle in high octave, else 0 */
    UWORD samplesPerSec;        /* data sampling rate */
    UBYTE ctOctave,             /* # of octaves of waveforms */
          sCompression;         /* data compression technique used */
    Fixed volume;               /* playback nominal volume from 0 to Unity
                                 * (full volume). Map this value into
                                 * the output hardware's dynamic range.
                                 */
    } Voice8Header;

/* ---------- NAME -----------------------------------------------------*/
/* NAME chunk contains a CHAR[], the voice's name. */

/* ---------- Copyright ------------------------------------------------*/
/* "(c) " chunk contains a CHAR[], the FORM's copyright notice. */

/* ---------- AUTH -----------------------------------------------------*/
/* AUTH chunk contains a CHAR[], the author's name. */

/* ---------- ANNO -----------------------------------------------------*/
/* ANNO chunk contains a CHAR[], the author's text annotations. */

/* ---------- Envelope ATAK & RLSE -------------------------------------*/
typedef struct {
    UWORD duration;     /* segment duration in milliseconds, > 0 */
    Fixed dest;         /* destination volume factor */
```



```
    } EGPoint;

/* ATAK and RLSE chunks contain an EGPoint[], piecewise-linear envelope. */

/* The envelope defines a function of time returning Fixed values.
 * It's used to scale the nominal volume specified in the Voice8Header.
 */

/* ---------- BODY -----------------------------------------------------*/
/* BODY chunk contains a BYTE[], array of audio data samples. */
/* (8-bit signed numbers, -128 through 127.) */


/* ---------- 8SVX Reader Support Routines -----------------------------*/

/* Just call this macro to read a VHDR chunk. */
#define GetVHDR(context, vHdr)  \
    IFFReadBytes(context, (BYTE *)vHdr, sizeof(Voice8Header))


/* ---------- 8SVX Writer Support Routines -----------------------------*/

/* Just call this macro to write a VHDR chunk. */
#define PutVHDR(context, vHdr)  \
    PutCk(context, ID_VHDR, sizeof(Voice8Header), (BYTE *)vHdr)

#endif
```

```
#ifndef COMPILER_H
#define COMPILER_H
/*** compiler.h ***********************************************************/
/*  Steve Shaw                                                    1/29/86 */
/*  Portability file to handle compiler idiosyncrasies.                   */
/*  Version: Lattice 3.03 cross-compiler for the Amiga from the IBM PC.   */
/*                                                                        */
/* This software is in the public domain.                                 */
/*                                                                        */
/**************************************************************************/

#ifndef EXEC_TYPES_H
#include "exec/types.h"
#endif


/* NOTE  --  NOTE  --  NOTE  --  NOTE  --  NOTE
 * Some C compilers can handle Function Declarations with Argument Types
 * (FDwAT) like this:
 *      extern LONG Seek(BPTR, LONG, LONG)
 * while others choke unless you just say
 *      extern LONG Seek()
 *
 * Comment out the #define FDwAT if you have a compiler that chokes. */



/* #define FDwAT        COMMENTED OUT BECAUSE GREENHILLS CANT TAKE IT */


#endif COMPILER_H
```



```
#ifndef GIO_H
#define GIO_H
/*----------------------------------------------------------------------*/
/* GIO.H  defs for Generic I/O Speed Up Package.               1/23/86 */
/* See GIOCall.C for an example of usage.                               */
/* Read not speeded-up yet.  Only one Write file buffered at a time.    */
/*                                                                      */
/* Note: The speed-up provided is ONLY significant for code such as IFF */
/* which does numerous small Writes and Seeks.                          */
/*                                                                      */
/* WARNING: If gio reports an error to you and you care what specific   */
/* Dos error was, you must call IoErr() BEFORE calling any other gio    */
/* functions.                                                           */
/*                                                                      */
/* By Jerry Morrison and Steve Shaw, Electronic Arts.                   */
/* This software is in the public domain.                               */
/*                                                                      */
/* This version for the Commodore-Amiga computer.                       */
/*                                                                      */
/*----------------------------------------------------------------------*/

/* Use this file interface in place of ALL Open,Close,Read,Write,Seek DOS
 * calls for an optional i/o speed-up via buffering.  You must use ONLY
 * these G routines for a file that is being buffered; e.g., call GClose
 * to Close the file, etc.
 * It is harmless though not necessary to use G routines for a file that
 * is not being buffered; e.g., GClose and Close are equivalent in that
 * case.
 * This Version only buffers one file at a time, and only for writing.
 * If you call GWriteDeclare for a second file before the first file
 * is GClosed, the first file becomes unbuffered.  This is harmless, no
 * data is lost, the first file is simply no longer speeded-up.
 */

/* Before compiling any modules that make G calls, or compiling gio.c,
 * you must set the GIO_ACTIVE flag below.
 *
 * To omit the speed-up code,
 *    #define GIO_ACTIVE 0
 *
 * To make the speed-up happen:
 * 1. #define GIO_ACTIVE 1
 * 2. link gio.o into your progrm
 * 3. GWriteDeclare(file, buffer, size)
 *    after GOpening the file and before doing
 *    any writing.
 * 4. ONLY use GRead, GWrite, GSeek, GClose -- do not use the DOS i/o
 *    routines directly.
 * 5. When done, do GClose.  Or to stop buffering without closing the
 *    file, do GWriteUndeclare(file).
 */
#define GIO_ACTIVE 0

#ifndef COMPILER_H
#include "iff/compiler.h"
#endif

#ifndef LIBRARIES_DOS_H
#include "libraries/dos.h"
#endif

#ifndef OFFSET_BEGINNING
#define OFFSET_BEGINNING OFFSET_BEGINING
#endif

#if GIO_ACTIVE

#ifdef FDwAT  /* Compiler handles Function Declaration with Argument Types */
```

```
/* Present for completeness in the interface.
 * "openmode" is either MODE_OLDFILE to read/write an existing file, or
 * MODE_NEWFILE to write a new file.
 * RETURNs a "file" pointer to a system-supplied structure that describes
 * the open file.  This pointer is passed in to the other routines below.*/
extern BPTR GOpen(char * /*filename*/, LONG /*openmode*/);

/* NOTE: Flushes & Frees the write buffer.
 * Returns -1 on error from Write.*/
extern LONG GClose(BPTR /*file*/);

/* Read not speeded-up yet.
 * GOpen the file, then do GReads to get successive chunks of data in
 * the file.  Assumes the system can handle any number of bytes in each
 * call, regardless of any block-structure of the device being read from.
 * When done, GClose to free any system resources associated with an
 * open file.*/
extern LONG GRead(BPTR /*file*/, BYTE * /*buffer*/, LONG /*nBytes*/);

/* Writes out any data in write buffer for file.
 * NOTE WHEN have Seeked into middle of buffer:
 * GWriteFlush causes current position to be the end of the data written.
 * -1 on error from Write.*/
extern LONG GWriteFlush(BPTR /*file*/);

/* Sets up variables to describe a write buffer for the file.*/
/* If the buffer already has data in it from an outstanding GWriteDeclare,
 * then that buffer must first be flushed.
 * RETURN -1 on error from Write for that previous buffer flush.
 * See also "GWriteUndeclare".*/
extern LONG GWriteDeclare(BPTR /*file*/, BYTE * /*buffer*/, LONG /*nBytes*/);

/* ANY PROGRAM WHICH USES "GWrite" MUST USE "GSeek" rather than "Seek"
 * TO SEEK ON A FILE BEING WRITTEN WITH "GWrite".
 * "Write" with Generic speed-up.
 * -1 on error from Write.  else returns # bytes written to disk.
 * Call GOpen, then do successive GWrites with GSeeks if required,
 * then GClose when done.  (IFF does require GSeek.)*/
extern LONG GWrite(BPTR /*file*/, BYTE * /*buffer*/, LONG /*nBytes*/);

/* "Seek" with Generic speed-up, for a file being written with GWrite.*/
/* Returns what Seek returns, which appears to be the position BEFORE
 * seeking, though the documentation says it returns the NEW position.
 * In fact, the code now explicitly returns the OLD position when
 * seeking within the buffer.
 * Eventually, will support two independent files, one being read, the
 * other being written.  Or could support even more.  Designed so is safe
 * to call even for files which aren't being buffered.*/
extern LONG GSeek(BPTR /*file*/, LONG /*position*/, LONG /*mode*/);

#else /*not FDwAT*/

extern BPTR GOpen();
extern LONG GClose();
extern LONG GRead();
extern LONG GWriteFlush();
extern LONG GWriteDeclare();
extern LONG GWrite();
extern LONG GSeek();

#endif FDwAT

#else /* not GIO_ACTIVE */

#define GOpen(filename, openmode)           Open(filename, openmode)
#define GClose(file)                        Close(file)
#define GRead(file, buffer, nBytes)         Read(file, buffer, nBytes)
#define GWriteFlush(file)                   (0)
#define GWriteDeclare(file, buffer, nBytes) (0)
```



```
#define GWrite(file, buffer, nBytes)        Write(file, buffer, nBytes)
#define GSeek(file, position, mode)         Seek(file, position, mode)

#endif GIO_ACTIVE


/* Release the buffer for that file, flushing it to disk if it has any
 * contents.  GWriteUndeclare(NULL) to release ALL buffers.
 * Currently, only one file can be buffered at a time anyway.*/
#define GWriteUndeclare(file)  GWriteDeclare(file, NULL, 0)


#endif
```

```
#ifndef IFF_H
#define IFF_H
/*----------------------------------------------------------------------*/
/* IFF.H  defs for IFF-85 Interchange Format Files.            1/22/86 */
/*                                                                      */
/* By Jerry Morrison and Steve Shaw, Electronic Arts.                   */
/* This software is in the public domain.                               */
/*----------------------------------------------------------------------*/

#ifndef COMPILER_H
#include "iff/compiler.h"
#endif

#ifndef LIBRARIES_DOS_H
#include "libraries/dos.h"
#endif

#ifndef OFFSET_BEGINNING
#define OFFSET_BEGINNING OFFSET_BEGINING
#endif

typedef LONG IFFP;      /* Status code result from an IFF procedure */
        /* LONG, because must be type compatable with ID for GetChunkHdr.*/
        /* Note that the error codes below are not legal IDs.*/
#define IFF_OKAY   0L   /* Keep going...*/
#define END_MARK  -1L   /* As if there was a chunk at end of group.*/
#define IFF_DONE  -2L   /* clientProc returns this when it has READ enough.
                         * It means return thru all levels. File is Okay.*/
#define DOS_ERROR -3L
#define NOT_IFF   -4L   /* not an IFF file.*/
#define NO_FILE   -5L   /* Tried to open file, DOS didn't find it.*/
#define CLIENT_ERROR -6L /* Client made invalid request, for instance, write
                         * a negative size chunk.*/
#define BAD_FORM  -7L   /* A client read proc complains about FORM semantics;
                         * e.g. valid IFF, but missing a required chunk.*/
#define SHORT_CHUNK -8L /* Client asked to IFFReadBytes more bytes than left
                         * in the chunk. Could be client bug or bad form.*/
#define BAD_IFF   -9L   /* mal-formed IFF file. [TBD] Expand this into a
                         * range of error codes.*/
#define LAST_ERROR BAD_IFF

/* This MACRO is used to RETURN immediately when a termination condition is
 * found. This is a pretty weird macro. It requires the caller to declare a
 * local "IFFP iffp" and assign it. This wouldn't work as a subroutine since
 * it returns for it's caller. */
#define CheckIFFP()   { if (iffp != IFF_OKAY) return(iffp); }


/* ---------- ID -------------------------------------------------------*/

typedef LONG ID;        /* An ID is four printable ASCII chars but
                         * stored as a LONG for efficient copy & compare.*/

/* Four-character IDentifier builder.*/
#define MakeID(a,b,c,d)  ( (LONG)(a)<<24L | (LONG)(b)<<16L | (c)<<8 | (d) )

/* Standard group IDs.  A chunk with one of these IDs contains a
   SubTypeID followed by zero or more chunks.*/
#define FORM MakeID('F','O','R','M')
#define PROP MakeID('P','R','O','P')
#define LIST MakeID('L','I','S','T')
#define CAT  MakeID('C','A','T',' ')
#define FILLER MakeID(' ',' ',' ',' ')
/* The IDs "FOR1".."FOR9", "LIS1".."LIS9", & "CAT1".."CAT9" are reserved
 * for future standardization.*/

/* Pseudo-ID used internally by chunk reader and writer.*/
#define NULL_CHUNK 0L          /* No current chunk.*/
```



```
/* ---------- Chunk ----------------------------------------------------*/

/* All chunks start with a type ID and a count of the data bytes that
   follow--the chunk's "logicl size" or "data size". If that number is odd,
   a 0 pad byte is written, too. */
typedef struct {
    ID    ckID;
    LONG  ckSize;
    } ChunkHeader;

typedef struct {
    ID    ckID;
    LONG  ckSize;
    UBYTE ckData[ 1 /*REALLY: ckSize*/ ];
    } Chunk;

/* Pass ckSize = szNotYetKnown to the writer to mean "compute the size".*/
#define szNotYetKnown 0x80000001L

/* Need to know whether a value is odd so can word-align.*/
#define IS_ODD(a)   ((a) & 1)

/* This macro rounds up to an even number. */
#define WordAlign(size)   ((size+1)&~1)

/* ALL CHUNKS MUST BE PADDED TO EVEN NUMBER OF BYTES.
 * ChunkPSize computes the total "physical size" of a padded chunk from
 * its "data size" or "logical size". */
#define ChunkPSize(dataSize)  (WordAlign(dataSize) + sizeof(ChunkHeader))

/* The Grouping chunks (LIST, FORM, PROP, & CAT) contain concatenations of
 * chunks after a subtype ID that identifies the content chunks.
 * "FORM type XXXX", "LIST of FORM type XXXX", "PROPerties associated
 * with FORM type XXXX", or "conCATenation of XXXX".*/
typedef struct {
    ID    ckID;
    LONG  ckSize;       /* this ckSize includes "grpSubID".*/
    ID    grpSubID;
    } GroupHeader;

typedef struct {
    ID    ckID;
    LONG  ckSize;
    ID    grpSubID;
    UBYTE grpData[ 1 /*REALLY: ckSize-sizeof(grpSubID)*/ ];
    } GroupChunk;


/* ---------- IFF Reader -----------------------------------------------*/

/******** Routines to support a stream-oriented IFF file reader *******
 *
 * These routines handle lots of details like error checking and skipping
 * over padding. They're also careful not to read past any containing context.
 *
 * These routines ASSUME they're the only ones reading from the file.
 * Client should check IFFP error codes. Don't press on after an error!
 * These routines try to have no side effects in the error case, except
 * partial I/O is sometimes unavoidable.
 *
 * All of these routines may return DOS_ERROR. In that case, ask DOS for the
 * specific error code.
 *
 * The overall scheme for the low level chunk reader is to open a "group read
 * context" with OpenRIFF or OpenRGroup, read the chunks with GetChunkHdr
 * (and its kin) and IFFReadBytes, and close the context with CloseRGroup.
 *
 * The overall scheme for reading an IFF file is to use ReadIFF, ReadIList,
```

```
 * and ReadICat to scan the file. See those procedures, ClientProc (below),
 * and the skeleton IFF reader. */

/* Client passes ptrs to procedures of this type to ReadIFF which call them
 * back to handle LISTs, FORMs, CATs, and PROPs.
 *
 * Use the GroupContext ptr when calling reader routines like GetChunkHdr.
 * Look inside the GroupContext ptr for your ClientFrame ptr. You'll
 * want to type cast it into a ptr to your containing struct to get your
 * private contextual data (stacked property settings). See below. */
#ifdef FDwAT
typedef IFFP ClientProc(struct _GroupContext *);
#else
typedef IFFP ClientProc();
#endif

/* Client's context for reading an IFF file or a group.
 * Client should actually make this the first component of a larger struct
 * (it's personal stack "frame") that has a field to store each "interesting"
 * property encountered.
 * Either initialize each such field to a global default or keep a boolean
 * indicating if you've read a property chunk into that field.
 * Your getList and getForm procs should allocate a new "frame" and copy the
 * parent frame's contents. The getProp procedure should store into the frame
 * allocated by getList for the containing LIST. */
typedef struct _ClientFrame {
   ClientProc *getList, *getProp, *getForm, *getCat;
    /* client's own data follows; place to stack property settings */
    } ClientFrame;

/* Our context for reading a group chunk. */
typedef struct _GroupContext {
    struct _GroupContext *parent; /* Containing group; NULL => whole file. */
    ClientFrame *clientFrame;     /* Reader data & client's context state. */
    BPTR file;             /* Byte-stream file handle. */
    LONG position;         /* The context's logical file position. */
    LONG bound;            /* File-absolute context bound
                            * or szNotYetKnown (writer only). */
    ChunkHeader ckHdr;     /* Current chunk header. ckHdr.ckSize = szNotYetKnown
                            * means we need to go back and set the size (writer only).
                            * See also Pseudo-IDs, above. */
    ID subtype;            /* Group's subtype ID when reading. */
    LONG bytesSoFar;       /* # bytes read/written of current chunk's data. */
    } GroupContext;

/* Computes the number of bytes not yet read from the current chunk, given
 * a group read context gc. */
#define ChunkMoreBytes(gc)  ((gc)->ckHdr.ckSize - (gc)->bytesSoFar)


/***** Low Level IFF Chunk Reader *****/

#ifdef FDwAT

/* Given an open file, open a read context spanning the whole file.
 * This is normally only called by ReadIFF.
 * This sets new->clientFrame = clientFrame.
 * ASSUME context allocated by caller but not initialized.
 * ASSUME caller doesn't deallocate the context before calling CloseRGroup.
 * NOT_IFF ERROR if the file is too short for even a chunk header.*/
extern IFFP OpenRIFF(BPTR, GroupContext *, ClientFrame *);
                 /*  file, new,            clientFrame  */

/* Open the remainder of the current chunk as a group read context.
 * This will be called just after the group's subtype ID has been read
 * (automatically by GetChunkHdr for LIST, FORM, PROP, and CAT) so the
 * remainder is a sequence of chunks.
 * This sets new->clientFrame = parent->clientFrame. The caller should repoint
 * it at a new clientFrame if opening a LIST context so it'll have a "stack
```



```
 * frame" to store PROPs for the LIST. (It's usually convenient to also
 * allocate a new Frame when you encounter FORM of the right type.)
 *
 * ASSUME new context allocated by caller but not initialized.
 * ASSUME caller doesn't deallocate the context or access the parent context
 * before calling CloseRGroup.
 * BAD_IFF ERROR if context end is odd or extends past parent. */
extern IFFP OpenRGroup(GroupContext *, GroupContext *);
                    /*  parent,         new  */

/* Close a group read context, updating its parent context.
 * After calling this, the old context may be deallocated and the parent
 * context can be accessed again. It's okay to call this particular procedure
 * after an error has occurred reading the group.
 * This always returns IFF_OKAY. */
extern IFFP CloseRGroup(GroupContext *);
                     /*  old  */

/* Skip any remaining bytes of the previous chunk and any padding, then
 * read the next chunk header into context.ckHdr.
 * If the ckID is LIST, FORM, CAT, or PROP, this automatically reads the
 * subtype ID into context->subtype.
 * Caller should dispatch on ckID (and subtype) to an appropriate handler.
 *
 * RETURNS context.ckHdr.ckID (the ID of the new chunk header); END_MARK
 * if there are no more chunks in this context; or NOT_IFF if the top level
 * file chunk isn't a FORM, LIST, or CAT; or BAD_IFF if malformed chunk, e.g.
 * ckSize is negative or too big for containing context, ckID isn't positive,
 * or we hit end-of-file.
 *
 * See also GetFChunkHdr, GetFlChunkHdr, and GetPChunkHdr, below.*/
extern ID       GetChunkHdr(GroupContext *);
  /*  context.ckHdr.ckID    context  */

/* Read nBytes number of data bytes of current chunk. (Use OpenGroup, etc.
 * instead to read the contents of a group chunk.) You can call this several
 * times to read the data piecemeal.
 * CLIENT_ERROR if nBytes < 0. SHORT_CHUNK if nBytes > ChunkMoreBytes(context)
 * which could be due to a client bug or a chunk that's shorter than it
 * ought to be (bad form). (on either CLIENT_ERROR or SHORT_CHUNK,
 * IFFReadBytes won't read any bytes.) */
extern IFFP IFFReadBytes(GroupContext *, BYTE *, LONG);
                     /*  context,        buffer, nBytes  */


/***** IFF File Reader *****/

/* This is a noop ClientProc that you can use for a getList, getForm, getProp,
 * or getCat procedure that just skips the group. A simple reader might just
 * implement getForm, store ReadICat in the getCat field of clientFrame, and
 * use SkipGroup for the getList and getProp procs.*/
extern IFFP SkipGroup(GroupContext *);

/* IFF file reader.
 * Given an open file, allocate a group context and use it to read the FORM,
 * LIST, or CAT and it's contents. The idea is to parse the file's contents,
 * and for each FORM, LIST, CAT, or PROP encountered, call the getForm,
 * getList, getCat, or getProp procedure in clientFrame, passing the
 * GroupContext ptr.
 * This is achieved with the aid of ReadIList (which your getList should
 * call) and ReadICat (which your getCat should call, if you don't just use
 * ReadICat for your getCat). If you want to handle FORMs, LISTs, and CATs
 * nested within FORMs, the getForm procedure must dispatch to getForm,
 * getList, and getCat (it can use GetFlChunkHdr to make this easy).
 *
 * Normal return is IFF_OKAY (if whole file scanned) or IFF_DONE (if a client
 * proc said "done" first).
 * See the skeletal getList, getForm, getCat, and getProp procedures. */
extern IFFP ReadIFF(BPTR, ClientFrame *);
```

```
                /*  file, clientFrame  */

/* IFF LIST reader.
 * Your "getList" procedure should allocate a ClientFrame, copy the parent's
 * ClientFrame, and then call this procedure to do all the work.
 *
 * Normal return is IFF_OKAY (if whole LIST scanned) or IFF_DONE (if a client
 * proc said "done" first).
 * BAD_IFF ERROR if a PROP appears after a non-PROP. */
extern IFFP ReadIList(GroupContext *, ClientFrame *);
                 /*  parent,         clientFrame  */

/* IFF CAT reader.
 * Most clients can simply use this to read their CATs. If you must do extra
 * setup work, put a ptr to your getCat procedure in the clientFrame, and
 * have that procedure call ReadICat to do the detail work.
 *
 * Normal return is IFF_OKAY (if whole CAT scanned) or IFF_DONE (if a client
 * proc said "done" first).
 * BAD_IFF ERROR if a PROP appears in the CAT. */
extern IFFP ReadICat(GroupContext *);
                /*  parent  */

/* Call GetFChunkHdr instead of GetChunkHdr to read each chunk inside a FORM.
 * It just calls GetChunkHdr and returns BAD_IFF if it gets a PROP chunk. */
extern ID       GetFChunkHdr(GroupContext *);
  /*  context.ckHdr.ckID    context  */

/* GetFlChunkHdr is like GetFChunkHdr, but it automatically dispatches to the
 * getForm, getList, and getCat procedure (and returns the result) if it
 * encounters a FORM, LIST, or CAT. */
extern ID       GetFlChunkHdr(GroupContext *);
  /*  context.ckHdr.ckID    context  */

/* Call GetPChunkHdr instead of GetChunkHdr to read each chunk inside a PROP.
 * It just calls GetChunkHdr and returns BAD_IFF if it gets a group chunk. */
extern ID       GetPChunkHdr(GroupContext *);
  /*  context.ckHdr.ckID    context  */

#else /* not FDwAT */

extern IFFP OpenRIFF();
extern IFFP OpenRGroup();
extern IFFP CloseRGroup();
extern ID   GetChunkHdr();
extern IFFP IFFReadBytes();
extern IFFP SkipGroup();
extern IFFP ReadIFF();
extern IFFP ReadIList();
extern IFFP ReadICat();
extern ID   GetFChunkHdr();
extern ID   GetFlChunkHdr();
extern ID   GetPChunkHdr();

#endif /* not FDwAT */

/* ---------- IFF Writer -----------------------------------------------*/

/******* Routines to support a stream-oriented IFF file writer *******
 *
 * These routines will random access back to set a chunk size value when the
 * caller doesn't know it ahead of time. They'll also do things automatically
 * like padding and error checking.
 *
 * These routines ASSUME they're the only ones writing to the file.
 * Client should check IFFP error codes. Don't press on after an error!
 * These routines try to have no side effects in the error case, except that
 * partial I/O is sometimes unavoidable.
 *
```



```
 * All of these routines may return DOS_ERROR. In that case, ask DOS for the
 * specific error code.
 *
 * The overall scheme is to open an output GroupContext via OpenWIFF or
 * OpenWGroup, call either PutCk or {PutCkHdr {IFFWriteBytes}* PutCkEnd} for
 * each chunk, then use CloseWGroup to close the GroupContext.
 *
 * To write a group (LIST, FORM, PROP, or CAT), call StartWGroup, write out
 * its chunks, then call EndWGroup. StartWGroup automatically writes the
 * group header and opens a nested context for writing the contents.
 * EndWGroup closes the nested context and completes the group chunk. */


#ifdef FDwAT

/* Given a file open for output, open a write context.
 * The "limit" arg imposes a fence or upper limit on the logical file
 * position for writing data in this context. Pass in szNotYetKnown to be
 * bounded only by disk capacity.
 * ASSUME new context structure allocated by caller but not initialized.
 * ASSUME caller doesn't deallocate the context before calling CloseWGroup.
 * The caller is only allowed to write out one FORM, LIST, or CAT in this top
 * level context (see StartWGroup and PutCkHdr).
 * CLIENT_ERROR if limit is odd.*/
extern IFFP OpenWIFF(BPTR, GroupContext *, LONG);
                /*  file, new,            limit {file position}  */

/* Start writing a group (presumably LIST, FORM, PROP, or CAT), opening a
 * nested context. The groupSize includes all nested chunks + the subtype ID.
 *
 * The subtype of a LIST or CAT is a hint at the contents' FORM type(s). Pass
 * in FILLER if it's a mixture of different kinds.
 *
 * This writes the chunk header via PutCkHdr, writes the subtype ID via
 * IFFWriteBytes, and calls OpenWGroup. The caller may then write the nested
 * chunks and finish by calling EndWGroup.
 * The OpenWGroup call sets new->clientFrame = parent->clientFrame.
 *
 * ASSUME new context structure allocated by caller but not initialized.
 * ASSUME caller doesn't deallocate the context or access the parent context
 * before calling CloseWGroup.
 * ERROR conditions: See PutCkHdr, IFFWriteBytes, OpenWGroup. */
extern IFFP StartWGroup(GroupContext *, ID, LONG, ID, GroupContext *);
                  /*  parent, groupType, groupSize, subtype, new  */

/* End a group started by StartWGroup.
 * This just calls CloseWGroup and PutCkEnd.
 * ERROR conditions: See CloseWGroup and PutCkEnd. */
extern IFFP EndWGroup(GroupContext *);
                  /*  old  */

/* Open the remainder of the current chunk as a group write context.
 * This is normally only called by StartWGroup.
 *
 * Any fixed limit to this group chunk or a containing context will impose
 * a limit on the new context.
 * This will be called just after the group's subtype ID has been written
 * so the remaining contents will be a sequence of chunks.
 * This sets new->clientFrame = parent->clientFrame.
 * ASSUME new context structure allocated by caller but not initialized.
 * ASSUME caller doesn't deallocate the context or access the parent context
 * before calling CloseWGroup.
 * CLIENT_ERROR if context end is odd or PutCkHdr wasn't called first. */
extern IFFP OpenWGroup(GroupContext *, GroupContext *);
                 /*  parent,        new  */

/* Close a write context and update its parent context.
 * This is normally only called by EndWGroup.
 *
```

```
 * If this is a top level context (created by OpenWIFF) we'll set the file's
 * EOF (end of file) but won't close the file.
 * After calling this, the old context may be deallocated and the parent
 * context can be accessed again.
 *
 * Amiga DOS Note: There's no call to set the EOF. We just position to the
 * desired end and return. Caller must Close file at that position.
 * CLIENT_ERROR if PutCkEnd wasn't called first. */
extern IFFP CloseWGroup(GroupContext *);
                    /*  old  */

/* Write a whole chunk to a GroupContext. This writes a chunk header, ckSize
 * data bytes, and (if needed) a pad byte. It also updates the GroupContext.
 * CLIENT_ERROR if ckSize == szNotYetKnown. See also PutCkHdr errors. */
extern IFFP PutCk(GroupContext *, ID,   LONG,    BYTE *);
             /*  context,        ckID, ckSize, *data  */

/* Write just a chunk header. Follow this will any number of calls to
 * IFFWriteBytes and finish with PutCkEnd.
 * If you don't yet know how big the chunk is, pass in ckSize = szNotYetKnown,
 * then PutCkEnd will set the ckSize for you later.
 * Otherwise, IFFWriteBytes and PutCkEnd will ensure that the specified
 * number of bytes get written.
 * CLIENT_ERROR if the chunk would overflow the GroupContext's bound, if
 * PutCkHdr was previously called without a matching PutCkEnd, if ckSize < 0
 * (except szNotYetKnown), if you're trying to write something other
 * than one FORM, LIST, or CAT in a top level (file level) context, or
 * if ckID <= 0 (these illegal ID values are used for error codes). */
extern IFFP PutCkHdr(GroupContext *, ID,   LONG);
                /*  context,        ckID, ckSize  */

/* Write nBytes number of data bytes for the current chunk and update
 * GroupContext.
 * CLIENT_ERROR if this would overflow the GroupContext's limit or the
 * current chunk's ckSize, or if PutCkHdr wasn't called first, or if
 * nBytes < 0. */
extern IFFP IFFWriteBytes(GroupContext *, BYTE *, LONG);
                     /*  context,        *data,  nBytes  */

/* Complete the current chunk, write a pad byte if needed, and update
 * GroupContext.
 * If current chunk's ckSize = szNotYetKnown, this goes back and sets the
 * ckSize in the file.
 * CLIENT_ERROR if PutCkHdr wasn't called first, or if client hasn't
 * written 'ckSize' number of bytes with IFFWriteBytes. */
extern IFFP PutCkEnd(GroupContext *);
                /*  context  */

#else /* not FDwAT */

extern IFFP OpenWIFF();
extern IFFP StartWGroup();
extern IFFP EndWGroup();
extern IFFP OpenWGroup();
extern IFFP CloseWGroup();
extern IFFP PutCk();
extern IFFP PutCkHdr();
extern IFFP IFFWriteBytes();
extern IFFP PutCkEnd();

#endif /* not FDwAT */

#endif IFF_H
```



```
#ifndef ILBM_H
#define ILBM_H
/*----------------------------------------------------------------------*
 * ILBM.H  Definitions for InterLeaved BitMap raster image.     1/23/86
 *    09/88 - added CAMG, CCRT, and CRNG typedefs and macros   (cs)
 *
 * By Jerry Morrison and Steve Shaw, Electronic Arts.
 * This software is in the public domain.
 *
 * This version for the Commodore-Amiga computer.
 *----------------------------------------------------------------------*/
#ifndef COMPILER_H
#include "iff/compiler.h"
#endif

#ifndef GRAPHICS_GFX_H
#include "graphics/gfx.h"
#endif

#include "iff/iff.h"

#define ID_ILBM MakeID('I','L','B','M')
#define ID_BMHD MakeID('B','M','H','D')
#define ID_CMAP MakeID('C','M','A','P')
#define ID_GRAB MakeID('G','R','A','B')
#define ID_DEST MakeID('D','E','S','T')
#define ID_SPRT MakeID('S','P','R','T')
#define ID_CAMG MakeID('C','A','M','G')
#define ID_CRNG MakeID('C','R','N','G')
#define ID_CCRT MakeID('C','C','R','T')
#define ID_BODY MakeID('B','O','D','Y')



/* ---------- BitMapHeader ---------------------------------------------*/

typedef UBYTE Masking;      /* Choice of masking technique.*/
#define mskNone                 0
#define mskHasMask              1
#define mskHasTransparentColor  2
#define mskLasso                3

typedef UBYTE Compression;   /* Choice of compression algorithm applied to
     * each row of the source and mask planes. "cmpByteRun1" is the byte run
     * encoding generated by Mac's PackBits. See Packer.h . */
#define cmpNone      0
#define cmpByteRun1  1

/* Aspect ratios: The proper fraction xAspect/yAspect represents the pixel
 * aspect ratio pixel_width/pixel_height.
 *
 * For the 4 Amiga display modes:
 *    320 x 200: 10/11  (these pixels are taller than they are wide)
 *    320 x 400: 20/11
 *    640 x 200:  5/11
 *    640 x 400: 10/11      */
#define x320x200Aspect 10
#define y320x200Aspect 11
#define x320x400Aspect 20
#define y320x400Aspect 11
#define x640x200Aspect  5
#define y640x200Aspect 11
#define x640x400Aspect 10
#define y640x400Aspect 11

/* A BitMapHeader is stored in a BMHD chunk. */
typedef struct {
    UWORD w, h;         /* raster width & height in pixels */
    WORD  x, y;         /* position for this image */
```

```
    UBYTE nPlanes;        /* # source bitplanes */
    Masking masking;        /* masking technique */
    Compression compression;    /* compression algoithm */
    UBYTE pad1;            /* UNUSED.  For consistency, put 0 here.*/
    UWORD transparentColor;   /* transparent "color number" */
    UBYTE xAspect, yAspect;   /* aspect ratio, a rational number x/y */
    WORD  pageWidth, pageHeight;  /* source "page" size in pixels */
    } BitMapHeader;

/* RowBytes computes the number of bytes in a row, from the width in pixels.*/
#define RowBytes(w)   (((w) + 15) >> 4 << 1)


/* ---------- ColorRegister ----------------------------------------------*/
/* A CMAP chunk is a packed array of ColorRegisters (3 bytes each). */
typedef struct {
    UBYTE red, green, blue;   /* MUST be UBYTEs so ">> 4" won't sign extend.*/
    } ColorRegister;

/* Use this constant instead of sizeof(ColorRegister). */
#define sizeofColorRegister  3

typedef WORD Color4;   /* Amiga RAM version of a color-register,
          * with 4 bits each RGB in low 12 bits.*/

/* Maximum number of bitplanes in RAM. Current Amiga max w/dual playfield. */
#define MaxAmDepth 6

/* ---------- Point2D ----------------------------------------------------*/
/* A Point2D is stored in a GRAB chunk. */
typedef struct {
    WORD x, y;      /* coordinates (pixels) */
    } Point2D;

/* ---------- DestMerge --------------------------------------------------*/
/* A DestMerge is stored in a DEST chunk. */
typedef struct {
    UBYTE depth;   /* # bitplanes in the original source */
    UBYTE pad1;      /* UNUSED; for consistency store 0 here */
    UWORD planePick;   /* how to scatter source bitplanes into destination */
    UWORD planeOnOff;   /* default bitplane data for planePick */
    UWORD planeMask;   /* selects which bitplanes to store into */
    } DestMerge;

/* ---------- SpritePrecedence -------------------------------------------*/
/* A SpritePrecedence is stored in a SPRT chunk. */
typedef UWORD SpritePrecedence;

/* ---------- Camg Amiga Viewport Mode -----------------------------------*/
/* A Commodore Amiga ViewPort->Modes is stored in a CAMG chunk. */
/* The chunk's content is declared as a LONG. */
typedef struct {
    ULONG ViewModes;
    } CamgChunk;

/* ---------- CRange cycling chunk ---------------------------------------*/
/* A CRange is store in a CRNG chunk. */
typedef struct {
    WORD  pad1;              /* reserved for future use; store 0 here */
    WORD  rate;      /* 60/sec=16384, 30/sec=8192, 1/sec=16384/60=273 */
    WORD  active;     /* bit0 set = active, bit 1 set = reverse */
    UBYTE low, high;   /* lower and upper color registers selected */
    } CRange;

/* ---------- Ccrt (Graphicraft) cycling chunk ---------------------------*/
/* A Ccrt is stored in a CCRT chunk. */
typedef struct {
   WORD  direction;  /* 0=don't cycle, 1=forward, -1=backwards */
   UBYTE start;      /* range lower */
```



```
   UBYTE end;         /* range upper */
   LONG  seconds;     /* seconds between cycling */
   LONG  microseconds; /* msecs between cycling */
   WORD  pad;         /* future exp - store 0 here */
   } CcrtChunk;


/* ---------- ILBM Writer Support Routines -------------------------------*/

/* Note: Just call PutCk to write a BMHD, GRAB, DEST, SPRT, or CAMG
 * chunk. As below. */
#define PutBMHD(context, bmHdr)  \
    PutCk(context, ID_BMHD, sizeof(BitMapHeader), (BYTE *)bmHdr)
#define PutGRAB(context, point2D)  \
    PutCk(context, ID_GRAB, sizeof(Point2D), (BYTE *)point2D)
#define PutDEST(context, destMerge)  \
    PutCk(context, ID_DEST, sizeof(DestMerge), (BYTE *)destMerge)
#define PutSPRT(context, spritePrec)  \
    PutCk(context, ID_SPRT, sizeof(SpritePrecedence), (BYTE *)spritePrec)
#define PutCAMG(context, camg)  \
    PutCk(context, ID_CAMG, sizeof(CamgChunk),(BYTE *)camg)
#define PutCRNG(context, crng)  \
    PutCk(context, ID_CRNG, sizeof(CRange),(BYTE *)crng)
#define PutCCRT(context, ccrt)  \
    PutCk(context, ID_CCRT, sizeof(CcrtChunk),(BYTE *)ccrt)

#ifdef FDwAT

/* Initialize a BitMapHeader record for a full-BitMap ILBM picture.
 * This gets w, h, and nPlanes from the BitMap fields BytesPerRow, Rows, and
 * Depth. It assumes you want  w = bitmap->BytesPerRow * 8 .
 * CLIENT_ERROR if bitmap->BytesPerRow isn't even, as required by ILBM format.
 *
 * If (pageWidth, pageHeight) is (320, 200), (320, 400), (640, 200), or
 * (640, 400) this sets (xAspect, yAspect) based on those 4 Amiga display
 * modes. Otherwise, it sets them to (1, 1).
 *
 * After calling this, store directly into the BitMapHeader if you want to
 * override any settings, e.g. to make nPlanes smaller, to reduce w a little,
 * or to set a position (x, y) other than (0, 0).*/
extern IFFP InitBMHdr(BitMapHeader *, struct BitMap *,
        /*  bmHdr,          bitmap  */
     int,     int,       int,            WORD,      WORD);
 /*  masking, compression, transparentColor, pageWidth, pageHeight */
 /*  Masking, Compression, UWORD -- are the desired types, but get
  *  compiler warnings if use them.            */

/* Output a CMAP chunk to an open FORM ILBM write context. */
extern IFFP PutCMAP(GroupContext *, WORD *,   UBYTE);
      /*  context,         colorMap, depth  */

/* This procedure outputs a BitMap as an ILBM's BODY chunk with
 * bitplane and mask data. Compressed if bmHdr->compression == cmpByteRun1.
 * If the "mask" argument isn't NULL, it merges in the mask plane, too.
 * (A fancier routine could write a rectangular portion of an image.)
 * This gets Planes (bitplane ptrs) from "bitmap".
 *
 * CLIENT_ERROR if bitmap->Rows != bmHdr->h, or if
 * bitmap->BytesPerRow != RowBytes(bmHdr->w), or if
 * bitmap->Depth < bmHdr->nPlanes, or if bmHdr->nPlanes > MaxAmDepth, or if
 * bufsize < MaxPackedSize(bitmap->BytesPerRow), or if
 * bmHdr->compression > cmpByteRun1. */
extern IFFP PutBODY(
    GroupContext *, struct BitMap *, BYTE *, BitMapHeader *, BYTE *, LONG);
    /*  context,           bitmap,   mask,   bmHdr,         buffer, bufsize */

#else /*not FDwAT*/

extern IFFP InitBMHdr();
```

```
extern IFFP PutCMAP();
extern IFFP PutBODY();

#endif FDwAT

/* ---------- ILBM Reader Support Routines ------------------------------*/

/* Note: Just call IFFReadBytes to read a BMHD, GRAB, DEST, SPRT, or CAMG
 * chunk. As below. */
#define GetBMHD(context, bmHdr)  \
    IFFReadBytes(context, (BYTE *)bmHdr, sizeof(BitMapHeader))

#define GetGRAB(context, point2D)  \
    IFFReadBytes(context, (BYTE *)point2D, sizeof(Point2D))
#define GetDEST(context, destMerge)  \
    IFFReadBytes(context, (BYTE *)destMerge, sizeof(DestMerge))
#define GetSPRT(context, spritePrec)  \
    IFFReadBytes(context, (BYTE *)spritePrec, sizeof(SpritePrecedence))
#define GetCAMG(context, camg)  \
    IFFReadBytes(context, (BYTE *)camg, sizeof(CamgChunk))
#define GetCRNG(context, crng)  \
    IFFReadBytes(context, (BYTE *)crng, sizeof(CRange))
#define GetCCRT(context, ccrt)  \
    IFFReadBytes(context, (BYTE *)ccrt, sizeof(CcrtChunk))


/* GetBODY can handle a file with up to 16 planes plus a mask.*/
#define MaxSrcPlanes 16+1

#ifdef FDwAT

/* Input a CMAP chunk from an open FORM ILBM read context.
 * This converts to an Amiga color map: 4 bits each of red, green, blue packed
 * into a 16 bit color register.
 * pNColorRegs is passed in as a pointer to a UBYTE variable that holds
 * the number of ColorRegisters the caller has space to hold. GetCMAP sets
 * that variable to the number of color registers actually read.*/
extern IFFP GetCMAP(GroupContext *, WORD *,   UBYTE *);
      /*  context,        colorMap, pNColorRegs  */

/* GetBODY reads an ILBM's BODY into a client's bitmap, de-interleaving and
 * decompressing.
 *
 * Caller should first compare bmHdr dimensions (rowWords, h, nPlanes) with
 * bitmap dimensions, and consider reallocating the bitmap.
 * If file has more bitplanes than bitmap, this reads first few planes (low
 * order ones). If bitmap has more bitplanes, the last few are untouched.
 * This reads the MIN(bmHdr->h, bitmap->Rows) rows, discarding the bottom
 * part of the source or leaving the bottom part of the bitmap untouched.
 *
 * GetBODY returns CLIENT_ERROR if asked to perform a conversion it doesn't
 * handle. It only understands compression algorithms cmpNone and cmpByteRun1.
 * The filed row width (# words) must agree with bitmap->BytesPerRow.
 *
 * Caller should use bmHdr.w; GetBODY only uses it to compute the row width
 * in words. Pixels to the right of bmHdr.w are not defined.
 *
 * [TBD] In the future, GetBODY could clip the stored image horizontally or
 * fill (with transparentColor) untouched parts of the destination bitmap.
 *
 * GetBODY stores the mask plane, if any, in the buffer pointed to by mask.
 * If mask == NULL, GetBODY will skip any mask plane. If
 * (bmHdr.masking != mskHasMask) GetBODY just leaves the caller's mask alone.
 *
 * GetBODY needs a buffer large enough for two compressed rows.
 * It returns CLIENT_ERROR if bufsize < 2 * MaxPackedSize(bmHdr.rowWords * 2).
 *
 * GetBODY can handle a file with up to MaxSrcPlanes planes. It returns
 * CLIENT_ERROR if the file has more. (Could be due to a bum file, though.)
```



```
 * If GetBODY fails, itt might've modified the client's bitmap. Sorry.*/
extern IFFP GetBODY(
    GroupContext *, struct BitMap *, BYTE *, BitMapHeader *, BYTE *, LONG);
    /*  context,           bitmap,   mask,   bmHdr,          buffer, bufsize */

/* [TBD] Add routine(s) to create masks when reading ILBMs whose
 * masking != mskHasMask. For mskNone, create a rectangular mask. For
 * mskHasTransparentColor, create a mask from transparentColor. For mskLasso,
 * create an "auto mask" by filling transparent color from the edges. */

#else /*not FDwAT*/

extern IFFP GetCMAP();
extern IFFP GetBODY();

#endif FDwAT

#endif ILBM_H
```

```
/*** intuall.h *****************************************************/
/*  intuall.h, Include lots of Amiga-provided header files.    1/22/86 */
/*  Plus the portability file "iff/compiler.h" which should be tailored */
/*  for your compiler.                                                */
/*                                                                    */
/* By Jerry Morrison and Steve Shaw, Electronic Arts.                 */
/* This software is in the public domain.                             */
/*                                                                    */
/* This version for the Commodore-Amiga computer.                     */
/*                                                                    */
/*********************************************************************/

#include "iff/compiler.h"       /* COMPILER-DEPENDENCIES */

/* Dummy definitions because some includes below are commented out.
 * This avoids 'undefined structure' warnings when compile.
 * This is safe as long as only use POINTERS to these structures.
 */

struct Region { int dummy; };
struct VSprite { int dummy; };
struct collTable { int dummy; };
struct CopList { int dummy; };
struct UCopList { int dummy; };
struct cprlist { int dummy; };
struct copinit { int dummy; };
struct TimeVal { int dummy; };

#include "exec/types.h"
#include "exec/nodes.h"
#include "exec/lists.h"
#include "exec/libraries.h"
#include "exec/ports.h"

#include "exec/tasks.h"
#include "exec/devices.h"


#include "exec/interrupts.h"

#include "exec/io.h"
#include "exec/memory.h"
#include "exec/alerts.h"

/* ALWAYS INCLUDE GFX.H before any other amiga includes */

#include "graphics/gfx.h"
/*#include "hardware/blit.h"*/

/*****
#include "graphics/collide.h"
#include "graphics/copper.h"
#include "graphics/display.h"
#include "hardware/dmabits.h"
#include "graphics/gels.h"
***/

#include "graphics/clip.h"

#include "graphics/rastport.h"
#include "graphics/view.h"
#include "graphics/gfxbase.h"
/*#include "hardware/intbits.h"*/
#include "graphics/gfxmacros.h"

#include "graphics/layers.h"

#include "graphics/text.h"
#include "graphics/sprite.h"
```



```
/*#include "hardware/custom.h"*/

/*#include "libraries/dos.h"*/
/*#include "libraries/dosextens.h"*/

#include "devices/timer.h"
#include "devices/inputevent.h"
#include "devices/keymap.h"

#include "intuition/intuition.h"

/*#include "intuitionbase.h"*/
/*#include "intuinternal.h"*/
```

```
#ifndef PACKER_H
#define PACKER_H
/*----------------------------------------------------------------------*
 * PACKER.H  typedefs for Data-Compresser.                    1/22/86
 *
 * This module implements the run compression algorithm "cmpByteRun1"; the
 * same encoding generated by Mac's PackBits.
 *
 * By Jerry Morrison and Steve Shaw, Electronic Arts.
 * This software is in the public domain.
 *
 * This version for the Commodore-Amiga computer.
 *----------------------------------------------------------------------*/

#ifndef COMPILER_H
#include "iff/compiler.h"
#endif

/* This macro computes the worst case packed size of a "row" of bytes. */
#define MaxPackedSize(rowSize)  ( (rowSize) + ( ((rowSize)+127) >> 7 ) )


#ifdef FDwAT  /* Compiler handles Function Declaration with Argument Types */

/* Given POINTERS to POINTER variables, packs one row, updating the source
 * and destination pointers. Returns the size in bytes of the packed row.
 * ASSUMES destination buffer is large enough for the packed row.
 * See MaxPackedSize. */
extern LONG PackRow(BYTE **, BYTE **, LONG);
                /*  pSource, pDest,   rowSize */

/* Given POINTERS to POINTER variables, unpacks one row, updating the source
 * and destination pointers until it produces dstBytes bytes (i.e., the
 * rowSize that went into PackRow).
 * If it would exceed the source's limit srcBytes or if a run would overrun
 * the destination buffer size dstBytes, it stops and returns TRUE.
 * Otherwise, it returns FALSE (no error). */
extern BOOL UnPackRow(BYTE **, BYTE **, WORD,     WORD);
                  /*  pSource, pDest,   srcBytes, dstBytes  */

#else /* not FDwAT */

extern LONG PackRow();
extern BOOL UnPackRow();

#endif /* FDwAT */

#endif
```



```
#ifndef PUTPICT_H
#define PUTPICT_H
/** putpict.h ********************************************************* */
/* PutPict().  Given a BitMap and a color map in RAM on the Amiga,      */
/* outputs as an ILBM.  See /iff/ilbm.h & /iff/ilbmw.c.       23-Jan-86 */
/*                                                                      */
/* By Jerry Morrison and Steve Shaw, Electronic Arts.                   */
/* This software is in the public domain.                               */
/*                                                                      */
/* This version for the Commodore-Amiga computer.                       */
/*                                                                      */
/************************************************************************/
#ifndef COMPILER_H
#include "iff/compiler.h"
#endif

#ifndef ILBM_H
#include "iff/ilbm.h"
#endif

#ifdef FDwAT

/****** IffErr ************************************************************/
/* Returns the iff error code and resets it to zero                        */
/**************************************************************************/
extern IFFP IffErr(void);

/****** PutPict ***********************************************************/
/* Put a picture into an IFF file                                          */
/* Pass in mask == NULL for no mask.                                       */
/*                                                                         */
/* Buffer should be big enough for one packed scan line                    */
/* Buffer used as temporary storage to speed-up writing.                   */
/* A large buffer, say 8KB, is useful for minimizing Write and Seek calls. */
/* (See /iff/gio.h & /iff/gio.c).                                          */
/**************************************************************************/
extern BOOL PutPict(LONG, struct BitMap *, WORD,WORD, WORD *, BYTE *, LONG);
                 /* file, bm,           pageW,pageH,colorMap, buffer,bufsize */

#else /*not FDwAT*/

extern IFFP IffErr();
extern BOOL PutPict();

#endif FDwAT

#endif PUTPICT_H
```

```
#ifndef READPICT_H
#define READPICT_H
/** ReadPict.h ***************************************************************/
/*                                                                          */
/* Read an ILBM raster image file into RAM.   1/23/86.                      */
/*                                                                          */
/* By Jerry Morrison, Steve Shaw, and Steve Hayes, Electronic Arts.         */
/* This software is in the public domain.                                   */
/*                                                                          */
/* USE THIS AS AN EXAMPLE PROGRAM FOR AN IFF READER.                        */
/*                                                                          */
/* The IFF reader portion is essentially a recursive-descent parser.        */
/****************************************************************************/

/* ILBMFrame is our "client frame" for reading FORMs ILBM in an IFF file.
 * We allocate one of these on the stack for every LIST or FORM encountered
 * in the file and use it to hold BMHD & CMAP properties. We also allocate
 * an initial one for the whole file. */
typedef struct {
   ClientFrame clientFrame;
   UBYTE foundBMHD;
   UBYTE nColorRegs;
   BitMapHeader bmHdr;
   Color4 colorMap[32 /*1<<MaxAmDepth*/ ];
   /* If you want to read any other property chunks, e.g. GRAB or CAMG, add
    * fields to this record to store them. */
   } ILBMFrame;

/** ReadPicture() ***********************************************************
 *
 * Read a picture from an IFF file, given a file handle open for reading.
 * Allocates BitMap RAM by calling (*Allocator)(size).
 *
 ****************************************************************************/

typedef UBYTE *UBytePtr;

#ifdef FDwAT

typedef UBytePtr Allocator(LONG);
   /* Allocator: a memory allocation procedure which only requires a size
    * argument. (No Amiga memory flags argument.) */

extern IFFP ReadPicture(LONG, struct BitMap *, ILBMFrame *, Allocator *);
                     /*  file, bm,             iFrame,       allocator  */
   /* iFrame is the top level "client frame". */
   /* allocator is a ptr to your allocation procedure. It must always
    *   allocate in Chip memory (for bitmap data). */

   /* PS: Notice how we used two "typedef"s above to make allocator's type
    * meaningful to humans.
    * Consider the usual C style: UBYTE *(*)(), or is it (UBYTE *)(*()) ? */

#else /* not FDwAT */

typedef UBytePtr Allocator();
extern IFFP ReadPicture();

#endif

#endif READPICT_H
```



```
/** RemAlloc.h **************************************************************/
/*  ChipAlloc(), ExtAlloc(), RemAlloc(), RemFree().                          */
/*  ALLOCators which REMember the size allocated, for simpler freeing.       */
/*                                                                           */
/* Date      Who Changes                                                     */
/* --------- --- ----------------------------------------------------------- */
/* 16-Jan-86 sss Created from DPaint/DAlloc.c                                */
/* 22-Jan-86 jhm Include Compiler.h                                          */
/* 25-Jan-86 sss Added ChipNoClearAlloc,ExtNoClearAlloc                      */
/*                                                                           */
/* By Jerry Morrison and Steve Shaw, Electronic Arts.                        */
/* This software is in the public domain.                                    */
/*                                                                           */
/* This version for the Commodore-Amiga computer.                            */
/*                                                                           */
/*****************************************************************************/
#ifndef REM_ALLOC_H
#define REM_ALLOC_H

#ifndef COMPILER_H
#include "iff/compiler.h"
#endif


/* How these allocators work:
 * The allocator procedures get the memory from the system allocator,
 * actually allocating 4 extra bytes. We store the length of the node in
 * the first 4 bytes then return a ptr to the rest of the storage. The
 * deallocator can then find the node size and free it. */


#ifdef FDwAT

/* RemAlloc allocates a node with "size" bytes of user data.
 * Example:
 *   struct BitMap *bm;
 *   bm = (struct BitMap *)RemAlloc( sizeof(struct BitMap), ...flags... );
 */
extern UBYTE *RemAlloc(LONG, LONG);
                     /* size, flags */

/* ALLOCator that remembers size, allocates in CHIP-accessable memory.
 * Use for all data to be displayed on screen, all sound data, all data to be
 * blitted, disk buffers, or access by any other DMA channel.
 * Does clear memory being allocated.*/
extern UBYTE *ChipAlloc(LONG);
                      /* size */

/* ChipAlloc, without clearing memory.  Purpose: speed when allocate
 * large area that will be overwritten anyway.*/
extern UBYTE *ChipNoClearAlloc(LONG);

/* ALLOCator that remembers size, allocates in extended memory.
 * Does clear memory being allocated.
 * NOTICE: does NOT declare "MEMF_FAST".  This allows machines
 * lacking extended memory to allocate within chip memory,
 * assuming there is enough memory left.*/
extern UBYTE *ExtAlloc(LONG);
                     /* size */

/* ExtAlloc, without clearing memory.  Purpose: speed when allocate
 * large area that will be overwritten anyway.*/
extern UBYTE *ExtNoClearAlloc(LONG);


/* FREEs either chip or extended memory, if allocated with an allocator
 * which REMembers size allocated.
 * Safe: won't attempt to de-allocate a NULL pointer.
 * Returns NULL so caller can do
```

```
 *   p = RemFree(p);
 */
extern UBYTE *RemFree(UBYTE *);
                  /*  p  */

#else /* not FDwAT */

extern UBYTE *RemAlloc();
extern UBYTE *ChipAlloc();
extern UBYTE *ExtAlloc();
extern UBYTE *RemFree();

#endif /* FDwAT */

#endif REM_ALLOC_H
```



```
/*----------------------------------------------------------------------*
 * SMUS.H  Definitions for Simple MUSical score.   2/12/86
 *
 * By Jerry Morrison and Steve Hayes, Electronic Arts.
 * This software is in the public domain.
 *
 * This version for the Commodore-Amiga computer.
 *----------------------------------------------------------------------*/
#ifndef SMUS_H
#define SMUS_H

#ifndef COMPILER_H
#include "iff/compiler.h"
#endif

#include "iff/iff.h"

#define ID_SMUS      MakeID('S', 'M', 'U', 'S')
#define ID_SHDR      MakeID('S', 'H', 'D', 'R')
#define ID_NAME      MakeID('N', 'A', 'M', 'E')
#define ID_Copyright MakeID('(', 'c', ')', ' ')
#define ID_AUTH      MakeID('A', 'U', 'T', 'H')
#define ID_ANNO      MakeID('A', 'N', 'N', 'O')

#define ID_INS1      MakeID('I', 'N', 'S', '1')
#define ID_TRAK      MakeID('T', 'R', 'A', 'K')

/* ---------- SScoreHeader ---------------------------------------------*/
typedef struct {
    UWORD tempo;        /* tempo, 128ths quarter note/minute */
    UBYTE volume;       /* playback volume 0 through 127 */
    UBYTE ctTrack;      /* count of tracks in the score */
    } SScoreHeader;

/* ---------- NAME -----------------------------------------------------*/
/* NAME chunk contains a CHAR[], the musical score's name. */

/* ---------- Copyright (c) --------------------------------------------*/
/* "(c) " chunk contains a CHAR[], the FORM's copyright notice. */

/* ---------- AUTH -----------------------------------------------------*/
/* AUTH chunk contains a CHAR[], the name of the score's author. */

/* ---------- ANNO -----------------------------------------------------*/
/* ANNO chunk contains a CHAR[], the author's text annotations. */

/* ---------- INS1 -----------------------------------------------------*/
/* Constants for the RefInstrument's "type" field. */
#define INS1_Name  0    /* just use the name; ignore data1, data2 */
#define INS1_MIDI  1    /* <data1, data2> = MIDI <channel, preset> */

typedef struct {
    UBYTE iRegister;    /* set this instrument register number */
    UBYTE type;         /* instrument reference type (see above) */
    UBYTE data1, data2; /* depends on the "type" field */
    char name[60];      /* instrument name */
    } RefInstrument;

/* ---------- TRAK -----------------------------------------------------*/
/* TRAK chunk contains an SEvent[]. */

/* SEvent: Simple musical event. */
typedef struct {
    UBYTE sID;          /* SEvent type code */
    UBYTE data;         /* sID-dependent data */
    } SEvent;

/* SEvent type codes "sID". */
#define SID_FirstNote     0
```

```
#define SID_LastNote     127      /* sIDs in the range SID_FirstNote through
                                   * SID_LastNote (sign bit = 0) are notes. The
                                   * sID is the MIDI tone number (pitch). */
#define SID_Rest         128      /* a rest; same data format as a note. */

#define SID_Instrument   129      /* set instrument number for this track. */
#define SID_TimeSig      130      /* set time signature for this track. */
#define SID_KeySig       131      /* set key signature for this track. */
#define SID_Dynamic      132      /* set volume for this track. */
#define SID_MIDI_Chnl    133      /* set MIDI channel number (sequencers) */
#define SID_MIDI_Preset  134      /* set MIDI preset number (sequencers) */
#define SID_Clef         135      /* inline clef change.
                                   * 0=Treble, 1=Bass, 2=Alto, 3=Tenor. */

#define SID_Tempo        136      /* Inline tempo change in beats per minute.*/

/* SID values 144 through 159: reserved for Instant Music SEvents. */

/* The remaining sID values up through 254: reserved for future
 * standardization. */
#define SID_Mark         255      /* SID reserved for an end-mark in RAM. */

/* ---------- SEvent FirstNote..LastNote or Rest -----------------------*/
typedef struct {
    unsigned tone      :8,        /* MIDI tone number 0 to 127; 128 = rest */
             chord     :1,        /* 1 = a chorded note */
             tieOut    :1,        /* 1 = tied to the next note or chord */
             nTuplet   :2,        /* 0 = none, 1 = triplet, 2 = quintuplet,
                                   * 3 = septuplet */
             dot       :1,        /* dotted note; multiply duration by 3/2 */
             division  :3;        /* basic note duration is 2**-division:
                                   * 0 = whole note, 1 = half note, 2 = quarter
                                   * note, ... 7 = 128th note */
    } SNote;

/* Warning: An SNote is supposed to be a 16-bit entity.
 * Some C compilers will not pack bit fields into anything smaller
 * than an int. So avoid the actual use of this type unless you are certain
 * that the compiler packs it into a 16-bit word.
 */

/* You may get better object code by masking, ORing, and shifting using the
 * following definitions rather than the bit-packed fields, above. */
#define noteChord  (1<<7)         /* note is chorded to next note */

#define noteTieOut (1<<6)         /* note/chord is tied to next note/chord */

#define noteNShift 4                      /* shift count for nTuplet field */
#define noteN3     (1<<noteNShift)        /* note is a triplet */
#define noteN5     (2<<noteNShift)        /* note is a quintuplet */
#define noteN7     (3<<noteNShift)        /* note is a septuplet */
#define noteNMask  noteN7                 /* bit mask for the nTuplet field */

#define noteDot    (1<<3)                 /* note is dotted */

#define noteDShift 0                      /* shift count for division field */
#define noteD1     (0<<noteDShift)        /* whole note division */
#define noteD2     (1<<noteDShift)        /* half note division */
#define noteD4     (2<<noteDShift)        /* quarter note division */
#define noteD8     (3<<noteDShift)        /* eighth note division */
#define noteD16    (4<<noteDShift)        /* sixteenth note division */
#define noteD32    (5<<noteDShift)        /* thirty-secondth note division */
#define noteD64    (6<<noteDShift)        /* sixty-fourth note division */
#define noteD128   (7<<noteDShift)        /* 1/128 note division */
#define noteDMask  noteD128               /* bit mask for the division field */

#define noteDurMask 0x3F                  /* bit mask for all duration fields
                                           * division, nTuplet, dot */

/* Field access: */
```



```
#define IsChord(snote)   (((UWORD)snote) & noteChord)
#define IsTied(snote)    (((UWORD)snote) & noteTieOut)
#define NTuplet(snote)   ((((UWORD)snote) & noteNMask) >> noteNShift)
#define IsDot(snote)     (((UWORD)snote) & noteDot)
#define Division(snote)  ((((UWORD)snote) & noteDMask) >> noteDShift)

/* ---------- TimeSig SEvent -------------------------------------------*/
typedef struct {
    unsigned type     :8,       /* = SID_TimeSig */
             timeNSig :5,       /* time signature "numerator" timeNSig + 1 */
             timeDSig :3;       /* time signature "denominator" is
                                 * 2**timeDSig: 0 = whole note, 1 = half
                                 * note, 2 = quarter note, ...
                                 * 7 = 128th note */
    } STimeSig;

#define timeNMask  0xF8         /* bit mask for timeNSig field */
#define timeNShift 3            /* shift count for timeNSig field */

#define timeDMask  0x07         /*  bit mask for timeDSig field */

/* Field access: */
#define TimeNSig(sTime)  ((((UWORD)sTime) & timeNMask) >> timeNShift)
#define TimeDSig(sTime)   (((UWORD)sTime) & timeDMask)

/* ---------- KeySig SEvent -------------------------------------------*/
/* "data" value 0 = Cmaj; 1 through 7 = G,D,A,E,B,F#,C#;
 * 8 through 14 = F,Bb,Eb,Ab,Db,Gb,Cb.                               */

/* ---------- Dynamic SEvent -------------------------------------------*/
/* "data" value is a MIDI key velocity 0..127. */


/* ---------- SMUS Reader Support Routines -----------------------------*/

/* Just call this to read a SHDR chunk. */
#define GetSHDR(context, ssHdr)  \
    IFFReadBytes(context, (BYTE *)ssHdr, sizeof(SScoreHeader))

/* ---------- SMUS Writer Support Routines -----------------------------*/

/* Just call this to write a SHDR chunk. */
#define PutSHDR(context, ssHdr)  \
    PutCk(context, ID_SHDR, sizeof(SScoreHeader), (BYTE *)ssHdr)

#endif
```

```
;  iffchecg.lnk
FROM lstartup.o,iffcheck.o,iffr.o,gio.o
LIBRARY lc.lib,amiga.lib
TO iffcheck

;  iffcheck.lnk
FROM lstartup.o,iffcheck.o,iffr.o
LIBRARY lc.lib,amiga.lib
TO iffcheck

;  ilbm2raw.lnk
FROM lstartup.o, ilbm2raw.o, readpict.o, ilbmr.o, unpacker.o, iffr.o*
remalloc.o
LIBRARY lc.lib, amiga.lib
TO ilbm2raw

;  ilbmdump.lnk
FROM lstartup.o, ilbmdump.o, readpict.o, ilbmr.o, unpacker.o, iffr.o*
remalloc.o, bmprintc.o
LIBRARY lc.lib, amiga.lib
TO ilbmdump

;  raw2ilbg.lnk
FROM lstartup.o, raw2ilbm.o, putpict.o, ilbmw.o, packer.o, iffw.o, gio.o
LIBRARY lc.lib, amiga.lib
TO raw2ilbm

;  raw2ilbm.lnk
FROM lstartup.o, raw2ilbm.o, putpict.o, ilbmw.o, packer.o, iffw.o
LIBRARY lc.lib, amiga.lib
TO raw2ilbm

;  showilbg.lnk
FROM lstartup.o,showilbm.o,readpict.o,ilbmr.o,unpacker.o,iffr.o,remalloc.o*
gio.o
LIBRARY lc.lib,amiga.lib
TO showilbm

;  showilbm.lnk
FROM lstartup.o,showilbm.o,readpict.o,ilbmr.o,unpacker.o,iffr.o,remalloc.o
TO showilbm
LIBRARY lc.lib,amiga.lib

;  read8svx.lnk
FROM      LIB:lstartup.obj, Read8svx.o, dUnpack.o, iffr.o
TO        Read8svx
LIBRARY   LIB:lc.lib, LIB:amiga.lib
```



```
/*----------------------------------------------------------------------- */
/* IFFCheck.C  Print out the structure of an IFF-85 file,      1/23/86  */
/* checking for structural errors.                                      */
/*                                                                      */
/* DO NOT USE THIS AS A SKELETAL PROGRAM FOR AN IFF READER!             */
/* See ShowILBM.C for a skeletal example.                               */
/*                                                                      */
/* By Jerry Morrison and Steve Shaw, Electronic Arts.                   */
/* This software is in the public domain.                               */
/*                                                                      */
/* This version for the Commodore-Amiga computer.                       */
/*                                                                      */
/* ---------------------------------------------------------------------*/
#include "iff/iff.h"


/* ---------- IFFCheck -------------------------------------------------*/
/* [TBD] More extensive checking could be done on the IDs encountered in the
 * file. Check that the reserved IDs "FOR1".."FOR9", "LIS1".."LIS9", and
 * "CAT1".."CAT9" aren't used. Check that reserved IDs aren't used as Form
 * types. Check that all IDs are made of 4 printable characters (trailing
 * spaces ok). */

typedef struct {
    ClientFrame clientFrame;
    int levels;          /* # groups currently nested within.*/
    } Frame;

char MsgOkay[] = { "----- (IFF_OKAY) A good IFF file." };
char MsgEndMark[] = {"----- (END_MARK) How did you get this message??" };
char MsgDone[] = { "----- (IFF_DONE) How did you get this message??" };
char MsgDos[] = { "----- (DOS_ERROR) The DOS gave back an error." };
char MsgNot[] = { "----- (NOT_IFF) not an IFF file." };
char MsgNoFile[] = { "----- (NO_FILE) no such file found." };
char MsgClientError[] = {"----- (CLIENT_ERROR) IFF Checker bug."};
char MsgForm[] = { "----- (BAD_FORM) How did you get this message??" };
char MsgShort[] = { "----- (SHORT_CHUNK) How did you get this message??" };
char MsgBad[] = { "----- (BAD_IFF) a mangled IFF file." };

/* MUST GET THESE IN RIGHT ORDER!!*/
char *IFFPMessages[-(int)LAST_ERROR+1] = {
    /*IFF_OKAY*/  MsgOkay,
    /*END_MARK*/  MsgEndMark,
    /*IFF_DONE*/  MsgDone,
    /*DOS_ERROR*/ MsgDos,
    /*NOT_IFF*/   MsgNot,
    /*NO_FILE*/   MsgNoFile,
    /*CLIENT_ERROR*/ MsgClientError,
    /*BAD_FORM*/  MsgForm,
    /*SHORT_CHUNK*/  MsgShort,
    /*BAD_IFF*/   MsgBad
    };

/* FORWARD REFERENCES */
extern IFFP GetList(GroupContext *);
extern IFFP GetForm(GroupContext *);
extern IFFP GetProp(GroupContext *);
extern IFFP GetCat (GroupContext *);

void IFFCheck(name)  char *name; {
    IFFP iffp;
    BPTR file = Open(name, MODE_OLDFILE);
    Frame frame;

    frame.levels = 0;
    frame.clientFrame.getList = GetList;
    frame.clientFrame.getForm = GetForm;
    frame.clientFrame.getProp = GetProp;
    frame.clientFrame.getCat  = GetCat ;
```

```
    printf("----- Checking file '%s' -----\n", name);
    if (file == 0)
        iffp = NO_FILE;
    else
        iffp = ReadIFF(file, (ClientFrame *)&frame);

    Close(file);
    printf("%s\n", IFFPMessages[-iffp]);
    }

main(argc, argv)   int argc;  char **argv; {
    if (argc != 1+1) {
        printf("Usage: 'iffcheck filename'\n");
        exit(0);
        }
    IFFCheck(argv[1]);
    }

/* ---------- Put... -----------------------------------------------------*/

PutLevels(count)   int count; {
    for ( ;  count > 0;  --count) {
        printf(".");
        }
    }

PutID(id)  ID id; {
    printf("%c%c%c%c",
           (char)((id>>24L) & 0x7f),
           (char)((id>>16L) & 0x7f),
           (char)((id>>8)   & 0x7f),
           (char)(id        & 0x7f) );
    }

PutN(n)   int n; {
    printf(" %d ", n);
    }

/* Put something like "...BMHD 14" or "...LIST 14 PLBM". */
PutHdr(context)  GroupContext *context; {
    PutLevels( ((Frame *)context->clientFrame)->levels );
    PutID(context->ckHdr.ckID);
    PutN(context->ckHdr.ckSize);

    if (context->subtype != NULL_CHUNK)
        PutID(context->subtype);

    printf("\n");
    }

/* ---------- AtLeaf -----------------------------------------------------*/

/* At Leaf chunk.  That is, a chunk which does NOT contain other chunks.
 * Print "ID size".*/
IFFP AtLeaf(context)  GroupContext *context; {

    PutHdr(context);
    /* A typical reader would read the chunk's contents, using the "Frame"
     * for local data, esp. shared property settings (PROP).*/
    /* IFFReadBytes(context, ...buffer, context->ckHdr->ckSize); */
    return(IFF_OKAY);
    }

/* ---------- GetList ----------------------------------------------------*/
/* Handle a LIST chunk.  Print "LIST size subTypeID".
 * Then dive into it.*/
IFFP GetList(parent)  GroupContext *parent; {
    Frame newFrame;
```



```
    newFrame = *(Frame *)parent->clientFrame;  /* copy parent's frame*/
    newFrame.levels++;

    PutHdr(parent);

    return( ReadIList(parent, (ClientFrame *)&newFrame) );
    }

/* ---------- GetForm ----------------------------------------------------*/
/* Handle a FORM chunk.  Print "FORM size subTypeID".
 * Then dive into it.*/
IFFP GetForm(parent)   GroupContext *parent; {
    /*CompilerBug register*/ IFFP iffp;
    GroupContext new;
    Frame newFrame;

    newFrame = *(Frame *)parent->clientFrame;  /* copy parent's frame*/
    newFrame.levels++;

    PutHdr(parent);

    iffp = OpenRGroup(parent, &new);
    CheckIFFP();
    new.clientFrame = (ClientFrame *)&newFrame;

    /* FORM reader for Checker. */
    /* LIST, FORM, PROP, CAT already handled by GetF1ChunkHdr. */
    do {if ( (iffp = GetF1ChunkHdr(&new)) > 0 )
            iffp = AtLeaf(&new);
        } while (iffp >= IFF_OKAY);

    CloseRGroup(&new);
    return(iffp == END_MARK ? IFF_OKAY : iffp);
    }

/* ---------- GetProp ----------------------------------------------------*/
/* Handle a PROP chunk.  Print "PROP size subTypeID".
 * Then dive into it.*/
IFFP GetProp(listContext)  GroupContext *listContext; {
    /*CompilerBug register*/ IFFP iffp;
    GroupContext new;

    PutHdr(listContext);

    iffp = OpenRGroup(listContext, &new);
    CheckIFFP();

    /* PROP reader for Checker. */
    ((Frame *)listContext->clientFrame)->levels++;

    do {if ( (iffp = GetPChunkHdr(&new)) > 0 )
            iffp = AtLeaf(&new);
        } while (iffp >= IFF_OKAY);

    ((Frame *)listContext->clientFrame)->levels--;

    CloseRGroup(&new);
    return(iffp == END_MARK ? IFF_OKAY : iffp);
    }

/* ---------- GetCat -----------------------------------------------------*/
/* Handle a CAT chunk.  Print "CAT size subTypeID".
 * Then dive into it.*/
IFFP GetCat(parent)  GroupContext *parent;  {
    IFFP iffp;

    ((Frame *)parent->clientFrame)->levels++;
```

```
    PutHdr(parent);

    iffp = ReadICat(parent);

    ((Frame *)parent->clientFrame)->levels--;
    return(iffp);
    }
```



```
/*----------------------------------------------------------------------*/
/* ilbm2raw.c                                                           */
/*                  2/4/86                                              */
/* Reads in ILBM, outputs raw format, which is                          */
/* just the planes of bitmap data followed by the color map             */
/*                                                                      */
/* By Jerry Morrison and Steve Shaw, Electronic Arts.                   */
/* This software is in the public domain.                               */
/*                                                                      */
/* This version for the Commodore-Amiga computer.                       */
/*                                                                      */
/*      Callable from CLI only                                          */
/*----------------------------------------------------------------------*/

#include "iff/intuall.h"
#include "libraries/dos.h"
#include "libraries/dosextens.h"
#include "iff/ilbm.h"
#include "iff/readpict.h"
#include "iff/remalloc.h"

#undef NULL
#include "lattice/stdio.h"
/*-------------------------------------------------------------------------*/
/*      Iff error messages                                                 */
/*-------------------------------------------------------------------------*/

char MsgOkay[] = { "----- (IFF_OKAY) A good IFF file." };
char MsgEndMark[] = {"----- (END_MARK) How did you get this message??" };
char MsgDone[] = { "----- (IFF_DONE) How did you get this message??" };
char MsgDos[] = { "----- (DOS_ERROR) The DOS gave back an error." };
char MsgNot[] = { "----- (NOT_IFF) not an IFF file." };
char MsgNoFile[] = { "----- (NO_FILE) no such file found." };
char MsgClientError[] = {"----- (CLIENT_ERROR) IFF Checker bug."};
char MsgForm[] = { "----- (BAD_FORM) How did you get this message??" };
char MsgShort[] = { "----- (SHORT_CHUNK) How did you get this message??" };
char MsgBad[] = { "----- (BAD_IFF) a mangled IFF file." };

/* MUST GET THESE IN RIGHT ORDER!!*/
char *IFFPMessages[-LAST_ERROR+1] = {
    /*IFF_OKAY*/  MsgOkay,
    /*END_MARK*/  MsgEndMark,
    /*IFF_DONE*/  MsgDone,
    /*DOS_ERROR*/ MsgDos,
    /*NOT_IFF*/   MsgNot,
    /*NO_FILE*/   MsgNoFile,
    /*CLIENT_ERROR*/ MsgClientError,
    /*BAD_FORM*/  MsgForm,
    /*SHORT_CHUNK*/  MsgShort,
    /*BAD_IFF*/   MsgBad
    };

LONG GfxBase;

/*----------------------------------------------------------------------*/

SaveBitMap(name,bm,cols)
    UBYTE *name;
    struct BitMap *bm;
    SHORT *cols;
    {
    SHORT i;
    LONG nb,plsize;
    LONG file = Open( name, MODE_NEWFILE);
    if( file == 0 )  {
        printf(" couldn't open %s \n",name);
        return (-1);    /* couldnt open a load-file */
        }
    plsize = bm->BytesPerRow*bm->Rows;
```

```
    for (i=0; i<bm->Depth; i++) {
        nb =  Write(file, bm->Planes[i], plsize);
        if (nb<plsize) break;
        }
    Write(file, cols, (1<<bm->Depth)*2);        /* save color map */
    Close(file);
    return(0);
    }

struct BitMap bitmap = {0};

char depthString[] = "0";       /* Replaced with desired digit below.*/

ILBMFrame ilbmFrame;    /* Top level "client frame".*/

/** main() ******************************************************************/

UBYTE defSwitch[] = "b";

void main(argc, argv)  int argc;  char **argv;  {
    LONG iffp, file;
    UBYTE fname[40];
    GfxBase = (LONG)OpenLibrary("graphics.library",0);
    if (GfxBase==NULL) exit(0);

    if (argc) {
        /* Invoked via CLI.  Make a lock for current directory. */
        if (argc < 2) {
            printf("Usage from CLI: 'ilbm2raw filename '\n");
            }
        else {

            file = Open(argv[1], MODE_OLDFILE);

            if (file) {
                iffp = ReadPicture(file, &bitmap, &ilbmFrame, ChipAlloc);
                Close(file);
                if (iffp != IFF_DONE) {
                    printf(" Couldn't read file %s \n", argv[1]);
                    printf("%s\n",IFFPMessages[-iffp]);
                    }
                else {

                    strcpy(fname,argv[1]);

                    if (ilbmFrame.bmHdr.pageWidth > 320) {
                        if (ilbmFrame.bmHdr.pageHeight > 200)
                             strcat(fname, ".hi");
                        else strcat(fname, ".me");
                        }
                    else     strcat(fname, ".lo");

                    depthString[0] = '0' + bitmap.Depth;
                    strcat(fname, depthString);

                    printf(" Creating file %s \n", fname);
                    SaveBitMap(fname, &bitmap, ilbmFrame.colorMap);
                    }
                }
            else printf(" Couldn't open file: %s. \n", argv[1]);

            if (bitmap.Planes[0])  RemFree(bitmap.Planes[0]);

            printf("\n");
            }
        }
    CloseLibrary(GfxBase);
    exit(0);
    }
```

```
/*----------------------------------------------------------------------*/
/*                                                                      */
/* ILBMDump.c: reads in ILBM, prints out ascii representation,         */
/*  for including in C files.                                           */
/*                                                                      */
/* By Jerry Morrison and Steve Shaw, Electronic Arts.                  */
/* This software is in the public domain.                               */
/*                                                                      */
/* This version for the Commodore-Amiga computer.                      */
/*                                                                      */
/*  Callable from CLI ONLY                                              */
/*  Jan 31, 1986                                                        */
/*----------------------------------------------------------------------*/


#include "iff/intuall.h"
#include "libraries/dos.h"
#include "libraries/dosextens.h"
#include "iff/ilbm.h"
#include "iff/readpict.h"
#include "iff/remalloc.h"

#undef NULL
#include "lattice/stdio.h"
/*----------------------------------------------------------------------*/
/*      Iff error messages                                              */
/*----------------------------------------------------------------------*/

char MsgOkay[] = { "----- (IFF_OKAY) A good IFF file." };
char MsgEndMark[] = {"----- (END_MARK) How did you get this message??" };
char MsgDone[] = { "----- (IFF_DONE) How did you get this message??" };
char MsgDos[] = { "----- (DOS_ERROR) The DOS gave back an error." };
char MsgNot[] = { "----- (NOT_IFF) not an IFF file." };
char MsgNoFile[] = { "----- (NO_FILE) no such file found." };
char MsgClientError[] = {"----- (CLIENT_ERROR) IFF Checker bug."};
char MsgForm[] = { "----- (BAD_FORM) How did you get this message??" };
char MsgShort[] = { "----- (SHORT_CHUNK) How did you get this message??" };
char MsgBad[] = { "----- (BAD_IFF) a mangled IFF file." };

/* MUST GET THESE IN RIGHT ORDER!!*/
char *IFFPMessages[-LAST_ERROR+1] = {
    /*IFF_OKAY*/  MsgOkay,
    /*END_MARK*/  MsgEndMark,
    /*IFF_DONE*/  MsgDone,
    /*DOS_ERROR*/ MsgDos,
    /*NOT_IFF*/   MsgNot,
    /*NO_FILE*/   MsgNoFile,
    /*CLIENT_ERROR*/ MsgClientError,
    /*BAD_FORM*/  MsgForm,
    /*SHORT_CHUNK*/  MsgShort,
    /*BAD_IFF*/   MsgBad
    };

/* this returns a string containing characters after the
         last '/' or ':' */
GetSuffix(to, fr) UBYTE *to, *fr; {
    int i;
    UBYTE c,*s = fr;
    for (i=0; ;i++) {
        c = *s++;
        if (c == 0) break;
        if (c == '/') fr = s;
        else if (c == ':') fr = s;
        }
    strcpy(to,fr);
    }

LONG GfxBase;
```



```
struct BitMap bitmap = {0};

ILBMFrame ilbmFrame;    /* Top level "client frame".*/

/** main() ******************************************************************/

UBYTE defSwitch[] = "b";

void main(argc, argv)  int argc;  char **argv;  {
    UBYTE *sw;
    FILE *fp;
    LONG iffp,file;
    UBYTE name[40], fname[40];
    GfxBase = (LONG)OpenLibrary("graphics.library",0);
    if (GfxBase==NULL) exit(0);

    if (argc) {
        /* Invoked via CLI.  Make a lock for current directory. */
        if (argc < 2) {
            printf("Usage from CLI: 'ILBMDump filename switch-string'\n");
            printf(" where switch-string = \n");
            printf("  <nothing> : Bob format (default)\n");
            printf("  s         : Sprite format (with header and trailer words)\n");
            printf("  sn        : Sprite format (No header and trailer words)\n");
            printf("  a         : Attached sprite (with header and trailer)\n");
            printf("  an        : Attached sprite (No header and trailer)\n");
            printf(" Add 'c' to switch list to output CR's with LF's   \n");
            }
        else {
            sw = (argc>2)? argv[2]: defSwitch;

            file = Open(argv[1], MODE_OLDFILE);

            if (file) {
                iffp = ReadPicture(file, &bitmap, &ilbmFrame, ChipAlloc);
                Close(file);
                if (iffp != IFF_DONE) {
                    printf(" Couldn't read file %s \n", argv[1]);
                    printf("%s\n",IFFPMessages[-iffp]);
                    }
                else {
                    printf(" Creating file %s.c \n",argv[1]);
                    GetSuffix(name,argv[1]);
                    strcpy(fname,argv[1]);
                    strcat(fname,".c");
                    fp = fopen(fname,"w");
                    BMPrintCRep(&bitmap,fp,name,sw);
                    fclose(fp);
                    }
                }
            else printf(" Couldn't open file: %s. \n", argv[1]);

            if (bitmap.Planes[0])  RemFree(bitmap.Planes[0]);

            printf("\n");
            }
        }
    CloseLibrary(GfxBase);
    exit(0);
    }
```

```
/** raw2ilbm.c *************************************************************
/*  Read in a "raw" bitmap (dump of the bitplanes in a screen)   */
/*  Display it, and write it out as an ILBM file.                */
/*  23-Jan-86                                                    */
/*                                                               */
/*  Usage from CLI: 'Raw2ILBM  source dest fmt(low,med,hi)       */
/*     nplanes'                                                  */
/*  Supports the three common Amiga screen formats.              */
/*              'low' is 320x200,                                */
/*              'med' is 640x200,                                */
/*              'hi' is 640x400.                                 */
/*               'nplanes' is the number of bitplanes.           */
/*  The default is low-resolution, 5 bitplanes                   */
/*              (32 colors per pixel).                           */
/*                                                               */
/* By Jerry Morrison and Steve Shaw, Electronic Arts.            */
/* This software is in the public domain.                        */
/*                                                               */
/* This version for the Commodore-Amiga computer.                */
/*                                                               */
/****************************************************************/

#include "iff/intuall.h"
#include "libraries/dos.h"
#include "libraries/dosextens.h"
#include "iff/ilbm.h"
#include "iff/putpict.h"

#define MIN(a,b) ((a)<(b)?(a):(b))
#define MAX(a,b) ((a)>(b)?(a):(b))

/* general usage pointers */
LONG IconBase;  /* Actually, "struct IconBase *" if you've got some ".h" file*/
struct GfxBase *GfxBase;


/* Globals for displaying an image */
struct RastPort rP;
struct RasInfo rasinfo;
struct View v = {0};
struct ViewPort vp = {0};
struct View *oldView = 0;       /* so we can restore it */

/* ----------------------------------- */
DisplayPic(bm, colorMap) struct BitMap *bm; UWORD *colorMap;  {

    oldView = GfxBase->ActiView;        /* so we can restore it */

    InitView(&v);
    InitVPort(&vp);
    v.ViewPort = &vp;
    InitRastPort(&rP);
    rP.BitMap = bm;
    rasinfo.BitMap = bm;

    /* Always show the upper left-hand corner of this picture. */
    rasinfo.RxOffset = 0;
    rasinfo.RyOffset = 0;

    vp.DWidth = bm->BytesPerRow*8;      /* Physical display WIDTH */
    vp.DHeight = bm->Rows;      /* Display height */

    /* Always display it in upper left corner of screen.*/

    if (vp.DWidth <= 320) vp.Modes = 0;
        else vp.Modes = HIRES;
    if (vp.DHeight > 200) {
        v.Modes |= LACE;
        vp.Modes |= LACE;
```



```
        }
    vp.RasInfo = &rasinfo;
    MakeVPort(&v,&vp);
    MrgCop(&v);
    LoadView(&v);       /* show the picture */
    WaitBlit();
    WaitTOF();
    if (colorMap) LoadRGB4(&vp, colorMap,(1 << bm->Depth));
    }

UnDispPict() {
    if (oldView) {
        LoadView(oldView);      /* switch back to old view */
        FreeVPortCopLists(&vp);
        FreeCprList(v.LOFCprList);
        }
    }

PrintS(msg)  char *msg; {   printf(msg);    }

void GoodBye(msg)  char *msg; {   PrintS(msg);   PrintS("\n");   exit(0);   }

struct BitMap bitmap = {0};
SHORT cmap[32];

AllocBitMap(bm) struct BitMap *bm; {
    int i;
    LONG psz = bm->BytesPerRow*bm->Rows;
    UBYTE *p = (UBYTE *)AllocMem(bm->Depth*psz, MEMF_CHIP|MEMF_PUBLIC);
    for (i=0; i<bm->Depth; i++)  {
        bm->Planes[i] = p;
        p += psz;
        }
    }

FreeBitMap(bm) struct BitMap *bm;  {
    if (bitmap.Planes[0])  {
        FreeMem(bitmap.Planes[0],
                bitmap.BytesPerRow * bitmap.Rows * bitmap.Depth);
        }
    }

BOOL LoadBitMap(file,bm,cols)
    LONG file;
    struct BitMap *bm;
    SHORT *cols;
    {
    SHORT i;
    LONG nb,plsize;
    plsize = bm->BytesPerRow*bm->Rows;
    for (i=0; i<bm->Depth; i++) {
        nb =  Read(file, bm->Planes[i], plsize);
        if (nb<plsize) BltClear(bm->Planes[i],plsize,1);
        }
    if (cols) {
        nb = Read(file, cols, (1<<bm->Depth)*2);        /* load color map */
        return( (BOOL) (nb == (1<<bm->Depth)*2) );
        }
    return((BOOL) FALSE);
    }


/** main() ****************************************************************/

UBYTE defSwitch[] = "b";

#define BUFSIZE  16000

static SHORT maxDepth[3] = {5,4,4};
```

```
void main(argc, argv)  int argc;  char **argv;  {
    SHORT fmt,depth,pwidth,pheight;
    UBYTE *buffer;
    BOOL hadCmap;
    LONG file;
    if( !(GfxBase = (struct GfxBase *)OpenLibrary("graphics.library",0)) )
        GoodBye("No graphics.library");
    if( !(IconBase = OpenLibrary("icon.library",0)) )
        GoodBye("No icon.library");
    if (argc) {
        if (argc < 3) {
            printf(
"Usage from CLI: 'Raw2ILBM  source dest fmt(low,med,hi) nplanes'\n");
            goto bailout;
            }
        fmt = 0;
        depth = 5;
        if (argc>3)
            switch(*argv[3]) {
                case 'l': fmt = 0; break;
                case 'm': fmt = 1; break;
                case 'h': fmt = 2; break;
                }
        if (argc>4) depth = *argv[4]-'0';
        depth = MAX(1, MIN(maxDepth[fmt],depth));
        pwidth = fmt? 640: 320;
        pheight = (fmt>1)? 400: 200;
        InitBitMap(&bitmap, depth, pwidth, pheight);
        AllocBitMap(&bitmap);

        file = Open(argv[1], MODE_OLDFILE);

        if (file)  {
            DisplayPic(&bitmap,NULL);
            hadCmap = LoadBitMap(file,&bitmap, cmap);
            if (hadCmap) LoadRGB4(&vp, cmap, 1<<bitmap.Depth);
            Close(file);
            file = Open(argv[2], MODE_NEWFILE);
            buffer = (UBYTE *)AllocMem(BUFSIZE, MEMF_CHIP|MEMF_PUBLIC);
            PutPict(file, &bitmap, pwidth, pheight,
                hadCmap? cmap: NULL, buffer, BUFSIZE);
            Close(file);
            FreeMem(buffer,BUFSIZE);
            }
        else printf(" Couldn't open file '%s' \n",argv[2]);
        }

    UnDispPict();
    FreeBitMap(&bitmap);

    bailout:
        CloseLibrary(GfxBase);
        CloseLibrary(IconBase);
        exit(0);
    }
```



```
/** Read8SVX.c ***************************************************************
 *
 * Read a sound sample from an IFF file.  21Jan85
 *
 * By Steve Hayes, Electronic Arts.
 * This software is in the public domain.
 *
 ****************************************************************************/

#include "exec/types.h"
#include "exec/exec.h"
#include "libraries/dos.h"
#include "iff/8svx.h"

/* Message strings for IFFP codes. */
char MsgOkay[]        = { "(IFF_OKAY) No FORM 8SVX in the file." };
char MsgEndMark[]     = { "(END_MARK) How did you get this message?" };
char MsgDone[]        = { "(IFF_DONE) All done."};
char MsgDos[]         = { "(DOS_ERROR) The DOS returned an error." };
char MsgNot[]         = { "(NOT_IFF) Not an IFF file." };
char MsgNoFile[]      = { "(NO_FILE) No such file found." };
char MsgClientError[] = { "(CLIENT_ERROR) Read8SVX bug or insufficient RAM."};
char MsgForm[]        = { "(BAD_FORM) A malformed FORM 8SVX." };
char MsgShort[]       = { "(SHORT_CHUNK) A malformed FORM 8SVX." };
char MsgBad[]         = { "(BAD_IFF) A mangled IFF file." };

/* THESE MUST APPEAR IN RIGHT ORDER!! */
char *IFFPMessages[-LAST_ERROR+1] = {
    /*IFF_OKAY*/  MsgOkay,
    /*END_MARK*/  MsgEndMark,
    /*IFF_DONE*/  MsgDone,
    /*DOS_ERROR*/ MsgDos,
    /*NOT_IFF*/   MsgNot,
    /*NO_FILE*/   MsgNoFile,
    /*CLIENT_ERROR*/ MsgClientError,
    /*BAD_FORM*/  MsgForm,
    /*SHORT_CHUNK*/  MsgShort,
    /*BAD_IFF*/   MsgBad
    };

typedef struct {
   ClientFrame clientFrame;
   UBYTE foundVHDR;
   UBYTE pad1;
   Voice8Header sampHdr;
   } SVXFrame;


/* NOTE: For a simple version of this program, set Fancy to 0.
 * That'll compile a program that skips all LISTs and PROPs in the input
 * file. It will look in CATs for FORMs 8SVX. That's suitable for most uses.
 *
 * For a fancy version that handles LISTs and PROPs, set Fancy to 1. */

#define Fancy  1

BYTE *buf;
int szBuf;

/** DoSomethingWithSample() **********************************************
 *
 * Interface to Amiga sound driver.
 *
 ************************************************************************/
DoSomethingWithSample(sampHdr)  Voice8Header *sampHdr;  {
    BYTE *t;
    printf("\noneShotHiSamples=%ld", sampHdr->oneShotHiSamples);
    printf("\nrepeatHiSamples=%ld", sampHdr->repeatHiSamples);
```

```
    printf("\nsamplesPerHiCycle=%ld", sampHdr->samplesPerHiCycle);
    printf("\nsamplesPerSec=%ld", sampHdr->samplesPerSec);
    printf("\nctOctave=%ld", sampHdr->ctOctave);
    printf("\nsCompression=%ld", sampHdr->sCompression);
    printf("\nvolume=0x%lx", sampHdr->volume);
    /* Decompress, if needed. */
    if (sampHdr->sCompression) {
        t = (BYTE *)AllocMem(szBuf<<1, MEMF_CHIP);
        DUnpack(buf, szBuf, t);
        FreeMem(buf, szBuf);
        buf = t;
        szBuf <<= 1;
        };
    printf("\nData = %3ld %3ld %3ld %3ld %3ld %3ld %3ld %3ld",
           buf[0],buf[1],buf[2],buf[3],buf[4],buf[5],buf[6],buf[7]);
    printf("\n        %3ld %3ld %3ld %3ld %3ld %3ld %3ld %3ld ...\n",
           buf[8+0],buf[8+1],buf[8+2],buf[8+3],buf[8+4],buf[8+5],
           buf[8+6],buf[8+ 7]);
    }

/** ReadBODY() ***********************************************************
 *
 * Read a BODY into RAM.
 *
 *************************************************************************/
IFFP ReadBODY(context)  GroupContext *context;  {
    IFFP iffp;

    szBuf  = ChunkMoreBytes(context);
    buf  = (BYTE *)AllocMem(szBuf, MEMF_CHIP);
    if (buf == NULL)
        iffp = CLIENT_ERROR;
    else
        iffp = IFFReadBytes(context, (BYTE *)buf, szBuf);
    CheckIFFP();
    }

/** GetFo8SVX() **********************************************************
 *
 * Called via ReadSample to handle every FORM encountered in an IFF file.
 * Reads FORMs 8SVX and skips all others.
 * Inside a FORM 8SVX, it reads BODY. It complains if it
 * doesn't find an VHDR before the BODY.
 *
 * [TBD] We could read and print out any NAME and "(c) " chunks.
 *
 *************************************************************************/
IFFP GetFo8SVX(parent)  GroupContext *parent;  {
   /*compilerBug register*/ IFFP iffp;
   GroupContext formContext;
   SVXFrame smusFrame;          /* only used for non-clientFrame fields.*/

   if (parent->subtype != ID_8SVX)
      return(IFF_OKAY); /* just continue scaning the file */

   smusFrame = *(SVXFrame *)parent->clientFrame;
   iffp = OpenRGroup(parent, &formContext);
   CheckIFFP();

   do switch (iffp = GetFChunkHdr(&formContext)) {
      case ID_VHDR: {
        smusFrame.foundVHDR = TRUE;
        iffp = GetVHDR(&formContext, &smusFrame.sampHdr);
        break; }
      case ID_BODY: {
        if (!smusFrame.foundVHDR)
            iffp = BAD_FORM;           /* Need an VHDR chunk first  */
        else iffp = ReadBODY(&formContext);
        break; }
```



```
      case END_MARK: {
        if (!smusFrame.foundVHDR)
            iffp = BAD_FORM;
        else
            iffp = IFF_DONE;
        break; }
      } while (iffp >= IFF_OKAY);  /* loop if valid ID of ignored chunk or a
                                    * subroutine returned IFF_OKAY (no errors).*/

    if (iffp != IFF_DONE)  return(iffp);

    /* If we get this far, there were no errors. */
    CloseRGroup(&formContext);
    DoSomethingWithSample(&smusFrame.sampHdr);
    FreeMem(buf, szBuf);
    return(iffp);
    }

/** Notes on extending GetFo8SVX ****************************************
 *
 * To read more kinds of chunks, just add clauses to the switch statement.
 * To read more kinds of property chunks (like NAME) add clauses to
 * the switch statement in GetPr8SVX, too.
 *
 *************************************************************************/

/** GetPr8SVX() **********************************************************
 *
 * Called via ReadSample to handle every PROP encountered in an IFF file.
 * Reads PROPs 8SVX and skips all others.
 *
 *************************************************************************/
#if Fancy
IFFP GetPr8SVX(parent)  GroupContext *parent;  {
   /*compilerBug register*/ IFFP iffp;
   GroupContext propContext;
   SVXFrame *svxFrame = (SVXFrame *)parent->clientFrame; /* Subclass */

   if (parent->subtype != ID_8SVX)
      return(IFF_OKAY); /* just continue scaning the file */

   iffp = OpenRGroup(parent, &propContext);
   CheckIFFP();

   do switch (iffp = GetPChunkHdr(&propContext)) {
      case ID_VHDR: {
        svxFrame->foundVHDR = TRUE;
        iffp = GetVHDR(&propContext, &svxFrame->sampHdr);
        break; }
      } while (iffp >= IFF_OKAY);  /* loop if valid ID of ignored chunk or a
                                    * subroutine returned IFF_OKAY (no errors).*/

   CloseRGroup(&propContext);
   return(iffp == END_MARK ? IFF_OKAY : iffp);
   }
#endif

/** GetLi8SVX() **********************************************************
 *
 * Called via ReadSample to handle every LIST encountered in an IFF file.
 *
 *************************************************************************/
#if Fancy
IFFP GetLi8SVX(parent)  GroupContext *parent;  {
    SVXFrame newFrame;  /* allocate a new Frame */

    newFrame = *(SVXFrame *)parent->clientFrame;  /* copy parent frame */

    return( ReadIList(parent, (ClientFrame *)&newFrame) );
```

```
    }
#endif

/** ReadSample() ***********************************************************
 *
 * Read IFF 8SVX, given a file handle open for reading.
 *
 ***************************************************************************/
IFFP ReadSample(file)  LONG file;  {
   SVXFrame sFrame;      /* Top level "client frame".*/
   IFFP iffp = IFF_OKAY;

#if Fancy
   sFrame.clientFrame.getList = GetLi8SVX;
   sFrame.clientFrame.getProp = GetPr8SVX;
#else
   sFrame.clientFrame.getList = SkipGroup;
   sFrame.clientFrame.getProp = SkipGroup;
#endif
   sFrame.clientFrame.getForm = GetFo8SVX;
   sFrame.clientFrame.getCat  = ReadICat ;

   /* Initialize the top-level client frame's property settings to the
    * program-wide defaults. This example just records that we haven't read
    * any VHDR properties yet.
    * If you want to read another property, init it's fields in sFrame. */
   sFrame.foundVHDR = FALSE;
   sFrame.pad1      = 0;

   iffp = ReadIFF(file, (ClientFrame *)&sFrame);

   return(iffp);
   }

/** main0() ****************************************************************/
void main0(filename)  char *filename;  {
    LONG file;
    IFFP iffp = NO_FILE;
    file = Open(filename, MODE_OLDFILE);
    if (file)
        iffp = ReadSample(file);
    Close(file);
    printf(" %s\n", IFFPMessages[-iffp]);
    }

/** main() *****************************************************************/
void main(argc, argv)  int argc;  char **argv;  {
    printf("Reading file '%s' ...", argv[1]);
    if (argc < 2)
        printf("\nfilename required\n");
    else
        main0(argv[1]);
    }
```



```
/** ShowILBM.c ************************************************************
 *
 * Read an ILBM raster image file and display it.       24-Jan-86.
 *
 * By Jerry Morrison, Steve Shaw, and Steve Hayes, Electronic Arts.
 * This software is in the public domain.
 *
 * USE THIS AS AN EXAMPLE PROGRAM FOR AN IFF READER.
 *
 * The IFF reader portion is essentially a recursive-descent parser.
 * The display portion is specific to the Commodore Amiga computer.
 *
 * NOTE: This program displays an image, pauses, then exits.
 *
 * Usage from CLI:
 *   showilbm picture1 [picture2] ...
 *
 * Usage from WorkBench:
 * Click on ShowILBM, hold down shift key, click on each picture to show,
 * Double-click on final picture to complete the selection, release the
 * shift key.
 *
 ***************************************************************************/

/* If you are constructing a Makefile, here are the names of the files
 * that you'll need to compile and link with to use showilbm:

        showilbm.c
        readpict.c
        remalloc.c
        ilbmr.c
        iffr.c
        unpacker.c
        gio.c

        and you'll have to get movmem() from lc.lib

 * robp.
 * *********************************************************************** */


#include "iff/intuall.h"
#include "libraries/dos.h"
#include "libraries/dosextens.h"
#include "iff/ilbm.h"
#include "workbench/workbench.h"
#include "workbench/startup.h"
#include "iff/readpict.h"
#include "iff/remalloc.h"

#define LOCAL static

#define MIN(a,b) ((a)<(b)?(a):(b))
#define MAX(a,b) ((a)>(b)?(a):(b))

/* general usage pointers */
struct GfxBase *GfxBase;
LONG IconBase;  /* Actually, "struct IconBase *" if you've got some ".h" file*/

/* For displaying an image */
LOCAL struct RastPort rP;
LOCAL struct BitMap bitmap0;
LOCAL struct RasInfo rasinfo;
LOCAL struct View v = {0};
LOCAL struct ViewPort vp = {0};

LOCAL ILBMFrame iFrame;

/* Define the size of a temporary buffer used in unscrambling the ILBM rows.*/
```

```
#define bufSz 512

/* Message strings for IFFP codes. */
LOCAL char MsgOkay[]         = {
        "(IFF_OKAY) Didn't find a FORM ILBM in the file." };
LOCAL char MsgEndMark[]      = { "(END_MARK) How did you get this message?" };
LOCAL char MsgDone[]         = { "(IFF_DONE) All done."};
LOCAL char MsgDos[]          = { "(DOS_ERROR) The DOS returned an error." };
LOCAL char MsgNot[]          = { "(NOT_IFF) Not an IFF file." };
LOCAL char MsgNoFile[]       = { "(NO_FILE) No such file found." };
LOCAL char MsgClientError[] = {
        "(CLIENT_ERROR) ShowILBM bug or insufficient RAM."};
LOCAL char MsgForm[]         = { "(BAD_FORM) A malformed FORM ILBM." };
LOCAL char MsgShort[]        = { "(SHORT_CHUNK) A malformed FORM ILBM." };
LOCAL char MsgBad[]          = { "(BAD_IFF) A mangled IFF file." };

/* THESE MUST APPEAR IN RIGHT ORDER!! */
LOCAL char *IFFPMessages[-(int)LAST_ERROR+1] = {
    /*IFF_OKAY*/  MsgOkay,
    /*END_MARK*/  MsgEndMark,
    /*IFF_DONE*/  MsgDone,
    /*DOS_ERROR*/ MsgDos,
    /*NOT_IFF*/   MsgNot,
    /*NO_FILE*/   MsgNoFile,
    /*CLIENT_ERROR*/ MsgClientError,
    /*BAD_FORM*/  MsgForm,
    /*SHORT_CHUNK*/  MsgShort,
    /*BAD_IFF*/   MsgBad
    };

/** DisplayPic() *************************************************************
 *
 * Interface to Amiga graphics ROM routines.
 *
 *****************************************************************************/
DisplayPic(bm, ptilbmFrame)
    struct BitMap *bm;  ILBMFrame *ptilbmFrame;  {
    int i;
    struct View *oldView = GfxBase->ActiView;   /* so we can restore it */

    InitView(&v);
    InitVPort(&vp);
    v.ViewPort = &vp;
    InitRastPort(&rP);
    rP.BitMap = bm;
    rasinfo.BitMap = bm;

    /* Always show the upper left-hand corner of this picture. */
    rasinfo.RxOffset = 0;
    rasinfo.RyOffset = 0;

    vp.DWidth = MAX(ptilbmFrame->bmHdr.w, 4*8);
    vp.DHeight = ptilbmFrame->bmHdr.h;

#if 0
    /* Specify where on screen to put the ViewPort. */
    vp.DxOffset = ptilbmFrame->bmHdr.x;
    vp.DyOffset = ptilbmFrame->bmHdr.y;
#else
    /* Always display it in upper left corner of screen.*/
#endif

    if (ptilbmFrame->bmHdr.pageWidth <= 320)
        vp.Modes = 0;
    else vp.Modes = HIRES;
    if (ptilbmFrame->bmHdr.pageHeight > 200) {
        v.Modes |= LACE;
        vp.Modes |= LACE;
        }
```



```
    vp.RasInfo = &rasinfo;
    MakeVPort(&v,&vp);
    MrgCop(&v);
    LoadView(&v);        /* show the picture */
    WaitBlit();
    WaitTOF();
    LoadRGB4(&vp, ptilbmFrame->colorMap, ptilbmFrame->nColorRegs);

    for (i = 0; i < 5*60; ++i)  WaitTOF();       /* Delay 5 seconds. */

    LoadView(oldView);  /* switch back to old view */
    }

/** stuff for main0() ********************************************************/
LOCAL struct WBStartup *wbStartup = 0;  /* 0 unless started from WorkBench.*/

PrintS(msg)  char *msg; {
    if (!wbStartup)  printf(msg);
    }

void GoodBye(msg)  char *msg; {
    PrintS(msg);   PrintS("\n");
    exit(0);
    }

/** OpenArg() ****************************************************************
 *  Given a "workbench argument" (a file reference) and an I/O mode.
 *  It opens the file.
 *****************************************************************************/
LONG OpenArg(wa, openmode)  struct WBArg *wa;   int openmode; {
    LONG olddir;
    LONG file;
    if (wa->wa_Lock)   olddir = CurrentDir(wa->wa_Lock);
    file = Open(wa->wa_Name, openmode);
    if (wa->wa_Lock)   CurrentDir(olddir);
    return(file);
    }

/** main0() ******************************************************************/
void main0(wa)  struct WBArg *wa;  {
    LONG file;
    IFFP iffp = NO_FILE;

    /* load and display the picture */
    file = OpenArg(wa, MODE_OLDFILE);
    if (file)
        iffp = ReadPicture(file, &bitmap0, &iFrame, ChipAlloc);
        /* Allocates BitMap using ChipAlloc().*/
    Close(file);
    if (iffp == IFF_DONE)
        DisplayPic(&bitmap0, &iFrame);

    PrintS(" ");   PrintS(IFFPMessages[-iffp]);   PrintS("\n");

    /* cleanup */
    if (bitmap0.Planes[0])  {
        RemFree(bitmap0.Planes[0]);
                /* ASSUMES allocated all planes via a single ChipAlloc call.*/
        FreeVPortCopLists(&vp);
        FreeCprList(v.LOFCprList);
        }
    }

/** main() *******************************************************************/

void main(argc, argv)  int argc;  char **argv;  {
    struct WBArg wbArg, *wbArgs;
    LONG olddir;
/*sss    struct Process *myProcess; */
```

```
    if( !(GfxBase = (struct GfxBase *)OpenLibrary("graphics.library",0)) )
        GoodBye("No graphics.library");
    if( !(IconBase = OpenLibrary("icon.library",0)) )
        GoodBye("No icon.library");
    if (!argc) {
        /* Invoked via workbench */
        wbStartup = (struct WBStartup *)argv;
        wbArgs = wbStartup->sm_ArgList;
        argc = wbStartup->sm_NumArgs;
        while (argc >= 2) {
            olddir = CurrentDir(wbArgs[1].wa_Lock);
            main0(&wbArgs[1]);
            argc--;   wbArgs = &wbArgs[1];
            }
#if 0
        /* [TBD] We want to get an error msg to the Workbench user... */
        if (argc < 2) {
            PrintS ("Usage from workbench:\n");
            PrintS (" Click mouse on Show-ILBM, Then hold 'SHIFT' key\n");
            GoodBye(" while double-click on file to display.");
            }
#endif
        }
    else {
        /* Invoked via CLI.  Make a lock for current directory.
         * Eventually, scan name, separate out directory reference?*/
        if (argc < 2)
            GoodBye("Usage from CLI: 'Show-ILBM filename'");
/*sss   myProcess = (struct Process *)FindTask(0); */
        wbArg.wa_Lock = 0; /*sss myProcess->pr_CurrentDir; */
        while (argc >= 2) {
            wbArg.wa_Name = argv[1];
            PrintS("Showing file ");   PrintS(wbArg.wa_Name);   PrintS(" ...");
            main0(&wbArg);
            PrintS("\n");
            argc--;   argv = &argv[1];
            }
        }
    CloseLibrary(GfxBase);
    CloseLibrary(IconBase);
    exit(0);
    }
```



```
/*----------------------------------------------------------------------*/
/*                                                                      */
/*                         bmprintc.c                                   */
/*                                                                      */
/* print out a C-language representation of data for bitmap             */
/*                                                                      */
/* By Jerry Morrison and Steve Shaw, Electronic Arts.                   */
/* This software is in the public domain.                               */
/*                                                                      */
/* This version for the Commodore-Amiga computer.                       */
/* Cleaned up and modified a bit by Chuck McManis, Aug 1988             */
/*                                                                      */
/*----------------------------------------------------------------------*/

#include <iff/intuall.h>
#undef NULL
#include <stdio.h>

#define NO 0
#define YES 1

static BOOL doCRLF;

void
PrCRLF(fp)
        FILE *fp;
{
        if (doCRLF)
                fprintf(fp, "%c%c", 0xD, 0xA);
        else
                fprintf(fp, "\n");
}

void
PrintBob(bm, fp, name)
        struct BitMap *bm;
        FILE *fp;
        UBYTE *name;
{
        register UWORD  *wp;    /* Pointer to the bitmap data */

        short   p,i,j,nb;       /* temporaries */
        short   nwords = (bm->BytesPerRow/2)*bm->Rows;

        fprintf(fp, "/*----- bitmap : w = %ld, h = %ld ------ */",
                        bm->BytesPerRow*8, bm->Rows);

        PrCRLF(fp);

        for (p = 0; p < bm->Depth; ++p) {       /* For each bit plane */
                wp = (UWORD *)bm->Planes[p];
                fprintf(fp, "/*------ plane # %ld: --------*/", p);
                PrCRLF(fp);
                fprintf(fp, "UWORD %s%c[%ld] = { ", name, (p?('0'+p):' '), nwords);
                PrCRLF(fp);
                for (j = 0; j < bm->Rows; j++, wp += (bm->BytesPerRow >> 1)) {
                        fprintf(fp, "    ");
                        for (nb = 0; nb < (bm->BytesPerRow) >> 1; nb++)
                                fprintf(fp, "0x%04x,", *(wp+nb));
                        if (bm->BytesPerRow <= 6) {
                                fprintf(fp, "\t/* ");
                                for (nb = 0; nb < (bm->BytesPerRow) >> 1; nb++)
                                        for (i=0, ; i<16; i++)
                                                fprintf(fp, "%c",
                                              (((*(wp+nb))>>(15-i))&1) ? '*' : '.'));
                                fprintf(fp, " */");
                        }
                        PrCRLF(fp);
```

```
			}
			fprintf(fp,"    };");
			PrCRLF(fp);
		}
}

static char     sp_colors[4] = ".oO@";
void
PSprite(bm, fp, name, p, dohead)
	struct BitMap   *bm;
	FILE            *fp;
	UBYTE           *name;
	int             p;
	BOOL            dohead;
{
	UWORD   *wp0, *wpl;     /* Pointer temporaries  */
	short   i, j, nwords,   /* Counter temporaries  */
		color;          /* pixel color          */
	short   wplen = bm->BytesPerRow/2;

	nwords =  2*bm->Rows + (dohead?4:0);
	wp0 = (UWORD *)bm->Planes[p];
	wpl = (UWORD *)bm->Planes[p+1];

	fprintf(fp, "UWORD %s[%ld] = {", name, nwords);
	PrCRLF(fp);

	if (dohead) {
		fprintf(fp,"  0x0000, 0x0000, /* VStart, VStop */");
		PrCRLF(fp);
	}
	for (j=0 ; j < bm->Rows; j++) {
		fprintf(fp, "  0x%04x, 0x%04x", *wp0, *wpl);
		if (dohead || (j != bm->Rows-1)) {
			fprintf(fp, ",");
		}
		fprintf(fp, "\t/*  ");
		for (i = 0; i < 16; i++) {
			color = ((*wpl >> (14-i)) & 2) + ((*wp0 >> (15-i)) & 1);
			fprintf(fp, "%c", sp_colors[color]);
		}
		fprintf(fp,"  */");
		PrCRLF(fp);
		wp0 += wplen;
		wpl += wplen;
	}
	if (dohead)
		fprintf(fp, "  0x0000, 0x0000 }; /* End of Sprite */");
	else
		fprintf(fp," };");
	PrCRLF(fp);
	PrCRLF(fp);
}

void
PrintSprite(bm, fp, name, attach, dohdr)
	struct BitMap   *bm;
	FILE            *fp;
	UBYTE           *name;
	BOOL            attach,
			dohdr;
{
	fprintf(fp,"/*----- Sprite format: h = %ld ------ */", bm->Rows);
	PrCRLF(fp);

	if (bm->Depth > 1) {
		fprintf(fp, "/*--Sprite containing lower order two planes:   */");
		PrCRLF(fp);
		PSprite(bm, fp, name, 0, dohdr);
```



```
	}
	if (attach && (bm->Depth > 3) ) {
		strcat(name, "1");
		fprintf(fp, "/*--Sprite containing higher order two planes:   */");
		PrCRLF(fp);
		PSprite(bm, fp, name, 2, dohdr);
	}
}

#define BOB     0
#define SPRITE  1

void
BMPrintCRep(bm, fp, name, fmt)
	struct BitMap *bm;      /* Contains the image data */
	FILE *fp;               /* file we will write to */
	UBYTE *name;            /* name associated with the bitmap */
	UBYTE *fmt;             /* string of characters describing output fmt*/
{
	BOOL attach, doHdr;
	char c;
	SHORT type;

	doCRLF = NO;
	doHdr = YES;
	type = BOB;
	attach = NO;
	while ( (c=*fmt++) != 0 )
		switch (c) {
			case 'b':
				type = BOB;
				break;
			case 's':
				type = SPRITE;
				attach = NO;
				break;
			case 'a':
				type = SPRITE;
				attach = YES;
				break;
			case 'n':
				doHdr = NO;
				break;
			case 'c':
				doCRLF = YES;
				break;
		}
	switch(type) {
		case BOB:
			PrintBob(bm, fp, name);
			break;
		case SPRITE:
			PrintSprite(bm, fp, name, attach, doHdr);
			break;
	}
}
```

```
/* DUnpack.c --- Fibonacci Delta decompression by Steve Hayes */

#include <exec/types.h>

/* Fibonacci delta encoding for sound data */
BYTE codeToDelta[16] = {-34,-21,-13,-8,-5,-3,-2,-1,0,1,2,3,5,8,13,21};

/* Unpack Fibonacci-delta encoded data from n byte source
 * buffer into 2*n byte dest buffer, given initial data
 * value x.  It returns the lats data value x so you can
 * call it several times to incrementally decompress the data.
 */

BYTE D1Unpack(source,n,dest,x)
BYTE source[], dest[];
LONG n;
BYTE x;
   {
   BYTE d;
   LONG i, lim;

   lim = n << 1;
   for (i=0; i < lim; ++i)
      {
      /* Decode a data nibble, high nibble then low nibble */
      d = source[i >> 1];    /* get a pair of nibbles */
      if (i & 1)             /* select low or high nibble */
         d &= 0xf;           /* mask to get the low nibble */
      else
         d >>= 4;            /* shift to get the high nibble */
      x += codeToDelta[d];   /* add in the decoded delta */
      dest[i] = x;           /* store a 1 byte sample */
      }
   return(x);
   }

/* Unpack Fibonacci-delta encoded data from n byte
 * source buffer into 2*(n-2) byte dest buffer.
 * Source buffer has a pad byte, an 8-bit initial
 * value, followed by n-2 bytes comprising 2*(n-2)
 * 4-bit encoded samples.
 */

void DUnpack(source, n, dest)
BYTE source[], dest[];
LONG n;
   {
   D1Unpack(source+2, n-2, dest, source[1]);
   }
```



```
/*----------------------------------------------------------------------*/
/* GIO.C  Generic I/O Speed Up Package                         1/23/86  */
/* See GIOCall.C for an example of usage.                               */
/* Read not speeded-up yet.  Only one Write file buffered at a time.    */
/* Note: The speed-up provided is ONLY significant for code such as IFF */
/* which does numerous small Writes and Seeks.                          */
/*                                                                      */
/* By Jerry Morrison and Steve Shaw, Electronic Arts.                   */
/* This software is in the public domain.                               */
/*                                                                      */
/* This version for the Commodore-Amiga computer.                       */
/*                                                                      */
/*----------------------------------------------------------------------*/
#include "iff/gio.h"    /* See comments here for explanation.*/

#if GIO_ACTIVE

#define local static


local BPTR wFile      = NULL;
local BYTE *wBuffer   = NULL;
local LONG wNBytes    = 0; /* buffer size in bytes.*/
local LONG wIndex     = 0; /* index of next available byte.*/
local LONG wWaterline = 0; /* Count of # bytes to be written.
                            * Different than wIndex because of GSeek.*/

/*---------- GOpen ------------------------------------------------------*/
LONG GOpen(filename, openmode)   char *filename;  LONG openmode; {
    return( Open(filename, openmode) );
    }

/*---------- GClose -----------------------------------------------------*/
LONG GClose(file)  BPTR file; {
    LONG signal = 0, signal2;
    if (file == wFile)
        signal = GWriteUndeclare(file);
    signal2 = Close(file);      /* Call Close even if trouble with write.*/
    if (signal2 < 0)
        signal = signal2;
    return( signal );
    }

/*---------- GRead ------------------------------------------------------*/
LONG GRead(file, buffer, nBytes)   BPTR file;  BYTE *buffer;  LONG nBytes; {
    LONG signal = 0;
    /* We don't yet read directly from the buffer, so flush it to disk and
     * let the DOS fetch it back. */
    if (file == wFile)
        signal = GWriteFlush(file);
    if (signal >= 0)
        signal = Read(file, buffer, nBytes);
    return( signal );
    }

/* ---------- GWriteFlush -----------------------------------------------*/
LONG GWriteFlush(file)  BPTR file; {
    LONG gWrite = 0;
    if (wFile != NULL  &&  wBuffer != NULL  &&  wIndex > 0)
        gWrite = Write(wFile, wBuffer, wWaterline);
    wWaterline = wIndex = 0;    /* No matter what, make sure this happens.*/
    return( gWrite );
    }

/* ---------- GWriteDeclare ---------------------------------------------*/
LONG GWriteDeclare(file, buffer, nBytes)
    BPTR file;  BYTE *buffer;  LONG nBytes; {
    LONG gWrite = GWriteFlush(wFile);  /* Finish any existing usage.*/
    if ( file==NULL  ||  (file==wFile  &&  buffer==NULL)  ||  nBytes<=3) {
```

```
        wFile = NULL;    wBuffer = NULL;      wNBytes = 0; }
    else {
        wFile = file;    wBuffer = buffer;    wNBytes = nBytes; }
    return( gWrite );
    }

/* ---------- GWrite ----------------------------------------------------*/
LONG GWrite(file, buffer, nBytes)   BPTR file;  BYTE *buffer;  LONG nBytes; {
    LONG gWrite = 0;

    if (file == wFile  &&  wBuffer != NULL) {
        if (wNBytes >= wIndex + nBytes) {
            /* Append to wBuffer.*/
            movmem(buffer, wBuffer+wIndex, nBytes);
            wIndex += nBytes;
            if (wIndex > wWaterline)
                wWaterline = wIndex;
            nBytes = 0;          /* Indicate data has been swallowed.*/
            }
        else {
            wWaterline = wIndex;     /* We are about to overwrite any
                * data above wIndex, up to at least the buffer end.*/
            gWrite = GWriteFlush(file);  /* Write data out in proper order.*/
            }
        }
    if (nBytes > 0  &&  gWrite >= 0)
        gWrite += Write(file, buffer, nBytes);
    return( gWrite );
    }

/* ---------- GSeek -----------------------------------------------------*/
LONG GSeek(file, position, mode)
    BPTR file;   LONG position;   LONG mode; {
    LONG gSeek = -2;
    LONG newWIndex = wIndex + position;

    if (file == wFile  &&  wBuffer != NULL) {
        if (mode == OFFSET_CURRENT  &&
            newWIndex >= 0  &&  newWIndex <= wWaterline) {
            gSeek = wIndex;      /* Okay; return *OLD* position */
            wIndex = newWIndex;
            }
        else {
            /* We don't even try to optimize the other cases.*/
            gSeek = GWriteFlush(file);
            if (gSeek >= 0)   gSeek = -2;  /* OK so far */
            }
        }
    if (gSeek == -2)
        gSeek = Seek(file, position, mode);
    return( gSeek );
    }

#else /* not GIO_ACTIVE */

void GIODummy() { }     /* to keep the compiler happy */

#endif GIO_ACTIVE
```



```
/*----------------------------------------------------------------------*/
/*  GIOCall.c:  An example of calling the Generic I/O Speed-up.  */
/*              1/23/86                                          */
/*                                                                */
/* By Jerry Morrison and Steve Shaw, Electronic Arts.            */
/* This software is in the public domain.                        */
/*                                                                */
/* This version for the Commodore-Amiga computer.                */
/*                                                                */
/*----------------------------------------------------------------------*/
    main(...) {
    LONG file;
    int success;
    ...
    success = (0 != (file = GOpen(...)));
    /* A TmpRas is a good buffer to use for a variety of short-term uses.*/
    if (success)
        success = PutObject(file, ob, tmpRas.RasPtr, tmpRas.Size);
    success &= (0 <= GClose(file));
    }

/*----- PutObject writes a DVCS object out as a disk file.------*/
BOOL PutObject(file, ob, buffer, bufsize)
    LONG file;  struct Object *ob;  BYTE *buffer;  LONG bufsize; {
    int success = TRUE;

    if (bufsize > 2*BODY_BUFSIZE) {
        /* Give buffer to speed-up writing.*/
        GWriteDeclare(file, buffer+BODY_BUFSIZE, bufsize-BODY_BUFSIZE);
        bufsize = BODY_BUFSIZE;  /* Used by PutObject for other purposes.*/
        }
    ...
        /* Use GWrite and GSeek instead of Write and Seek.*/
    success &= (0 <= GWrite(file, address, length));
    ...
    success &= (0 <= GWriteUndeclare(file));
                /* Release the speed-up buffer.*/
                /* This is not necessary if GClose is used to close the file,
                 * but it can't hurt.*/
    return( (BOOL)success );
    }
```

```
/*----------------------------------------------------------------------*
 * IFFR.C  Support routines for reading IFF-85 files.          1/23/86
 * (IFF is Interchange Format File.)
 *
 * By Jerry Morrison and Steve Shaw, Electronic Arts.
 * This software is in the public domain.
 *
 * This version for the Commodore-Amiga computer.
 *
 * Uses "gio".  Either link with gio.c, or set the GIO_ACTIVE flag to 0
 * in gio.h.
 *----------------------------------------------------------------------*/
#include "iff/gio.h"
#include "iff/iff.h"

/* ----- Private subroutine FileLength() --------------------------------*/
/* Returns the length of the file or else a negative IFFP error code
 * (NO_FILE or DOS_ERROR). AmigaDOS-specific implementation.
 * SIDE EFFECT: Thanks to AmigaDOS, we have to change the file's position
 * to find its length.
 * Now if Amiga DOS maintained fh_End, we'd just do this:
 *    fileLength = (FileHandle *)BADDR(file)->fh_End; */
LONG FileLength(file)  BPTR file;  {
    LONG fileLength = NO_FILE;

    if (file > 0)  {
        GSeek(file, 0, OFFSET_END);     /* Seek to end of file.*/
        fileLength = GSeek(file, 0, OFFSET_CURRENT);
            /* Returns position BEFORE the seek, which is #bytes in file. */
        if (fileLength < 0)
            fileLength = DOS_ERROR;     /* DOS being absurd.*/
        }

    return(fileLength);
    }

/* ---------- Read ------------------------------------------------------*/

/* ---------- OpenRIFF --------------------------------------------------*/
IFFP OpenRIFF(file0, new0, clientFrame)
        BPTR file0;   GroupContext *new0;  ClientFrame *clientFrame; {
    register BPTR file = file0;
    register GroupContext *new = new0;
    IFFP iffp = IFF_OKAY;

    new->parent       = NULL;          /* "whole file" has no parent.*/
    new->clientFrame  = clientFrame;
    new->file         = file;
    new->position     = 0;
    new->ckHdr.ckID   = new->subtype    = NULL_CHUNK;
    new->ckHdr.ckSize = new->bytesSoFar = 0;

    /* Set new->bound and go to the file's beginning. */
    new->bound = FileLength(file);
    if (new->bound < 0)
        iffp = new->bound;                /* File system error! */
    else if ( new->bound < sizeof(ChunkHeader) )
        iffp = NOT_IFF;                   /* Too small for an IFF file. */
    else
        GSeek(file, 0, OFFSET_BEGINNING);  /* Go to file start. */

    return(iffp);
    }

/* ---------- OpenRGroup ------------------------------------------------*/
IFFP OpenRGroup(parent0, new0)   GroupContext *parent0, *new0; {
    register GroupContext *parent = parent0;
    register GroupContext *new    = new0;
    IFFP iffp = IFF_OKAY;
```



```
    new->parent       = parent;
    new->clientFrame  = parent->clientFrame;
    new->file         = parent->file;
    new->position     = parent->position;
    new->bound        = parent->position + ChunkMoreBytes(parent);
    new->ckHdr.ckID   = new->subtype    = NULL_CHUNK;
    new->ckHdr.ckSize = new->bytesSoFar = 0;

    if ( new->bound > parent->bound  ||  IS_ODD(new->bound) )
        iffp = BAD_IFF;
    return(iffp);
    }

/* ---------- CloseRGroup -----------------------------------------------*/
IFFP CloseRGroup(context)   GroupContext *context; {
    register LONG position;

    if (context->parent == NULL) {
        }  /* Context for whole file.*/
    else {
        position = context->position;
        context->parent->bytesSoFar += position - context->parent->position;
        context->parent->position = position;
        }
    return(IFF_OKAY);
    }

/* ---------- SkipFwd ---------------------------------------------------*/
/* Skip over bytes in a context. Won't go backwards.*/
/* Updates context->position but not context->bytesSoFar.*/
/* This implementation is AmigaDOS specific.*/
IFFP SkipFwd(context, bytes)   GroupContext *context;  LONG bytes; {
    IFFP iffp = IFF_OKAY;

    if (bytes > 0) {
        if (-1 == GSeek(context->file, bytes, OFFSET_CURRENT))
            iffp = BAD_IFF;     /* Ran out of bytes before chunk complete.*/
        else
            context->position += bytes;
        }
    return(iffp);
    }

/* ---------- GetChunkHdr -----------------------------------------------*/
ID GetChunkHdr(context0)   GroupContext *context0;  {
    register GroupContext *context = context0;
    register IFFP iffp;
    LONG remaining;

    /* Skip remainder of previous chunk & padding. */
    iffp = SkipFwd(context,
        ChunkMoreBytes(context) + IS_ODD(context->ckHdr.ckSize));
    CheckIFFP();

    /* Set up to read the new header. */
    context->ckHdr.ckID = BAD_IFF;      /* Until we know it's okay, mark it BAD.*/
    context->subtype    = NULL_CHUNK;
    context->bytesSoFar = 0;

    /* Generate a psuedo-chunk if at end-of-context. */
    remaining = context->bound - context->position;
    if (remaining == 0) {
        context->ckHdr.ckSize = 0;
        context->ckHdr.ckID   = END_MARK;
        }

    /* BAD_IFF if not enough bytes in the context for a ChunkHeader.*/
    else if (sizeof(ChunkHeader) > remaining) {
```

```
        context->ckHdr.ckSize = remaining;
        }

    /* Read the chunk header (finally). */
    else {
        switch (
            GRead(context->file, (BYTE *)&context->ckHdr, sizeof(ChunkHeader))
            ) {
            case -1: return(context->ckHdr.ckID = DOS_ERROR);
            case 0:  return(context->ckHdr.ckID = BAD_IFF);
            }

        /* Check: Top level chunk must be LIST or FORM or CAT. */
        if (context->parent == NULL)
            switch(context->ckHdr.ckID) {
                case FORM:  case LIST:  case CAT:  break;
                default:    return(context->ckHdr.ckID = NOT_IFF);
                }

        /* Update the context. */
        context->position += sizeof(ChunkHeader);
        remaining         -= sizeof(ChunkHeader);

        /* Non-positive ID values are illegal and used for error codes.*/
        /* We could check for other illegal IDs...*/
        if (context->ckHdr.ckID <= 0)
             context->ckHdr.ckID = BAD_IFF;

        /* Check: ckSize negative or larger than # bytes left in context? */
        else if (context->ckHdr.ckSize < 0  ||
                 context->ckHdr.ckSize > remaining) {
            context->ckHdr.ckSize = remaining;
            context->ckHdr.ckID   = BAD_IFF;
            }

        /* Automatically read the LIST, FORM, PROP, or CAT subtype ID */
        else switch (context->ckHdr.ckID) {
            case LIST:  case FORM:  case PROP:  case CAT:  {
                iffp = IFFReadBytes(context,
                                    (BYTE *)&context->subtype,
                                    sizeof(ID));
                if (iffp != IFF_OKAY)
                    context->ckHdr.ckID = iffp;
                break; }
            }

        }
    return(context->ckHdr.ckID);
    }

/* ---------- IFFReadBytes ---------------------------------------------*/
IFFP IFFReadBytes(context, buffer, nBytes)
    GroupContext *context;   BYTE *buffer;   LONG nBytes; {
    register IFFP iffp = IFF_OKAY;

    if (nBytes < 0)
        iffp = CLIENT_ERROR;
    else if (nBytes > ChunkMoreBytes(context))
        iffp = SHORT_CHUNK;
    else if (nBytes > 0)
        switch ( GRead(context->file, buffer, nBytes) ) {
            case -1: {iffp = DOS_ERROR; break; }
            case 0:  {iffp = BAD_IFF;   break; }
            default: {
                context->position   += nBytes;
                context->bytesSoFar += nBytes;
                }
            }
```



```
    return(iffp);
    }

/* ---------- SkipGroup ------------------------------------------------*/
IFFP SkipGroup(context)  GroupContext *context;  {
    }  /* Nothing to do, thanks to GetChunkHdr */

/* ---------- ReadIFF --------------------------------------------------*/
IFFP ReadIFF(file, clientFrame)  BPTR file;  ClientFrame *clientFrame;  {
    /*CompilerBug register*/ IFFP iffp;
    GroupContext context;

    iffp = OpenRIFF(file, &context);
    context.clientFrame = clientFrame;

    if (iffp == IFF_OKAY)
        switch (iffp = GetChunkHdr(&context)) {
            case FORM: { iffp = (*clientFrame->getForm)(&context); break; }
            case LIST: { iffp = (*clientFrame->getList)(&context); break; }
            case CAT : { iffp = (*clientFrame->getCat )(&context); break; }
            /* default: Includes IFF_DONE, BAD_IFF, NOT_IFF... */
            }

    CloseRGroup(&context);

    if (iffp > 0)               /* Make sure we don't return an ID.*/
        iffp = NOT_IFF;         /* GetChunkHdr should've caught this.*/
    return(iffp);
    }

/* ---------- ReadIList ------------------------------------------------*/
IFFP ReadIList(parent, clientFrame)
    GroupContext *parent;  ClientFrame *clientFrame; {
    GroupContext listContext;
    IFFP iffp;
    BOOL propOk = TRUE;

    iffp = OpenRGroup(parent, &listContext);
    CheckIFFP();

    /* One special case test lets us handle CATs as well as LISTs.*/
    if (parent->ckHdr.ckID == CAT)
        propOk = FALSE;
    else
        listContext.clientFrame = clientFrame;

    do {
        switch (iffp = GetChunkHdr(&listContext)) {
            case PROP: {
                if (propOk)
                    iffp = (*clientFrame->getProp)(&listContext);
                else
                    iffp = BAD_IFF;
                break;
                }
            case FORM: { iffp = (*clientFrame->getForm)(&listContext); break; }
            case LIST: { iffp = (*clientFrame->getList)(&listContext); break; }
            case CAT : { iffp = (*clientFrame->getCat )(&listContext); break; }
            /* default: Includes END_MARK, IFF_DONE, BAD_IFF, NOT_IFF... */
            }
        if (listContext.ckHdr.ckID != PROP)
            propOk = FALSE;     /* No PROPs allowed after this point.*/
        } while (iffp == IFF_OKAY);

    CloseRGroup(&listContext);

    if (iffp > 0)       /* Only chunk types above are allowed in a LIST/CAT.*/
        iffp = BAD_IFF;
    return(iffp == END_MARK ? IFF_OKAY : iffp);
```

```
    }

/* ---------- ReadICat -------------------------------------------------*/
/* By special arrangement with the ReadIList implement'n, this is trivial.*/
IFFP ReadICat(parent)  GroupContext *parent;  {
    return( ReadIList(parent, NULL) );
    }

/* ---------- GetFChunkHdr ---------------------------------------------*/
ID GetFChunkHdr(context)   GroupContext *context; {
    register ID id;

    id = GetChunkHdr(context);
    if (id == PROP)
        context->ckHdr.ckID = id = BAD_IFF;
    return(id);
    }

/* ---------- GetF1ChunkHdr ---------------------------------------------*/
ID GetF1ChunkHdr(context)   GroupContext *context; {
    register ID id;
    register ClientFrame *clientFrame = context->clientFrame;

    switch (id = GetChunkHdr(context))  {
        case PROP: { id = BAD_IFF; break; }
        case FORM: { id = (*clientFrame->getForm)(context); break; }
        case LIST: { id = (*clientFrame->getList)(context); break; }
        case CAT : { id = (*clientFrame->getCat )(context); break; }
        /* Default: let the caller handle other chunks */
        }
    return(context->ckHdr.ckID = id);
    }

/* ---------- GetPChunkHdr ---------------------------------------------*/
ID GetPChunkHdr(context)   GroupContext *context; {
    register ID id;

    id = GetChunkHdr(context);
    switch (id) {
        case LIST:  case FORM:  case PROP:  case CAT:  {
            id = context->ckHdr.ckID = BAD_IFF;
            break; }
        }
    return(id);
    }
```



```
/*----------------------------------------------------------------------*
 * IFFW.C  Support routines for writing IFF-85 files.          1/23/86
 * (IFF is Interchange Format File.)
 *
 * By Jerry Morrison and Steve Shaw, Electronic Arts.
 * This software is in the public domain.
 *
 * This version for the Commodore-Amiga computer.
 *----------------------------------------------------------------------*/
#include "iff/iff.h"
#include "iff/gio.h"

/* ---------- IFF Writer -----------------------------------------------*/

/* A macro to test if a chunk size is definite, i.e. not szNotYetKnown.*/
#define Known(size)   ( (size) != szNotYetKnown )

/* Yet another weird macro to make the source code simpler...*/
#define IfIffp(expr)  {if (iffp == IFF_OKAY)  iffp = (expr);}

/* ---------- OpenWIFF -------------------------------------------------*/

IFFP OpenWIFF(file, new0, limit)  BPTR file; GroupContext *new0; LONG limit; {
    register GroupContext *new = new0;
    register IFFP iffp = IFF_OKAY;

    new->parent       = NULL;
    new->clientFrame  = NULL;
    new->file         = file;
    new->position     = 0;
    new->bound        = limit;
    new->ckHdr.ckID   = NULL_CHUNK;  /* indicates no current chunk */
    new->ckHdr.ckSize = new->bytesSoFar = 0;

    if (0 > Seek(file, 0, OFFSET_BEGINNING))    /* Go to start of the file.*/
        iffp = DOS_ERROR;
    else if ( Known(limit) && IS_ODD(limit) )
        iffp = CLIENT_ERROR;
    return(iffp);
    }

/* ---------- StartWGroup ----------------------------------------------*/
IFFP StartWGroup(parent, groupType, groupSize, subtype, new)
      GroupContext *parent, *new; ID groupType, subtype; LONG groupSize;  {
    register IFFP iffp;

    iffp = PutCkHdr(parent, groupType, groupSize);
    IfIffp( IFFWriteBytes(parent, (BYTE *)&subtype, sizeof(ID)) );
    IfIffp( OpenWGroup(parent, new) );
    return(iffp);
    }

/* ---------- OpenWGroup -----------------------------------------------*/
IFFP OpenWGroup(parent0, new0)  GroupContext *parent0, *new0; {
    register GroupContext *parent = parent0;
    register GroupContext *new    = new0;
    register LONG ckEnd;
    register IFFP iffp = IFF_OKAY;

    new->parent       = parent;
    new->clientFrame  = parent->clientFrame;
    new->file         = parent->file;
    new->position     = parent->position;
    new->bound        = parent->bound;
    new->ckHdr.ckID   = NULL_CHUNK;
    new->ckHdr.ckSize = new->bytesSoFar = 0;

    if ( Known(parent->ckHdr.ckSize) ) {
        ckEnd = new->position + ChunkMoreBytes(parent);
```

```
    if ( new->bound == szNotYetKnown || new->bound > ckEnd )
        new->bound = ckEnd;
    };

    if ( parent->ckHdr.ckID == NULL_CHUNK || /* not currently writing a chunk*/
         IS_ODD(new->position) ||
         (Known(new->bound) && IS_ODD(new->bound)) )
        iffp = CLIENT_ERROR;
    return(iffp);
    }

/* ---------- CloseWGroup ----------------------------------------------*/
IFFP CloseWGroup(old0)  GroupContext *old0; {
    register GroupContext *old = old0;
    IFFP iffp = IFF_OKAY;

    if ( old->ckHdr.ckID != NULL_CHUNK )  /* didn't close the last chunk */
        iffp = CLIENT_ERROR;
    else if ( old->parent == NULL ) {     /* top level file context */
        if (GWriteFlush(old->file) < 0)  iffp = DOS_ERROR;
        }
    else {                                /* update parent context */
        old->parent->bytesSoFar += old->position - old->parent->position;
        old->parent->position = old->position;
        };
    return(iffp);
    }

/* ---------- EndWGroup ------------------------------------------------*/
IFFP EndWGroup(old)  GroupContext *old;  {
    register GroupContext *parent = old->parent;
    register IFFP iffp;

    iffp = CloseWGroup(old);
    IfIffp( PutCkEnd(parent) );
    return(iffp);
    }

/* ---------- PutCk ----------------------------------------------------*/
IFFP PutCk(context, ckID, ckSize, data)
      GroupContext *context; ID ckID; LONG ckSize; BYTE *data; {
    register IFFP iffp = IFF_OKAY;

    if ( ckSize == szNotYetKnown )
        iffp = CLIENT_ERROR;
    IfIffp( PutCkHdr(context, ckID, ckSize) );
    IfIffp( IFFWriteBytes(context, data, ckSize) );
    IfIffp( PutCkEnd(context) );
    return(iffp);
    }

/* ---------- PutCkHdr -------------------------------------------------*/
IFFP PutCkHdr(context0, ckID, ckSize)
      GroupContext *context0;  ID ckID;  LONG ckSize; {
    register GroupContext *context = context0;
    LONG minPSize = sizeof(ChunkHeader); /* physical chunk >= minPSize bytes*/

    /* CLIENT_ERROR if we're already inside a chunk or asked to write
     * other than one FORM, LIST, or CAT at the top level of a file */
    /* Also, non-positive ID values are illegal and used for error codes.*/
    /* (We could check for other illegal IDs...)*/
    if ( context->ckHdr.ckID != NULL_CHUNK  ||  ckID <= 0 )
        return(CLIENT_ERROR);
    else if (context->parent == NULL)  {
        switch (ckID)  {
            case FORM:  case LIST:  case CAT:  break;
            default: return(CLIENT_ERROR);
            }
        if (context->position != 0)
```



```
            return(CLIENT_ERROR);
        }

    if ( Known(ckSize) ) {
        if ( ckSize < 0 )
            return(CLIENT_ERROR);
        minPSize += ckSize;
        };
    if ( Known(context->bound)  &&
         context->position + minPSize > context->bound )
        return(CLIENT_ERROR);

    context->ckHdr.ckID   = ckID;
    context->ckHdr.ckSize = ckSize;
    context->bytesSoFar   = 0;
    if (0 >
        GWrite(context->file, (BYTE *)&context->ckHdr, sizeof(ChunkHeader))
        )
        return(DOS_ERROR);
    context->position += sizeof(ChunkHeader);
    return(IFF_OKAY);
    }

/* ---------- IFFWriteBytes --------------------------------------------*/
IFFP IFFWriteBytes(context0, data, nBytes)
      GroupContext *context0;  BYTE *data;  LONG nBytes; {
    register GroupContext *context = context0;

    if ( context->ckHdr.ckID == NULL_CHUNK  ||      /* not in a chunk */
         nBytes < 0  ||                             /* negative nBytes */
         (Known(context->bound)  &&                 /* overflow context */
            context->position + nBytes > context->bound)  ||
         (Known(context->ckHdr.ckSize)  &&          /* overflow chunk */
            context->bytesSoFar + nBytes > context->ckHdr.ckSize) )
        return(CLIENT_ERROR);

    if (0 > GWrite(context->file, data, nBytes))
        return(DOS_ERROR);

    context->bytesSoFar += nBytes;
    context->position   += nBytes;
    return(IFF_OKAY);
    }

/* ---------- PutCkEnd -------------------------------------------------*/
IFFP PutCkEnd(context0)  GroupContext *context0; {
    register GroupContext *context = context0;
    WORD zero = 0;      /* padding source */

    if ( context->ckHdr.ckID == NULL_CHUNK )  /* not in a chunk */
        return(CLIENT_ERROR);

    if ( context->ckHdr.ckSize == szNotYetKnown ) {
        /* go back and set the chunk size to bytesSoFar */
        if ( 0 >
GSeek(context->file, -(context->bytesSoFar + sizeof(LONG)), OFFSET_CURRENT) ||
             0 >
GWrite(context->file, (BYTE *)&context->bytesSoFar, sizeof(LONG))  ||
             0 >
GSeek(context->file, context->bytesSoFar, OFFSET_CURRENT)  )
            return(DOS_ERROR);
        }
    else {  /* make sure the client wrote as many bytes as planned */
        if ( context->ckHdr.ckSize != context->bytesSoFar )
            return(CLIENT_ERROR);
        };

    /* Write a pad byte if needed to bring us up to an even boundary.
     * Since the context end must be even, and since we haven't
```

```
   * overwritten the context, if we're on an odd position there must
   * be room for a pad byte. */
  if ( IS_ODD(context->bytesSoFar) ) {
      if ( 0 > GWrite(context->file, (BYTE *)&zero, 1) )
          return(DOS_ERROR);
      context->position += 1;
      };

  context->ckHdr.ckID   = NULL_CHUNK;
  context->ckHdr.ckSize = context->bytesSoFar = 0;
  return(IFF_OKAY);
  }
```



```
/*----------------------------------------------------------------------*
 * ILBMR.C  Support routines for reading ILBM files.          11/27/85
 * (IFF is Interchange Format File.)
 *
 * By Jerry Morrison and Steve Shaw, Electronic Arts.
 * This software is in the public domain.
 *
 * This version for the Commodore-Amiga computer.
 *----------------------------------------------------------------------*/
#include "iff/packer.h"
#include "iff/ilbm.h"


/* ---------- GetCMAP ------------------------------------------------*/
/* pNColorRegs is passed in as a pointer to the number of ColorRegisters
 * caller has space to hold.  GetCMAP sets to the number actually read.*/
IFFP GetCMAP(ilbmContext, colorMap, pNColorRegs)
      GroupContext *ilbmContext;  WORD *colorMap;  UBYTE *pNColorRegs;
   {
   register int nColorRegs;
   register IFFP iffp;
   ColorRegister colorReg;

   nColorRegs = ilbmContext->ckHdr.ckSize / sizeofColorRegister;
   if (*pNColorRegs < nColorRegs)   nColorRegs = *pNColorRegs;
   *pNColorRegs = nColorRegs;   /* Set to the number actually there.*/

   for ( ;  nColorRegs > 0;  --nColorRegs)  {
      iffp = IFFReadBytes(ilbmContext, (BYTE *)&colorReg,sizeofColorRegister);
      CheckIFFP();
      *colorMap++ = ( ( colorReg.red   >> 4 ) << 8 ) |
                    ( ( colorReg.green >> 4 ) << 4 ) |
                    ( ( colorReg.blue  >> 4 )      );
      }
   return(IFF_OKAY);
   }

/*---------- GetBODY ---------------------------------------------------*/
/* NOTE: This implementation could be a LOT faster if it used more of the
 * supplied buffer. It would make far fewer calls to IFFReadBytes (and
 * therefore to DOS Read) and to movemem. */
IFFP GetBODY(context, bitmap, mask, bmHdr, buffer, bufsize)
      GroupContext *context;  struct BitMap *bitmap;  BYTE *mask;
      BitMapHeader *bmHdr;  BYTE *buffer;  LONG bufsize;
   {
   register IFFP iffp;
   UBYTE srcPlaneCnt = bmHdr->nPlanes;   /* Haven't counted for mask plane yet*/
   WORD srcRowBytes = RowBytes(bmHdr->w);
   LONG bufRowBytes = MaxPackedSize(srcRowBytes);
   int nRows = bmHdr->h;
   Compression compression = bmHdr->compression;
   register int iPlane, iRow, nEmpty;
   register WORD nFilled;
   BYTE *buf, *nullDest, *nullBuf, **pDest;
   BYTE *planes[MaxSrcPlanes]; /* array of ptrs to planes & mask */

   if (compression > cmpByteRun1)
      return(CLIENT_ERROR);

   /* Complain if client asked for a conversion GetBODY doesn't handle.*/
   if ( srcRowBytes  !=  bitmap->BytesPerRow  ||
         bufsize < bufRowBytes * 2  ||
         srcPlaneCnt > MaxSrcPlanes )
      return(CLIENT_ERROR);

   if (nRows > bitmap->Rows)
      nRows = bitmap->Rows;

   /* Initialize array "planes" with bitmap ptrs; NULL in empty slots.*/
```

```
    for (iPlane = 0; iPlane < bitmap->Depth; iPlane++)
       planes[iPlane] = (BYTE *)bitmap->Planes[iPlane];
    for ( ;  iPlane < MaxSrcPlanes;  iPlane++)
       planes[iPlane] = NULL;

    /* Copy any mask plane ptr into corresponding "planes" slot.*/
    if (bmHdr->masking == mskHasMask) {
       if (mask != NULL)
          planes[srcPlaneCnt] = mask;  /* If there are more srcPlanes than
                * dstPlanes, there will be NULL plane-pointers before this.*/
       else
          planes[srcPlaneCnt] = NULL;  /* In case more dstPlanes than src.*/
       srcPlaneCnt += 1;  /* Include mask plane in count.*/
       }

    /* Setup a sink for dummy destination of rows from unwanted planes.*/
    nullDest = buffer;
    buffer  += srcRowBytes;
    bufsize -= srcRowBytes;

    /* Read the BODY contents into client's bitmap.
     * De-interleave planes and decompress rows.
     * MODIFIES: Last iteration modifies bufsize.*/
    buf = buffer + bufsize;  /* Buffer is currently empty.*/
    for (iRow = nRows; iRow > 0; iRow--)  {
       for (iPlane = 0; iPlane < srcPlaneCnt; iPlane++)  {

          pDest = &planes[iPlane];

          /* Establish a sink for any unwanted plane.*/
          if (*pDest == NULL) {
             nullBuf = nullDest;
             pDest   = &nullBuf;
             }

          /* Read in at least enough bytes to uncompress next row.*/
          nEmpty  = buf - buffer;          /* size of empty part of buffer.*/
          nFilled = bufsize - nEmpty;      /* this part has data.*/
          if (nFilled < bufRowBytes) {
             /* Need to read more.*/

             /* Move the existing data to the front of the buffer.*/
             /* Now covers range buffer[0]..buffer[nFilled-1].*/
             movmem(buf, buffer, nFilled);  /* Could be moving 0 bytes.*/

             if (nEmpty > ChunkMoreBytes(context)) {
                /* There aren't enough bytes left to fill the buffer.*/
                nEmpty = ChunkMoreBytes(context);
                bufsize = nFilled + nEmpty;  /* heh-heh */
                }

             /* Append new data to the existing data.*/
             iffp = IFFReadBytes(context, &buffer[nFilled], nEmpty);
             CheckIFFP();

             buf     = buffer;
             nFilled = bufsize;
             nEmpty  = 0;
             }

          /* Copy uncompressed row to destination plane.*/
          if (compression == cmpNone) {
             if (nFilled < srcRowBytes)  return(BAD_FORM);
             movmem(buf, *pDest, srcRowBytes);
             buf    += srcRowBytes;
             *pDest += srcRowBytes;
             }
          else
          /* Decompress row to destination plane.*/
```



```
             if ( UnPackRow(&buf, pDest, nFilled,  srcRowBytes) )
                    /*  pSource, pDest, srcBytes, dstBytes  */
                return(BAD_FORM);
          }
       }

    return(IFF_OKAY);
    }
```

```
/*----------------------------------------------------------------------*
 * ILBMW.C  Support routines for writing ILBM files.           1/23/86
 * (IFF is Interchange Format File.)
 *
 * By Jerry Morrison and Steve Shaw, Electronic Arts.
 * This software is in the public domain.
 *
 * This version for the Commodore-Amiga computer.
 *----------------------------------------------------------------------*/
#include "iff/packer.h"
#include "iff/ilbm.h"

/*---------- InitBMHdr -------------------------------------------------*/
IFFP InitBMHdr(bmHdr0, bitmap, masking, compression, transparentColor,
            pageWidth, pageHeight)
        BitMapHeader *bmHdr0;  struct BitMap *bitmap;
        WORD masking;           /* Masking */
        WORD compression;       /* Compression */
        WORD transparentColor;  /* UWORD */
        WORD pageWidth, pageHeight;
    {
    register BitMapHeader *bmHdr = bmHdr0;
    register WORD rowBytes = bitmap->BytesPerRow;

    bmHdr->w = rowBytes << 3;
    bmHdr->h = bitmap->Rows;
    bmHdr->x = bmHdr->y = 0;    /* Default position is (0,0).*/
    bmHdr->nPlanes = bitmap->Depth;
    bmHdr->masking = masking;
    bmHdr->compression = compression;
    bmHdr->pad1 = 0;
    bmHdr->transparentColor = transparentColor;
    bmHdr->xAspect = bmHdr->yAspect = 1;
    bmHdr->pageWidth = pageWidth;
    bmHdr->pageHeight = pageHeight;

    if (pageWidth = 320)
        switch (pageHeight) {
            case 200: {bmHdr->xAspect = x320x200Aspect;
                       bmHdr->yAspect = y320x200Aspect; break;}
            case 400: {bmHdr->xAspect = x320x400Aspect;
                       bmHdr->yAspect = y320x400Aspect; break;}
            }
    else if (pageWidth = 640)
        switch (pageHeight) {
            case 200: {bmHdr->xAspect = x640x200Aspect;
                       bmHdr->yAspect = y640x200Aspect; break;}
            case 400: {bmHdr->xAspect = x640x400Aspect;
                       bmHdr->yAspect = y640x400Aspect; break;}
            }

    return( IS_ODD(rowBytes) ? CLIENT_ERROR : IFF_OKAY );
    }

/*---------- PutCMAP ---------------------------------------------------*/
IFFP PutCMAP(context, colorMap, depth)
      GroupContext *context;  WORD *colorMap;  UBYTE depth;
   {
   register LONG nColorRegs;
   IFFP iffp;
   ColorRegister colorReg;

   if (depth > MaxAmDepth)   depth = MaxAmDepth;
   nColorRegs = 1 << depth;

   iffp = PutCkHdr(context, ID_CMAP, nColorRegs * sizeofColorRegister);
   CheckIFFP();

   for ( ;  nColorRegs;  --nColorRegs)  {
```



```
      colorReg.red   = ( *colorMap >> 4 ) & 0xf0;
      colorReg.green = ( *colorMap      ) & 0xf0;
      colorReg.blue  = ( *colorMap << 4 ) & 0xf0;
      iffp = IFFWriteBytes(context, (BYTE *)&colorReg, sizeofColorRegister);
      CheckIFFP();
      ++colorMap;
      }

   iffp = PutCkEnd(context);
   return(iffp);
   }

/*---------- PutBODY ---------------------------------------------------*/
/* NOTE: This implementation could be a LOT faster if it used more of the
 * supplied buffer. It would make far fewer calls to IFFWriteBytes (and
 * therefore to DOS Write). */
IFFP PutBODY(context, bitmap, mask, bmHdr, buffer, bufsize)
      GroupContext *context;  struct BitMap *bitmap;  BYTE *mask;
      BitMapHeader *bmHdr;  BYTE *buffer;  LONG bufsize;
   {
   IFFP iffp;
   LONG rowBytes = bitmap->BytesPerRow;
   int dstDepth = bmHdr->nPlanes;
   Compression compression = bmHdr->compression;
   int planeCnt;              /* number of bit planes including mask */
   register int iPlane, iRow;
   register LONG packedRowBytes;
   BYTE *buf;
   BYTE *planes[MaxAmDepth + 1]; /* array of ptrs to planes & mask */

   if ( bufsize < MaxPackedSize(rowBytes)  ||    /* Must buffer a comprsd row*/
        compression > cmpByteRun1  ||            /* bad arg */
        bitmap->Rows != bmHdr->h   ||            /* inconsistent */
        rowBytes != RowBytes(bmHdr->w)  ||       /* inconsistent*/
        bitmap->Depth < dstDepth   ||            /* inconsistent */
        dstDepth > MaxAmDepth )                  /* too many for this routine*/
      return(CLIENT_ERROR);

   planeCnt = dstDepth + (mask == NULL ? 0 : 1);

   /* Copy the ptrs to bit & mask planes into local array "planes" */
   for (iPlane = 0; iPlane < dstDepth; iPlane++)
      planes[iPlane] = (BYTE *)bitmap->Planes[iPlane];
   if (mask != NULL)
      planes[dstDepth] = mask;

   /* Write out a BODY chunk header */
   iffp = PutCkHdr(context, ID_BODY, szNotYetKnown);
   CheckIFFP();

   /* Write out the BODY contents */
   for (iRow = bmHdr->h; iRow > 0; iRow--)  {
      for (iPlane = 0; iPlane < planeCnt; iPlane++)  {

         /* Write next row.*/
         if (compression == cmpNone) {
            iffp = IFFWriteBytes(context, planes[iPlane], rowBytes);
            planes[iPlane] += rowBytes;
            }

         /* Compress and write next row.*/
         else {
            buf = buffer;
            packedRowBytes = PackRow(&planes[iPlane], &buf, rowBytes);
            iffp = IFFWriteBytes(context, buffer, packedRowBytes);
            }

         CheckIFFP();
         }
```

```
    }

/* Finish the chunk */
iffp = PutCkEnd(context);
return(iffp);
}
```



```
/*----------------------------------------------------------------------*
 * packer.c Convert data to "cmpByteRun1" run compression.     11/15/85
 *
 * By Jerry Morrison and Steve Shaw, Electronic Arts.
 * This software is in the public domain.
 *
 *      control bytes:
 *       [0..127]   : followed by n+1 bytes of data.
 *       [-1..-127] : followed by byte to be repeated (-n)+1 times.
 *       -128       : NOOP.
 *
 * This version for the Commodore-Amiga computer.
 *----------------------------------------------------------------------*/
#include "iff/packer.h"

#define DUMP    0
#define RUN     1

#define MinRun 3
#define MaxRun 128
#define MaxDat 128

LONG putSize;
#define GetByte()       (*source++)
#define PutByte(c)      { *dest++ = (c);   ++putSize; }

char buf[256];  /* [TBD] should be 128?  on stack?*/

BYTE *PutDump(dest, nn)  BYTE *dest;  int nn; {
        int i;

        PutByte(nn-1);
        for(i = 0;  i < nn;  i++)   PutByte(buf[i]);
        return(dest);
        }

BYTE *PutRun(dest, nn, cc)   BYTE *dest;  int nn, cc; {
        PutByte(-(nn-1));
        PutByte(cc);
        return(dest);
        }

#define OutDump(nn)   dest = PutDump(dest, nn)
#define OutRun(nn,cc) dest = PutRun(dest, nn, cc)

/*----------- PackRow --------------------------------------------------*/
/* Given POINTERS TO POINTERS, packs one row, updating the source and
   destination pointers.  RETURNs count of packed bytes.*/
LONG PackRow(pSource, pDest, rowSize)
    BYTE **pSource, **pDest;   LONG rowSize; {
    BYTE *source, *dest;
    char c,lastc = '\0';
    BOOL mode = DUMP;
    short nbuf = 0;             /* number of chars in buffer */
    short rstart = 0;           /* buffer index current run starts */

    source = *pSource;
    dest = *pDest;
    putSize = 0;
    buf[0] = lastc = c = GetByte();  /* so have valid lastc */
    nbuf = 1;   rowSize--;      /* since one byte eaten.*/


    for (;  rowSize;  --rowSize) {
        buf[nbuf++] = c = GetByte();
        switch (mode) {
                case DUMP:
                        /* If the buffer is full, write the length byte,
                           then the data */
```

```
                    if (nbuf>MaxDat) {
                            OutDump(nbuf-1);
                            buf[0] = c;
                            nbuf = 1;   rstart = 0;
                            break;
                            }

                    if (c == lastc) {
                        if (nbuf-rstart >= MinRun) {
                            if (rstart > 0) OutDump(rstart);
                            mode = RUN;
                            }
                        else if (rstart == 0)
                            mode = RUN;     /* no dump in progress,
                            so can't lose by making these 2 a run.*/
                        }
                    else  rstart = nbuf-1;          /* first of run */
                    break;

            case RUN: if ( (c != lastc)|| ( nbuf-rstart > MaxRun)) {
                    /* output run */
                    OutRun(nbuf-1-rstart,lastc);
                    buf[0] = c;
                    nbuf = 1; rstart = 0;
                    mode = DUMP;
                    }
                    break;
            }

        lastc = c;
        }

    switch (mode) {
        case DUMP: OutDump(nbuf); break;
        case RUN: OutRun(nbuf-rstart,lastc); break;
        }
    *pSource = source;
    *pDest = dest;
    return(putSize);
    }
```



```
/** putpict.c ****************************************************/
/* PutPict().  Given a BitMap and a color map in RAM on the     */
/* Amiga, outputs as an ILBM.  See /iff/ilbm.h & /iff/ilbmw.c.  */
/*                     23-Jan-86                                */
/*                                                              */
/* By Jerry Morrison and Steve Shaw, Electronic Arts.           */
/* This software is in the public domain.                       */
/*                                                              */
/* This version for the Commodore-Amiga computer.               */
/*                                                              */
/****************************************************************/
#include "iff/intuall.h"
#include "iff/gio.h"
#include "iff/ilbm.h"
#include "iff/putpict.h"

#define MaxDepth 5
static IFFP ifferror = 0;

#define CkErr(expression)  {if (ifferror == IFF_OKAY) ifferror = (expression);}

/*****************************************************************************/
/* IffErr                                                                    */
/*                                                                           */
/* Returns the iff error code and resets it to zero                          */
/*                                                                           */
/*****************************************************************************/
IFFP IffErr()
   {
   IFFP i;
   i = ifferror;
   ifferror = 0;
   return(i);
   }

/*****************************************************************************/
/* PutPict()                                                                 */
/*                                                                           */
/* Put a picture into an IFF file                                            */
/* Pass in mask == NULL for no mask.                                         */
/*                                                                           */
/* Buffer should be big enough for one packed scan line                      */
/* Buffer used as temporary storage to speed-up writing.                     */
/* A large buffer, say 8KB, is useful for minimizing Write and Seek calls.   */
/* (See /iff/gio.h & /iff/gio.c).                                            */
/*****************************************************************************/

BOOL PutPict(file, bm, pageW, pageH, colorMap, buffer, bufsize)
      LONG file; struct BitMap *bm;
        WORD pageW,pageH;
        WORD *colorMap;
      BYTE *buffer;  LONG bufsize;
    {
    BitMapHeader bmHdr;
    GroupContext fileContext, formContext;

    ifferror = InitBMHdr(&bmHdr,
        bm,
        mskNone,
        cmpByteRun1,
        0,
        pageW,
        pageH );

/* use buffered write for speedup, if it is big-enough for both
 * PutBODY's buffer and a gio buffer.*/
#define BODY_BUFSIZE 512
    if (ifferror == IFF_OKAY  &&  bufsize > 2*BODY_BUFSIZE) {
        if (GWriteDeclare(file, buffer+BODY_BUFSIZE, bufsize-BODY_BUFSIZE) < 0)
```

```
        ifferror = DOS_ERROR;
    bufsize = BODY_BUFSIZE;
    }

CkErr(OpenWIFF(file, &fileContext, szNotYetKnown) );
CkErr(StartWGroup(&fileContext, FORM, szNotYetKnown, ID_ILBM, &formContext) );

CkErr(PutCk(&formContext, ID_BMHD, sizeof(BitMapHeader), (BYTE *)&bmHdr));

if (colorMap!=NULL)
    CkErr( PutCMAP(&formContext, colorMap, (UBYTE)bm->Depth) );
CkErr( PutBODY(&formContext, bm, NULL, &bmHdr, buffer, bufsize) );

CkErr( EndWGroup(&formContext) );
CkErr( CloseWGroup(&fileContext) );
if (GWriteUndeclare(file) < 0  &&  ifferror == IFF_OKAY)
    ifferror = DOS_ERROR;
return( (BOOL)(ifferror != IFF_OKAY) );
}
```



```
/** ReadPict.c *****************************************************************
 *
 * Read an ILBM raster image file.                                23-Jan-86.
 *
 * By Jerry Morrison, Steve Shaw, and Steve Hayes, Electronic Arts.
 * This software is in the public domain.
 *
 * USE THIS AS AN EXAMPLE PROGRAM FOR AN IFF READER.
 *
 * The IFF reader portion is essentially a recursive-descent parser.
 ******************************************************************************/

#define LOCAL   static

#include "iff/intuall.h"
#include "libraries/dos.h"
#include "libraries/dosextens.h"
#include "iff/ilbm.h"
#include "iff/readpict.h"

/* This example's max number of planes in a bitmap. Could use MaxAmDepth. */
#define EXDepth 5
#define maxColorReg (1<<EXDepth)
#define MIN(a,b) ((a)<(b)?(a):(b))

#define SafeFreeMem(p,q) {if(p)FreeMem(p,q);}

/* Define the size of a temporary buffer used in unscrambling the ILBM rows.*/
#define bufSz 512

/*------------ ILBM reader -----------------------------------------------*/
/* ILBMFrame is our "client frame" for reading FORMs ILBM in an IFF file.
 * We allocate one of these on the stack for every LIST or FORM encountered
 * in the file and use it to hold BMHD & CMAP properties. We also allocate
 * an initial one for the whole file.
 * We allocate a new GroupContext (and initialize it by OpenRIFF or
 * OpenRGroup) for every group (FORM, CAT, LIST, or PROP) encountered. It's
 * just a context for reading (nested) chunks.
 *
 * If we were to scan the entire example file outlined below:
 *    reading            proc(s)                new             new
 *
 * --whole file--   ReadPicture+ReadIFF   GroupContext        ILBMFrame
 * CAT              ReadICat                GroupContext
 *   LIST           GetLiILBM+ReadIList       GroupContext        ILBMFrame
 *     PROP ILBM    GetPrILBM                   GroupContext
 *       CMAP       GetCMAP
 *       BMHD       GetBMHD
 *     FORM ILBM    GetFoILBM                   GroupContext        ILBMFrame
 *       BODY       GetBODY
 *     FORM ILBM    GetFoILBM                   GroupContext        ILBMFrame
 *       BODY       GetBODY
 *   FORM ILBM      GetFoILBM                 GroupContext        ILBMFrame
 */

/* NOTE: For a small version of this program, set Fancy to 0.
 * That'll compile a program that reads a single FORM ILBM in a file, which
 * is what DeluxePaint produces. It'll skip all LISTs and PROPs in the input
 * file. It will, however, look inside a CAT for a FORM ILBM.
 * That's suitable for 90% of the uses.
 *
 * For a fancier version that handles LISTs and PROPs, set Fancy to 1.
 * That'll compile a program that dives into a LIST, if present, to read
 * the first FORM ILBM. E.g. a DeluxePrint library of images is a LIST of
 * FORMs ILBM.
 *
 * For an even fancier version, set Fancy to 2. That'll compile a program
 * that dives into non-ILBM FORMs, if present, looking for a nested FORM ILBM.
 * E.g. a DeluxeVideo C.S. animated object file is a FORM ANBM containing a
```

```
 * FORM ILBM for each image frame. */
#define Fancy  0

/* Global access to client-provided pointers.*/
LOCAL Allocator *gAllocator = NULL;
LOCAL struct BitMap *gBM = NULL;        /* client's bitmap.*/
LOCAL ILBMFrame *giFrame = NULL;        /* "client frame".*/

/** GetFoILBM() *************************************************************
 *
 * Called via ReadPicture to han?le every FORM encountered in an IFF file.
 * Reads FORMs ILBM and skips all others.
 * Inside a FORM ILBM, it stops once it reads a BODY. It complains if it
 * finds no BODY or if it has no BMHD to decode the BODY.
 *
 * Once we find a BODY chunk, we'll allocate the BitMap and read the image.
 *
 ****************************************************************************/
LOCAL BYTE bodyBuffer[bufSz];
IFFP GetFoILBM(parent)  GroupContext *parent;  {
   /*compilerBug register*/ IFFP iffp;
   GroupContext formContext;
   ILBMFrame ilbmFrame;          /* only used for non-clientFrame fields.*/
   register int i;
   LONG plsize; /* Plane size in bytes. */
   int nPlanes; /* number of planes in our display image */

    /* Handle a non-ILBM FORM. */
    if (parent->subtype != ID_ILBM) {
#if Fancy >= 2
        /* Open a non-ILBM FORM and recursively scan it for ILBMs.*/
        iffp = OpenRGroup(parent, &formContext);
        CheckIFFP();
        do {
            iffp = GetF1ChunkHdr(&formContext);
            } while (iffp >= IFF_OKAY);
        if (iffp == END_MARK)
            iffp = IFF_OKAY;     /* then continue scanning the file */
        CloseRGroup(&formContext);
        return(iffp);
#else
        return(IFF_OKAY); /* Just skip this FORM and keep scanning the file.*/
#endif
        }

   ilbmFrame = *(ILBMFrame *)parent->clientFrame;
   iffp = OpenRGroup(parent, &formContext);
   CheckIFFP();

   do switch (iffp = GetFChunkHdr(&formContext)) {
      case ID_BMHD: {
        ilbmFrame.foundBMHD = TRUE;
        iffp = GetBMHD(&formContext, &ilbmFrame.bmHdr);
        break; }
      case ID_CMAP: {
        ilbmFrame.nColorRegs = maxColorReg;  /* we have room for this many */
        iffp = GetCMAP(
           &formContext, (WORD *)&ilbmFrame.colorMap[0], &ilbmFrame.nColorRegs);
                     /* was &ilbmFrame.colorMap, (fixed) robp. */
        break; }
      case ID_BODY: {
         if (!ilbmFrame.foundBMHD)  return(BAD_FORM);   /* No BMHD chunk! */

         nPlanes = MIN(ilbmFrame.bmHdr.nPlanes, EXDepth);
         InitBitMap(
            gBM,
            nPlanes,
            ilbmFrame.bmHdr.w,
            ilbmFrame.bmHdr.h);
```



```
         plsize = RowBytes(ilbmFrame.bmHdr.w) * ilbmFrame.bmHdr.h;
         /* Allocate all planes contiguously.  Not really necessary,
          * but it avoids writing code to back-out if only enough memory
          * for some of the planes.
          * WARNING: Don't change this without changing the code that
          * Frees these planes.
          */
         if (gBM->Planes[0] =
                 (PLANEPTR)(*gAllocator)(nPlanes * plsize))
            {
            for (i = 1; i < nPlanes; i++)
                 gBM->Planes[i] = (PLANEPTR) gBM->Planes[0] + plsize*i;
            iffp = GetBODY(
                 &formContext,
                 gBM,
                 NULL,
                 &ilbmFrame.bmHdr,
                 bodyBuffer,
                 bufSz);
            if (iffp == IFF_OKAY) iffp = IFF_DONE;      /* Eureka */
            *giFrame = ilbmFrame;  /* Copy fields to client's frame.*/
            }
         else
            iffp = CLIENT_ERROR;        /* not enough RAM for the bitmap */
         break; }
      case END_MARK: { iffp = BAD_FORM; break; } /* No BODY chunk! */
      } while (iffp >= IFF_OKAY);  /* loop if valid ID of ignored chunk or a
                            * subroutine returned IFF_OKAY (no errors).*/

   if (iffp != IFF_DONE)  return(iffp);

   /* If we get this far, there were no errors. */
   CloseRGroup(&formContext);
   return(iffp);
   }

/** Notes on extending GetFoILBM ********************************************
 *
 * To read more kinds of chunks, just add clauses to the switch statement.
 * To read more kinds of property chunks (GRAB, CAMG, etc.) add clauses to
 * the switch statement in GetPrILBM, too.
 *
 * To read a FORM type that contains a variable number of data chunks--e.g.
 * a FORM FTXT with any number of CHRS chunks--replace the ID_BODY case with
 * an ID_CHRS case that doesn't set iffp = IFF_DONE, and make the END_MARK
 * case do whatever cleanup you need.
 *
 ****************************************************************************/

/** GetPrILBM() *************************************************************
 *
 * Called via ReadPicture to handle every PROP encountered in an IFF file.
 * Reads PROPs ILBM and skips all others.
 *
 ****************************************************************************/
#if Fancy
IFFP GetPrILBM(parent)  GroupContext *parent;  {
   /*compilerBug register*/ IFFP iffp;
   GroupContext propContext;
   ILBMFrame *ilbmFrame = (ILBMFrame *)parent->clientFrame;

   if (parent->subtype != ID_ILBM)
      return(IFF_OKAY); /* just continue scaning the file */

   iffp = OpenRGroup(parent, &propContext);
   CheckIFFP();

   do switch (iffp = GetPChunkHdr(&propContext)) {
      case ID_BMHD: {
```

```
        ilbmFrame->foundBMHD = TRUE;
        iffp = GetBMHD(&propContext, &ilbmFrame->bmHdr);
        break; }
      case ID_CMAP: {
        ilbmFrame->nColorRegs = maxColorReg; /* we have room for this many */
        iffp = GetCMAP(
          &propContext, (WORD *)&ilbmFrame->colorMap, &ilbmFrame->nColorRegs);
        break; }
      } while (iffp >= IFF_OKAY);  /* loop if valid ID of ignored chunk or a
                                  * subroutine returned IFF_OKAY (no errors).*/

   CloseRGroup(&propContext);
   return(iffp == END_MARK ? IFF_OKAY : iffp);
   }
#endif

/** GetLiILBM() *******************************************************
 *
 * Called via ReadPicture to handle every LIST encountered in an IFF file.
 *
 ***********************************************************************/
#if Fancy
IFFP GetLiILBM(parent)  GroupContext *parent;  {
    ILBMFrame newFrame; /* allocate a new Frame */

    newFrame = *(ILBMFrame *)parent->clientFrame;  /* copy parent frame */

    return( ReadIList(parent, (ClientFrame *)&newFrame) );
    }
#endif

/** ReadPicture() *****************************************************/
IFFP ReadPicture(file, bm, iFrame, allocator)
   LONG file;
   struct BitMap *bm;
   ILBMFrame *iFrame;   /* Top level "client frame".*/

        /* **** ERROR IN SOURCE CODE, WAS jFrame, now iFrame */
        /* fixed */

   Allocator *allocator;
   {
   IFFP iffp = IFF_OKAY;

#if Fancy
   iFrame->clientFrame.getList = GetLiILBM;
   iFrame->clientFrame.getProp = GetPrILBM;
#else
   iFrame->clientFrame.getList = SkipGroup;
   iFrame->clientFrame.getProp = SkipGroup;
#endif
   iFrame->clientFrame.getForm = GetFoILBM;
   iFrame->clientFrame.getCat  = ReadICat ;

   /* Initialize the top-level client frame's property settings to the
    * program-wide defaults. This example just records that we haven't read
    * any BMHD property or CMAP color registers yet. For the color map, that
    * means the default is to leave the machine's color registers alone.
    * If you want to read a property like GRAB, init it here to (0, 0). */
   iFrame->foundBMHD  = FALSE;
   iFrame->nColorRegs = 0;

   gAllocator = allocator;
   gBM = bm;
   giFrame = iFrame;
  /* Store a pointer to the client's frame in a global variable so that
   * GetFoILBM can update client's frame when done.  Why do we have so
   * many frames & frame pointers floating around causing confusion?
   * Because IFF supports PROPs which apply to all FORMs in a LIST,
```



```
   * unless a given FORM overrides some property.
   * When you write code to read several FORMs,
   * it is ssential to maintain a frame at each level of the syntax
   * so that the properties for the LIST don't get overwritten by any
   * properties specified by individual FORMs.
   * We decided it was best to put that complexity into this one-FORM example,
   * so that those who need it later will have a useful starting place.
   */

   iffp = ReadIFF(file, (ClientFrame *)iFrame);
   return(iffp);
   }
```

```
/** RemAlloc.c ****************************************************************/
/*  ChipAlloc(), ExtAlloc(), RemAlloc(), RemFree().                          */
/*  ALLOCators which REMember the size allocated, for simpler freeing.       */
/*                                                                            */
/* Date      Who Changes                                                      */
/* --------- --- ---------------------------------------------------------------*/
/* 16-Jan-86 sss Created from DPaint/DAlloc.c                                */
/* 23-Jan-86 jhm Include Compiler.h, check for size > 0 in RemAlloc.        */
/* 25-Jan-86 sss Added ChipNoClearAlloc,ExtNoClearAlloc                      */
/*                                                                            */
/* By Jerry Morrison and Steve Shaw, Electronic Arts.                        */
/* This software is in the public domain.                                    */
/*                                                                            */
/* This version for the Commodore-Amiga computer.                            */
/*                                                                            */
/******************************************************************************/
#ifndef COMPILER_H
#include "iff/compiler.h"
#endif

#include "exec/nodes.h"
#include "exec/memory.h"
#include "iff/remalloc.h"

/** RemAlloc ******************************************************************/
UBYTE *RemAlloc(size,flags) LONG size, flags; {
    register LONG *p = NULL;     /* (LONG *) for the sake of p++, below */
    register LONG asize = size+4;
    if (size > 0)
        p = (LONG *)AllocMem(asize,flags);
    if (p != NULL)
        *p++ = asize;   /* post-bump p to point at clients area*/
    return((UBYTE *)p);
    }

/** ChipAlloc *****************************************************************/
UBYTE *ChipAlloc(size) LONG size; {
    return(RemAlloc(size, MEMF_CLEAR|MEMF_PUBLIC|MEMF_CHIP));
    }

/** ChipNoClearAlloc **********************************************************/
UBYTE *ChipNoClearAlloc(size) LONG size; {
    return(RemAlloc(size, MEMF_PUBLIC|MEMF_CHIP));
    }

/** ExtAlloc ******************************************************************/
UBYTE *ExtAlloc(size) LONG size; {
    return(RemAlloc(size, MEMF_CLEAR|MEMF_PUBLIC));
    }

/** ExtNoClearAlloc ***********************************************************/
UBYTE *ExtNoClearAlloc(size) LONG size; {
    return(RemAlloc(size, MEMF_PUBLIC));
    }

/** RemFree *******************************************************************/
UBYTE *RemFree(p) UBYTE *p; {
    if (p != NULL) {
        p -= 4;
        FreeMem(p, *((LONG *)p));
        }
    return(NULL);
    }
```



```
/*----------------------------------------------------------------------*
 * unpacker.c Convert data from "cmpByteRun1" run compression. 11/15/85
 *
 * By Jerry Morrison and Steve Shaw, Electronic Arts.
 * This software is in the public domain.
 *
 *      control bytes:
 *       [0..127]   : followed by n+1 bytes of data.
 *       [-1..-127] : followed by byte to be repeated (-n)+1 times.
 *       -128       : NOOP.
 *
 * This version for the Commodore-Amiga computer.
 *----------------------------------------------------------------------*/
#include "iff/packer.h"


/*----------- UnPackRow ------------------------------------------------*/

#define UGetByte()      (*source++)
#define UPutByte(c)     (*dest++ = (c))

/* Given POINTERS to POINTER variables, unpacks one row, updating the source
 * and destination pointers until it produces dstBytes bytes. */
BOOL UnPackRow(pSource, pDest, srcBytes0, dstBytes0)
        BYTE **pSource, **pDest;  WORD srcBytes0, dstBytes0; {
    register BYTE *source = *pSource;
    register BYTE *dest   = *pDest;
    register WORD n;
    register BYTE c;
    register WORD srcBytes = srcBytes0, dstBytes = dstBytes0;
    BOOL error = TRUE;  /* assume error until we make it through the loop */
    WORD minus128 = -128;  /* get the compiler to generate a CMP.W */

    while( dstBytes > 0 )  {
        if ( (srcBytes -= 1) < 0 )  goto ErrorExit;
        n = UGetByte();

        if (n >= 0) {
            n += 1;
            if ( (srcBytes -= n) < 0 )  goto ErrorExit;
            if ( (dstBytes -= n) < 0 )  goto ErrorExit;
            do {  UPutByte(UGetByte());  } while (--n > 0);
            }

        else if (n != minus128) {
            n = -n + 1;
            if ( (srcBytes -= 1) < 0 )  goto ErrorExit;
            if ( (dstBytes -= n) < 0 )  goto ErrorExit;
            c = UGetByte();
            do {  UPutByte(c);  } while (--n > 0);
            }
        }
    error = FALSE;      /* success! */

  ErrorExit:
    *pSource = source;  *pDest = dest;
    return(error);
    }
```

Additional IFF Examples

This section contains source code listings of additional IFF examples provided by Commodore and third parties.

Display	;Displays an ILBM graphic file in an Amiga screen
PGTB	;The include file for use with PGTB
ScreenSave.c	;Save the frontmost Amiga screen to a file
apack.asm	;68000 version of the ILBM run length encoding routines
cycvb.c	;Color cycling interrupt example

Note:

Source code examples for ANIM are available on the Byte Information Exchange (BIX) in amiga.dev/listings and on other bulletin boards, along with the modified IFF includes and modules required to compile and link the ANIM examples. Also, the Software Distillery has provided a PGTB viewer and catcher with source which should be available shortly.

```
/*
 * Display v1.06 - 11/88 Carolyn Scheppner   CBM
 *
 *   Read an ILBM file and display as a screen/window until closed.
 *   Simulated close gadget in upper left corner of window.
 *   Clicking below title bar area toggles screen bar for dragging.
 *   Handles normal and HAM ILBM's
 *   Now has options for backscreen, timer, cycling, printing
 *
 *   Options:
 *
 *     opt  b     means come up behind other screens
 *          c     means cycle colors
 *          p     where P means dump to printer
 *          e     default 6 planes to extra-halfbrite
 *          t=n   where n = display time in seconds (without or after dump)
 *
 *  By Carolyn Scheppner   CBM  01/15/88
 *
 *  Modified 09/02/86 - Only global frame is iFrame
 *                      Use message->MouseX and Y
 *                      Wait() for IDCMP
 *  Modified 10/15/86 - For HAM
 *                      Name changed from SeeILBM to ViewILBM
 *  Modified 11/01/86 - Revised for linkage with myreadpict.c
 *  Modified 11/18/86 - For Astartup ... Amiga.lib, LC.lib linkage
 *  Modified 12/12/86 - Added color cycling at request of Mimetics
 *  Modified 01/06/87 - Tab toggles cycling
 *  Modified 03/03/87 - Recognizes RNG_NORATE (36) as non-active DP CRNG
 *                      Changed name to Display
 *  Modified 03/13/87 - Accepts display time in seconds as 2nd CLI arg
 *  Modified 01/15/88 - New command line options, now prints
 *  Modified 04/20/88 - Mask troublesome flags from Viewmodes
 *  Modified 05/06/88 - (v1.04) Add CTRL/D to exit returning failure, e flag
 *  Modified 09/27/88 - (v1.05) Use CAMG, CRNG, and CCRT defs in new ilbm.h
 *  Modified 11/08/88 - (v1.06) Explicitly mask high word of CAMG
 *
 *     Display supports cycling, timed display, printing, and backscreen.
 *     See usage lines. Type Display<RET> or double-click Display for help.
 *     If the command line opt c or picture tooltype CYCLE=TRUE are used,
 *     this viewer will cycle any ILBM that contains cycling chunks
 *     (CCRT or CRNG) which are marked as active and do not have a CRNG
 *     cycle rate of 36. (To DPaint, rate 36 = don't cycle).  Note that
 *     by default, DPaint saves its pics with CRNG (cycling) chunks
 *     flagged as active and with a rate not equal to 36.
 *
 * Based on ShowILBM.c, readpict.c    1/86
 *  By Jerry Morrison, Steve Shaw, and Steve Hayes, Electronic Arts.
 *  This software is in the public domain.
 *
 * >>NOTE<<: This example must be linked with additional IFF rtn files.
 *           See linkage information below.
 *
 * The display portion is specific to the Commodore Amiga computer.
 *
 * Linkage Information:
 *  (NOTE: All modules including iff stuff compiled with -v on LC2)
 *
 * FROM     LIB:AStartup.obj,Display.o,myreadpict.o,dump.o,iffmsgs.o*
 *          iffr.o,ilbmr.o,unpacker.o
 * TO       Display
 * LIBRARY  LIB:Amiga.lib, LIB:LC.lib
 *
 */

#include <exec/types.h>
#include <exec/memory.h>
#include <exec/tasks.h>
#include <libraries/dos.h>
```



```
#include <libraries/dosextens.h>
#include <workbench/startup.h>
#include <workbench/workbench.h>
#include <intuition/intuition.h>
#include <graphics/gfxbase.h>

#include "iff/ilbm.h"
#include "myreadpict.h"

#ifndef MIN
#define MIN(a,b) ((a)<(b)?(a):(b))
#endif  MIN

#define TOUPPER(c)      ((c)>='a'&&(c)<='z'?(c)-'a'+'A':(c))

/* Bits we must mask out of CAMG.Viewmodes */
#define BADFLAGS   (SPRITES|VP_HIDE|GENLOCK_AUDIO|GENLOCK_VIDEO)
#define FLAGMASK   (~BADFLAGS)
#define CAMGMASK   (FLAGMASK & 0x0000FFFFL)

/* The screendump routine */
extern int dump();

/* For wbStdio rtns */
extern LONG stdin, stdout, stderr;  /* in Astartup.obj */

char conSpec[] = "CON:0/40/640/140/";
BOOL wbHasStdio = NULL;


/* general usage pointers */
struct GfxBase       *GfxBase;
struct IntuitionBase *IntuitionBase;
ULONG  IconBase = 0;

/* Globals for displaying an image */
struct Screen   *screen1;
struct Window   *window1;
struct RastPort *rport1;
struct ViewPort *vport1;

struct BitMap   tBitMap;      /* Temp BitMap struct for small pics  */

/* For WorkBench startup */
extern struct WBStartup *WBenchMsg;
struct FileLock *startLock, *newLock;

/* Other globals */
BOOL  FromWb, TBtoggle, Done;
BOOL  Cycle=FALSE, Print=FALSE, Timer=FALSE, Back=FALSE, EHB=FALSE;

char ul[]  = "\nDISPLAY   v1.06  C. Scheppner  CBM  11/88\n";

char ulc[] = "\nCLI Usage: Display ilbmfile [opt [b][c][e][p] [t=n]]\n";
char u2c[] =  "     opts: b=backscreen c=cycle e=ehb p=print t=seconds\n";

char ulw[] = "\n WB Usage: Click this icon, SHIFT and DoubleClick on pic\n";
char u2w[] =  "ToolTypes: Display  TIMER=n,PRINT=TRUE,BACK=TRUE\n";
char u3w[] =  "           Picture  CYCLE=TRUE, EHB=TRUE\n";

char u2[]  = "\nClick toggles bar, Tab toggles cycling, P prints screen\n";
char u3[]  = "Close upper left or CTRL/C, or CTRL/D to break a script\n";

char *cliUsage[] = {ul,ulc,u2c,u2,u3,""};
char *wbUsage[]  = {ul,ulw,u2w,u3w,u2,u3,""};

/* Structures for new Screen, new Window */

struct   TextAttr       TextFont = {
```

```
   "topaz.font",                  /* Font Name   */
   TOPAZ_EIGHTY,                  /* Font Height */
   FS_NORMAL,                     /* Style       */
   FPF_ROMFONT,                   /* Preferences */
   };

struct   NewScreen      ns = {
   0, 0,                               /* LeftEdge and TopEdge   */
   0, 0,                               /* Width and Height       */
   0,                                  /* Depth                  */
   1, 0,                               /* DetailPen and BlockPen */
   NULL,                               /* Special display modes  */
   CUSTOMSCREEN,                       /* Screen Type            */
   &TextFont,                          /* Use my font            */
   " <- Close here after clicking below",          /* Title */
   NULL,                               /* No gadgets yet         */
   NULL,                               /* Ptr to CustomBitmap    */
   };

struct   NewWindow      nw = {
   0, 0,                               /* LeftEdge and TopEdge */
   0, 0,                               /* Width and Height */
   -1, -1,                             /* DetailPen and BlockPen */
   MOUSEBUTTONS|VANILLAKEY,            /* IDCMP Flags */
   BACKDROP                            /* Flags */
   |BORDERLESS,                        /* Gadget and Image pointers */
   NULL, NULL,                         /* Title string */
   NULL,                               /* Put Screen ptr here */
   NULL,                               /* SuperBitMap pointer */
   NULL,                               /* MinWidth and MinHeight */
   0, 0,                               /* MaxWidth and MaxHeight */
   0, 0,                               /* Type of window */
   CUSTOMSCREEN,
   };

USHORT  allBlack[maxColorReg] = {0};

/* For alloc to define new pointer */
#define PDATASZ 12
UWORD   *pdata;

#ifndef MIN
#define MIN(a,b) ((a)<(b)?(a):(b))
#endif  MIN

extern char *IFFPMessages[];
ILBMFrame   iFrame;          /* my global frame */


/* Cycle Task stuff */
#define CYCLETIME   16384L
#define REVERSE     0x02
#define ACTIVE      0x01

extern VOID cycleTask();
char *cyTaskName = "CAS_D1.04cyTask";
struct Task *cyTask;

/* Data shared with cycle/timer Task */
CRange *cyCrngs;
struct ViewPort *cyVport;
int    cyRegs, cyCnt;
USHORT cyMap[maxColorReg];
LONG   cyClocks[maxCycles];
LONG   cyRates[maxCycles];
LONG   dTimer;
BOOL   TimerOn, CycleOn, PrepareToDie;
struct Task *mainTask;
LONG   tSigNum = -1, retcode = RETURN_OK;
```



```
ULONG  tSig;

/*
 *  main
 */

main(argc, argv)
int argc;
char **argv;
   {
   ULONG           signals, wSig;
   LONG            file;
   IFFP            iffp = NO_FILE;
   struct WBArg    *arg;
   char            *filename;
   int error;

   FromWb = (argc==0) ? TRUE : FALSE;
   TimerOn = FALSE;

   if((FromWb)&&(WBenchMsg->sm_NumArgs > 1))
      {
      /* Passed filename via Workbench */
      arg = WBenchMsg->sm_ArgList;
      arg++;
      filename   = (char *)arg->wa_Name;
      newLock    = (struct FileLock *)arg->wa_Lock;
      startLock  = (struct FileLock *)CurrentDir(newLock);
      /* Get ToolTypes */
      getWbOpts(WBenchMsg);
      }
   else if((!FromWb)&&(argc>1)&&(*argv[1] != '?'))
      {
      /* Passed filename via command line */
      filename = argv[1];

      if(argc>2)
         {
         if(strEqu(argv[2],"opt"))  getCliOpts(argc,argv);
         else  cleanexit("Bad args\n",RETURN_FAIL);
         }
      }
   else
      {
      usage();
      cleanexit(" ",RETURN_OK); /* Space forces wait for keypress if WB */
      }


   if(!(GfxBase = (struct GfxBase *)OpenLibrary("graphics.library",0)))
      cleanexit("Can't open graphics",RETURN_FAIL);

   if(!(IntuitionBase=
         (struct IntuitionBase *)OpenLibrary("intuition.library",0)))
      cleanexit("Can't open intuition",RETURN_FAIL);

   if(!(file = Open(filename, MODE_OLDFILE)))
      cleanexit("Picture file not found",RETURN_WARN);

   iffp = myReadPicture(file,&iFrame);
   Close(file);

   if (!(iffp == IFF_DONE))
      cleanexit("Not an IFF ILBM",RETURN_WARN);


   error = DisplayPic(&iFrame);
   if(error)  cleanexit("Can't open screen or window",RETURN_WARN);
```

```
   if(pdata = (UWORD *)AllocMem(PDATASZ,MEMF_CHIP|MEMF_CLEAR))
      {
      pdata[2] = 0x8000;  /* 1 pixel */
      SetPointer(window1,pdata,1,16,0,0);
      }

   /* Set up cycle/timer task */

   mainTask = (struct Task *)FindTask(NULL);
   if((tSigNum = AllocSignal(-1)) == -1)
      cleanexit("Can't alloc timerSig",RETURN_FAIL);
   tSig = 1 << tSigNum;
   wSig = 1<<window1->UserPort->mp_SigBit;

   initCycle(&iFrame,vport1);
   cyTask = (struct Task *)CreateTask(cyTaskName,0,cycleTask,4000);
   if(!cyTask)  cleanexit("Can't create timimg task",RETURN_FAIL);

   /* Dump screen if requested before starting timer */
   if(Print)  dump(screen1);

   if(Timer)  TimerOn = TRUE;
   if(Cycle)  CycleOn = TRUE;

   TBtoggle   = FALSE;      /* Title bar toggle */
   Done       = FALSE;      /* Close flag       */

   while (!Done)
      {
      signals = Wait(SIGBREAKF_CTRL_D|SIGBREAKF_CTRL_C|wSig|tSig);
      if(signals & wSig)  chkmsg();
      if(signals & tSig)  Done = TRUE;
      if(signals & SIGBREAKF_CTRL_C)  Done = TRUE;
      if(signals & SIGBREAKF_CTRL_D)  Done = TRUE, retcode=RETURN_FAIL;
      }
   cleanexit("",retcode);
   }


getCliOpts(argc,argv)
int  argc;
char **argv;
   {
   int k,i;
   UBYTE c;

   for(k=3; k<argc; k++)
      {
      c = argv[k][0] | 0x20;
      switch(c)
         {
         case 't':
            i=0;
            while((argv[k][i])&&(argv[k][i] != '=')) i++;
            i++;
            dTimer = 60 * atoi(&argv[k][i]);
            Timer = TRUE;
            break;
         default:
            for(i=0; argv[k][i]; i++)
               {
               c = argv[k][i] | 0x20;
               switch(c)
                  {
                  case 'b':
                     Back = TRUE;
                     break;
                  case 'p':
                     Print = TRUE;
```



```
                     break;
                  case 'c':
                     Cycle = TRUE;
                     break;
                  case 'e':
                     EHB = TRUE;
                     break;
                  default:
                     break;
                  }
               }

         }
      }
   }


getWbOpts(wbMsg)
struct WBStartup *wbMsg;
   {
   struct WBArg  *wbArg;
   struct DiskObject *diskobj;
   char **toolarray;
   char *s;

   if((IconBase = OpenLibrary("icon.library", 0)))
      {
      /* First get ToolTypes from Display.info */
      wbArg = wbMsg->sm_ArgList;
      diskobj=(struct DiskObject *)GetDiskObject(wbArg->wa_Name);
      if(diskobj)
         {
         toolarray = (char **)diskobj->do_ToolTypes;

         if(s=(char *)FindToolType(toolarray,"PRINT"))
            {
            if(strEqu(s,"TRUE"))  Print = TRUE;
            }
         if(s=(char *)FindToolType(toolarray,"BACK"))
            {
            if(strEqu(s,"TRUE"))  Back = TRUE;
            }
         if(s=(char *)FindToolType(toolarray,"TIMER"))
            {
            Timer = TRUE;
            dTimer = 60 * atoi(s);
            }
         FreeDiskObject(diskobj);
         }

      if(wbMsg->sm_NumArgs > 1)
         {
         wbArg++;

         diskobj=(struct DiskObject *)GetDiskObject(wbArg->wa_Name);
         if(diskobj)
            {
            toolarray = (char **)diskobj->do_ToolTypes;

            if(s=(char *)FindToolType(toolarray,"CYCLE"))
               {
               if(strEqu(s,"TRUE"))  Cycle = TRUE;
               }
            if(s=(char *)FindToolType(toolarray,"EHB"))
               {
               if(strEqu(s,"TRUE"))  EHB = TRUE;
               }
            FreeDiskObject(diskobj);
```

```
            }
         }
      CloseLibrary(IconBase);
      }
   }


initCycle(ptFrame,vp)
ILBMFrame *ptFrame;
struct ViewPort *vp;
   {
   int k;

   CycleOn   = FALSE;
   PrepareToDie = FALSE;
   cyCrngs   = ptFrame->crngChunks;
   cyVport   = vp;
   cyRegs    = ptFrame->nColorRegs;
   cyCnt     = ptFrame->cycleCnt;

   for(k=0; k<cyRegs; k++)
      {
      cyMap[k] = ptFrame->colorMap[k];
      }

   /* Init Rates and Clocks */
   for(k=0; k<cyCnt; k++)
      {
      /* In DPaint CRNG, rate = RNG_NORATE (36) means don't cycle */
      if(cyCrngs[k].rate == RNG_NORATE)
         {
         cyCrngs[k].rate = 0;
         cyCrngs[k].active &= ~ACTIVE;
         }

      if((cyCrngs[k].active & ACTIVE)&&(cyCrngs[k].rate))
         {
         cyRates[k] = cyCrngs[k].rate;
         }
      else
         {
         cyRates[k] = 0;  /* Means don't cycle to my cycleTask */
         }
      cyClocks[k] = 0;
      }
   }


VOID cycleTask()
   {
   int    k, i, j;
   UBYTE  low, high;
   USHORT cyTmp;
   BOOL   Cycled;

   while(!PrepareToDie)
      {
      WaitTOF();
      if(CycleOn)
         {
         Cycled = FALSE;
         for(k=0; k<cyCnt; k++)
            {
            if(cyRates[k])  /* cyRate 0 = inactive */
               {
               cyClocks[k] += cyRates[k];
               if(cyClocks[k] >= CYCLETIME)
                  {
                  Cycled = TRUE;
```



```
                  cyClocks[k] -= CYCLETIME;
                  low = cyCrngs[k].low;
                  high= cyCrngs[k].high;
                  if(cyCrngs[k].active & REVERSE)  /* Reverse cycle */
                     {
                     cyTmp = cyMap[low];
                     for(i=low,j=low+1; i < high; i++,j++)
                        {
                        cyMap[i] = cyMap[j];
                        }
                     cyMap[high] = cyTmp;
                     }
                  else     /* Forward cycle */
                     {
                     cyTmp = cyMap[high];
                     for(i=high,j=high-1; i > low; i--,j--)
                        {
                        cyMap[i] = cyMap[j];
                        }
                     cyMap[low] = cyTmp;
                     }
                  }
               }
            }
         if(Cycled)
            {
            LoadRGB4(cyVport,cyMap,cyRegs);
            }
         }
      if(TimerOn)
         {
         if(--dTimer <= 0)  Signal(mainTask,tSig);
         }
      }
   PrepareToDie = FALSE;
   Wait(0L);  /* Wait to die */
   }


chkmsg()
   {
   struct IntuiMessage *msg;
   ULONG class, code;
   SHORT mouseX, mouseY;

   while(msg=(struct IntuiMessage *)GetMsg(window1->UserPort))
      {
      class = msg->Class;
      code  = msg->Code;
      mouseX = msg->MouseX;
      mouseY = msg->MouseY;

      ReplyMsg(msg);
      switch(class)
         {
         case MOUSEBUTTONS:
            if ((code == SELECTDOWN)&&
                  (mouseX < 10)&&(mouseY<10))
               {
               Done = TRUE;
               }
            else if ((code == SELECTDOWN)&&
                        ((mouseY>10)||(mouseX>10))&&
                           (TBtoggle==FALSE))
               {
               TBtoggle = TRUE;
               ShowTitle(screen1,TRUE);
               ClearPointer(window1);
               }
```

```
            else if ((code == SELECTDOWN)&&
                       (mouseY>10)&&(TBtoggle==TRUE))
               {
               TBtoggle = FALSE;
               ShowTitle(screen1,FALSE);
               SetPointer(window1,pdata,1,16,0,0);
               }
            break;
         case VANILLAKEY:
            switch(code)
               {
               case 0x03:    /* CTRL/C */
                  Done = TRUE;
                  break;
               case 0x04:    /* CTRL/D */
                  Done = TRUE;
                  retcode = RETURN_FAIL;
                  break;
               case 'p': case 'P':
                  dump(screen1);
                  break;
               case 0x09:    /* Tab toggles Cycle */
                  if(CycleOn)
                     {
                     CycleOn = FALSE;
                     WaitTOF();          /* Make sure cyTask saw FALSE */
                     WaitBOVP(vport1);
                     LoadRGB4(vport1,iFrame.colorMap,maxColorReg);
                     }
                  else
                     {
                     initCycle(&iFrame,vport1);
                     CycleOn = TRUE;
                     }
                  break;
               default:
                  break;
               }
            break;
         default:
            break;
         }
      }
   }


usage()
   {
   char **ulines;
   int k;

   if((FromWb)&&(! wbHasStdio))  wbHasStdio = openStdio(conSpec);

   if((!FromWb)||(wbHasStdio))
      {
      ulines = FromWb ? wbUsage : cliUsage;
      for(k=0; ulines[k][0]; k++)
         {
         Write(stdout,ulines[k],strlen(ulines[k]));
         }
      }
   }


cleanexit(s,rcode)
char  *s;
LONG  rcode;
   {
   if(*s)
```



```
      {
      if((FromWb)&&(!wbHasStdio))  wbHasStdio = openStdio(conSpec);

      if((!FromWb)||(wbHasStdio))
         {
         Write(stdout,s,strlen(s));
         Write(stdout,"\n",1);
         }
      if(wbHasStdio)
         {
         Write(stdout,"\nPRESS RETURN TO EXIT\n",22);
         while (getchar() != '\n');
         }
      }
   cleanup();
   if(wbHasStdio) closeStdio();
   exit(rcode);
   }


cleanup()
   {
   struct IntuiMessage *msg;

   if(cyTask)
      {
      CycleOn = FALSE;
      PrepareToDie = TRUE;
      while(PrepareToDie)  Delay(10);
      DeleteTask(cyTask);
      }

   /* Free timer signal */
   if (tSigNum > -1)  FreeSignal(tSigNum);

   /* Note - tBitMap planes were deallocated in DisplayPic() */
   if (window1)
      {
      while(msg=(struct IntuiMessage *)GetMsg(window1->UserPort))
         {
         ReplyMsg(msg);
         }
      CloseWindow(window1);
      }
   if (screen1) CloseScreen(screen1);
   if (pdata)   FreeMem(pdata,PDATASZ);
   if (IntuitionBase) CloseLibrary(IntuitionBase);
   if (GfxBase)       CloseLibrary(GfxBase);
   if (newLock != startLock)  CurrentDir(startLock);
   }


strlen(s)
char *s;
   {
   int i = 0;
   while(*s++) i++;
   return(i);
   }


/** getBitMap() *********************************************************
 *
 * Open screen or temp bitmap.
 *   Returns ptr destBitMap  or  0 = error
 *
 ************************************************************************/
struct BitMap *getBitMap(ptilbmFrame)
```

```
ILBMFrame *ptilbmFrame;
{
int     i, nPlanes, plsize;
SHORT  sWidth, sHeight, dWidth, dHeight;
struct BitMap *destBitMap;

sWidth  = ptilbmFrame->bmHdr.w;
sHeight = ptilbmFrame->bmHdr.h;
dWidth  = ptilbmFrame->bmHdr.pageWidth;
dHeight = ptilbmFrame->bmHdr.pageHeight;
nPlanes = MIN(ptilbmFrame->bmHdr.nPlanes, EXDepth);

ns.Width  = dWidth;
ns.Height = dHeight;
ns.Depth  = nPlanes;

if (ptilbmFrame->foundCAMG)
   {
   ns.ViewModes = ptilbmFrame->camgChunk.ViewModes & CAMGMASK;
   }
else
   {
   if (ptilbmFrame->bmHdr.pageWidth >= 640)
      ns.ViewModes = HIRES;
   else
      ns.ViewModes = 0;

   if (ptilbmFrame->bmHdr.pageHeight >= 400)
      ns.ViewModes |= LACE;

   /* EHB is kludgey flag for ExtraHalbrite ILBMs with no CAMG */
   if(ns.Depth == 6)
      {
      if(EHB) ns.ViewModes |= EXTRA_HALFBRITE;
      else ns.ViewModes |= HAM;
      }
   }


if(Back) ns.Type |= SCREENBEHIND;

if ((screen1 = (struct Screen *)OpenScreen(&ns))==NULL)    return(0);

vport1 = &screen1->ViewPort;
LoadRGB4(vport1, &allBlack[0], MIN(1<<ns.Depth,maxColorReg));

if((ns.ViewModes)&(HAM))  setHam(screen1,FALSE);

nw.Width  = dWidth;
nw.Height = dHeight;
nw.Screen = screen1;

if(!Back)  nw.Flags |= ACTIVATE;

if ((window1 = (struct Window *)OpenWindow(&nw))==NULL)
   {
   CloseScreen(screen1);
   screen1 = NULL;
   return(0);
   }

ShowTitle(screen1, FALSE);

if ((sWidth == dWidth) && (sHeight == dHeight))
   {
   destBitMap = (struct BitMap *)screen1->RastPort.BitMap;
   }
else
   {
```



```
   InitBitMap( &tBitMap,
               nPlanes,
               sWidth,
               sHeight);

   plsize = RowBytes(ptilbmFrame->bmHdr.w) * ptilbmFrame->bmHdr.h;
   if (tBitMap.Planes[0] =
    (PLANEPTR)AllocMem(nPlanes * plsize, MEMF_CHIP))
      {
      for (i = 1; i < nPlanes; i++)
         tBitMap.Planes[i] = (PLANEPTR)tBitMap.Planes[0] + plsize*i;
      destBitMap = &tBitMap;
      }
   else
      {
      CloseWindow(window1);
      window1 = NULL;
      CloseScreen(screen1);
      screen1 = NULL;
      return(0);  /* can't allocate temp BitMap */
      }
   }
return(destBitMap);          /* destBitMap allocated */
}


/** DisplayPic() *************************************************************
 *
 * Display loaded bitmap.  If tBitMap, first transfer to screen.
 *
 ****************************************************************************/
DisplayPic(ptilbmFrame)
   ILBMFrame *ptilbmFrame;
   {
   int    i, row, byte, nrows, nbytes;
   struct BitMap  *tbp, *sbp; /* temp and screen BitMap ptrs */
   UBYTE  *tpp, *spp;         /* temp and screen plane ptrs  */

   if (tBitMap.Planes[0])     /* transfer from tBitMap if nec. */
      {
      tbp = &tBitMap;
      sbp = screen1->RastPort.BitMap;
      nrows  = MIN(tbp->Rows, sbp->Rows);
      nbytes = MIN(tbp->BytesPerRow, sbp->BytesPerRow);

      for (i = 0; i < sbp->Depth; i++)
         {
         tpp = (UBYTE *)tbp->Planes[i];
         spp = (UBYTE *)sbp->Planes[i];
         for (row = 0; row < nrows; row++)
            {
            tpp = tbp->Planes[i] + (row * tbp->BytesPerRow);
            spp = sbp->Planes[i] + (row * sbp->BytesPerRow);
            for (byte = 0; byte < nbytes; byte++)
               {
               *spp++ = *tpp++;
               }
            }
         }
      /*  Can now deallocate the temp BitMap  */
      FreeMem(tBitMap.Planes[0],
                 tBitMap.BytesPerRow * tBitMap.Rows * tBitMap.Depth);
      }

   vport1 = &screen1->ViewPort;
   LoadRGB4(vport1, ptilbmFrame->colorMap, ptilbmFrame->nColorRegs);
   if((ns.ViewModes)&(HAM))  setHam(screen1,TRUE);

   return(0);
```

```
   }


/* setHam --- For toggling HAM so HAM pic invisible while loading */
setHam(scr,toggle)
struct Screen *scr;
BOOL   toggle;
   {
   struct ViewPort *vp;
   struct View     *v;

   vp = &(scr->ViewPort);
   v = (struct View *)ViewAddress();
   Forbid();
   if(toggle)
      {
      v->Modes   |= HAM;
      vp->Modes  |= HAM;
      }
   else
      {
      v->Modes  &= ~HAM;
      vp->Modes &= ~HAM;
      }
   MakeScreen(scr);
   RethinkDisplay();
   Permit();
   }

strEqu(p, q)
TEXT *p, *q;
   {
   while(TOUPPER(*p) == TOUPPER(*q))
      {
      if (*(p++) == 0)  return(TRUE);
      ++q;
      }
   return(FALSE);
   }

/* wbStdio.c --- Open an Amiga stdio window under workbench
 *               For use with AStartup.obj
 */

openStdio(conspec)
char *conspec;
   {
   LONG wfile;
   struct Process *proc;
   struct FileHandle *handle;

   if (wbHasStdio)  return(1);

   if (!(wfile = Open(conspec,MODE_NEWFILE)))  return(0);
   stdin  = wfile;
   stdout = wfile;
   stderr = wfile;
   handle = (struct FileHandle *)(wfile << 2);
   proc = (struct Process *)FindTask(NULL);

   proc->pr_ConsoleTask = (APTR)(handle->fh_Type);
   proc->pr_CIS = (BPTR)stdin;
   proc->pr_COS = (BPTR)stdout;
   return(1);
   }

closeStdio()
   {
   struct Process *proc;
```



```
   struct FileHandle *handle;

   if (! wbHasStdio) return(0);

   if (stdin > 0)  Close(stdin);
   stdin  = -1;
   stdout = -1;
   stderr = -1;
   handle = (struct FileHandle *)(stdin << 2);
   proc = (struct Process *)FindTask(NULL);
   proc->pr_ConsoleTask = NULL;
   proc->pr_CIS = NULL;
   proc->pr_COS = NULL;
   wbHasStdio = NULL;
   }
```

Nov 10 17:19 1988 additional_examples/Display/dump.c Page 1

```
/*
 * dump.c     - routine to dump rastport
 *
 */


#include "exec/types.h"
#include "intuition/intuiticn.h"
#include "devices/printer.h"

extern struct IODRPReq  *CreateExtIO();
extern struct MsgPort   *CreatePort();

dump(screen)
struct Screen *screen;
   {
   struct IODRPReq *iodrp;
   struct MsgPort  *printerPort;
   struct ViewPort *vp;
   int error = 1;

   if(printerPort = CreatePort("CAS_ddmp",0))
      {
      if(iodrp=CreateExtIO(printerPort,sizeof(struct IODRPReq)))
         {
         if(!(error=OpenDevice("printer.device",0,iodrp,0)))
            {
            vp = &screen->ViewPort;
            iodrp->io_Command = PRD_DUMPRPORT;
            iodrp->io_RastPort = &screen->RastPort;
            iodrp->io_ColorMap = vp->ColorMap;
            iodrp->io_Modes = (ULONG)vp->Modes;
     /*     iodrp->io_SrcX = 0;      MEMF_CLEAR zeroed this   */
     /*     iodrp->io_SrcY = 0;      MEMF_CLEAR zeroed this   */
            iodrp->io_SrcWidth = screen->Width;
            iodrp->io_SrcHeight = screen->Height;
     /*     iodrp->io_DestCols = 0; MEMF_CLEAR zeroed this   */
     /*     iodrp->io_DestRows = 0; MEMF_CLEAR zeroed this   */
            iodrp->io_Special = SPECIAL_FULLCOLS|SPECIAL_ASPECT;

            error = DoIO(iodrp);
            CloseDevice(iodrp);
            }
         DeleteExtIO(iodrp, sizeof(struct IODRPReq));
         }
      DeletePort(printerPort);
      }
   return(error);
   }
```

Nov 10 17:19 1988 additional_examples/Display/iffmsgs.c Page 1

```
/* iffmsgs.c --- The IFF error msgs indexed by iffp
 * Use:  extern char *IFFPMessages[];  in application to access
 */

#ifndef IFF_H
#include "iff/iff.h"
#endif

/* Message strings for IFFP codes. */
char MsgOkay[]        = {"(IFF_OKAY) No FORM of correct type in file." };
char MsgEndMark[]     = {"(END_MARK) How did you get this message?" };
char MsgDone[]        = {"(IFF_DONE) All done."};
char MsgDos[]         = {"(DOS_ERROR) The DOS returned an error." };
char MsgNot[]         = {"(NOT_IFF) Not an IFF file." };
char MsgNoFile[]      = {"(NO_FILE) No such file found." };
char MsgClientError[] = {"(CLIENT_ERROR) Probably insufficient RAM."};
char MsgForm[]        = {"(BAD_FORM) File contains a malformed FORM." };
char MsgShort[]       = {"(SHORT_CHUNK) File contains a short Chunk." };
char MsgBad[]         = {"(BAD_IFF) A mangled IFF file." };

/* THESE MUST APPEAR IN RIGHT ORDER!! */
char *IFFPMessages[-LAST_ERROR+1] = {
    /*IFF_OKAY*/  MsgOkay,
    /*END_MARK*/  MsgEndMark,
    /*IFF_DONE*/  MsgDone,
    /*DOS_ERROR*/ MsgDos,
    /*NOT_IFF*/   MsgNot,
    /*NO_FILE*/   MsgNoFile,
    /*CLIENT_ERROR*/ MsgClientError,
    /*BAD_FORM*/  MsgForm,
    /*SHORT_CHUNK*/  MsgShort,
    /*BAD_IFF*/   MsgBad
    };
```

```
/** myReadPict.c ****************************************************************
 *
 * Read an ILBM raster image file.              23-Jan-86.
 *
 * Modified version of ReadPict.c
 *   by Jerry Morrison, Steve Shaw, and Steve Hayes, Electronic Arts.
 *   This software is in the public domain.
 *
 * Modified by C. Scheppner  11/86
 *   Handles CAMG chunks for HAM, etc.
 *   Calls user defined routine getBitMap(ilbmFramePtr) when it
 *      reaches the BODY.
 *   getBitMap() can open a screen of the correct size using
 *      information this rtn places in the ilbmFrame, and returns
 *      a pointer to a BitMap structure.  The BitMap structure
 *      tells myReadPicture where it should load the bit planes.
 *
 * Modified by C. Scheppner  12/86
 *   Loads in CCRT or CRNG chunks (converts CCRT to CRNG)
 * Modified 11-88 to use CCRT, CAMG defs and macros added to ilbm.h
 *                and existing CRange (not CrngChunk) def in ilbm.h
 ******************************************************************************/

#define LOCAL   static

#include "intuition/intuition.h"
#include "libraries/dos.h"
#include "libraries/dosextens.h"
#include "iff/ilbm.h"
#include "myreadpict.h"    /* cs */

/* Define size of a temporary buffer used in unscrambling the ILBM rows.*/
#define bufSz 512

/*------------ ILBM reader -----------------------------------------------*/
/* ILBMFrame is our "client frame" for reading FORMs ILBM in an IFF file.
 * We allocate one of these on the stack for every LIST or FORM encountered
 * in the file and use it to hold BMHD & CMAP properties. We also allocate
 * an initial one for the whole file.
 * We allocate a new GroupContext (and initialize it by OpenRIFF or
 * OpenRGroup) for every group (FORM, CAT, LIST, or PROP) encountered. It's
 * just a context for reading (nested) chunks.
 *
 * If we were to scan the entire example file outlined below:
 *    reading          proc(s)                new                  new
 *
 * --whole file--   myReadPicture+ReadIFF GroupContext        ILBMFrame
 * CAT              ReadICat                GroupContext
 *   LIST           GetLiILBM+ReadIList       GroupContext        ILBMFrame
 *     PROP ILBM    GetPrILBM                   GroupContext
 *       CMAP       GetCMAP
 *       BMHD       GetBMHD
 *     FORM ILBM    GetFoILBM                   GroupContext        ILBMFrame
 *       BODY       GetBODY
 *     FORM ILBM    GetFoILBM                   GroupContext        ILBMFrame
 *       BODY       GetBODY
 *   FORM ILBM      GetFoILBM                 GroupContext        ILBMFrame
 */

/* NOTE: For a small version of this program, set Fancy to 0.
 * That'll compile a program that reads a single FORM ILBM in a file, which
 * is what DeluxePaint produces. It'll skip all LISTs and PROPs in the input
 * file. It will, however, look inside a CAT for a FORM ILBM.
 * That's suitable for 90% of the uses.
 *
 * For a fancier version that handles LISTs and PROPs, set Fancy to 1.
 * That'll compile a program that dives into a LIST, if present, to read
 * the first FORM ILBM. E.g. a DeluxePrint library of images is a LIST of
 * FORMs ILBM.
```



```
 *
 * For an even fancier version, set Fancy to 2. That'll compile a program
 * that dives into non-ILBM FORMs, if present, looking for a nested FORM ILBM.
 * E.g. a DeluxeVideo C.S. animated object file is a FORM ANBM containing a
 * FORM ILBM for each image frame. */
#define Fancy  0

/* Global access to client-provided pointers.*/
LOCAL ILBMFrame *giFrame = NULL;   /* "client frame".*/


IFFP handleCAMG(context,frame)
GroupContext *context;
ILBMFrame    *frame;
   {
   IFFP iffp = IFF_OKAY;

   frame->foundCAMG = TRUE;
   iffp = GetCAMG(context, &frame->camgChunk);
   return(iffp);
   }

IFFP handleCRNG(context,frame)
GroupContext *context;
ILBMFrame    *frame;
   {
   IFFP iffp = IFF_OKAY;

   if(frame->cycleCnt < maxCycles)
      {
      iffp = GetCRNG(context,&(frame->crngChunks[frame->cycleCnt]));
      frame->cycleCnt++;
      }
   return(iffp);
   }


IFFP handleCCRT(context,frame)
GroupContext *context;
ILBMFrame    *frame;
   {
   CcrtChunk  ccrtTmp;
   CRange  *ptCrng;
   IFFP iffp = IFF_OKAY;

   if(frame->cycleCnt < maxCycles)
      {
      iffp = GetCCRT(context, &ccrtTmp);
      ptCrng = &(frame->crngChunks[frame->cycleCnt]);
      if(ccrtTmp.direction)  ccrtTmp.direction = -ccrtTmp.direction;
      ptCrng->active = ccrtTmp.direction & 0x03;
      ptCrng->low = ccrtTmp.start;
      ptCrng->high = ccrtTmp.end;

      /* Convert  CCRT secs/msecs to CRNG timimg
       * 0x4000 = max CRNG rate  (cycle every 1 60th sec)
       * This must be divided by # 60th's between cycles
       * seconds to 60th's is easy
       * msecs to 60th's requires division by 16667
       * this is int math so I add 8334 (half 16667) first for rounding
       */
      ptCrng->rate = 0x4000 /
         ((ccrtTmp.seconds * 60)+((ccrtTmp.microseconds+8334)/16667));
      frame->cycleCnt++;
      }
   return(iffp);
   }
```

```
/** GetFoILBM() *************************************************************
 *
 * Called via myReadPictureto handle every FORM encountered in an IFF file.
 * Reads FORMs ILBM and skips all others.
 * Inside a FORM ILBM, it stops once it reads a BODY. It complains if it
 * finds no BODY or if it has no BMHD to decode the BODY.
 *
 * Once we find a BODY chunk, we'll call user rtn getBitMap() to
 *    allocate the bitmap and planes (or screen) and then read
 *    the BODY into the planes.
 *
 ***************************************************************************/
LOCAL BYTE bodyBuffer[bufSz];
IFFP GetFoILBM(parent)  GroupContext *parent;
   {
   /*compilerBug register*/ IFFP iffp;
   GroupContext formContext;
   ILBMFrame ilbmFrame;      /* only used for non-clientFrame fields.*/
   struct BitMap *destBitMap;    /* cs */

   /* Handle a non-ILBM FORM. */
   if (parent->subtype != ID_ILBM)
      {
#if Fancy >= 2
      /* Open a non-ILBM FORM and recursively scan it for ILBMs.*/
      iffp = OpenRGroup(parent, &formContext);
      CheckIFFP();
      do {
         iffp = GetF1ChunkHdr(&formContext);
         } while (iffp >= IFF_OKAY);
      if (iffp == END_MARK)
         {
         iffp = IFF_OKAY;   /* then continue scanning the file */
         }
      CloseRGroup(&formContext);
      return(iffp);
#else
      return(IFF_OKAY); /* Just skip this FORM and keep scanning the file.*/
#endif
      }

   ilbmFrame = *(ILBMFrame *)parent->clientFrame;
   iffp = OpenRGroup(parent, &formContext);
   CheckIFFP();

   do switch (iffp = GetFChunkHdr(&formContext)) {
      case ID_BMHD: {
         ilbmFrame.foundBMHD = TRUE;
         iffp = GetBMHD(&formContext, &ilbmFrame.bmHdr);
         break; }
      case ID_CAMG: {        /* cs */
         iffp = handleCAMG(&formContext, &ilbmFrame);
         break; }
      case ID_CRNG: {        /* cs */
         iffp = handleCRNG(&formContext, &ilbmFrame);
         break; }
      case ID_CCRT: {        /* cs */
         iffp = handleCCRT(&formContext, &ilbmFrame);
         break; }
      case ID_CMAP: {
         ilbmFrame.nColorRegs = maxColorReg; /* room for this many */
         iffp = GetCMAP(&formContext, (WORD *)ilbmFrame.colorMap,
                        &ilbmFrame.nColorRegs);
         break; }
      case ID_BODY: {        /* cs */
         if (!ilbmFrame.foundBMHD)
            {
            iffp = BAD_FORM;    /* No BMHD chunk! */
```



```
            }
         else
            {
            if(destBitMap=(struct BitMap *)getBitMap(&ilbmFrame))
               {
               iffp = GetBODY( &formContext,
                               destBitMap,
                               NULL,
                               &ilbmFrame.bmHdr,
                               bodyBuffer,
                               bufSz);
               if (iffp == IFF_OKAY) iffp = IFF_DONE;   /* Eureka */
               *giFrame = ilbmFrame; /* copy fields to client frame */
               }
            else
               {
               iffp = CLIENT_ERROR;   /* not enough RAM for the bitmap */
               }
            }
         break; }

      case END_MARK: {
         iffp = BAD_FORM;
         break; }

      } while (iffp >= IFF_OKAY);
      /* loop if valid ID of ignored chunk or a
       * subroutine returned IFF_OKAY (no errors).*/

   if (iffp != IFF_DONE)  return(iffp);

   CloseRGroup(&formContext);
   return(iffp);
   }

/** Notes on extending GetFoILBM ********************************************
 *
 * To read more kinds of chunks, just add clauses to the switch statement.
 * To read more kinds of property chunks (GRAB, CAMG, etc.) add clauses to
 * the switch statement in GetPrILBM, too.
 *
 * To read a FORM type that contains a variable number of data chunks--e.g.
 * a FORM FTXT with any number of CHRS chunks--replace the ID_BODY case with
 * an ID_CHRS case that doesn't set iffp = IFF_DONE, and make the END_MARK
 * case do whatever cleanup you need.
 *
 ***************************************************************************/


/** GetPrILBM() *************************************************************
 *
 * Called via myReadPicture to handle every PROP encountered in an IFF file.
 * Reads PROPs ILBM and skips all others.
 *
 ***************************************************************************/
#if Fancy
IFFP GetPrILBM(parent)  GroupContext *parent;  {
   /*compilerBug register*/ IFFP iffp;
   GroupContext propContext;
   ILBMFrame *ilbmFrame = (ILBMFrame *)parent->clientFrame;

   if (parent->subtype != ID_ILBM)
      return(IFF_OKAY);   /* just continue scaning the file */

   iffp = OpenRGroup(parent, &propContext);
   CheckIFFP();

   do switch (iffp = GetPChunkHdr(&propContext)) {
      case ID_BMHD: {
```

```
         ilbmFrame->foundBMHD = TRUE;
         iffp = GetBMHD(&propContext, &ilbmFrame->bmHdr);
         break; }
      case ID_CAMG: {        /* cs */
         iffp = handleCAMG(&propContext, ilbmFrame);
         break; }
      case ID_CRNG: {        /* cs */
         iffp = handleCRNG(&propContext, ilbmFrame);
         break; }
      case ID_CCRT: {        /* cs */
         iffp = handleCCRT(&propContext, ilbmFrame);
         break; }
      case ID_CMAP: {
         ilbmFrame->nColorRegs = maxColorReg; /* room for this many */
         iffp = GetCMAP(&propContext,
                        (WORD *)&ilbmFrame->colorMap,
                           &ilbmFrame->nColorRegs);
         break; }
      } while (iffp >= IFF_OKAY);
        /* loop if valid ID of ignored chunk or a
         * subroutine returned IFF_OKAY (no errors).*/

   CloseRGroup(&propContext);
   return(iffp == END_MARK ? IFF_OKAY : iffp);
   }
#endif

/** GetLiILBM() ***********************************************************
 *
 * Called via myReadPicture to handle every LIST encountered in an IFF file.
 *
 ***************************************************************************/
#if Fancy
IFFP GetLiILBM(parent)  GroupContext *parent;  {
    ILBMFrame newFrame;    /* allocate a new Frame */

    newFrame = *(ILBMFrame *)parent->clientFrame;  /* copy parent frame */

    return( ReadIList(parent, (ClientFrame *)&newFrame) );
    }
#endif

/** myReadPicture() *******************************************************/
IFFP myReadPicture(file,iFrame)
   LONG file;
   ILBMFrame *iFrame;   /* Top level "client frame".*/
   {
   IFFP iffp = IFF_OKAY;

#if Fancy
   iFrame->clientFrame.getList = GetLiILBM;
   iFrame->clientFrame.getProp = GetPrILBM;
#else
   iFrame->clientFrame.getList = SkipGroup;
   iFrame->clientFrame.getProp = SkipGroup;
#endif
   iFrame->clientFrame.getForm = GetFoILBM;
   iFrame->clientFrame.getCat  = ReadICat ;

   /* Initialize the top-level client frame's property settings to the
    * program-wide defaults. This example just records that we haven't read
    * any BMHD property or CMAP color registers yet. For the color map, that
    * means the default is to leave the machine's color registers alone.
    * If you want to read a property like GRAB, init it here to (0, 0). */

   iFrame->foundBMHD  = FALSE;
   iFrame->nColorRegs = 0;
   iFrame->foundCAMG  = FALSE;     /* cs */
   iFrame->cycleCnt   = 0;         /* cs */
```



```
   giFrame = iFrame;

  /* Store a pointer to the client's frame in a global variable so that
   * GetFoILBM can update client's frame when done.  Why do we have so
   * many frames & frame pointers floating around causing confusion?
   * Because IFF supports PROPs which apply to all FORMs in a LIST,
   * unless a given FORM overrides some property.
   * When you write code to read several FORMs,
   * it is ssential to maintain a frame at each level of the syntax
   * so that the properties for the LIST don't get overwritten by any
   * properties specified by individual FORMs.
   * We decided it was best to put that complexity into this one-FORM example,
   * so that those who need it later will have a useful starting place.
   */

   iffp = ReadIFF(file, (ClientFrame *)iFrame);
   return(iffp);
   }
```

```
/* myreadpict.h
 * Modified 12/88 - removed Camg, Ccrt, Crng defs (now in ilbm.h)
 */

#ifndef MYREADPICT_H
#define MYREADPICT_H


#ifndef GRAPHICS_GFX_H
#include <graphics/gfx.h>
#endif

#ifndef ILBM_H
#include <iff/ilbm.h>
#endif


#define EXDepth 6         /* Maximum depth (6=HAM) */
#define maxColorReg 32
#define maxCycles   8
#define RNG_NORATE  36    /* Dpaint uses this rate to mean non-active */

typedef struct {
   ClientFrame clientFrame;
   UBYTE foundBMHD;
   UBYTE nColorRegs;
   BitMapHeader bmHdr;
   Color4 colorMap[maxColorReg];
   /* If you want to read any other property chunks, e.g. GRAB or CAMG, add
    * fields to this record to store them. */
   UBYTE foundCAMG;
   CamgChunk camgChunk;
   UBYTE cycleCnt;
   CRange crngChunks[maxCycles]; /* I'll convert CCRT to this */
   } ILBMFrame;

typedef UBYTE *UBytePtr;

#ifdef FDwAT
extern IFFP myReadPicture(LONG, ILBMFrame *);
extern struct BitMap *getBitMap(ILBMFrame *);
#else
extern IFFP myReadPicture();
extern struct BitMap *getBitMap();
#endif

#endif MYREADPICT_H
```

```
/* * * * * * * * * * * * * * * * * * * * * * * * * * * * * * * * * * * * * * */
/* |_o_o|\\   The Software Distillery                                        */
/* |. o.| ||  Made available for the Amiga development community             */
/* | .  | ||   author:                                            BBS:       */
/* | o  | ||   John Mainwaring                          (919)-471-6436       */
/* |  . |//                                                                  */
/* ======                                                                    */
/* * * * * * * * * * * * * * * * * * * * * * * * * * * * * * * * * * * * * * */

/* global definitions for traceback dump utility */

#include "exec/types.h"
#include "exec/memory.h"
#include "proto/exec.h"
#include "stdio.h"
#include "string.h"
#include "stdlib.h"

#define FATAL 20

/* bit flags for dump options */
#define SYMFLG          1<<0
#define FAILFLG         1<<1
#define REGFLG          1<<2
#define ENVFLG          1<<3
#define STAKFLG         1<<4
#define UDATFLG         1<<5
#define FMEMFLG         1<<6
#define TRACEFLG        1<<7

struct symbol_node {
   struct symbol_node * sn_next;
   long sn_memsize;
   ULONG sn_value;
   char sn_sym[4]; /* real length determined when allocated */
   };

struct line_elem {
   ULONG le_line;
   ULONG le_off;
   };

struct line_node {
   struct line_node * ln_next;
   ULONG ln_size;       /* byte size of this block                        */
   ULONG ln_codesize;   /* byte size of this object file                  */
   ULONG ln_letabsize;  /* number of line_elems for this object file      */
   ULONG ln_offset;     /* offset into segment of this object file        */
   ULONG ln_nsize;      /* length of name (in longwords)                  */
   char  ln_name[4];    /* name of object file lines belong to            */
                        /* a table of line_elem comes after full name     */
   };

/* element of table of seglist descriptors */
struct segment {
   long addr;
   long size;
   struct symbol_node *symbols;
   struct line_node *lines;
   };

/* element of UDAT chain */
struct udata {
   struct udata *udptr;
   long udsize;
   long udat[1];  /* actual length of array given by udsize */
   };

/* data structure to hold contents of PGTB traceback file */
```



```
struct tbtemplate {
   /* FAIL stuff */
   long  gotfail;         /* found FAIL chunk              */
   char *taskname;        /* name from task block          */
   ULONG environ,         /* H/W environment               */
         vbfreq,          /* Vertical Blank                */
         psfreq,          /* Power Supply                  */
         starter,         /* 0 = WB else CLI               */
         guru,            /* defined in alerts.h           */
         segcount;        /* longword count                */
   struct segment *segments; /* seglist                    */
   /* REGS stuff */
   long  gotregs;         /* found REGS chunk              */
   ULONG pc,              /* program counter               */
         cc,              /* condition code reg            */
         dregs[8],        /* D0-D7                         */
         aregs[8];        /* A0-A7                         */
   /* VERS stuff */
   long  gotvers;         /* found VERS chunk              */
   ULONG ver,             /* version of catch.o            */
         rev;             /* revision of catch.o           */
   char *filename;        /* name of catch.o               */
   /* FMEM stuff */
   long  gotfmem;         /* got FMEM chunk                */
   ULONG memca,           /* available chip                */
         memcm,           /* max chip                      */
         memcl,           /* largest chip                  */
         memfa,           /* available fast                */
         memfm,           /* max fast                      */
         memfl;           /* largest fast                  */
   /* STAK stuff (pointer to data chain) */
   ULONG staktop,         /* top of stack                  */
         stakptr,/* saved stack pointer                    */
         staklen,         /* bottom of stack               */
         topseg,          /* bool top present              */
         botseg,          /* bool bot present              */
         seglen,          /* else entire size*/
         stak[2048];      /* stack data, 8K bytes          */
   /* UDAT stuff */
   struct udata *udhead;
   };

struct addrinfo {
   long hunknum;
   long offset;
   char *name;
   char *objname;
   long line;
   long lineoff;
   };

/* templates for functions called from outside defining section */

/* defined in tdrutil.c */
long getlong(FILE *);
long forcegetlong(FILE *);
void getblock(FILE *, ULONG *, long);
void getbytes(FILE *, ULONG *, long);
ULONG getascii(FILE *, char **);
void skiplong(FILE *, long);
void skipbytes(FILE *, long);

/* defined in tdread.h */
int  tdread(FILE *);

/* defined in tdsym.h */
int  readsym(FILE *);

/* defined in tdump.c */
```

```
void tdump(int);

/* defined in tdwutil.c */
void hexdump(FILE *, unsigned char *, long, long);
void longtoascii(ULONG, char *);
int  locaddr(ULONG, struct addrinfo *);
```

```c
/*
 *  ScreenSave.c --   v1.06 Carolyn Scheppner  CBM
 *                    Saves front screen as ILBM file
 *                    Saves a CAMG chunk for HAM, etc.
 *                    Creates icon for ILBM file
 *  Original 10/86
 *  Modified 9/88 - To mask out unwanted ViewMode bits in CAMG
 *                  and use CAMG defs in new ilbm.h
 *
 *     Uses IFF rtns by J.Morrison and S.Shaw of Electronic Arts
 *
 *       (all C code including IFF modules compiled with -v on LC2)
 * Linkage information:
 * FROM     AStartup.obj, ScreenSave.o, iffw.o, ilbmw.o, packer.o
 * TO       ScreenSave
 * LIBRARY  Amiga.lib, LC.lib
 *
 */

#include <exec/types.h>
#include <exec/memory.h>
#include <libraries/dos.h>
#include <libraries/dosextens.h>
#include <graphics/gfxbase.h>
#include <graphics/rastport.h>
#include <graphics/gfx.h>
#include <graphics/view.h>

#include <intuition/intuition.h>
#include <intuition/intuitionbase.h>
#include <workbench/workbench.h>
#include <workbench/startup.h>

#include "iff/ilbm.h"

/* From AStartup - used to create stdio on WB startup */
extern  LONG  stdin, stdout, stderr;

/* For masking unwanted Viewmodes bits */
#define BADFLAGS  (SPRITES|VP_HIDE|GENLOCK_AUDIO|GENLOCK_VIDEO)
#define FLAGMASK  (~BADFLAGS)
#define CAMGMASK  (FLAGMASK & 0x0000FFFFL)

/* Other Stuff */

#define bufSize 512

struct IntuitionBase *IntuitionBase;
struct GfxBase       *GfxBase;
ULONG  IconBase;

struct Screen   *frontScreen;

struct ViewPort *picViewPort;
struct BitMap   *picBitMap;
WORD            *picColorTable;
ULONG            picViewModes;
BOOL fromWB, newStdio;

#define INBUFSZ 40
char sbuf[INBUFSZ];
char nbuf[INBUFSZ];

char conSpec[] = "CON:0/40/639/160/ ScreenSave v1.06 ";

/* Definitions for ILBM Icon */
USHORT  ILBMimagedata[] = {
 0xFFFF, 0xFFFC,
 0xC000, 0x000C,
```



```c
 0xC000, 0x000C,
 0xC1E7, 0x9E0C,
 0xC1F8, 0x7E0C,
 0xC078, 0x780C,
 0xC187, 0x860C,
 0xC078, 0x780C,
 0xC1F8, 0x7E0C,
 0xC1E7, 0x9E0C,
 0xC000, 0x000C,
 0xC000, 0x000C,
 0xFFFF, 0xFFFC,
 0x0000, 0x0000,
 0x0000, 0x0000,
/**/
 0xFFFF, 0xFFFC,
 0xFFFF, 0xFFFC,
 0xF800, 0x007C,
 0xF9E0, 0x1E7C,
 0xF980, 0x067C,
 0xF807, 0x807C,
 0xF81F, 0xE07C,
 0xF807, 0x807C,
 0xF980, 0x067C,
 0xF9E0, 0x1E7C,
 0xF800, 0x007C,
 0xFFFF, 0xFFFC,
 0xFFFF, 0xFFFC,
 0x0000, 0x0000,
 0x0000, 0x0000,
/**/
 };

struct Image ILBMimage = {
   0,0,                        /* Leftedge, Topedge */
   30,15,                      /* Width Height */
   2,                          /* Depth */
   &ILBMimagedata[0],          /* Data for image */
   3,0                         /* PlanePick, PlaneOnOff */
   };

struct DiskObject ILBMobject = {
   WB_DISKMAGIC,
   WB_DISKVERSION,

   /* Gadget Structure */
   NULL,                       /* Ptr to next gadget */
   0,0,                        /* Leftedge, Topedge */
   30,15,                      /* Width, Height */
   GADGHBOX|GADGIMAGE,         /* Flags */
   RELVERIFY|GADGIMMEDIATE,    /* Activation */
   BOOLGADGET,                 /* Type */
   (APTR)&ILBMimage,           /* Render */
   NULL,                       /* Select Render */
   NULL,                       /* Text */
   NULL,NULL,NULL,NULL,        /* Exclude, Special, ID, UserData */

   4,                          /* WBObject type */
   ":Display",                 /* Default tool */
   NULL,                       /* Tool Types */
   NO_ICON_POSITION,           /* Current X */
   NO_ICON_POSITION,           /* Current Y */
   NULL,NULL,NULL,             /* Drawer, ToolWindow, Stack */
   };


main(argc, argv)
int argc;
char **argv;
   {
```

```
   LONG            file;
   IFFP            iffp = NO_FILE;
   char            *filename;
   int l;

   newStdio = FALSE;
   fromWB = (argc==0) ? TRUE : FALSE;

   if((fromWB) && (!(newStdio = openStdio(&conSpec[0]))))
      {
      return(0);
      }

   if ((IntuitionBase =
      (struct IntuitionBase *)OpenLibrary("intuition.library",0))==NULL)
         cleanexit("Can't open intuition.library\n");

   if ((GfxBase =
      (struct GfxBase *)OpenLibrary("graphics.library",0))==NULL)
      cleanexit("Can't open graphics.library\n");

   if ((IconBase = OpenLibrary("icon.library",0))==NULL )
      cleanexit("Can't open icon.library\n");

   printf("ScreenSave v 1.06 --- C. Scheppner  CBM  9/88\n");
   printf("   Saves the front screen as an IFF ILBM file\n");
   printf("   A CAMG chunk is saved (for HAM pics, etc.)\n\n");

   if(argc>1)                /* Passed filename via command line  */
      {
      filename = argv[1];
      }
   else
      {
      printf("Enter filename for save: ");
      l = gets(&nbuf[0]);

      if(l==0)               /* No filename - Exit */
         {
         cleanexit("\nScreen not saved, filename required\n");
         }
      else
         {
         filename = &nbuf[0];
         }
      }

   if (!(file = Open(filename, MODE_NEWFILE)))
      cleanexit("Can't open output file\n");

   Write(file,"x",1);  /* 1.1 so Seek to beginning works ? */

   printf("Click here and press <RETURN> when ready: ");
   gets(&sbuf[0]);
   printf("Front screen will be saved in 10 seconds\n");
   Delay(500);

   Forbid();
   frontScreen  = IntuitionBase->FirstScreen;
   Permit();

   picViewPort = &( frontScreen->ViewPort );
   picBitMap = (struct BitMap*)picViewPort->RasInfo->BitMap;
   picColorTable = (WORD *)picViewPort->ColorMap->ColorTable;
   picViewModes = (ULONG)picViewPort->Modes;

   printf("\nSaving...\n");

   iffp = PutPicture(file, picBitMap, picColorTable, picViewModes);
```



```
   Close(file);

   if (iffp == IFF_OKAY)
      {
      printf("Screen saved\n");
      if(!(PutDiskObject(filename,&ILBMobject)))
         {
         cleanexit("Error saving icon\n");
         }
      printf("Icon saved\n");
      }
   cleanexit("Done\n");
   }


cleanexit(s)
   char  *s;
   {
   if(*s) printf(s);
   if ((fromWB)&&(*s))    /* Wait so user can read messages */
      {
      printf("\nPRESS RETURN TO EXIT\n");
      gets(&sbuf[0]);
      }
   cleanup();
   exit();
   }

cleanup()
   {
   if (newStdio)  closeStdio();
   if (GfxBase) CloseLibrary(GfxBase);
   if (IntuitionBase) CloseLibrary(IntuitionBase);
   if (IconBase) CloseLibrary(IconBase);
   }


openStdio(conspec)
char *conspec;
   {
   LONG wfile;
   struct Process *proc;
   struct FileHandle *handle;

   if (!(wfile = Open(conspec,MODE_NEWFILE)))  return(0);
   stdin  = wfile;
   stdout = wfile;
   stderr = wfile;
   handle = (struct FileHandle *)(wfile << 2);
   proc = (struct Process *)FindTask(NULL);
   proc->pr_ConsoleTask = (APTR)(handle->fh_Type);
   proc->pr_CIS = (BPTR)stdin;
   proc->pr_COS = (BPTR)stdout;
   return(1);
   }

closeStdio()
   {
   struct Process *proc;
   struct FileHandle *handle;

   if (stdin > 0)  Close(stdin);
   stdin  = -1;
   stdout = -1;
   stderr = -1;
   handle = (struct FileHandle *)(stdin << 2);
   proc = (struct Process *)FindTask(NULL);
   proc->pr_ConsoleTask = NULL;
   proc->pr_CIS = NULL;
```

```
   proc->pr_COS = NULL;
   }


gets(s)
char *s;
   {
   int l = 0, max = INBUFSZ - 1;

   while (((*s = getchar()) !='\n' )&&(l < max)) s++, l++;
   *s = NULL;
   return(l);
   }


/* String Functions */

strlen(s)
char *s;
   {
   int i = 0;
   while(*s++) i++;
   return(i);
   }

strcpy(to,from)
char *to, *from;
   {
   do
      {
      *to++ = *from;
      }
   while(*from++);
   }


/** PutPicture() ***********************************************************
 *
 * Put a picture into an IFF file.
 * This procedure calls PutAnILBM, passing in an <x, y> location of <0, 0>,
 * a NULL mask, and a locally-allocated buffer. It also assumes you want to
 * write out all the bitplanes in the BitMap.
 *
 ***************************************************************************/
Point2D nullPoint = {0, 0};

IFFP PutPicture(file, bitmap, colorMap, viewmodes)
      LONG file;  struct BitMap *bitmap;
      WORD *colorMap;  ULONG viewmodes;
   {
   BYTE buffer[bufSize];
   return( PutAnILBM(file, bitmap, NULL,
           colorMap, bitmap->Depth, viewmodes,
           &nullPoint, buffer, bufSize) );
   }


/** PutAnILBM() ************************************************************
 *
 * Write an entire BitMap as a FORM ILBM in an IFF file.
 * This version works for any display mode (C. Scheppner).
 *
 * Normal return result is IFF_OKAY.
 *
 * The utility program IFFCheck would print the following outline of the
 * resulting file:
 *
 *   FORM ILBM
 *     BMHD
```



```
 *     CAMG
 *     CMAP
 *     BODY       (compressed)
 *
 ***************************************************************************/
#define CkErr(expression)  {if (ifferr == IFF_OKAY) ifferr = (expression);}

IFFP PutAnILBM(file, bitmap, mask, colorMap, depth,
                                viewmodes, xy, buffer, bufsize)
      LONG file;
      struct BitMap *bitmap;
      BYTE *mask;  WORD *colorMap; UBYTE depth;
      ULONG viewmodes;
      Point2D *xy; BYTE *buffer;  LONG bufsize;
   {
   BitMapHeader bmHdr;
   CamgChunk    camgChunk;
   GroupContext fileContext, formContext;
   IFFP ifferr;
   WORD pageWidth, pageHeight;

   pageWidth  = (bitmap->BytesPerRow) << 3;
   pageHeight = bitmap->Rows;

   ifferr = InitBMHdr(&bmHdr, bitmap, mskNone,
                      cmpByteRun1, 0, pageWidth, pageHeight);
   /* You could write an uncompressed image by passing cmpNone instead
    * of cmpByteRun1 to InitBMHdr. */
   bmHdr.nPlanes = depth;   /* This must be  <= bitmap->Depth */
   if (mask != NULL) bmHdr.masking = mskHasMask;
   bmHdr.x = xy->x;   bmHdr.y = xy->y;

   camgChunk.ViewModes = viewmodes & CAMGMASK; /* Mask out unwanted bits! */

   CkErr( OpenWIFF(file, &fileContext, szNotYetKnown) );
   CkErr(StartWGroup(&fileContext, FORM, szNotYetKnown, ID_ILBM, &formContext));

   CkErr( PutBMHD(&formContext, &bmHdr) );
   CkErr( PutCAMG(&formContext, &camgChunk) );
   CkErr( PutCMAP(&formContext, colorMap, depth) );
   CkErr( PutBODY(&formContext, bitmap, mask, &bmHdr, buffer, bufsize) );

   CkErr( EndWGroup(&formContext) );
   CkErr( CloseWGroup(&fileContext) );
   return( ifferr );
   }
```

```
/*
 * cycvb.c --- Dan Silva's DPaint color cycling interrupt code
 *
 *    Use this as an example for interrupt driven color cycling
 *    If compiled with Lattice, use -v flag on LC2
 *    For an example of subtask cycling, see Display.c
 */

#include <exec/types.h>
#include <exec/interrupts.h>
#include <graphics/view.h>
#include <iff/compiler.h>

#define MAXNCYCS 4
#define NO  FALSE
#define YES TRUE
#define LOCAL static

typedef struct {
    SHORT count;
    SHORT rate;
    SHORT flags;
    UBYTE low, high;  /* bounds of range */
    } Range;

/* Range flags values */
#define RNG_ACTIVE  1
#define RNG_REVERSE 2
#define RNG_NORATE 36  /* if rate == NORATE, don't cycle */

/* cycling frame rates */
#define OnePerTick   16384
#define OnePerSec    OnePerTick/60

extern Range  cycles[];
extern BOOL   cycling[];
extern WORD   cycols[];
extern struct ViewPort *vport;
extern SHORT  nColors;


MyVBlank()  {
   int i,j;
   LOCAL  Range *cyc;
   LOCAL  WORD  temp;
   LOCAL  BOOL  anyChange;

#ifdef IS_AZTEC
#asm
       movem.l  a2-a7/d2-d7,-(sp)
       move.l   a1,a4
#endasm
#endif

   if (cycling)  {
      anyChange = NO;
      for (i=0; i<MAXNCYCS; i++)  {
         cyc = &cycles[i];
         if ( (cyc->low == cyc->high) ||
              ((cyc->flags&RNG_ACTIVE) == 0) ||
              (cyc->rate == RNG_NORATE) )
                 continue;

         cyc->count += cyc->rate;
         if (cyc->count >= OnePerTick)  {
            anyChange = YES;
            cyc->count -= OnePerTick;

            if (cyc->flags&RNG_REVERSE)  {
```



```
               temp = cycols[cyc->low];
               for (j=cyc->low; j < cyc->high; j++)
                  cycols[j] = cycols[j+1];
               cycols[cyc->low] = temp;
               }
            else  {
               temp = cycols[cyc->high];
               for (j=cyc->high; j > cyc->low; j--)
                  cycols[j] = cycols[j-1];
               cycols[cyc->low] = temp;
               }
            }
         }
      if (anyChange) LoadRGB4(vport,cycols,nColors);
      }

#ifdef IS_AZTEC
      ;   /* this is necessary */
#asm
      movem.l  (sp)+,a2-a7/d2-d7
#endasm
#endif

   return(0);  /* interrupt routines have to do this */
   }


/*
 *  Code to install/remove cycling interrupt handler
 */

LOCAL char myname[] = "MyVB";  /* Name of interrupt handler */
LOCAL struct Interrupt intServ;

typedef void (*VoidFunc)();

StartVBlank()  {
#ifdef IS_AZTEC
   intServ.is_Data = GETAZTEC();  /* returns contents of register a4 */
#else
   intServ.is_Data = NULL;
#endif
   intServ.is_Code = (VoidFunc)&MyVBlank;
   intServ.is_Node.ln_Succ = NULL;
   intServ.is_Node.ln_Pred = NULL;
   intServ.is_Node.ln_Type = NT_INTERRUPT;
   intServ.is_Node.ln_Pri  = 0;
   intServ.is_Node.ln_Name = myname;
   AddIntServer(5,&intServ);
   }

StopVBlank() { RemIntServer(5,&intServ); }

/**/
```

```
****************************************************************
*
*  Copyright 1988 by CREATIVE FOCUS.  This code is freely
*  distributable as long as this notice is retained and no
*  other conditions are imposed upon its redistribution.
*
*
*  APACK.ASM --
*
*  A fully compatible replacement for Electronic Arts' PACKER.C
*  routine.  Converts data according to the IFF ILBM cmpByteRun1
*  compression protocol:
*
*     control bytes:
*
*        n =  0.. 127:   followed by n+1 bytes of data;
*        n = -1..-127:   followed by byte to be repeated -n+1 times;
*        n =     -128:   don't do no nada.
*
*     calling format:
*
*        long PackRow(from, too, amt)
*           char **from, /* pointer to source data pointer */
*                **too;  /* pointer to destination data pointer */
*           long amt;    /* number of bytes to compress */
*
*        return(number of bytes written to destination);
*
*     effects:
*
*         *from = *from + amt, and *too = *too + return;
*         return is "smart," that is, not greater than
*         MaxPackedSize = amt + ((amt+127) >> 7).
*
*     By commenting out CHECK (below) you disable checking for runs
*     exceeding 128 bytes.  That CHECK is not needed if you are sure
*     the amt to be compressed is always 128 or less.
*
*  !!! DISCLAIMER !!!  You use this code entirely at your own
*  risk.  I don't warrantee its fitness for any purpose.  I
*  can't even guarantee the accuracy of anything I've said
*  about it, though I've tried my damndest to get it right.
*  I may, in fact, be completely out of my tiny little mind :-).
*
*  That being said, I can be reached for questions, comments,
*  or concerns at:
*
*        Dr. Gerald Hull
*        CREATIVE FOCUS
*        12 White Street
*        Binghamton, N.Y.  13901
*        (607) 648-4082
*
*        bix:    ghull
*        PLink:  DRJERRY
*
****************************************************************

      xdef  _PackRow

PT    equr  a0                    -> beginning of replicate run (if any)
IX    equr  a1                    -> end+1 of input line
IP    equr  a2                    -> beginning of literal run (if any)
IQ    equr  a3                    -> end+1 of lit and/or rep run (if any)
OP    equr  a4                    -> end+1 of output line current pos
FP    equr  a6                    frame pointer
SP    equr  a7                    stack pointer
```



```
RT    equr  d0                    return value
MX    equr  d1                    check for maximum run = MAX
AM    equr  d2                    amount
CH    equr  d3                    character

REGS  reg   AM/CH/IP/IQ/OP

FRM   equ   8                     input line address
TOO   equ   12                    output line address
AMT   equ   16                    length of input line

MAX   equ   128                   maximum encodable output run
* CHECK equ  1                      turns on maximum row checking


_PackRow


***************     CASE 0:    GRAB PARAMS & INITIALIZE
CAS0
      link     FP,#0
      movem.l  REGS,-(SP)
      movea.l  FRM(FP),IP
      movea.l  (IP),IP            IP = *from
      movea.l  IP,IQ              IQ = IP
      movea.l  IQ,IX
      adda.l   AMT(FP),IX         IX = IP + amt
      movea.l  TOO(FP),OP
      movea.l  (OP),OP            OP = *too


***************     CASE 1:    LITERAL RUN
CAS1
      movea.l  IQ,PT              adjust PT (no replicates yet!)
      move.b   (IQ)+,CH           grab character
      cmpa.l   IQ,IX              if input is finished
      beq.s    CAS5                  branch to case 5

      ifd      CHECK
      move.l   IQ,MX
      sub.l    IP,MX
      cmpi     #MAX,MX            if run has reached MAX
      beq.s    CAS6                  branch to case 6
      endc

      cmp.b    (IQ),CH            if next character != CH
      bne.s    CAS1                  stay in case 1

*                                 else fall into case 2


***************     CASE 2:    AT LEAST 2 BYTE REPEAT
CAS2
      move.b   (IQ)+,CH           grab character
      cmpa.l   IQ,IX              if input is finished
      beq.s    CAS7                  branch to case 7

      ifd      CHECK
      move.l   IQ,MX
      sub.l    IP,MX
      cmpi     #MAX,MX            if run has reached MAX
      beq.s    CAS6                  branch to case 6
      endc

      cmp.b    (IQ),CH            if next character != CH
      bne.s    CAS1                  branch to case 1

*                                 else fall into case 3
```

```
***************     CASE 3:    REPLICATE RUN
CAS3
        move.b   (IQ)+,CH      grab character
        cmpa.l   IQ,IX         if input is finished
        beq.s    CAS7             branch to case 7

        ifd      CHECK
        move.l   IQ,MX
        sub.l    PT,MX
        cmpi     #MAX,MX       if run has reached MAX
        beq.s    CAS4             branch to case 4
        endc

        cmp.b    (IQ),CH       if next character = CH
        beq.s    CAS3             stay in case 3

*                              else fall into case 4

***************     CASE 4:    LIT AND/OR REP DUMP & CONTINUE
CAS4
        move.l   PT,AM
        sub.l    IP,AM         AM = PT - IP
*                              if no literal run
        beq.s    C41              branch to replicate run

        subq     #1,AM         AM = AM - 1
        move.b   AM,(OP)+      output literal control byte

C40     move.b   (IP)+,(OP)+   output literal run
        dbra     AM,C40

C41     move.l   PT,AM
        sub.l    IQ,AM         AM = PT - IQ (negative result!)
        addq     #1,AM         AM = AM + 1
        move.b   AM,(OP)+      output replicate control byte
        move.b   CH,(OP)+      output repeated character
        movea.l  IQ,IP         reset IP
        bra.s    CAS1          branch to case 1 (not done)

***************     CASE 5:    LITERAL DUMP & QUIT
CAS5
        move.l   IQ,AM
        sub.l    IP,AM         AM = IQ - IP (positive result > 0)
        subq     #1,AM         AM = AM - 1
        move.b   AM,(OP)+      output literal control byte

C50     move.b   (IP)+,(OP)+   output literal run
        dbra     AM,C50

        bra.s    CAS8          branch to case 8 (done)


        ifd      CHECK

***************     CASE 6:    LITERAL DUMP & CONTINUE
CAS6
        move.l   IQ,AM
        sub.l    IP,AM         AM = IQ - IP (positive result > 0)
        subq     #1,AM         AM = AM - 1
        move.b   AM,(OP)+      output literal control byte

C60     move.b   (IP)+,(OP)+   output literal run
        dbra     AM,C60

        bra      CAS1          branch to case 1 (not done)
```



```
        endc

***************     CASE 7:    LIT AND/OR REP DUMP & FINISH
CAS7
        move.l   PT,AM
        sub.l    IP,AM         AM = PT - IP (positive result > 0)
*                              if no literal run
        beq.s    C71              branch to replicate run

        subq     #1,AM         AM = AM - 1
        move.b   AM,(OP)+      output literal control byte

C70     move.b   (IP)+,(OP)+   output literal run
        dbra     AM,C70

C71     move.l   PT,AM
        sub.l    IQ,AM         AM = PT - IQ (negative result)
        addq     #1,AM         AM = AM + 1
        move.b   AM,(OP)+      output replicate control byte
        move.b   CH,(OP)+      output repeated character

*                              fall into case 8

***************     CASE 8:    ADJUST PARAMS & RETURN VALUE
CAS8
        movea.l  FRM(FP),PT    PT = **from
        move.l   IQ,(PT)       *from = *from + amt
        movea.l  TOO(FP),PT    PT = **too

        move.l   OP,RT
        sub.l    (PT),RT      return = OP - *too

        move.l   OP,(PT)      *too = *too + return
        movem.l  (SP)+,REGS
        UNLK     FP
        rts

        end
```

Section J

Function Index

This section contains an alphabetical listing of system functions. Use this when you know the name of a function, but not what system module the function is a part of.

CMD_START	parallel.device	B-41
CMD_STOP	audio.device	B-1
CMD_STOP	serial.device	B-58
CMD_STOP	printer.device	B-47
CMD_STOP	narrator.device	B-36
CMD_STOP	parallel.device	B-41
CMD_UPDATE	audio.device	B-1
CMD_UPDATE	clipboard.device	B-11
CMD_WRITE	audio.device	B-1
CMD_WRITE	serial.device	B-58
CMD_WRITE	console.device	B-15
CMD_WRITE	printer.device	B-47
CMD_WRITE	narrator.device	B-36
CMD_WRITE	parallel.device	B-41
CMD_WRITE	clipboard.device	B-11
CMOVE	graphics.library	A-64
CmpTime	timer.device	B-66
ConfigBoard	expansion.library	A-52
ConfigChain	expansion.library	A-52
CopyMem	exec.library	A-4
CopyMemQuick	exec.library	A-4
CopySBitMap	graphics.library	A-64
CreateBehindLayer	layers.library	A-166
CreateDir	dos.library	**
CreateExtIO	amiga.lib	F-1
CreatePort	amiga.lib	F-1
CreateProc	dos.library	**
CreateTask	amiga.lib	F-1
CreateUpfrontLayer	layers.library	A-166
CurrentDir	dos.library	**
CurrentTime	intuition.library	A-124
CWAIT	graphics.library	A-64
DateStamp	dos.library	**
dbf	amiga.lib/math	F-1
Deallocate	exec.library	A-4
Debug	exec.library	A-4
Delay	dos.library	**
DeleteExtIO	amiga.lib	F-1
DeleteFile	dos.library	**
DeleteLayer	layers.library	A-166
DeletePort	amiga.lib	F-1
DeleteTask	amiga.lib	F-1
DeviceProc	dos.library	**
Disable	exec.library	A-4
DisownBlitter	graphics.library	A-64
DisplayAlert	intuition.library	A-124
DisplayBeep	intuition.library	A-124
DisposeFontContents	diskfont.library	A-1
DisposeLayerInfo	layers.library	A-166
DisposeRegion	graphics.library	A-64
DoCollision	graphics.library	A-64
DoIO	exec.library	A-4
DoubleClick	intuition.library	A-124
Draw	graphics.library	A-64
DrawBorder	intuition.library	A-124
DrawEllipse	graphics.library	A-64
DrawGList	graphics.library	A-64
DrawImage	intuition.library	A-124
DupLock	dos.library	**
Enable	exec.library	A-4
EndRefresh	intuition.library	A-124
EndRequest	intuition.library	A-124
EndUpdate	layers.library	A-166
Enqueue	exec.library	A-4
Examine	dos.library	**
Execute	dos.library	**
Exit	dos.library	**
ExNext	dos.library	**
FastRand	amiga.lib	F-1
FattenLayerInfo	layers.library	A-166
FindConfigDev	expansion.library	A-52
FindName	exec.library	A-4
FindPort	exec.library	A-4
FindResident	exec.library	A-4
FindSemaphore	exec.library	A-4
FindTask	exec.library	A-4
FindToolType	icon.library	A-119
Flood	graphics.library	A-64
Forbid	exec.library	A-4
fpa	amiga.lib/math	F-1
fpbcd	amiga.lib/math	F-1
FreeBoardMem	expansion.library	A-52
FreeColorMap	graphics.library	A-64
FreeConfigDev	expansion.library	A-52
FreeCopList	graphics.library	A-64
FreeCprList	graphics.library	A-64
FreeDiskObject	icon.library	A-119
FreeEntry	exec.library	A-4
FreeExpansionMem	expansion.library	A-52
FreeFreeList	icon.library	A-119
FreeGBuffers	graphics.library	A-64
FreeMem	exec.library	A-4
FreePotBits	potgo.resource	C-9
FreeRaster	graphics.library	A-64
FreeRemember	intuition.library	A-124
FreeSignal	exec.library	A-4
FreeSprite	graphics.library	A-64
FreeSysRequest	intuition.library	A-124
FreeTrap	exec.library	A-4
FreeUnit	disk.resource	C-4
FreeVPortCopLists	graphics.library	A-64
GetCC	exec.library	A-4
GetColorMap	graphics.library	A-64
GetCurrentBinding	expansion.library	A-52
GetDefPrefs	intuition.library	A-124
GetDiskObject	icon.library	A-119
GetGBuffers	graphics.library	A-64
GetMsg	exec.library	A-4
GetPrefs	intuition.library	A-124
GetRGB4	graphics.library	A-64
GetScreenData	intuition.library	A-124
GetSprite	graphics.library	A-64
GetUnit	disk.resource	C-4
GetUnitID	disk.resource	C-4
GiveUnit	disk.resource	C-4
GPD_ASKCTYPE	gameport.device	B-22
GPD_ASKTRIGGER	gameport.device	B-22
GPD_READEVENT	gameport.device	B-22
GPD_SETCTYPE	gameport.device	B-22
GPD_SETTRIGGER	gameport.device	B-22
IEEEDPAbs	mathieeedoubbas.library	A-196
IEEEDPAcos	mathieeedoubtrans.library	A-193
IEEEDPAdd	mathieeedoubbas.library	A-196
IEEEDPAsin	mathieeedoubtrans.library	A-193
IEEEDPAtan	mathieeedoubtrans.library	A-193
IEEEDPCeil	mathieeedoubbas.library	A-196
IEEEDPCmp	mathieeedoubbas.library	A-196
IEEEDPCos	mathieeedoubtrans.library	A-193
IEEEDPCosh	mathieeedoubtrans.library	A-193
IEEEDPDiv	mathieeedoubbas.library	A-196
IEEEDPExp	mathieeedoubtrans.library	A-193
IEEEDPFieee	mathieeedoubtrans.library	A-193
IEEEDPFix	mathieeedoubbas.library	A-196
IEEEDPFloor	mathieeedoubbas.library	A-196
IEEEDPFlt	mathieeedoubbas.library	A-196
IEEEDPLog	mathieeedoubtrans.library	A-193
IEEEDPLog10	mathieeedoubtrans.library	A-193
IEEEDPMul	mathieeedoubbas.library	A-196
IEEEDPNeg	mathieeedoubbas.library	A-196
IEEEDPPow	mathieeedoubtrans.library	A-193
IEEEDPSin	mathieeedoubtrans.library	A-193
IEEEDPSincos	mathieeedoubtrans.library	A-193
IEEEDPSinh	mathieeedoubtrans.library	A-193
IEEEDPSqrt	mathieeedoubtrans.library	A-193

** dos.library is documented in the AmigaDOS Manual